FOUNDATIONS
of Restaurant Management
& Culinary Arts
Level Two

Teacher's Wraparound Edition

National Restaurant Association

Prentice Hall

Boston   Columbus   Indianapolis   New York   San Francisco   Upper Saddle River   Amsterdam

Cape Town   Dubai   London   Madrid   Milan   Munich   Paris   Montreal   Toronto

Delhi   Mexico City   Sao Paulo   Sydney   Hong Kong   Seoul   Singapore   Taipei   Tokyo

Editorial Director: Vernon Anthony
Executive Editor: Wendy Craven
Director of Marketing: David Gesell
Campaign Marketing Manager: Leigh Ann Sims
School Marketing Manager: Laura Cutone
Senior Marketing Assistant: Les Roberts
Associate Managing Editor: Alexandrina Benedicto Wolf
Project Manager: Kris Roach
Senior Operations Supervisor: Pat Tonneman
Operations Specialist: Deidra Skahill
Cover Designer: Jane Diane Ricciardi
Manager, Rights and Permissions: Zina Arabia

Cover Art: Kipling Swehla
NRAS Product Management Team: Janet Benoit, Megan Meyer, William Nolan, Rachel Peña, and Wendi Safstrom
Product Development and Project Management: Emergent Learning, LLC
Writing and Text Development: Kristine Westover, Michelle Graas, Michelle Somody, Tom Finn
Editorial and Composition: Claire Hunter and Abshier House
Printer/Binder: Courier Kendallville
Cover Printer: Phoenix Color

Credits and acknowledgments borrowed from other sources and reproduced, with permission, in this textbook appear on appropriate page within text (or on page 828).

2 3 4 5 6 7 8 9 10 V011 15 14 13 12 11

Prentice Hall
an imprint of

PearsonSchool.com/careertech

ISBN 13: 978-0-13-138101-8
ISBN 10: 0-13-138101-6

Brief Table of Contents

Level 1

This is the first book in a two-book series covering the Foundations of Restaurant Management & Culinary Arts.

Level 2

Table of Contents for the second book of this two-book series covering the Foundations of Restaurant Management & Culinary Arts. The ISBN for the Level 2 book is 0-13-138022-2.

Can students using this book receive recognition from the National Restaurant Association?

Yes!

The *Foundations of Restaurant Management & Culinary Arts*–Levels 1 and 2 curriculum teaches students the fundamental skills they will need to begin a career in the industry. What's more, after completing each level of this industry-driven curriculum, students can sit for the National Restaurant Association's exam for that level. Students who pass both the Level 1 and Level 2 exams receive certificates from the National Restaurant Association.

Welcome Teachers!

Dear Teachers:

Thank you for choosing *Foundations of Restaurant Management & Culinary Arts* for your classroom!

We at the National Restaurant Association are thrilled to take this journey with you and your students as they learn more about the restaurant and foodservice industry. Restaurant and foodservice operations make up one of the most dynamic industries in the United States today. They are a shining example of the entrepreneurial spirit and a place where employees become owners every day.

Millions of opportunities: As the nation's second-largest private-sector employer, the restaurant and foodservice industry creates opportunity for millions of Americans. The industry employs nearly 13 million people today and is expected to add almost 2 million positions over the next decade.

This means there are many opportunities and career paths ahead for your students. Whether it's a quick-service restaurant, a family operation, or a multi-million-dollar company providing on-site foodservice at schools or hospitals, our industry is the place for them to build their career. Please encourage them to explore all that the industry has to offer.

Industry-backed learning materials matter: *Foundations of Restaurant Management & Culinary Arts* was developed with input from industry leaders. We believe that an industry-backed education is the best way to prepare your students to lead the industry into the future. Working with industry and academia, we have identified the management, operational, and culinary skills critical to success in the industry. The skills you teach in Level 1 and Level 2 will give your students a competitive advantage and solid foundation upon which to build their careers or further their educations.

We are proud that you have chosen to partner with the National Restaurant Association to prepare your students for their futures. As the leading business association for the restaurant industry, the Association works to lead America's restaurant industry into a new era of prosperity, prominence, and participation, enhancing the quality of life for all we serve. Our philanthropic foundation, the National Restaurant Association Educational Foundation, enhances the restaurant industry's service to the public through education, community engagement, and promotion of career opportunities.

We invite you to learn more about us at www.restaurant.org and www.nraef.org, and be sure to check out Overview of the ProStart® Program on page vi to learn more about the ProStart program and its benefits for students and educators.

Overview of the ProStart® Program

The National Restaurant Association Educational Foundation's (NRAEF) ProStart® program teaches high school students the management and culinary skills needed for a career in the restaurant and foodservice industry. Throughout an exciting two-year period, they study in the classroom, participate in mentored work experiences, and test their skills in local and national competitions. Whether students are looking to enter the job market directly after graduation or plan to attend college, a ProStart graduate makes a solid candidate for success.

The heart of the ProStart program is the connection with the restaurant and foodservice industry. The career-building program was developed by the National Restaurant Association Educational Foundation and is supported by partnerships with state restaurant associations across the United States. The program is designed to:

- Increase and strengthen industry involvement in high school classrooms

- Set the standard for restaurant and foodservice career education

- Improve the image of restaurant and foodservice management as a career

- Recruit and train students to become the next industry leaders

How the ProStart Program Works

Classroom Experience
The Foundations of Restaurant Management & Culinary Arts–Levels 1 and 2 curriculum teaches students the fundamental skills they will need to begin a career in the industry. After completing each level of the industry-driven curriculum, students sit for the National Restaurant Association's exam for that level.

Mentored Work Experience
ProStart students put classroom learning to work on the job in qualified industry operations. In their work experience, students receive mentor support, character development, and real-world skills that help launch their careers. Working with industry mentors, they demonstrate that they have mastered a series of competencies defined as critical to success by the industry.

ProStart National Certificate of Achievement
Students who pass both the Level 1 and Level 2 exams and complete the 400-hour mentored work experience are eligible to earn the ProStart National Certificate of Achievement. ProStart graduates who earn this prestigious certificate possess a solid foundation for their future careers, and are eligible to earn special scholarships and college credit from colleges and universities across the country. It also opens the door to our vibrant and growing industry.

National ProStart Invitational

During their two years in the program, students have the opportunity to put their skills to the ultimate test in the National ProStart Invitational. This demanding culinary and management competition invites top students to represent their state, with winning teams competing for scholarships. To compete at the National ProStart Invitational, teams must first win at the state level competition hosted by their state restaurant association.

How the ProStart Program Benefits Students

Students who earn the ProStart National Certificate of Achievement have access to numerous scholarship and articulation opportunities to put them on the fast track to a college degree. The NRAEF offers special scholarships to students who earn the certificate, as well as to winning teams at the National ProStart Invitational. Annually, more than $1.5 million in scholarships are awarded to competition winners at the state and national levels. In addition, many colleges and universities across the country have articulation agreements with ProStart that award students scholarships, class credits, or work hour credits when they enroll.

Students in the ProStart program have access to support and resources from the National Restaurant Association, the NRAEF, and their state restaurant association. They join a network of restaurateurs and chefs who recognize the students as the future of the industry and are committed to helping them succeed. The National Restaurant Association also offers a complimentary student membership to ProStart students.

How the ProStart Program Benefits Educators

ProStart program educators benefit from professional development opportunities, ranging from state-wide training hosted by state restaurant associations to national webinars. The NRAEF also sponsors the Educator Training & Development Awards. Recipients are hosted for a week of management training, alongside the company's own managers, by ProStart sponsor companies.

Each participating state restaurant association employs a ProStart Coordinator to work with ProStart educators in the state. The coordinator helps connect educators and classrooms with local industry. These connections can aid in securing mentored work experience for students, classroom supplies and equipment, and classroom demonstrations, among others. ProStart educators also have access to support and resources from the National Restaurant Association and NRAEF, including a complimentary Association membership.

How to Get Involved

To learn more about joining the ProStart program, contact your state restaurant association. For more information on the program or to locate your state ProStart Coordinator, visit www.prostart. restaurant.org.

Learning Objectives

Chapter 1:
Breakfast Food and Sandwiches
Section 1.1

1.1 List the characteristics of milk and identify ways to keep it safe.

1.2 Identify the different forms of cream and their fat contents.

1.3 Differentiate between butter and butter substitutes and recognize the characteristics of each.

1.4 Identify the different types of cheese and give examples of each.

1.5 List the characteristics of eggs and identify ways to keep them safe.

1.6 Prepare and serve eggs using a variety of cooking methods.

Section 1.2

1.7 Prepare pancakes, crêpes, waffles, and French toast.

1.8 Prepare ham, hash, grits, cold cereals, oatmeal, and sausage.

1.9 Prepare coffee, tea, and cocoa.

Section 1.3

1.10 Give examples of different types of sandwiches, including simple hot, open-faced, hors d'oeuvres, grilled, deep-fried, and simple cold.

1.11 Explain the roles of the three components of a sandwich: bread, spread, and filling

1.12 Prepare common sandwich spreads and fillings.

1.13 List the necessary tools and equipment to make sandwiches at a sandwich station.

1.14 Demonstrate preparation of several types of sandwiches.

Chapter 2:
Nutrition
Section 2.1

2.1 Explain why nutrition is important to the food-service industry.

2.2 List the six basic types of nutrients found in food.

2.3 Describe how phytochemicals and fiber function in the body.

2.4 Name the types of carbohydrates and fats and describe their function in the body.

2.5 Identify food sources of carbohydrates and fats.

2.6 Describe cholesterol and identify its food sources.

2.7 Describe the makeup of proteins and their function in the body.

2.8 Identify food sources of proteins.

2.9 Describe the three major vegetarian diets.

2.10 List the functions of vitamins, minerals, and water in the body.

2.11 Identify food sources of vitamins, minerals, and water.

2.12 Explain what food additives are and how they function in food.

2.13 Explain the role of digestion in nutrition and health.

Section 2.2

2.14 List and describe techniques for food preparation that preserve nutrients.

2.15 Suggest ways to make menus and recipes more healthful.

2.16 Suggest healthful substitutes for high-fat items.

2.17 List and define recent developments in food production that may affect nutrition.

Chapter 3:
Cost Control
Section 3.1

3.1 Identify the types of costs incurred by a foodservice business and give examples of each.

3.2 Explain the purposes of a budget.

3.3 Explain the purpose of a profit-and-loss report.

3.4 Identify methods for analyzing profit-and-loss reports.

3.5 Explain the purpose of invoices in a foodservice business.

3.6 Identify tools to help control costs.

Section 3.2

3.7 Define and calculate food cost and food cost percentage.

Preface

Our objective with this program is simple yet significant:

Provide an industry-driven curriculum that prepares students for a career in restaurant and foodservice management.

To achieve that objective, *Foundations of Restaurant Management & Culinary Arts* was meticulously developed by the National Restaurant Association with input and contributions from countless representatives from both industry and education. That balanced perspective is important in helping students make the connection between classrooms and careers.

The visual tour that follows summarizes many of this textbook's most distinguishing and remarkable features. *Foundations of Restaurant Management & Culinary Arts,* Level 1 and Level 2, provide the following benefits:

- Comprehensive coverage of culinary and management topics

- An industry-infused approach

- Pedagogy that supports 21st Century Learning

- Relevant and timely topics from global cuisines to sustainability

- Content aligned to certificates and ProStart program opportunities

- Certificate opportunities that meet Carl Perkins funding requirements

- Supplements and technologies that help educators do more in less time

We offer a pedagogy that is fortified by 21st Century Learning themes and objectives:

- Critical thinking and problem solving

- Communication and collaboration

- Creativity and innovation

- Global awareness

- Health literacy

Thank you for considering *Foundations of Restaurant Management & Culinary Arts!*

Features of the Teacher's Wraparound Edition Include:

Chapter Overview–This includes summary information on the sections in each chapter. Teachers can use this material as an introduction to what students are about to learn.

Advance Preparation–A table is included on the opening page of each chapter, with suggestions for steps instructors may take to prepare for the class.

Customized Instruction Options–These list the pages where teachers can look for instructional materials customized for different levels of learning.

Chapter Tools–Directs teachers to activities that include 21st-Century Skills, Mathematics, Science, or Literacy.

ServSafe Connection–This points teachers to where this content is covered.

Focus and Engage–Introductory text helps teachers get the students introduced in what they are about to learn.

Introduce the Section–This includes a list of important facts covered in the chapter that can be used to introduce content to come.

Vocabulary Terms–Key terms and definitions introduced on the current page are supplied.

Discuss–These discussion topics relate directly and indirectly to the content on the current page.

Reinforce and Review–Topics covered in the previous section, or in previous chapters, that instructors may want to review before continuing are provided.

Teaching Tips–These items help explain the content and provide additional information for instructors to use in the classroom.

Customized Instruction Boxes–These include accommodations and additional activities for More Advanced, Less Advanced, ESOL, Special Needs, and At-Risk Students.

Figure Focus–Every figure in the student edition has a corresponding Figure Focus feature in the Teacher's Wraparound Edition, to provide additional information for discussion and instruction.

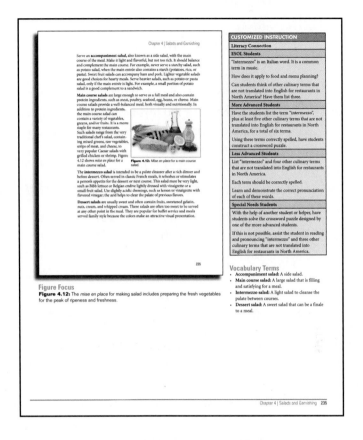

In-Class and Homework Activity Boxes–These original activities are not in the student edition textbook. They are designed to encourage students to use critical-thinking skill and to promote teamwork, cooperation, and leadership skills.

Feature Focuses–Every feature and box in the student edition has a corresponding feature in the Teacher's Wraparound Edition, to provide answers, discussion prompts, and additional teaching tips.

End-of-Section and Chapter Activities–Answers, additional teaching tips, discussion points, and supplemental activities relating to the end of chapter activities are provided.

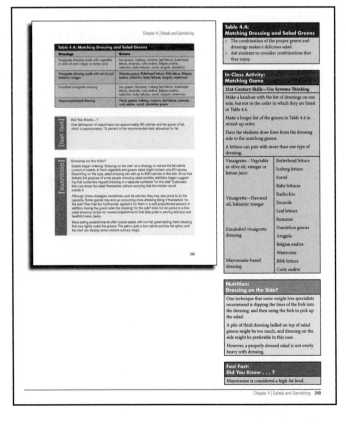

Supplements:

Activity Guide

The Activity Guide contains a wealth of additional lab and classroom activities to supplement the activities in the Student Edition. It includes critical-thinking activities that review and enhance the text learning, as well as hands-on application activities that give students more opportunities to experience the course content interactively. Separate books for Level 1 and Level 2.

Test Book with ExamView® Assessment Suite CD-ROM

The comprehensive test bank includes objective and short answer questions for both levels of the Student Text. Questions are provided in print format for duplication with separate answer keys, as well as on CD in ExamView® software for creating randomized and customized exams. Separate books for Level 1 and Level 2.

Teacher's Resource CD

A complete media CD supports the teaching package. It includes PowerPoint® presentations, videos, and interactive media for each chapter, as well as point-of-use teaching notes and tips, answers, and class/lab set-up information for the activities in the student Activity Guide. Separate CDs for Level 1 and Level 2.

CourseSmart Textbooks Online

The CourseSmart Textbooks Online enable students to access the textbook they use in class from home or anywhere with an Internet connection. CourseSmart eTextbooks give schools an affordable alternative to providing students with the essential learning resources they need to succeed. And, with a CourseSmart eTextbook, students can search the text, make notes online, print out reading assignments that incorporate lecture notes, and bookmark important passages for later review. For more information, visit www.coursesmart.com.

Additional Supplements

The Companion Web site includes student resources and additional activities such as crossword puzzles, essay questions, and self-grading quizzes. To access the Companion Web site, please visit http://www.pearsonhighered.com/nra. Recipe Cards are printed on laminated cards for durability and ease of use.

Acknowledgements

The development of Level 1 and Level 2 of *Foundations of Restaurant Management & Culinary Arts* would not have been possible without the expertise and guidance of our many advisors, contributors, and reviewers. We would like to thank the thousands of educators who have been involved in the ProStart program and given us invaluable support and feedback as they have taught the National Restaurant Association's curriculum. Additionally, we offer our thanks to the following individuals and organizations for their time, effort, and dedication in creating these first editions.

Curt Archambault
Jack in the Box, Inc.

Linda Bacin and the staff
of Bella Bacinos, Chicago, IL

Allen Bild
Hammond Area Career Center
Hammond, IN

Brian Bergquist
University of Wisconsin-Stout

Scott Brecher
Long Beach High School
Long Beach, NY

Barbara Jean Bruin
The Collins College of Hospitality Management

Nancy Caldarola
Concept Associates, Inc.

Jerald Chesser
The Collins College of Hospitality Management

Billie DeNunzio
Eastside High School
Gainesville, FL

Mary K. Drayer
Trotwood-Madison High School
Trotwood, OH

John A. Drysdale
Johnson County Community College, Emeritus

Therese Duffy
Warren High School
Downey, CA

Michael Edwards
EHOVE Career Center
Huron, OH

Annette Gabert
Ft. Bend ISD Technical Education Center
Sugar Land, TX

Elizabeth Hales
Compass Group North America

Abbie Hall
Lithia Springs High School
Douglasville, GA

Nancy Haney
Tri-County Regional Vocational High School
Medfield, MA

Lyle Hildahl
Washington Restaurant Association Education
Foundation

Tanya Hill
Golden Corral Corporation

Steven M. Hinnant, II
National Academy Foundation High School
Baltimore, MD

Nancy Iannacone
Capital Region BOCES Career and
Technical School
Schoharie, NY

Gary E. Jones
Walt Disney World

Mary June
Adams Twelve Five Star School District Magnet
Program
Thornton, CO

Betty Kaye
The Ohio State University

Thomas Kaltenecker
McHenry County College

Lauren Krzystofiak
Lake Park High School
Roselle, IL

Terri Kuebler
Eureka CUSD #140 High School
Goodfield, IL

Lettuce Entertain You Enterprises
and the staff of Wildfire, Chicago, IL

Michael Levin
Peabody Veterans Memorial High School
Peabody, MA

Paul Malcolm
Johnson & Wales University Charlotte

Edward Manville
Apex High School
Apex, NC

Victor Martinez
Hospitality Industry Education Foundation

Timothy Michitsch
Lorain County JVS
Oberlin, OH

Patricia A. Plavcan
Le Cordon Bleu College of Culinary Arts

Mark Molinaro
New England Culinary Institute

Scott Rudolph
The Collins College of Hospitality Management

Michael Santos
Micatrotto Restaurant Group

Greg Schaub
Aramark Corporation

Susan G. Seay
North Carolina Hospitality Education Foundation

Ed Sherwin
Sherwin Food Safety

Rudy Speckamp
Culinary Institute of America

John Stephens
Compass Group North America

Karl Titz
University of Houston

Laura Walsh
Walsh Nutrition Group, Inc.

Anthony Wietek
The Cooking and Hospitality Institute of Chicago

LaDeana Wentzel
Restaurant Association of Maryland Education
Foundation

Michael Yip
Tulsa Technology Center
Tulsa, OK

Michael Zema
Elgin Community College, Emeritus

Table of Contents

Guy "Guido" Fieri

Restaurateur, Celebrity Chef, Food Network Host

Johnny Garlic's California Italian Restaurants (3 locations), Tex Wasabi's Restaurant (2 locations), Knuckle Sandwich, LLC

Three years ago, I won the second season of The Next Food Network Star. Today, as the "Bad Boy" of the Food Network, I host three popular shows—*Guy's Big Bite*; *Ultimate Recipe Showdown*; and *Diners, Drive-Ins, and Dives*.

The Story Behind the Man

I actively chose this career. I started cooking at about ten. In my house, the rule was that "whoever cooks makes the decision (on what to have)…" I was such a pest that mom made a rule that you couldn't ask "what's for dinner" until after lunch.

I began my love affair with food at the age of ten, selling soft pretzels from a three-wheeled bicycle cart I built with my father. I named the cart "The Awesome Pretzel." Through selling pretzels and washing dishes, I earned enough money in six years to study abroad as an exchange student in Chantilly, France. While there, I gained a true appreciation not only for international cuisine, but the culture and lifestyle associated with it. I also realized that if you go to the point of origin and eat a food there, that's where you get the best experience. So, for example, go to France to have a baguette, go to Philly to have a cheesesteak.

I learned the way I recommend everyone should learn…you need to try lots of things, even if you aren't crazy about them. I'd rather have ten two-bite meals than one big one.

After graduating from the University of Nevada-Las Vegas with a bachelor's degree in hospitality management, I went to work for Stouffers, managing its flagship restaurant in Long

Beach, California. After three years, I became district manager of Louise's Trattoria, overseeing six restaurants and responsible for recruiting and training for the growing chain.

In 1996, my business partner Steve Gruber and I opened Johnny Garlic's, an Italian restaurant in Santa Rosa. We soon had two more sites for that concept, and then moved on to develop Tex Wasabi's, a Southern BBQ and California sushi restaurant. (See what I mean about trying things?)

Although he is busy with so many enterprises, Guy believes in using his celebrity to help others. In the fall of 2007, the Navy flew him to the Persian Gulf to entertain and cook for the troops.

Keys to Success

I believe that to succeed in this industry you need to take calculated risks. You can't be hesitant to try things. Food is the common denominator of all people from all walks of life. So experience everything…eat everything you can. Listen to anybody that cooks. Challenge yourself to enjoy food that is not normal to you. Try everything! And then "Own it! ……Do you own it?"

In all aspects of this industry, food is an emotional experience… whether you're in the kitchen or out in front, on the restaurant floor or the management floor. And we all need to understand it.

We've skipped a few generations of food at home…ever since the advent of the two-person working family in the 1970s. We're not learning pass-downs from grandma and mom anymore. Instead, we've moved to home replacement meals. There's been a huge influx of midmarket family restaurants.

We're also wising up. We eat for different reasons….palate and health. But we all want better food. Remember, we are what we eat, and we're moving back to basics. That will be the focus of the industry in years to come.

It's a smarter chef's game. We need to be creative; we need to take risks. But we also have to be supremely aware of food safety and cost management.

So, to be successful, experiment and apply. Study hard and use this program. If you want a broad awareness of food, this is your program. If you want to be a professional, this is where you start. If you want to be a legend, this is a great foundation.

Guy Fieri

Chapter 1 Overview

Chapter 1 presents dairy products and eggs; breakfast food and drinks; and sandwiches.

Section 1: This section reviews milk and milk products, cream, butter and butter substitutes, cheese, and eggs.

Section 2: This section covers pancakes, waffles, crêpes, and French toast; preparing breakfast meats and starches; hot breakfast beverages; and matching sauces to foods.

Section 3: This section covers the types of sandwiches, primary sandwich components, and sandwich stations.

Advance Preparation	
Review	Sections 1.1–1.3
	Level 1, Chapter 2: Food Safety
Contact	Grocer, deli, or cheese shop
	Computer lab
	Bakery or bread company
Prepare	Eggs for students to cook
	Soft ball or beanbag
	Reference book, software, or Web site for caloric values of common foods (USDA Web site offers this)
	Ingredients for the recipes at the end of the chapter, or other recipes you choose

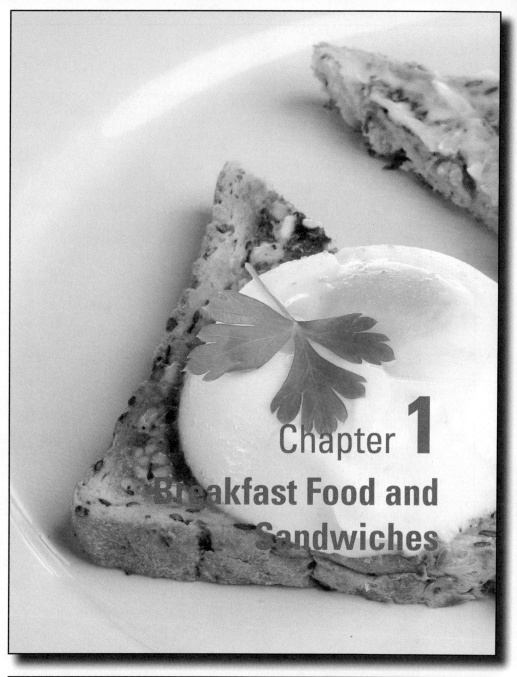

Chapter 1
Breakfast Food and Sandwiches

CUSTOMIZED INSTRUCTION OPTIONS

Less Advanced Students	More Advanced Students	ESOL Students	Special Needs Students
Page 16	Page 16	Page 16	Page 16

CHAPTER TOOLS

21st-Century Skills	Mathematics	Science	Literacy
Pages 3, 17, 19, 34, 40, 44, 58, 59, 60, 64	Pages 40, 59, 60	Pages 19, 59, 64	Pages 3, 17, 44

ServSafe Connection

Pages 7, 15, 19, 44, 47, 56, 59

Case Study *Following a Hunch for Brunch*

Having recently expanded Kabob's service to include weekday lunch with profitable results, Miguel wants to try opening up for weekend brunch as well. But Chef Kate is skeptical of the idea. The two of them have been exchanging ideas on the issue for the past few weeks.

Miguel feels that opening up for brunch would further increase their visibility in the neighborhood. It would allow them to showcase another elegant variation on their already successful lunch and dinner menus, and would help them gain exposure with people who may not yet know about Kabob. In addition, the cost of breakfast food, such as eggs and pancakes, typically comes with a higher margin of profit. Miguel sees all potential and very little risk involved in giving this a try.

Chef Kate, on the other hand, isn't as comfortable with the idea of serving breakfast foods. It's been years since she's focused on that kind of service, and she's concerned about the product she'll be able to put out. She doesn't want the reputation of the restaurant to be tarnished with a substandard brunch service. And, since a traditional brunch menu offers a very broad range of items, from eggs to sandwiches to steaks, timing would be crucial. Can she comfortably put together a menu to meet all of these concerns and demands?

Chef Kate also is concerned about start-up and service costs. Would they need to hire a brunch chef? Would table-service specs need to be revised for the front of the house? Would this require new waitstaff training or hiring? Would they need to buy new table setups to fit the brunch atmosphere? Chef Kate is seeing much more risk than potential benefit to this endeavor.

As you read this chapter, think about the following questions:

1. How might you balance Miguel's enthusiasm with Chef Kate's concerns? How could you make this endeavor work so that everyone was happy?

2. What would your biggest concerns be in starting up a brunch service?

Case Study
Following a Hunch for Brunch

- Miguel sees the potential to increase revenue by offering weekend brunch.
- Chef Kate understands the complicated logistics, which are the realities of serving brunch.
- The logistics will have an impact on the profitability of the tactic.
- Note that there are follow-up questions about the case study at the end of the chapter.
- This activity could be done in groups, as a class, or as a homework assignment.

In-Class Activity: KWL Chart

Literacy Connection, 21st-Century Skills—Be Self-Directed Learners

Students might feel that there is not much to learn about breakfast foods and sandwiches.

Most students have had some experience with these topics, and they might seem straightforward.

However, the students might have a few questions that arise as they consider the various aspects of the case study and their own experiences.

Have the students fold a piece of paper in thirds, lengthwise, making three columns. Label the columns, from left to right, "Know," "Want to Know," and "Learned."

In the Know column, have the students list all the facts they feel confident about concerning breakfast foods and sandwiches. In the Want to Know column, have the students list all the questions they have concerning this topic.

At the end of the chapter, after the students have learned the material, have them fill in the Learned column. They will write the answers to their questions. They will also write the facts they learned that are new, plus any facts that were mistaken from the Know column that are now correct.

Perhaps students will be surprised at how much new information they learned.

Discuss these results as a class.

Students can keep this chart in their notebooks for later review.

Professional Profile

Discuss	Chef Nims encourages experience and training. Discuss the importance of both. Do any of the students work in the restaurant and foodservice industry, or have they?
Reinforce and Review	Chef Nims has a creative take on Eggs Benedict. Are the students familiar with Eggs Benedict? Many will be: toasted English muffin half, Canadian bacon slice, and a poached egg, topped with hollandaise sauce.
	Are the students familiar with a grilled Reuben sandwich? How does it differ from a regular corned beef sandwich? Perhaps the students are aware that a Reuben is corned beef, Swiss cheese, and sauerkraut on rye bread, grilled.
Teaching Tips	Do not assume that all the students have experience with even classic cuisine.
	Be sure that the students can express their need to learn in a nonthreatening atmosphere.

[professional profile]

Morgan L. Nims

Chef Instructor
Le Cordon Bleu College of Culinary Art, Miramar, Florida

I have always loved to cook. To be able to make a living at what you love is magical!

I graduated magna cum laude with a bachelor's degree in culinary arts from Johnson & Wales University in Providence, Rhode Island. Additionally, I studied classical French cuisine at the École Supérieure De Cuisine De Françoise in Paris, France. I've won both gold and silver medals in the American Culinary Federation Hot Food Competitions and was also a participant in the 2000 World Culinary Olympics held in Erfurt, Germany.

Specializing in International Cuisine, I believe in using the freshest ingredients to perform your best artwork. You should cook to impress and season to leave an impression. Make sure you know the regional and ethnic culinary flavors of the area in which you work and live.

I worked for five years for the Walt Disney World Resort restaurants, including the Biergarten Restaurant, The Coral Reef, Epcot Events, Germany Pavilion, and the African Outpost . . . a really wide range of flavors and dishes.

Here I found out that there's always time for fun. For instance, each year at Walt Disney World, we had a food and wine festival. One year, when working at the Biergarten, I was bringing food out to the tented area used for the festival. This included a new wheel of Raclette cheese, which usually weighs about 13 pounds. This cheese wheel was large, and here I was, carrying it out on my shoulder. A young man—a resort guest—was looking at me quizzically. So, I smiled and said: "This is Mickey's lunch. Gotta' run!"

By the way, most recently, Chef Morgan was the personal chef for Shaquille "Shaq" O'Neal when he played with the Miami Heat. She has created many dishes for the Heat star and has traveled with him extensively.

On a more serious note, however, it was during this experience in Walt Disney World that I found my passion for foods of the sea and preparing them in their ethnic tradition. My classical training provided a wonderful base to create my signature fusion of flavors.

For those of you interested in entering this field, I say that the combination of education and experience is priceless. We must continually reinvent ourselves in order to contribute excellence to our craft.

4

Remember:

❝ *Always cook from your heart.* **❞**

About Breakfast Food and Sandwiches

My favorite breakfast dish is Classic Eggs Benedict: I am a classic chef and this dish mirrors perfection and versatility. It takes talent and skill to perfect the hollandaise that finishes the dish. This dish also is very versatile. You can make lots of different Benedicts—lobster, smoked salmon, even spinach for vegetarians.

There's an interesting story here, though. Originally, I actually didn't like Eggs Benedict. I kept thinking "eggs and eggs?" (Chef Morgan is referring to the eggs in the hollandaise sauce.) But once I actually started making the sauce—the delicacy of it, the blends of flavors—it was gorgeous! So, now I have "palate respect" for this wonderful dish. And since I love seafood as well, I've leaned toward things like Lobster Benedict with shrimp in the sauce. The sweetness of the lobster paired with the lemon zing of the sauce . . . wonderful!

My favorite sandwich is the Grilled Reuben sandwich: Once again, it's a classic dish. But this time, it is the flavor profile—the mix of ingredients—that appeals to me. When in high school in Detroit, Michigan, I remember going out to get a corned beef sandwich piled five inches high with corned beef. So, this is like coming home.

1.1 Dairy Products and Eggs	1.2 Breakfast Foods and Drinks	1.3 Sandwiches
• Milk and milk products	• Pancakes, waffles, crêpes, and French toast	• Basic kinds of sandwiches
• Receiving and storing milk		• Primary sandwich components: bread, spread, and filling
• Creams	• Preparing breakfasts meat and starches	• Sandwich stations
• Butter and butter substitutes	• Hot breakfast beverages: coffee, tea, and cocoa	
• Cheese		
• Eggs		

SECTION 1.1 DAIRY PRODUCTS AND EGGS

Do you think that you know everything you need to know about eggs and dairy products, such as milk, cream, butter, and cheese? Do you recall the slogan, "It's not just for breakfast anymore?" Well, that's true. These products are actually the basis of almost every meal.

5

Focus and Engage

Discuss
- The information in this section is visual and hands-on.
- The emphasis is "how-to" for useful culinary skills.

Section 1.1
Dairy Products and Eggs

Introduce the Section
a. This section will specifically teach techniques for cooking eggs.
b. The students will learn about dairy processes that affect culinary decisions.

Vocabulary Review
a. Direct students to the key terms.
b. Pronounce each word, and have the students repeat the pronunciation aloud.
c. Discuss the definition of each word.

Teach

Discuss
- Ask the students collectively if they eat breakfast before school.
- Breakfast is essential to good health and well-being. It should be part of a daily routine.

Discuss

- Not too many people die of undulant fever (Brucellosis) in the United States today because dairy products are pasteurized.

- Although undulant fever is no longer a threat due to the advances in food science and food safety, if pasteurization practices were abandoned, the disease could become a threat again.

- Homogenization is not done for safety, but for convenience and mouthfeel.

Vocabulary Terms

- **Pasteurization:** Heat processing to kill microbes.

- **Homogenization:** Blending fat uniformly throughout milk.

Study Questions

After studying Section 1.1, you should be able to answer the following questions:

- What are the basic differences between milk, cream, and butter?

- What is the proper procedure for handling and storing milk and milk products?

- What are the basic parts of cheese, and what are the primary kinds of cheese?

- What are the various grades and sizes of eggs?

- What are the different ways to cook an egg?

Milk and Milk Products

Some milk is available in raw form, but most milk products are processed to remove harmful bacteria that could make people sick. Two processes applied to milk products are **pasteurization** (pass-cher-i-ZAY-shun) and **homogenization** (huh-MAH-juh-ni-ZAY-shun):

- **Pasteurization**: Milk is heated to kill microorganisms that cause spoilage and disease without affecting its nutritional value.

- **Homogenization**: Milk is strained through very fine holes to break down fat and then is blended into one fluid.

6

[ServSafe Connection]

The Pasteurization Process

Dairies use basically two methods of pasteurization today: batch and continuous flow. In the batch process, a large quantity of milk is held in a large heated vat at 149°F for 30 minutes and then cooled quickly to about 39°F. In the continuous flow, or HTST (High Temperature, Short Time) method, milk is forced through small pipes that are heated on the outside by hot water. While flowing through the pipes, the milk is heated to 161°F for at least 16 seconds. It then gets cooled down gradually until it is chilled and stored at 39°F. Most milk in the United States is pasteurized using the continuous flow method. Figure 1.1 shows this process.

Pasteurization kills most, if not all, of the disease-causing bacteria that can be found in raw milk. The pasteurization process makes milk and milk products safer for human consumption. The process also increases the length of time the milk is acceptable for use. Pasteurized milk can be shelved for up to 16 days.

Figure 1.1: The process of pasteurization was named after its developer Louis Pasteur.

The type of milk utilized is often based on the nutritional value. For example, lactose-intolerant customers may want lactose-reduced or lactose-free milk. While some people call lactose intolerance a milk allergy, that is not an entirely accurate description. This common condition is digestive and is a reaction to many cultured dairy products, not just milk. While lactose intolerance is sometimes called a milk allergy, it is not one. A casein allergy is a true protein-sensitive allergy and all dairy foods must be avoided. Dairy alternatives, such as soy milk and rice milk, can be used instead. Table 1.1 on the following page shows a variety of different types of milk.

7

ServSafe Connection: The Pasteurization Process

Sophisticated and complex dairy machinery can handle very large quantities of milk.

Discuss

- Lactose is the sugar found in milk.

- Lactose intolerance is often a genetic condition.

- Casein allergy is unrelated to lactose intolerance. It is an allergy triggered by a milk protein called casein.

Figure Focus

Figure 1.1: A pasteurization machinery line this efficient and intricate would probably have been beyond Louis Pasteur's imagination in the 1860s.

Table 1.1: Types of Milk

- Some fat-free milks have additional milk solids added.

- Some fat-free milks are modified with texturizing agent to more closely match the mouthfeel of milk with butterfat.

- If milk is not homog enized, the fat will float to the top as cream, and the remaining milk will be low in fat.

- Fat-free milk is sometimes called skim milk because it was the milk that remained after all the cream was skimmed off the top of nonhomogenized milk.

- Buttermilk is a fermented product that lactose-intolerant people can use.

- Evaporated milk was used for homemade infant formula before commercial formulas were developed.

- Condensed milk is often marketed as "sweetened condensed milk."

- UHT milk has a distinctive flavor that not everyone appreciates.

- Reconstituted powdered milk must be carefully mixed to avoid lumps.

- Lactose-free milk is often called "acidophilus milk."

- The mineral calcium needs to be added to soy milk to make it a nutritional substitute for fresh milk.

Table 1.1: Types of Milk

Type of Milk	Fat Content	Notes
Whole	At least 3.25%	
Low fat	Available in 1% and 2%	
Skim	Less than 0.5% (usually 0.1%)	
Buttermilk	Depends on the type of fresh milk used	Made from fresh liquid milk that has bacteria added to it to create a sour taste Doesn't actually contain butter Has a rich, thick texture and tangy acid taste that is valued in baking and the preparation of many items, such as salad dressings
Evaporated	At least 6.5%	Made from milk by removing 60% of the water Has a slight cooked flavor from its canning process Usually used in baking; helps bring richness without excess moisture
Condensed	At least 8.5%	Tastes richer and sweeter than evaporated milk Made from whole milk by removing 60% of the water and then sweetening with sugar Used in specialty baking when richness and sweetness are desired Cannot replace evaporated or other milk products unless the recipe's sugar content and fat content are adjusted
UHT (ultra-high temperature)	Depends on the type of fresh milk used	Processed with high heat, cooled, and then packaged in a sterile environment to avoid contamination Doesn't need refrigeration Has a shelf life of 9 months
Powdered	Depends on the type of fresh milk used	Usually made from whole or skim milk Made from milk by removing all of the water Can improve the reconstituted flavor by serving the milk very cold Often used in baking
Lactose-free milk	Depends on the type of fresh milk used	Made by adding enzymes to milk to break down the lactose
Soy milk (nondairy)	Four grams of fat per eight-ounce serving (fortified)	Often fortified with vitamins (including calcium, and perhaps vitamin D and riboflavin) and offered in low-fat forms Has a slightly nutty flavor with a rich texture Is available in different flavors Good source of protein; has no cholesterol

(continued)

8

Table 1.1: Types of Milk continued

Type of Milk	Fat Content	Note
Rice milk (nondairy)	Three grams or less per eight-ounce serving	Often fortified with vitamins (check for the addition of calcium, vitamin D, and riboflavin)
		Usually made with water, brown rice syrup, starch, and other thickeners
		Has a sweet flavor and a thin texture
		Is available in different flavors
		Has less protein than milk or soy milk

It's also important to recognize that low-fat and skim milks behave differently in cooking than whole milk does. Fat brings flavor, body, and mouthfeel to a dish. If a chef reduces the fat in the milk, the ingredient will perform differently in the recipe.

[nutrition]

Lactose Intolerance

People who are lactose intolerant can't easily digest lactose, which is a natural sugar found in milk and dairy products. Undigested lactose moving through the body can cause uncomfortable symptoms such as gas, bloating, nausea, diarrhea, or stomach pain.

Some people who are lactose intolerant can't digest any lactose at all. Others who are lactose intolerant can digest small amounts. While lactose intolerance is not life threatening, it can cause quite a bit of distress for those who suffer from it. A big challenge for those who suffer from lactose intolerance is finding foods that can be digested easily while still providing a full range of proper nutrients in their diets.

Soy and rice milk are great alternatives to milk for people who are lactose intolerant. If fortified with calcium, they provide many essential vitamins and nutrients, while also avoiding the higher fat and cholesterol content found in whole dairy products. It is a good strategy to use lactose-free dairy products, including cheese, Swiss cheese, and yogurt, rather than turning away from dairy foods completely.

To further supplement the calcium found in dairy products, menu planners should keep in mind other calcium-rich foods, including kale, canned fish (such as tuna and salmon), and chickpeas. Note though, that while these foods have a higher-than-normal calcium content, they are not calcium rich when compared to dairy.

Table 1.1 (cont.)

- Like soy milk, rice milk needs calcium to be a nutritional substitute for fresh milk. Soy milk provides protein, but rice milk does not provide much of it, so rice milk also needs added protein to be a good substitute. If someone has a casein allergy, he or she should make sure that the protein added to rice milk is not casein.

Discuss

- Ask, "If you drink milk, can you tell the difference between whole milk and skim without seeing the label?"

- If the students respond positively, ask them how they can tell.

- They are probably referring to mouthfeel.

- The mouth can perceive a slight difference in viscosity (thickness of flow) between the two types.

- There is a subtle difference in aroma from butterfat in whole milk as well.

Nutrition: Lactose Intolerance

Only fermented dairy products are lactose free.

Nondairy calcium sources include dark green, leafy vegetables that are gently cooked and fish canned with the bones (such as sardines).

9

Vocabulary Terms

- **Cream:** The high-fat fraction of milk before homogenization, usually skimmed from the top and processed separately.

Receiving and Storing Milk

Milk products should be received at 41°F or lower unless otherwise specified by regulatory requirement. (Some areas may require a different receiving temperature.) All milk and milk products should be labeled "Grade A." This means that the product meets standards for quality and safety set by the FDA and the U.S. Public Health Service. Milk should have a sweetish flavor. It should be rejected if it is too sweet or if it has a sour, bitter, or moldy taste.

Milk products should be stored at 41°F or lower. Always use the FIFO (first in, first out) method of stock rotation for milk. With the FIFO method, foodhandlers store products to ensure that the older products are used first. For example, they place products with an earlier use-by or expiration date in front of products with later dates. Any milk that has passed its use-by or expiration date should be thrown away (see Figure 1.2).

Figure 1.2: The first in, first out (FIFO) food rotation method ensures serving safe food and eliminates spoiled food waste.

Creams

Cream contains far more fat than milk. Chefs use it based primarily on its fat content, which provides richness. Creams with more than 30 percent fat are stable when whipped. They add elegance and flavor to many desserts. The heavy creams also bring richness and a silky texture to sauces and dressings. Table 1.2 on the following page shows the common types of cream.

10

Figure Focus

Figure 1.2: Even with a FIFO system, it is important to pay careful attention to expiration dates.

Table 1.2: Types of Cream

Type of Cream	Amount of Fat	Notes
Light whipping cream	About 30%	
Heavy whipping cream	36 to 38%	
Very heavy whipping cream	40%	Produces a greater yield and a longer shelf life for the products made with it
Light cream	18 to 30%	Sometimes called coffee cream
Half-and-half	10.5 to 18%	One part milk/one part cream; technically half-and-half doesn't have enough fat in it to be called cream
Sour cream	At least 18%	Tangy flavor and thick texture due to the culturing the cream receives

Butter and Butter Substitutes

Different types of butter are chosen based on their flavor and consistency. The best grades of butter are either Grade AA or Grade A. Butter is most commonly used to add flavor, richness, or smoothness to a dish.

Butter is made by mixing cream containing between 30 percent and 45 percent milkfat at a high speed. The finished butter must contain at least 80 percent butterfat content. The remaining 20 percent of the butter is milk solids and water:

- Sweet butter is butter made only from pasteurized fresh cream. It is typically pale yellow and may be salted or unsalted.

- Cultured butter (European butter) is made from fermented cream and has a higher butterfat content and lower salt content than regular butter.

While butter has traditionally been produced in sticks or blocks, spreadable butter and whipped butter are now available. Both have been chemically formulated to spread more easily.

Table 1.2: Types of Cream

- "Culturing" means adding bacteria to ferment the lactose. This gives a tangy flavor to sour cream, yogurt, and buttermilk.

Discuss

- Ask the students if they can taste the difference between butter and margarine.

- Have the students read and compare the labels of butter, whipped butter, and spreadable butter.

11

Discuss

- Butter's appealing flavor comes from milk fat and milk solids.

- Margarine does not contain milk fat, so it has a different flavor.

- Some margarine has milk solids or even some butterfat added for flavor, but then it is no longer true margarine.

- Margarine and butter have the same amount of fat and calories.

- The fat in margarine might be more heart-healthy than the fat in butter.

- Butter is usually more expensive than margarine.

Vocabulary Terms

- **Clarified:** To make butter or fat clear by gently heating it and removing any impurities.

- **Smoke point:** The temperature at which the decomposition products of frying oils become visible as bluish smoke.

- **Butter substitute:** Any of a variety of alternate ingredients that can be used instead of oil or butter in the preparation of foods, such as fruit oils, nut oils, vegetable oils, and oils from grains. These products are available as reduced fat, no fat, and in different forms such as spreadable and liquid oils.

- **Margarine:** A butter substitute often consisting of a blend of hydrogenated vegetable oils mixed with emulsifiers, vitamins, coloring matter, and other ingredients.

[fast fact]

Did You Know...?

European-style butter is low in moisture and high in butterfat. Plugrá (ploo-gra) is one example of this type of butter. While regular butter is 80 percent butterfat and 20 percent water and milk solids, Plugrá is 82 percent butterfat. It is slow-churned, which helps to create a creamy texture.

European-style butter is preferred by bakers because the lower water content results in flakier pie crusts and crisper cookies. Chefs sometimes use this type of butter to add a rich texture to food. For example, you can make Alfredo sauce without using cream if you use a European-style butter and *Parmigiano-Reggiano* cheese.

Butter is available salted or unsalted. Most commercially sold butter is lightly salted. Manufacturers add salt to butter as a preservative and sometimes to enhance flavor, but butter should contain no more than 2 percent salt. Chefs often use unsalted butter in desserts and some cooking, because it gives them more precise control over the amount of salt in a dish.

Butter is good for cooking because it adds color and flavor to food. Butter for cooking is often **clarified**, which means either the chef or the manufacturer has heated it and removed the milk solids and water. Clarified butter is better for many cooking processes because the milk solids in whole, or unclarified, butter burn easily (the point at which an oil or fat begins to burn is called the **smoke point**). Clarified butter has a higher smoke point, which makes it less likely to burn when heated.

A **butter substitute** is any alternative used to replace butter in a recipe. Examples include margarine, olive oils, and soy-based oils, which are all used to avoid cholesterol but not fat. (Some of these alternatives are more heart healthy than butter, but still flavorful.) Additionally, rice-based oils have less fat content and less cholesterol.

Margarine is one of the most common butter substitutes, but it is a manufactured food product that often contains no milk products. Margarine is made of vegetable oils and animal fats with added flavoring, emulsifiers, colors, preservatives, and vitamins. Contrary to what many people believe, margarine is not much lower in fat than butter. At least 80 percent of margarine's calories must come from fat. Solid margarine is the most popular form. Liquid margarine is often used in sautéing and grilling. One benefit of margarine is that it usually has a higher smoke point than butter.

12

[fast fact]

Did You Know...?

Margarine was first made in France in 1870. French chemist Hippolyte Mège-Mouriés invented oleomargarine for Emperor Louis Napoleon III. The emperor was looking for a suitable substitute for butter for use by his military.

[nutrition]

Trans Fat

It's hard to talk about margarine without thinking of trans fats. When margarine was first created, it had a significant amount of trans fats because of the hydrogenation process—the process used to solidify liquid vegetable oil into a spread. These fats are created when manufacturers hydrogenate (that is, combine with, treat with, or expose to the action of, hydrogen) liquid oils to make the oils solid so that they have longer shelf lives. Research has shown trans fats to raise LDL ("bad" cholesterol) and lower HDL ("good" cholesterol). This combination can increase the risk of heart disease.

Both butter and margarine must be stored in tightly sealed containers to prevent them from absorbing the flavors of other foods.

Essential Skills
Clarifying Butter

❶ To make 1 cup of clarified butter, put 1¼ cups of butter in a saucepan over very low heat.

❷ The butter will slowly melt into three separate layers—water and milk solids sink to the bottom; liquid butterfat in the middle; and foam on top. Do not stir butter as it melts.

❸ Skim foam off the top. See Figure 1.3a on the following page.

❹ Remove the saucepan from the heat to let the butter cool a bit. This will allow any remaining milk solids to sink to the bottom.

❺ Slowly and carefully pour the butterfat into a separate container, being very careful to not let the water or milk solids slip out of the bottom and into the butterfat container.

13

**Fast Fact:
Did You Know . . . ?**

Many food science innovations have come from military pursuits, including canned food, margarine (both for the French military), and even instant orange breakfast drink (from NASA).

**Nutrition:
Trans Fat**

Trans fats have become an increased problem in the years since manufacturers have replaced saturated animal fats in food processing and cooking operations with hydrogenated vegetable fats.

**Essential Skills:
Clarifying Butter**

The product that remains after clarifying butter is pure butterfat. When melted, it is clear.

Discuss

- Many cheeses are begun by curdling milk with an enzyme called rennet. The whey remains unfermented.

- Other cheeses are begun by curdling milk by friendly bacterial fermentation, which makes the whey sour.

Vocabulary Terms

- **Parmigiano:** A hard cheese made near Parma and other places in Italy, sometimes called Parmigiano-Reggiano, sometimes called Parmesan.

- **Curdling:** Enzyme or bacterial separation of milk proteins (curds) from liquid, other protein, and carbohydrate fractions (whey).

❻ Alternatively, you can try to ladle the butterfat from the saucepan and into a separate container. See Figure 1.3b.

Figure 1.3a: Step 3—Skim the foam off the top.

Figure 1.3b: Step 6—Ladle the butterfat from the saucepan into a separate container.

Cheese

All cheeses have three basic parts: water, fat, and protein. The amounts vary depending on the type of cheese, several varieties of which are shown in Figure 1.4. For example, cottage cheese can have up to 80 percent water and little fat. On the other hand, a hard cheese like **Parmigiano** (pahr-*muh*-ZHAH-*noh*) might have as little as 30 percent water but a high percentage of fat.

Dairies make cheese by separating a milk's solids from its liquid in a process called **curdling**. The proteins, or curds, that form are then usually processed in some way to make a particular type of cheese. Some are then ripened. Because curdling separates the solids from the lactose portion of milk, lactose-intolerant people can eat ripened cheese. Cheese is rich in calcium. There is a wide variety of processing techniques, ripening methods, and types of milk used to make cheese.

Figure 1.4: There are many types of cheese.

14

Figure Focus

Figure 1.3a: The foam contains the nonfat fraction.

Figure 1.3b: The butterfat will be clear when melted, but will not remain liquid when chilled. It will return to a solid because butterfat is a saturated fat.

Figure 1.4: Each type of cheese has a distinctive flavor, yet each ones starts with milk or cream. If possible, have a cheese tasting in class.

Receiving Cheese

When inspecting cheese for receiving, make sure it has a uniform color and the typical flavor and texture for the cheese. Also, if it has a rind, be sure that the rind is clean and unbroken.

The types of milk used in cheese include the following:

• Cow

• Goat

• Sheep

[fast fact]

Did You Know...?

A tour through the heartland of America, whether it's dairy country, Amish country, or both, can be a great restaurant experience. One special treat is cottage cheese, freshly made on-site.

Cottage cheese, historically, was cheese made in the cottage, at home. It is not a complicated process to make the dry curds of cottage cheese. It involves gently heating and holding milk, and then adding a small amount of culture starter. After the curds form, they are strained and separated. A very small amount of whey tends to remain. Traditionally, the dry curds are then mixed with fresh, thick, sweet cream to create the final dish.

Some establishments purchase just the dry curds from a dairy processor, and mix them with cream before serving. New cream cottage cheese has a fresher and more delicate flavor than commercial cottage cheese. It can be served alone, with salt and pepper and tomatoes, or with fruit.

Cheese can be **unripened** or **ripened**. Unripened, or fresh, cheeses include cream cheese and cottage cheese. Some cheeses are ripened by external bacteria put into curds (Brie, bleu, Roquefort, Camembert). Others are ripened by bacteria naturally in the curds (Swiss, Havarti). The variety of cheese ranges from mild to sharp to pungent (very sharp). Table 1.3 on the following page provides a comparison of a variety of cheeses.

15

ServSafe Connection: Receiving Cheese

Cheese is not "spoiled" unless it is rotten.

Rotten cheese grows microorganisms that are not desirable or typical of the variety of cheese.

Friendly microorganisms are often part of the manufacturing process for cheese.

Fast Fact: Did You Know . . . ?

The cream that holds the curds together is fresh, not fermented.

Creamed cottage cheese is actually a cheese "dish" made of cheese, salt, and a cream or milk liquid.

Discuss

• Each type of cheese has a flavor and texture that is unique.

• Bacterial cultures usually are responsible for the particular characteristics of a cheese.

• Cultures might grow best in certain locales, which is why certain cheeses are made only in certain regions.

• Other cheeses could be made elsewhere, but the cultures are carefully guarded as trade secrets.

Vocabulary Terms

• **Unripened cheese:** Fresh cheeses that are not aged, and can be made with bacteria, rennet, or both.

• **Ripened cheese:** Cheeses that are aged or ripened by bacteria.

Table 1.3:
Varieties of Cheese

- Cheese varieties are exciting to taste. If possible, bring in a variety of cheeses for students to sample.

Fast Fact:
Did You Know . . . ?

Edam is coated with red wax.

Gouda may be coated with red or yellow wax.

These are traditions from The Netherlands, where these cheeses are made.

The wax protects the cheese from drying out.

Vocabulary Terms

Processed cheese: A cheese product with noncheese ingredients.

Homework Activity:
Becoming Cheese-Savvy

CUSTOMIZED INSTRUCTION

Special Needs Students

Tailor the activity to suit the students' limitations. For students with learning differences, have them be "cheese critics."

Students will taste five different types of common cheeses (cheddar, Swiss, Colby, Monterey Jack, etc.) and describe the flavor of each.

The descriptions can be verbal, written, sign language, or whatever is the most helpful for the students.

Descriptors might include words like "salty," "robust," "mild," "biting," "tangy," "nutty," etc. Students might have other descriptors that suit the project.

Less Advanced Students

The students will make a very simple cheese, beginning the process with milk, rennet, and salt. The resulting cheese will be a fresh cheese that is strained in cheesecloth.

Encourage the students to research and choose a recipe for a fresh homemade cheese. This project is not done in class, but at home. It can be done alone or in study groups. As part of the homework, the students should taste the cheese and describe the result.

The students can bring in a sample for documentation, but the teacher does not need to taste the cheese because it might not have been under correct temperature controls in transport.

Table 1.3: Varieties of Cheese

Type of Ripening	Characteristics	Examples
Unripened, fresh	Soft and white Should be eaten soon after purchase	Cottage cheese Cream cheese Ricotta
Soft-ripened	Ripened from the outside (or rind) into the center Rinds are powdery white or golden orange Can be semisoft to creamy in texture Mold and bacterial cultures provide flavor, body, and texture	Brie Camembert
Semisoft, ripened	Mild cheeses, some with buttery flavor Smooth, sliceable texture Ripen outward from the interior and sometimes ripen from the surface	Gouda Munster
Blue-veined, mold-ripened	Mold is injected or sprayed into the cheese to spread throughout it while it ages (typically blue or green) Creamy texture and a somewhat strong flavor	Maytag Blue Gorgonzola Roquefort
Firm, ripened	Bacterial cultures help to ripen the cheese, and curing usually takes a long time Firm texture Mild to sharp flavor, depending on how long it's been aged	Cheddar Gruyère Emmenthal
Very hard, ripened	Ripened with bacterial culture and enzymes Very slow process (at least 2 years in most cases) Hard and dry texture; good for grating	Asiago Parmigiano-Reggiano Pecorino Romano

[fast fact]

Did You Know...?
Other than cheese rinds made from cloth or wax, such as those found on Edam or Gouda, all naturally formed cheese rinds are completely edible.

Manufacturers make **processed cheese** by grinding, blending, and forming one or more natural cheeses. Emulsifiers help to make the product uniform. It's also pasteurized to prevent it from aging. It can have many flavors, including port wine, herbed, and plain processed (such as American). The taste is usually mild compared to aged cheese.

16

ESOL Students

ESOL students can do either of the activities listed at left.

Another option would be to have ESOL students introduce a cheese or cheese dish from his or her native culture to the class.

The teacher's discretion should be used as to whether or not ESOL students like to be featured for their native culture or would rather learn the local culture.

More Advanced Students

Students should research the number of cheese varieties produced in France.

Why is France known for its cheese industry?

Are there characteristics that make French cheese superior to other cheeses?

Have students learn the names and characteristics of five new cheeses they have not yet tasted.

If possible, in cooperation with a local grocer or deli, have the students taste these five cheeses and describe them.

Help the special needs students present their findings to the class at the same time the more advanced students present their findings.

Essential Skills
Considerations in Storing Cheese

❶ Wrap cheese in waxed or parchment paper so cheese can still breathe without drying out. New wrapping should be used each time a cheese is rewrapped. See Figure 1.5.

❷ Optimal temperature for storing cheese is 35°F to 45°F at a high humidity level, which typically means toward the bottom of the refrigeration system.

❸ Double wrap pungent cheeses, such as bleu cheeses, so the aroma doesn't permeate other foods, and so other food aromas don't permeate the cheese. Alternatively, cheese can be wrapped and held in an airtight plastic container or plastic bag.

❹ Do not freeze cheeses, as they may lose their texture and flavor profile.

❺ If stored cheese is overly dry or slimy or if it lets off a strong odor, discard it immediately.

Figure 1.5: Step 1—Wrap cheese in waxed or parchment paper so that it can breathe without drying out.

Eggs

An egg is composed of the outer shell, the white (**albumen**), and the yolk. The white consists of protein and water. The **yolk** contains protein, fat, and lecithin, a natural emulsifier (thickener). The membranes that hold the egg yolk in place are called **chalazae** (*kuh*-LEY-*zuh*). See Figure 1.6 for an illustration of the main parts of an egg.

There are USDA grades for shell eggs—Grades AA, A, and B. Buyers purchase the top two grades (Grade AA and Grade A) for menu items in which the egg's

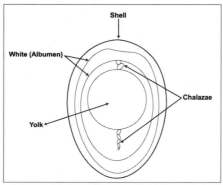

Figure 1.6: The parts of an egg are: the outer shell, the white (albumen), the chalazae, and the yolk.

17

Figure Focus

Figure 1.5: If cheese wrapping is completely airtight, pathogens can grow.

Figure 1.6: Eggs have an anatomy. They are large single cells.

Discuss

- Perhaps the students have had "grilled cheese sandwiches" or "macaroni and cheese" made with processed cheese-food products.

- Do they have opinions about how processed cheeses taste as compared to natural cheeses?

- Can the students identify different melting or mouthfeel characteristics of processed cheese products and natural cheeses?

Essential Skills: Considerations in Storing Cheese

The seventeenth-century composer J. S. Bach used a parchment-type paper for writing his music.

Before his music was fully appreciated, some of his original written compositions were used as cheese wrappers.

In-Class Activity: Poetry Corner

Literacy Connection, 21st-Century Skills—Think Creatively, Access and Evaluate Information

In 1987 a large slab of ancient cheese was found in a peat bog in Ireland. It was 1,400 years old and brave people tasted it. They did not get ill, but it didn't taste very good. It probably tasted like a peat bog.

Have the students do some quick online research about this story. Do not give them the details.

This cheese was not found in the Irish county of Limerick. However, have the students compose a limerick-style poem about it (G-rated).

Have the students share their poems with one another in a lighthearted poetry reading format.

Vocabulary Terms

- **Albumen:** Egg white.

- **Yolk:** The cell nucleus of an egg; contains protein, emulsifier, cholesterol, and fat.

- **Chalazae:** Tissue that suspends the yolk within the egg.

Discuss

- Most commercially sold eggs are white chicken eggs.

- Chicken eggs are also available in brown, green, blue, and pink.

- White eggs come from white chickens, and brown eggs come from brownish chickens.

- Auracauna chickens lay green eggs because they possess the pigment oocyanin, which causes the green/blue eggs.

- The color of the shell has nothing to do with egg quality, nutritional value, or flavor

- Most of the eggs in your supermarket come from the following breeds of chickens: the White Leghorn, the Rhode Island Red, the New Hampshire, and the Plymouth Rock.

appearance is important. A USDA Grade AA egg means that the yolk is high and the white will not spread much when the shell is broken. A USDA Grade A egg means that the yolk is fairly high and the white will still not spread too much when the shell is broken. Both Grade AA and A eggs have generally clean, unbroken shells. Grade B eggs are not usually purchased fresh by operations, but might be bought refrigerated or frozen. Grade B eggs are good for use in menu items that will hide their appearance, such as baked items. As eggs age, they lose density. This means the thick part of the white becomes larger, and the egg spreads over a larger area when it is broken. Figure 1.7 shows the differences in how eggs should look according to grade.

Figure 1.7: Eggs look different depending upon the grade.

Buyers must choose eggs by size—ranging from peewee (15 ounces per dozen) to jumbo (30 ounces per dozen). Figure 1.8 shows the range of actual egg sizes. Many operations use large eggs (24 ounces per dozen) for all purposes. In fact, most recipes are based on this size. Size and grade together determine the cost of eggs. What if the recipe calls for jumbo eggs and you only have medium eggs in stock? You'll find that many recipes call for a certain number of ounces of egg. So, if you know how many ounces are in a jumbo egg and a medium egg, you can calculate how many medium eggs you will need to equal the amount called for in the recipe.

18

Figure Focus

Figure 1.7: Use the best-looking eggs for sunny-side up and over-easy fried eggs.

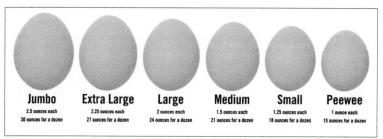

Jumbo
2.5 ounces each
30 ounces for a dozen

Extra Large
2.25 ounces each
27 ounces for a dozen

Large
2 ounces each
24 ounces for a dozen

Medium
1.5 ounces each
21 ounces for a dozen

Small
1.25 ounces each
18 ounces for a dozen

Peewee
1 ounce each
15 ounces for a dozen

Figure 1.8: Egg sizes vary from peewee to jumbo.

[ServSafe Connection]

Cooking with Eggs

1. Consider using pasteurized shell eggs or egg products when prepping egg dishes that need little or no cooking, such as hollandaise sauce, tiramisu, and Caesar salad dressing.

2. Cook eggs for immediate service to 145°F for 15 seconds. Cook eggs that will be hot-held for service to 155°F for 15 seconds.

Young hens produce smaller eggs, which are generally of a better quality than larger eggs. Medium eggs are best for breakfast cooking because the appearance of the cooked eggs is important.

19

Figure Focus

Figure 1.8: Chicken eggs come in various sizes and colors. If possible, bring a variety of eggs to class for the students to examine.

Eggs come in a variety of forms, as shown in Table 1.4.

Table 1.4: Market Forms of Eggs

Form	Usage
Fresh (shell) eggs	These are most often used for breakfast cooking or instances in which a whole shell egg is required. Use pasteurized shell eggs if the operation mainly serves high-risk populations, such as those in hospitals or senior-care centers.
Frozen eggs • Whole eggs • Whites • Yolks • Whole eggs with extra yolks	Frozen eggs are usually made from high-quality fresh eggs and are excellent for use in scrambled eggs, omelets, French toast, and baking. They are pasteurized and are usually purchased in 30 lb cans or milk carton-style containers. Frozen eggs take at least 2 days to thaw at refrigerated temperatures.
Dried eggs • Whole eggs • Yolks • Whites	Use dried eggs primarily for baking. They are not good for breakfast cooking. Dried eggs do not store well, so keep them refrigerated or frozen and tightly sealed.
Egg substitutes	Egg substitutes may be entirely egg-free or made from egg whites, with dairy or vegetable products substituted for the yolks. These substitutes are important for people with cholesterol-free diet requirements.
Organic and other alternatives	Many customers now look for organic products and/or products that indicate humane treatment of the animals that produced the items. Organic eggs come from chickens that have been raised without the use of antibiotics, pesticides, or hormones. Some organic eggs receive certification through the USDA's National Organic Program, which confirms the processes used by the producer. Customers may also look for the use of cage-free and free-range eggs. These descriptors refer to the way the chickens were treated on the farms and are related to how much space and outdoor access they have; however, the terms are not regulated legally and their definitions vary by farm. An operation that wants to purchase these types of eggs should research the producer before doing so. Hens that are fed only vegetable-based food products produce vegetarian eggs. Omega-3 eggs are another kind of egg that has been appearing in the market in the past few years. Eggs naturally have some omega-3 fatty acids, but some egg companies feed their hens special diets to ensure their eggs have even more of the substance.

Nutrition:
Good Egg or Bad Egg?

Like all foods, there is a place for the egg in most healthy diet plans.

Like all purchased items, evaluate and order eggs based on characteristics such as their color, form, packaging, intended use, and preservation method. Figure 1.9 depicts uses of fresh, frozen, or dried eggs.

Figure 1.9: Fresh or frozen eggs are most often used to make omelets (top left). Frozen or dried eggs are frequently used for baking cakes (top right).

[nutrition]

Good Egg or Bad Egg?

Cholesterol is a waxy substance that is found in certain foods, such as meat, dairy products, and eggs. In recent years, there has been a lot of news coverage about how much cholesterol should be in a healthy diet and what foods to eat or avoid to maintain a healthy diet. Eggs are often at the center of this coverage, with conflicting reports about their nutritional effects. How can you be sure what eggs contribute to your diet?

First, eggs are definitely high in cholesterol, but all of the cholesterol is contained in the yolk. However, research has not found that plasma cholesterol (that is, cholesterol in the blood stream) increases significantly when people include egg yolks in their diets. Also, blood plasma HDL (the "good cholesterol") levels tend to rise a little when eggs are the cholesterol source, which is a good thing. It should also be noted that any egg dish prepared with only egg whites is cholesterol-free (in terms of the egg component, that is).

Second, the average healthy person should limit daily cholesterol intake to 300 milligrams. One whole large egg contains approximately 213 milligrams of cholesterol, or 71 percent of the recommended daily allowance. So, limiting cholesterol intake from other food sources on days when you eat eggs is a good idea.

Finally, on the sunnier upside of eggs, they are a good source of protein and are very low in fat. One large egg contains 6 grams of protein, which is 12 percent of the recommended daily intake. As with all foods, knowing the nutritional values of eggs will help you make better, wiser choices.

Figure Focus

Figure 1.9: Cooked eggs should look good, but eggs used in baked goods and other products don't show.

Discuss

- Eggs are checked at the farm processing plant for slight cracks and problems.

- This process used to be done one egg at a time by a farmer looking at each egg in front of a candle.

- This old technique is no longer used, but the process is still called "candling."

**Essential Skills:
Cracking and Opening an Egg**

Practice cracking an egg.

It is not necessary to be fast at first.

Keep shells out.

One-handed egg cracking is not necessary.

Receiving and Storing Eggs

Purchasers should use suppliers that can deliver eggs within a few days of the packing date in refrigerated trucks that are capable of recording air temperature during transport. When the eggs arrive, the truck's air temperature should be 45°F or lower. Store the eggs immediately in refrigeration at an air temperature of 45°F or lower.

To be acceptable, shell eggs must also meet the following criteria:

- No odor
- Clean and unbroken shells

Reject any shell eggs with an off odor, a sulfur smell, or dirty or cracked shells.

Liquid, frozen, and dehydrated eggs must be pasteurized by law. They also must have a USDA inspection mark. When delivered, refrigerate liquid and frozen eggs at or below 45°F unless the eggs should stay frozen. Check packages for damage or signs of refreezing, and make sure that the use-by date has not passed. Reject any packages that are damaged or have an expired use-by date.

Fresh eggs must be stored at an air temperature of 45°F or lower. Store liquid eggs according to the manufacturer's recommendations. Place dried egg products in a cool, dry storeroom. Once eggs have been mixed with water, store them at 41°F or lower.

Essential Skills
Cracking and Opening an Egg

❶ Crack the egg using a sharp snap of the wrist, striking the egg against a hard, flat surface. This leaves a dent in the shell. Too hard, and you have a mess. Too soft, and the shell doesn't break. See Figure 1.10a on the following page.

❷ When you make the dent, use two thumbs in the dent and pull the two sides of the egg apart. See Figure 1.10b

❸ Let the egg drop into a small bowl. Always crack eggs into a bowl instead of directly into the product. See Figure 1.10c

❹ Inspect the egg for small bits of shell. Fix the problem. See Figure 1.10d

❺ Then, add the egg to the product. See Figure 1.10e

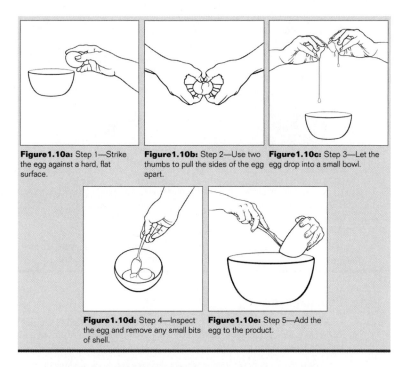

Figure1.10a: Step 1—Strike the egg against a hard, flat surface.

Figure1.10b: Step 2—Use two thumbs to pull the sides of the egg apart.

Figure1.10c: Step 3—Let the egg drop into a small bowl.

Figure1.10d: Step 4—Inspect the egg and remove any small bits of shell.

Figure1.10e: Step 5—Add the egg to the product.

Essential Skills
Separating Egg Whites and Yolks

❶ Crack the egg using a sharp snap of the wrist, striking the egg against a hard, flat surface. This leaves a dent in the shell. Too hard, and you have a mess. Too soft, and the shell doesn't break.

❷ When you've made the dent, use two thumbs in the dent and open the egg carefully, allowing the unbroken yolk to settle into one side of the shell as the white pours off into the bowl.

23

Figure Focus

Figure 1.10a: A flat surface will dent and flatten a small area of the shell.

Figure 1.10b: Make sure your hands are always clean.

Figure 1.10c: The separate bowl is very important, in case shell falls into it.

Figure 1.10d: Even expert egg crackers can get a tiny bit of shell into the egg.

Figure 1.10e: If you add the egg after inspection, there won't be any surprises.

Separated yolks are also used for their particular characteristics.

The yolk's have fat in them and the whites do not, so when the whites are whipped they produce air bubbles, which help the cake or whatever you're making to rise. If there are any yolks in the whites when they are whipped, the fat separates between the bubbles, causing it to stay flat.

Vocabulary Terms

- **Hard-cooked eggs:** Eggs cooked in the shell, in simmering water, until the white and yolk are both set and cooked through but not overcooked and discolored.

- **Shocking:** Placing hard-cooked eggs into cold water to stop the cooking process.

❸ Gently move the egg to the other open shell half, allowing the rest of the white to flow out. See Figure 1.11a.

❹ There should be no speck of yolk in the white.

❺ Put the yolk into a separate dish. See Figure 1.11b.

Figure 1.11a: Step 3—Move the egg to the other open shell half.

Figure 1.11b: Step 5—Put the yolk into a separate dish.

Note: An egg separator or spoon can help with this process.

If the shell is clean, bacteria will not enter the egg by cracking it open. Make sure the eggshells are clean. See Figure 1.10, which illustrates the process.

Cooking Eggs

Chefs can cook eggs in many ways, from hard cooked to scrambled to soufflés. Different egg preparations, from hard cooking to coddling, require different cooking times. When preparing eggs, it is important to time the cooking.

A grayish-green color can develop when a shell egg is cooked too long or a scrambled egg is held too long before service; this comes from the development of iron sulfide. It is a natural reaction that occurs between the iron content in the yolk and the sulfur content in the egg white. While the color does not generally develop sufficiently to impact the flavor quality of the egg, it reduces the eye appeal of the egg.

Make **hard-cooked eggs** by simmering and then **shocking** the eggs. Shocking is putting the eggs into cold water immediately after cooking to stop the cooking and make them easier to peel. Eggs should be simmered, rather than boiled, because boiling can cause fragile eggshells to crack and make the egg tough. In addition to breakfast dishes, hard-cooked eggs are an important ingredient in a number of other popular preparations, such as cold hors d'oeuvres, canapés, salads, and garnishes.

24

Figure Focus

Figure 1.11a: Moving the yolk from one shell half to the other is a delicate process.

Figure 1.11b: Separated yolks should be whole and unbroken.

Essential Skills
Simmering or Hard Cooking an Egg in Shell

❶ Select an egg free of cracks; cracked eggs will leak in cooking and not be useable for service.

❷ Bring enough water to completely cover the egg to a rapid boil; then reduce the heat to a simmer, 180°F to 185°F.

❸ Carefully lower an egg into the water. See Figure 1.12a.

❹ Cook for 3 to 8 minutes for soft-boiled eggs; cook for 10 minutes for hard-boiled eggs. (Excess cooking time will result in a grayish-green tone developing in the outer edge of the yolk.) See Figure 1.12b.

❺ Serve immediately or cool immediately to be used cold later.

Tip: Cool and peel hard-cooked eggs immediately after they have finished cooking. This prevents a green ring from forming around the yolk.

Cooking times for shell eggs:

- **Coddled** (or slightly cooked): 30 seconds; lower cold eggs into already simmering water.

- Soft-cooked: 1 to 2 minutes

- Medium-cooked: 3 to 5 minutes

- Hard-cooked: 10 minutes

Figure 1.12a: Step 3—Lower the egg into the water.

Figure 1.12b: Step 4—Cook the eggs.

Combine baked eggs with a number of additional ingredients to create a fun, satisfying breakfast. To bake eggs, place the shelled eggs into individual **ramekins** (RAM-uh-kins), small, ceramic oven-proof dishes. Combine them with other ingredients, such as butter, cream, or cooked bacon. Or, layer them on top

25

Discuss

- Eggs are part of many favorite and famous restaurant menu items.

- Some guests will come to a restaurant simply to have eggs that are cooked to order.

- Guests might be very particular and specific with their instructions for how they want their eggs prepared.

- Skillful preparation of eggs will be a valuable career asset.

Teaching Tips

- The following pages involve egg skills.

- The skills require practice, and students should attempt them in the classroom, at home, or both.

- The instructions are simple.

Essential Skills:
Simmering or Hard Cooking an Egg in Shell

Please note that the eggs are not involved in a rolling boil.

Vocabulary Terms

- **Coddled:** Eggs cooked slowly and gently just below the boiling point.

- **Ramekins:** Small, individual, ceramic, oven-proof dishes.

Figure Focus

Figure 1.12a: Be careful not to drop the eggs as the shell might crack.

Figure 1.12b: Boiling eggs makes them tough and rubbery. Eggs should be cooked in simmering or hot water.

Essential Skills: Baking an Egg

Baked eggs are often served in the ramekins in which they are baked.

Consider this when plating the egg: The ramekin will still be too hot for the guest to touch.

Essential Skills: Cooking a Shirred Egg

Hot fat helps cook a shirred egg.

Vocabulary Terms

- **Shirred eggs:** Eggs baked in ramekins, perhaps in butter or cream.

of cooked food, such as mashed potatoes or a thick tomato sauce. Then, bake the eggs until the whites are fully cooked.

Essential Skills
Baking an Egg

❶ Prepare the baking dish by buttering it generously.

❷ Add any additional ingredients in an even layer to the baking dish.

❸ Bake the eggs at 325°F until the whites are set and milky in appearance.

❹ Unmold the eggs, if desired, garnish, and serve hot. See Figure 1.13.

Figure 1.13: Step 4—Garnish the dish and serve it hot.

Shirred eggs are a variety of baked egg. Like baked eggs, cook shirred eggs with other ingredients, such as cheese, vegetables, meats, and sauces. Cook shirred eggs in butter (and sometimes cream) in a ramekin. The size, shape, and material of the baking dish can affect the texture of the finished item. The egg must be fresh because its appearance is very important in the service of this dish. Most important, freshness will prevent the yolk from breaking.

Essential Skills
Cooking a Shirred Egg

❶ Butter a baking dish and place it on a hot stovetop.

❷ Break an egg into a separate dish, and then slide it into the shirred dish when butter has slightly browned. See Figure 1.14a on the following page.

❸ Finish the egg in an oven set to 325°F to set the white portion and produce a hot but liquid yolk.

26

Figure Focus

Figure 1.13: Garnishes can add visual appeal, texture, and flavor to egg dishes.

❹ Serve immediately. See Figure 1.14b.

Figure 1.14a: Step 2—Break the egg into a separate dish.

Figure 1.14b: Step 4—Serve shirred eggs immediately.

To **poach eggs**, shell them (remove from the shell) and simmer the eggs in water. Poached eggs are popular in classic dishes, such as eggs Benedict and eggs Florentine, and as toppings for hash or baked potatoes. A properly poached egg should be tender and well-shaped, meaning the yolk is centered and the white is not rough or ragged.

Essential Skills
Poaching an Egg

❶ Combine water, salt, and vinegar in a shallow skillet or pan and bring it to a simmer.

❷ Break the eggs into a clean cup and slide the egg carefully into the poaching water. Cook until the whites are set and opaque. See Figure 1.15a.

❸ Remove the eggs from the water with a slotted spoon and blot them on an absorbent towel.

❹ Trim, if desired, and serve hot. See Figure 1.15b.

Figure 1.15a: Step 2—Break the egg and slide the egg carefully into the boiling water.

Figure 1.15b: Serve poached eggs hot.

27

Vocabulary Terms

- **Poached eggs:** Eggs simmered in water without the shell.

Figure Focus

Figure 1.14a: Breaking the eggs in a separate dish and then sliding them into the browned butter helps to ensure that they will cook evenly.

Figure 1.14b: Shirred eggs taste best when served hot, as they congeal when they cool.

Figure 1.15a: Breaking the eggs into a clean cup and carefully sliding them into boiling water helps to prevent the yolks from breaking. This also can prevent you from using a "bad" egg.

Figure 1.15b: To ensure the best flavor and maintain the consistency of the yolk, serve poached eggs hot.

Essential Skills: Scrambling Eggs

Eggs may be scrambled alone, with milk, or with water.

Experiment to determine your preferred method.

Vocabulary Terms

- **Scrambled eggs:** Eggs that are shelled and have the yolks and whites mixed together before cooking.

- **Fried eggs:** Raw eggs cracked onto a hot cooking surface and cooked until the white is set.

- **Up or sunny-side up:** Eggs fried without flipping.

- **Over or over-easy:** Fried eggs flipped over briefly to slightly cook the top before serving.

- **Basted eggs:** Fried eggs that are also slightly steamed to barely cook the albumin over the yolk.

Scrambled eggs should have a light texture, creamy consistency, and delicate flavor. They are best when served very hot. Blend the eggs just until the yolks and whites are combined, and then add any seasonings. Cook scrambled eggs over gentle heat while constantly stirring and scraping from the bottom and sides of the pan to keep them creamy and prevent them from burning.

Essential Skills
Scrambling Eggs

1. Beat eggs until they're well blended; if adding milk, the standard proportion is ½ cup per six eggs. See Figure 1.16a.

2. Heat the frying pan and add fat.

3. When the fat bubbles, add the beaten eggs to the pan.

4. Stir eggs, shaking the pan to keep the eggs moving. Cook to a creamy consistency with no white showing. It's best to remove the eggs from the pan slightly undercooked, because carryover heat will finish setting the eggs. See Figure 1.16b.

5. Serve immediately on a warm plate. If they're being held for service, place the eggs in a lightly oiled (preferably buttered) warm pan. Holding eggs for an excessive time will result in a grayish-green color on the bottom and sides of the eggs. See Figure 1.16c.

Figure 1.16a: Step 1—Beat the eggs until blended.   **Figure 1.16b:** Step 4—Stir the eggs.   **Figure 1.16c:** Step 5—Serve the eggs immediately.

Fried eggs are quick and easy to prepare. To make sure that eggs are fried with the yolks high and centered, use fresh eggs and an appropriate amount of cooking fat, cook the eggs at 145°F for at least 15 seconds, and serve immediately. If they are going to be held for a few minutes, cook them at 155°F. The yolk should be cooked to whatever doneness the customer requests. Eggs fried **up**, sometimes called sunny-side up, are fried only on the bottom. Eggs fried **over easy** are fried on the bottom, then turned over and fried very lightly on their top sides. **Basted eggs** are fried and then steamed in a covered pan.

28

Figure Focus

Figure 1.16a: Beating or whisking the eggs ensures that they will be light and fluffy.

Figure 1.16b: Gently stir the eggs to prevent separating and clumping.

Figure 1.16c: Serve hot for best flavor and consistency.

Essential Skills
Making a Fried Egg

❶ Heat a frying pan and add fat (such as clarified butter, bacon fat, shortening, oil, or margarine).

❷ Break an egg into a small dish.

❸ When the fat in the frying pan bubbles, slip the egg into the pan. See Figure 1.17.

Over-easy:

- Cook the egg until the white is set.
- Flip the egg by pushing the pan forward and pulling back sharply, or use a spatula.
- Continue to cook until the white is firmly set with a soft yolk.

Hard-fried:

- Cook the egg until the white is set.
- Puncture the yolk and then flip the egg.
- Continue to cook it until the white and the yolk are firmly set.

Basted:

- Fry the egg on one side.
- Do not flip the egg.
- Moisten it during cooking with hot fat or cover the pan, allowing the egg to steam slightly until the yolk is slightly whitened.
- Cook until the white is firmly set and the yolk is hot but soft.

Figure 1.17: Step 3—Cook an egg until the white is set.

Sunnny-side up:

- Cook the egg, without flipping or basting, until the white is set.

❹ Serve eggs immediately on a warm plate.

Essential Skills: Making a Fried Egg

Yolks should remain intact.

Only break the yolk if the guest specifically requests it.

Figure Focus

Figure 1.17: An egg white is thoroughly cooked and set when it solidifies from transparency into snow-white cream.

Essential Skills: Rolled Omelet

Rolling an omelet requires practice.

If the omelet sticks to the pan, it will break.

If the omelet has too much filling, it will ooze out of the ends and not plate properly.

Vocabulary Terms

- **Omelets:** Eggs that are beaten and set in a pan, but not scrambled. They are filled with cheese or other items and folded in half before serving.

- **Frittata:** An omelet that might have the cheese or other items with the eggs, or added to the top after the eggs have set, and not folded.

Make **omelets** by slightly beating eggs and then cooking them in a skillet with a filling, such as cheese, mushrooms, onions, or ham. Omelets are either rolled, flat, or souffléed. A rolled omelet should be golden yellow with a creamy, moist interior and must be made to order. Flat omelets (also called **frittatas**) may be made in individual portions or in larger quantities. Souffléed omelets have a light, fluffy texture because the egg whites are whipped before cooking.

Essential Skills
Rolled Omelet

❶ Blend the eggs, liquid (milk, cream, and/or water), and seasonings.

❷ Pour the egg mixture into a heated and oiled pan.

❸ Swirl the pan over the heat, stirring and scraping the eggs simultaneously until curds begin to form. See Figure 1.18a.

❹ Add a filling, if desired.

❺ Cook the omelet until it is set.

❻ Roll the omelet—completely encasing the filling—out of the pan directly onto a heated plate. Shape it, using a clean towel, if necessary. See Figure 1.18b.

❼ Rub the surface with butter, if desired.

Figure 1.18a: Step 3—Stir the eggs.

Figure 1.18b: Step 6—Place the omelet on a heated plate.

30

Figure Focus

Figure 1.18a: Stirring the eggs helps to prevent clumping.

Figure 1.18b: Serving omelets on heated plates keeps the food flavorful and warm for a longer period of time.

Essential Skills
Flat Omelet (Frittata)

❶ Blend the eggs, liquid (milk, cream, and/or water), and seasoning.

❷ Sauté any garnish ingredients. See Figure 1.19a.

❸ Pour the egg mixture into a hot, oiled pan over the garnish, swirling the pan so the egg mixture covers the entire bottom of the pan.

❹ Cook, without stirring, until the edges are set.

❺ Finish the omelet in a hot oven, adding other garnish ingredients, such as grated cheese. See Figure 1.19b.

❻ Brown under a broiler, if desired.

Figure 1.19a: Step 2—Sauté any garnish, such as mushrooms.

Figure 1.19b: Step 5—Finish the omelet in a hot oven.

Essential Skills:
Flat Omelet (Frittata)

Ingredients can be added to the top as garnish, after the omelet is set.

Ingredients can also be added to the egg mixture and cooked into the omelet, as in a Spanish omelet.

Figure Focus

Figure 1.19a: Sautéing garnishes brings out the full flavor.

Figure 1.19b: Finishing the omelet in a hot oven helps it to set evenly.

Essential Skills:
Souffléed Omelet

Beaten egg whites make this omelet very light and fluffy.

Vocabulary Terms

- **Quiche:** A savory egg custard pie.

- **Soufflés:** Sweet or savory egg dishes made with beaten egg whites.

Essential Skills
Souffléed Omelet

❶ Whip the eggs until they are frothy. Add any seasonings and garnish ingredients. See Figure 1.20a.

❷ Pour the egg mixture into a heated and oiled pan.

❸ Cook the omelet until the edges and bottom are set. See Figure 1.20b.

❹ Finish in a hot oven.

Tips for perfect omelets include the following:

- Always use high heat.

- Use the appropriate omelet pan (8 or 10 inches).

Figure 1.20a: Step 1—Whip the eggs.

Figure 1.20b: Step 3—Cook the omelet until the edges and bottom are set.

Other favorite egg dishes that can be carried over to lunch or dinner include quiche (KEESH) and soufflés (soo-FLAYS). **Quiche** is a savory egg custard baked in a crust. Blend eggs with milk or cream until smooth and then add a variety of other ingredients. In one traditional quiche, the Florentine, blend the eggs with onion or spinach, cheese (usually Gruyere or Swiss, but other cheese can be used), and crisp bacon or cooked ham. Regardless of ingredients, season the mixture of eggs and other ingredients, pour it into an uncooked pie crust, bake it in a moderately heated oven, and serve it hot. Quiches are easy to reheat in a microwave oven just before serving.

Soufflés are made of eggs and can be both savory and sweet. While they can be served at any meal, they take time to bake and must be made to order. Make a soufflé by enriching a sauce base (generally béchamel) with egg yolk, whipped egg whites, and flavorings. The egg whites cause the soufflé to puff during cooking. Soufflés are not difficult to prepare, but timing is everything. The kitchen staff and the serving staff must work together very closely to assure that the customer receives the soufflé while it is still hot and puffy. Cheese soufflés are very popular.

32

Figure Focus

Figure 1.20a: Whipping the eggs helps to make the omelet light and fluffy.

Figure 1.20b: When the edges are set, they will pull away from the side of the pan.

Essential Skills
Making Soufflés

❶ Prepare a base and add the flavoring.

❷ Whip egg whites and fold the whites into the base. See Figure 1.21a.

❸ Fill the molds. See Figure 1.21b.

❹ Place them in a hot oven.

❺ Once they are done, serve the soufflés immediately. See Figure 1.21c.

Figure 1.21a: Step 2— Whip the egg whites.   **Figure 1.21b:** Step 3— Fill the molds.   **Figure 1.21c:** Step 5— Serve the soufflé immediately.

[fast fact]

Did You Know...?

Chicken eggs are the most common type of egg and are commonly found in food stores. Their shells are usually either white or brown. But there are many other types of eggs including the ostrich egg, quail egg, duck egg, goose egg, and turkey egg.

The ostrich egg is the largest of all eggs. It weighs about 3½ to 5 pounds and is equivalent to two dozen chicken eggs. The ivory-colored shell is very thick, and it takes a knife to crack it. They are fluffier than chicken eggs, which makes them good for baking and pastries. It takes one hour to soft cook a fresh ostrich egg and 1½ hours to hard cook one. Unless there is an ostrich breeder in the neighborhood, ostrich eggs are hard to find.

Quail eggs are popular with gourmets. They are small and oval with a speckled outer shell. Quail eggs taste similar to chicken eggs, but they have a thin shell that cracks very easily compared to chicken eggs. Since the shell is so thin, the moisture in the egg white evaporates as the egg ages. Five quail eggs equal the weight of one chicken egg. Quail eggs are mostly hard-boiled and served as a food garnish, hors d'oeuvre, or an accompaniment for salads. Quail eggs are often found in Asian stores.

Duck eggs are larger than chicken eggs and range in size from small to jumbo. The egg white is more transparent, containing less yellow than a chicken egg. Duck eggs have more protein, flavor, and richness, are higher in fat, and have more cholesterol than chicken eggs. The richness of duck eggs makes them well suited for desserts.

33

Figure Focus

Figure 1.21a: Whipping the egg whites is like blowing air into a balloon. Egg whites are mostly protein and can whip up to seven times the original volume.

Figure 1.21b: Container or mold size is important. The soufflé can increase two to three times in volume. If the mold is too big, the mixture will not rise above the rim. If it is too small, it will overflow.

Figure 1.21c: Serve the soufflé immediately, so that you can watch it "fall."

21st-Century Skills—Produce Results

Have individuals or groups of students each learn how to make a particular kind of egg.

Use the Essential Skills boxes in this chapter for the instructions.

Allow each student or group to practice cooking their assigned type of egg.

When the students are proficient, have each one demonstrate his or her method to the class.

If possible, have students set up in separate kitchen stations in the classroom so that they can display their entire preparation and process, start to finish.

Students can learn how to demonstrate clearly as they learn how to cook their eggs.

Vocabulary Terms

- **Pooled eggs:** Opened, shelled eggs in a container.

Goose eggs are four times larger than chicken eggs. They are rich in flavor and best suited for dessert dishes. They can be used in any recipe calling for chicken eggs. One goose egg is equal to two chicken eggs. Because goose eggs are very high in fat and cholesterol, they should be used sparingly.

Turkey eggs are 1½ times larger than a jumbo chicken egg. They have a brown shell and are rich in flavor. They are also high in fat and cholesterol. Generally, farmers do not sell turkey eggs commercially because turkeys produce 100 to 120 eggs per year, compared to commercial egg-producing chickens that lay over 300 eggs per year. In addition, a turkey doesn't start laying eggs until she is 32 weeks old, whereas a chicken starts laying eggs at around 19 weeks of age. It takes more money and time to produce turkey eggs.

No matter how they are prepared, always follow safety steps to ensure properly cooked eggs:

- Handle pooled eggs carefully. **Pooled eggs** are eggs that are cracked open and combined in a container. Cook them immediately after mixing, or store them at 41°F or lower. Wash and sanitize the containers used to hold pooled eggs before making a new batch.

- Keep shell eggs in cold storage until ready for use. Take out only as many eggs as needed for immediate use. Figure 1.22 shows well-made egg dishes.

Figure 1.22a: Hard-cooked eggs.

Figure 1.22b: Baked eggs.

Figure 1.22c: Poached eggs.

Figure 1.22d: Scrambled eggs.

Figure Focus

Figure 1.22a: There should be no green showing around a hard-cooked yolk.

Figure1.22b: The eggs are both baked and served in the ramekin.

Figure 1.22c: Poached eggs require expert handling to be perfectly prepared.

Figure 1.22d: Scrambled eggs should not leak fluid.

Summary

- Remind students to review the following:
  1. Milk and milk products
  2. Receiving and storing milk
  3. Creams
  4. Butter and butter substitutes
  5. Cheese
  6. Eggs

Figure 1.22e: Fried eggs.

Figure 1.22f: Omelet.

Figure 1.22g: Quiche.

Figure 1.22h: Soufflé.

Summary

In this section, you learned the following:

- There are many types of milk; the type of milk you use is often based on the nutritional value you want. Cream contains far more fat than milk. It must have at least 18 percent fat content just to be considered light cream, and heavy whipping cream can be 40 percent fat or higher. The type of cream used is based primarily on its fat content. Butter is made by mixing heavy cream at a very high speed. Butter itself must have at least 80 percent butterfat content; the remaining 20 percent is milk solids and water.

- The pasteurization process is what kills the bacteria in milk that could make people sick. All milk and milk products should be labeled Grade A, stored at 41°F or lower, and handled using the FIFO (first in, first out) method. Any milk that has passed its use-by or expiration date should be thrown away.

- All cheese has three basic parts: water, fat, and protein. The amounts vary depending on the type of cheese. There are three different types of milk used in cheese: cow's milk, goat's milk, and sheep's milk. Cheese comes in three primary textures: soft, semisoft, and hard. Cheese can also be either fresh (unripened) or aged (ripened).

35

Figure Focus

Figure 1.22e: High-grade eggs should be used for frying.

Figure 1.22f: Omelets require skill to plate properly.

Figure 1.22g: Quiche is an excellent menu item for brunch, lunch, or a buffet.

Figure 1.22h: Soufflés are also covered in Chapter 8.

- Eggs are chosen by their grade (AA, A, or B) and size (ranging from peewee, the smallest, to jumbo, the largest).

- Eggs can be cooked using many different methods, including simmering, frying, poaching, and baking.

Section 1.1 Review Questions

1. Define each of the following terms:
   a. Homogenization
   b. Jumbo
   c. Pasteurization
   d. Clarified
   e. Peewee
   f. Ripened

2. List the three basic parts of cheese.

3. What is the best way to handle and store milk?

4. What determines if cream will be stable when whipped?

5. Chef Nims' favorite breakfast dish is Classic Eggs Benedict. She says that this dish "mirrors perfection and versatility." What does that mean to you? Do you agree?

6. Eggs would definitely be on any brunch menu. Taking into account Chef Kate's concern about quality, timing, and efficiency, what egg dishes would you put on the Kabob brunch menu?

7. Investigate the many differences in dairy products between Jersey and Guernsey cows.

8. What are the costs and benefits to using organic products? How do you yourself weigh the pros and cons? Which type of products would you choose for your restaurant: conventional or organic?

37

Section 1.1 Review Questions

1. Definitions:
   a. Blending fat uniformly throughout milk.
   b. 30 ounces per dozen eggs.
   c. Heat processing to kill microbes.
   d. For butter, removing milk solids and water. The butter appears clear and pale yellow when melted.
   e. 15 ounces per dozen eggs.
   f. Aged, matured with bacteria.

2. Water, fat, and protein.

3. Keep the milk at 41°F or colder, follow the FIFO method of stock rotation, and be sure to use the product before its expiration date.

4. Cream will be stable after being whipped as long as its fat content is greater than 30 percent.

5. Each student will have a unique answer. Make sure students understand what Eggs Benedict is.

6. Each student will have different ideas about this.

7. This requires some outside research by the students. Milk from Guernsey cows is sometimes called "golden Guernsey" because it has a slightly yellowish color from the presence of the anti-oxidant beta-carotene (a precursor to vitamin A). It also has a high protein and fat content (5 percent), so it tastes rich. Jersey milk has a white color and an even higher fat content (6 percent) and protein content and tastes very rich. The students might find that there are differences in the cream, ice cream, and cheeses made from these types of cows' milk as well.

8. Each student will have an opinion about this. Encourage the students to cite their resources.

Section 1.1 Activities

1. Encourage the students to look at fairly recent centuries first, when better records were kept. It might also be of interest to examine ancient historical uses of dairy foods, and information might be available for this area of study as well, especially in frequently studied ancient civilizations. Hint: Not all milk and milk products have always come from cows.

2. Milk is a colloidal suspension, so, in theory, in time it would eventually settle out of suspension. However, it doesn't happen easily in the time frame before the milk spoils and curdles on its own. Curdling and falling out of suspension are not the same thing. Curdling is a coagulation of the milk protein. Cheese making is an ancient art form and craft. Understanding it, at least a little bit, can add to a chef's appreciation of cheese and its role in cuisine.

3. A graphic will provide a picture that can help the students mentally organize the information for further understanding. Each student will have an idea of how to do this.

Section 1.1 Activities

1. Study Skills/Group Activity: The History of Dairy

Working alone or in a group, select a century. Research the production and use of dairy products in that time period. Pick a specific location: France, the United States, China, etc. Chart the production and usage of milk, eggs, and cheese in that time frame and area.

Compare your charts in class. Are there differences in usage based on area or ethnicity? Were these products used more by the upper or lower classes? How were they used?

2. Activity: No Whey!

Cheese is made from the solid components of milk with the liquid whey removed. How does this work? Why does fresh milk remain liquid without solid particles falling out of the solution? How is cheese made? How long does it take? What are some of the potential pitfalls? Research cheese making in both small independent and large commercial operations.

3. Critical Thinking: Breaking Down Milk

When milk comes out of the cow, it is all one liquid. Milkfat, or cream, rises to the top and is skimmed off. Nonfat milk is sometimes called "skim milk" for this reason. Cream is collected and used for various recipes, including butter production. The difference between each of these is fat content. What are the fat limits on milk, cream, and butter? Create a graphic that shows the relationship between milk, cream, and butter.

38

1.1 Dairy Products and Eggs	1.2 Breakfast Foods and Drinks	1.3 Sandwiches
• Milk and milk products • Receiving and storing milk • Creams • Butter and butter substitutes • Cheese • Eggs	• Pancakes, waffles, crêpes, and French toast • Preparing breakfasts meat and starches • Hot breakfast beverages: coffee, tea, and cocoa	• Basic kinds of sandwiches • Primary sandwich components: bread, spread, and filling • Sandwich stations

SECTION 1.2 BREAKFAST FOODS AND DRINKS

Breakfast foods are wholesome and satisfying. That's why some places serve breakfast all day long. In addition, an entire food culture has developed around the drinks that normally accompany breakfast—coffee bars and tea rooms.

Study Questions

After studying Section 1.2, you should be able to answer the following questions:

- What are other popular breakfast foods aside from eggs?
- What are the primary breakfast proteins and how should they be handled for service?
- What is hash and how is it prepared?
- What are the basic types of breakfast potatoes and how is each prepared?
- What are the two basic types of breakfast cereal?
- What are the traditional hot breakfast beverages and how is each served?

Pancakes, Waffles, Crêpes, and French Toast

Other popular breakfast foods include pancakes, crêpes, waffles, and French toast. The batters for these items are simple to make. Many can be cooked in a few minutes.

Make **pancakes** with a medium-weight pour batter, and cook them on an open, lightly oiled griddle. See Figure 1.23 on the following page. **Crêpes** (CRAPES or CREPPS) are very thin pancake-type items with a high egg content. The result is a delicate, unleavened griddlecake. Crêpes are traditionally cooked in a lightly oiled, very hot sauté pan. Make **Swedish pancakes** with a slightly sweetened batter that is a bit heavier than a crêpe batter. Cook these pancakes on a flat griddle or in a special fluted pan.

39

Section 1.2
Breakfast Foods and Drinks

Introduce the Section

a. Eggs and milk are main ingredients in many batter-based breakfast foods.

b. This section covers a variety of dishes that have similar batters and features.

c. The food items in this section are most often served for breakfast or brunch.

d. This section encourages hands-on practice of the skills.

e. Many of the foods in the section are often served with syrup, but the students can think of other accompaniments.

Vocabulary Review

a. Direct students to the key terms.

b. Pronounce each word, and have the students repeat the pronunciation out loud.

c. Discuss the definition of each word.

Teach

Discuss

- Ask students if they have a favorite special breakfast food.

- Breakfast foods made with batter (e.g., pancakes, waffles, and French toast) are very popular restaurant items.

- These foods are inexpensive to make, yet guests will often come to a restaurant just to order them.

- These breakfast foods can also be combined for service with breakfast meat, eggs, potatoes, and other selections.

Vocabulary Terms

- **Pancakes:** A milk-egg batter food that is poured and cooked on a griddle in round cakes, usually served in stacks.

- **Crêpes:** Made with a milk-egg batter with a high egg content that cooks into a thin pancake; usually cooked one at a time in a specialized pan with curved sides. They can be rolled around fillings, both sweet and savory.

- **Swedish pancakes:** Similar to crêpes, but the batter is a bit sweeter and heavier.

Essential Skills:
Making Pancakes, Crêpes, Waffles, and French Toast

A common element of all of these batter items is their golden brown color when they are perfectly ready to eat.

In-Class Activity:
Zen Venn, or Thinking Outside the Box about Pancakes

Math Connection, 21st-Century Skills—Global Awareness

Pancakes or some sort of egg-batter griddle cakes are found in many, many cuisines of the world.

The students will make a modified Venn diagram, with the common elements of the cakes written inside a square box.

Outside the box, the students will write the various differences and names for these cakes: blintzes, crêpes, hotcakes, flapjacks, pancakes, *pannekuchen*, and any other name or dish they can learn about.

Each of these names should include a brief description, such as "rolled around a fruit filling" or "topped with sour cream." These differences will be "floating" around the central box.

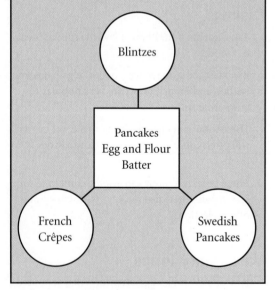

Vocabulary Terms

- **Waffles:** Made with batter similar to a pancake batter, with added egg and oil; cooked on a special iron grid, both sides at the same time, until golden.

Figure 1.23: A cook prepares pancakes on the grill.

For **waffles**, use a medium-weight pour batter similar to pancake batter, but with more egg and oil. Cook waffles in a specially designed waffle maker, or iron, that creates grid-like holes or specialty designs.

French toast is sliced bread (preferably a day old) dipped in an egg-and-milk mixture. Chefs often season the mixture lightly with cinnamon and nutmeg. Cook French toast on a lightly oiled griddle or flat pan, or pan-fry it in clarified butter in a hot sauté pan.

Serve pancakes, crêpes, waffles, and French toast with butter and syrup, powdered sugar, fresh fruit, or whipped cream. For additional variety, add ingredients such as chocolate chips or blueberries to pancake or waffle batters.

Essential Skills
Making Pancakes, Crêpes, Waffles, and French Toast

❶ Prepare the batter according to the particular recipe. See Figure 1.24a.

❷ While letting the batter rest, heat the pan, griddle, or waffle iron.

❸ Lightly coat the pan or griddle with oil, clarified butter, or a nonstick spray.

❹ When the surface is hot, pour the batter in or on it. In the case of French toast, first dip the bread in the egg-milk mixture, and then place it on a heated surface. See Figure 1.24b.

❺ Turn the item and completely cook it on the other side. When using a waffle iron, do not turn the item.

Figure 1.24a: Step 1—Prepare the batter.

Figure 1.24b: Step 4—Pour the batter on the hot surface.

Figure Focus

Figure 1.23: A grill or griddle is the best method of cooking pancakes. They can be easily flipped at just the correct time without an awkward wrist movement.

Figure 1.24a: All breakfast batters should be smooth and light, without lumps.

Figure 1.24b: Another common element when preparing breakfast batters is that the cooking surface should be preheated and nonstick, ready to cook.

Preparing Breakfast Meats and Starches

Operations often include breakfast meats, such as bacon, sausage, ham, Canadian bacon, and hash, to complete the breakfast meal.

Bacon and Sausage

Food preparers can cook bacon and sausage in advance. Bacon is about 70 percent fat and shrinks quite a bit. Cook bacon until it is crisp, and then drain it of fat. Cook sausage completely through. It should be slightly browned on the outside but juicy on the inside. Some operations have begun using precooked bacon and sausage. These items help to reduce labor cost and equipment requirements.

Essential Skills
Cooking Bacon or Sausage

❶ Cook it in a fry pan or on a griddle on a medium heat. See Figure 1.25a.

❷ Alternatively, place it on sheet pans and bake it at 375°F in a standard oven until it is crisp and brown as desired. See Figure 1.25b.

❸ Monitor it and turn it as needed to ensure even cooking and browning.

Figure 1.25a: Step 1—Cook bacon or sausage in a fry pan or griddle.

Figure 1.25b: Step 1—Or, place the meat on sheets and bake it.

41

Discuss

- Bacon and sausage are both usually made from pork. They are salty and high in fat, so they are usually served in small portions.

- Ask students if they prefer bacon crispy, crunchy, or oily.

- Cooked properly, bacon should be crisp and brown, not raw in thick sections or crunchy in thin sections.

- What ideas do the students have about bacon thickness?

Essential Skills:
Cooking Bacon or Sausage

Undercooked bacon or sausage is unappealing and perhaps even unsafe.

Although most pork products today are safe, complete cooking is key to ensuring the safety of your guests.

Figure Focus
Figure 1.25a: Make sure that the thickest sections of fat cook through.

Figure 1.25b: When baking bacon, watch for it curling up and make sure the thickest sections of fat cook through.

Discuss

- Canadian bacon is used for breakfast as a meat with eggs and hash browns. It is also the meat element of Eggs Benedict and is popular as a pizza topping, often paired with fresh tomatoes.

- Fish is an essential part of a breakfast buffet in many parts of Asia, Europe, and Scandinavia. The fish is sometimes smoked, brined, or pickled, and served cold.

- Hash is a dish that originated by using leftovers before there were microwaves. It was a "second-day" dish.

- "Scrapple" is another name for breakfast hash. It might have apples mixed in with the meat, potatoes, and onions.

Vocabulary Terms

- **Hashed brown potatoes:** Two-stage potato dish made by steaming or simmering potatoes, shredding them, and pan-frying them.

Ham and Canadian Bacon

Ham for breakfast service is a smoked or cured item that only needs to be heated and browned slightly on a griddle or under the broiler. Canadian bacon is boneless pork loin that has been cured and smoked. Cook it the same way as ham, by heating and browning it. Ham and Canadian bacon don't hold well. Cook them as close to service as is practical.

Fish

Operations often offer fish, such as smoked salmon or trout, on breakfast and brunch menus. See Figure 1.26. Generally, these items are served cold; all such fish items should remain properly refrigerated until as close to service as is practical. Items such as broiled trout are particularly popular for breakfast at certain types of resorts.

Figure 1.26: Bagels can be served with cream cheese, lox, and dill.

Hash

Hash is a mixture of chopped meat (fresh, smoked, or cured), potatoes, and onions. The ratio of meat to vegetable is not an exact one, and the chef can include a wide variety of vegetables to give the dish color and flavor. The goal of the dish is to achieve a flavorful balance of meat, potatoes, and onion. Hash can be prepared from leftover meat. The meat should always be of high quality; otherwise, the result will not be a quality product. Hash is often formed into patties and fried.

Potatoes

Potatoes are prepared in a variety of ways for breakfast and brunch. Most often chefs make them into hashed brown potatoes or home fries. Prepare **hashed brown potatoes**, or hash browns, by steaming or simmering them in lightly salted water and then peeling, chilling, and shredding the potatoes. Cook the shredded potato on a lightly oiled griddle on medium heat to a light golden

42

Figure Focus

Figure 1.26: Lox are a form of brined or smoked salmon, usually kosher. If the lox are from Nova Scotia, they may be called "Nova."

brown on both sides. **Home fries** are raw potatoes that have been peeled and then sliced, diced, or shredded. Cook them on a well-oiled griddle, or pan-fry them until golden brown and cooked through. Season hash browns and home-fried potatoes well during cooking.

Cereals

Hot and cold cereals have become more popular as breakfast entrées. A wide variety of cold cereals featuring oat bran and granola are common breakfast requests. Cold, prepackaged cereals need no formal preparation. Serve cold cereals with accompanying milk or cream, sugar (brown sugar is attractive), and fresh fruit, such as sliced bananas or strawberries. Some kitchens prefer to make their own granola, often serving it with yogurt and fresh or stewed fruit.

There are two types of hot cereal: whole, cracked, or flaked (oatmeal and cracked wheat) and granular (farina and cornmeal). When preparing hot cereal, be sure to measure the correct amount of water, salt, and cereal according to package directions. Adding milk makes the cereal creamier—and more expensive. When using milk, take care not to boil or scorch it. Always add the cereal to the liquid slowly, stirring constantly to prevent lumps. "Instant" hot cereals are precooked and dried cereals that are reconstituted in hot water or milk. These cereals have become popular in homes and commercial kitchens because they need little preparation time and do not lump easily. To prevent hot cereals from drying out, keep them covered until they are served. Oatmeal, cream of wheat or rice, grits, and cornmeal mush are all typical hot cereals. Figure 1.27 shows examples of hot and cold cereals.

Figure 1.27: Hot and cold cereals are popular breakfast entrées.

Discuss

- Students might not understand why someone would go out to breakfast and order hot oatmeal. Help the students understand that many breakfast guests are eating "on the road" for business reasons. This is especially true at hotels. Guests who travel for business often have menu preferences that are different than those of people who eat out for social reasons or celebration.

- Guests who eat many breakfasts in the same place on consecutive days might have specific requests of the kitchen. It is nice to accommodate the guest when possible.

Vocabulary Terms

- **Home fries:** Similar to hashed brown potatoes, but made from raw potatoes.

Figure Focus

Figure 1.27: Hot cereal, such as oatmeal, should be available on any breakfast menu for guests who prefer it to heavier breakfasts. Cold cereal assortments will also satisfy some guests.

Discuss

- Guests might also have specific requests for toast, including type of bread, light toast or dark, and butter, spread, or dry. Accommodate the guest if possible.

- The same is true of fruit. Guests might request specific fruits with their breakfast.

- Breakfast is perhaps the most individualized meal a restaurant will serve.

- Offerings might or might not be creative, unusual, or exotic, but many guests will have very specific requests. These are often due to health or well-being concerns. The food a guest eats first thing in the morning could affect how he or she feels throughout the day.

ServSafe Connection:
Breakfast Buffet: Considerations When Presenting Cold Fish and Meat

Keeping cold foods away from hot foods on a buffet prevents heat transfer from hot foods that could warm cold foods to temperatures within the danger zone.

Fast Fact:
Did You Know . . . ?

The temperature danger zone was thoroughly covered in Level 1, Chapter 2: Food Safety.

It is important to maintain proper temperature controls on all TCS foods.

In-Class Activity:
Granny's Advice for a Happy Life

Literacy Connection, 21st-Century Skills—Work Creatively with Others

"Remember to butter the toast all the way to the edges." Some people find great meaning in this expression.

What could it possibly mean? Is it a metaphor for living? Is it culinary advice?

Divide the students into two groups. Have each group prepare and present a skit based on this expression. After the performances, discuss how this might apply to a philosophy of cooking for and serving guests.

Breads and Pastries

The most common breakfast bread in the United States is probably the simple slice of toast—white, wheat, and sourdough, for example, grace many tables. Other bread and pastry options include bagels, biscuits, muffins, croissants, doughnuts, cornbread, coffeecake, English muffins, and sweet rolls, among many others. Chefs typically serve breakfast breads hot or warm, accompanied by butter, honey, cream cheese, or jam.

Fruit

A number of fruits are commonly associated with the breakfast table. Halved grapefruit, either raw or broiled with brown sugar, is very popular on breakfast menus. Although fresh fruits—whole or sliced, depending on the type—may appear with cereals, many people enjoy a light fruit salad as part of this meal. Compotes and jams made of fresh or dried fruits also play a role: for instance, slather apples cooked in cinnamon on top of a stack of pancakes. Fruit juices, especially orange and tomato, are traditional at this time as well.

[ServSafe Connection]

Breakfast Buffet: Considerations when Presenting Cold Fish and Meat

1. Always keep cold foods separate from hot foods.
2. Hold cold foods at 41°F or colder.
3. Keep all cold foods refrigerated until ready to serve.
4. Display cold foods upon ice beds.
5. Make ice beds by filling bowls or chafing dishes with ice and placing small shallow trays of cold food items on top of the ice. See Figure 1.28.
6. Use smaller rather than larger trays and frequently rotate in new trays from the refrigerator.
7. Check food temperatures at least once every two hours, which will leave time to fix a problem before you must throw out the food.
8. Replace empty food platters with new platters rather than reusing the previous ones.

Figure 1.28: Cold foods are displayed upon ice beds.

[fast fact]

Did You Know...?

The CDC estimates that 76 million people in the United States become ill from foodborne pathogens every year, and 5,000 of these people die. Pathogens that cause foodborne illness grow rapidly at room temperature (70°F). The temperature danger zone is 41°F to 135°F.

Figure Focus
Figure 1.28: Fish can look spectacular and beautiful presented on trays of ice.

[trends]

Coffee in Schools

The coffee culture in the United States began its renaissance in the 1990s, and it's still in full bloom almost a full two decades later. There aren't any signs of it slowing down either—especially since the market for coffee and coffee-based drinks continues to get younger.

Coffee houses are now a staple on most college campuses, but an ever-increasing number of college campuses are taking it a step further by building a coffee shop right into the college library. More and more teens are using coffee houses to gather and socialize as well. In 2007, Starbucks Corp. officially recognized that its customer base had expanded to include teenagers and children, which was a reversal from its previous stance. This trend seems to be taking hold in high schools. Foodservice contractor Aramark, for example, has opened 15 coffee shops in high schools across the country.

There may be nutritional perils associated with this trend. Most young people do not simply have a small cup of black coffee. Many popular coffee drinks are high in fat and sugar, and the caffeine can be habit forming.

What does all this mean? Well, if nothing else, it means that the next generation of coffee drinkers promises to be better versed and more selective in their coffee tastes, preferences, and service. This is an industry trend that any foodservice professional would do well to be aware of.

Coffee drinks consumed by teens are often "dessert"-type beverages, hot or cold, that are high in sugar and fat in addition to being an addictive stimulant. Make sure that students understand that.

Discuss

- Ask the students how they feel about coffee being sold in schools to minors.

- Are the students aware that caffeine is an addictive stimulant? Perhaps they are not aware that caffeine does not create any energy for the person who drinks coffee. Caffeine can also make a person very jittery.

- Caffeine stimulates the body to burn energy more rapidly, in a feeling of awake energy. The feeling lasts until the person becomes even more tired and sleepy than he or she would normally be.

- Do the students realize that a lack of caffeine in an addicted person can cause headaches?

- Do students think that caffeine makes them better students?

- Many guests like to have a cup of black coffee in the morning.

- Sugar and cream are the usual coffee enhancers, and can be offered at the table for guests to add for themselves.

- Some guests like to have coffee with dessert after a nice dinner.

- Coffee bars with barista service are a unique type of foodservice operation. Some are drive-thrus.

- Coffee shops can be gathering places for social interaction and relaxation.

Hot Breakfast Beverages: Coffee, Tea, and Cocoa

Traditional breakfast beverages include coffee, tea, and hot cocoa. Always serve hot beverages very hot and steaming. Both coffee and tea contain **caffeine,** which is a stimulant. People who are sensitive to the effects of caffeine will often ask for decaffeinated options. Figure 1.29 shows a variety of hot breakfast beverages.

Coffee beans are the berries of a tropical shrub that are roasted to develop their flavor. The degree of roasting, which can be light, medium, or dark, affects the flavor of the coffee. Americans generally prefer medium roast, while dark roast coffee is popular in Europe. Coffee is often

Figure 1.29: Hot breakfast beverages include coffee, tea, and hot cocoa.

45

Figure Focus

Figure 1.29: There are several different beverages served hot at breakfast. Ask the students which hot beverages they enjoy.

Vocabulary Terms

- **Caffeine:** The active stimulant in coffee and tea. It gets its name from the word coffee.

Discuss

- Encourage the students to understand coffee service. If they work as servers, they might need to know how to serve a tray full of hot coffee cups and saucers.

- Coffee cups are often monitored by servers to keep them full and warm.

- Coffee should be well made and fresh in urns and insulated pitchers. Coffee urns need to be properly cleaned.

- Some guests will want decaffeinated coffee.

Vocabulary Terms

- **Tea:** A caffeinated drink made from steeping tea leaves. Herbal teas that have no caffeine are made from herbs such as mint.

- **Black tea:** Made from fermented tea leaves.

- **Green tea:** Made from nonfermented tea leaves.

served at every meal. Flavored coffee—ranging from hazelnut, almond, mint, and chocolate to blueberry and strawberry—is also popular at any meal.

Many times, a sip of coffee is the first and last impression a customer has of a restaurant. Because these impressions are very important, always purchase, brew, and pour good-quality coffee. Avoid holding brewed coffee for over an hour. After that time, the loss of flavor is considerable. Serve coffee hot and steaming. Plan coffee production so that coffee is always fresh.

For the best-tasting coffee, use the right proportion of water to coffee. Always start with fresh, cold water, and heat it to a proper brewing temperature of 195°F to 200°F. Take into account proper timing, equipment, filters, and holding procedures as well.

Clean coffee urns regularly to avoid calcium buildup and to ensure good-tasting coffee. To clean urns, run a solution of one part white vinegar and four parts water through the brewing cycle. Rinse the system by running plain cold water through the brewing cycle three times.

Cold coffee drinks are also very popular now. Iced coffee, which is the coffee counterpart to iced tea, is made by putting brewed coffee over ice. Fancier frozen coffee drinks are also very popular and often come in different flavors such as mocha, caramel, or peppermint.

Tea is generally less expensive than coffee, although some rare teas can be quite expensive. One cup of tea has about half the caffeine contained in a cup of coffee. Tea is served either very hot or iced. There are **black teas** (tea leaves that have been fermented) and **green teas** (tea leaves that are not fermented). Oolong tea is partially fermented. Herbal tea (technically called a tisane because there is no actual tea in the blend) is made from many different fruits and herbs and is naturally caffeine-free. After tea is graded, which depends on its level of bruising, wilting, and oxidation, it is blended to ensure consistency and uniformity. Some tea blends may contain as many as 30 individual teas. Figure 1.30 shows a well-presented table-side tea service.

Figure 1.30: A personal tea service includes the brewed tea, sugar, and honey.

Figure Focus

Figure 1.30: Most guests steep their own tea in a small pitcher or a cup. They will also add their sweetener, cream, or lemon themselves.

[fast fact]

Did You Know...?

Fermentation is the term used in the tea industry for the treatment of tea leaves that breaks down certain unwanted chemicals and modifies others to develop the flavor of the tea.

[ServSafe Connection]

Tea, Anyone?

Dry tea leaves contain low levels of bacteria, yeast, and mold (like most plant-derived food). Tea must be handled properly to ensure its safety:

- When steeping tea, make sure the tea leaves are exposed to water at least 175°F for at least 5 minutes. When preparing tea in automated machines, make sure the leaves remain in contact with water at least 175°F for 1 minute.

- Brew only as much tea as you reasonably expect to sell within a few hours.

- Never hold tea brewed for iced tea at room temperature for more than 12 hours. Throw out the tea at the end of the 12 hours.

- To protect tea flavor and avoid pathogen contamination and growth, clean and sanitize tea brewing, storage, and dispensing equipment at least once a day. Equipment should be disassembled, washed, rinsed, and sanitized. Urn spigots should be replaced at the end of each day with freshly cleaned and sanitized ones.

Hot cocoa is also a popular breakfast drink. It is made from cocoa powder or shaved chocolate and sugar stirred into heated milk or water. The terms "hot chocolate" and "hot cocoa" are often used interchangeably, but there is a difference. Hot chocolate is made from actual chocolate bars. Hot cocoa is made from the powder of the cacao bean. Hot cocoa is much lower in fat than hot chocolate because the cocoa butter, added back in when chocolate bars are manufactured, is extracted when the cocoa powder is ground from the cacao bean.

Hot cocoa is usually made from its instant form, a dry mix of cocoa powder, sugar, and dry milk, mixed with hot milk or water. Hot cocoa drinks can be topped with small marshmallows or whipped cream.

47

**Fast Fact:
Did You Know . . . ?**

The fermentation of tea means the leaves have been oxidized.

**ServSafe Connection:
Tea, Anyone?**

Chill tea for iced tea soon after steeping.

Discuss

- Hot cocoa does not have as much caffeine as a coffee drink.

- Hot cocoa does have theobromine, a substance similar to caffeine that is found in chocolate. Theobromine might have mildly stimulating properties, but it is not as strong as caffeine.

Vocabulary Terms

- **Hot cocoa:** A beverage made from cocoa powder, milk, and sugar.

Nutrition: Caffeine

A caffeine "crash" or fatigue can occur after the dose wears off.

Also, withdrawal symptoms may begin to occur between doses.

High school students can experience difficulty concentrating and insomnia from caffeine, so this should be considered when offering caffeine drinks on campus.

What's New: Honey Straws

Originally, a honey salesman thought of filling straws with honey for convenience, then invented a machine for this and filled the straws as a home industry.

[nutrition]

Caffeine

Caffeine is a stimulant, and it is the most popular drug in the world. Every day, over 90 percent of Americans use caffeine in some form. Caffeine is found in chocolate, colas and other carbonated beverages, coffee, and tea. Today, many "high-energy" drinks are specially formulated to increase the caffeine content so as to increase drinkers' energy during the day.

Caffeine acts as a stimulant by causing chemical changes in the brain. One effect it has is to raise the level of dopamine in the brain. Dopamine increases feelings of well-being and enhances mood. This reaction is one of the primary reasons why caffeine is also addictive.

Because of its addictive quality, people who drink caffeine regularly can experience withdrawal symptoms such as irritability, restlessness, muscle stiffness, headache, and difficulty concentrating.

Contrary to popular belief, light-roasted coffee has a higher caffeine content than dark-roasted coffee. The longer roasting process in dark-roast coffee literally roasts more caffeine out of the coffee beans. In terms of caffeine content, though, coffee tends to have higher caffeine content than other caffeinated beverages, aside from high-energy drinks.

[what's new]

Honey Straws

Honey is a traditional accompaniment to hot tea. The problem with using honey is that it can be messy—hard to get out of its container, hard to dispense into a cup, and easy to get all over hands and table surfaces. This is not desirable or practical for restaurant service.

The new trend of using honey straws solves a lot of these problems. They come in a variety of flavors and are easy to use, carry, and dispense. The customer cuts the end off of the straw and pushes the honey into a cup of tea without getting sticky. See Figure 1.31.

Figure 1.31: Honey straws are a convenient accompaniment to hot tea.

Figure Focus

Figure 1.31: Honey straws come in various flavors and colors, which are added to regular honey.

Essential Skills
Making Hot Tea with Tea Leaves

❶ Put tea leaves into a preheated, empty pot. Use 1 teaspoon loose tea or one single service tea bag for each 6 ounces of water.

❷ Pour boiling water into the pot. See Figure 1.32a.

❸ Let the tea steep (soak) for at least 3 to 5 minutes.

❹ Serve immediately after steeping. Tea will become bitter if left to steep too long. See Figure 1.32b.

Figure 1.32a: Step 2—Pour boiling water into the pot.

Figure 1.32b: Step 4—Serve tea immediately after steeping.

Being a Barista

[on the job]

With an exponential increase in the numbers of coffee bars, a new group of server opportunities has arisen… the baristas.

In English, barista is a name applied to a person who prepares and serves espresso-based coffee drinks. The word barista is Italian, where a barista is a male or female "bartender" who typically works behind a counter, serving both hot drinks (such as espresso) and cold alcoholic and nonalcoholic beverages.

However, many employers, such as Starbucks, officially use this title for their employees. Among coffee fans, the term is often reserved for someone who has acquired a level of expertise in the preparation of such drinks. In fact, some consider a true barista to be a type of "coffee sommelier," a professional who is highly skilled in coffee preparation, with a comprehensive understanding of coffee, coffee blends, espresso, quality, coffee varieties, roast degree, and espresso equipment and maintenance.

49

Essential Skills:
Making Hot Tea with Tea Leaves

Tea made from leaves that are not bagged needs to be strained.

Another option would be to use a tea ball or a tea infuser spoon.

On The Job:
Being a Barista

Baristas have specific skills, talents, and training. Ask students what skills they think are necessary to be a good barista.

Figure Focus

Figure 1.32a: Be careful of burns.

Figure 1.32b: Serve tea before it becomes stale or bitter.

Summary

- Remind students to review the following:
  1. Pancakes, waffles, crêpes, and French toast
  2. Preparing breakfast meats and starches
  3. Hot breakfast beverages—coffee, tea, and cocoa

Summary

In this section, you learned the following:

- Pancakes, waffles, crêpes, and French toast make up the primary breakfast foods aside from eggs, and these items have similar preparation methods. Crêpes are thinner and have a higher egg content than the basic pancake.

- Bacon, sausage, ham, Canadian bacon, and fish make up the traditional breakfast meats. Bacon and sausage hold well for service, but ham, Canadian bacon, and fish should always be prepared as close to service as is practical.

- Hash is traditionally a combination of meat, potatoes, and onion, but chefs can include other items to give the dish color and flavor.

- Potatoes have two traditional forms for breakfast: hashed brown (steamed or simmered before being shredded and fried) and home-fried (shredded or chopped raw before being fried). Season both versions liberally during preparation.

- Both hot and cold cereals are popular breakfast entrées. They are healthy and relatively easy to prepare. Hot breakfast cereals come in two basic forms: whole, cracked, or flaked (such as oatmeal or cracked wheat) and granular (such as farina and cornmeal).

- Traditional hot beverages are coffee, tea, and cocoa. Coffee and tea can also be served cold over ice, and are available either caffeinated or decaffeinated. Cocoa is lower in fat than hot chocolate and typically made in the United States by mixing hot milk or water with a prepackaged blend of cocoa powder, sugar, and dry milk. All of these beverages in their hot form should be served within an hour after brewing.

Section 1.2 Review Questions

1. What is the difference between a crêpe and a regular pancake?

2. Name two breakfast meats that hold well before service.

3. Describe the two basic forms of hot breakfast cereals.

4. How long can coffee or tea be held before it starts losing flavor?

5. Chef Nims says that you should "cook to impress, and season to leave an impression." How would you prepare a breakfast meal of pancakes or crêpes, meat items, and beverages that would impress a group of culinary students?

6. Breakfast food items tend to be high in fat and calories. Knowing that Kabob makes a concerted effort to keep its menu options healthful and heart-healthy, what breakfast dishes can they put on their brunch menu that will maintain their usual standards?

7. This chapter pointed out that the market for coffee drinkers continues to get larger and more selective and that coffee houses, both independent and corporate chains, continue to multiply. Would these facts make you more or less inclined to focus on coffee service at your own establishment? Given how saturated the coffee market is, how much time and money would you invest in your coffee service?

8. Would you use instant cereals in your restaurant? Why or why not?

51

Section 1.2 Review Questions

1. A crêpe is made from a thinner batter with more eggs than pancakes.

2. Bacon and sausage hold better than Canadian bacon and ham.

3. The two basic forms are granular and whole, cracked, or flaked.

4. Coffee should be served within an hour of brewing. Tea should be served immediately.

5. Each student will have his or her own ideas about this.

6. Each student will come up with ideas for this. They should avoid options very high in fat and calories, like Eggs Benedict, and very sweet and rich fried items.

7. Each student will have an opinion about this.

8. Each student will have an opinion about this, and it will depend on the type of operation the student considers. A hotel self-service breakfast operation would have a completely different requirement than a luxury brunch buffet, for example.

Section 1.2 Activities

1. This will require some outside research by the students. Encourage them to research a food they have never heard of or considered for breakfast.

2. Perhaps the finest way to serve cocoa is in a small pot given with a cup and saucer, as is done in Europe. However, a mug of hot chocolate garnished with whipped cream is also a popular mode of service. Giving a guest an envelope of dry mix and some hot water is not especially nice, and could be messy and result in lumpy cocoa.

3. Each student will have original ideas for this activity. The wedding menus should be created with both the guests and the celebration of the event in mind.

Section 1.2 Activities

1. Study Skills/Group Activity: A Puzzling Way to Start the Day

Work within a group to research a specific breakfast food. Selections may include grits, scrapple, fried mush, hash browns, fried tomatoes, or any other breakfast food that might be new to the class. Groups can present their findings to the class.

2. Activity: Investigation: The Cocoa Case

Investigate cocoa service in a restaurant setting. What is the best way to make cocoa? Does it hold well? How is cocoa best served? Should guests make their own from a mix at the table?

3. Critical Thinking: Wedding Brunch

Create two complete breakfast menu options for a wedding brunch. Your menu must include the main course, side dishes, and the beverage. Explain why you chose those specific menu options for the event.

52

1.1 Dairy Products and Eggs	1.2 Breakfast Foods and Drinks	1.3 Sandwiches
• Milk and milk products • Receiving and storing milk • Creams • Butter and butter substitutes • Cheese • Eggs	• Pancakes, waffles, crêpes, and French toast • Preparing breakfasts meat and starches • Hot breakfast beverages: coffee, tea, and cocoa	• Basic kinds of sandwiches • Primary sandwich components: bread, spread, and filling • Sandwich stations

SECTION 1.3 SANDWICHES

Peanut butter and jelly? Grilled cheese? You probably grew up eating these kinds of sandwiches. Now, take a look at how sandwiches have changed.

Study Questions

After studying Section 1.3, you should be able to answer the following questions:

- What are the basic kinds of sandwiches and what are the basic components?
- What role does each of the three main elements of a sandwich play?
- What are the necessary tools and equipment needed at a sandwich station?

Basic Kinds of Sandwiches

When making sandwiches, consider the combinations of flavors and textures created by different breads, condiments, and meat and vegetable additions. For example, how does the texture of the bread blend with the texture of the filling? Do the flavors work together? Decide whether to serve the sandwich hot or cold, and consider the ratio of bread to the quantity and flavors of the other ingredients.

All sandwiches fall into one of two general categories: hot or cold. A simple hot sandwich consists of hot fillings, such as hot roast beef or grilled vegetables, between two slices of bread or two halves of a roll. Additional items such as fresh tomato, lettuce, or onion may be added for flavor. In the United States, hamburgers and hot dogs are among the most popular hot sandwiches.

In the broadest sense of the word, sandwiches may be served in a variety of ways: open-faced on one slice of bread, rolled up in a piece of bread (such as a wrap sandwich), or even on a flat crust (such as pizza).

53

Section 1.3 Sandwiches

Introduce the Section

a. Help the students understand how important sandwiches are to the lunch trade.
b. There are classic and basic rules about sandwiches.
c. There are traditional main ingredients that serve functional purposes beyond just flavor.
d. Sandwiches can be built efficiently at a station equipped with necessary equipment and foods, like a *mise en place*.

Vocabulary Review

a. Direct students to the key terms.
b. Pronounce each word, and have the students repeat the pronunciation out loud.
c. Discuss the definition of each word.

Teach

Discuss

- Sandwiches are usually handheld, but not always.
- Some hot sandwiches, such as an open-faced hot turkey sandwich, are eaten with a fork and knife.
- Some bread, flat bread, or crust component is universal to a sandwich-type item.
- Hamburgers and hot dogs are hot sandwiches, and pizza is a hot open-faced sandwich.

Teaching Tips

- Help the students to see sandwiches as a category, and not a single item.

- It might challenge the students' food beliefs to think of pizza as a sandwich item.

- This sort of challenge can help students experiment and be imaginative with creating sandwiches.

Vocabulary Terms

- **Open-faced hot sandwiches:** Open-faced means that the filling does not have a second piece of bread or crust over it. When grilled, heated, or covered with melted cheese or gravy, these sandwiches can be served hot.

- **Hors d'oeuvres:** Often based on sandwich concepts, these are bite-sized hot or cold finger foods served as appetizers.

- **Grilled (or toasted) sandwiches:** Sandwiches with buttered bread cooked on a grill or heated in the oven. The filling heats and any cheese in it melts.

- **Panini:** A grilled sandwich that is not buttered and is heated in a panini press, or a two-sided grill.

- **Deep-fried sandwich:** A sandwich dipped in egg and deep-fried.

- **Pizza:** A yeast pie crust topped with a pizza sauce, mozzarella cheese, and a variety of other items; served open-faced.

[fast fact]

Did You Know...?
The popular explanation for the term "sandwich" is that John Montagu, the Fourth Earl of Sandwich, asked his valet to bring him meat between two pieces of bread that he could eat (maybe at his desk, maybe at a card table). Today, a sandwich is defined as two or more slices of bread with a filling of meat, fish, cheese, jam, or pretty much anything else.

Hot Sandwiches

Make **open-faced hot sandwiches** by placing one slice of buttered or unbuttered bread or roll on a serving plate with hot meat or other filling and covering it with a hot topping, such as sauce or cheese. Broil the sandwich quickly if the cheese needs melting. Make smaller versions of some types of open-faced hot sandwiches for **hors d'oeuvres** (or DERVS), the hot or cold bite-sized finger foods that are served before a meal.

Grilled (or **toasted**) **sandwiches** are another type of hot sandwich. Butter the outside of the bread and brown on the griddle or in a hot oven. Grilled cheese, grilled ham and cheese, and tuna melt (grilled tuna salad and cheese) are popular varieties. Make panini sandwiches by grilling sandwiches on a **panini** (PAH-nee-nee) press. This compresses the sandwich and warms the ingredients without adding additional fat to the outside of the sandwich. Figure 1.33 provides an example of a well-made panini sandwich.

Figure 1.33: A panini sandwich is grilled on a panini press.

Make **deep-fried sandwiches** by dipping the sandwich in beaten egg (sometimes with bread crumbs) and then deep-frying it. Cook the sandwich on the griddle or in the oven to reduce fat and make it less greasy. One example is a Monte Cristo sandwich, which is filled with turkey or chicken breast, ham, and Swiss cheese.

Pizza, while not a typical sandwich, is hot, open-faced Italian pie with a crisp yeast dough bottom. Bake pizza with flavored or seasoned tomato sauce and

54

Figure Focus

Figure 1.33: A panini press not only heats the sandwich through while toasting the bread, but it also compresses the filling a bit, making the sandwich easier to eat.

additional toppings, such as cheese, meat, and vegetables. Pizza comes in a wide variety of crusts, such as thin, thick, and pan. There is a tremendous variety of toppings and sauces as well. Examples include chicken alfredo, Hawaiian with pineapple and Canadian bacon, and taco pizza. Pizzas can also be wood-fired, roasted, or kiln-baked.

Cold Sandwiches

A simple **cold sandwich** consists of two slices of bread or two halves of a roll, a spread, and a filling. As with hot sandwiches, the choices for fillings are many. The most common fillings are meat and cheese or a salad, such as egg salad or tuna salad.

A **submarine sandwich** usually refers to a cold sandwich served on a long, sliced roll with several types of cheese, meat, lettuce, tomato, onion, and various other toppings. These sandwiches may also be referred to as subs, grinders, heroes, or hoagies. In some instances, the filling may be hot, such as in a meatball sub.

A **wrap sandwich** is made on any type of flat bread—for example, tortillas, cracker bread, or rice paper wrappers—and spread with a hot or cold sandwich filling. It is then rolled up.

A **multi-decker sandwich** has more than two slices of bread (or rolls) with several ingredients in the filling. The club sandwich is one example of a multi-decker sandwich. A traditional **club sandwich** is three slices of toasted bread spread with mayonnaise and filled with an assortment of sliced chicken and/or turkey, ham, bacon, cheese, lettuce, and tomato. Serve club sandwiches cut into four triangles.

Open-faced sandwiches can also be cold sandwiches, made with a single slice of bread, with the filling or topping attractively arranged and garnished. A version of the open-faced cold sandwich is a **canapé** (CAN-uh-pay), a type of hors d'oeuvre. See Figure 1.34. Make canapés from bread or toast cutouts, English muffins, crackers, melba toasts, or tiny unsweetened pastry shells. Spreads can be as simple as flavored butter or softened cream cheese. Use meat or fish spreads to give a zestier

Figure 1.34: A pantry chef may prepare canapés using crackers with an attractive topping.

Discuss

- Ask the students what they had for lunch yesterday. Chances are a few will say "sandwich." Help the students to see that many of their favorite handheld food items are really based on the sandwich concept.

Vocabulary Terms

- **Cold sandwich:** Made up of cold sandwich components, handheld.

- **Submarine sandwich:** Sometimes called a poor boy or a hoagie; a roll filled with mixed sandwich fillings, hot or cold, handheld.

- **Wrap sandwich:** A sandwich rolled into a flat bread like a tortilla.

- **Multi-decker sandwich:** Several slices of bread or toast layered with filling.

- **Club sandwich:** A layered meat sandwich sliced into triangles and secured with a pick.

- **Canapé:** Small hors d'oeuvres sandwiches that are visually attractive, open-faced, and often cut into decorative shapes.

Figure Focus

Figure 1.34: Very small cookie cutters can also be used to prepare canapé bread. The canapés are bite-sized.

Discuss

- Tea sandwiches are not made with tea, of course. They are served with tea, traditionally at afternoon "tea time" in Great Britain, which is served as a refreshing afternoon restorative, not a full meal.

- Tea sandwiches have a light filling such as cucumbers, watercress, egg salad, or a light ham salad with celery.

**Fast Fact:
Did You Know . . . ?**

Although all burgers can be wholesome, the quality of burgers varies. Some might be from a mixed beef product with a small patty, whereas others could be ground Angus sirloin loaded with condiments.

**ServSafe Connection:
Tips for Salads and Sandwiches Containing TCS Food**

Ongoing sandwich prep stations should have refrigerated containers or ingredients packed in ice.

Discuss

- Preparing sandwiches to order ensures a good texture of the bread. Advance preparation of sandwiches can result in soggy or stale bread, unless precautions are taken to avoid these problems.

Vocabulary Terms

- **Tea sandwiches:** Always served cold on bread without crusts, usually small. Fillings are usually light, fresh, and delicate.

---

flavor. Or use fruit, vegetables, and meat cut into bite sizes as the base for canapés. An attractive garnish is the finishing touch to any canapé.

Tea sandwiches are small, cold sandwiches usually served on bread or toast, trimmed of crusts, and cut into shapes. The filling and spread may be the same as those for canapés. Tea sandwiches may also be served open faced.

[fast fact]

Did You Know...?
The hamburger is the most popular sandwich in the United States. In this country, there are primarily two types of burgers: quick-service hamburgers and individually prepared burgers made in homes and restaurants. Common toppings include lettuce, tomatoes, onions, sliced pickles, and/or cheese.

[ServSafe Connection]

Tips for Salads and Sandwiches Containing TCS Food
- Make sure TCS food such as tuna, eggs, ham, and chicken is properly cooked before mixing it into sandwich filling.
- Always refrigerate salad sandwiches at 41°F or lower. Remember that pathogens can grow in food that is in the temperature danger zone. *NOTE:* This should also be done for potato and pasta salads made with mayonnaise (which contains eggs).
- Remove from the cooler only as much food as you can prepare in a short period of time, and prepare food in small batches. This keeps ingredients from sitting out for long periods of time.
- Many sandwiches have ready-to-eat food as their ingredients; for example, deli meat, cheese, and vegetables. Remember to wash your hands before putting on gloves when handling ready-to-eat food.

Primary Sandwich Components: Bread, Spread, and Filling

Preparing hot and cold sandwiches to order is an important skill for anyone who works in foodservice. Many operations prepare sandwiches to order to ensure their freshness. Cover sandwiches prepared ahead of time with a sheet of plastic wrap and store in a refrigerator for service within three hours, or wrap them individually and refrigerate for two to three days.

56

The basic components of a sandwich are bread, spread, and filling. While **bread** serves as an edible container for the food inside, it also provides bulk and nutrients. **Pullman loaves**, sandwich loaves of sliced white bread, are still the most frequently used sandwich bread. But a variety of hard rolls, pita bread, French bread, tortillas, flatbreads, and multigrain or cinnamon and raisin bread are also very popular. Many operations also offer a variety of whole wheat, marbled ryes, and non-wheat or gluten-free breads. Regardless of the type, any bread or roll must be served fresh.

There are many different types of spreads that can be used when preparing a sandwich. A **spread** serves three main purposes: to prevent the bread from soaking up the filling, to add flavor, and to add moisture. Butter and mayonnaise are the most common spreads. Butter must be soft enough to spread easily without tearing the bread. Butter can be softened by whipping it in a mixer or letting it stand at room temperature for about 30 minutes. Butter flavored with lemon, chive, mustard, honey, or other ingredients is often used to add a unique flavor to a sandwich.

While mayonnaise is often used instead of butter because it has more flavor, it actually adds moisture to the bread and can make it soggy. Commercially prepared mayonnaise has been made with pasteurized eggs and is, therefore, less hazardous than homemade mayonnaise. Raw, unpasteurized eggs should never be used to make mayonnaise in kitchens catering primarily to high-risk individuals.

The **filling** of the sandwich is the main attraction. The purpose of the filling is to provide the primary flavor to the sandwich. Generally, the filling is protein-based, but it doesn't have to be. Vegetable-based sandwiches are popular today, such as Caesar salad wraps or portobello sandwiches. Fillings can vary from sliced or grilled meat and cheeses to salad mixtures such as egg or tuna. The filling may be sliced, ground, blended, or tossed—any form that fits the type of sandwich being prepared. The flavors of a sandwich are limited only by the creativity of the sandwich chef.

Sandwiches are often served with accompaniments. These vary from additional condiments, such as ketchup, mustard, or horseradish sauce to fresh and pickled vegetables, such as lettuce, onion, tomato, and sweet or dill pickles. French fries or chips are also a popular accompaniment, as are potato salads and slaws.

Pizza is generally composed of a crust, sauce, and toppings. All of these ingredients are affected by customer tastes and local demands for a particular pizza or toppings. For example, New York-style pizza has a thin, flexible crust with a small amount of sauce. Chicago-style deep-dish pizza, on the other hand, has a very thick crust and much more sauce and cheese. Pizzas may be extremely

57

Discuss

- Mayonnaise-type salad dressing spreads are usually thickened with starch rather than emulsified by an egg, which changes the performance and the flavor a little bit. They can make bread a bit soggier than mayonnaise if sandwiches need to be held refrigerated for a long period of time. However, they are still oil based and can serve as a barrier. Some individuals prefer these spreads to mayonnaise.

- Because sandwiches are considered handheld and easy to eat, the accompaniments are often easy to eat as well. French fries are handheld. Potato salad and cole slaw can be eaten easily with a plastic fork for a picnic or take-out lunch. Although definitely not handheld, soup is often paired with sandwiches for a lunch menu.

Vocabulary Terms

- **Bread:** Allows sandwiches to be edible as handheld items.

- **Pullman loaves:** Square bread slices, ideal for simple sandwiches.

- **Spread:** Usually fat based, serves as a barrier between the filling and the bread to prevent soggy bread. Also adds moisture, texture, and appealing mouthfeel to the sandwich.

- **Filling:** The main ingredient that identifies the sandwich, often protein.

Table 1.5:
Primary Sandwich Components

- Sandwich fillings are often classics that appeal to many people. New ideas are always arriving on the scene as well.

- Have students invent their own sandwiches.

Discuss

- Pizza is such a ubiquitous food item in the United States today that it almost is a food category unto itself. Ask the students to discuss their favorite type of pizza. Many of the students will have strong opinions about this topic. Limit the discussion to fit the time allowed.

In-Class Activity:
The Name Game

21st-Century Skills—Work Creatively with Others

Students will learn the names of classic sandwiches.

Find a soft ball or beanbag for the students to toss.

Have each student in the room adopt the name of a classic sandwich: Monte Cristo, club, Reuben, BLT, patty melt, grilled cheese, hamburger, hot dog, pizza, calzone, PB&J, egg salad, Philly cheesesteak, French dip, and any other classic names you can think of.

Once a student has a name, have that student compose a one-line description of that sandwich.

Arrange students in a circle. The student with the ball introduces himself by saying the name of the sandwich and the description: "Hello! My name is _____ (name the sandwich), and I am a _____ (description)."

The student then tosses the ball to another student who must reply: "Hello _____ (whichever the last sandwich was). It's nice to meet a (describe the last sandwich). My name is _____ (his or her sandwich name), and I am a _____ (description)."

Continue around the room until each person has caught the ball. After each has been introduced, keep going as the game goes faster and faster. At the end, quiz the students to see if they remember the descriptions that go with the names.

simple or contain a number of complex ingredients; as with sandwiches, it largely depends on customer desires and the chef's creativity.

Table 1.5 reviews the various primary sandwich components.

Table 1.5: Primary Sandwich Components	
Beef	Roast beef slices, cold or hot; hamburger patties; small steaks; corned beef; pastrami
Mayonnaise-based salads	Egg salad; tuna salad; chicken salad; turkey salad; crabmeat salad; ham salad
Fish and shellfish	Tuna; sardines; smoked salmon and lox; shrimp; anchovies; fried fish
Pork products	Roast pork; ham; bacon; Canadian bacon
Poultry	Turkey breast; chicken breast
Cheeses	Cheddar; Swiss; monterey jack; mozzarella; pepper jack; provolone; American; cream cheese
Pickled vegetables	Dill and sweet pickles; olives; peppers; artichoke hearts
Condiments	Mustard; horseradish sauce; ketchup; hot sauce; relish
Vegetables	Lettuce; tomatoes; onions, raw or grilled; sprouts (alfalfa, bean, etc.); spinach and other greens
Other fillings	Peanut butter and other nut butters; jelly; hard-cooked eggs; fruits, fresh or dried; hummus; tabbouleh
Popular pizza toppings	**Meat, poultry, and seafood** Pepperoni; sausage; bacon; chicken; anchovies; shrimp **Cheese** Mozzarella; Parmesan; ricotta; gorgonzola; feta **Vegetables** Mushrooms; olives; tomatoes; eggplant; peppers; onions; broccoli; spinach; arugula

58

[ServSafe Connection]

Sandwiches and Ready-to-Eat Foods

Any food that will not be thoroughly cooked or reheated after it is prepared should not be touched with bare hands. Most sandwich items fall into this category. Pathogens from the human body can be transmitted by direct contact and contaminate food. So it is recommended that single-use gloves (also known as disposable gloves) be worn when handling sandwich ingredients and making sandwiches. Alternatively, tongs, forks, spatulas, and waxed paper can also be used to handle sandwich ingredients.

Gloves can be contaminated by sneezing, coughing, preparing raw or undercooked meat, or touching anything that is not food-preparation equipment, such as money or the telephone. Remember to wash hands thoroughly before putting on a pair of new gloves.

In addition, even with gloves, frequent handwashing is required to prevent food contamination. Handwashing is required after doing anything that may result in the contamination of hands, such as using the bathroom, smoking, handling raw or undercooked meat, coughing, sneezing, touching money, or using the telephone.

Handwashing and wearing gloves are two safe, easy ways to reduce food contamination and foodborne illness.

[fast fact]

Did You Know...?

The average child in the United States eats approximately 1,500 peanut butter and jelly sandwiches by the time he or she graduates from high school. In the United States, we refer to peanut butter and jelly sandwiches as PB&J. In England, though, PB&J stands for peanut butter and jam sandwiches.

Sandwich Stations

Sandwich preparation involves a great deal of handwork, precision, and speed. It is important to reduce hand motions whether preparing sandwiches in quantity or to order. The setup for a sandwich station depends on the operation's menu and on available equipment and space. Like every other station in a professional kitchen, the sandwich station needs two basic things: ingredients and equipment. Figure 1.35 shows a well-supplied sandwich station.

Figure 1.35: A well-supplied sandwich station depends on the operation's menu and available equipment and space.

59

Figure Focus

Figure 1.35: Any TCS food in the station should be held at safe temperatures, hot or cold.

Nutrition:
Why Do Sandwiches Get a Bad Rep?

To keep sandwiches lower in calories, reduce the use of fat-based spreads and high-fat deli meats and deli cheeses.

Some types of breads, like croissants, also are very calorie rich.

Pay attention to ingredients, because a sandwich is the sum total of its ingredients.

In-Class Activity:
Totaling Sandwich Calories

Math Connection, 21st-Century Skills—Use Systems Thinking

Choose two sandwiches from the list of classic sandwiches the students learned for the Name Game activity earlier in this chapter.

Have the students research the calorie content of each ingredient in the sandwich. Using this data, have the students add the calories together for a total calorie content of the sandwich.

Please keep in mind that calories must be added for oil or butter if a sandwich is buttered before grilling (like a grilled cheese), or if it is deep-fried (like a Monte Cristo).

Vocabulary Terms

- *Mise en place:* Prepared ingredients and assembled equipment, ready for preparing and cooking a dish.

- **Work table:** A dedicated work space with enough room for *mise en place* and preparations.

Ingredients

Many sandwich ingredients must be prepared ahead of time. This is called *mise en place:* everything needed to prepare a particular item or for a particular service period is ready and at hand. Depending on the sandwich, this could mean separating and cleaning lettuce leaves, slicing tomatoes, preparing garnishes, slicing meats and cheeses, mixing fillings, or preparing spreads.

Arrange and store the ingredients to reduce hand movement. All the items should be within reach so you can work quickly and safely.

In a busy sandwich station, every second counts. Portion sliced items by count and by weight. Portion fillings by weight as well. To keep recipes accurate, each ingredient must be counted or weighed properly. As always, following the recipe is essential to maintaining the quality of the sandwich and meeting the expectations of the customer.

Pizza should have its own preparation area, because the flour needed could contaminate other ingredients. Ingredients on the pizza should be evenly distributed across the top of it. The sauce and other ingredients should come to within a half inch to an inch of the edge of the pizza, depending on the size of the pie.

[nutrition]

Why Do Sandwiches Get a Bad Rep?
Many people don't think of sandwiches as a low calorie, nutritious meal. How many people do you know who opt for a salad at lunch? Are sandwiches inherently a "less" healthful choice?

Of course not! Sandwiches can be hearty and nutritious—a great source of energy. Not all sandwiches are overstuffed, filled with mayonnaise or butter, or loaded with high-fat cheese and large amounts of meat. You can use whole-grain breads or flatbreads, olive oil as a spread, and vegetables, grilled chicken, or meats and cheeses that are low in saturated fat and sodium as fillers.

So, if you want a "bigger" sandwich, add more lettuce, tomato, onions, and pickles.

Equipment

The type of equipment needed in a sandwich station depends on the size of the menu and the operation. An efficient sandwich station makes it easier to prepare sandwiches in large quantities. Most stations have the following:

- **Work table:** It must be big enough to spread out ingredients and do work.

60

- **Storage facilities:** This includes refrigeration equipment for cold ingredients, a steam table for hot ingredients, and dry storage for breads and dry goods as well as paper products, plates, etc.

- **Storage materials:** This includes plastic wrap, deli paper, and labels.

- **Hand tools:** This includes a spreader, spatula, serrated knife, chef's knife, cutting board, and power slicer (power slicer may be needed for any slicing not done ahead of time).

- **Portion-control equipment:** This includes scoops for fillings and a portion scale for measuring ingredients.

- **Cooking equipment for hot sandwiches:** This includes griddles, grills, broilers, deep-fryers, and microwave ovens.

Pizza equipment is similar to that of sandwich equipment but varies based on cooking needs. Conveyer ovens, deck ovens, or wood-fired pizza kilns/ovens can all be used. Metal or wooden peels (as shown in Figure 1.36) for moving the pizzas in and out of the ovens are needed, as well as cutting equipment for finished pizzas. There are several methods and knives to choose from to cut pizza. Possibilities include a rotary cutter (pizza wheel) or a large curved pizza knife that cuts across the entire pizza at once. Let the pizza rest for a brief time before cutting or slicing to allow the ingredients to set. Quick, clean cuts are best. Slices should be even in size.

Figure 1.36: A pizza peel is used to transfer pizza in and out of the oven.

61

Discuss

- Portion controls are a house concern, not a guest concern.

- Measure meat or cheese by weight before guests are involved. Do not allow guests to see the house removing meat or cheese from a portion, as this does not appear generous.

- Specific-sized scoops can portion salad fillings like tuna.

Vocabulary Terms

- **Storage facilities:** The proper storage for any sandwich component, protecting flavor, quality, and safety.

- **Storage materials:** Items that can wrap or cover sandwiches or their components.

- **Hand tools:** Sandwich-making equipment.

- **Portion-control equipment:** Tools that help measure correct portions for quality control.

- **Cooking equipment for hot sandwiches:** Various cooking surfaces and grills or ovens that can cook or toast a sandwich, its bread, or its fillings, including a panini press.

Figure Focus

Figure 1.36: It is not called a "pizza paddle" or a "slider." It is called a "pizza peel" and is often sprinkled with cornmeal to help the crusts slide.

Essential Skills: Sandwich Presentation

Very tall sandwiches are cut with sharp angles so the guest has a corner that will fit in his or her mouth.

Essential Skills: Making a Sandwich (The Basics)

Tomatoes can make bread soggy. Protect the bread with avocado, cheese, mayonnaise, or other fat. Place the tomato between the filling and the fat, never right against the bread.

Essential Skills
Sandwich Presentation

Except for hamburgers and hot dogs, sandwiches are usually cut before serving. Cutting a sandwich in half makes it easier to hold and eat. Cutting a sandwich also makes a more attractive presentation. Cut sandwiches diagonally to create a more angular, sharp look. Cut large, multi-decker sandwiches or very thick sandwiches into quarters, with each section held in place with a toothpick. The customer can easily see the ingredients, and the sandwich looks appealing and appetizing. Serve hamburgers and other uncut sandwiches open-faced to showcase their ingredients.

Pizzas are normally cut before serving as well. Cut smaller, personal-sized pizzas into quarters and larger pizzas into eighths (cut four times across instead of two). For the most attractive presentation, always serve pizza piping hot from the oven when the cheese is still bright and bubbly.

Essential Skills
Making a Sandwich (the Basics)

❶ Pick a type of bread. It can be white, wheat, whole grain, rye, a roll, pita bread, or any other selection. If desired, toast the bread. See Figure 1.37a on the following page.

❷ Choose a spread that will make the bread stick together. Margarine, mayonnaise, or avocado are some choices. Combine the spreads for a different taste. See Figure 1.37b.

❸ Assemble the filling(s). Jam, peanut butter, ham, cheese, lettuce, tomato, vegetables, pickles, bacon bits, onions, turkey, beef, and chicken are just some options. The fillings of the sandwich are really up to the chef's imagination and preference. See Figure 1.37c.

❹ When you finish putting together the foods, slice the sandwich for easier handling. See Figure 1.37d.

Figure 1.37a: Step 1—Select a type of bread.

Figure 1.37b: Step 2—Choose a spread.

Figure 1.37c: Step 3—Assemble the fillings.

Figure 1.37d: Step 4—Slice the sandwich.

Essential Skills
Cutting a Club Sandwich

❶ Place four long, frilled toothpicks in the middle of each side of the sandwich.

❷ Cut the sandwich into quarters from corner to corner. Place the sandwich with the points facing upward. See Figures 1.38a and 1.38b.

Figure 1.38a: Step 2—Cut the sandwich into quarters from corner to corner.

Figure 1.38b: Step 2—Place the sandwich with the points facing upward.

63

Discuss

- There are several traditional layering condiments that can be included with a sandwich, and each can serve a purpose. Ask the students to discuss the function of onion slices, tomato slices, pickle slices, and lettuce leaves.

Teaching Tip

- Students should be encouraged to brainstorm. Even something that might seem funny, like "Lettuce helps keep the bread from sticking in your teeth" might actually be correct (guests probably don't want bread stuck in their teeth).

Figure Focus

Figure 1.37a: The type of bread will determine much about the flavor and texture of the sandwich.

Figure 1.37b: Spreads should complement the bread and the filling.

Figure 1.37c: Keep in mind the importance and function of different layering options.

Figure 1.37d: A sliced sandwich should display the filling.

Figure 1.38a: Use a good knife. Don't saw the sandwich.

Figure 1.38b: The fillings are displayed.

Essential Skills:
Some Guidelines for Making Canapés

Canapés are served as much to invoke a feeling of lavishness as to satisfy hunger.

They should look beautiful and taste fresh and interesting.

Essential Skills:
Tips for Keeping Bread Fresh

Bread can become stale long before it becomes unsafe to eat.

Homework Activity:
Stale Bread—When Does It Become Unsafe?

Science Connection, 21st-Century Skills— Make Judgments and Decisions

When bread is stale, it is beginning to lose quality but is still safe. At some point, bread will begin to grow mold.

What does stale mean? Is it a quantifiable word, or just a description?

What day does mold begin to form? Is mold visible as soon as it has begun to grow?

Should day-old bread be eaten? How about week-old bread? When should it be discarded?

Students can perform their research online or by contacting a bakery.

Students can draw a time line of the quality and safety of one type of bread (brand specific is fine).

Specifically tell the students not to sample a taste of moldy bread. Moldy bread should be discarded, wrapped, in an outside garbage container. Do not handle moldy bread with bare hands.

Mold spores are thought to be potentially carcinogenic or in other ways harmful to humans.

Essential Skills
Some Guidelines for Making Canapés

❶ Pre-preparation is essential. All bases, spreads, and garnishes must be ready ahead of time.

❷ Use quality ingredients. These do not necessarily have to be expensive, but they must be purchased, stored, and prepared with an eye to creating the best-tasting and most attractive-looking product possible.

❸ Assemble canapés as close as possible to serving time. Bases quickly become soggy, and spreads and garnishes dry out easily. As trays are completed, they can be covered lightly with plastic and refrigerated for a short time. Always follow time and temperature rules for safe foodhandling.

❹ Keep spreads and garnishes simple and neat. Elaborate garnishes can fall apart on the tray or in the guests' hands.

❺ Use flavor combinations in spreads and garnishes that are appealing both in taste and in appearance. The ingredients must blend well together and look attractive.

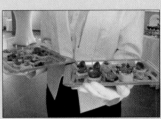

❻ Use spicy or flavorful ingredients. Offer a variety of canapés, including vegetarian and low-fat options to meet the needs of all guests.

❼ Arrange the canapés carefully and attractively on trays. See Figure 1.39.

Figure 1.39: Step 7—Arrange canapés on trays.

Essential Skills
Tips for Keeping Bread Fresh

❶ Bread should be delivered daily, if possible. See Figure 1.40a on the following page.

❷ Keep bread wrapped in moisture-proof wrapping until it is used. See Figure 1.40b.

❸ Store bread between 75°F and 85°F rather than in a refrigerator.

❹ Use French bread and other hard-crusted bread the day it is delivered or baked. See Figure 1.40c.

64

Figure Focus
Figure 1.39: Canapés on trays can be a beautiful work of art, much like a mosaic.

❺ If bread must be kept more than one day, store it in the freezer. Thaw frozen bread inside its wrapping.

❻ Day-old bread can be used for toasting without loss of quality. See Figure 1.40d.

Figure 1.40a: Step 1—Bread is delivered daily.

Figure 1.40b: Step 2—Keep bread wrapped.

Figure 1.40c: Step 4—Use French or hard-crusted bread the same day it is delivered.

Figure 1.40d: Step 6—Day-old bread can be toasted or used to make croutons.

Summary

In this section, you learned the following:

- There are two basic kinds of sandwiches—hot and cold. There are three primary components to all sandwiches—bread, spread, and filling.

- The bread serves as an edible container for the food inside and provides bulk and nutrients. The spread prevents the bread from soaking up the filling and adds flavor and moisture. The filling is the main attraction and is generally the primary flavor of the sandwich.

- Every sandwich station needs two basic things: ingredients and equipment. If possible, ingredients should be prepared ahead of time to cut down on preparation time and hand movement. Equipment should include a work table, storage facility, hand tools, portion-control equipment, and heating equipment.

65

Summary

- Remind students to review the following:
  1. Basic kinds of sandwiches
  2. Primary sandwich components—bread, spread, and filling
  3. Sandwich stations

Figure Focus

Figure 1.40a: Operations can have relationships with local bakers.

Figure 1.40b: Air will cause bread to dry out.

Figure 1.40c: The crust is part of the appeal. As the bread's moisture redistributes in storage, the crust softens.

Figure 1.40d: Day-old bread is still safe.

Section 1.3
Review Questions

1. The spread prevents bread from soaking up the filling, adds flavor, and adds moisture.

2. Any of the following would be correct: work table, storage facilities, storage materials, hand tools (students could specify by name), portion-control equipment (students could specify by name), and cooking equipment (students could specify by name).

3. Students could discuss efficiency, portion control, and service-to-order.

4. Flour is used in the pizza station, which can contaminate other sandwich fillings.

5. This will involve the students' creativity.

6. Students should keep in mind Kabob's healthy-menu philosophy in answering this question.

7. Students should see that certain sandwiches become classics because they work well and taste good. Not all ingredients combine well, but some combinations are excellent.

8. The student should make a solid case for choices here. There could be several good answers, but each one must be supportable.

Section 1.3 Review Questions

❶ What three purposes does the spread in a sandwich serve?

❷ List three pieces of equipment that should be included in an efficient sandwich station.

❸ Why should ingredients in a sandwich station be prepared ahead of time if possible?

❹ Why is it important that the pizza station be separate from the traditional sandwich station?

❺ Chef Nims chose her favorite sandwich, a Grilled Reuben, because of the mix of flavors. What sandwich would you create that would also offer a mix of flavors? Be specific about the ingredients in the sandwich.

❻ For Kabob's new brunch menu, Miguel really wants to offer a pizza item. If you could only put one pizza on the menu, what kind would you put together? Why?

❼ What is the origin of the "sandwich"? Why are there classic sandwiches, like a "patty melt" or a "BLT"? What is the role of creativity and innovation in sandwich making?

❽ Sometimes in an operation, you must make choices based on budget and availability. Keeping that in mind, reexamine the main components of the typical sandwich station. If you had to go without two of the items listed, which would they be? Why did you select the items you did? What would be your work-around for not having access to these tools?

66

Section 1.3 Activities

1. Study Skills/Group Activity: Jigsaw Sandwich

In groups, for homework or in the school kitchen, set up rotating sandwich ingredient stations (bread station, meat station, spread section, cheese station, vegetable/other station, etc.). These could be hypothetical stations with paper "ingredients" if necessary. Each group should determine the options offered at each station. Then, see what sorts of sandwiches could be created by assembling components from each station. Your group should create a table or chart for sandwich suggestions.

2. Activity: Sandwich Flowchart

Create a flowchart that illustrates the most efficient way to make a hot sandwich, such as the Monte Cristo, and a cold sandwich, such as a multi-decker club. Your chart should start with the initial prepping of main ingredients and progress to final assembly of the sandwich on the plate. Where would the components be, and how would they be arranged? How would you control temperatures? How much space would be required?

3. Critical Thinking: One-Cook Show

Imagine you are the sole owner and employee of a sandwich shop. Because you are the only one who can handle all the orders, you need a limited menu that you can serve efficiently. Your menu consists of four sandwiches: two hot sandwiches and two cold sandwiches. Obviously, since your menu is so small, the menu items must be of the best quality while also appealing to a broad range of people. What four sandwiches would you choose to put on your menu and why? Make sure to take into consideration such factors as preparation time, cost, taste appeal, trends, health and nutrition, etc.

67

Section 1.3 Activities

1. This creates a "mix-and-match" format for innovation.

2. Because the requirements of this assignment are detailed, each student should do only one sandwich. However, in a real operation, every sandwich on the menu would require all of these considerations.

3. Because no help is available in the hypothetical sandwich shop, the student will have to consider logistics.

Case Study Follow-Up

1. Each student will have ideas on this. They could include using fresh fruits, whole grains, and low-fat options.

2. Each student will have an opinion about this. Issues such as personnel, logistics, temperature controls, and selection could be included.

3. There is a case for each. Optimism comes from the idea of the exciting new tactic. Skepticism comes from the reality of the logistics. Every good idea requires logistics to enact.

4. Using eggs cuts costs because they are a relatively inexpensive protein. Using local fresh produce in season is usually more cost-effective than off-season selections that must be shipped. The students will also have ideas for this problem.

5. Miguel and Chef Kate will need to use marketing strategies locally, including publicity, to inform and motivate the public to come and eat. Perhaps an introductory campaign or special event could help get it started. Students might have more creative ideas for an opening.

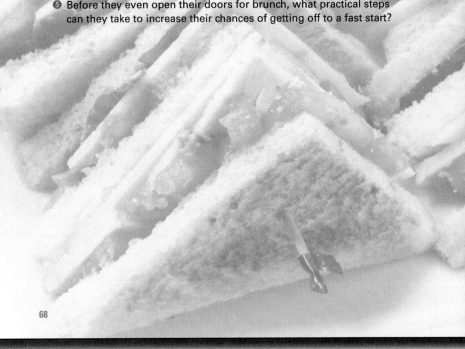

Case Study Follow-Up *Following a Hunch for Brunch*

At the beginning of the chapter, we mentioned that Kabob wanted to open for brunch. Miguel was very excited about the idea, but Chef Kate was more skeptical.

❶ What can Kabob do to make sure the menu still has a healthful, nutritious look and appeal even though some breakfast item selections will necessarily present challenges toward that end?

❷ What do you feel are the biggest obstacles and concerns in putting together a brunch menu?

❸ Do you tend to agree more with Miguel's optimism or Chef Kate's skepticism in opening for brunch? Why?

❹ What steps would you suggest they take to keep their costs down?

❺ Before they even open their doors for brunch, what practical steps can they take to increase their chances of getting off to a fast start?

68

Apply Your Learning

Pricing a Sandwich

As with the price of any menu item, the price of a sandwich takes into account far more than just the ingredients. List all the different elements that go into the price of a sandwich. Then surf the Web for three popular sandwich shops and delis in your area to find the price of a basic cold turkey sandwich, a cold cheese sandwich, and a hot grilled chicken sandwich at each one. Is there a difference in price between the types of sandwiches? If so, what factors account for any differences you find? Is there a difference in the price of the same sandwich at different shops? If so, what factors might account for those differences?

The Many Faces of Pizza

Pizza used to be fairly standard fare: dough, tomato sauce, cheese, and maybe an additional topping or two. But in recent years, pizza has become one of the most versatile food items in the world. Research one specific aspect of this diverse food. Look into its origins, regional differences, sauces, toppings, latest trends, types of crust, cooking methods, etc. Then, write a report on what you find.

Green Eggs and Chem

Eggs have iron in the egg yolk, while the protein of the egg has some amino acids that contain sulfur. The sulfur is released during cooking. Free sulfur reacts with the iron to form a green compound called "iron sulfide". When an egg is hard-cooked, the longer the egg simmers in the cooking water, the more sulfur is liberated. This drives the reaction and the greenish iron sulfide appears at the borders of the yolk. The discoloration can be avoided by using correct cooking times for the altitude, removing the eggs promptly to a pan of cold water, and peeling them as soon as they can be handled. Cook three hard-cooked eggs. Cook one exactly as recommended, and then move the egg to cold water. Cook another three minutes longer. Cook another the correct amount of time, but simply remove the pan from heat, leaving the egg in the hot water. After all three eggs have cooled, peel them and observe any differences in the color of the yolk.

69

Apply Your Learning

Pricing a Sandwich

The student should consider factors like the overhead of the sandwich shop or deli. Space in the middle of a successful urban high-rent financial district will be more expensive than a more remote location.

Each ingredient must be priced and added to the total. The various modes of service must be considered and priced. Will the sandwiches be served on washable dishes or disposable plates? How will this affect the cost?

If the operation has a larger sit-down lunch menu and wait staff, does that affect the price of a simple sandwich?

The Many Faces of Pizza

Students should start their research with Italy, or at least mention Italy. They should also mention New York and Chicago-style pizzas, if they are talking about pizza in the United States.

Green Eggs and Chem

The egg cooked exactly right using the correct method is called the "control." The other eggs are the "test" eggs, and are evaluated as compared to the control.

If there is access to camera equipment, photograph each of the different egg cooking methods and the eggs that result.

Critical Thinking Restaurants and Consumer Health

Each student will have a different opinion. This is a complex and real issue. Is the operation responsible for the guest's food choices?

Are there good foods and bad foods? Or can any food fit into a healthy diet?

Teenagers need a lot of calories if they are active and growing. Is it the place of an operation to determine that certain menu items are too high in calories for a "reference guest"?

Would nutrition information be accurate and consistent? Why or why not? Some of these ideas might help students consider this problem.

Critical Thinking Restaurants and Consumer Health

What responsibility do restaurants have for the health of consumers? Some American cities have banned the use of trans fats in all restaurants. Food options and cooking methods, for breakfast foods in particular, can be very high-fat and high-calorie, especially short-order cooking with fat on the grill. Should nutritional information be provided alongside every menu item? If so, what information should be given? How should foodservice industry professionals balance the role of flavor, texture, and enjoyment of food when it might conflict with consumer health? For an example, consider a 1,000+ calorie egg, sausage, and hash brown breakfast.

70

Exam Prep Questions

1. The purpose of pasteurizing milk is to
   A. kill pathogens.
   B. break down milkfat.
   C. add vitamins and minerals.
   D. prevent spoilage by sunlight.

2. Two nondairy milk options are
   A. rice and soy milk.
   B. skim and rice milk.
   C. soy and lactose-free milk.
   D. lactose-free and evaporated milk.

3. All milk products should be received and stored at what temperature?
   A. 41°F or lower
   B. 43°F or lower
   C. 47°F or lower
   D. 51°F or lower

4. What is the difference between ripened and unripened cheese?
   A. Ripened cheese is typically sweeter than unripened cheese.
   B. Ripened cheese is better for cooking than unripened cheese.
   C. Ripened cheese is aged with bacteria, while unripened cheese is fresh.
   D. Ripened cheese is processed and pasteurized, while unripened cheese is not.

5. Most recipes are based on what size of egg?
   A. Small
   B. Medium
   C. Large
   D. Extra large

6. Pooled eggs should be stored at
   A. 41°F or lower.
   B. 43°F or lower.
   C. 47°F or lower.
   D. 50°F or lower.

7. Baking is typically used in the cooking of which two types of eggs?
   A. Shirred eggs and soufflés
   B. Souffles and coddled eggs
   C. Poached and shirred eggs
   D. Scrambled eggs and omelets

8. The two traditional breakfast meats that hold the best for service are
   A. ham and bacon.
   B. fish and sausage.
   C. sausage and bacon.
   D. bacon and Canadian bacon.

Exam Prep Answers

1. A
2. A
3. A
4. C
5. C
6. A
7. A
8. C
9. C
10. C

9 What is the optimal water temperature for brewing coffee?

A. 175°F to 180°F

B. 185°F to 190°F

C. 195°F to 200°F

D. 210°F to 215°F

10 The two basic components of an efficient sandwich station are

A. bread and meat.

B. condiments and containers.

C. ingredients and equipment.

D. a refrigerator and a microwave.

Farmer–Style Omelet with Asparagus and Mushrooms

Yield: 10 servings

Ingredients

10 oz	Bacon, diced		30	Eggs
10 oz	Onions, minced		1 tsp	Salt
20 oz	Mushrooms, sliced		½ tsp	Ground black pepper
10 oz	Asparagus, cooked and sliced			

Directions

1. Render 1 ounce bacon in a small nonstick skillet until crisp.
2. Add 1 ounce of onions and 2 ounces of mushrooms. Sauté over medium heat, stirring occasionally until light golden brown, about 10-12 minutes.
3. Add 1 ounce of asparagus. Sauté until hot, 5 minutes or more.
4. Beat 3 eggs together and season them with salt and pepper to taste. Pour over ingredients in skillet and stir gently.
5. Reduce heat to low, cover skillet, and cook until eggs are nearly set.
6. Remove cover and place skillet under the broiler to lightly brown the omelet. Serve immediately on a heated plate.

Recipe Nutritional Content

Calories	370	Cholesterol	655 mg	Protein	25 g
Calories from fat	250	Sodium	690 mg	Vitamin A	20%
Total fat	28 g	Carbohydrates	7 g	Vitamin C	10%
Saturated fat	9 g	Dietary fiber	2 g	Calcium	10%
Trans fat	0 g	Sugars	4 g	Iron	20%

Nutritional analysis provided by FoodCalc®, www.foodcalc.com

73

Recipe

Farmer-Style Omelet with Asparagus and Mushrooms

- Note that this item is much lower in calories than the French Toast on the next page, but not a lot lower in fat.

Recipe

French Toast

- Note that even though this is a sweet, rich breakfast item, it actually has less cholesterol than the omelet with asparagus and mushrooms. It is lower in fat, but has twice the calories.

French Toast
Yield: 10 servings

Ingredients

30	Slices challah or brioche (¼ to ½ in thick)	Pinch	Ground cinnamon
		Pinch	Ground nutmeg
1 qt	Milk	½ tsp	Salt
8	Eggs	3 fl oz	Melted butter or vegetable oil
2 oz	Sugar		

Directions

1. Lay slices of bread in single layers on sheet pans and allow to dry overnight, or in a 200°F oven for 1 hour.
2. Combine the milk, eggs, sugar, cinnamon, and nutmeg. Add salt, and then mix well with a whisk until smooth. Refrigerate until needed.
3. Heat a skillet or nonstick pan over medium heat and brush with small amount of butter or vegetable oil.
4. Dip bread slices into batter, coating them evenly. Cook slices on one side until evenly browned, then turn and do the same thing on the other side.
5. Serve at once on heated plates.

NOTE: You may garnish with powdered sugar, cinnamon sugar, or berries, should you choose.

Recipe Nutritional Content

Calories	660	Cholesterol	250 mg	Protein	23 g
Calories from fat	210	Sodium	1060 mg	Vitamin A	20%
Total fat	23 g	Carbohydrates	90 g	Vitamin C	2%
Saturated fat	10 g	Dietary fiber	4 g	Calcium	30%
Trans fat	0 g	Sugars	8 g	Iron	30%

Nutritional analysis provided by FoodCalc®, www.foodcalc.com

74

Open-Faced Turkey Sandwich with Sweet and Sour Onions

Yield: 10 servings

Ingredients

1 lb 4 oz	Onions, sliced	½ tsp	Salt
4 fl oz	Clarified butter	¼ tsp	Ground black pepper
4 fl oz	Soy sauce	10 slices	White Pullman bread
8 fl oz	Plum sauce (prepared)	2 lbs 8 oz	Roasted turkey, thinly sliced
4 fl oz	Water	20	Tomato slices
½ tsp	Garlic powder	1 lb 4 oz	Swiss cheese, thinly sliced
½ tsp	Ground ginger		

Directions

1. Sauté the onions in clarified butter until translucent.
2. Add soy sauce, plum sauce, and water. Simmer until onions are fully cooked and dry.
3. Season with garlic powder, ginger, salt, and pepper to taste.
4. For each sandwich, spread some of the onion mixture on a slice of toast.
5. Cover with about 4½ ounces of turkey.
6. Spread additional onion mix over turkey.
7. Place 2 slices of tomato on top of onion mix, then cover with 2 ounces of Swiss cheese.
8. Bake in 350°F oven until sandwich is heated through and the cheese is melted.
9. Serve immediately.

Recipe Nutritional Content

Calories	620	Cholesterol	190 mg	Protein	53 g
Calories from fat	260	Sodium	1390 mg	Vitamin A	20%
Total fat	29 g	Carbohydrates	36 g	Vitamin C	15%
Saturated fat	17 g	Dietary fiber	2 g	Calcium	50%
Trans fat	0 g	Sugars	5 g	Iron	20%

Nutritional analysis provided by FoodCalc®, www.foodcalc.com

75

Recipe

Open-Faced Turkey Sandwich with Sweet and Sour Onions

- It might interest the students to compare the calories and fat of this item to that in a hamburger or hot dog.

Chapter 2 Overview

Food provides the body with essential nutrients. Proper nutrition helps the body and mind work effectively and efficiently, so it's important for students to learn how to create more nutritious menus.

Section 1: This section reviews the basics of nutrition, including nutrients, the digestive system, and the problems associated with a poor diet.

Section 2: This section reviews food preparation, making menus more healthful, reducing excessive fats, and types of produce (from a grower's point of view).

Advance Preparation	
Review	Sections 2.1–2.2
Contact	Computer lab
	Math department
	Chemistry department
Prepare	Baking soda
	Red cabbage
	Various types of salt to taste
	Raw eggs
	Petri dishes
	Pipettes
	Hydrochloric acid
	Sulfuric acid
	Acetic acid (vinegar)
	Ascorbic acid (vitamin C)

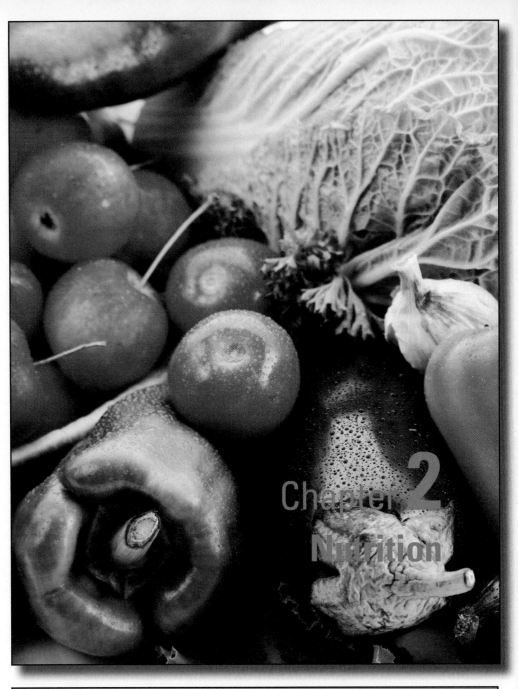

Chapter 2
Nutrition

CUSTOMIZED INSTRUCTION OPTIONS

Less Advanced Students	More Advanced Students	ESOL Students	Special Needs Students
Pages 95, 119	Pages 95, 119	Pages 95, 119	Pages 95, 119

CHAPTER TOOLS

21st-Century Skills	Mathematics	Science	Literacy
Pages 78, 88, 95, 102, 117, 119, 127	Page 102	Pages 93, 123	Pages 119, 127

ServSafe Connection

Pages 84, 87, 111

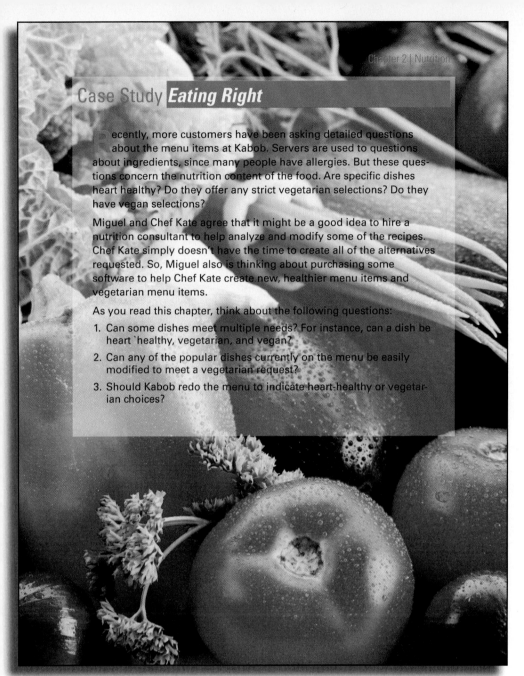

Case Study *Eating Right*

Recently, more customers have been asking detailed questions about the menu items at Kabob. Servers are used to questions about ingredients, since many people have allergies. But these questions concern the nutrition content of the food. Are specific dishes heart healthy? Do they offer any strict vegetarian selections? Do they have vegan selections?

Miguel and Chef Kate agree that it might be a good idea to hire a nutrition consultant to help analyze and modify some of the recipes. Chef Kate simply doesn't have the time to create all of the alternatives requested. So, Miguel also is thinking about purchasing some software to help Chef Kate create new, healthier menu items and vegetarian menu items.

As you read this chapter, think about the following questions:

1. Can some dishes meet multiple needs? For instance, can a dish be heart `healthy, vegetarian, and vegan?

2. Can any of the popular dishes currently on the menu be easily modified to meet a vegetarian request?

3. Should Kabob redo the menu to indicate heart-healthy or vegetarian choices?

Case Study
Eating Right

- What is the difference between "vegetarian" and "vegan"?

- Does this make a difference in the restaurant and foodservice industry?

- How would a chef modify recipes for various nutritional modifications?

- Is this the responsibility of the restaurant? Why or why not?

- This is a topic of much debate lately.

- Note that there are follow-up questions about the case study at the end of the chapter.

- This activity could be done in groups, as a class, or as a homework assignment.

Professional Profile

Discuss	How the experiences of Laura Walsh differ from those of a traditional chef.
Reinforce and Review	Dietetics is a science career, based around nutrients. It integrates food science with foodservice, all within the framework of human physiology and biochemistry.
Teaching Tips	Help students to understand how specialized, yet how broad, the field of nutrition is. Are any of them interested in this field? Find out why. If students are interested in dietetics or food science, they should work hard in their high school math and science courses.

In-Class Activity: Dietetics Careers

21st-Century Skills—Financial, Economic, Business, and Entrepreneurial Literacy

Visit the Web site of the American Dietetic Association at www.eatright.org.

Click the For Health Professionals tab.

Click RD = Nutrition Experts, and then click Qualifications of a Registered Dietitian and read the text.

Click What Services Do RD's Provide and read the text.

Next, click Collaborating for Success, then click ADA Groups and Networks, and then click Dietetic Practice Groups.

Have the students select three practice groups that interest them. Click the group name and visit the Web site for that group.

Have the students write a paragraph about each dietetic area of practice they explored.

If the URL for the Web site has changed since the publication of this book, use a search engine to find The American Dietetic Association, Chicago, Illinois.

[professional profile]

Laura Walsh, RD, LDN

President/Food and Nutrition Consultant
Walsh Nutrition Group, Inc.

I always liked to cook and bake and loved trying new recipes. As I got older I became more health conscious. I worked in a test kitchen for a few years when I first graduated from college, after majoring in Foods in Business, which strengthened my culinary skills. I enjoyed the culinary path but also wanted to learn more about nutrition and how to eat well and help others do the same. After my job in the test kitchen, I went back to school for a degree in nutrition—a B.S. in human nutrition and dietetics. This helped link my interests in food and nutrition and started me on my current career path.

My career started out in a test kitchen developing recipes. This was a great first job and it helped to develop my culinary skills. But I wanted my career to have a health focus. After I graduated with a degree in nutrition and dietetics, I realized my education had prepared me for a job in clinical dietetics, which I knew wasn't the right fit for me. I wanted to incorporate the knowledge I had gained about nutrition in the food industry. And I also wanted to be my own boss.

Laura started her career in the test kitchens of The Pampered Chef working as a Certified Home Economist developing recipes and cookbooks.

But I knew that before opening my own business I needed experience to build my skill set and help me figure out my strengths and weaknesses. So, I started working on weekends as an outpatient dietitian to keep up my clinical skills while working full-time in a nontraditional job in the dietetics field.

I worked very hard at jobs I didn't really like that much. But I knew that they were just part of the plan. I gained invaluable experience, and that is what I needed to run my own business.

Looking back on my path, I am thankful I took each of these jobs seriously even though they weren't my dream jobs. I always gave 100 percent because I knew that these were building blocks to get me to where I wanted to be.

Remember to always try your best—whether you are washing dishes, taking orders, or doing any job. You just never know who you may meet or what skill you might develop along the way. My earlier jobs were not ideal for me, but they helped me develop a varied skill set, learn how to interact with others, and make a lot of contacts along the way. This has served me well in my business. I would certainly not be where I am today without the experience of yesterday.

78

So, if you want to enter this field, always follow your dreams and find a niche that excites you. But remember that many things worth having in life aren't easy to obtain and maintain. Expect to work hard and then appreciate your success.

Remember:

"*We are what we repeatedly do. Excellence, therefore, is not an act, but a habit.***"**
—Aristotle

About Nutrition

A solid knowledge of basic nutrition is so important for someone entering a career in foodservice. Consumers are becoming more health-conscious and the demand for specialized meals and nutrition information on menu items has increased. Understanding nutrition can help you have a dialogue with consumers about their food needs and develop and market items to meet consumer demand.

Providing consumers with more healthful options or disclosing nutrition on menu items can help increase an establishment's appeal to health-conscious consumers. It can also help distinguish an establishment from others by meeting consumers' growing demand for nutrition information. Consumers are growing more interested in nutrition and aren't afraid to ask for what they want. Basic nutrition knowledge will only serve you well by giving you a cutting edge in the food industry.

2.1 The Basics of Nutrition
- The importance of nutrition
- Nutrients
- The digestive system
- Food additives
- A healthy diet

2.2 Making Menu Items More Nutritious
- Food preparation techniques
- Making menus more healthful
- Reducing excessive fats
- Types of produce (from a grower's point of view)

SECTION 2.1 THE BASICS OF NUTRITION

What is food? People often think of food as a way to satisfy their hunger or give them pleasure. But food also provides the body with essential nutrients for energy. Without these nutrients, the body would not be able to function. In the restaurant and foodservice business, having a basic knowledge of proper nutrition and its importance will help in giving customers food that tastes good and is good for them.

79

Focus and Engage

Discuss

- Nutrition is for everyone, because everyone eats and has a body.
- Nutrition can seem tedious to learn and teach.
- Help the students to see it as exciting.
- Discuss real food that tastes good.

Section 2.1
The Basics of Nutrition

Introduce the Section
a. Nutrition is important to understand.
b. There are essential nutrient categories.
c. The digestion of food by the human body is part of the nutrition process.
d. Poor nutrition choices can lead to poor health.

Vocabulary Review
a. Direct students to the key terms.
b. Pronounce each word, and have the students repeat the pronunciation out loud.
c. Discuss the definition of each word.

Teach

Discuss
- Nourishing your guests is part of the enriching experience of feeding them good food.

Discuss

- The several categories of chemicals that are the major nutrients are outlined in this section.
- What is the difference between diet and nutrition? The students might have opinions about this.

Teaching Tips

- Students might need a bit of support if the science concepts are new to them.
- Students require only an awareness and exposure to the molecular nature of nutrition in this lesson.
- Students should always be brought back around to the practical nature of the food itself.
- Food is the beginning and end of the nutrition story. Keep the food as the focus for this class.

Vocabulary Terms

- **Nutrition:** The study of nutrients in food and how they nourish the body.
- **Nutrients:** Molecules from food that are used to maintain the human body.

Study Questions

After studying Section 2.1, you should be able to answer the following questions:

- Why is nutrition important to the restaurant and foodservice industry?
- What are the six basic types of nutrients found in food?
- How do phytochemicals and fiber function in the body?
- What role do carbohydrates have in people's diets?
- What is the role of fats in people's diets?
- What is the role of proteins in people's diets?
- What is the role of vitamins and minerals in people's diets?
- What is the role of water in people's diets?
- What are food additives and how do they function in food?
- What is the role of digestion in nutrition and health?

The Importance of Nutrition

After restaurant and foodservice employees learn about nutrition, they can begin to plan menus and recipes that incorporate nutrition principles and meet customers' expectations for healthy, tasty cuisine. People need certain nutrients on a regular basis to maintain health and prevent disease. The roles of the different types of nutrients vary. The body needs nutrients to do the following:

- Provide energy
- Build and repair cells
- Keep the different systems in the body working smoothly, such as breathing, digesting food, and building red blood cells

Nutrition is the study of the nutrients in food and how they nourish the body. **Nutrients** are components of food that are needed for the body to function. After consuming nutrients, people digest, absorb, transport, and use them to build and maintain the body. People receive nutrients almost entirely through the food they eat.

80

Did You Know...?

Daily metabolism issues are primarily those concerning carbohydrates (CHO) and water. Protein and fat also contribute to daily, even hourly, management of blood sugar. Water-soluble vitamins are needed daily, but not for survival. A day without vitamin C will not be risky if it isn't the norm. But we do need CHO and water on a daily basis to stay healthy.

Everyone needs to receive nutrients on a regular basis and in the correct amounts. This does not have to occur at each meal. It can happen over a period of time, such as several days or a week. Malnutrition is caused by a lack of nutrients or an imbalance of nutrients. Malnutrition can lead to the following:

- Decreased energy
- Developmental problems
- Decreased focus
- Long-term disease
- Death

[nutrition]

Nutrients Provide Energy

Eat the nutrients that provide energy (fat, carbohydrate, and protein) in balance with energy demands every day. Bodies are constantly burning fuel and need a steady supply. Not enough fuel, and the body burns muscle for fuel. Too much, and the body stores fat. Also, drink an adequate supply of water daily. Dehydration can be dangerous. Provide the other nutrients (vitamins, minerals, and fiber) adequately over a longer period. Eat well every day, but recognize that the body can store some vitamins and minerals for later use. Too long without a particular nutrient, and problems will begin.

What people eat is usually a matter of choice. Most people in the United States eat food from a restaurant or foodservice operation at least five times a week. Almost all Americans depend on restaurant and foodservice operations for some of their meals. As a result, restaurant and foodservice professionals supply at least some of the nutrients that people need. To do this well, they need to understand the nutritional needs of their customers. This allows restaurant and foodservice professionals to help their customers follow a balanced, nutritious diet plan. However, no one can force their customers to choose food wisely and balance their diets. Each person has the responsibility to make smart food choices. The good news is that today's operations can and often do provide menu items that make balanced, nutritious choices possible. Figure 2.1 on the following page shows a family dining together at a casual foodservice operation. It is important to be well nourished emotionally as well. Family dinner is one way to provide this, either at home or in a restaurant.

81

Fast Fact:
Did You Know . . . ?

Metabolism means "running the engine."

Everything that happens in a living body is part of metabolism.

Discuss

- In the United States and much of the developed world, the problems of overnutrition are the greatest malnutrition risk. Malnutrition just means "bad nutrition." Ask the students if they know what overnutrition causes.

- They will probably be aware that overweight or even obesity are caused by eating more than the body needs and uses.

- The students might be aware that overweight and obesity can cause serious and life-threatening health problems.

- With increasingly more families and individuals eating meals from restaurant and foodservice operations, is it the responsibility of the operations to protect their guests from overnutrition? How would this be done?

- What sells well in a restaurant or foodservice operation? Let the students discuss and explore this area for awhile.

Nutrition:
Nutrients Provide Energy

Make sure the students understand that vitamins do not provide energy, and neither do minerals. Vitamins and minerals aren't "fuel," they are regulators.

Discuss

- Perhaps the students realize that some of these nutrition claim phrases have criteria established by the U.S. government.

- This area changes, so a restaurant or foodservice operator would be advised to work with a consulting nutritionist before making claims.

- Laura Walsh is this type of nutritionist. There are both national and local nutritionists (dietitians) in this field.

What's New: Heart-Healthy Menu Symbols

An item's recipe is analyzed for the criteria.

The chef must be faithful to the recipe and not increase the fat, sodium, or cholesterol content during preparation.

Reinforce and Review

- No matter how good a food is for the body, if it doesn't taste good, no one will want to eat it.

- Humans develop a palate for nutritious, health-promoting food if it tastes good.

- Help your guests to truly enjoy what is going to be good for them.

Increasingly, restaurants are adding more options that fit into a healthy lifestyle. Some restaurants use marketing to highlight the nutrients in their meals. "Low calorie," "heart healthy," "low fat," "high fiber," and "low sodium" are all examples of some of the claims a restaurant and foodservice operation might make about a menu item.

Figure 2.1: Families can get nutritious, healthy meals at foodservice operations.

[what's new]

Heart-Healthy Menu Symbols

The American Heart Association can certify products that provide fewer than 3 grams of fat, less than 1 gram of saturated fat and fewer than 20 milligrams of cholesterol per serving. A product with a heart-check designation must be consistently reliable to meet these criteria.

Customers also want food that is aromatic, colorful, and flavorful. They need nutritious food, but they don't want to compromise taste. Healthful, fresh food filled with nutrients is a feast for both the eye and the palate. When restaurant and foodservice professionals understand how to combine nutrition science and culinary arts, they are able to provide food that is both delicious and healthful. Nutritious cooking also sells well when it looks and smells appetizing.

The opportunities for providing nutritious, tasty menu selections will only continue to grow. This may, however, require some operational adjustments.

82

Figure Focus

Figure 2.1: The act of sharing food together is a bonding experience for a family.

An operation must balance processes that help provide healthier options with the need to make a profit. For example, an operation that decides to switch from canned fruit and vegetables to fresh items might need to do the following things:

- Increase refrigerated storage space
- Schedule more frequent deliveries
- Add equipment, such as a steamer
- Hire another employee to help with prep

Sales can increase when an operation provides healthier options, but management must also consider the costs to make sure the dishes will still make a profit.

Scientific knowledge continues to grow as scientists learn more about food and nutrition. Each advance has changed the way people look at food, not only for pleasure, but for good health. It is challenging to follow advances in nutrition, but it is necessary. Understanding and staying current on the latest nutrition principles will help you to meet the growing demands of customers for healthy, tasty food. Relying on reputable information sources and resources can help avoid confusion as nutrition science continues to evolve.

Nutrients

There are six basic categories of nutrients that are important to the body:

- Carbohydrates
- Lipids (fats)
- Proteins
- Vitamins
- Minerals
- Water

All six groups are necessary for good health, and all must work as a team. Each nutrient plays an essential role. Each individual is his or her own nutrition coach and must choose the food that will provide all the nutrients his or her body needs. If just one nutrient category is missing in a day, the rest of the team cannot work properly. Figure 2.2 shows the six major nutrient categories.

Figure 2.2: The six basic categories of nutrients are all necessary for good health.

83

Discuss

- How can students keep up with changes in nutrition?
- Are there any fundamental themes that never change? Perhaps the students can think of some.

Reinforce and Review

- Each group is related by chemistry and by function.
- Carbohydrates all have similar types of molecules. The same is true for lipids and proteins.
- Vitamins have very different types of molecules. There are many different shapes and structures.
- Vitamins are all in the same category because they help regulate the body but cannot be made by the body.
- Minerals are all elements on the periodic table of the elements.
- Water is used for lubrication, transport, temperature control, chemical reactions, and structure.

Figure Focus

Figure 2.2: A person cannot live without all of the nutrient categories in the diet.

ServSafe Connection: Keeping Purple Food Purple

Although the color alterations described are not harmful, they are distasteful.

If they are distasteful, the food won't be eaten and the nourishment from it will be lost.

The red cabbage demonstration described is very simple and easy to do.

Vocabulary Terms

- **Fiber:** Nondigestible carbohydrate that provides bulk and roughage to the diet.

- **Phytochemicals:** Nutrients from colorful fruits and vegetables that as yet do not have established nutrient requirements.

Figure 2.3: Fresh, colorful fruits and vegetables are loaded with phytochemicals, which aid the body in preventing disease.

Other important substances are in food, including fiber and chemical substances called phytochemicals. **Fiber** promotes digestive health and regularity. It is found in plant food, such as whole grains, fruit, vegetables, nuts, and legumes.

Phytochemicals (also known as phyto-nutrients) are chemicals that aid the body in fighting or preventing diseases. Phyto-chemicals can be identified by the color pigment they provide to certain types of food, such as the anthocyanins in blueberries.

Nutrients, phytochemicals, and fiber are found in food items in different amounts. No food contains all the nutrients that people need. People who want to be well nourished must eat a diet with a large variety of food items. Figure 2.3 shows a variety of fresh, colorful fruits and vegetables.

[ServSafe Connection]

Keeping Purple Food Purple

Get ready for a new word—anthocyanins (an tho-SI-a-ninz). Cyan, part of the word, means "blue." These are naturally occurring blue nutrient chemicals in a group called phytochemicals. Phytochemicals are nonnutritive plant chemicals that have protective or disease-preventing properties. Many of the bright purple, red, yellow, orange, and green colors of fruits and vegetables are caused by phytochemicals. Eating lots of fresh, color-ful produce can ensure that you receive plenty of these phytochemicals.

Not too many foods are actually "blue;" even blueberries are sort of purple. Most an-thocyanin foods are purple. They are also subject to change depending upon handling. When cooked in a mild acid, they turn magenta pink. When cooked in a mild alkali, they turn very blue and even can go turquoise. Try soaking a little cooked red cabbage in either vinegar or baking soda-water solution and see what happens. Take care to avoid anything alkaline in the preparation of anthocyanin foods, or they will lose their pretty purple color.

Carbohydrates

Carbohydrates are the body's main energy source. They help the body use protein and fat efficiently. Sugar, starch, and fiber are the main forms of these

84

Figure Focus

Figure 2.3: The main pigments in fruits and vegetables act as nutrients in the body.

carbohydrates. Carbohydrates, except fiber, provide the body with 4 kilocalories of energy per gram of food eaten. A **kilocalorie** is the energy needed to heat 1 kilogram (about 2.2 pounds) of water by approximately 39°F. In nutrition, the unit of measurement for energy is the kilocalorie, but it is more commonly called a **calorie.** In addition to calories, carbohydrate food items add vitamins, minerals, and fiber to the diet.

Some examples of foods that are good sources of carbohydrates are following:

- Pasta
- Rice
- Tortillas
- Cereal
- Baked potato
- Honey
- Table sugar

Figure 2.4 is a graphic of a long, branched carbohydrate molecule of starch.

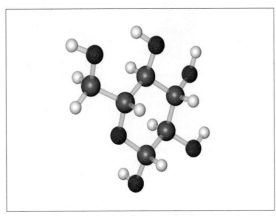

Figure 2.4: The branched carbohydrate molecule helps make up rice, wheat, and corn, which are the major sources of starch in the human diet.

Teaching Tips

- There might be some confusion between "calories" and "kilocalories." In nutrition, "calorie" means a kilocalorie, which is really 1,000 calories. Dietitians sometimes call them "kaycalz," meaning the plural of "kcal," which is the abbreviation for kilocalorie. Nutrition Facts panels and nutrient labels use the term calorie and kilocalorie interchangeably. When speaking about the kcal. content of food, use the term calorie. Only nutrition lab chemists need to worry about the difference.

Vocabulary Terms

- **Kilocalorie:** 1,000 calories. In food, it is called simply a "calorie."

- **Calorie:** Energy needed to heat 1 kilogram (about 2.2 pounds) of water by approximately 1°C. In nutrition, the unit of measurement for energy is the kilocalorie, but it is more commonly called a calorie.

Figure Focus

Figure 2.4: Starch is a polymer, which means it is a continuous chain of molecules.

3,500 kilocalories is more than most people need in a day for all functions, including heartbeat and breathing.

This means that even if you starve yourself completely for a day, you won't burn off a pound of fat. You might dehydrate and weigh less, but it isn't fat loss.

Reinforce and Review

- The basic molecular building block of carbohydrates is a molecule of glucose (or a few other types of sugar), which has six carbon atoms along with hydrogen and oxygen.

- "Carbo-" means carbon, "-hydr-" means hydrogen, and "-ate" means oxygen.

Vocabulary Terms

- **Simple carbohydrates:** Sugar, or carbohydrate, molecules made of no more than two sugar molecules. Not a polymer, but a monomer or a dimer.

[fast fact]

Did You Know...?

The number of calories per pound is 3,500. This is for a pound of stored body fat. Not all flesh on a human body is fat. Water, muscle, bone, and other tissues comprise most of a healthy, non-obese person's body weight.

If a person consumes 3,500 more dietary calories than the body needs for energy, the body stores it as one pound of fat. To lose the pound of fat, the body must burn all the food eaten plus a few other things, and then go after the fat stores— 3,500 caloriesworth. Losing this pound won't happen overnight no matter how badly a person wants to lose it.

The two types of carbohydrates are simple carbohydrates and complex carbohydrates. Carbohydrates are differentiated by their chemical structure. Figure 2.5 shows examples of simple and complex carbohydrates.

Figure 2.5a: Simple carbohydrates include oranges and soft drinks.

Figure 2.5b: Complex carbohydrates include bread, cereal, and rice.

Simple Carbohydrates

Simple carbohydrates contain one or two sugars. Sugars are called simple carbohydrates because their chemical structure is relatively simple compared to starch and fiber, which are complex carbohydrates. Sugars are found in fruit, milk, and the simple carbohydrates that are used in the kitchen or bakery, such as white sugar, brown sugar, molasses, and honey. Simple carbohydrates are digested and absorbed quickly. They provide a short burst of energy.

Figure Focus

Figure 2.5a: Fruits contain the monomers glucose, fructose (which is a little different with five carbons), or both. Soft drinks contain sucrose, which is a dimer that tastes sweet (table sugar), or high-fructose corn syrup.

Figure 2.5b: Starches are made of the same sugar molecule building blocks, but they are assembled into long chains.

Glucose is a very important simple sugar. It is the primary source of energy. It's also the only source of energy for the brain and nervous system. Good sources of glucose are fruit, vegetables, and honey. Figure 2.6 is a graphic of glucose and sucrose.

Figure 2.6a: Glucose, also known as monosaccharide, has this molecular structure.

Figure 2.6b: Surcrose, also known as disaccharide, has this molecular structure.

[ServSafe Connection]

Everyone Likes Sugar!

Glucose is the source of energy for all animals. Even bacteria use glucose to meet their requirements. Ants are attracted to table sugar. Roaches want to feed on crumbs of bread. Weevils want pasta and flour. Bacteria will ferment juices to alcohol or vinegar. These organisms are competing with humans (you!) for glucose.

Don't let them win in the commercial kitchen:

- Store starch and sugar foods properly so that the competition does not get a chance.
- Keep shelves and cupboards clean and free of crumbs.
- Keep sugar, flour, and other carbohydrate foods in covered and closed containers.
- Keep opened juices refrigerated or frozen.
- Store food in the storeroom at least 6 inches off of the floor.

Hormones are special chemical messengers made by bodies that regulate different body functions. The digestive process is not possible without a hormone called **insulin,** which is produced in the pancreas. It allows glucose, or blood sugar, to travel throughout the body for energy use. Problems with insulin production and blood sugar levels can be symptoms of diabetes or other diseases that put stress on the body, causing weakness and fatigue.

Complex Carbohydrates

Complex carbohydrates contain long chains that include many glucose molecules. They are found in plant-based foods such as grains, legumes, and

87

Figure Focus

Figure 2.6a: This is a flat drawing of a three-dimensional molecule that has an interesting shape. Most molecules do.

Figure 2.6b: Note that the ring on the left is like the glucose in Figure 2.6a. It is linked to a five-member ring of fructose.

Teaching Tips

- Although students might not need to know the exact chemistry of these sugars, the rings are important.
- Each ring of glucose is three-dimensional and has almost a zig-zag appearance around the line of carbons.
- Just like bigger things in life, tiny molecules have shape and take up space accordingly, similar to items in the kitchen that have to fit someplace, but still be useful.
- Students might realize that this is part of understanding food.
- For example, many, many sucrose dimer molecules shown in Figure 2.6b can arrange themselves into crystals, which is why table sugar is crystalline.
- There are many examples of how molecular shape influences ingredients in foods. Shape also influences nutrition, digestion, absorption, and physiology.
- This might help students further understand how foods and ingredients perform.

ServSafe Connection: Everyone Likes Sugar!

Members of the animal kingdom all need glucose and oxygen. Waste products are carbon dioxide and water.

Species in the plant kingdom provide glucose and oxygen and need water and carbon dioxide to make glucose.

This is called the carbon cycle. If it stops, humans will not survive.

Vocabulary Terms

- **Glucose:** A six-carbon ring molecule of simple sugar. This is the sugar that is found in human blood and used by humans for fuel.
- **Hormones:** Chemical regulators of metabolism.
- **Insulin:** A hormone made by the pancreas that moves glucose molecules from the bloodstream into individual cells to be used as fuel.
- **Complex carbohydrates:** Long-chain polymers of glucose molecules.

Reinforce and Review

- Fiber is a very similar molecule to starch.

- If fiber is boiled long enough, much of it will turn into starch. For example, a raw carrot is high in fiber and doesn't have much starch. A cooked carrot is lower in fiber and now has more starch.

- Too much cooking or boiling can break down the fiber.

- Bran fiber does not break down under cooking or baking conditions.

In-Class Activity: Recipes for Nutrition

21st-Century Skills—Collaborate with Others

Oatmeal is a source of soluble fiber, which can help reduce cholesterol levels. Adding more oats to the diet is recommended for individuals at risk.

Have the class work together to collect five recipes that are based on oats or oatmeal.

If possible, try one recipe in class.

Vocabulary Terms

- **Fiber:** A nondigestible type of plant starch that provides bulk and cleansing to the gut.

- **Soluble fiber:** Fiber that dissolves in water, usually forming a gel, like pectin. Oatmeal has soluble fiber.

- **Insoluble fiber:** Fiber that does not dissolve in water, like grain husks and the cell walls of vegetables and fruits. Bran is an insoluble fiber. Celery is an example of a food with insoluble fiber from cell walls.

vegetables. They provide a long-lasting source of energy. Complex carbohydrates take longer to digest than simple carbohydrates.

Good sources of complex carbohydrates include the following:

- Dry beans and peas
- Starchy vegetables, such as potatoes and corn
- Rice
- Grits
- Pasta
- Oatmeal
- Cornmeal
- Breads and cereals

Starch is also found in some fruit, such as bananas. To maintain good health, it is important to eat lots of complex carbohydrates every day.

Fiber is found only in plant food along with starch and sugar. It is the part of the plant that cannot be digested by people. Because it cannot be broken down, fiber is not absorbed in the intestines and is eliminated. Fiber is a chemical cousin to complex carbohydrates, but cannot be digested for energy needs. High-fiber food includes bran, legumes, fruit, vegetables, and whole grains. Like nutrients, dietary fiber is essential for good health. The two types of fiber each provide a valuable function:

- **Soluble fiber** dissolves in water. When we eat foods that contain soluble fiber, we feel full for a longer time. Soluble fiber also slows down the release of sugar into the blood and helps lower cholesterol levels in the blood.

- **Insoluble fiber** does not dissolve in water. It was once referred to as roughage (RUFF-ij) because it is rough. It acts like a stiff broom to clean and scrub the digestive tract so we can eliminate wastes from our systems more easily.

Figure 2.7: High-fiber foods include celery, wheat, oats, and apples.

Figure 2.7 shows an array of high-fiber foods.

Figure Focus

Figure 2.7: Plant foods are the sources of fiber.

Although in recent years carbohydrates have been identified as the source of many people's weight problems, this is not entirely true. Most people shouldn't fear carbohydrates as a food category. If a person uses all of the energy from the calories he or she eats, it's unlikely that the person will gain weight when eating normal amounts of carbohydrates. Excess calories from *all* nutrient sources and a lack of exercise are the actual causes in weight gain.

Lipids

Lipids is another word for fat. Lipids are a group of molecules that include fats, oils, waxes, steroids, and other compounds. Many people want to reduce the amount of fat in their diets, although a certain amount of fat is needed for good nutrition. **Fat** usually refers to both fats and oils, although basic differences exist between the two. Fats are solid at room temperature and often come from animals. Oils are liquid at room temperature. Fat is an essential nutrient with many functions, including the following:

- Carrying vitamins A, D, E, and K through the body
- Cushioning the body's vital organs
- Protecting the body from extreme temperatures
- Providing a reserve supply of energy (when the body stores it)
- Supplying nutrients called essential fatty acids, such as omega 3-fatty acid (linolenic) and omega-6 fatty acid (linoleic)

The three types of fatty acids are the following:

1. Saturated
2. Monounsaturated
3. Polyunsaturated

All fat in food is made up of different combinations of the three types of fatty acids. Some foods have no saturated fats. If a food contains mostly saturated fatty acids, it is considered a saturated fat. If a food contains mostly polyunsaturated fatty acids, it is a polyunsaturated fat. Animal fats generally are more saturated than liquid vegetable oils. Food such as seafood, poultry, and meat contain saturated fats. Polyunsaturated and monounsaturated fats are found in vegetable oils and foods such as peanuts, olives, and avocados. Figure 2.8 on the following page shows examples of the different types of foods with fatty acids.

89

Reinforce and Review

- Fats are extremely important in both cooking and nutrition.
- Fats provide lots of energy (calories) and can be stored as body fat.
- Too much fat in the diet can make a person fat.
- Too much sugar in the diet can also be stored as fat.
- Overweight individuals should thus be careful of their fat and sugar intake.
- The melting point determines when a fat will become liquid (oil). It determines whether a fat will be liquid at room temperature (an oil) or will be solid at room temperature (a solid fat, also called a "plastic" fat in food science, because it can be shaped).
- Saturated fats have a higher melting point than monounsaturated and polyunsaturated fats.

Vocabulary Terms

- **Lipids:** Fats, oils, and other compounds that repel water.
- **Fat:** Molecules made from glycerol and fatty acids, both solid fats and oils.

Reinforce and Review

- There are three fatty acids on a typical molecule of dietary fat. These are long chains connected to a backbone, sort of in the shape of an E.

- The fatty acids determine the type of fat: saturated, monounsaturated, or polyunsaturated.

- They are either saturated with hydrogen or not.

- Fats can oxidize, or go rancid, during storage, especially without refrigeration. Sunlight accelerates the process, and polyunsaturated fats are prone to this. Saturated fats can also oxidize, but not as quickly.

- Oxidation destroys the fat and its flavor. In some cases, oxidation can make the fat unsafe to use and consume.

- Cholesterol is a lipid, but not a fat.

- Cholesterol is a sterol, which is a complex molecule with several carbon rings.

- Sex hormones, bile, and vitamin D are all made from cholesterol.

- Too much cholesterol can form a harmful waxy substance in the arteries.

Vocabulary Terms

- **Essential fatty acids:** Specific fatty acids that are required for human health but not made by the body.

- **Oxidation:** The destruction of a molecule, or combustion, by oxygen. This process can be fast and hot (fire) or slow and barely noticeable over time (rust).

- **Cholesterol:** A sterol lipid, naturally occurring in the body to make other steroids.

- **Trans fatty acids:** Unsaturated fats with a trans configuration.

- **Hydrogenation:** Further saturating a polyunsaturated fatty acid with hydrogen to make it more solid at room temperature.

Figure 2.8: Foods that contain fatty acids include butter, olive oil, and cooking oil.

Essential fatty acids are just a few specific ones that are required for good nutrition. They are used to make substances that regulate vital body functions, such as blood pressure, muscle contraction, blood clotting, and immune responses. They are also needed for normal growth, healthy skin, and healthy cells.

Oxidation is a chemical process that causes unsaturated fats to spoil. Heat, light, salt, and moisture help speed up oxidation. It is best to store fats and oils in tightly closed containers kept in a refrigerator or a cool, dark place.

Cholesterol is a white, waxy substance that helps the body carry out its many processes. Cholesterol is made in the liver. It's an important part of all cell membranes and is found in large amounts throughout the nervous system. In the body, cholesterol also helps to make substances such as bile acids, vitamin D, and hormones. Cholesterol is a natural component of the body. People don't need it in the food they eat.

Cholesterol is found only in animal foods such as egg yolks, dairy products, meat, poultry, seafood, liver, and other organ meats. Although cholesterol is essential for body functions, high levels of cholesterol in the blood are linked with heart disease. The greatest concern with cholesterol is absorbing extra amounts from the diet into the bloodstream.

Trans fatty acids are the result of taking a liquid fat and making it solid. This is achieved through a process called hydrogenation. **Hydrogenation** of fats alters their physical properties and makes them stay fresh longer. This is beneficial from a merchandising standpoint. Hydrogenation also increases the smoking point, which makes these fats suitable for frying. The disadvantage of hydrogenation is that it may be more harmful to a person's health than saturated fats in relation to the development of heart disease. Processed food, especially baked goods, can be sources of trans fat. Table 2.1 on the following page shows food sources of fats and cholesterol.

90

Figure Focus

Figure 2.8: Fatty acids are part of fats and oils.

Table 2.1: Food Sources of Fats and Cholesterol

Type of Fat	Food Sources
Saturated fat	Meat, poultry, fish, dairy products, butter, lard, palm oil, palm kernel oil, coconut oil
Monounsaturated fat	Olive, canola, peanut, avocado, and nut oils
Polyunsaturated fat	Safflower, sunflower, soybean, corn, cottonseed, and sesame oils and fish oils
Cholesterol	Egg yolk; liver and other organ meats such as brains, kidneys, and tongue; whole milk and whole milk cheeses; cream; ice cream; butter; meat; poultry; fish; and some shellfish

[nutrition]

Saturated Fat and Unsaturated Fat

Fats are long molecules made of carbon and hydrogen. Long chains of carbon and hydrogen are called "hydrocarbons." Hydrocarbons exist in automobile fuel, but people don't often think about them in the oils and fats they eat. However, it is the same type of molecule. A lot of energy is stored in carbon chains. Fats are an important part of a healthy diet.

When hydrogen exists in every single place on the chain, it is "saturated fat" and is solid at room temperature. Remove one hydrogen atom or more, and it becomes "unsaturated" and more flexible.

- There are fats in many foods. Most animal fats are saturated.

Nutrition:
Saturated Fat and Unsaturated Fat

Hydrocarbons are chain polymer molecules that get their name from hydrogen ("hydro-") and carbon.

All fats, whether they are food fats or petroleum, are hydrocarbon chains.

Discuss

- Point out to the students the double bond on the unsaturated fatty acid molecular drawing. The double bond is a site where two additional hydrogens could bond.

- This unsaturated fatty acid is a cis configuration.

- The trans configuration would look like this:

$$O = C - C - C - C - C - C - C = C - C - C - H$$

- Note that the double bond has the hydrogens on either side of the chain.

Fats that tend to be solid also tend to be solid in the bloodstream. They form clumps of fat that must be transported in the blood.

Liquid oils are easier for the body to process.

Teaching Tips

- Students might have studied amino acids in a biology course.
- DNA codes for the assembly of amino acids into specific proteins.
- This is called protein synthesis.
- Formally or informally assess the students for prior knowledge of protein synthesis.

Fast Fact:
Did You Know . . . ?

Americans tend to eat more protein than they need.

Typical restaurant or foodservice operation servings of beef, chicken, or fish often contain more protein than a guest needs in the entire day.

Discuss

- "Protein is expensive." Have the students discuss what this means. There are many global, economic, agricultural, environmental, and other reasons why protein is expensive.
- Remind the students that excess protein that is eaten is stored as fat or burned instead of cheaper carbohydrates.

Vocabulary Terms

- **Proteins:** The polymer molecule nutrients that build and repair the body.
- **Amino acids:** The specific nitrogen-containing molecules that link together to make protein.
- **Essential amino acids:** Amino acids that are needed for life, but are not made by the body. They must be eaten.

Most food sources of fat have a mixture of both kinds, unless they have been specially prepared to exclude one. For example, no saturated fat exists in polyunsaturated liquid vegetable oil. But, both kinds of fat occur in salmon, butter, or steak. Most fats from animal sources are saturated. Most fats from vegetable sources are not.

Health-wise, saturated fats can take a toll on the heart. It's best to limit the use of these fats. Unsaturated fats are usually better. But the bottom line is that a high-fat diet is not healthful for most people. Reducing total dietary fat is a good strategy. Increasing unsaturated fats while decreasing saturated fats within the lower-fat target are additional positive strategies.

Protein

Proteins are another class of nutrients that can supply energy to the body. They are needed to build new cells and repair injured ones. Proteins provide the building blocks, in the form of amino acids, that the body uses for a variety of things, including muscles, tissues, enzymes, and hormones. Proteins are large complex molecules that contain long chains of amino acids. If used for energy, proteins can provide four calories of energy per gram to the body.

[fast fact]

Did You Know...?

Most Americans eat much more protein than their bodies actually need. Most healthy adults need about 50 milligrams a day (a little less for women, a little more for men). That is roughly the amount in one 6-ounce cut of meat. There are 6 grams of protein in a single egg, 8 grams in a cup of milk, 28 in a 3-ounce (small) portion of meat. Any extra protein the body doesn't need in a day is stored as fat, not as muscle.

Amino acids are chemical compounds that have special functions in the body. One of the primary functions of amino acids is to supply nitrogen for growth and maintenance. Amino acids also maintain fluids, keep the body from getting too acidic or basic, and act as transporters when in the form of lipoproteins (molecules combining a lipid and a protein). Twenty amino acids can be found in food. Only nine of them, known as **essential amino acids**, have to be obtained from food each day. The others can be made by the body.

92

Proteins can be found in large quantity in meat, eggs, cheese, beans, nuts, legumes, and milk. Vegetables and grains also contain protein. Vegetarian customers may want diets that draw mostly or solely from these vegetables and grains. Figure 2.9 shows protein sources.

Skin, hair, nails, muscles, and tendons are all made of protein. When tissues are destroyed—for example, when someone gets burned, has surgery, or has an infection—more protein than usual is needed. Extra protein is also required during pregnancy and times of physical growth.

Figure 2.9: Protein-rich foods include salmon, nuts, eggs, and pulses, such as beans and lentils.

[fast fact]

Did You Know...?

About one-fifth of your body's total weight is protein.

Some of the body parts that are protein-based include muscle, brain cells, skin, hair, and nails. Interestingly, the human body can't store protein. It has to be supplied on a daily basis from the foods we eat.

Complete proteins are called complete because they contain all the essential amino acids in the right amount. Good sources of complete proteins are meat, poultry, fish, eggs, and dairy products.

Incomplete proteins lack one or more of the essential amino acids. Foods from plant sources are incomplete proteins. Dried beans, dried peas, grains, and nuts have more protein than other vegetables and fruits. To get complete proteins from plant food, combine them with other food. For example, combine cooked dry beans or peas with a grain product (such as lentils and rice), or combine a plant food with an animal protein (such as macaroni and cheese).

Complementary proteins are two or more incomplete protein sources that together provide adequate amounts of all the essential amino acids. Examples of complementary proteins include peanut butter sandwich, macaroni and cheese, tofu with rice, and beans and tortillas.

93

Figure Focus
Figure 2.9: Soybeans are also protein rich.

**In-Class Activity:
Protein and Acid Demonstration**

Science Connection

Acids will denature protein. Denature means to change or alter the nature of something.

Using raw egg white (albumen), show the effect of various strengths of acid.

Contact the chemistry department for assistance with this.

Rehearse this lab.

Determine with the help of the chemistry teacher how to transport and dispense the acid.

Be especially careful and use eye, hand, and clothing protection when working with the acids.

Needed:

- 4 Petri dishes
- Pipettes
- 4 raw eggs
- Samples of acids:
  - Hydrochloric acid
  - Sulfuric acid
  - Acetic acid (vinegar)
  - Ascorbic acid (dissolved vitamin C tablet in ¼ cup water)

Crack an egg into each Petri dish.

Drop a pipette of acid onto an egg. Observe the results.

This is not a quantified experiment. It is merely a demonstration that acids will coagulate protein as effectively as heat.

Inform the students that human stomach acid is the same as hydrochloric acid.

Vocabulary Terms

- **Complete protein:** A food that contains all the essential amino acids.
- **Incomplete protein:** A food that contains some essential amino acids, but not all of them.
- **Complementary proteins:** Two or more incomplete proteins that are eaten together to provide all essential amino acids.

It is interesting that cultures discovered the principle long before the science was understood. Their survival depended on it.

Reinforce and Review

- Vitamins were discovered because people without a certain vitamin got sick. This is called deficiency. When the vitamin was added they got better.

- The requirements for the vitamin were based on the amount required to prevent sickness.

- Too much of a vitamin can also make you sick, which is called toxicity.

- Lately we realize that there might be optimal levels of vitamins, somewhere between deficiency and toxicity.

Discuss

- "Vitamin B" is actually a misnomer.

- Vitamins were discovered and got their names early in the twentieth century. At the time, they thought there was one that they called B. Now we realize that there are as many as 17 B vitamins, now called the B complex. They include thiamin, niacin, riboflavin, pyridoxine, B_{12}, and others.

- There are still other vitamins that are not included in this text.

Vocabulary Terms

- **Vitamins:** Necessary molecules that are catalysts and regulators the body needs, but are not made by the body.

- **Water-soluble vitamins:** Vitamin C and the B complex vitamins can dissolve in water and should be eaten daily.

- **Fat-soluble vitamins:** Vitamins A, D, E, and K do not dissolve in water and can be stored in the body in reserve.

[nutrition]

Complementary Proteins in Traditional Cuisines
Long before vegetarianism was a personal philosophy in the United States, ancient cultures the world over discovered complementary proteins. To have meat and animal products required a successful hunt, which didn't always happen. The rest of the time, protein needs were met by combining vegetable (crop) foods—beans and corn, peanut butter and bread, soy and anything. All of the necessary amino acids for protein needs must be eaten at the same meal to be useful. However, this does not mean they need to be eaten in the same food.

Vitamins and Minerals

Vitamins and minerals help in growth, reproduction, and the operation and maintenance of the body. In addition, certain minerals, such as the calcium in bones, provide some of the body's structure.

Without the right amounts of vitamins and minerals, people may become deficient and develop deficiency-related diseases. Food should be the primary source for vitamins and minerals. If this isn't possible, a vitamin-mineral supplement may be helpful. However, too great an amount of a vitamin can be toxic.

Vitamins are chemical compounds found in food. They're needed for regulating metabolic processes, such as digestion and the absorption of nutrients. They are essential for life. Vitamins must be obtained from food because the human body makes insufficient amounts or, in some cases, none at all. The amounts of vitamins and minerals needed by the body are very small when compared to its need for carbohydrates, proteins, and fats. However, vitamins help carbohydrates, proteins, fats, and minerals to work properly. The two types of vitamins are water soluble and fat soluble. Water-soluble vitamins mix only with water, and fat-soluble vitamins mix only with fat:

- **Water-soluble vitamins** (vitamins C and B) are found in food such as oranges and grapefruit. The body needs these vitamin sources every day. These vitamins are vulnerable to cooking and may be destroyed by heat or washed away by steam or water.

- **Fat-soluble vitamins** (vitamins A, D, E, and K) are found in food containing fat. They're stored in the liver and body fat. The body draws on these stored vitamins when needed.

Figure 2.10 on the following page shows water-soluble and fat-soluble vitamins.

94

Figure 2.10: Water-soluable vitamins include B and C. Fat-soluable vitamins include A, D, E, and K.

Minerals are classified as major or trace, according to how much is needed in the diet. Some examples of major minerals are calcium, phosphorus, potassium, sodium, and magnesium. Calcium and phosphorus help build strong bones and teeth. Potassium and sodium are needed for maintaining the body's water balance. Iron, copper, zinc, and iodine are examples of trace minerals. Although they are as important as major minerals, only tiny amounts of trace minerals are required. Iron is essential for replenishing red blood cells. Even though some minerals are needed in very tiny amounts, getting the right amount is important to good health. Minerals are part of body structures and are also needed for body functions.

Vitamins work as chemical keys or triggers for body functions. Some of these involve a body's energy. Vitamins do not provide any energy. The sources of energy, or calories, are carbohydrate, protein, and fat. In addition to all the other things vitamins do, they also help the body to use energy from food as fuel.

How much energy do carbohydrate, protein, and fat supply? Here is the breakdown:

One gram of carbohydrate = four calories

One gram of protein = four calories

One gram of fat = nine calories

[fast fact]

Did You Know...?

Early British sailors were called "limies" because they ate limes on board their ships. Eating limes, which are high in vitamin C, helped prevent scurvy, a disease caused by a lack of vitamin C. Scurvy produces spongy, bleeding gums, bleeding under the skin, and weakness and fatigue. Fresh fruit was not plentiful on ships, so sailors were very susceptible to this disease.

95

Figure Focus

Figure 2.10: There are many B vitamins. There are actually more water-soluble vitamins than fat-soluble ones.

Discuss

- Where can you get advice on nutrition?

- Who can tell you what vitamins or minerals you might need?

- Students should mention the dietitian and the physician.

- The term "nutritionist" usually refers to a dietitian.

- There are no such terms as "nutritionalist" or "dietologist." Please gently correct the use of these.

Fast Fact:
Did You Know . . . ?

Scurvy is sometimes referenced in pirate or seafarer books and movies. A bad case of scurvy can make your teeth fall out.

CUSTOMIZED INSTRUCTION

21st-Century Skills—Health Literacy

More Advanced Students

Choose one of the following diseases: pellagra, beriberi, or ariboflavinosis.

Ask students to look up the nature of the disease, the symptoms, the occurrence (when, where, who), and the treatment.

What foods would help prevent the disease?

Have students write a one-page report.

Less Advanced Students and ESOL Students

Learn the names of vitamins B_1, B_2, and B_3 (thiamin, riboflavin, and niacin).

Learn two food sources of each vitamin.

Learn to correctly spell the names of the vitamins.

Special Needs Students

Prepare three cards: B_1, B_2, and B_3.

Prepare three more cards: Thiamin, Riboflavin, and Niacin.

Play a matching game with the cards.

Vocabulary Terms

- **Minerals:** Elements found on the periodic table, and naturally occurring in the earth.

Discuss

- Help the students to recognize water as a nutrient.

- Some beverages, like those including caffeine and sugar, actually cause the body to lose water rather than increase it.

- Plain water is a good beverage throughout the day.

**Fast Fact:
Did You Know . . . ?**

Plan for ways to include fresh water during the day.

Water

Water is an essential nutrient, and its importance is often overlooked. Water is essential to all forms of life. People can't live without it. See Figure 2.11. About 55 to 65 percent of the human body is water by weight. It enables a tremendous number of chemical reactions in the body to take place. Cells, tissues, and organs need water to function.

[fast fact]

Did You Know...?

How much water should a person drink every day? Young adult males need 13 cups of fluid; young adult females need 9 cups of fluid. The remaining amount the body needs comes from food. Although all beverages count toward this fluid intake, make smart choices about what to drink, such as water or milk.

Water has many important roles, including the following:

- Helping with the digestion, absorption, and transportation of nutrients

- Helping with the elimination of wastes through the kidneys, colon, and lungs

- Distributing heat throughout the body and allowing heat to be released through the skin by evaporation (sweating)

- Lubricating joints and cushioning body tissues

Besides water itself, other beverages and some types of food (such as fruits and vegetables) contain water. The human body can live a long time without many other nutrients, but only a few days without water. As you can see, offering customers a cold glass or bottle of water is more than just a courtesy; it is important for their health.

Figure 2.11: Water is an essential nutrient and helps with digestion and absorption.

96

Figure Focus

Figure 2.11: Think of the human body as you would a plant. You can see the plant wilt without water. People are mostly water, too.

[nutrition]

Calories in Beverages

Beverage	Calories per 8-ounce serving
Bottled water	0
Brewed coffee or tea	0
Diet cola, decaffeinated	0
Diet cola, caffeinated	8
Sports drinks	64
Latte with nonfat milk	80
Nonfat milk	88
Cola, caffeinated	88
Cola, decaffeinated	104
Orange juice	112
Energy drinks	112
Apple juice	120
Cranberry juice	136
Latte with whole milk	136

[trends]

Caffeinated Beverages

Although no "bad foods" exist—meaning everything can fit into a healthy diet plan if the serving sizes are appropriate—an alarming trend has occurred. The water craze of a few years ago (highly profitable, by the way) is giving way to an increase in caffeinated beverages, even caffeinated water. Caffeine has a diuretic effect, which causes the body to shed water through the urine, meaning more work and stress for the kidneys. Caffeine is addictive, so once introduced, the person can become dependent. In addition to being habit forming, it is also thirst forming, defeating the purpose of the beverage.

97

Nutrition: Calories in Beverages

Even fruit juices are a concentrated source of energy and can contribute a lot of extra calories to the diet.

Trends: Caffeinated Beverages

There are many problems associated with the drug caffeine, which is so readily available in hot and cold beverages.

One of the problems is water loss. It does not "quench" thirst, but does the opposite.

Reinforce and Review

- The body is actually like a giant doughnut with a hole in the middle. The alimentary canal (mouth to anus) is like the doughnut hole.

- Food doesn't actually enter the body until it crosses over from the alimentary canal into the bloodstream and on to the cells. So food in the stomach and intestines hasn't yet been digested or absorbed.

- The process of digestion begins in the mouth and ends in the small intestine. Absorption of water and alcohol begin in the stomach; the rest happens in the small intestine.

- The large intestine is for absorbing more water, and collecting and passing solid wastes.

- There are several organs involved in the entire process.

Discuss

- What are students' perceptions of food additives? How did they form those opinions?

- Flavorings, colorings, and seasonings are all additives.

- Encourage students to discuss the roles of various types of additives.

Vocabulary Terms

- **Food additive:** A chemical added to a food for a purpose.

- **Additive:** Any chemical that might be added for any purpose.

The Digestive System

Digestion is the process of breaking down food into its simplest parts so that it can be absorbed. It is carried out by the digestive system, which starts at the mouth and ends at the anus. Figure 2.12 shows the digestive system.

Start chewing food, and digestion begins in the mouth. The teeth grind it into smaller pieces and mix it with saliva. Swallow the food, and the stomach breaks

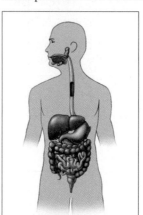

Figure 2.12: Digestion is the process of turning the food we eat into energy.

it down with the aid of enzymes and acids, turning it into a fluid called chyme (KIME). The chyme moves to the small intestine, where the majority of digestion and absorption of nutrients occurs. Other organs help to digest the nutrients fully. For example, bile from the gall bladder helps to break down fats into fatty acids.

As the digestive system sends the nutrients to parts of the body to be used, the wastes of digestion are sent to the large intestine. The large intestine absorbs water and stores feces for elimination through the colon and anus.

The absorption of nutrients needed by the body is what nutrition is really about. Now you can see why people say, "You are what you eat."

Food Additives

A **food additive** is a substance or combination of substances present in food as a result of processing, production, or packaging. An **additive** is a chemical, just as nutrients are chemicals. Many additives occur naturally or are extracted from food. For example, carotene (a form of vitamin A), which is used as a yellow food coloring, contains orange or red crystalline pigments found in plants.

Other additives are synthetic, but chemically identical to natural substances. For example, ascorbic acid (identical to vitamin C) is used as an antioxidant to prevent certain fruit from becoming brown when exposed to air.

Food additives include familiar ingredients such as salt, baking soda, vanilla, and yeast. However, most people tend to think only of other chemicals added

98

Figure Focus

Figure 2.12: This is the human alimentary canal and accessory organs that make up the digestive system.

to food items as additives. All food additives are carefully regulated by the Food and Drug Administration.

Food additives perform many functions in food:

- Improve flavor, color, and texture
- Retain nutritional value
- Prevent spoilage
- Extend shelf life

Some of these additives perform functions that are often taken for granted. Because most people no longer live on farms, additives help keep food wholesome and appealing during transport to markets. Without additives, many food items would be less attractive, less flavorful, less nutritious, more likely to spoil, and more costly. Without them, people would not enjoy a variety of safe and tasty food items year-round, and many convenient food items would not be available.

[fast fact]

Did You Know...?

The Food and Drug Administration of the United States compiles and maintains a list of food additives called the GRAS list. GRAS is an acronym for "Generally Recognized As Safe." It is the work of the FDA's Center for Food Safety and Applied Nutrition and governs preservatives, colors, flavors, conditions, thickeners, stabilizers, and artificial sweeteners. The database has been expanded to include "Everything Added to Food in the United States" (or EAFUS) and includes more than 3,000 ingredients. The safety of additives is determined scientifically to protect the U.S. population from harm. Individuals may still have sensitivities and allergies to any food component.

A Healthy Diet

According to the Dietary Guidelines for Americans, a healthy diet should have the following:

- An emphasis on fruits, vegetables, whole grains, and fat-free or low-fat milk and milk products
- Lean meats, poultry, fish, beans, eggs, and nuts
- Low amounts of in saturated fats, trans fats, cholesterol, salt (sodium), and added sugars

In the United States, nutrition professionals use standards and guidelines to teach people about and help them achieve a healthy diet. **Dietary Reference Intakes (DRIs)** are recommended daily nutrient and energy intake amounts

99

Fast Fact:
Did You Know . . . ?

The U.S. food supply is the safest, most varied, and most available in the history of the world.

Vocabulary Terms

- **Dietary Reference Intakes (DRIs):** Recommended daily intakes of nutrients.

Discuss

- It seems that RDAs, DRIs, and AIs are all the same thing. These guides have developed over years of trying to determine several things:
  - How much of a nutrient is required to prevent a deficiency disease?
  - How much of a nutrient will cause a toxicity reaction?
  - How much do people of different sizes, shapes, genders, and ages differ in their nutrient needs?
  - How much of a nutrient is truly optimal?
- All these assessment systems attempt to answer these questions with research data that can be easily used.
- Help students understand the effect that veganism has recently had on cuisine.
- These are some examples of food products that a strict vegan would avoid:
  - Soup or sauce thickened with a butter roux
  - Any foods that have lard in them, or those that are fried in lard
  - Any food that is colored with carmine, because it is made from beetles
  - Any food that contains gelatin
  - Honey
- Some vegans reject foods that have animal products used in their cultivation, such as bone meal or whey proteins.
- Vegans must be very careful with their dietary planning to consume adequate protein, calories, fats, iron, and vitamin B_{12}.
- In a foodservice operation setting, do not position a menu item as vegan unless it is completely compliant with veganism.

Vocabulary Terms

- **Recommended Dietary Allowances (RDAs):** Recommended daily allowances of nutrients.
- **Adequate intakes (AIs):** Nutrient daily intake levels for healthy people.
- **Vegetarian:** An individual who chooses to consume only vegetable and plant foods.
- **Lacto-vegetarian:** A vegetarian who will include milk and dairy foods.
- **Lacto-ovo-vegetarian:** A vegetarian who will include dairy foods and eggs.
- **Vegan:** A vegetarian who will use no animal products.
- **The Dietary Guidelines for Americans 2005:** Government dietary advice.

(that is, what a person needs to consume) for healthy people of a particular age range and gender. They are the guides for nutrition and food selection.

Two important Dietary Reference Intakes are Recommended Dietary Allowances (RDAs) and Adequate Intakes (AIs). **Recommended Dietary Allowances** are daily nutrient standards established by the U.S. government, the average daily intakes that meet the nutrient requirement of nearly all healthy individuals of a particular age and gender group. The nutrients recommended are protein, eleven vitamins, and seven minerals. **Adequate intakes** are similar to RDAs. They also identify daily intake levels for healthy people. AIs are typically assigned when scientists don't have enough information to set an RDA.

Vegetarian Diets

People choose to eat vegetarian diets for many reasons, including the following:

- Religious beliefs
- Concern for the environment
- Economics
- Health considerations
- Animal welfare factors
- Ethical considerations related to world hunger issues

A **vegetarian** is a person who consumes no meat, fish, or poultry products. The different types of vegetarians include **lacto-vegetarians,** who consume vegetarian items plus dairy products, and **lacto-ovo-vegetarians,** who consume vegetarian items plus dairy products and eggs. A **vegan** follows the strictest diet of all and will consume no dairy, eggs, meat, poultry, fish, or anything containing an animal product or byproduct. They consume only grains, legumes, vegetables, fruit, nuts, and seeds.

A vegetarian diet can meet all nutrient requirements. Vegetarians need to eat a varied diet that includes enough calories to maintain weight. Most vegetarian diets have less fat, less cholesterol, and more fiber because no meat is included in the diet. Because vegans do not eat any animal-based foods and there are no natural plant sources of vitamin B, vegans need to supplement their diet with a source of this vitamin.

Dietary Guidelines for Americans

The Dietary Guidelines for Americans 2005 is a document published jointly by the Department of Health and Human Services and the USDA. This report offers science-based advice for healthy people over the age of two about food choices to promote health and reduce risk for major chronic diseases. Like the recommended dietary allowances, these dietary guidelines apply to diets eaten over several days, not to single food items or meals.

If you do not follow a healthy diet, a number of conditions might occur.

Diseases Caused By Malnutrition

Malnutrition is a condition that occurs when a body does not get enough nutrients. It can result from not having enough of the right food or from making poor food choices, including eating too much food. Food insecurity, for example, is when circumstances do not allow people to get enough food to meet their nutritional needs. Major causes of disease and death in the United States are related to poor food choices and not getting enough exercise.

Obesity

Overweight and obesity are health problems that people can overcome with an improved diet and exercise plan. A person who is **overweight** or **obese** has a weight that is greater than what is generally considered healthy. These terms also identify ranges of weight that have been shown to increase the likelihood of certain diseases and other health problems. Figure 2.13 shows the growth of obesity rates in the United States.

Teen and childhood obesity continues to grow at an alarming rate. According to the U.S. Centers for Disease Control and Prevention (CDC), about 16 percent of U.S. children and teens, aged 6 to 19, are obese.

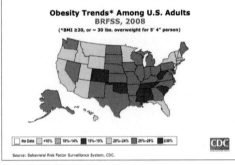

Figure 2.13: Obesity rates continue to grow.

Osteoporosis

Osteoporosis is a condition in which the bones gradually lose their minerals and become weak and fragile. See Figure 2.14 on the following page. It is more prevalent in Asian and Caucasian women, although men can also get the disease. Factors that contribute to development of this disease include inadequate sources of calcium and vitamin D, heredity, lack of exercise, being underweight, and smoking.

101

Reinforce and Review

- Obesity is one of the greatest health risks in the world right now.

- Obesity in the United States contributes to many deaths every year.

- Obesity in children is becoming an epidemic and reduces a child's life expectancy.

- Excluding obesity, the United States has the population with the longest life expectancy of any other in recorded history.

Discuss

- What do you think about childhood obesity? What can be done about it?

- Why is childhood obesity becoming an epidemic? What can you do to prevent it in your own family?

- How can you protect yourself from becoming obese?

- What can obese people do to become healthier?

- Let the students discuss these and other issues related to obesity.

Vocabulary Terms

- **Malnutrition:** Poor nutrition for any reason.

- **Overweight:** A person who weighs more than is recommended for health (BMI > 25).

- **Obese:** A person who has too much body fat to be healthy (BMI > 30).

- **Osteoporosis:** A disease that causes bones to lose their calcium deposits and become brittle.

Figure Focus

Figure 2.13: It is easy to see that there is too much obesity in the United States. Colorado is the most successful state in the United States in terms of residents with appropriate body weights.

For strong bones, drink milk and exercise. Ask students what foods are high in calcium.

Reinforce and Review

- Women are especially vulnerable to osteoporosis as they age and their estrogen production decreases.

- Women are also especially vulnerable to iron-deficiency anemia due to menstrual blood loss.

- Women can first get anemia, and then after menopause they can get osteoporosis.

- Women can also have very high nutrient demands during pregnancy and lactation.

- Women need to build stores of nutrients during their childhood and teenage years.

- Women need to eat well and exercise from their childhood and teen years onward.

In-Class Activity:
BMI Calculation

Math Connection, 21st-Century Skills—Solve Problems

$$BMI = \frac{mass\ (lb) \times 703}{(height\,(in))^2}$$

This equation is used to calculate body mass index (BMI), an evaluation of weight for height.

Have students use this equation to determine their own BMIs.

A BMI over 25 (approximately) is considered overweight.

A BMI over 30 (approximately) is considered obese.

Have the students evaluate their status.

There are more sophisticated and accurate measures and calculations, but these will be useful for this course.

Vocabulary Terms

- **Iron-deficiency anemia:** Not enough iron to make enough red blood cells to carry oxygen, causing fatigue.

Figure 2.14: Osteoporosis is the thinning of bone tissue and loss of bone density over time.

Young adults have the ability to prevent osteoporosis. They can build strong bones and reach peak bone density by getting adequate sources of calcium and vitamin D and exercising daily.

[nutrition]

Bone Density

The teen years through age 18 are the best time to make strong bones. The strength of bones depends upon their density. Density depends upon the amount of calcium held in a bone's protein framework. Calcium comes from the diet. Although other processes are involved, eating enough calcium during the teen years develops bones that will remain stronger all life long. Ninety-two percent of bone mass is present by the time you turn 19.

That said, calcium is continually replaced and recycled in those bones throughout your whole life. Therefore, it is important to eat enough calcium throughout the entire life cycle.

Iron-deficiency Anemia

Iron-deficiency anemia is a lack of iron in a person's blood. It is often caused by eating a diet poor in iron or having problems with absorption. Meat, fortified grains, eggs, and milk are products rich in iron. Iron-deficiency anemia causes weakness, irritability, headaches, pale skin, and sensitivity to cold temperatures. It is more common in women and children than men, and is a common condition in the world.

102

Figure Focus
Figure 2.14: This is a microscopic image of bone tissue that has become porous due to osteoporosis.

Eating a proper diet with foods high in iron and taking an iron supplement are ways to treat iron-deficiency anemia.

Dental Cavities

Tooth decay is a predisposition to cavities that can be caused by high-sugar diets and poor dental care. Dental fluoride treatments and fluoride in the water or in a supplement can help strengthen teeth.

Cardiovascular Diseases

Cardiovascular diseases affect the heart and blood vessels. They include hypertension, strokes, and heart attacks. Collectively, they are the number one cause of death in the United States. Risk factors for cardiovascular disease include the following:

- A sedentary lifestyle
- Smoking
- Overweight and obesity
- High cholesterol
- High saturated/trans-fat diets
- Diabetes

To decrease your risk for cardiovascular diseases, you should do the following:

- Stop smoking.
- Eat a healthy diet.
- Reduce blood cholesterol.
- Lower high blood pressure.
- Be physically active every day.
- Maintain a healthy weight.
- Manage diabetes.
- Reduce stress.

103

Reinforce and Review

- Children and teens might be more affected by dental cavities than by other nutritional illnesses that show up in middle age.

- Proper diet, along with good dental hygiene, helps protect the teeth.

- Untreated dental problems can create illness and problems elsewhere in the body, including the heart.

- Students might not be serious about preventing cardiovascular diseases while in high school.

- American Heart Association studies have reported a rise in arterial plaque formation in obese children and teenagers, which until recently was seen only in people in their middle age (40+).

- Help students to understand that fatal heart attacks can occur without any outward physical warning.

- Strokes might not be fatal to the entire body, but can permanently damage areas of the brain.

- It is best to live a healthy lifestyle all the time, from childhood.

Vocabulary Terms

- **Cardiovascular diseases:** Diseases that involve the circulatory system.

Nutrition: Good and Bad Cholesterol

Cholesterol must be moved through the body via the blood.

It is packaged for this, in either low-density complexes (which can be gooey), or high-density complexes (which are hard and move more easily).

Discuss

- It would be a disservice to imply that cardio-vascular disease, diabetes mellitus, and cancer can be completely avoided with proper lifestyle choices. Genetics can be a factor.

- Research helps us understand what might put us at risk for the disease.

- If we reduce the risk factors over which we have control, we reduce our risk.

- Even so, some of us can develop cardiovascular disease, diabetes mellitus, and cancer.

- Lifestyle can definitely improve the management of diabetes.

- Poorly managed diabetes can cause the loss of feet and legs.

Teaching Tips

- Encourage students to consider reducing their intake of soda, energy drinks, candy, and other foods that are high in sugar and/or fat.

- Encourage the students to be physically active and to exercise.

Vocabulary Terms

- **Diabetes mellitus:** A disease caused by problems with the regulation of insulin and blood sugar; it affects every system of the body and must be managed every day.

[nutrition]

Good and Bad Cholesterol

LDL, low-density lipoprotein, is the "bad" cholesterol. When too much LDL circulates in the blood, it slowly builds on the inner walls of the arteries that feed the heart and brain. It then forms plaque, which are hard, thick deposits that narrow and irritate the arteries. If the plaque clots and blocks the artery, a heart attack or stroke is possible.

To decrease LDL, minimize intake of saturated fats and trans fat. Include foods with soluble fiber, soy proteins, omega 3-rich foods (salmon, fish oils, flaxseed), and garlic into your diet. Also, maintain a healthy weight and active lifestyle.

HDL, high-density lipoprotein, is the "good" cholesterol. HDL takes excess cholesterol away and carries it back to the liver to be excreted. High levels of HDL protect against heart attacks. Low levels of HDL increase the risk of heart disease. To maintain high levels of HDL, stay active, quit smoking, include omega 3-rich foods in your diet, and reduce total fat intake to less than 30 percent.

Diabetes Mellitus

Diabetes mellitus is a condition in which the body cannot regulate blood sugar properly. Diabetes is on the rise in the United States. According to the Centers for Disease Control, approximately 23.6 million people, or 7.8 percent of the population, have this disease. Diabetes is treatable with diet, physical activity, and medication. If untreated or poorly treated, it can lead to blindness, seizures, kidney failure, heart disease, amputation of limbs, coma, and death.

Although not always the cause, obesity is a major contributor to both the incidence and severity of diabetes symptoms. Maintaining a healthy body weight through good nutrition and exercise is the best strategy for controlling the risk of diabetes. People who are diagnosed with diabetes should manage their dietary carbohydrates with the help of a registered dietitian in their clinic or hospital. They must also properly use their diabetes medications under the direction of their physician.

Cancer

Scientists are studying the role of nutrition in cancer prevention and treatment. The American Institute for Cancer Research believes obesity increases the likelihood of developing the following cancers:

- Breast
- Colon
- Endometrial (also known as uterine)
- Esophageal

104

- Kidney

- Prostate

To reduce the risk of cancer, eat a diet rich in fruits and vegetables, limit red meat, and be sure to exercise.

Proper nutrition is also important during and following a battle with cancer. Certain cancer therapies decrease appetite and produce nausea. Eating well, even when it's difficult, helps the body fight the disease.

Summary

In this section, you learned the following:

- Nutrition is the study of nutrients in food and how they nourish the body. Nutrition is important to the restaurant and foodservice industry because people depend on restaurant and foodservice operations for some of their meals. Operations should strive to provide menu items that make balanced, nutritious choices possible.

- The six basic nutrients found in food are carbohydrates, proteins, lipids, vitamins, minerals, and water.

- Phytochemicals aid the body in fighting or preventing diseases.

- Fiber promotes digestive health and regularity.

- Carbohydrates provide the body with energy. They help the body use protein and fat efficiently.

- Fat carries vitamins A, D, E, and K through the body, cushions the body's vital organs, protects the body from extreme temperatures, provides a reserve supply of energy when the body stores it, and supplies chemicals called essential fatty acids.

- Proteins supply energy to the body and provide the building blocks the body uses for muscles, tissues, enzymes, and hormones.

- Vitamins and minerals help in growth, reproduction, and the operations and maintenance of the body.

- Water is essential to the body. It helps with digestion, absorption, and transportation of nutrients; helps with elimination of waste through the kidneys, colon, and lungs; distributes heat throughout the body and allows heat to be released through the skin by evaporation; and lubricates joints and cushions body tissues.

105

Summary

- Remind students to review the following:
  1. The importance of nutrition
  2. Nutrients
  3. The digestive system
  4. Food additives
  5. A healthy diet
  6. Diseases caused by malnutrition

- Food additives improve flavor, color, and texture; retain nutritional value; prevent spoilage; and extend shelf life.

- Digestion breaks down food into its simplest parts.

- A healthy diet emphasizes fruits, vegetables, whole grains, and fat-free or low-fat milk and milk products. It includes lean meats, poultry, fish, beans, eggs, and nuts. And, it is low in saturated fats, trans fats, cholesterol, salt, and added sugars.

- Malnutrition is the condition that occurs when your body does not get enough nutrients. The major diseases caused by malnutrition include the following:

  - **Obesity**: Can be prevented by eating a healthy diet, exercising, and eating fewer calories.

  - **Osteoporosis:** Can be prevented by building strong bones and reaching peak bone density by getting adequate sources of calcium and vitamin D and exercising daily.

  - **Iron-deficiency anemia**: Can be prevented by eating a healthy diet of iron-rich foods.

  - **Dental cavities**: Can be prevented by avoiding high-sugar foods and using fluoride.

  - **Diabetes mellitus**: Can be prevented by eating a healthy diet and exercising.

  - **Cancer**: May be partially prevented by eating a healthy diet and exercising.

Section 2.1 Review Questions

1. As a restaurant and foodservice professional, why should you be concerned about nutrition?

2. Why is water important to the body?

3. Describe the 6 groups of nutrients that are necessary for good health.

4. Why are carbohydrates important in a person's diet?

5. Why does Laura Walsh believe that it is important to have an understanding of nutrition if you plan on a career in foodservice?

6. Chef Kate needs to create a 4-course dinner menu that is heart healthy. What are the criteria? Explain any modifications you would make to create a heart-healthy menu.

7. What is the difference between amino acids and protein?

8. How can a small amount of fat in a meal prevent you from overeating?

107

Section 2.1 Review Questions

1. The students should realize that they will receive inquiries about nutrition.

2. Water is the major component of the body and gives structure, provides lubrication, and helps with reactions and transport.

3. (1) Proteins: structure of tissues, repair, other molecules used by the body like enzymes and some hormones, and energy; (2) Carbohydrates: energy for the body to function; (3) Fats: energy storage, storage of vitamins A, D, E, and K, cushioning and insulation of the body, some transport, essential fatty acids, satiety; (4) Vitamins: molecules that work as catalysts or regulators in body processes; (5) Minerals: earth elements that are used in making molecules in the body, and also are involved in some reactions; (6) Water: the main component of the body (see answer to Question 2). The students might also include fiber and phytochemicals.

4. Carbohydrates provide energy for the body in the form of glucose that is carried in the bloodstream to the individual cells of the body.

5. Laura Walsh is correct in believing that consumers are becoming more interested in nutrition. Any restaurant or foodservice operation should be able to answer questions about the nutrient content of the foods served. It will also be a marketing tool. The students might also glean other information from the Professional Profile.

6. Each student will have his or her own ideas and creation for this assignment.

7. Amino acids are the nitrogen-containing building blocks of proteins. Proteins are polymer molecules made of amino acids. The students might know from prior learning that proteins are made by assembling amino acids according to a genetic DNA code.

8. Students might realize that fat contributes to satiety, which is the feeling of being full and satisfied with a meal.

Section 2.1
Activities

1. The information in the chapter might be enough to create this presentation. If not, have students use the American Dietetic Association Web site, the USDA Web site, or other reliable sources. Have students cite the sources they use.

2. Keeping an accurate food journal is an enlightening experience. Students might actually alter and improve their eating habits because they are writing them down. Instruct them to include everything, including water, breath mints, gum, and so on.

3. This will generate some interesting arguments. Help students to remember the various aspects, such as the high price of lifestyle illnesses. Whose right is it to tell you how to care for your own body? Whose right is it to rely on others for assistance?

Section 2.1 Activities

1. Study Skills/Group Activity: Nutrient Jigsaw

Work with 5 other classmates to create a presentation that includes the type, major function, and a food source for each of the 6 main nutrient categories.

2. Activity: Food Journal

Begin a food journal and keep it for one week. Record everything you eat and drink, not just meals. Include calories, serving sizes, time of day, motivation for eating, where you were, and who you were with.

3. Study Skills/Group: What's Good for You?

Should the government be allowed to decide what fats are used in a restaurant? Why or why not? Research this debate.

108

2.1 The Basics of Nutrition	2.2 Making Menu Items More
• The importance of nutrition	Nutritious
• Nutrients	• Food preparation techniques
• The digestive system	• Making menus more healthful
• Food additives	• Reducing excessive fats
• A healthy diet	• Types of produce (from a grower's point of view)

SECTION 2.2 MAKING MENU ITEMS MORE NUTRITIOUS

Eating a variety of foods is a good way to get all the nutrients the body needs. Nutrition experts have developed guidelines to help people make healthy food choices. But there's more to nutrition than choosing the proper selection of foods. Cook the food properly, present it attractively, and vary choices.

Study Questions

After studying Section 2.2, you should be able to answer the following questions:

- What techniques for food preparation preserve nutrients?
- How can menus and recipes be more healthful?
- What are healthful substitutes for high-fat items?
- What recent developments in food production affect nutrition?

Food Preparation Techniques

Cooking foods changes their nutritional values. Sometimes the change is small, but other times it is quite significant. Healthy menus require techniques that keep as many nutrients as possible. Keeping food safe throughout the flow of food helps to preserve nutrients.

Purchasing and Receiving

Purchasing high-quality products is the first step toward providing nutritious meals. Maintaining the nutritional value of this food after it enters an operation

109

Section 2.2 Making Menu Items More Nutritious

Introduce the Section

a. Some food-preparation techniques can preserve nutrient content.
b. Healthful choices can be delicious and well planned.
c. Fats in foods can be reduced.
d. Follow current trends in food and nutrition to remain aware of new techniques.

Vocabulary Review

a. Direct students to the key terms.
b. Pronounce each word, and have the students repeat the pronunciation out loud.
c. Discuss the definition of each word.

Teach

Discuss

- The choice to improve nutrition begins with planning.
- Menu planning, recipe selection, and purchasing decisions all grow out of a commitment to good nutrition choices.
- Follow all food safety guidelines for receiving and storing foods.
- Nutrition is protected while safety is maintained.
- If safety and quality are overlooked, nutrition will suffer as well.

- Help the students to see the positive correlation between food safety and nutrient protection.

- It will be a negative correlation if food safety principles are neglected.

is critical. Long storage times and warm temperatures can be damaging to both safety and nutritional value. When receiving food, do the following:

- Make sure frozen products are received frozen.

- Receive cold food at 41°F or lower without signs of freezing.

- Receive dry goods and other food products, like onions and potatoes, at room temperature and in clean and dry condition.

- Check fruit and vegetables for insect infestation, mold, cuts, discoloration and dull appearance, and unpleasant odors and tastes.

- Make sure produce feels heavy for its size and is free from wilting and wrinkling.

Storing

Nutrients are destroyed by heat and light (oxidation) and humidity (causes ripening and decay). Over time, food in storage can dry, rot, or grow mold or fungus. The best way to prevent deterioration is to maintain a low inventory of food products and use a quick turnaround system. FIFO is a good way to make sure inventory is used efficiently. Figure 2.15 shows moldy, rotten strawberries.

As a general rule, order only what the restaurant or foodservice operation needs in the short term. When possible, have frequent, smaller deliveries rather than large, infrequent orders. It is important to maintain proper storage temperatures:

- Keep dry goods at a cool room temperature.

- Store food at 41°F for refrigeration.

- Keep frozen foods frozen at 32°F or less.

Figure 2.15: Use the FIFO method to eliminate the risk of moldy and rotten food.

Figure Focus
Figure 2.15: FIFO only works if you use the "first in" products before they spoil.

Dry Storage
- Keep storerooms cool and dry. The temperature for the storeroom should be between 50°F and 70°F.
- Make sure storerooms are well ventilated. Keep temperature and humidity constant during storage.
- Store dry food away from walls and at least six inches off the floor.
- Keep dry food out of direct sunlight.

Refrigerated Storage
- Set refrigerators to the proper temperature. The setting must keep the internal temperature of the food at 41°F or lower. Check the temperature once during each shift.
- Monitor food temperature regularly. Use a calibrated thermometer placed in the warmest part of the unit to ensure proper temperature.
- Schedule regular maintenance for refrigerators.
- Do not overload refrigerators.
- Use open shelving.
- Keep refrigerator doors closed as much as possible.
- Wrap or cover all food properly.
- Store raw meat, poultry, and seafood separately from ready-to-eat foods.

Frozen Storage
- Set freezers to a temperature that will keep products frozen.
- Check freezer temperatures regularly.
- Place frozen food deliveries in freezers as soon as they have been inspected.
- Ensure good airflow inside freezers.
- Defrost freezer units on a regular basis.
- Clearly label food prepared on-site that is intended for frozen storage.
- Keep the unit closed as much as possible.

Prepping Food

When preparing vegetables, wash them quickly and thoroughly. Letting produce soak causes some vitamins to wash off or seep out and threatens food safety. Excessive trimming can also waste a lot of nutrients. For example, skins and leaves are rich in many vitamins and minerals. Using vegetable trimmings in stock or a soup base is one way to recover some of these nutrients.

111

Reinforce and Review
- Water and oil can dissolve vitamins and minerals out of foods.
- Soaking foods in water for long periods and then discarding the water can result in lost nutrients.

ServSafe Connection: Dry Storage, Refrigerated Storage, and Frozen Storage

Help the students note that these recommendations are not limited to nutrition.

They are the same as recommendations for food safety.

Could concern for safety and concern for health be related?

Discuss

- Help students understand that the goal is still delicious, beautiful food.

- If food doesn't taste good, people won't choose to eat it.

- Nutritious food should never be boring or bland.

Nutrition:
Nutrients and Heat

"Bioavailable" means the body can absorb food and use it as a nutrient.

Sometimes a nutrient is found in food, but cannot be absorbed by a human, or it is not in a usable form. These nutrients are not bioavailable.

Nutrients should be served in a bioavailable form to be considered in the nutritional intake.

Fast Fact:
Did You Know . . . ?

The best solution is to eat a widely varied and well-prepared diet.

Discuss

- Is the goal to eat for sensory experience, or to eat for nutrition? Are the two mutually exclusive?

- Have students debate, give ideas, make suggestions, share experiences, and so on.

In addition, cutting produce exposes surface areas to air and heat that destroy vitamin C. It is best to prepare vegetables and fruit close to serving time and to keep them intact as much as possible until ready for use. When cooking, try to use whole vegetables or cut larger pieces. Using sharp knives prevents bruising produce, which can quicken the loss of vitamin C.

[nutrition]

Nutrients and Heat

During the processing of food, the nutrients are vulnerable yet still stable (unless you boil the food too long). Overboiling destroys the color, alters the fresh flavor, and reduces the vitamin content of some fresh foods. The foods do not become useless, but fresh, seasonal, and local is the best option. Some nutrients are more bioavailable when cooked than when raw and fresh. Careful cooking!

[fast fact]

Did You Know...?

Clean, raw foods are often considered more whole or wholesome, and therefore more nutritious than cooked varieties. This is sometimes the case, but not always. Some nutrients are improved by cooking. Also, some anti-nutrients are deactivated by cooking. An anti-nutrient is a chemical that blocks the absorption of a nutrient from food. For example, oxalic acid (an anti-nutrient) is found in raw spinach and other green leafies. It "locks up" iron, calcium, magnesium, zinc, and other nutrient minerals, preventing them from being absorbed in the digestive system. When the greens are cooked, they may lose some fresh nutrients (like some vitamin C), but they become a better source of nutrient minerals. Figure 2.16 on the following page shows a photo of spinach being gently cooked.

Cooking Food

When cooking any food, remember that the lower the temperature and the shorter the cooking period, the less nutrient loss there will be.

A good adaptation can produce a dish that is not only acceptable, but potentially delicious. Using modifications sensibly and artistically can result in tasty fare that guests love. Think of healthy cooking as simply good cooking with good ingredients, rather than as an unwelcome adaptation of classical cooking.

Cooking Grains and Legumes

Be careful not to overwash grains. Some imported or bulk grains may contain dirt and impurities and will need to be rinsed. But washing can greatly affect vitamin content. For example, white rice can lose 25 percent of its thiamin, and brown rice can lose 10 percent. The best way to preserve vitamins in grains is by not overcooking them and keeping grains covered.

112

Figure 2.16: Gentle cooking can enhance the nutrients of some greens.

Some food products like rice, yucca, grains, and dry beans must be cooked to make their nutrients available to the body. For example, when the starch in these food items cooks, water is absorbed and the starch is gelatinized, making the item edible and nutritious.

Cooking Meat, Fish, and Poultry

Meat, fish, and poultry are at their best and most healthful when served close to the time they are cooked. During cooking, nutrients in meats are lost primarily through water, which evaporates or goes into the drippings. Protein losses are minimal. The longer meat is cooked, the more thiamin and vitamin B_6 are lost.

Other ways to optimize the flavor and nutritive qualities are to grill, broil, steam, bake, poach, or sauté these foods and then serve them immediately. Tough cuts are best when slowly cooked by either braising or using them in a soup or stew. They can be served with the broth, which is a good way to retain some of the nutrients lost in the cooking process. Cooking meat or vegetables in an acid sauce (such as a tomato sauce) in an iron pan is also useful, as it adds iron to the diet.

When cooking meat, fish, and poultry, the protein in the flesh **coagulates** (thickens and congeals) when heat is applied. With tender food like fish, shellfish, and chicken breasts, the protein coagulation as well as temperature

113

Discuss

- Protein isn't easily destroyed by cooking.

- Meat, fish, and poultry are usually consumed for protein nutrition.

- These foods contain other vitamins and minerals as well, which might be lost in overcooking.

- Is overcooking ever a desirable culinary strategy?

- Proper cooking benefits both taste and nutrition.

Vocabulary Terms

- **Coagulates:** Denatures and becomes thick, firm, and opaque.

Figure Focus

Figure 2.16: This spinach is ready to serve very soon after it is heated through. It still has its bright color.

- Help students to understand that adding baking soda isn't a good strategy.

Reinforce and Review

- Baking soda is good for baking, but not for produce.
- The ideal pH range for foods is slightly acidic, or below 7.
- This enhances acceptability for flavor and absorbability for nutrition.
- Baking soda can raise the pH above 7, into the alkaline range.
- Alkaline foods taste soapy.
- Vitamin C is best obtained from fresh, raw fruits and vegetables.
- Citrus fruits are the best source of vitamin C, but other fruits and vegetables have vitamin C.
- Cooked foods shouldn't be relied on for vitamin C. Include raw produce for this purpose.

indicates doneness. For tougher meat, the initial protein coagulation is only one step in the cooking process. When moisture is added, the tough connective tissue in the meat can break down to form gelatin. In addition, fat in the meat slowly melts, or renders, during the cooking process. This adds flavor and moistness. When adding fats to a dish, choose monounsaturated fats rather than saturated fats when possible and when consistent with the desired flavor of the dish. Avoid reusing cooking oil, because the fat becomes rancid and unhealthy with overuse. Figure 2.17 shows salmon served over a baby greens salad.

Figure 2.17: Salmon served over a baby greens salad.

Cooking Fruit and Vegetables

Fruits and vegetables should be served raw where appropriate. When cooking, cook quickly in minimal liquid and serve immediately with the cooking liquid where possible. Steaming in the microwave or on the stove by pan-steaming are ideal methods of cooking fruits and vegetables. Pan-steaming is done by placing the vegetable in a sauté pan with a bit of water or stock and then covering and cooking over high heat until the vegetable is tender, but not soft.

Another way to maintain the maximum amount of nutrients is to season lightly. One common, but not advisable, practice is to add baking soda to enhance the color of green vegetables. While this works for color, it destroys the texture of the vegetable and the fragile vitamin C. Frying can be similarly damaging to vitamin C and other nutrients and, of course, adds fat to the dish.

114

Figure Focus
Figure 2.17: This plate of food is loaded with many desirable nutrients.

With vegetables, the size of the vegetable and the amount of water used are also important. If less water is used, more vitamin B and C are retained. Stir-frying and brief steaming are good methods to use. Also, baking root vegetables in their skins retains nutrients better than peeling, cutting, and boiling. Figure 2.18 shows a cook stir-frying vegetables.

Figure 2.18: Cooking fresh vegetables quickly reduces nutrient loss.

Holding

The key to cooking nutritious food is to manage time and temperature so that food is cooked only as much as necessary and served as soon as possible. The longer the food sits on the stove or in the steam table, the fewer vitamins may remain for the guest. Multistage cooking, such as precooking vegetables, shocking them in water, chilling until service, reheating at service, and storing in a steam table, may be useful from a timing perspective, but it also causes a noticeable decrease in some vitamins. A noticeable decrease occurs because the vegetable is exposed to so much heat during two cooking periods and a potentially extended holding period. Heat breaks down many nutrients.

One way you might be able to avoid long holding times is to cook food in smaller batches. Figure 2.19 on the following page shows a cook preparing food in batches.

Discuss

- Vitamin B is actually several vitamins with numerical subscripts (B_1, B_2, B_3, etc.).

- The most common ones also have other names: thiamin is B_1, riboflavin is B_2, niacin is B_3, pantothenic acid is B_5, pyridoxine is B_6, biotin is B_7, folic acid is B_9, and cobalamin is B_{12}.

- Each has a different role in maintaining metabolism, but the specifics are beyond the scope of this chapter.

- Not all B vitamins are found in the same foods.

- A wide variety of foods ensures good B vitamin nutrition.

- There are other B vitamins as well, but over time some of them have not turned out to be necessary nutrients.

- Originally there was one for each number, in order, up to 17.

Reinforce and Review

- Color is a good indication of what is happening with cooked foods.

- If the color is going dull, nutrients are probably being lost as well.

- Hold foods only for short periods of time, while quality can be maintained.

Figure Focus

Figure 2.18: A quick stir-fry can keep vegetables appealing and colorful.

Essential Skills:
Batch Cooking for Vegetables

Batch cooking can be efficient if it is well planned and carefully prepped.

Vocabulary Terms

- **Batch cooking:** Cooking amounts as they are needed, rather than large amounts for holding.

Figure 2.19: Cook food in batches to avoid long holding times.

Batch cooking is the process of reheating or finishing a small batch of food, as needed, or preparing a small amount of food several times during a service period, so that a fresh supply of cooked items is always available. This process improves the nutritional value, flavor, color, and texture of food.

Essential Skills
Batch Cooking for Vegetables

1. Rinse, trim, and peel vegetables properly.
2. Cut vegetables into even pieces, as directed in the recipe. See Figure 2.20a.
3. Blanch or parcook vegetables by boiling or steaming them.
4. Shock vegetables in an ice bath. See Figure 2.20b.
5. Drain vegetables thoroughly. See Figure 2.20c.
6. Refrigerate blanched or parcooked vegetables until ready to prepare a batch.
7. Reheat small batches of vegetables in simmering water or sauté them.

Figure 2.20a: Step 2—Cut the vegetables into even pieces.

Figure 2.20b: Step 4—Shock the vegetables in an ice bath.

Figure 2.20c: Step 5—Drain the vegetables.

116

Figure Focus

Figure 2.19: Smaller batches can help preserve fresh nutrients.

Figure 2.20a: Careful handling of a raw carrot.

Figure 2.20b: Shocking blanched vegetables stops the cooking process.

Figure 2.20c: Drain the water so the vegetables don't soak.

Making Menus More Healthful

Many people think healthy cooking is only about removing less desirable ingredients from a menu item. But that's simply not true. One easy way to make a dish more healthful is to modify its portion size. **Portion control** means controlling the quantity of particular foods by using appropriately sized servings. Consider offering a variety of portions, such as lunch, half, light, or senior sizes.

Healthy cooking also can be about adding healthful ingredients. Most people in the United States do not get sufficient fiber from their diet. Adding fresh fruit and vegetables, whole grains, and legumes to dishes is a good way to increase the nutrient content of food. It can increase fiber and add interest to a dish. For example, add amaranth, quinoa, or millet to a menu to accomplish these goals.

[fast fact]

Did You Know...?

Tabouleh (tah-BOOL-lee) is a Middle Eastern salad made from finely chopped parsley, bulgur, tomato, scallions, mint, and other herbs with lemon juice, olive oil, and various seasonings. It is eaten around the world, especially in vegetarian or vegan cuisines.

Tabouleh is a national dish in Lebanon, where it is believed to have originated. In Lebanon, it is commonly scooped onto lettuce leaves from a large bowl and eaten.

After understanding the purpose of the ingredients, begin to modify recipes to be lower in fat, sugar, and salt. Figure 2.21 shows a small serving of a rich dessert with a low-calorie garnish on top.

Figure 2.21: A small serving of a rich dessert provides fewer calories.

117

Discuss

- What difference does portion size make?

- Help the students to see that portion control is key to good nutrition.

- In the current civilized world, overnutrition is a major problem, but it could be solved with appropriate portion choices.

**Fast Fact:
Did You Know . . . ?**

Give tabouleh a try. It's very fresh tasting and very good. If possible, find a recipe to make in class.

Teaching Tip

- Note that the plate shown in Figure 2.21 has a plate garnish that gives volume to the menu item. It makes the item fill the plate better, giving the illusion of a larger portion. The visual appeal can increase customer satisfaction with the portion size.

Vocabulary Terms

- **Portion control:** Keeping serving sizes appropriate and consistent.

Figure Focus
Figure 2.21: A small bite can be more satisfying than a large helping of a substitute.

Essential Skills: Modifications in Baking

Experiment with various modifications to see which ones you like.

Try new things in the quest for a more nutritious menu.

Reinforce and Review

- Fat is not always visible in a soup, sauce, or gravy. In fact, if properly made, the fat will be invisible.

- Fats and oils will pool on the top of sauces, soups, and gravies if they are poorly made with roux.

- Cream is very high in fat, so when used as an ingredient, fat is added to a dish.

- Some alternatives can reduce fat while maintaining the character of the dish.

- Experiment with different thickeners to see the result. If this is not possible, smaller portions can help reduce the total fat of the meal.

Essential Skills
Modifications in Baking

❶ Reduce half of the fat in many recipes by using fruit pureés such as applesauce in place of butter or oil. This results in a moist, denser cake, and the crumb will still be tender. See Figure 2.22.

❷ To lower cholesterol, use an egg substitute instead of an egg. The rule of thumb is ¼ cup of egg substitute equals 1 egg. Egg substitutes are egg whites with a small amount of vegetable oil added to replace the egg yolk. Yellow food coloring is usually added.

❸ To lower sugar, replace it with a sugar substitute following the manufacturer's directions.

Figure 2.22: Step 1—Replace butter with applesauce in many recipes to reduce fat.

Modifications in Soups, Sauces, and Gravies

Much culinary creativity and experimentation comes in the soup, sauce, and gravy categories. Classic sauces are flavorful but tend to have a lot of fat. Many are thickened with roux, a cooked mixture of fat and flour. Others are emulsion sauces, such as hollandaise and mayonnaise that consist of egg yolk and butter or oil. The result is a sauce made predominantly of fat.

There are several ways to reduce the fat content of soups, sauces, and gravies:

- Use a reduction of stock. Start with a stock made from vegetables, meat, poultry, or fish and simmer until it is about one-third of the original volume. Stock and broth are nearly fat free because the fat rises to the top and can be skimmed off. In the process of reduction, the stock will develop body and its flavors will intensify. Then, less thickener is needed.

- Use a slurry. In place of a traditional flour-and-fat roux, a slurry (a thin paste made from water or stock mixed with starch, such as cornstarch) can be a thickening alternative. To use a slurry, dissolve starch in cold water and incorporate it into the hot sauce.

118

Figure Focus
Figure 2.22: Applesauce or other puréed fruit can provide moisture for a baked product with reduced fat or oil.

- Use skimmed stock. Rather than using a premade mother sauce (a classic sauce from which other sauces are made), make a sauce of pan drippings, wine, broth, or stock, and skim the fat from the top.

- Use less oil in salad dressings by replacing bland salad oils with intensely flavored nut oils, olive oils, or infused oils (oils that have been heated with seasonings for flavor). Also, replace 25 percent of the oil with slightly thickened stock. *Note:* Remember to disclose the type of nut oil, in case of food allergies.

- To mimic a creamy sauce for macaroni and cheese, for example, blend cottage cheese and strained yogurt, using corn starch as a thickener, if heating.

- In place of heavy cream, use canned evaporated skimmed milk, which mimics the body of cream.

- In a braise or soup, puréeing the vegetables in the cooking liquid thickens the sauce, retaining all the nutrients.

- In place of gravy, fruit coulis (thick puréed sauces), salsas, and chutneys make excellent sauces for meats.

- In béchamel sauce, use skim milk and trans-fat-free margarine.

- Two teaspoons of sour cream or plain yogurt can be added as a garnish on low-fat cream soup to give it the mouthfeel of full-fat cream soup.

- Vegetable jus (the French term for juice) and consommé make great sauces.

- Remember that margarine has the same fat as butter, but doesn't taste as nice.

[nutrition]

Sauce Bourguignon

A lot is said about sauces being a lavish extra that weight-conscious individuals should have on the side. However, a sauce is a beautiful, flavorful, and important part of a dish and its presentation. Some sauces improve the nutrition of an item. One is Sauce Bourguignon, which uses the red wine Bourgogne to deglaze.

In the deglazing and gentle cooking, the alcohol content of the wine is decreased. The nutrient content of the wine remains, boosting the nutrition of the entire dish, whether it is *boeuf bourguignonne* or coq au vin. Red wine provides antioxidants, flavonoids (like anthocyanins), procyanidins, and resveratrol. These long-name chemicals fight both cancer and heart disease.

Discuss

- Each of these modifications is used throughout the culinary world.

- Some famous chefs specialize in health-conscious cuisine adaptations.

- Their food does not taste "substituted," but tastes delicious in its own right.

Nutrition: Sauce Bourguignon

Red wine and red grape juice do not lose their pigments under fermentation or cooking.

Fermentation does not make the grape more red.

Red grape juice provides the same advantages without alcohol.

CUSTOMIZED INSTRUCTION

Literacy Connection, 21st-Century Skills— Analyze Media

Special Needs Students

Have students act the part of a TV chef making a modification to a recipe to make it more healthful. Choose one in the text. Rehearse as needed.

ESOL Students

In English, have student(s) explain and demonstrate how to make a modification that is listed in the text. Rehearse as needed.

Less Advanced Students

Research a TV chef, past or present, who taught an example of how to modify a recipe for health purposes. If possible, show a clip of this chef making the modification in a demonstration. If not, describe the event and show a still photo of the chef.

More Advanced Students

Research at least two famous chefs who have created healthful recipes using classic culinary principles. One chef to consider is Graham Kerr, who began early as a TV chef with a popular show, and eventually devoted his time to health-promoting modifications of cuisine.

Create a PowerPoint presentation and show it to the class.

Essential Skills: Modifications for Meat

Lean meat should be cooked for tenderness.

Some lean cuts can be tough if improperly cooked.

Essential Skills: Modifications for Seafood

Omega-3 fatty acids are a type of mono-unsaturated fat that is especially good for the heart and cardiovascular system.

Essential Skills
Modifications for Meat

1. Choose low-fat meat such as beef or pork tenderloin, beef eye of round, beef flank steak, beef sirloin steak, pork loin chops, turkey breast, ostrich, buffalo, venison, or rabbit.

2. Trim visible fat, and cook the meat using a low-fat cooking technique such as dry-sautéing, stir-frying, grilling, broiling, pan-smoking, or roasting. See Figure 2.23a.

3. For poultry, select white-meat chicken instead of the dark meat legs and thighs, which have a higher fat content.

4. When cooking chicken, leave the skin on and remove it just before serving. See Figure 2.23b.

5. If using a marinade, boneless, skinless chicken breast will work well.

Figure 2.23a: Step 2—Trim visible fat from meat.

Figure 2.23b: Step 4—Cook chicken with the skin on and remove it just before serving.

Essential Skills
Modifications for Seafood

1. Care should be taken not to overcook fish and seafood, thus ruining their delicate flavors.

2. Dry-sautéing, grilling, and poaching are the best cooking methods. See Figure 2.24a on the following page.

3. Using swordfish, mackerel, salmon, and tuna provides customers with omega-3 fatty acids, which may help prevent heart disease. See Figure 2.24b on the following page.

4. Shellfish, such as shrimp, lobster, and crawfish have high cholesterol but no saturated fat, so they are nutritious choices. See Figure 2.24c on the following page.

120

Figure Focus

Figure 2.23a: Remove visible fat.

Figure 2.23b: Protect the chicken meat, but remove the excess fat before serving.

Essential Skills:
Modifications for Vegetables

Try to find an alternative for fat-dependent cooking methods.

The flavor of a small amount of fat can be added in limited quantity as a garnish.

Figure 2.24a: Step 2—Dry-sautéing, grilling, and poaching are the best cooking methods for seafood.

Figure 2.24b: Step 3—Salmon has omega-3 fatty acids, which may help to prevent heart disease.

Figure 2.24c: Step 4—Shrimp has high cholesterol, but no saturated fat, so it is a nutritious choice.

Essential Skills
Modifications for Vegetables

❶ Instead of sautéing vegetables in oil, sweat them in a little stock. This extracts flavor from the vegetables and is a good foundation for the rest of the dish. See Figure 2.25a.

❷ To finish a vegetable, a small amount of butter or flavored nut oil can be added. See Figure 2.25b. Remember to disclose the type of nut oil in case of allergies.

❸ Use any fat at the end, so its flavor still can be perceived.

Figure 2.25a: Step 1—Sweat vegetables in stock.

Figure 2.25b: Step 2—Add a small amount of butter to finish the vegetables.

121

Figure Focus

Figure 2.24a: Some fish is too dry or delicate for dry cooking. It does work well with salmon and halibut.

Figure 2.24b: Presentation maintains the beautiful quality of the food.

Figure 2.24c: A mix of vegetables, grains, and seafood can be low in fat and nutritious.

Figure 2.25a: Sweating brings out the flavor. Use fat-free, low-sodium stock.

Figure 2.25b: Rather than cooking with butter, simply garnish dishes with a little butter.

Essential Skills:
Modifications for Desserts

The goal is for dessert to be a delicious finish to a meal.

A dessert can be delicious without undermining nutrition efforts and good health.

Essential Skills:
Modifications for Garnishes

Microgreens are an excellent trend in garnishes.

They are not only edible, but they add further nutrients to the item.

Essential Skills
Modifications for Desserts

Know the function of a dessert's ingredients. If an ingredient substitute will change the integrity of the dessert, then do not make the substitution, as in pie crust.

❶ Use low-fat and fat-free cottage cheese, ricotta cheese, yogurt, or cream cheese. If fat-free items are used, it is important to use some type of starch to protect the proteins from heat when baking, or they will curdle. See Figure 2.26a.

❷ The fat in a pie crust is there to make it flaky. To reduce or change the fat, it would be necessary to change the nature of the dessert from a pie to a strudel or a cobbler. If making a strudel, phyllo (also spelled filo) dough can be used as the pastry by spraying it with atomized oil before baking to reduce the fat significantly. If making a cobbler, little or no fat is needed. See Figure 2.26b.

Figure 2.26a: Use low-fat and fat-free cottage, rocotta, or cream cheese or yogurt.

Figure 2.26b: Step 2—Replace pie with a strudel or cobbler to reduce fat.

Essential Skills
Modifications for Garnishes

❶ Instead of using small pieces of fried items, such as shallots or potatoes, use thinly sliced pieces of vegetables or microgreens. See Figure 2.27a on the following page.

❷ Cheese adds nutrition but also fat and calories and should be computed with any calorie/nutrient analysis.

❸ Foams: Make by aerating a sauce and spooning just the foam onto the dish. See Figure 2.27b on the following page.

❹ Salsa: Bind perfectly brunoised fruit or vegetables with a light vegetable sauce so it can be shaped into a quenelle; crispy, savory tuile; or cracker.

122

Figure Focus

Figure 2.26a: Low-fat dairy foods can still taste very full and rich.

Figure 2.26b: There is not as much pastry in a strudel or cobbler.

Figure 2.27a: Step 1—Use thinly sliced pieces of vegetables or microgreens as alternate garnish.

Figure 2.27b: Step 3—Make foam by aerating a sauce and spooning just the foam onto the dish.

[fast fact]

Did You Know...?

To decrease salt but add a salty flavor, increase the use of herbs and spices. Use citrus and vinegar to season.

[nutrition]

Types of Salt

The most commonly used types of salt include the following:

Table salt is the most common salt found on every table. It is refined to remove other minerals and impurities. It is processed to give it a fine, even grain, and a small amount of starch to keep it from forming clumps.

Kosher salt has no additives, so it has a purer flavor than table salt. It is usually coarser than table salt, which means it has larger crystals. To substitute kosher salt for table salt, use twice as much kosher salt as called for in the recipe. It is the most common salt found in professional kitchens.

Sea salt is extracted from the ocean using evaporation techniques. It is usually not refined, so it contains additional minerals and other elements found in sea water, which affect the flavor.

Iodized salt is table salt that has been enriched with iodine as a nutritional supplement.

Rock salt is less refined than table salt and not meant to be eaten. It is used in ice cream makers and as a bed for certain items, such as oysters or clams on their shells.

123

Figure Focus

Figure 2.27a: Microgreens, mint leaves, lavender, and other herbs are beautiful garnishes.

Figure 2.27b: Make sure the aerated sauce does not look like soap bubbles.

- This is a very important topic, given the overnutrition and obesity problem in our society.

- Too many calories from fats and simple sugars are a serious problem.

- Not everyone understands, or cares about, what they are eating.

- Long-term consequences might not be immediately motivating when someone is hungry and wants something to eat.

Discuss

- Do you contemplate the implications of long-term nutrition decisions when you are looking in the refrigerator for a snack?

- Encourage students to discuss tactics to improve nutritional decisions and choices for wellness and improved health.

When making modifications, remember to keep flavor in mind at all times. If fat is the contributing factor to flavor, then a strong flavor alternative must be substituted. Be creative and use modifications as an opportunity to make food memorable.

Reducing Excessive Fats

Saturated fats (butter, lard, tropical oils) and trans fats (margarine, shortening) can be reduced by using less and replacing them with alternative products. For example, margarine made with saturated fats can be replaced by margarine made with monounsaturated fats, such as canola oil that hasn't been hydrogenated. Fats are typically found in high amounts in food such as meat, full-fat dairy products, sauces, nuts, oils, salad dressings, and baked goods (often made with trans fats). Figure 2.28 shows foods that contain saturated fats.

Figure 2.28: Many baked goods and fried foods can contain high levels of saturated fats.

Using high-quality lean meat is a good strategy for replacing the large amounts of fat found in prime cuts. For example, USDA Choice can be used in place of USDA Prime beef. Although USDA Choice is a leaner grade of beef because it has less fat marbling than USDA Prime, it is still of high quality and sufficiently juicy to broil or grill. USDA Select beef is lean because it has the least fat marbling. Prepare it by using a moist method of cooking to ensure tenderness. Maintain moisture in lean meat by cooking in parchment, foil, or vegetable leaves. Basting lean meat with stock will also prevent it from drying out when cooking and will keep the fat content of the resulting dish low. When sautéing, brush a little oil on the meat and cook it in a nonstick pan.

For some food items that can't be changed, limit the frequency with which they are eaten or decrease the portion size that is served. When making substitutions to reduce fat in a dish, remember why the fat is in the dish in the first place. Butter, rendered bacon, duck fat, and goose fat have flavors that are appealing

Figure Focus
Figure 2.28: Baked goods and fried foods often have a lot of fat in them or are fried in fat.

to consumers and cooking properties that are difficult to imitate. A pie crust can easily be made with lard or shortening. When substituting vegetable oil for shortening, it is difficult to obtain a comparable result. When making substitutions, remember the purpose for the substitution and the role that fat plays in the food item. Not all fats can be reduced, removed, or replaced. Table 2.2 is a list of common ingredient substitutions.

Table 2.2: Recipe Substitutions

Instead of:	Use:
Whole milk	2%, 1%, or fat-free milk
Eggs, whole or yolks	Egg whites or a commercial egg substitute, fruit or vegetable purée
Butter	Trans-fat-free margarine (some of these spreads are not appropriate for baking), olive oil, nut oils, avocado
Coconut and palm oil	Canola oil, soybean oil, safflower oil, grape seed oil, applesauce, low-fat plain yogurt
Cheese	Low-fat varieties
Yogurt	Low or non-fat
Bacon	Turkey bacon, Canadian bacon, lean ham
Sausage	Turkey sausage, seasoned ground turkey, soy crumbles
Ground beef	Ground sirloin, ground turkey breast, ground soy
Chocolate	Cocoa
Heavy cream	Equal portions of half-and-half and canned evaporated skim milk

[nutrition]

Saturated Fats

In the 1980s, businessman Phil Sokolof was concerned about the levels of high-cholesterol and saturated fats in the U.S. food supply. He launched a media campaign about it, stating that these fats in foods were destroying the heart health of the American public.

Through his efforts, saturated tropical oils and beef tallows (lard) were removed from many popular food preparations, like snack crackers and French fries. They were replaced with vegetable oils that were hydrogenated for processing. Unfortunately, processing foods with hydrogenated vegetable oils can create trans fats, which also are not healthy for the heart. The answer? Reduce total dietary fat, increase heart-healthy foods, and get some exercise.

Table 2.2: Recipe Substitutions

- Use reliable substitutions unless you have a lot of time to experiment and possibly fail.

Teaching Tips

- Help students to understand that substitutions will not taste the same as the original recipe.

- The new item will vary in flavor, mouthfeel, smoothness, or other sensory qualities.

- However, help students consider that the new item can be just as delicious, and perhaps even more so.

Nutrition: Saturated Fats

Unintended consequences can create interesting problems. Mr. Sokolof was trying to help the American people by increasing the heart-healthy quality of the diet by reducing saturated fat in processed foods. However, his campaign was based upon faulty and incomplete knowledge of food science and nutrition, and the way fats work in processing. Unintentionally, the problem with fat actually worsened.

125

Discuss

- Do students understand the nature of scientific studies, like the Alar studies?

- Rat studies deal with experimentation and trials. The results deal with risks and probabilities. The results of rat research are published, and the connection between rats and humans is suggested by the research.

- Remind students that research is not absolute, but trends can be seen over time in most cases.

Vocabulary Terms

- **Pesticides:** Chemicals that kill insects.

- **Herbicides:** Chemicals that kill plants.

- **Hormones:** Proteins or steroids that regulate and control metabolism.

- **Antibiotics:** Chemicals that kill bacteria.

- **GMOs (genetically modified organisms):** Plant or animal whose genetic makeup has been altered.

Types of Produce (From a Grower's Point of View)

Although a foodservice operation serves food that is safe, wholesome, and nutritious, some customers may be concerned about the following:

- **Pesticides:** Chemicals that kill insects and other plant pests
- **Herbicides:** Weed killers
- **Hormones:** Often injected into animals to make them grow
- **Antibiotics:** Medicines that prevent infections
- **GMOs:** Genetically modified organisms, which are plants or animals whose genetic makeup has been changed
- Feed made from animal products

These concerns aren't actually new. For example, a chemical known as Alar, that helped apples to grow, was commonly used for decades. But in 1989, it was removed from the market when studies showed that it caused tumors in mice. See Figure 2.29.

Figure 2.29: Some people are concerned about the chemicals used to help produce grow.

Figure Focus

Figure 2.29: This apple is grown in an orchard. Is the orchard safe? Most farmers want their food to be safe and are careful.

Some of the products currently used in farming are now also being studied:

- If bovine growth hormone (BGH) is used to cause dairy cows to produce more milk, will drinking the milk pass the hormone to people's bodies and cause harm?

- If bacteria become resistant to antibiotics, will eating an animal that has been given an antibiotic affect people's resistance?

- If an animal is sick, will using its bones in animal feed cause other animals to get the same disease?

The answers to these kinds of questions are not yet clear. But many consumers take a "better safe than sorry" approach. They want food produced without using any of the products listed previously, and they will pay more money to get it.

To meet these needs, many restaurant and foodservice operations have started to choose organic food products. As a professional, it is important to know what this means. Restaurant and foodservice employees must be able to identify the differences among the various types of products available:

- **Conventional:** These products are grown using approved USDA and FDA agricultural methods. The methods allow the use of certain fertilizers, pesticides, hormones, and drugs that are recognized as safe. Most of the food in the supermarket and from restaurant and foodservice suppliers comes from conventional producers.

- **Organic:** Generally, these products have been produced without pesticides or synthetic fertilizers. Soil and water are also usually conserved. Animals don't receive antibiotics or growth hormones.

- **Certified organic:** These products meet the requirements of their certifying organization. In the United States, the National Organic Program of the USDA certifies products as "100 percent organic," "organic" (95 percent organic), or "made with organic ingredients" (70 percent organic). While all foods are technically "organic" as far as their chemistry is concerned, the term implies much more. The "certified organic" name applies to farming and processing techniques that are simple, nontoxic, and sustainable. If a label is USDA "certified organic," it will apply to these standards.

- **Local:** Products made by local producers can be either conventional or organic.

- **Natural:** The term "natural" is legally meaningless. Food products labeled as "natural" may or may not have any organic ingredients or processing.

127

Discuss

- "Organic" means many things.

- Have the students discuss the various marketing terms and why they are used.

Teaching Tips

- Some of the terms on this page are descriptors of production standards. Some are marketing terms. Help the students to see the difference.

In-Class Activity: KIM Chart

Literacy Connection, 21st-Century Skills—Use and Manage Information

Help the students learn the concepts behind the vocabulary words/concepts on pp. 126 and 127. Help the students to understand the information and develop a memory cue to remember the information so it will be useful.

Have the students fold a piece of paper lengthwise in thirds.

Label the columns "K" for Key Term, "I" for Information, and "M" for Memory Cue.

Write the term in the K column and the definition and textbook information in the I column.

In the M column, invent a memory cue. This could be a little picture, a key word, a rhyme, a sound-alike, or a mnemonic device of some sort.

Give the students a period of time to use their KIM chart: 10 minutes, overnight, a week, or whatever is appropriate for your classroom.

Without the help of the chart, quiz the students on the terms.

Have students keep the KIM chart in their notes for future reference.

Vocabulary Terms

- **Conventional:** A food product available for purchase with no special modifications or claims.

- **Organic:** A food product without added chemicals.

- **Certified organic:** A specific set of standards for organic food production.

- **Local:** Made within a relatively close radius.

- **Natural:** Anything occurring in nature, but not a specific food term.

Discuss

- The NOP develops and administers national production, handling, and labeling standards for organic agriculture products.

- There are many reasons to make philosophical choices about foods and processes.

- Help students realize that investigation is a personal responsibility.

Vocabulary Terms

- **Genetically modified organisms (GMOs):** Organisms with altered DNA to emphasize certain desirable traits; genetic engineering.

Figure 2.30: A USDA organic logo indicates that agricultural products have met specific standards.

Figure 2.30 displays the USDA (United States Department of Agriculture) organic logo. This National Organic Program (NOP) develops and administers national production, handling, and labeling standards for organic agricultural products.

A common misperception about organic food products is that they have more nutrients than conventionally grown food. Another is that organic food products are made by small producers, while conventional food products are made by large producers. Actually, both large and small producers grow organic and conventional food products. Their finished food products are quite similar nutritionally. People also choose organic food because of its impact on the environment.

Genetically modified food organisms need a special mention in any discussion about today's farming. **Genetically modified organisms (GMOs)** are plants or animals whose genetic makeup has been altered. This results in a change in the genetic code of the receiving plant or animal, which becomes permanent. In addition, the offspring of the plant or animal also has that altered genetic makeup.

What could be the benefits of a GMO? For plants, these might include the following:

- Better resistance to insects, weeds, or fungi
- Improved nutritional value
- Able to withstand extreme heat, cold, or drought
- Better resistance to specific herbicides or pesticides (most common)
- Better flavor

Figure Focus

Figure 2.30: Ask students if they prefer products that have this logo.

Of course, not all of these benefits are consistent. For example, tomatoes have been bred for storage and transport to the grocers. They have also been bred to reduce acidity. In the process, though, they have lost flavor and juiciness. Now, the industry is experiencing a demand for "heirloom" tomato seed stock, a high-acid juicy tomato.

Some consumers express concern about GMOs that are resistant to herbicides. If a plant, such as soybeans, is resistant to a specific herbicide, then the field may be sprayed with that herbicide to kill the weeds. However, this leaves the growing soybean plants with herbicide still on them. In the minds of these consumers, both the modification and the remaining herbicide are issues.

Genetic modification is one form of biotechnology and bioengineering. These fields of science apply technology to living organisms in order to produce something of use. A more common example is how biological organisms are put in fresh cheese to age it.

From a nutritional standpoint, genetically modified food products do not differ much from unmodified food products. In fact, some may have been modified to increase nutrients. No conclusive evidence shows that genetically modified food products are harmful to people's health.

Ultimately, the products a restaurant or foodservice organization chooses to serve will depend on what their customers want.

Summary

In this section, you learned the following:

- Correctly purchasing, receiving, storing, prepping, cooking, and holding food helps preserve nutrients.

- Menus and recipes can be made more healthful by modifying portion size, adding healthful ingredients, and substituting healthier ingredients.

- Healthy substitutes for high-fat items include the following:

  - When baking, use fruit purées.

  - When cooking soups, sauces, and gravies, use a reduction of stock, slurry, skimmed stock, canned evaporated skimmed milk, or vegetable jus.

  - When cooking meat, choose low-fat meat, trim visible fat, cook meat using a low-fat cooking technique, use white-meat chicken instead of the legs and thighs, and leave the skin on chicken, and remove the skin just before serving.

129

Discuss

- Do students have ideas about where they can obtain information about nutrition decisions?

- Help students find reliable scientific information that they can understand.

- Encourage students to look beyond popular culture for word-of-mouth information about their important choices.

Summary

- Remind students to review the following:
  1. Food preparation techniques
  2. Making menus more helpful
  3. Reducing excessive fats
  4. Types of produce (from a grower's point of view)

- • When cooking seafood, do not overcook fish, and use dry-sautéing, grilling, and poaching methods.

- • When cooking vegetables, sweat vegetables in a little stock, and add a small amount of butter or flavored nut oil to finish vegetables. Use fat at the end (if necessary).

- • When cooking desserts, use low-fat and fat-free cottage cheese, ricotta cheese, yogurt, or cream cheese.

- • When using garnishes, use thinly sliced pieces of vegetables.

- • When using salt, decrease salt and increase the use of herbs and spices.

- • When making salad dressings, use less oil.

■ Organic foods and genetically modified food are recent developments in food production that affect nutrition in different ways.

Section 2.2 Review Questions

1. How can you retain nutrients when cooking the following?
   a. Grains and legumes
   b. Fruits and vegetables
   c. Meat, fish, and poultry

2. What concerns do customers have about farming techniques that might affect their food choices?

3. Define genetically modified foods.

4. List 10 ways to reduce fat when cooking.

5. Do you think that Laura Walsh would prefer specific methods of cooking to retain nutrients? How might she choose to cook legumes? Fish? Vegetables?

6. Chef Kate is considering the purchase of different software applications. One helps formulate recipes and provides nutrition information for those recipes. Another prints the nutrition information of the order on the receipt. Still another suggests changes for vegan, heart healthy, hypoallergenic, and other modifications. Which applications do you think would be the best for Kabob?

7. Why is batch cooking a healthy cooking method?

8. What are the benefits of using organic foods? Is there a downside?

131

Section 2.2 Review Questions

1. You retain nutrients when cooking by doing the following:
   a. Do not overrinse or cook grains and legumes too long; however, cook enough to soften. Use yeast in leavening whole grain flours. The students might not be aware of all of these options from the chapter.
   b. Use local, ripe, colorful, fresh produce, and prepare it raw or gently cooked.
   c. Cook meat, fish, and poultry according to directions; do not overcook.

2. This answer would include a debate about organic versus certified organic or conventional farming techniques, GMOs, and so on. Encourage students to be thoughtful.

3. The DNA sequence has been changed to provide for improved features.

4. Students will find these in the chapter. Answers include cooking in stock, substituting applesauce for oil, reducing butter in sauces, substituting a starch slurry for a roux, and other strategies found on pp. 118 and 119.

5. The students can determine the most healthful technique for each from the information in the chapter: Legumes—cook thoroughly but do not overcook; fish—grill, steam, or poach; vegetables—eat raw or quickly steam or sauté in stock.

6. Each student will have an opinion about this. There are pros and cons to each program. The best option would be a software solution that provides all three applications.

7. Batch cooking prevents the food from being held too long and losing nutrients.

8. Each student will have a feeling about this, based partly in philosophy and partly in science. The nutrient content of conventional and organic foods is about the same.

Section 2.2 Activities

1. This will be a unique result for each group.

2. Students should visit www.eatright.org to locate information.

3. Students might get a feeling for the wide variety of reliable and unreliable information available on the Web.

Section 2.2 Activities

1. Study Skills/Group Activity: Nutritional Selling Points

With a partner, choose a regional cuisine of the United States and identify two signature foods of that area. Identify their nutrition selling points (strengths, such as "low in fat" or "complete protein"). Identify their nutrition shortcomings (weaknesses, such as "high in fat" or "high in sugar").

2. Activity: American Dietetic Association

Explore the Web site of the American Dietetic Association. What is its mission statement? What information is there on topics of nutrition? How is it accessed?

3. Study Skills/Group: Diseases with Nutritional Implications

Choose a disease or condition that has nutrition implications (diabetes, heart disease, kidney disease, obesity, failure to thrive, and so on). Find three Web sources of diet and nutrition information pertaining to this condition. One of the sources should be the American Dietetic Association. Does the advice given from the three sources agree and align?

132

Case Study Follow-Up *Eating Right*

At the beginning of the chapter, Miguel and Chef Kate were discussing hiring a nutrition consultant to help analyze and modify some of the recipes. They wanted to know the following:

❶ Will some dishes meet multiple needs? For instance, can a dish be heart healthy, vegetarian, and vegan?

❷ Can any of the popular dishes currently on the menu be easily modified to meet a vegetarian request?

❸ Should Kabob redo the menu to indicate heart-healthy or vegetarian choices?

What suggestions do you think the consultant might offer?

133

Case Study Follow-Up

1. Each student will have ideas on this. They could include using fresh fruits, whole grains, and lower fat options.

2. Each student will have ideas on this. For example, they could substitute vegetables for meat in lasagna. The American Dietetic Association Web site, the National Restaurant Association Web site, or Laura Walsh's Web site might also give the students some ideas they could use.

3. There is a case for each. You might want to check the American Heart Association Web site.

Apply Your Learning

 Fat Budget

1. Assume the calorie requirement is 2,000 kcal per day.

2. Assume 30 percent, which would be 667 (approx. 2,000 × .3 = 600).

3. 600 ÷ 9 = 67 grams of fat; 6.7 grams of saturated fat is 10 percent.

4. There are approximately 5 grams per teaspoon, so this is less than 2 teaspoons of saturated fat per day.

For the next aspect of the activity, students will need to use information about foods available in tables that are online (USDA.gov) or in published books.

Encourage students to plan a very simple menu without too many ingredients, or they might be overwhelmed.

Please be aware that this assignment is rather time-consuming, but is very educational.

This is how the work is done in this field of dietetics.

Apply Your Learning

Fat Budget

Since there are no bad foods, how do you include butter in the daily diet? The same way you include playtime in your busy school schedule or get a little spending money from your paycheck—a budget!

1. Determine your daily calorie requirements at www.MyPyramid.gov.

2. Then determine your daily proportion of those calories from fat (if you stay at or below 30 percent, you are being conservative).

3. Now, divide those fat calories, determine the number of grams of fat by dividing by 9 calories per gram of fat. Ten percent or less of those fat grams should come from saturated fat.

4. So, how many grams of butter, chocolate, bacon, or other saturated fat is that? It might not be very many, but it's not zero. You are discovering your fat budget.

Using this same math technique, determine the number of grams of fat in a luncheon menu of your own design:

1. Determine the menu and recipes.

2. Research and total the number of fat grams of the entire menu.

3. Multiply this number by 9 kilocalorie/gram. This gives you calories from fat.

4. Research and total the number of calories in the entire menu.

5. Divide the number of fat calories by the number of total calories. This gives you the percentage of calories from fat.

6. Consider that you want your menu to provide no more than 15 percent of calories from fat.

7. Do you need to modify the menu to meet this goal?

8. Suggest menu changes and recalculate until you reach 15 percent of calories from fat.

134

Mercury in the Water

A bad environmental poison can damage generations of individuals. In Minamata, Japan, in the mid-twentieth century, a local industry dumped mercury-containing toxic waste into the local waters. Fish feeding in those waters carried mercury to all who consumed them. Local animals and children born during that time exhibited birth defects at a very alarming rate, traced to mercury poisoning. This led authorities to investigate and discover the problem. The problem still affects the local population of that Japanese bay community.

A safe food supply begins before the food ever arrives at the table. Write a report that answers the following questions:

- What environmental concerns do you have for your local food supply?
- Are these concerns local or global?
- Can you investigate whether or not they are valid concerns?
- How many differing opinions should you gather?
- What can you do to ensure that the food you consume is safe from toxins and pathogens?

Bone Density

The teen years are prime time for building the strong, sturdy bones you will need throughout your life. Bones are built with protein, calcium, vitamin D (the best source is sunlight), some phosphorus, minerals, vitamins, and exercise. The best exercises are those that require the long bones of the legs to bear weight: running, walking, team sports, and dancing. Bones are a protein "honeycomb" that continues to lengthen until the long-bone end-plates "close" and you reach your adult height. The little compartments of the honeycomb are filled with a crystal of calcium that makes them white and solid. They are not entirely solid. Nutrients, hormones, and red blood cells flow in and out of the center (marrow) of your bones all the time. However, the density of the calcium crystals is important. The denser, the better. Don't worry about the marrow functions. They can squeeze through even the strongest bones. The key to building strong bones in childhood and teens is a healthy lifestyle. Two recommendations: Drink lots of milk and play outside.

Determine your personal needs for protein, calcium, and vitamin D on MyPyramid.gov. Determine how many servings of various foods you need each day to meet these goals. Compare this to your food journal and see how you are doing. Write a sentence about your actual intake as compared to your goal. Write down one goal you can use to improve your bone-health nutrition.

135

Mercury in the Water

This case is real. There are not many such cases in the world, fortunately.

Students should not broaden the scope of this to fear seafood from other sources. Seafood in the United States is a safe food.

Bone Density

MyPyramid.gov is useful for students who know their own height and weight and other data. It says that height and weight data are optional, but students should provide it.

Help them to navigate this Web site. There is no right answer to this problem. The purpose is for students to become familiar with the site.

They can view the dietary guidelines link and recommendations.

There are aspects of the site that require a log-in. This should be optional.

Critical Thinking | Substitutions to Reduce Fat and Sugar

Students will each have different feelings and opinions about this.

Personal health issues help motivate individuals. For example, if a young person is sick with Type I diabetes mellitus, certain dietary modifications might be more motivating than they would be for another young person.

Take a look at your lifestyle. Write down any and all weight-bearing exercise activities you have participated in during the time you kept your food journal. Include walking to and from school and around the school, but total the number of minutes. How are you doing? Could you improve in this area as well?

Critical Thinking | Substitutions to Reduce Fat and Sugar

What substitutions would you be willing to live with to reduce your sugar and fat intake? Would you enjoy cream soup made with evaporated milk? Would you care if you had Canadian bacon and boiled eggs instead of fried bacon strips and eggs? Take a critical look at the high-fat foods in your food journal from your homework. Decide what you can change, what you can live without, and what you want to keep the same and account for in your fat budget. Do the same for the high-sugar foods in the journal (not all of them will be the same). Research and find one commercial restaurant or foodservice menu item that has been modified based upon fat-reducing ingredient substitutions. Write a paragraph about this item in your food journal.

Exam Prep Questions

1. A class of nutrients that includes starches, sugar, and dietary fiber is
   A. lipids.
   B. proteins.
   C. vitamins.
   D. carbohydrates.

2. The building blocks of protein are
   A. calories.
   B. vitamins.
   C. amino acids.
   D. carbohydrates.

3. What type of vitamin is vitamin C?
   A. Fat-soluble
   B. Fiber-soluble
   C. Water-soluble
   D. Phytochemical-soluble

4. What typically makes up 55 to 65 percent of the human body?
   A. Fat
   B. Water
   C. Vitamins
   D. Cholesterol

5. A vegetarian is best described as someone who does not eat
   A. dairy products.
   B. red meat and eggs.
   C. any animal products.
   D. meat, poultry, and fish.

6. What condition causes bones to gradually lose their minerals and become weak and fragile?
   A. Obesity
   B. Osteoporosis
   C. Diabetes mellitus
   D. Iron-deficiency anemia

7. What is the most common nutritional deficiency in the world?
   A. Vitamin C
   B. Vitamin D
   C. Diabetes mellitus
   D. Iron-deficiency anemia

8. At what temperature should cold, fresh food be received?
   A. 0°F with signs of freezing
   B. 32°F with signs of freezing
   C. 41°F with no signs of freezing
   D. 50°F with no signs of freezing

Exam Prep Answers

1. D
2. C
3. C
4. B
5. D
6. B
7. D
8. C
9. D
10. C

9. Which products have been produced without pesticides or synthetic fertilizers?

A. Local

B. Natural

C. Conventional

D. Certified organic

10. To function, the human body turns carbohydrates into

A. fat.

B. fiber.

C. glucose.

D. protein.

Chapter 2: Nutrition Appendix

The following tables offer additional information on vitamins, minerals, and food additives.

Table 2.3: Vitamins and Minerals		
Vitamin	**Vegetable Sources**	**Animal Sources**
A	Dark orange and green vegetables, sweet potatoes, mangos	Fortified milk or dairy products, liver, eggs
B_1	Whole grains, enriched products, fortified products, nuts, legumes	Pork
B_2	Whole grains or enriched grains	Milk and milk products
B_3	Whole grains, enriched products, nuts	Milk, eggs, meat, poultry, and fish
B_5	Most	Most
B_6	Green vegetables, green leafy vegetables, fruit, whole grains	Meat, fish, poultry
B_7	Most vegetable sources; people make small amounts in their intestines	Most animal sources
B_9	Green leafy vegetables, legumes, seeds, enriched products	Liver
B_{12}	None naturally; may be fortified in cereals	All
C	Citrus fruit, peppers, strawberries, tomatoes, potatoes	None
D	None, but made with the help of sunlight	Fortified milk, fatty fish, some fish-liver oils, eggs
E	Green leafy vegetables, mayonnaise made with vegetable oil, nuts, peanut butter, sunflower seeds, sea buckthorn berries, seeds, vegetables oils (palm, sunflower, canola, corn, soybean, and olive), wheat germ, whole grains	Fish, only small amounts in some, not a good source
K	Green, leafy cabbage-type vegetables, collards, spinach, also made by bacteria in the intestine	Minimal amounts in liver and eggs

139

Nutrition Appendix

Table 2.3:
Vitamins and Minerals

- This table is for use during this chapter and for future reference.

Table 2.3 (cont.)

- Minerals are also very important nutrients.

Table 2.4:
Food Additives and Their Functions

- These are all added to food for a reason.
- Each additive solves a problem.

Mineral	Function
Calcium	Bone health, helps maintain normal blood pressure, muscle contraction
Chloride	Maintains fluid and electrolyte balance in the body
Chromium	Required for carbohydrate metabolism
Copper	Part of various enzymes; used for electron transport
Fluorine	Bone and tooth health
Iron	Part of hemoglobin
Magnesium	Part of bones and teeth; makes protein; helps muscle activity; activates metabolism of carbohydrates, fats, and proteins
Manganese	Part of many enzymes
Molybdenum	Necessary for purine degradation and formation of uric acid and used in many enzyme reactions
Phosphorus	Part of the bones and teeth
Potassium	Maintains fluid and electrolyte balance in the body
Selenium	Antioxidant
Sodium	Maintains the fluid and electrolyte balance in the body
Zinc	Taste perception, coenzyme

Table 2.4: Food Additives and Their Functions

Food Additive	Function
Antioxidants	Antioxidants slow the oxidation process that turns fats rotten. Some fats, especially vegetable oils, do not become rancid as quickly because they contain naturally occurring antioxidants such as tocopherol.
Benzoates	Benzoates are used as preservatives in acidic food items such as fruit juices and syrups, pie fillings, pickles, pickled vegetables, and sauces. Benzoates occur naturally in cranberries.
Colorants	Food colors (or colorants) fall into three groups: natural pigments extracted from plant materials, inorganic pigments and lakes (metals combined with organic colors), and synthetic coal-tar dyes.
Emulsifiers	Emulsifiers enable the formation of water-fat mixtures. They are a common ingredient in baked items because they help integrate the fat. Examples of some emulsifiers are gums, egg yolks, albumin, casein, and lecithin. All these substances help disperse oil in water uniformly. Emulsifiers also interact with fats to modify their crystal structure, which reduces viscosity or increases aeration (as in whipped cream). Emulsifiers interact with starch to reduce stickiness and to slow the staling of bread. They interact with gluten and improve the baking quality of wheat flour, resulting in better texture and volume in packed goods.

(continued)

140

Table 2.4: Food Additives and Their Functions *continued*

Food Additive	Function
Gums	Gums are substances that form a sticky mass in water. Gums help to keep emulsions from separating into constituent parts and are widely used in salad dressings, processed cheese, and confections.
Monosodium glutamate (MSG)	MSG is probably one of the best known and widely used flavor enhancers. MSG occurs naturally in food items and is often added to canned soups and meats. MSG gives some people headaches and a bloated feeling.
Nitrates	Nitrates are natural constituents of plants and, together with nitrites, are used in the pickling of meats. Nitrate is converted into nitrite in the process.
Nitrites	Used in canned meats, nitrite is the essential agent in preserving meat by pickling. They slow the growth of *Clostridium botulinum* and prevent botulism. Nitrites also preserve the desirable color and flavor of canned meat products.
Phosphates	Phosphates are used widely within food processing and have several applications. For baked goods, phosphates are used as leavening agents. Phosphates are also used in the tenderizing of meats and in the processing of meats and seafood to improve texture.
Stabilizers	Stabilizers help maintain the structure of emulsions. They are often used in meringues and marshmallows to produce body and mouthfeel.
Thickeners	Thickeners add body to a food product without imparting flavor. Modified starches are used as thickeners in commercial baking, as they work well with acidic ingredients, tolerate high temperatures, and do not cause pie fillings to "weep" during storage.

141

Table 2.4 (cont.)

- Some additives have drawbacks. Help students understand that there are trade-offs to consider in many instances.

Chapter 3 Overview

Chapter 3 introduces the student to basic notions of foodservice costing mechanisms, explaining basic economic and financial concepts that are critical to understanding business in the restaurant and foodservice industry.

Section 1: The first section explains some basic costs that are incurred by restaurant and foodservice operations as well as some common tools used to track and control these expenses.

Section 2: Next, this section discusses how to control foodservice costs in greater detail, such as by correctly determining food costs and menu pricing.

Section 3: This section addresses labor costs and how these can be scheduled and controlled.

Section 4: This section describes some quality standards used throughout the restaurant and foodservice industry.

Advance Preparation	
Review	Sections 3.1–3.4
	Chapter 5
	Level 1, Chapters 2, 4, 5, 7, 8, 10, 12
Contact	A guest speaker from a local restaurant who can discuss how his or her operation controls costs
	A guest speaker from the campus foodservice staff
Prepare	Sample menus from a variety of restaurants
	Sample purchase orders and invoices

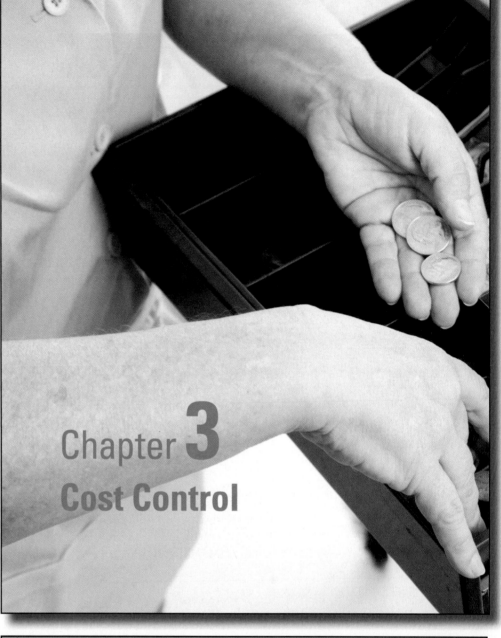

Chapter 3
Cost Control

CUSTOMIZED INSTRUCTION OPTIONS			
Less Advanced Students	**More Advanced Students**	**ESOL Students**	**Special Needs Students**
Pages 144, 149, 187	Pages 145, 191	Pages 144, 193	Pages 149, 189

CHAPTER TOOLS			
21st-Century Skills	**Mathematics**	**Science**	**Literacy**
Pages 143, 144, 145, 147, 149, 154, 155, 165, 166, 169, 172, 173, 174, 175, 180, 181, 185, 186, 187, 188, 189, 191, 192, 193, 199, 200, 204	Pages 169, 172, 173, 174, 181	Pages 172, 175, 200	Pages 143, 144, 145, 147, 149, 154, 155, 165, 166, 169, 172, 173, 174, 175, 180, 181, 185, 186, 187, 188, 189, 191, 192, 193, 199, 200, 204

Case Study *Costly Costs*

Chef Kate and Miguel, co-owners of Kabob, have recently been trying to expand and improve their operation. They started serving brunch, which has been fairly successful in terms of the amount of sales it's generating. By successfully expanding their operation, they were thinking they would see a marked increase in profit, but that hasn't been the case. Chef Kate and Miguel are both concerned and confused. How could they be increasing sales but not increasing profit?

When they started to look closely at their business, they realized that maybe they hadn't planned the brunch expansion as efficiently as they could have. As a result, they are incurring higher costs for food and labor than they should be. After they started looking at their brunch service, they realized that they should evaluate all elements of their operation, from purchasing to service. While Chef Kate and Miguel know it will be a big undertaking, they feel that taking better measures to control costs will be well worth it when the difference shows up on their bottom line. The only question now is where to begin.

As you read this chapter, think about the following questions:

1. What additional costs could have arisen from their new brunch service?

2. How should the menus for each service be synchronized to eliminate waste and redundancies?

3. Have they properly calculated yields for newly added recipes, such as pancake batter?

4. What other aspects of their business might be made more efficient to control costs and increase profit?

Case Study
Costly Costs

- What additional steps should Miguel and Chef Kate have taken before deciding to expand by adding brunch service? Why might a successful dinner operation have determined to offer brunch in the first place? In what other ways could the co-owners have chosen to expand?

- What role does labor cost play in Kabob's difficulties? Encourage students to consider all costs involved with the interviewing, hiring, and training process, as discussed in Level 1.

- What do students perceive as the biggest reason why sales have increased but profits have not?

- Note that there are follow-up questions about the case study at the end of the chapter.

- This activity could be done in groups, as a class, or as a homework assignment.

Homework Activity: Delicious Dish

Literacy Connection, 21st-Century Skills— Work Independently, Solve Problems, Reason Effectively, Communicate Clearly

Kabob's most popular brunch item is its French Toast Napoleon, made with brioche and layered with orange-scented pastry cream and fresh strawberries. This substantial portion—many guests can't eat the entire portion, although an equal number praise the generous serving—sells for $11.95, which is not quite enough to cover all the costs associated with producing the dish and operating the restaurant.

Before reading the chapter, answer the following questions:

What changes can Chef Kate and Miguel make that might make this popular item more profitable?

What advantages and disadvantages are associated with each of those proposed changes?

Consider the problem-solving model described in Level 1, Chapter 8. How can it help Miguel and Chef Kate decide what to do?

Answer these questions in a one-page essay.

Professional Profile

Discuss	Encourage students to discuss how successful recruitment is an important component of running any business. How does the recruiting process affect a business's costs?
	Why is it important to understand a company's culture? What are some ways to learn about this culture? Ask students to relate this to the material on vision and mission statements learned from Level 1.
	In addition to the questions that Sherie Valderrama suggests asking current employees about their companies, what other questions do students consider important?
Reinforce and Review	To succeed in the restaurant and foodservice industry, you must have a passion for service and a commitment to excellence.
	Each company has a distinct culture that can play a key role in professional satisfaction.
	Students should research potential employers as thoroughly as possible, opening their minds to unexplored career opportunities.
Teaching Tips	Point out that almost every professional profile has described the importance of passion. Encourage students to consider their own professional and personal passions and how these can help them identify appropriate career choices.
	Refer to Level 1, Chapter 12 for more information on helping students identify and prepare for potential careers.

[professional profile]

Sherie Valderrama

Senior Director, Talent Acquisition
Sodexo

I love my profession. For me, work has always been about being able to make a difference in the world. Being able to help individuals find their dream jobs and build their careers has always been joyful. Then, seeing the impact that these individuals have on the company and the world at large is so satisfying.

I received my B.A. in international affairs and completed graduate coursework in economics. Then I began my career at George Washington University, advising students and alumni on how to develop job search strategies. I transitioned into working with a leading international development consulting firm, directing recruiting operations for its projects in more than 70 developing countries and transitioning economies.

Five years ago, I joined Sodexo, the leading food and facilities management company, which is very much in alignment with my service orientation. I chose this industry because of my passion for service and have now been able to combine it with my love of food.

To be successful in this field, you must have a passion for service and a commitment to excellence. I would suggest learning as much as possible about the industry and the various career paths it offers as well as the companies that are known for excellence. Research the companies that might be of interest to you to learn more about their services, their career opportunities, and the potential for professional and personal growth. Try to learn about the corporate culture, as each company has a distinct culture that can play a key role in professional satisfaction. To do this, you can research the company's Web site, any company blogs, and its presence on social media sites such as Facebook, LinkedIn, YouTube, and Twitter.

You can also identify individuals currently working with the company and talk to them about their experiences and perceptions. Some questions to explore might include:

- How does this company value its customers and employees?
- Is this a company that embraces a diverse and inclusive workforce?
- Does this company invest in its employees through mentoring and professional development programs and tuition reimbursement?
- Does this company have a corporate social responsibility program?
- Does this company give back to society in the form of philanthropic activity?

Another consideration is the segment that the company represents. Many of you readily recognize the career opportunities in hotels and restaurants but have not

144

CUSTOMIZED INSTRUCTION

Literacy Connection, 21st-Century Skills—Work Independently, Think Creatively, Reason Effectively, Communicate Clearly, Create Media Products

ESOL Students and Less Advanced Students

What are you passionate about? How can you translate your passions into a career that can help you thrive?

List three potential career paths that interest you and involve your passions. What must you do to prepare for each career? What qualifications will you need?

Prepare a poster or slide show describing each career path and present it to the class.

explored the exciting and varied opportunities that exist within contract management. For example, companies like Sodexo offer exciting hospitality careers within a contract management environment, working in hospitals, educational institutions, long-term career facilities, and private sector businesses.

After you have identified a company of interest, I would encourage you to seek out an internship opportunity with that company. That will help you to validate that the company truly fulfills your expectations. It will also position you for an offer of full-time employment upon graduation. Even if the company does not live up to expectations, you will still gain valuable industry experience, which will be an advantage in the job search.

Remember:

❝What I know is, that if you do work that you love, and the work fulfills you, the rest will come.**❞**
—Oprah Winfrey

And another favorite is:

❝We make a living by what we get; we make a life by what we give.**❞**
—Winston Churchill

About Cost Control

Cost control in our industry has many facets. The key is to understand your business needs and ensure the effective alignment and utilization of all of your resources—human, financial, and technology. So, we need to understand the optimum staffing needs for a unit, ensure careful attention to purchasing and supply chain management, and reduce the potential for waste. The key consideration when looking at cost control is to have the commitment to maintain quality and operate in a responsible and sustainable manner. Here are a few examples:

1. This year, we eliminated tray service at most of our college campuses. This decision resulted in a major reduction in the use of water and energy to wash the trays, but also had the added benefit of reducing food waste. We found that without the trays, students took fewer items and, therefore, wasted less.

2. Our Supply Management department focuses on efficient purchasing, inventory management, and effective invoicing. Utilizing technology to aid with uniform tracking and analysis has a major impact on our ability to contain costs, yet maintain the high quality of our products. It also helps to leverage our ability to negotiate with vendors, and therefore reduce our overall costs.

3. Our staffing model ensures that we have the right talent at the right levels within each unit. This helps us to control labor costs by ensuring that we are not over-staffed and that we have the correct mix of senior, midlevel, and entry-level talent to provide quality services to our clients and customers.

145

Professional Profile (cont.)

Discuss	Sherie Valderrama quotes Winston Churchill in her profile. How is this quote applicable to employees in the restaurant and foodservice industry? Sherie Valderrama also quotes Oprah Winfrey. How is this quote applicable to employees in the restaurant and foodservice industry? Ask students to identify the similarities and differences between these two quotes. Building from Sodexo's example, what are some other ways that controlling foodservice costs can increase efficiency and decrease wastefulness? What is the relationship between controlling costs and maintaining quality?
Reinforce and Review	A corporate internship can provide invaluable industry experience and position a student for postgraduation employment opportunities. The key to effective cost control is to organize and use all of a company's resources efficiently, directing efforts toward a common goal. Maintaining quality and operating responsibly and sustainably are not incompatible with controlling costs.
Teaching Tips	Encourage students to learn more about contract management. If campus foodservices are provided by a contractor, consider asking a representative of that company to address the class. Make sure students understand the roles played by both human and technological resources in controlling costs. Suggest that interested students speak with the school's guidance or career counselors to learn about internship opportunities.

CUSTOMIZED INSTRUCTION

Literacy Connection, 21st-Century Skills—Work Independently, Think Creatively, Reason Effectively, Communicate Clearly

More Advanced Students

Have you ever considered an internship? Paid or unpaid, these opportunities can provide invaluable experience in the professional world. You can make excellent contacts while assessing various career paths from the inside.

Identify three companies where you would be like to work as an intern. Research each company and prepare cover letters, résumés, and portfolio materials. Use the material in Level 1, Chapter 12 for assistance, or consult your campus's career counselor.

Whether or not you choose to apply for these internship positions, prepare yourself and your application materials as though you want the job. Submit the finished products to your teacher.

Focus and Engage

Discuss

- Why is it essential for a manager or owner in the restaurant and foodservice industry to understand how to control and plan for necessary costs?

- In what ways are kitchen or dining-room team members responsible for controlling costs?

- Why is it important to maintain appropriate quality standards in all steps of the food flow process?

Teaching Tips

- Students without any background classes in economics or accounting might find some of the material covered in this chapter challenging. This could prove especially difficult for those students who struggled with the mathematics concepts presented in Level 1, Chapter 4. To the extent possible, the text has been simplified to prevent confusion, but the Teachers' Wrap addresses these concepts in greater detail.

Section 3.1 Introduction to Cost Control

Introduce the Section
a. Review the difference between sales and profit.
b. Identify some common tools for assessing a company's financial picture.
c. Discuss the objectives for the section.

Vocabulary Review
a. Direct students to the key terms.
b. Pronounce each word, and have the students repeat the pronunciation out loud.
c. Discuss the definition of each word.

Teach

Discuss

- What is cost control? How is it relevant to all industries, not just the restaurant and foodservice industry?

- "Every action that takes place in a restaurant costs money." Do students agree with this statement? Encourage a debate between those who support and those who oppose this assertion.

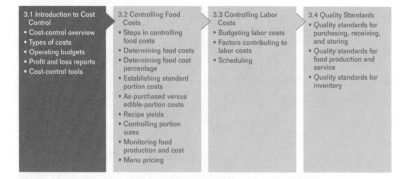

3.1 Introduction to Cost Control	3.2 Controlling Food Costs	3.3 Controlling Labor Costs	3.4 Quality Standards
• Cost-control overview • Types of costs • Operating budgets • Profit and loss reports • Cost-control tools	• Steps in controlling food costs • Determining food costs • Determining food cost percentage • Establishing standard portion costs • As-purchased versus edible-portion costs • Recipe yields • Controlling portion sizes • Monitoring food production and cost • Menu pricing	• Budgeting labor costs • Factors contributing to labor costs • Scheduling	• Quality standards for purchasing, receiving, and storing • Quality standards for food production and service • Quality standards for inventory

SECTION 3.1 INTRODUCTION TO COST CONTROL

Here's a little known secret about running a successful operation: You can put out a great product and have a really high sales volume, but if you don't run the business with a great deal of efficiency, you still won't turn a profit. In the restaurant and foodservice industry, efficiency often translates as cost control. A successful operation must keep costs down to stay in business, but that's no easy task given the number of expenses a restaurant and foodservice operation incurs. Running a restaurant and foodservice operation requires kitchen staff, service staff, and people to manage them; food to serve and equipment to prepare it; and, of course, a place to serve the food. In addition to the mortgage or lease on the property, costs include all the insurance and utility expenses that go along with the property. In short, there are a lot of costs to consider and control. This chapter sets you on your way to doing just that.

Study Questions

After studying Section 3.1, you should be able to answer the following questions:

- What is cost control, and why is it important?
- What are the different types of costs?
- What is an operating budget?

146

- What costs are incurred by both a five-star restaurant and a local waffle cart? What costs might one face that the other does not?

Reinforce and Review

- In the restaurant and foodservice industry, efficiency often translates as cost control.

- A successful operation must control costs to stay in business. High sales volume alone is no guarantee of a profit.

Teaching Tips

- If students are concerned about their mathematics skills as they prepare to study this chapter, encourage them to seek any outside help that might be available on campus.

- What is a profit-and-loss report?
- What different tools are used to control costs?

Cost Control Overview

Every business needs to obey one basic principle in order to survive: it must make more money than it spends. In other words, its sales, or revenue, have to be higher than its costs. **Revenue** is the income from sales before expenses, or costs, are subtracted. **Cost** is the price an operation pays out in the purchasing and preparation of its products or the providing of its service.

If at any point a business's costs are higher than its sales, that business is losing money. And if its costs remain higher than its sales for a long time, the operation will likely go out of business. In fact, a business can actually have a high sales volume—meaning, it is earning a lot of money—but still ultimately fail if it doesn't properly manage its costs. This is why it is so important that an operation keep costs as low as possible. **Cost control** is a business's efforts to manage how much it spends (see Figure 3.1).

Figure 3.1: Cutting costs is the simplest way to improve your bottom line.

Types of Costs

In the restaurant and foodservice industry, a successful operation needs to effectively manage and control many costs. The four main categories break down as follows (see Figure 3.2 on the following page):

1. Food costs
2. Beverage costs
3. Labor costs
4. Overhead costs

147

Figure Focus

Figure 3.1: How else might a restaurant choose to account for increased winter heating costs, besides cutting employee hours? Why might cutting employee hours be the most appropriate step to take for this restaurant?

Discuss

- What are some reasons that a popular, well-regarded restaurant might be losing money?

- Is there a point at which a restaurant or foodservice operation might have cut too many costs? How can the management identify this point? What about the employees? What about the guests? What changes might each group notice when costs are cut?

Reinforce and Review

- Each business must obey the same basic principle: Make more money than it spends.

- When costs (expenses) are higher than sales (income), the business is losing money.

- The four main categories of costs are food costs, beverage costs, labor costs, and overhead costs.

Vocabulary Terms

- **Revenue:** The income from sales before expenses, or costs, are subtracted.

- **Cost:** The price an operation pays out in the purchasing and preparation of its products or the providing of its service.

- **Cost control:** A business's efforts to manage how much it spends.

Homework Activity: Spending and Saving

Literacy Connection, 21st-Century Skills— Work Independently, Think Creatively, Reason Effectively, Communicate Clearly

In one's personal life, costs don't only involve money; they often involve time. But we still use the same terms: We talk about "spending" time or "wasting" time. The first suggests that time has been used in a positive way, whereas the second suggests that time has been used in a negative way. We also talk about "saving" time, "free" time, and "paying" attention. How does this language affect the way we think about time?

Students should identify some ways in which they can control their use of both money and time in their own lives. What unnecessary expenses can they identify in either category? How does wastefulness play a role?

Over the next week, students should consider how they use their "free" time and money. How does simply being aware of how time and money are spent affect their perspectives on how these resources are used?

Students should write a brief essay describing how their behaviors and emotions were affected by this week-long process.

Discuss

- What is the difference between controllable and noncontrollable costs? What examples of each do students experience in their own lives?

- Which of the four categories of costs do students think is the most important for a restaurant or foodservice operation to control? Why?

Reinforce and Review

- Food costs, beverage costs, and labor costs each have components related to sales levels and are subject to change based on sales; therefore, they are considered controllable costs.

- Overhead costs do not change based on an operation's sales and are therefore considered noncontrollable costs.

- Two methods by which operations monitor, assess, and try to control costs are the operating budget and the profit-and-loss report.

Teaching Tips

- Overhead costs also include items such as new carpets or artwork for a restaurant's dining room. These expenses are not "fixed" in the same way that rent is set at the same amount each month, regardless of sales; however, they are considered fixed costs in that they do not relate to sales. In fact, a restaurant that has experienced low sales might choose to change its menu, service style, and ambiance, in which case new floor coverings or artwork might be important components of the restaurant's new "look."

- Similarly, utility bills do not always stay the same from month to month: Figure 3.1 uses the example of rising heating costs during winter. However, because the increased heating bill is not affected by the sales volume, it is considered a "fixed" cost even though it does change.

Vocabulary Terms

- **Food cost:** The total cost of food purchased by an operation.

- **Beverage cost:** The total cost of beverages purchased by an operation.

- **Labor cost:** The total cost associated with staff members employed by an operation.

- **Variable cost:** A cost that changes, depending on sales.

- **Semivariable cost:** A cost with some components that change depending on sales and some that do not.

Figure 3.2: There are various categories of costs, including fixed and variable costs.

Food costs, beverage costs, and **labor costs** each have components that are related to sales levels. These are either **variable** or **semivariable costs**, which means that they can change based on sales. Because costs such as these are subject to change based on how the operation is doing, they are **controllable costs**; the operation has a certain amount of control in how it spends on these aspects of the operation.

The fourth cost on the list is the **overhead cost**, which is also a **fixed** or **noncontrollable cost**. These costs can include insurance, utilities, or an operation's lease or mortgage on the building. Such costs are fixed, meaning they need to be paid regardless of whether the operation is making or losing money. Fixed costs, in contrast to variable costs, do not change based on the operation's sales. Because costs such as these do not change, they are often referred to as noncontrollable costs. Table 3.1 helps further illustrate and break down these costs.

Table 3.1: Controllable versus Noncontrollable Costs

Controllable costs	Noncontrollable costs
Variable and semivariable costs	Overhead/fixed costs
Food, beverage, and labor	Lease/mortgage, insurance, utilities

It's very important for an operation to understand the differences in how all of these costs work and how these costs can (and cannot) be managed. This chapter discusses elements of both controllable and noncontrollable costs. The primary focus is on controllable costs, most notably food and labor costs. But before the discussion gets into the specifics of managing controllable costs, this chapter covers two broad methods by which operations monitor, assess, and try to control costs: the operating budget and the profit-and-loss report.

148

- **Controllable cost:** A cost that is subject to change based on an operation's financial performance; in other words, the operation has some control over these costs and can adjust spending based on its changing needs.

- **Overhead costs:** Ongoing expenses, such as rent and utilities, that are necessary to continued operation but do not directly relate to sales or profits.

- **Fixed costs:** Costs that must be paid regardless of actual business performance and cannot be controlled or altered based on changing needs.

- **Noncontrollable cost:** Fixed cost.

Figure Focus

Figure 3.2: Which of these four components do students think accounts for the greatest part of an operation's expenses?

Examples of Cost Classifications

Controllable Costs

An example of a controllable cost is food cost. Management can control this cost by using standardized recipes or exercising standard procedures for portion control, menu listing, and pricing, or by one of several other restraints. For example, if the price of chicken increases and no action is taken, the restaurant's food cost will increase. At this point, management can either raise the selling price of all chicken entrées, reduce portions, reposition the items on the menu, or eliminate chicken from the menu altogether. By taking action, management has controlled the effect of the increased cost of chicken, resulting in no increase in the restaurant's food cost.

Another example of a controllable cost is the hourly wage portion of labor cost. By changing the number of hours worked on an employee's schedule, a manager can affect labor costs. For example, if an operation's workweek is reduced because of holidays and no other action is taken, payroll cost as a percentage of sales decreases. See Figure 3.3. By reducing the number of hours worked by employees, this percentage could be brought back into line.

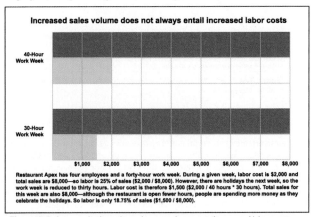

Increased sales volume does not always entail increased labor costs

Restaurant Apex has four employees and a forty-hour work week. During a given week, total sales are $8,000—so labor is 25% of sales ($2,000 / $8,000). However, there are holidays the next week, so the work week is reduced to thirty hours. Labor cost is therefore $1,500 ($2,000 / 40 hours * 30 hours). Total sales for this week are also $8,000—although the restaurant is open fewer hours, people are spending more money as they celebrate the holidays. So labor is only 18.75% of sales ($1,500 / $8,000).

Figure 3.3: Increased sales volume does not always entail increased labor costs.

Two subsets of controllable costs are variable and semivariable costs.

Variable Costs

Variable costs are those costs that go up and down as sales go up and down, and do so in direct proportion. An example of a variable cost is food cost. As sales go up, more food is purchased to replenish inventory. As sales go down, less

149

Figure Focus

Figure 3.3: In this figure, sales volume stays the same over a two-week period although labor cost declines over that same period, so the labor cost falls as a percentage of sales. What if labor cost had increased and sales had remained the same?

Discuss

- Variable costs increase or decrease in proportion to sales, but it is not always a one-to-one relationship. That is, sometimes when sales increase by $5,000, a particular variable cost might only increase by $1,000; conversely, when sales decrease by $5,000, a different variable cost might only decrease by $2,000.

- The student text (Figure 3.4) has been simplified to facilitate understanding. It assumes that variable costs rise and fall in direct proportion to sales, suggesting that sales and costs are fixed in a one-to-one relationship.

- Semivariable costs contain one or more variable components, which means that they also increase or decrease when sales increase or decrease. However, semivariable costs also contain one or more fixed components, which are not affected by sales. In the following example, each increase of $5,000 in sales corresponds to a $2,000 increase in hourly wages; management salaries are fixed at $2,000, regardless of sales. The horizontal axis represents sales volume, and the vertical axis represents labor cost. Because management costs are fixed, every $5,000 increase in sales corresponds to a $2,000 increase in labor cost, as represented by the blue diagonal.

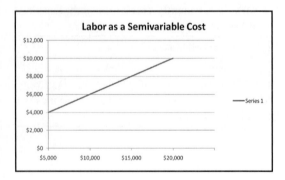

food is bought. If adequate cost controls are in place, little waste exists, and no theft occurs, then the amount of food used should be in direct proportion to sales. See Figure 3.4.

As total sales increase, food cost also increases. More food must be purchased, because more food is being ordered and eaten by customers.

Figure 3.4: As total sales increase, food cost also increases since more food must be purchased.

Semivariable Costs

Semivariable costs go up and down as sales go up and down, but not in direct proportion. Semivariable costs are made up of both fixed costs and variable costs. An example of a semivariable cost is labor. Management is normally paid a salary. The salary remains the same regardless of the operation's sales volume. If the general manager, assistant manager, and chef are collectively paid $160,000 per year, they will receive that amount regardless of what the restaurant makes for a year. Thus, management's salary is a fixed cost. That is, it remains the same regardless of volume.

On the other hand, staff members such as the waitstaff and line cooks are often paid an hourly wage and are scheduled according to anticipated sales. As a result, the cost of hourly employees goes up as sales go up and goes down as sales go down. If proper scheduling is used, the cost will go up and down in direct proportion to sales levels. Putting this all together, labor is considered a

150

Figure Focus

Figure 3.4: This graph represents an ideal environment, without food waste or theft. How might waste, theft, poor cooking skills, mismanagement, or other factors affect the environment? How would that new environment be graphed?

semivariable cost because there is a fixed cost component (management's salary) and a variable cost component (hourly staff wages).

Noncontrollable Costs

An example of a noncontrollable cost is insurance. After an insurance policy has been negotiated, management has no control over the cost of that policy. Another example is the operation's lease or mortgage. After management signs the lease, it has virtually no control over this cost. A subset of noncontrollable costs is the fixed, or overhead, cost.

Fixed Costs

Fixed costs are those costs that remain the same regardless of sales volume. Insurance is an example of a fixed cost. As previously mentioned, after the insurance policies have been negotiated, the cost remains the same throughout the term of the policy. For example, if the cost of insuring the business is $1,000 per month, it will remain at $1,000 every month, regardless of how much money the operation makes or loses. That cost would not change because sales levels have changed.

[fast fact]

Did You Know...?
Restaurants can easily spend as much on the cost of food and beverages as they do on payroll. According to the National Restaurant Association, on average, restaurants operate on profit margins of 4 to 6 percent, which means every dollar saved is crucial to the health and sustainability of the operation.

Operating Budgets

An **operating budget** is a financial plan for a specific period of time. It is an essential tool for managing an operation's many costs. An operating budget lists the anticipated sales revenue and projected costs and gives an estimate of the profit or loss expected for the period. Management often prepares operating budgets monthly, but it can prepare them for shorter or longer periods depending on the structure of the organization. Operating budgets serve many purposes in the management of a restaurant or foodservice operation. These purposes include the following:

1. Analyzing controllable cost needs, such as labor, food and beverages, and supplies

2. Outlining operating goals and managers' performance responsibilities

3. Measuring *actual* performance against *anticipated* performance

151

Discuss

- How can an operating budget help a business anticipate future expenses? What are some other steps a business can take to predict upcoming costs?

- Encourage students to discuss the differences between actual and anticipated performance. Why do differences between the two exist at all? How can actual performance improve to match anticipated performance?

Reinforce and Review

- An operating budget lists an operation's anticipated sales revenue and projected costs and gives an estimate of the profit or loss expected for the period.

- Operating budgets have three major roles: They analyze controllable cost needs, outline operating goals and managerial responsibilities, and measure actual performance against anticipated performance.

Vocabulary Terms

- **Operating budget:** A financial plan for a specific period of time.

Discuss

- Encourage students to discuss the role of forecasts in budgeting. What is the difference between a forecast and a guess?

- What types of historical data are used to plan restaurant operations? How are historical data relevant in students' lives?

Reinforce and Review

- An operating budget takes into account all aspects of an operation's finances, including all sales, controllable and noncontrollable costs, employee benefits, and depreciation.

- Most operating budgets are based on forecasts.

- Budgets and P & L statements are very similar; however, budgets project what managers expect to happen, whereas P & L statements record what has actually happened.

Teaching Tips

- Explain the operating budget shown in Figure 3.5.

Vocabulary Terms

- **Forecast:** A prediction of sales levels or costs that will occur during a specific time period.

- **Historical data:** Past information about a restaurant and its operations, used to predict future needs.

- **Average sales per customer:** The total dollar sales divided by the total number of customers, used to help calculate revenue forecasts.

Although an operating budget is a necessary tool for restaurant and foodservice managers, preparing one is not a simple process. Putting together a useful and accurate budget requires time and care. See Figure 3.5 for a sample operating budget. An operating budget takes into account all aspects of an operation's finances, including all sales, controllable and noncontrollable costs, employee benefits, and depreciation.

Figure 3.5: Sample operating budget.

Most operating budgets are based on forecasts. A **forecast** is a prediction of sales levels or costs that will occur during a specific time period. A variety of methods are used to forecast foodservice sales and costs, and most of them rely directly on having accurate **historical data** for the operation. To plan for the future, a manager must look at what has occurred in the past. The most common foodservice revenue forecasting techniques are based on the number of customers and **average sales per customer**, which are calculated by the total dollar sales divided by the total number of customers. Operational records, such as sales histories and production sheets, provide this valuable information.

152

Figure Focus

Figure 3.5: Do students think this operating budget puts enough money toward promotional expenses? Why or why not?

A **sales history** is a record of the number of portions of every item sold on a menu. A **production sheet** lists all menu items that are going to be prepared for a given date (see Figure 3.6). The sheets will vary according to an operation's individual needs and forecasts. Use these kinds of operational records to calculate what has happened in the past, including trends related to menu item popularity.

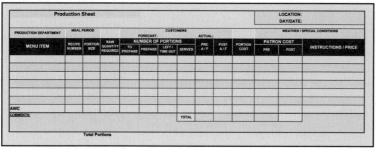

Figure 3.6: Sample production sheet.

Several software products are available that can also help calculate sales forecasts. Most operations can run historical sales and production reports from their **point-of-sale (POS) systems**. Use the information on these reports to anticipate what is likely to occur moving forward. But be careful. Sales one week don't necessarily translate into the same sales the next week. Outside factors, such as weather, time of year, local construction, and so on, always need to be accounted for as well.

One way to forecast in spite of such fluctuations is to use the **moving average technique,** also called the smoothing technique. Using this technique, sales information for two or three recent and similar periods is averaged together. The average can produce a forecast that is more likely to be accurate, since it is not based solely on one period that might have had unique circumstances.

153

Discuss

- How is a sales history related to a production sheet? Which do students think is the more important document?

- Encourage students to identify factors that could affect an operation's sales.

Reinforce and Review

- Operational records, such as sales histories and production sheets, are used to determine what happened in the past and to predict future needs.

- It's important to be careful when forecasting needs. Sales one week do not necessarily translate into the same sales next week.

- The moving average technique averages together sales information for two or three recent and similar sales period to determine a more accurate prediction of future sales.

Teaching Tips

- Relate the moving average technique to student academic performance. For instance, an illness or family emergency might have prevented a student from performing as well as usual on an exam; using this smoothing technique balances out that incident with other, more typical grades.

Vocabulary Terms

- **Sales history:** A record of the number of portions of every item sold on a menu.

- **Production sheet:** A list of all menu items that are going to be prepared for a given date, based on forecasts.

- **Point-of-sale (POS) system:** Computer software that helps managers track sales, employee activity, and other information, as well as facilitating guest orders.

- **Moving average technique:** A forecasting technique that averages together sales information for two or three recent and similar periods to predict future sales.

Figure Focus

Figure 3.6: The menu items and number of portions to be made of each is recorded on a production sheet, which is based on manager forecasts.

Trends:
Beverage Boon!

Encourage students to discuss the following:

- Pairing specific menu items with certain alcoholic beverages is common at many operations. It is less common to pair nonalcoholic beverages with particular dishes, but many consumers enjoy these drinks as well. What are some nonalcoholic beverages that could be paired with the following dishes, and why would each drink be an appropriate complement?

  - Hamburger with sweet potato fries

  - Chicken parmigiana with egg noodles

  - Green salad with blue cheese and candied pecans

- Are operations that don't serve alcoholic beverages at a disadvantage against those that do? Consider some examples in your community.

- In what ways can an operation's beverage program help maintain and reinforce its image? How might the beverage program attract certain guests?

Essential Skills:
How to Develop an Operating Budget

Encourage students to discuss the following:

- Making a budget is the first step in planning a company's financial future. What are some other steps in this process?

- What type of operation might succeed in each of the following areas?

  - A quiet suburb, near schools and away from major shopping malls

  - Downtown in a large city, near a mix of high-rise offices and apartment buildings

  - A peaceful rural environment, away from large towns and surrounded by farmland

- Does Kabob's operating budget in Figure 3.5 seem realistic? Why or why not? What information would help you make a better assessment?

Figure Focus

Figure 3.7: Is this table tent an effective advertisement for this restaurant's special offer? To whom do you think this ad is directed?

[trends]

Beverage Boon!

Offering alcoholic beverages to customers is an integral part of the dining experience at many restaurants. Many customers regard it as an enjoyable accompaniment to their food. If alcoholic beverage service is in keeping with the character of the operation, pairing items from the food and alcoholic beverage menus that complement each other can enhance the diners' experiences. Offering alcoholic beverage service also plays a very important role in the profitability of an operation, so it comes as no surprise that many restaurants want to offer alcoholic beverage service to their guests.

Meeting the needs and expectations of customers is just as important to alcoholic beverage service as it is to the selection of food offerings. The alcoholic beverage menu may be limited or extensive and can be provided to customers in many ways, such as table tents, separate menus, or as part of the food menu (see Figure 3.7). Because beverage service makes such a strong contribution to the operation's profit margin, the operation's staff must be well trained and knowledgeable in the alcoholic beverages offered.

Figure 3.7: Sample alcoholic beverage tent.

The average markup for alcoholic beverages typically falls between 300 and 400 percent; food items have a much lower markup, between 100 and 200 percent. Because of this substantially higher markup, alcoholic beverages generate much greater gross margin and net profit than food items. Additionally, when customers order alcoholic beverages, it is reflected in an increase in the total guest check. The result for the restaurant is greater revenues and higher profits.

Essential Skills
How to Develop an Operating Budget

Making a budget is the first step to planning a company's financial future. Make this as accurate and realistic as possible. If the restaurant is in a small town, for instance, don't expect 300 guests for dinner each night. Over the years, most managers refine their budgeting skills, perhaps through practice and experience, perhaps by taking classes in business management.

154

In-Class Activity:
Advertising Age

Literacy Connection, 21st-Century Skills—Work Creatively with Others, Create Media Products, Reason Effectively, Communicate Clearly, Work Effectively in Diverse Teams

Working in groups of three or four, design an advertising campaign for a special offer at an imaginary foodservice operation. You will need to write up a plan describing your campaign and create at least two media products to advertise the special program; these could include table tents, flyers, audio or visual "commercials," and so forth.

Your plan should clearly describe the program or event you are advertising, why you have chosen to design these specific media products, the group of people you wish to attract, and why you think that group of people will be attracted to your advertising and to the operation's special offer.

Refer back to Figure 3.5, and use this basic overview to get started:

❶ Collect all available historical and demographic data: If this isn't your first year in business, then you have records—invoices, sales information, and payroll figures—that you can look at when making a budget. If you are preparing to open a new business, look around the community for information. Ask the local Chamber of Commerce about other similar businesses, research property values and income levels in your community, and study the area to see where people live and work. The National Restaurant Association can also provide data about your area. (See the What's New box in the "Profit-and-Loss Report" section.) A lunch-only restaurant near a number of offices might do very well; whereas the same restaurant might fail in a residential neighborhood. Do your homework!

❷ Forecast revenues: Realistically predict how much money the business will earn in the coming year. Is the restaurant planning to cater a number of big events? Is a housing boom bringing newcomers to the area? Is a big marketing campaign in the works, or is the restaurant introducing a new menu concept? All of these can affect potential income. Make sure to create categories of revenue, such as dinner sales, wedding catering, and so on, and list realistic amounts of earnings in each category.

❸ Forecast costs: Realistically predict how much money the business will spend during the coming year. Are wage increases due to the employees? Is the rent going up? What about the price of gas—will that affect delivery costs? Does the restaurant plan to expand the outdoor seating area? Again, all of these can affect costs. Create cost categories, like payroll, rent, and utilities and predict how much the operation will spend on each.

It may be difficult to make an accurate budget the first year of business, but each following year, as better historical data becomes available and management skills improve, the estimates will get better and better.

Essential Skills
How to Forecast Sales Volume

Forecasting means using previous experience to foresee future occurrences. Restaurants use forecasting to predict everything from next year's budget to how busy Saturday night will be. These "guesstimates" help management and staff know what to expect so they can plan the work.

Essential Skills:
How to Develop an Operating Budget (cont.)

Encourage students to discuss the following:

- What other demographic information should a prospective restaurateur research? Where would he or she collect this information?

- What type of operation would do well near your high school? What type might do poorly? In each case, explain your answer.

- Many new operations fail because they overestimate potential revenues and underestimate potential costs. Why do these errors occur?

Essential Skills:
How to Forecast Sales Volume

Encourage students to discuss the following:

- Which type of forecast do you think is easier to "get right": a short-term prediction or a long-term prediction? Why?

- Are any problems associated with underestimating sales? Why might this be an issue for an operation and its staff?

In-Class Activity:
Student Selections

Literacy Connection, 21st-Century Skills— Social and Cultural Skills, Work Creatively with Others, Reason Effectively, Communicate Clearly

Working with two or three other students, design a restaurant or foodservice operation that you think would appeal to other students and become a financial success. Describe the menu choices, service style, and ambiance. What in particular would attract students?

Present your design to the class, using any visual aids you think appropriate. After all the groups have given their presentations, vote as a class on which operation would be the biggest success.

Encourage students to discuss the following:

- What are some other examples of external factors that could affect sales volume?

- How can the reservation book be an important tool in predicting sales volume?

- Why is it important for managers and staff to use the sales mix in planning their work? What are some possible results if the sales mix is a poor prediction of actual customer choices during a particular service period?

Discuss

- Encourage students to discuss what categories a profit-and-loss report for a typical household might have.

- What does it mean when the profit-and-loss report provides information that is significantly different from the budget's original predictions? How can the situation be remedied?

Reinforce and Review

- A profit-and-loss report, or income statement, helps managers gauge an operation's profitability as well as compare actual results to expected goals.

- A profit-and-loss report reflects what actually happened during a particular time period, whereas a budget predicts what is expected to happen during that period.

- For an operation to be profitable, sales must exceed costs.

Teaching Tips

- Relate the profit-and-loss report to household budgeting.

Vocabulary Terms

- **Profit-and-loss report:** A compilation of sales and cost information for a specific period of time.

These are the steps involved in forecasting:

❶ Analyze the sales history: Knowing what items were popular at what times yields a lot of information. Consider changing the menu price for an item that is consistently in high demand or removing a poorly selling dish. If Saturday nights are always slow in January, reduce inventory and schedule fewer staff members.

❷ Account for externalities: If a blizzard is predicted, consider closing early. On the other hand, if the restaurant has air conditioning during an August heat wave, consider increasing supplies and scheduling more staff to account for more customers.

❸ Predict sales volume: Based on all this information, estimate how busy the operation will be for a particular service or time period. Schedule staff and deliveries of perishables accordingly.

❹ Predict sales mix: Anticipating how many the restaurant will sell of each menu item helps to plan work. For instance, if the seared duck breast accounts for 5 percent of dinner entrée sales and the restaurant expects 100 guests this evening, expect to sell five duck breasts. (Of course, have more than five prepared, just to be safe—this isn't an exact science.)

Profit-and-Loss Reports

Another way of helping an operation to manage and control its overall costs is through a **profit-and-loss report** (see Figure 3.8 on the following page). A profit-and-loss report is a compilation of sales and cost information for a specific period of time. This report shows whether an operation has made or lost money during the time period covered by the report. The profit-and-loss report, which is also called the income statement, is a valuable management tool. It helps managers gauge an operation's profitability as well as compare actual results to expected goals. Carefully monitoring this information monthly or quarterly helps management determine areas where adjustments must be made to bring business operations in line with established financial goals. It is a useful tool in helping to assess how accurate an operation's operating budget has been.

A profit-and-loss report lists sales income first and then lists all expenses. The end of the report reflects the amount of profit or loss for the period covered. For an operation to be profitable, sales must exceed costs.

156

Kabob Restaurant
Profit and Loss Report

Sales			
Food	$	40,000	
Beverage	$	10,000	
Total sales			$ 50,000
Cost of Sales			
Food	$	16,000	
Beverage	$	2,500	
Total cost of sales			$ 18,500
Gross Profit			
Food	$	24,000	
Beverage	$	7,500	
Total gross profit			$ 31,500
Controllable Expenses			
Salaries and wages	$	13,000	
Employee benefits	$	2,000	
Legal/accounting	$	500	
Marketing	$	250	
Utility services	$	1,650	
General and administrative	$	2,200	
Repairs and maintenance	$	1,100	
Other income	$	300	
Total controllable expenses			$ 21,000
Fixed Expenses			
Rent	$	3,500	
Depreication	$	475	
Utility services	$	100	
Insurance	$	1,200	
Loan payments	$	1,500	
Total fixed expenses			$ 6,775
Profit/(Loss)*			$ 3,725
Income Taxes			$ 250
Net Earning (Loss)			$ 3,475
*before income taxes			

Figure 3.8: Sample profit-and-loss statement.

Use the reports to judge the efficiency of an operation, to determine where costs have gotten out of line, and to make basic management decisions. For larger organizations, investors, owners, and managers use the reports to determine the profitability of an operation.

Take several approaches to analyzing a profit-and-loss report. When comparing a recent profit-and-loss report to the budget, company standards, industry standards, or historical trends, look for any **variances** or changes that have occurred. This is a good way to check how the operation is running and can prevent future problems by catching them early. As soon as he detects variances, a manager can analyze what happened and develop a plan of how to correct the problem. This is a little like using progress reports and report cards.

157

Discuss

• Managers look for variances when assessing an operation's performance. Are all variances significant? Why or why not?

• How do managers know which variances need to be addressed and which do not? What potential variances can students identify that probably don't need correcting?

Reinforce and Review

• Looking for variances can indicate how the operation is running and can prevent future problems by catching them early.

• When variances are detected, managers can analyze the situation and develop a plan for corrective action.

• Some approaches to analyzing a profit-and-loss report include comparing it to the operating budget, comparing it to company or industry standards, and comparing it to the operation's own historical trends.

Teaching Tips

• Discuss various common evaluation techniques. For instance, report cards, progress reports, and daily grades are used in schools, and businesses often use performance reviews and self-evaluation forms to track progress. What elements do all these share? How do they differ?

Vocabulary Terms

• **Variance:** A change that has occurred, reflecting a difference between actual performance and the standards against which performance is being measured.

Figure Focus

Figure 3.8: This profit-and-loss report shows what actually happened at Kabob Restaurant during a particular month. What does it tell you about the restaurant? (Note: The categories on the operating budget shown in Figure 3.5 and the profit-and-loss report shown in Figure 3.8 are intentionally different, to give students some idea of how different managers operate.)

Encourage students to discuss the following:

- Why is it important for the National Restaurant Association to gather information from its members about their business practices? What possible uses are there for this data?

- Explain why operations should compare themselves to similar operations when assessing their costs. Why would comparing dissimilar restaurants result in relatively useless information?

- According to a recent survey, full-service operations with an average check of below $15 spend between 28.4 percent and 37.8 percent of their budgets on employee wages and benefits. Using Figure 3.8, calculate the percentage of its total sales that Kabob spends on employee wages and benefits. What might this indicate about the operation?

Discuss

- The National Restaurant Association represents more than 380,000 businesses in the United States, so their member surveys can provide detailed information about various segments of the restaurant and foodservice industry.

- How can portioning and measuring equipment help control costs? What can happen if the equipment is being used incorrectly?

- How can the proper use of schedules both control labor costs and improve employee relations?

- How can managers make sure that all employees are following house policies that have been installed to control costs?

Reinforce and Review

- In the kitchen, measuring, monitoring, portioning, and weighing equipment can be used to help control costs.

- Time clocks and POS systems can help control labor costs throughout the operation.

- POS systems also help track sales, as do cash registers.

[what's new]

National Restaurant Association Industry Surveys

The National Restaurant Association regularly surveys its members to collect information about the American restaurant industry. Some of this material is used to develop ranges for certain costs, such as labor or utilities. These ranges serve as the general standards for the industry and can be used for an individual operation when analyzing its own profit-and-loss report.

For example, a recent survey found that full-service restaurants with an average check of under $15.00 spend between 28.4 and 37.8 percent of their total budgets on employee wages and benefits, with a median of 32.5 percent. If a restaurant or foodservice operation's costs are significantly lower than 28.4 percent, they may not be attracting the best employees or might not have enough staff to perform the necessary work. On the other hand, if their costs are much higher than 37.8 percent, they might be paying out more in wages and benefits than the restaurant sales can support. The report gives similar information for both quick-service and full-service operations at a variety of price points, providing ranges for food costs, marketing expenses, profits, and other financial essentials.

It's important to remember that restaurants should compare themselves to similar establishments when determining whether their costs fall within general industry standards. For instance, a quick-service restaurant with a check average of $10.00 is a radically different operation from a full-service restaurant with a check average of $50.00. One is not inherently better or worse than the other, but they are apples and oranges as far as labor, operational, and other costs.

Cost-Control Tools

Many tools are available to restaurant and foodservice managers to help them control foodservice costs. For example, in the kitchen, portioning equipment, such as ladles and scoops, helps to ensure consistent quality and portion sizes. Receiving and portion scales also serve the same purpose but for larger-volume items. To help control staffing and labor costs, time clocks and POS (point-of-sale) systems also can serve the same purpose. Cash registers and POS systems also keep track of sales during the day, and equipment-monitoring systems can help ensure that an operation's equipment is functioning properly to keep efficiency high.

Advances in technology have also drastically increased the number of options available to operations in controlling costs. Email, the Internet, and numerous software programs all aid managers in closely monitoring sales. **Full-line supplier** companies (that is, one-stop shops that provide equipment, food, and supplies) have programs available to their customers that help with controlling

158

Teaching Tips

- Refer students to the discussions of measuring equipment in Level 1, Chapter 4 and Chapter 5.

- Refer students to Level 1, Chapter 7, on the importance of communication, and to Level 1, Chapter 8, on key management responsibilities.

Vocabulary Terms

- **Full-line supplier:** A one-stop shop that provides equipment, food, and supplies to the restaurant and foodservice industry.

costs. Programs can be used to complete the calculations required in cost planning, controlling sales, controlling inventory, and focusing on the menu. Software programs can easily provide better access to information, more accurate and more convenient collection of information, and improved analysis of that information. See Figure 3.9.

Figure 3.9: Accounting software programs provide accurate information and analysis.

But going overboard with all of the options available today can also be counterproductive. If not put to good use, they'll amount to nothing more than additional costs to the operation, and some of this technology are expensive. When choosing technology, answer the following questions:

- Will it help enhance guest satisfaction?

- Will it help increase revenue?

- Will it help reduce costs?

- Will it increase employee or management productivity?

- Will it improve communication?

If used effectively, technology can be a real help in running an operation more efficiently and helping to reduce and effectively control costs. Changes and advances in what's available on the market for this purpose are never ending, so operations need to continually stay up to date with the latest trends in both technological hardware and software.

159

Discuss

- Advances in computer software can help managers obtain accurate, timely information, but only if the data have been entered correctly into the program. What are some other potential flaws?

- How can managers select the technology that is most appropriate for their operation? Do all operations need computer software to run their business? Why or why not?

- In what ways can using technological advances increase revenues and decrease costs?

Reinforce and Review

- Email, the Internet, and numerous software programs all aid managers in closely monitoring sales.

- Programs can be used to complete the calculations required in cost planning, controlling sales and inventory, and focusing on the menu.

- When choosing technology, managers should ask the following: Will it help enhance guest satisfaction? Will it help increase revenue? Will it help reduce costs? Will it increase employee or management productivity? Will it improve communications?

- If used effectively, technology can help control costs, increasing an operation's efficiency.

Figure Focus

Figure 3.9: A variety of computer programs can help managers organize and track income and expenses.

Summary

- Remind students to review the following:
  1. Cost control
  2. Operating budgets
  3. Profit-and-loss reports
  4. Cost-control tools

Summary

In this section, you learned the following:

- Every business needs to obey one basic principle in order to survive: it must make more money than it spends. In other words, its sales, or revenue, must be higher than its costs. Revenue is the income from sales before expenses, or costs, are subtracted. Cost is the price an operation pays out in purchasing and preparing products or providing services. Cost control is the process by which an operation tries to keep its costs as low as possible.

- Food costs, beverage costs, and labor costs each have components that are related to sales levels. These costs are either variable or semivariable, which means that they can change based on sales. Because such costs are subject to change based on how the operation is doing, they are controllable; the operation has a certain amount of control in how it spends on these aspects of the operation. The overhead cost is a fixed or noncontrollable cost. These costs can include insurance, utilities, or a lease or mortgage on a building. Such costs are fixed, meaning they won't change. Because fixed costs do not change, they are often referred to as noncontrollable costs.

- An operating budget is a financial plan for a specific period of time. It lists the anticipated sales revenue and projected costs and gives an estimate of the profit or loss expected for the period. Operating budgets serve many purposes in the management of a restaurant or foodservice operation. They can be used to analyze controllable costs, such as labor, food and beverage, and supplies; to outline operating goals and managers' performance responsibilities; and to measure *actual* performance against *anticipated* performance.

- A profit-and-loss report is a compilation of sales and cost information for a specific period of time. This report shows whether an operation has made or lost money during the time period covered by the report. The profit-and-loss report, which is also called the income statement, is a valuable management tool. It helps managers gauge an operation's profitability as well as compare actual results to expected goals.

■ Many tools are available to restaurant and foodservice managers to help them control foodservice costs. For example, the kitchen offers portioning equipment, such as ladles and scoops, to ensure consistent quality and portion sizes. Receiving and portion scales serve the same purpose but for larger-volume items. To help control staffing and labor costs, use time clocks and POS (point-of-sale) systems. Cash registers and POS systems keep track of sales during the day, and equipment-monitoring systems can help ensure that an operation's equipment is functioning properly to keep efficiency high. Email, the Internet, and numerous software programs all aid managers in closely monitoring sales. Programs can be used to complete the calculations required in cost planning, controlling sales, controlling inventory, and focusing on the menu.

Section 3.1
Review Questions

1. Cost control is a business's efforts to manage how much it spends.

2. Controllable costs include food costs, beverage costs, and labor costs.

3. Examples of noncontrollable costs include insurance, utilities, and an operation's lease or mortgage on its building.

4. An operating budget helps manage an operation by analyzing controllable cost needs, outlining operating goals and managers' performance responsibilities, and measuring actual performance against anticipated performance.

5. Sherie Valderrama believes that the key consideration when looking at cost control is to have the commitment to maintain quality and operate in a responsible and sustainable manner.

6. Student responses may vary, as long as they defend their answers in a clear and logical manner.

7. Students should be creative in their list-making; their answers should not come solely from the examples provided in the text.

8. Student responses may vary, as long as they defend their answers in a clear and logical manner. However, they should include portioning tools, staffing tools, and POS systems in their responses, as these are all common in quick-service operations.

Section 3.1 Review Questions

1. What is cost control?

2. What are two controllable costs?

3. Provide two examples of a noncontrollable cost.

4. List two ways in which an operating budget helps manage an operation.

5. Why would Sherie Valderrama agree that cost control is critical to the success of a restaurant or foodservice operation?

6. Given what you just learned in this section, what would you suggest to Chef Kate and Miguel regarding where they should start their cost-control efforts?

7. Try to list as many foodservice costs as you can according to whether they are controllable or noncontrollable.

8. What cost-control tools do you think you would rely on most if you were running a quick-service operation? Explain your answer.

162

Section 3.1 Activities

1. Study Skills/Group Activity: Quick-Service Budgeting

Working with two or three other students, think of a quick-service restaurant with which you are all familiar. Then, begin to create an operating budget for that establishment. In doing so, highlight the top five factors that you would need to consider and explain your rationale in choosing them.

2. Independent Activity: Profit-and-Loss Analysis

Imagine you are running your own operation. Briefly describe what it would be like. Then, consider the three methods of analyzing profit-and-loss reports. Which do you think would be most useful to you and why?

3. Critical Thinking: Start-Up Costs

Select a city or town and research its characteristics: population, major industries, and other elements that affect its character. What kind of restaurant would succeed there? In what way would you try to allocate costs? For example, would you want to spend more on labor and better service, or more on food? Would you think allotting more money for overhead expenses like a lease or mortgage on a location would be more significant than either food or labor? Write a one-page proposal, detailing your broad cost outline.

163

Section 3.1 Activities

1. Students should identify a local quick-service restaurant and determine some of its expense categories. The factors they highlight could include such elements as staffing, food costs, or insurance, so long as they give solid reasons why these are among the top five elements.

2. Students should describe the foodservice operation they run and which method of analyzing profit-and-loss reports is preferable. Student responses may vary so long as they are convincingly argued.

3. Students will need to research demographic and economic information for the community they select. They should be sure to describe why they believe a particular type of restaurant would succeed and defend their expense allocations.

Section 3.2
Controlling Food Costs

Introduce the Section

a. Explain the importance of determining food cost and food cost percentage as a step in controlling costs.

b. Reiterate the need to calculate portion costs, AP versus EP costs, and recipe yields when determining menu pricing.

c. Discuss the objectives for the section.

Vocabulary Review

a. Direct students to the key terms.

b. Pronounce each word, and have the students repeat the pronunciation out loud.

c. Discuss the definition of each word.

Teach

Discuss

- When guests patronize an operation, what are they really buying? Is it "worth it" to pay more for a different atmosphere, level of service, quality of ingredients, convenience, and so forth? In what sense is the customer really buying an experience, not a meal?

- How do customer expectations of a meal vary depending on where it is purchased? Is a glass of soda "always" a glass of soda?

Reinforce and Review

- The quality of ingredients, care of preparation, expertise in cooking, and quality of service can all add up to a higher, and just, price point on a menu.

- Not all extra expenses are legitimate. Some operations might try to compensate for other inefficiencies when pricing their dishes, or they might not understand the pricing process.

- Essential skills in controlling food costs include calculating the price of food, assessing the cost of recipes, and valuing food appropriately on the menu.

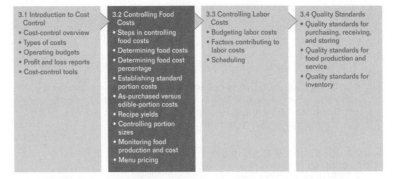

3.1 Introduction to Cost Control	3.2 Controlling Food Costs	3.3 Controlling Labor Costs	3.4 Quality Standards
• Cost-control overview • Types of costs • Operating budgets • Profit and loss reports • Cost-control tools	• Steps in controlling food costs • Determining food costs • Determining food cost percentage • Establishing standard portion costs • As-purchased versus edible-portion costs • Recipe yields • Controlling portion sizes • Monitoring food production and cost • Menu pricing	• Budgeting labor costs • Factors contributing to labor costs • Scheduling	• Quality standards for purchasing, receiving, and storing • Quality standards for food production and service • Quality standards for inventory

SECTION 3.2 CONTROLLING FOOD COSTS

How can a burger and fries at one place cost $5.00 but cost $10.00 at another place. Why does one establishment charge $2.00 for a cup of coffee, while another shop down the road only charges $1.50? Why do prices vary so much for what seem like similar items?

The pricing of food is a complicated process. Sometimes the extra expense is fair and well worth paying for. The quality of ingredients, care in preparation, expertise in cooking, and quality of service can all add up to a higher, and just, **price point** on a menu. Sometimes, though, such quality isn't evident at all. When that happens, either the operation is trying to compensate for inefficiencies somewhere else in the business, or it simply doesn't understand how to correctly price its product. Neither adds up to a successful operation.

This section discusses the various elements that go into figuring out the price of food, how to accurately assess what recipes cost an operation, and how to properly value it on the menu. All three are essential skills in not only controlling food costs, but running a successful operation in general.

Study Questions

After studying Section 3.2, you should be able to answer the following questions:

- What are the steps in the food flow process?
- How is food cost determined?

164

Teaching Tips

- Provide sample menus from two restaurants that serve dishes with similar titles, but at different price points. For instance, the menu from a quick-service hamburger restaurant could be compared with the menu from a full-service hamburger restaurant. Encourage students to discuss why the prices might differ.

Vocabulary Terms

- **Price point:** The selling price of a menu item.

- How is food cost percentage determined?

- How are standard portion costs established?

- What is the difference between as-purchased cost and edible-portion cost?

- What is a recipe yield?

- What tools can be used in controlling portion sizes?

- In what way can an operation monitor food production and cost?

- What methods can be used to price a menu?

Steps in Controlling Food Costs

Food costs must be controlled during all seven stages of the food flow process; from the actual purchasing of food items to how they are served to customers. Figure 3.10 shows a diagram of the food flow process. Following is a list of each of the seven stages:

- **Purchasing:** An operation must be spending wisely and getting good quality product for cost. Establishing quality standards is essential in acquiring and producing consistent, top-quality product. An operation that is spending too much for a product is wasting money and ultimately losing potential revenue. For more on purchasing, see *Chapter 5: Purchasing and Inventory*.

- **Receiving:** An operation must be sure that it is getting what it's paying for, both in quality and quantity, from its vendors. Management or well-trained staff need to be in charge of receiving to ensure quality standards and accuracy of orders. For more on receiving, see *Chapter 5*.

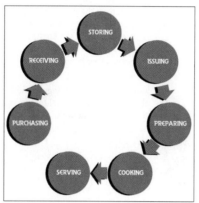

Figure 3.10: The seven stages of the food flow process.

165

Discuss

- How can following proper food safety principles help control food costs? How can kitchen staff help control food costs before they have even begun to prepare the food?

Reinforce and Review

- The seven stages in the food flow process are purchasing, receiving, storing, issuing, preparing, cooking, and serving.

- Establishing quality standards in purchasing is essential in acquiring and producing consistent, top-quality product.

- Receiving only those products that meet quality standards and accurately fulfill an order is an important component of controlling costs.

Teaching Tips

- Encourage students to review the material in Level 1, Chapter 2 about proper food safety and the flow of food.

Homework Activity: Family Food Finances

Literacy Connection, 21st-Century Skills— Work Independently, Collaborate with Others, Reason Effectively, Think Creatively, Implement Innovations

Controlling costs isn't only an issue in the workplace: it's equally important at home.

Consider your family's food spending. Identify five ways in which spending can be controlled and food purchases can be made more efficiently. You might wish to consult with the person in your household who purchases the bulk of the family's food to gain some insights.

Write a brief report describing your findings and how they can help your household finances.

Figure Focus

Figure 3.10: The flow of food is as important in controlling food costs as it is in controlling food safety.

Discuss

- Close attention to the flow of food is helpful in controlling food costs. At what steps in this process are costs most vulnerable; that is, at what points is the operation most likely to spend money on food that will not earn money?

- Consider how food is prepared in the classroom kitchen. What examples of waste and inefficiency have you noticed? How could these be eliminated?

Reinforce and Review

- Proper storage prevents loss of food through spoilage and waste.

- Efficient issuing systems, or inventory controls, record what product is being used when, by whom, and for what purpose, thereby tracking sales and reducing opportunities for pilferage.

- Accurate preparation, production, and portioning of food all help to prevent inefficiency and waste.

- Mistakes made at the service level can both directly and indirectly contribute to increased food costs.

Teaching Tips

- Encourage students to review Level 1, Chapter 10 on the importance of providing good customer service.

Fast Fact: Did You Know . . . ?

Encourage students to discuss the following:

- How can restaurant and foodservice operations reduce waste? How can food be repurposed for internal or external consumption?

- In what ways can inefficiencies in the flow of food be eliminated in households, as they can be in restaurant and foodservice operations? How can this keep consumers from wasting food as well as lower their costs?

- What do you think is the single biggest step operations can take to prevent wasting food?

Vocabulary Terms

- **Pilfering:** Theft of food, usually in reference to staff members.

- **Storage:** Proper storage of goods is essential. Storage facilities must be safe, sanitary, and efficient. Operations must continually monitor freezers and refrigerated storage units to make sure they are running as they should be. Improperly stored food will be wasted, and wasted food increases food costs. For more on storage, see *Chapter 5.*

- **Issuing:** An efficient issuing system, also known as inventory control, allows operations to control food costs in a number of ways. It keeps a record of what product is being used most frequently (that is, what is selling), and it also helps prevent **pilfering.** For more on issuing, see *Chapter 5.*

- **Preparation:** Efficient food preparation is crucial to controlling food costs. All product should be used to the fullest, so operations should have detailed specifications as to exactly how every food item should be prepared for cooking.

- **Cooking (production):** The way in which food is prepared and portioned is obviously an important stage in the food flow process. Incorrectly cooked food goes to waste, and incorrectly portioned food also results in waste, both of which add to food costs.

- **Service (sale):** Service is the final stage in the process, but no less important than the previous stages. Good service is crucial to moving product that needs to be moved, as well as correctly taking orders so that mistakes aren't made in the kitchen. Any mistakes made at the service level can both directly and indirectly contribute to increased food costs. For more on service, see *Foundations of Restaurant Management & Culinary Arts, Level One, Chapter 10: Serving Your Guests.*

Inefficiencies at any stage of the food flow process result in foodservice costs that go up, so it's crucial for any operation to closely monitor all aspects of how the business functions.

[fast fact]

Did You Know...?
In the United States as a whole, an estimated 30 percent of food is wasted. This waste is from grocery stores (because of spoilage or blemishes), restaurants (food that isn't used), and consumers (leftovers and food that is spoiling). That amounts to an annual loss of approximately $50 billion of food.

166

Homework Activity: Shaker Your Plate

Literacy Connection, 21st-Century Skills—Reason Effectively, Work Independently, Communicate Clearly

There is an old saying, "Shaker your plate," which means to eat every crumb of what is served to you. The spirit of this adage goes further: To "shaker your plate" means to use all your resources as effectively as possible, wasting nothing and utilizing everything.

How can restaurant and foodservice operations use this proverb to inspire employees and managers to reduce waste and cut costs in the kitchen and dining room? Is this a useful approach, or could it backfire?

Write a brief essay describing how and why restaurant and foodservice operations might use "shaker your plate" to motivate their employees.

Determining Food Cost

Food cost is the actual dollar value of the food used by an operation during a certain period. It includes the cost incurred when food is consumed for any reason. Food cost includes the cost of food sold, given away, wasted, spoiled, incorrectly prepped, overportioned, overproduced, or pilfered. Fortunately, the formula for figuring food cost takes into account the multiple purchases and uses of food items in a typical operation.

Opening and closing inventory data are needed to determine the value of the food cost. **Inventory** represents the dollar value of a food product in storage and can be expressed in terms of units, values, or both. **Opening inventory** is the physical inventory at the beginning of a given period (such as the month of April). The **closing inventory** is the inventory at the end of a given period. Most operations do inventory and figure food cost monthly, but some do it weekly. Rarely is it done on a daily, quarterly, or annual basis.

The formula for calculating food cost starts with adding the opening inventory together with the purchases made during that period. The total of these two numbers equals the total food available, or the dollar amount of all food available for sale. Then, subtract the closing inventory from the total food available, resulting in the total food cost.

This method is the only accurate way to obtain an actual food cost:

(Opening inventory + Purchases = Total food available) – Closing inventory = Total food cost

Some operations further refine the cost of food sold to get a more accurate number of how all the food is being used. To do this, the operation subtracts these items from its cost of food sold:

- Employee meals
- Complimentary items to customers
- Transferring food to another location (used by hotels and chain operations)

Determining Food Cost Percentage

Total food cost percentage is the relationship between sales and the cost of food to achieve those sales. Food cost percentage is often the standard against which food cost is judged. Analyze food cost percentage by comparing it to company standards, historical costs, or even industry standards. In most cases, the standard food cost percentage is a target determined by management.

167

Discuss

- Is it really possible for managers and employees to keep track of every mouthful of food, when opportunities for waste are so abundant in many kitchens? How accurate is the food cost?

- Why do students think that inventory is rarely taken on a daily, quarterly, or annual basis?

Reinforce and Review

- Food cost includes the cost of food sold, given away, wasted, spoiled, incorrectly prepped, overportioned, overproduced, or pilfered.

- Opening and closing inventory data are used to determine the value of the food cost.

- The total food available for sale includes the opening inventory and the purchases made during that period.

- The total food available for sale, minus the closing inventory, equals the total food cost.

- Some operations include staff meals, complimentary items, and transfers of food when calculating the total food cost.

- Total food cost percentage is often the standard against which food cost is judged and is usually a target determined by management.

Teaching Tips

- Encourage students to practice calculating total food cost.

Vocabulary Terms

- **Food cost:** The actual dollar value of the food used by an operation during a certain period.

- **Inventory:** The dollar value of a food product in storage; it can be expressed in terms of units, values, or both.

- **Opening inventory:** The physical inventory at the beginning of a given period.

- **Closing inventory:** The physical inventory at the end of a given period.

- **Total food cost percentage:** The relationship between sales and the cost of food used to achieve those sales.

Discuss

- Each time the purchasing price of an ingredient increases, the standard portion costs of all the standardized recipes using that ingredient also increase. What techniques can managers use to track changes in purchasing prices and production costs?

- How can managers ensure that employees are following the standardized recipes at all times, even when preparing dishes they have made multiple times?

Reinforce and Review

- To determine the food cost percentage, divide total food cost by sales.

- Food cost is a variable cost, which means it should increase or decrease in direct proportion to an increase or decrease in sales, all other things being equal.

- When all cost controls are followed properly, food cost and sales will be proportionate.

- If an operation does not cost out its standardized recipes, then the selling price will be only a guess.

Teaching Tips

- Encourage students to practice calculating total food cost percentage.

Vocabulary Terms

- **Standardized recipe:** A recipe followed every time that menu item is prepared.

- **Standard portion cost:** The exact amount that one serving of a food item should cost when prepared according to its standardized recipe.

- **Recipe cost card:** A table of ingredient costs for each item in the standardized recipe.

To determine the percentage, divide the total food cost by the sales. This sets it up as a ratio relationship. Doing the math and dividing it out makes it a percentage. By expressing the cost of food sold in percentages, it can be compared on a month-to-month or week-to-week basis regardless of any fluctuation in sales. Controlling the food cost percentage becomes the most important priority if the operation is to be profitable.

Total food cost ÷ Sales = Food cost percentage

Food cost is a variable cost, which means it should increase or decrease in direct proportion to an increase or decrease in sales if all of the standards and food controls are followed correctly. In contrast, if the cost controls are *not* followed correctly, food costs and sales will not be in proportion to each other. Therefore, if an operation meets its standard food cost percentage month after month, its standards are set properly, and the control system is working. If it does not meet its standard, then either the standards are set incorrectly, the controls are not working, or both.

Establishing Standard Portion Costs

Most every operation has **standardized recipes** that are followed every time a menu item is prepared. For every standardized recipe, an operation should establish a **standard portion cost**, which is the exact amount that one serving, or portion, of a food item should cost when prepared according to the item's standardized recipe.

A key control in getting the proper relationship between a menu item's cost and its selling price is through the use of a recipe cost card. A **recipe cost card** is a tool used to calculate the standard portion cost for a menu item. See Figure 3.11 on the following page. It is a table of ingredient costs for each item in the standardized recipe. If recipe cost cards are not used, the selling price is nothing more than a guess. Operations must understand and use recipe cost cards since they are critical to the accurate figuring of selling prices.

As with the standardized recipe, a recipe cost card should exist for every multiple-ingredient item listed on the menu.

MACARONI AND CHEESE				
Amount needed	Unit of measurement	Ingredient	Cost per unit	Total cost
3	lbs	macaroni, raw	$2.00	$6.00
2	qts	white sauce	$3.00	$6.00
2	c	cheese, grated	$1.50	$3.00
4	oz	butter	$0.25	$1.00
1	tbsp	salt	$0.01	$0.01
1	tsp	paprika	$0.01	$0.01
4	oz	breadcrumbs	$0.25	$1.00
			RECIPE	$17.02
			SERVINGS	26
			COST PER SERVING	$0.65

Figure 3.11: Sample recipe cost card.

Essential Skills
How to Determine Standard Portion Cost

Before you can decide how much to charge for an item on your menu, you must know how much it costs to make. Follow these steps to determine how much the ingredients to make a single portion of tomato sauce will cost, assuming you need 1 cup of tomato paste to make the recipe, which serves 6 people.

❶ Using the standardized recipe, list all the ingredients.

❷ For each ingredient, list both the amount needed and the unit of measurement you'll use:

1 cup tomato paste

("1" is the amount needed, and "cup" is the unit of measurement you'll use.)

❸ For each ingredient, list the cost (the amount you paid) and the unit of measurement the seller used (these should be on the invoice from the seller):

$15/quart

("$15" is the cost to purchase the tomato paste, and "quart" is the unit of measurement the seller used, so 1 quart of tomato paste costs $15.)

Figure Focus
Figure 3.11: What is the easiest way to determine how large each portion should be?

Essential Skills:
How to Determine Standard Portion Cost (cont.)

Encourage students to discuss the following:

- Why is it important for all culinary professionals to understand basic mathematic operations, such as the calculations needed to determine standard portion cost?

- In what ways might knowing the standard portion and standard portion cost of a given item affect the cook preparing the dish?

- This tomato sauce recipe costs $2.785 per person to produce. Do students think this is too high, too low, or just right? How much does a can of store-bought tomato sauce cost per portion?

❹ Convert the seller's unit of measurement to your recipe's unit of measurement:

1 quart = 4 cups.

(If 1 quart of tomato paste costs $15, then 4 cups of tomato paste also cost $15.)

❺ Convert the cost for the seller's unit of measurement to the cost of your unit of measurement:

$15 ÷ 4 cups = $3.75.

("$15" is the cost of all 4 cups of the tomato paste, and "$3.75" is the cost of a single cup.)

❻ Multiply the number of units needed for the recipe by the cost per unit:

1 cup × $3.75 = $3.75.

(So 1 cup of tomato paste costs you $3.75.)

❼ Follow the same steps for all the other ingredients in the recipe. For instance, 8 ounces of basil costs you $12, and 1.5 pounds of onion costs you $0.96.

❽ Add together all the costs you pay for the ingredients in this recipe.

For instance, $3.75 + $12 + $0.96 = $16.71.

If tomato paste, basil, and onion are the only ingredients in this recipe, then the recipe cost will be $16.71.

❾ Divide the recipe cost by the number of portions the recipe yields:

$16.71 ÷ 6 = $2.785.

The standard portion cost of this recipe is $2.79.

Discuss

- The "Essential Skills: How to Determine Standard Portion Cost" box above uses the example of a tomato sauce recipe. Does this example use the AP method or the EP method? How can you tell? Why might one be a better choice than the other?

Reinforce and Review

- Standard portion cost is the exact amount that one serving of a food item should cost when prepared according to the item's standardized recipe.

- The AP or "as-purchased" method and the EP or "edible portion" method are the two techniques used to determine the cost of ingredients in a standardized recipe.

- In the AP method, all ingredient quantities are listed on the standardized recipe in the form in which they are purchased.

As-Purchased versus Edible-Portion Costs

As mentioned earlier, standard portion cost is the exact amount that one serving, or portion, of a food item should cost when prepared according to the item's standardized recipe. Two methods are used to determine the cost of ingredients in a standardized recipe: the AP method, which means "as purchased;" and the EP method, which stands for "edible portion." A big difference between these two methods affects both the quality of the recipe and the costs of the ingredients. See Figure 3.12 on the following page.

The **as-purchased (AP) method** is used to cost an ingredient at the purchase price *before* any trim or waste is taken into account. In the AP method, all ingredient quantities are listed on the standardized recipe in the form in which

Teaching Tips

- Encourage students to review the basic math operations in Level 1, Chapter 4. The examples provided in the Teachers' Wrap for Level 1, Chapter 4 might also be helpful.

Vocabulary Terms

- **As-purchased method:** A method used to determine the cost of ingredients in a standardized recipe at the purchase price, before any time or waste is taken into account.

Figure 3.12 : The onions on the left are in EP form, while the onions on the right are in AP form.

they are purchased. "Ten pounds of onion, diced" is an example of AP, as the recipe is calling for ten pounds of onion, as purchased. In this case, the chef would start with ten pounds of whole onion, then peel and dice it, and add the onion to the recipe. Ten pounds of onions wouldn't actually be used in the recipe itself, which is why it falls under the AP method.

The **edible-portion (EP) method** is used to cost an ingredient *after* trimming and removing waste so that only the usable portion of the item is reflected. Using the EP method to cost an ingredient, the quantity is listed on the standardized recipe using only the edible portion of that particular ingredient. For example, "ten pounds of diced onion" involves taking some quantity of onion, and then peeling, dicing, and weighing the results until there are ten pounds of peeled, diced onion. This ingredient would be costed using the EP method because the recipe is based on the edible portion of the onion only.

To obtain a cost in this case, use the original weight of the product. If you started with eleven pounds of onion in order to obtain ten pounds EP of diced onion, you would use the cost for eleven pounds to determine the cost of the onion used in the recipe.

Recipe Yields

Occasionally a recipe will not yield the number of portions that it is supposed to yield, or an operation will opt to serve a different portion size than what is listed on the recipe card. In such cases, the operation needs to determine exactly what kind of yield the recipe is making or change the yield according to the operation's needs. A **recipe yield** is the process of determining the number of portions that a recipe produces.

171

Figure Focus

Figure 3.12: Can students tell which product is in AP form and which is in EP form? Why must culinary professionals understand the difference between products in AP form and products in EP form?

Discuss

- The EP method assumes that the item has been trimmed, so only the usable portion remains. However, a usable portion for one recipe is not necessarily a usable portion for another recipe. For instance, one recipe might call for peeling and trimming the tops from whole carrots before roasting them; another recipe might call for peeling and trimming the tops from the whole carrots, but then cutting the carrots into batonnets. In this case, all the scrap carrot produced when cutting the carrots into shape is considered waste. Why is this important when figuring out how many pounds of carrots to order?

- Sometimes, the waste produced from one application can be used in another. For instance, the carrot scraps produced from cutting batonnets in the previous discussion can be used to make chicken stock. How can this help to control costs?

Reinforce and Review

- The EP method of costing assumes that some preparation has taken place after the ingredient arrived in the kitchen.

- To obtain the true cost of an ingredient using the EP method, use the original weight of the ingredient that was needed to produce the necessary amount for the recipe.

Teaching Tips

- Discuss how recipes are often written with an eye to either AP or EP costing. For example, a recipe calling for "10 pounds of celery, diced" will require less celery than a recipe calling for "10 pounds of diced celery."

Vocabulary Terms

- **Edible-portion method:** A method used to determine the cost of ingredients in a standardized recipe after trimming and removing waste, so that only the usable portion of the item is reflected.

- **Recipe yield:** The process of determining the number of portions that a recipe produces.

Discuss

- Encourage students to suggest other recipes that will be affected either by cooking loss or by cooking gain. Why is it important to understand how different ingredients behave when cooked? How can this affect recipe cost?

Reinforce and Review

- To determine how many portions a recipe yields, calculate the total yield of the recipe either by weight or by volume.

- Weigh or measure only the major ingredients in a recipe, and remember to factor in cooking loss as well as cooking gain.

Teaching Tips

- Students should divide into groups to make this recipe, weighing the raw ingredients (including those used to make the white sauce) as well as the final product. How do student results vary from the text's example? Why might this be the case?

Homework Activity:
The Weight of Things

Mathematics Connection, Science Connection, Literacy Connection, 21st-Century Skills— Work Independently, Reason Effectively, Communicate Clearly

Weigh a whole apple; this provides its AP, or as-purchased, weight. Now peel the apple, remove its core, and cut it into wedges. Weigh the wedges. What is the EP weight of the prepared raw apple? What is the apple's yield percentage?

Place the apple wedges in a pan with 2 fluid ounces of water. Cook the apples until they can be easily pierced with a fork. Now weigh the cooked apples. Compare the weight of the cooked apple to that of the raw apple: What is the ratio between the cooked apple's weight and its AP weight? What is the ratio between the cooked apple's weight and its EP weight?

Research the scientific explanation for these changes between the apple's raw and cooked weight. Describe your results and findings in a one-page report.

To determine how many portions a recipe yields, calculate the total yield of the recipe either by weight or by volume, depending on how the portion size is calculated. Weigh or measure only the major ingredients. Remember to take cooking loss into account, especially for meat, vegetables, and fruit. To determine the total number of eight-ounce portions available from a macaroni and cheese recipe, for example, an operation must first look at the recipe's list of ingredients and their volume, such as the list for macaroni and cheese as shown in Figure 3.13.

3 pounds raw macaroni

2 quarts white sauce

2 cups grated cheese

4 ounces butter

1 tablespoon salt

1 teaspoon paprika

4 ounces breadcrumbs

In this particular recipe, only the volume of the macaroni and the white sauce must be calculated. The cheese is not calculated, since it is absorbed into the white sauce. Butter, salt, paprika, and breadcrumbs are negligible and also are not counted. Three pounds of raw macaroni yields 24 cups of cooked macaroni. On average, a cup of cooked pasta weighs between 5 and 6 ounces. Therefore, 24 cups of pasta multiplied by 5.5 ounces equals 132 ounces or 8.25 pounds of cooked macaroni. This converts to 192 fluid ounces. Two quarts converts to 64 ounces (32 ounces per quart, so 2 × 32 = 64).

Figure 3.13 : Sample recipe yield.

Figure Focus

Figure 3.13: The weight of a finished product is not always the same as the weight of the raw ingredients used to produce the recipe. In this example, cooked macaroni will weigh more than raw macaroni, because the pasta absorbs water while cooking.

The total volume of the macaroni and cheese recipe is:

192 fluid ounces macaroni + 64 fluid ounces white sauce = 256 fluid ounces of finished macaroni and cheese.

Then, divide the total volume by the portion size to provide the yield of the recipe:

256 fluid ounces product ÷ 8 ounces portion = 32 servings.

Understanding recipe yields is one of the keys to successful food preparation and controlling food costs. The measurements given in recipes must be followed exactly. If the number of portions a recipe yields is unknown, or if a recipe isn't being portioned properly, it can cost an operation substantial amounts of revenue.

Finally, keep in mind that once a yield is known and properly followed, it's easier to increase or decrease the size of the recipe based upon the operation's changing needs. Most recipes, even those for baked goods, can be doubled successfully. Many recipes for casseroles and soups can be doubled, and even halved, tripled, and so on. See Table 3.2 on converting yields. Accurate recipe yields are crucial for an operation to effectively manage inventory, revenues, and costs.

Table 3.2: Converting Recipe Yields

Formula for increasing or decreasing recipe yields:

1. Decide how many servings you need (desired yield).

2. Use the following formula: Desired yield ÷ Original yield = Conversion factor (number to multiply ingredients by). For example, if your chili recipe serves 80 and you need to serve 40: 40 ÷ 80 = 0.5. The conversion factor is 0.5.

3. Multiply each ingredient amount by the conversion factor. This keeps all the ingredients in the same proportion to each other as they were in the original recipe.

4. As needed, convert answers to logical, measurable amounts. Think about the equipment you will use for measuring. For example: 6/4 cups flour = 1½ cups; 12 tablespoons brown sugar = ¾ cups.

5. Make any necessary adjustments to equipment, temperature, and time. The depth of food in a pan affects how fast it will cook. Use pans that are the right size for the amount of food—neither too large nor too small.

173

Discuss

- The text notes that negligible ingredients, such as salt and seasonings, are not typically included when calculating recipe yields. Why not? How does a cook or manager determine what ingredients are negligible and which are not?

- If negligible ingredients are not important enough to factor into a recipe's yield, why are they used to calculate a recipe's cost?

Reinforce and Review

- Negligible ingredients, like salt, are not typically used to calculate recipe yields, although they are important in calculating recipe costs.

- Employees at successful restaurant and food-service operations must know how to properly calculate recipe yields. This helps an operation effectively manage its inventory, revenues, and costs.

- Once a yield is known and properly followed, it's easier to increase or decrease the size of the recipe, based on operational needs.

Teaching Tips

- Review the differences between weight and volume measurements with students, as in Level 1, Chapter 4.

Table 3.2:
Converting Recipe Yields

- Cooks and managers often increase or decrease recipe yields to meet an operation's needs. What are some ways in which this can affect costs? For instance, might there be discounts for ordering in bulk, or penalties for ordering too little of a particular product? Encourage students to think broadly about cost structures. Chapter 5 addresses purchasing in greater detail.

- Using the recipe for macaroni and cheese presented on the previous page, calculate the following recipe yields:
  - 18 servings
  - 100 servings
  - 200 servings

Encourage students to discuss the following:

- Why is it important for recipe testers to take notes while preparing recipes? What information should he or she write down?

- Why is there a need for recipe testers? If the instructions are written clearly, shouldn't all cooks follow the recipe in the same way?

- What types of recipes do students think require the most testing? What audiences might need the most information about recipes?

In-Class Activity:
The Perils of Improper Portioning

Mathematics Connection, Literacy Connection, 21st-Century Skills—Work Independently, Reason Effectively, Communicate Clearly, Solve Problems

Haiya's Place recently added a beef tenderloin dish to its menu. The dish, which includes a 5-ounce portion of beef, sells for $21.

On the first day this item was offered, the butcher looked at the food production chart to see how many portions of beef she needed to prepare for service. The manager who had completed the form had been in a hurry, and her handwriting had smeared: the "5-oz portion" looked like "8-oz portion." So the butcher proceeded to cut 8-ounce portions of beef.

The fifteenth and final 8-ounce portion of beef tenderloin was being plated for a guest before the sous chef realized that the portion size was incorrect.

How many 5-ounce portions of tenderloin could have been obtained from the fifteen 8-ounce portions served? How much revenue did the restaurant lose by not selling those additional portions?

How could this problem have been prevented? What aftereffects might this situation have on staff and guests?

Discuss

- How can failing to control portion size jeopardize an operation's entire financial status?

- How can failing to control portion size affect customers and their expectations?

- What are some examples of portions typically controlled by weight? By volume? By count?

[on the job]

Recipe Tester

Ever tried out a recipe, even for something as seemingly straightforward as a grilled cheese sandwich, and considered various ways to make the finished product even better? This is the basic principle of a recipe tester's job. These individuals work with recipes that are to be published in cookbooks, magazines, and newspapers to ensure that they are clear and easy to follow, produce consistent outcomes, and, of course, taste good.

A recipe taster needs good communication skills because he or she is the bridge between the chef who created the recipe and the consumer who will eventually read and try the published version at home. The tester must work hard to make sure everything in the recipe is easy to understand and can't be confused or misread. Depending on what publication the recipe will appear in, the tester will provide more or less information to the reader. A newspaper's food section may require brief, easy-to-prepare recipes geared to busy home cooks, while advanced cookbooks may need highly detailed material for professional chefs.

A typical day of testing may involve extended purchasing trips, several hours of cooking and note taking, and often meetings with editors and managers to taste and discuss the finished products. A broad range of education and career choices can be suited to this work.

Controlling Portion Sizes

Controlling portions is very important for a restaurant to meet its standard food cost. Portions can be controlled by weight, volume, or count: for example, an 8-ounce portion of steak, a 1-ounce ladle of dressing, or 12 shrimp. Although some staff in the kitchen may believe that they have a "feel" for exact portion sizes, it is important that staff use portion-control devices rather than guessing. Without using portioning equipment, staff may be serving portions that are bigger than the menu price has been calculated for, which will result in the operation losing money. On top of that, inconsistent portioning can lead to inconsistent products. Tools that are essential for accurate portion control include the following (see Figure 3.14 on the following page):

- Scoops
- Ladles
- Serving spoons
- Serving dishes
- Ramekins, bowls, cups, and so on
- Portion scales

Reinforce and Review

- Although some employees might believe they "know" exact portion sizes, it's critical to use portioning devices to ensure that dishes are consistently prepared and that cost structures are being followed.

- Inconsistent portioning can lead to inconsistent products.

- Portions can be controlled by weight, volume, or count.

Teaching Tips

- Review the information on portioning equipment, referring to the material in Level 1, Chapter 4.

Figure 3.14: Portions can be controlled by weight, volume, or count. Portion control tools include scoops, serving dishes, bowls, and scales.

Another mechanism for ensuring that portions are the right size is to preportion any item that can be preportioned before serving. For example, during a rush period, the cook's line can get hectic, and errors are more prone to happen. Therefore, preportioning items will not only save time but will also improve accuracy. Deli meats, which can be precut, weighed, and sealed in plastic bags until used for sandwiches are a good example of preportioning. The more preportioning that can be done, the smoother the rush period will be, the fewer errors that will be made, and the more food costs will be controlled in both the short and long run.

Monitoring Production Volume and Cost

While not adhering to standard recipes is a major cause of increased food cost in production, preparing the incorrect amount of product is also a problem. Every operation should strive to produce quantities as close to the quantity actually needed in order to maintain standard food costs and sales. If the operation produces too much food, leftovers are the result.

Quite often, these leftovers aren't suitable for sale because their appearance and taste do not meet company standards. Sometimes adding leftovers to other recipes, such as adding leftover beef to beef vegetable soup, can salvage the extra product. However, the leftovers rarely bring the same markup as the original product.

Conversely, not producing enough product and running out of an item can disappoint customers and runs the risk that they will not return to your establishment. Either of these situations is a lose-lose for the restaurant. Produce too much and food cost goes up; produce too little and sales are lost. The answer to this dilemma resides in the food production chart.

175

Figure Focus

Figure 3.14: How are each of these portioning tools used? Give examples of some foods that would be portioned using each device.

Discuss

- What are some foods that could and should be preportioned? What are some foods that should not be preportioned? What are the differences between the two categories?

- How can leftover mashed potatoes be reused? What about raw chicken breasts? Cooked carrots?

Reinforce and Review

- When possible, preportion items before service; however, this should only be done in cases when quality will not be diminished.

- In general, the more preportioning that can be done, the more control the kitchen will have over its food costs.

- Every operation should strive to produce quantities as close to the quantity actually needed to maintain standard food costs and sales.

- Although leftovers often represent a waste in terms of food cost, running out of products during service can be equally dangerous for an operation's finances.

- Correctly using a food production chart can help prevent producing too much or too little food.

Teaching Tips

- Discuss the food safety issues that could be involved in reusing food, such as cross-contamination and time–temperature abuse.

Homework Activity: The Purpose of Repurposing

Science Connection, Literacy Connection, 21st-Century Skills—Work Independently, Information Literacy, Reason Effectively, Communicate Clearly

Select three raw or cooked foods—a protein, a starch, and a vegetable—that might be left over from an operation's service period. For each, identify appropriate ways that they can be repurposed.

What are some food safety issues that could be involved with these repurposed foods? How can they be avoided?

Write a one-page report discussing your ideas for repurposing the selected foods and the relevant food safety issues.

Discuss

- Besides sales history, what other tools do managers have to help forecast sales volume?

- Why is it important to estimate what sales will be for a given service period? How can this estimate affect an operation's food costs?

Reinforce and Review

- A well-structured food production chart can ensure product quality, avoid product shortages, and minimize waste, spoilage, theft, energy costs, and administrative costs.

- Sales history is critical in helping management forecast how many portions of each menu item to produce on a given day, but it is a prediction, not a guarantee.

Teaching Tips

- Ask a member of the campus foodservice staff to talk with the class about how they determine how many portions of each dish to provide on a given day.

Vocabulary Terms

- **Food production chart:** A form that shows how much product should be produced by the kitchen during a given meal period.

A **food production chart** (see Figure 3.15) is a form that shows how much product should be produced by the kitchen during a given meal period. A well-structured chart can ensure product quality, avoid product shortages, and minimize waste, spoilage, theft, energy costs, and administrative costs.

Figure 3.15: Sample food production chart.

Sales history is critical in helping management forecast how many portions of each menu item to produce on a given day. Management determines what percentage of the total sales each menu item provides. Then management multiplies the percentages by the customer forecast to predict how many portions of each menu item to produce. For example, a restaurant runs these items every Monday on its menu:

- Chicken á la king in a puff-pastry shell
- Roast loin of pork with dressing
- Broiled salmon with lemon butter sauce
- Roast sirloin of beef au jus
- Vegetable lasagna

Figure Focus

Figure 3.15: How can busy operations keep accurate records of what was made and what was sold?

Having run these items for a while, the restaurant has a sales history. From the sales history, management knows that when this menu runs, the following percentages are sold:

- Chicken á la king in a puff-pastry shell   22 percent
- Roast loin of pork with dressing   18 percent
- Broiled salmon with lemon butter sauce   15 percent
- Roast sirloin of beef au jus   35 percent
- Vegetable lasagna   10 percent

Management then predicts how many customers will come in on that Monday. One hundred eighty customers are expected, so the following portions of each item should be produced:

- Chicken á la king in a puff-pastry shell $(180 \times .22) = 40$
- Roast loin of pork with dressing $(180 \times .18) = 32$
- Broiled salmon with lemon butter sauce $(180 \times .15) = 27$
- Roast sirloin of beef au jus $(180 \times .35) = 63$
- Vegetable lasagna $(180 \times .10) = 18$

       Total portions: 180

Of course, these are estimated projections, not exact figures. So an operation would want to make slightly more or less depending on the circumstances at that exact time (for example, weather, construction, time of season, and so on).

Menu Pricing

The menu is the primary sales tool in most restaurant and foodservice operations. Since food costs influence what goes on the menu and how those menu items are priced, operations must be aware of all the factors that affect food costs. The menu would ideally reflect the overall cost of running the operation. That means the price of an item should include all of the costs needed to purchase, prepare, and serve it, along with other costs such as labor, rent, utilities, etc. In short, the success of the operation hinges on proper menu pricing. A manager can use a number of methods in menu pricing:

- Contribution margin method
- Straight markup pricing

Discuss

- If the chicken dish usually represents 22 percent of sales, and 180 guests are expected, how many orders of chicken should the staff prepare to avoid running out of the item? Why? Explain how many orders of each of the other dishes should be prepared as well.

- Explain how and why the menu is an operation's primary sales tool.

Reinforce and Review

- A sales history is generated by tracking sales of a particular item over time.

- The menu is the primary sales tool in most restaurant and foodservice operations and should reflect the overall cost of running the operation.

- The price of an item should include all of the costs associated with purchasing, preparing, and serving the item, as well as costs such as utilities, labor, and rent.

- The success of an operation hinges on proper menu pricing.

Teaching Tips

- Display a number of menus from various restaurants. Encourage students to predict how much each would spend on food, labor, rent, and other costs, based on the information they glean from the menus.

Discuss

- Which of the four methods of pricing a menu seems to be the easiest? Which seems to be most difficult? Which is most likely to yield accurate results? Why?

- How would a manager using the straight markup method decide what fraction to use in determining menu prices? Discuss the various costs an operation incurs and what fractions might be realistic to cover costs without overcharging customers.

Reinforce and Review

- The four methods commonly used to determine menu prices are the contribution margin pricing method, the straight markup pricing method, the average check pricing method, and the food cost percentage pricing method.

- To use the contribution margin method, an operation must know the portion costs for each item sold; this is why using standardized recipes, recipe cost cards, and correct portioning techniques is so important to an operation's finances.

- The food cost percentage is equal to the food cost divided by food sales.

Teaching Tips

- Practice these calculations with students to make sure they understand how each works.

Vocabulary Terms

- **Contribution margin:** The portion of dollars that a particular menu item contributes to overall profits.

- **Contribution margin pricing method:** This pricing method uses the portion costs for each item sold to determine how much money the average customer contributes to overhead and profit; this dollar amount is then added to each menu item.

- **Straight markup pricing method:** This pricing method multiplies raw food cost by a predetermined fraction to determine the dollar amount to be added to each food item.

- **Average check pricing method:** This pricing method divides the operation's total revenue by the number of seats, average seat turnover, and number of days open each year; this yields the average check amount, which is then used with the approximate food cost amount to determine menu prices.

- Average check method
- Food cost percentage method

Contribution Margin Method

A **contribution margin** is the portion of dollars that a particular menu item contributes to overall profits. To use the **contribution margin method** of pricing a menu, an operation must know the portion costs for each item sold. This is why recipe portion cost cards are so important. Then an operation can determine the average contribution margin needed to cover overhead and yield a desired profit at an expected level of sales volume. Let's say 30,000 customers are served in the following example:

$100,000 gross food sale – $40,000 cost of food sold = $60,000 gross profit (total contribution margin)

$60,000 – $50,000 overhead/fixed costs = $10,000 net profit

Each customer spent an average of $3.33 ($100,000 sales / 30,000 customers) and contributed an average of $2.00 (60,000 total contribution margin / 30,000 customers) to overhead and profit. Using the contribution margin method, the operation would then price each menu item at $2.00 above cost.

Straight Markup Method

In the **straight markup pricing method**, multiply raw food costs by a predetermined fraction. For example, if an operation pricing a menu item with a raw food cost of $0.63 uses a straight two-thirds markup, the menu is calculated as follows:

$0.63 × 2/3 = 0.42

0.42 + $0.63 = $1.05

Average Check Method

With the **average check method**, the total revenue is divided by the number of seats, average seat turnover, and days open in one year. The average check gives managers an idea of the price range of items on the menu. Use this range, along with an approximate food cost percentage, to determine each item's selling price.

178

Food Cost Percentage Method

As discussed earlier in the chapter, the food cost percentage is equal to the food cost divided by food sales. If an operation projects monthly food costs to be $18,000 and monthly food sales to be $62,000, the food cost percentage will be 29 percent ($18,000 / $62,000). Based on this figure, an operation can price all food items on the menu. For example, if an item costs $1.12, determine its selling price using this pricing formula:

Item cost ÷ Food cost percentage = Price

$1.12 ÷ 0.29 = 3.86 (which can be used to price the item at $3.86, or rounded up to $4.00)

(*Note:* .29 is the decimal equivalent of 29 percent.)

Summary

In this section, you learned the following:

- Food costs must be controlled during all seven stages of the food flow process, from the actual purchasing of food items to how they are served to customers. The seven stages are purchasing, receiving, storage, issuing, preparation, cooking, and service.

- Food cost is the actual dollar value of the food used by an operation during a certain period. It includes the cost incurred when food is consumed for any reason. Food cost includes the cost of food sold, given away, wasted, spoiled, incorrectly prepped, overportioned, overproduced, or pilfered. Opening and closing inventory data is needed to determine the value of the food cost. Inventory represents the dollar value of a food product in storage and can be expressed in terms of units, values, or both. Opening inventory is the physical inventory at the beginning of a given period (such as the month of April). The closing inventory is the inventory at the end of a given period. The following method is the only accurate way to obtain an actual food cost: (Opening inventory + Purchases = Total food available) – Closing inventory = Total food cost.

- Food cost percentage is the relationship between sales and the cost of food to achieve those sales. Food cost percentage is often the standard against which food cost is judged. Analyze food cost percentage by comparing it to company standards, historical costs, or even industry standards. In most cases, the standard food cost percentage is a target determined by management. By expressing the cost of food sold in percentages, it can be compared on a month-to-month or week-to-week basis regardless of any fluctuation

179

Summary

- Remind students to review the following:
  1. Steps in controlling food costs
  2. Determining food cost
  3. Determining food cost percentage
  4. Establishing standard portion cost
  5. AP (as purchased) and EP (edible portion) costs
  6. Recipe yields
  7. Controlling portion sizes
  8. Monitoring production volume and cost
  9. Menu pricing

Homework Activity: It's Gonna Cost Ya!

Literacy Connection, 21st-Century Skills— Work Independently, Reason Effectively, Communicate Clearly

Sometimes, when criticizing restaurants for perceived overcharges, people say, "I could buy this cheaper somewhere else." To what extent might this be a true statement—for instance, when comparing menus at family-style restaurants and fine-dining restaurants? What factors besides the actual food cost are involved in establishing menu prices?

Write a brief essay assessing this statement, both positively and negatively.

in sales. Controlling the food cost percentage becomes the most important priority if the operation is to be profitable. The food cost percentage formula is as follows: Food cost ÷ Sales = Food cost percentage.

- Most every operation has standardized recipes that are followed every time a menu item is prepared. For every standardized recipe, an operation should establish a standard portion cost, which is the exact amount that one serving, or portion, of a food item should cost when prepared according to the item's standardized recipe. A key control in getting the proper relationship between a menu item's cost and its selling price is through the use of a recipe cost card. A recipe cost card is a tool used to calculate standard portion cost for a menu item. It is a table of ingredient costs for each item in the standardized recipe. If recipe cost cards are not used, the selling price is nothing more than a guess. It is essential that operations understand and use recipe cost cards since they are critical to the accurate figuring of selling prices.

- Two methods used to determine the cost of ingredients in a standardized recipe are the AP method, which means "as purchased," and the EP method, which stands for "edible portion." Use the as-purchased (AP) method to cost an ingredient at the purchase price *before* any trim or waste is being taken into account. In the AP method, list all ingredient quantities on the standardized recipe in the form in which they are purchased. "Ten pounds of onion, diced" is an example of AP, as the recipe is calling for ten pounds of onion, as purchased. In this case, the chef would start with ten pounds of whole onion, then peel and dice it, and add the onion to the recipe. Use the edible-portion (EP) method to cost an ingredient *after* trimming and removing waste so that only the usable portion of the item is reflected. Using the EP method to cost an ingredient, list the quantity on the standardized recipe using only the edible portion of that particular ingredient. For example, "ten pounds of diced onion" involves taking some quantity of onion, and then peeling, dicing, and weighing the results until there are ten pounds of peeled, diced onion.

- A recipe yield is the process of determining the number of portions that a recipe will produce. To determine how many portions a recipe yields, calculate the total volume of the recipe either by weight or by volume, depending on how the portion size is calculated. Weigh or measure only the major ingredients. Remember to take cooking loss into account, especially for meat, vegetables, and fruit.

180

- Controlling portions is very important for a restaurant to meet its standard food cost. Portions can be controlled by weight, volume, or count; for example, an 8-ounce portion of steak, a 1-ounce ladle of dressing, or 12 shrimp. It is important that staff use portion control devices rather than guessing. Without using portioning equipment, staff may be serving portions that are bigger than the menu price has been calculated for, which will result in the operation losing money. In addition to that, inconsistent portioning can lead to inconsistent products. Tools that are essential for accurate portion control include scoops, ladles, serving spoons, serving dishes, ramekins, bowls, cups, and portion scales.

- Every operation should strive to produce quantities as close to the quantity actually needed in order to maintain standard food costs and sales. If the operation produces too much food, leftovers result. Conversely, not producing enough product and running out of an item can disappoint customers and runs the risk that they will not return to the establishment. Either of these situations is a lose-lose for the operation. Produce too much and food cost goes up; produce too little and sales are lost. The answer to this dilemma resides in the food production chart.

- A food production chart is a form that shows how much product should be produced by the kitchen during a given meal period. A well-structured chart can ensure product quality, avoid product shortages, and minimize waste, spoilage, theft, energy costs, and administrative costs.

- The menu is the primary sales tool in most restaurant and foodservice operations. Since food costs influence what goes on the menu and how those menu items are priced, operations must be aware of all the factors that affect food costs. The menu would ideally reflect the overall cost of running the operation. That means the price of an item should include all of the costs needed to purchase, prepare, and serve it, along with other costs such as labor, rent, utilities, and so on. In short, the success of the operation hinges on proper menu pricing. Use a number of methods in menu pricing: contribution margin method, straight markup pricing, average check method, and food cost percentage method.

**Homework Activity:
Charting a Course**

Mathematics Connection, Literacy Connection, 21st-Century Skills—Work Independently, Reason Effectively, Communicate Clearly, Create Media Products

You are the kitchen manager for a 90-seat operation that expects to serve 215 guests during service this evening. The menu has seven entrées, with the percentage each typically contributes to the sales history in parentheses: rockfish (12 percent), salmon (15 percent), venison (19 percent), pork (13 percent), beef (22 percent), duck (9 percent), and rabbit (10 percent). Standard practice is to prepare 10 percent more of each dish than the sales history suggests, to avoid running out of food during service.

Draw up a food production chart, using the example in Figure 3.16 as a template. How many of each entrée should be prepared?

Section 3.2
Review Questions

1. The formula for determining actual food cost is (Opening inventory + Purchases = Total food available) – Closing inventory = Total food cost.

2. Determining food cost percentage is important because it is often the standard against which food cost is judged. Controlling the food cost percentage is the most important priority for an operation to be profitable.

3. Controlling portion sizes is important for an operation to meet its standard food cost and to ensure product consistency.

4. $0.50 \times \frac{2}{3}$ = $0.33; $0.33 + $0.50 = $0.83.

5. Efficient purchasing involves identifying suppliers with an appropriate quality and consistency of product at the most appropriate price (for instance, if high-quality customer service is important to a manager, he or she might choose to pay slightly higher prices). Purchasing from these companies helps ensure consistency and maintain costs.

6. Students will need to research these dishes to determine the ingredients used to make them, as well as the typical costs for each ingredient. The format should follow the example given in Figure 3.11.

7. Using a standard portion size ensures that a restaurant's actual practices accurately reflect the standardized recipes and recipe cost cards used to predict food cost and food cost percentages. If an operation serves portions that are too large or too small, then the food cost will increase or decrease accordingly; consistency will suffer, as could patronage.

8. Student answers will vary but should be well defended.

Section 3.2 Review Questions

1. What is the formula for determining actual food cost?
2. Why is determining food cost percentage important?
3. Why is it important to control portion sizes?
4. Use the straight markup method to determine the price of a menu item with a raw food cost of $0.50 at a two-thirds markup.
5. Sherie Valderrama noted that the supply management department focuses on efficient purchasing, which has a major impact on their ability to contain costs, yet maintain the high quality of their products. Why is this true?
6. Chef Kate and Miguel never sat down and made up recipe cards for their new brunch menu. Write up a recipe card for one of the following three dishes to get them started: eggs Benedict; omelet with spinach, feta, and tomato; or Belgian waffle with fresh blueberries.
7. How does using a standard portion size affect a restaurant's costs and profits? What if an operation does not use a standard size?
8. Look at the four methods of menu pricing and determine which you think would be the most effective. Which would you use if you were managing an operation? Why? Explain your rationale in two paragraphs.

182

Section 3.2 Activities

1. Study Skills/Group Activity: Cost-Control Poster

Working in small groups, create a poster showing the various steps in the food flow process at which you can control food costs in your restaurant. Include two or three methods for controlling costs at each step.

2. Independent Activity: A Tale of Two Recipes

Find a recipe online and write it two ways: edible-portion and as-purchased. When do you think it would be better to use each version?

3. Critical Thinking: Converting Recipes

Select a recipe from this book. Using a conversion factor of 2.3, convert the recipe to the new yield.

183

Section 3.2 Activities

1. Students should include all steps of the food flow process in their posters and clearly identify cost-controlling measures at each.

2. Students should clearly identify the pros and cons of using either the EP or the AP methods of recipe writing. They should demonstrate understanding of the different writing styles required by each method, using the examples on p. 171 for assistance. Also, they should attach a copy of the recipe to their work before submission.

3. Students can use any recipe in the text so long as their mathematic operations are correct.

Section 3.3
Controlling Labor Costs

Introduce the Section

a. Describe the concept of labor cost and the various factors affecting it.
b. Consider the role of scheduling in determining labor cost, relating this material to the content in Level 1, Chapter 8.
c. Discuss the objectives for the section.

Vocabulary Review

a. Direct students to the key terms.
b. Pronounce each word, and have the students repeat the pronunciation out loud.
c. Discuss the definition of each word.

Teach

Discuss

- In what ways can inappropriate employee behavior cost the employer money?

- How can employees be part of a successful operation without sacrificing their personal and professional goals and needs?

- How can controlling labor costs be compatible with a positive work environment, as discussed in Level 1, Chapter 8?

Reinforce and Review

- Employees need guidance and training to make significant contributions to the operation; any deviation from established policies can cost the employer.

- Businesses must be vigilant in establishing goals, keeping lines of communication open, and being flexible to the needs of staff members.

- Foodservice managers typically have less control over their labor cost and their employees than over other aspects of the business.

Teaching Tips

- Relate this material to the content in Level 1, Chapter 8.

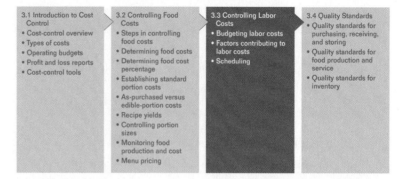

3.1 Introduction to Cost Control	3.2 Controlling Food Costs	3.3 Controlling Labor Costs	3.4 Quality Standards
• Cost-control overview • Types of costs • Operating budgets • Profit and loss reports • Cost-control tools	• Steps in controlling food costs • Determining food costs • Determining food cost percentage • Establishing standard portion costs • As-purchased versus edible-portion costs • Recipe yields • Controlling portion sizes • Monitoring food production and cost • Menu pricing	• Budgeting labor costs • Factors contributing to labor costs • Scheduling	• Quality standards for purchasing, receiving, and storing • Quality standards for food production and service • Quality standards for inventory

SECTION 3.3 CONTROLLING LABOR COSTS

A foodservice manager can know a location or an area for an operation really well. They can also know food really well. And if he or she has expert knowledge in both of these foodservice costs, they're off to a great start. But in some ways that's the easy part because there aren't an endless number of variables to account for. For example, T-bone steaks don't call in sick, one broccoli floret can't decide to be less productive than another broccoli floret, and locations don't suddenly and unexpectedly move away without notice. When it comes to location and food products, the foodservice manager has a certain amount of control. The same consistency can't necessarily be said for the staff.

People and their productivity levels can vary greatly with regard to experience, motivations, personalities, and overall work ethics. People need guidance and training, both in general foodservice skills and the particular rules and procedures of a specific operation. Any deviation from established skill sets or operation specifications can cost the business money, which is why controlling labor costs can be so difficult, but also so important. It's not as easy to quantify how much an operation is getting for its money, so it needs to be vigilant in establishing goals, keeping lines of communication open, and being flexible to the needs of its staff. These aspects of controlling labor costs are covered in this section.

184

Study Questions

After studying Section 3.3, you should be able to answer the following questions:

- How do labor costs affect cost control?
- What factors affect labor costs?
- How is effective scheduling achieved?

Budgeting Labor Costs

As discussed earlier in the chapter, labor is a semivariable, controllable cost. Labor costs are tied to sales, but not directly. Most operations have full-time staff, such as a manager and chef, and also part-time staff, such as servers, greeters, and sometimes line cooks (see Figure 3.16). Full-time employees are often salaried, so they will work and be paid regardless of how busy the operation is on a daily or weekly basis. But part-time employees are staffed according to sales volume, or how busy or slow an operation is at a given time or during a particular season.

Operations must be aware of the fluctuations in their sales so as to have just the right amount of staff on hand to handle customers efficiently. Having too few staff results in poor quality product and service. Having too many staff results in money wasted. Additionally, inefficient and/or inconsistent staffing on the part of management will likely lead to disgruntled employees, which could then result in even more cost-control problems, such as increased employee turnover.

For an operation to achieve its budgeted profit, the sales projections listed in its budget must be met. Additionally, the operation's costs must be held to its standards,

Figure 3.16: Restaurant and foodservice operation staff.

185

Discuss

- It's often said that people are the most important resources a company has. In what ways do students agree and disagree with this statement? Why?

- How can managers staff appropriately while maintaining a harmonious workplace, even when times are hard and sales are down?

Reinforce and Review

- Labor is a semivariable, controllable cost. Labor costs are tied to sales, but not directly.

- Operations are staffed based on their needs. They must have enough staff working to meet customer needs in an efficient and appropriate manner, but having unnecessary staff members working is inefficient.

- Inefficient and inconsistent staffing impedes staff morale. Staff members are likely to feel mistreated and are more likely to engage in behaviors like turnover and poor performance.

- For an operation to achieve the profit it expects, it must meet its sales projections and control costs.

Teaching Tips

- Encourage students to share their experiences with scheduling, either at work or at school. What happens when people don't get the schedules they desire? How can that affect their relationship with employers and coworkers or teachers and students?

- Make sure students understand that managers are not being malicious when they cut employee hours or change shifts; in virtually all cases, they are trying to save the company money to help it remain profitable during a slow period.

Figure Focus

Figure 3.16: What can you infer about the workplace from this photograph?

Homework Activity:
Hard Times, Hard Talks

Literacy Connection, 21st-Century Skills—Work Independently, Think Creatively, Reason Effectively, Communicate Clearly

You manage a local restaurant that is undergoing tough times. Although your operation has consistently provided excellent service and food, the city has a high unemployment rate, so sales volume has slowed dramatically. To avoid laying employees off, you have decided to reduce everyone's hours so as to share the burden as evenly as possible.

You need to explain to your staff why you will have to reduce their working hours, due to the low volume. What is the best way of doing this so that staff morale suffers as little as possible and service quality remains high? Create an action plan for talking with your employees about the upcoming changes.

Consider referring to the material In Level 1, Chapters 7 and 8 for assistance.

Discuss

- How do managers determine the ideal labor cost for a new operation? What factors might they use in their predictions?

- What are some ways that managers can work with employees to reduce labor costs without creating a negative work environment?

Reinforce and Review

- An operation's standards are the budgeted dollar amount of percentage for each type of cost incurred.

- When labor cost falls below the standard, quality of food or service might suffer; when labor cost exceeds the standard, the profit might suffer.

- Actual labor cost is rarely the same as ideal labor cost. Ideal labor cost is what management predicts, whereas actual labor cost is the true cost of the workforce.

Homework Activity: Standards and Practices

Literacy Connection, 21st-Century Skills—Work Independently, Reason Effectively, Communicate Clearly

Some restaurateurs claim that the secret to a successful operation is to have 30 percent food cost, 30 percent labor cost, 30 percent operational and administrative costs, and a 10 percent profit. Do you think that these standards are achievable and/or desirable for all operations? Why or why not?

Write a brief report, defending your position.

which is the budgeted dollar amount or percentage for each type of cost. It is an important part of the management function to make sure that payroll cost is in line with the budgeted standard. If the cost goes below the standard, the quality of food or service could suffer, resulting in lost sales. If the cost is above the standard, the profit suffers. In short, an operation must know all of the factors that contribute to labor costs as well as how to create effective schedules for all employees.

In Figure 3.17, the blue line represents the restaurant's ideal labor cost. Of course, the restaurant can rarely stick to that exact ideal on any given day: more or fewer customers arrive than are expected, a new employee may be less skilled and therefore slower than the long-term employee he or she has replaced, employees call in sick, and so forth. So, usually a restaurant will spend either a little above or a little below the line—as represented by the red line.

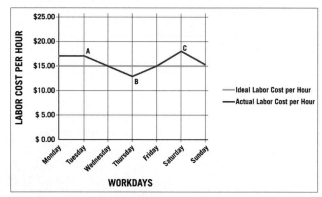

Figure 3.17: The X-axis represents hours worked and the Y-axis represents wages paid.

If the restaurant spends too much on labor—in other words, if it is spending money above the blue line—then it is losing profit by paying more staff than are needed to perform the necessary work. If the restaurant spends too little on labor—if it is spending money below the blue line—then the quality of the employees' work will deteriorate because there are too few staff members to perform the necessary work.

The ideal labor cost is the standard the restaurant uses to budget for staffing needs; it represents what the restaurant management predicts will happen. The actual labor cost varies above or below the ideal cost from day to day, since the management's prediction cannot be 100 percent accurate.

186

Figure Focus

Figure 3.17: Can students envision a situation in which actual labor cost matches ideal labor cost for a period of time? What elements would be involved?

Factors Contributing to Labor Costs

Many factors go into the labor costs. All of the following affect labor costs:

- Business volume
- Employee turnover
- Quality standards
- Operational standards

Business volume, or the amount of sales an operation is doing for a given time period, impacts labor costs. When business volume increases, the fixed elements (salaried employees such as managers) of labor cost decrease by a percentage (see Figure 3.18). The variable elements of labor cost go up and down in direct relation to sales volume. An increase in sales means more hours needed; a decrease in sales means fewer hours. Staffing needs to correspond to the given need of the operation for it to function efficiently and cost effectively.

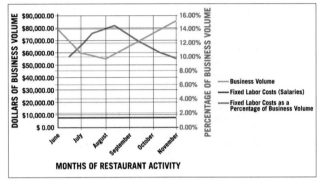

Figure 3.18: As business volume increases, fixed labor cost decreases as a percentage of business volume because salaried employees are paid the same regardless of how many hours they may work.

Labor cost has both fixed and variable components. As business volume increases, fixed labor costs *decrease* as a percentage of business volume because employees who are on salary can be required to work more hours for the same pay. But variable costs as a percentage of business volume may increase or decrease. If employees who are paid hourly work more hours to deal with increased business volume, then variable labor costs will *increase* as a percentage of business volume. But what if management wants to take greater advantage of the increased business volume? They might choose to keep the same

Discuss

- Why might a business owner expect more hours of work from salaried staff than from hourly staff? In what ways can this be a positive or a negative development?

- Besides working fewer hours, how are hourly employees affected by business slowdowns? How do rapid increases in business affect hourly employees?

Reinforce and Review

- Four main factors that contribute to labor cost are business volume, employee turnover, quality standards, and operational standards.

- The variable elements of labor cost generally increase and decrease in direct relation to sales volume.

- The fixed elements of labor cost vary as a percentage of business volume: Generally, when sales increase, fixed labor costs as a percentage of sales decrease.

- Staffing must correspond to the operation's needs to be efficient and cost-effective.

Teaching Tips

- These concepts can be difficult for students to understand, so consider spending additional time on this section until students are confident.

Vocabulary Terms

- **Business volume:** The amount of sales an operation is doing for a given time period.

CUSTOMIZED INSTRUCTION
Literacy Connection, 21st-Century Skills— Work Independently, Make Judgments and Decisions, Reason Effectively, Communicate Clearly
Less Advanced Students
Which restaurant jobs are typically salaried positions, and which are typically hourly? Why might this be the case?

Figure Focus

Figure 3.18: Fixed labor costs, like salaries, do not change when business volume changes.

Discuss

- Consider the discussion of employee hiring and training in Level 1, Chapter 8. What expenses are involved with employee turnover that can increase labor costs? Are these expenses "lost," or are they investments in a successful business model?

- How might the labor costs of a quick-service restaurant be similar to and different from those of a full-service, fine-dining restaurant?

Reinforce and Review

- Typically, the higher an operation's turnover rate, the higher its labor costs.

- The type of operation and its menu determine the number and skill level of its employees.

- New staff members require time and training before they can meet the employer's quality standards.

amount of hourly labor as before and rely on salaried employees to take more shifts. This will decrease the amount of *total* labor costs (fixed and variable).

The period just before Valentine's Day at Julio's Bistro can be a useful illustration. Julio knows that business volume will increase significantly as guests celebrate the holiday. He also knows that his salaried staff can be asked to work more hours during that time. In this case, Julio's fixed labor costs decrease as a percentage of business volume. The more sales Julio makes, the less his salaried employees cost him. In Figure 3.18 on the previous page, the X-axis represents business volume and the Y-axis represents months of restaurant activity. See the green line that represents fixed labor costs as a percentage of business volume.

Julio has two options regarding his hourly employees. He can increase their hours (and therefore their paychecks) to cope with the increased business volume; or he can keep their hours (and therefore their paychecks) the same, and rely on his salaried employees to handle the increased business volume. In the first scenario, these variable labor costs will increase as a percentage of business volume. In the second scenario, these variable labor costs will decrease as a percentage of business volume. In Figure 3.19, the X-axis represents business volume and the Y-axis represents variable labor costs.

Figure 3.19: If hourly employees work more to meet the demands of increased business volume, then variable labor costs may increase as a percentage of business volume. If hourly workers work the "normal" amount of hours, or fewer hours, despite increased business volume, then variable labor cost will decrease as a percentage of business volume.

Homework Activity: Turnover Tactics

Literacy Connection, 21st-Century Skills— Work Independently, Think Creatively, Reason Effectively, Communicate Clearly

As discussed in Level 1, Chapter 8, turnover can be very expensive to an operation. Hiring and effectively training new employees is often costly. What can an operation do to keep its best employees, maintaining a loyal, enthusiastic, and well-trained staff?

Write an essay on how you would maintain a positive work establishment in your operation, keeping a high-quality staff.

Figure Focus

Figure 3.19: How can variable labor costs affect a business's profit margin?

Employee turnover is the number of employees hired to fill one position in a year's time. It directly impacts labor cost. Typically, the higher the turnover rate of a given operation, the higher the labor costs. This results primarily from the training costs involved in bringing on new staff. For example, an operation's current employees are often responsible for teaching and tutoring new trainees; at the same time, the new trainee is getting paid for very little or no productivity while learning the ins and outs of the operation. Every time an operation hires someone, labor costs go up because it takes a new employee a period of time to achieve the productivity level of an experienced employee.

Quality standards also affect labor cost. As discussed in *Chapter 5,* quality standards are the specifications of the operation with regard to products and service. The type of operation and the type of menu it has determine the number of staff and the skill level required of that staff to meet the operation's needs. For example, a fine-dining operation might have higher menu prices and higher service specifications than a quick-service restaurant. Employee skill levels will then need to be higher, which will require more training, more experience, and, consequently, higher labor costs.

Regardless of the operation's quality standards for service, it also must meet **operational standards**. If an employee does not prepare a product that meets the operation's standards, the item must be redone. This costs money, not only in terms of wasted product that increases food cost, but also in terms of productivity that increases labor cost. If a line cook at a fine-dining steakhouse, for example, overcooks one steak priced at $30.00 on the menu, all of that potential revenue is wasted. Likewise, if a quick-service line cook overcooks an entire batch of fries, that would yield 10 servings at $3.00 a serving, $30.00 in potential revenue is lost. The quality standards for these establishments are likely different, but the operational standards for each were not met, resulting in lost revenue and, ultimately, increased labor costs to compensate for mistakes made.

[fast fact]

Did You Know...?
The restaurant industry employs approximately 13 million people nationwide in the United States. It is the nation's biggest employer outside of the government. By 2019, the restaurant industry is expected to add another 1.8 million jobs.

189

Discuss

- In what ways are employees who continually fail to meet operational standards expensive? How can such situations be resolved?

- How do operational standards help to define a restaurant's image?

Reinforce and Review

- When an operation's requirements for employee skill levels increase, its costs also increase.

- When an employee performs a task that does not meet operational standards, the task must be redone, costing the operation in wasted labor, wasted product, and wasted potential revenue.

Teaching Tips

- Review the differences between quality standards and operational standards to ensure students clearly understand these concepts.

Fast Facts: Did You Know . . . ?

Encourage students to discuss the following:

- How might adding so many jobs to a single industry within a relatively short span of time affect the U.S. economy as a whole?

- What factors have combined to make the restaurant and foodservice industry the nation's largest employer?

- Does the restaurant and foodservice industry's status as the largest private employer give it any particular influence or opportunities? What might be some examples?

CUSTOMIZED INSTRUCTION

Literacy Connection, 21st-Century Skills— Think Creatively, Reason Effectively, Communicate Clearly

Special Needs Students

The restaurant and foodservice industry is projected to add millions of jobs during this decade. What types of jobs do you think will be most in demand? Why? Which jobs do you find appealing?

Vocabulary Terms

- **Employee turnover:** The number of employees hired to fill one position in a year's time.

- **Quality standards:** The specifications of the operation with regard to products and services.

- **Operational standards:** Specifications of an operation with regard to products. If an item must be redone to meet standards, this costs money, not only in terms of wasted product that increases food cost, but also in terms of productivity that increases labor cost.

Discuss

- What are some factors that could radically change an operation's projection of its future sales? What effects would these have on staffing levels and labor costs?

- How can a properly constructed master schedule help to control labor costs and contribute to a positive work environment?

Reinforce and Review

- Scheduling depends both on how much revenue an operation is bringing in and how much revenue the same operation is expected to bring in.

- An operation should consider both historical data and current trends when predicting sales.

- Generally, as projected sales increase, the number of employees will increase, and vice versa.

Teaching Tips

- Compare an operation's master schedule to the school's schedule in terms of what classes are available at what times, in what classrooms, and for how many students having completed what prerequisites.

- Consider inviting a restaurant or foodservice manager to discuss the role of scheduling with the class.

Vocabulary Terms

- **Master schedule:** A template showing the number of people needed in each position to run the restaurant or foodservice operation for a given time period.

Scheduling

Scheduling depends greatly on how much revenue an operation is bringing in and how much revenue an operation is *expected* to bring in. Such sales projections are an estimate of future sales based largely on historical sales records. The historical sales records are used as a baseline. This baseline is either increased or decreased based on current, local, and national trends.

As projected sales increase, the number of employees will increase, and as projected sales decrease, the number of employees will decrease. Therefore, a **master schedule** is based on a norm (see Figure 3.20). It is a template, usually a spreadsheet, showing the number of people needed in each position to run the restaurant or foodservice operation for a given time period. List no names on the master schedule, simply the positions and the number of employees in those positions. Create it with the idea that a certain sales level will likely be reached. As sales change from that norm, either up or down, adjust the master schedule accordingly.

Job Title	Monday HRS	# Hours	Tuesday HRS	# Hours	Wednesday HRS	# Hours	Thursday HRS	# Hours	Friday HRS	# Hours	Saturday HRS	# Hours	Sunday HRS	# Hours
Server	9-5	8	9-5	8	9-5	8	9-5	8	9-5	8	9-5	8	9-5	8
Server	9-3	6	9-3	6	9-3	6	9-3	6	9-3	6			9-3	6
Server	10-3	5	10-3	5	10-3	5	10-3	5			10-3	5		
Server	10-3	5			10-3	5							10-3	5
Server	10-3	5	10-3	5			10-3	5	10-3	5	10-3	5	10-3	5
Server			11-8	9			11-8	9	11-8	9	11-8	9	11-8	9
Server	4-10	6	4-10	8	4-10	6	4-10	6	4-10	6	4-10	6	4-10	6
Server	4-11	7			4-11	7			4-11	7	4-11	7	4-11	7
Server			5-11	6			5-11	6	5-11	6	5-11	6		
Grill	8-4	8	8-4	8	8-4	8	8-4	8	8-4	8	8-4	8	8-4	8
Grill	4-11	7	4-11	7	4-11	7	4-11	7	4-11	7	4-11	7	4-11	7
Grill	12-8	8	12-8	8	12-8	8	12-8	8	12-8	8	12-8	8	12-8	8
Fry	9-3	6	9-3	6	9-3	6	9-3	6	9-3	6	9-3	6	9-3	6
Fry	3-11	8	3-11	8	3-11	8	3-11	8	3-11	8	3-11	8	3-11	8
Dishes	8-4	8	8-4	8	8-4	8	8-4	8	8-4	8	8-4	8	8-4	8
Dishes	4-11	7	4-11	7	4-11	7	4-11	7	4-11	7	4-11	7	4-11	7
TOTALS	Mon	94	Tues	99	Wed	95	Thur	102	Fri	99	Sat	104	Sun	98

Figure 3.20: A sample master schedule.

For example, if a new office park is slated to open across the street from a restaurant, project lunch sales to show an increase over the previous year. Conversely, if a manufacturing plant in town is expected to shut down, lower the projections, as some residents will have little or no income to spend on eating out.

An operation needs to examine more than just the previous year's sales information when calculating future sales projections. To make the best estimates for a reasonable master schedule, it also needs to consider current trends. Although

190

Figure Focus

Figure 3.20: Based on the number of employees needed, their work schedules, and their job titles, how would students characterize this restaurant?

local trends are more important than national ones, the latter should not be overlooked. The economy, unemployment, and other national and international events all affect a person's desire or ability to eat out. For example, in 2008-09, the national financial crisis impacted restaurant and foodservice operations across the country. If an operation failed to account for this national economic downturn, perhaps by cutting back on hourly staff, it likely suffered more financially throughout this period.

After determining the anticipated sales, management must determine the payroll dollars, which are the number of dollars available for payroll for a scheduling period. After the dollars available for labor scheduling are known, management can begin to create a crew schedule. A **crew schedule** is a chart that shows employees' names and the days and times they are to work. Figure 3.21 is a sample crew schedule. Create the crew schedule by using the master schedule as a template. Develop it with flexibility in mind. Employees are unhappy when their schedule conflicts with important events in their personal lives. It will often seem to the employees as if their needs and concerns are being disregarded by management. Likewise, managers become unhappy when an employee cannot, or will not, work a shift when he or she is desperately needed. Most of these types of situations can be avoided by having clear policies, making the schedule far enough ahead so that your employees can plan, and maintaining open, two-way communication in the scheduling process.

Crew Schedule

S = Server   G = Grill   F = Fry   D = Dishes

Week of 10/2/10

Saturday	8 a.m.	9	10	11	12	1	2	3	4	5	6	7	8	9	10	11
Michele		S	S	S	S	S	S	S	S	S						
Ron		S	S	S	S	S	S	S								
Alisa			S	S	S	S	S	S								
Marcia			S	S	S	S	S	S								
Randy			S	S	S	S	S									
Maxwell				S	S	S	S		S	S						
Claire									S	S	S	S	S	S	S	
Manuella									S	S	S	S	S	S	S	S
Hunter										S	S	S	S	S	S	S
Jacob	G	G	G	G	G	G	G	G	G							
Isabella										G	G	G	G	G	G	G
Ethan					G	G	G	G	G	G	G	G				
David	F	F	F	F	F	F	F	F								
Meghan								F	F	F	F	F	F	F	F	F
Zachary	D	D	D	D	D	D	D	D	D							
Hannah									D	D	D	D	D	D	D	D

Figure 3.21: A sample crew schedule.

191

Figure Focus

Figure 3.21: Based on this crew schedule, when do you think this restaurant is busiest?

- How can restaurant and foodservice operations maintain or increase sales during periods of local, national, or international uncertainty? How can these uncertainties affect employees?

- Managers and staff are all part of the same team, but sometimes conflicts can arise, making it seem that each "side" has its own interests. How can everyone work together to overcome these conflicts?

Reinforce and Review

- The economy, unemployment, and other national and international trends all affect a person's ability or desire to dine out, which can cause restaurant and foodservice operations to suffer.

- A crew schedule should be developed with the master schedule in mind but should also account for individual employee needs to the extent possible.

- Scheduling conflicts can often be avoided or mitigated by having clear policies, making schedules far in advance, and maintaining open communication between management and staff.

- Contingency plans help operations remain efficient and productive even during adverse conditions.

Teaching Tips

- Review Level 1, Chapter 8 with students and discuss appropriate resolution of workplace conflicts.

CUSTOMIZED INSTRUCTION

Literacy Connection, 21st-Century Skills—Work Independently, Think Creatively, Reason Effectively, Communicate Clearly

More Advanced Students

Can managers create crew schedules that meet operational needs while also meeting staff needs, or are the two incompatible?

Write a one-page report, defending one of these two positions.

Vocabulary Terms

- **Crew schedule:** A chart that shows employees' names and the days and times they are to work.

Discuss

- What are some examples of situations that might require contingency plans?

- Why would an experienced, qualified individual choose to work as an on-call employee for Restaurant A as opposed to working full-time for Restaurant B?

- Do properly staffed workplaces always result in "happy crews and contented management"? What other factors might play a role?

Reinforce and Review

- A good contingency plan should include cross-training employees, identifying shift leaders, and having on-call employees.

- Properly staffed operations generally result in lower labor costs and increased productivity.

Teaching Tips

- Refer students to Level 1, Chapter 3 for more information on contingency plans in the workplace.

Homework Activity: Pros and Cons

Literacy Connection, 21st-Century Skills—Work Independently, Think Creatively, Reason Effectively, Communicate Clearly

During periods in which business volume is slow, managers are often faced with a difficult decision: Should they lay off employees, which will cause a few to suffer but keep the rest fully employed; or should they simply reduce everyone's hours, so everyone suffers a little but everyone keeps his or her job?

As an employee, which situation would you rather face, and why? Consider all the potential ramifications of either path. For instance, would you rather be laid off so you can have the free time to look for another job, or would you rather work fewer hours at your original job?

Write an essay stating and defending your position.

Of course, things don't always go according to plan, so develop a contingency plan. Such a plan helps the operation remain efficient and productive even during adverse conditions, such as power outages, weather issues, employee absences, and so on. A good contingency plan should include the following:

- **Cross-training employees:** These employees can handle responsibilities in sections of the operation aside from their primary work responsibilities.

- **Identifying shift leaders:** Train new hires and take the lead when plans need to change on the fly during the course of a work shift.

- **Having on-call employees:** A certain number of employees must call their operation at a predetermined time to find out whether they have to work that day; this way an operation will have staff ready and available should a particular work shift require more hands, regardless of the reason why (see Figure 3.22).

Figure 3.22: A manager using an on-call list.

Having all of these provisions in place will lead to properly staffed operations with happy crews and contented management. Such conditions will invariably produce lower labor costs overall, as turnover, negligence, and pilfering will be down, while productivity will be up—the ideal cost-controlling scenario.

Essential Skills
How to Develop a Contingency Plan

Contingency plans give both managers and employees peace of mind by providing roadmaps to resolve any unusual situation. These plans are especially valuable in case of emergency, such as a fire or an outbreak of foodborne illness, which requires working with outside agencies. The following components should all be involved:

- Make a telephone tree. These make it easier to contact all staff, including on-call employees, in a short period of time. See Figure 3.23.

  Note: Depending on the establishment, you might use a mass voice-mail, email, or text message that reaches everyone simultaneously.

192

Figure Focus

Figure 3.22: How can an operation develop and maintain a list of on-call employees who are both qualified and available on short notice?

- Cross-train employees. Every recipe, technique, or task used in the establishment should be practiced and understood by at least three employees.

- Create and test an emergency plan. See *Foundations of Restaurant Management & Culinary Arts, Level One, Chapter 3, Workplace Safety.*

- Identify and train leaders. Do this among different shifts or kitchens.

- Develop an employee handbook. This will codify emergency and contingency plans.

- Communicate with staff. Be sure everyone understands what he or she should do in case problems arise.

Figure 3.23: Sample telephone tree.

[on the job]

Scheduling Staff and Calling "Audibles"

Managers who make up the crew schedule are sometimes like quarterbacks in football: they may have to change plans and call an "audible" at the last minute to adapt to new situations. Both employees and employers need some flexibility in scheduling. We're all human, and personal and working lives can change quickly. Accordingly, many restaurant and foodservice establishments have carefully developed staffing policies to help prepare for unexpected situations, such as staff illnesses and lower-than-anticipated business. One common component is the audible, the ability either to call staff members in to work or to cancel their shifts without much notice in order to meet changing needs. Often, front-of-the-house members will be on call for certain shifts, usually days on which little business is expected. This flexibility allows restaurants and managers to control their labor costs without sacrificing customer service.

193

Figure Focus

Figure 3.23: How can telephone trees be effective means of communication? What are the potential flaws?

Summary

- Remind students to review the following:
  1. Budgeting labor costs
  2. Scheduling

Summary

In this section, you learned the following:

- Operations must be aware of the fluctuations in their sales so as to have just the right amount of staff on hand to handle customers efficiently. Having too few staff results in poor-quality product and service. Having too many staff results in money wasted. Inefficient and/or inconsistent staffing on the part of management will likely lead to disgruntled employees. This could then result in even more cost-control problems such as increased employee turnover.

- For an operation to achieve its budgeted profit, the sales projections listed in its budget must be met. Additionally, the operation's costs must be held to its standards, which is the budgeted dollar amount or percentage for each type of cost. It is an important part of the management function to make sure that payroll cost is in line with the budgeted standard. If the cost goes below the standard, the quality of food or service could suffer, resulting in lost sales. If the cost is above the standard, the profit will suffer.

- Four primary factors affect labor costs:

  - Business volume, or the amount of sales an operation is doing for a given time period, impacts labor costs. The variable elements of labor cost go up and down in direct relation to sales volume (increase in sales means more hours needed; a decrease in sales needs fewer hours).

  - Employee turnover is the number of employees hired to fill one position in a year's time. It directly impacts labor costs. Typically, the higher the turnover rate of a given operation, the higher the labor costs. This results primarily from the training costs involved in bringing on new staff.

  - Quality standards also affect labor costs. Quality standards are the specifications of the operation with regard to products and service. The type of operation and the type of menu it has determines the number of staff and the skill level required of that staff to meet the operation's needs.

  - Operational standards also need to be met. If an employee does not prepare a product that meets the operation's standards, the employee must redo that item. This costs money, not only in terms of wasted product that increases food cost, but also in terms of productivity and increasing labor cost.

194

■ Scheduling depends greatly on how much revenue an operation is bringing in and how much revenue an operation *expects* to bring in. Such sales projections are an estimate of future sales based largely on historical sales records. The historical sales records are used as a baseline. This baseline is either increased or decreased based on current, local, and national trends. As projected sales increase, the number of employees will increase; and as projected sales decrease, the number of employees will decrease. Therefore, a master schedule is based on a norm. It is a template, usually a spreadsheet, showing the number of people needed in each position to run the restaurant or foodservice operation for a given time period. List no names on the master schedule, simply the positions and the number of employees in those positions. It is created with the idea that a certain sales level will likely be reached. After determining the anticipated sales, management must determine the payroll dollars, which are the number of dollars available for payroll for a scheduling period. After the dollars available for labor scheduling are known, management can begin to create a crew schedule. A crew schedule is a chart that shows employees' names and the days and times they are to work. The crew schedule is created by using the master schedule as a template. Develop it with flexibility in mind.

195

Section 3.3
Review Questions

1. If payroll costs fall below the budgeted standard, the quality of food or service could suffer, resulting in lost sales. If payroll costs exceed the standard, the profit suffers.

2. The four factors that influence labor cost are business volume, employee turnover, quality standards, and operational standards.

3. A master schedule represents the ideal staffing situation and is used as a template; the crew schedule is based on the master schedule and represents the actual labor schedule for a period of time.

4. Strategies that can be included in a contingency plan include making a telephone tree, cross-training employees, creating and testing an emergency plan, identifying and training leaders among different shifts or kitchens, developing an employee handbook to codify emergency and contingency plans, and communicating with staff to ensure everyone understands his or her role when problems arise.

5. Having the right talent at the right levels means that employees have the appropriate skills for their positions and that the appropriate number of them are working at any given time, thereby helping to control labor costs.

6. Students can answer in a variety of ways, as long as they present clear and relevant ideas for controlling labor costs.

7. Students can respond with any of the four major factors affecting labor costs, as long as they defend their answer appropriately.

8. Students should explain the advantages and disadvantages of cross-training; answers may vary when discussing why they might or might not cross-train their own employees.

Section 3.3 Review Questions

1. What could happen if the payroll cost falls out of line with the budgeted standard?

2. List the four factors that influence labor costs.

3. How does a master schedule differ from a crew schedule?

4. What are two strategies that can be included in a contingency plan?

5. Sherie Valderrama noted that Sodexo's staffing model ensures that it has the right talent at the right levels within each unit. Why is this critical to the success of an operation?

6. Part of the problem that Chef Kate and Miguel discovered is that they are often overstaffed, and so while the service is good, their labor costs are very high. Present them with options as to how to go about controlling their labor costs. Write a one-page proposal of your ideas.

7. What factor affecting labor costs do you think is the most important to control? Why? Explain your answer in a two-paragraph report.

8. Why is cross-training important? Are there any disadvantages to it? Would you use it in your operation? Explain your rationale.

196

Section 3.3 Activities

1. Study Skills/Group Activity: Creating a Crew Schedule

Working with two or three other students, create a one-week crew schedule for a restaurant open six days a week for lunch and dinner that employs eight full-time cooks, four part-time cooks, two full-time dishwashers, and two part-time dishwashers. Assume all the cooks are equally skilled and that the restaurant's service periods are 11:30 a.m. to 2:00 p.m. for lunch, and 5:30 p.m. to 9:00 p.m. for dinner.

2. Independent Activity: Employee Policies and Cost Control

Research the employee policies of two different restaurant or foodservice operations. What do they offer employees in terms of scheduling, benefits, and pay? Write a paragraph for summarizing each of the two employee policies, and then, in an additional paragraph, explain which one you think is better in terms of controlling labor costs and why.

3. Critical Thinking: Turning Around Turnover

Your restaurant suffers from a high turnover rate, which is increasing your labor costs and bringing down productivity. As the manager, you need to solve this problem. Put together a one-page plan that will address the turnover issue. What steps can you take to reduce turnover in your restaurant or foodservice establishment?

197

Section 3.3 Activities

1. Students can use the sample crew schedule on p. 191 or any other format they find appropriate, so long as they schedule staff to meet the restaurant's needs.

2. Students should research two different restaurant or foodservice operations and accurately summarize their employee policies. Their rationales for supporting one over the other may vary as long as they adequately defend their positions.

3. Students can answer in a variety of ways so long as they effectively explain the effect of turnover on labor cost and how it can be controlled.

Section 3.4 Controlling Quality Standards

Introduce the Section

a. Explain the importance of establishing and meeting quality standards throughout the food flow process.

b. Introduce the basic principles of appropriate purchasing, to be discussed more fully in Chapter 5.

c. Discuss the objectives for the section.

Vocabulary Review

a. Direct students to the key terms.

b. Pronounce each word, and have the students repeat the pronunciation out loud.

c. Discuss the definition of each word.

Teach

Discuss

- In what part of the food flow process is controlling costs the most important? In what part is it easiest?

- How is controlling food costs similar to controlling labor costs? What are the significant differences?

Reinforce and Review

- To control costs throughout the food flow process, appropriate quality standards must be developed and maintained.

- An operation's demand for high-quality standards is the surest way to reduce costs across all facets of foodservice delivery.

Teaching Tips

- Review Level 1, Chapter 2 with students to refresh understanding of the food flow process.

3.1 Introduction to Cost Control	3.2 Controlling Food Costs	3.3 Controlling Labor Costs	3.4 Quality Standards
• Cost-control overview	• Steps in controlling food costs	• Budgeting labor costs	• Quality standards for purchasing, receiving, and storing
• Types of costs	• Determining food costs	• Factors contributing to labor costs	• Quality standards for food production and service
• Operating budgets	• Determining food cost percentage	• Scheduling	• Quality standards for inventory
• Profit and loss reports	• Establishing standard portion costs		
• Cost-control tools	• As-purchased versus edible-portion costs		
	• Recipe yields		
	• Controlling portion sizes		
	• Monitoring food production and cost		
	• Menu pricing		

SECTION 3.4 CONTROLLING QUALITY STANDARDS

As mentioned earlier in the chapter, take cost-control measures in all aspects of the food flow process, from purchasing to service. In order to control costs through all of these stages, establish quality standards and strictly follow them for each and every step. This section discusses the quality standards to be implemented for not only food production, but also receiving and storing food and taking accurate inventory. An operation's demand for high quality standards is the surest way to reduce costs across all facets of foodservice.

Study Questions

After studying Section 3.4, you should be able to answer the following questions:

- How can quality standards for purchasing, receiving, and storing help control costs?

- How can quality standards for food production and service help control costs?

- How can quality standards for inventory help control costs?

198

Quality Standards for Purchasing, Receiving, and Storing

Purchasing

Prior to ordering, receiving, and storing quality products, consider where the products were grown or produced. Even the best receiving and storing policies and procedures cannot make a poor-quality product better after it is in the establishment. So, choosing a credible supplier is key. Those with purchasing responsibility should seek suppliers who are considered to be ethical, reliable, and financially stable or deemed to be part of an approved supplier list, based on food safety, product quality, and price.

Understanding what items are necessary for an operation stems from ensuring that the item's intended use is clearly defined. The intended use describes how a product or service is meant to be used, developed, or consumed. A product's intended use is its most important characteristic to consider when specifying quality standards. The way a product is to be used drives all decisions for selecting the product and its supplier. Draw up specification sheets according to these criteria.

Receiving

Once purchase orders have been made, the next step is to receive the item in the most efficient, safe, and effective way possible. Deliveries should be designated to times when the operation is slow. An operation does not want staff to worry about receiving and putting away products at the same time they are serving customers. Proper delivery timing can only be accomplished by establishing a good relationship with vendors so that an operation can count on them to consistently deliver food when wanted. Figure 3.24 shows an employee checking a delivery.

The frequency of deliveries can help preserve food quality. Some food must be delivered daily, while other food can safely be delivered weekly. An operation

Figure 3.24: An employee inspects a delivery.

199

Discuss

- Many suppliers can provide similar products. What are the qualities that a manager should look for when choosing suppliers?

- Should operations always purchase the highest quality ingredients, regardless of the items' intended uses? What are some situations in which the "best" might not be the best choice?

Reinforce and Review

- Choosing a credible supplier is key to obtaining high-quality products.

- Before ordering a product, managers should identify its intended use, or how it will be used, developed, or consumed; this is the product's most important characteristic.

- Specification sheets describing the criteria a given product must meet should be developed in accordance with the product's intended use.

- Products should be received in the most efficient, safe, and effective way possible.

- Deliveries should be scheduled for times when the operation is slow, so employees do not have to choose between caring for food and serving guests.

- The frequency of deliveries can help preserve food quality.

Teaching Tips

- Consider asking a representative from the campus foodservice department to discuss the department's purchasing standards and practices.

- If possible, enable students to observe the receiving process in the campus foodservice department.

Figure Focus
Figure 3.24: What is this employee doing to maintain quality standards?

**Homework Activity:
Special Specs**

**Literacy Connection, 21st-Century Skills—
Work Independently, Information Literacy,
Reason Effectively, Communicate Clearly**

Select three ingredients commonly used in a restaurant kitchen. Draw up product specification sheets for each, describing the qualities and characteristics you want each product to have. For instance, if you select butter, you would need to specify salted or unsalted, frozen or fresh, clarified or whole, package size, and name of the dairy. You might need to research the ingredients you select to make sure you include all the relevant characteristics.

Discuss

- Employees should be trained on proper receiving practices. What should this training involve?
- Some guidelines for delivery specifications are listed on p. 200. What is the rationale for each specification? Why should some items be ordered more frequently than others?

Reinforce and Review

- The operation's menu and service style affect the frequency of deliveries. Freshness is important, but so is the cost of the labor used to receive products.
- Well-defined receiving procedures ensure that an operation receives only the products that meet its established standards for quality and quantity and rejects products that do not meet these standards.
- Implementing appropriate receiving practices helps prevent product deterioration, which can lead to spoilage and higher food costs.

Teaching Tips

- Encourage students to draw up guidelines for receiving products for the classroom kitchen.

Homework Activity:
Food Safety and the Food Flow Process

Science Connection, Literacy Connection, 21st-Century Skills—Work Independently, Use Systems Thinking, Information Literacy, Communicate Clearly

An important component of controlling costs is keeping a close eye on anything that could become a potential problem, because problems cost money. From a food safety perspective, what problems could arise during the food flow process? In particular, what illnesses can spread to customers and employees as a result of errors made?

Write a two-page report on food safety issues in the flow of food and how these can increase a restaurant's costs. Consider the costs of waste, spoilage, negative publicity, lost customers, and legal fees, as well as any other relevant costs, in your answer.

---

may need to weigh the advantage of daily and weekly deliveries for freshness against the added time that receiving takes. The menu and service style of the operation factor into decisions such as these. Following are guidelines for delivery specifications:

- **Fish:** Fresh fish should be delivered daily. Frozen fish can be delivered only weekly.
- **Produce:** Certain fresh produce should be delivered daily. Bulk and hardy vegetables should be delivered weekly.
- **Specialty produce:** Delicate or specialty produce, such as wild mushrooms, mesclun mix lettuce, and tropical fruit (mangoes, kumquats) with a short shelf life, should be ordered daily according to its specifications sheet.
- **Dried goods:** Specialty products exist that are shelf stable and do not need to be ordered daily. Gain a financial advantage by bulk ordering some specialty sauces or specialty items for the pastry department, such as chocolates, flours, and decorations. But when ordering bulk, an operation also must consider financial savings versus storage space and the potential loss due to pilfering or pest infestation.
- **Meat:** Regardless if it is dry- or wet-aged, meat should be ordered and delivered at least two or three times per week. This will depend mostly on the establishment's usage and storage capacity.
- **Dairy:** Order dairy product at least twice a week. Milk and eggs have a good shelf life, but do not stretch the time too far. Most cheeses are very shelf stable as long as they are kept in the cooler.

Well-defined receiving procedures ensure that an operation receives only the products that meet its established standards for quality and quantity and rejects product that does not meet these standards. The operation's manager has the responsibility for establishing appropriate procedures for receiving and storing food, training the designated staff members in these procedures, and monitoring the receiving function. Implementing appropriate procedures helps to prevent product deterioration that can lead to spoiled food and a higher food cost for the operation. Such procedures can include the following:

1. Have the delivery person put the order in a designated "receiving area" of the kitchen. The receiving area should be clean, well lit, and easily accessible.
2. Obtain a copy of the purchase order.
3. Have a copy of the purchasing specifications available.

200

4. Check the delivery quantity against both the purchase order and **invoice**, which is a document from a vendor that lists such details as items purchased, date of order, purchaser, and sales price. An invoice is also called a bill. Find out whether any unauthorized items were added to the order by checking the purchase order and invoice. See Figure 3.25.

Figure 3.25: A sample invoice.

5. If the items are purchased by count, count them. If purchased by weight, weigh them, particularly meat and produce.

6. Open the shipment boxes and check for freshness and accuracy for all items.

7. Compare the prices on the invoice to those on the purchase order to ensure that they match. Check the math on the invoice, even if it is a computer-generated invoice.

201

Discuss

- Why is it important to examine all deliveries carefully? What are the potential ramifications of accepting products that should have been rejected?

- Unfortunately, sometimes deliveries arrive when all staff members are busy with service. Which should take precedence, proper receiving practices or quality guest service? Why?

Reinforce and Review

- Receiving staff should check deliveries against both the original purchase order and the invoice before accepting products.

- All deliveries should be inspected for accuracy and quality, and prices should be double-checked.

Teaching Tips

- Display sample invoices and purchase orders so that students can learn more about these documents.

Vocabulary Terms

- **Invoice:** A document from a supplier that lists such details as items purchased, date of order, purchaser, and sales price.

Figure Focus

Figure 3.25: How might the information provided on an invoice differ from the information provided on a purchase order?

Discuss

- Which is more important to a restaurant or foodservice operation's food cost: receiving or storing?

- Explain the FIFO system. How does it help control food cost?

Reinforce and Review

- Even if the delivery person is in a hurry, employees should not speed through the receiving process.

- The goal of proper receiving is to ensure the correct product, quality, and quantity at the correct price.

- Perishable foods should be monitored daily to ensure freshness; schedules should be followed regularly to ensure that every product is being used safely and efficiently.

- Storage facilities should also be monitored regularly to ensure that they are clean and functioning properly.

Teaching Tips

- Encourage students to examine storage procedures in the classroom kitchen.

8. If everything is in order, sign the invoice. If something must be returned, have the driver write out a credit memo for the item or circle the item on the invoice and state the reason for the return. Use the same procedure if an item is missing. The driver may want to rush through this procedure. Do not rush! The objective here is to ensure you have the correct product, quality, and quantity at the correct price. If any of these elements are missing, the food cost will likely increase, and the profit will subsequently decrease.

9. Put the goods away promptly: dairy, meat, fresh poultry, and fresh seafood first; then frozen food, produce, and dry goods. Prompt storage protects against food spoilage and theft. Secure the storage area when everything is in its place.

10. Process the paperwork by sending copies of the signed purchase order and the signed invoice to the accounting department.

Storing

After purchasing and properly receiving orders, safely store them. Poor storage procedures and facilities can greatly increase food costs due to waste and increased labor costs, so it's critical that operations create quality standards for proper storage.

Obviously, monitor perishable food daily to preserve its quality. Some food items have manufacturer's recommendations for storing the product. One example is a recommended storage temperature. Air circulation in any storage area is critical to keep food cool or frozen or to prevent food from getting moldy. Store food with proper labels and rotate all products in storage following the FIFO (first in, first out) system. Each establishment should have inventory schedules for the freezer, cooler, and dry goods sections of its storage. Schedules should be followed regularly to ensure that every product is being used safely and efficiently and so that no product is going to waste.

In addition to checking the food in the storage facilities, the storage facilities themselves should be checked regularly to make sure they are clean and functioning properly and efficiently. Following is a list of items to monitor for each storage unit:

- **Freezers:** These must be at a temperature that will keep food frozen solid. Freezers are usually either walk-in or have front door or trunk openings. Walk-in freezers should have speed racks, or shelving, to provide enough space for items to have enough room to freeze properly. Air movement is crucial in both the freezer and cooler. Clean freezers at least once a week.

202

- **Coolers:** These must be able to hold food at 41°F or lower. Coolers and freezers have a fan blowing the cold air around in the room. Again, it is very important to keep the air moving between products. Avoid placing product on sheet pans, since this hampers air circulation. The cooler should be monitored on a daily basis to ensure cleanliness.

- **Temperature:** Both freezers and coolers must be tested for the correct temperature regularly. Establishments with a HACCP program might test freezer and cooler temperatures every two hours or at least twice a day.

- **Dry storage:** Moisture and heat are the biggest dangers to dry and canned food. The temperature of the storeroom should be between 50°F and 70°F. Keep relative humidity at 50 to 60 percent, if possible. All shelving in any of the areas must be at least 6 inches off the ground. This space is necessary to make access difficult for rodents and to provide enough space to clean underneath the shelving on a daily basis.

Quality Standards for Food Production and Service

As discussed earlier, standard portion sizes, standardized recipes, and standard portion costs are all food production standards. Such standardizing of food production helps to ensure quality standards as well because each item is measured against one standard. Customers receive the same quality of food on each visit to the operation, which, in turn, helps ensure the success of the business by building the operation's reputation and creating regular customers. It also helps to keep costs consistent. It is important that managers ensure these standards are met throughout the foodservice cycle, from menu planning to table service. In larger operations with multiple locations, these standard procedures ensure that the meal served in one location is comparable to the same meal in another location with regard to quality, taste, and presentation.

But having these standards doesn't guarantee that mistakes won't get made from time to time. So it is important that operations have quality assurance measures in place right up to the service stage of the food flow process. Prior to service, managers should taste each item to ensure it meets the operation's standard. For any item that could suffer a quality problem during holding (such as a sauce breaking), check periodically to verify its quality. Check the appearance of a dish before serving it. Visual evaluation before serving a dish catches problems that can be corrected easily, such as a lack of garnish or a dish that has not been held at a specified serving temperature (see Figure 3.26 on the following page). Some operations have specifications for exactly how a plate should look when it leaves the kitchen. Another reason visual evaluation is important is that it is

203

(see Figure 3.26 on the following page)

Discuss

- What are some examples of foods that should be checked or freshly made periodically throughout service?

- Managers sometimes identify problems with dishes just before they are served. What are their options at this stage of service? Why might one option be chosen over another?

- Are dishes with quality problems ever served? Why? How can this affect a restaurant's reputation? What effect can this have on employee morale?

Reinforce and Review

- Moisture and heat are the biggest dangers to dry and canned foods.

- Standard portion sizes, standardized recipes, and standard portion costs are all food production standards, but they also ensure consistent quality standards.

- Prior to service, managers should taste each item to ensure that it meets the operation's standards; certain fragile items should be checked throughout service as well.

- Visual evaluation before serving a dish allows management to correct minor problems and identify larger ones.

Teaching Tips

- Review Level 1, Chapter 2 with reference to safe storage procedures.

- Review Level 1, Chapter 4 with reference to professionalism.

Discuss

- If all staff members are actively engaged in providing quality service in all its forms, how do problems occur in the first place?

Reinforce and Review

- The key to identifying deviations from standard recipes and presentations is regular monitoring and the understanding by the staff that it is the responsibility of everyone in the operation to ensure quality.

- When a problem's cause or causes are diagnosed, the manager must work with the entire staff to implement the correction.

- Failure to find the root cause of a problem will lead to increased cost through food waste, lower staff productivity, and possibly loss of customer base.

- The faster a problem is identified and a correction is made, the more costs will be kept under control.

Teaching Tips

- Refer students to the problem-solving model described in Level 1, Chapter 8.

Homework Activity: Problem-Solving Skills

Literacy Connection, 21st-Century Skills— Work Independently, Solve Problems, Reason Effectively, Communicate Clearly

A local operation has recently experienced a significant increase in the number of dishes being returned to the kitchen by irate guests. Due to financial troubles, many of the kitchen and dining-room staff members are new, and the managers are overworked and stressed by the situation. Morale is low, and sales volume has fallen.

The operation has hired you as a consultant. Using the seven-step problem-solving model, help identify the root cause of the operation's troubles and find workable solutions. Describe your process in a one-page essay.

Vocabulary Terms

- **Physical inventory:** Counting and recording the number of each item in the dry-storage area.

---

usually the first clue that there may be a larger problem to be solved.

The key to identifying deviations from standard recipes and presentations is regular monitoring and the understanding by the staff that it is the responsibility of everyone in the establishment to ensure quality. Constantly monitoring food quality is not difficult to do, but it may take time to turn it into a habit for everyone. It is also essential that all staff—management, the executive chef, waitstaff, front-of-the-house staff, and kitchen staff—are involved and that their opinions are considered and valued.

Figure 3.26: Before food leaves the kitchen for service, it must be inspected.

When a problem's cause or causes are discovered, the manager must work with the entire staff to implement the correction. It is important to discover the root cause, or true cause, of a problem. A problem can be internal or external, meaning it might be caused by something happening inside the operation or by something happening outside the operation, such as a vendor delivering the wrong item. Failure to identify the root of a problem will lead to increased costs by way of food waste, lower staff productivity, and perhaps even loss of customer base. If everyone is responsible for the product being delivered, then the chances are greater that deviations from quality standards will not occur; or if a deviation does occur, that it will be corrected more quickly.

Examples of corrections could include revising product specifications, revising a procedure, revising a recipe, or selecting a new vendor. The faster a problem is identified and a correction is made, the more costs will be kept under control.

Quality Standards for Inventory

Taking inventory is yet another way to ensure quality standards that will ultimately serve as a cost-control measure. Taking **physical inventory** means counting and recording the number of each item in the storeroom. Literally count each item or scan bar codes with handheld scanners (see Figure 3.27 on the following page).

204

Figure Focus

Figure 3.26: Inspecting dishes before service is a key component in identifying problems with the food, such as poor cooking practices or an incorrect garnish.

Figure 3.27: An employee monitors inventory.

Closely monitor inventory to ensure that products are ordered more efficiently as they are needed. Operations are less likely to run out of product, which could disrupt food production and, ultimately, the satisfaction of the guests' experience. Closely monitoring inventory also helps ensure that no product goes to waste. Operations that know what products have been purchased, when they were purchased, and how long they've been in-house are more likely to effectively use the FIFO system. Minimizing waste keeps costs down as the use of only the freshest products helps keep sales up.

Determine actual food costs by opening and closing inventories for a given period. These costs can't be properly calculated without an operation closely monitoring the products being purchased and used. At the start, or opening, of a given inventory period, calculate total values of each item by multiplying the unit cost of the item by the number of items in inventory. For example, if 18 cans of peaches are in inventory and each can costs $2.38, the total value of canned peaches is $42.84 (18 × $2.38 = $42.84).

After calculating a total count for each inventory item, calculate the closing inventory or the total dollar value of the inventory at the end of a period. The value of the closing inventory can be determined using any of the following four methods:

1. **Latest purchase price (FIFO):** Multiply the number of units of each item by the most recent price paid for the item.

2. **Actual purchase price:** Multiply the number of units of each item by the price actually paid for each unit.

205

Figure Focus
Figure 3.27: Monitoring inventory not only guards against pilferage, but ensures that all products are being used in an appropriate and timely manner.

Discuss

- What are the advantages and disadvantages of using each method of calculating closing inventory? Which technique seems most accurate?

Reinforce and Review

- Closely monitor inventory to ensure that products are ordered as they are needed.

- Operations that know what products have been purchased, when they were purchased, and how long they've been in-house are more likely to effectively use the FIFO system.

- Minimizing waste keeps costs down as the use of only the freshest products keeps sales high.

- Determining food costs relies on knowledge of the opening and closing inventory figures for each period.

- There are four methods to calculate closing inventory: latest purchase price, actual purchase price, weighted average purchase price, and last in, first out.

- Depending on the technique used to calculate closing inventory, values will vary slightly.

Teaching Tips

- Students should understand the relationship between monitoring inventories and determining actual food cost.

- Each method of calculating closing inventory is valid, but establishments should use the same technique each time inventory is taken to avoid confusion.

Vocabulary Terms

- **Latest purchase price:** A method of calculating closing inventory by multiplying the number of units of each item by the most recent price paid for the item.

- **Actual purchase price:** A method of calculating closing inventory by multiplying the number of units of each item by the price actually paid for each unit.

- **Weighted average purchase price:** A method of calculating closing inventory by multiplying the number of units of each item in the opening inventory and later purchases by the price actually paid for each item, adding all the prices together, and dividing by the total number of items.

- **Last in, first out:** A method of calculating closing inventory by multiplying the number of units of each item by the earliest price paid for the item.

On the Job:
Cost of Food Sold Does Not Equal "Sold" Food

Encourage students to discuss the following:

- What percentage of the food that a restaurant orders and receives is actually prepared and served to guests? Consider all the variables that could be involved.

- How does a restaurant determine which guests will receive special items, either complimentary or not?

- What are some ways a restaurant can prevent pilferage?

Fast Fact:
Did You Know . . . ?

Encourage students to discuss the following:

- Nearly 75 percent of all inventory shortages are due to employee theft. Why do some employees and managers steal? How might they try to justify their actions?

- How can improved training and communication reduce pilferage?

- Why might some establishments have far lower rates of employee theft than others?

3. **Weighted average purchase price:** Multiply the number of units of each item in the opening inventory and later purchases by the price actually paid for each unit, add the prices all together, and divide by the total number of items.

4. **Last in, first out (LIFO):** Multiply the number of units of each item by the earliest price paid for the item.

It is important to note that closing inventory values will usually differ slightly, depending on which method is used.

[on the job]

Cost of Food Sold Does Not Equal "Sold" Food

The true cost of food is not the same as the cost of the ingredients that go into the menu items that a restaurant may sell on a given day. That's because a lot of the food that the operation purchases never makes it onto a customer's plate. For instance, some ingredients are made into employee meals or become special items for favored guests. Other foods, like herbs and fruit, are used to create specialty drinks at the bar. Unfortunately, some food is wasted through burning or being allowed to spoil, or it may even be pilfered. The restaurant's food cost must account for all this extra food somehow.

That means that the prices on the menu must be high enough to pay for not only the components used to create each dish—ingredients, labor, electricity, and so on—but also for this extra food. And remember, the restaurant must also make a profit! That's why the manager in charge of inventory needs to closely monitor both inventory and sales. Only in this way can the operation know whether the menu prices are both high enough to cover costs and low enough to attract customers. Inventory may seem like a mundane part of the business, but good control of inventory is the only way an operation can stay in business.

[fast fact]

Did You Know...?

The National Restaurant Association estimates that nearly 75 percent of all inventory shortages are due to employee theft. That amounts to approximately 4 percent of total restaurant sales. Many operations are using sophisticated, computerized, point-of-sale (POS) registers to keep track of inventory and food costs and to monitor when and how food is issued from the kitchen, but management still needs to monitor the situation carefully.

Summary

In this section, you learned the following:

- It is important to take cost-control measures in all aspects of the food flow process, from purchasing to service. In order to control costs through all of these stages, establish and strictly follow quality standards for each and every step. Quality standards for purchasing, receiving, and storing all contribute to cost control. An operation's demand for high-quality standards is the surest way to reduce costs across all facets of foodservice.

- Understanding what items are necessary for an operation stems from ensuring that the item's intended use is clearly defined. The way a product is to be used drives all decisions for selecting the product and its supplier. Draw up specifications sheets according to these criteria. After making purchase orders, the next step is to receive product in the most efficient, safe, and effective way possible. Designate deliveries to times when the operation is slow. The frequency of deliveries can help preserve food quality. Some food must be delivered daily, and other food can safely be delivered weekly. An operation may need to weigh the advantage of daily and weekly deliveries for freshness against the added time that receiving takes. After purchasing and properly receiving an order, safely store the product. Poor storage procedures and facilities can greatly increase food costs due to waste and increased labor costs, so it's critical that operations create quality standards for proper storage.

- Standardizing food production helps to ensure quality standards because each item is gauged on one standard. Customers receive the same quality of food on each visit to the operation. This in turn helps ensure the success of the business by building the operation's reputation, creating regular customers, and keeping costs consistent. Managers ensure these standards are met through the foodservice cycle, from menu planning to table service. In larger operations with multiple locations, these standard procedures ensure that the meal served in one location is comparable to the same meal in another location with regard to quality, taste, and presentation. But having these standards doesn't guarantee that mistakes won't be made from time to time, and it is important that operations have quality assurance measures in place right up to the service stage of the food flow process. Prior to service, managers should taste each item to ensure it meets the operation's standard. For any item that could suffer a quality problem during holding, check periodically to verify its quality.

207

Summary

- Remind students to review the following:
  1. Quality standards for purchasing, receiving, and storing
  2. Quality standards for food production and service
  3. Quality standards for inventory

- Closely monitor inventory to ensure that products will be ordered more efficiently as they are needed. This means that operations are less likely to run out of product, which could disrupt food production and, ultimately, the satisfaction of the guests' experience. Closely monitoring inventory also helps ensure that no product goes to waste. Operations that know what products have been purchased, when they were purchased, and how long they've been in-house, are more likely to effectively use the FIFO system. Minimizing waste keeps costs down just as the use of only the freshest products helps keep sales up—this is a recipe for a successful operation.

Section 3.4 Review Questions

1. Provide one way in which quality standards help with cost control for each of the following aspects of foodservice:

   a. Purchasing

   b. Receiving

   c. Storing

2. When receiving orders, why is it a good idea to check the delivery against the purchase order and the invoice?

3. Why is standardizing food production a good quality control measure?

4. Explain one way that closing inventory can be taken.

5. Do you think that Sherie Valderrama would agree that closely monitoring inventory is important? Why?

6. Chef Kate and Miguel haven't implemented a standard way of doing inventory. Of the four methods you learned about, which would you suggest to them and why?

7. What kind of procedure would you employ for quality assurance when food is already plated? Who would you have check the dish? Would you utilize multiple people? Write a paragraph summarizing your thoughts on this.

8. If you had to focus your attention on one of the following aspects of the food flow process, which would it be and why? Receiving or storing? Explain your answer in a two-paragraph report.

209

Section 3.4
Review Questions

1. **Purchasing:** Choosing a credible supplier; carefully defining each product's intended use.

   Receiving: Receiving deliveries when it is convenient for the operation; ordering items as needed to maintain quality; rejecting food that does not meet the operation's criteria or was not actually ordered.

   Storing: Storing all accepted goods promptly and appropriately; monitoring perishable items regularly; inspecting storage facilities regularly.

2. The delivery should be checked against the purchase order and the invoice to ensure that all the items ordered were actually delivered, with no additions or substitutions, and that the prices are correct.

3. Standardizing food production is a good quality control measure because it ensures that guests will receive meals that are of a consistently high quality and that food costs will not be affected by over- or underportioning.

4. Students may describe any of the four ways of calculating closing inventory, as long as their responses are accurate.

5. Sherie Valderrama would probably agree that closely monitoring inventory is essential, as it plays an important role in controlling overall costs and determining actual food cost.

6. Students may suggest any of the four ways of calculating closing inventory, so long as they defend their answers appropriately.

7. Student answers may vary but should reflect the material found in the text.

8. Students may discuss either receiving or storing so long as their answers are accurate and well-reasoned.

Section 3.4
Activities

1. Students may suggest a variety of answers so long as they are properly defended, accurately described, and correctly represented on the flow chart.

2. **FIFO method:** 20 pounds of all-purpose flour multiplied by $4.50 per pound equals $90.00. **LIFO method:** 20 pounds of all-purpose flour multiplied by $4.00 per pound equals $80.00. The two answers differ because they are based on different prices for the same item, purchased at different times.

3. Student answers will vary widely but should include all the information requested by the activity. This information might most easily be recorded in a spreadsheet.

Section 3.4 Activities

1. Study Skills/Group Activity: Cost Controls for Purchasing, Receiving, and Storing

Working with two or three other students, consider the purchasing, receiving, and storage process. What are some ways you can manage your restaurant to make this part of the food flow process more cost effective and efficient? Write a flowchart with your group that will detail the entire process and provide specifications for each stage.

2. Independent Activity: Comparing Inventory Methods

Your closing inventory includes 20 pounds of all-purpose flour purchased at $4.00 per pound and now selling for $4.50 per pound. Calculate the value of this flour based on the first-in, first-out method (FIFO) and the last-in, first-out method (LIFO). How do your results differ?

3. Critical Thinking: Taking Inventory of Your Home

Take a physical inventory of a kitchen cupboard in your home. First, guess the total cost of the contents. Then, begin taking your inventory. What information do you need to obtain for each item? Create a detailed list for your inventory and calculate the total cost. Was your guess higher, lower, or right on target with the actual cost?

210

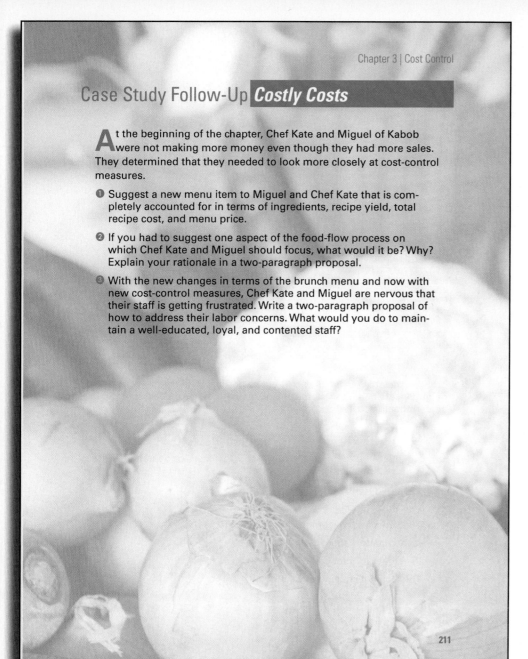

Case Study Follow-Up *Costly Costs*

At the beginning of the chapter, Chef Kate and Miguel of Kabob were not making more money even though they had more sales. They determined that they needed to look more closely at cost-control measures.

❶ Suggest a new menu item to Miguel and Chef Kate that is completely accounted for in terms of ingredients, recipe yield, total recipe cost, and menu price.

❷ If you had to suggest one aspect of the food-flow process on which Chef Kate and Miguel should focus, what would it be? Why? Explain your rationale in a two-paragraph proposal.

❸ With the new changes in terms of the brunch menu and now with new cost-control measures, Chef Kate and Miguel are nervous that their staff is getting frustrated. Write a two-paragraph proposal of how to address their labor concerns. What would you do to maintain a well-educated, loyal, and contented staff?

211

Case Study Follow-Up

1. Students should develop and cost out an original recipe.

2. Student answers may vary so long as they are properly supported.

3. Student answers may vary so long as they are properly supported. Students might wish to review the information in Level 1, Chapter 8 for assistance.

Apply Your Learning

 Converting Marinara Sauce

Students should perform the mathematic and measuring operations accurately to demonstrate that they understand this process.

 Research the Expenses of a National Chain

Students may use a variety of research materials, including the National Restaurant Association's Web site, www.restaurant.org. They should be sure to include all the requested information in their report.

Apply Your Learning

Converting Marinara Sauce

Calculate the number of 4-ounce portions of spicy marinara sauce yielded by the following recipe:

Amount	Ingredient	Purchase price
12 pounds	Canned crushed tomatoes	6-pound can = $9
2 tablespoons	Dried basil	8-ounce jar = $16
2 tablespoons	Dried oregano	8-ounce jar = $14
1 tablespoon	Salt	3-pound box = $2.50
4 ounces	Celery	1 pound = $0.98
4 ounces	Carrot	1 pound = $0.47
8 ounces	Onion	1 pound = $0.39
2 tablespoons	Olive oil	1 gallon = $24
1 tablespoon	Crushed red pepper	8-ounce jar = $12

Now, calculate the cost of each 4-ounce portion. Where ingredient amounts are given as volume, weigh the ingredients if necessary to determine the cost of each item.

Research the Expenses of a National Chain

Research a national restaurant or foodservice operation. Write a report covering the following:

- The organization's mission
- The type of food it serves
- The service style it employs
- Its budget for labor
- Its budget for food
- The locations it generally seeks out

212

The Weight of Food

Most cooking processes change the ingredient—its color, appearance, size, texture, and taste. After all, that's a big part of why we cook. But cooking an item can also change its weight and/or volume in important ways, which can make significant differences in your recipe costing and portioning.

Weigh the following raw ingredients:

- 1 cup long-grain white rice
- 1 cup long-grain brown rice
- 1 cup polenta
- 1 cup barley
- 1 chicken breast
- 1 hamburger patty
- 1 slice of bacon
- 1 fish fillet

Write two paragraphs (one on the starches, one on the proteins) on the changes in weight and volume that you anticipate will occur in these ingredients during cooking. Now cook the items and weigh the finished products; also measure the volume of the cooked starches. Do your results match your predictions? Write two paragraphs describing your findings.

Critical Thinking   AP versus EP

It is critical to understand whether a recipe calls for as-purchased (AP) or edible-portion (EP) ingredients. Listed here are an AP and an EP version of each of three ingredients. How could using one or the other option change a recipe?

- 10 pounds white onion versus 10 pounds diced white onion—for a chili recipe
- 8 pounds watermelon versus 8 pounds watermelon balls—for a fruit salad
- 4 pounds apples versus 4 pounds apple purée—for a cake

Write one paragraph on each variation, explaining how the finished dishes could differ, based on the AP or EP ingredient.

The Weight of Food

The measurement and cooking of these ingredients should be done in class to maintain consistency of products, but students should each write their own reports and make their own predictions.

Critical Thinking   AP versus EP

Students should demonstrate understanding of the differences between AP and EP ingredients as they explain how using one or the other can affect the outcome of each of the three recipes.

Exam Prep Answers

1. D
2. D
3. D
4. D
5. B
6. C
7. D
8. B
9. A
10. A

Chapter 3 | Foundations of Restaurant Management & Culinary Arts

Exam Prep Questions

1. Revenue is defined as income
   - A. used only for advertising.
   - B. lost by poor cost-control measures.
   - C. from sales after expenses are subtracted.
   - D. from sales before expenses are subtracted.

2. Food and labor can be designated as what cost?
   - A. Fixed
   - B. Overhead
   - C. Secondary
   - D. Controllable

3. Taking sales information for two or three recent and similar periods and averaging it together is a forecasting method called
   - A. the 3-2-1 strategy.
   - B. the median method.
   - C. consolidated budgeting.
   - D. the moving average technique.

4. Total food cost is calculated by what formula?
   - A. (Opening inventory / Purchases = Total food available) – Closing inventory
   - B. (Opening inventory × Purchases = Total food available) – Closing inventory
   - C. (Opening inventory – Purchases = Total food available) – Closing inventory
   - D. (Opening inventory + Purchases = Total food available) – Closing inventory

5. Food cost ÷ _____ = Food cost percentage.
   - A. Labor
   - B. Sales
   - C. Gross profit
   - D. Overhead cost

6. A tool used to calculate standard portion cost for a menu item is called a
   - A. vendor invoice.
   - B. production sheet.
   - C. recipe cost card.
   - D. food production chart.

7. What form shows how much product should be produced by the kitchen during a given meal period?
   - A. Vendor invoice
   - B. Production sheet
   - C. Recipe cost card
   - D. Food production chart

8. Which method calculates a menu price by multiplying raw food costs by a predetermined fraction?
   - A. Check average
   - B. Straight markup
   - C. Contribution margin
   - D. Food cost percentage

214

⑨ At what temperature should foodservice freezer units be held?

A. 0°F

B. 15°F

C. 25°F

D. 32°F

⑩ A document that a receiving employee uses to verify a delivery is called a

A. vendor invoice.

B. production sheet.

C. recipe cost card.

D. food production chart.

215

Chapter 4 Overview

Chapter 4 presents salads, dressings and dips, and garnishes.

Section 1: This section reviews the ingredients and types of salads, as well as how to clean, serve, and store them.

Section 2: This section covers various dressings and dips.

Section 3: This section covers the how and why of garnishes, as well as garnishes for desserts and soups.

Advance Preparation	
Review	Sections 4.1–4.3
Contact	Chemistry or physics teacher for a laser beam or pointer
	Computer lab
Prepare	Blank cards for memory game
	Pictures of greens and salad dressings and ingredients
	Pictures of garnishes
	Paper
	Egg yolks, oil, and vinegar
	Greens or vegetables from a field, still dirty
	Various types of greens to see and taste
	Various types of oils and vinegars to see and taste
	Ingredients for practicing garnishes:
	Cucumbers
	Carrots
	Scallions
	Leeks
	Radishes
	Chocolate
	Mint leaves
	Equipment for practicing garnishes

Chapter 4
Salads and Garnishing

CUSTOMIZED INSTRUCTION OPTIONS

Less Advanced Students	More Advanced Students	ESOL Students	Special Needs Students
Page 235	Page 235	Page 235	Page 235

CHAPTER TOOLS

21st-Century Skills	Mathematics	Science	Literacy
Pages 218, 222, 228, 249, 270	Page 234	Pages 238, 245	Pages 221, 223, 235

ServSafe Connection

Pages 237, 248, 268

Case Study | *Looks Can Be Appealing*

Miguel and Chef Kate of Kabob recently gathered customer feedback from their patrons in an attempt to increase efficiency and raise profits. The feedback they received indicated that customer service and food quality were good, but that the restaurant didn't have enough light and healthful menu options. Some patrons noted that the presentation of the food was mediocre. As one patron said, "This reminds me of home. I want to feel eating out is a treat."

Miguel and Chef Kate now have some tough decisions to make. Miguel wants to focus on changing the menu, but Chef Kate is equally concerned with the presentation of food. She knows that eating involves more than just taste. How can they make the menu healthier without diminishing food quality and taste? And how can they add more visual appeal to their menu options without spending more money on each dish? The purpose of the customer feedback was to raise profits, not cut into them.

As you read this chapter, think about the following questions:

1. What types of food items can Kabob put on the menu to respond to customer preferences?

2. How can healthier food be attractive in terms of both taste and flavor?

3. How can food presentations be made more attractive without increasing costs?

Case Study
Looks Can Be Appealing

- Miguel and Chef Kate are looking at "the bottom line."

- They want to please their guests even more than they have been.

- Their ultimate goal is to improve the profitability of Kabob.

- A business must be successful to continue.

- Miguel and Chef Kate have a vision for Kabob, and a desire to serve outstanding food.

- It is in the best interests of the guests and employees of Kabob for it to be profitable.

- Note that there are follow-up questions about the case study at the end of the chapter.

- This activity could be done in groups, as a class, or as a homework assignment.

Professional Profile

Discuss	Debra Olson comes to a culinary career through the portals of science and engineering.
Reinforce and Review	Review the areas of study including food science, food packaging, nutrition, and menu development.
Teaching Tips	Perhaps the students are not aware that R&D means research and development. R&D is usually the first part of new product development, and it starts with an idea.

In-Class Activity: Debra Olson's Education and Career

21st-Century Skills—Financial, Economic, Business, and Entrepreneurial Literacy

The students might be interested in culinary arts and food science careers.

There are more careers in the field than they might realize.

Have the students investigate the college majors mentioned in this profile:

- Food science
- Food packaging
- Nutrition
- Menu development

What sorts of classes are required for these areas? What types of jobs are available? What colleges offer these programs? Which college is the closest to your high school?

[professional profile]

Debra Olson

Senior Manager of Recipe Development

Golden Corral

❝ *The best is what we're all about.* **❞**
— *Golden Corral Corporate Culture*

I have a passion for food and have always worked in restaurants. When I went to college, I majored in food science with a minor in food packaging. I was originally interested in nutrition and didn't even know that menu development was a career option.

Since the discipline of culinology has emerged, blending both culinary arts and food science, we've seen many new career opportunities for those interested in this industry. The whole approach of this science is to make food taste better, be more consistent and safer. So, start working. Go to work, continue your education, and keep an open mind.

I started in menu development at Arby's Incorporated and remained there almost seven years. After that position, I joined Hardees Food Systems. Currently, and for the past 13 years, I've been with Golden Corral. It's a privately held company run by a president/CEO who knows and loves food. He pays a lot of attention to details, even down to the recipes. And that's helped to bring Golden Corral from a steak-and-potatoes chain to the largest buffet in the United States in about 30 years.

I love that I work with someone who is innovative. I love that we don't waiver on quality. That's important to me. We do a lot in the back of the house so that we maintain versatility and control. For instance, we don't buy processed meat—we do a lot of our own butchering.

My personal focus is to ensure that the R&D prototype menu options approved in development can be equally successful in mass production so that all of our stores can duplicate it. There's such an excitement in developing products that are tested and then rolled out nationally...products that then drive the business! Our company mission is "Making pleasurable dining affordable." It's something I believe in. So, as you look ahead, find something that you believe in...and go for it.

About Salads and Garnishes

Salads are an interesting focus for me—creating recipes that add value, stimulate interest, and offer both traditional and nontraditional choices. Considering that the hot bar drives business 80 percent of the time, we need to add other menu items that both complement the hot bar and offer alternatives. Salads can be a side or a main meal; if they're a main meal, they need to fill you up!

218

We prepare our salads daily—hand chopping the lettuce for freshness. We focus on fresh and seasonal produce. That's not something that all restaurants do. We even make three of our dressings on-site.

I think salads offer versatility and healthy options. So, I want them to be tasty, attractive, and creative—in our restaurants, we use ingredients such as fresh spinach, spring salad, pine nuts, raisins, mandarin oranges, watermelon, and strawberries.

4.1 Salads	4.2 Salad Dressings and Dips	4.3 Garnishes
• Ingredients and parts of a salad	• Types of dressings	• Garnishing: why and how
• Types of salads	• Dips	• Garnishing desserts
• Salads and service		• Garnishing soups
• Cleaning and storing salads		

SECTION 4.1 SALADS

Do you think of salads as iceberg lettuce with tomato wedges and rings of green pepper? That's what the idea of a side salad used to bring to mind. But salads are one of the most versatile menu offerings. Today they can be served for any course and can include anything from vegetables to fruits and nuts, to meat and fish.

In this section, the main ingredients and parts of a salad are discussed first. Then the major types of salads are explained. After that, the kinds of salads that can be served during various courses of a meal are covered. And finally, the section concludes by illustrating the proper way to clean and store salads and salad greens.

Study Questions

After studying Section 4.1, you should be able to answer the following questions:

- What are the ingredients and parts to a salad?
- What are the various types of salad?
- What are the different types of salad that can be served throughout the courses of a meal?
- What is the best way to clean and store salad?

219

Discuss	Debra Olson says, "I think salads offer versatility and healthy options." What options? How are they versatile? Have the students discuss these concepts.
Reinforce and Review	Discuss the various uses and roles of salads.
Teaching Tips	What do students think of when they first think of salads?

Focus and Engage

- This section involves lots of practical instruction.
- The more practice with the "Essential Skills" the better.
- Most of the teaching support for this section should be hands-on.
- If funds are too limited to purchase food for every skill, paper replicas or food models can be used for some tasks.

Discuss

- Not all cuisine is cooked.
- Some of the finest menu items are artistically assembled from fresh, raw ingredients.
- Salads are a category of fresh food creations.

Section 4.1 Salads

Introduce the Section

a. Salads have quality expectations.
b. Freshness is expected.
c. Lack of freshness will be detected immediately by most guests.

Vocabulary Review

a. Direct students to the key terms.
b. Pronounce each word, and have the students repeat the pronunciation out loud.
c. Discuss the definition of each word.

Encourage students to discuss the following:

- Greens are leaf vegetables.

- Some can also be eaten cooked.

- They are used raw in most salads.

Teaching Tips

- The best way for the students to learn about greens is to see and taste them.

- If at all possible, have samples for the classroom.

- Perhaps the students would like to raise some of these greens in their own gardens or containers over the summer. Many are easy to cultivate.

Ingredients and Parts of a Salad

Most salads consist of a lettuce base, but a wide variety of ingredients can go into a salad. Meat, fish, vegetables, fruits, and starches, such as potatoes or pasta, can all go into a salad. A salad is defined as a single food or a mix of different foods accompanied by or held together with a dressing.

The three keys to ensuring a quality salad, regardless of the ingredients used, are as follows:

- The freshness of ingredients

- Having all the ingredients blend together in harmony

- Making sure the salad is appealing to the eye

Always consider freshness, flavor, and eye appeal when making any type of salad. See Table 4.1 for examples of salad green types.

Table 4.1: Kinds of Salad Greens	
Salad Green	Description
Arugula	Pungent, distinctive flavor
Belgain endive	Also known as witloof, witlof, or French endive. Related to endive; slightly bitter but pleasant flavor; used solo for salad or mixed with other greens; can be steamed, simmered, or grilled
Butterhead lettuce	Bibb (limestone) lettuce has a tender, delicate flavor. Boston lettuce has a buttery texture; does not keep well; cup-shaped leaves are excellent for salad bases; mild yet flavorful leaves
Crisphead lettuce	Iceberg (head) lettuce is a most popular American salad green; can be served alone or mixed with other greens, such as romaine. Romaine lettuce has a crisp texture and full, sweet, mild flavor; keeps well; easy to handle; essential ingredient in Caesar salad
Curly endive	Also known as frisee or chicoree frisee. Slightly bitter flavor; generally used with other greens
Escarole	Strength and bitterness of flavor diminishes as color lightens
Green cabbage	Slightly tough leaf; slightly strong flavor
Leaf lettuce	Leaf lettuce has red or green leaves; grows in bunches; wilts easily; gives mild flavor, variety, and color to salads. Oak leaf lettuce has a slightly bitter flavor
Micro greens	Plant's first true leaves formed between sprouting seed stage and baby stage; mild, delicate flavor; adds color and flavor; many types including arugula, broccoli, green and red cabbage, kohlrabi, Swiss chard, radish, beetroot, and red kale

220

Table 4.1: Kinds of Salad Greens *continued*

Salad Green	Description
Napa cabbage	Milder flavor than Savoy cabbage
Raddichio	Common chicory; Italian variety of chicory; crunchy texture; slightly bitter flavor; generally used in a mixture with other greens for flavor and color; can be cooked like collard or other greens
Red cabbage	Slightly tough leaf; mild flavor
Savoy cabbage	Milder flavor than green cabbage
Sorrel	Contains oxalic acid yielding a slightly acidic and bitter flavor; smaller leaves are preferred for their milder flavor
Spinach	Good alone or mixed with other greens; must be washed very thoroughly; remove coarse stems before service; baby spinach is highly regarded for its mild, fresh flavor
Watercress	Pungent, peppery flavor; used as garnish and in salads

Arugula · Bibb lettuce · Curly endive · Escarole · Green cabbage

Leaf lettuce · Radicchio · Red cabbage · Romaine lettuce · Spinach · Watercress

Although salads are made up of many ingredients and vary greatly in appearance, the four basic parts to most any salad follow (see Figure 4.1 on the following page for the basic parts of a salad):

1. Base
2. Body
3. Garnish
4. Dressing

The **base** of a salad is usually a layer of salad greens that line the plate or bowl in which the salad will be served. Use smaller leafy greens, cup-shaped Boston lettuce, or iceberg lettuce leaves to give height to salads and form edible containers. Also use romaine, Belgian endive, and leaf lettuce as a salad base.

221

Table 4.1 (cont.)

- More information is provided, with photos of some of the greens.

In-Class Activity: Tossed Salad Memory Game

Literacy Connection

There might be many types of salad "greens" (some are red) that are new to the students. Not every teenager is familiar with raddichio, arugula, or other greens.

Help the students to create a memory game of the greens.

Divide the number of greens by the number of students (or vice versa, depending on the size of your class). Have each student or team work on the same number of greens.

Have the student or team make a card for each green. It should be plain on the back. On the front it should have a picture of the green and a brief description of the green from Table 4.1. Use every example from Table 4.1.

Make a second identical set. There will be two cards for each green.

Combine the sets of cards. Shuffle them and spread them out face-down in a grid. This is like a memory game or Concentration.

Have students turn over two cards, attempting to find a match.

If the two do not match, turn them face-down again. It is now another student's turn.

If the two match, the student takes the pair and shows the card picture to the class. The student then reads the description aloud to the class. Successful pairing gives the student another turn.

The game gets easier as it progresses. Score it however you choose. If the students are divided into two teams, the teams can compete against each other and the students can receive team points for pairs.

Vocabulary Terms

- **Base:** The bottom foundation layer of a salad service.

21st-Century Skills—Make Judgments and Decisions

Have the students analyze several salad recipes.

They should be able to identify the four components:

- Base
- Body
- Garnish
- Dressing

Using the following chart, write the recipe component in the appropriate section.

Figure 4.1: A salad develops from the base to the body to the garnish and dressing.

The **body** of the salad consists of the main ingredients. The body can be a mixture of vegetables, such as lettuce, tomatoes, carrots, etc.; meats, such as turkey breast or ham; or cheeses and various fruits, such as mandarin oranges or apples. Use mayonnaise-based salads, such as tuna salad or crabmeat salad, as a salad body placed on a base of lettuce. Salad ingredients can vary by season or occasion, but freshness is always important.

Garnish enhances the appearance of the salad while also complementing the overall taste. A garnish should be something that will be eaten with the body, functioning as a flavor component. Simple garnishes are the best. Mix them with the other salad ingredients or add garnishes at the very end. For example, mix shredded carrot or a fine julienne of red bell pepper with salad greens, or lightly toss them with seasoning and then place them on top of the greens. This garnish is decorative as well as tasty. Always consider the components and overall taste of the salad when choosing a garnish.

Salad dressings are liquids or semiliquids used to flavor salads. They act as a sauce that holds the salad together. Dressings can range from mayonnaise for potato- or macaroni-based salads to vinaigrettes for lettuce-based salads. Sometimes dressings are called cold sauces because their purpose is to flavor, moisten, and enrich food. Use tart or sour dressings for green salads and vegetable salads. Use slightly sweetened dressings for fruit salads. Mix some dressings with the ingredients ahead of time, such as for "bound salad." Add some dressings at plating and service to bring an additional flavor aspect to the final product.

See Table 4.2 on the following page for examples of traditional salad vegetables.

Reinforce and Review

- Garnishes may be a signature part of the salad. For example, a Crab Louis seafood salad is often garnished with a sliced beet cut into the shape of a flower or a star.
- Crumbled hard-cooked egg yolk is often used to garnish a spinach salad.

Discuss

- Can the students think of any other examples of garnishes?
- Are there any classic and popular restaurant salads that are always garnished the same way?.

Vocabulary Terms

- **Body:** Main ingredients of a salad.
- **Garnish:** An element that enhances a salad's appearance.
- **Salad dressings:** Viscous liquids used to flavor and bind a salad.

Table 4.2: Other Traditional Salad Vegetables

Salad Vegetable	Description
Bulbs	Garden beets: Thickened lower part of the stem and upper part of the root; sweet, pungent flavor; may be used in addition to baby beet leaves
	Onion: Edible bulb; pungent flavor and aroma; sweet varieties increasing in availability and popularity; are the most widely used bulb to add flavor
	Scallion: Can be any shoot from the white onion variety pulled before the bulb has formed
Celery	Long stalk; mild flavor and crisp texture
Cucumber	Botanically a berry, more than 20 different species; mild, slightly watery flavor with light melon notes
	European or English cucumbers: Seedless, lighter green in color; 2 to 2¼ inches in diameter
	Japanese cucumber: Mild flavor, slender, deep green color, bumpy, ridged skin
Fruits	Berries and citrus fruits
Mushrooms	Wide variety available with varying textures, colors, and flavors; includes common mushroom, enoki, portabella, crimini, cepe, morel, shiitake, chanterelle; mushrooms are used in raw, cooked, or pickled forms
Peppers	Sweet/mild peppers and hot/pungent categories; sweet/mild are traditionally associated with salads
	Sweet/mild peppers:
	Bell pepper: Crisp juicy flesh; most are a rich, bright green when young. As they ripen, the color changes and the flesh sweetens; colors include yellow, orange, purple, red, and brown
	Pimiento: Familiar red stuffing found in green olives
	Banana pepper: Long banana shape
Tomato	A berry, pulpy; contains one or more seeds and no stones; vary in shape and flavor; wide variety of small, younger variations coming to market
Tuber	Carrot: Early summer carrots are long and cylindrical; winter carrots have a large fleshy root
	Radish: Commonly round, red bulb; other varieties include bicolored or white and have longish, blunt, or pointed roots (called daikon); mild to peppery flavor

Celery | Cucumber | Garden beets | Mushrooms | Radish | Sweet/mild peppers | Tomato

Table 4.2: Other Traditional Salad Vegetables

Encourage students to discuss the following:

- Lettuce and greens aren't the only vegetables (or fruit) in classic salads. Have students discuss some of their favorite salad elements.

In-Class Activity: Tossed Salad Memory Game

Literacy Connection

The vegetables in Table 4.2 can be added to the memory game started earlier.

Make two cards for each vegetable, or for each category.

Discuss

- Have the students discuss examples of each type of salad.
- Perhaps they can contribute salads from the recipe analysis assignment.

[fast fact]

Did You Know...?
Arugula, roquette, rocket, and rucola are all names for the same thing—a slightly peppery/bitter green found in salads all over the world!

[nutrition]

Greens and Oxalic Acid
Raw, green leafy vegetables are a great source of minerals, such as magnesium, iron, and calcium. In the world of chemistry, these minerals occur as ions that carry a 2+ charge. So they should be a great source of nutrients, right? Not necessarily.

An acid in the same kinds of vegetables prevents all of the nutrients from being absorbed by the body. Raw greens like sorrel and spinach contain this acid, known as oxalic acid. Unfortunately, oxalic acid latches on to minerals with a 2+ charge, preventing absorption in the intestine and making the minerals useless as nutrients.

So what's the answer? How do you get these valuable minerals into your body? Cook the vegetables! A little heat releases the minerals from the acid and allows them to be absorbed into our digestive system.

This doesn't mean that you should never eat raw spinach. Lots of nutrients are in the raw leaf. Some are even better raw than cooked. Just remember to use variety in the things you eat and the cooking methods you use to eat them.

Types of Salad

Because salads are not cooked, it is especially important to be extra careful about proper handwashing when preparing them. Remember that many health departments require single-use gloves to be worn—and changed frequently—whenever working with products that will not be cooked before service. Figure 4.2 on the following page shows the main types of salad:

- Green—tossed and composed
- Bound
- Vegetable
- Fruit
- Combination

224

Green tossed   Green composed   Bound

Combination   Fruit   Vegetable

Figure 4.2: Salad is a combination of raw or cooked ingredients that is served cold or warm.

The two types of green salad are **tossed** and **composed** (or mixed). Prepare all ingredients individually for either salad. Mix (toss) together the ingredients of a tossed green salad prior to plating. Place a tossed salad on a base or serve without further garnish. Do not toss together the ingredients for a composed salad. Arrange the ingredients on the base separately to create the desired taste experience and achieve a high level of visual appeal.

Prepare the **bound salad** from cooked primary ingredients such as meat, poultry, fish, egg, or starch such as potato, pasta, or rice. The ingredients are "bound" with some type of heavy dressing such as mayonnaise.

Prepare a **vegetable salad** from cooked and/or raw vegetables. Use a heavy dressing to bind this type of salad or toss with a lighter dressing. For example, bind the cabbage for coleslaw with a heavier mayonnaise-based dressing or a lighter vinegar and oil dressing. As part of the preparation, allow the ingredients in a vegetable salad to rest for a period of time to increase flavor and change texture in the mixture of ingredients.

Prepare a **fruit salad** from fruit using a slightly sweet or sweet/sour dressing to enhance the flavor. Handle the fruit carefully, and prepare the salad close to service to prevent the cut fruit from softening, browning, or losing moisture.

Discuss

- Can students think of an example of each type of salad?
  - Tossed: Caesar
  - Composed: Cobb
  - Bound: Potato
  - Vegetable: Coleslaw
  - Fruit salad: Tropical fruit cocktail
  - Combination: Tomato salad with a scoop of tuna salad
- Students might be able to think of several examples.
- Ask them to describe salads that can be used for a main dish.
- After discussing this, ask them to mention some salads that are best for a side salad or first course.

Vocabulary Terms

- **Tossed:** A salad that is mixed together with large utensils before serving.
- **Composed:** A salad with the ingredients carefully arranged in a display.
- **Bound salad:** A salad made from ingredients and dressings that can stick together.
- **Vegetable salad:** A nonlettuce raw vegetable salad.
- **Fruit salad:** A salad made of a mixture of fresh or canned fruits. Usually sweet, but not a dessert.

Figure Focus

Figure 4.2: Various examples of salads. Ask students what their favorite salads are.

Essential Skills:
Designing an Attractive Salad

Freshness, color, composition, dimension, and presentation are all factors in the attractiveness of a salad. An attractive salad is appetizing.

Vocabulary Terms

- **Combination salad:** A salad made of two or more of the basic types of salads.

A **combination salad** incorporates a combination of any of the four salad types discussed previously. When making a combination salad, prepare the different components according to their individual guidelines. Be sure to follow the guidelines for attractive salad arrangement.

Essential Skills
Designing an Attractive Salad

❶ Look at the plate or bowl as a picture frame. Select the right dish for the portion size. Keep the salad off the rim of the dish.

❷ Maintain a good balance of colors. Spark up plain iceberg lettuce with shredded carrots, red cabbage, another colored vegetable, or darker greens. Remember, three colors are usually enough. Too many colors are unappetizing.

❸ Height makes a salad more attractive. Ingredients that are mounded on a plate are more interesting and appealing than if they are spread flat over it. Place tomato or fruit wedges so that they overlap or lean on each other.

❹ Always cut the ingredients neatly and uniformly.

❺ Make sure every ingredient can be easily identified. Cut every ingredient into large enough pieces so that the customer can recognize them immediately. Use bite-sized pieces unless the food item can be cut with a fork.

❻ Finely chop items used as seasoning, such as onions.

❼ Keep the arrangement of ingredients simple. Using too many ingredients in an effort to make a salad more visually attractive may end up muddling the taste of the salad. See Figure 4.3.

Figure 4.3a: A good salad presentation: pasta and scallop salad.

Figure 4.3b: A better salad arrangement: garden vegetables and pasta salad.

Figure 4.3c: The best arrangement of salad: fresh tuna pasta salad niçoise.

226

Figure Focus

Figure 4.3a: The pasta and scallop salad looks small in the dish.

Figure 4.3b: This salad is more colorful and ample.

Figure 4.3c: This composed salad is colorful and abundant.

[fast fact]

Did You Know...?
The average 10-ounce tossed salad dressed with oil and vinegar has approximately 170 calories.

Essential Skills
Preparing a Green Salad

❶ Choose the ingredients. Try using one or more types of greens with flavors that will enhance the combination: some sweet and some bitter; some crisp and some soft; and some light in color and some dark in color.

❷ Wash and clean ingredients. Discard all withered, wilted, moldy, discolored, or rotten pieces. See Figure 4.4a.

❸ Remove all bitter and/or woody stems and cores. See Figure 4.4b.

❹ Use a salad spinner to spin the ingredients completely dry.

❺ Cut as required, making sure the cuts are uniform. See Figure 4.4c.

❻ Store any ingredients that you aren't using immediately.

❼ Tear or cut the greens into bite-size pieces. Customers should not have to cut the greens. The preferred serving size for a piece of lettuce is about the size of half of a dollar bill. If time does not allow for tearing greens, be sure to use sharp, stainless-steel knives to cut them.

Figure 4.4a: Step 2—Discard wilted or rotten pieces. **Figure 4.4b:** Step 3— Remove stems and cores. **Figure 4.4c:** Step 5—Make uniform cuts.

Fast Fact:
Did You Know . . . ?

More oil results in more calories. More vinegar doesn't add more calories. Vegetables add very few calories.

Essential Skills:
Preparing a Green Salad

Always keep in mind that a salad should be easy to eat with a fork and not require a knife if at all possible. Also, each leaf should look fresh.

227

Figure Focus

Figure 4.4a: Look inside the head of lettuce in case some wilted leaves are hidden.

Figure 4.4b: Some ribs are "woody," so discard them.

Figure 4.4c: Keep guests in mind and don't make bites too big or too small.

Essential Skills:
Preparing a Green Salad (cont.)

Very delicate items, like tomato or avocado slices, should be added after tossing to prevent them from falling apart.

In-Class Activity:
Nontraditional Salads

21st-Century Skills—Flexibility and Adaptability

Meat salads?

In Germany, a dish called *Fleischsalat* (meat salad) is made of strips of cold sausages similar to bologna, mixed together with pickles and bound with mayonnaise. It is served cold with bread and sliced cheese.

Wilted salads?

Bacon, sugar, and vinegar recipes can make a glaze "dressing" in a sauté pan. While the glaze is warm, some spinach leaves can be very quickly tossed in it and then plated with the bacon, warm goat cheese, nuts, or other ingredients for a wilted salad.

Warm salads?

Retired basketball great Karl Malone is famous for having sensitive teeth, but a taste for green salads. He always had his salad and salad plate briefly microwaved as part of his pregame restaurant dinner order.

Divide students into two groups.

Have each group discuss and brainstorm about different types of nontraditional salads.

- What is actually defined as a salad?

- What are the limits of the definition?

- How can salads be altered slightly to accommodate guests?

When ready for assembly:

Tossed Green Salad

❶ Combine all ingredients in a stainless-steel bowl and toss gently (being careful not to break apart delicate items) until well blended. Toss the greens gently until they are uniformly mixed. It's acceptable to add a nonjuicy raw vegetable garnish, such as julienne of green pepper or carrot shreds. Cut the garnish into broad, thin slices or shreds. See Figure 4.5a.

❷ Garnish with tomato wedges, cherry tomatoes, cucumber slices, radishes, and pepper rings, as desired. Garnishes that will become soggy or discolored, such as croutons or avocados, should be added just before service.

❸ Refrigerate.

❹ Dress the greens appropriately with only enough dressing to lightly coat the greens as close to service time as possible. The normal ratio is one-third ounce of dressing per ounce of greens.

❺ Place the salad on cold plates, using a base if necessary. Avoid putting salad ingredients on plates more than an hour or two before service, because they will wilt or dry. See Figure 4.5b.

❻ Serve chilled with chilled fork and dressing as required. See Figure 4.5c.

Figure 4.5a: Step 1—Toss gently until blended.

Figure 4.5b: Step 5—Place salad on cold plates.

Figure 4.5c: Step 6—Serve chilled.

Composed Green Salad

❶ Place desired base on a chilled plate or bowl. See Figure 4.6a on the following page.

❷ If serving immediately, pre-toss each ingredient with a small amount of dressing or olive oil and lightly season. If not serving immediately, skip this step to avoid wilting and loss of color. The flavor of the finished dish will not be as complete, but the texture and color of the ingredients will be fresher.

228

Figure Focus

Figure 4.5a: Tossing is usually a two-handed job, but can be done one-handed with tongs.

Figure 4.5b: Warm plates will wilt the leaves. Cold plates help keep them crisp, and are delightful for the presentation.

Figure 4.5c: Do not try to hold leaves too long or they will wilt or discolor.

Essential Skills:
Preparing Vegetable Salads

Cooked or raw, color and texture are very important to vegetable salads.

❸ Place ingredients as planned.

❹ Garnish and dress in accordance with the recipe or service need.

❺ Serve chilled with a chilled fork. See Figure 4.6b.

Figure 4.6a: Step 1—Place base on chilled plates.

Figure 4.6b: Step 5—Serve chilled.

Essential Skills
Preparing Vegetable Salads

❶ Gather all ingredients, including dressing.

❷ Cut all ingredients neatly. The shapes of the vegetables are important to the appearance of the salad (see Figure 4.7a on the following page):

• Cut vegetables in a uniform size.

• Cut the fresh vegetables as close to service time as possible.

❸ Cooked vegetables should be firm, with a crisp texture and good color.

❹ Cook vegetables in accordance with the recipe, but always protect the color and texture.

❺ Thoroughly drain and chill cooked vegetables before mixing them with the other ingredients.

❻ Toss all ingredients in a stainless-steel bowl and chill thoroughly. See Figure 4.7b on the following page.

229

Figure Focus

Figure 4.6a: The base should be completely edible and appear fresh.

Figure 4.6b: Layer upon layer, a composed salad is a work of art.

Essential Skills: Preparing Vegetable Salads (cont.)

Endive can be used as a base for plating many cold foods. It is especially nice on serving platters. In large pieces, it is not as desirable to eat as other milder greens.

On a guest's plate, iceberg or romaine are good choices.

Essential Skills: Preparing Bound Salads

Have all ingredients salad-ready before beginning to assemble the salad.

Pasta or potatoes should be cooked and chilled before assembling the salad.

Plan timing accordingly.

❼ Plate on a chilled plate or bowl with base and garnish in accordance with recipe or service need (see Figure 4.7c):

- Do not plate vegetable salads in acidic dressings too far ahead of time.
- Use sturdy, crisp greens for the base—iceberg, romaine, or endive—because these greens will not wilt easily.

Figure 4.7a: Step 1—Cut all ingredients in a uniform size. **Figure 4.7b:** Step 6—Toss all ingredients. **Figure 4.7c:** Step 7—Place on a chilled plate or bowl.

Essential Skills
Preparing Bound Salads

❶ Cook main ingredients correctly:
- Ensure pasta is cooked al dente.
- Ensure potatoes are cooked until soft in the center, but not falling apart.
- Ensure proteins are fully cooked, but still moist and tender.

❷ Cut cooked and raw ingredients to a uniform size. See Figure 4.8a on the following page.

❸ Cut ingredients in attractive shapes to enhance the appearance of the finished dish.

❹ Ensure all dressing is well-blended and seasoned.

❺ Keep all ingredients chilled during preparation:
- Make sure that cooked ingredients are well chilled before mixing with mayonnaise or mayonnaise-based dressing.
- Keep the completed salad out of the temperature danger zone at all times to avoid any danger of foodborne illness.

230

Figure Focus

Figure 4.7a: Grating raw vegetables keeps them uniform in size.

Figure 4.7b: Toss salad in a bowl with high sides.

Figure 4.7c: Transfer the salad to another bowl, platter, or plate for service.

❻ Add crisp foods for flavor and interest, such as celery, carrots, green peppers, chopped pickles, onions, water chestnuts, or apples. Be sure that the flavors complement each other.

❼ Marinate potatoes and seafood in light vinaigrette before mixing with other salad ingredients. Be sure to drain excess liquid first.

❽ Fold in thick dressings gently to avoid crushing or mashing the main ingredient, as with potato or egg salad.

❾ Portion cooked salads with a utensil such as a scoop to provide portion control and give height and shape to the salad.

❿ Serve on chilled plates with an appropriate base and garnish in accordance with the recipe and service needs. See Figure 4.8b.

Figure 4.8a: Step 2—Cook uniform-sized potatoes.

Figure 4.8b: Step 10—Serve on chilled plates with garnish.

Essential Skills
Prepping Gelatin Salads

❶ Use the right amount of gelatin for the volume of liquid in the recipe:

- Basic proportions for unflavored gelatin are below:
  - 2 ounces of dry, unsweetened gelatin per gallon of liquid (19 grams per liter) for a soft gel (molded gelatins)
  - 8 ounces dry, unsweetened gelatin per gallon for medium texture (sliceable)
  - 2½ ounces dry, unsweetened gelatin per gallon for hard texture (glazing only)
  - Basic proportions for sweetened, flavored gelatin are 24 ounces of gelatin per gallon of liquid (180 grams per liter).

231

Essential Skills:
Preparing Bound Salads (cont.)

Carefully fold dressing into ingredients.

A bound salad should not appear mashed or gluey.

Essential Skills:
Prepping Gelatin Salads

Just a little too much or too little water will doom a set salad.

Dissolve the gelatin in a different container than it is set in.

Figure Focus

Figure 4.8a: Keep potatoes of uniform size so they cook uniformly.

Figure 4.8b: Have the appropriate serving utensils for the type of salad.

Essential Skills:
Prepping Gelatin Salads (cont.)

The enzymes in pineapple and papaya "digest" the gelatin protein, preventing the structure from forming.

Because the enzyme is also a protein, cooking the fruit denatures or alters the protein so it is no longer an active enzyme.

❷ Altering the standard recipe in any way (using fruit, whipping, etc.) changes the way gelatin sets. Test each recipe before using it on the menu.

❸ Gelatin dissolves at about 100°F, but will dissolve faster at higher temperatures. To dissolve unflavored gelatin, stir it into cold liquid to avoid lumping. Let it stand for 5 minutes to absorb water. Heat it until dissolved, or add hot liquid and stir until dissolved. To dissolve sweetened, flavored gelatin, stir it into boiling water. Use half cold water or crushed ice for a quick set.

❹ Raw pineapple or papaya contains enzymes that dissolve the gelatin; the gelatin will not set. Cooked or canned pineapple or papaya may be used.

❺ Add solid ingredients when the gelatin is partially set to keep them evenly mixed and prevent settling to the bottom.

❻ Always drain canned fruit well. Measure the drained liquid and include in the added liquid.

❼ Pour into pans or individual molds and allow to set. Then cut into equal portions and garnish.

❽ To unmold gelatin:

- Run a thin knife blade around the top edges of the mold to loosen the salad.
- Dip the mold three-quarters of the way into hot water (120°F to 140°F) for one or two seconds only.
- Quickly wipe the bottom of the mold. Invert the salad plate over the mold and carefully flip the plate and mold over together.

❾ Always refrigerate gelatin salads until just before serving to keep them firm (see Figure 4.9):

- Add unflavored gelatin to vegetable or fruit salads, such as shredded cabbage and carrots to achieve a desired texture and appearance. Although flavored, sweetened gelatins can be used with fruits, unflavored gelatin does not compete with the natural flavor of the vegetable or fruit. Gelatin is also essential in aspics and other savory creations.

Figure 4.9: Step 9—Refrigerate gelatin salads until serving.

232

Figure Focus

Figure 4.9: Temperature control is essential. Do not place a set salad near a hot food.

Essential Skills
Preparing Fruit Salads

❶ Fruit salads may be either tossed or composed.

❷ Save the best pieces of fruit for the top. Place broken or less attractive pieces of fruit on the bottom of the salad. See Figure 4.10a.

❸ Some fruit discolors after it is peeled and cut, such as bananas and apples. Dip these fruits in a combination of lemon juice and water to keep their fresh appearance. Do not soak the fruit in the mixture or it will ruin the flavor of the fruit.

❹ Fruit does not hold well after it has been cut and peeled. Prepare fruit salads as close to service as possible.

❺ Drain canned fruit well before mixing it into a salad. Some of the liquid can be saved and used in fruit salad dressings or in other preparations.

❻ Dressings for fruit salads are usually sweet, but a little tartness gives additional flavor. Use fruit juices in the dressings. See Figure 4.10b.

Figure 4.10a: Step 2—Save the best pieces of fruit for the top.

Figure 4.10b: Step 6—Use fruit juices in the dressings.

Salads and Service

Today the salad section on most menus goes beyond the simple dinner salad. The salad, once typically served as a first course, is now also a main entrée at either lunch or dinner. Salads can incorporate various types of meat and fish, pastas and potatoes, as well as cheeses, vegetables, and fresh fruit.

233

Essential Skills: Preparing Fruit Salads

Keep color mixtures in mind.

For example, orange-yellow fruit and purple fruit might not mix to form a nice color.

Sometimes fruit juices mix to look gray or brown.

To include them in the same salad, mix right before serving.

Reinforce and Review

- Creativity with salads is popular.

- A great salad can set a restaurant apart from the competition.

- Salads require skill in the kitchen.

Figure Focus

Figure 4.10a: Fruit can be an ingredient and a self-garnish.

Figure 4.10b: Be careful of color combinations.

Mathematics Connection

Students will come to understand that fresh ingredients are important for salads.

Freshness varies from ingredient to ingredient. So does shelf life.

The most delicate ingredient is the "limiting factor" in the timeline of salad ingredient receiving and storage. The salad must be made while the most delicate ingredient is still fresh.

Have the students consider the limiting factor. What is it? What does it mean?

Assign students to each choose a salad recipe. Have them identify the most delicate ingredient, the limiting factor.

Have them specify the receiving, storage, and handling guidelines of their limiting factor ingredient.

Vocabulary Terms

- **Starter salad:** A salad given as the beginning course of a meal.

Salads can be used in five different ways during the service courses (see Figure 4.11 for visual examples of each):

1. Starter (or appetizer)
2. Accompaniment
3. Main course
4. Intermezzo (palate cleanser before dessert or cheese course)
5. Dessert

A **starter salad**, served as an appetizer to the main meal, is smaller in portion and consists of light, fresh, crisp ingredients to stimulate the appetite. Generally, salad greens and other vegetables lightly coated with a tangy, flavorful dressing work well as starter salads. A starter salad can also include small portions of protein such as seared tuna. A satisfying, attractive salad can set the tone for the rest of the meal.

Starter

Accompaniment

Main course

Intermezzo

Dessert

Figure 4.11: Salads contain many ingredients and can be more than just the first course.

234

Figure Focus

Figure 4.11: Each type of salad serves a different purpose in the presentation of the entire meal. Ask students what type of salads they enjoy.

Serve an **accompaniment salad,** also known as a side salad, with the main course of the meal. Make it light and flavorful, but not too rich. It should balance and complement the main course. For example, never serve a starchy salad, such as potato salad, when the main entrée also contains a starch (potatoes, rice, or pasta). Sweet fruit salads can accompany ham and pork. Lighter vegetable salads are good choices for hearty meals. Serve heavier salads, such as potato or pasta salad, only if the main entrée is light. For example, a small portion of potato salad is a good complement to a sandwich.

Main course salads are large enough to serve as a full meal and also contain protein ingredients, such as meat, poultry, seafood, egg, beans, or cheese. Main course salads provide a well-balanced meal, both visually and nutritionally. In addition to protein ingredients, the main course salad can contain a variety of vegetables, greens, and/or fruits. It is a menu staple for many restaurants. Such salads range from the very traditional chef's salad, containing mixed greens, raw vegetables, strips of meat, and cheese, to very popular Caesar salads with grilled chicken or shrimp. Figure 4.12 shows *mise en place* for a main course salad.

Figure 4.12: *Mise en place* for a main course salad.

The **intermezzo salad** is intended to be a palate cleanser after a rich dinner and before dessert. Often served in classic French meals, it refreshes or stimulates a person's appetite for the dessert or next course. This salad must be very light, such as Bibb lettuce or Belgian endive lightly dressed with vinaigrette or a small fruit salad. Use slightly acidic dressings, such as lemon or vinaigrette with flavored vinegar; the acid helps to clear the palate of previous flavors.

Dessert salads are usually sweet and often contain fruits, sweetened gelatin, nuts, cream, and whipped cream. These salads are often too sweet to be served at any other point in the meal. They are popular for buffet service and meals served family style because the colors make an attractive visual presentation.

235

Figure Focus
Figure 4.12: The *mise en place* for making salad includes preparing the fresh vegetables for the peak of ripeness and freshness.

Vocabulary Terms

- **Accompaniment salad:** A side salad.

- **Main course salad:** A large salad that is filling and satisfying for a meal.

- **Intermezzo salad:** A light salad to cleanse the palate between courses.

- **Dessert salad:** A sweet salad that can be a finale to a meal.

Essential Skills: Plating Salads

"Road-test" menu items when considering the plating.

Sit down and eat it, paying close attention to how easy it is to eat gracefully.

The last thing you want to do is make a guest feel overwhelmed and frustrated.

Also, take a "bird's-eye" view of the salad plate, as if you were a guest looking down on it.

It should be beautiful and inviting.

Teaching Tips

- If possible, have students gather together to clean spinach or chard fresh from the field.

- The best way to understand the need to clean greens is to clean mud off of them.

- Students should all get their hands dirty.

Essentials Skills
Plating Salads

What does the foodhandler use to serve an intermezzo salad? A platter? A bowl? A plate? It all depends upon the salad. The most important thing is to make it easy for the customer to eat gracefully.

Using the proper plate and utensil, a customer should never have to put his/her fingers in a salad when eating. Whatever the dish, it should be large enough to "frame" the food on top of it. This means that the outside rim of the plate should be free of food. Present the salad neatly within the frame created by the plate rim. See Figure 4.13.

If the salad is very large, the serving plate should be larger. Mound a bound salad like a crab Louis on a flat plate; the customer can eat it easily with a fork. A large composed salad like a cobb salad is difficult to mix and eat if the lettuce is piled onto a flat plate with the other ingredients stacked there as well, so use a large flat soup bowl or a plate with curved sides, which still displays the salad. The sides of the bowl give the customer someplace to contain the pieces and leverage the fork for graceful, hands-free dining.

Figure 4.13: Proper plating for an intermezzo salad.

Cleaning and Storing Salads

As discussed earlier, a key to preparing good-tasting, interesting, attractive salads is to start with clean, fresh ingredients. Always thoroughly wash greens, because dirt can lodge between leaves. When preparing salads, be careful not to handle ingredients too much.

236

Figure Focus

Figure 4.13: Note how the garnish and ingredients are part of the complete picture.

[ServSafe Connection]

Storing Loose Salad Greens

❶ Place clean greens on metal or plastic trays or tubs.

❷ Cover the greens loosely with lightly dampened paper towels. See Figure 4.14.

❸ Date, label, and refrigerate at 41°F or lower, but not lower than 36°F, for quality reasons.

❹ Remember that all salads/greens are highly perishable. Hold them for no more than 24 hours.

❺ Don't store greens with tomatoes, apples, or fruit that emits ethylene gas. This gas causes the greens to wilt.

Figure 4.14: Step 2—Cover greens with lightly dampened paper towels.

Storing Freshly Prepared Salads and Prepackaged Salads
Prepared Salads

❶ After preparation of a salad is complete, immediately place the salad in a suitably sized container with a tight lid. See Figure 4.15.

❷ Make sure the container is shallow enough to allow rapid chilling.

❸ Date, label, and refrigerate at 41°F or lower.

Figure 4.15: Step 1—Place the salad in a suitably sized container with a tight lid.

Prepackaged Salads

❶ Store in the original container at 41°F or lower until opened.

❷ Monitor the expiration date and rotate stock to make sure that product is used prior to its expiration date. Follow FIFO.

237

ServSafe Connection: Storing Loose Salad Greens

Salad greens need careful handling.

They might come with dirt, insects, and even compost on them.

It is important to completely clean greens without wilting them with too much water.

Properly storing them actually improves their crispness.

Figure Focus

Figure 4.14: New paper towels are clean and sterile.

Figure 4.15: The airtight lid keeps the leaves crisp and fresh.

Reinforce and Review

- Prepackaged greens might seem ready-to-serve, but even these need rinsing before serving.

- They are flushed and gassed with chemicals that preserve them a bit longer than otherwise.

- Some produce is irradiated to extend its shelf life.

- Be aware of these treatments in case customers inquire.

- These processes are considered safe, but some guests might be philosophically opposed to the treatments.

After the greens are clean, proper storage is essential to keeping them fresh. Proper storage ensures the quality of the product served to the guest. Remember, the quality of the salad is determined just as much by its wholesomeness (if it is safe to eat) and freshness, as by the quality of its ingredients and preparation.

Figure 4.16 shows prepackaged greens in a commercial kitchen.

All labels on stored containers should include the name of the item, weight, date received, name of person storing the product, and the original use-by date, if any. Do not open the containers of produce until you are ready to use them. Unopened produce can be stored for two to three days. Always test the quality of the product before serving it to customers.

Figure 4.16: Prepackaged greens in a commercial kitchen.

Homework Activity: Research MAP

Science Connection

Modified atmosphere packaging (MAP) is a process of preparing foods, including salad greens, for shipment and storage.

Have students investigate this process.

Why is it important?

Is it a widespread practice in the United States?

Have them write two paragraphs about the process, to the extent of their science understanding.

The process inhibits spoilage and increases storage life.

Airtight bags are filled with a special mix of gases to surround the produce. These gases, which might include carbon dioxide and nitrogen, reduce oxidation and decrease the growth of microbes. Both actions delay spoilage and prolong the shelf life of the produce until the bag is opened.

Nitrogen gas (N_2) is inert, and inhibits oxidation, which requires oxygen.

Carbon dioxide gas (CO_2) creates an acidic environment that can inhibit bacterial growth. Carbon dioxide can form carbonic acid with the water in the produce, which can slightly lower the pH.

What's New: Drying Greens on Spin Cycle: The Salad Spinner

Do the students understand centrifugal force?

This should have been part of their middle school science curriculum.

Assess for prior knowledge and understanding.

A salad spinner might improve their understanding.

[what's new]

Drying Greens on Spin Cycle: The Salad Spinner

Drying salad greens can be a long, tedious chore. In the past, chefs had to lay the greens out flat on a counter and pat them dry with paper towels, which not only takes a lot of time, but also creates a lot of paper waste. Both lost time and excess waste cost money. In addition, the irregular shapes and textures of salad greens make it difficult to get all of the leaves completely dry with even the best effort. If greens are not dried completely, any remaining water on the leaves prevents the salad dressing from clinging properly to the leaves. This results in soggy salads with diluted flavors.

A much easier solution to drying greens is the salad spinner (see Figure 4.17), and it couldn't be easier to use. Put wet greens into a basket with holes in it (like a colander). Place the basket inside a solid plastic container, and then add the lid with a spinning mechanism on top. The mechanism spins the basket around inside the solid plastic container, creating centrifugal force. Centrifugal force is the outward pressure created from the center of a spinning object. The pressure created from the spinning motion forces all of the loose droplets of water from the leaves and into the solid plastic container. After a few short spins, only dry greens are left in the basket, and all the water is dumped into the plastic container. Fully dried greens in less than a minute!

Figure 4.17: The spinning motion of a salad spinner pulls excess water from the lettuce.

238

Figure Focus

Figure 4.16: This lettuce is packaged for improved storage life.

Figure 4.17: The water is spun off into the outer container of the salad spinner and discarded.

Essential Skills
Cleaning Greens

❶ Keep greens refrigerated until they are ready to be prepared and served. Cover them with a damp paper towel to keep them crisp and fresh.

❷ When ready to use, greens need to be cleaned thoroughly.

❸ Remove the outer leaves and discard.

❹ Pull greens completely apart into separate leaves.

❺ Rinse each leaf thoroughly until all traces of dirt, grit, and insects are completely removed. See Figure 4.18a.

❻ Water should be a little warmer than the greens being washed.

❼ If possible, avoid soaking greens because they tend to absorb water.

❽ Dry the greens as thoroughly as possible after rinsing. Spinning the greens in a salad spinner is highly recommended. Water on the greens will not allow dressing to adhere to the leaf and will dilute the consistency and flavor of the dressing, so it's important that leaves are completely dry. Using a colander or patting with paper towels are also options. See Figure 4.18b.

❾ Remove any tough stems or wilted spots. Tearing is preferred for delicate greens, but be careful not to bruise the leaves.

❿ When the greens have been rinsed and dried, you can refrigerate them for a few hours. Sturdy greens, such as iceberg lettuce or romaine lettuce, can be held for as long as 24 hours.

Figure 4.18a: Step 5—Thoroughly wash all greens.   **Figure 4.18b:** Step 8—Dry greens after rinsing and pat them with paper towel.

Essential Skills: Cleaning Greens

Follow these instructions specifically to assure safety.

Drying the greens is as important as washing them, as it helps prevent wilting.

Use tap water to clean only if the tap water in your area is safe (e.g., the United States).

Local authorities announce any temporary problems with a water supply.

Figure Focus

Figure 4.18a: Even tiny leaves and spaces need to be clean.

Figure 4.18b: Allow for personnel to spend the time required to clean the greens properly.

Summary

- Remind students to review the following:
  1. Ingredients and parts of a salad
  2. Types of salad
  3. Salads and service
  4. Cleaning and storing salads

Summary

In this section, you learned the following:

■ Lettuce is frequently used as a salad base, but any number of ingredients can be used in a salad, including meat, fish, starches (such as pasta or potatoes), vegetables, cheeses, and fruit. The basic parts of a salad are the base, the body, the garnish, and the dressing.

■ The five basic types of salad are green salads (tossed or composed), bound, vegetable, fruit, and combination.

■ The five basic salads that can be served throughout the course of a meal are starter, accompaniment, main course, intermezzo, and dessert. Starter salads are small, light salads that stir the appetite for the main meal. Accompaniment, or side, salads are small salads served along with the main meal. These salads balance and complement the main ingredients of the meal. Main course salads are larger salads that can be main meals in themselves. Main course salads often have a protein along with a variety of vegetables, cheeses, greens, and even sometimes fruit. Intermezzo salads are small salads used to clear the palate for the next course. Dessert salads are sweeter than the others and often consist of fruit as the primary ingredient.

■ To clean salads, remove the outer leaves of greens, pull apart the remaining leaves, and rinse them thoroughly to remove any and all dirt, grit, and insects. Rinsing is preferred to soaking because leaves can absorb water, making the lettuce soggy. Store loose greens with dampened paper towels at a temperature between 36°F and 41°F. Store prepared salads in a tightly sealed container that is shallow enough to allow for rapid chilling. Properly label and rotate the greens for service using the FIFO method for all salad ingredients.

Section 4.1 Review Questions

1. What are the four parts of any salad?

2. What are the five basic salad types?

3. Describe the different kinds of salad that can be served during the course of a meal.

4. Explain the proper way to clean lettuce for salads.

5. Debra Olson notes that she finds it interesting to create salad recipes that add value, stimulate interest, and offer both traditional and nontraditional choices. Research a traditional and nontraditional salad recipe that are interesting and that use reasonably priced produce.

6. How can salads help Miguel and Chef Kate meet the demands of their customers? Create a salad for each of the five courses that would be tasty, healthy, and have eye appeal.

7. How does timing affect fruit salad production? What must be considered when making a fruit salad? What are the nutritional differences between fresh and canned fruit salads?

8. Why do you think salad greens should not be stored below a temperature of 36°F? How might lower temperatures affect the product?

241

Section 4.1 Review Questions

1. The four parts are base, body, garnish, and dressing.

2. The five basic types are green, bound, vegetable, fruit, and combination.

3. The kinds of salad are starter, accompaniment, main course, intermezzo, and dessert.

4. See the Essential Skills box on p. 239.

5. Each student will have a unique set of discoveries.

6. Students will use their creativity.

7. Freshness and limiting factors will influence when food can be served. The nutritional differences involve some loss of vitamin C and other water-soluble vitamins. Colors that stay fresh and bright maintain their phytochemical qualities. Minerals tend to be stable. Some minerals are better used from canned or cooked produce than from raw.

8. If produce freezes, the water in cells expands. That makes the cell walls burst, resulting in wilting or mushiness.

Section 4.1 Activities

1. Each group will learn new salads. The more the students learn about various salads, the better.

2. This will result in more information and thinking about salads. Creativity should prevail.

3. The students will have their own opinions about this.

Section 4.1 Activities

1. Study Skills/Group Activity: The Classics

In a small group, have each member research a classic salad. Some examples include salade niçoise, waldorf salad, crab Louis, coleslaw, German potato salad, and caprese salad. Feel free to think of others. Learn the ingredients and preparation of this salad and a little of its history. Then, present your findings to the class as a group.

2. Independent Activity: Bowl or Platter?

Some composed salads are served in a bowl, and others are served on a platter. Present an opinion piece about this. What are the pros and cons of each? Then, based on your analysis, propose a plate presentation for three of the classic salads researched for the Group Activity.

3. Critical Thinking: Choosing Salads

This section reviewed the five kinds of salads that can be served during the course of a meal: starter, accompaniment, main course, intermezzo, and dessert. If you were running a restaurant, on which kinds of salads would you focus when making your menu? Choose two and explain your reasoning.

242

4.1 Salads	4.2 Salad Dressings and Dips	4.3 Garnishes
• Ingredients and parts of a salad	• Types of dressings	• Garnishing: why and how
• Types of salads	• Dips	• Garnishing desserts
• Salads and service		• Garnishing soups
• Cleaning and storing salads		

SECTION 4.2 SALAD DRESSINGS AND DIPS

You don't often think of salad without thinking of salad dressing. A well-seasoned dressing added in the right proportions can lift a salad to new heights. A bland dressing added to excess can completely ruin a salad. Striking the right balance is key. In order to do that, knowledge of the consistency and ingredients of the main salad dressing types is very important, as are the types of ingredients with which each dressing is best paired. The same is true of various kinds of dips. In this section, you learn about both. First, you learn about the major types of dressings, how they're made, and what they're made of. Then, you learn about the basic kinds of dips, their ingredients, and what the best pairings are.

Study Questions

After studying Section 4.2, you should be able to answer the following questions:

- What are the different types of dressings?
- What is the emulsion process?
- What is the difference between an emulsion and a suspension mixture?
- How are the different types of dressings used?
- What is a dip, and how is it like a salad dressing?
- What are some different kinds of dips?

Types of Dressing

The flavor of a salad dressing complements or enhances the salad ingredients. For example, when working with a slightly bitter green such as arugula or radicchio, give the dressing a hint of sweetness (as well as a slight acidity) to work with the bitterness of the green. The type of dressing also depends on the texture of the salad ingredients. Use lighter dressings on more delicate ingredients; use heavier dressings on more robust, heartier ingredients.

243

Section 4.2
Salad Dressings and Dips

Introduce the Section

a. There are many different types of dressings.
b. Emulsions and suspensions are the chemical aspects of dressings and dips.
c. Dips and salad dressings are chemically similar, but not quite the same.

Vocabulary Review

a. Direct students to the key terms.
b. Pronounce each word, and have the students repeat the pronunciation out loud.
c. Discuss the definition of each word.

Teach

Discuss

- Dressings can identify a salad.

- Asian chicken salad has a very specific, ginger-laced dressing.

- Crab Louis has Louis dressing, which is a mayonnaise dressing to which red chili sauce, minced green onion, and minced green chili peppers have been added. There are slight variations on the sauce.

- Caesar salad is only a regular green salad without the dressing. Caesar dressing has parmesan cheese, lemon juice, olive oil, egg, anchovy, Worcestershire sauce, and black pepper. It may be prepared tableside.

- Ranch dressing and ranch dip are essentially the same thing, but differ in viscosity. Both consist of buttermilk or sour cream, mayonnaise, minced green onion, garlic powder, and other seasonings.

- Demonstrate mixing oil and vinegar.

- Use a stopwatch to time how long it takes for the oil and vinegar to separate again.

- Help students understand that dressing should be shaken right before it is poured on the salad.

- Help students understand that nonemulsified dressing should be added right before serving.

- The dressing will separate even after it is on the lettuce.

Vocabulary Terms

- **Vinaigrette dressing:** Oil and vinegar dressing.

- **Suspension:** The phase mixture between two or more nonmixing liquids, usually achieved by agitating.

Dressings can be made from a number of different ingredients, but the primary dressings are listed below:

- Vinaigrette
- Emulsified vinaigrette
- Mayonnaise-based
- Mayonnaise

Vinaigrette (vin-uh-GRETT) **dressing** in its simplest form is made of oil and vinegar. Vinaigrettes are lighter, thinner dressings often used on more delicate ingredients, such as greens and vegetables. The standard recipe for a basic vinaigrette is three parts oil to one part vinegar. Substitute acidic juices like lemon, lime, or orange for part or all of the vinegar. When shaken together, these ingredients form a suspension. A **suspension** is a temporary mixture of ingredients that eventually separates back into its unique parts. The ingredients in vinaigrette will separate after nonuse; remix them before every service.

Figure 4.19: A vinaigrette is a salad dressing made by combining vinegar and oil.

Figure 4.19 is an illustration of oil and vinegar.

Use certain vinegars with sharp flavors, such as tarragon or balsamic vinegar, sparingly. Strongly flavored oils, such as extra virgin or virgin olive oils (which are made from the first pressing of the olives) and nut oils, contribute a flavor of their own and can overpower the other flavors in the dressing and the salad if not used in moderation. Generally, add other flavoring ingredients to the vinegar and oil mixture. Table 4.3 on the following page lists the types of oil and vinegar.

244

Figure Focus
Figure 4.19: The flavor of the oil and the flavor of the vinegar should be considered when choosing which ones to use.

Table 4.3: Types of Oil and Vinegar

Types of Oil	
Canola	Light in color and very mild in flavor; very low in saturated fat; high in monounsaturated fat content; has a good omega-3 fatty acid profile.
Corn	Light golden color; nearly tasteless.
Cottonseed Soybean Safflower	Bland; nearly tasteless.
Olive	Distinctive, fruity flavor; greenish color; not an all-purpose oil, but brings a distinctive flavor.
Peanut	Mild but distinctive flavor; somewhat expensive; must disclose use in menu items because of allergies.
Walnut	Distinctive flavor; expensive; used mostly in elegant restaurants with specialty salads; must disclose use in menu items because of allergies.
Types of Vinegar	
Balsamic	Special wine vinegar aged in wooden barrels for 4–50 years; dark brown color and sweet taste; sticky consistency due to high sugar content.
Cider	Made from apples; brown color; slightly sweet taste.
Flavored	Have flavor of other products added to them, such as tarragon, garlic, or raspberries.
Sherry	Made from sherry wine; has sherry flavor.
Specialty	Malt, rice vinegar, and vinegars flavored with fruits, such as raspberry; sometimes lemon juice or other citrus juices are used in place of or in addition to vinegar in some salad dressings.
White or Distilled	Distilled and purified to give it a neutral flavor.
Wine or Champagne	White or red color; usually made from wines.

Compared to the suspension mixture of regular vinaigrettes, **emulsified** (uh-MUL-si-fide) **vinaigrettes** have gone through the emulsion process. An **emulsion** is a mixture of ingredients that permanently stays together, unlike a suspension that eventually separates. In order to create an emulsion, you

245

Table 4.3: Types of Oil and Vinegar

- Oils and vinegars have distinctive flavors. They lend character to salads and other dishes. They should be carefully chosen for their purpose.

Teaching Tips

- Be aware of any student peanut or walnut allergies before tasting any oils.

In-Class Activity: Emulsifiers

Science Connection

Oil (lipid) doesn't mix with water. It is called "hydrophobic," or afraid of water. Vinegar is a water solution of an acid. Acid mixes just fine with water. It's called "hydrophilic," or water-loving.

There are molecules that have a lipophilic or lipid-loving end that can mix just fine with oil. The other end of the same molecule is hydrophilic, and can mix with water. These molecules are emulsifiers. They can emulsify, or mix, lipid and water—oil and vinegar. Think of them as helping hands or negotiators.

One such emulsifier is soap. No one wants to eat soap, or make salad dressing from it. But it cleans grease off skin by connecting its lipophilic end with grease and making it water soluble with the hydrophilic end. Grease is removed with all the bubbles and water.

An edible emulsifier is lecithin, found in egg yolk. Lecithin has far more culinary potential than soap!

Later in this chapter there are Essential Skills boxes for making emulsified vinaigrette and for making mayonnaise. They are emulsified with egg yolks.

Teach this lesson about emulsifiers. Then have the class or groups make emulsified vinaigrette, mayonnaise, or both.

Assess their success in the kitchen lab as you usually do.

Vocabulary Terms

- **Emulsified vinaigrette:** An oil and vinegar mixture that remains blended due to the addition of a chemical that can keep them mixed and stable.
- **Emulsion:** A stable mixture of two or more non-mixing phases with the help of an emulsifier.

Essential Skills:
How To Make a Vinaigrette

This dressing is not emulsified.

As suggested previously, time how long it takes for the mixture to separate.

Vocabulary Terms

- **Emulsifier:** A chemical that can bind nonmixable ingredients.

need an emulsifier. An **emulsifier** is an ingredient that can permanently bind dissimilar ingredients, such as oil and vinegar, together on a molecular level. Eggs are good emulsifiers. Eggs bind together oil and vinegar permanently, so these three ingredients make up the base of many emulsified vinaigrettes. Emulsified vinaigrettes are thicker than suspension vinaigrettes and coat ingredients more heavily. They are good dressings for salads containing sturdier, more robust ingredients, such as pastas, meats, or fish.

Essential Skills
How to Make Vinaigrette Dressing

1. Combine the vinegar and seasonings in an appropriately sized stainless-steel bowl.

2. Slowly whisk in the oil until a homogeneous mixture is formed (the suspension). See Figure 4.20.

3. Serve the dressing immediately or refrigerate it.

4. Before dressing the salad, thoroughly recombine all of the ingredients by stirring or shaking vigorously.

Figure 4.20: Step 2—Whisk together the oil until mixture is formed (suspension).

[fast fact]

Did You Know...?
The trend in restaurants is to use balsamic vinegar with brown sugar on fruit salads. This is probably because the flavor of the balsamic vinegar is rich and sweet. The finest grades are the product of years of aging in a successive number of casks made of various types of wood (including oak, mulberry, chestnut, cherry, juniper, ash, and acacia). It is a perfect complement to fruit.

246

Figure Focus
Figure 4.20: A whisk will mix the dressing. A shaker bottle works as well.

Mayonnaise-based dressings are typically creamy dressings, such as Russian, thousand island, and blue cheese. They are often thicker than emulsified vinaigrettes (but not always). These dressings are versatile in that foodhandlers can use them to dress lighter greens or heartier proteins. Apply them like the vinaigrettes, as close to service as possible.

Essential Skills
How to Make Emulsified Vinaigrette Dressing

❶ Beat the egg yolks until they are frothy. Add a little water if the yolks are very thick.

❷ Add a small amount of the vinegar or lemon juice.

❸ Gradually mix in two-thirds of the oil, whisking the mixture constantly. See Figure 4.21a.

❹ Add the remainder of the vinegar or lemon juice and blend well.

❺ Gradually mix in the remainder of the oil and any additional seasonings or flavoring ingredients.

❻ Serve the dressing at once or store it in refrigeration. See Figure 4.21b.

Figure 4.21a: Step 3—Mix two-thirds of the oil.

Figure 4.21b: Step 6—Serve the dressing immediately or refrigerate.

Essential Skills: How To Make Emulsified Vinaigrette Dressing

The egg yolk proteins are denatured by the acid (vinegar or lemon juice).

Therefore, they are not quite "raw," even though they are not cooked.

Reinforce and Review

- Viscosity is the thickness of a liquid, which affects the flow of that liquid.

- The viscosity of a dressing should match the needs of the salad.

- A very thick dressing does not work for a very light, tender green like Bibb lettuce.

- The mouthfeel of a thick dressing is different than that of a thin dressing.

Vocabulary Terms

- **Mayonnaise-based:** Salad dressings made from mayonnaise.

247

Figure Focus

Figure 4.21a: Mix the oil in slowly.

Figure 4.21b: Because of the egg yolks, refrigerate the dressing.

Most mayonnaise foods are safe, but keep them refrigerated to avoid possible problems.

Reinforce and Review

- Mayonnaise is as safe as its ingredients. However, because pathogens can grow in mayonnaise, proper handling is crucial.

- The weight of the dressing determines the weight of the ingredients it can dress.

- A thick, stable dressing can bind potatoes, chicken, or other foods.

- If bound properly, a bound salad can be scooped.

Vocabulary Terms

- **Mayonnaise:** An emulsified and stable thick oil, vinegar, and egg yolk dressing.

[ServSafe Connection]

Mayonnaise and TCS Food

Bound salads are often held together with mayonnaise. This includes potato salad, egg salad, tuna salad, and macaroni salad. Also, many dressings for tossed salads have a mayonnaise base. Homemade mayonnaise is made with raw eggs, although commercial operations usually use prepared mayonnaise.

Anything containing mayonnaise is a TCS food. These types of foods are usually not cooked after preparation, resulting in no chance to get rid of any pathogens. The temperature of these foods must be monitored very carefully.

Watch the temperature carefully so that mayonnaise-containing foods do not enter the danger zone (41°F–135°F). Keep these stored at 41°F or lower until ready to serve. Don't let these items sit out longer than two hours. And be sure to use the FIFO method of storage rotation.

Mayonnaise is the most stable and thickest emulsified dressing. It contains a higher ratio of oil to vinegar and a greater quantity of egg yolks than is required for emulsified vinaigrette. Use mayonnaise to bind and hold together heartier ingredients, such as potatoes, tuna, or chicken. Use it in the preparation of a salad before service. Add other ingredients to the mayonnaise to create different flavor profiles. Mustard is a common addition to mayonnaise dressings, as are fresh herbs and garlic.

Also use other ingredients, such as sour cream, yogurt, and fruit juices as the main dressing ingredients. Since most salad dressing is served fresh, without cooking, the dressing quality depends directly on the quality of ingredients used to prepare it. Higher-quality ingredients typically improve the overall quality of the dressing, and lower-quality ingredients detract from the overall quality. Table 4.4 on the following page matches dressing with the appropriate salad greens.

Table 4.4: Matching Dressing and Salad Greens

Dressings	Greens
Vinaigrette dressing made with vegetable or olive oil and vinegar or lemon juice	Any greens: Iceberg, romaine, leaf lettuce, butterhead lettuce, escarole, curly endive, Belgian endive, radicchio, baby lettuces, sorrel, arugula, dandelion
Vinaigrette dressing made with nut oil and balsamic vinegar	Delicate greens: Butterhead lettuce, Bibb lettuce, Belgian endive, radicchio, baby lettuces, arugula, watercress
Emulsified vinaigrette dressing	Any greens: Romaine, iceberg leaf lettuce, butterhead lettuce, escarole, curly endive, Belgian endive, radicchio, baby lettuces, sorrel, arugula, watercress
Mayonnaise-based dressing	Hardy greens: Iceberg, romaine, leaf lettuce, escarole, curly endive, sorrel, dandelion greens

[fast fact]

Did You Know…?
One tablespoon of mayonnaise has approximately 90 calories and ten grams of fat, which is approximately 15 percent of the recommended daily allowance for fat.

[nutrition]

Dressing on the Side?
Guests began ordering "dressing on the side" as a strategy to reduce the fat calorie content of salads. A fresh vegetable and greens salad might contain only 50 calories. Depending on the type, salad dressing can add up to 600 calories to the dish. Since that defeats the purpose of some people choosing salad entrées, dietitians began suggesting that customers request dressing in a separate container "on the side." Customers then can dress the salad themselves without worrying that the kitchen would overdo it.

Although these strategies sometimes save fat calories, they may also prove to do the opposite. Some guests may end up consuming more dressing doing it themselves "on the side" than had the foodhandler applied it for them in a well-proportioned amount. In addition, having the guest order the dressing "on the side" does not do justice to a fine salad dressing recipe nor reward establishments that take pride in serving delicious and healthful menu items.

Many eating establishments offer tossed salads with low-fat, great-tasting, fresh dressing that very lightly coats the greens. The patron gets a low-calorie and low-fat option, and the chef can display some creative culinary magic.

249

Table 4.4: Matching Dressing and Salad Greens

- The combination of the proper greens and dressings makes a delicious salad.
- Ask students to consider combinations that they enjoy.

In-Class Activity: Matching Game

21st-Century Skills—Use Systems Thinking

Make a handout with the list of dressings on one side, but not in the order in which they are listed in Table 4.4.

Make a longer list of the greens in Table 4.4 in mixed-up order.

Have the students draw lines from the dressing side to the matching greens.

A lettuce can pair with more than one type of dressing.

Vinaigrette—Vegetable or olive oil, vinegar or lemon juice	Butterhead lettuce
	Iceberg lettuce
	Sorrel
	Baby lettuces
Vinaigrette—Flavored oil, balsamic vinegar	Radicchio
	Escarole
	Leaf lettuce
	Romaine
Emulsified vinaigrette dressing	Dandelion greens
	Arugula
	Belgian endive
	Watercress
Mayonnaise-based dressing	Bibb lettuce
	Curly endive

Nutrition: Dressing on the Side?

One technique that some weight loss specialists recommend is dipping the tines of the fork into the dressing, and then using the fork to pick up the salad.

A pile of thick dressing ladled on top of salad greens might be too much, and dressing on the side might be preferable in this case.

However, a properly dressed salad is not overly heavy with dressing.

Fast Fact: Did You Know . . . ?

Mayonnaise is considered a high-fat food.

Essential Skills: How to Make Mayonnaise

Teach the lesson on emulsifiers prior to making mayonnaise.

Discuss

- When the students think of Famous Dave's Barbeque and pulled pork, they probably don't envision a salad.

- Yet there is just such a salad available at the outlets of this chain. They feature salads with barbequed pulled pork, beef brisket, and fried chicken.

- Perhaps the students can think of other unusual salads they have tried or heard of at restaurants.

Essential Skills
How to Make Mayonnaise

1. Place egg yolks in an appropriately sized stainless-steel bowl.

2. Add dry ingredients and whisk until frothy and well blended. See Figure 4.22a.

3. Drizzle oil slowly into mixture, whisking rapidly.

4. As mixture thickens, slowly alternate adding small amounts of vinegar or lemon juice and oil until all are used.

5. Check seasoning.

6. Serve the dressing at once or refrigerate it. See Figure 4.22b.

Although house-made mayonnaise is fresh-tasting, it is usually best to use commercially prepared mayonnaise in a restaurant or foodservice operation because the acidity in commercially prepared versions has been raised to make them less susceptible to pathogen growth. If using house-made mayonnaise, use pasteurized yolks.

Figure 4.22a: Step 2—Whip the eggs until frothy.

Figure 4.22b: Step 6—Serve the dressing immediately or refrigerate.

250

Figure Focus

Figure 4.22a: The bowl for beating yolks should be large enough to hold all of the mayonnaise that is made.

Figure 4.22b: If mayonnaise is to be used warm or at room temperature, serve it freshly made.

[fast fact]

Did You Know...?

Oil and water don't mix—unless, that is, they're in an emulsifier. An emulsifier is a molecule that attracts water to one of its ends (hydrophilic) and oil to the other end (lipophilic). A common emulsifier is lecithin in egg yolk. Soy beans also have some emulsifying qualities. The emulsifier molecule permanently mixes the two liquids that could not otherwise stay mixed. See Figure 4.23.

Without the emulsifier, two liquids of different densities, like oil and vinegar, will not stay mixed. But shake them together, and they are mixed temporarily in a suspension, like a vinaigrette dressing. Tiny droplets of oil are suspended throughout the vinegar for awhile. Before long, the oil drops float to the top and join into an oil layer once again. See Figure 4.24.

A colloid is similar to a suspension, but the droplets are much smaller and cannot usually be seen with the naked eye. The mixture occurs on the molecular level. Many colloids exist among food products, including whipped topping, homogenized milk, marshmallows, and gelatin. Given enough time, colloids can separate. Usually, the colloidal food grows stale before this happens. See Figure 4.25.

A solution is a mixture that is not going to separate. It is chemically changed and cannot be changed back without a chemical reaction, often involving heat. For example, after salt has dissolved into water, it's pretty tough to get the salt crystals back out. They do not settle to the bottom because they have chemically changed. See Figure 4.26.

Figure 4.23: Common emulsifier —lecithin in egg yolk.

Figure 4.24: Vinaigrette dressing.

Figure 4.25: Common colloid— marshmallow.

Figure 4.26: Solutions—salt crystals.

Dips

A dip is a flavorful mixture that accompanies certain food items. Like salad dressings, dips should complement or enhance a food's flavor. Depending on their ingredients and purpose, dips can be served hot or cold. Cold dips often

251

Fast Fact:
Did You Know . . . ?

A colloid can be two phase liquids, or two states like air and liquid.

Discuss

- Dips usually have increased viscosity for being carried on chips, vegetables, or crackers.

- Students might be familiar with salsa as a dip for tortilla chips.

- A dip should not be gluey, gloppy, or runny.

Figure Focus

Figure 4.23: Eggs must be separated.

Figure 4.24: Vinaigrette will mix by suspension, but only for a little while.

Figure 4.25: Air is suspended within marshmallows, but it is so fine that it is a colloid that will not fall out of suspension.

Figure 4.26: Salt crystals will dissolve in water, which is actually a chemical change rather than a mixture.

Reinforce and Review

- Dips, like soups, sauces, and other classics, appear in ancient cuisines from around the world.

- Tahini is a sesame seed paste.

Discuss

- Chips and dip have historically been a popular party food.

- Potato chips and onion dip or clam dip are typically found on a snack buffet.

- Discuss chips and dips with the students. Do they see them at social functions they attend?

Vocabulary Terms

- **Guacamole:** A dip made of mashed avocados.

- **Salsa:** A fresh relish-type sauce or dip.

- **Hummus:** A Middle Eastern dip of mashed legumes.

use mayonnaise, sour cream, or cream cheese as a base. Make cold dips the same way as mayonnaise-based salad dressings, although dips are normally thicker than salad dressings. Thin many cold dips for use as salad dressing.

It's important for a dip to have the proper consistency. Any dip should be soft enough to scoop up with a cracker, chip, or vegetable, but thick enough to stay on it. Serve each dip at the proper consistency and serving temperature. Most dips become thicker as they are held in the refrigerator. Some dips are heated in the oven or microwave before serving.

Ethnic variations of special salads and accompaniments are very popular as dips. Some examples include the following:

- **Guacamole** (gwah-kuh-MOE-lee): This is an avocado dip (of Aztec origin).

- **Salsa:** This is made from peppers, such as jalapeño or serrano, onions, and tomatoes (from Mexico).

- **Hummus:** This is made with chick peas, garlic, and tahini (from the Middle East).

Their texture and flavors are bold and unique, as well as nutritious. See Figure 4.27 for examples of each.

Figure 4.27: Guacamole, fresh salsa, and hummus.

Figure Focus

Figure 4.27: These are completely different types of dips, from different parts of the world. If possible, have students create some of the dips discussed.

Essential Skills
Making a Simple Cold Dip

❶ Select your base, such as mayonnaise, sour cream, or cream cheese. If cream cheese is the base, first soften it by mixing in an electric mixer.

❷ Add the selection of flavoring ingredients (chopped cooked vegetables, chopped cold vegetables, chopped cold cooked fish, seafood, herbs, spices, etc.).

❸ Blend all ingredients well.

❹ Adjust the consistency by adding milk, buttermilk, cream, sour cream, or another liquid that is suitable for the dip.

❺ Serve immediately or refrigerate until service. See Figure 4.28.

Figure 4.28: Step 5—Serve cold dip immediately or refrigerate.

Summary

In this section, you learned the following:

■ Many ingredients can be used to make salad dressings, but the four main salad dressings are vinaigrette, emulsified vinaigrette, mayonnaise-based, and mayonnaise.

■ An emulsion is the permanent blending of dissimilar ingredients, such as oil and vinegar. An emulsion requires an emulsifier, an ingredient that can permanently bind ingredients together on a molecular level. Eggs are good

253

Summary

- Remind students to review the following:
  1. Types of dressing
  2. Types of dips

Figure Focus
Figure 4.28: Cold dip should be cold, but not frigid.

emulsifiers and are often used in emulsified vinaigrettes to permanently bind oil and vinegar together. A suspension is a temporary blending of unlike ingredients, such as oil and vinegar. In a suspension, the ingredients will eventually come apart and separate. Vinaigrette is a suspension mixture, and mayonnaise is a classic emulsion.

- Vinaigrettes are lighter dressings used on more delicate ingredients, like salad greens. Emulsified vinaigrettes tend to be thicker and can be used on increasingly sturdier ingredients. Mayonnaise-based dressings are often thicker and creamy and can be used on heartier lettuce, proteins, and pastas. Finally, mayonnaise is the sturdiest emulsion and is used to bind ingredients, such as meat, fish, and starches together.

- A dip is a mixture served as an accompaniment to certain food items. Like salad dressings, dips are meant to complement or enhance the food items they are served with, not hide the flavor of the food.

- Salsa, guacamole, and hummus are examples of popular ethnic dips.

Section 4.2 Review Questions

❶ What are the four primary types of salad dressing?

❷ Explain what an emulsion is and how the process of emulsion works.

❸ List and differentiate between three different types of oil and three different types of vinegar.

❹ What are the three main ingredients that make up mayonnaise?

❺ Debra Olson says that, currently, Golden Corral makes three dressings on-site. Why would a restaurant choose to make its own dressings rather than purchase prepared products?

❻ Most of Kabob's salad dressing choices are high in fat and calories. The lack of more healthful dressing options is one reason why the customers aren't as happy as they could be. Add five new low-fat and low-calorie dressing options to Miguel and Chef Kate's menu. Provide nutritional information for each of the five items.

❼ Many people naturally associate dips with chips. But what are some other, more healthful food items that can be paired with dips? Come up with 10 items that might make an attractive menu option.

❽ Vinaigrettes are often paired with greens. But what other food items might pair well with vinaigrette? Try to think of three types of salad that might go well with a vinaigrette but do not have greens as the main ingredient.

255

Section 4.2 Review Questions

1. The primary types of salad dressing are vinaigrette, emulsified vinaigrette, mayonnaise-based, and mayonnaise.

2. An emulsion is made by chemically bonding nonmixable liquids by means of an emulsifier, which forms a link between separate ingredients.

3. See Table 4.3 on p. 245.

4. Oil, vinegar, and egg yolk are the three main ingredients in mayonnaise.

5. The students might have interesting answers to this. If a restaurant has a delicate emulsion, they might want to make it on-site. Perhaps they have a proprietary recipe that they want to protect.

6. The students can find purchased dressings with published nutritionals. They could also analyze a recipe by ingredients. The USDA Web site can help with the analysis.

7. The students will probably mention various crunchy raw vegetables, crisp fruit, whole grain breads, toasts, crusts, and crackers.

8. Even fruit, pastas, potatoes, or fish can pair with vinaigrettes.

Section 4.2 Activities

1. Be sure to use distilled water first; it will seem like the beam goes straight through. Second, use distilled water with one drop of milk; it will look clear, but will deflect the beam off of the milk molecules. Third, tap water will appear clear but will deflect the light off of particles even without adding milk. A chemistry or physics teacher might have a laser beam or pointer. Students can write a paragraph of observations.

2. Hummus is actually a source of legume protein. There is some oil added with the tahini or any added oil, but the chickpeas are fat-free. The information can be found online, but each recipe will be slightly different.

3. Low-fat dressings are usually thickened with starch, gums, or other additive gel formers. Perhaps the students will discover other low-fat dressing processes in their research.

Section 4.2 Activities

1. Study Skills/Group Activity: Demonstrating Colloids

Fill a 250 mL beaker with distilled water (or use a clear measuring cup with 250 mL capacity, or approximately 1 cup). Shine a laser beam or laser pointer beam through the water. Observe. Add one drop of milk to the water and stir with a clean spoon or glass rod. Shine the laser beam through the water again. What do you observe this time? The molecules of milk should be finely dispersed throughout the water as a colloid. Eventually, they will fall to the bottom. After observing, fill another beaker or clear cup with tap water. Shine the laser through. What does this tell you about tap water?

2. Independent Activity: Digging into Hummus

Do some research on hummus. What is hummus? Where did it originate? How is it made? What is its nutritional value? Write a one-page report on your findings.

3. Critical Thinking: The Skinny on Dressings

Dressings are often made with ingredients that are higher in fat, such as oil and mayonnaise. This, of course, makes the dressing higher in fat. But increasingly, tasty lower-fat, lower-calorie alternatives are becoming available. How is this being done? What in these dressings allows them to be low in fat, but still taste good? Look into the ingredients of three popular low-fat, low-calorie dressings at your local supermarket. What are the common ingredients? How do the ingredients of low-fat dressings differ from regular dressings?

4.1 Salads	4.2 Salad Dressings and Dips	4.3 Garnishes
• Ingredients and parts of a salad • Types of salads • Salads and service • Cleaning and storing salads	• Types of dressings • Dips	• Garnishing: why and how • Garnishing desserts • Garnishing soups

SECTION 4.3 GARNISHES

The way to a diner's stomach often starts through his or her eyes. Enjoyment of a meal depends greatly on how it looks. In this section, you learn about garnishes: why and how they're used, as well as the best ways to garnish desserts and soups.

Study Questions

After studying Section 4.3, you should be able to answer the following questions:

- Why and how is garnish used?
- How should desserts be garnished?
- What are the three ways that soups can be garnished?

Garnishing: Why and How

Enjoyment of the meal is more likely if the food has eye appeal. If food is unattractive, the customer is more likely to expect a poor meal. This is why garnishing properly is essential when presenting food.

Proper garnish complements the main dish in color, flavor, and texture. The placement of extraneous items on a plate just to add color and heighten appearance is not proper garnishment. Garnish should enhance the flavor of a dish as well its eye appeal.

For example, finishing an item with a sprinkle of micro greens may sound good, but if the flavor of the greens does not enhance the food being served, then the goal has not been achieved. Adding the stronger flavor of watercress or arugula to a delicate dish does nothing to enhance the dining experience.

Finishing a side of broccoli with lightly sautéed red pepper enhances both its eye appeal and flavor. On the other hand, sprinkling *brunoise* (BROON-wah)—cuts of uncooked, unseasoned red pepper—adds color, but does nothing to enhance the flavor.

257

Section 4.3 Garnishes

Introduce the Section

a. Garnishes are used to add a final appetizing finish to a plate.

b. A garnish should be edible and enhance the flavor and style of the item.

c. Soups have their own rules for garnishing.

Vocabulary Review

a. Direct students to the key terms.

b. Pronounce each word, and have the students repeat the pronunciation out loud.

c. Discuss the definition of each word.

Teach

Discuss

- Perhaps the best way to teach garnishes is to get students excited about discussing it.

- Ask students for bad examples; they will probably come up with several.

- When they have gotten creative and outlandish describing ridiculous garnishes, bring them around again.

- Have them describe beautiful and creative garnishes.

- Be prepared with examples or pictures of nicely garnished plates.

Vocabulary Terms

- *Brunoise:* Cutting technique—julienne cut, quarter turn, then cross-cut into small cubes.

Essential Skills:
Garnish as an Important Part of the Complete Dish

The garnish goes on last, right before service. It should never look stale or wilted.

Reinforce and Review

- When planning menus and recipes, plan the garnishes as well.

- The perfect garnish might require some work and prior planning, but could set the restaurant apart as distinctive.

- Rehearse the garnish when you rehearse the menu item.

Essential Skills
Garnish as an Important Part of the Complete Dish

Garnishing brings new personality to a dish.

❶ Always garnish dishes right before serving.

❷ Remember that one of the purposes of a garnish is to add personality to a plain dish. See Figure 4.29a.

❸ Use contrasting colors of the food and garnish for a beautiful presentation. See Figure 4.29b.

Figure 4.29a: Step 2—Ungarnished broccoli looks plain.

Figure 4.29b: Step 3—Use contrasting colors.

Preparation of garnishes is not an "extra" part of a dish. It is an essential part of the dish. Some garnishes can be prepared in bulk for use when plating and finishing both hot and cold items. (See Figure 4.30 on the following page.) Examples of these include the following:

- Lettuce, tomato, onion, etc., served on the side of the plate for a sandwich
- Finely minced herbs used to top items at service
- Micro greens used to top items at service
- Glazed nuts, grated cheese, or grated vegetables used to finish salads for service
- Sautéed vegetables used to top proteins and vegetables at service
- Sauces used to finish proteins and vegetables at service

258

Figure Focus

Figure 4.29a: Beautiful broccoli, without a garnish.

Figure 4.29b: Garnished broccoli ready for service.

What garnish to use depends not only on the food being served, but also on how the food is laid out on the plate. Plate presentation is something of an art. The question becomes, "to KIS or not to KIS," and the answer is definitely, "KIS." KIS stands for, "Keep It Simple." The purpose of plate presentation is to enhance the eye appeal of the food. Poor plate presentation diminishes rather than enhances the appeal of the food. The goal is simple, but elegant. Build appetizing, elegant, easily consumable food presentations, not architectural wonders. For a list of basic plate presentations guidelines, see Table 4.5. Used properly, garnish "brings the dish together," both to the palate and to the eye.

Figure 4.30: Vegetables shaped into tiny delicate flowers, stars, circles, and other intricate designs.

Discuss

- "Keep it simple" is a good rule of thumb.
- However, a garnish that is too simple (e.g., a sprig of parsley) might not be quite enough.
- Encourage the students to think of garnishes by discussing techniques that can be used.
- Creativity and simplicity can go hand-in-hand.

Table 4.5:
The Basics of Plate Presentation

- This table is a useful primer for garnishing skills.
- Have students practice creating garnishes.

Teaching Tips

- Use Table 4.5 for lesson planning and practice.
- The more students practice and try preparing garnishes themselves, the better their skills will be.
- The most important skill students can develop is an eye for what looks good.
- Even a simple, easy garnish needs to look right.
- Looks are very important where garnishing a plate is concerned.

Table 4.5: The Basics of Plate Presentation	
Color	• Variety • Balance • Freshness
Shapes	• Variety • Complementary • Balance
Texture	• Variety • Physical: smooth, coarse, solid • Visual: puréed, speckled, patchy • Balance
Plate, bowl, platter	• Appropriate size • Appropriate color
Design	• Appropriate to time and temperature constraints • Appropriate for available equipment, staff, and facility • Easy for guest to eat • Uses the dish as a canvas and its rim as a frame; meaning, generally an artist's painting doesn't extend to the frame but stays inside it. The same idea applies here.

continues

259

Figure Focus

Figure 4.30: Beautiful garnishes can be made with inexpensive vegetables. Have students practice creating garnishes.

Discuss

- Discuss dimension in presentation and garnishing.

- Perhaps students have seen (or seen pictures of) osso bucco, lamp chops on the bone, lobster Newberg in a puff pastry cup, or other dimensional items.

- Whether or not the dish or the garnish is dimensional, it should be easy and inviting to eat. It should not look like a fortress of food.

Vocabulary Terms

- **Timbale:** An elaborate dish of vegetables baked in a springform pan or timbale mold.

- *Dauphinoise:* Baked au gratin potato.

- **Duchesse:** Mashed, seasoned, piped, and baked potatoes.

Table 4.5: The Basics of Plate Presentation *continued*	

Principles of arrangement	• Keep food off the rim of the plate. The well of the plate is where the food is meant to be. If too much food exists for the well of the plate, get a larger plate or reduce the amount of food.
	• Arrange the food in unity. The plate should look like one meal made up of several items. Do not have the food spread to all parts of the plate. The customer's eye should focus on the center of the plate, not the edge.
	• Place food on the plate in the most attractive manner possible.
	• Place the best side of the meat forward.
	• Face the back part of the duck or chicken half away from the customer.
	• Face the bone of a chop away from the customer.
	• Sauces can improve plate presentation when used properly. See Figure 4.31 on the following page.
	• In arranging the plate, do the following:
	   Serve sauce around or under food.
	   Do not disguise or mask products that are served in the sauce.
	   For sauce meant to be put on top of a meat or vegetable, place a thin ribbon for color and serve additional sauce on the side.
	   Be careful not to oversauce. Sauce is meant to complement and enhance the flavor of food, not hide the flavor.
	   Sauces should be kept light and more natural, not thick and pasty.
	• Refrain from using the same pattern over and over again. Particularly for buffet presentation, variety in platter arrangement is as important as color variation.
	• Use nonintegral garnish only when necessary. Only add a garnish to a plate or platter for balance; it must be functional.
	• Simplicity is the key.

Adding height to your plate or platter	• Use the gross piece, natural bone, or add a seasoned cracker to achieve height. See Figure 4.32 on the following page.
	• Relishes or marinated vegetables can be used to create ramps to elevate slices on platters and plates.
	• Utilize vegetable cuts or seasoned croutons to achieve height in salad presentations.
	• Mold or shape starches and vegetables to achieve height in plate and platter presentation. Possibilities include the use of the following:
	   A vegetable **timbale** (tim-buh), which is a kind of dish of various ingredients baked in a round mold
	   A *dauphinoise* (doh-fan-WAZ) potato (baked with cream, garlic, and cheese, also called French gratin) cut into rounds or triangles
	   Duchesse potatoes (doo-CHEZ), potatoes that have been boiled and mashed, and then baked with butter and egg yolks
	   Piped puréed vegetables
	   Shredded potatoes formed as a basket and fried
	   Bundles of vegetables such as haricot vert and yellow pepper tied with leek strips

260

Table 4.5: The Basics of Plate Presentation *continued*

	• Use the natural shapes of bones, such as a chop or breastbone, to achieve height in the plate presentation of entrées and appetizers. • Cut vegetables to achieve height, such as a **tourner** (tour-NYAY), a football or barrel shape that forms six or seven sides on the length of the vegetable. • Building a composite plate by placing the starch or vegetable under the entrée can bring height to a plate presentation.
Tips	• Respect the food. • Respect the borders of the plate. • Balance colors, textures, shapes, and flavors. • Allow the guests to see what they are eating. • When appropriate, try to garnish with ingredients with which the particular dish is prepared.

Figure 4.31: Sauces improve plate presentation.

Figure 4.32: Natural bone adds height to a plate.

Essential Skills
Preparing Common Garnishes

Many ingredients can be used as garnish, and there are many ways to prepare each one. Following are some common garnish preparations. The key is to practice with each one, and then practice some more! Garnishes not only add flavor and eye appeal to a dish, they can also become a chef's signature.

Fried Parsley

❶ Separate sprigs and remove coarse stems. See Figure 4.33 on the following page.

❷ Wash and dry thoroughly.

❸ Deep-fry at about 375°F for just a few seconds, until crisp but still green.

261

Table 4.5 (cont.)

Food is beautiful to the human eye, and is even more beautiful when it is garnished.

The table says "Respect the food."

The entire goal of a garnish is to invite the guest to eat.

Essential Skills: Preparing Common Garnishes

Parsley is the classic plate garnish.

Always remember that parsley is edible and has a distinct flavor.

Does the flavor work with the menu item?

Vocabulary Terms

• **Tourner:** An oblong or football-shaped cut for a vegetable.

Figure Focus

Figure 4.31: A sauce can be part of the presentation. It must be exactly where the chef wants it to be, and should not be messy.

Figure 4.32: A bone is not edible and is very bold. It must be roasted to look and smell good. When it is, it can add a delicious aroma and visual dimension.

Leeks add an earthy, grassy, onion flavor and aroma, so keep that in mind.

The aroma will be delightful with the right dish.

❹ Drain on absorbent paper. Serve immediately.

Figure 4.33: Step 1—
Separate sprigs and
remove coarse stems.

Fried Leeks

❶ Clean and slice leeks fine julienne. See Figure 4.34a.

❷ Dust with corn starch.

❸ Deep-fry at about 375°F for just a few seconds, until crisp.

❹ Drain on absorbent paper. Serve immediately. See Figure 4.34b.

See Figure 4.34a: **Figure 4.34b:**
Step 1—Slice leeks Step 4—Serve
fine julienne. immediately.

Cucumbers

❶ For slices, score unpeeled cucumber with a fork or flute with a channel knife, and then slice. See Figure 4.35a on the following page.

❷ For twists, cut slices three-fourths of the way across, twist open, and stand them on a plate. See Figure 4.35b.

❸ For cups, cut fluted cucumber in 1-inch sections, hollow them out slightly with a melon ball cutter or spoon, and fill them with an appropriate condiment sauce. See Figure 4.35c.

NOTE: A cucumber is a good item on which to practice. See Essential Skills "Cucumber Fans" for a step-by-step tutorial on cucumber garnish.

262

Figure Focus

Figure 4.33: Parsley sprigs should be very fresh and perky.

Figure 4.34a: Hold the layers of the leek together as you julienne.

Figure 4.34b: The crisp fried leek will become soft if left to sit too long.

Figure 4.35:
Step 1—Peel the cucumber in strips with a channel knife.

Figure 4.35b:
Step 2—Cut slices three-fourths of the way across.

Figure 4.35c:
Step 3—Hollow out slightly with a melon ball cutter.

Mushroom Caps

❶ Cut the stem out and scoop out any remaining stem without breaking the cap. See Figure 4.36.

❷ To keep mushrooms white, simmer 2 to 3 minutes in salted water with a little butter and lemon juice.

Figure 4.36: Step 1—Cut the stem out.

Radishes

❶ Radishes can be cut in many ways to make decorative garnishes. See Figure 4.37.

❷ After cutting, soak the radishes in ice water until they open.

Figure 4.37: Step 1—Use radishes as decorative garnish.

NOTE: This is a good item on which to practice.

263

Essential Skills:
Preparing Common Garnishes (cont.)
Help the students to practice with real produce.

Teaching Tips

- Have students practice making garnishes with radishes.

- Radishes are a good place to begin.

- Radishes can be split, blemished, or stained in the field. Choose radishes that will clean up nicely.

Figure Focus

Figure 4.35a: The outside of the cucumber must be completely clean.

Figure 4.35b: Do not cut all the way through.

Figure 4.35c: A cucumber cup can be filled with something else, like a dollop of a seasoned dip.

Figure 4.36: Mushrooms should be completely clean.

Figure 4.37: Use radishes that are not too big. Make sure they are completely clean and not stained.

Essential Skills: Preparing Common Garnishes (cont.)

Cold water can keep vegetables fresh and crisp.

It will also curl the ends of the scallions, which makes a fancy garnish.

Scallion Brushes

❶ Cut off the root ends of the scallions, including the little hard core. Cut the white part into 2-inch sections.

❷ With a thin-bladed knife, split both ends of the scallion pieces with cuts ½-inch deep. Make enough cuts to separate the ends into fine shreds. See Figure 4.38.

❸ Soak in cold water until the ends curl.

Figure 4.38: Step 2—Split both ends of scallion pieces.

Pickles

❶ To make fans, with the stem end of the pickle away from you, make a series of thin vertical slices the length of the pickle, but do not cut through the stem end.

❷ Spread the pickle into a fan shape. See Figure 4.39.

Figure 4.39: Step 2—Spread the pickle into a fan.

NOTE: This is a good item on which to practice.

Frosted Grapes

❶ Separate grapes into small bunches.

❷ Brush with water.

❸ Sprinkle with granulated sugar. See Figure 4.40 on the following page.

❹ Let them dry before serving.

264

Figure Focus

Figure 4.38: Get all the field dirt and outer layers off of the scallion.

Figure 4.39: Pickle fans are good with dishes that need a pickle, like a hamburger or sandwich platter.

Essential Skills:
Preparing Common Garnishes (cont.)

Lemon garnish accompanies seafood dishes.

The lemon is part of the expected condiments for the dish.

If the lemon is wrapped in cheesecloth, or has the pips removed, it will be more user-friendly.

Figure 4.40: Step 3—
Sprinkle grapes with
granulated sugar.

Lemons

❶ Cut fluted lemon slices and twisted slices in the same way as cucumbers. Cut slices placed directly on fish or meat from peeled lemons. See Figure 4.41a.

❷ Dip half the lemon slice in paprika or finely chopped parsley for a colorful effect. For just a line of paprika down the center, bend the lemon slice between the fingers and dip lightly in paprika.

❸ Wedges are often more attractive if the ends of the lemons are cut off first. For added color, dip the edge of the lemon wedge in paprika.

❹ For lemon halves, first cut a thin slice from each end of the lemon so the halves will stand straight. Then, cut the lemon in half. Cut a long strip of rind from the outer edge of the lemon half but do not detach it. Tie a decorative knot in the strip, being careful not to break it, or cut two strips, one from either side, and make two knots. Decorate with parsley. See Figure 4.41b.

❺ For a sawtooth edge, cut a sawtooth pattern, piercing all the way to the center of the lemon with the knife. Separate the two halves. Decorate with parsley, or dip the points of the teeth in paprika. See Figure 4.41c.

Figure 4.41: Step 1—Twist slices. **Figure 4.41b:** Step 4—Tie a decorative knot. **Figure 4.41c:** Step 5—Cut a sawtooth pattern.

NOTE: This is a good item on which to practice.

265

Figure Focus

Figure 4.40: Red grapes can also be used.

Figure 4.41a: Make sure the outside of the lemon is completely clean.

Figure 4.41b: Making ties is labor intensive, but might be just the right look.

Figure 4.41c: A sawtooth pattern can be used to cut a lemon in half, leaving two decorated halves to use as garnish.

Even the photo stimulates the appetite, because the presentation of the platter is so nice.

Essential Skills
Garnishing Platters

Platter garnish does not have to be elaborate to be effective. A simple assortment of colorful fresh vegetables, cooked to perfection, is an elegant garnish to the most sophisticated platter presentation. A succulent roast beef adorned with a colorful variety of fresh garden vegetables is always appealing for banquet crowds. The arrangement of the main food item, complete with accompaniments of colorful vegetables and starches, may not require additional garnish. Always avoid cluttering a plate. See Figure 4.42.

Figure 4.42: Succulent beef with crisp, bright vegetables.

Plating and Garnishing Hot Platters

❶ Vegetables should be arranged in ways that are simple and practical. A mound of peas on a platter is unattractive and difficult to serve. Instead, choose vegetables that are available in easy-to-handle pieces, such as cauliflower, broccoli, whole green beans, etc.

❷ Arrange the garnishes around the platter for the best effect, emphasizing different sizes and colors.

❸ Be careful that the platter garnish isn't too elaborate. The attractiveness of the main food item should not be overshadowed by garnish.

❹ Any extra sauce or gravy should be served in a sauce boat. Only use a small amount of gravy or sauce when preparing a platter of meat, fish, or poultry.

❺ Serve hot food on a hot platter. Serve cold food on a cold platter.

266

Figure Focus
Figure 4.42: The vegetables serve as both side dish and garnish.

Coloring the Appetite

Color plays a big role in nutrition. The compounds that give fruits and vegetables yellow, orange, green, and purple tones are nutrients called phytochemicals. In addition, the visual color of food can enhance or diminish the appetite. Warm food colors are instinctively inviting. Brown, red, orange, yellow, green, and warm reddish-purple are all appealing to the appetite centers of the brain. Bluish or cool tones are not instinctively seen as food colors. Use this knowledge when designing garnishes. Grated cheddar cheese, finely chopped red pepper, brown chocolate shavings, and red strawberries all enhance the visual impact of the food, which improves the appetite and encourages nourishment.

[nutrition]

Essential Skills
Cucumber Fans

❶ Select a firm, blemish-free cucumber.

❷ Wash and dry.

❸ Using a channel knife, score the cucumber vertically from end to end. Space the cuts evenly around the cucumber.

❹ Cut off both ends with a chef's knife.

❺ Begin slicing ⅛-inch to ¼-inch-thick slices, but don't cut all the way through the cucumber. Leave ¼-inch of the flesh connected on the side to hold the rounds together.

❻ Slice off the length of fan you want and place on a plate, spreading the fan open. See Figure 4.43 for how it should look when finished.

Figure 4.43: Step 6—Cucumber fan.

Figure Focus

Figure 4.43: Notice the even, consistent size of each slice.

ServSafe Connection: Allergy Disclosures

Major allergens include peanuts, tree nuts, shellfish, and berries.

If these are included in a garnish, they should be disclosed in the menu description.

The server should be aware of this as well, in case he or she is asked.

Fast Fact: Did You Know . . . ?

If the menu uses the traditional term, make sure the server knows what it means, to be able to inform guests who inquire.

[ServSafe Connection]

Allergy Disclosures

If a customer has an allergy or food sensitivity, he or she might ask the server about the ingredients in a particular menu item. The server answers based upon his or her knowledge of the recipe and preparation. However, if the garnish is not standard, an allergen can be inadvertently added to the dish.

Therefore, remember to disclose the ingredients of garnishes in any ingredients list. Sprinkling a few unexpected chopped nuts on top of a salad can be a huge problem for a customer, even life-threatening. And, if the customer has an allergic reaction after the server states that the food does not contain a specific allergen, an enormous problem exists for the establishment.

Take three practical steps to avoid this problem:

1. Do not use major allergens in garnishes.
2. Standardize the garnish with every dish.
3. Disclose the garnish ingredients with the rest of the menu item.

[fast fact]

Did You Know...?

Classical French garnish is what many modern chefs call accompaniments, or side dishes, to a main entrée. Accompaniments include potatoes, rice, or vegetables, to name just a few. During the eighteenth and nineteenth centuries, one French handbook listed more than 209 classical garnishes. Some of these classic terms have carried over to the modern professional kitchen.

The classical French terms for garnishes that are listed here have been revised to refer to a specific type of vegetable used to garnish an item, rather than the original complete side dish. An example of this is the use of the term *doria*. Often today, to state that a dish is *á la doria* is to indicate that it has been garnished with cucumber. The actual classical garnish *doria* consists of cucumber slices trimmed in an olive shape and stewed in butter combined with sliced, peeled, and depipped lemon. This preparation was used as a garnish for fish prepared á la meunière. In a truly classical French kitchen, these terms are applied as originally created. Use caution when using French terms, because they usually indicate specific ingredients and techniques relating to the food being prepared.

Bouquetière	Bouquet of vegetables
Clamart	Peas
Crécy	Carrots
Doria	Cucumbers cooked in butter
Dubarry	Cauliflower
Fermière	Carrots, turnips, onions, and celery cut into uniform slices
Florentine	Spinach
Forestière	Mushrooms
Jardinière	Garden vegetables

Judic	Braised lettuce
Lyonnaise	Onions
Parmentier	Potatoes
Printanière	Spring vegetables
Provençale	Tomatoes, mushrooms, garlic, and herbs
Vichy	Carrots, cooled and glazed

Garnishing Desserts

As with any course, consider the flavor, texture, and appearance of the item being garnished when garnishing desserts. For example, using chocolate **string work** to garnish a piece of apple pie may create a striking appearance, but does not achieve the goal of enhancing the apple pie's flavor and eye appeal. Garnishing a piece of apple pie with shredded cheddar cheese and a small dollop of applejack brandy whipped cream, however, can achieve the goal.

Numerous items can be used to properly garnish desserts, including the following:

- Fruit coulis in many varieties
- Whipped cream, flavored and unflavored
- Frosted mint leaves
- Chocolate work in the form of string work or formed pieces
- Spun sugar work
- Sweet sauces

The overall impact of the garnish on the appearance of the dessert is driven by the way the garnish is presented. To simply place a pool of raspberry coulis on a plate and set a piece of cheesecake in the middle achieves enhanced flavor but does not greatly enhance the appearance. Creating a design on the plate with the coulis and **napping** (drizzling a design) the cheesecake with the coulis improves both flavor and appearance. Application techniques include the following:

- String work (a design made with very fine piping) with a single item on the plate surface
- Artistic design work with one item placed in another item on the plate's surface
- String work done separately and then transferred to the plate

269

Reinforce and Review

- Garnishes can become elaborate with desserts.
- The garnishes for desserts can be part of the dessert itself.
- For example, a berry coulis with a slice of cheesecake will make it berry cheesecake.

Vocabulary Terms

- **String work:** Chocolate piped into a bead in a design that hardens and can be lifted and used upright as a garnish.
- **Napping:** To expertly dress or pour a sauce over an item.

- Piping of cream or other accompaniments directly on the plate or the dessert item
- Placement of multiple types of dessert items on the plate, each with its own garnish or an interconnecting garnish

Figure 4.44 illustrates these application techniques.

Figure 4.44: Use light pressure to pipe melted chocolate onto the paper; pull the knife or toothpick through the sauces in different directions; spun sugar on a rolling pin.

Additional garnishes for dessert that add to both the appearance and flavor include the following:

- Herbs, such as mint and tarragon
- Thin slices of fruit
- Citrus curls, sugared rinds, and segments
- Chocolate shapes, curls, and shavings
- Glazes added to poached fruits used in tarts and tortes add sheen to the finished product and protect the fruit
- Roasted fruits enhance natural flavors, textures, and the final appearance
- Slightly broiled meringue peaks on lemon meringue pie

[fast fact]

Did You Know...?
Newborn infants prefer sweet tastes over sour or bitter ones. The next time you feel guilty about your love of desserts, take comfort in the fact that it's not your fault. You were born to love sweets!

270

Figure Focus
Figure 4.44: Creating garnishes requires a careful and steady hand.

Garnishing Soups

Garnishes for soups are classified into three groups:

- Garnishes *in* the soup
- Garnishes *topping* the soup
- Garnishes that *accompany* the soup on the side

Garnishes *in* the soup are the actual ingredients. For example, the vegetables in a clear vegetable soup are considered garnish. All garnishes must enhance both the flavor and appearance of the soup. **Consommés** (CON-suh-mays), rich, clarified stocks or broths, are named after their garnishes. For example, consommé julienne is made of carrot, celery, and onion or leeks cut into julienne shapes. Vegetable cream soups traditionally are garnished with carefully cut pieces of the vegetable that is the main ingredient.

Add *toppings* to soups as a garnish as well. Toppings for thick soups (such as cream of potato, cream of mushroom, and cream of leek) may include the following:

- Chopped parsley or chives
- Toasted, sliced almonds
- Grated cheese
- Sieved egg yolks
- Chopped hard-cooked eggs
- Croutons
- Crumbled bacon
- Paprika
- A swirl or **dollop** (DOLL-up) of sour cream or whipped cream
- Toasted seeds, such as pumpkin or squash
- Fresh herbs and dried herbs

Place any topping on the soup immediately before service because it will either melt or sink to the bottom. Be sure the flavor of the topping is appropriate to the flavor of the soup.

Garnishes in the form of *accompaniments* with soups include crackers, melba toast, corn chips, breadsticks, cheese straws, whole-grain wafers, and **gougères** (GOO-jere) (small, finger-sized pastries, filled with ingredients such as mushrooms, beef, or ham). Figure 4.45 on the following page shows examples of each of these three types of soup garnishes.

271

Reinforce and Review

- Soups have their own traditional garnishes.
- They might actually be ingredients in the soup.
- They can be traditional for the specific soup, or creative. For example, borscht is usually garnished with sour cream. Seafood chowders are often garnished with small oyster crackers, but these are offered on the side.

Teaching Tips

- Toasted, sliced almonds are allergens and should be disclosed.

Vocabulary Terms

- **Consommés:** Clarified broths eaten as soup.
- **Dollop:** A spoonful, usually dropped on.
- **Gougères:** Small pastries with savory fillings, often including cheese.

Figure 4.45: Garnish in soup, on top of soup, and on the side of soup.

[trends]

Fresh Flowers: On the Table and Now in the Plate

Thirty-five years ago, few besides the extremely creative chef Alice Waters of Chez Panisse used real flowers in salads and garnishes. Now it is becoming an industry trend, even reaching out into home cuisine. Small edible flowers are beautiful on a plate, colorful, and delightful.

Not every flower is suitable. Some make people ill when ingested, so only work from a list of edible flowers with suitable flavors. Pansies, nasturtiums, and calendulas all work well. The flowering tops of edible field greens, like arugula and basil, are also edible. Add the flowers of the onion family, like chive blossoms, to food items for an onion-y appeal. Purchase or raise only culinary flowers that are completely free of pesticides.

Keep in mind that even though this is a trend, using flowers as food is not necessarily new. Broccoli and cauliflower are flowers as well!

[on the job]

Squirt Bottles and Scoops: Not Just for Ketchup and Ice Cream Anymore

Outside of the commercial kitchen, squirt bottles with pointed tips are for mustard and ketchup. In the commercial kitchen, they are for anything with the right viscosity (thickness) for staying in a bead. Easily dispense a fruit coulis, a chocolate sauce, a salad dressing, or thickened syrup through a squirt bottle. Use the tip the same way as a frosting tip on a pastry bag—to make designs or "write."

Outside the commercial kitchen, a half-globe scoop is used for ice cream. In the commercial kitchen, the scoop is used for anything viscous enough to mound up and stick to a spoon. Dispense bound salads, mashed potatoes, and portions of unbaked dough with a scoop. Scoops come in various standard sizes to aid in portion control. They create a dimensional and attractive dome shape on the plate. And, they can be operated with one hand to allow for multitasking.

272

Trends: Fresh Flowers: On the Table and Now in the Plate

Nasturtiums taste peppery, almost like a radish.

Taste any edible flower before you use it as a garnish.

Also, check the inside of the flowers for tiny insects.

On The Job: Squirt Bottles and Scoops: Not Just for Ketchup and Ice Cream Anymore

Students will need practice with the squirt bottle.

They will need to have just the right size hole in the tip for whatever they are dispensing, dependent on the viscosity of the liquid.

Scoops add dimension and a pretty half-globe shape to a "plastic" (or moldable) item.

Figure Focus

Figure 4.45: Various types of soup garnishes. More than one type can be used for a soup serving.

Summary

In this section, you learned the following:

- Enjoyment of a meal is affected by how it looks. If food has eye appeal, then enjoyment of the meal tends to increase. This is why garnishing properly is essential when presenting food. The garnish will complement the main dish in color, flavor, and texture. Garnish enhances the flavor of a dish as well its eye appeal.

- As with any course, garnishing desserts requires consideration of the flavor, texture, and appearance of the item being garnished. Garnish should not be added for eye appeal alone. It should enhance the flavor of the dessert as a whole.

- Garnishes for soups are classified into three groups—garnishes *in* the soup, garnishes *topping* the soup, and garnishes that *accompany* the soup on the side. Garnishes in the soup may be the vegetables in a clear broth. Some examples of garnish topping a soup are grated cheese, croutons, or a dollop of sour cream. And garnishes that frequently accompany soup are crackers, melba toast, and breadsticks.

273

Summary

- Remind students to review the following:
  1. The why and how of garnishing
  2. Garnishing desserts
  3. Garnishing soups

Section 4.3
Review Questions

1. Garnishes are used to enhance the visual appeal of a food and to enhance the flavor of a food.

2. Students could list any five of the many listed in this chapter, plus others they might think of. Hopefully they will get beyond parsley sprigs, parsley leaves, and other more common garnishes.

3. There are several items listed on p. 269, plus they can add other items like candy, crushed candy, sprinkled candy bits, piped icing, stencils, and so on.

4. Soups are garnished with ingredients in the broth, a garnish added to the top of the soup in the bowl, or something added alongside on the plate.

5. Garnish draws the guest into the food and makes it look inviting.

6. Each student will have ideas about this. They might include inexpensive garnish ingredients like carrots, cucumbers, and onions, plus other more creative ones. They could also include labor-intensive choices like chocolate string work or delicate cocoa stencils.

7. Students will express an opinion, and hopefully support it. One additional note: The fried tortilla adds a lot of fat and calories to the salad, making it a very high-calorie menu item if the bowl is eaten.

8. It will be interesting to see what the students choose, perhaps something red.

Section 4.3 Review Questions

1. What are the two primary reasons to garnish?

2. List five popular garnishes.

3. Name three popular items that can be used to garnish dessert.

4. Describe the three ways in which to garnish a soup.

5. Debra Olson would agree that presentation is important in buffet service. If the food is well prepared, then why would it be necessary to garnish food served on a buffet?

6. As Miguel and Chef Kate know, some customers were dissatisfied with the presentation of food at Kabob. Comments overheard included that the food was "drab" and the appearance "lackluster." Provide Miguel and Chef Kate with five low-cost garnishing ingredients that can be applied to a number of different dishes and courses to enhance taste and eye appeal. Remember, they don't want to increase costs, so you'll have to pick staple ingredients that Kabob might have stocked already.

7. Taco salads are sometimes served in a large, golden brown, bowl-shaped, fried flour tortilla. Is this the base, the bowl, or the garnish? Make an argument for each.

8. Create the perfect garnish for a plate of lightly pan-fried fillet of sole with butter-tossed steamed wide green beans and wild rice pilaf. What would complement the presentation?

274

Section 4.3 Activities

1. Study Skills/Group Activity: 16-Carrot Gold!

In teams of two or three, using a few carrots for each team, make as many garnishes from carrots as you can, safely using any hand tool in the kitchen. You have a 15-minute time limit. Score a point for every idea you successfully create. The team with the most points wins.

2. Independent Activity: Stringing Dessert Along

Working alone, practice chocolate string-work garnishes on a dessert, or even on an empty dessert plate. Experiment with various shapes, techniques, and styles. Share your best creation with the class.

3. Critical Thinking: Keeping Garnish Afloat

How can you garnish a soup without having the garnish sink to the bottom? List five strategies for successful soup garnishing. How would each garnish be made?

275

Section 4.3 Activities

1. The students might be tempted to be hasty or silly. Each garnish item should look good and be something that could be used.

2. This activity will require equipment for each student, or another activity that could be done while waiting to share.

3. Adding fat through buttered toast points, croutons, fried vegetables, and the like will help a garnish to float because fat floats (hydrophobic). Also, items light in weight for a large surface area, like croutons or oyster crackers, are buoyant and will float until saturated. Items so lightweight that they do not break the surface tension of the soup, like tiny microgreens, will also float. Grated cheese will float cold or melted until it is stirred in because of its high fat content. Sour cream will float for a while, but will melt and disperse out of a dollop.

Case Study Follow-Up

1. Each student will have his or her own answer to this problem.

2. Students will have their own ideas about this. French onion should, by definition, have the crust of bread and melted cheese. It could also use a little bit of scallion for a touch of green. The cream of broccoli might benefit from some crumbled bacon or shredded cheese. Perhaps the students might try microgreens on the cream of broccoli. They could also look nice on the chicken noodle. They would have to be added right before service so they wouldn't wilt. The possibilities are many, but should include something that pairs well with the flavor of the soup.

3. The important aspect of this is for students to understand the process and support their decisions. They should have more reasons for proposing an item for sale than a heartfelt desire for it. There should be some real justification for it.

Case Study Follow-Up *Looks Can Be Appealing*

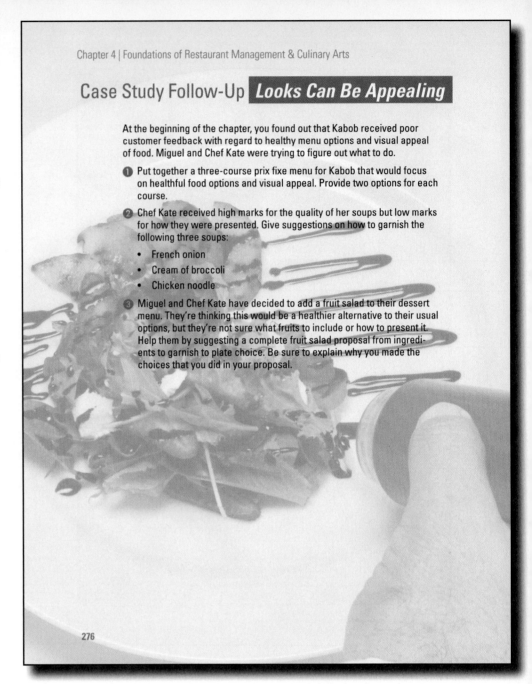

At the beginning of the chapter, you found out that Kabob received poor customer feedback with regard to healthy menu options and visual appeal of food. Miguel and Chef Kate were trying to figure out what to do.

❶ Put together a three-course prix fixe menu for Kabob that would focus on healthful food options and visual appeal. Provide two options for each course.

❷ Chef Kate received high marks for the quality of her soups but low marks for how they were presented. Give suggestions on how to garnish the following three soups:

- French onion
- Cream of broccoli
- Chicken noodle

❸ Miguel and Chef Kate have decided to add a fruit salad to their dessert menu. They're thinking this would be a healthier alternative to their usual options, but they're not sure what fruits to include or how to present it. Help them by suggesting a complete fruit salad proposal from ingredients to garnish to plate choice. Be sure to explain why you made the choices that you did in your proposal.

Apply Your Learning

Pricing Cobb Salad

The Brown Derby's cobb salad was first invented and served out of a culinary necessity from items in the refrigerator. It met with rave reviews and was put on the menu after many requests. How would you price a cobb salad? Research cobb salad, its ingredients, dressing, and traditional plating. Determine a price and outline your reasoning.

Visiting Florentine

"Florentine" is the name of something from Florence, Italy. It is also a culinary term. How did the name come to be used for food? What does it mean? How is it used? What are some examples of dishes? Write two paragraphs about it.

Oil Salesperson

Research canola oil. Create a brochure about canola oil as if you owned a canola oil company and wanted to sell your product to a restaurant supply broker. Present as much information as possible in a visually appealing way. When researching, consider the following questions: What type of oil is it? Where is it from? How is it used? What does it taste like? What types of fatty acids are in a molecule of canola oil, and why is this important? Is it healthy? How can canola oil be used in a commercial establishment?

Critical Thinking — The Main Event

You're creating a new section on your menu for main-course salads. You want them to be lower-fat, lower-calorie alternatives to your traditional main courses, but you still want them to taste great. Come up with three main-course salads to be served on this menu. Remember, main-course salads must be a meal in themselves. Detail all aspects of these new menu options, including main ingredients, dressing, garnish, base, and plate. Why did you choose the salads that you did?

277

Apply Your Learning

Pricing Cobb Salad

The students need to know all the ingredients in a Cobb salad and their portion sizes. Classic ingredients are lettuce, bacon, blue or Roquefort cheese, tomatoes, chicken, hard-cooked eggs, avocado, and chives with a vinaigrette dressing.

Visiting Florentine

"Florentine" often means something is made with spinach or arugula. However, there is an entire Italian country cuisine from the region of Florence, which is in Tuscany. The students can research and learn something about this region and its local foods and dishes.

Oil Salesperson

The students might want to refer back to Chapter 2 when considering the type of fatty acids that are provided by canola oil. The name "canola" means "Canada oil." It is made from the rapeseed crop, but rapeseed is not a good marketing name, even though the oil is good. It is raised in the farmlands of Alberta and other regions in the Canadian plains and the United States and Australia.

Critical Thinking — The Main Event

Each student will have unique choices of salad ideas. Encourage students to support and defend their selections.

Exam Prep Answers

1. D
2. A
3. C
4. D
5. A
6. A
7. B
8. C
9. D
10. D

Exam Prep Questions

1 The part of a bound salad that holds everything together is the

A. body.

B. base.

C. garnish.

D. dressing.

2 Which part of a salad is the main ingredient?

A. Body

B. Base

C. Garnish

D. Dressing

3 Which type of food typically makes up the base of a salad?

A. Unleavened bread

B. A creamy dressing

C. Leafy or heartier greens

D. A protein, such as chicken

4 The three keys to a quality salad are

A. texture, taste, and cost.

B. sweet, bitter, and tart flavors.

C. eye appeal, cost, and heartiness.

D. freshness, flavor, and eye appeal.

5 Which salad most often uses slightly sweeter or sweet/sour dressing to enhance its flavor?

A. Fruit

B. Bound

C. Starter

D. Tossed

6 Which salad is served after dinner and before dessert?

A. Intermezzo

B. After dinner

C. Intermediate

D. Accompaniment

7 Salads are best stored between

A. 33°F–38°F.

B. 36°F–41°F.

C. 39°F–44°F.

D. 41°F–46°F.

8 The four basic types of salad dressing are

A. mayonnaise, mayonnaise-based, vinaigrette, and cheese vinaigrette.

B. braised vinaigrette, vinaigrette, mayonnaise, and emulsified vinaigrette.

C. vinaigrette, emulsified vinaigrette, mayonnaise-based, and mayonnaise.

D. emulsified vinaigrette, braised vinaigrette, vinaigrette, and cheese vinaigrette.

9 What is most likely to happen to a dip the longer it is held in a refrigerator?

A. It will curdle.

B. It will get runny.

C. It will evaporate.

D. It will get thicker.

10 The purpose of garnishing is to

A. mask bland-tasting food.

B. increase the price of a meal.

C. show off a chef's culinary skills.

D. enhance food's taste and eye appeal.

278

Creamy Coleslaw

Cooking time: 20 minutes
Yield: 8–10 servings

Ingredients

8 oz	Mayonnaise		1 lb	Green cabbage (shredded)
4 oz	Sour cream		8 oz	Red cabbage (shredded)
1 oz	Granulated sugar		4 oz	Carrot (shredded)
1 oz	Cider vinegar		To taste	Salt and pepper
1 clove	Garlic (minced)			

Directions

1. Combine the mayonnaise, sour cream, sugar, vinegar, and garlic in a bowl; whisk together.
2. Add the shredded cabbages and carrot to the dressing and mix well. Season to taste with salt and pepper.

Recipe Nutritional Content

Calories	240	Cholesterol	15 mg	Protein	2 g
Calories from fat	200	Sodium	330 mg	Vitamin A	50%
Total fat	22 g	Carbohydrates	10 g	Vitamin C	55%
Saturated fat	4.5 g	Dietary fiber	2 g	Calcium	6%
Trans fat	0 g	Sugars	7 g	Iron	4%

Nutritional analysis provided by FoodCalc®, www.foodcalc.com

279

Recipe

Creamy Coleslaw

- Tell students that the word coleslaw is a rough translation from the Dutch term *koolsla* (short for *koolsalade*), which means cabbage salad.

- Do students just think of coleslaw as a side dish? Do any of them eat coleslaw in other ways, such as putting it on a sandwich?

Recipe

Basic Vinaigrette Dressing

- Time how long this dressing remains in suspension after it is agitated.

Basic Vinaigrette Dressing

Cooking time: 5 minutes
Yield: 1 quart

Ingredients

8 fl oz	Wine vinegar	2 tsp	Salt
24 fl oz	Salad oil	To taste	Pepper

Directions

Combine the vinegar, salt, and pepper and mix well. Whisk in the oil gradually. Store at room temperature.

Recipe Nutritional Content

Calories	120	Cholesterol	0 mg	Protein	0 g
Calories from fat	120	Sodium	100 mg	Vitamin A	0%
Total fat	14 g	Carbohydrates	0 g	Vitamin C	0%
Saturated fat	1 g	Dietary fiber	0 g	Calcium	0%
Trans fat	0 g	Sugars	0 g	Iron	0%

Nutritional analysis provided by FoodCalc®, www.foodcalc.com

Raspberry Sauce

Cooking time: 15 minutes
Yield: 1 quart

Ingredients

2 lb	Raspberries, fresh or IQF (individually quick frozen)	1 lb	Granulated sugar
		1 fl oz	Lemon juice

Directions

1. Purée the berries and strain through a fine *chinois*.
2. Stir in the sugar and lemon juice.
3. Adjust the flavor with additional sugar if necessary.

Recipe Nutritional Content

Calories	120	Cholesterol	0 mg	Protein	0 g
Calories from fat	120	Sodium	100 mg	Vitamin A	0%
Total fat	14 g	Carbohydrates	0 g	Vitamin C	0%
Saturated fat	1 g	Dietary fiber	0 g	Calcium	0%
Trans fat	0 g	Sugars	0 g	Iron	0%

Nutritional analysis provided by FoodCalc®, www.foodcalc.com

Recipe

Raspberry Sauce

- If time and money allow, it might be nice to make another dish that could be garnished with this sauce.

- There is a flourless chocolate cake recipe in Chapter 8.

- Vanilla ice cream would be another good way to taste the sauce as part of a dessert.

Chapter 5 Overview

Chapter 5 follows from the material addressed in Chapter 3, focusing on purchasing and inventory management as a means of controlling costs.

Section 1: The first section covers basic purchasing concepts, such as distribution, and encourages students to consider the broad range of goods and services purchased in the restaurant and foodservice industry.

Section 2: This section focuses on purchasing decisions: how an operation determines what it needs to provide a certain level of service.

Section 3: Finally, this section looks at caring for purchases: receiving, storing, and inventory practices.

Advance Preparation	
Review	Sections 5.1–5.3
	Chapters 3, 9
	Level 1, Chapters 2, 7, 8, 10
Contact	A representative from a food distributor
	A purchaser with responsibilities for multiple foodservice outlets
	A member of the campus foodservice team
Prepare	Samples of nonfood items, such as linens, candles, and paper goods
	A copy of any ethical code of conduct governing campus behavior

ServSafe Connection
Pages 329, 333

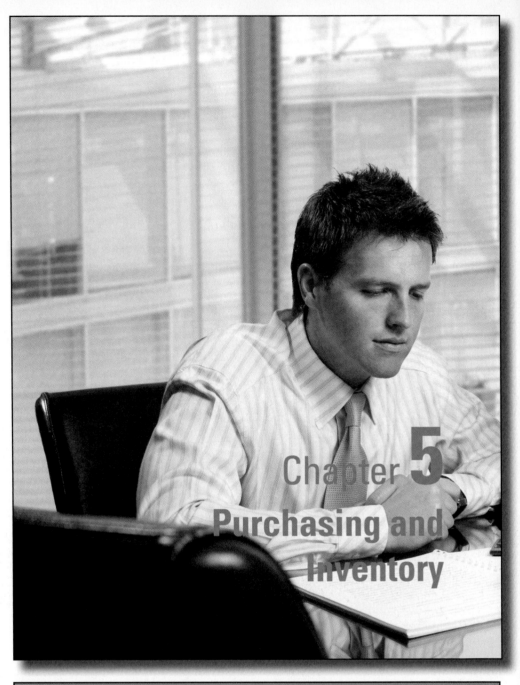

Chapter 5
Purchasing and Inventory

CUSTOMIZED INSTRUCTION OPTIONS			
Less Advanced Students	More Advanced Students	ESOL Students	Special Needs Students
Pages 292, 306	Pages 288, 307	Pages 292, 317	Pages 287, 295

CHAPTER TOOLS			
21st-Century Skills	Mathematics	Science	Literacy
Pages 286, 287, 288, 289, 290, 292, 295, 302, 306, 307, 308, 309, 311, 312, 313, 317, 319, 321, 331, 332, 334, 335, 338	Pages 312, 313	Pages 306, 312, 331, 332	Pages 286, 287, 288, 289, 290, 292, 295, 302, 306, 307, 308, 309, 311, 312, 313, 317, 319, 321, 331, 332, 334, 335, 338

Case Study *Purchasing More Profit*

Chef Kate and Miguel share the buying duties for Kabob Restaurant. As the buyers, they know what to expect in terms of volume of business, regulations, production, processing, and safety. Ever since a downturn in the economy, the volume of customers has gone down. Fewer people are going out for dinner. They've tried various promotions, but nothing seems to be working. They've spoken to people who used to be regulars, and they all say the same thing: people simply don't have as much money to spend on eating out right now.

So Chef Kate and Miguel are now looking at the internal workings of Kabob—namely, their purchasing practices. They are trying to find ways to cut expenses but also maintain the quality of the food. To do so, they'll need to carefully examine their entire system of purchasing, from what goods and services they buy, to how they make their purchasing decisions, to how they store and track those purchases. It won't be easy, but by reevaluating the purchasing process, they may be able to maintain the quality of food and service while still making a better profit during this tough economic time.

As you read this chapter, think about the following questions:

1. Why is it important for Chef Kate and Miguel to understand the economic factors that affect product price?

2. How will quality standards affect pricing and consistency?

3. How can a reevaluation of their relationships with suppliers help Chef Kate and Miguel cut costs?

Reinforce and Review	To succeed in the restaurant and foodservice industry, stay abreast of evolving consumer food trends while remaining focused on the specific population you serve.
	Always be sure to offer value for money, so customers and potential customers feel that doing business with you is worthwhile.
	Don't enter the restaurant and foodservice industry for the wrong reasons.
	Purchasing is a key driver in successfully operating a profitable operation.
Teaching Tips	Does Al Gaylor seem passionate about his career? Why or why not?
	Relate this material to Level 1, Chapter 7 to explain the importance of good communication skills to the purchasing process.

Case Study
Purchasing More Profit

- What did students learn in Chapter 3 that might help Chef Kate and Miguel succeed in cutting their operational costs?

- What risks might Chef Kate and Miguel need to manage by changing their purchasing practices?

- What role does employee training play in cutting purchasing costs?

- What other tactics could Chef Kate and Miguel try? Why might these succeed?

- Note that there are follow-up questions about the case study at the end of the chapter.

- This activity could be done in groups, as a class, or as a homework assignment.

Professional Profile	
Discuss	Why do only 20 percent of dissatisfied customers complain about the problems they have experienced? Based on the material students have learned throughout this program, what are some ways to increase customer feedback?
	What are some common complaints customers have about an operation? How can these problems be resolved?
	How is purchasing a component of quality guest service?
	In what ways is purchasing related to professionalism?
	Think about your most recent foodservice purchases. How did they make you feel? What was the business doing correctly or incorrectly?
	Explain the role of communication in the purchasing process. What are some effects poor communication can have on a restaurant?

Discuss	Why does Al Gaylor suggest that restaurant and foodservice managers work with a limited number of distributors and suppliers?
	Why is it important for operations to do business with "full-service" suppliers?
	Why should an operation's suppliers understand all of the operation's costs? What are some advantages and disadvantages of this strategy?
Reinforce and Review	It is essential to establish a positive relationship with distributors and suppliers.
	Professional distributors and their employees can help restaurant and foodservice operations find the goods and services that are best suited for their needs.
	A variety of purchasing resources are available to professionals in the restaurant and foodservice industry.
Teaching Tips	Consider inviting a purchaser or foodservice distributor to speak to the class.

Focus and Engage

Discuss

- What are the key components to purchasing? Why is it essential in controlling an operation's costs?

- How are student purchases from a restaurant or foodservice operation related to the operation's purchasing decisions?

Teaching Tips

- Encourage students to see the relationship between their purchases from a restaurant or foodservice operation and that operation's purchases from its suppliers and distributors.

[professional profile]

Al Gaylor

Vice President, Industry Relations and Diversity
Sysco Corporation

Professionally, I've always had a very strong interest in marketing and marketing-related functions. My current and previous assignments have allowed me the opportunity to work with in all of the disciplines involving the marketing function.

I received a BS in marketing from Southern University and an MBA from Central Oklahoma State University. As a student, I had a keen interest in the food business, and upon graduating from college, started my career with a consumer package goods food company. Later, I transitioned to the foodservice/distribution side of the business and have enjoyed working with foodservice operators, manufacturers, and Sysco operating companies.

For students interested in this field, remember to stay abreast of overall evolving consumer food trends. However, you should remain focused on the specific segment that you are serving. Make sure that you offer customers value for the dollars they spend, especially in today's difficult economic environment.

Above all, be careful not to go into this industry for the wrong reasons. This is a difficult business, and everyone who enters it will not become a celebrity chef.

Remember:

" For every one customer who communicates to you concerning a problem, four customers will not....they will simply not return to your restaurant. You must find a way to stay in touch with customers and determine their impressions of your operation. **"**

About Purchasing and Inventory

Operators—especially independent restaurant owners—often place a primary focus on the culinary aspect of their business while relegating purchasing to a secondary position. Purchasing, by its very nature, is a key driver in successfully operating a profitable restaurant.

284

One key to developing a successful purchasing strategy is establishing a positive relationship with a limited number of distributor/supplier partners. Be certain at least one of the distributors is a "full-service," broad-line supplier; and work with your suppliers to clearly understand all of your purchasing-related costs, including menu costs, inventory costs, labor costs, and more.

Professional distributors employ highly trained and knowledgeable associates that can assist you. Additionally, there are valuable foodservice purchasing resources that are available online, either free from food manufacturers and distributors, or for a nominal cost from foodservice consultants. Again, whether you are an experienced operator or just getting started in the restaurant business, effective purchasing is critical to the long-term success of any operation.

5.1 Introduction to Purchasing	5.2 Making Purchasing Decisions	5.3 Managing Purchases
• Purchasing overview	• Determining quality standards	• Receiving orders
• Channels of distribution flow	• Writing product specifications	• Storing orders
• Goods and services: what's being purchased	• Ordering	• Taking inventory
• Buyers: who's doing the purchasing	• Ordering forms	
	• Knowing food prices	

SECTION 5.1 INTRODUCTION TO PURCHASING

Some people think that restaurant and foodservice purchasing is like shopping at a mall—just make a list of things you want, go buy them, and you're done. Easy, right? In reality, it's not quite that simple. In fact, the purchasing process is a lot more complex than that, and smart restaurant and foodservice managers know this. The successful operation must fully understand its budget, identity, standards, storage capacity, and customers' wants and needs, to name just a few factors. An operation must also be able to develop and maintain strong vendor relationships for goods as well as services. In short, there's a lot more to the purchasing process than might initially meet the eye. This chapter is dedicated to giving you a behind-the-scenes look at the processes and procedures that make for smart purchases and successful operations.

This section will start by providing an overview of the purchasing process in general and then discuss in greater detail goods and services, and finally buyers, offering a glimpse at the buying process.

285

Introduce the Section

a. Review the purchasing function with students, addressing the various channels of distribution.

b. Note the wide range of goods and services required in the restaurant and foodservice industry.

c. Explain the role of the buyer and what the position requires.

d. Discuss the objectives for the section.

Vocabulary Review

a. Direct students to the key terms.

b. Pronounce each word, and have the students repeat the pronunciation out loud.

c. Discuss the definition of each word.

Teach

Discuss

- How does an operation's chosen identity affect its purchasing decisions?

Reinforce and Review

- The successful operation must fully understand its budget, identity, standards, storage capacity, and customers' wants and needs, among other things.

- An operation must also be able to develop and maintain strong supplier relationships.

Discuss

- Which of the five parts of the purchasing process is most important? Why?

- Human error can affect each stage of the purchasing process. Encourage students to give examples of how things can go wrong.

Reinforce and Review

- The purchasing process is everything involved in buying products and services for an operation.

- The five parts of the purchasing process are determining what the operation wants and needs to buy, identifying quality standards, ordering products and services, receiving deliveries, and storing and issuing products.

- Buyers and managers usually work together to determine what should be ordered and in what quantities.

- Product specifications, or specs, are the standards for the quality of the products and services necessary to meet operational goals; suppliers use these specs to meet the operation's needs.

- Employees must check the quality, as well as the price and the amount, of all goods being received.

- Once received, products should be stored swiftly and appropriately to prevent food safety problems and spoilage.

Teaching Tips

- Divide students into five groups and assign each group one of the five components of the purchasing process to defend in a class debate. Students should develop arguments to support why their component is the most important one of the five.

- Relate this material to Chapter 3, Section 4.

Study Questions

After studying Section 5.1, you should be able to answer the following questions:

- What are the five major steps in the purchasing process?

- What are the four basic goals of purchasing?

- What are the main layers in the channels of distribution?

- What are the major categories of goods and services?

- What does a buyer do?

Purchasing Overview

The purchasing process is everything involved in buying products and services for an operation. This process has five major steps that we will discuss in detail throughout this chapter. The basic procurement steps are listed here and illustrated in Figure 5.1 on the following page:

1. Determine what an operation wants and needs to buy. Buyers work with managers to understand what they should order. This step usually happens on a regular basis. It includes products that need to be ordered frequently as well as major, one-time purchases like new ovens.

2. Identify quality standards. Buyers and managers determine standards for the quality of the products and services based on the operation's goals. The standards help to build product specifications, or specs, which suppliers need to provide the right products and services.

3. Order products and services. The way an operation orders products and services depends on its size. Independently owned restaurants might place orders by phone. Larger companies have more formal procedures, which might include using computer software and purchase orders.

4. Receive deliveries. A foodhandler must check all deliveries before they are either accepted or refused. Receiving employees must verify that the products being delivered meet the operation's specifications. Buyers need to schedule deliveries to ensure that someone will be available to check them.

5. Store and issue products. The employee who receives products must store them as quickly as possible to prevent food safety problems and spoilage. An issuing system helps an operation track which areas are using which products. It also helps to control theft. Many operations use requisitions that managers must approve.

286

Homework Activity: Special Specs

Literacy Connection, 21st-Century Skills—Think Creatively, Critical Thinking and Problem Solving, Communicate Clearly, Work Independently

Develop a spec sheet for something you purchase regularly, such as a cup of coffee or school supplies. What information do you need to provide to make sure that, if someone else were buying the product for you, you would receive the correct item?

Make out a spec sheet that presents this information in a clear, logical fashion.

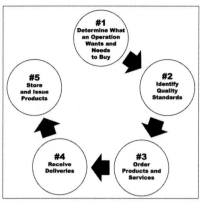

Figure 5.1: The five steps of the purchasing process.

How effective an operation is in executing these steps directly affects its success. The number of factors involved in purchasing decisions can be confusing, and it's easy for even a seasoned buyer to lose focus. So, it's good to have a few clear goals to keep in mind whenever considering the purchase of any item. Having a set of goals will help keep buyers focused on making only smart purchases. The four goals are listed here and illustrated in Figure 5.2:

1. Maintain the right supply of products and services.

2. Maintain the quality standards of the operation.

3. Minimize the amount of money the operation spends.

4. Stay competitive with similar operations.

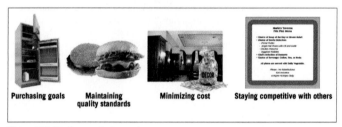

Figure 5.2: The four purchasing goals.

287

Figure Focus

Figure 5.1: In what ways does the purchasing process shape other aspects of an operation's business?

Figure 5.2: Achieving the four purchasing goals is a buyer's primary objective; however, they are broad overviews. What specific goals might a buyer also bear in mind?

Discuss

- Which of the four purchasing goals is most important to an operation's success? Why?

- What challenges might a buyer face when making purchasing decisions? How can relying on these goals help?

Reinforce and Review

- An operation's success is directly affected by the efficiency and effectiveness of its purchasing process.

- The four purchasing goals can help clarify the overall process for the buyer by limiting distractions.

- The purchasing goals are to maintain the right supply of products and services, maintain the quality standards of the operation, minimize the amount of money the operation spends, and stay competitive with similar operations.

CUSTOMIZED INSTRUCTION
Literacy Connection, 21st-Century Skills— Reason Effectively, Communicate Clearly, Interact Effectively with Others
Special Needs Students
What is your favorite food? What are some qualities you expect it to have? Why?

Homework Activity: Quality Standards
Literacy Connection, 21st-Century Skills—Use Systems Thinking, Communicate Clearly, Work Independently
Select one of the following items: a cheeseburger, a black-bean burrito, or a cupcake. Now develop quality standards for the selected item. Explain why each quality standard is important.

Discuss

- Encourage students to share experiences in which a restaurant or foodservice operation has run out of the dish or product they had hoped to purchase. How did the operation respond?

- Identify some examples of an outside influence that can affect an operation's sales.

- What is the relationship between the popularity index and the food production chart? In what ways are both used to forecast sales?

- Ralph Waldo Emerson once said that, "A foolish consistency is the hobgoblin of little minds." What does this quote mean? In what cases is consistency essential, and in what cases are variations acceptable?

Reinforce and Review

- The first goal of purchasing is to make sure that the operation has enough product to sell.

- Some tools to help buyers purchase appropriate quantities include customer-count histories, popularity indexes, vendor delivery schedules, availability of items, and awareness of outside influences that can affect an operation.

- A customer-count history tracks how many customers have been served during specific time periods.

- The popularity of a particular menu item is a determining factor in how frequently its ingredients must be ordered.

- Every item an operation produces must meet its quality standards.

- Consistency is the key to drawing repeat business, and it often begins with consistently purchasing high-quality products.

- Specifications are simple to follow in some cases, but fresh food can pose challenges: Freshness, seasonality, and availability often change.

Vocabulary Terms

- **Quality standards:** An operation's expectations about the quality of the goods and services it plans to purchase.

- **Specifications/specs:** An operation's purchasing requirements for a particular good or service.

Maintain the Right Supply of Products and Services

There aren't many things more disappointing to diners than ordering an item only to be told, "I'm sorry. We're out of that right now." The first goal of purchasing is to make sure that an operation has enough product to sell.

There are many tools available to help purchasers buy the right amount of product:

- **Customer-count histories:** This tracks how many customers an operation has served during specific time periods in the past.

- **Popularity index of items sold:** This identifies which menu items have been most popular.

- **Vendor delivery schedules:** This tracks how frequently or infrequently a particular vendor makes deliveries.

- **Availability of items from vendors:** This tracks when a vendor has particular products available for sale.

- **Recognizing outside influences that might affect an operation:** Being aware of this helps identify what events or conditions might help or hurt an operation during a particular time period (for example, conventions, festivals, weather forecasts, construction, etc.).

Maintain the Quality Standards of the Operation

Every item an operation produces must meet that operation's standards for quality. A guest who enjoyed a cheeseburger last week expects the same cheeseburger this week. Substituting ground beef of an inferior grade this week will directly affect this customer's experience and satisfaction. Consistency is the key to drawing repeat customers, and consistency often starts with consistently purchasing high-quality product.

An operation therefore must have established **quality standards** for each item or service and clearly communicate these standards to potential vendors in the form of **specifications**, or **specs**. Specifications are set by the chef, manager, and/or owner, and are easy to follow when purchasing brand-name items such as alcohol or condiments. Fresh food, however, can be challenging. Freshness, seasonality, and availability frequently change.

CUSTOMIZED INSTRUCTION

Literacy Connection, 21st-Century Skills—Think Creatively, Critical Thinking and Problem Solving, Communicate Clearly, Work Independently

More Advanced Students

You operate an independent foodservice operation that specializes in local produce. From late spring until mid-autumn, you have abundant produce opportunities; the rest of the year, your options are severely limited. As a result, purchasing produce is a more complicated process for your operation than for some of your competitors.

How can the challenges you face when specifying and ordering particular fresh ingredients be turned into a marketable asset?

Write a one-page essay on the marketing opportunities available to you and how you would capitalize on them.

Minimize the Amount of Money an Operation Spends

No operation has unlimited funds. An operation must carefully weigh the value of a potential purchase against the operation's **cash position**—the amount of funds available to it at any given time. Tying up large amounts of money in products that will make a profit at a date too far in the future can cripple a restaurant or foodservice operation's ability to function in the present. Buying too much product can be just as damaging as buying too little. To minimize spending, an operation needs to consider some important factors:

- **Customer-count forecasts:** This is the number of customers expected for a given time period.

- **Available storage capacity for new product:** Only purchase what you are able to store and use.

- **Forecasts of future costs of particular products:** For example, fresh produce prices may go up or down seasonally, so an operation needs to take such price fluctuations into account when making purchases.

Stay Competitive with Similar Operations

Most people shop around for the best prices for products they want to buy. For example, there is no reason to buy a new flat-screen TV from Store A when Store B sells the same TV for $100 cheaper. Restaurant and foodservice purchasers look for good deals on the market, too, but they must also compete against one another for the best prices on goods and services.

For any operation, all costs must be controlled and the restaurant must be able to attract customers. This is how an operation maintains its **competitive position** with other operations. If Restaurant A can get better pricing and/or services than Restaurant B for similar items, Restaurant A will have a competitive advantage because it is spending less money for the supplies it needs. Although simple in concept, achieving this advantage in practice is difficult. Competitors rarely talk about their costs. Vendors often have different pricing levels among operations. Larger, higher-volume clients typically have an advantage in pricing and added services.

For an operation to stay competitive in such a market, it must do the following:

- Shop around for vendors who will provide the best combination of price *and* service for the operation's needs. Vendors sell more than products. They sell their services—frequency of delivery, emergency and odd-hour deliveries, flexible payment terms, low minimum orders, and consistency. Some larger vendors also include added services such as menu printing, free samples, and consulting services.

289

Discuss

- How can a restaurant or foodservice operation improve its competitive position?

- In what cases might a purchaser choose to pay a higher price for an item from a particular supplier?

- What are some examples of products that have fluctuating prices?

Reinforce and Review

- Tying up large amounts of money in products that will make a profit at a date too far in the future can cripple an operation's ability to function in the present.

- Buying too much of a product can be as damaging to an operation as buying too little.

- Buyers can minimize spending by considering the customer-count forecast, the available storage capacity, and forecasts of future product costs.

- In a successful operation, all costs must be controlled and the operation must be able to attract customers.

- Larger, higher volume clients typically have an advantage in pricing and added services, as they purchase more goods.

- To stay competitive, an operation must shop around, get the lowest possible EP or AS price, and obtain total utilization from products purchased.

Teaching Tips

- Relate these four purchasing goals to the material on controlling costs in Chapter 3.

Vocabulary Terms

- **Cash position:** The amount of funds available to an operation at any given time.

- **Customer-count forecast:** The number of customers expected for a given time period.

- **Competitive position:** An operation's ability to attract customers, relative to another operation's ability to attract customers.

Homework Activity:
Competitive Advantage

Literacy Connection, 21st-Century Skills—Think Creatively, Make Judgments and Decisions, Communicate Clearly, Be Self-Directed Learners

What attracts you to a particular restaurant or store? Is it the service, the aromas, the products, the prices, or something else? The elements that draw you to Operation A rather than Operation B are Operation A's competitive advantages. Explain how these advantages can affect all aspects of Operation A—its profits, its sales, its identity, and so on—in a one-page report.

Discuss

- What are some food safety concerns that could arise during the distribution flow? How can they be prevented?

Reinforce and Review

- Getting the lowest possible EP (edible-portion) or AS (as-served) price for a given item can help an operation obtain its competitive advantage.

- Distribution refers to the journey products make as they move from where they were grown or made to their final destination in a restaurant or foodservice operation.

- The three main layers in the channel of distribution are the primary source, the intermediary source, and the retailer.

Teaching Tips

- Review the difference among AP, EP, and AS products and prices, referring to the material in Chapter 3 and in Level 1, Chapter 4 as necessary.

Table 5.1: Channels of Distribution

- What are some situations in which a primary source might sell directly to a retailer, without the involvement of an intermediary?

- Explain how primary sources affect retail prices.

- Discuss the role of intermediate sources in facilitating trade. In what ways can they benefit both primary and retail sources?

- At what point in the channels of distribution are items like French fries or peeled carrots produced?

Vocabulary Terms

- **Channel of distribution:** The particular businesses that buy and sell a product as it makes its way from its original source to a retailer.

- Try to get the lowest possible edible-portion (EP) price (the cost of an item after all trimming and fabrication but before cooking) or as-served (AS) price (the cost of an item as it is served to the customer). EP and AS can vary considerably from the as-purchased (AP) product.

- Try to get the maximum yield, or the total utilization, from products purchased.

Channels of Distribution Flow

So how do products get from the farm or manufacturing plant to the restaurant? Distribution refers to the journey products make as they move from where they are grown or made to their final destination in a restaurant. Many businesses are involved in this effort. A **channel of distribution** includes the particular businesses that buy and sell a product as it makes its way from its original source to a retailer. The channel of distribution for a crate of tomatoes is different than the channel for a box of cereal, and both are different than the channel for a fax machine.

There are three main layers in any channel of distribution:

- Primary sources
- Intermediary sources
- Retailers

Knowing the function of each layer will help in making better purchasing decisions. See Table 5.1 for examples of each of the three layers in the channel of distribution.

Table 5.1: Channels of Distribution

Primary Sources
- Farmers
- Ranchers
- Manufacturers
- Distillers

Intermediaries
- Wholesalers
- Distributors
- Suppliers

Retailers
- Restaurants
- School cafeterias
- Caterers

Homework Activity: Go with the Flow

Literacy Connection, 21st-Century Skills—Think Creatively, Use Systems Thinking, Communicate Clearly, Create Media Products, Work Independently

Select a product that a restaurant or foodservice operation might use, such as frozen chicken thighs or large white onions. Identify the channels of distribution through which it must pass before it reaches the public.

Develop a flow chart demonstrating how the product moves from source to source.

Primary sources include the farmers and ranchers who raise produce and livestock. This group also includes manufacturers (businesses that make products like kitchen equipment from raw materials) and distillers (businesses that produce alcoholic beverages from raw materials like grapes and grains).

Intermediary sources include wholesalers, distributors, and suppliers. These various businesses are sometimes referred to as middlemen because they don't actually alter the products in any way. Instead, these businesses buy products from primary sources and sell them to their final destination: the retailer. Figure 5.3 shows a typical distributor's warehouse.

Figure 5.3: Warehouses store goods until they are needed.

Retailers sell their products directly to the public. All restaurants are considered retailers. Most restaurant and foodservice operations deal directly with primary sources only when they are buying new equipment or locally grown specialty foods. Otherwise they use intermediary sources. Following are specific examples of how purchasing works in various operations:

- Karen Giotto learned purchasing from one of the best buyers in the business—her father. Her control over the business is typical of most independent restaurant or foodservice operations. Karen's two brothers each operate their own versions of Giotto's in the suburbs. A few years back, the three businesses began combining their orders to get lower prices from their suppliers. This type of working together is often called cooperative, or co-op, buying.

291

Figure Focus

Figure 5.3: Storing goods can be expensive, so most intermediary sources resell goods as quickly as possible.

Discuss

- Name some other examples of foodservice retailers, besides the ones listed in the text.

Reinforce and Review

- Primary sources include farmers, ranchers, distillers, and manufacturers.

- Intermediary sources include wholesalers, distributors, and suppliers; they are often known as middlemen because they do not alter the products in any way.

- Retailers include restaurants, school cafeterias, and caterers; all restaurants are retail businesses.

- Most restaurant and foodservice operations deal directly with primary sources only when buying new equipment or locally grown specialty foods.

Teaching Tips

- Make sure students understand that multiple primary sources can be involved in the distribution of a single product. For instance, the farmer who grows carrots is a primary source, as is the company that peels, trims, and packages the carrots.

- Ask students why can cooperative purchasing result in lower prices? How is this related to the concept of competitive advantage?

- What are some advantages and disadvantages of family businesses?

- In what ways can cooperative purchasing help or hurt small businesses?

Vocabulary Terms

- **Primary source:** The origin of raw materials, such as ingredients, or of items made from raw materials, such as kitchen equipment.

- **Intermediary source:** A business that purchases products from primary sources and resells them to retail sources.

- **Retailer:** A business that sells products directly to the public.

Discuss

- What other examples of "economies of scale" can students identify? How can they help obtain or maintain a competitive advantage?

- In what ways can the use of a central commissary lower a chain's costs and improve efficiency?

- In what other ways can chains work together to save costs and improve customer service?

- Ask students what is the difference between a franchise and a chain? With a franchise, people are granted a license to market a company's goods or services in a certain area. A chain is a set of related restaurants with the same name in many different locations that are either under shared corporate ownership (e.g., In-N-Out Burgers in the United States) or franchising agreements.

- What costs might arise from maintaining a central commissary?

- Why might a franchisee choose to purchase from a central commissary or from an independent supplier?

Trends:
Farm-to-Chef Programs

Encourage students to discuss the following:

- How can "farm-to-chef" programs benefit both farmers and retailers?

- "Farm-to-chef" programs replace traditional intermediary sources. How might this affect how intermediary sources operate? Why?

- Are these programs more than a passing trend? Why or why not?

CUSTOMIZED INSTRUCTION

Literacy Connection, 21st-Century Skills— Reason Effectively, Communicate Clearly, Information Literacy, Work Independently

ESOL Students

Are there any notable restaurant chains or franchises in your country of origin? If so, research and present a brief oral report to the class on one example. If not, select a restaurant chain or franchise in another country for your report.

- Bob's Burgers is a highly successful quick-service chain. Like other chains, Bob's Burgers benefits from its economies of scale—the savings that a multiunit business creates for itself by sharing the cost of purchasing expenses. In the case of Bob's Burgers, its size allows the company to maintain a central commissary—a distribution warehouse that provides goods to each individual location. A director of purchasing is responsible for keeping the commissary filled with Bob's Burgers products. When a Bob's Burgers location needs hamburger, the store manager contacts the commissary to place an order.

- Sonny's Morning Café is a popular chain of breakfast-based restaurants. A franchise is a legal business relationship in which an independent owner buys the right to use a company's name, products, and logo. Franchise examples include Boston Market, McDonald's, and KFC. Franchise restaurant and foodservice operations can choose to buy from a central commissary run by the franchisor or from any supplier that meets the company's standards.

[trends]

Farm-to-Chef Programs

Not so long ago, a chef wishing to add heirloom tomatoes or Berkshire pork to a menu had to build relationships with individual farmers, a challenging and time-consuming task, especially in urban areas. Today, however, "farm-to-chef" programs across the country are changing the way restaurant and foodservice operations purchase ingredients. These programs, now found in a number of states, serve as the intermediary between farmers and chefs, giving farmers a new market for their crops and chefs a source of new ingredients.

Many benefits arise from these new relationships. For one thing, restaurants can offer unique, high-quality ingredients to their diners. In some cases, a chef can even have a particular farmer grow a specialty crop for a single restaurant, which can be a great attraction for customers. Additionally, giving farms new markets gives them a stronger economic base: the increased demand helps them stay in business and keep rural areas healthy. Finally, when the farms are named directly on menus, diners feel a stronger connection to the food they are about to eat and a closer connection to their community. This is a winning situation for farmers, chefs, and consumers alike!

CUSTOMIZED INSTRUCTION

Literacy Connection, 21st-Century Skills—Reason Effectively, Communicate Clearly, Work Independently

Less Advanced Students

In some cases, retailers can also be primary sources. What are some examples of this practice? Are there any such suppliers in your community?

Did You Know...?
Recent studies have found that approximately 25 percent of new restaurants fail in the first year and that 50 percent of restaurants fail within the first three years. An entirely separate general business study has found that over 80 percent of small businesses fail as a result of forces within the control of the operation—meaning that owners and operators truly do control their own fates. And part of that control is understanding the purchasing process.

Goods and Services: What's Being Purchased

When thinking about restaurant and foodservice purchases, it makes sense that one might automatically think of buying food. But in fact, food is just one of many goods and services that a successful operation needs to function efficiently. Having an understanding of each category and how they are all connected is essential not only to making smart purchases, but to running the operation as a whole. The major categories of purchases are outlined and described in this section:

- Food and beverages
- Nonfood items
- Smallwares and equipment
- Technology
- Furniture, fixtures, and equipment
- Business supplies and services
- Support services
- Maintenance services
- Utilities

Food and Beverages

These are items that operations actually prepare and sell. This is to say that these items are what goes into the profit-making aspect of a given restaurant or foodservice operation. Quality and consistency are absolutely key to delivering a desirable product that will attract repeat customers. Purchasing lower- or inconsistent-quality food items can quickly lead to the failure of an operation. Table 5.2 lists some examples of the kinds of food that operations might purchase.

293

Fast Fact:
Did You Know . . . ?

Encourage students to discuss the following:

- Why do so many restaurants fail within the first three years?

- How can understanding the purchasing process save a business from failure?

- What are some hallmarks of a successful business model?

Discuss

- Identify at least one good or service in each category that the typical restaurant or foodservice operation must purchase.

- Why do restaurant and foodservice operations purchase so many goods and services that they cannot directly sell?

Reinforce and Review

- Food is only one of the goods and services that a successful operation needs to function.

- The major categories of foodservice purchases include food and beverages; nonfood items; smallwares and equipment; technology; furniture, fixtures, and equipment; business supplies and services; support services; maintenance services; and utilities.

- Quality and consistency are absolutely key to delivering a desirable product that will attract repeat customers.

- Purchasing food items that are of inconsistent or lower quality than consumers expect can cause a restaurant or foodservice operation to fail.

Teaching Tips

- Remind students that the costs of purchasing all these goods and services must be covered by food and beverage sales, so menu prices must be high enough to cover these costs.

Table 5.2:
Food and Beverages that Restaurant and Foodservice Operations Purchase

- Is this list of food and beverages comprehensive? What items might be missing?

- In what ways does an operation's style of service, its cuisine, or its guests affect its food and beverage purchases?

- Identify food items from each category that the campus foodservice operations might purchase.

Discuss

- Describe how an operation's service style affects its purchase of nonfood items.

- What nonfood items might be purchased by what types of restaurant and foodservice operations?

Reinforce and Review

- Nonfood items are directly tied to the sale of food and beverages.

- Purchasers should identify how best to support the operation's theme and style of service when making decisions about their purchases of nonfood items.

- Nonfood items include linens, uniforms, candles, music, and other goods that support an operation's atmosphere and style of service, thereby affecting its sales of food and beverages.

Teaching Tips

- Provide examples of nonfood items and encourage students to identify service styles for which they would be appropriate.

Table 5.2: Food and Beverages that Restaurant and Foodservice Operations Purchase

Beverages, alcoholic	• Spirits (liquor) • Beer • Wine
Beverages, nonalcoholic	• Soda (pop) • Coffee and tea • Juices • Bottled waters
Food items	• Meat • Poultry • Eggs • Processed food • Fish • Dairy • Produce • Dry and canned goods

Nonfood Items

These items are *directly* tied to the sale of food and beverages. For example, operations use linen, candles, and flowers for tabletops, and paper bags and plastic containers for take-out orders. This is a particularly tricky category for an operation to negotiate because service style, or what an operation wants its service style to be, comes into play. Purchasers need to ask a lot of questions when making purchases in this category. How much is enough? If an operation is a full-service restaurant, is it casual, semiformal, or upscale? And then how does the purchaser support that atmosphere? What will the costs be in the long run for using linen tablecloths instead of a bare tabletop? Is it worthwhile to provide a sturdier plastic take-out container or is a plain, foldable container sufficient? There are a lot of hidden costs in the answers to these questions, and an operation needs to be aware of them all. Figure 5.4 shows some examples of nonfood items a restaurant or foodservice operation might need to purchase; some of these are listed here as well:

- Linen and uniforms
- Bar supplies
- Paper goods
- Cleaning supplies
- Menus and beverage lists

294

- Candles
- Flowers
- Music

Figure 5.4: Restaurant and foodservice operations have to purchase many nonfood items.

Smallwares and Equipment

Smallwares and small equipment are items that an individual can generally move from location to location easily and that require replacement fairly often—but *how* often is a key question here. Is an operation better off buying cheaper equipment but replacing it more frequently, or should the operation buy more expensive equipment that will last longer? To answer this question, an operation will likely have to consider how often the equipment will be in use, how important the product is to the operation, and what the long-term costs of the cheaper products will be against the up-front costs of the more expensive products. Here are some examples of smallwares and catering equipment:

- China and glassware
- Silverware
- Kitchen utensils and supplies
- Tabletop mixers
- Blenders
- Food processors

295

Discuss

- What smallwares and small equipment are available in the classroom kitchen?
- Under what circumstances should operations purchase inexpensive and lower quality equipment instead of expensive and higher quality equipment?
- How might an operation's style of service or menu dictate its purchases of smallwares and small equipment?

Reinforce and Review

- Smallwares and small equipment are items that an individual can generally move from location to location easily and that require replacement fairly often.
- To determine whether to purchase inexpensive or expensive equipment, an operation must consider how often the equipment will be in use, how important the product is to the operation, and what the long-term and up-front costs will be.
- Smallwares and small equipment include china, silverware, and food processors.

CUSTOMIZED INSTRUCTION
Literacy Connection, 21st-Century Skills—Solve Problems, Communicate Clearly, Use and Manage Information
Special Needs Students
What are some smallwares and small equipment that you have in your household? How are they used?

Figure Focus

Figure 5.4: What nonfood items can students identify in this photograph?

Discuss

- What technologies are found in most restaurant and foodservice operations? What do these technologies have in common?

- How can an operation's style of service affect its purchase or lease of FFE?

- How can a new operation reduce its start-up costs?

Reinforce and Review

- Managers and employees use technology throughout many restaurant and foodservice operations.

- An important consideration for purchasers is whether implementing new technology will improve the operation's bottom line.

- Technology includes computers, POS systems, and credit-card processing systems.

- The category of furniture, fixtures, and equipment is also known as capital expenditures or FFE.

- FFE items are often leased and not purchased, as they are expensive and can require expensive maintenance and repair.

- FFE includes dining-room tables, cooking equipment, and plumbing fixtures.

Teaching Tips

- Make sure that students understand the distinction between FFE and technology, despite the proliferation of "smart" equipment.

Technology

Management and employees use technology throughout the modern restaurant or foodservice operation, from the computer in the office to the printer for the point-of-sale (POS) system in the kitchen. A crucial question here is whether implementing technology will improve the bottom line of the operation. When considering any new technology, a purchaser must calculate how soon, or whether, the savings an operation gets from the new tool will exceed its cost. Here are some examples of purchases that fall in this category:

- Computers
- Printers
- Fax machines
- Point-of-sale systems
- Phone systems
- Credit card processing systems
- Security systems

Furniture, Fixtures, and Equipment

This category is also known as FFE, or capital expenditures. An operation might purchase or lease some of the items in this category, as is often the case with warewashing machines, ice machines, and beverage dispensing equipment. These big-ticket appliances require a lot of maintenance and expensive repair. To reduce up-front expenses (especially during the start-up phase) and future maintenance and repair costs, many operations choose to lease these items rather than buy them. This list includes some other examples of FFE, and Figure 5.5 on the following page illustrates the issue:

- Tables, chairs, and barstools
- Lighting fixtures
- Bars
- Cooking equipment
- Refrigeration
- Plumbing fixtures
- HVAC

Figure 5.5: An operation must decide to purchase higher-end or lower-end items, or simply lease furniture, fixtures, and equipment.

Business Supplies and Services

These supplies and services support the management or marketing of an operation. The size of the operation is often a factor in what services an operation may use. Management might make the decision to use an outside marketing service, for example, based on the amount of **capital**, or assets, an operation has at its disposal. As with any purchase, purchasers must carefully weigh the potential profit of such an **investment** (the use of money for future profit) against the costs. Here are some examples:

- Office supplies and equipment
- Financial and legal services
- Insurance
- Marketing and advertising

Support Services

These support services are tied to the operational aspect of the business. As with nonfood item purchases, many of the support service options have to do with an operation's chosen service style and how far that operation wants to go in emphasizing that service style. For example, if an operation wants fresh-cut flowers on every table, is it more cost efficient to manage this in-house, or

297

Discuss

- How are business supplies and technology related? How do managers decide where to put items that appear to belong in both categories?
- Explain the role of capital in opening and operating a restaurant.
- Generally speaking, are restaurant and foodservice operations good investments? Why or why not? What types of operations might be less risky than others?

Reinforce and Review

- Business supplies and services support an operation's management or marketing.
- An operation's size is often a factor in determining what supplies and services it requires.
- Purchasers must carefully weigh the potential profits of any investment against its costs.
- Business supplies and services include office supplies and equipment, professional services, and insurance.
- Support services are tied to the operational aspect of the business; they often are related to the operation's chosen service style.

Teaching Tips

- Make sure students understand how capital and investment are related.

Vocabulary Terms

- **Capital:** Assets.
- **Investment:** The use of money for future profit.

Figure Focus

Figure 5.5: What are the advantages and disadvantages to purchasing rather than leasing FFE?

Discuss

- What factors are involved in an operation's decision to manage certain responsibilities itself, rather than employing an outside service?
- Consider the typical restaurant. What maintenance services need to be performed?

Reinforce and Review

- Relying on support services to perform some work that would otherwise have to be done by an operation's staff might cost more, but it could also free employees to focus on more important aspects of their work.
- Examples of support services include garbage removal, pest control, and parking services.
- Maintenance services help keep the facility in good shape and are essential to efficient operations.
- Managers must plan for both short- and long-term maintenance costs.
- Maintenance services include security system support, groundskeeping, and equipment repair.

Teaching Tips

- Encourage students to identify examples of each category of goods and services covered in this chapter that the school or school district purchases.

would hiring a flower service be a wise purchasing decision? The service will obviously be more costly, but it could free up employees of an operation to do other, more productive, things. Here are some examples of support services:

- Credit card processing service
- Linen and uniform rental
- Garbage removal
- Flower services
- Music services
- Pest control
- Parking and valet services

Maintenance Services

Maintenance services help keep the facility in good shape. These are often overlooked by start-up operations, but many of these services are essential to the efficient functioning of an operation. Like any of the other categories discussed, maintenance service costs need to be accounted for on both short-term and long-term bases. Here are some examples:

- Point-of-sale (POS) system support
- Security system support
- Cleaning services
- Plumbing and heating maintenance and repair
- Groundskeeping
- Painting and carpentry
- Equipment repair and maintenance

298

Utilities

In many areas of the country, operations can choose among competing utility suppliers. Careful negotiation of the various utilities in a given area will end up saving an operation money. Cutting costs on utilities frees up money that might be better spent on other aspects of the operation. Figure 5.6 shows a utility service person. Here is a list of the utilities that most operations will use:

Figure 5.6: A service utility person at work.

- Gas

- Heat

- Electricity

- Telephone

- Internet service

Essential Skills
Vendor Shopping

When selecting a vendor, you need to do your homework! This isn't simply a matter of getting the best price: as in any other situation, quality can be expensive—and worth it. There are a lot of other things an operation should consider when shopping around. There are three main steps in the process:

❶ Consider your establishment's needs:

- Quality standards

- Type of restaurant

- Number of guests

- Service periods

- Availability of skilled labor

- Budget and menu pricing

299

Discuss

- In what ways are a restaurant or foodservice operation's utility needs similar to that of a typical household?

- How do an operation's utility costs affect its overall business plan?

Reinforce and Review

- When operations can choose among competing utility providers, they can often negotiate cost savings.

- Cutting utility costs frees up money that might be better spent on other aspects of an operation.

- Most operations use gas, heat, electricity, telephone, and Internet services.

Teaching Tips

- Utility costs and ways to contain them will be discussed in greater detail in Chapter 9.

Essential Skills: Vendor Shopping

Encourage students to discuss the following:

- Under what circumstances might an operation choose to spend more money for a particular good or service?

- How do an operation's quality standards determine its choice of suppliers?

- Explain how the availability of skilled labor can affect an operation's choice of suppliers.

Figure Focus

Figure 5.6: How can restaurant and foodservice operations lower their utility costs? How might these efforts affect guest service?

Encourage students to discuss the following:

- What other questions should restaurant and foodservice managers ask prospective suppliers?

- How can restaurant and foodservice managers research the suppliers that they are considering?

- What is the most important aspect of building positive relationships with suppliers? Why?

Discuss

- Why do some operations use the formal purchasing method, whereas others use the informal method? How do operations determine which method is appropriate for their needs?

- How do bids differ from quotes?

Reinforce and Review

- The buyer for an independent or single-unit operation might be its owner or manager; in larger operations, purchasing responsibilities might be overseen by a purchasing vice president, agent, or director.

- The head of the purchasing chain might perform all purchasing tasks or might review purchasing decisions and assist with purchasing for multiple units or franchises.

- Buyers use either formal or informal purchasing methods to obtain goods and services.

Vocabulary Terms

- **Buyer:** The employee responsible for an operation's purchasing activities.

- **Franchisees:** Those people granted a franchise to market a company's goods or services in a given area.

- **Formal purchasing method:** A process through which buyers prepare purchase specifications for the items they wish to buy; these specifications are then sent to various suppliers, who prepare bids.

- **Bids:** Specialized, written priced lists created for an operation by a supplier.

- **Informal purchasing method:** A process through which managers or owners request verbal price quotes from a variety of suppliers.

- **Quote:** Notice of a price that a supplier gives to a buyer during the purchasing process.

❷ Once you know your needs, you can research vendors. Some areas to investigate include the following:

- Price ranges for items you use frequently
- Quality of customer service
- Delivery schedule plus availability of emergency deliveries
- Ease of ordering
- Satisfaction level of long-term customers

❸ Finally, start building relationships with the vendors that look promising:

- Try out sample products.
- Talk with your peers and check references.
- Make small orders at first to see how they deliver.

Buyers: Who's Doing the Purchasing

In independent or single-unit operations, the **buyer** of an operation's product might be the owner or manager. In some medium-sized independent operations, purchasing may be divided among the owner and various unit managers. For example, the owner might be responsible for purchasing food items, while the bar manager might be responsible for beverage purchasing. The purchasing structure in chain operations might include a purchasing vice-president, director, or agent. This person in some cases performs all purchasing activities. Other times, the individual in this position reviews purchasing decisions and provides assistance with purchasing for all units and/or franchisees. **Franchisees** are those people who are granted a franchise to market a company's goods or services in a certain area.

Buyers engage in two types of purchasing methods: formal or informal, as illustrated in Figure 5.7 on the following page. Hotels, large restaurants, and chains use the **formal purchasing method** to order goods and services. In the formal purchasing method, buyers prepare purchase specifications for the items they want. These specifications are then sent to several suppliers for bids. **Bids** are specialized, written price lists created for the restaurant by a supplier. Smaller operations use an **informal purchasing method**. For example, when the owner of a small diner needs a new supplier, he or she simply asks for verbal price quotes from a variety of suppliers before making a decision. A **quote** is notice of a price that a supplier gives to a buyer during the purchasing process.

300

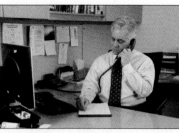

Figure 5.7: There are both formal and informal purchasing methods.

Like any other position in the restaurant and foodservice industry, a good deal of training may be required to become a buyer. A buyer must know everything about the operation—from the items on the menu and their current prices to the expected volume of business. Buyers must also understand federal and state regulations that oversee food quality, production, processing, labeling, transportation, and safety. For an operation to run effectively, buyers must have a full understanding of the purchasing process and be familiar with the technology available for simplifying and improving the process.

Purchasing decisions affect all of an operation's employees. Anyone responsible for purchasing must cooperate and communicate with other employees to be sure he or she buys the right goods and services. For example, a chef or production manager who purchases fruit and other food items for the entire operation should check with the bar manager to see what that area needs. Likewise, the bar manager might purchase the wines and spirits used in the kitchen and should check with the chef to see what's needed. Making assumptions about what other aspects of an operation want or need can often result in having too much or too little of an item, or even getting the wrong products altogether. Cooperation in purchasing is very important.

A buyer must also have integrity. Most operations have a written code of ethics that buyers must agree to follow. These rules help guide a buyer's behavior if he or she faces a situation that threatens the honesty of the relationship to the vendor or with the operation itself. One type of this situation is illustrated in Figure 5.8 on the following page. **Kickbacks** are money or other goods received by a person in exchange for purchasing from a specific vendor. Receiving a

301

Discuss

- How can poor communication affect the buyer's ability to obtain the correct products? How can this affect the operation's reputation?

- Why is it important for purchasers to understand all applicable laws and regulations governing food-related issues?

- Explain the concept of integrity. How is it related to the concept of professionalism?

- What are some opportunities for students to demonstrate integrity?

Reinforce and Review

- A buyer must know everything about the establishment as well as understand relevant federal and state regulations.

- Buyers must also fully understand the purchasing process and be familiar with available technology that can assist in the process.

- Anyone responsible for purchasing must cooperate and communicate with other employees to be sure he or she buys the right goods and services.

- Many restaurant and foodservice operations have a written code of ethics that help guide a purchaser's behavior.

- Buyers are sometimes faced with situations that threaten their honesty.

Teaching Tips

- Reiterate the importance of integrity throughout the professional world.

Vocabulary Terms

- **Kickback:** Money or other goods received by a person in exchange for purchasing from a specific supplier.

Figure Focus

Figure 5.7: In what ways does the use of either formal or informal purchasing methods require professionalism?

Discuss

- How does an operation or a person determine an ethical code of conduct? What considerations are involved?

- What are some opportunities for people to engage in ethical behavior in their personal lives?

Reinforce and Review

- Some suppliers may offer gifts to buyers that are not expressly linked to an order, but these gifts can cause feelings of obligation.

- Buyers should always follow the operation's code of conduct and avoid anything that might cause a personal conflict.

- Ethical behavior is not an option: It is necessary for any operation to run successfully.

Teaching Tips

- If there is an ethical code of conduct in place on campus, review and discuss it with students.

On the Job:
Buyers: Responsibilities, Education, and Skills

Encourage students to discuss the following:

- What aspects of the buyer's job appear particularly interesting or especially challenging? Why?

- Explain why buyers must have excellent communication skills.

- Is it important for a foodservice buyer to have a foodservice background? Why or why not?

Homework Activity:
The Right Stuff

Literacy Connection, 21st-Century Skills—Make Judgments and Decisions, Communicate Clearly, Be Self-Directed Learners

Describe a situation in which you felt pressured to do what you knew was wrong. What did you do? Were you able to maintain your integrity? What was the outcome?

Discuss the situation in a one-page report.

kickback is obviously wrong (and illegal). Some vendors may offer buyers gifts without an express expectation of an order. But accepting a gift from a generous vendor might cause a buyer to feel obligated to that company, even if he or she didn't feel that way at the time the gift was accepted. The best course of action for buyers, therefore, is to follow the operation's code of conduct and to avoid anything that might cause a personal conflict. Ethical behavior is not an option; it is necessary for any operation to run successfully.

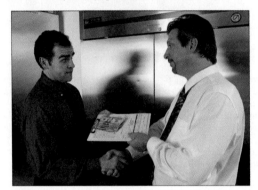

Figure 5.8: Kickbacks are payments or an offering of services with the intent to influence or gain something from a company or a person.

[on the job]

Buyers: Responsibilities, Education, and Skills

Larger restaurant organizations and other foodservice establishments often hire buyers to handle business relationships with outside vendors. These individuals are responsible for purchasing perishable and nonperishable goods and services, while maintaining appropriate quality standards and adhering to a budget. Buyers negotiate contracts with suppliers, often working with vendors to provide novel or unusual products. While it is important for buyers to find good deals, it is equally important to build good relationships with vendors. Internally, buyers work with research and development teams and marketers as well as chefs and managers to coordinate business needs.

Typically, a bachelor's degree is required to become a buyer, though this is not always the case. More importantly, a buyer must have excellent communication and negotiation skills and must work well with a variety of personality types. Financial skills, especially accounting and budgeting, are also key.

Figure Focus

Figure 5.8: What are some more discreet ways of offering or accepting a kickback? Why is it important for owners and managers to know about these techniques?

Summary

In this section, you learned the following:

- There are five basic steps to the procurement process: determine what an operation wants and needs to buy; identify quality standards; order products and services; receive deliveries; and store and issue products.

- There are four major goals of purchasing: maintain the right supply of products and services, maintain the quality standards of the operation, minimize the amount of money the operation spends, and stay competitive with similar operations. Purchasers need to fully understand and strive to achieve these purchasing goals to run a successful operation.

- There are three main layers in any channel of distribution: primary sources, intermediary sources, and retailers. Primary sources are the producers, such as farmers, manufacturers, and distillers. Intermediary sources include wholesalers, distributors, and suppliers. These businesses buy products from primary sources and sell them to their final destination: the retailer. Retailers sell their products directly to the public. All restaurants are considered retailers.

- There are nine major categories of goods and services: food and beverage; nonfood items; smallwares and equipment; technology; furniture, fixtures, and equipment; business supplies and services; support services; maintenance services; and utilities. Restaurant and foodservice operations need to carefully negotiate what they spend money on in each of these categories, looking closely at both the short-term and long-term costs for each purchase.

- A buyer must know everything about an operation—from the items on the menu and their current prices to the expected volume of business. Buyers must also understand federal and state regulations that oversee food quality, production, processing, labeling, transportation, and safety. For an operation to run effectively, buyers must have a full understanding of the purchasing process and be familiar with the technology available for simplifying and improving the process. Buyers engage in two types of purchasing methods: formal or informal.

- Buyers must have integrity to avoid forming relationships with vendors that could either compromise the relationship with that vendor or compromise the best interests of the operation the buyer is making purchases for.

303

Summary
- Remind students to review the following:
  1. The overview of purchasing
  2. Channels of distribution flow
  3. What goods and service are being purchased
  4. Who's doing the purchasing

Section 5.1
Review Questions

1. Student responses may vary so long as they provide clear and logical answers.

2. Primary sources include farmers, ranchers, manufacturers, and distillers. Intermediary sources include wholesalers, suppliers, and distributors. Retail sources include restaurants, school cafeterias, and caterers.

3. Student responses may vary so long as the examples they identify are appropriate.

4. Student responses may vary so long as they explain both a potential situation and how it could be avoided.

5. Students should explain why they do or do not agree with this statement.

6. Students may identify any of a number of methods to maintain the restaurant's ambiance; they should select at least three methods.

7. Students should identify the objective they consider most important and provide a logical explanation.

8. Students should identify and defend their choice.

Section 5.1 Review Questions

❶ Pick two of the four goals of purchasing and explain why each is important, using an example for each to illustrate your point.

❷ Give an example of a primary source, an intermediary source, and a retail source.

❸ Name four of the nine goods and services categories, and provide an example of a good or service for each category you name.

❹ Explain a situation in which a buyer's integrity might be compromised and how a buyer might avoid such a situation.

❺ Al Gaylor comments that "purchasing, by its very nature, is a key driver in successfully operating a profitable restaurant." Do you agree that this is true? Why or why not?

❻ In going over the purchases, Miguel and Chef Kate found that they are spending way too much on nonfood items. Kabob has a classy, intimate feel, and they want to keep that atmosphere. Can you think of ways to achieve that style without spending a lot of money?

❼ Of the four major objectives of the purchasing function, which do you believe is the most important and why?

❽ You are the owner of a medium-sized restaurant. You often do the buying for the restaurant, but you also have assistant managers who sometimes do the buying as well. What kind of purchasing method would you implement—formal or informal? Explain your decision.

$250.00

304

Section 5.1 Activities

1. Study Skills/Group Activity: Buyers Beware!

Working with two or three other students, take the information you learned in this chapter about the buying process and what buyers do, and develop a written code of ethics for buyers to follow. Then share your list of ethics with the rest of the class.

2. Activity: Two Tools

Review the various tools available to maintain the right supply of products and services. What two tools do you think would prove most effective? Write a one-page report explaining your rationale.

3. Critical Thinking: An Interlude with an Intermediary

Research a real-life example of an intermediary source. First, discuss the role of the intermediary in the distribution channel. Then, look into how your example functions and the service it provides its customers. Then, prepare a three-minute presentation to explain your findings to the class.

305

Section 5.1 Activities

1. Students can research codes of ethics and refer to Level 1, Chapter 8 in developing their code of ethics.

2. Students should research planning and purchasing tools online to determine which might be most effective.

3. Students should identify and research an intermediary source and how it operates.

Section 5.2
Making Purchasing Decisions

Introduce the Section

a. Explain how a restaurant or foodservice operation determines its quality standards and product specifications.

b. Describe the ordering process and how restaurant and foodservice operations decide how and what to order.

c. Discuss the objectives for the section.

Vocabulary Review

a. Direct students to the key terms.

b. Pronounce each word, and have the students repeat the pronunciation out loud.

c. Discuss the definition of each word.

Teach

Discuss

- Encourage students to explain some purchasing decisions they face or have faced in their own lives. What information is helpful in making these decisions?

- Why might people make poor decisions?

Reinforce and Review

- An operation's purchasing decisions affect whether or not the operation will be successful or even viable.

- The major elements of foodservice purchasing decisions are quality standards, product specifications, and the ordering process.

CUSTOMIZED INSTRUCTION

Science Connection, Literacy Connection, 21st-Century Skills—Think Creatively, Reason Effectively, Communicate Clearly, Create Media Products, Work Independently

Less Advanced Students

Imagine a restaurant as a body, in which purchasing is the brain and service is the heart. Identify some other important restaurant concepts. What body parts would these be and why?

5.1 Introduction to Purchasing	5.2 Making Purchasing Decisions	5.3 Managing Purchases
• Purchasing overview	• Determining quality standards	• Receiving orders
• Channels of distribution flow	• Writing product specifications	• Storing orders
• Goods and services: what's being purchased	• Ordering	• Taking inventory
• Buyers: who's doing the purchasing	• Ordering forms	
	• Knowing food prices	

SECTION 5.2 MAKING PURCHASING DECISIONS

Everyone makes purchasing decisions every day. The questions are endless: Buy lunch out, or bring it from home? Buy this bottle of water, this candy bar, this apple? Or, save the money for something down the road? Do I need a new pair of jeans, or are mine okay for a few more months? Should I go to this movie in the theater, or should I just wait until it comes out on DVD? The purchasing decisions we make for ourselves will hopefully lead to happier, healthier, more satisfying lives. We all have our own set of quality standards that guide our decisions, but it's a delicate balance.

The same is true for the life of restaurants and foodservice operations. The purchasing decisions an operation makes will ultimately affect whether it is healthy and successful, or not. Just as with an individual's purchasing decisions, a restaurant or foodservice operation needs to strike a good balance. Buying too much or too little of something can affect the health of the business in other areas, or, worse yet, it can affect its potential for long-term success. This section discusses the major elements of making restaurant and foodservice purchasing decisions: quality standards, product specifications, and the ordering process.

Study Questions

After studying Section 5.2, you should be able to answer the following questions:

- What are the factors that go into determining quality standards?

- What needs to be considered in writing product specifications?

- What is a make-or-buy analysis?

- What tools do operations use to help determine what to purchase?

- What are the typical ordering forms?

- What factors influence food prices?

306

Determining Quality Standards

One of the keys to purchasing the right products is **quality standards**. *Quality*, in this sense, refers to the value or worth that customers place on a product or service. For example, no one expects the highest grade of beef in a $2.00 hamburger. But people do expect the $2.00 hamburger to be cooked properly and to taste good. So, an operation that wants to sell this kind of hamburger needs to have a quality standard for the beef it uses that meets its customers' expectations while controlling costs.

Establishing solid quality standard specifications helps an operation create the consistency that customers grow to expect when they purchase their favorite food items. Successful operations select the best products early on by determining the quality standards for *every* product purchased and used at the operation. Putting together quality standards is a complex process. Managers and buyers usually work together to create them, along with input from vendors and other employees. The following are some of the factors that need to be taken into account when figuring out an operation's quality standards:

- Item's intended use
- Operation's concept and goals
- The menu
- Employee skill level
- Budgetary constraints
- Equipment constraints
- Customers' wants and needs
- Seasonal availability
- Storage capacity

The Item's Intended Use

Knowing how an item will be prepared and served is the most influential factor in determining quality standards. For example, fruit used for accenting or garnishing plates should be a different quality than that used to make dessert sauces. That is, chefs choose fruit used for garnishing based on its appearance; it needs to look good on the plate. Chefs can use fruit that is overripe or even damaged in a sauce, though, because it won't be used in its natural form.

307

Discuss

- Why are employee skill levels a factor in establishing quality standards?

- The "best product available" and the "most appropriate product" are both important purchasing concepts. How do they differ? How might they overlap?

Reinforce and Review

- In terms of purchasing, "quality" refers to the value or worth that customers place on a product or service.

- Establishing quality standard specifications helps an operation maintain the consistency that its guests expect.

- Successful operations determine the quality standards for every item that they purchase and use.

- Some factors that should be considered when determining an operation's quality standards include the item's intended use, the menu, and customers' wants and needs.

- Knowing how an item will be prepared and served is the most influential factor in determining quality standards.

Teaching Tips

- Refer students back to the "Quality Standards" activity on p. 287. If they had to repeat that task now, what additional information would they consider?

Vocabulary Terms

- **Quality standards:** An operation's expectations about the quality of the goods and services it plans to purchase.

CUSTOMIZED INSTRUCTION

Literacy Connection, 21st-Century Skills—Think Creatively, Critical Thinking and Problem Solving, Communicate Clearly, Information Literacy, Work Independently

More Advanced Students

Have you ever heard the phrase "value for your money"? It relates to the purchasing process: A good or service with a perceived level of value is exchanged for an amount of money. If the amount of money given is greater than the perceived value of the good or service, then the purchaser received poor value (at least in his or her eyes). On the other hand, if the amount of money given is less than the perceived value of the good or service, then the purchaser received good value, or a bargain.

How does perception affect value? Research this topic and write a one-page report discussing this relationship.

Discuss

- A quick-service restaurant's need for bread (for instance, frozen heat-and-serve hamburger buns) might differ from a fine-dining restaurant's need for bread (for instance, freshly baked baguettes from a local bakery). Give some other examples of how an operation's concept can affect its purchases.

- How is an item's intended use related to the concept of total utilization?

Reinforce and Review

- The overall concept and goals of the operation guide all decisions.

- Operations with different concepts have different equipment—and therefore different purchasing needs—in their kitchens.

- An operation's purchases must accurately reflect its menu; otherwise, the operation could be committing fraud.

Teaching Tips

- Students should be aware from previous discussions that operations with different concepts will also have different equipment and therefore different purchasing needs.

Homework Activity: Eggs Not-So-Easy

Literacy Connection, 21st-Century Skills—Think Creatively, Solve Problems, Communicate Clearly, Flexibility and Adaptability, Work Independently, Guide and Lead Others

Your operation always serves eggs from nearby Albina Farms, which has such a sterling reputation that you list "Albina Farms eggs" on your menu. However, your purchaser has forgotten to specify "Albina Farms eggs," and eggs from another source were mistakenly purchased, received, stored, and used.

As the owner, what is your obligation to the guests? Do you exchange eggs? Do you change your menu? Do you ask your servers to explain that the operation is temporarily substituting eggs from another source? What other options might you have?

In a one-page paper, explain how you would handle this situation and what you would do to prevent a similar occurrence in the future.

The Operation's Concept and Goals

The overall concept and goals of the operation guides all decisions. Figure 5.9 illustrates how operations with different concepts have different equipment in their kitchens. For example, if an operation is a fast-casual restaurant, it must serve premium items in a fraction of the time it takes at an upscale dining restaurant. Such an operation is promising speed, convenience, reasonable prices, and premium menu items. So which products will help to achieve these goals? One option might be an impinger oven—a conveyer-belt-style oven used to toast bread products. These ovens quickly toast sandwiches, bagels, and small pizzas. This type of oven may get rid of the need to employ a full-time baker, which will cut labor costs and allow the operation to provide a lower price to its customers. A buyer must consider these kinds of goals before creating quality standards.

Figure 5.9: Operations with different concepts have differences in quality standards and purchasing.

The Menu

If the menu specifies "whole Cornish hens," the buyer must specify in the quality standard, "whole Cornish hens." If a name brand is mentioned on the menu, then the buyer must specify only the name-brand item on the operation's list of quality standards. The section *Writing Product Specifications* covers this in more detail.

Homework Activity: Conceptual Concerns

Literacy Connection, 21st-Century Skills—Think Creatively, Reason Effectively, Communicate Clearly, Work Independently

You plan to open your own restaurant. What is its concept, and what are its goals? How will these affect what and from whom you will purchase?

Describe your concept, goals, and purchasing plan in a one-page paper.

Figure Focus

Figure 5.9: What information can students deduce about each operation concept from looking at these photographs?

Employee Skill Level

If an operation offers items that require extensive preparation, the operation will need highly skilled employees. Of course, higher skill levels mean higher wages. When employees have lower skill levels, an operation must buy easy-to-use or easy-to-prepare convenience products. Although an operation can pay less-skilled employees lower wages than highly skilled employees, it will likely be paying more for such easy-to-prepare convenience products, which often come with higher costs. So again, an operation needs to look at all the different angles of how it is spending its money.

Budgetary Constraints

Operations in highly competitive markets may need to include cost limits in their quality standards. Restaurant or foodservice operations can't change prices on the menu every week to reflect the changing costs of the items it purchases. Their prices should be fairly consistent or customers will get upset, and they have to stay competitive with their competitors' prices. Operations may need to avoid purchasing products whose prices go up and down wildly. Drastic changes in an item's price can cut into the business's profit and make budgets difficult to project.

Customers' Wants and Needs

It's very important to look closely at what customers want and why they choose to eat at an operation. Analyze and track trends by providing surveys and feedback forms. Smart operations respond to their customers' wants and needs by providing goods and services that meet those needs and produce a profit. In many cases, these wants and needs are influenced by industry and consumer trends. Purchasers and management may need to update quality specifications from time to time to reflect these trends.

Seasonal Availability

The seasonal nature of produce and other items affects price and availability, as illustrated in Figure 5.10 on the following page. The need for certain products (especially produce) may more than double during certain months. Managers and chefs will need to determine if the season will affect a change in quality standards. Some operations may also change menus to reflect the seasonal availability of some products.

309

Discuss

- As an owner, under what circumstances would you choose to have an operation that employs low-skilled employees and relies on easy-to-prepare convenience items? Under what circumstances would you choose to have highly skilled employees and rely on raw products?

- Why do some foodservice goods experience significant price fluctuations? Give some examples.

- What are some restaurant and foodservice trends? How do they affect consumer demands?

- When dealing with seasonal produce that may become more expensive or lower in quality at certain times of the year, is it better to keep the items on the menu but change their quality standards, or to remove the items from the menu altogether? Under what circumstances might either solution be correct?

Reinforce and Review

- If an operation offers items that require extensive preparation, the operation will need highly skilled employees, so labor costs will increase; alternatively, the operation can save on labor by employing less skilled workers and relying on convenience products, but these are more expensive and will increase food costs.

- Operations in highly competitive markets might need to include cost limits in their quality standards; although prices for goods may fluctuate, restaurant menu prices must remain fairly consistent.

- Drastic changes in an item's price can cut into the operation's profit and make budgets difficult to project.

- Smart operations respond to their customers' needs and wants by providing goods and services that meet those needs and produce a profit.

- The seasonal nature of produce and other items can affect their price, availability, and quality.

**Homework Activity:
Value**

Literacy Connection, 21st-Century Skills—Reason Effectively, Make Judgments and Decisions, Communicate Clearly, Work Independently

What constitutes a "good value" to you? Why? How do you determine what is and is not a good value? Why do some people find certain goods or services to be more valuable than other people do?

Discuss your responses to these questions in a brief essay.

Discuss

- What problems can arise if purchasers do not thoroughly research their potential suppliers?

- What are some reasons that operations often have relatively limited storage space?

Reinforce and Review

- An operation's storage space—both the amount of space and the type of space—limits the amount of product it can purchase.

- Product specifications are based on quality standards and include the details that will help a product or service meet the operation's quality standards.

- Smaller companies might use informal specifications, giving few details about the desired product, whereas larger companies often develop formal, precise specifications.

- Buyers should always work with approved, reputable suppliers.

Teaching Tips

- Relate this material to Chapter 3.

Vocabulary Terms

- **Product specifications/specs:** An operation's purchasing requirements for a particular good or service.

Figure 5.10: The seasonal nature of produce and the transportation needed to bring it to market results in higher costs for restaurants.

Storage Capacity

An operation's storage space limits the amount of product it can purchase. If an operation has limited freezer space, a limited amount of food can be maintained at the required temperature levels. Purchasers may prefer to order fresh, ready-to-use products if additional freezer storage is not bought. On the other hand, if plenty of shelf space in dry storage is available, some items, such as corn, may be ordered in a can instead of frozen—which may then affect the quality of some menu items.

[fast fact]

Did you Know...?
A recent study published in the *Cornell Hotel and Restaurant Administration Quarterly* determined that restaurants are more likely to succeed when the operation has a clear concept that it executes consistently. This same study found that maintaining and fostering connections with customers and the community proved to be more valuable to an operation's success than spending money on advertising and promotions.

Writing Product Specifications

Once managers and purchasers decide on quality standards, they need to create product specifications. **Product specifications**, or **specs**, describe the requirements for a particular product or service that an operation wants to buy. Specifications include the details that help a product or service meet the operation's quality standards. Operations should always document product specifications. Smaller operations may use informal specifications that include only a few details. But specifications in larger companies are usually formal and precise. It's also important to remember that buyers should always work with approved, reputable suppliers.

310

Figure Focus
Figure 5.10: Why do most restaurant and foodservice operations use produce that is out of season?

Buyers must be very familiar with the operation's quality standards and product specifications. They also must communicate these standards and specifications to both staff and vendors. Managers and receiving employees must then be trained to make sure that vendors have followed product specifications, so that the quality standards are met.

Example:

Quality standard: Crushed tomatoes

Product specification: Finley® crushed tomatoes, six to a case, #10 can

Well-written specifications, like the one shown in Figure 5.11, prevent buyers from receiving low-quality or wrong items. Possible specifications are shown in Table 5.3 on the following page. However, it's possible to write specs that are too rigid. Demanding an out-of-season melon may force a supplier to ship by air and greatly increase the price. Instead, a buyer should review the menu or allow for substitutions. But, keep in mind that customers will easily notice changes in some products. Substitutions shouldn't mean a drop-off in quality.

Figure 5.11: Sample product specification sheet.

Many suppliers have their own product code numbers, which helps to ensure that customers are receiving specifically what they need. The product code numbers relate to particular quality standards and name brands.

311

Figure Focus

Figure 5.11: What makes this product specification sheet a good example?

Discuss

- How can an operation write a comprehensive product specification without being too rigid?

- What role does employee training play in the purchasing and receiving process?

Reinforce and Review

- Buyers must be very familiar with the operation's quality standards and product specifications when speaking with suppliers or purchasing goods and services.

- Managers and receiving employees must be trained to make sure that suppliers have followed product specifications, so that the operation's quality standards are met.

- Well-written specifications prevent purchasers from obtaining low-quality or wrong items.

- Sometimes a buyer must make substitutions to obtain quality products at an appropriate price, but customers should not suffer because of these decisions.

- Using a product code number, which relates to particular quality standards and name brands, can help both suppliers and purchasers ensure that the right product is being provided.

Teaching Tips

- Students should clearly understand the differences between quality standards and product specification sheets.

Homework Activity: Specs Revisited

Literacy Connection, 21st-Century Skills— Make Judgments and Decisions, Communicate Clearly, Flexibility and Adaptability, Work Independently

Compare the information provided in the product specification sheet shown in Figure 5.11 with the specs you developed for earlier assignments in this chapter and in Chapter 3. Looking back, what would you change about your previous work and why?

Discuss your reaction in a one-paragraph report.

- Explain why a product's intended use is the primary factor involved in selection decisions.

- Why is it important to specify the desired "market form" of an item?

- In an increasingly globalized society, why is specifying an item's place of origin relevant?

- Why is it important for the buyer, the chef, and other management personnel to communicate and collaborate when developing purchasing specifications?

Homework Activity:
Caesar Dressing

Mathematics Connection, Literacy Connection, 21st-Century Skills—Critical Thinking and Problem Solving, Communicate Clearly, Work Independently

Convert the recipe for Caesar dressing on p. 344 to make 1-quart, 1-gallon, and 2.5-gallon batches. What is the recipe cost for each?

Write a brief report discussing how labor and equipment needs might be affected by the increased production and how this could increase costs.

Homework Activity:
Food Safety Around the World

Science Connection, Literacy Connection, 21st-Century Skills—Critical Thinking and Problem Solving, Communicate Clearly, Information Literacy, Work Independently

Select another country and research its food safety policies. How do they differ from regulations in your community? Why might this be the case?

Table 5.3: Possible Specifications

Specification	Notes
Acceptable substitutes	• List alternative products that an operation will accept if an order can't be filled. • Providing acceptable substitutes saves time and money and prevents last-minute menu changes, but it also takes time to identify alternatives that don't compromise the operation's quality standards.
Acceptable trim	• Indicate the maximum amount of waste acceptable in a received product. • Use for fresh products like lettuce, which may have some rotting on its outer layers.
Brand name	• Brand names often indicate a quality level. • Packer's brand names are the supplier's own labeled products. These products often have many quality levels available. Packer's brands usually place a high value on consistency, and they're also the most familiar brands among produce suppliers.
Color	• If an item is available in different colors, then the buyer must specify the right color. Green beans and yellow beans are one example. Be aware that color can also mean a different flavor, which is important in recipes. For example, green grapes are sweeter than red grapes.
Exact name	• Prevent confusion by listing the exact name of the product desired; for example, saying "grapes, Thompson seedless" is better than just saying "grapes."
Intended use	• Describe how a product will be used, prepared, or consumed. • Intended use drives all selection decisions.
Market form	• Market forms identify how an item has been processed before being packaged. For example, "shredded" is a market form of carrots. Other types of market forms include fresh, canned, and dried.
Packaging	• Intended use is the most important factor for choosing packaging; for example, a take-out lunch counter needs packets of ketchup, not bottles. • Some packaging is standardized based on product needs. For example, eggs need special protective packaging.
Place of origin	• This is important to note for products that have textures and flavors specific to a region. • Some operations' policies may require that products come from certain places, such as local farms.

(continued)

Table 5.3: Possible Specifications *continued*

Specification	Notes
Pricing	• List the maximum amount an operation will pay for an item. If an item exceeds the maximum price, then the vendor can't ship it to the operation.
Size	• Identify size in terms of weight, volume, or count (quantity). • Specify some items in exact weights, such as the flour for baking. Order other items, such as a whole turkey or a side of beef, using an acceptable range of weights. • Buyers and suppliers must work together to decide what kinds of units are listed in product specifications. One supplier may provide 150-count boxes, while another provides 12-dozen boxes.
Temperature	• Identify the temperature requirements for receiving an item. For example, an operation may specify that all fresh poultry must be delivered at 39°F. • Train all managers and receiving employees to check temperatures of deliveries.
USDA grade of the item	• The USDA grades over 300 food and agricultural items. Different terms are used for different products. For example, the best beef is Prime, but the best milk is Grade A. • Grading stamps are not the same as inspection stamps. USDA inspections are required for some types of food, but USDA grading is voluntary.

Ordering

Make it or Buy it?

Before placing an order, operations first need to figure out what items they can make themselves versus what items it makes more sense to purchase. To do this, buyers conduct a **make-or-buy analysis** to decide if an operation should make an item from scratch or buy a ready-made version. This analysis helps to balance how much food a kitchen produces with the quality standards of the operation.

There are advantages to buying a ready-made product. Such a product will likely provide consistency; a buyer will know exactly what the operation is getting with each purchase. It also reduces prep time and labor costs. And finally, it reduces the need for certain types of equipment and storage space that might be otherwise necessary to make something from scratch.

313

Table 5.3 (cont.)

• What factors must a buyer consider when specifying a purchase price for a particular item?

• Why is specifying size important? How can ordering the correct amount, but the wrong size, affect a menu?

• How can correct specifications help avoid some concerns about food safety?

• What other product specifications can students envision? Why would each be a helpful addition?

Discuss

• Under what circumstances should products be made in-house or purchased ready-made? Why do many operations combine the two methods?

Reinforce and Review

• Before placing orders, purchasers must determine what items will be purchased or made in-house by conducting a make-or-buy analysis.

• Make-or-buy analyses help balance how much food a kitchen produces with the operation's quality standards.

• Purchasing ready-made products can be advantageous in terms of consistency, reducing prep time and labor costs, and reducing or eliminating certain pieces of equipment or storage space.

Teaching Tips

• Relate the make-or-buy analysis to recipe costing to demonstrate the importance of knowing how much it costs to make each item on the menu.

Vocabulary Terms

• **Make-or-buy analysis:** The process through which a purchaser, often with the assistance of the chef or sous chef, determines whether an operation should make certain items from scratch or purchase ready-made versions.

**Homework Activity:
Make-or-Buy Analyses**

Mathematics Connection, Literacy Connection, 21st-Century Skills—Critical Thinking and Problem Solving, Communicate Clearly, Information Literacy, Be Self-Directed Learners

Select a recipe from this textbook or from Level 1 and determine its cost, based on prices at a local grocer. How much does it cost to purchase the same amount of a similar item from a retail establishment, such as a deli or takeout restaurant? Which is financially a better deal?

Describe your findings in a brief report.

Discuss

- Describe the relationship between production sheets and the food cost percentage.

- Is cost the primary factor in determining whether to make or buy a given product? What role does taste play? Can a great-tasting product be made inexpensively?

Reinforce and Review

- Ready-made products are typically more expensive than raw goods; moreover, many operations pride themselves on their house-made recipes and prefer to serve fresh foods.

- To decide whether to make or buy an item, a buyer must first determine the total cost of making the item in-house and then compare this to the cost of purchasing the item ready-made.

- Knowing exactly what and when to order is at the heart of purchasing.

- Because many operations do not order every day, managers and purchasers rely on quality forecasting to predict future needs as accurately as possible.

- Buyers combine the establishment's production records with their own knowledge and experience to plan purchasing needs.

- Production sheets not only provide an accurate snapshot of predicted and actual production for a given day, but enable buyers to see signs of both stockouts and overproduction.

Teaching Tips

- Chapter 3 introduced students to this material, presented here in greater detail.

Vocabulary Terms

- **Production records:** Documents that provide information about past production and utilization; these include production sheets, daily food cost sheets, and sales mix records.

- **Production sheet:** A list of all menu items that a kitchen will prepare on a given day.

- **Stockout:** Running out of a particular menu item.

- **Overproduction:** Making too much food.

Of course, ready-made products cost more money than items that must be prepared, and such items may also have other drawbacks. Many operations pride themselves in making specialty dishes that require more prep time.

Ultimately, the decision to make or buy must be based on which option provides the most benefits to the operation. To decide whether to make or buy an item, a buyer must first determine the total cost of making the item in-house. This calculation must include all ingredients, processing, labor, and any other directly associated costs. The total of these costs should then be closely compared to the best price of the ready-made item.

Determining What to Order

Determining whether to make an item or buy one ready made is just the start of the ordering process. Knowing exactly what and when to order is at the center of purchasing. Operations don't place orders daily. They have to buy products with some understanding of what they'll need in the days, or perhaps even a week, ahead. So, how does the buyer or manager predict the future? While no method is absolutely certain, quality forecasting, based on good data, greatly reduces errors. Buyers and managers use **production records** to forecast their buying needs. Production records include three elements:

- Production sheets
- Daily food cost sheets
- Sales mix records

By combining this information with years of personal experience, buyers can effectively plan their restaurant's purchasing needs.

In most restaurant and foodservice operations, the chef fills out production sheets for the upcoming weeks. A **production sheet** lists all menu items that the chefs will prepare on a given day. At the end of the day, the chef adjusts the information to reflect actual production and gives the sheets to the buyer. Compiled over a period of time, production sheets become a very important forecasting tool.

Buyers also use production sheets to spot signs of **stockouts** (running out of a menu item) and **overproduction** (making too much food). Overproduction often leads to food waste, which affects food cost percentage. Figure 5.12 on the following page illustrates the problem of stockouts and overproduction.

Figure 5.12: Good planning can reduce waste and lower costs.

One of the most important ways managers try to limit food waste is by keeping accurate **daily food cost sheets**, or ongoing records of daily and monthly food costs for an operation. Daily food cost is determined by adding up the requisitions from the storeroom and the daily purchases. This number, divided by the daily sales figure, is the daily food cost percentage.

Managers use this information to compare costs over a period of time. Most managers try to stay at or below 33 percent, as shown in Table 5.4. While minor fluctuations do occur, a large change will help a manager quickly identify problems such as overproduction, food waste, or theft.

Table 5.4: Food and Beverage Costs by Operation

- Full-service restaurants, average check per person under $15: 31.9%
- Full-service restaurants, average check per person $15–$24.99: 33.1%
- Full-service restaurants, average check per person above $25: 32.4%
- Limited-service restaurants: 30.4%

Source: National Restaurant Association 2007–2008, Restaurant Operation's Report

Managers also keep **sales mix records** that track each item sold from the menu. This can be done on a daily, weekly, or monthly basis. This record shows which items sell well, called **leaders**, or ones that don't sell well, called **losers**. By recognizing leaders and losers, buyers can order more effectively.

315

Figure Focus

Figure 5.12: How can both stockouts and overproduction affect an operation's food cost percentage? How can each affect an operation's reputation?

- Is it realistic to expect all restaurant and foodservice operations to keep track of this information? Why or why not?

- Why do most restaurant and foodservice managers try to keep food costs at or below 33 percent?

Reinforce and Review

- Keeping accurate daily food cost sheets can help managers limit food waste.

- Daily food cost is determined by adding up the requisitions from the dry-storage area and the daily purchases.

- Daily food cost percentage is determined by dividing daily food cost by the daily sales figure.

- Significant changes in the daily food cost can help managers identify problems, such as overproduction, waste, or theft.

- Accurate sales mix records can help buyers identify leaders and losers, enabling them to purchase more effectively.

Teaching Tips

- Review important math skills with students as needed.

Table 5.4:
Food and Beverage Costs by Operation

- Why do limited-service restaurants have the lowest food cost percentage of any category in this table?

- Why do the most expensive restaurants shown here have a lower food cost percentage than moderately priced full-service restaurants?

- Why do the least expensive full-service restaurants have a food cost percentage that is so much higher than that of the limited-service restaurants?

Vocabulary Terms

- **Daily food cost sheets:** Ongoing records of an operation's daily and monthly food costs.

- **Sales mix records:** Documents that track each menu item sold.

- **Leaders:** Menu items that sell strongly.

- **Losers:** Menu items that sell poorly.

Discuss

- How can using the par stock approach to ordering, a reorder point, or both help control foodservice costs?

Reinforce and Review

- Sales mix records help managers determine and track changes in an item's popularity.

- Over time, operations learn their customers' demands and can predict par stock levels so that they never run out of anything.

- To use the par stock approach to ordering, operations must agree to the supplier's ordering process and delivery schedule, determine a par stock level for each inventory item, and calculate what to order by subtracting the amount of an item in hand from its par stock level.

- Using either the par stock approach or an established reorder point can help operations maintain the proper level of inventory at all times.

- Whichever inventory tracking method managers select should be followed closely to prevent purchasing errors.

- Purchase orders are legally binding documents and should be carefully planned.

Teaching Tips

- Describe the ordering process used in the classroom kitchen.

- Consider asking a member of the campus foodservice team to describe the purchasing process it uses.

Vocabulary Terms

- **Par stock:** The ideal amounts of inventory items that an operation should have at all times.

- **Reorder point (ROP):** The point at which an item's inventory has fallen low enough to trigger a reorder.

- **Purchase order:** A legally binding written document that details exactly what the buyer is ordering from the supplier.

Sales mix records help managers determine an item's popularity. When sales for a popular chicken entrée drop off suddenly, a manager might use the sales mix record to explore possible causes. Does the meal sell better in the summer? Are production problems or poor sales techniques responsible? The sales mix record gives managers clues to answer these important questions.

Many operations use the par stock approach to ordering. **Par stock** levels are the ideal amounts of inventory items that an operation should have at all times. Over time, operations learn their customers' demands and can predict these levels so that they never run out of anything. To use the par stock approach, operations must do the following:

1. Agree to the supplier's ordering process and delivery schedule. This is the simplest way to avoid extra costs for changing delivery times or making special requests.

2. Determine a par stock level for each inventory item. This can be done by using sales projections to estimate how much product the operation needs.

3. Calculate what to order by subtracting what is currently in stock from the par stock. Par stock – Amount in stock = Amount to be ordered

Another way to ensure that an operation always has the proper level of stock on hand is to establish a **reorder point,** or **ROP**, for each item. If the reorder point for 50-pound sacks of flour is 2, and there are only 2 sacks left in the storeroom, then the buyer knows that he or she has to order more flour. A reorder point is like a warning bell; it alerts an operation to make orders immediately. The reorder point can be used with the par stock figure to help maintain proper inventory when suppliers do not deliver regularly.

Managers should decide which inventory tracking method is most appropriate for their operation and then maintain it very carefully to avoid overpurchasing or underpurchasing.

Ordering Forms

A **purchase order** is a legally binding written document that details exactly what the buyer is ordering from the vendor. Figure 5.13 shows an example of a purchase order form. Buyers place purchase orders in a number of ways. Some buyers phone in an order, others use the Internet, and still others fax their orders.

316

Figure 5.13: Sample purchase order form.

Every purchase order should include the following pieces of information:

- Operation's name, address, and phone number
- Buyer's name
- Supplier's name, address, and phone number
- Supplier's contact person
- Date of the order
- Desired date of receipt/how long the purchase order is good
- Shipping method
- Quantity for each item

317

Discuss

- Why is it important to know that purchase orders are legally binding?

Reinforce and Review

- Every purchase order should contain contact information for both parties; the date of the order as well as either the desired date of receipt or an expiration date; the shipping method used to transport the items; the item's name and description, the quantity desired, and both the unit and total price; the price of the order; and any special information about the order.

Homework Activity: Purchasing Power
Literacy Connection, 21st-Century Skills—Critical Thinking and Problem Solving, Communicate Clearly, Information Literacy, Work Independently
Write a purchase order for some good, using either an imaginary or an actual supplier. Be sure to include all the necessary information, using Figure 5.13 for assistance.

CUSTOMIZED INSTRUCTION
Literacy Connection, 21st-Century Skills—Critical Thinking and Problem Solving, Communicate Clearly, Information Literacy, Work Independently
ESOL Students
How is the American legal system similar to or different from that of your country of origin? How can this affect the restaurant and foodservice industry?
Write a brief report discussing your findings.

Figure Focus

Figure 5.13: Purchase orders can be used when receiving goods to confirm that no errors were made in the process.

Discuss

- What are some examples of goods that might be cheaper purchased in bulk?

- Why might an operation choose to pay a higher price to a supplier in exchange for the ability to receive deliveries at a convenient time?

- In your area, which goods do you think might have a high or low place value? Why?

Reinforce and Review

- Purchase orders are generally less detailed than product specifications, which suppliers should already have on file.

- In larger restaurant and foodservice operations, upper management must approve certain purchases before the buyer can make them; typically, a requisition form is used in these circumstances.

- Purchasers must understand the various factors that cause an item's price to fluctuate.

- The channels of distribution, time, form, place, transportation, and service all affect a product's value and therefore its price.

Vocabulary Terms

- **Requisition form:** In larger operations, a document describing a good or service that would constitute a major and atypical expense that must be approved by upper management before the buyer can purchase it.

- **Time value:** The price retailers pay for the convenience of selecting the time when suppliers will deliver goods.

- **Form value:** The price savings created when a buyer purchases an item in bulk instead of portions.

- **Place value:** The differences in a product's price, depending on where it must be shipped.

- Brief description of each item
- Size of each item
- Unit price for each item
- Total price for all items
- Total price for entire order (including sales tax, shipping, and any other special charges)
- Any special information regarding the item or delivery

Keeping track of all this information helps the buyer control products and services. Purchase orders are generally less detailed than specs, but remember: purchase orders are legal contracts between buyers and suppliers.

Occasionally, an operation will need to purchase expensive new equipment. In large restaurant and foodservice organizations, upper management must approve the purchase before the buyer can order the item. For instance, if the chef believes that a deep-fat fryer should be replaced, the chef must first fill out a **requisition** (WREK-kwi-ZI-shun) **form** that lists the item or service needed and send it to company headquarters. Once headquarters approves the purchase and notifies the buyer, then the buyer can place the order.

Knowing Food Prices

Part of the homework a buyer must do is understanding and keeping track of the factors that affect food prices. There are many economic factors that influence the price of an item. As a product moves through the channels of distribution, such factors as time, form, place, transportation, and service can all affect its value:

- **Time value:** The price retailers pay for the convenience of selecting the time of delivery from suppliers.

- **Form value:** The price savings created when a buyer purchases bulk quantities of food instead of individually portioned servings. For example, blocks of butter cost less than individual pats because less packaging and processing goes into making the block of butter.

- **Place value:** The price differences of a product depend on where it needs to be shipped. Delivering fresh fish from New England to a market in Kansas City is more expensive than having that same fish delivered to a market in New York.

318

- **Transportation value:** The cost of choosing a quick but expensive form of transport to get goods delivered. Shipping seafood by air is much more expensive than by truck, but the increased price may be worth the added freshness of the product.

- **Service value:** Additional convenience services that a vendor provides to its customers. This could include customer services that make ordering easier, such as a 24-hour, toll-free number, or it might include things that stream-line kitchen prep like pre-coring lettuce or providing special cuts of meat. These services often result in higher prices for an item, but these higher prices are often offset by reduced food-preparation costs.

Less obvious factors can affect food prices as well. Political efforts both in this country and abroad often affect price. Federal laws permitting or banning certain imported products will directly affect prices. Weather can also be a factor. A bad coffee crop in Brazil will decrease the supply of coffee beans. While the supply decreases, the number of buyers who want these goods remains the same. As a result, the price of coffee goes up. This imbalance is an example of an economic reality known as supply and demand, as illustrated in Figure 5.14.

D: demand for coffee beans, which remains static over the period observed

S: original supply of coffee beans

S₁: reduced supply of coffee beans, cue to poor weather in Brazil

S₂: enlarged supply of coffee beans, due to excellent weather in Brazil

E: original equilibrium point between demand for & supply of coffee beans

E₁: new equilibrium point between demand for & supply of coffee beans; note that the price has increased and the quantity sold has decreased

E₂: new equilibrium point between demand for and large supply of coffee beans; note that the price has decreased and the quantity sold has increased

Figure 5.14: Example showing supply and demand.

319

Discuss

- When might it be a good idea to pay a higher price for faster transportation? Why?

- Is it always a good idea to pay higher prices in exchange for more and better service? Why or why not?

- Why might federal laws in various countries ban or restrict the import of certain goods?

Reinforce and Review

- Faster transportation and increased convenience are often available in exchange for a premium.

- Other factors that can affect food prices include political activities and weather.

Teaching Tips

- Work with students to help them understand the basic principles of supply and demand.

Homework Activity: Food Politics

Literacy Connection, 21st-Century Skills— Make Judgments and Decisions, Communicate Clearly, Information Literacy, Work Independently

Identify a food item that cannot be imported into the United States due to a federal ban. Explain the history and rationale for the policy. Do you think the ban is justified? Why or why not?

Discuss your findings in a one-page report, defending your opinion.

Vocabulary Terms

- **Transportation value:** The cost of choosing a quick but expensive form of transportation.

- **Service value:** Additional convenience services that a supplier provides to its customers.

Figure Focus

Figure 5.14: When supplies of coffee beans increase, their price typically decreases, and more are sold. When supplies decrease, their price typically increases, so fewer are sold.

Discuss

- What are some examples of how supply and demand can affect an item's price?

Reinforce and Review

- When supply falls, prices typically increase and fewer items are sold; when supply increases, prices typically decrease and more items are sold.

- When demand falls, prices typically decrease and fewer items are sold; when demand increases, prices typically increase and more items are sold.

Teaching Tips

- Suggest goods and conditions, such as "frozen treats in summer" or "pumpkins in October," and ask students to identify whether either supply or demand for the item would rise or fall under those conditions.

What's New: Ordering Software Systems

Encourage students to discuss the following:

- Why do many establishments choose to pay increased prices for the "service value" their suppliers provide?

- How can the availability of ordering software make a purchaser's work more efficient? What other benefits does it offer?

- Explain how using a single buyer to make purchases for all a company's outlets can serve as a competitive advantage.

Essential Skills: Conducting a Make-or-Buy Analysis

Encourage students to discuss the following:

- Why is it important for chefs and buyers to understand labor costs when determining whether to make or buy an item?

- In what ways could a chef's aspirations or goals affect the make-or-buy analysis?

- What tools might a chef use when conducting a make-or-buy analysis?

Supply and demand can also drive prices down. Strawberries sold in June are less expensive than those sold in January because June is the time of year when most farmers' crops are ready for picking. In January, only warm climates like California or Florida are able to grow the crop, and the price of the fruit goes up.

[what's new]

Ordering Software Systems

Advances in computer technologies have made it easier than ever for restaurant and foodservice operations to order goods and services from their vendors. Some of these options are provided by the vendors themselves.

Several major suppliers offer secure Web sites where buyers can place orders, track the delivery truck, monitor their purchase and payment histories, and control inventories. Alternately, ordering software can be installed on a chef's or manager's own computer that can communicate directly with a supplier. In addition to offering many of the same benefits as supplier Web sites, ordering software can be used to build recipe databases, cost menu items, and calculate nutritional data. Some of these software packages are available directly from restaurant and foodservice suppliers, while others can be purchased from software companies.

Larger organizations may have multiple service points. Ordering software can enable one person to order all the inventory that is needed without having to place separate orders for each outlet. One person can then possibly handle all the administrative tasks involved with routing invoices and payments. Ordering all at once may also enable the buyer to take advantage of bulk discounts.

Essential Skills
Conducting a Make-or-Buy Analysis

Chefs conduct make-or-buy analyses when they need to decide whether it makes better financial sense to purchase a ready-made product or to make the item from scratch. The chef will need to consider the following questions in the decision-making process:

- Is the quality of the ready-made item equal to or superior than the item my staff can make?

- What is the true cost of buying the raw materials and making the item here, bearing in mind the cost of labor and the time taken away from other tasks?

- Do I have enough storage space for the ready-made item or for the ingredients to make it?

320

- How frequently would the item have to be either purchased or made, given the level of business in the restaurant?
- Are my employees skilled enough to make this product consistently each time?

The answers to these questions will vary, depending on the item needed or the situation. For instance, a chef may feel comfortable making a quart of mayonnaise every day or so to meet a restaurant's needs, but he or she might choose to order a five-gallon bucket of mayonnaise to cater a large picnic. Be aware, and be flexible!

Summary

In this section, you learned the following:

- Quality standards refers to the value or worth that customers place on a product or service. Establishing solid quality standard specifications helps an operation to create consistency. Successful operations select the best products early on by determining the quality standards for every product purchased and used at the operation. Putting together quality standards is a complex process. Managers and buyers usually work together to create them, along with input from vendors and other employees. The following are some of the factors to consider when establishing quality standards: item's intended use, operation's concept and goals, the menu, employee skill level, budgetary constraints, customers' wants and needs, seasonal availability, and storage capacity.

- Product specifications describe the requirements for a particular product or service that an operation wants to buy. They include the details that help a product or service to meet the operation's quality standards. Buyers should always document product specifications. Smaller operations may use informal specifications that include only a few details. But specifications in larger companies are usually formal and precise. It's also important to remember to purchase products from approved, reputable suppliers.

- Buyers conduct a make-or-buy analysis to decide if an operation should make an item from scratch or buy a ready-made version. This analysis helps to balance how much food a kitchen produces with the quality standards of the operation. There are advantages to buying a ready-made product, such as consistency, reduced prep time and labor costs, and reduced needs for certain types of equipment and storage space. But ready-made products cost more money than items that must be prepared, and such items may

---

Essential Skills:
Conducting a Make-or-Buy Analysis (cont.)

Encourage students to discuss the following:

- How might the make-or-buy analysis yield different results, depending on which employee is making the product?

- Why does the frequency at which the item would need to be purchased or made play a role in the make-or-buy analysis?

- Is it better to purchase a ready-made product or to train employees to make the product more efficiently? Why?

Homework Activity:
Make vs. Buy

Literacy Connection, 21st-Century Skills—Use Systems Thinking, Communicate Clearly, Information Literacy, Create Media Products, Work Independently

Consider the process of conducting a make-or-buy analysis. What are the critical steps in this process?

Develop a flow chart of the make-or-buy process, demonstrating the steps you have identified.

Summary

- Remind students to review the following:
  1. Determining quality standards
  2. Writing product specifications
  3. Ordering and ordering forms
  4. The factors that impact food prices

also have other drawbacks. Ultimately, the decision to make or buy must be based on which option provides the most benefits to the operation.

■ Buyers use production sheets, daily food cost sheets, and sales mix records to help with purchasing decisions. A production sheet lists all menu items that chefs will prepare on a given day. At the end of the day, the chef adjusts the information to reflect actual production and gives the sheets to the buyer. Compiled over a period of time, production sheets become a very important forecasting tool. Daily food cost sheets are ongoing records of daily and monthly food costs for an operation. Daily food cost is determined by adding all the requisitions from the storeroom and the daily purchases. This number, divided by the daily sales figure, is the daily food cost percentage. Sales mix records track each item sold from the menu on a daily, weekly, or monthly basis. This record shows which items sell well, called leaders, or ones that don't sell well, called losers. By recognizing leaders and losers, buyers can order more effectively.

■ There are many economic factors that influence the price of an item. As a product moves through the channels of distribution, such factors as time, form, place, transportation, and service affect the value of an item.

Section 5.2 Review Questions

1. What is the relationship between quality standards and product specifications?

2. What is one advantage and one disadvantage to buying a ready-made product?

3. List the three tools used in helping to make purchasing decisions, and then explain how one of them works.

4. List three factors that influence food pricing.

5. Al Gaylor notes that "one key to developing a successful purchasing strategy is establishing a positive relationship with a limited number of distributor/supplier partners." Why is this important?

6. Miguel and Chef Kate prided themselves on knowing food prices—at least, they used to know food prices. They realized in looking at their supplier invoices that they're spending far more than they used to. Look at the five factors that affect food pricing and suggest ways to cut costs on fish, meat, and produce, all ingredients that Kabob uses in its menu.

7. How can product specifications affect a restaurant's costs?

8. Look back at the five factors that can affect food prices. Write a one-page plan explaining how you would get the best price for your produce, detailing how you would account for each of the five factors.

323

Section 5.2 Review Questions

1. Product specifications are based on quality standards.

2. Advantages to purchasing ready-made food include consistency, reducing prep time and labor costs, and reducing or eliminating certain pieces of equipment or storage space. Disadvantages include increased food cost, less nutritional or tasty food, and limits on specializing in particular dishes.

3. Three tools used in making purchasing decisions are production sheets, daily food cost sheets, and sales mix records. Production sheets provide predicted and actual sales information for each service period and can help identify stockouts and overproduction. Daily food cost sheets record actual food costs, allowing for comparisons and helping to eliminate waste or theft. Sales mix records help determine and track the popularity of each menu item.

4. Factors that influence food pricing include time, form, place, transportation, service, political issues, and weather.

5. Students should explain how this statement affects purchasing and supplier relations.

6. Students should use the factors that influence food prices to determine logical methods by which Kabob can cut its food costs.

7. Student responses should focus on the quality that the particular operation demands.

8. Student responses may vary but should clearly and logically address how they would obtain ideal prices when purchasing produce, using the five primary factors affecting food prices (omitting political issues and weather).

Section 5.2 Activities

1. Students should research meat substitutes, such as gluten or seitan products, and how they are commonly used in recipes. They should develop appropriate product specifications for each ingredient in the recipe they select.

2. Students do not actually need to make each item on their menu to conduct the make-or-buy analysis. They should use their best judgment of their employees' skills and their customer base to determine which ingredients to make and which to purchase.

3. Students should refer to the list of items to include in a purchase order, as shown on pp. 317–318.

Section 5.2 Activities

1. Study Skills/Group Activity: Product Specifications for a Vegetarian Menu Item

Working in small groups, imagine you're the buyers for a vegetarian restaurant. Do some research on the various ways to make and season a popular vegetarian meat substitute. Then, pick a recipe and write product specifications for your recipe. Make sure to account for every ingredient in the dish. Use Table 5.3, the list of possible specifications criteria, on p. 312 to assist you. Compare and contrast your specifications with those of other groups.

2. Independent Activity: Make-or-Buy Analysis for a Lunch Menu

You run a hot dog and burger joint. Make up a lunch menu of five items, making sure to list every ingredient you will use, including the condiments. Then look at your menu and do a make-or-buy purchasing analysis. Divide your ingredients into those that you will make yourself and those that you will buy ready made. Share your menu and your analysis with the class.

3. Critical Thinking: Purchase Order for a Cobb Salad

You own a 200-seat fine-dining restaurant that is renowned for its cobb salads. Write a purchase order for spring mix lettuce.

324

5.1 Introduction to Purchasing	5.2 Making Purchasing Decisions	5.3 Managing Purchases
• Purchasing overview	• Determining quality standards	• Receiving orders
• Channels of distribution flow	• Writing product specifications	• Storing orders
• Goods and services: what's being purchased	• Ordering	• Taking inventory
• Buyers: who's doing the purchasing	• Ordering forms	
	• Knowing food prices	

SECTION 5.3 MANAGING PURCHASES

Did you ever make a purchase at a drive-thru window, drive away without checking the order, and then find out later that it's all wrong? Perhaps you were missing an order of French fries, or a few tacos were left out, or a container of soup was improperly packed and leaking all over the inside of the bag. It's a frustrating experience and one that ultimately cost you money. You're easily out five bucks or maybe even more.

Now, think about the amount of money that a restaurant or foodservice operation could lose by being shorted 20 pounds of poultry, or if it orders pork tenderloin but finds out right before dinner service that it received pork shoulder instead. Or, think about buying an entire crate of steaks and then storing them incorrectly so that they all spoil before ever being used. The money adds up fast, as does the damage to a restaurant or foodservice operation that doesn't properly manage its purchases. Making smart purchases is very important, but it won't matter at all if foodhandlers do not take care to properly receive, store, and inventory the products. This section discusses all three of those aspects in detail.

Study Questions

After studying Section 5.3, you should be able to answer the following questions:

- What are the best guidelines for receiving purchases?

- What are perishable versus nonperishable items?

- What are proper storage guidelines?

- What are the two basic methods of taking inventory, and why is taking inventory important?

325

Section 5.3
Managing Purchases

Introduce the Section

a. Review the correct processes for receiving and storing goods.

b. Describe common methods for taking inventory.

c. Discuss the objectives for the section.

Vocabulary Review

a. Direct students to the key terms.

b. Pronounce each word, and have the students repeat the pronunciation out loud.

c. Discuss the definition of each word.

Teach

Discuss

- Encourage students to share examples of incidents involving poor receiving or storage practices.

Reinforce and Review

- Making smart purchases is critical, but proper receiving, storage, and inventory practices are equally important.

- Failing to manage purchases appropriately can cause a restaurant or foodservice operation to close.

Teaching Tips

- Relate the material covered in this section to the content of Chapter 3.

Discuss

- What staff members should be trained to receive deliveries? Why?

- Why is it important to check the delivered goods against both the invoice and the original purchase order?

Reinforce and Review

- The first step in establishing good receiving procedures is to make sure that only employees who have been trained in proper receiving do the job.

- Any savings generated by careful purchasing can be erased if an operation's receiving and storage practices are sloppy or inconsistent.

- Successful operations establish receiving procedures and strictly follow them before accepting any product.

- Written invoices should accompany all deliveries.

- When receiving items, staff members should use the original purchase order, the supplier's invoice, and the product specifications to ensure that only the correct items are received.

Vocabulary Terms

- **Receiving:** Inspecting, accepting, and sometimes rejecting deliveries of goods and services.

- **Invoice:** The supplier's bill listing the exact goods delivered by the supplier.

Receiving Orders

Receiving means inspecting, accepting, and, in some cases, rejecting deliveries of goods and services. The first, and perhaps most important, step in setting up good receiving procedures is to make sure that only employees who have been trained in proper receiving techniques do the job. With nearly 40 percent of annual revenue spent on food and supplies, a restaurant or foodservice operation cannot afford to allow products to go to waste, disappear, or be delivered in substandard form. Any savings generated by the most careful purchasing can quickly be erased if an operation's receiving and storage procedures are sloppy or inconsistent. Successful operations establish receiving procedures and strictly follow them before accepting any product. If all trained employees are busy when a delivery shows up, have the delivery person wait.

A written **invoice** should accompany every delivery. The invoice is the supplier's bill listing the actual goods delivered by the supplier. The person responsible for receiving at the operation—the receiver—should always check the invoice against the operation's original purchase order to make sure that the quantity and cost of the goods has not changed. The receiver should also have a copy of the original specs to confirm that the delivery meets the operation's quality standards. Any discrepancies on the invoice should be noted and signed by both the receiver and the delivery person.

A restaurant or foodservice operation should have a clean, well-maintained receiving area, like the one shown in Figure 5.15. Here are some additional guidelines for efficient receiving procedures:

Figure 5.15: A clean, well-maintained receiving area.

Figure Focus

Figure 5.15: Staff members responsible for receiving goods must check the contents of each package to be sure that the proper items have arrived in the desired condition.

- Plan ahead for shipments. Have clean hand trucks, carts, dollies, and containers available in the receiving area. Make sure enough space is available in walk-ins and storerooms before receiving times. If products need to be washed or broken down and rewrapped, make work space available as close to the receiving area as possible.

- Inspect and store each delivery before receiving another one. This will prevent time-temperature abuse in the receiving area.

- Inspect deliveries immediately. Visually inspect items to count quantities, check for damaged products, and look for items that might have been repacked or mishandled. Spot-check weights of items such as meats and take sample temperatures of all refrigerated food. Check product expiration dates. Always check the lower layers in a package to make sure they are of the same quality as the top layers.

- Record items on a receiving sheet. This helps to keep inventories accurate. See Figure 5.16 for a sample receiving sheet.

- Correct mistakes immediately. If any products are damaged, at the wrong temperature, or of the wrong quality, do not accept them.

- Put products away as quickly as possible. This is especially important for cold or frozen TCS food.

- Maintain the receiving area. Keep the area clean and well lighted to discourage pests.

Date	Time Delivered	Quantity	Invoice #	Supplier
3/3/10	7:10 a.m.	3.00	2864	ABC
3/4/10	8.30 a.m.	2.00	K314	Eastern
3/5/10	7:45 a.m.	4.00	9881	Smith

Figure 5.16: Sample receiving sheet.

Receivers have the right to refuse any delivery that doesn't meet the operation's standards. All receiving employees should know and follow the company's policy on returns. Figure 5.17 on the following page illustrates the kinds of items that should be refused.

Follow a basic procedure to reject a product or shipment:

- Set the rejected item aside. Keep it separate from other food and supplies.

- Tell the delivery person exactly what is wrong with the rejected item. Use the purchase agreement with the supplier and company standards to back up a decision to reject the product.

327

Discuss

- Is it a good idea to provide a receiving area away from kitchen workspace, to limit dirt, infestation, and other concerns, or would that prevent the timely storing of food?

- Under what circumstances should deliveries be refused due to food safety issues?

Reinforce and Review

- Guidelines for good receiving include planning ahead, inspecting and storing each delivery before receiving the next, inspecting deliveries immediately, recording deliveries on receiving sheets, correcting all mistakes immediately, storing products as quickly as possible, and maintaining the receiving area.

- All deliveries must be checked thoroughly to ensure that the appropriate food arrives in the appropriate condition.

- Products that are damaged, at the wrong temperature, or of the wrong quality should be rejected immediately.

- Receivers have the right to refuse any deliveries that do not meet the operation's quality standards.

- To reject an item, set it aside, tell the delivery person exactly why the item is being refused, get a signed adjustment or credit memo from the delivery person, and log the incident on the supplier's invoice.

Teaching Tips

- Relate this to the material in Level 1, Chapter 2.

Figure Focus

Figure 5.16: Receiving sheets provide a record of deliveries and when they arrive.

Discuss

- What are terms of service? How do they help protect both purchasers and suppliers?

Reinforce and Review

- The purchaser must identify the terms of service with the supplier before placing an initial order.

- The buyer must keep track of the supplier's behavior to ensure that the operation is receiving the appropriate level of service.

- Buyers should always insist on good service from suppliers and should speak up when problems arise.

Fast Fact:
Did You Know . . . ?

Encourage students to discuss the following:

- How can proper receiving and storage practices help prevent the spread of foodborne illness?

- What role can purchasing play in preventing the spread of foodborne illness?

- What effects can foodborne illnesses have on restaurant and foodservice operations implicated in an outbreak?

Vocabulary Terms

- **Credit memo:** A written record that ensures that the vendor will credit the operation for the rejected item.

- Get a signed adjustment or credit memo from the delivery person. A **credit memo** is a written record that ensures the vendor will credit the operation for the rejected item. After receiving the memo, allow the delivery person to remove the rejected item or throw it away.

- Log the incident on the invoice. Note the item involved, the standard that wasn't met, and the action that was taken.

Figure 5.17: From left to right, you should reject the moldy strawberries and accept the clean, colorful ones. You should also accept the clean, sealed bag of flour and reject the water-stained bag.

Remember, the buyer must identify the terms of service with a supplier *before* placing an order. Establish delivery schedules, product consistency, and specifications for substitutions in a contract. It's then up to the buyer to keep track of how the vendor is doing to make sure that the operation is getting what it asked for. Talk with the receiving employees regularly. They're the best source of information for how a vendor is doing—if trucks are on time, delivery temperatures are safe, etc. Stay in contact with the vendor, and be sure to report any issues with shipments.

Finally, insist on good service from suppliers. If they cannot deliver to the operation's standards, there is almost always another supplier who can.

[fast fact]

Did You Know...?
According to the CDC, there are approximately 325,000 hospitalizations and 5,000 deaths from foodborne-related diseases every year in the United States.

328

Figure Focus

Figure 5.17: What are some health hazards associated with moldy strawberries and water-damaged flour?

Receiving: Rules and Guidelines

Reject frozen food for these reasons, because any one of these may be signs of thawing and refreezing:

- Fluids or frozen liquids in case bottoms
- Ice crystals on the product or the packaging
- Water stains on the packaging

Follow these steps to check the temperature of packaged food:

1. Open the package and insert the thermometer stem or probe into the food.
2. Immerse the sensing area fully into the food.
3. Do not let the stem or probe touch the packaging.

Reject any food or nonfood items with the following packaging problems:

- Tears, holes, or punctures
- Cans with swollen ends, rust, or dents
- Broken cartons or seals
- Dirty wrappers

Storing Orders

After a receiver accepts a delivery, he or she must then move the goods to either the kitchen production area or the storage facility. When items go into storage, foodhandlers must follow proper storage procedures. Proper storage management requires good planning. Health requirements for storing food items are very exact, and cleanliness is essential at all times.

The most basic aspect of storage starts with an understanding of what needs to go where. More specifically, foodhandlers must know what needs to be refrigerated, what needs to be frozen, and what can go into dry storage. There are two major categories here: perishable versus nonperishable products.

Perishable products are food products sold or distributed in a form that will spoil or decay within a limited period of time. They can be damaged by bacteria, light, or air. Perishable products include meat, fish, poultry, dairy, eggs, produce, and alcoholic beverages. Operations purchase these items more often than nonperishable items. Buyers should purchase perishable items in a **JIT ("just in time") format** whenever possible. This means that buyers should take great care to determine the amount needed prior to the next delivery, with the goal that the chefs will have used up the majority of the previous order by the time the new delivery arrives. The difficulty is solidly predicting the point at

329

ServSafe Connection: Receiving: Rules and Guidelines

Encourage students to discuss the following:

- Why should frozen items be rejected if they demonstrate signs of having thawed and refrozen?
- Why is it important to check the temperature of packaged food?
- Why should nonfood items with dirty wrappers be rejected?

Discuss

- What are some storage limitations in the classroom kitchen? How might they affect purchasing decisions?
- What common techniques for preventing time-temperature abuse or cross-contamination are appropriate in the classroom kitchen?
- What tools can help purchasers use the JIT format most effectively?

Reinforce and Review

- Proper storage management requires good planning and begins with an understanding of what needs to go where.
- Health requirements for storing food items are very exact, and cleanliness is essential at all times.
- Perishable items can readily be damaged by bacteria, light, or air, and they are time-sensitive. As a result, they are typically purchased more frequently than nonperishable items.
- Ordering goods with a JIT goal requires the buyer to predict as accurately as possible the point at which a new delivery of each good will be required.

Teaching Tips

- Make sure students understand the possible hazards of the JIT format as well as its benefits.

Vocabulary Terms

- **Perishable products:** Food products sold or distributed in a form that will spoil or decay within a limited period of time.
- **"Just in time" (JIT) format:** Products should be ordered so that their delivery will coincide with the point at which most of the previous delivery will have been used.

Discuss

- Why are nonperishable items generally purchased in bulk?

Reinforce and Review

- To use the JIT format, buyers must keep very good records and make accurate predictions, so that operations almost run out of food instead of actually running out of food.

- Buyers generally purchase nonperishable items in large quantities and with less frequency than they do perishable foods.

- Most operations have refrigerated storage, frozen storage, and dry storage on site.

- Refrigerated storage space should always maintain appropriate temperatures and should be checked regularly.

- All refrigerated devices must be maintained regularly; Ensuring proper air flow is critical to efficiency.

- All refrigerated foods should be properly wrapped or covered to prevent cross-contamination.

Teaching Tips

- Review with students the proper procedure for calibrating a thermometer.

Vocabulary Terms

- **Nonperishable products:** Items that do not readily support the growth of bacteria, generally due to their packaging or processing.

- **Refrigerated storage:** Storage areas for perishable food items, kept at 41°F or below.

- **Frozen storage:** Storage areas for frozen items.

- **Dry storage:** Storage areas for nonperishable items, such as dry and canned foods.

---

which the operation will *almost run out* without actually *running out*. Buyers must keep very good records and practice careful forecasting of food use.

Nonperishable products are items that, generally due to packaging or processing, do not readily support the growth of bacteria. They include processed and canned or bottled products and dried goods. Buyers generally purchase nonperishable food in large quantities and less often than perishable food. The price of nonperishable items fluctuates with the market (because of availability and demand) but less often than the perishable items. Restaurants often purchase many of these items weekly, biweekly, or monthly to streamline the buyer's activities.

Most operations have three types of storage areas in their facilities:

- **Refrigerated storage:** These areas typically hold TCS food at 41°F or lower.
- **Frozen storage:** These areas hold frozen food at temperatures that will keep it frozen.
- **Dry storage:** These areas hold dry and canned food.

Refrigerated Storage

Foodhandlers should remember several things when storing items in refrigerated storage:

- Set refrigerators to the correct temperature. The setting must keep the internal temperature of the food at 41°F or lower. Check the temperature of the unit at least once during a shift. See Table 5.5 for proper food storage temperatures and humidity levels.
- Monitor food temperature regularly. Take temperatures of coolers regularly, in different parts of the cooler
- Schedule regular maintenance of coolers.
- Don't overload coolers. Storing too many products prevents good airflow and makes units work harder to stay cold.
- Use open shelving. Lining shelves with aluminum foil, sheet pans, or paper restricts circulation of cold air in the unit.
- Keep cooler doors closed as much as possible. Frequent opening lets warm air inside, which can affect food safety and make the unit work harder.
- Wrap or cover all food properly. Leaving food uncovered can lead to cross-contamination.

330

Table 5.5: Food Storage Temperatures and Humidity Levels

Item	Temperature	Humidity Level
Meat and poultry	41°F or lower	75% to 85%
Fish	41°F or lower	75% to 85%
Live shellfish	45°F	75% to 85%
Eggs in shell	45°F or lower	75% to 85%
Dairy products	41°F or lower	75% to 85%
Most fruits and vegetables	41°F or lower	85% to 95%

Frozen Storage

Foodhandlers should remember several things when storing items in frozen storage:

- Set freezers to the correct temperature. The setting must keep all products frozen.

- Check freezer temperatures regularly.

- Place frozen food deliveries in freezers as soon as they have been inspected. Never leave these items at room temperature.

- Ensure good airflow inside freezers. Use open shelving, avoid overloading, and keep the door closed as much as possible.

- Defrost freezers on a regular basis if necessary. They will operate more efficiently when free of frost. Move food to another freezer during defrosting.

- Clearly label food prepared on-site that is intended for frozen storage.

331

Table 5.5: Food Storage Temperatures and Humidity Levels

- Why do most fruit and vegetables require a higher humidity level than most animal proteins?

- How can live, unshucked shellfish and shell eggs tolerate warmer temperatures than the other items in this table?

- Why should live shellfish not be stored below an air temperature of 45°F? What is the best way to maintain their quality?

Discuss

- Why might some foods deteriorate in the freezer, especially if stored over a long period of time?

- What are the only safe ways to thaw frozen foods?

Reinforce and Review

- Freezer temperatures should be checked regularly to maintain consistently frozen products.

- If necessary, freezers should be defrosted regularly to maintain efficiency.

- Carefully label all foods prepared in-house before freezing.

Homework Activity: Home Storage

Science Connection, Literacy Connection, 21st-Century Skills—Use Systems Thinking, Communicate Clearly, Information Literacy, Work Independently

Evaluate your household refrigerator, based on the guidelines for professionally maintained refrigerated storage. For instance, at what temperature is it kept? Are the shelves overloaded, or can cool air circulate freely? Are open shelves used? How might these conditions affect the quality of the food stored there?

Discuss your answers in a brief report.

Discuss

- What are some other steps that restaurant and foodservice operators can take to prevent pest infestation?

- Why is it important to maintain proper air circulation in all storage areas?

Reinforce and Review

- Dry-storage areas should be kept clean and dry, with the temperature maintained between 50°F and 70°F and proper ventilation.

- Food should be stored in containers that are clean, durable, leakproof, sealable, and airtight.

- All storage areas should be cleaned daily.

- Proper steps should be taken to prevent infestation by pests and vermin, with professional pest control scheduled regularly.

- Different areas of a cooler have different levels of humidity.

Teaching Tips

- Review the material covered in Level 1, Chapter 2 on proper food storage.

Homework Activity: Pest Prevention

Science Connection, Literacy Connection, 21st-Century Skills—Reason Effectively, Communicate Clearly, Information Literacy, Work Independently

Identify one pest that is associated with the restaurant and foodservice industry. Describe its habits, its habitats, and why it poses a threat to food safety.

Discuss your findings in a one-page report.

Vocabulary Terms

- **Staples:** Items for which demand is constant.

- **Vermin:** Small, disease-carrying animals that are difficult to control.

- **Humidity:** The amount of water moisture in the air or in a contained space, such as within a refrigerator.

Dry Storage

Foodhandlers should remember several things when storing items in dry storage:

- Keep storerooms clean and dry. For the best quality and to assure safety, the temperature of the storeroom should be between 50°F and 70°F.

- Make sure storerooms are well ventilated. This will help to keep the temperature and humidity (the amount of water moisture in the air) constant throughout the area.

- Store dry food away from walls and at least six inches off of the floor.

- Keep food out of direct sunlight.

Here are some important general points to remember when storing goods:

- Store food in containers intended for food. The containers should be durable, leakproof, and able to be sealed or covered. Never use empty food containers to store chemicals. Never put food in empty chemical containers.

- Create proper air circulation around goods by keeping shelves about six inches from the floor, ceiling, and walls.

- Keep food stored far away from soaps, pesticides, chemicals, etc.

- Try to purchase **staples** (items for which the demand is constant) in airtight containers.

- Transfer items purchased in unsealed containers into airtight containers to protect them against insects and **vermin** (small disease-carrying animals, such as lice, fleas, or mice that are difficult to control).

- Use strong shelving for all nonperishables.

- Clean and sweep storage areas daily to eliminate spoiled food and to discourage insects and vermin.

- Have a professional pest control operator come in and spray regularly.

- Store perishable food, such as meat and produce, at its proper temperature and humidity level. **Humidity** refers to the amount of water moisture in the air or in a contained space such as a refrigerator. Different areas of a cooler have different levels of humidity. Areas close to the cooler's blower have higher humidity levels, while areas away from it have lower humidity levels.

332

[ServSafe Connection]

Preventing Spoilage and Cross-Contamination

Preventing spoilage and cross-contamination are the two primary goals of proper storage. All food should be wrapped or covered. If possible, ready-to-eat foods should be stored separately from raw meats, seafood, and poultry. If such items must share the same refrigerated space, ready-to-eat items should be shelved separately and above raw meat, seafood, and poultry. Figure 5.18 shows food organized properly in a refrigerator. The items sharing refrigerated space should be stored in the following order from top to bottom:

Top shelf: Ready-to-eat foods

Then: Seafood

Then: Whole cuts of beef and pork

Then: Ground meat and ground fish

Bottom: Whole and ground poultry

Figure 5.18: Food organized properly in a refrigerator.

Taking Inventory

An **inventory** is a record of all products an operation has in storage and in the kitchen. Ideally, a restaurant or foodservice operation will have only the amounts of food and nonfood items it needs to meet customer demand. Having too little inventory means customers don't get what they want. Having too much inventory means food spoils and storage costs go up.

There are two common methods for purchasing nonperishable food:

- Physical inventory method
- Perpetual inventory method

333

Figure Focus

Figure 5.18: Proper storage of perishable items is essential to controlling costs.

Discuss

- What are some ways a restaurant or foodservice operation can keep from having excessive inventory?

- How can having too little inventory increase an operation's costs?

Reinforce and Review

- Ideally, a restaurant or foodservice operation will have on hand only those goods it needs to meet guest demands.

- Having too little inventory means guests might not receive the items they would like to have.

- Having too much inventory means that food could spoil before use and storage costs will increase.

- The two common methods for purchasing nonperishable food are the physical inventory method and the perpetual inventory method.

Teaching Tips

- Remind students of the earlier discussion of par stock and reorder points.

Vocabulary Terms

- **Inventory:** A record of all products an operation has in storage and in the kitchen.

Discuss

- How does the FIFO system of stock rotation help to control an operation's costs?

- Should all restaurant and foodservice operations follow formal issuing procedures? Why or why not?

Reinforce and Review

- A physical inventory is an actual count of all items in stock, whereas a perpetual inventory is an estimate of stock on hand.

- Formal issuing procedures record all items when they are removed from the dry-storage area for use in the kitchen.

- Formal issuing procedures both keep accurate inventory records and reduce pilfering.

- Pilfering is both a serious problem and a serious offense; it typically results in termination of employment and could end in conviction for theft.

Teaching Tips

- Reiterate the gravity of pilfering. Relate it to the earlier discussion of integrity.

Homework Activity: Requisition Forms

Literacy Connection, 21st-Century Skills— Critical Thinking and Problem Solving, Communicate Clearly, Create Media Products, Work Independently

Create your own version of a product requisition form, including all information that you think a restaurant or foodservice operation might typically include.

Vocabulary Terms

- **Physical inventory method:** The entire stock is physically reviewed on a regular basis.

- **Perpetual inventory method:** Employees record items when they are received and when they are used.

- **Issuing:** The official procedures employees use when taking an item out of the dry-storage area and putting it into production.

- **Pilfering:** Stealing; the illegal removal of inventory items for personal use.

In the **physical inventory method**, the entire stock is physically reviewed on a regular basis. From this review, the operation determines the reorder point for each inventory item. In the **perpetual inventory method**, employees record items when they are received and then when they are used up. This information is kept on receiving and issuing sheets or logs, or electronically on a combined form. Figure 5.19 shows a screen shot of an electronic form.

November 10	Cost/cs	Units/cs	Cost/unit	Selling $	COS	Beginning	Purchased	Ending	Sales	Variance	Variance $	Value
Canned Tomatoes												
Whole	$37.00	12	$1.12	$6.00	18.67%	1.00	0.00	1.00	0.00	0.00	$ -	$1.12
Paste	$21.00	12	$1.12	$5.00	22.40%	32.00	72.00	47.00	57.00	0.00	$ -	$52.64
Chopped	$23.00	12	$1.92	$7.00	27.36%	9.00	48.00	28.00	29.00	0.00	$ -	$53.67
Chopped with basil	$26.00	12	$1.39	$5.00	27.80%	22.00	24.00	27.00	19.00	0.00	$ -	$37.53
Crushed	$44.00	12	$3.67	$6.00	61.11%	15.00	0.00	0.00	16.00	-1.00	$ (3.67)	$0.00
Sun-dried	$45.00	12	$1.25	$6.00	20.83%	17.00	48.00	35.00	30.00	0.00	$ -	$43.75

Figure 5.19: Sample combined form used in the perpetual inventory method.

A very important difference between physical inventory and perpetual inventory is that a physical inventory is an *actual* count of all items in stock while a perpetual inventory is not. Therefore, managers use physical inventory to calculate reliable financial data such as actual costs and inventory value. In contrast, the perpetual inventory is an *estimate* of stock on hand, based on data entry. Managers should not use perpetual inventory to calculate actual costs or inventory value. There are computer programs available for managing purchasing and inventory control. There are also programs that integrate the information from inventory and point-of-sale to provide a constantly updated perpetual inventory.

All items in the storeroom need to be accounted for when foodhandlers take them from the storeroom and use them in the restaurant. **Issuing** refers to the official procedures employees use when taking an item out of the storeroom and putting it into production. In a standard issuing situation, kitchen employees fill out product requisition forms indicating exactly what items they need, and then give the forms to the manager or whoever is in charge of inventory. Employees should observe the first in, first out (FIFO) system of stock rotation, both when the items first go into stock and when they are issued. In the FIFO system, foodhandlers place the oldest stock in front of or on top of the newer stock. FIFO makes sure that chefs use older items before newer items.

Many large restaurants and foodservice operations use a formal issuing procedure both as a way to keep accurate inventory records and to prevent pilfering. **Pilfering** is stealing (see Figure 5.20 on the following page). It is when employees illegally take inventory items for their personal use. In the restaurant and foodservice industry, pilfering is both a serious problem and a serious offense. Employees caught pilfering are usually fired. In more extreme cases, employees have been arrested and convicted of theft.

334

Figure Focus

Figure 5.19: What might have caused the variance in canned crushed tomatoes?

Figure 5.20: Pilfering is another word for stealing.

Calculation of Usage

Using an inventory system helps a buyer calculate product usage, food cost, and losses.

Tracking the amount of a product used during a set period of time helps the buyer calculate how much of the item needs to be ordered and how often. The first step is to select the period for the calculation (for example, day, week, month). Then, a buyer will follow these steps:

1. Note the amount of the item in inventory at the start of the period.

2. Note all new orders of the item received during the period.

3. Finally, note the amount of the item in inventory at the end of the period.

4. To figure out usage, add the starting inventory to the amount of the item received, and then deduct the ending inventory from the total.

5. The sum of the calculation is the amount of the item used. Here is an example of the calculation:

    Beginning inventory of item: 18 cases

    Amount received: +22 cases

    Total: 40 cases

    Ending inventory: -32 cases

    Total use for period: 8 cases

335

Figure Focus

Figure 5.20: Is taking a can of soda different from taking money? Why or why not?

Discuss

- Why should all restaurant and foodservice operations, regardless of size or style, determine and follow good practices for inventory control?

Reinforce and Review

- Using an inventory system helps a buyer calculate product usage, food cost, and losses.

- Tracking the amount of product used during a given period of time helps the buyer determine when and how much of an item to order.

- Calculating an item's usage requires knowing both the opening and closing inventories.

Teaching Tips

- Relate the information in this section to the material in Chapter 3.

In-Class Activity: Pilfer Problems
Literacy Connection, 21st-Century Skills— Critical Thinking and Problem Solving, Communicate Clearly, Work Independently
Discuss the relationship between pilfering and professionalism. Under what circumstances is it acceptable to pilfer? Why? Have the class discuss these issues.

Homework Activity: Do You Have Issues?
Literacy Connection, 21st-Century Skills— Critical Thinking and Problem Solving, Communicate Clearly, Create Media Products, Work Independently, Interact Effectively with Others
Create a document that you think would help a restaurant or foodservice operation keep better track of the goods it issues. Include any information that you think would help the business cut costs while reducing waste and pilferage.

In class, compare the document you have created with those from the rest of the class and discuss what features all agree are important. |

Discuss

- If a restaurant operates at a gross profit, does that mean that it is a success? Why or why not?

- Explain the importance of formal issuing procedures to the accurate calculation of potential losses.

Reinforce and Review

- Buyers calculate the total cost of food for the restaurant or foodservice operation the same way they calculate usage, only instead of looking at single items, they look at the operation's entire inventory.

- The food cost for a given period is determined by dividing the percentage of food by the food sales.

- If sales of food for a given period are less than the cost of food sold, the operation is operating at a loss.

- If sales of food for a given period are greater than the cost of food sold, the operation is operating at a gross profit.

- Managers determine the value of goods issued by auditing the issuing records; if the total cost of food is more than the total cost of food issued, inventory shrinkage has occurred.

Teaching Tips

- Relate this material to the discussion in Chapter 3.

- Encourage students to practice their math skills by calculating food costs, usage, and loss.

Vocabulary Terms

- **Gross profit:** Total sales minus the total cost of sales.

- **Inventory shrinkage:** The difference between the total cost of food and the cost of goods issued during a given period.

Calculate Food Cost

Buyers calculate the total cost of food for the restaurant or foodservice operations the same way they calculate item usage, except that they use the figures for total restaurant food inventory value. An example calculation is shown here:

09/01/11	Beginning Inventory:	$32,333
09/07/11	Cost of Goods Received:	+$ 8,563
09/14/11	Cost of Goods Received:	+$10,265
09/21/11	Cost of Goods Received:	+$11,378
09/28/11	Cost of Goods Received:	+$ 9,245
	Total:	$71,784
10/01/11	Ending Inventory:	-$30,577
(09/01/11–09/30/11)	Total Cost of Food:	$41,207

A buyer would use this figure to calculate the food cost percentage for the restaurant for the month of September. For example, if the restaurant had $125,000 in food sales, the food cost for the period would be 33 percent (cost of food divided by food sales).

Calculate Loss

It is also possible to determine if a restaurant or foodservice operation is operating at a loss or potential profit based on food sales. In the previous example, the total cost of food for September was $41,207. If sales of food for the period equal less than the cost of food sold, then the operation is operating at a loss. For example, if the restaurant had food sales of $39,866 for September, the loss in just food cost would be $1,341. However, based on the previous example of $125,000 in sales, the restaurant has a **gross profit** (profit on this portion before all other costs are deducted) of $83,793.

Another type of loss that managers can calculate using inventory value and receiving and issuing information is **inventory shrinkage**. This is the difference between the total cost of food and the cost of goods issued during the period. Managers determine the value of goods issued by auditing issuing records. Here is an example calculation:

Total Cost of Food: $41,207

Total Cost of Food Issued: -$40,763

Difference (+/-): -$ 444

Management must then account for the difference between the value of goods gone from inventory and the value of goods issued.

Remember that taking inventory, calculating inventory usage, compiling food costs, and determining potential losses or profits are critical management tools for restaurant and foodservice operations. Proper inventory management contributes to the success of any operation. Table 5.6 reviews the ten steps of purchasing.

Table 5.6: Summarizing the Ten Steps of Purchasing
1. Begin the purchasing process: • Review or plan all menus. • Determine the quality and quantity needed to produce menus. • Determine purchase amounts needed to maintain par stock levels. • Review, approve, or write specifications.
2. Check inventory records to determine supplies on hand and supplies that need to be reordered.
3. Request written price bids or verbal quotes from suppliers.
4. Select the supplier based on three factors: • Supplier services • Optimal price • Product quality
5. Prepare purchase order(s) and place the order(s).
6. Use proper receiving procedures when an order is delivered: • Review the invoice to check quantity, quality, and price of items delivered. • Accept delivery and sign or initial the invoice, or reject items and get a request for a credit memo. • Record each item in the receiving log. Date perishable food. Remember to save seafood tags in case of a foodborne illness.
7. Store items properly, observing all sanitation guidelines.
8. Store items properly, using the FIFO principle for stock rotation.
9. Have employees fill out requisition forms as they need supplies.
10. Following par stock guidelines, reorder supplies and begin the process again.

Discuss

- What procedures could restaurant and foodservice operations establish that would help account for inventory shrinkage?

- Why does inventory shrinkage occur?

- What is the relationship between inventory shrinkage and controlling costs?

Reinforce and Review

- Managers must determine the reasons for inventory shrinkage.

Table 5.6: Summarizing the Ten Steps of Purchasing
• How does the purchasing process help to determine the success or failure of a restaurant or foodservice operation?
• Is purchasing a full-time job? Why or why not? How can employing a buyer function as a competitive advantage?
• Why is so much documentation required by the purchasing process? Is it realistic to expect that all restaurant and foodservice operations will follow all these guidelines? Why or why not?

337

On the Job:
Preventing Pilfering Before It Starts

Encourage students to discuss the following:

- Explain how a positive work environment can reduce pilfering, referring to Level 1, Chapters 7 and 8 as needed.

- What are some other reasons employees might pilfer? How can these be handled proactively?

- When employees notice other employees pilfering, what actions should they take? Why?

Essential Skills:
Formal Issuing Procedures

Encourage students to discuss the following:

- In a busy operation, should there be a single employee who gathers requisitioned items? What are the advantages and disadvantages of this policy?

- How can managers keep emergency requisitions from becoming everyday affairs?

- What problems can arise if managers and employees do not follow established issuing procedures? How can this affect an operation's costs?

Homework Activity:
Issues

Literacy Connection, 21st-Century Skills—Critical Thinking and Problem Solving, Communicate Clearly, Work Independently

What formal issuing procedures would you establish for your operation? Why are these steps appropriate for your business model?

Discuss your conclusions in a one-page report.

[on the job]

Preventing Pilfering Before It Starts

Employee pilfering is a major problem in all businesses, and the restaurant and foodservice industry is no exception. Good managers can take steps to prevent pilfering before it starts by opening up lines of communication with employees. No manager can stop all pilfering, of course, but below are proactive steps that can help keep it to a minimum:

- Do thorough research on employees during the hiring process, including background checks.

- Make it difficult to steal by keeping precise inventory records and holding employees accountable for doing the same.

- Train employees on how to spot pilfering and actions to take if they do spot it.

- Be sure to periodically revisit the operation's policy on pilfering, and make sure to underscore that no one—even management—is exempt from it.

- Serve as a role model. Don't take advantage of your position. Obey the same rules that you communicate to all employees.

- Last but not least, be accessible. Make sure employees know that they can come to you if they are having problems outside of work. Employees are less likely to feel as if they have no other choice if you provide them with one.

Essential Skills
Formal Issuing Procedures

Operations with multiple foodservice outlets, such as conference centers or country clubs, typically have one buyer and one centralized storage space from which food and other items are issued to the other kitchens and preparation areas. Developing formal issuing procedures helps maintain inventory while reducing waste and theft. There are various ways to issue product; the following is one method:

- Create a product requisition form.

- Identify the individual from each shift and each kitchen or preparation area responsible for completing and submitting the requisition form and for collecting the items required.

- Identify a manager who will accept the completed requisition forms and oversee the collection process.

- Identify the individual who will gather the requisitioned items.

- Train all employees on the requisition process.

- Develop a policy for emergency requisitions.

338

If properly developed and observed, formal issuing procedures can save time and money. However, once put in place, employees must follow them consistently.

Summary

In this section, you learned the following:

- Receiving means inspecting, accepting, and, in some cases, rejecting deliveries of goods and services. The first step in setting up good receiving procedures is to make sure that only employees who have been trained in proper receiving techniques do the job. A written invoice should accompany every delivery. The invoice is the supplier's bill listing the actual goods delivered by the supplier. The person responsible for receiving at the restaurant—the receiver—should always check the invoice against the restaurant's original purchase order to make sure that the quantity and cost of the goods has not changed. The receiver should also have a copy of the original specs to confirm that the delivery meets the operation's quality standards. Any discrepancies on the invoice should be noted and signed by both the receiver and the delivery person. Additional guidelines include the following:

  - Plan ahead for shipments.

  - Inspect and store each delivery before receiving another one.

  - Inspect deliveries immediately.

  - Record items on a receiving sheet.

  - Correct mistakes immediately.

  - Put products away as quickly as possible.

  - Maintain the receiving area.

- Perishable products are food products sold or distributed in a form that will spoil or decay within a limited period of time. They can be damaged by bacteria, light, or air. Perishable products include meat, fish, poultry, dairy, eggs, produce, and alcoholic beverages. These items are purchased more often than nonperishable items. Perishable items should be purchased in a JIT (just in time) format whenever possible. This means that great effort must be taken to determine the amount needed prior to the next delivery with the goal that when the new delivery arrives, the majority of the previous order has been used. Nonperishable products are items that, generally due to packaging or processing, do not readily support the growth of pathogens. They include processed and canned or bottled products and dried

339

Summary

- Remind students to review the following:
  1. Receiving orders
  2. Storing orders
  3. Taking inventory

goods. Nonperishable food is generally purchased in large quantities and less often than perishable food.

■ Food should be stored according to whether it's perishable or nonperishable. There are three types of storage available in most foodservice establishments: refrigeration, freezer, and dry storage. Other guidelines for storage include the following:

- Store food in containers intended for food.

- Create proper air circulation around goods by keeping shelves about six inches from the floor, ceiling, and walls.

- Keep food stored far away from soaps, pesticides, chemicals, etc.

- Try to purchase staples (items for which the demand is constant) in airtight containers.

- Transfer items purchased in unsealed containers into airtight containers to protect them against insects and vermin.

- Use strong shelving for all nonperishables.

- Clean and sweep storage areas daily to eliminate spoiled food and to discourage insects and vermin.

- Have a professional pest control operator come in and spray regularly.

- Store perishable food, such as meat and produce, at its proper temperature and humidity level.

■ An inventory is a record of all products an operation has in storage and in the kitchen. Ideally, a foodservice operation will have only the needed amounts of food and nonfood items it needs to meet customer demand. Having too little inventory means customers don't get what they want. Having too much inventory means food spoils and storage costs go up. The two most common methods for purchasing nonperishable food are the physical inventory method and the perpetual inventory method. In the physical inventory method, the entire stock is physically reviewed on a regular basis. From this review, the operation determines the reorder point for each inventory item. The perpetual inventory method is the recording of items when received and again when issued.

Section 5.3 Review Questions

1. Why does the receiver use an invoice in the receiving process?

2. How does a nonperishable item differ from a perishable item, and how does the storage of each differ accordingly?

3. List three guidelines for food storage, and explain why each is important.

4. How does the physical inventory method differ from the perpetual inventory method?

5. Al Gaylor says that it helps if at least one of the distributors is a "full-service," broad-line supplier. How might a full-service distributor help you manage your purchases?

6. Lately, Chef Kate and Miguel have been letting their employees do the receiving, but they're wondering if these employees are doing it correctly. Chef Kate and Miguel have decided they need written guidelines. Write up a list of receiving guidelines they can use for their employees.

7. If you were in charge of receiving at a restaurant, what three receiving guidelines would you make sure you always followed? Explain why you chose these three.

8. A vendor drops off a delivery that has many mistakes and unacceptable products. You like this vendor, which is normally reliable and delivers items correctly and in good condition. Explain what you should do to address the situation constructively.

341

Section 5.3 Review Questions

1. Receivers check invoices against purchasing orders to ensure that the quantity and cost of the purchased goods have not changed.

2. Perishable items are food products sold or distributed in a form that will spoil or decay within a limited period of time, so they typically must be stored under refrigeration or frozen. Nonperishable items are items that do not readily support bacterial growth, usually as a result of processing or packaging; they are typically stored in dry-storage areas.

3. Students should select any of the three guidelines for refrigerated, frozen, or dry storage and explain why each guideline is important.

4. The physical inventory method counts actual items that the establishment possesses, whereas the perpetual inventory estimates the items that the establishment possesses.

5. Students should identify ways in which full-service suppliers can assist their customers.

6. Students should clearly identify appropriate guidelines for the receiving process.

7. Student responses will vary but should clearly explain why they have selected these particular receiving guidelines.

8. Students should rely on good communication skills but should also identify ways in which they could obtain acceptable products quickly to avoid interruptions in service.

Section 5.3 Activities

1. Students should develop a clear and logical flow chart describing the purchasing process.

2. Students should clearly explain how each category of people is affected by pilfering.

3. Students should identify factors that could produce inventory shortages, including excessive waste, poor forecasting, incorrect ordering, and pilferage. Their policies should directly address the causes they identified.

Section 5.3 Activities

1. Study Skills/Group Activity: Going with the Flow—Charting the Purchasing Process

Working in a small group, create a detailed flow chart that illustrates the entire purchasing process. Share the chart with the rest of the class. The class will vote on which chart explains the process the best.

2. Independent Activity: The Effects of Pilfering

You're working at a restaurant where a lot of pilfering is going on. Explain how pilfering affects each of the following groups:

a. Other employees

b. The owner

c. The managers

d. The guests

3. Critical Thinking: Investigating Shortages

In the past three months at your 50-seat, fine-dining restaurant, you've seen a consistent and alarming gap between what you expected to have in your food and beverage inventory and what you actually physically counted. Most of your kitchen staff has been with the restaurant for a long time, but two of your servers are new. Additionally, you've recently added three new entrées to the dinner menu.

Considering these factors and what you learned in this chapter, identify three possible reasons why you have a gap in your expected inventory. Then, draft new policies for your operation to follow to help close the gaps in future months.

NET WT 5 LB (2.26 kg)

Case Study Follow-Up **Purchasing More Profit**

At the beginning of the chapter, we mentioned Miguel and Chef Kate were trying to cut costs by looking closely at their entire purchasing process.

❶ After having read this chapter, do you think it's possible for an operation to significantly cut costs without reducing food quality? Why or why not? Explain your answer.

❷ If you had to suggest one aspect of the purchasing process for Miguel and Chef Kate to focus on, which aspect of purchasing would it be? Why? Explain your answer.

❸ Obviously, Chef Kate and Miguel got into some bad habits in their purchasing procedures. Based on what you've learned from this chapter, which three aspects of purchasing do you think could be most frequently overlooked in a restaurant? Why do you feel this would be so?

343

Case Study Follow-Up

1. Students should defend their positions in a clear, reasoned manner.

2. Students should identify one step in the purchasing process and explain how focusing on it can help Kabob lower its costs.

3. Students should select three aspects of purchasing and explain why some restaurants might neglect them.

Apply Your Learning

Make or Buy Caesar Dressing?

Students should accurately calculate the total cost of making the dressing, including labor cost. They should identify which product is financially a better deal as well as explain why they would choose one dressing over the other.

Apply Your Learning

Make or Buy Caesar Dressing?

Your restaurant is known for its excellent Caesar salads, made with your secret salad dressing recipe. The recipe takes about 15 minutes to prepare, and the cook who usually makes it is paid $12.00/hour. One of your trusted specialty suppliers, who understands your high standards and attention to detail, brings you a sample of a prepared Caesar dressing to try. Both the prepared product and the homemade recipe are of similar quality, although the flavor is somewhat different. Conduct a make-or-buy analysis to determine which product is a better financial deal. Regardless of the cost, which dressing do you choose to use and why?

Jacqui's Famous Caesar Dressing: makes 1.5 quarts			Freshmaker Direct Caesar Dressing
(Housemade dressing)			(Purchased from vendor) $32/gallon
Amount	**Ingredient**	**Total Cost**	
2 tablespoons	Pasteurized egg yolk	$1.00	
1 cup	Olive oil	$3.25	
3 cups	Canola oil	$4.00	
½ ounce	Garlic	$0.15	
2 each	Anchovies	$0.90	
1 teaspoon	Dijon mustard	$0.10	
½ each	Lemon	$0.12	
4 ounces	Parmesan cheese	$2.00	
To taste	Hot sauce	–	
To taste	Worcestershire sauce	–	
To taste	Black pepper	–	

2008 Food Shortages

During 2008, there were a number of concerns about world-wide food shortages, especially of staples like corn and rice. These fears affected the prices of these foods. Research an ingredient that was expected to be in short supply during that year and write three paragraphs about why a shortage was feared, how the price was affected, and what the current availability and price of the item is now.

The Science of Rejection

In this chapter, we discussed the reasons for rejecting damaged deliveries in the context of food safety. But why would we reject damaged items from a scientific standpoint? How has the food itself changed? For example:

- What is freezer burn?
- Why do canned goods sometimes bulge?
- How does milk turn sour?

Select one of these or another reason for rejecting a damaged food item and research the underlying science behind the rejection. Be sure to cover both food safety concerns and physical changes to the product in your response, which should be one page in length.

Critical Thinking — Finding Time in the Day

Developing quality standards and writing product specifications is an important part of maintaining consistency, but it can be time consuming. How can busy chefs and managers integrate this work into their busy schedules? Write a paragraph for each.

2008 Food Shortages

Students should identify and research a food that was expected to be in short supply, explaining what happened in 2008 and describing current supplies and prices.

The Science of Rejection

Students should select a reason to reject a damaged food item and describe why it is valid, both in terms of food safety and of physical changes to the product.

Critical Thinking — Finding Time in the Day

Students should write one paragraph on chefs and one on managers, both identifying ways in which these individuals can make time to develop standards and write specifications.

Exam Prep Answers

1. D
2. B
3. A
4. A
5. A
6. A
7. C
8. D
9. B
10. A

Exam Prep Questions

1 The three main layers in the channel of distribution are

A. peripheral, central, and focal.

B. primary, secondary, and tertiary.

C. peripheral, retail, and secondary.

D. primary, intermediary, and retail.

2 The buying process that smaller operations tend to use is a(n)

A. formal method.

B. informal method.

C. allocated method.

D. three-pronged method.

3 The goods and services category that includes gas or heating is

A. utilities.

B. technology.

C. maintenance service.

D. smallwares and equipment.

4 Storage capacity, budgetary constraints, and an operation's concept and goals are some factors that go into establishing

A. quality standards.

B. employee scheduling.

C. inventory procedures.

D. the name of a restaurant.

5 A production sheet lists all of the items that will be prepared

A. daily.

B. weekly.

C. monthly.

D. bimonthly.

6 The ideal amount of inventory items that an operation should have at all times is called

A. par stock.

B. optimal stock.

C. premium balance.

D. storage equilibrium.

7 The legally binding written document that details exactly what the buyer is ordering from the vendor is called a(n)

A. invoice.

B. daily cost sheet.

C. purchase order.

D. issuing statement.

8 In the restaurant and foodservice industry, the term receiving refers to the process of

A. servers taking plated food from the kitchen line.

B. accepting bids from various vendors for an operation's business.

C. working directly with primary sources for goods and services.

D. inspecting and accepting or rejecting deliveries of goods and services.

346

9 The temperature of the dry-storage area should be between

A. 40°F and 60°F.

B. 50°F and 70°F.

C. 60°F and 80°F.

D. 70°F and 90°F.

10 The official procedures employees use when taking an item out of the store-room and putting it into production is called

A. issuing.

B. receiving.

C. invoicing.

D. expediting.

347

Chapter 6 Overview

This chapter covers meat, poultry, and seafood.

Section 1: This section covers the grades and cuts of meat, as well as purchasing, storing, and cooking meat.

Section 2: This section covers the grades and forms of poultry, as well as purchasing, fabricating, storing, and cooking poultry.

Section 3: This section covers seafood inspection and the grades and forms of seafood, as well as purchasing, fabricating, storing, and cooking seafood.

Section 4: This section covers the definitions of charcuterie and garde manger as well as the types of charcuterie.

Advance Preparation	
Review	Sections 6.1–6.4
Contact	Computer lab
	Contact library
Prepare	Paper (large, like butcher paper)
	Egg white
	White fish
	Lime juice
	One or more whole chickens
	Cards or card stock
	Pictures of foods,
	Cooking equipment (if needed)

ServSafe Connection
Pages 386, 418

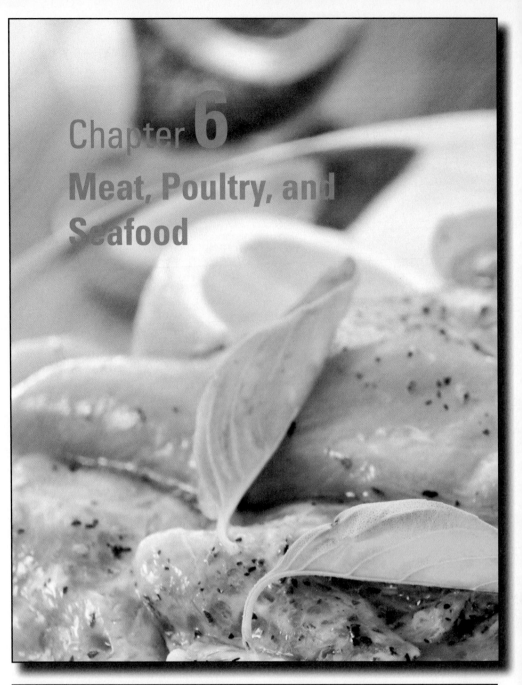

Chapter 6
Meat, Poultry, and Seafood

CUSTOMIZED INSTRUCTION OPTIONS			
Less Advanced Students	More Advanced Students	ESOL Students	Special Needs Students
Pages 361, 411	Pages 361, 411	Pages 361, 411	Pages 361, 411

CHAPTER TOOLS			
21st-Century Skills	Mathematics	Science	Literacy
Pages 356, 361, 369, 384, 390, 392, 407, 411	Pages 369, 407	Page 365	Pages 361, 390, 407

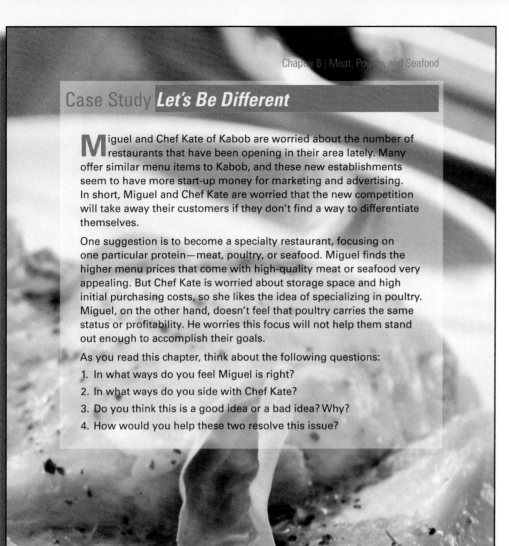

Case Study *Let's Be Different*

Miguel and Chef Kate of Kabob are worried about the number of restaurants that have been opening in their area lately. Many offer similar menu items to Kabob, and these new establishments seem to have more start-up money for marketing and advertising. In short, Miguel and Chef Kate are worried that the new competition will take away their customers if they don't find a way to differentiate themselves.

One suggestion is to become a specialty restaurant, focusing on one particular protein—meat, poultry, or seafood. Miguel finds the higher menu prices that come with high-quality meat or seafood very appealing. But Chef Kate is worried about storage space and high initial purchasing costs, so she likes the idea of specializing in poultry. Miguel, on the other hand, doesn't feel that poultry carries the same status or profitability. He worries this focus will not help them stand out enough to accomplish their goals.

As you read this chapter, think about the following questions:

1. In what ways do you feel Miguel is right?
2. In what ways do you side with Chef Kate?
3. Do you think this is a good idea or a bad idea? Why?
4. How would you help these two resolve this issue?

Case Study
Let's Be Different

- The protein foods are often the most expensive part of the menu.

- This aspect of a restaurant requires serious consideration.

- The students should discuss and formulate a preliminary opinion upon first reading the case study.

- Encourage the students to write down their first ideas.

- After they have read the chapter, have them compare their first opinion to their current one.

- Do the students have an idea of how these two could resolve their feelings?

- Note that there are follow-up questions about the case study at the end of the chapter.

- This activity could be done in groups, as a class, or as a homework assignment.

[professional profile]

Charleen Obal

Owner, Saphron Restaurant,
Prince Frederick, Maryland

Owning a restaurant is really my fifth career. When I graduated high school, I joined the U.S. Army and served seven years, including assignments in West Germany and South Korea. My educational background is in speech communication. I've also been in the retail business and taught elementary school. So, I certainly have diverse interests!

I began catering in the 1990s. In 2006, when searching for a commercial catering kitchen, I decided to open a restaurant.

I've always thought, in any endeavor, that you begin by selling yourself. If your customers trust and believe in you, all the rest is easy. As a matter of fact, I took this philosophy further than just my customers. When I applied for the restaurant's liquor license, I decided to speak for myself instead of hiring a lawyer as many other establishments do. The board members were a bit taken aback by this and they asked me, "If we don't grant you a liquor license, are you still going to open a restaurant?" I was speechless for a bit since it never entered my mind that anything would deter me from opening. I told them that nothing would stop me. You open a restaurant to serve food. Wine and cocktails are menu items that enhance the enjoyment of the dining experience. Your restaurant operations begin as soon as a diner comes through the front door. This means an inviting foyer, a sincere welcome, and congenial greeting. The ambiance in the restaurant must also be welcoming and comfortable. The restaurant and restrooms must be clean. The servers must be attentive, knowledgeable, and courteous. Food preparation and presentation are also integral, as customers first enjoy the food with their eyes.

I also believe in a personal touch and try to visit each table and talk with the customers at some point during the meal. The kitchen staff is the foundation for the food service and must be prepared to operate efficiently and correctly any time the restaurant doors are open. I'm also a firm believer in using local ingredients and resources whenever possible. I purchase many of my fruits and vegetables (in season) from local growers, use local wineries on my wine list, and buy from local bakeries and coffee roasteries.

People in this industry must be passionate about what they do; whether it be the front or back of the house. Without passion, the food industry is just another job. You must also do your homework to learn everything you can about your role in the industry.

350

Remember:

" *If you can't stand the heat, stay out of the kitchen!* **"**

About Meat, Poultry, and Seafood

I love the versatility and variety of all three of these groups. They can be used as entrées, soups, parts of salads, appetizers, and accompaniments. They can be cooked in innumerable ways: baked, fried, poached, raw (sometimes), grilled, and any way your imagination takes you. They are also adaptable to many cuisine styles: Low Country (as in my restaurant), Asian, European, Tex-Mex, etc. The variations are endless. All groups can be served at breakfast, lunch, or dinner.

In the meat category, I'm particularly fond of braised short ribs. They are easy to prepare, hearty, and can presented in a variety of ways with a variety of accompanying vegetables and starches. They're ideal in the winter season and surprise diners when they appear on the menu.

In the chicken category, I am partial to fried chicken. It's a great comfort food when accompanied by mashed potatoes. You can season them in a variety of ways and even serve them with waffles.

In the seafood category, I return to my South Carolina roots with a strong preference for shrimp and grits. This is a signature dish in my restaurant and can be prepared in any number of ways. It's particularly good at breakfast, but works well as a dinner entrée also. If preparing it for yourself, you can customize the grits to your personal style. You can also vary the shrimp preparation, either choosing to flour coat it or not. You can also vary the aromatics and other meat (for example, sausage or bacon) that compose the gravy that you place atop the grits with the shrimp. This is a truly unique and versatile dish.

351

Professional Profile (cont.)

Discuss	Charleen Obal thinks that, in any endeavor, you begin by selling yourself. "If your customers trust and believe in you, all the rest is easy." What do students think about this philosophy?
Reinforce and Review	Review the versatility of these products—meat, poultry, and seafood.
Teaching Tips	Perhaps some research into shrimp and grits would help the students be familiar with this dish. It's a low-country Southern dish. This cuisine will be introduced in Chapter 10.

Focus and Engage

Discuss

- Cuts of meat, pieces of poultry, and seafood are often the focal point of a meal.

- What do meat, poultry, and seafood have in common?

- They are all significant protein sources.

- They are referred to simply as "protein" in the professional kitchen.

- They are not referred to that way by nutritionists, but that doesn't make it wrong; it just signifies two different nomenclatures.

Section 6.1 Meat

Introduce the Section

a. It helps to be educated about how to purchase meat.
b. Meat comes in various grades and cuts.
c. Each cut and type of meat has recommended cooking methods.

Vocabulary Review

a. Direct students to the key terms.
b. Pronounce each word, and have the students repeat the pronunciation out loud.
c. Discuss the definition of each word.

Teach

Reinforce and Review

- Meat grades are determined by the USDA standards.

- Inspection stamps are only awarded to safe, wholesome meat.

- The grades help determine the quality of the tenderness and flavor.

- Cooking methods are often suggested by the grade as well.

Vocabulary Terms

- **Meat:** Muscle flesh of edible mammals.

6.1 Meat	6.2 Poultry	6.3 Seafood	6.4 Charcuterie and Garde Manger
• Grades of meat • Cuts of meat • Purchasing and storing meat • Cooking techniques for meat • Determining doneness	• Grades of poultry • Two forms of poultry: white and dark • Purchasing, fabricating, and storing poultry • Cooking techniques for poultry	• Seafood inspections and grades • Forms of seafood • Purchasing, fabricating, and storing seafood • Cooking techniques for seafood • Determining doneness	• Definitions of charcuterie and garde manger • Types of charcuterie

SECTION 6.1 MEAT

Foodservice industry professionals use "**meat**" to refer to beef, veal, lamb, mutton, or pork. A T-bone steak or pork tenderloin is almost certain to be the main attraction of any plate on which it appears, so it is crucial that the product on the plate is of high quality and is properly prepared. The main dish determines the success of most meals. If that dish is prepared well, the meal will likely be a success.

Study Questions

After studying Section 6.1, you should be able to answer the following questions:

- What are the grades of meat?
- What are the primary cuts of meat?
- What factors go into purchasing meat?
- What is the best way to cook and prepare meat?

Grades of Meat

Meat inspection is mandatory in the United States. The Food Safety and Inspection Service, a division of the USDA, conducts these inspections. It ensures that meat is wholesome and that the processing facilities and equipment meet food safety standards. Products that pass inspection receive a USDA stamp, which means that the product is approved for wholesomeness and is safe for people to eat. See Figure 6.1 for a picture of what the stamp looks like.

Figure 6.1: A USDA stamp means that a product is approved for wholesomeness and is safe for people to eat.

Figure Focus

Figure 6.1: Look for this stamp for meat sold in the United States.

Only meat products that are approved for wholesomeness may be **graded**. Grading refers to the meat's quality. The quality of meat is based primarily on its overall flavor characteristics and tenderness.

Although it is voluntary, many processors and packers pay a fee to the USDA to have meat products graded to ensure their quality. USDA grades are based on nationally uniform federal standards. The USDA assigns two grades for most types of meat:

- Quality grade
- Yield grade

Some types of meat may have one of these grades, and other types may have both.

Quality grade measures the flavor characteristics of meat products. The USDA evaluates meat for traits that indicate its tenderness, juiciness, and flavor. Quality grades for beef, lamb, and veal can include Prime, Choice, Select, Standard, Commercial, Utility, Cutter, Cull, or Canner. Unlike other types of meat, pork does not receive a quality grade. Although the USDA inspects pork for wholesomeness, pork is graded only for yield and receives a yield grade stamp. See Table 6.1.

Yield grade measures the proportion of edible or usable meat after it has been trimmed of bones or fat. You can get yield grades for beef, pork, and lamb products. This is helpful because the differences in the amount of fat on the outside of the meat can cause the yield of usable product to vary.

Use the lower grades to make ground beef and other processed products. Institutions also sometimes use these grades. Use the lowest grades for canning.

Table 6.1: Quality Grades for Beef, Lamb, and Veal

Grade	Description
Prime	This is the highest quality available for beef, veal, and lamb. Usually found in only the finest restaurants, hotels, and markets. A lot of marbling and a cover of firm fat, which enhances flavor and juiciness. Only a small percentage of beef products meet this standard.
Choice	This is also a high grade for most meat and readily available for restaurant use and the general consumer. Choice beef is very tender, juicy, and flavorful, but has less marbling than Prime.
Select	This is a slightly lower grade for beef, but still suitable for restaurant use depending on the desired end product. These cuts will be considerably lower in overall marbling content. Can be tender and tasty if cooked properly. Often processed, ground, or canned.

(continued)

353

Teaching Tips

- Have a cut of meat or label with an inspection stamp and a grade stamp on it for the students to see.

- Help students understand the concept of "yield" and how it impacts pricing and portioning.

Table 6.1: Quality Grades for Beef, Lamb, and Veal

- The various grades only indicate uses and cooking methods.

- All inspected meat is safe to use.

Vocabulary Terms

- **Graded:** Evaluation of meat against established standards.

- **Quality grades:** The standards for flavor and texture of meat.

- **Yield grades:** The amount of edible meat after trimming.

Table 6.1 (cont.)

- There is a reason why canned meat does not have the same quality as fresh, select cuts, but it is still safe and nutritious.

What's New:
Lower-Fat Pork

Pork can be a nice alternative to other low-fat proteins.

Teaching Tips

- For this chapter, you should find out if any of the students keep kosher or are religiously vegetarian.

- This could be a difficult section, and consulting with parents might be helpful.

Table 6.1: Quality Grades for Beef, Lamb, and Veal *continued*

Grade	Description
Good	This is comparable to the Select grade for beef but is used only for veal and lamb.
Lower grades for beef	These are: Standard, Commercial, Utility, Cutter, and Canner.
Lower grades for lamb	These are Utility and Cull.
Lower grades for veal	These are Standard and Utility.

Figure 6.2 shows the differences between graded cuts of meat.

Figure 6.2: Graded cuts of meat, from left to right, based on the amount of marbling, are Prime, Choice, and Select.

[what's new]

Lower-Fat Pork

Pork used to be a high-fat meat product. Pigs' diets and lifestyles promoted a very thick fat collar around the carcass and high marbling. When cardiac health became an issue in the latter part of the twentieth century, people began to eat less pork. To combat this, pork producers developed a variety of pig with a lower-fat carcass. Changes in food, lifestyle, genetics, and handling produced a pig with a thin collar layer of fat and reduced marbling.

Trimmed pork is now lower in fat than most beef. The slogan, "Pork: The Other White Meat" was launched to show that pork compares favorably to white chicken as a low-fat protein choice. A public perception advertising campaign increased pork consumption. Pork is still widely consumed and, when trimmed, still lower in fat than other meat.

354

Figure Focus

Figure 6.2: You can often visually see the difference between cuts of meat.

Cuts of Meat

Before a chef can determine the right cooking method for a cut of meat, he or she needs to understand the various cuts of meat, the physical composition of the muscle tissue, and how it is affected by heat.

Muscle tissue consists of about 75 percent water, 20 percent protein, and 5 percent fat and is made up of a network of muscle fibers bound together in bundles. Each of the fibers is surrounded by connective tissue. The amount of connective tissue in a muscle increases as the animal ages and with the amount the animal is exercised. This tissue makes the meat tougher but also more flavorful.

Cuts of meat taken from the shoulder and flanks are examples of cuts that have a lot of connective tissue. Figure 6.3 shows a cut of meat that tends to be tougher. The two types of connective tissue are collagen and elastin. Collagen breaks down during long, slow, moist-heat cooking. Elastin connects the meat to the bone and will not break down during cooking; trim it away by hand before cooking.

Figure 6.3: Tough connective tissue is cut from meat using a sharp knife.

The tenderest cuts of meat come from those muscle groups that receive the least amount of exercise. These cuts also have more marbling, or fat, which builds up between the muscle fibers. Tenderloins and roasts from the sirloin are naturally juicier because they contain more marbling. Figure 6.4 on the following page shows beef primal cuts.

355

Reinforce and Review

- Collagen is a type of protein molecule.

- It is found in fascia, the thin covering over a muscle.

- It is also found between muscle fiber bundles.

- Elastin is found in ligaments and tendons and is fibrous and tough.

- It is a protein molecule that is cross-linked and insoluble in water.

- Elastin is sometimes called "gristle." It is inedible. It is not poisonous, but it is unchewable.

Figure Focus

Figure 6.3: A good knife is essential for trimming tough tissues from cuts of meat.

Reinforce and Review

- Cuts of meat come from various places on the carcass.

- An animal carcass has primal cuts that work well for flavor and cooking.

- The psoas major muscle is long and can be sliced into various sizes and cuts, all tender.

- The muscles that receive the most use, like the legs, are the toughest.

In-Class Activity: Pin the Sirloin on the Bovine

21st-Century Skills—Use Systems Thinking

Make large paper cutouts of the various primal cuts of beef.

Divide the students into two groups.

Play a game to assemble the entire carcass.

Each team gets a chance to put a cut on the board in the correct place.

If they do this incorrectly, the other team has a turn.

When the students are done, there should be a reconstructed bovine carcass model on the board.

Vocabulary Terms

- **Primal cuts:** The initial butchering cuts of an animal carcass.

- **Aging:** A chance for meat to overcome postmortem rigor. Muscle fibers lengthen and relax.

Figure 6.4: Primal cuts are a larger section of a carcass from which retail cuts are made.

Before a cut of meat becomes available for purchase by a restaurant or foodservice operation, several stages of butchering need to take place. After harvesting (slaughtering), the processor cuts the whole carcass into large sections. The number of sections depends on the type of animal:

- The processor cuts cattle butchered for beef into four sections.

- The processor cuts cattle that are butchered from the age of 1 day up to 14 or 15 weeks into two halves and sells this meat as veal, which has a pale flesh and delicate flavor.

- The processor cuts slaughtered hogs into two halves in facilities that handle no other type of meat in order to prevent foodborne illness.

- Sheep slaughtered under the age of one year are considered lamb. After that age, they must be labeled mutton. The processor cuts lamb directly into primal cuts. **Primal cuts** are the primary divisions of meat produced by the initial butchering of animal carcasses.

Butchers then must age meat between 48 and 72 hours to allow the muscles to relax. Butchers hang the meat during **aging** to help lengthen the muscle fibers and increase the tenderness of the meat, as shown in Figure 6.5 on the following page. When butchers age meat for longer periods of time, the meat continues to darken, and the flavor improves. It also becomes more expensive because the meat loses a significant amount of moisture that reduces its yield.

Figure Focus

Figure 6.4: Ask the students which cuts of meat are the most tender. A tenderloin is the psoas major muscle that resides along the back. It is tender.

Figure 6.5: Butchers hang meat during the aging process to let the muscles lengthen and relax.

At the end of the aging period, the butcher cuts the carcass into primal cuts. These cuts also depend on the types of animal. See Figure 6.6 for an illustration of primal cuts. After the butcher makes primal cuts, fabrication can take place. **Fabrication** is the process of butchering primal cuts into usable portions, such as roasts or steaks.

Figure 6.6: Primal cuts for beef, veal, pork, and lamb.

Retail cuts of meat are those cuts that are ready for sale. They can be primal cuts or fabricated portions. The amount of cutting or butchering necessary to prepare a retail cut affects its price. For example, the more time the butcher spends cutting or butchering a piece of meat, the more expensive it will be. Foodservice purchasers can choose to purchase retail cuts that are primal cuts and then fabricate them for their own use or buy fabricated portions. They make this determination based on the needs of the restaurant.

357

Reinforce and Review

- Meat is aged under refrigeration to prevent the growth of pathogens.

- Under proper refrigeration, meat can be aged up to six weeks.

- The longer the aging process, the more flavorful the meat.

- The longer the aging process, the greater the moisture loss and shrinkage.

- If the meat shrinks, it decreases the yield, and decreased yield means increased price.

- The price for aged meat must also reflect the price of the aging facility, the refrigeration, and other expenses to prepare the meat.

- The psoas major muscle is not very large in comparison to the rest of the carcass.

- An aged piece of tenderloin, therefore, is very flavorful and quite expensive.

Vocabulary Terms

- **Fabrication:** Butchering operation, cutting primal cuts into market cuts.

- **Retail cuts:** Market cuts with established names and criteria.

Figure Focus

Figure 6.5: The aging and hanging process is done under refrigeration to protect the meat.

Figure 6.6: Primal cuts are large portions of the carcass.

Reinforce and Review

- A butterfly cut opens like a book, or like the wings of a butterfly.

- This cut can make a small, tender cut have more surface area.

- Various cuts of meat are sometimes tied together because they can fall apart during cooking.

- The connective tissue holding muscle fibers together can disconnect during cooking.

- Tying solves this problem. Use cotton string.

- Silverskin (the tough elastin connective tissue fascia of muscles of a carcass) and gristle (the tough elastin connective tissue cartilage) should be sliced off, as it is tough.

Essential Skills: Trimming and Butterflying a Tenderloin

A tenderloin must be properly butchered for the most profitable yield.

Vocabulary Terms

- **Butterflying:** Slicing a cut of meat crossways, not all the way through, and opening it up.

- **Medallions:** A small, bound, and cut circular fillet.

An operation can save money on its meat purchases by fabricating its own meat from retail primal cuts. Fabrication procedures for beef, veal, lamb, pork, and large game are similar and require practice but very few tools. A fabricator needs only a sharp knife and a clean cutting board. An easy fabrication method is tying a roast, which ensures even cooking and keeps the shape of the meat. Trimming and **butterflying** tenderloin is also a popular technique.

Essential Skills
Trimming and Butterflying a Tenderloin

Butchers and chefs must trim tenderloin very carefully because it is one of the most expensive cuts. To do so properly:

❶ Remove only the silverskin (the tough membrane that surrounds the meat), fat, and gristle. See Figure 6.7a.

❷ Cut away the fat. See Figure 6.7b.

❸ Use a chef's knife to make an even cut through the center of the meat.

❹ Open the meat using a butterfly cut. Butterflying means to cut a piece of meat lengthwise nearly in half so that it opens out and lies flat. This cut speeds up the cooking process by increasing the surface area of the meat. See Figure 6.7c.

Figure 6.7a: Step 1—Remove the silverskin, fat, and gristle.

Figure 6.7b: Step 2—Cut away the fat.

Figure 6.7c: Step 4—Open the meat using a butterfly cut.

Fabricators make cuts from the boneless loin or tenderloin of beef, veal, lamb, or pork into a variety of menu cuts:

- **Medallions:** Small, round pieces molded by wrapping them in cheesecloth. (See Figure 6.8 on the following page.)

358

Figure Focus

Figure 6.7a: Gristle and silverskin are tough and inedible. Fat is unappealing to eat.

Figure 6.7b: Fat should be removed from the collar, but not marbled fat.

Figure 6.7c: Butterfly after the entire cut is prepared.

- **Noisettes** (nwah-ZET): Small, usually round portion of meat; the French word for hazelnut. Sometimes the terms "medallions" and "noisettes" are both used to describe small, boneless, tender cuts of meat.

- **Scallops:** Thin, boneless cuts that are lightly pounded. (See Figure 6.9.)

- *Emincé* (eh-manss-AY): Thin strips of meat used for sautéing.

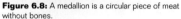

Figure 6.8: A medallion is a circular piece of meat without bones.

Figure 6.9: Turkey scallopini with capers and lemon.

Historically, people needed to make full use of every part of the animals they raised for food. **Offal** (OH-fel) **meat** is organ meat from hogs, cattle, or sheep (see Figure 6.10). It includes sweetbreads (thymus glands), liver, kidney, tripe (muscular stomach lining), heart, and brain. Though no longer very popular in the United States, offal meat is still enjoyed in other regions of the world and is a great source of essential vitamins and minerals.

Figure 6.10a: Liver and *rucola* (a salad green).

Figure 6.10b: Sweetbreads.

Figure 6.10c: Lamb's liver and caramelized onions.

359

Reinforce and Review

- Deer meet is called "venison."

- When game meat is taken from the wild, the meat is from an active animal. Therefore, the muscles are used, and the fat content is low.

- Game meat might not be as tender as beef from a feedlot.

- Slow cooking is usually recommended.

- Game meat can have very strongly flavored offal, so be careful to taste-test before using.

- The psoas major muscle of elk, moose, and deer is more tender than the leg muscles, just as in other animals.

Trends:
Home on the Range

Venison is deer. Ask if any of the students have tried deer meat.

Trends:
Is This Kosher?

Kosher guidelines should be respected. Being familiar with kosher principles is important in the restaurant and foodservice industry, especially in areas with a large Jewish population.

Vocabulary Terms

- **Game meat:** Meat from undomesticated animals.

Figure 6.10d: Steak and kidney pie with chips and peas.

Figure 6.10e: Polish tripe soup.

Figure 6.10f: Veal heart.

Game meat is meat from animals that are not raised domestically. This includes deer, wild boar, moose, and elk. Chefs prepare many distinctly different dishes with game meat. However, the same preparation guidelines for red meat apply to game meat.

[trends]
Home on the Range

Some game is now raised domestically. So, the venison served in a restaurant may not be from the forest any more. To learn more about farm-raised game meat, check out www.fossilfarms.com.

Kosher meat is specially slaughtered to comply with Jewish dietary laws. A rabbi visits the slaughterhouse and processing plant for kosher approval. In the United States, only beef and veal forequarters, poultry, and some game are used for kosher preparations.

[trends]
Is This Kosher?

Kosher law flatly prohibits the eating of pork, but specific rules within other meat groups determine which can be used, which cannot, and when. Seafood, for example, is limited to fish with scales and fins, so shellfish as a whole are not kosher. Wild birds of prey are not kosher, but domestic birds, like chickens, are kosher. For meat to be kosher, the animal's death must be painless, and meat cannot be served or prepared with milk products. These are just a few of the rules of kosher law.

Acceptable food products have a label designation of a "circle-U," a "U," a Hebraic-appearing "K," a scroll, and other symbols provided by commercial kosher regulatory services. In order to carry the designation, the food must first be an acceptable food with acceptable ingredients. Then the processing plant must be visited by a rabbi. The rabbi examines the cleanliness, the ingredients, the equipment, the process, and the types of foods that are prepared together. When the rabbi is satisfied that the entire process will satisfy kosher principles, the designation is approved. Any changes in the ingredients or processing procedures must be reviewed by the rabbi to maintain the kosher designation.

360

Figure Focus

Figure 6.10d: Steak and kidney pie, a favorite in the United Kingdom.

Figure 6.10e: Tripe is stomach. Menudo, a Mexican dish, is also tripe soup.

Figure 6.10f: Veal heart is a very useful piece of meat, and does not have as strong a flavor as liver.

[trends]

Take a look at some food labels of breakfast cereals, pickles, and other food products. See whether you can find a kosher designation, as shown in Figure 6.11, somewhere on the label. It is usually on the front and very small. If your establishment has Jewish guests, you may be asked whether your restaurant is kosher. Be aware of what will be required to say "Yes."

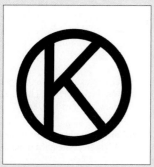

Figure 6.11: Kosher may be used only on the labels of products prepared under rabbinical supervision.

[on the job]

Butchering

Butchers are trained professionals in meat distribution. A master butcher can train apprentices in the trade. Some schools teach the butcher trade and specialty vocational jobs in butchering, such as "slaughterer" or "sausage-maker." These positions require less specialized training.

Butchers must understand the health and anatomy of edible animals. They need the skills to recognize and choose a quality animal or carcass and prepare it for sale. They must cut it into specific market cuts without damaging the tissue. Butchers use hand tools and power tools to accomplish this.

Butchers used to own shops and do all the work from carcass to sale. Now, it is more common for meat to be sold in grocery stores and supermarkets. Restaurants may purchase meat products from a broker or a restaurant butcher. Some butchering may be done on-site in a commercial kitchen. The safety considerations are the same for butchers and for chefs cutting meat in the kitchen.

Serious injuries used to be common in the profession. In current times, improved safety considerations are available for the butcher. He or she wears a belly guard and safety glove made of chain mail and kevlar, the material used for bulletproof vests. A commercial chef also uses these if he or she uses power cutting tools in the kitchen. Otherwise, butchers and chefs must take care with the hand tools and knives used for slicing, deboning, etc. All parts of the body should be guarded from blades. Work should proceed without the distraction of having to "multitask."

361

On the Job: Butchering

A butcher is a professional who specializes in meat. Butcher shops used to be a common feature in most towns, but now many supermarkets have full-service butchers. Ask students if they've ever been to a butcher shop.

CUSTOMIZED INSTRUCTION

Literacy Connection, 21st Century Skills—Be Self-Directed Learners

More Advanced Students

Have students create a game, puzzle, or other group activity based on the names of various cuts of meat and their descriptions. Once they have created the game, try it out!

Less Advanced Students

Have students invent a game called "Name That Meat." The goal is to have names of different cuts of meat in the game, to help students learn the names.

ESOL Students

Compare the names of different cuts to the names used in the primary language, using words and pictures. Are the names the same? Connecting the new language to the familiar primary language can help students to learn. Students should create a translation tool that uses pictures to connect the two languages.

Special Needs Students

Encourage students to learn the names and spelling of various cuts of meat. Have students create—or create for them if necessary—a spelling worksheet for the names of various cuts.

Figure Focus

Figure 6.11: Many different products are kosher certified. The Hebrew alphabet K and the circle U are also commonly used to indicate that a product is kosher.

All tenderizing involves breaking down tough proteins. Cutting them works.

Reinforce and Review

- Students might realize that ground meat is tender because the pieces of muscle fiber are very short.

- A little fat helps bind ground meat together.

- Ground meat is often made from tough cuts and scraps, but it is just as nutritious as larger cuts.

Essential Skills
Tenderizing Meat

Food preparers can tenderize meat in a number of ways. They can use mechanical means, chemical means, or cooking means. Following are guidelines for each method.

Mechanical Tenderizing
Pulverizing

❶ Place the meat between two pieces of plastic wrap or wax paper to keep meat contained while tenderizing.

❷ Take a tenderizing mallet, the bottom of a pan, or another heavier blunt object and beat meat until it has an even thickness throughout. This will help break up tougher muscle fiber, sinew, and cartilage. See Figure 6.12a.

Scoring
With a sharp knife, make cuts along the meat's tougher fibers and sinew. This not only helps tenderize the meat cut, but also frees the meat to lie flat on a heating surface for even cooking. See Figure 6.12b.

Grinding or Grounding
Run very tough cuts of meat through a grinder to make ground meat. Then form and cook the ground product in a number of different ways. See Figure 6.12c.

Figure 6.12a: Step 2—Tenderize the meat.

Figure 6.12b: Make cuts along the meat's tougher fibers and sinew.

Figure 6.12c: Ground meat through a grinder.

362

Figure Focus

Figure 6.12a: Pounding will break connective tissues and sinuous muscle fibers.

Figure 6.12b: Scoring cuts shorten the fibrous strands.

Figure 6.12c: Grinding chops the fibers into very small pieces.

Essential Skills
Chemical Tenderizing

❶ A number of chemically processed, powdered tenderizers are on the market. Apply the powder to the exterior of the meat.

❷ Some of these tenderizers work instantly, and others require time for the meat to sit. While such powdered tenderizers may work to a degree, many cooks avoid them because they can make the exterior mushy without ever penetrating the core of the meat. They can leave an unpleasant, chemical odor, and sometimes leech juice out of the meat, drying it out in the process of tenderizing.

Marinades

❶ As discussed in the text, a marinade not only tenderizes the meat, it also adds flavor. See Figure 6.13a.

❷ To tenderize, the marinade must contain an acid of some sort. The acid denatures, or unwinds, the longer protein fibers, thus tenderizing the meat. See Figure 6.13b.

❸ Marinating often requires a wait time for the acid to penetrate the meat and denature protein fibers, so allow time for this process before cooking.

❹ Marinades have the same drawbacks as powdered tenderizers: they may not penetrate deeply enough into the center of the meat. Special injectors are on the market to help with this problem. See Figure 6.13c.

Figure 6.13a: Step 1—Chili, lime and garlic, horseradish and lime, sesame oil and grainy mustard, tamarind and five spice, yogurt and ginger marinades.

Figure 6.13b: Step 2—Use an acid when tenderizing.

Figure 6.13c: Step 4—Marinades and powdered tenderizers may not penetrate deeply.

363

Essential Skills: Chemical Tenderizing

Enzymes and acids can break down and denature protein molecules.

Reinforce and Review

- pH is the measure of acidity.
- The lower the pH value, the more acidic a substance is.
- Water is neutral at pH 7.
- Lemon juice and lime juice are about pH 2 and will denature protein.
- Lime juice is the juice of the lime fruit.
- This is not to be confused with limewater, which does not include lime juice.
- "Lime" is another name for calcium hydroxide, an alkaline substance rather than an acid.
- Limewater is alkaline, about pH 12.
- It is used to break down corn for tortillas, a process discussed in Chapter 10.

Figure Focus

Figure 6.13a: All tenderizing marinades have an acid component.

Figure 6.13b: Lemon juice and vinegar are both about pH 3 or lower, strong enough to tenderize.

Figure 6.13c: Chemical tenderizers only tenderize by contact.

Discuss

- What is meant by "Time is money"?

- How would this relate to serving meat at a restaurant or foodservice operation?

- Help students realize that paying personnel to prepare meat is a cost to consider when comparing the prices of various methods of butchering and purchasing.

Vocabulary Terms

- **Contribution margin:** The amount of profit actually realized by the sale of an item, after all expenses are considered.

Essential Skills
Cooking, Stewing, or Braising

❶ Moist-heat cooking methods, such as stewing or braising, are also very good tenderizers, perhaps even the best method of tenderizing available.

❷ To properly tenderize through these methods, the meat must cook for an extended period of time to break down the collagen that composes the connective tissue. See Figure 6.14.

Figure 6.14: Step 2—Cook meat for an extended period to properly tenderize it.

Purchasing and Storing Meat

Purchase meat from processing plants inspected by the USDA or a state department of agriculture. Meat products that have been inspected will be stamped. These stamps don't appear on every single cut of meat, but one should be on every inspected carcass and on packaging.

The two highest cost areas of a restaurant and foodservice operation are labor and food costs. The lower each of these costs is in relation to the menu prices, the higher the operation's profit. It is a very delicate balancing act for any operation to manage. For example, an item with high initial cost, such as filet mignon, may require less kitchen labor to prepare, so the food cost and labor cost balance out. Items with high initial costs also may generate a higher retail value on the menu regardless of labor cost, which may make such high up-front costs worth it in the long run. This **contribution margin** is the marginal profit per unit sale. So, the successful operator will have a menu that balances the raw costs and menu prices for maximum profit.

The success of a meat dish often depends on choosing the right form or cut of meat for the intended use. Some types of meat are better suited to certain cooking methods than others. Consider the following general guidelines when purchasing meat:

- **Cost:** Fabrication is a way to reduce meat costs. The more fabricating an operation does itself, the more money it can save. Most restaurant and foodservice operations do not have the space, equipment, or time to butcher

364

Figure Focus
Figure 6.14: If moist cooking is too fast, the meat won't tenderize as well, and won't be as flavorful.

whole cuts of meat. Yet some operations purchase certain types of meat in partially fabricated forms to control the cost of buying premium-priced, uniform pieces.

- **Freshness**: Often, high-quality frozen meat does not appear that different from fresh meat products. Any quality lost is usually due to improper handling. For example, freezer burn occurs when an item is loosely wrapped. Ice crystals form on the surface and dry out the meat. Any product with freezer burn should be rejected at delivery because freezer burn reduces the texture and flavor of meat. In general, all meat products should be used within two to three days of purchase.

- **Fat content**: The fat content of meat products often influences the cooking method used. Meat with a higher fat content generally take to dry-heat cooking methods, such as grilling, broiling, and sautéing. Cuts of meat with greater **marbling** (lines of fat within the lean flesh portion of the meat) or a thicker skin or fat cap produce juices that keep the meat moist while cooking, even in dry heat. See Figure 6.15 for an example of meat with good marbling. Prepare meat with less fat or more tendons and tough fibers using a combination or moist-heat cooking methods, such as braising, stewing, or poaching. Meat with less fat comes from animal muscles that are used a lot, such as shanks, shoulders, or breasts. These items require long, slow cooking to break down the muscle fibers and render them tender.

Figure 6.15: Rib beef roast with good marbling.

- **Equipment**: Consider the types of equipment an operation has before deciding what types of meat products to purchase. Small restaurants may not have the space and variety of cooking equipment found in a large hotel or commercial foodservice establishment. Refrigeration and freezer space is also critical in that the operator may not have the space to purchase larger cuts or greater quantities of product.

- **Vendors**: It is always a good idea for an operation to shop around to ensure getting the best price for its needs. Check out the equipment, storage capabilities, labor costs, and transportation costs of competing vendors. It is important that an operation is paying for the quality of the product rather than the overhead of the vendor.

365

Figure Focus
Figure 6.15: Marbling helps keep meat moist and tender.

Reinforce and Review

- There are many cost considerations when purchasing and preparing meat.
- Meat is one of the most expensive food purchases a foodservice operation will make.
- Meat purchasing strategies—the right cuts and the right amount—have an impact on an operation's profitability.

In-Class Activity: Denaturing Protein Demonstration

Science Connection

Protein is made of assembled amino acid molecules. These types of chemical assemblies are called polymers.

If the protein is exposed to heat or acid, the amino acid polymer chains unravel. This is called denaturing, which means the nature has changed. Another word for it is cooked.

Using egg white and white fish, demonstrate denaturing of protein. Use heat in a frying pan and show the cooking process.

Next, use acid to denature protein. Lime juice is strongly acidic and will demonstrate the principle. Demonstrate the changes that occur by mixing egg white in lime juice.

Put the fish in lime juice. If the denaturing process is not visible during the class period, refrigerate it overnight and observe it during the next class meeting.

Teaching Tips

- If the students have taken biology, they have studied DNA replication and protein synthesis.
- This will build on their prior knowledge of proteins.

Vocabulary Terms

- **Marbling:** Lines of fat within the lean flesh portion of the meat.

Reinforce and Review

- Do not accept delivery or purchase of meat that is not excellent and fresh.

- Food safety is at risk if the storage temperature has ever been too high.

- Even if the meat is safe, it should be flavorful and high quality for serving guests.

- The cut should fit within the price point of the menu item for which the meat is intended.

In addition to considering all these criteria in making the initial meat purchase, carefully inspect the meat product before finalizing the transaction. Fresh meat must be delivered at 41°F or lower.

To be accepted during delivery, meat must meet the following criteria:

- **Color:**
  - **Beef:** Bright cherry red; aged beef may be darker in color; vacuum-packed beef will appear purplish in color
  - **Lamb:** Light red
  - **Pork:** Light pink meat; white fat
- **Texture:** Firm flesh that springs back when touched
- **Odor:** No odor
- **Packaging:** Intact and clean

Reject meat based on the following criteria:

- **Color** (see Figure 6.16):
  - **Beef:** Brown or green
  - **Lamb:** Brown, whitish surface covering the lean meat
  - **Pork:** Excessively dark color; soft or rancid fat

Figure 6.16a: A piece of browned and tainted meat as a result of freezer burn.

Figure 6.16b: A nicely colored red and tasty steak.

366

Figure Focus

Figure 6.16a: Freezer burn desiccates protein fibers by crystallizing the water as it freezes.

Figure 6.16b: Meat should look appetizing when raw so that it will look even more so when cooked.

■ **Texture**: Slimy, sticky, or dry

■ **Odor**: Sour odor

■ **Packaging**: Broken cartons; dirty wrappers; torn packaging; vacuum packaging with broken seal

■ **Freezer burn** (see Figure 6.17): Any signs of frost, ice, or leakage of the package

Finally, after purchasing the product and accepting it for delivery, properly store it. Proper storage guidelines are as follows:

■ Store meat immediately after delivery and inspection in its own storage unit or in the coldest part of the cooler. See Figure 6.18 for a picture of properly organized storage area.

■ Hold fresh meat at an internal temperature of 41°F or lower.

■ Store frozen meat at a temperature that will keep it frozen.

■ If storing meat in the same cooler as ready-to-eat food, be sure to store the meat *below* the ready-to-eat food.

■ Follow the FIFO method of stock rotation.

Figure 6.17: A hamburger patty with freezer burn. Freezer burn occurs when moisture on the surface evaporates.

Figure 6.18: If storing meat in the same cooler as ready-to-eat food, be sure to store the meat below the ready-to-eat food.

367

Reinforce and Review

· Freezer burn does not necessarily make meat unsafe, just unappealing.

· The water contained in the meat crystallizes and separates from the meat protein.

· Then, the water evaporates, leaving the meat "burned" and dehydrated.

· However, if meat was frozen, then thawed, and entered the temperature danger zone, then refrozen, it can harbor pathogens.

· Thawing and refreezing can cause the water to crystallize and cause freezer burn as well.

· Properly wrapped meat that displays freezer burn might be evidence of thawing during freezing.

· Keep frozen foods solid during frozen storage.

· When thawing, keep meat under refrigeration until cooked.

Figure Focus

Figure 6.17: Brown color is not necessarily caused by freezer burn, but the grayish color is.

Figure 6.18: Meat can express juices that can run into foods stored below the meat.

Discuss

- Can you "ruin" a filet mignon?

- What if you boiled it?

- The meat would still be wholesome and nutritious, but it would be wasted for the uniquely flavorful and tender qualities of the cut.

- The price of the meat would not be worth the finished product.

- Some meat should be cooked using a dry method. Very hot (high BTUs) is usually the best way to cook a tender cut. The idea is to stay out of the way of the meat

Cooking Techniques for Meat

The chef's goal while cooking meat is to maximize flavor and tenderness while minimizing the loss of moisture. As heat molecules attack the meat during cooking, the collagen breaks down into gelatin and water. This reduction in collagen increases the tenderness of the meat, but at the same time, the loss of moisture dries it out. A tough cut of meat cooked too quickly will still be too tough to serve when done. This is also true for a tender cut of meat cooked too long. This section summarizes the various ways of cooking meat so that it comes out tender, moist, and delicious.

Dry-heat Cooking

Because the tenderest cuts are the most expensive, cooking them in a slow, moist-heat method is not cost efficient, because a cheaper cut of meat would produce a quality product and actually offer more flavor. That is why dry-heat methods, which quickly cook meats, are best for naturally tender cuts. (See Figure 6.19 for meats that are cooked with the dry-heat method.)

Figure 6.19: Steaks and chops are best cooked with dry heat.

The dry-heat methods of broiling and grilling are best for tender meat. Such meat normally has enough fat to keep it moist through the dry-heat process. It is important to master these two basic cooking techniques. Steaks and chops are two cuts that hold up well to the dry heat of broiling and grilling.

Roasting is also a dry-heat cooking method. The tender cuts from the rib or tenderloin are ideal for roasting. Trim most of the visible fat to ensure even cooking. Then, sear the meat. Searing caramelizes the outside of the meat and improves the flavor and appearance of the finished product (see Figure 6.20 on the following page). You can also season roasts before cooking by marinating, barding, or stuffing, which is discussed at greater length later in this section.

While cooking, the roast should sit uncovered on an elevated rack inside a pan to ensure even cooking. To test for doneness, insert a bimetallic, stemmed, instant-reading thermometer at an angle into the thickest part of the meat at

Figure Focus
Figure 6.19: Let the tender cuts "speak for themselves."

any time during the cooking process. Roast meat uncovered until the proper internal temperature is reached. Degrees of doneness and internal temperatures are discussed later in this section.

Add a **mirepoix** (meer-PWAH), a combination of chopped aromatic vegetables—two parts onion, one part carrot, and one part celery—to the roasting pan during the final half-hour of roasting time to add flavor to the gravy. When finished, the roast should have a golden-brown exterior and an interior that is tender and moist.

Figure 6.20: A roast being seared.

Dry-heat Cooking with Fat and Oil

Another way to prepare meat is to use dry-heat cooking methods with fat and oil. These methods include sautéing, stir-frying, pan-frying, and deep-frying. Sautéing and stir-frying use a small amount of oil. Pan-frying uses a larger amount of oil and a coating. These methods cook meat quickly, use high heat, and require tender, portion-sized or smaller pieces of meat.

Serve sautéed meat with a sauce prepared while the food is cooking or by deglazing the pan after cooking. The sauce is an important element because it contains the food's flavor lost during cooking, introduces new flavor, and adds moisture. If meat strips are to be sautéed, lightly dust them with flour and be sure to shake off any excess flour before adding the item to the pan. Flour helps the meat retain moisture and promotes even browning. Beef Stroganoff is an example of preparing meat by sautéing.

Cut meat for stir-frying into small pieces, with all the fat, gristle, or silverskin removed. In stir-frying, cook food over very high heat, using little fat or cooking oil (see Figure 6.21 on the following page). Stir-fried meat should be moist and tender. An example is stir-fried beef with vegetables. (See Figure 6.22 on the following page for meats that are cooked using dry heat with fat and oil.)

369

Reinforce and Review

- High heat and fast cooking maintains the moisture of the meat.

- Meats with a high fat content can add calories to the dish.

- Stir-fry meat should be in pieces small enough to cook quickly in the wok.

- Searing creates a flavorful crust that helps develop the flavor and texture of a piece of meat.

In-Class Activity: "Time Is Money" and Other Profit Considerations

Mathematics Connection, 21st-Century Skills—Manage Goals and Time

In pairs, have the students strategize the most profitable way to use an entire beef carcass.

Your restaurant has been able to purchase an entire beef carcass at a very good price of $100.

There will be 50 guests in the restaurant over the weekend.

Using the entire carcass, feed the 50 guests. Develop a strategy for maximizing the profitability of the carcass.

Which pair can generate the most income from the carcass?

They must consider meat cost, cost of other ingredients, time, and personnel.

Have students present their strategies to one another. Which pair of students made the most money from their carcass?

Vocabulary Terms

- **Mirepoix:** A combination of chopped aromatic vegetables added to the roasting pan during the final half-hour of roasting time to add flavor to the gravy.

Figure Focus

Figure 6.20: Searing is best done in the same pan a roast will be cooked in, to fully develop the flavor.

Reinforce and Review

- Moist heat methods can use a lot of water or broth, or just a little.

- Water or broth cooking methods should enhance the flavor, not dilute it.

Figure 6.21: Chopped red peppers, carrots, and green onions being stir-fried in a wok.

Figure 6.22: Veal and pork are meats that are best cooked using dry heat with fat and oil.

Moist-heat Cooking

Moist-heat cooking techniques produce food that is delicately flavored and moist with a rich broth. Poach, simmer, or boil tougher cuts of meat. Cook an entire boiled dinner, complete with vegetables and meat, in one pot. A New England boiled dinner is one example using the boiling method. Yankee pot roast is an example of cooking with the simmering method. This method is also used heavily in ethnic cuisines, such as a North African *tagine*. (See Figure 6.23 for meat that is cooked with the moist-heat method.)

Figure 6.23: Ham is best cooked with the moist-heat method.

370

Figure Focus

Figure 6.21: Wok cooking is quick and hot in either oil or water.

Figure 6.22: Veal and pork can be delicate and prone to drying out.

Figure 6.23: Ham can become stringy if it dries out.

Combination Cooking

The combination cooking methods, braising and stewing, use both dry and moist heat to cook food that is not very tender. First, sear the meat in hot oil and then slowly cook it with a small amount of liquid in the oven or on the stove. Stewing is very much like braising, except the meat or other major ingredient is cut into bite-size pieces before it is seared (see Figure 6.24).

Figure 6.24: Meat being prepared using combination cooking.

Supplemental Cooking Techniques: Marinades, Rubs, and Barding

A number of techniques have been developed to impart additional flavor while reducing moisture loss during all of the cooking processes described previously. One of the most popular methods is to soak the raw meat in a marinade—a liquid made of oil, an acid such as vinegar or wine, and herbs and spices. The acid in the marinade breaks down the collagen along the surface of the meat and allows the flavoring from the aromatics to enter. Refrigerate the meat while marinating and turn it on occasion to equally distribute the marinade. This method will not turn a tough piece of meat into tenderloin, but it will improve the flavor of the cooked meat.

Another method used to impart additional flavor is called a dry marinade or spice rub, which is a combination of dry herbs, spices, and salt that give the exterior of the meat an attractive look and flavorful taste. Use caution because the salt, while breaking down the surface structure, also pulls moisture from the meat.

Figure 6.25: To bard, tie some type of fat (bacon or fatback) around what is being cooked to prevent it from drying out while roasting. Barding bastes the meat while it is cooking.

Game meat has much less fat in its muscle than domesticated animals. It may be necessary to **bard** meat that has little or no natural fat cover in order to protect and moisten them during cooking. Tie a layer of fat (bacon or pork fatback) around the roast. Also use this technique on leaner roasts, such as veal tenderloin. Figure 6.25 shows the process of barding.

371

Discuss

- Is dry meat ever a good thing?

- Most ideal cooking methods are chosen to protect moisture content, tenderness, and texture.

- Barding meat or adding fat can protect delicate meat.

- Have the students ever used a dry rub for flavoring meat?

- Perhaps they have used barbeque sauce. If so, have they discovered that barbeque sauce burns during cooking?

- Barbeque sauce is not a marinade or basting sauce; it is a condiment.

Vocabulary Terms

- **Bard:** Add a layer of fat for roasting to maintain moisture.

Figure Focus

Figure 6.24: More than one method might be the best for certain cuts.

Figure 6.25: Basting means bathing the meat in moisture as it cooks.

Discuss

- If you went to a restaurant and ordered a steak well done, what would you expect?

- What if it were served pink in the middle?

- What should a guest do if the meat is not cooked as he or she ordered it?

- What impact will refused or redone food have on the bottom line?

- Cooking meat orders correctly helps improve profitability.

- Always keep carryover cooking in mind when determining doneness.

- Gain experience cooking meat to be accurate.

Table 6.2: Determining Doneness

- The standards for doneness are well established. They need to be consistently understood by guests.

Vocabulary Terms

- **Carryover cooking:** Meat continues to cook with retained heat even after being removed from a heat source.

Determining Doneness

One of the most important steps in cooking meat is determining the doneness. Food preparers can cook beef, lamb, and some game meat to a wide range of doneness. A beef roast is rare when the internal temperature is 130°F. The meat appears red inside with a thin layer of brown on the outside. At an internal temperature of 145°F, the roast is medium. The meat is pink inside with a well-browned surface. The surface of meat cooked to medium is firmer than rare meat. Well-done meat is completely cooked, leaving little or no juice. The cooked surface of the meat is firm and dry, and the internal temperature is 160°F. In general, as meat cooks, the exterior should develop a deep brown color. Allow a roast to rest for 15 to 30 minutes after removing from the oven. This allows less juice to be lost during carving. See Table 6.2 for a complete chart of determining doneness.

Table 6.2: Determining Doneness

Some common terms indicate a degree of doneness for a product.

Rare	• The item has been seared on both sides. • Meat offers no resistance when pressed. • Cut meat is red to almost blue in color. • Warm all the way through.
Medium rare	• Cook until drops of blood rise to the upper surface; turn and brown on the other side. • When pressed, the meat should have a spongy feel. • Color should be bright pink to red when cut.
Medium	• Turn meat when drops of juice are visible on surface; brown other side until meat resists when pressed. • When cut, the meat should be pink in the center.
Well done	• Turn meat when drops of juice are clearly visible on surface; then cook until firm to the touch. • Heat fully penetrates to the center of the meat. • When cut, there should be no trace of pink.

Note that the heat absorbed during the cooking process continues to cook the meat even after it is removed from the oven. This is called **carryover cooking.** The larger the item, the greater the amount of heat it retains, and the more carryover cooking takes place. For example, the temperature of a top round of beef may increase as much as 15°F degrees after being taken out of the oven. For this reason, it is a good idea to take the meat out of the oven just before it reaches the desired temperature.

Cook white meat, such as veal and pork, all the way through, but do not over-cook it. When it is done, the meat gives slightly when pressed with the back of a fork. As white meat cooks, the meat changes from pink to white or off-white. The meat is generally cooked well done, although many cuts of veal are considered done while still slightly pink in the center. Remember to be careful, since carryover heat can have a large impact on these thin pieces of meat. Table 6.3 lists the best cooking method for each type of meat.

Table 6.3: Meat Cuts and Cooking Method	
Type of Meat	**Cut and Cooking Method That Can Be Used**
Beef	Steaks: Dry heat (broil or grill) Rib roast: Dry heat (roast) Short ribs: Combination (braise) Top round: Dry heat (roast) or combination (braise) Brisket: Moist heat (simmer)
Veal	Foreshank: Combination (braise) Hotel rack: Dry heat (grill, broil, or roast) Loin chop: Dry heat (grill or broil) or dry heat with fat/oil (sauté) Hindshank: Moist heat (simmer) or combination (braise) Tenderloin: Dry heat (grill, broil, roast) or dry heat with fat/oil (sauté)
Lamb	Lamb rack: Dry heat (grill, broil, roast) or dry heat with fat/oil (sauté) Loin chops: Dry heat (grill, broil) or dry heat with fat/oil (sauté) Leg of lamb: Dry heat (grill, broil, roast) Breast: Combination (braise)
Pork	Spare ribs: Combination (steam, then grill) Pork loin: Dry heat (roast) or combination (braise) Pork tenderloin: Dry heat (broil, grill, roast) or dry heat with fat/oil (sauté) Pork loin chop: Dry heat (broil or grill) or combination (braise) Fresh ham: Dry heat (roast)

[fast fact]

Did You Know...?
Did you know that jus (ZHEW) is a sauce that incorporates drippings released during roasting? Make jus by deglazing the roasting pan with brown stock or water. Deglazing means to swirl a liquid in a pan to dissolve cooked particles or food remaining on the bottom. Food served with this juice is said to be served au jus (oh ZHEW); for example, roast beef au jus. When the jus from the drippings is thickened with arrowroot or cornstarch, it is known as *jus lié* (zhew lee-AY). Sauce thickened with a roux incorporating the fat from a roast and additional water or stock is called pan gravy.

373

**Nutrition:
Marbling**

Students might find it interesting to realize that their muscles "marble," too.

**Essential Skills:
Rendering Fat**

Rendered fat is melted to liquid and runs out. It can then be saved separately.

Marbling

Animals store excess energy in fatty deposits within muscles. These deposits are referred to as marbling. The streaks of whitish-yellow fat within the red muscle look a bit like red marble stone, hence the name. The fat is actually around and between the individual muscle fibers and between connective tissues. The type of feed and exercise of the animal determines the amount of fat marbling.

Generally speaking, the greater the marbling in the meat, the higher the quality grade of the meat. Marbling does not necessarily indicate tenderness, but well-marbled meat is the most flavorful and juicy. This means that the higher quality grades may actually be less attractive from a nutrition perspective because of a higher fat content. Large and/or frequent portions of high-fat meat increases the saturated fat and cholesterol in the diet, which puts more stress on the heart and circulation. As with most any food, moderation is the best strategy.

Essential Skills
Rendering Fat

Use animal fat directly from the meat or render it, extracting the fat from the physical structure of the meat. Use rendered fat to flavor other dishes.

❶ Cut the fat from the meat into uniform 1-inch cubes. See Figure 6.26a.

❷ Place the fat in a pot and add enough water to come halfway up the fat.

❸ Cook on low heat until the fat is melted and all the water has evaporated. See Figure 6.26b.

❹ Remove the fat from the heat and let it cool for 10 minutes.

❺ Strain the fat into containers and place in a cooler.

Figure 6.26a: Step 1—Cut the fat from the meat.

Figure 6.26b: Step 3—Cook on low heat.

374

Figure Focus

Figure 6.26a: Cutting away visible fat.

Figure 6.26b: Melt away the remaining fat.

Summary

In this section, you learned the following:

- The two grades of meat are quality grade and yield grade. Quality grade measures the flavor characteristics of meat products. Meat is evaluated for traits that indicate its tenderness, juiciness, and flavor. Quality grades for beef, lamb, and veal can include Prime, Choice, Select, Standard, Commercial, Utility, Cutter, Cull, or Canner. Yield grade measures the proportion of edible or usable meat after it has been trimmed of bones or fat. You can get yield grades for beef, pork, and lamb products. This can be helpful because the differences in the amount of fat on the outside of the meat can cause the yield of usable product to vary.

- A number of butchering processes take place with meat. The first is called primal cuts. Primal cuts are the primary divisions of meat produced by the initial butchering of animal carcasses. After primal cuts are made, fabrication can take place. Fabrication is the process of butchering primal cuts into usable portions, such as roasts or steaks. Retail cuts of meat are those cuts that are ready for sale. They can be primal cuts or fabricated portions. The amount of cutting or butchering necessary to prepare a retail cut affects its price. Use cuts from the boneless loin or tenderloin of beef, veal, lamb, or pork to make a variety of menu cuts, including medallions, noisettes, scallops, and eminé. Offal meat is organ meat cut from hogs, cattle, or sheep. It includes sweetbreads, liver, kidney, tripe, heart, and brains.

- Meat must be purchased from plants inspected by the USDA or a state department of agriculture. Meat products that have been inspected will be stamped. In addition to USDA inspection approval, a number of other factors should be considered when purchasing meat:

  - **Cost**: Fabrication is a way to reduce meat costs. The more fabricating an operation does itself, the more money it can save.

  - **Freshness**: Often, high-quality frozen meat does not appear that different from a fresh meat product. Any quality lost is usually due to improper handling. In general, all meat products should be used within two to three days of purchase.

  - **Fat content**: The fat content of meat products often influences the cooking method used. Meat with a higher fat content generally takes to dry-heat cooking methods, such as grilling, broiling, and sautéing. Meat with less fat or more tendons and tough fibers can be prepared using moist-heat cooking methods, such as braising, stewing, and poaching.

375

Summary

- Remind students to review the following:
  1. Grades of meat
  2. Cuts of meat
  3. Purchasing and storing meat
  4. Cooking techniques for meat
  5. Determining doneness

- **Equipment:** Deciding what types of meat products to purchase is often determined by the types of equipment an operation has. Refrigeration and freezer space are also critical in determining what type of meat to purchase.

- **Vendors**: Check out the equipment, storage capabilities, labor costs, and transportation costs of competing vendors. It is important that an operation is paying for the quality of the product rather than the overhead of the vendor from which it is buying.

■ Before a chef can determine the right cooking method for a cut of meat, he or she must understand the physical composition of the muscle tissue and how it is affected by heat. A good cook must also be aware of the numerous flavorings that he or she can add when cooking meat. The chef's goal while cooking meat is to maximize flavor and tenderness while minimizing the loss of moisture. Do this in a number of ways, such as by using marinades, dry rubs, and barding. The main cooking methods are moist heat, dry heat, dry heat with oil or fat, and combination cooking. Carryover cooking is the heat that continues to cook the meat even after the chef pulls it from the heat source.

Section 6.1 Review Questions

1. What are the two primary grades of meat? Describe them.

2. What is the name of the meat cut made in the initial butchering process? What happens after that step?

3. List three factors that should be considered when purchasing meat and explain why each is important.

4. On what types of meat cuts should the moist-heat cooking method be used?

5. Charleen Obal likes braised short ribs. What kind of meat is used for short ribs? How is the meat cooked to maximize flavor and tenderness while minimizing the loss of moisture?

6. What will Miguel and Chef Kate have to seriously think about if they want to focus on serving meat? List three factors you feel they must consider and explain why each is so important.

7. What is your philosophy about eating meat? Why? Explain and defend your position. Explain and defend the opposing view.

8. Of the five main factors listed for purchasing meat, which three do you think are the most important? Why? Explain your rationale for each choice.

377

Section 6.1 Review Questions

1. Prime is the highest grade available, often only to restaurants. Choice is the next grade, still excellent, and available to all foodservice and grocery store customers.

2. This is the primal cut, which is further butchered into retail cuts.

3. There are several factors that can be used. They are found on pp. 365 and 366.

4. Less tender cuts are best cooked by moist-heat cooking.

5. Ribs from the chuck primal plate are used for short ribs that are braised. They are cooked using moist heat.

6. Each student will have his or her own opinion on this. They can use the issues on pp. 365 and 366 to help determine real pricing of beef for their restaurant.

7. Let students decide why they feel the way they do. Help them to thoughtfully consider another point of view.

8. The students will each have an opinion about this. The items are on pp. 365 and 366.

Section 6.1 Activities

1. The various groups' contributions will make a complete lesson.

2. Searing does not "seal in juices," but it does caramelize and develop flavor both on the outside of the meat and in the pan for flavoring the water or broth.

3. The students should develop an understanding of the material with this project.

Section 6.1 Activities

1. Study Skills/Group Activity: Researching Meat

Divide into groups. Each group researches a type of meat: beef, pork, lamb, etc. Then, create a brochure about each type, showing and naming the different market cuts of this type. Present the information to the class.

2. Activity: Behind the Sear

What is "searing"? Why is it done? Investigate searing and write a paragraph about what is happening when food is seared. Write a second paragraph about the role searing plays in properly cooking meat, making sure to distinguish fact versus fiction.

3. Critical Thinking: Matching Cuts with Cooking

List all the different cuts of beef from one carcass. Then indicate whether dry heat or moist heat is best for each cut. Finally, create a menu item description for a dry-heat cut. Do the same for a moist-heat cut.

6.1 Meat	6.2 Poultry	6.3 Seafood	6.4 Charcuterie and Garde Manger
• Grades of meat	• Grades of poultry	• Seafood inspections and grades	• Definitions of charcuterie and garde manger
• Cuts of meat	• Two forms of poultry: white and dark	• Forms of seafood	• Types of charcuterie
• Purchasing and storing meat	• Purchasing, fabricating, and storing poultry	• Purchasing, fabricating, and storing seafood	
• Cooking techniques for meat	• Cooking techniques for poultry	• Cooking techniques for seafood	
• Determining doneness		• Determining doneness	

SECTION 6.2 POULTRY

Poultry is arguably the most versatile protein. You can find it on the menu of virtually all restaurants and foodservice establishments, from less expensive to more expensive. Poultry can be served as a main course, in a casserole, in a sandwich, even on pizza. It is a truly versatile protein.

Study Questions

After studying Section 6.2, you should be able to answer the following questions:

- What are the various grades of poultry?

- What are the forms of poultry?

- What are the guidelines for purchasing, fabricating, and storing poultry?

- What are the basic cooking techniques used to prepare poultry?

Grades of Poultry

U.S. poultry grades apply to chicken, turkey, duck, geese, guinea, and pigeon. Quality grades are available for whole poultry, poultry roasts, poultry tenderloins, and poultry parts, including those with or without skin or bone, and either fresh or frozen. The USDA (see Figure 6.27 on the following page) is responsible for both inspecting and grading poultry.

Poultry receives a Grade of A, B, or C (A being the highest), based upon a number of guidelines:

- Poultry must have a good conformation, structure, and shape, and be free of deformity in the natural form of the product, such as a bent leg or curved backbone.

- Other factors taken into account involve flesh, fat covering, defeathering, discolorations, signs of broken or disjointed bones, and freezing defects.

379

Section 6.2
Poultry

Introduce the Section

a. Poultry is more than chicken, turkey, and game birds.

b. Poultry is graded.

c. Poultry must be handled properly for safety.

d. Poultry has recommended cooking techniques.

Vocabulary Review

a. Direct students to the key terms.

b. Pronounce each word, and have the students repeat the pronunciation out loud.

c. Discuss the definition of each word.

Teach

Discuss

- Poultry of all grades is wholesome and safe.

- Physical characteristics are considered when grading poultry.

Vocabulary Terms

- **Poultry**: Domesticated birds raised for food.

Discuss

- Ask the students, "Would you eat grade B or C poultry?" They probably already do.

- Grade A is more attractive poultry for plating.

Reinforce and Review

- Poultry should be thoroughly cooked until the juices run clear.

- Poultry should not be overcooked or dried out.

■ Boneless poultry roasts should be free of all bone, cartilage, tendons, visible bruises, and blood clots. Tenderloin, a boneless portion of poultry cut from the breast area, is expected to have tendons; however, the tendons must not extend more than one-half inch beyond the meat tissue.

Use Grade A poultry as is, meaning cook the bird and its parts and consume them in their entirety, without processing. Use Grades B and C poultry in processed products where the poultry meat is cut up, chopped, or ground. Products sold at retail are usually not grade identified. Although all poultry must be inspected, no grade standards exist for some poultry parts, such as neck, wing tip, tail, and giblets.

Figure 6.27: The USDA (U.S. Department of Agriculture) inspects and grades poultry.

Within the grade levels, select poultry by class. The class of poultry is defined mostly by the age and gender of the bird. A bird's age generally affects the tenderness, look, and feel of the bird. It also affects the cooking methods necessary to obtain maximum flavor quality. Older birds are less tender than their younger counterparts and are best prepared using moist-heat cooking methods, such as stewing and braising. More tender, younger birds are suitable for all cooking methods, including barbecuing and frying.

Two Forms of Poultry: White and Dark

The two distinct differences in poultry forms are white meat and dark meat (see Figure 6.28 on the following page). Each type of meat holds different nutrition values.

White meat is from the areas of the fowl where little muscle use takes place, such as the breast. As a result, white meat is low in calories and fat content. White meat also cooks faster, which can result in a dryer product if the chef is not careful. Chefs can both grill and sauté white meat. When roasting poultry, chefs can add fat under or over the skin, or they can baste it with stock or melted butter to help retain moistness.

380

Figure Focus

Figure 6.27: All the grades of poultry are wholesome and safe.

Figure 6.28a: White meat.

Figure 6.28b: Dark meat.

Dark meat, on the other hand, is from areas where the bird's muscles are used more heavily, such as the leg and thigh region. Dark meat is higher in calories and fat. Dark meat also tends to be the richer, more flavorful meat. It requires more time to cook. Chefs may cook dark meat with either dry-heat or moist-heat cooking methods, depending on the amount of tendon and fiber in these parts. For example, they may grill or sauté the thighs, whereas the drumstick lends itself to braising or to roasting.

[trends]

Want More Chicken?
Chicken consumption in the United States has risen by approximately 3 times in the last 40 years. In 1960, Americans annually consumed approximately 30 pounds of chicken per person. Today, that number is up to approximately 90 pounds.

Purchasing, Fabricating, and Storing Poultry

Domestic poultry is readily available and less costly than most other meat. A recent change in the market is the greater availability of free-range poultry, which is raised in large yards and given a lot of space to roam and get some exercise. The meat is darker in color than other poultry and has a slightly different flavor and texture.

New interest also exists in game birds—wild birds such as partridge, pheasant, squab, duck, goose, and quail—that are hunted for sport or food. Many game birds are now raised on farms year-round in conditions similar to those for free-range poultry. These birds are still considered "wild" and are at their best for purchasing from October through December or January. They should have

381

Reinforce and Review

- There are several types of poultry besides chicken.

- Game birds are quite popular.

- Free range poultry can have a delicious flavor.

- Ratite birds, such as emu, ostrich, and rhea, have red meat.

Trends:
Want More Chicken?

Chicken is nutritious and tends to be lower in fat than most red meat.

Figure Focus

Figure 6.28a: White meat is from the breast, which does not carry the weight of the bird.

Figure 6.28b: Dark meat is from muscle that is used more during the bird's life.

Reinforce and Review

- The purchasing considerations are the same for poultry as for other meat.

- Birds can be purchased whole and fabricated in house.

- Birds can also be roasted whole.

- Sometimes it is cost effective to purchase poultry already fabricated.

Vocabulary Terms

- **Boning:** Removing the bones.

soft, smooth, pliable skin. The breastbone cartilage should be flexible, as it is for domestic fowl. The flesh should be tender, with a slightly "gamey" taste.

Take the first basic step in purchasing poultry by deciding on the type and quality of product that is needed for the particular menu item, the intended use of the poultry. Restaurant and foodservice operations usually use U.S. Grade A quality for poultry. Many of the same guidelines for poultry purchasing are similar to those discussed earlier for meat purchasing. They are summarized here:

- **Freshness:** As with meat products, high-quality frozen poultry does not look different from a fresh poultry product. Any quality lost, such as through freezer burn, is usually due to improper handling; reject these products upon delivery. In general, use all poultry products within two to three days of purchase.

- **Form:** The operation determines whether dark meat or white meat is preferable depending on its particular needs and makes purchases accordingly.

- **Equipment:** An operation decides what types of poultry products to purchase and how much to purchase by considering the types of equipment it has. For example, refrigeration space, freezer space, and adequate workspace areas for fabrication.

- **Vendors:** Check out the equipment, storage capabilities, labor costs, and transportation costs of competing vendors. An operation is paying for the quality of the product rather than the overhead of the vendor from which it is buying.

- **Cost:** As with meat purchases, in-house fabrication is a way to reduce costs. Operations finds it easier to fabricate poultry because the birds are smaller in size and easier to butcher. The more fabricating an operation does itself, the better the quality and the better the price. Also, the operation can use the trim for stocks, soups, sauces, hors d'oeuvres, and forcemeats.

Poultry fabrication includes disjointing and **boning** (separating meat from bones), and cutting a bird into pieces. Fabricating poultry is easier than fabricating other meat because poultry bones are smaller and easier to cut through. Essential tools include a clean work surface, boning knife, and chef's knife.

Breaking down poultry into pieces is a useful technique for both small and large birds. The size of the cut depends on the size of the bird and the method of cooking. Knowing how to disjoint and bone chicken breasts is also an important part of fabricating poultry. Not all birds are fabricated or cut into smaller pieces. Larger birds are often roasted whole.

382

Essential Skills
Cutting a Whole Bird Into Pieces

Fabrication of a whole chicken into eight parts is a basic skill needed in the professional kitchen. The skill allows the chef to prepare many dishes as well as save money by buying whole birds.

❶ The first step is to square up the bird by placing it on its back and pressing on the legs and breast to create a uniform appearance. See Figure 6.29a.

❷ Next remove the leg and thigh from the body by cutting between the joints close to bones in the back of the bird. Repeat for the other side. See Figure 6.29b.

❸ Place the bird on its breast and cut through the skin and straight down along either side of the backbone from tail to head.

❹ Cut the ribs that connect the backbone removing the backbone. See Figure 6.29c.

❺ To cut the breast in two pieces, place the chicken skin side down and starting at the wishbone cut through separating breasts into two halves. Bending the sides of the bird backwards before hand will make it easier to cut. See Figure 6.29d.

❻ To separate the leg potion from the thigh, make a cut following the line of fat on the inside of the thigh. This is done with skin side down and cutting through the joint. See Figure 6.29e.

❼ To separate the wings from the breast pull the wing away form body and cut inside each wing along the joint. See Figure 6.29f.

❽ You now have two wings, two breasts, two legs, and two thighs

Figure 6.29a: Step 1—Square up the bird.

Figure 6.29b: Step 2—Remove leg and thigh by cutting between the joints.

Figure 6.29c: Step 4—Cut the ribs that connect the backbone, removing the backbone.

Essential Skills:
Cutting a Whole Bird into Pieces
It might be cost effective for an establishment to fabricate whole fowl.

Figure Focus
Figures 6.29a–6.29f: Review the steps used to cut a whole bird into pieces.

Reinforce and Review

- There are standards for wholesomeness for poultry delivery.

- Refuse poultry that does not meet safety standards.

Figure 6.29d: Step 5—Cut the breast in two pieces.

Figure 6.29e: Step 6—Separate the leg from the thigh.

Figure 6.29f: Step 7—Pull the wing away from the body and cut each wing along the joint.

Essential Skills
Fabricating Boneless Chicken Breasts

❶ Make a cut along the side of the breastbone and following the line of the bone use you thumb or boning knife and separate the breast from the rib bones. See Figure 6.30a.

❷ Pull the meat gently away as you cut being careful to leave the tender pieces known as the tenderloins attached to the breast meat. Remove the breast meat from the bird by making a cut to separate the breast from the wing. See Figure 6.30b.

Figure 6.30a: Step 1—Make a cut along the side of the breast-bone.

Figure 6.30b: Step 2—Remove breast meat by making a cut to separate the breast from the wing.

384

Figure Focus
Figures 6.30a–6.30b: Review the steps taken to fabricate chicken breasts.

Fresh poultry should be delivered at 41°F or lower. Frozen poultry should be received frozen. Accept a delivery of poultry when it meets the following criteria:

- **Color**: No discoloration
- **Texture**: Firm flesh that springs back when touched
- **Odor**: No odor

Reject a delivery of poultry for the following reasons:

- **Color**: Purple or green discoloration around the neck; dark wing tips (red tips are acceptable)
- **Texture**: Stickiness under the wings and around the joints
- **Odor**: Abnormal, unpleasant odor
- **Freezer burn**: Any signs of frost, ice, or leakage of the package

Store fresh, raw poultry at an internal temperature of 41°F or lower. Store frozen poultry at a temperature that keeps it frozen. If poultry has been removed from its original packaging, place it in airtight containers or wrap it in airtight material. Remember to store poultry below ready-to-eat food if they are both stored in the same cooler. Finally, be sure to follow FIFO. Table 6.4 describes the different bird types.

Table 6.4: Bird Types

Bird	Description
Chicken	Young chicken: rock Cornish hen, broiler, fryer, roaster, capon Mature chicken: hen, fowl, baking chicken, stewing chicken
Turkey	Young turkey: fryer-roaster, young hen, young tom Yearling turkey: mature turkey, old turkey
Duck	Young duck: duckling, young duckling, broiler duckling, fryer duckling, roaster duckling Old duck: mature

(continued)

385

ServSafe Connection: Safely Storing and Fabricating Poultry

Carefully follow foodhandling guidelines for poultry.

ServSafe Connection: Maintaining Safe Cutting Boards

Wooden cutting boards can be safe, effective tools. Chefs interested in using them must first make sure they are allowed according to local food safety laws.

Table 6.4: Bird Types *continued*	
Bird	**Description**
Goose/Guinea	Young goose: guinea Old goose: mature
Pigeon	Young pigeon: squab Old pigeon: pigeon

[ServSafe Connection]

Safely Storing and Fabricating Poultry

Strictly observe the following food safety rules in poultry fabrication to prevent cross-contamination:

❶ Clean and sanitize cutting boards and all cutting utensils before and after fabrication.

❷ Refrigerate poultry when it is not being fabricated.

❸ Store poultry in clear, leakproof containers at 41°F or lower.

❹ Never store uncooked poultry above cooked meat, and never store uncooked poultry above ready-to-eat foods.

[ServSafe Connection]

Maintaining Safe Cutting Boards

A "butcher block" is a hardwood cutting surface used for food preparation. See Figure 6.31. Some states have banned the use of these types of wooden cutting boards and other surfaces (such as a butcher-block table) in food-related operations. But many butchers and foodservice professionals appreciate the quality, appearance, and tradition of these materials. Where butcher-block surfaces are allowed, they can be used safely as long as you treat them with the proper care to prevent pathogen growth and cross-contamination.

Figure 6.31: Butcher block.

Most acceptable butcher blocks are made of hard maple. The surface should be cleaned and sanitized following the same guidelines for any other food-contact surface. Some

386

Figure Focus

Figure 6.31: Ask students if they agree that butcher-block cutting surfaces should be banned.

companies create special cleaners for butcher block surfaces; be sure that these cleaners follow regulatory guidelines before using them. The surfaces also must be planed (its top layer removed) or sanded regularly. The surface can be "sanded" by rubbing it with coarse salt. This is far better than sandpaper, which is not recommended for culinary equipment. The gentle abrasion of the salt wears down the cuts and slits caused by knives, which can harbor pathogens. Additionally, the surface should be "seasoned" quarterly with a rubdown of food-grade mineral oil that is fresh and free from aroma or flavor.

The remaining surface must be free of pits, grooves, or cracks. Health inspectors look for any split in the wood or an uneven surface level where pathogens might be able to grow. If they find a problem, the item must be thrown out. Similarly, plastic cutting boards must also be replaced when they have been worn down or cut or scored too often.

All cutting boards should be dedicated for a type for food (some are color coded for this purpose). For example, there should be one board for meat products and a different one for vegetables. The boards should be cleaned and sanitized immediately after use. Never use a soiled board without properly cleaning and sanitizing it. And never use a meat or poultry board to chop raw vegetables.

[what's new]

Exotic Birds

Ratites are birds with wings that are inadequate for flight. Emu and ostrich are ratites. They lay edible eggs like other birds, and the meat of the bird is edible as well. In fact, their dark meat seems more like red meat than any other poultry. Emu is classified as a red meat in the United States. Ostrich meat is higher in iron than even beef, and much higher than turkey or other, more common, poultry. Emu, ostrich, and other ratites are finding their way onto restaurant menus around the world.

Cooking Techniques for Poultry
Dry-heat Cooking

Poultry is especially suited to the dry-heat cooking techniques of grilling, broiling, and roasting. When grilling poultry, cook it through or *à point* (ah PWAH), but do not overcook. Pressing the meat with the back of a form yields a slight amount of "give." Any juices are colorless. The grilled flavor and aroma should enhance the food, not overpower its natural flavor. One example of chicken prepared using this method is mesquite-grilled chicken breast.

Roasting requires a longer cooking time because this technique is used to cook the whole bird. For roasting, **truss**—which means the legs and wings are tied to the bird's body—the bird so it cooks evenly and stays moist. The chef can season, stuff, marinate, bard, and/or sear the bird over direct heat or in a hot oven before roasting. Then place it on an elevated rack in a roasting pan so that hot

387

**What's New:
Exotic Birds**

Ratites are considered exotic birds, and are eaten throughout the world.

Reinforce and Review

- Most poultry does not carry *Salmonella* spp. but some does.

- Handle all poultry with food safety in mind.

- Poultry should be cooked until there is no pink and the juices run clear.

- A roasting bird should smell very good and appetizing.

Vocabulary Terms

- *À point:* Correct cooking for poultry.

- **Truss:** To tie a bird's body for cooking.

- Make sure students understand the difference between opaque, translucent, and transparent.

- Raw chicken is translucent, whereas cooked chicken is opaque. When chicken is undercooked, there is still a translucence in the thicker parts.

air can reach all sides. Roast the bird uncovered until the desired internal temperature is reached (see Figure 6.32).

Cook poultry until well done (165°F) to kill all traces of *Salmonella* spp. Bake dressing and stuffing for poultry separately for food safety; however, food preparers can safely stuff small birds (Cornish hens and quail) and serve them as single portions. Also, cook the stuffing in these birds to 165°F. The skin should be crisp, creating a contrast with the meat's texture. Roasted herb chicken with natural gravy is one example of using the roasting cooking method.

Figure 6.32: A whole roast turkey cooked to desired doneness.

Dry-heat Cooking with Fat and Oil

Poultry is especially well suited to dry-heat cooking with fat and oil. These techniques—sautéing, stir-frying, pan-frying, and deep-frying—require tender, portion-size pieces.

Combine chicken with a variety of vegetables and other food to create a stir-fry dish. Pat marinated chicken until dry before adding it to the cooking oil. One example of using this technique is stir-fried chicken with vegetables. (See Figure 6.33 for poultry that is cooked using dry heat with fat and oil.)

One of the most traditional methods for preparing chicken is deep-frying. Chicken that is deep-fried must be naturally tender. Food prepared by deep-frying is breaded or batter coated and then boiled in hot fat or oil. The result is a nice combination of flavors and textures. Always observe sanitation guidelines when you are working with batter.

Figure 6.33: Vegetables and chicken being cooked using dry heat.

388

Figure Focus

Figure 6.32: The beautiful roasted skin of the turkey is part of the delicacy.

Figure 6.33: Dry heat can be excellent for a stir-fry preparation.

Moist-heat Cooking

Steaming is a healthy way to pre-pare poultry because nutrients are not washed away or drawn out of the food during cooking. Steamed poultry is done when it has an evenly **opaque** (oh-PAKE) appearance, which means you should not be able to see through it when done. Also, the flesh offers little resistance when pressed. (See Figure 6.34 for poultry that is cooked with the moist-heat method.)

Simmering and poaching are also excellent ways to prepare chicken. Simmered chicken has a rich, flavorful broth and can be used for soups, creamed dishes, casseroles, and salads.

Figure 6.34: Chicken being cooked with the moist-heat method.

Combination Cooking

Chicken is a natural ingredient for the combination cooking methods of stew-ing and braising. These two methods produce dishes with exceptional sauces and flavor concentrations. In addition, these are very healthy choices because the proteins and other nutrients lost from other cooking techniques are retained in the sauce. *Mole poblano,* a popular Mexican sauce, is used to make Chicken Mole. This is one example of poultry prepared with moist-heat cook-ing. Table 6.5 describes various methods of cooking poultry.

Table 6.5: Cooking Poultry	
Type of Poultry	**Class and Cooking Method That Can Be Used**
Chicken	Game hen: Dry heat (broil, grill, or roast) Broiler/fryer: Any cooking method Roaster: Any cooking method
Duck	Broiler/fryer: Dry heat (roast) Roaster: Dry heat (roast) Mature: Combination (braise)

(continued)

389

Reinforce and Review

- Nearly any cooking technique can be successful for chicken and other poultry.

- Combination techniques are often used with poultry dishes.

- It is wise to learn tried-and-true techniques before attempting experimentation with poultry cooking.

Table 6.5: Cooking Poultry

- There are different cooking methods that work well for various types of poultry.

Vocabulary Terms

- **Opaque:** Does not allow any light to be seen through it.

- *Mole poblano:* A popular Mexican sauce.

Figure Focus
Figure 6.34: Chicken can also be cooked with moist methods without losing flavor.

Essential Skills:
Stuffing Poultry

Stuffing can be served as a side dish even without being cooked inside the bird.

In-Class Activity:
How Do I Cook Thee? Let Me Count the Ways

Literacy Connection, 21st-Century Skills— Work Independently, Think Creatively, Reason Efectively, Communicate Clearly

Chicken is one of the most versatile of all proteins.

It can be cooked with dry heat, moist heat, pan fried, deep fried, grilled, stir fried, stewed, boiled, barbequed, scalloped, pressure-cooked, and cooked other ways as well.

Challenge students to come up with a long list of different cooking methods that will work for chicken. See if they can name ten methods. Maybe they can name twenty.

Have them write the methods down on paper and then award a point for each method named.

Table 6.5: Cooking Poultry *continued*	
Type of Poultry	**Class and Cooking Method That Can Be Used**
Goose	Young: Dry heat (roast)
	Mature: Combination (braise or stew)
Turkey	Fryer/roaster: Dry heat (roast) or dry heat with fat/oil (sauté)
	Young: Dry heat (roast) or combination (stew)
	Mature: Combination (stew)

[nutrition]

Steaming Foods

Steaming food is often credited with maintaining nutrients better than other cooking methods. Some believe that all the nutrients remain in the food and are not drawn out in the cooking liquid, as in boiling or poaching. This is not entirely true, and a misunderstanding of the science is the problem.

Water does not become a gas until it is an invisible vapor, after it steams or evaporates. Steam is still liquid water in very fine droplets, still dissolves water-soluble vitamins, and can still carry them away as the steam drops collect elsewhere in the cooking system.

In defense of steam cooking, it requires less water so food does not soak or tumble in a boiling bath, which can draw out even more nutrients. It is a closed system that maintains moisture. Also, it uses relatively low cooking temperatures at or above 213°F, which also helps maintain nutrients. Steam cooking is still a great option, but for slightly different reasons than one might think.

Essential Skills
Stuffing Poultry

Stuffing can be a breeding ground for pathogens. For this reason, stuff only smaller birds, such as Cornish game hens, squab, or small chickens. Take care, even in stuffing these smaller birds, to ensure that food safety risks are kept to the absolute minimum.

❶ First, mix together all of the stuffing ingredients when cold. The mixture's temperature should never be allowed to rise above 45°F. See Figure 6.35a.

❷ Stuff the raw bird as close to roasting time as possible.

❸ Stuff the neck and main body cavities loosely because the stuffing expands during cooking. See Figure 6.35b.

❹ After filling cavities, secure their openings with skewers and butcher's twine or by trussing. See Figure 6.35c.

❺ After cooking, remove the stuffing from the bird and store separately.

390

Figure 6.35a: Step 1—Mix together stuffing ingredients.

Figure 6.35b: Step 3—Stuff the neck and main cavities.

Figure 6.35c: Step 4—Secure cavities with twine or trussing.

Summary

In this section, you learned the following:

- The three grades of poultry are USDA A, B, and C. A is the highest grade, and C is the lowest grade. Serve Grade A poultry in whole, unprocessed portions. Grades B and C poultry are often processed and used in other forms. Guidelines for distinguishing between grades are as follows:

  - Poultry must have a good conformation—structure and shape—and be free of deformity in the natural form of the product, such as a bent leg or curved backbone.

  - Other factors taken into account involve flesh, fat covering, defeathering, discolorations, signs of broken or disjointed bones, and freezing defects.

  - Boneless poultry roasts should be free of all bone, cartilage, tendons, visible bruises, and blood clots.

- The two distinct differences in poultry forms are white meat and dark meat. Each type of meat holds different nutrition values. White meat is low in calories and fat content and cooks faster. Dark meat, on the other hand, is generally higher in calories and fat. Dark meat also tends to be the richer, more flavorful meat and requires more time to cook.

- Domestic poultry is readily available and is less costly than most other meats. A recent change in the market is the greater availability of free-range poultry and more demand for game birds.

391

Summary

- Remind students to review the following:
  1. Grades of poultry
  2. Differences between white and dark meat
  3. Purchasing, fabricating, and storing poultry
  4. Cooking techniques for poultry

Figure Focus

Figure 6.35a: Stuffing ingredients usually start with cubed bread.

Figure 6.35b: Clean the cavity and then stuff the bird.

Figure 6.35c: Trussing keeps the stuffing in the cavity.

In-Class Activity: Chicken Match Game

21st-Century Skills—Global Awareness

Chicken dishes are found the world over, in nearly every nonvegan cuisine.

The following table lists the name of a few chicken dishes next to their countries of origin.

Using this table, play a match game with the students in class, or make a worksheet.

Have students try to match the chicken dish to its country of origin. Students could also name a country and try to think of a chicken dish from that country. Or they could learn the name of the dish and the country and try to locate it on a world map. There are many games to play with this information.

More information about this is given in Chapters 10 and 11. This is meant as a fun introduction rather than a definitive assignment.

Chicken Paprikash	Hungary
General Tso's chicken	China
Chicken cacciatore	Italy
Chicken enchilada	Mexico
Chicken Kiev	Russia
Chicken cordon bleu	United States
Chicken fajitas	Texas (Tex-Mex)
Chicken Marsala	Italy
Chicken Tandoori	India
Chicken sate (satay)	Indonesia
Chicken rice (Khao man kai)	Thailand
Southern fried chicken	United States
Chicken fricassee	France
Chicken soup	Nearly every cuisine of the world

- The first basic step in purchasing poultry is to decide on the type and quality of product that is needed for the particular menu item. Many of the same guidelines for poultry purchasing are similar to those discussed earlier for meat purchasing:
  - **Freshness:** As with meat products, high-quality frozen poultry should not appear different from a fresh poultry product. In general, all poultry products should be used within two to three days of purchase.
  - **Form:** The operation should determine whether dark meat or white meat is preferable—depending on its particular needs—and make purchases accordingly.
  - **Equipment:** Deciding what types of poultry products to purchase and how much to purchase is often determined by the types of equipment an operation has.
  - **Vendors:** Check out the equipment, storage capabilities, labor costs, and transportation costs of competing vendors.
  - **Cost:** As with meat purchases, in-house fabrication is a way to reduce costs. It is easier for an operation to fabricate poultry because the birds are smaller in size and easier to butcher.
- Poultry fabrication includes disjointing, boning (separating meat from bones), and cutting a bird into pieces. Essential tools include a clean work surface, boning knife, and chef's knife. Store fresh, raw poultry at an internal temperature of 41°F or lower. Store frozen poultry at a temperature that keeps it frozen. If poultry has been removed from its original packaging, place it in airtight containers or wrap it in airtight material. Remember that poultry should be stored below ready-to-eat food if they are both stored in the same cooler. Finally, be sure to follow FIFO.
- Poultry is a durable meat that lends itself to multiple cooking methods, such as dry-heat, dry-heat with fat or oil, moist-heat, and combination cooking methods.

392

Section 6.2 Review Questions

1. What are the three grades that can be assigned to poultry? What does each grade signify?

2. What are the two primary forms of poultry and what are the nutritional differences between the two?

3. How does the fabrication of poultry differ from the fabrication of meat?

4. List and describe three cooking methods for poultry.

5. Charleen Obal is partial to fried chicken. Research three different recipes that would use fried chicken as a component.

6. Chef Kate was more in favor of specializing in poultry dishes than was Miguel. Come up with three reasons why Chef Kate may be on to something. What would three benefits be to making poultry an operation's specialty? What would one drawback be?

7. Chicken is the most commonly consumed poultry in the United States. How many chicken items or dishes can you list? Try to list at least 20.

8. Which type of poultry form do you prefer: white meat or dark meat? Provide three reasons in support of your choice and then one reason why it may not be the best choice to make.

393

Section 6.2 Review Questions

1. The grades are A, B, and C. They represent variations and quality in conformation and flesh.

2. White meat and dark meat are the two forms. White meat is lower in fat than dark meat.

3. Poultry can be fabricated in the kitchen. It only requires a knife, rather than bone-cutting saws.

4. Poultry can be cooked in a variety of ways, both dry and moist. Also, combination methods will work.

5. Each student will have different findings.

6. Poultry is versatile and can be used in many dishes. It can be cooked a variety of ways. It is moderately priced, and can be more affordable for guests. Poultry is also nutritious and can be lower in fat.

7. Students should be able to come up with 20. They might need to refer to a cookbook or do some research.

8. Each student's opinion will be unique.

Section 6.2
Activities

1. As students practice, their trussing skills will improve and they will become faster at it.

2. Students should consider various options inspired by other cuisines; for example, turkey in Italian dishes or Asian dishes.

3. Such a menu would allow an operation to completely use the chicken they purchase.

Section 6.2 Activities

1. Study Skills/Group Activity: Trust in Your Trussing

Working in small groups, properly truss a whole chicken for roasting. Each person should take a turn completely trussing the same bird. Make a written note of any areas of difficulty and how your group worked around the problem. When everyone in the group has become comfortable with trussing, play a game between groups: Who can truss the fastest?

2. Independent Activity: Turkey Day Every Day!

Turkey is often thought of as a Thanksgiving dish. It is served every November in the United States with traditional side dishes. Create two menu item ideas using the excess turkey that is available the day after Thanksgiving. Create two more turkey menu items that could be featured at other times of the year.

3. Critical Thinking: The WHOLE Chicken

Create a menu that uses every usable part of a chicken. Name and describe each menu item. Keep in mind that these menu offerings should be suitable for a real, current restaurant to serve in your local market.

6.1 Meat	6.2 Poultry	6.3 Seafood	6.4 Charcuterie and Garde Manger
• Grades of meat	• Grades of poultry	• Seafood inspections and grades	• Definitions of charcuterie and garde manger
• Cuts of meat	• Two forms of poultry: white and dark	• Forms of seafood	• Types of charcuterie
• Purchasing and storing meat	• Purchasing, fabricating, and storing poultry	• Purchasing, fabricating, and storing seafood	
• Cooking techniques for meat	• Cooking techniques for poultry	• Cooking techniques for seafood	
• Determining doneness		• Determining doneness	

SECTION 6.3 SEAFOOD

Many seafood lovers salivate at the thought of a perfectly broiled lobster tail accompanied by salty-sweet drawn butter. Others prefer the delicate flaky texture of sole or flounder poached in wine and fresh herbs. And still others seek the heartier steaks of salmon, tuna, or swordfish grilled to perfection. It is for this reason that serving well-prepared seafood can be a boon for an operation, and why serving substandard seafood can be just as perilous to an operation.

Study Questions

After studying Section 6.3, you should be able to answer the following questions:

- What is the inspection and grading process for seafood?
- What are the various forms of seafood?
- What are the purchasing guidelines for seafood?
- What is the best way to fabricate and store seafood?
- What are the basic cooking methods for seafood?

Seafood Inspections and Grades

The U.S. Food and Drug Administration (FDA) monitors interstate fish shipments and also requires fish processors to adopt a Hazard Analysis and Critical Control Point (HACCP) program. The FDA does not inspect seafood when it is caught. Instead, many processors participate in the voluntary seafood inspection program conducted by the U.S. Department of Commerce (USDC). Products that have been inspected under this program carry a Processed Under Federal Inspection (PUFI) mark. This mark means that the product is safe and wholesome and has been packed in an establishment that meets the sanitary guidelines required by the National Marine Fisheries Service (NMFS), a division of the USDC.

395

Section 6.3 Seafood

Introduce the Section

a. Seafood is subject to strict safety and quality standards.

b. Seafood all falls into established categories.

c. Seafood should be purchased according to well-established standards.

Vocabulary Review

a. Direct students to the key terms.

b. Pronounce each word, and have the students repeat the pronunciation out loud.

c. Discuss the definition of each word.

Teach

Discuss

- Help the students to appreciate seafood as a menu selection.
- Are there seafood specialties from your geographic area?

Reinforce and Review

- The term "seafood" usually refers to protein foods that come from salt or fresh water sources.
- Although seafood is very popular in restaurants, there are folks who have an aversion to a "fishy" taste.
- Seafood is not regulated by the USDA, like meat and poultry are. It is monitored by the FDA.
- Processing inspections are done by the USDC.
- Sanitary handling and packing guidelines are from the NMFS.
- Clearly, fish is carefully monitored for safety and quality in the United States.

Reinforce and Review

- When seafood is evaluated for odor, it is for a strong fish smell as opposed to a sweeter, fresher ocean or lake smell.

- A spoiled or rancid smell is never acceptable.

- The flesh of fine fish is tight-grained and plump.

- If the flesh divides or appears mushy, it is not as appealing.

- The flesh should never be slimy or gooey.

The NMFS also publishes grades for seafood that has been inspected, although not all types of seafood are included. Both fresh and processed seafood items can be graded. Items are typically graded as A, B, C, or Below Standard, based on the grading factors that follow:

- Appearance
- Blemishes and damage
- Color
- Dehydration
- Flavor
- Odor
- Texture
- Uniformity

Grade A is the highest quality seafood available. These items have an excellent appearance, good flavor and odor, and are free of blemishes or defects. Grade B items have good quality, but usually have blemishes or other defects. Grade C items have relatively good quality, but these items are only appropriate for dishes that do not require an attractive appearance. Below Standard items do not have good quality.

Only Grade A seafood is marked with a stamp (see Figure 6.36). Most seafood items sold to restaurant and foodservice establishments are Grade A, but some Grade B products might be appropriate, depending on their usage. To ensure ordering the proper quality of seafood items, an operation should specify which grade it wants as part of the buying specifications to the vendor.

Figure 6.36: Grade A fish is of the highest quality, with good shape, flavor, and aroma.

Forms of Seafood

Seafood is divided into two major categories:

- Fin fish
- Shellfish

396

Figure Focus
Figure 6.36: Grade A fish will look attractive as a featured item on a plate.

Fin fish have a backbone and can live in fresh water or in the ocean. They are classified according to their shape, either round or flat. **Round fish** have a round body shape and one eye on each side of the head, and they swim upright in salt water or fresh water. Some examples are cod, sea bass, mahi-mahi, tuna, and trout. **Flatfish** are oval and flat in shape and have two eyes on the front part of the head. Examples include flounder, halibut, and turbot. Flat and round fish can have either fat or lean characteristics. Table 6.6 provides a detailed list of the fish that are fat or lean, which is indicated by an F for fat or an L for lean. All types of fin fish are available in fresh or processed forms.

Table 6.6: Fat and Lean Classifications for Varieties of Fin Fish

Flatfish	Round Fish
Flounder-L	Black sea bass-L
Halibut-L	Catfish-L
Sole-L	Cod-L
	Grouper-L
	Haddock-L
	Mackerel-F
	Monkfish-L
	Ocean perch-L
	Perch-L
	Pike-L
	Pompano-F
	Red snapper-L
	Salmon-F
	Shark-F
	Striped bass-L
	Swordfish-L
	Trout-L
	Tuna-F
	Whitefish-L
	Whiting bluefish-F

Shellfish have an outer shell but no backbone and live primarily in salt water. They are further categorized into **crustaceans, mollusks,** and **cephalopods.** Crustaceans have an outer skeleton and jointed appendages. Examples are shrimp, lobster, and crab. Mollusks have one or two hard shells. Univalves (one shell) include abalone. Bivalves (two hinged shells) include clams, oysters, mussels, and scallops. Cephalopods have a single internal shell and tentacles. Examples are octopus and squid. All types of shellfish are available in fresh or processed forms.

397

Discuss
- Informally survey students to see if they eat shellfish.
- What experience do they have with various types of shellfish?
- Are shellfish available regionally in your area?
- Do shellfish only grow in the ocean salt water?

Table 6.6:
Fat and Lean Classifications for Varieties of Fin Fish
- Flat fish are lean, but the fat they do have is also health-promoting omega-3 fatty acids.

Vocabulary Terms
- **Fin fish:** Fish species with an internal skeleton and fins.
- **Round fish:** Fish with an eye on each side of the head and a tube-shaped body.
- **Flatfish:** Fish with both eyes on the same side of the head and a flat body.
- **Shellfish:** Fish with an outer shell and meaty flesh inside.
- **Crustaceans:** Shellfish with an exoskeleton made of chitin.
- **Mollusks:** Hard single or double shell.
- **Cephalopods:** Tentacles and an interior shell.

The nutritional benefits of seafood would make it important to eat, even if it wasn't delicious.

Teaching Tips

- Note that these are essentially the same considerations as for meat and poultry.

- The students will realize that savvy shopping considers not just price, but profitability.

[nutrition]

Is Seafood Really "Brain Food"?

People often refer to seafood as "brain food" because it was thought to build brain tissue. Although this may not be exactly accurate, seafood truly is a great source of protein and other nutrients needed by the entire body. Seafood is usually low in fat. In addition, the fat in seafood is full of omega-3 fatty acids. The main omega-3 is linolenic acid, an essential human nutrient. It is also very good for the circulatory system and the heart. Additionally, seafood is a great source of many trace mineral nutrients that are sometimes hard to find in other foods, like iodine and selenium.

On the other hand, shellfish have a reputation for being very high in cholesterol, but this is not really true according to current research. Shellfish is about as high in cholesterol as red meat, but without the fat of meat. Even so, while shrimp and other shellfish may contribute some cholesterol to the body, cholesterol is also used extensively in building nerve and brain tissue. Maybe it's truly "brain food" after all.

Purchasing, Fabricating, and Storing Seafood

The most important step in purchasing seafood is deciding on the type and quality of seafood that is needed for particular menu items—the intended use of the seafood. If an operation does not market itself as serving fresh seafood, then it could purchase processed items. But being well-versed in all types of seafood is always ideal. Following are guidelines for purchasing fresh seafood. Many of these guidelines are similar to that of purchasing meat and poultry:

- **Market form:** Vendors can supply seafood to an operation in a number of ways. Purchase fresh seafood in the market form that best suits the operation's needs. For example, buy some types of fish already portioned, saving preparation time and ensuring uniform dishes. On the other hand, if the kitchen staff has the skills to cut up whole fish, consider whether the operation could use the trimmings and bones.

- **Storage capabilities:** Fresh seafood is highly perishable; therefore, adequate storage facilities are a must for seafood items to ensure as long a shelf life as possible. Temperature control is particularly important since fresh fish should be received packed in ice and maintained that way in storage. Careless storage of seafood leads to poor appearance, texture, and odor, as well as food safety issues, all of which ultimately result in wasted product.

- **Vendor selection:** Considering the vast variety of seafood available, a reliable, reputable supplier is crucial. Verify that your supplier is an approved food source that has been inspected and is in compliance with all applicable laws. Doing this helps ensure that seafood is safe and of consistent good quality.

398

Processed seafood might be an appropriate choice for an operation if it does not market menu items as "fresh caught." Customer perception is often negative toward processed food items, but many types of processed seafood—from frozen to cured—offer excellent flavor. Some factors to consider about processed seafood include the following:

- **Processing method**: Various types of seafood are available in frozen, canned, and cured forms. Choose the method that best matches the item and its intended usage.

- **Convenience**: By purchasing processed seafood, an operation might achieve significant cost reductions for equipment and space, as well as in preparation time and labor skills. Yet these savings must be balanced with the typically higher unit cost as well as the chance that the quality of the menu item might decline.

- **Storage capabilities**: Although processed seafood has a slightly longer shelf life than fresh seafood, it is still highly perishable. Operations must have the appropriate amount of storage equipment and space. Frozen seafood, for example, must be stored frozen. Accidental thawing will result in food safety issues and poor quality.

Many forms of fin fish can be purchased, and a smart foodservice operator will know the various categories and the distinctions between each. The market forms of fin fish are as follows (see Figure 6.37):

- **Whole or round**: The fish just as it was caught

- **Drawn**: Only viscera (guts) removed

- **Dressed**: Viscera, scales, fins, and often the head removed

- **Fish fillet**: Boneless pieces cut from the sides

- **Butterfly fillet**: Two sides cut away from the backbone

- **Steak**: Cross section cut, generally from large fish

Figure 6.37: Fish are available in six market forms.

Reinforce and Review

- Fish bones are a problem for both guests and chefs.
- Choose fish market forms for the least amount of bone interference.
- Servers can become expert in boning whole round fish.
- Some canned fishes have the bones in; for example, sardines are too small to bone and salmon is canned with large bones that need to be pulled out.
- Fish bones, like other bones, are full of calcium.
- Fish canned with bones provides calcium, whereas other fish is not especially high in calcium.
- Help provide guests with graceful ways to remove and discard bones.
- Crusty bread can help guests swallow small fish bones that they might accidentally eat.
- Stomach acid will digest the fish bones.

Vocabulary Terms

- **Drawn:** Internal organs removed.
- **Dressed:** Internal and external structures removed.
- **Butterfly fillet:** Bone removed from flesh, open.
- **Fish fillet:** Boneless side pieces.
- **Steak:** Cut across the spine, cross-section.

399

Figure Focus
Figure 6.37: Market forms of fish should be chosen for the best menu item option.

Reinforce and Review

- Crustaceans should be served with the guest in mind.

- It is difficult to eat them without making a mess, but tools, bibs, and washing supplies can make it easier.

- Raw crustaceans should be purchased and cooked while alive. When they die first, they can develop toxic substances.

- Lobsters don't "yell" when dropped in boiling water, but trapped air inside the shell can whistle and squeal.

Vocabulary Terms

- **IQF (individually quick frozen):** Each piece is frozen or ice glazed separately.

In addition to these, each of the market forms of fin fish may be purchased either fresh or frozen (see Figure 6.38). Some fin fish are sold in a dried form. An example would be cod sold as dried cod or bacalao. Many small fish are sold dried in either whole or fillet forms. Many dried fish are found in Asian or other ethnic markets.

Shellfish also come in different forms. As mentioned in the last section, shellfish have hard outer shells and have no backbones or internal skeletons. The two classifications of shellfish are mollusks and crustaceans. Both forms can be purchased as live, fresh, frozen, dried, canned, cooked fresh, cooked frozen, **IQF (individually quick frozen)**, or block frozen and in various states of preparation.

The most common types of mollusks found in commercial kitchens are oysters, clams, mussels, scallops, squid, and octopus. Purchase them live, in the shell, shucked (fresh or frozen), or canned.

Figure 6.38: A variety of fish and mollusks.

The most common types of crustaceans found in commercial kitchens are lobsters, shrimp, crabs, and crayfish.

Lobsters are classified by weight: chicken lobsters weigh approximately 1 pound; quarters lobsters weigh approximately 1¼ pounds; select lobsters weigh approximately 1½ to 2¼ pounds; jumbo lobsters weigh over 2½ pounds. The rock lobster, also known as the spiny or langouste lobster, is another type on the market. Purchase lobsters live, as cooked meat (fresh or frozen), IQF (individually quick frozen), or canned.

The six kinds of crabs typically found in commercial restaurant and foodservice operations are Alaskan king crab, Alaskan snow crab, Dungeness crab, blue crab, soft-shell crab, and stone crab. Purchase crabs live, frozen in the shell (cooked), as cooked frozen meat, or canned.

The different varieties of shrimp refer to where they are caught and include Gulf whites, pink, browns, and black tigers. These are the most popular varieties used in commercial foodservice. Prawn and scampi are terms commonly used to refer to shrimp, but neither term identifies an actual type of shrimp. Scampi is also considered a type of cooking recipe in which shrimp is sautéed in garlic butter.

400

Figure Focus

Figure 6.38: If possible, have students go to a fish market to see all the varieties of fish. Have them take photos with a digital camera.

Some of the most popular market forms of shrimp are fresh, head-on, raw, and head-off (also known as green headless) with shell on. In commercial food-service, most shrimp are deheaded and frozen at sea to preserve freshness. Additional market forms include raw, peeled, and deveined; cooked, peeled, and deveined; and IQF. Shrimp can be purchased with some processing (cooked whole or pieces, breaded, and canned). Shrimp are classified by count per pound.

Fabricating Fin Fish and Shellfish

Fin Fish

Fin fish fabrication techniques consist of scaling, trimming, gutting, and filleting the fish. Scaling methods are the same for both round and flatfish, but the way you gut and fillet them is slightly different. The tools needed for fin fish fabrication are a sharp, flexible filleting knife and a clean cutting board. When fabricating fin fish, put much of the trim to use in a mousseline, filling, canapé, soup, or sauce.

When scaling fin fish, scrape off the scales from tail to head. Once the fish has been scaled and trimmed, it should be gutted.

When gutting round fish, make a slit in the fish's belly and pull out the guts, or insides. Gutting a flatfish is a bit easier. Make the cuts around the head. As the head is pulled away from the body, the guts come away with the head.

Filleting a fish is the step that separates the flesh of the fish from the bones. Flatfish produce four fillets, and round fish produce two fillets. It is important to remove all of the bones from the fillet.

Once the fish has been filleted, make it into various cuts, such as *goujonettes* (goo-sha-NET) or small strips, or **paupiettes (po-pee-EHT),** thin, rolled fillets filled with stuffing; steaks; or, most commonly, individual fillet portions of varying weights depending on the desired use.

Shellfish

Unlike fin fish, shellfish do not have bones or a skeletal system. They do, however, need to be fabricated.

Mollusks, such as clams and oysters, are often served on the half shell, so it is important not to destroy the shell when **shucking**. Shucking is the opening or removing of a mollusk's shell. Scrub all mollusks well under cold running water before opening them to remove sand and grit.

When fabricating lobsters, removing the meat from the shell is easier when the lobster has been partially or fully cooked. Blanching the lobster lightly in

401

Reinforce and Review

- Careful fabrication of fish fillets will maintain the integrity of the delicate flesh.

- There are many varieties of menu items that can be made from fish fillets. Fried fillets include regional favorites such as fiddlers (catfish fillets) and seared Alaskan halibut; rolled fillets include stuffed salmon; Asian techniques, such as Japanese tempura, can be used for fish fillets; and Jamaican jerk-spice or Southern blackened fish begin with a fillet.

- Mollusks need very little fabrication, but require careful cleaning. The meat comes out of the mollusk whole, so trimming and cutting are not required. However, bacterial contamination is possible with mollusks so they must be handled and recorded properly.

- Abalone might need to be pounded. Abalone is a barnacle "foot" meat that is a very strong muscle. It can be thick, tough, and chewy. Pounding it tenderizes the meat.

- Lobster can become tough if overcooked, and it is far too valuable a food to risk overcooking. Careful attention should be paid to making sure it is cooked properly.

- Lobster shells can be used for the presentation. Lobster shells turn a glorious coral color as they are cooked. The entire "bug" makes an impressive display on a platter, with the claws ominously reaching toward the guest. If only the lobster tail is served, it can be loosened for the guest, but then replaced in the shell for an attractive presentation.

Vocabulary Terms

- *Goujonettes:* Finger-sized slices of fillet.

- **Paupiettes:** Thin slices of fillet wrapped around a filling.

- **Shucking:** Opening a shell, like an oyster.

Discuss

- If you were receiving a delivery of fish, what would you look for?

- How could you tell if it was good or bad?

- The eyes are a good way to identify freshness. Look for bright, clear eyes. Dull-eyed fish may be safe to eat, but they are past their prime.

- Fish is very good food, and should look and smell inviting, even when raw.

- When high-quality raw fish is cooked, the smell is appetizing.

Vocabulary Terms

- **Deveining:** Removing a shrimp vein along the outer edge.

---

a steam bath, in boiling water, or in a hot oven is all that is necessary to make removing the flesh easier.

Shrimp are cleaned by removing the shell and **deveining** them. Deveining is the process of removing a shrimp's digestive tract.

Storing Fish

Fin Fish

Fresh fish is very sensitive to time-temperature abuse and can spoil quickly if it isn't handled correctly. At delivery, it should be received at a temperature of 41°F or lower. Frozen fish should be received frozen; don't accept a delivery if there are any signs that it has been allowed to thaw, such as ice crystals, or if it has freezer burn.

To be acceptable, fresh fish must also meet the following criteria:

Figure 6.39: Fresh fish with bright, shiny skin.

- **Color**: Bright red gills; bright shiny skin (see Figure 6.39)

- **Texture**: Firm flesh that springs back when touched

- **Odor**: Mild ocean or seaweed smell

- **Eyes**: Bright, clear, and full

- **Packaging**: Product should be surrounded by crushed, self-draining ice

Reject fresh fish based on the following criteria:

- **Color**: Dull, gray gills; dull, dry skin

- **Texture**: Soft flesh that leaves an imprint when touched

- **Odor**: Strong fishy or ammonia smell

- **Eyes**: Cloudy, red-rimmed, sunken

Figure Focus

Figure 6.39: Have students learn to identify the criteria for fresh fish. The skin should look metallic and clean, and the fish should smell like fresh water or a little briny.

Shellfish

Receive live shellfish on ice or at an air temperature of 45°F or lower. Receive shucked product at an internal temperature of 41°F or lower. Shellfish must have shellstock identification tags, which document where the shellfish were harvested. These tags must remain attached to the delivery container until all of the shellfish have been used, and then retained for 90 days after the last item from the delivery has been served (see Figure 6.40).

Figure 6.40: Sample shellstock identification tag.

To be acceptable, shellfish must meet the following criteria:

- **Condition**: If fresh, then received alive

- **Smell**: Mild ocean or seaweed smell

- **Shells**: Closed and unbroken for mollusk shells

Reject shellfish based on the following criteria:

- **Condition**: If shipped fresh, dead on arrival

- **Odor**: Strong fishy smell

- **Texture**: For mollusks, slimy, sticky, or dry

- **Shells**: For mollusks, muddy or broken

- **Freezer burn:** If the shellfish was frozen, any signs of frost, ice, or leakage of the package

If the delivery is accepted for purchase, use the following criteria for safe and proper storage. Fish items are highly perishable and so proper storage is very important:

Fin Fish

- Store fresh fish at an internal temperature of 41°F or lower.

- Pack fresh, whole fish in beds of flaked or crushed ice.

- Ice beds must be self-draining, and the containers should be cleaned and sanitized regularly (see Figure 6.41 on the following page).

- Change the ice regularly (crushed ice works best).

- Store frozen fish at a temperature that will keep it frozen.

403

Reinforce and Review

- Help students understand that foodborne pathogens or biological toxins can be present in shellfish.

- Knowing where and when the shellfish were harvested can prevent any further problem with that batch.

- Also, if someone becomes ill, knowing the origin of the shellfish can help with treatment.

- As always, handle shellfish as a TCS food.

- Odor is a main indicator of freshness.

- Serve any cold fish or shellfish on ice beds that can drain away the water.

- Do not let fish dry out.

- For raw fish, such as sushi, only use fresh sushi-grade fish.

- Sushi fish tastes fresh and almost sweet and mild.

Figure Focus
Figure 6.40: Shellfish are tracked and identified.

Reinforce and Review

- Shellfish is always stored in the original container.

- The identification information should remain on the container.

Essential Skills: Shucking Clams

Working with bivalve shellfish can result in cut hands. It requires strength, skill, and protection for hands.

Discuss

- Author Ian Fleming created the character of James Bond. One of Fleming's favorite dishes was potted shrimp.

- Potted shrimp is made of shrimp spiced with mace and cayenne pepper and set in a little clarified butter, chilled in a ramekin.

- To serve, it is inverted and unmolded, or served in the ramekin, on a plate with slices of crusty bread.

- Fleming also described this dish in his books as a favorite of James Bond.

Figure 6.41: Self-draining ice bed.

Shellfish

- Store live shellfish in its original container at an air temperature of 45°F or lower.

- Keep the shellstock identification tags on file for 90 days from the date the last shellfish was sold or served.

- Store frozen shellfish at a temperature that will keep them frozen.

Essential Skills
Shucking Clams

Clams have a top shell and a bottom shell that are firmly held together with a tight, muscular hinge. Cutting open this hinge is the key to opening the clam swiftly and without breaking the shell.

❶ With a stiff brush, scrub the outside of the shell vigorously under cold running water until all sand and grit have been removed. See Figure 6.42a on the following page.

❷ Put a wire mesh glove on the hand that will hold the clam. See Figure 6.42b.

❸ Hold the clam firmly in your protected hand and insert the clam knife between the top shell and the bottom shell.

❹ Work the knife around the opening to cut the hinged muscle.

❺ Open the shell and slide the knife under the clam meat and the shell to detach the clam meat. See Figure 6.42c.

404

Figure Focus

Figure 6.41: Ice beds serve a food safety function, in addition to making fish appear fresh and appealing.

Figure 6.42a: Step 1—Scrub the outside shell.

Figure 6.42b: Step 2—Put a wire mesh glove on your hand.

Figure 6.42c: Step 5—Open the shell and slide the knife under the clam meat and the shell to detach the clam meat.

Essential Skills
Filleting a Round Fish

❶ Make a cut behind the head and then run the knife down the length of the fish, from head to tail of the first side. See Figure 6.43a.

❷ Turn the fish to the second side and work from the tail to the head. See Figure 6.43b.

❸ Trim away the belly bones. See Figure 6.43c on the following page.

❹ Lay the fillet near the edge of the surface and run the blade of a fillet knife or boning knife between the skin and the flesh. Angle the blade downward slightly when doing this.

❺ Use a sawing motion and hold the skin taut to make it easier to remove. See Figure 6.43d.

Figure 6.43a: Step 1—Make a cut behind the head and run the knife down the length of the fish.

Figure 6.43b: Step 2—Turn the fish to the second side and work from tail to head.

405

Figure Focus

Figure 6.42a: Be sure to remove all sand from the outside.

Figure 6.42b: The wire mesh protects the hand from scratches and cuts.

Figure 6.42c: There is a little prying action required to open the shell.

Figure 6.43a: Start at the head, not the tail.

Figure 6.43b: On the second side, slice from tail to head.

Essential Skills:
Peeling and Deveining Shrimp

Shrimp are sort of like water bugs, so remove the bug-like portions and the dark vein.

Shrimp should be plump, pink, and appealing.

Fast Fact:
Did You Know . . . ?

Lobster is quite expensive, and quite delicious. They are typically harvested from the ocean, rather than farmed, which is another factor contributing to their price.

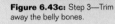

Figure 6.43c: Step 3—Trim away the belly bones.

Figure 6.43d: Step 5—Use a sawing motion and hold the skin taut to make it easier to remove.

Essential Skills
Peeling and Deveining Shrimp

❶ Pull away the shell. See Figure 6.44a.

❷ Cut along the back vein with a knife or a shrimp deveiner. See Figure 6.44b.

❸ Remove the intestinal tract. See Figure 6.44c.

Figure 6.44a: Step 1—Pull away the shell.

Figure 6.44b: Step 2—Cut along the back vein.

Figure 6.44c: Step 3—Remove the intestinal tract.

[fast fact]

Did You Know...?
It can take a Maine lobster anywhere from four to seven years to grow just one pound. This may partially explain why lobsters tend to be very expensive.

406

Figure Focus

Figure 6.43c: When removing bones, take care not to break them.

Figure 6.43d: A sawing motion can aid in removing the skin without tearing the flesh.

Figure 6.44a: This step can make your hands sticky.

Figure 6.44b: Take care not to cut too far into the shrimp.

Figure 6.44c: Pull out the vein gently so it doesn't break.

Cooking Techniques for Seafood

The best way to pair a fish with a cooking technique is to consider the flesh of the fish. For example, mackerel (an oily fish), cooks best with a dry-heat technique, such as grilling or broiling. Prepare tuna and salmon, which contain a moderate amount of fat, using any cooking method. Very lean fish, such as sole and flounder, have the most flavor when they are poached or sautéed.

Dry-heat Cooking

Fatty fish cut into fillets or steaks are the best cuts to bake, broil, and grill. Most fish are baked between 350°F and 400°F. Bake larger fish at the low end of this range so they cook evenly. To retain moistness, coat fish with bread crumbs, crushed nuts, or thinly sliced vegetables or meat, such as prosciutto, and bake it on an oiled or buttered baking sheet. *NOTE*: If using nuts, always remember to disclose the type of nuts on the menu to prevent possible allergic reactions.

Dry-heat Cooking with Fat and Oil

Lean fin fish and shellfish are best when using dry-heat cooking with fat and oil, such as sautéing, stir-frying, pan-frying, and deep-frying. Coat fish with flour or a breading before cooking in either clarified butter or oil. Small items, such as shrimp and scallops, are extremely delicate and must be quickly sautéed, stir-fried, or pan-fried over very high heat. Larger items require lower heat for even cooking.

When deep-frying, the fish should be very fresh; the fat used to deep-fry should be of high quality; and the item should be served immediately after cooking. Breading the fish before cooking will protect it from the hot fat and provide a crispy coating. It is necessary to follow sanitation rules when working with the batter.

Moist-heat Cooking

Moist-heat cooking techniques—poaching, simmering, and steaming—are excellent ways to cook fish, especially the lean varieties. To enhance the flavor of the fish, poach it in **court bouillon** (cort boo-YON), a stock made of vegetables and an acid such as vinegar or wine. Also poach fish in **fumet** (foo-MAY), a rich fish stock made with wine, or simmer it in its own juices with a little added liquid. Another method in use today is poaching in olive oil or butter, which may or may not be infused with other flavorings. The principles for poaching in olive oil or butter are the same as for poaching in other liquids regarding time and temperature.

407

Reinforce and Review

- All cooking methods for fish should help retain moisture and texture.

- Fragile fish can dry out easily.

- Fish that are more sturdy and meaty can be cooked over an open flame or other dry heat.

- Very tender lean fish can be simmered gently in court bouillon or fumet.

Homework Activity: Making Protein Decisions

Mathematics Connection, Literacy Connection, 21st-Century Skills—Financial, Business, Economic and Entrepreneurial Literacy

A successful business executive for a large foods company once said, "It's easy to make a million dollars. The trick is to not spend a million dollars doing it."

Have students consider this statement. How might this relate to protein decisions for a restaurant?

Have students write at least two paragraphs of their thoughts and strategies for profitability, with specific consideration of the protein foods that could be featured at a restaurant.

Their writing should include real-world profitability topics, and not just general concepts about good ideas for menu items.

Vocabulary Terms

- **Court bouillon:** An acid and vegetable stock.
- **Fumet:** Fish stock.

- Students might enjoy wrapping fish in some parchment and cooking it.

- Help students realize that the delicate fish is not only protected by the parchment, but can be seasoned by steaming it with aromatics.

Vocabulary Terms

- *En papillote*: Steaming fish in a parchment wrap.

- **Bouillabaisse**: French seafood stew.

Shallow-poached fish and shellfish should be opaque. The flesh of oysters, clams, and mussels should show curling on the edges. No white deposits should show on the flesh of fin fish or shellfish as this indicates cooking at too high a temperature or for too long. The finished item should be moist and extremely tender. Any stringiness, dryness, or excessive flaking indicates that the food was cooked too long or at too high a temperature.

En papillote (en paw-pee-YOTE) is one classical moist-heat cooking technique that is especially suited to fish. In this cooking method, encase the fish, herbs, vegetables, and/or sauce in parchment paper and steam in a hot oven. Fish cooked *en papillote* should be naturally tender (see Figure 6.45). Sear thicker cuts of fish first to ensure even cooking. Modern versions of this technique include wrapping the fish in banana leaves.

Combination Cooking

The combination cooking methods, stewing and braising, use both dry and moist heat. These methods have produced some very popular fish recipes over the years. Some of the best-known recipes include **bouillabaisse** (BOO-ya-base), a French seafood stew made with assorted fish and shellfish, onions, tomatoes, white wine, olive oil, garlic, saffron, and herbs; cioppino, a San Francisco version of seafood stew made with local seafood; and jambalaya (jam-bo-LIE-ah), a Creole stew from Louisiana made with rice, shellfish, and vegetables (see Figure 6.46).

Figure 6.45: Seafood papillote.

Figure 6.46: Spicy Cajun jambalaya with sausage, shrimp, and chicken.

408

Figure Focus

Figure 6.45: The parchment is discarded and not eaten with the fish.

Figure 6.46: Jambalaya is a Cajun fish stew that is served with rice.

Determining Doneness

Most all fin fish and shellfish are naturally tender, so do not undercook or overcook fish for tenderizing purposes. Cook all fish just until done. Following are guidelines to follow in determining doneness:

1. **Flesh turns from translucent to opaque:** Raw flesh of most fish is translucent. When the flesh turns a denser, more opaque shade, the fish is done.

2. **Flesh becomes firm:** Raw fish is somewhat mushy. As the flesh cooks, it becomes firmer and springs back to the touch when done.

3. **Flesh pulls easily away from bone:** As the fish cooks, the flesh loosens and can be effortlessly separated from the bone when done.

4. **Flesh begins to flake:** As the fish cooks, connective tissue breaks down and muscle fibers begin to separate from each other, or flake. The fish is done as soon as flaking starts to occur.

Finally, carryover cooking applies to seafood as well as meat. With this in mind, it is better to slightly undercook the fish and allow carryover cooking to bring it to doneness. Not taking the residual heat of carryover cooking into account often leads to overcooked fish and a less satisfying dish for guests.

[on the job]

The Pressure-Cooking Cook

A cook has many techniques available for preparing food. Sautéing, broiling, baking, and grilling are examples of cooking methods that are frequently talked about. One method that is not as well known, but highly effective, is called pressure cooking.

Water boils at 212°F at sea level. If the air pressure on top of the water increases, it pushes against the water and prevents bubbles of steam and vapor from escaping the surface. The water must increase in heat energy to overcome the increased pressure and form rolling bubbles. Water under pressure must reach an even greater temperature in order to boil.

A pressure cooker is a closed system that allows air or steam pressure to increase inside the system. This increases the atmospheric pressure, which also increases the boiling point. Pressure is measured in pounds per square inch. At 5 pounds of pressure, water boils at 228°F. At 15 pounds, water doesn't boil until it reaches 250°F.

Pressure cooking requires special equipment. Consider safety, as the system must remain closed and locked not only to build pressure, but to prevent the machinery from flying apart. Pressure is released through a petcock or other device designed for this purpose. Do not open the cooker until the pressure is back to local atmospheric pressure once again.

409

Teaching Tips

- The very best way to teach about doneness is to demonstrate it.

- Students should see a piece of fish cooked in the classroom to the proper doneness.

- Students can assess the translucency or opacity of the fish.

- Perhaps students can touch the fish before and after cooking.

- Flaking properly cooked fish can be demonstrated with a fork.

On the Job:
The Pressure-Cooking Cook

A pressure cooker can keep chicken or fish very moist inside a crispy skin.

There are safety considerations when pressure cooking. Equipment must be properly made, used, and maintained so that it holds together.

Summary

- Remind students to review the following:
  1. Seafood inspections and grades
  2. Forms of seafood
  3. Purchasing, fabricating, and storing seafood
  4. Cooking techniques for seafood
  5. Determining doneness

Foods cooked under pressure cook hotter in a moist environment without drying or burning. This makes them cook more quickly, with the heat being distributed more evenly throughout the food. Also, the system is closed so the steam and cooking juices remain in the system and recycle back into the foods. Pressure cooked foods taste like they have gone through a long, slow, moist, flavorful cooking method, but the process takes much less time.

Summary

In this section, you learned the following:

- Seafood is not inspected when it is caught. Instead, many processors participate in the voluntary seafood inspection program conducted by the U.S. Department of Commerce (USDC). Products that have been inspected under this program carry a Processed Under Federal Inspection (PUFI) mark. This mark means that the product is safe and wholesome and has been packed in an establishment that meets the sanitary guidelines required by the National Marine Fisheries Service (NMFS), a division of the USDC. The NMFS also publishes grades for seafood that has been inspected, although not all types of seafood are included.

- Both fresh and processed seafood items can be graded. Items are typically graded as A, B, C, or Below Standard, based on these grading factors: appearance, blemishes and damage, color, dehydration, flavor, odor, texture, and uniformity. Grade A is the highest-quality seafood available. These items have an excellent appearance, have good flavor and odor, and are free of blemishes or defects. Grade B items have good quality, but usually have blemishes or other defects. Grade C items have relatively good quality, but these items are only appropriate for dishes that do not require an attractive appearance. Below Standard items do not have good quality.

- The two main forms of seafood are fin fish and shellfish. Fin fish have a backbone and can live in fresh water or in the ocean. They can be classified according to their shape, either round or flat. Shellfish have an outer shell but no backbone and live primarily in salt water. Shellfish can be categorized further into three categories: crustaceans, mollusks, and cephalopods.

- The most important step in purchasing seafood is deciding on the type and quality of seafood that is needed for particular menu items—the intended use of the seafood. If an operation does not market itself as serving fresh seafood, then it could purchase processed items. But being well versed in

410

all types of seafood is always ideal. Following are guidelines for purchasing fresh seafood. Many of these guidelines are similar to those for purchasing meat and poultry:

- **Market form**: Vendors can supply seafood to an operation in a number of ways. Purchase fresh seafood in the market form that best suits your operation's needs.

- **Storage capabilities**: Fresh seafood is highly perishable; therefore, adequate storage facilities for seafood items are a must to ensure as long a shelf life as possible.

- **Vendor selection**: Considering the vast variety of seafood available, a reliable, reputable supplier is crucial. Verify that your supplier is an approved food source that has been inspected and is in compliance with all applicable laws.

■ Processed seafood might be an appropriate choice for an operation if it does not market its menu items as "fresh caught." Customer perception is often negative toward processed food items, but many types of processed seafood—from frozen to cured—offer excellent flavor. Some factors to consider about processed seafood include processing method, convenience, and storage capabilities.

■ Many different forms of fin fish can be purchased, and a smart foodservice operator will know the various categories and the distinctions between them. The market forms of fin fish are as follows: whole or round, drawn, dressed, butterfly fillet, fish fillet, and steak.

■ Fin fish fabrication techniques consist of scaling, trimming, gutting, and filleting the fish. Scaling methods are the same for both round and flatfish, but the way you gut and fillet them is slightly different. The tools needed for fin fish fabrication are a sharp, flexible filleting knife and a clean cutting board. When fabricating fin fish, put much of the trim to use in a mousseline, filling, canapé, soup, or sauce.

■ Unlike fin fish, shellfish do not have bones or a skeletal system. They do, however, need to be fabricated. Mollusks, such as clams and oysters, are often served on the half shell, so do not destroy the shell when shucking, which is the opening or removing of a mollusk's shell. When fabricating lobsters, it is easier to remove the meat from the shell when the lobster has been partially or fully cooked. Blanch the lobster lightly in a steam bath, in boiling water, or in a hot oven, which is all that is necessary to make removing the flesh easier.

411

CUSTOMIZED INSTRUCTION

More Advanced Students

Give the student the name of a protein. He or she must think of an appropriate cooking technique for it.

Less Advanced Students

Students can confer with team members before answering. This can be done only for a limited number of turns during the game. For example, each team can confer twice.

Special Needs Students

Depending on the disability, the student might need to see pictures of the foods and the cooking equipment. Or perhaps the student will need the support of team members to answer the questions. Adapt as needed.

ESOL Students

Include pictures of the meat cuts and the cooking equipment on the cards. Show the student the pictures while he or she reads the card as you say the word aloud.

In-Class Activity: Speedy Responses

21st-Century Skills—Flexibility and Adaptability

There are many ways to cook meat, poultry, sausages, and seafood. There are also inappropriate ways to cook things. For example, boiling pork loin chops would not be correct, but boiling would be appropriate for crab.

Play a quiz game. Divide the class into two teams.

There will be two types of cards, each with one word on each card.

Make a stack of cards with these cooking techniques: boil, roast, grill, broil, stew, bake, sauté, pan-fry, deep-fry, stir-fry, poach, *en papillote*, pressure-cook, denature with acid, braise, steam, simmer, consume raw (this would be sushi and tartare, and can be left out if you prefer).

Make another stack of cards with cuts of meat, types of poultry, seafood, and sausages. Use anything from this chapter, including items from Table 6.3, Table 6.4, Table 6.5, and Table 6.6; and other lists from the text, such as crab, shrimp, lobster, clams, scallops, crayfish, sausage, pâté, terrine, and galatine.

Place both stacks of cards face down.

Taking turns, the MC, or teacher, picks up the top card of each stack and reads them. For example: "Shrimp" and "Grill." The student must quickly say "Yes" or "No," indicating whether or not this cooking technique would be appropriate for this protein item. If the answer is correct, the student wins a point for his or her team, and it is the other team's turn. If the answer is wrong, the other team gets a point, and then still gets the next turn.

This game will put students "on the spot" to answer in the heat of the moment.

- Fish items are highly perishable and so proper storage is very important. Store fresh fish at an internal temperature of 41°F or lower. Pack fresh, whole fish in beds of flaked or crushed ice. Ice beds must be self-draining. Clean and sanitize the containers regularly. Change the ice regularly. Store frozen fish and shellfish at a temperature that will keep it frozen. Store live shellfish in its original container at an air temperature of 45°F or lower. Keep the shellstock identification tags on file for 90 days from the date the last shellfish was sold or served.

- Cooking methods for seafood include dry-heat, dry-heat cooking with oil or fat, moist-heat, and combination technique, using both dry and moist-heat methods.

412

Section 6.3 Review Questions

1. Compare and contrast the inspection and grading process for seafood with that for meat and poultry. How is it similar? What are the differences?

2. What are the two main forms of seafood? What is one primary difference between the two forms?

3. Explain how to fabricate the following two fish: a round fish and a mollusk.

4. At what temperature should fresh fish be stored?

5. One of Charleen Obal's favorite seafood dishes is shrimp and grits. She can serve this for breakfast or dinner. What other seafood dish can be served both at breakfast and dinner?

6. One of Chef Kate's concerns about specializing in seafood is storage issues. She's just not sure of all that's entailed in the storing of seafood. Now that you have learned all about the storing of seafood, write a one-page memo to Chef Kate explaining the basics of what she'll need to know in order to make an informed decision.

7. Why is seafood not inspected when it is caught, and why is the inspection program voluntary? Should it be? Explain this process and defend your opinion in a one-page report.

8. Given all that you know now about seafood, if you were running a restaurant, would you prefer to specialize in shellfish or fin fish? Explain your answer.

413

Section 6.3 Review Questions

1. Students should note that the USDA is not involved with seafood as it is for meat and poultry. They should also note that seafood inspection is voluntary, whereas meat inspection is mandatory. Also, there are many more agencies involved in fish regulation than in meat and poultry regulation.

2. There are fin fish and shellfish. Fin fish have the skeleton on the inside, and shellfish have it on the outside.

3. A round fish should have the guts removed and then be filleted. A mollusk should be opened and the meat removed.

4. It should be stored at or below 41°F.

5. Students might not be familiar with seafood for breakfast, but there are several examples. Kippers, lox, sardines, or even cold, whole, cooked fin fishes on ice can be used for breakfast. This is not unusual in England, Europe, Scandinavia, and Asia. Students might have other ideas as well.

6. Food safety and quality of seafood are strongly determined by the storage of the seafood. It must be adequate and appropriate.

7. Students will have opinions, but the voluntary program works well because it is a marketing tool for fish vendors. Compliance will help maintain business.

8. Students' ideas will be interesting, and could be influenced by their personal prior experiences eating seafood.

Section 6.3
Activities

1. Experience is the best teacher here, and students might discover keys to success that they can share.

2. Shellfish like shrimp, crab, and lobster are most typically involved in food allergies. Scallops can also trigger food allergies. All such ingredients or menu items should be fully disclosed on the menu. The serving staff should be aware of their presence in all dishes, even a new item or a special

3. Local research is valuable. Fresh seafood is especially nice when it is brought to the table very soon after the catch. Local fish makes this possible.

Section 6.3 Activities

1. Study Skills/Group Activity: Prepping Fish

Working with two or three other students, fillet a fish together from start to finish. Then shuck one clam each. Take note of tricks that any group members discover along the way. Write them down and share them with the rest of the class when you're finished.

2. Independent Activity: Research Seafood Allergies

Research seafood allergies. What foods typically cause problems? How would you deal with this when writing a menu? How would the servers at your establishment help a guest to deal with a seafood allergy?

3. Critical Thinking: Service with a Style!

Go to a local fish market, fishmonger, or grocery store meat/fish department. Talk to an employee about the current local catch. Learn what is fresh and plentiful in your locale. Learn about the seasons of fish in your area. Report your finding in a one-page paper.

414

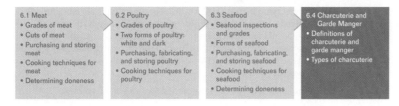

6.1 Meat	6.2 Poultry	6.3 Seafood	6.4 Charcuterie and Garde Manger
• Grades of meat • Cuts of meat • Purchasing and storing meat • Cooking techniques for meat • Determining doneness	• Grades of poultry • Two forms of poultry: white and dark • Purchasing, fabricating, and storing poultry • Cooking techniques for poultry	• Seafood inspections and grades • Forms of seafood • Purchasing, fabricating, and storing seafood • Cooking techniques for seafood • Determining doneness	• Definitions of charcuterie and garde manger • Types of charcuterie

SECTION 6.4 CHARCUTERIE AND GARDE MANGER

Charcuterie has been around for centuries, and it has recently had a resurgence. Restaurants across the United States are putting a renewed emphasis on this age-old culinary art. From fresh sausage stuffed with quality meat and herbs to fine pâtés to beautifully smoked meat, charcuterie is not only here to stay, it is a vital part of twenty-first-century cuisine.

In this section, you will learn what exactly charcuterie and garde manger are, as well as the various types of charcuterie and how they are prepared.

Study Questions

After studying Section 6.4, you should be able to answer the following questions:

- What is charcuterie and garde manger?
- What are the main types of charcuterie?

Definitions of Charcuterie and Garde Manger

The term **charcuterie**, which in French means "cooked flesh," refers to specially prepared pork products, including sausage, smoked ham, bacon, pâté, and terrine (see Figure 6.47). Charcuterie refers to the production of pâtés, terrines, galantines, sausages, and similar foods. Serve these food items cold; they are generally provided by the garde manger department.

Figure 6.47: Speciality prepared meats.

415

Section 6.4
Charcuterie and Garde Manger

Introduce the Section

a. Charcuterie involves the production of mixed or smoked meat dishes.

b. Garde manger is the department that manages cold foods, not just meat.

Vocabulary Review

a. Direct students to the key terms.

b. Pronounce each word, and have the students repeat the pronunciation out loud.

c. Discuss the definition of each word.

Teach

Discuss

- There are many types of sausages and foods that can be used in sausages.

- Smoked meat is popular, and not just for breakfast.

- The meat of the charcuterie can be used for many different dishes at any meal.

Vocabulary Terms

- **Charcuterie:** "Cooked flesh" and meat-based foods.

Figure Focus

Figure 6.47: Ask students if they can identify the meats in the photo.

Discuss

- Ask if students are aware that sausages are made inside a thin layer of pig intestines.

- Every usable part of a hog can be made into food.

- Small scraps of meat, ground meat, fat, and spices are used in making sausage.

- What types of sausages can students name?

Fast Fact:
Did You Know . . . ?

The word "chef" means chief or military leader.

On the Job:
The Guardian of the Garde Manger

Some of the foods of this department are very artistically produced and presented.

Vocabulary Terms

- **Garde manger:** Kitchen brigade department that deals with cold foods and charcuterie.

- **Sausages:** Ground and spiced meat in a tube casing.

Garde manger (gard mawn-ZHAY) is the department typically found in a classical brigade system kitchen and/or the chef who is responsible for the preparation of cold foods, including salads and salad dressings, cold appetizers, charcuterie items, and similar dishes. Most of the decorative buffet work would come from the garde manger department. The garde manger department is also referred to as the pantry.

Charcuterie consists of two main categories: sausages and forcemeat.

[fast fact]

Did You Know…?
The garde manger department is part of the classic brigade kitchen. The brigade kitchen was created in late nineteenth-century France by Georges Auguste Escoffier, who wanted the kitchen to operate in the same way as the French military. There was a distinct hierarchy: cooks answered to a direct supervisor, who answered to a sous chef, who answered to the chef de cuisine, who answered to the executive chef.

[on the job]

The Guardian of the Garde Manger
The garde manger is the chef station responsible for the presentation, garnish, and preparation of cold foods. Because most of the food is uncooked, and because so many types of food are used in this station, chances for cross-contamination are plentiful. Food safety considerations are extremely important in this capacity. For example, a fruit platter with a beautifully carved exterior of a watermelon may look gorgeous, but might harbor pathogens unless properly cleaned and handled in the kitchen.

The fruit platter must be created with a cutting board that is clean and sanitized. A cold pâté must be held at the proper temperature for safety, even when served on a tray with a sliced baguette on a buffet table. The garde manger knows how to manage these various aspects of presentation. The garde manger must be very aware of food safety requirements.

Types of Charcuterie

Sausages

Traditionally, **sausages** were ground pork that the preparer forced into a casing made from the lining of animal intestines. Today, many other ingredients are used to make sausage, including game, beef, veal, poultry, fish, shellfish, and even vegetables. The three main types of sausage (see Figure 6.48 on the following page) are as follows:

- Fresh sausage

- Smoked or cooked sausage

- Dried or hard sausage

416

Figure 6.48a: Fresh sausage.　　**Figure 6.48b:** Smoked sausage.　　**Figure 6.48c:** Hard sausage.

Make fresh sausage with raw ingredients that have not been cured or smoked. Cook fresh sausage before serving. Fresh sausage includes breakfast sausage links and Italian sausage. Polish kielbasa, Mexican chorizo, and French andouille are other examples of fresh sausage.

Make smoked and cooked sausage with raw meat products treated with preservatives. German knackwurst, frankfurter, and bratwurst are examples of smoked and cooked sausage.

Make dried or hard sausage with cured meat and then air-dry it under sanitary, controlled conditions. Italian salami and pepperoni are examples of dried or hard sausage.

Forcemeat

Forcemeat is a mixture of lean ground meat and fat that is emulsified, or forced together, in a food grinder and then pushed through a sieve to create a very smooth paste. How did forcemeat get its name? The word forcemeat is from the French word **farce** (FAHRS), which means stuffing. Forcemeat is the main ingredient used to make **pâté** (pah-TAY), a rich loaf made of meat, game, poultry, seafood, and/or vegetables baked in a mold.

Create straight forcemeat by very finely grinding the meat, seasoning it with herbs and spices, and then cooking it in an earthenware mold called a **terrine** (tehr-REEN). Cook the terrine in a hot-water bath to an internal temperature of 145°F to 155°F. In a country-style forcemeat, or *pâté de campagne* (pah-TAY de kom-PAN-yuh), a cured meat is usually the main ingredient. The texture is slightly coarser than in straight forcemeat, which allows the flavor of the meat to dominate.

Sometimes the forcemeat is wrapped in a pâté dough that may contain herbs, spices, or lemon zest. A pâté dough is much stronger than pie dough because it must stand up to the liquid released during cooking. This dish is referred to as a *pâté en croûte* (pah-TAY on kroot).

417

Discuss

- Students might not be familiar with charcuterie.
- However, many students have eaten pepperoni, bacon, and sausage.
- Discuss and describe the various meat dishes described in this section.
- If at all possible, have a sample of a forcemeat or sausage for them to taste.

Vocabulary Terms

- **Forcemeat:** A meat paste made of meat and fat.
- **Farce:** Stuffing.
- **Pâté:** A meat paste baked in a mold.
- **Terrine:** Earthenware mold.
- *Pâté de campagne:* A slightly coarse, country-style forcemeat.
- *Pâté en croûte:* Forcemeat wrapped in a dough and baked.

Figure Focus

Figure 6.48a: Sausage made of a meat mixture that isn't smoked.

Figure 6.48b: Sausage that has been cured with smoke.

Figure 6.48c: Sausage that has been aged and dried.

Teaching Tips

- A vegetable mixture can also be created and used, meat-free.

Nutrition:
Benefits of Liver

Liver should be prepared very fresh to reduce graininess.

ServSafe Connection:
Food Safety Reminders for This Chapter

Be sure to follow internal temperature guidelines for cooking.

Vocabulary Terms

- **Mousseline:** A white meat forcemeat mixed with egg whites and cream.

Inventive chefs have created new recipes, such as spring vegetable terrine, which no longer require meat, but because they are cooked in the same mold, they are still called a terrine.

A forcemeat made of veal, poultry, or fish is called a **mousseline** (moose-uh-LEEN). A *mousseline* is delicately flavored and lightened with cream and egg whites. Shape the *mousseline* into small, dumpling-shaped ovals and poach it in a rich stock or court bouillon to make *quenelles* (kuh-nel).

[nutrition]

Benefits of Liver

"Sweetbreads," "variety meats," or "poultry giblets" all refer to liver and other organ meats. Various organ meats are used in cuisine, but liver may be the most common in the United States. Use liver in *pâté de foie gras,* liverwurst, and giblet gravy, or serve it as an entrée.

Liver is an excellent source of dietary iron. The iron in liver is also very well absorbed and used. It is called "heme" iron because it comes from the hemoglobin of the animal. Additionally, liver and other meat sources contain MFP factor, which improves the absorption of iron from other non-heme sources (like bread) in the same meal. Iron is sometimes difficult to obtain in the diet, especially for women, so it is useful to include some foods that contain liver in the diet. Many forcemeat dishes accomplish this goal.

The one downside is that liver is quite high in cholesterol, so that must be taken into consideration when including it in the diet.

[ServSafe Connection]

Food Safety Reminders for this Chapter

- To check the temperature of meat, poultry, or seafood during receiving, insert the thermometer stem or probe into the thickest part of the food. The center is usually the thickest part.

- To help prevent cross-contamination during preparation, use separate equipment for each type of food. For example, use one set of cutting boards, utensils, and containers for raw poultry. Use another for meat. Use a third set for seafood.

- Remember the minimum internal temperatures required for cooking TCS food:

  - Poultry: 165°F for 15 seconds

  - Ground meat, including beef and seafood: 155°F for 15 seconds

  - Seafood and steaks/chops of pork, beef, veal, and lamb: 145°F for 15 seconds

  - Roasts of pork, beef, veal, and lamb: 145°F for four minutes

418

Summary

In this section, you learned the following:

- The term charcuterie, which in French means "cooked flesh," refers to specially prepared pork products, including sausage, smoked ham, bacon, pâté, and terrine. Charcuterie refers to the production of pates, terrines, galantines, sausages, and similar foods. These food items are served cold and generally provided by the garde manger department. Garde manger is the department typically found in a classical brigade system kitchen and/ or the chef that is responsible for the preparation of cold foods, including salads and salad dressings, cold appetizers, charcuterie items, and similar dishes. Most of the decorative buffet work would come from the garde manger department. The garde manger department is also referred to as the pantry.

- Charcuterie consists of two main categories: sausages and forcemeat. The three main types of sausage are fresh, smoked, or dried. A number of dishes can be made using forcemeat. The two main types of forcemeat are straight forcemeat, which is very finely ground, seasoned with herbs and spices, and then cooked in an earthenware mold called a terrine; and a country-style forcemeat, which is usually made of a cured meat and has a slightly coarser texture.

419

Summary

- Remind students to review the following:
  1. Definitions of charcuterie and garde manger
  2. The types of charcuterie

Section 6.4
Review Questions

1. Charcuterie is meat mixture foods and force-meat, and includes sausage.

2. Garde manger is the kitchen brigade responsible for cold foods, buffets, and charcuterie.

3. Sausages can be fresh, smoked, or dried.

4. Country style forcemeat is not ground as fine; it is more coarse and cured.

5. Each student will have an interpretation of the professional profile.

6. Perhaps there would be an advantage to making menu items ahead of time. There could be a signature flavor or recipe for a fresh sausage that would be special.

7. The students will have their own treatments of the concept. They might mention the popularity of sausages and sausage dishes.

8. The three types are fresh sausage, smoked sausage, or dried sausage. Students answers will vary.

Section 6.4 Review Questions

1. What is charcuterie?
2. What is garde manger?
3. What are the three types of sausages?
4. What is the difference between straight forcemeat and country-style forcemeat?
5. Based on Charlene Obal's preferences, how might charcuterie fit in to the menu at Saphron Restaurant? Why?
6. Miguel and Chef Kate aren't really considering specializing in charcuterie. Is this a mistake? Give one reason why such a specialty might be beneficial and one reason why it may not.
7. There was a time not too long ago when garde manger was said to be a thing of the past, but it has recently had a resurgence. Do you think garde manger is a vital part of the dining experience or not? Explain your opinion.
8. Come up with a menu item for each of the three types of sausage. Write up each item as if you were putting it on a real menu.

420

Section 6.4 Activities

1. Study Skills/Group Activity: Making Pâté

In a group, use ingredients to make a liver pâté appetizer. Make the dish in a mold, as directed. The next class period, turn it out of the mold and garnish it for service. Taste the product and share it with the class. What have you learned about this type of product? Verbally explain to the class what your group created.

2. Independent Activity: Cruise Ship Garde Manger

Imagine that you are the garde manger (pantry chef) on a luxurious cruise ship. You are asked to present an afternoon class for the passengers. You want to talk about buffet displays that they see onboard the ship. Write an outline for your 20-minute class. Include descriptions of your displays.

3. Critical Thinking: Sausage Diagram

Create a Venn diagram showing the similarities and differences between various types of dried, smoked, and cooked sausages.

421

Section 6.4 Activities

1. The best way for students to understand these concepts is to try making and tasting them.

2. Cruise ships are famous for having fancy and elaborate food displays. Students can consider elaborate displays of carved watermelons and other fruit and vegetables, ice sculpture, beautiful fish on beds of ice, sausages, pâtés, and so on.

3. The students only need two or three circles in their Venn diagrams. Each diagram might be different because the students might choose different types of sausages.

Case Study Follow-Up

- All three questions will have answers based on the student's opinions and feelings after studying the chapter. Each will be different.

- The results of this follow-up could make for some very interesting classroom discussions.

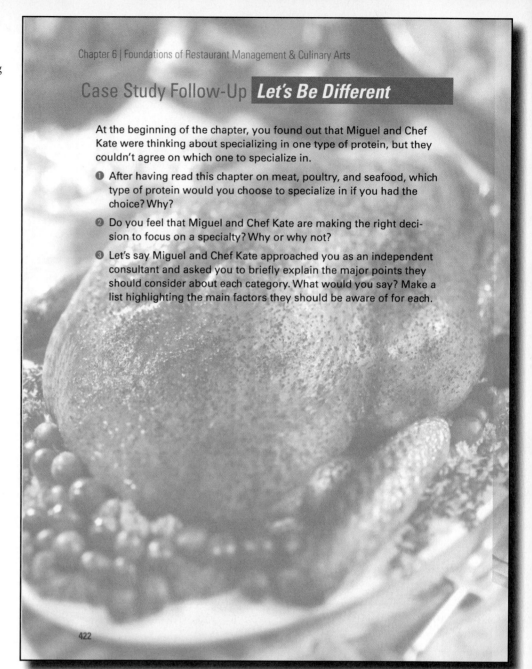

Case Study Follow-Up *Let's Be Different*

At the beginning of the chapter, you found out that Miguel and Chef Kate were thinking about specializing in one type of protein, but they couldn't agree on which one to specialize in.

❶ After having read this chapter on meat, poultry, and seafood, which type of protein would you choose to specialize in if you had the choice? Why?

❷ Do you feel that Miguel and Chef Kate are making the right decision to focus on a specialty? Why or why not?

❸ Let's say Miguel and Chef Kate approached you as an independent consultant and asked you to briefly explain the major points they should consider about each category. What would you say? Make a list highlighting the main factors they should be aware of for each.

422

Apply Your Learning

Figuring Out Profit Margins

Serving fresh lobster requires little labor. But it is expensive to buy, so it is usually very high priced on a menu. Sometimes high cost can generate profit for a restaurant. Profit margin is the price of an item minus the cost of serving it (including the cost of the food, the overhead for the establishment, and the servers).

A lobster may cost $25 to serve. However, you can charge the guest $50 for the item. That is a profit of $25.

If you divide the profit by the price, you have the profit margin: $25 ÷ $50 = 0.5. 0.5 can also be called 50 percent. The profit is $25. The profit margin on the lobster dish is 50 percent.

Suppose your menu offered a chicken breast that cost $4 to serve. You charge $20 for it. What is the profit for the chicken breast? What is the profit margin for the chicken breast?

Which menu item, lobster or chicken, has a greater profit margin? Which item earns the restaurant more money?

Crayfish in Literature

Crayfish are freshwater crustaceans found in parts of the United States and other parts of the world. In the United States they are called "crayfish," "crawfish," or "crawdads." You can find cultural references to them in literature. Research online and find at least one reference to them in American literature. Then continue your research into the role of crayfish in American cuisine. Name three menu crayfish.

Apply Your Learning

Figuring Out Profit Margins

The profit on the chicken is $20 − $4 = $16, and the profit margin is 16 ÷ 20 = 0.8 or 80 percent. The profit margin for the chicken (80 percent) is greater than that for the lobster (50 percent). However, the lobster makes more profit ($25) than the chicken ($16).

Crayfish in Literature

Encourage the students to check literature from the Southern or Midwestern United States. However, crayfish are found in the Pacific Northwest and other regions as well.

Examining Water Molecules

When water is solid it is an ordered lattice like this:

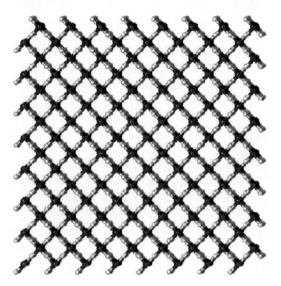

Liquid water molecules have a shape that allows them to flow freely. When they freeze, they form a rigid structure that actually has more space between the molecules than when the water is liquid. This makes ice less dense than water, so ice cubes float in water. Most solids sink in the liquid medium of the same compound, because most solids are more dense than the liquid forms.

When water temperature drops below 32°F, the ice forms and it feels very cold and is solid. The molecules still vibrate, but they do not move out of the lattice until the temperature rises above 32°F, the pressure on the ice increases, or there is friction on it. However, the incomplete lattice at the edge of the structure remains nearly liquid and slippery. Ice is slippery.

When heat is applied, the molecules start to move around. When the water molecules are boiling and releasing as steam, they move apart and fly away from each other. Steam feels very hot because it is made of little water droplets moving away from boiling water. Keep in mind, however, that these little visible water droplets in steam are not actually water vapor, but still liquid water. The molecules get further apart and become invisible as steam vaporizes.

However, as they further separate into water vapor in the air they are not necessarily hot. They can cool down until they reach the dew point and condense again. There is water vapor in the air all around us.

Examining Water Molecules

Heat is energy. Energy makes molecules move faster. When molecules move faster, they create friction, which is felt as heat. This heat energy can alter protein molecules, which cooks meat.

Cut and color paper models of ten water molecules to match this drawing.

Research images of water in various forms in textbooks or online.

Assemble the models as they appear in a solid form. When water is a solid, does it feel hot or cold? What is the temperature range? How much do the molecules move?

Now, assemble the water molecule models as they would appear in a liquid form. When water is a liquid, does it feel hot or cold? What is the temperature range? How much do the molecules move?

Finally, assemble the models as they would appear when heated to boiling and vaporizing. When heated water is a gas (vapor), does it feel hot or cold? What is the temperature range? How much do the molecules move?

A heat source causes motion in food molecules. This motion changes and heats (cooks) the food.

Critical Thinking A Selling Script

What role has poultry played in traditional U.S. cuisine? What is the connection of wild poultry to the Native Americans and the first European settlers on the American continent? What role did wild game birds play in the presidential-inauguration festivities of Barack Obama or other U.S. presidents? How could this relate to a restaurant establishment in the United States? Write a report at least two paragraphs long about these questions.

424

Critical Thinking A Selling Script

Wild game birds were served at the inaugural luncheon of President Barack Obama: duck breast with cherry chutney and herb-roasted pheasant with wild rice stuffing. Abraham Lincoln also had game birds at his inauguration. Ronald Reagan had chicken breast in white wine and caper sauce. George W. Bush's menu featured quail. Franklin D. Roosevelt served a chicken salad.

Exam Prep Questions

1 The grade of meat that measures the edible or usable portion of meat after being trimmed is called

A. yield.

B. quality.

C. USDA A.

D. USDA C.

2 Meat must be aged _____ hours to allow for the muscles to relax.

A. 6 to 24

B. 24 to 48

C. 48 to 72

D. 72 to 96

3 Thin, boneless cuts of meat that are lightly pounded are called

A. emincé.

B. scallops.

C. noisettes.

D. medallions.

4 How is dark meat poultry different than white meat poultry?

A. Dark meat is lower in calories than white meat.

B. Dark meat is harder to come by than white meat.

C. Dark meat tends to be more expensive than white meat.

D. Dark meat tends to be juicier and more flavorful than white meat.

5 What are the three essential tools needed for fabricating poultry?

A. Hand saw, boning knife, and bucket

B. Rubber mallet, fork, and paring knife

C. Paring knife, chef's knife, and tourné knife

D. Work surface, boning knife, and chef's knife

6 Sautéing is a _____ cooking method used for cooking meat, poultry, or seafood.

A. dry-heat

B. moist-heat

C. combination

D. dry-heat with fat and oil

7 What are the two main types of fin fish?

A. Shell and flat

B. Round and flat

C. Crustaceans and mollusks

D. Mollusks and cephalopods

8 When fabricating a lobster, it is easier to remove the meat from the shell

A. after steaming or boiling it first.

B. if it is cut in half when still semi-frozen.

C. by cutting the lobster in half lengthwise.

D. if the knife is first heated and then dipped in olive oil.

425

Exam Prep Answers

1. A
2. C
3. B
4. D
5. D
6. D
7. B
8. A
9. B
10. C

9 Live shellfish must be received on ice or at an air temperature of _____ or lower.

A. 30°F

B. 45°F

C. 50°F

D. 60°F

10 Garde manger is the department in the kitchen that is typically in charge of

A. desserts.

B. hot foods.

C. cold foods.

D. expediting food service.

Minute Steak Dijonaise

Cooking time: 6 minutes
Yield: 2 servings

Ingredients

Two 6-oz	Sirloin steaks, trimmed	3 fl oz	Heavy cream
1 oz	Dijon mustard	1 oz	Whole butter
2 oz	Onion, small dice	To taste	Salt and pepper
1 fl oz	Clarified butter		

Directions

1. Pound the steaks to a ¼-inch thickness.
2. Cover one side of each sirloin first with 1½ teaspoons of the mustard and then half of the onion, pressing the onion firmly into the steak.
3. Sauté the steaks in the clarified butter, presentation (onion) side down first for 2 to 3 minutes per side. Remove and hold in warm place.
4. Degrease the pan. Add the cream and reduce by half. Add the rest of the mustard.
5. Adjust the seasonings. Serve each portion with some of the sauce.

Recipe Nutritional Content

Calories	750	Cholesterol	245 mg	Protein	52 g
Calories from fat	510	Sodium	1220 mg	Vitamin A	30%
Total fat	57 g	Carbohydrates	6 g	Vitamin C	4%
Saturated fat	31 g	Dietary fiber	1 g	Calcium	10%
Trans fat	0 g	Sugars	1 g	Iron	20%

Nutritional analysis provided by FoodCalc®, www.foodcalc.com

427

Recipe

Minute Steak Dijonaise

- This recipe is cooked with dry heat with fat. A sauce is made as an accompaniment.

Recipe

Braised Chicken with Apple Cider and Cashew Butter

- This recipe uses a moist cooking process.

Braised Chicken with Apple Cider and Cashew Butter

Cooking time: 30 minutes
Yield: 8 Servings

Ingredients

2 oz	Shallots, minced	As needed	Flour
2½ fl oz	Clarified butter	12 oz	Mirepoix
12 fl oz	Calvados	1	Garlic head, cut in half
2 tsp	Fresh thyme, chopped	1 pint	Apple cider
3 oz	Cashews	1 Tbsp	Cider vinegar
1 Tbsp	Honey	3 pints	Chicken stock
1 lb	Unsalted butter	2	Bay leaves
To taste	Salt and pepper	1 sprig	Fresh thyme
Two 3 lb, 8-oz each Chickens, quartered		As needed	Blond roux

Directions

1. To make the cashew butter, lightly sauté the shallots in 1 tablespoon clarified butter. Add 4 ounces of the calvados and the chopped thyme and reduce the mixture. Remove from the heat and cool.
2. Place the cashews in a food processor and process to a medium-fine consistency. Add the cooled shallots, honey, and unsalted butter. Season with salt and pepper and process well.
3. Season the chicken with salt and pepper and dredge in flour.
4. Brown the chicken evenly in the clarified butter for about 6 minutes per side.
5. Remove the chicken. Add the mirepoix and garlic to the pan; sauté for 1 minute.
6. Add the remaining calvados, cider, and vinegar; reduce by half.
7. Return the chicken to the pan and add the stock and herbs. Cover and braise until done, approximately 15 minutes. Remove the chicken from the pan. (The breast and wings will cook more quickly and must be removed before the thigh and leg pieces.)
8. Reduce the stock by half. Use the roux to thicken to a light consistency.
9. Strain the sauce, mix with the cashew butter, and season to taste with salt and pepper. Ladle the sauce over the chicken and serve at once.

Recipe Nutritional Content

Calories	1710	Cholesterol	455 mg	Protein	83 g
Calories from fat	1110	Sodium	800 mg	Vitamin A	100%
Total fat	124 g	Carbohydrates	37 g	Vitamin C	20%
Saturated fat	55 g	Dietary fiber	2 g	Calcium	10%
Trans fat	0 g	Sugars	14 g	Iron	35%

Nutritional analysis provided by FoodCalc®, www.foodcalc.com

428

Sautéed Trout Meuniére

Cooking time: 15 minutes
Yield: 10 servings

Ingredients

10	Pan-dressed trout (10-ounces each)	10 oz	Butter (for sauce)
To taste	Salt and pepper	2 fl oz	Lemon juice
As needed	Flour	3 Tbsp	Parsley
2 fl oz	Butter (for sauté)		

Directions

1. Rinse the trout.
2. Trim the trout as necessary, removing the head and tail if desired.
3. When ready to sauté, blot dry and season with salt and pepper.
4. Dredge the fish in flour, shaking off excess.
5. Heat a sauté pan to medium-high.
6. Add the butter.
7. Sauté the trout until the flesh is opaque and firm, about 3 minutes per side.
8. Remove the trout from the pan. Keep warm on side.
9. Pour excess fat from pan.
10. Add whole butter.
11. Cook until the butter begins to brown and has a nutty aroma.
12. Add the lemon juice.
13. Swirl the pan to deglaze.
14. Add the parsley and immediately spoon over trout.
15. Serve immediately.

Recipe Nutritional Content

Calories	810	Cholesterol	285 mg	Protein	76 g
Calories from fat	460	Sodium	500 mg	Vitamin A	20%
Total fat	52 g	Carbohydrates	5 g	Vitamin C	10%
Saturated fat	22 g	Dietary fiber	0 g	Calcium	20%
Trans fat	0 g	Sugars	0 g	Iron	30%

Nutritional analysis provided by FoodCalc®, www.foodcalc.com

429

Recipe

Sautéed Trout Meuniére

- This recipe uses dry heat with fat.

Chapter 7 Overview

Chapter 7 builds on the other management principles addressed throughout the program, explaining how to create and manage a marketing plan and conduct a market analysis. It also discusses the role of the menu in marketing a restaurant or foodservice operation.

Section 1: This section introduces students to basic marketing concepts and explains how to create a marketing plan.

Section 2: This section focuses on the specifics of marketing: analyzing markets, building an identity, and communicating that identity to the community.

Section 3: Finally, this section looks at the menu. After describing the various types of menus, it discusses how to build and analyze a menu as part of the greater marketing scheme.

Advance Preparation	
Review	Sections 7.1–7.3
	Chapters 3, 5
	Level 1, Chapters 1, 4, 7, 8, 10
Contact	A restaurant or foodservice professional who specializes in marketing
Prepare	Samples of market communications from a variety of restaurant or foodservice operations
	Samples of promotional items from a variety of restaurant or foodservice operations
	Sample menus from a variety of restaurants that display a range of menu types

Chapter 7
Marketing

CUSTOMIZED INSTRUCTION OPTIONS

Less Advanced Students	More Advanced Students	ESOL Students	Special Needs Students
Pages 438, 474	Pages 437, 479	Pages 435, 469	Pages 441, 458

CHAPTER TOOLS

21st-Century Skills	Mathematics	Science	Literacy
Pages 434, 435, 437, 438, 441, 442, 448, 449, 451, 456, 458, 459, 460, 461, 462, 463, 469, 471, 474, 479, 480, 481, 482, 484, 485, 486, 488	Pages 484, 485, 486	Pages 479, 482, 488	Pages 434, 435, 437, 438, 441, 442, 448, 449, 451, 456, 458, 459, 460, 461, 462, 463, 469, 471, 474, 479, 480, 481, 482, 484, 485, 486, 488

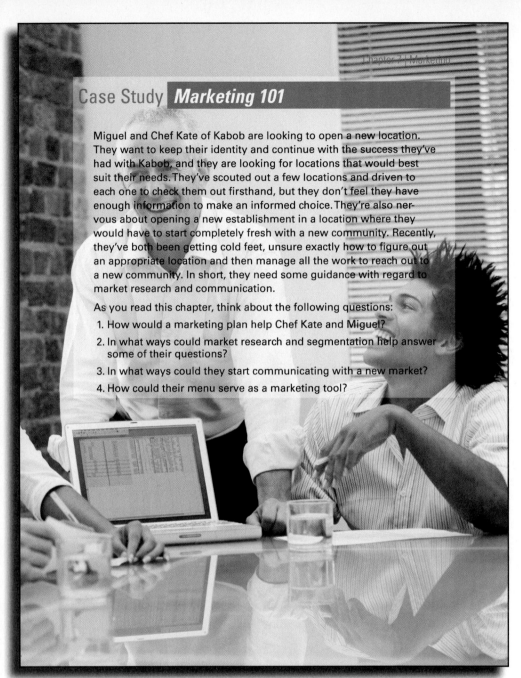

Miguel and Chef Kate of Kabob are looking to open a new location. They want to keep their identity and continue with the success they've had with Kabob, and they are looking for locations that would best suit their needs. They've scouted out a few locations and driven to each one to check them out firsthand, but they don't feel they have enough information to make an informed choice. They're also nervous about opening a new establishment in a location where they would have to start completely fresh with a new community. Recently, they've both been getting cold feet, unsure exactly how to figure out an appropriate location and then manage all the work to reach out to a new community. In short, they need some guidance with regard to market research and communication.

As you read this chapter, think about the following questions:

1. How would a marketing plan help Chef Kate and Miguel?

2. In what ways could market research and segmentation help answer some of their questions?

3. In what ways could they start communicating with a new market?

4. How could their menu serve as a marketing tool?

Case Study
Marketing 101

- Discuss the implications of opening a second location. For instance, how can Miguel and Chef Kate be sure that the level of guest service and the quality of food will not suffer if their attention is divided between two locations?

- What are some advantages and disadvantages to opening multiple locations?

- What role does communication play in opening a new operation, both within the business and within the community it will serve?

- How can employee training and staff development help mitigate some of the worries associated with opening a new operation?

- Note that there are follow-up questions about the case study at the end of the chapter.

- This activity could be done in groups, as a class, or as a homework assignment.

Discuss	Tania Haigh says, "Working in foodservice is so much fun!" How do students respond to this statement?
	What might "a company that is dedicated to its employees" look like? What are some characteristics it might have?
	When considering your career path and opportunities that might arise, how can you decide whether or not to take specific risks? What information do you consider in these decisions?
	What is grassroots marketing? Why is it important in helping a company identify consumer needs?
Reinforce and Review	To be successful in marketing, you should first find a company that is dedicated to its employees and provides substantial career development opportunities.
	Taking risks and trying something different can be very rewarding, both personally and professionally.
	Excel in every assignment you get, no matter how big or small the task might be.
Teaching Tips	Like most of the other subjects of these Professional Profiles, Haigh describes her passion for her career.
	Taking advantage of both formal and informal learning opportunities is crucial to a successful marketing career.

[professional profile]

Tania M. Haigh

Marketing Manager, McDonald's USA, LLC

I knew early on, with my parents' encouragement, that a career in business—specifically marketing—was the right path for me. My marketing courses at Texas Christian University in Fort Worth, Texas, really whetted my appetite, and I knew I could excel in this industry. Following four years at the university, I received a B.S. in business administration with a major in international marketing. Working in foodservice is so much fun! We provide on-the-go solutions for busy customers every day, and there's something available for everyone.

To be successful in marketing, you should first find a company that is dedicated to its employees and provides substantial career development opportunities. Once you find your place, have passion for your job. Excel in every assignment you get, no matter how big or small the task may be.

I remember a time early on in my marketing career, when an opportunity came up to go on a mobile promotional marketing tour around the country. At the time, I was working in the comfort of an office. This new challenge meant I'd be driving a promotional vehicle along with one other person. We'd be on the road for long hours and would stay in hotels for five months. Even though this job would upset my routine and take me outside my comfort zone, away from friends and family, I jumped at the opportunity to be able to learn about grassroots marketing. It allowed me to travel to different parts of the country and be exposed to many different kinds of consumers. At the time, I didn't know how this job was going to fit into the grand scheme of things. But, it turned out that taking the risk—trying something different—proved to be very rewarding.

In 2005, I joined McDonald's® as a regional marketing supervisor in the Chicago region. There, I gathered an in-depth knowledge of McDonald's business while leading the development of local market marketing strategies in the Chicagoland area, including programs for the Hispanic consumer market.

As a first-generation American who spent her childhood in Honduras, the Dominican Republic, and the United States, Tania's Italian and Honduran background combined with a childhood spent in different countries has provided her a unique perspective that has carried her into a successful marketing career at McDonald's U.S.A.

432

In 2007, I was promoted to manager and joined McDonald's National Marketing team at McDonald's U.S. headquarters in Oak Brook, Illinois. In this current role, I manage the company's brand trust marketing efforts for McDonald's employment brand as well as the company's support of McDonald's charity of choice, Ronald McDonald House Charities® (RMHC®), which includes the company's worldwide RMHC fundraiser benefiting children's charities across the globe, McHappy Day®.

Remember:

❝*If you do it first class, you never have to do it again.* **❞**
—Ray Kroc, Founder, McDonald's

About Marketing

For me, the most important aspect of marketing is always putting the customer first. Working for McDonald's, I've learned that keeping the customer at the fore-front of a range of activities, from product development to advertising campaigns, will help you succeed in giving customers what they want.

Marketing should matter to you because you are a valuable consumer. Once you have more awareness of what marketing is and what it means for a business, you will find it interesting how many brands continually strive to get your attention and keep you interested in their products! This can range from TV shows to clothing lines to—yes—food! I hope that more of you will become interested in pursuing a career in marketing. You're in a position to add a lot of value by sharing your per-spective.

7.1 Introduction to Marketing	7.2 Market Analysis, Identity, and Communication	7.3 The Menu as Marketing Tool
• Marketing overview	• Market research methods	• Menu overview
• Basic marketing concepts	• Market segmentation	• Menu types
• Marketing plan	• Creating a market identity	• Organizing a menu
• SWOT	• Market communications	• Creating a menu
	• Types of sales promotions	• Pricing the menu
	• Public relations: Engaging the community	• Analyzing the menu

SECTION 7.1 INTRODUCTION TO MARKETING

Did you ever have a really good idea only to have it fizzle out by presenting it at the wrong time or to the wrong audience? For example, did you ever ask your parents for something big, something you were really excited about—like an expensive clothing item or to go to a party with friends—only to have them say no because they were in a bad mood? Or maybe you were dying to go to a

433

Professional Profile (cont.)

Discuss	Haigh states, "The most important part of marketing is always putting the customer first." Explain how this relates to both quality guest service and professionalism.
	"If you do it first class, you never have to do it again." Do students agree or disagree with this statement? How does it apply to the restaurant and foodservice industry?
	What are some examples of restaurant and foodservice marketing? How do they affect you personally?
	McDonald's food is very popular with consumers worldwide, attracting huge numbers of customers daily. Why does it continue to operate large marketing campaigns, if it already has a solid and assured customer base?
Reinforce and Review	Becoming aware of what marketing is and what it means to a business can help consumers identify the ways in which businesses market to them each day.
	Keeping the customer at the forefront of a range of activities can help a company succeed in giving customers what they want.
Teaching Tips	While studying this chapter, encourage students to identify any marketing practices that they might not have observed before.

Section 7.1
Introduction to Marketing

Introduce the Section
a. Provide a general overview of the marketing function and identify specific marketing concepts.
b. Explain why a thorough marketing plan is essential to the success of a restaurant or foodservice operation.
c. Note that before a company moves forward, it must understand its strengths and weaknesses so it can capitalize on the former and minimize the damage caused by the latter.
d. Discuss the objectives for the section.

Vocabulary Review
a. Direct students to the key terms.
b. Pronounce each word, and have the students repeat the pronunciation out loud.
c. Discuss the definition of each word.

Focus and Engage

Discuss
- Why is marketing an important part of the res-taurant and foodservice industry?
- How do marketing campaigns target specific de-mographic groups? What examples are particu-larly directed toward teenagers?

Teaching Tips
- Throughout this chapter, students should con-sider the importance of a defined public image to the success of a restaurant or foodservice operation.

Teach

Discuss

- In what ways does marketing involve communication?

- How do you engage in marketing in your daily life?

Reinforce and Review

- For a business to profitably provide a product or service, there must first be a market for that product or service.

- Marketing and advertising are not the same thing; rather, advertising is a component of a successful marketing strategy.

- Marketing includes determining what products and services to offer, how to position them in the marketplace, how to promote them to potential buyers, how to price them so people will buy them, and how to deliver the products and services to the purchasers.

Teaching Tips

- Encourage students to share opportunities in which they have successfully or unsuccessfully marketed themselves.

Homework Activity: To Market, To Market

Literacy Connection, 21st-Century Skills—Critical Thinking and Problem Solving, Communicate Clearly, Work Independently

Consider the five parts of the marketing function. How can you use each to gain a positive outcome in your daily life? Identify a goal you wish to attain and explain how you would use each component of marketing to succeed.

Vocabulary Terms

- **Market:** A group of people who desire a particular product or service; also known as customers.

- **Marketing:** The process of communicating a business's message to its market.

movie, but asked a friend who had absolutely no money at the time and so you were stuck watching TV all night. If you've ever had an experience like this, it is likely that you can attribute it to bad marketing. In the first example, you mistimed the market (asking your parents when they were in a bad mood), and in the second example, you failed to do proper research, asking a penniless friend to spend what he or she didn't have. Better timing or better research would have likely resulted in better outcomes for you. In all likelihood, you *have* had better outcomes. And that's probably because you did a better job marketing yourself.

Marketing might sound like a big, important business term—and it most definitely is—but it's also something that you're probably more familiar with than you think. People, like operations, need to do their research, figure out their market, and determine how best to present themselves in an effort to achieve their desired goals. Marketing is the process by which people and operations accomplish these goals.

Study Questions

After studying Section 7.1, you should be able to answer the following questions:

- What is marketing and how is it different from advertising?

- What is the contemporary market mix?

- What is a market plan?

- What is the purpose of SWOT?

Marketing Overview

In order for a business to profitably provide a product or a service, there must be a group of people who desire that product or service. That group of people, also called customers, is called a **market**. But having a product or service and a market that desires it is only half the battle. A business also needs to find a way to reach its ideal market; the business has to communicate that its product or service is available for purchase. **Marketing** is the process of communicating a business's message to its market.

People often talk about advertising and marketing as if they are the same thing. They are not. Advertising is just one component of a successful marketing strategy. Marketing includes determining what products and services to offer, how to position them in the marketplace, how to promote them to potential buyers, how to price them so people will buy them, and how to get the goods to these buyers. These concepts are illustrated in Figure 7.1 on the following page.

434

MARKETING FUNCTIONS

1 determine what products and services to offer

2 position them in the marketplace

3 promote them to potential buyers

4 price them so people will buy them

5 get the goods to these buyers

Figure 7.1: Marketing functions address many issues.

In the current business environment, marketing drives the operation. Managers now ask, "What do people want that we can provide at a profit?" This means that an operation has to do the following:

- Determine customer needs and wants before doing anything else.

- Determine the costs, prices, and profitability of products and services before starting to produce them.

- Organize all aspects of the operation to provide what the customers want.

This approach is called the marketing concept. It puts marketing into, and sometimes in charge of, areas of the company and the product development process that used to belong exclusively to other specialties. For example, in a large corporation or operation, a marketing department might be more influential than people outside the organization would think because of the following:

- The research and development department is no longer in charge of inventing whatever it wants. The marketing department now tells it what products are needed and what their characteristics should be.

- The production department is no longer in charge of deciding how to produce the product. Marketing now puts parameters in place that control costs, locations, and timing of production.

- The sales department is no longer in control of pricing; the marketing department is now in control.

435

Discuss

- What does it mean to say that "Marketing drives the operation"?

- Identify some advantages and disadvantages to the marketing concept approach to business.

Reinforce and Review

- Determining customer wants and needs is the first step a business must take.

- Before production can begin, management must determine the costs, prices, and profitability of the goods and services it plans to provide.

- The marketing concept puts marketing into, and sometimes in charge of, areas of the company and the product development process that used to belong exclusively to other specialties.

Teaching Tips

- Encourage students to explore ways in which a business could change, based on which department is prioritized. For instance, if the production department is in charge of the business, how might that affect the marketing department, or the sales department?

CUSTOMIZED INSTRUCTION
Literacy Connection, 21st-Century Skills— Think Creatively, Reason Effectively, Communicate Clearly, Work Independently
ESOL Students
Are there any goods and services offered in your country of origin that are less available here? Could any of these be profitably marketed in your current community? Why or why not?
Write a brief essay outlining your thoughts.

Figure Focus

Figure 7.1: Although advertising and promotion are often the only components of marketing that consumers notice, they represent only a fraction of the overall marketing function.

Discuss

- Identify a current marketing campaign. What are its four Ps? Do they provide all the information that potential consumers need when deciding whether to purchase the good or service? Why or why not?

- Is the contemporary marketing mix only relevant to the restaurant and foodservice industry? Why or why not?

Reinforce and Review

- All businesses need to engage in vigorous marketing activity.

- The conventional marketing mix involves the four Ps: place, product, price, and promotion.

- The contemporary marketing mix expands the four Ps to include other elements that help distinguish a product or service in an era of fierce competition.

Teaching Tips

- Relate the contemporary marketing mix to the concept of quality guest service.

Vocabulary Terms

- **Marketing mix:** The combination of all the factors that go into creating, developing, and selling a product.

- **Contemporary marketing mix:** A model of business operations that relies on the product-service mix, the presentation mix, and the communication mix.

In smaller operations, all of these "departments" might be one or two people, but decisions about research and development, production, and sales will all be influenced by marketing concerns and priorities.

Basic Marketing Concepts

All businesses need to engage in vigorous marketing activity. Such marketing activity is frequently called the **marketing mix**, which is the combination of all the factors that go into creating, developing, and selling a product. For decades, the conventional marketing mix was highlighted by what's known as "the four P's": place, product, price, and promotion. This framework is very similar to what was covered in the Marketing Overview section, and it all still applies today. But in today's highly competitive restaurant and foodservice industry, marketers have modified this standard model somewhat to reflect the complexities and challenges that operations now face. This new model is called the **contemporary marketing mix**, and it consists of three primary elements, as illustrated in Figure 7.2:

- Product-service mix

- Presentation mix

- Communication mix

Figure 7.2: Examples of the contemporary marketing mix include activities designed to create, develop, and sell a product.

436

Figure Focus

Figure 7.2: What does each photograph suggest to you about the products and services being offered?

The **product-service mix** consists of all of the food and services offered to customers. Restaurant and foodservice operations are often thought of by the food, or product, they offer. But the way they provide it, the service, is also a huge aspect of an operation's marketing. As discussed in *Foundations of Restaurant Management & Culinary Arts, Level One, Chapter 10, Serving Your Guests*, operations can often gain a competitive edge in today's restaurant and foodservice industry by offering a greater variety of services provided with better efficiency. Operations serving similar food products at similar prices will often need to enhance their services to gain an advantage on the competition. Enhanced tableside service, delivery service, takeout service, and even new trends in curbside takeout services all factor into the product-service mix.

The **presentation mix** consists of all the elements that make the operation look unique. The layout of the operation, its size, the type of furniture it uses, the decorations, color scheme, lighting, and service uniforms all contribute to the identity of the operation. All of these elements contribute to an operation's **aesthetic**, or the way it looks and feels to the customers. Dim lighting with a subdued color scheme, for example, will generate a much different impression than a brightly lit establishment that employs a vibrant, energetic color scheme. The choices that an operation makes with regard to how it actually presents itself to customers are critical factors in its marketing strategy.

The **communication mix** includes all of the ways an operation actively tries to reach, or communicate, with its desired customers. An operation communicates with its customers through advertising such as television, radio, newspapers, flyers, or Web sites. But it also communicates with its customers through its menu, customer survey requests and other customer feedback requests, local community outreach, and perhaps even Internet social networking sites. Employing an effective communication mix is crucial to monitoring, maintaining, and improving an operation's relationship with the market that it serves.

These aspects of the contemporary marketing mix are constantly changing. An operation must continually evolve with the times. In order to do so, operations need to be aware of what's going on in the immediate community as well as the surrounding areas. In short, a successful operation needs to keep up with consumer trends, also known as **market trends**. Market trends, such as the one illustrated in Figure 7.3 on the following page, may be responses to consumers' changing attitudes about food, service, or aesthetics. They can also be responses to broader, farther-reaching trends, such as political issues to do with energy conservation and recycling, or economic upswings or downturns that can greatly affect the behavior of a given market.

437

CUSTOMIZED INSTRUCTION

Literacy Connection, 21st-Century Skills—Critical Thinking and Problem Solving, Communicate Clearly, Information Literacy, Work Independently

More Advanced Students

A branch of philosophy known as aesthetics considers the nature and meaning of beauty; similarly, the science of aesthetics works to uncover why and how humans perceive beauty and make value-driven judgments.

Research aesthetics, from a scientific or a philosophical standpoint. Explain this concept, its origins, current trends of thought, and any other material you find relevant in a two-page report.

Discuss

- What products and services are important to you as a consumer? How do you make decisions about what to purchase and from whom to purchase it?

- What types of aesthetic appeal to you? Does your choice depend on what goods and services you intend to purchase?

- What are the most effective ways in which a restaurant or foodservice operation could communicate its message to you? Why?

- How can smaller operations stay abreast of changing market trends and thereby stay competitive with larger operations?

Reinforce and Review

- Restaurant and foodservice operations can often gain a competitive edge by offering a greater variety of services provided with better efficiency.

- Operations selling similar items at similar prices must differentiate themselves from their competitors.

- The ways in which an operation chooses to present itself are critical parts of its marketing strategy.

- Employing an effective communication mix is crucial to monitoring, maintaining, and improving an operation's relationship with the market it serves.

- Restaurant and foodservice operations need to keep up with market trends and be aware of changing consumer needs.

Teaching Tips

- Relate this discussion to the concept of competitive advantage, as discussed in Chapter 5 and in Level 1, Chapter 10.

Vocabulary Terms

- **Product-service mix:** All the food and services offered to customers.

- **Presentation mix:** All the elements that make a restaurant appears to be unique.

- **Aesthetic:** The way a particular operation looks and feels to customers.

- **Communication mix:** All the ways an operation actively tries to communicate with its desired customers.

- **Market trends:** Changing consumer habits.

Discuss

- What local restaurant or foodservice operations successfully observe changing trends? Does this make these operations more or less attractive to students? Why?

Reinforce and Review

- To manage the contemporary marketing mix and stay current with changing trends, restaurant and foodservice operations need to develop marketing plans.

- The five components of the marketing plan are researching the market, establishing objectives, developing a market strategy, implementing an action plan, and evaluating and modifying the action plan as needed.

Teaching Tips

- Consider inviting a restaurant or foodservice professional who specializes in marketing to speak with the class.

Vocabulary Terms

- **Marketing plan:** A list of steps an operation must take to sell a product or service to a specific market.

Figure 7.3: Curbside takeout is an example of a market trend. Market trends are constantly changing.

Any operation that isn't current with the latest trends is going to be, literally, behind the times, which isn't often a recipe for success. To efficiently manage the contemporary marketing mix and to effectively keep up with ever-changing local and national trends, operations need a plan. More specifically, every operation needs a marketing plan, which is the subject of the next section.

Marketing Plan

A **marketing plan** is a list of steps an operation must take to sell a product or service to a specific market. There are multiple steps to any plan, but every marketing plan will have five main components, as Figure 7.4 on the following page illustrates:

1. Research the market.
2. Establish objectives.
3. Develop a market strategy.
4. Implement an action plan.
5. Evaluate/modify the action plan as needed.

438

Figure Focus

Figure 7.3: How does offering reserved parking for takeout customers become a competitive advantage?

Figure 7.4: The components of a marketing plan include researching the market, establishing objectives, developing a strategy, implementing an action plan, and evaluating or modifying the action plan.

Research the Market

Gathering research must be the first step in any market plan. After all, it's very difficult to play a game without knowing the rules or the other players. Running a business is very similar in that managers need to know the ins and outs of the market and what they are up against. Marketers can gather information from a variety of reliable sources, such as customers, employees, the community, sales records, trade journals, and government offices. Through intensive research, marketers can figure out the strengths and weaknesses of their own operations as well as those of the competition. Marketers can also figure out the strengths and weaknesses of the products and services that their operation offers, as well as those that the competition offers. The market research an operation's marketer conducts will form the foundation from which management will make all other decisions.

Establish Objectives

Once marketers have completed a thorough research phase, the next step is to establish organizational objectives or goals. These objectives should clearly state what it is the operation wants to accomplish within a set time frame. Providing not only goals but also deadlines for achieving those goals will give the operation something to work toward. The goal and the time line for achieving it will also help shape the marketing strategy the operation will use.

439

Discuss

- How frequently should a business conduct market research? Why?

- In what ways are an organization's goals related to its vision and mission statements?

Reinforce and Review

- Gathering information must always be the first step in developing a marketing plan.

- Research can not only provide information about local and regional characteristics and competitors, but can help a company determine its own strengths and weaknesses.

- Market research forms the foundation on which management will make all subsequent decisions.

- Organizational goals should clearly state what it is the operation wishes to accomplish within a set time frame.

- Both organizational goals and the timelines for achieving these goals help to shape the operation's marketing strategy.

Teaching Tips

- Vision statements, mission statements, and organizational goals are discussed in Level 1, Chapter 8.

Figure Focus

Figure 7.4: In what ways does the marketing plan model resemble the problem-solving model introduced in Level 1, Chapter 8? How are the two related?

Discuss

- How can the development of a market strategy be used to strengthen employee relationships and enhance career skills?

- How frequently should the action plan be modified? Should managers always respond quickly to customer feedback? Why or why not?

Reinforce and Review

- An open-ended, collaborative approach to developing a market strategy will likely result in a better exchange of ideas and allow for more creativity.

- The best strategy is often a hybrid of the various strategies proposed.

- The action plan is the way in which the market strategy is implemented and is guided by the three prior steps.

- Finally, continuous monitoring is necessary to determine the success of an operation's marketing plan and to identify ways to modify the plan to meet evolving consumer demands.

Teaching Tips

- Relate this to the discussion of customer feedback in Level 1, Chapter 10.

Essential Skills:
Monitoring a Promotion Scheme

Encourage students to discuss the following:

- What are some promotions that would attract you to a particular restaurant or foodservice operation? Are these promotions that the operation could reasonably take? Why or why not?

- How are particular promotions part of the greater action plan?

- What are some reasons that a promotion might fail? How can these be avoided in future promotions?

Develop a Market Strategy

Once the operation's goals have been set and a time line laid out, the managers and marketers must brainstorm ways to achieve the objectives. It is helpful at this stage to come up with a number of different strategies and then evaluate the pros and cons of each. An open-ended, collaborative effort will likely result in a better exchange of ideas and allow for more creativity than if only one plan was thought up and immediately decided upon. Once you weigh the pros and cons of all the ideas, choose the best strategy. Often this will be a hybrid of the various strategies proposed.

Implement an Action Plan

The action plan is the way the market strategy is put into action. The action plan is guided by all the steps that have come before it: researching the market, establishing objectives and deadlines, and developing a market strategy. With an action plan, management and marketers take market strategy theory and actually put it into practice by making menu changes, adjusting pricing, purchasing advertising, and so on.

Evaluate/Modify the Action Plan

This stage is an ongoing process of monitoring the actions taken by the operation and gauging how successful they are. Management and marketers must continually be asking, "Is the plan working? Are there ways it is missing the mark? How can it be improved? What can we be doing better?" The answers to these questions will help management determine how to modify or revise the plan to meet the needs and trends of an ever-changing marketplace.

Essential Skills
Monitoring a Promotion Scheme

Promotions can really drive your business, bringing in new customers and encouraging existing customers to return more frequently. But simply assuming that more people are coming through the door and therefore the promotion must be working isn't enough. In order to know how well a promotion is working, you must constantly monitor its results.

❶ Develop a promotional scheme, making sure to bring other members of your team into the planning process. Many business owners work with public relations firms as well. Figure 7.5 illustrates a team at work.

❷ Plan how you will implement the new promotion: When will it begin and end? What other changes might occur? For instance, if you are offering two cheeseburgers for the price of one, should you expect a decrease in sales of other menu items? Can your suppliers meet your anticipated demands?

❸ Once the new promotion has begun, carefully track sales of not only the promotional items, but of all menu items. What unforeseen changes have arisen?

❹ Meet regularly with your staff to discuss the promotion: How is it working? What have customers reported? Have staff members experienced any problems with the promotion? Is the promotion successful enough that it should be extended? You may need to adjust the promotion slightly, but be careful with this; it could anger both potential and long-term customers if it appears that you aren't living up to the implicit bargain of the original promotion.

❺ Once the promotion has ended, discuss the entire process with your staff and public relations firm. What positive and negative aspects of the promotion did they observe? How could the promotion be fine-tuned in the future? Have the new customers attracted by the promotion continued to visit your restaurant? How have overall sales been, both during the promotion and after its completion?

This may all seem like a lot of work—and a lot of time to find in a busy day. But without careful monitoring, you may as well not offer a promotion at all, because you won't be able to calculate its results in a meaningful way that can help you make your business grow.

Figure 7.5: Step 1—Develop a promotional scheme.

441

Figure Focus

Figure 7.5: What inferences can students draw about the marketing team depicted in this photograph?

Discuss

- Should companies perform their own SWOT analyses or hire outside contractors? Why?

- When should a SWOT analysis be performed? How frequently should these analyses be conducted?

Reinforce and Review

- A SWOT analysis can help management better understand and respond to its current situation.

- Performing a SWOT analysis enables management and marketers to focus on the key issues affecting an operation.

- Management must be realistic about an operation's strengths and weaknesses to respond appropriately to the changing environment.

Vocabulary Terms

- **SWOT analysis:** An assessment of an operation's strengths, weaknesses, opportunities, and threats; also known as a situation assessment.

- **Strength:** An area in which an operation excels.

SWOT

To do a **SWOT analysis** (also called a situation assessment), identify a restaurant or foodservice operation's **S**trengths, **W**eaknesses, **O**pportunities, and **T**hreats. These concepts are illustrated in Figure 7.6. Doing a SWOT analysis is a simple way for the management of an operation to understand its current situation and take advantage of the opportunities open to it. SWOT analysis is very important to the process of preparing a marketing plan and to the success of an operation overall because it helps managers and marketers stay focused on key issues. To have a successful SWOT analysis, managers must be realistic about the operation's strengths and weaknesses and clearly separate its present conditions from where they want to be in the future.

Figure 7.6: The four elements of SWOT are strengths, weaknesses, obstacles, and threats.

At every stage of the marketing process, marketers can use a SWOT analysis as a good assessment tool to evaluate whether a particular plan is working and to gauge what is currently going on in a market:

- **Strengths:** List all of the strengths of the operation—areas where it excels. Examples of strengths include a well-trained staff, a good location, well-kept and clean facilities, high food quality, and service that exceeds customer expectations.

442

Figure Focus
Figure 7.6: What are some barriers to conducting a successful SWOT analysis?

- **Weaknesses:** Identify the operation's weaknesses. Do this so that weaknesses can eventually be eliminated or even turned into strengths. Some examples of weaknesses could be a boring menu, dirty facilities, limited abilities or resources, poor service, high staff turnover, or poor reputation.

- **Opportunities:** These are areas where the operation could either increase revenues or decrease costs. Examples might include launching a delivery or takeout service, recognizing weak competition, or gaining a volume discount from a supplier. One goal in any operation's marketing plan should be to make the most use of identified opportunities.

- **Threats:** These are the factors outside the operation that could decrease revenues or increase costs. Identifying threats helps to control them. Examples of possible threats include increased competition, increased taxes or costs of certain products, or even road construction.

Management should evaluate the different elements of the operation to identify which need improving to support the marketing plan and which are working well. After a full evaluation has been completed, management will know how successful its past efforts have been and have good ideas about where to invest money and energy in the future. It will also know what aspects should be improved to result in more benefits to customers, to employees, and to the operation as a whole.

Summary

In this section, you learned the following:

- In order for a business to profitably provide a product or a service, there must be a group of people who desire that product or service. That group of people, also called customers, is called a market. But having a viable product or service and a market that desires that product or service is only half the battle. A business also needs to find a way to reach its ideal market; the business has to communicate that its product or service is available for purchase. Marketing is the process of communicating a business's message to its respective market. People often refer to advertising and marketing as if they are the same thing. They are not. Advertising is only one component of a successful marketing strategy.

- In today's highly competitive restaurant and foodservice industry, operations employ a new marketing mix model called the contemporary marketing mix. It consists of three primary elements: product-service mix, presentation mix, and communication mix. The product-service mix consists of all of the food and services offered to customers. The presentation mix consists

443

Discuss

- What are some weaknesses that students have identified in restaurant and foodservice operations? How could they be eliminated?

- Suggest examples of threats that could face a restaurant or foodservice operation. What are some ways to control these threats?

Reinforce and Review

- Identifying weaknesses can help an operation eliminate them or even turn them into strengths.

- Identifying opportunities can help an operation increase its revenues or decrease its costs.

- Identifying threats can help an operation control them.

- Evaluations can help management identify appropriate areas for future investment and improvement.

Vocabulary Terms

- **Weakness:** An area in which an operation performs poorly.

- **Opportunity:** An area in which an operation could either increase revenues or decrease costs.

- **Threat:** An external factor that could either decrease revenues or increase costs.

Summary

- Remind students to review the following:
    1. The overview of marketing
    2. Basic marketing concepts
    3. The marketing plan
    4. SWOT

of all the elements that make the operation look unique. The communication mix includes all of the ways an operation actively tries to reach, or communicate, with its desired customers.

- A marketing plan is a list of the steps an operation must take to sell a product or service to a specific market. There are multiple steps to any plan, but every marketing plan will have five main components: research the market, establish objectives, develop a market strategy, implement an action plan, and evaluate or modify the action plan as needed.

- In a SWOT analysis (or a situation assessment), you identify your restaurant's Strengths, Weaknesses, Opportunities, and Threats. Doing a SWOT analysis is a simple way for management to understand the operation's current situation and take advantage of the opportunities open to it. A SWOT analysis is very important to the preparation of a marketing plan and to the success of an operation overall because it helps management stay focused on key issues. To have a successful SWOT analysis, management must be realistic about an operation's strengths and weaknesses and clearly separate its present conditions from where it wants to be in the future.

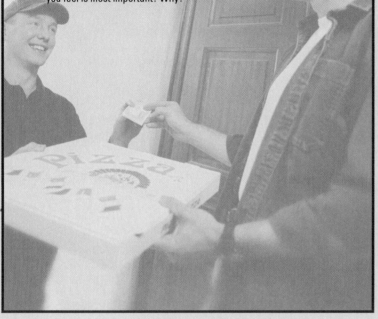

Section 7.1 Review Questions

1. What is the primary purpose of marketing?

2. What are the three primary elements of the contemporary marketing mix?

3. List the five components of a marketing plan.

4. What is SWOT?

5. What would Tania Haigh identify as the most important aspect of marketing?

6. Walk Chef Kate and Miguel through the five main components of a marketing plan, briefly explaining how they should proceed through each step.

7. What is the difference between marketing and advertising?

8. Which of the three primary elements of the contemporary marketing mix do you feel is most important? Why?

445

Section 7.1 Review Questions

1. The primary purpose of marketing is communicating a business's message to its market.

2. The three primary elements of the contemporary marketing mix are the product-service mix, the presentation mix, and the communication mix.

3. The five components of a marketing plan are researching the market, establishing objectives, developing a market strategy, implementing an action plan, and evaluating or modifying the action plan as needed.

4. SWOT stands for strengths, weaknesses, opportunities, threats.

5. Tania Haigh identifies always putting the customer first as the most important aspect of marketing.

6. Student responses will vary but should be clear and logical.

7. Advertising is a component of a successful marketing strategy.

8. Student responses will vary but should clearly defend one of the three elements of the contemporary marketing mix.

Section 7.1
Activities

1. Students should develop a cohesive and coherent marketing plan for the chosen restaurant category, taking care to follow the five steps of a marketing plan.

2. Students should logically explain the advantages and disadvantages of the communication methods they select.

3. Students should use any resources available to them to determine what type of restaurant would be a successful addition to the community and to make a sound case for their opinions.

Section 7.1 Activities

1. Study Skills/Group Activity: Marketing Plan

Working in small groups, come up with a marketing plan for one of the following types of restaurants: quick service, family, or fine dining. All of the restaurants are operating in the same type of location: a moderately dense, middle-income suburb of a big city. Be sure to follow the five steps as you create the marketing plan for your operation.

2. Independent Activity: Can You Hear Me Now?

Imagine you are running your own operation. Consider the communication mix, and decide on two ways to communicate your message. What methods would you choose? Explain the possible pros and cons of each method.

3. Critical Thinking: Your Local Market

Research trends in your community's population and economic growth. What type of restaurant might be a successful addition to your area and why?

446

7.1 Introduction to Marketing
• Marketing overview
• Basic marketing concepts
• Marketing plan
• SWOT

7.2 Market Analysis, Identity, and Communication
• Market research methods
• Market segmentation
• Creating a market identity
• Market communications
• Types of sales promotions
• Public relations: Engaging the community

7.3 The Menu as Marketing Tool
• Menu overview
• Menu types
• Organizing a menu
• Creating a menu
• Pricing the menu
" Analyzing the menu

SECTION 7.2 MARKET ANALYSIS, IDENTITY, AND COMMUNICATION

With ever-increasing competition in the restaurant and foodservice industry, it isn't enough any longer to just produce a good product. Many operations will put out a good product, yet not all of them will succeed. Often, the difference between success and failure in the restaurant and foodservice industry is determined by how well an operation markets itself. But success in marketing is much easier said than done. To launch a successful marketing campaign, an operation must know the smaller steps that are essential to any marketing endeavor. An operation must know how to conduct accurate and productive research, be able to create a market identity based on that research, and then communicate that identity through effective use of the various methods of market communication. All of these important aspects of marketing are covered in this section.

Study Questions

After studying Section 7.2, you should be able to answer the following questions:

■ What are the basic types of research methods used to gather information?

■ What is market segmentation?

■ How can an operation create a unique market identity?

■ What are the various ways to communicate a message to the market?

Market Research Methods

The sections so far have addressed how important research is; now this section will look at the actual methods that are used to conduct and gather market research. There are four basic methods marketers use to gather research:

447

Section 7.2 Market Analysis, Identity, and Communication

Introduce the Section

a. Identify and explain the four basic methods of market research.
b. Relate the concept of market segmentation to the concept of market identity.
c. Demonstrate how businesses communicate and engage with their markets.
d. Discuss the objectives for the section.

Vocabulary Review

a. Direct students to the key terms.
b. Pronounce each word, and have the students repeat the pronunciation out loud.
c. Discuss the definition of each word.

Teach

Discuss

• How can marketing make the difference between success and failure? How is this related to competitive advantage?

Reinforce and Review

• The difference between success and failure in the restaurant and foodservice industry is often determined by how well an operation markets itself.

• To launch a successful marketing campaign, an operation must know how to conduct accurate and productive research, be able to create a market identity based on that research, and then communicate that identity through effective use of the various methods of market communication.

Discuss

- What are some advantages and disadvantages to each method of research?

- How are these research methods related to customer feedback, as discussed in Level 1, Chapter 10?

- In what situations would each method of research be most useful? Why?

Reinforce and Review

- The experimental method allows operations to test a new product in limited amounts before deciding whether or not to expand its offerings.

- The observational method lets staff members directly observe guest responses to new products.

- Questionnaires can be administered in a variety of ways, depending on the information that management requires.

Vocabulary Terms

- **Experimental method:** An operation offers a product or promotion for a limited time or with a limited group of people.

- **Observational method:** An operation observes how customers react toward a product in a natural setting.

- **Survey method:** An operation gathers information using questionnaires.

Homework Activity:
Survey Success

Literacy Connection, 21st-Century Skills—Think Creatively, Use Systems Thinking, Communicate Clearly, Work Independently

Develop a survey on some restaurant- or foodservice-related topic. It should contain at least five questions, and you should administer it to at least ten people.

What information did you obtain? How can it be useful to you or to someone else? Write a short report on your findings, attaching your survey and its results.

- Experimental method
- Observational method
- Survey method
- Sampling method

In the **experimental method**, an operation might try out a product for a limited time or with a limited group of people. If the response to the product is favorable, the operation might think more seriously about using the product on a larger scale. However, if the product is not well received, then the operation knows right away that more work will be required.

The **observational method** involves observing how customers react in a natural setting toward a product. Figure 7.7 shows an observer watching customers. For example, a manager might tell the service staff to present the daily specials in three different ways, and then require them to record how many specials were sold, to track sales in relation to the different presentations. Based on the results, management gains a better idea of how to train servers in the future. The research about what worked and what did not work can guide decisions.

Figure 7.7: The observational method.

With the **survey method**, a marketer gathers information using questionnaires. Figure 7.8 on the following page shows a sample questionnaire that might be used to survey customers. Marketers can administer these questionnaires in a number of ways, such as by telephone, email, or even feedback cards presented tableside. For example, if a marketer wanted to know how strongly customers felt about the operation serving brunch or changing store hours, the marketer could simply ask such questions directly. Sometimes, management offers an

Figure Focus
Figure 7.7: What are some benefits of the observational method of research?

incentive, such as coupons for a free dessert to encourage customer participation. Management could then use this information to figure out how best to shape its market strategy moving forward.

Kabob Restaurant *Customer Survey*

We're conducting a short survey to find out about your dining experience and what we might do to improve. Please help us by completing this short survey.

	Circle One
Please rate the following:	POOR GREAT
The menu had an extensive selection	1 2 3 4
The food was served hot and fresh	1 2 3 4
The food was tasty and colorful	1 2 3 4
How would you rate your experience with the host/hostess?	1 2 3 4
How would you rate the employees' friendliness and courteousness?	1 2 3 4
Would you recommend Kabob Restaurant to a friend?	Yes No

Comments or suggestions: _____

_____

Kabob Restaurant would like to hear from you. Email us at xxcomments@xyz.com

Figure 7.8: A questionnaire is a simple tool that provides feedback from both existing and potential customers.

Sampling involves testing a product with a specific, small group of people, sometimes called a **focus group**. Figure 7.9 on the following page shows a focus group at work. A marketer performing a sampling trial, for example, might present a new dessert item to a preselected group of people. Based on this group's response to the dessert, the chef might consider putting it on the menu or trying something altogether different. Again, the market strategy is guided by the research results.

449

Discuss

- How does the sampling method differ from the experimental method?
- How does the sampling method resemble the observational method?

Reinforce and Review

- Incentives offered during the survey process can increase customer participation.
- The market strategy should always be guided by the research results.
- The sampling method usually involves a focus group.

Vocabulary Terms

- **Sampling:** The operation tests a product with a small, specific group of people.
- **Focus group:** A small, specific group of people on whom a particular product is tested.

In-Class Activity: Focus on Foodstuffs

Literacy Connection, 21st-Century Skills—Creativity and Innovation, Use Systems Thinking, Communication and Collaboration, Social and Cross-Cultural Skills

Working in small groups, develop an idea for a new food or beverage product and describe its characteristics. If you were to assemble a focus group to test this product, who would you enlist and why?

Prepare an oral report to describe your new product and the group you would bring together to test it.

Figure Focus

Figure 7.8: How can this survey help Kabob learn more about its customer needs? What other questions would students ask and why?

Discuss

- Why is it important for operations to be customer-driven?

- In students' experiences, which operations tend to be customer-driven and which do not? Why?

- Does a customer-driven model mean that the customer is always right? Why or why not?

- How is a target market different from a market segment?

Reinforce and Review

- The selection of the target market is an important element of an operation's marketing strategy.

- Identifying a target market enables an operation to avoid mass marketing and instead focus on target marketing.

- Understanding the target market enables an operation to provide the products and services that are needed by a particular group of people and to focus its marketing resources toward that group of people.

- An operation chooses to focus on a particular market segment based on its plans.

Vocabulary Terms

- **Target market:** The people an operation intends to pursue as customers.

- **Customer driven:** An operation's market strategy is determined by its customers' wants and needs.

- **Mass marketing:** A marketing strategy that treats everyone in the market as having the same wants and needs.

- **Target marketing:** A marketing strategy that makes a focused appeal to a distinct group of customers.

- **Market segmentation:** The process of breaking down a large market into smaller groups of similar individuals.

- **Demographics:** The ways in which researchers categorize or group people.

Figure 7.9: An example of a focus group that is sampling a product.

Market Segmentation

An important element of marketing strategy is the selection of the **target market** or markets: the people an operation intends to pursue as customers. Every operation should be **customer driven**; that is, making sure that satisfying the wants and needs of the customer drives the market strategy.

Identifying a target market enables an operation to avoid mass marketing and instead focus on target marketing. **Mass marketing** treats everyone in the market as having the same needs and wants. Restaurant and foodservice operations, however, deal with people's tastes for food, drink, and services; these definitely are not the same for everyone. **Target marketing** treats people as different from each other and tries to make a focused appeal to a distinct group of customers. Understanding the target market enables an operation to provide the products and services that are needed. It also helps an operation focus marketing resources toward the people who buy its products. This is where the process of market segmentation comes in.

Market segmentation is when marketers break down a large market into smaller groups of similar individuals that make up that market. It's like looking at the market through a microscope to see what parts make up the whole. Segmenting the market into smaller groups will help identify target demographics in any given location. **Demographics** refer to the ways in which researchers categorize or group people, and it can be done in any number of ways. What segments of the market an operation chooses to focus on depends largely on

450

Figure Focus

Figure 7.9: What are some disadvantages of using a focus group to test a new product?

what kind of operation it is and/or what kind of operation it wants to be—in short, what its plans are.

An operation can start segmenting the market in four basic ways, as listed here:

- Demographic segmentation
- Geographic segmentation
- Product usage segmentation
- Lifestyle segmentation

Demographic segmentation, as illustrated in Figure 7.10, looks at the personal makeup of individuals in a given location. This could include such criteria as age, gender, ethnicity, marital status, income, size of household, education level, etc. Different types of people have different interests, preferences, and needs, so understanding these details might help an operation better serve its potential customers. For example, a restaurant operating in a community with a lot of young families (determined using criteria such as age, marital status, size of household) might want to implement family-friendly service practices and offer kid-friendly menu items.

Figure 7.10: Examples of demographic segmentation reflect different preferences and interests.

Geographic segmentation includes such factors as where consumers live, where they work, and what kind of transportation they use to get around. Knowing, for example, that most of the residents of a suburb commute into the city for work each day might dissuade an operation in that suburb from opening for lunch service on weekdays, and convince a restaurant in the city not to stay open for dinner.

Segmenting a market by **product usage** can also shed light on how best to serve a community. For example, if there are a lot of successful coffee houses in a given area, an operation might be well served to capitalize on the community's

451

Figure Focus
Figure 7.10: How do these market segmentations overlap?

Discuss

- Consider the discussion of stereotyping in Level 1, Chapter 8. Why is demographic segmentation acceptable, when stereotyping is not?

- How can understanding geographic segmentation help operations determine where to open new locations?

Reinforce and Review

- Market segmentation helps identify target markets.

- The four basic types of market segmentation are demographic, geographic, product usage, and lifestyle.

- Different types of people have different preferences; understanding these differences can help an operation better serve its potential customers.

Teaching Tips

- Students should understand that a given individual can be part of multiple overlapping market segments at any given time.

Homework Activity: Segmentation

Literacy Connection, 21st-Century Skills—Critical Thinking and Problem Solving, Communicate Clearly, Work Independently

Each person has thousands of characteristics that make him or her unique: Hair color, hobbies, and favorite foods are just a few of these. Many of these characteristics can be used by marketers to sell specific goods and services. They identify market segments to help them make focused appeals to specific groups of consumers and potential consumers.

Think about where you live and what you like to do. If a marketer were to look at you, what market segments might he or she put you into? Why?

Vocabulary Terms

- **Demographic segmentation:** Market segmentation based on the personal makeup of individuals in a given location.

- **Geographic segmentation:** Market segmentation based on where customers are located at particular times of day as well as how they arrive at those locations.

- **Product usage segmentation:** Market segmentation based on what products and services are popular in a particular area.

Discuss

- How do students decide whether the benefits are worth the cost of the purchases they make in their daily lives?

Reinforce and Review

- Product usage segmentation helps managers make informed decisions about future operational plans.

- Marketers can combine data from different categories to enhance an operation's knowledge of its marketplace.

- The more an operation knows about its potential customers, the more successful it will likely be in satisfying their needs.

- The question that the value proposition must answer for its target market is this: "Are the benefits worth the cost?"

- Each target market values different things, so operations must tailor different value propositions for each group.

Teaching Tips

- Relate this information to the discussion of how individuals make purchasing decisions in Chapter 5.

Essential Skills: Target Marketing

Encourage students to discuss the following:

- Why do restaurant and foodservice operations determine target markets?

- How might a restaurant's target market differ from its actual customers? In these situations, how should the restaurant respond and why?

Vocabulary Terms

- **Lifestyle segmentation:** Market segmentation based on the activities, hobbies, interests, and opinions of a given target market.

- **Value proposition:** A statement of the value an operation's target market will experience when they purchase its products and services.

love of coffee. It could start offering its own coffee service to try to catch some of the competitors' business, or perhaps it could add dessert items that incorporate coffee flavors, or it may want to avoid the coffee trade altogether. The bottom line is that the managers of the operation need this segmented market information to make informed decisions about the direction it will take.

Finally, **lifestyle segmentation** looks at the activities, hobbies, interests, and opinions of a given target market. A highly active, athletic community, for example, might be inclined to patronize operations that offer a more healthful menu. Knowing this aspect of its target market will serve an operation well.

Of course, these are broad categories that should only serve as a starting point. Many of these categories eventually overlap, and marketers can combine data from different categories to even further enhance an operation's knowledge of the marketplace it hopes to serve. Ultimately, the more an operation knows about its potential customers, the more successful it will likely be in satisfying their needs.

Once marketers and management have identified a target market or markets, an operation can work to establish a value proposition. A **value proposition** is a statement of the value an operation's target customers will experience when they purchase its products and services. The question that the value proposition must answer for its target market is, "Are the benefits worth the cost?" In other words, what benefits does the product provide that the target market considers worth purchasing?

An operation must specify which target market its value proposition is for because each target market values different things. Preparing a value proposition for each target market defines the way an operation is going to promote its products and services to this market.

Essential Skills
Target Marketing

Target marketing helps you to focus your promotion and advertising efforts on specific groups. This sounds like an easy process, but it can be a challenge. These are the basic steps to success:

❶ Identify the groups you want to serve: who are the customers you want to attract and why?

❷ Identify the groups you are actually serving: who currently buys your products and why? Customer surveys and comment cards can be useful market research tools. See Figure 7.11 on the following page.

❸ Perform a situation assessment of your business. It may be that you should change your targets to reflect the reality of your situation. For instance, a burger joint may not succeed located in an area where there are a number of senior centers and assisted-living facilities.

❹ Using the results of your situation assessment, change either your marketing or your menu to attract the desired targets, working with a public-relations firm as necessary. This is your customer profile.

❺ Continually work to refine your message and your promotions—your customer base and your resources will change over time, so your business plan must stay flexible and adaptable.

A single restaurant can't be "all things to all people." Trying to do everything at once will only muddy your message. Knowing your target market and how to market to it will save you time, money, and effort.

Kabob Restaurant

100 Main Street   Anywhere, CT 00000

Phone: 555-555-1234

Comment Card

Kabob Restaurant is committed to fulfilling the wishes and needs of our guests, each and every time you dine with us. Please tell us how we're doing. Your feedback is very important to us.

Date of service: _____

Server's name: _____

	Excellent	Good	Average	Fair	Poor
Service					
Food					
Atmosphere					

How likely are you to return to our restaurant?

Very likely   Likely   Unlikely   Very unlikely   Not sure

Are there any suggestions you can make that would improve your dining experience?

Figure 7.11: Step 2—A sample comment card.

Creating a Market Identity

Once a target market has been identified through market segmentation, marketers and managers will need to figure out how to best position their operation within that market. **Positioning** means creating within the marketplace

453

Reinforce and Review

- Once the target market has been identified, restaurant and foodservice managers must determine how to position their operation within that market.

Vocabulary Terms

- **Positioning:** Creating within the marketplace a clear, specific identity for both a product and the operation that offers that product.

Figure Focus

Figure 7.11: Compare this comment card to the customer survey in Figure 7.8.

Discuss

- What are some ways in which students' favorite restaurants "stand out in a crowd"? How does this relate to the restaurants' identities?

- What non-foodservice examples of positioning can students identify?

Reinforce and Review

- Positioning consists of three steps: identifying ways to create a unique identity, selecting the right mix of differentiating aspects, and communicating the chosen identity to a specific target market.

- An operation's differentiating aspects include its product, physical appearance and aesthetics, service, location, and image.

- An operation's ability to position itself in a competitive market is essential to its long-term success.

Table 7.1:
Ways to Attract Customers

- Innovation and creativity are essential to attracting guests to a restaurant or foodservice operation. However, the quality of the food and service is often what turns a one-time customer into a regular guest. How can successful operations integrate these different elements?

- How can special events and themes enhance an operation's identity?

- What steps must restaurant and foodservice operations take to ensure that they do not lose money on successful or unsuccessful promotions?

- What are some other tactics operations can use to differentiate themselves from the competition and attract more customers?

a clear, specific identity for both a product and the operation that offers that product. In the restaurant and foodservice industry, it is all about standing out in a crowd. If an operation is just one of many, then its chances of being successful are greatly diminished. But if an operation can stand out from the crowd by offering a product that no one else does, or by offering a product in a way that no one else does, then its chances of success are far greater. So how exactly do managers, marketers, and chefs go about positioning an operation in such a way?

Positioning consists of the following three steps:

1. Identify possible ways to differentiate the operation within the market and create a unique identity.

2. Select the right mix of differentiating aspects.

3. Communicate the chosen identity to a specific target market.

Ways to Differentiate an Operation

There are a number of ways that managers can differentiate an operation from its competitors to create a unique identity:

- Product
- Physical appearance/aesthetics
- Service
- Location
- Image

Table 7.1 lists a number of ways to attract customers.

Table 7.1: Ways to Attract Customers
Innovation and creativity are the keys to attracting customers and growing the business. Here are some examples of methods that operations use to attract customers:
• Merchandising techniques at the table, such as unique garnishing or flambé
• Themes, both as operation-wide celebrations and special events
• Frequent shopper cards that offer discounts or other incentives
• Signature items, such as special desserts or "secret" recipes
• Specials, such as "buy one, get one free" nights
• Educational promotions, such as wine tastings

Teaching Tips

- Level 1, Chapter 1 describes the breadth of the restaurant and foodservice industry. Encourage students to relate this discussion of positioning to that material.

Product: The first and most obvious way to position an operation in the market is through the product it offers. Unique menu items or traditional menu items prepared in a unique way are time-tested ways to create a market identity. The danger in relying on this aspect of positioning alone is that it is difficult to produce something so unique, and so much better than the competition that the product alone can establish an operation's identity. Often, operations need to explore other options as well.

Physical appearance/aesthetics: Use the actual physical space of an operation to create an image. For example, will the aesthetics, or look of the place, be sleek and modern, or quaint and cozy? Will there be a lot of wall decorations or very few? Will it go for a sophisticated vibe or a down-to-earth, cheerful one?

Service: Service is also a differentiating point. How will the service staff be dressed? Will the uniforms be formal or informal? See Figure 7.12. What should the greeter say when a customer arrives? What will tableside service be like? Will you offer delivery? Will you have a separate area for takeout? All of these aspects of service work to create an identity for an operation.

Figure 7.12: Examples of service.

Location: Location can play a big part in creating an identity. This is why it's important to fully understand the various segments of a particular market. Positioning an operation as the ultimate steakhouse in a location with a high population of vegetarians might not be the best idea. However, if the goal is to appeal to a segment of that market that has potentially been overlooked in that area, positioning the operation as "the alternative" might actually work.

455

Discuss

- Chapter 5 discussed the prominent role of purchasing in the success of any restaurant or foodservice operation. Which is more important: purchasing or marketing? Why?

- Explain the relationship between purchasing and marketing. How can smart purchasing help an establishment create and reinforce its identity?

Reinforce and Review

- Unique menu items or preparation techniques can help to create an operation's market identity; generally, however, this differentiation tactic is used in conjunction with other methods.

- A restaurant or foodservice operation's physical space helps to create its identity.

- The level and quality of service available in a restaurant or foodservice operation helps to determine its identity.

- Restaurants and foodservice operations should first decide on the image they wish to present and then make product and service decisions based on achieving and maintaining that image.

Teaching Tips

- An activity in Chapter 5 encouraged students to consider purchasing as the "head" and service as the "heart" of a restaurant or foodservice operation. What role do students believe marketing plays? Why?

Figure Focus

Figure 7.12: Pho, a beef noodle soup of Vietnamese origin, is increasingly popular in certain market segments.

Discuss

- How can restaurant and foodservice operations determine which differentiation points to use in developing their identities?

Reinforce and Review

- Once managers have determined which differentiating aspects are available to them, they have to decide how best to utilize these aspects.

- Focusing on a single differentiation point might not be enough for an operation to establish a unique identity, but focusing on too many points can dilute the overall message.

- The way an operation communicates its position in the market is as important as how the position is initially determined.

- Restaurant and foodservice operations must send clear messages to their target markets.

Trends:
Marketing and Celebrity Chefs

Encourage students to discuss the following:

- What do students consider to be the primary characteristics of a celebrity chef?

- What food-related media sources do students use? What attracts them to each?

- How is technology related to marketing? How can the restaurant and foodservice industry use emerging technologies to enhance its marketing techniques?

Homework Activity:
Celebrity Chefs

Literacy Connection, 21st-Century Skills—Use Systems Thinking, Communicate Clearly, Information Literacy, Create Media Products, Work Independently

Research someone you consider to be a celebrity chef and create a poster noting the highlights of his or her career.

Image: Finally, image is yet another way to differentiate an operation. Decide on an image first, then make product and service decisions that work toward achieving that image. For example, maybe management wants to present an operation as environmentally and ecologically responsible. The products it offers and the way it prepares these products will need to correspond to that intended image.

Selecting the Right Mix

Once marketers and managers have laid all the potential options for positioning an operation in the marketplace, they will have to decide the best route to take. This may lead an operation to fully dedicate itself to one differentiation point, or to try to achieve a number of points. Any choice an operation makes comes with risks. Focusing exclusively on one point may not be enough to create a unique identity, but choosing too many points of positioning may end up diluting any message an operation wants to present to the market. Finding the right positioning mix requires a lot of time and research.

Communicating Chosen Identity

The way managers and marketers communicate an operation's position in the market is just as important as choosing the right positioning tactics in the first place. For example, the managers of an operation that wants to present itself as a green, eco-friendly restaurant might buy all organic products, prepare all items in the most environmentally friendly ways, and then do their best to recycle and compost all waste materials. But if they fail to let the market know about all the operation does to be a responsible citizen in the community, their hard work will not contribute to the operation's identity or its success. If the message isn't clear, positioning efforts will ultimately not be realized.

[trends]

Marketing and Celebrity Chefs

The last several years have seen a dramatic increase in the popularity of virtually all things food related. Much of this trend is due to the marketing techniques discussed in this chapter coupled with advances in technology that allow for more communication and access between businesses and the public.

Today, individual chefs and cooks have found fame on a scale that was almost unheard of just a few years ago. The term "celebrity chef" describes this new generation of chefs. There is no real consensus on what a celebrity chef is. It can refer to a chef seen often on television (or who even has his or her own program), or a chef with multiple restaurant and foodservice operations, or a chef who has published several cookbooks—or even a combination of all three. There are many celebrity chefs around now, and each has his or her own market identity. Personality, target market, or simply cuisine all contribute to differentiation among chefs and the products they are selling.

456

The increase in the number of television channels, and access to those channels, has given rise to segmenting the market to cater to those who love all things food. The Food Network is a great example of this. The Internet has also played a role in connecting "foodies," via Web pages, chat rooms, and blogs, to each other as well as to chefs and restaurant and foodservice operations. Creating a line of foods under a celebrity chef's name increases exposure. Celebrity chefs have both come from and capitalized on these advances in technology, which is what any smart operation has to do as well. For example, many celebrity chefs then create a line of foods under their name that is sold in grocery stores.

Market Communications

There are many ways to communicate with an operation's market. The ways an operation goes about this process of communication is called the **promotional mix**. The promotional mix can consist of any or all of the following, as listed here and illustrated in Figure 7.13:

- Advertising
- Sales promotions
- Personal selling
- Public relations
- Direct marketing

Figure 7.13: The elements of a promotional mix.

Advertising: Paying to present or promote an operation's products, services, or identity. Advertising can be conducted through multiple mediums. Television, radio, newspapers, storefront, and Internet are all viable options for advertising. Though there are costs involved with advertising, effective ads can be a powerful communication tool for any operation.

Sales promotions: Limited, or short-term, incentives to entice customers to patronize an operation. For example, offering two-for-one entrées is a sales

457

Figure Focus

Figure 7.13: What elements of the promotional mix are represented here?

Discuss

- What types of market communications are appropriate for what target markets? Why?
- What are some popular sales promotions? What makes them successful?

Reinforce and Review

- The promotional mix can consist of any or all of the following: advertising, sales promotions, personal selling, public relations, and direct marketing.
- Advertising can be conducted through multiple media and, if effective, can be a powerful communication tool.
- An operation's identity might be tied to specific sales promotions.

Teaching Tips

- Provide samples of communication material from a variety of restaurant and foodservice operations.

Vocabulary Terms

- **Promotional mix:** The ways in which an operation communicates with its market.

- **Advertising:** Paying to present or promote an operation's products, services, or identity.
- **Sales promotions:** Limited or short-term incentives to entice customers to patronize an operation.

Discuss

- What local restaurant and foodservice operations do a good job of building community relations? How do they do this?

- Which of the five components of the promotional mix do students think is most important? Why?

Reinforce and Review

- Well-trained service staff should be able to communicate an operation's message to its guests.

- Personal selling might be the best way to solidify an operation's credibility and identity in a competitive market.

- Building good relations with the community can help an operation gain favorable publicity and enhance its image.

- Successful direct marketing both elicits immediate responses from customers and builds long-term relationships.

Teaching Tips

- Relate personal selling to the discussion of suggestive selling in Level 1, Chapter 10.

On the Job:
Restaurant PR Specialists (RPRSs)

Encourage students to discuss the following:

- In what ways does the increased number of restaurant PR specialists benefit the entire restaurant and foodservice industry?

- Why is it important for restaurant PR specialists to have excellent communication skills? With whom do they need to communicate?

- As a restaurateur, would you choose to work with a restaurant PR specialist? Why or why not?

Vocabulary Terms

- **Personal selling:** Face-to-face interactions between staff members and guests.

- **Public relations (PR):** The process by which an operation interacts with the community at large.

- **Direct marketing:** Making a concerted effort to connect directly with a certain segment of the market.

promotion. Sometimes an operation's identity can actually be based on sales promotions. An operation might become known for specific reoccurring promotions, such as half-priced appetizers during certain hours or themed nights during the week. Creativity in coming up with smart sales promotions can greatly enhance business. A later section in this chapter covers sales promotions at greater length.

Personal selling: Always key to an operation's financial success, but well-trained service staff can also go a long way in communicating an operation's message. Professionalism, politeness, and efficiency can be easily and powerfully conveyed by front-of-house staff. In fact, face-to-face interactions between service staff and guests may be the very best way to solidify an operation's credibility and identity in a competitive market.

Public relations (PR): The process by which an operation interacts with the community at large. Building good relations with the community can help an operation gain favorable publicity and enhance an operation's image. For example, sponsoring local Little League teams or holding a charity event at an operation are both ways to build bridges with the public. Public relations are discussed at greater length later in this chapter.

Direct marketing: Making a concerted effort to connect directly with a certain segment of the market. Such connections could help garner immediate responses from customers as well as build longer-term relationships. Direct mailing or emails, telephone calls, Web site feedback or interaction, and even tableside feedback are all ways to direct market.

[on the job]

Restaurant PR Specialists (RPRSs)

It seems that more than ever, the American public is increasingly interested in food: where it comes from, how it's prepared, and where they can get it. As a result, the number of public relations specialists focusing on restaurant and foodservice operations has increased as operations compete for newly savvy diners. These specialists work to promote operations by producing press releases, organizing events, and generally building positive relationships with local, regional, and even national media outlets.

Restaurant PR specialists have a number of tools in their arsenals, including social-networking outlets. Their job is to create opportunities to showcase the restaurant, such as cooperating with nonprofit agencies or staging community activities. Ultimately, an RPRS gets people through the door of the operation. After that, it's the operation's job to keep them coming back.

RPRSs typically hold degrees from four-year colleges, often majoring in public relations, but also in communications, journalism, or related fields. A background in the restaurant and foodservice industry is not uncommon. Accreditation is available from both the Universal Accreditation Board and the International Association of Business Communicators.

458

CUSTOMIZED INSTRUCTION

Literacy Connection, 21st-Century Skills—Use Systems Thinking, Communicate Clearly
Special Needs Students
What advertisements particularly appeal to you? Why?

Types of Sales Promotions

Sales promotions provide special incentives for customers to patronize an operation. There are many types of sales promotions and different tools or materials that can be used in a sales promotion. All are designed to give customers that extra "boost" to get them into an operation or to purchase certain items. However, sales promotions are only useful when customers know about them, which is why they are often the focus of advertising.

Here are some types of sales promotions:

- **Special pricing**: Limited-time reduced prices offered through specials, deals, coupons, or other programs; saves customers money and creates a low-risk opportunity to try a new item.

- **Frequent shopper program**: Provides a benefit in exchange for continuing patronage—often free food items or substantial discounts. Figure 7.14 shows some frequent shopper cards.

- **Premiums**: Free or reduced-price merchandise, such as a pen or cup that shows the name and location of the restaurant, usually given away or sold for a reduced price with the purchase of a food item.

- **Special events**: One-time or periodic occasions that provide a special incentive for the customer to patronize your restaurant. These events vary a great deal, but include things like bringing in celebrities or offering special entertainment.

Figure 7.14: Here are several samples of frequent shopper cards.

459

Figure Focus
Figure 7.14: How can frequent shopper programs increase overall revenues?

Discuss
- What makes a sales promotion effective?

Reinforce and Review
- Sales promotions provide special incentives for customers to patronize an establishment.

- Promotions are designed to give customers an additional incentive to enter an operation or to purchase certain items.

Vocabulary Terms
- **Special pricing:** Limited-time reduced prices offered through specials, deals, coupons, or other programs.

- **Frequent shopper program:** Provides a benefit in exchange for continuing patronage.

- **Premiums:** Free or reduced-price merchandise.

- **Special events:** One-time or periodic occasions that provide a special incentive for customers to patronize an operation.

Discuss

- What sales promotions are appropriate for what types of restaurant and foodservice operations? Why?

- How do take-home promotional items, such as carryout menus or branded merchandise, help reinforce an operation's identity?

- What types of promotional materials are commonly used by local restaurant and foodservice operations? Why?

Reinforce and Review

- Promotional materials can be designed either to enhance a particular program or to promote the operation whether or not an active promotion program is being offered.

- Promotional materials increase public awareness of an operation without necessarily offering incentives to patronize it.

- Typical promotional items include signage, branded merchandise, and email.

Teaching Tips

- Provide samples of promotional materials from a variety of restaurant and foodservice operations.

Homework Activity:
See Food

Literacy Connection, 21st-Century Skills— Think Creatively, Critical Thinking and Problem Solving, Communicate Clearly, Work Independently

The management of a local seafood restaurant has asked you to develop a sales promotion based on the upcoming wild salmon season. Develop a sales promotion and identify at least three types of promotional materials you will use to promote the event.

Vocabulary Terms

- **Samples:** Small, free tastes of food items.

- **Contests and sweepstakes:** Games and other programs that involve the customer and provide prizes.

- **Samples:** Free, small tastes of food items, providing customers a risk-free opportunity to try a new item.
- **Contests and sweepstakes:** Games and other programs that involve the customer and provide a prize.

Some sales promotion methods use materials such as coupons for special pricing programs or toys for premiums. However, other promotion materials support a marketing plan by continuously promoting an operation even when it is not running an active promotion program. Promotion materials are miscellaneous items that do not necessarily offer incentives for visiting an operation, but they increase awareness of an establishment. A menu board placed outside an operation is an example of a promotion material.

Some typical promotional materials are listed here and shown in Figure 7.15:

- **Signage:** Menu boards, directional signs, and other signs that indicate where the operation is located and/or the items it serves
- **Flyers:** Paper notices that are distributed in a specific location or to a targeted group to create awareness of a certain promotion or menu item
- **Premiums:** Token gifts or giveaway items, such as pens, stationery, children's toys, mugs, T-shirts, or magnets that display the restaurant name and location or phone number
- **Carryout and door hanger menus:** Paper menus for customers to use outside of the restaurant; door hanger menus for hanging on doorknobs or handles
- **Apparel and branded merchandise:** An operation's name and/or logo on T-shirts or other garments, mugs, pencils, stuffed animals, etc.
- **Point-of-purchase (POP) materials:** Menu boards, video, print pieces, and other display items near the point of purchase where customers make their decisions about what to buy; can be at the counter, or at the table
- **Merchandising materials:** Table tents and other display items in the restaurant
- **Direct mail:** Mass mailing of coupons, menus, advertising about a promotion, etc., to customers in a particular area
- **Email:** Electronic mail targeted to particular market

460

Yet another type of promotion is the cooperative sales promotion. **Cooperative sales promotions** are when two or more sponsors develop complementary promotions or offer complementary promotional materials. For example, a restaurant hands out coupons for free admission to a sports event, and the sports arena hands out coupons for a free appetizer at the restaurant.

Figure 7.15: Typical promotional materials.

Public Relations: Engaging the Community

The purpose of public relations is to generate positive publicity. **Publicity** is the attention an operation receives; one way to get good publicity is by engaging in the affairs of the community. A major benefit of this kind of publicity is that people respond positively to local support. Marketers and managers should focus on two types of relationships as they incorporate public relations in their promotion mix: media relations and community relations.

Community relations involve interacting with the people in the local area to create awareness of and trust for an operation. Activities such as hosting charity events, giving tours, and sponsoring sports teams are examples of community relations. These types of activities are a way to "give back" to the community. They also provide many benefits for both a restaurant and its management:

- Creating a positive image within the community
- Building credibility within the community
- Building relationships with other community leaders
- Creating a network with other restaurant and foodservice professionals
- Generating positive publicity
- Promoting the restaurant

461

Figure Focus
Figure 7.15: How does each promotional item reinforce the establishment's brand identity?

- What examples of cooperative sales promotions can students identify? How is each successful?
- Is it true that, "There is no such thing as bad publicity"? Why or why not?
- How can community support help a restaurant or foodservice operation thrive? Can operations without such support succeed?

Reinforce and Review

- Cooperative sales promotions involve at least two sponsors, who work in tandem to increase patronage and revenues.
- The purpose of public relations is to generate publicity.
- A major benefit of engaging in local affairs is that people respond positively to local support.
- Media relations and community relations should be an important part of the promotional mix.
- Community relations provide an opportunity to "give back" to the local area.
- The benefits of positive community relations include creating a positive image within the community, building credibility within the community, building relationships with community leaders, creating a network with other restaurant and foodservice professionals, generating positive publicity, and promoting the operation.

Homework Activity: Community Communications

Literacy Connection, 21st-Century Skills—Use Systems Thinking, Communicate Clearly, Work Independently

Select one of the benefits of community relations and discuss its importance to restaurant and foodservice operations in a one-page essay. Be sure to consider how positive community relations can increase a business's revenues.

Vocabulary Terms

- **Cooperative sales promotions:** An opportunity in which two or more sponsors develop complementary promotions or offer complementary promotional materials.
- **Publicity:** The attention an operation receives.
- **Community relations:** The ways in which an operation interacts with the people in the local area to create awareness of and trust in an operation.

Discuss

- What community relations opportunities might be appropriate for what types of restaurant and foodservice operations to participate in? Why?

- Explain the importance of good communication skills and thorough employee training in developing a public relations program.

Reinforce and Review

- The cost of being involved in organizations and events can vary but should be viewed as an investment in the community and in the business.

- Once marketers have identified community relations opportunities that align with their marketing plans, they can determine how to become involved in a way that generates good publicity.

- Proactive community engagement helps shape an operation's identity within the community and can affect people's likelihood of patronizing the operation.

- Marketers can directly generate media publicity by sending out press releases or media kits.

- Well-written press releases present marketing information as news.

Teaching Tips

- Refer students to the content on communication skills and employee training in Level 1, Chapters 7 and 8.

Homework Activity: Full-Court Press

Literacy Connection, 21st-Century Skills—Use Systems Thinking, Communicate Clearly, Create Media Products, Work Independently

Write a press release about a real or imaginary event in which a restaurant or foodservice operation participates. Pose as the marketer for that establishment. The press release should be at least one-page long and should answer the "Five Ws and How" questions.

Vocabulary Terms

- **Media relations:** The relationships that marketers maintain with media outlets.

- **Press release:** A brief presentation of promotional information written to sound like a news article.

The cost of becoming involved in organizations and events can vary. An operation may need to pay yearly dues or meeting fees to be involved with some organizations. But it probably will not need to pay anything to volunteer at other organizations, such as a local homeless shelter. If managers choose to support an organization with donations of food, labor, money, or space, some of these costs may be tax deductible. However, owners and managers should view any costs that are incurred as an investment in both the community and the business.

Once marketers have identified community relations opportunities that align with their operations' marketing plans, they can begin thinking about how to become involved in a way that generates good publicity. For example, they can develop promotions or sales, such as the following, that support their chosen organization or event while generating business for their operation:

- Offering discounts to schoolchildren who have good grades or attendance

- Donating a percentage of sales to a charity for a given item or period of time (for instance, all lunch sales)

- Offering customers a discount when they bring in a donation for charity

- Sponsoring a local children's sports team and offering incentives for winning a game

- Offering the operation's facility or providing the catering for a fundraiser or meeting

Other types of programs may not generate direct business but can still provide excellent opportunities for publicity; for example, being part of an ongoing charity program that donates food, labor, or equipment to a soup kitchen. Such proactive engagement in the community goes a long way toward shaping an operation's identity within the community, and, directly or indirectly, people's likelihood of patronizing the establishment.

Media relations are the relationships that marketers maintain with media outlets, which in this context include newspapers, magazines, television, and radio. One way that marketers directly generate publicity through the media is by sending out press releases and/or media kits. A **press release**, or news release, is a brief presentation of promotional information written to sound like a news article. Well-written press releases present marketing information as news. If an operation is lucky, the information in the press release will be published or read "as is," but more often, the information will be incorporated into a story. A press

462

release may be sent by itself or as part of a press kit. A **press kit**, also called a media kit, is a packet of information given to media representatives to answer questions they might have about a business or organization. (Press kits also may be given to prospective customers, employees, or investors.) Some restaurant and foodservice operations also provide their press kits in an electronic format, often through a Web site or CD-ROM.

Typically, a press kit for a restaurant or foodservice operation is a folder that contains the following:

- General information about the operation
- Menus
- Any recent articles or press releases
- A list of any recent awards
- Photos of the operation and its menu items
- The operation's mission or goal statement
- Contact information for the operation's spokesperson
- Other promotional materials

With any form of marketing communications, marketers need to focus their efforts on reaching the target market. In media relations, marketers need to evaluate potential types of media and **media vehicles**, such as particular publications or radio stations, by considering the following questions:

- Does the media vehicle reach the target market or people who can influence the target market? If so, how much of the target market does it reach? The same criteria should be used to evaluate the media vehicle for an advertising campaign.
- How likely is it that the media vehicle will be interested in the stories being submitted? Is there a story that may interest the target market or community?
- With any form of marketing communications, marketers need to focus their efforts on reaching the target market. In media relations, marketers need to evaluate potential types of media and media vehicles, such as particular publications or radio stations, by considering the following questions:
- Does the media vehicle reach the target market or people who can influence the target market? If so, how much of the target market does it reach? The same criteria should be used to evaluate the media vehicle for an advertising campaign.

463

Discuss

- What media vehicles might be appropriate to reach what target markets? Why?
- How do restaurant and foodservice operations determine what information to include in their press kits?

Reinforce and Review

- Typically, a restaurant press kit contains a wide variety of information about the operation, including menus, current promotional materials, and contact information for the restaurant's spokesperson.
- With any form of marketing communications, marketers need to focus their efforts on reaching their target markets.

Homework Activity: Im-PRESS-ive!

Literacy Connection, 21st-Century Skills— Think Creatively, Reason Effectively, Communicate Clearly, Create Media Products, Work Independently

Your restaurant has an important public-relations event next week. Develop two items that you will include in the media kit that you distribute to members of the press.

Vocabulary Terms

- **Press kit/media kit:** A packet of information given to media representatives to answer questions they might have about a business or organization.
- **Media vehicle:** A particular media outlet.

Summary

- Remind students to review the following:
  1. Market research techniques
  2. Market segmentation
  3. Creating a market identity
  4. Market communications
  5. Types of sales promotions
  6. Public relations and engaging the community

- How likely is it that the media vehicle will be interested in the stories being submitted? Is there a story that may interest the target market or community?

- With any form of marketing communications, marketers need to focus their efforts on reaching the target market. In media relations, marketers need to evaluate potential types of media and media vehicles, such as particular publications or radio stations.

Summary

In this section, you learned the following:

- There are four basic methods marketers use to gather research:

  - Experimental method, where an operation might try out a product for a limited time or to a limited group of people

  - Observational method, which involves observing how customers react in a natural setting towards a product

  - Survey method, which gathers information using questionnaires that can be administered in different ways such as telephone, email, or feedback cards

  - Sampling method, which involves testing a product with a specific, small group of people, sometimes called a focus group

- Market segmentation is breaking down a larger market into smaller groups of similar individuals to help identify target demographics in any given location. Demographics refer to the ways in which people are categorized or grouped. What segments of the market marketers and managers choose to focus on depends largely on what kind of operation they have and/or what kind of operation they want to be. Marketers can start segmenting the market in four basic ways: demographic segmentation, geographic segmentation, product usage segmentation, and lifestyle segmentation.

- Positioning means creating within the marketplace a clear, specific identity for both a product and the operation that offers that product. In the restaurant and foodservice industry, it's all about standing out in a crowd. Positioning consists of three steps: 1) Identify possible ways to differentiate the operation within the market and create a unique identity; 2) Select the right mix of differentiating aspects; and 3) Communicate the chosen identity to a specific target market. There are a number of ways that an operation can differentiate itself from its competitors to create its own identity, including product, physical appearance/aesthetics, service, location, and image.

464

- There are many ways for marketers and managers to communicate with their market. The various ways they go about this process of communication is called the promotional mix. The promotional mix can consist of any or all of the following: advertising, sales promotions, personal selling, public relations, and direct marketing.

- Sales promotions provide special incentives for customers to patronize an operation. There are many types of sales promotions and different tools or materials that can be used in a sales promotion. However, sales promotions are only useful when customers know about them, which is why they are often the focus of advertising. Some sales promotion methods use materials such as coupons for special pricing programs or toys for premiums. However, other promotion materials, such as a menu board placed outside an operation, support a marketing plan by continuously promoting an operation even when it is not running an active promotion program by increasing awareness of an establishment.

- The purpose of public relations is to generate positive publicity. Publicity is the attention an operation receives; one way to get good publicity is by engaging in the affairs of the community. A major benefit of this kind of publicity is that people respond positively to local support. Marketers and managers should focus on two types of relationships as they incorporate public relations in their promotion mix: media relations and community relations. Community relations involve interacting with the people in a local area to create awareness of and trust for an operation. Activities such as hosting charity events, giving tours, and sponsoring sports teams are examples of community relations. A press kit, also called a media kit, is a packet of information given to media representatives to answer questions they might have about a business or organization. Press kits are a great help in building and maintaining strong media relations.

Section 7.2
Review Questions

1. The four basic research methods are experimental, observational, survey, and sampling.

2. Four general ways to segment a market are by demographics, by geography, by product usage, and by lifestyle.

3. Five ways to differentiate within a market are by product, by physical appearance or aesthetics, by service, by location, and by image.

4. The five elements of a promotional mix are advertising, sales promotions, personal selling, public relations, and direct marketing.

5. Student answers will vary but should clearly state why students are attracted to particular promotions.

6. Students should identify ways in which Miguel and Chef Kate can communicate with appropriate markets.

7. Students should logically explain why the criteria they have selected is the most important.

8. Students should clearly defend their chosen research method.

Section 7.2 Review Questions

1. List the four basic research methods.

2. What are four general ways to segment a market?

3. List five ways to differentiate within a market.

4. What are the five elements of a promotional mix?

5. Tania Haigh works for McDonald's, a company that offers many promotions. What types of promotions are most appealing to you? Why?

6. Talk to Miguel and Chef Kate about market segmentation. Suggest two markets that you feel might be desirable for their business. Then suggest two ways they might communicate with those markets.

7. What do you think is the most important criteria for an operation to differentiate itself? Explain your answer in a paragraph.

8. What research method do you think is best for gathering vital information? Why do you think it would be a better method than the others discussed in this chapter?

466

Section 7.2 Activities

1. Study Skills/Group Activity: Promotional Poster

Working with two or three other students, decide how you will integrate nutritional and health concerns into your promotions for your 40-seat, fine-dining restaurant. Prepare a poster and a presentation detailing your efforts.

2. Independent Activity: Segmenting the Market

If you were to open your own operation, which segment of the population would you most like to serve? Why? Write a one-page report explaining your rationale, along with possible challenges that your chosen market segment might present.

3. Critical Thinking: Public Relations in Your Community

How do local businesses in your area try to engage the community? Select a local business and discuss its efforts to reach out to and make ties with the community where it does business. For this exercise, you do not necessarily have to choose a restaurant or foodservice operation.

467

Section 7.2 Activities

1. Student posters and presentations should emphasize the role of nutritional and health issues in their operations.

2. Student reports should detail the advantages and disadvantages of serving the chosen target market.

3. Students should research a local business and its community relations. This might involve interviewing a staff member of that business.

Section 7.3
The Menu as Marketing Tool

Introduce the Section
a. Explain the importance of the menu as a marketing tool.
b. Describe the various types of menus and how menus can be organized.
c. Discuss how menus are created and priced, as well as the role of menu analysis.
d. Discuss the objectives for the section.

Vocabulary Review
a. Direct students to the key terms.
b. Pronounce each word, and have the students repeat the pronunciation out loud.
c. Discuss the definition of each word.

Teach

Discuss
- What restaurant or foodservice operations have menus that are particularly attractive to students? What elements are especially appealing?
- What would make a menu unappealing? Why?

Reinforce and Review
- The menu helps plan an operation's goals and helps communicate those goals to the operation's target market.
- Menus are sales tools that help managers assess the operation's strengths and weaknesses.
- The most important interaction consumers have with a given operation is through the menu.
- If a potential customer isn't influenced enough by the menu to order something, then the quality of the food and service becomes irrelevant.

7.1 Introduction to Marketing	7.2 Market Analysis, Identity, and Communication	7.3 The Menu as Marketing Tool
• Marketing overview	• Market research methods	• Menu overview
• Basic marketing concepts	• Market segmentation	• Menu types
• Marketing plan	• Creating a market identity	• Organizing a menu
• SWOT	• Market communications	• Creating a menu
	• Types of sales promotions	• Pricing the menu
	• Public relations: Engaging the community	• Analyzing the menu

SECTION 7.3 THE MENU AS MARKETING TOOL

The menu may not be the first thing that comes to mind when thinking of ways to market a restaurant or foodservice operation, yet no other marketing tool may be as important. The menu serves to help plan the goals of an operation as well as being a means to communicate those goals to the operation's target market. It also serves as a sales tool and can help managers assess the operation's strengths and weaknesses. In short, the menu is an indispensible jack-of-all-trades that needs to be given special attention and consideration. This section is dedicated to doing just that.

Study Questions

After studying Section 7.3, you should be able to answer the following questions:

- What functions does a menu serve?
- What are the different types of menus?
- What factors must be considered when creating a menu?
- What are the various methods used to price a menu?
- How can menu sales be analyzed?

Menu Overview

There may be no other stronger marketing tool than the menu. The most important interaction consumers have with a given operation is through the menu, as illustrated in Figure 7.16. It's where sales are initially won or lost. If, for example, customers like what's on the menu, and the prices seem fair, then they're likely to place an order. If, on the other hand, any of these elements are not pleasing for the customer, then the operation may lose business. Of course, the execution of preparing and delivering what's on the menu matters greatly, but if a consumer isn't enticed enough to order something from the menu in the first place, then the product itself doesn't matter.

468

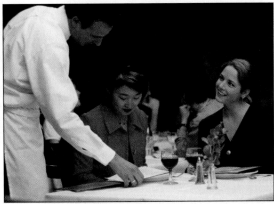

Figure 7.16: The menu is an important marketing tool.

The menu functions in two ways: planning purposes and communication purposes. For the planning function, the menu gives an operation an end goal to work toward. The chefs gear all the stages of food production toward putting out the best product at the best prices, and the menu helps all the staff members of an operation to organize themselves. The menu forces the staff to ask a number of important questions:

- What is the target market? What segments are we aiming to serve?
- What types of food and service do these segments of the market expect?
- Are the ingredients for the menu items readily available and cost effective?
- Can the menu items be prepared in the most appealing way possible?
- Is the menu best serving the needs of our target market?
- Is the menu best serving the goals of the operation?

Using the menu as a planning tool, then, helps employees stay focused on all the behind-the-scenes work and how to best accomplish the goals of the operation.

As a marketing and communication tool, the menu functions in three ways:

- Informing customers about what the operation offers
- Selling products
- Creating identity

469

Discuss

- How does a menu address the needs of the operation's target market?
- How does the menu communicate both with potential customers and staff members?
- How can managers ensure that an operation's menu will help it fulfill its objectives?
- In what ways does a menu provide a competitive advantage?

Reinforce and Review

- The menu facilitates planning by giving an operation an end goal around which purchasing, staffing, and training can be organized.
- The menu also informs customers about what the operation offers, sells products, and creates an identity for the operation.

Teaching Tips

- Provide sample menus from a variety of restaurants that display a range of menu types. Encourage students to identify the message that each communicates.

CUSTOMIZED INSTRUCTION
Literacy Connection, 21st-Century Skills— Reason Effectively, Communicate Clearly, Work Independently
ESOL Students
Obtain menus from restaurant or foodservice establishments in your country of origin. How are these similar to or different from the menus discussed in this section? Why?

Figure Focus

Figure 7.16: When serving staff have been properly trained, they can increase the menu's effectiveness.

Discuss

- How might the message communicated by a multiple-page menu be different from the message communicated by a single-page menu? Why?

- Why is it important to have both an informative menu and a well-informed staff?

Reinforce and Review

- The most basic function of a menu is to tell customers what an operation has to offer, but it also presents an opportunity to distinguish an operation's items from those of the competition.

- The menu informs customers about potential health concerns and provides details about how different items are prepared.

- The description and placement of each menu item helps determine a customer's impression of each dish and therefore what he or she will order.

- The more visual attention certain items attract, the more likely customers are to order them.

- The menu's presentation—the choice and color of font, the quality of paper, and the number of items offered—communicates information about the operation's identity.

Informing Customers

The most basic function of the menu is to tell customers what the operation has to offer, but the menu also presents an opportunity to distinguish an operation's items from those of the competition. Many places serve a burger of some sort, but a chef can use the menu to describe exactly how a burger is prepared and why it is better than any of the competitors' burgers. Do the chefs use a particular kind of meat or spice? Do they cook it in a different way? Do they offer different condiments for the dish? Chefs can provide such a level of detail only on the menu itself. In addition, the menu informs customers about potential health concerns, such as the risks of eating undercooked food, ingredients that may cause allergic reactions (for example, nuts), or particularities of specific dishes (for example, degrees of spiciness).

Selling Products

The menu may be an operation's best sales tool. It can greatly influence what customers decide to order. Descriptions are very helpful for this purpose. Appeal to the appetites of customers through well-written descriptions of menu items. The placement of items on the menu can influence sales as well. Marketers and chefs may choose to highlight the items they most want to sell by placing those items at the top of the menu, putting them in a bolder or bigger font, or even by boxing off the items altogether in a separate category. The more visual attention certain items attract, the more likely customers are to consider and order them. A "Daily Specials" page is one way to use the menu to sell product.

Creating Identity

The menu also helps create the image or identity of an operation. The items listed on a menu say a lot about an operation, but so does the way the menu is laid out. The font, color scheme, and material or paper stock the menu is printed on all help communicate the identity of an operation. For example, a menu using a heavy paper stock, bound in a leather cover, and listing menu items in a script font may give the impression of a high-end, formal operation, whereas a menu presented on one sheet of regular paper stock with menu items printed in a large, colored font may create the impression of an informal, casual operation. The menu itself goes a long way in communicating the identity of an operation even before a word is spoken by any service personnel.

Menu Types

There are many types of menus. An understanding of these broad categories of menus is a good first step in determining or identifying an operation's goals and function in the marketplace. The different menu types are listed below:

- À la carte (AH le CART)
- Du jour (doo-ZHEUR)
- Cyclical
- Limited
- Fixed
- California
- Prix fixe (PREE FIX)
- Table d'hôte (tah-buhl DOHT)

À la carte menu: This menu prices each item separately. Everything on the menu has its own price and is paid for separately, per order. For example, on an à la carte menu, a typical meal, such as steak, potatoes, and a vegetable, will have separate prices for each item, and they need to be ordered individually. In short, nothing on an à la carte menu comes with anything else. See Figure 7.17.

KABOB RESTAURANT
LUNCH MENU

APPETIZERS
Mozzarella Sticks	$6.95
Chicken Fingers	$6.75
Buffalo Wings	$8.95
Clams on the Half Shell	$9.95
Jumbo Shrimp Cocktail	$8.75

SOUPS
Lobster Bisque	$4.75
Minestrone	$3.50
New England Clam Chowder	$4.25

SALADS
House Salad	$4.75
House Salad with Mozzarella	$5.75
Chef Salad	$6.75
Cobb Salad	$7.75
Caesar Salad	$8.25
Grilled Chicken Caesar Salad	$9.75

SANDWICHES/WRAPS/WEDGES (served with homemade chips)
Grilled Chicken	$7.50
Tuna/Egg/Chicken	$5.75
Turkey Club	$6.00
Grilled Cheese	$3.50
Chicken Parmigiana	$7.50
Eggplant Parmigiana	$7.50
Meatball	$7.50
Sausage and Peppers	$7.50

SIDE ORDERS
French Fries	$2.50
Onion Rings	$3.00
Cole Slaw	$1.50
Potato Salad	$1.50
Pasta Salad	$1.75

Figure 7.17: An à la carte menu.

471

Figure Focus

Figure 7.17: What can you tell about Kabob just by examining its lunch menu?

Discuss

- For guests, what are the advantages and disadvantages of an á la carte menu? Why?
- For restaurant employees, what are the advantages and disadvantages of an á la carte menu? Why?

Reinforce and Review

- Identifying the type of menu an operation uses can help identify the operation's goals.
- Common menu types include á la carte, cyclical, and limited.

Teaching Tips

- Students should decide on three terms they would use to describe Kabob, based on the menu depicted in Figure 7.17.

In-Class Activity: Menu Mania

Literacy Connection, 21st-Century Skills—Work Creatively with Others, Critical Thinking and Problem Solving, Communication and Collaboration, Social and Cultural Skills

Working in small groups, consider Kabob's lunch menu, shown in Figure 7.17. Does it give you a clear picture of the restaurant's identity? Why or why not?

Building on the current menu, eliminate some lunch items and replace them with others of your choice. How have your choices either strengthened the restaurant's identity or changed it altogether? If your choices have changed the identity, what is the restaurant's new image?

Each group should share its work with the class to discuss the importance of the menu in shaping a restaurant's public face.

Vocabulary Term

- **Á la carte menu:** A menu that prices each item separately.

Discuss

- How can the use of either a du jour menu or a cyclical menu reinforce the message that a particular operation serves the freshest seafood in the community?

- How can the use of a cyclical menu be tied to seasonality? What other characteristics might you expect restaurants offering this message to have?

Reinforce and Review

- In the United States, du jour menus are commonly used to offer daily specials and might be presented verbally by staff members.

- Cyclical menus give chefs and managers the flexibility to offer new dishes, ingredients, and cooking techniques at certain intervals throughout the year.

Teaching Tips

- Students should decide on three terms they would use to describe the restaurant offering the menu depicted in Figure 7.18.

Vocabulary Terms

- **Du jour menu:** A menu listing the menu items that are available on a particular day.

- **Cyclical menu:** A menu that is changed after a certain period of time.

Du jour menu: *Du jour* is a French term that means "of the day," and so a du jour menu simply lists the menu items that are available on a particular day. In the United States, this kind of menu is often presented as a Daily Specials menu and is presented as an insert in the standard menu or written on a blackboard within the operation. Sometimes, a chef or manager might choose not to print the du jour menu at all, but opt to have the service staff verbally present the menu items of the day instead. See Figure 7.18.

Figure 7.18: A du jour menu.

Cyclical menu: With this type of menu, chefs or managers change menu items after a certain period of time. For example, an operation might serve four different menus that correspond to the four seasons. Cyclical menus can change on a daily, weekly, or monthly basis as well; it all depends on the management's objectives in catering to their target market. See Figure 7.19 on the following page.

Figure Focus

Figure 7.18: What types of restaurant or foodservice operations might offer du jour menus? Why?

Cyclical Menu

Monday, 9/13	Portion		Thursday, 9/16	Portion
Chili with Beans & Cheese	1 cup		Sliced Turkey	4 oz
Mixed Greens Salad	½ cup		Whipped Potatoes	½ cup
Cherry Apple Juice	6 oz		Garden Peas	½ cup
Sesame Crackers	8		Raisin Spice Bar	1
Peanut Butter Cookie	1		Low-Fat Milk	½ pt
Low-Fat Milk	½ pt			
Tuesday, 9/14	**Portion**		**Friday, 9/17**	**Portion**
Vegetable Pizza	1 Slice		Lasagna	3 oz
Seasoned Green Beans	½ cup		Applesauce	½ cup
Fresh Apple	½ cup		Sweet Corn	½ cup
Low-Fat Milk	½ pt		Sourdough Roll	1
			Low-Fat Milk	½ pt
Wednesday, 9/15	**Portion**			
Cheeseburger/Bun	3½ oz			
French Fries	½ cup			
Chilled Peaches	½ cup			
Low-Fat Milk	½ pt			

Figure 7.19: A cyclical menu.

Limited menu: A limited menu is just that—limited. There are typically only a few items offered on a limited menu. Quick-service operations frequently offer a limited menu. Such a menu makes it easy to keep track of costs because there are fewer ingredients to account for, and those ingredients are usually the same through inventory cycles, making it easier to track and monitor pricing.

Fixed menu: This menu offers the same items every day. A particular advantage to a menu such as this is that customers know what to expect every time they return. Many chefs work with a fixed menu to offer customers consistency, but then supplement the fixed menu with a du jour menu to offer variety.

California menu: This menu lists all meals available at any time of day. Diners that are open 24 hours might use a California menu. This accommodates a wider variety of customers who may differ in lifestyle and work schedules. Working people might have night shifts and therefore want breakfast at the same time that younger kids in school are hanging out with friends for late-night snacking. An operation that uses a California menu can accommodate both segments of the market at once.

Prix fixe menu: This is the opposite of an à la carte menu in that it offers multiple menu items at one price. Often, customers are offered multiple courses for a single set price. For example, a choice of appetizer, full entrée with sides,

473

Discuss

- Why might an operation choose to combine menu types or offer multiple menus? How would this work?

- How can offering a limited menu help a restaurant or foodservice operation become more efficient in all of its activities?

- How can the consistency offered by a fixed menu help reinforce the operation's identity?

- What types of restaurants are most likely to offer California menus? Why?

- What message does a prix fixe menu send? Why?

Reinforce and Review

- Quick-service restaurants commonly offer limited menus, which facilitate cost control, purchasing, preparation, and service.

- Fixed menus are often coupled with du jour menus to offer both variety and consistency.

- California menus enable operations to serve multiple market segments simultaneously.

- Prix fixe menus offer multiple courses for a set price.

Teaching Tips

- Students should decide on three terms they would use to describe the restaurant offering the menu depicted in Figure 7.19.

Vocabulary Terms

- **Limited menu:** A menu that offers only a few items.

- **Fixed menu:** A menu that offers the same items every day.

- **California menu:** A menu that lists all meals and items available at all times of day.

- **Prix fixe menu:** A menu that offers multiple items at one price.

Figure Focus

Figure 7.19: What are some advantages and disadvantages of offering a cyclical menu? Why?

Discuss

- Explain how prix fixe and table d'hôte menus are similar and different.

- Why might a restaurant or foodservice operation choose to offer a table d'hôte menu? What benefits does it offer to guests and to staff?

Reinforce and Review

- Prix fixe menus increase the check total while providing a discount on the food items ordered, benefiting both operation and guest.

- Table d'hôte menus offer a variety of options and multiple courses for a fixed price.

Teaching Tips

- Students should decide on three terms they would use to describe the restaurants offering the menus depicted in Figures 7.20 and 7.21.

- Students should compare the descriptive terms they have selected for the restaurants whose menus appear in Figures 7.17-7.21. Is there any overlap? Why or why not?

Vocabulary Terms

- **Table d'hôte menu:** A menu offering multiple courses, with multiple choices within each course, for a set price.

and a dessert might be offered for one price, and that price is often slightly lower than if each course or item were purchased separately. This type of menu arrangement presents a win-win for both customer and operation. The operation ensures a higher check total by bundling multiple courses together, while the customer receives a discount on that higher total. Both casual and formal operations utilize prix fixe menus. See Figure 7.20.

Prix Fixe Menu

French onion au gratin

Classic Caesar salad with Romaine lettuce, herbed croutons, grated Parmesan cheese, and Caesar dressing

Surf and turf with filet mignon and a lobster tail served with drawn butter

Carrot cake with coconut frosting

$45

Figure 7.20: A prix fixe menu.

Table d'hôte menu: This menu is similar to a prix fixe menu in that it bundles various elements of the menu into one package. For example, such a menu might present in advance four meals, and each would include a number of courses and possibly even beverages all for one price. Banquets frequently offer such a menu. See Figure 7.21.

CHAR STEAKHOUSE
Table d'hôte

$65

Starters

Clams on the Half Shell   Fried Calamari
Oysters on the Half Shell   Fresh Mozzarella and Tomato

Entrées (all entrées served with tossed salad)

Filet Mignon   Broiled Swordfish
Prime Rib of Beef   Grilled Salmon
King Veal Chop   Chicken Marsala
Two Loin Lamb Chops   Veal Piccata

Desserts

Apple Pie   Cheesecake
Carrot Cake   Chocolate Layer Cake
Tiramisu   Sorbet

Figure 7.21: A table d'hôte menu.

474

Figure Focus

Figure 7.20: What are some advantages and disadvantages of offering a prix fixe menu?

Figure 7.21: How do the menu offerings enhance the "steakhouse" message?

Organizing a Menu

Most menus organize foods according to the order in which they are usually eaten, as illustrated in Figure 7.22, and listed below:

Figure 7.22: A menu organized by the order of courses.

1. Appetizers

2. Soups

3. Salads

4. Sandwiches (sandwiches can be offered before or after salads)

5. Entrées

6. Vegetables

7. Desserts

8. Beverages

Variations in these categories depend on what an operation offers and the image management wants to promote. For example, an Italian restaurant might offer a pasta course separate from the rest of the entrées.

475

Discuss

- Which of the courses could be grouped into a single category? Why?

- What other categories might a menu include that could help an operation differentiate itself from the competition?

Reinforce and Review

- Most menus organize foods according to the order in which they are usually eaten.

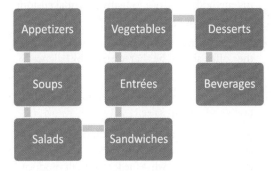

- Variations in these categories depend on what an operation offers and the image it wishes to promote.

Figure Focus

Figure 7.22: What information does the Kabob Restaurant dinner menu provide? Is the message conveyed by the dinner menu different from that conveyed by the lunch menu in Figure 7.17?

Discuss

- Why should foods within a major classification, such as appetizers or entrées, be prepared using a variety of cooking methods?

- How many different entrées should a fine-dining restaurant offer? How many should a family-style restaurant offer? Why?

Reinforce and Review

- Menus should vary tastes, textures, and seasoning methods to attract as many potential customers as possible.

- Menus, no matter how many or how few dishes they offer, should be characterized by balance and variety.

- Dessert choices should be based on customers' tastes and on past sales.

- A menu should reflect the operation's character and goals, but it should also reflect a realistic understanding of what the kitchen can produce in an efficient and cost-effective way.

- The two main steps in menu creation are planning and design.

Prepare foods within a major classification using a variety of cooking methods, such as poaching, roasting, grilling, frying, and baking. Vary tastes, textures, and seasoning for contrast to meet the tastes of a variety of customers.

Chefs or managers can divide entrées by categories such as beef, pork, chicken, lamb, veal, ham, shellfish, fish, pasta, egg, cheese, and vegetarian dishes. Maintain balance in the choice of vegetables, sauces, and potatoes used to complement entrées. For example, if a menu contains ham and chicken, offering sweet potatoes or yellow winter squash is a good balance. Four to six vegetables, including potatoes, should meet most menu needs. Salads and salad dressings also should reflect balance and variety.

The number of desserts on the menu depends on customers' tastes and past sales. Some operations may need to serve only ice cream or sherbet to satisfy their customers. Others may need to combine these with a limited number of pies or cakes; add puddings and fruit to extend dessert selections.

Creating a Menu

A menu should reflect the operation's character and goals. It also needs to reflect a realistic understanding of what chefs are capable of producing in a cost-effective way. There are two separate steps in menu creation: planning and design. There are various elements that must be considered with each step.

Planning

In the planning phase, managers and chefs must keep the following elements in mind:

- Physical layout of facility
- Skill of personnel
- Availability of ingredients
- Target market's wants and needs
- Target market's expectations
- Profit margin

Physical layout: Planners must take the physical layout, or space, of the actual operation into account when they design a menu. For example, planners must take into consideration the size of storage facilities, preparation and cooking areas, and the service and dining areas. An operation's physical layout often determines the kind of menu the chefs will be most capable of producing efficiently. An operation might not succeed if planners put out a menu that the chefs cannot produce efficiently.

Personnel: Planners must also consider the staff of an operation. If management wants to offer a menu of food items that require highly skilled, delicate preparation, then it needs to have cooks on staff that can fulfill those needs. On the other hand, if managers want a menu with ingredients that are easy to work with and inexpensive to produce, then it would be a mistake to employ a kitchen staff that is highly trained and experienced and therefore more costly. In short, the operation's personnel must fit the menu that planners create.

Ingredients: Ideally, managers and chefs want to create a menu that best reflects fresh, seasonal ingredients. But those ingredients can be expensive to acquire, so planners need to be aware of the availability of ingredients when making the menu. Making a menu consisting of many high-priced ingredients might end up losing money for the operation because food costs will make the items unprofitable. Planners need to consider not only what their operation can produce well, but also how cost efficient items are to produce. The availability of ingredients throughout the course of the year is also a factor.

Wants and needs of the target market: Sometimes, the personal desires of an operation's owners or managers overtake the wants and needs of the market they want to serve. This is a mistake. Management can never forget who the operation is supposed to be serving, and never fail to account for the wants and needs of its market.

Expectations of the target market: Expectations are closely related to the market's wants and needs. But the expectations of the market are more important after an operation has become established. Not meeting expectations becomes more dangerous the longer an operation exists. An operation can become complacent over time. But it is critical for managers to make sure the operation is staying true to the expectations of its customers. A change or loss of quality in the menu items or identity that initially brought success can hurt an operation. Consistency is one of the cornerstones of success in the restaurant and foodservice industry. When customers no longer know what to expect from a certain operation, they may decide to stop coming to it and spend their money elsewhere.

Profit margin: No business can survive if it is not producing at profitable levels. Planners must create the menu with profitability in mind throughout the entire process. Chefs and managers must compose dishes and design the menu itself with this in mind. An unprofitable operation will soon not be an operation at all.

477

Discuss

- How might an operation's physical layout make some proposed menu items "off limits"? Here are some examples: Operations with little space between guest tables probably will not be able to perform flambéing or other tableside cooking tasks; kitchens with a single, small deep-fryer probably will not be able to handle a menu that relies heavily on fried seafood and chicken; kitchens without freezers that are accessible during service probably cannot offer ice creams, sorbets, and other frozen desserts.

- Why might some restaurant or foodservice operations choose to purchase fresh, seasonal ingredients, whereas other similar operations do not?

Reinforce and Review

- In the planning phase of menu creation, managers and chefs must consider the physical layout of the facility, staff skills, ingredient availability, the target market's wants and needs, the target market's expectations, and the profit margin.

- An operation's physical layout often determines the kind of menu that the chefs will be most capable of producing efficiently.

- Staff skills should be in line with the menu demands: skilled enough to do the work, but not too skilled to do it.

- Planners must consider both what items the operation can produce well and how cost-effectively those items can be produced.

- When planning a menu, availability of the desired ingredients at an appropriate price should be considered.

- Management and staff should place the target market's wants and needs above their own desires when planning a menu.

Teaching Tips

- Relate this material to the discussion of purchasing in Chapter 5.

Discuss

- Why do the target market's expectations become especially important after the restaurant or food-service operation has been established?

- What information do planners need to develop a profitable menu?

- Why is menu design so important to an operation's image and success?

Reinforce and Review

- Not meeting expectations becomes more dangerous the longer an operation exists.

- A deviation from or loss of quality in the menu items or identity that originally attracted customers can cause an operation to fail.

- When operations become inconsistent, customers no longer know what to expect from them and stop patronizing them.

- Chefs and managers must plan the menu with profitability in mind.

- Once the menu items have been determined, the menu itself can be designed.

- Well-designed menus are pleasing to read, easy to understand, and clearly express the identity and character of the operation as a whole.

- Five elements to consider when designing a menu include medium, layout, color, font, and art.

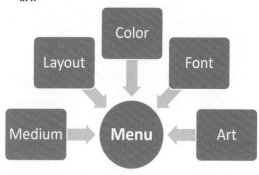

- Most menus are presented on some form of paper. Lightweight papers are more often used by casual operations, whereas more formal operations commonly use heavier paper.

Designing

Once chefs and managers have decided upon all of the items to be included on a menu in the planning phase, the design phase can begin. In the design phase, management must consider how the menu will actually look. Well-designed menus are pleasing to read, easy to understand, and clearly express the identity and character of the operation as a whole. But how do designers actually accomplish this? Designers must consider the following elements when laying out a menu:

- Medium
- Layout
- Color
- Font
- Art

Medium: An operation's menu can be presented in a number of ways, as illustrated in Figure 7.23. Most use some sort of paper with the menu items printed on it. The paper stock that designers use can help to express the identity of the operation. Thick, heavy paper stock feels more expensive in the hand and is more durable, which may help create an impression of elegance. Lightweight paper stock might signal to customers that the operation is more casual or carefree. Sometimes, an operation may opt to put its menu on a different medium altogether. For example, a menu can be written with chalk on a blackboard that is visible to all the patrons in a dining room, or even on a wall in the dining room. These types of menus are called **menu boards**. Finally, at some operations, the servers memorize the menu and relay it verbally to the customers. This is called a **spoken menu**, and it can help personalize the menu and create a more intimate feel for the operation as a whole.

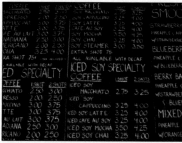

Figure 7.23: Media for menus.

Figure Focus

Figure 7.23: What types of media are most appropriate for menus in what types of restaurant or foodservice establishments? Why?

Layout: How the menu is categorized and sequenced also adds to the identity of an operation. Is everything all on one page, or are the items spaced out over multiple pages? Are the items crammed together in a busy, hectic way, or are they spaced wide apart in a calmer, more subdued manner? Answers to these questions will say a lot about an operation's personality. In addition, the layout can help emphasize aspects of the menu that management wants customers to notice, and order, most frequently. The layout, in short, can help further an operation's identity and work to sell menu items all at the same time.

Color: Color is obviously very important to any business. The colors chosen by an operation could be the difference between being considered romantic or rowdy; sophisticated or casual; expensive or inexpensive. Sometimes the color can even signal to patrons what type of food will be served. For example, various blue tones could signal seafood to customers, while a blend of orange and red may signal a spicier cuisine, such as barbeque. When planning the colors of a menu, designers should think about the feeling they want customers to get when considering the operation. Figure 7.24 shows some menus' color schemes.

Figure 7.24: Sample menu color schemes.

Font: Like many elements of design, fonts can work in different ways. A font can, of course, highlight certain elements on the menu. Italic or bold fonts will stand out on the page and draw customers' attention. A large, dark font might be helpful for an operation catering to segments of the market who might appreciate easy-to-read print, and sometimes using italics helps provide contrast between the name of the menu item and its description. Fonts can also signal the personality of an operation. Flowing, bubbly fonts might be appropriate for a kids' menu, for example. A font that mimics handwriting signals a more informal, casual establishment. Scripted fonts create a classical

479

Figure Focus

Figure 7.24: Why might an operation choose one of these color schemes over another? How might that choice affect sales?

Discuss

- What are some advantages and disadvantages of relying on a spoken menu? How can a spoken menu be used in tandem with a printed menu?

- How are these elements of menu design also used on other promotional materials? How can these other materials reinforce the identity presented by the menu?

- What colors do students associate with which restaurant or foodservice operations? Why? How does this connect to the operations' images?

Reinforce and Review

- Menu boards and spoken menus are also important ways of communicating an operation's offerings to its guests.

- The layout of a menu can help emphasize particular dishes that the management wants guests to order most frequently.

- A proper layout can both reinforce the operation's identity and work to sell particular menu items.

- The colors selected for a menu should reflect the image that the operation wishes to present.

CUSTOMIZED INSTRUCTION

Science Connection, Literacy Connection, 21st-Century Skills—Critical Thinking and Problem Solving, Communicate Clearly, Information Literacy, Work Independently

More Advanced Students

How can color affect human behavior? The study of color psychology seeks to answer this question, looking into the ways in which preferences, behavior, and choices are affected by the colors we see. Because marketers know that color plays a role in perception, they use different colors for different purposes and to project different images.

Research the ways in which color can affect preferences and write a one-page report discussing your findings and explaining how marketing can capitalize on this information.

Vocabulary Terms

- **Menu board:** A menu presented on blackboards, whiteboards, or directly on the walls or fixtures of an operation.

- **Spoken menu:** A menu that is verbally presented to guests by staff members.

Discuss

- What are some other ways in which an operation can use art to reinforce its identity?

Reinforce and Review

- Fonts can both highlight particular menu items or categories and signal the operation's "personality."

- The choice of art selected for a menu—as well as the absence of art—can reinforce the operation's identity.

Homework Activity: Negative Space

Literacy Connection, 21st-Century Skills— Reason Effectively, Communicate Clearly, Work Independently

Negative space is the empty space left around artwork or text. It helps emphasize the image, drawing the eye to a particular place.

How is negative space used in menu design? Explain how negative space can be used to highlight a particular menu item or category, increasing its sales. Discuss your findings in a one-page paper.

Homework Activity: Competition

Literacy Connection, 21st-Century Skills— Reason Effectively, Communicate Clearly, Work Independently

In what ways can small operations gain a competitive advantage over larger ones through their menu planning and design, and vice versa? Explain your answers in a two-paragraph report.

feel, while clean, rigid lines speak to a more modern approach. Menu designers must be careful when choosing a font for all of these reasons. Figure 7.25 shows a variety of fonts.

Art: Finally, the art on a menu can say a lot about an operation. Clowns and smiley faces say kid-friendly to many people, while no art at all might say the opposite. A picture of an old 1950s car will say diner to some customers, while flames might say barbeque or spicy cuisine to others. The borders that divide various segments of the menu also fall under the category of art. What kinds of lines are incorporated in the menu? Straight lines with lots of angles give off a different vibe than borders with more arcs and curves.

Figure 7.25: Different fonts have different connotations.

Essential Skills
Planning a Menu

Planning a menu isn't as easy as simply listing all your favorite dishes or all the dishes that you find easy to cook. Instead, it takes quite a bit of thought and planning to ensure that you are presenting the right mix of food to the desired customers. Here is a process that can help you develop a successful menu:

❶ List all the menu items that you think might be successful. Take into account customer preferences, goods available from your suppliers and their prices, the time of year, and any other factors that you think could be important.

❷ Eliminate items from the list that might not work on the finished menu. For instance, look for garnishes that take too long to prepare or multiple dishes featuring the same main item. Unless your operation is a steakhouse, how many steaks do you really need on the menu?

Figure Focus

Figure 7.25: Which of these fonts is appropriate for what types of restaurant or foodservice operations? Why?

❸ Fine-tune the remaining items to fit your restaurant. Figure 7.26 shows a menu in the fine-tuning phase. For example, if your operation has a New Italian theme, then your award-winning chili really doesn't belong on the menu.

❹ Make sure that all the items can be successfully prepared within your existing structure at an appropriate cost. No matter how elegant and delicious your potato *tuiles* may be, if it takes one chef two hours each day to make them and you only have two other chefs, the *tuiles* might be too expensive for your menu. Save special presentations like this for major events, such as wine dinners or private parties.

❺ Identify the winning selections and create your menu. If these items are new to your restaurant, or you have hired new staff who have not prepared or seen any of these dishes, make sure to build some training time into your schedule. Plan both to teach the cooks how to make the items and to teach the service staff how to describe them properly.

❻ Save the documents you've created when coming up with the final menu. It may be that a dish that would be unsuccessful now will be a hit in a year or two. Don't waste all your work.

❼ Once you've fully planned out the content of your menu, it's time to design it!

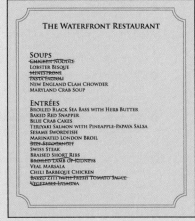

THE WATERFRONT RESTAURANT

SOUPS
~~CHICKEN NOODLE~~
LOBSTER BISQUE
~~MINESTRONE~~
~~PASTA FAGIOLI~~
NEW ENGLAND CLAM CHOWDER
MARYLAND CRAB SOUP

ENTRÉES
BROILED BLACK SEA BASS WITH HERB BUTTER
BAKED RED SNAPPER
BLUE CRAB CAKES
TERIYAKI SALMON WITH PINEAPPLE-PAPAYA SALSA
SESAME SWORDFISH
MARINATED LONDON BROIL
~~BEEF STROGANOFF~~
SWISS STEAK
BRAISED SHORT RIBS
~~BROILED LAMB OF KIDNEYS~~
VEAL MARSALA
CHILI BARBEQUE CHICKEN
~~BAKED ZITI WITH FRESH TOMATO SAUCE~~
~~VEGETABLE LASAGNA~~

Figure 7.26: Step 3—A menu in the fine-tuning phase.

481

Figure Focus

Figure 7.26: Restaurant and foodservice operations must carefully prune their menus so that the remaining dishes reinforce the operation's image and can be consistently prepared under prevailing conditions.

Encourage students to discuss the following:

- How can chefs and managers ensure balance and variety in the menu?

- What might result if the New Italian restaurant did choose to offer the chef's award-winning chili?

- If the operation itself is still in the planning stage, how can chefs and managers accurately predict labor costs that might affect the ability to serve certain items?

Homework Activity: Designing Menus

Literacy Connection, 21st-Century Skills—Think Creatively, Reason Effectively, Communicate Clearly, Work Independently

If you were to open a restaurant, how would you design your menu? Explain your choices of medium, layout, color, font, and art. How would these reinforce your identity and attract your target market?

Write a one-page essay describing your menu design and discussing how it fits your overall marketing plan.

Reinforce and Review

- A menu's borders can also reinforce the operation's identity.

Teaching Tips

- Present students with the sample menus they examined and discussed earlier in this section. How have their impressions of each menu changed? What new information can they extract from each?

Essential Skills: Planning a Menu (cont.)

Encourage students to discuss the following:

- Is it cost-effective and efficient to train staff members to prepare new dishes, or should chefs and managers stick with the "old standards"? Why?

- What role can service staff play in the menu-planning process? How can their input strengthen a menu's appeal to its target market?

- How can the process of menu planning help chefs and managers to think more deeply about the image that the operation presents?

Essential Skills
Testing New Menu Items

Encourage students to discuss the following:

- Relate this material to the discussion of customer feedback in Level 1, Chapter 10.

- Which of these feedback methods might be most productive? Why?

- Which feedback methods are appropriate for use with which target markets? Why?

Homework Activity:
Feeding Back

Science Connection, Literacy Connection, 21st-Century Skills—Critical Thinking and Problem Solving, Communicate Clearly, Work Independently

Feedback is the use of information about some past event to influence similar events in the future. Feedback is an important concept in the restaurant and foodservice industry, but it is also relevant throughout the natural and social sciences.

Select a branch of science that interests you, such as biology or economics. Explain how feedback plays a role in this field in a one-page report.

Essential Skills
Testing New Menu Items

When creating or changing a menu, it's important to get as much direct feedback as possible. Below is a list of ways the managers of an operation can get feedback about new menu items:

1. New menu items can be tested using clip-ons or table-tent points of sale, as shown in Figure 7.27.

2. New items should be run for a limited time only; for example, as daily or weekly specials.

3. Servers can suggest the items and then get feedback from the customers to help evaluate the items' success.

4. The sales of new items can be compared to sales of established items to evaluate if they would be profitable additions to the regular menu.

5. Offer small tastings of new items for free and then solicit feedback from customers who try them.

Figure 7.27: Step 1—Use a table-tent menu.

Pricing the Menu

Pricing the menu is a critical process for any operation. Price serves two main roles: it provides information to customers, and it determines profitability.

Price provides information to customers about how much menu items cost, but it also reveals much more about an operation. The price of items on a menu also speaks to the market category in which the restaurant falls; indicating quality of the food, level of service, atmosphere to expect, etc. Customers, for example, will expect more by way of service, quality, and atmosphere for a $50.00 steak than for a $10.00 steak. With increased customer expectations comes the need to execute all levels of food preparation and service on a higher level as well. Management needs to make sure that pricing aligns with the goals of the operation and the skill level of the staff.

482

Figure Focus

Figure 7.27: What image does this promotional item reinforce? How do its layout, color scheme, font, and artwork all combine to present a uniform message?

Price also determines profitability by ensuring that an operation is bringing in more dollars than the sum of all the costs for the product or service. **Profitability** is defined as the amount of money remaining for an operation after expenses, or costs, are paid. Profitability in restaurant and foodservice operations is determined by the amount of money left over from the sale of food or beverages after the cost to prepare them and pay for other overhead expenses like rent and heat has been subtracted. This difference is also called the **margin**; most restaurant and foodservice operations set a target margin for their operation.

The price of a menu item must account for all of the costs involved in producing that item for the customer. Food costs, labor costs, and overhead costs must all be factored into the price of any item. Then, management must build into the price how much money it wants, and can reasonably get, in profit. An item that is overpriced in a particular market will likely not sell enough to be profitable. In contrast, an item that is underpriced may sell well but will lose money because it costs the operation more than it is bringing in. Striking the right balance requires careful planning and consideration.

There are many methods of pricing menu items. *Chapter 3, Cost Control,* discussed in detail the food cost percentage method, contribution margin method, the straight markup method, and the average check method. This section will review these methods briefly:

- **Food percentage method:** Set the percentage of menu price that the food cost must be, and then calculate the price that will provide this percentage using the following formula:

  Item food cost ÷ Food cost percentage = Menu price

  Because food cost percentage is dependent on the costs of the food and its preparation within the restaurant or foodservice operation, an accurate food cost percentage will be different for each menu category: appetizers, salads, entrées, signature dishes, specials, desserts, beverages, etc.

- **Contribution margin method:** This is a pricing method that works for à la carte menu items as well as menu items that comprise a meal (soup, salad, entrée, etc.). This method uses operation-wide data to determine a dollar amount that must be added to each major menu item's food cost. The managers of a restaurant or foodservice operation can use the same contribution margin for all menu items, or they can calculate separate contribution margins for different menu categories. There are two steps to the formula:

  (Total nonfood cost + Target profit) ÷ Number of customers = Contribution margin

  Contribution margin + Food cost = Menu price

483

- **Contribution margin method:** This pricing method uses the portion costs for each item sold to determine how much money the average customer contributes to overhead and profit; this dollar amount is then added to each menu item.

Discuss

- How do student expectations of a restaurant or foodservice operation vary according to the operation's menu prices? Is this reasonable? Why or why not?

- What role does the operation's target market play in its menu pricing?

Reinforce and Review

- Menu prices have two main roles: They provide information to customers and they determine profitability.

- Menu prices not only tell customers how much particular items cost, but also indicate important information about quality levels, ambiance, and other characteristics of the operation.

- Customer expectations increase with price; therefore, higher menu prices place greater pressure on all staff members to perform at their best.

- Management should ensure that menu prices are aligned with both operational goals and staff skills.

- Price determines profitability by ensuring that revenues are greater than costs.

- The price of a menu item must account for all the costs involved in producing and serving that item, including food, labor, and overhead.

- Overpriced items will usually not sell enough to be profitable, whereas underpriced items might sell too well and lose money.

- The four most common methods of pricing a menu are the food cost percentage method, contribution margin method, straight markup method, and average check method.

Teaching Tips

- Encourage students to review Chapter 3.

Vocabulary Terms

- **Profitability:** The amount of money remaining for an operation after expenses have been paid.

- **Margin:** The difference between the amount of revenue remaining after the cost of food and beverage sales and overhead has been subtracted; another way of indicating "profitability."

- **Food percentage method:** This pricing method sets the percentage of menu price that the food cost must be and then divides the item's food cost by that percentage to develop the menu price.

Discuss

- How will menu prices vary, depending on the method management uses to determine the prices?

- What is the most appropriate method for determining menu prices? Why?

- What factors are involved in the decision to use one method of pricing a menu and not another?

Reinforce and Review

- Because food cost percentage is dependent on the cost of food and preparation, it will vary for each menu category.

- The contribution margin method uses operation-wide data to determine a dollar amount that must be added to the food cost of each major item to establish the menu price.

- The straight markup pricing method allows managers to mark up the costs of an item by some predetermined amount to establish the selling price; an underlying assumption of this method is that each customer will help pay for labor, operating costs, food costs, and some portion of the profit.

- The average check pricing method uses the average check amount to determine the price range of menu items, which is then used in tandem with the food cost percentage to determine the menu price for each item.

- Two other menu pricing methods that operations can use, but only for major menu items, are the set dollar amount markup and the set percentage increase markup.

Vocabulary Terms

- **Straight markup pricing method:** This pricing method multiplies raw food cost by a predetermined fraction to determine the dollar amount to be added to each food item.

- **Average check method:** This pricing method divides the operation's total revenue by the number of seats, average seat turnover, and number of days open each year; this yields the average check amount, which is then used with the approximate food cost amount to determine menu prices.

- **Set dollar amount markup:** This pricing method adds a fixed dollar amount to the food cost of an item to determine menu prices.

- **Set percentage increase method:** This pricing method enables managers to add a fixed percentage to the food cost of each item to determine menu prices.

- **Straight markup pricing:** This refers to a pricing method where managers mark up the costs according to a formula to obtain the selling price. A margin is defined in terms of the selling price; a markup is determined in terms of the cost.

  Ideally, the dollar amount of the markup should be large enough to cover the operating costs of the restaurant or foodservice operation and include a reasonable profit; however, this is not a requirement. An underlying assumption of this method is that each customer will help pay for labor, operating costs, and the cost of food, as well as contribute to profit.

- **Average check method:** For this method, managers divide the total revenue by the number of seats, average seat turnover, and days open in one year. The result is an average check amount, which gives managers an idea of the price range of items on the menu. Managers can then use this range, along with an approximate food cost percentage, to determine each item's selling price.

In addition to these methods, there are two other methods that an operation can use, but only for major menu items. These methods are the set dollar amount markup and the set percentage increase method:

- **Set dollar amount markup:** This method simply adds a fixed dollar amount to the food cost of an item. In order to utilize this method, you must know the food cost and the dollar amount of the markup. The equation works as follows:

  Food cost + Markup = Menu price

  The markup is calculated based on the following:

  Profit per menu item + Labor cost per menu item + Operating cost per menu item = Markup

- **Set percentage increase method:** This method builds on the set dollar amount markup method and takes it a step further. Basically, managers calculate the markup as described for the set dollar amount markup for one or several menu items. Then they determine what the percentage markup is in comparison to the items' food costs.

  Food cost × Percentage = Markup

  Markup ÷ Food cost = Percentage

Using the markup and food costs from the set dollar amount markup method model allows managers to calculate a percentage markup for all menu items.

484

Homework Activity: Lunch Is Served

Mathematics Connection, Literacy Connection, 21st-Century Skills—Solve Problems, Communicate Clearly, Work Independently

During today's lunch service at Jimmy's Café, the three most popular dishes were chicken-fried steak (25 orders at $10 apiece), cheeseburger (20 orders at $8 apiece), and Reuben sandwich (18 orders at $7.50 apiece). 100 guests were served, and the restaurant took in $900 on the sale of food alone.

How much does the average guest spend on food? ($9.00)

What percentage of revenue was earned on each of the three bestselling items? (Steak, 27.78 percent; cheeseburger, 17.78 percent; Reuben, 15 percent)

What was the average menu price of the other items on the menu? ($9.60)

Essential Skills
Pricing the Extras

To determine accurate pricing and food costs, restaurant and foodservice operations must take into account not just the food the guests order, but the food that the guests don't order but receive anyway: the salt and pepper on the table, the bread and butter or olive oil provided, the amuse-bouche or pre-dessert, the ketchup, the jelly packets—the list is long. And all those little things can add up quickly. The total cost of these items is often called the Q factor and is usually factored into the cost of each entrée on the menu. Here's how to calculate the Q factor:

❶ List all the possible foods that you may provide guests for "free." In addition to the items already mentioned, include half-and-half, sugar cubes, sliced lemon, and so on.

❷ Determine how much of each item would be used by a typical consumer (for instance, 1 ounce of butter or ⅛ teaspoon of salt). An easy way to do this is to keep track of how much of each item is served over a period of time, and then divide by the number of entrées sold during this period. For instance, if you serve 800 entrées in a two-week period and you use 100 lemons during this time, placing a half-slice of lemon in each glass of water served, you would divide 100 lemons by 800 entrées to obtain .125 (or ⅛) lemons served per entrée.

❸ Calculate the cost of each item based on the average portion used. If each lemon costs $0.10, then the cost of each serving of lemon is $0.0125.

❹ Once you determine the cost of each serving of each item, add them all together. This total is your Q factor.

❺ When costing your entrées, add the Q factor as an ingredient in each.

Using the Q factor is the most efficient and accurate way to determine your costs and prices. Otherwise, you will be basing your prices on incorrect costs and are likely to lose profits.

Analyzing the Menu

It is crucial to the success of an operation that the managers have the knowledge and means to analyze how well items on the menu are performing. Managers can determine the sales performance of each menu item after the restaurant has been open for some time and they have enough sales data to analyze. Gathering information for three months or longer provides more useful results than data from a shorter time period.

485

- Why might managers choose to use the set dollar amount markup or the set percentage increase method instead of one of the four more common methods of menu pricing?

Reinforce and Review

- The set percentage increase method marks up each menu item by a percentage, based on the information provided by the set dollar amount markup.

- For example, if an item's food cost is $5 and the markup is $1, then the percentage of the markup is 20 percent; therefore, the food costs of other major menu items should be increased by 20 percent to determine the appropriate menu prices.

Teaching Tips

- Work with students to review math skills as needed.

Essential Skills
Pricing the Extras

Encourage students to discuss the following:

- Why is it important to consider the Q factor when determining food costs?

- Guests usually pay indirectly for items like condiments, bread, and butter. What difference might charging directly for these items make to customers? How might this affect the operation's image?

- Which types of operations would probably benefit most from using the Q factor? Why?

- Why is the Q factor only included when calculating the food costs of entrées?

- Can the Q factor be estimated, or should it be accurately determined? What are the advantages and disadvantages to either strategy?

- If an operation begins to incorporate the Q factor into its costing and pricing procedures, are prices likely to change enough that regular guests will notice? Why or why not?

Homework Activity:
Q-ing up for Breakfast

Mathematics Connection, Literacy Connection, 21st-Century Skills—Solve Problems, Communicate Clearly, Work Independently

In a given week, your breakfast restaurant provides the following items for "free": 40 lemons ($0.20 apiece), 300 ramekins of homemade jam ($0.12 apiece), and 8 oz of homemade hot chili paste ($0.95). During this time, 400 entrées are served.

What is the average portion of each item? (Lemon, 1/10 of a lemon; jam, 75 percent of a ramekin; hot chili paste, 0.02 oz)

What is the cost per average portion of each item? (Lemon, $0.02; jam, $0.09; hot chili paste, $0.02)

What is the Q factor? ($0.13)

Discuss

- Do all menu items that have a high sales volume earn money for the restaurant or foodservice operation? Why or why not?

- Conversely, can menu items with relatively low sales volume earn money for the operation? Why or why not?

Reinforce and Review

- One way management can gauge performance is by examining sales volume and sales volume percentage.

- The sales mix analysis compares menu items in terms of sales and profitability, determining which are most frequently ordered and which earn the most money.

- Menu engineering can help managers make decisions about which menu items to leave alone, which to increase or decrease in selling price, which to promote, and which to eliminate.

Homework Activity: Voluminous Volume

Mathematics Connection, Literacy Connection, 21st-Century Skills—Solve Problems, Communicate Clearly, Work Independently

Mako's restaurant is open five days per week and offers a cyclical menu that currently offers six entrées. This week, she sold 80 portions of lamb, 60 of chicken, 57 of pork, 28 of mushroom, 74 of beef, and 36 of shrimp. Entrée revenues were $5,025.

For each entrée, what was the average sales volume per day? (Lamb, 16; chicken, 12; pork, 11.4; mushroom, 5.6; beef, 14.8, shrimp, 7.2)

For each entrée, what percentage of the week's sales volume did it represent? (Lamb, 23.9 percent; chicken, 17.9 percent; pork, 17 percent; mushroom, 8.4 percent; beef, 22.1 percent; shrimp, 10.8 percent)

What is the average price per entrée? ($15)

Vocabulary Terms

- **Sales volume:** The number of times a given item is sold during a particular time period.

- **Sales volume percentage:** The expression of each item's sales as a percentage of total sales.

- **Sales mix analysis:** An analysis of the popularity and profitability of a group of menu items.

- **Menu engineering:** The systematic breakdown of a menu's components to analyze which items are making money and which are selling well.

Management can start to gauge performance by looking at **sales volume**. The sales volume of a menu item is the number of times the item is sold in a time period. Generally, managers sort the sales of items by category, such as appetizers, entrées, and so forth. The quantity of each menu item sold can be recorded by hand or by many of the point-of-sale (POS) systems now used in restaurants. Managers can also use sales volume information to compare the number of each menu item sold to the total number of items sold on the entire menu in the same time period, which means each menu item's sales can be expressed as a percentage of total sales. This is called the **sales volume percentage**.

Managers need to monitor the effectiveness of menu items to maximize profits. A method called the sales mix analysis helps do that. A **sales mix analysis** is an analysis of the popularity and the profitability of a group of menu items. To effectively do this, the analysis should be done at least four times per year. The analysis includes determining which menu items are most popular and which contribute the most money to expenses and profit. It involves comparing menu items in terms of sales and profitability. The results of the menu sales mix analysis help determine whether managers need to make changes in menu pricing, content, or design.

While there are several methods available to do menu analysis, one of the most popular is **menu engineering**. It systematically breaks down a menu's components to analyze which items are making money and which items are selling. This analysis then helps management to make decisions about which menu items to leave alone, which to increase or decrease in selling price, which ones to promote, and which ones to eliminate.

Menu engineering involves a large number of computations. While managers have to know a few of the calculations, it is usually not necessary to perform all of the math in the analysis. Understanding these few formulas, though, provides a better understanding of how menu engineering works. Table 7.28 on the following page reflects the steps of this process:

1. First, list all of the menu entrées in column A. List only entrée items. Do not list appetizers, desserts, and other side items.

2. List the total number of purchases for each item in column B. List all purchases on a per-person basis or covers (purchases) sold. Obtain this number from the point-of-sale (POS) data or from a tally sheet showing the number of items purchased by each guest on the guest's check. Then, total the purchases for each item at the bottom of column B.

Menu Engineering Worksheet

The Galleon

Meal Period—Month of May

June 1, 2011

A Menu Item	B Number Sold	C Menu Mix % (B÷ΣB)	D Selling Price	E Item Food Cost	F Item Contribution Margin (D−E)	G Total Revenue (B×D)	H Total Food Cost (B×E)	I Total Item Contribution Margin (G−H)	J Contribution Margin Category (high or low)	K MM% Category (high or low)	L Menu Item Classification (dog, plow horse, puzzle, or star)
Skewered Shrimp	37	19.6	$12.95	$4.51	$8.44	$479.15	$166.87	$312.28	Low	High	Plow horse
Pork Medallions	25	13.3	15.50	5.71	9.79	387.50	142.75	244.75	High	High	Star
Rib Eye Steak	42	22.2	14.95	5.38	9.57	627.90	225.96	401.94	High	High	Star
Herbed Chicken	29	15.3	12.95	3.37	9.58	375.55	97.73	277.82	High	High	Star
Planked Salmon	14	7.4	15.95	5.90	10.05	223.30	82.60	140.70	High	Low	Puzzle
Beef Stroganoff	21	11.1	11.50	4.18	7.32	241.50	87.78	153.72	Low	High	Plow horse
Veal Piccata	10	5.3	13.50	7.15	6.35	135.00	71.50	63.50	Low	Low	Dog
Filet Oscar	11	5.8	15.95	7.82	8.13	175.45	86.02	89.43	Low	Low	Dog
Totals	189					$2,645.35	$961.21	$1,684.14			

Figure 7.28: A menu engineering sheet.

Discuss

- Why is it important to understand how menu engineering works? Can similar results be obtained simply by observing how many portions of each item are sold during a given period of time? Why or why not?

Reinforce and Review

- To conduct a menu analysis by menu engineering, first list all of the menu items in a given category and the number of purchases of each.

- The menu mix percentage is the percentage of total sales accounted for by each item.

Figure Focus

Figure 7.28: Using a computerized spreadsheet will simplify the process of menu engineering.

Discuss

- Why is it essential to know the true cost of a given item before calculating its menu price?
- Why is 70 percent the cutoff point for determining an item's popularity? Is this reasonable? Why or why not?

Reinforce and Review

- In menu engineering, a menu item is considered popular if it sells at least 70 percent of the menu mix average.
- Each menu item is classified as "high" or "low" based on whether it sells at least 70 percent of the menu mix average.
- The contribution margin is calculated by subtracting the item's standard food cost from its selling price.
- A target margin is a planned price based on how much money the business wants to make on each item sold.
- Total menu revenue is determined by multiplying the number of each item sold by its selling price and then summing the results for each item.

Homework Activity: Menu Engineering

Science Connection, Literacy Connection, 21st-Century Skills—Critical Thinking and Problem Solving, Communicate Clearly, Work Independently

The concept of menu engineering isn't strictly limited to the restaurant and foodservice industry: Any industry that offers a range of goods or services to its clients can use menu engineering to increase profitability.

First, research the concept of menu engineering to learn more about its applications in the non-foodservice world. Then identify an industry or a company that you think would benefit from the use of menu engineering and explain why. Write a one-page report discussing your findings.

Vocabulary Terms

- **Menu mix percentage:** The number of the menu items sold divided by the total number of purchases.
- **Mix percent rate:** The menu mix percentage multiplied by 70 percent.

3. Divide each item's sales by the total number of purchases (covers) to determine each item's **menu mix percentage**.

   Item number sold ÷ total number of purchases = menu mix percentage

   For example: Skewered Shrimp sold 37 covers out of a total of 189 covers, resulting in a menu mix percentage of 19.6.

   37 covers ÷ 189 total number sold = 19.6 percent

4. Now, jump to column K. In column K, categorize each item's menu mix percentage as either high or low. In menu engineering, consider a menu item popular if it sells at least 70 percent of the menu mix average. Therefore, consider low any menu item that is lower than 70 percent of the menu mix average percentage. Call a menu item high that is 70 percent or above. To determine menu mix percentage, take 100 percent (1.00) and divide by the number of items listed in the test (in this case, 8 items are being tested).

   100 percent or 1.00 ÷ 8 = 12.5 percent

   Therefore, on this 8-item menu, each item is 12.5 percent of the mix. Multiply the mix percentage by 70 percent to get the **mix percent rate**.

   12.5 percent × 70 percent = 8.75 percent

   Any item selling 8.75 percent or higher is considered high. Any item selling less than 8.75 percent is low. It is not necessary to complete the calculation for each menu item, but it is important to know that each menu item is classified in column K based on achieving 70 percent of the average menu mix.

   Look at each item on the chart and compare its menu mix to the 8.75 percent figure and then look at column K to see how it was classified.

5. List each item's selling price in column D. The selling price is obtained from the menu.

6. List each item's standard food cost in column E. Find an item's standard food cost on the cost card; it comes from the standard recipe cost, garnish cost, and the cost of accompanying items. Note that not all items have all three cost components.

7. List the contribution margin for each item in column F. Determine the contribution margin by subtracting the item's standard food cost (column E) from its selling price (column D).

   Selling price – Item food cost = Contribution margin

   This formula may look familiar. It is the same formula that is used to figure gross profit and target margin. Contribution margin and gross profit are the same thing, just different terminology. A target margin is a planned price based on how much money the business wants to make off of each item.

8. In column G, record the total revenue. Determine total menu revenue by multiplying the number sold of each item (column B) by its selling price (column D).

Number sold × Selling price = Total revenue

Total this column at the bottom of the column.

9. In column H, list the total item food cost. To obtain this figure, multiply each item's food cost (column E) by the number sold (column B) to obtain total food cost (column H).

Item food cost × Number sold = Total food cost

Total this column at the bottom of the column.

10. List the total item contribution margin in column I. Determine this value by multiplying each item's contribution margin (column F) times the number sold of each item (column B).

Item contribution margin × Number sold = Total item contribution margin

12. Categorize each item's contribution margin as either high or low in column J, depending on whether or not the item exceeds the menu's average contribution margin. Determine the menu's average contribution margin by dividing the total contribution margin ($1,684.14) in column I by the total number of items sold (189) in column B.

Total contribution margin of all menu items ÷ Total number sold = Average contribution margin

The average contribution margin for The Galleon is $8.91.

$1,684.14 ÷ 189 = $8.91

Categorize any item whose contribution margin (column F) is greater than $8.91 as high, and any item whose contribution margin (column F) is lower than $8.91 as low. Look at columns F and J to see how each item was classified.

13. Use all the data gathered to classify each item into categories in column L. Classify each menu item as a star, plow horse, puzzle, or dog.

Using the Classifications

After grouping all the menu items into one of the four key categories, it is time to make decisions. When making decisions, refer to how close on the graph an item is to the next category. For example, an item that falls into the Puzzle

Reinforce and Review

- Obtain the total item food cost by multiplying each item's food cost by the number of that item sold.
- Determine the total item contribution margin by multiplying each item's contribution margin by the number of that item sold.
- Any item that has a contribution margin greater than the average contribution margin is considered "high"; the remaining items are considered "low."
- Classify each menu item as a star, plow horse, puzzle, or dog.

Vocabulary Terms

- **Average contribution margin:** The average amount that each menu item contributes to gross profit.

Discuss

- How does an item's location on the menu affect its popularity?

Reinforce and Review

- Stars should be located in a highly visible area of the menu to increase orders.

- Stars should be tested occasionally for price rigidity, because they are likely to be less price sensitive than other menu items.

- Plow horses may be highly price-sensitive, so increasing the price might lead to a significant drop in orders; if only slightly profitable, these items should be removed from the menu, despite their popularity.

- If a particular menu item is an image maker or signature dish, hold its current price as long as possible to avoid alienating customers.

Vocabulary Terms

- **Star:** A menu item that is both popular and profitable.

- **Plow horse:** A menu item that is popular, but less profitable than a star.

- **Puzzle:** A menu item that is unpopular but very profitable.

category but has a popularity number very close to the Star category should be handled differently than one that has popularity numbers far below the Star category. The following are the four categories:

- **Stars:** These items are both popular and profitable. For the most part, stars should be left alone. Locate them in a highly visible position on the menu. Test them occasionally for price rigidity; that is, are guests willing to pay more for these items and still buy them in significant quantity? If so, these items may be able to carry a larger portion of any increase in cost of food and labor. They are the celebrities of the menu, the highest-priced stars, and may be less price sensitive than any other items on the menu.

- **Plow horses:** These items are popular but less profitable. These items are often an important reason for a restaurant's popularity. Because they are less profitable, one solution may be to increase their price. However, this should be done very carefully. If a plow horse is highly price sensitive; that is, if customers see it as a good price-value and that is the reason they come to your restaurant, then attempt to pass on only food cost increases of the item to the menu price. If it is only marginally profitable (close to the dog on the graph), drop it from the menu and make a substitution for it.

  When increasing the price, always test for a negative effect on sales. Make any price increase in stages (from $4.55 to $4.75, then $4.95). If the item is an image maker or signature item, hold its current price as long as possible. On the other hand, if the listing is a nonsignature item with a low contribution margin, move the plow horse to a lower-profile position on the menu. Attempt to shift demand to more profitable items through merchandising and menu positioning. Another solution might be to reduce the item's standard portion without making the difference noticeable. Also, try adding value to the item through menu packaging. In other words, merchandise the plow horse by packaging it with side items to increase its contribution margin.

- **Puzzles:** These items are unpopular but very profitable. One of the best solutions to helping out a puzzle is to decrease its price. While this may appear counterproductive to making a profit, consider that the customer may not perceive it as a fair value. If an item isn't selling, no profit is being made anyway. Another option is to leave its price alone and reposition it on the menu, perhaps featuring it in a more popular location. Additionally, merchandise it by using table tents, chalkboards, or suggestive selling. Rename it. A puzzle's popularity can be affected by what it is called, especially if it is unfamiliar to customers. Remember that even if a puzzle is not selling well, it is making a lot of money, relatively speaking. If sales can be substantially increased without decreasing the price, the item could easily become a star.

Limit the number of puzzles on a menu. Puzzles can create difficulties in quality consistency, slow production down, and cause inventory and cost problems. Accurately evaluate the effect puzzle items have on the operation's image. Do they enhance the image? A final option is to take them off the menu, particularly if a puzzle is low in popularity, requires costly or additional inventory, has poor shelf life, requires skilled or labor-intensive preparation, or is of inconsistent quality.

■ **Dogs:** These items are unpopular and unprofitable. Eliminate all dog items if possible. Replace them with more popular items. Take advantage of hot, trendy, or cutting-edge listings. Restaurant and foodservice operations are sometimes intimidated by influential guests to continue carrying a dog item on the menu. The way to solve this problem is to carry the item in inventory (assuming it has a shelf life) but not on the menu. Offer the special guest the opportunity to have the item made to order on request. Charge extra for this service. Raise the dog's price to puzzle status.

Some items in the dog category may have market potential. These tend to be the more popular dogs, and may be converted to puzzles by increasing prices. Another detail to consider is that the menu may have too many items. It is not unusual to discover a number of highly unpopular menu listings that have little, if any, relation to other more popular and profitable items held in inventory. Do not be afraid to eliminate dogs, especially when demand is not satisfactory.

[what's new]

Menu Engineering

The whole purpose of menu engineering is to sell more of the menu items that will earn the restaurant more money. While food cost percentage is important, menu engineering is about the actual dollars earned for the restaurant with each food sale. Carefully describe and strategically place food items on the menu in ways calculated to increase total sales by highlighting the dishes that will earn the most, based on the food cost and contribution margin. A number of software packages and Web sites are available to help with this.

Determining how to write or change a menu—for instance, how to change a puzzle into a star by changing a menu description, a price, or a preparation—is also a crucial aspect of menu engineering. For instance, researchers have recently been doing a lot of work to help clarify the psychological factors behind customer preferences: such subtle elements as size or type of font can significantly change customer choices. Small restaurants that change their menus frequently can readily adapt to consumer demand, eliminating dogs and tweaking puzzles. Larger restaurants, especially those with a nationwide presence, have a harder time making such changes.

491

Discuss

- How many items are "too many"? How can a restaurant decide whether to abbreviate or lengthen its menu?

- Is it possible to have a menu that is all stars? Why or why not?

Reinforce and Review

- Two ways to reduce demand for a plow horse are moving the item to a lower profile position on the menu and slightly reducing its portion size.

- Plow horses can be packaged with side items to increase their contribution margins and therefore their profitability.

- One solution to a puzzle is decreasing its price. Another tactic is to place it in a more favorable position on the menu.

- Even though a puzzle is unpopular, it makes a lot of money; take steps to increase sales and turn the item into a star.

- Dogs should be eliminated where possible, although the key ingredients can be kept in inventory for special requests.

- Dogs can often be turned into puzzles with price increases.

Vocabulary Terms

- **Dog:** A menu item that is both unpopular and unprofitable.

- Which is more important, the food cost percentage or the dollars earned per order? Why?

- How can training service staff help to change a dish's status? Why?

- Menu engineering is a fairly recent phenomenon, and restaurants have existed for hundreds of years. Does this mean that menu engineering is not important to the success or failure of an operation, or that the conditions under which contemporary restaurants operate are different? Why?

Fast Fact:
Did You Know . . . ?

Encourage students to discuss the following:

- What are some advantages and disadvantages to serving carbonated soft drinks in a restaurant or foodservice operation?

- How can maximizing the use of star menu items help subsidize items that don't sell as well?

- What are some other popular nonalcoholic beverages? Into which of the four menu engineering categories would you place them?

It's important for restaurant and foodservice operations of all shapes and sizes to pay attention to advances in menu engineering, though. Why? Because ultimately menu engineering, and management's ability to master it, will determine the operation's long-term success. If management can't adapt a menu to address changing customer needs, especially in the fast-paced twenty-first century, they will be unable to make a profit and stay in business. Fortunately, many resources exist to help managers and owners stay abreast of current research, such as industry publications and online sources. The National Restaurant Association is an excellent resource for further information.

Did You Know...?

One of the most frequently ordered items in the United States is carbonated soft drinks. Their low production cost and high profitability make such items a star on any menu.

Summary

In this section, you learned the following:

- The menu serves two purposes: planning and communication. For the planning function, the menu gives an operation an end goal to work toward. Using the menu as a planning tool helps managers stay focused on all the behind-the-scenes work and how to best accomplish an operation's goals. In the role of marketing communication tool, the menu functions in three ways: informing the market about what the operation offers, selling products, and creating identity.

- There are many types of menus. An à la carte menu prices each menu item separately. A du jour menu simply lists the menu items that are available on a particular day. A cyclical menu changes menu items after a certain period of time. A limited menu typically offers only a few items. Quick-service operations frequently offer a limited menu. Fixed menus offer the same items every day. A California menu is one that lists all meals available at any time of day. A prix fixe menu is the opposite of an à la carte menu in that it includes multiple menu items at one price. A table d'hôte menu is similar to a prix fixe menu in that it bundles various elements of menus into one package.

492

- Most menus organize foods according to the order in which they are eaten: appetizers, soups, salads, sandwiches (which can be offered before or after salads), entrées, vegetables, desserts, and beverages.

- A menu should reflect the operation's character and goals and a realistic understanding of what the operation is capable of producing in a cost effective way. There are two steps in menu creation: planning and design. In the planning phase, keep the following elements in mind: physical layout of the facility, skill of personnel, availability of ingredients, target market's wants and needs, target market's expectations, and profit margin. Consider the following elements when designing a menu: medium, layout, color, font, and art.

- Pricing the menu is a critical process for any operation. Price serves two main roles: it provides information to customers, and it determines profitability. Price provides information to customers not only about the price of the menu item, but it also speaks to the market category in which the restaurant falls. Price determines profitability by bringing in more dollars than the sum of all the costs for the product or service. The food cost percentage method, contribution margin method, straight markup method, average check method, set dollar amount markup, and set percentage increase method are all ways to price menu items.

- It is crucial to the success of an operation that management have the knowledge and means to analyze how well items on its menu are performing. While there are several methods available to do menu analysis, one of the most popular is menu engineering. It systematically breaks down a menu's components to analyze which items are making money and which items are selling. This analysis then helps management make decisions as to which menu items to leave alone, which to increase or decrease in selling price, which ones to promote, and which ones to eliminate. The classifications that come from menu engineering are star, plow horse, puzzle, and dog.

Summary
- Remind students to review the following:
  1. The overview of a menu
  2. Menu types
  3. Organizing a menu
  4. Creating a menu
  5. Pricing the menu
  6. Analyzing the menu

Section 7.3
Review Questions

1. The two primary functions of the menu are to plan and to communicate.

2. Types of menus include á la carte, du jour, cyclical, limited, fixed, California, prix fixe, and table d'hôte.

3. The two steps in creating a menu are planning and design.

4. The four main menu categories derived from menu engineering are star, plow horse, puzzle, and dog.

5. Quick-service restaurants might offer a number of menus, including limited, fixed, á la carte, and prix fixe.

6. Student responses will vary but should accurately discuss menu analysis and engineering and the ways in which use of these techniques can increase profitability.

7. Student answers will vary but should defend their answers clearly and logically.

8. Student responses will vary but should demonstrate an understanding of the menu engineering process.

Section 7.3 Review Questions

1. What are the two primary functions of the menu?

2. List five different types of menus.

3. What are the two basic steps that need to be considered when creating a menu?

4. What are the four menu item categories derived from menu engineering?

5. What types of menus do you see at a quick-service restaurant such as McDonald's?

6. In their new place, Miguel and Chef Kate want to start with a limited menu, but, of course, they want it to be as profitable as possible. Explain the process of menu analysis and engineering and how this could help maximize their chances for a profitable limited menu.

7. Do you think a menu functions more as a planning tool or a communication tool? Explain your answer in a paragraph.

8. What would be your first option for turning a plow horse into a star?

494

Section 7.3 Activities

1. Study Skills/Group Activity: Targeting Teens

Working with two or three other students, create a menu that appeals to the teenage target market. Make sure to include at least eight menu items.

2. Independent Activity: Menu Comparison

Obtain and compare menus from two restaurant and foodservice operations. You might even be able to find sample menus online. What information about the restaurant does each provide? What kind of message is the menu communicating? Who appears to be the target market of each restaurant? How does each menu work as a selling tool?

3. Critical Thinking: Determining Menu Prices

Deciding the appropriate markup for menu prices can be difficult. What is the best way to determine selling prices? Defend your answer in two paragraphs.

Indulge!

$4.99

495

Section 7.3 Activities

1. Students should be able to explain and defend their menu selections and prices.

2. Students should respond to each question, building on the material addressed in Section 7.3.

3. Students should identify one of the six techniques of pricing menus discussed in Section 7.3 and explain why it is the best way to determine selling prices.

Case Study Follow-Up

1. Students should identify and describe techniques for improving community relations.

2. Students should select and justify the use of two media choices to advertise Kabob's new location.

3. Students should write at least one page addressing menu function and design.

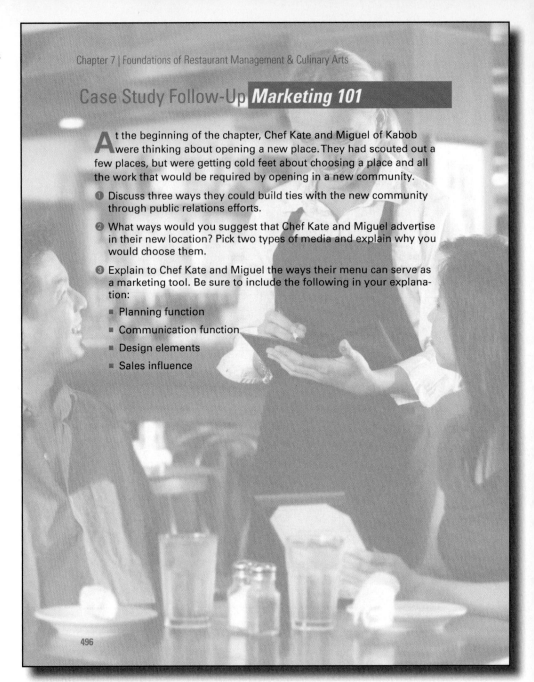

Case Study Follow-Up *Marketing 101*

At the beginning of the chapter, Chef Kate and Miguel of Kabob were thinking about opening a new place. They had scouted out a few places, but were getting cold feet about choosing a place and all the work that would be required by opening in a new community.

❶ Discuss three ways they could build ties with the new community through public relations efforts.

❷ What ways would you suggest that Chef Kate and Miguel advertise in their new location? Pick two types of media and explain why you would choose them.

❸ Explain to Chef Kate and Miguel the ways their menu can serve as a marketing tool. Be sure to include the following in your explanation:

- Planning function
- Communication function
- Design elements
- Sales influence

496

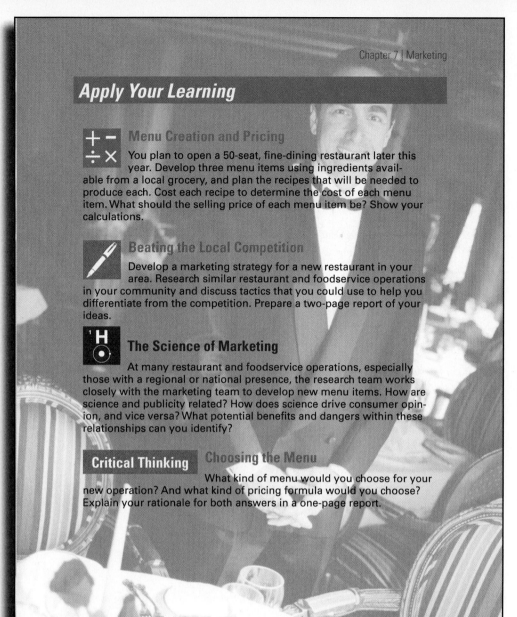

Apply Your Learning

Menu Creation and Pricing

You plan to open a 50-seat, fine-dining restaurant later this year. Develop three menu items using ingredients available from a local grocery, and plan the recipes that will be needed to produce each. Cost each recipe to determine the cost of each menu item. What should the selling price of each menu item be? Show your calculations.

Beating the Local Competition

Develop a marketing strategy for a new restaurant in your area. Research similar restaurant and foodservice operations in your community and discuss tactics that you could use to help you differentiate from the competition. Prepare a two-page report of your ideas.

The Science of Marketing

At many restaurant and foodservice operations, especially those with a regional or national presence, the research team works closely with the marketing team to develop new menu items. How are science and publicity related? How does science drive consumer opinion, and vice versa? What potential benefits and dangers within these relationships can you identify?

Critical Thinking Choosing the Menu

What kind of menu would you choose for your new operation? And what kind of pricing formula would you choose? Explain your rationale for both answers in a one-page report.

497

Apply Your Learning

Menu Creation and Pricing

Students should describe the selected menu items, develop and cost appropriate recipes, and determine an appropriate selling price based on one of the six menu pricing methods discussed in the chapter.

Beating the Local Competition

Students will need to explain some ways in which their proposed restaurants can establish competitive advantages. Researching other local restaurants, as well as relevant community factors, is an important part of determining the ways in which a new restaurant can stand out from the competition.

The Science of Marketing

Students should research links between science and publicity and the relationship between science and consumer opinion. They should justify their responses.

Critical Thinking Choosing the Menu

Students should select a menu type (or types) and a pricing formula that they consider appropriate, and explain their choices.

Exam Prep Answers

1. B
2. C
3. C
4. B
5. B
6. B
7. C
8. D
9. A
10. C

Exam Prep Questions

1 The comprehensive process of communicating an operation's message to potential customers is

A. selling.

B. marketing.

C. fashioning.

D. advertising.

2 What is a marketing plan?

A. The way marketers research a market

B. The way marketers execute their market strategy

C. The steps marketers must take to sell a product or service

D. The way marketers advertise an operation's product or service

3 What are the four research methods used to gather market information?

A. Survey, sampling, experimental, informal

B. Experimental, formal, informal, mathematical

C. Experimental, observational, survey, sampling

D. Formal, observational, mathematical, sampling

4 Creating within the marketplace a clear, specific identity for both a product and the operation that offers that product is called

A. elbowing.

B. positioning.

C. identification.

D. market carving.

5 Advertising, sales promotions, personal selling, public relations, and direct marketing are all elements of what's called the

A. product mix.

B. promotional mix.

C. experimental method.

D. lifestyle segmentation.

6 Informing customers, selling products, and creating identity are all functions performed simultaneously by

A. greeters.

B. the menu.

C. Web sites.

D. direct marketing.

7 A menu that prices all items separately is called

A. limited.

B. prix fixe.

C. à la carte.

D. California.

8 A menu that lists all meals available at any time of day is called

A. fixed.

B. du jour.

C. à la carte.

D. California.

9 The difference between revenue minus preparation and service costs is known as the

A. margin.

B. wage factor.

C. lost revenue.

D. money gap.

10 Add a fixed dollar amount to the food cost of an item to calculate the

A. average cover.

B. set dollar markup.

C. contribution margin.

D. set percentage increase.

Chapter 8 Overview

Chapter 8 introduces the principles and skills needed to successfully produce quality desserts and baked goods for guests.

Section 1: This section covers bakeshop basics, including baker's ingredients and measurements.

Section 2: This section covers yeast breads—the types of dough and yeast bread preparation.

Section 3: This section covers quick breads and cakes, including batters, icing, steamed puddings, and soufflés.

Section 4: This section covers pies, pastries, and cookies.

Section 5: This section reviews chocolate—preparation and products, storage, and tempering chocolate.

Section 6: This section covers specialty desserts, including frozen desserts, poached fruit and tortes, dessert sauces and creams, and plating and presenting desserts.

Advance Preparation

Review	Sections 8.1–8.6 Level 1, Chapter 11: Potatoes and Grains
Contact	Math teacher, if needed Chemistry teacher, if needed Chocolatier to visit, if possible, or a field trip
Prepare	Paper strips for display Flour and sugar for teaching Scale for weighing flour and sugar 1 lb flour 3 bowls Scales (sensitive, or gram scales from the science department) 1 cup dry measuring cups Paper towel Blade spatula for leveling flour Sifter Chocolate samples Muffin batter for examples

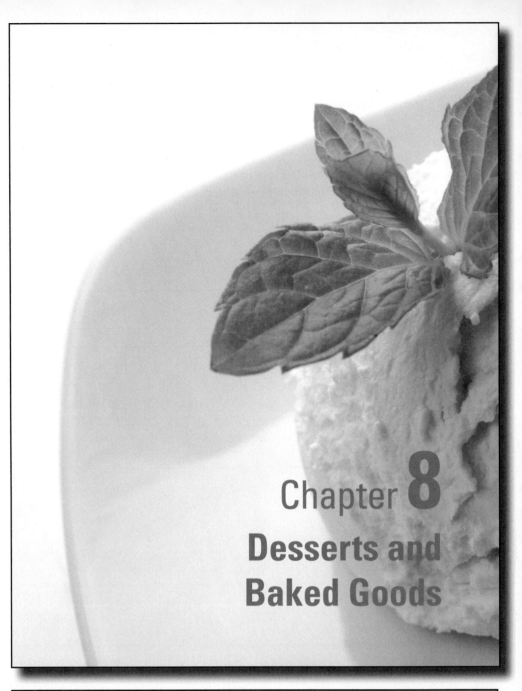

Chapter 8
Desserts and Baked Goods

CUSTOMIZED INSTRUCTION OPTIONS

Less Advanced Students	More Advanced Students	ESOL Students	Special Needs Students
Pages 513, 527, 552	Pages 509, 513, 552	Pages 513, 527, 552	Pages 513, 552

CHAPTER TOOLS

21st-Century Skills	Mathematics	Science	Literacy
Pages 502, 505, 506, 514, 525, 535, 552, 555	Pages 504, 506, 509	Pages 505, 513, 546	Pages 505, 506, 514, 516, 527, 552

ServSafe Connection

Pages 509, 517, 529, 538, 546

Case Study | *Dessert Dilemma*

In recent customer feedback surveys, Miguel and Chef Kate learned that many guests were disappointed by their final dinner course, dessert. On the whole, guests felt that their desserts were "unimaginative," "mediocre," "outdated," and "too limited in choice." The truth is, when Chef Kate and Miguel opened Kabob, they never paid much attention to desserts, as they didn't feel they were as important to customers as other aspects of their operation. They are starting to reconsider their position now.

The problem Chef Kate and Miguel are confronting is that they aren't well versed in dessert items. They don't have a pastry chef on staff, and they can't afford to hire one. Miguel handles front-of-the-house and Chef Kate has her hands full with managing the kitchen staff and making sure their existing menu is up to quality standards. In short, they're not exactly sure what to do to improve the quality of their dessert menu or how to go about doing it.

As you read this chapter, think about the following questions:

1. What dessert items would be the most appealing to a wide variety of people, while also being relatively light on labor?

2. What does it mean to have an "unimaginative" dessert menu, and how would you go about making it "imaginative" instead?

3. Is dessert as important as other aspects of foodservice? As you go through the chapter, think of some arguments for and against this question.

4. Use the knowledge you gained about make-or-buy analysis in *Chapter 5*, and apply it to solving Miguel and Chef Kate's dessert dilemma.

Case Study
Dessert Dilemma

- By not giving full attention to dessert-menu offerings, Kabob could be losing money. Guests who might otherwise purchase dessert after a meal might be skipping it.

- The students might not know the various ways available to restaurateurs to find new dessert ideas.

- Without a pastry chef, they will also need to consider the different sources of dessert items.

- The questions listed can help direct preliminary discussion in the classroom.

- Use the Chapter 5 make-or-buy analysis as a way to demonstrate the usefulness of the skills the students are learning and building on.

- Note that there are follow-up questions about the case study at the end of the chapter.

- This activity could be done in groups, as a class, or as a homework assignment.

Professional Profile

Discuss	Chef Gale Gand has very positive messages for the students. Help them to identify the various positive messages and approaches.
Reinforce and Review	What helps students decide to become pastry chefs?
Teaching Tips	Focus on the role of pastries and desserts in a variety of restaurant and foodservice operations.

In-Class Activity: Case Study Affirmations

21st-Century Skills—Guide and Lead Others, Create Media Products

Choose one or two of Chef Gale Gand's positive statements as a motto.

If computers are available, have each student create an image of his or her motto. Compile all of the students' results into a classroom PowerPoint presentation.

If computers are not available, make a poster or word strip to display in the classroom.

Have the students present their choices to the class, explaining how they relate to a culinary career.

[professional profile]

Gale Gand

Executive Pastry Chef and Partner: Tru in Chicago

Cookbook Author: Artisanal Root Beer Maker

Television personality and host of the Food Network show, Sweet Dreams

❝ *Really, I feel as if my career chose me. But what I love about it is how it has everything. No two days are the same. It's entertainment, a form of nurturing, a creative art and craft. It's chemistry and physics, psychology, mentoring, motivating. It's like dance and theatre together, plus you get to help people take time to mark and celebrate important moments in their lives.* ❞

I have a Bachelor of Fine Arts from the Rochester Institute of Technologies School for American Craftsmen. Always interested in creative pursuits, I majored in metalsmithing (silver and goldsmithing, jewelry making) and minored in painting. I also went to La Varenne in Paris for cooking school and the French Pastry School in Chicago.

When I think about my career, I think about how long it's gone on, how it continues to grow, and how diverse the field has become. Being a pastry chef has allowed me to cook for queens, sultans, sheiks, princes and princesses, rock stars, movie stars, comedians, presidents, mayors, cancer survivors, newlyweds, and new parents. I've been on television with Julia Child, Al Roker, Harry Smith, and Oprah; in culinary school with Jacques Pepin (he was a student!); at culinary festivals, grocery stores, bookstores, and on the radio (cooking on the radio-what next?). I've worked in France, England, Spain, Greece, Croatia, and Italy, with kids in schools, with families, and with my own children. What great choices and variety!

If you do a job because you love it, you will be successful. The more you do something, the better you'll get at it, and the more fun it will be to do it. And if you're interested in this industry, remember to always wear comfortable shoes. When your chef asks if you know how to make something; say "yes" now and then go home that night and figure out how to do it, even if it means staying up all night and making croissants seven times over till you get it absolutely perfect! (Ask me how I know that.) Finally, eat a lot at a lot of restaurants—nothing will open your eyes more than that!

Remember:

❝ *If you think you can or you think you can't either way, you're probably right.* ❞
— Rich Melman

He also said:

❝ *When it comes to improving your restaurant, it's not one big thing. It's 100 little things.* ❞

502

Discuss	What does Chef Gand teach about pastry and desserts in this section of her profile?
Reinforce and Review	Ask them to discuss this idea: ". . . trying to make each one more perfect than the last, while conserving as much motion as possible so that you can work as efficiently as possible."
Teaching Tips	Review how this would relate to other back-of-the-house positions.

About Desserts and Baking

I absolutely love the ingredients, how reliable they are, how predictable pastry is, and all the precision it requires. I like the fact that my pastry kitchen makes the first impression of the meal (bread, *gougere* as hors d'oeuvres, etc.) and the last (cheese, dessert, petit fours).

My favorite dishes involve taking recipes that have roots in tradition—pie, layer cake, banana split—and then doing a new take on it. It's sort of an improvisation on an idea, like a culinary sketch. I like to rely on really ripe, flavorful fruit. That way you don't have to do much to it; the ingredients do all the work for you.

While I don't have one favorite dessert, my husband says the day I'm rolling out and crimping the 100 or so pie crusts for pumpkin pies just before Thanksgiving is the day I come home the happiest. I love working with the ingredients of the pastry kitchen, combining them, and shaping them…whether it's making a meringue, piping some buttercream, or rolling out pie dough. And there's something about the repetition of dipping truffle after truffle in melted chocolate, and then placing it just so in dark, rich cocoa powder…trying to make each one more perfect than the last, while conserving as much motion as possible so that you can work as efficiently as possible.

8.1 Bakeshop Basics • Baker's ingredients • Baker's measurements → 8.2 Yeast Breads • Types of dough • Yeast bread preparation → 8.3 Quick Breads and Cakes • Quick bread and cake batters • Icing • Steamed puddings and soufflés → 8.4 Pies, Pastries, and Cookies • Pies • Pastries • Cookies → 8.5 Chocolate • Chocolate preparation and products • Chocolate storage • Tempering chocolate → 8.6 Specialty Desserts • Frozen desserts • Poached fruit and tortes • Dessert sauces and creams • Plating and presenting desserts

SECTION 8.1 BAKESHOP BASICS

Most everyone loves a good dessert. A perfectly moist, rich slice of chocolate cake or a warm piece of pie with a light, flaky crust are the perfect ending to a meal. But no small amount of time, effort, and precision go into creating such delicious desserts. And it all starts with knowing the basics. How is milk used in baked goods? Is an egg a strengthener, a liquid, a leavening agent, or all three? How many types of flour are there? While many people may know the general ingredients that go into baked goods, not many know exactly how they're used or in what proportions. This section will start you off with the baking basics: ingredients and measurements.

503

Focus and Engage

Discuss

- What does dessert mean to people?
- What are the range of ingredients that go into the broad category of desserts?
- Can you think of desserts in other ways than "rich and sinful"?

Section 8.1 Bakeshop Basics

Introduce the Section

a. Chef Gand remarks that the pastry kitchen makes the first and last impression of the meal, from bread to dessert.
b. There are essential and classic ingredients and techniques in baking.
c. Baking involves food science in every step.

Vocabulary Review

a. Direct students to the key terms.
b. Pronounce each word, and have the students repeat the pronunciation out loud.
c. Discuss the definition of each word.

Teach

Discuss

- Desserts set operations above the ordinary.
- The chance for a special dessert after a meal is one of the reasons people celebrate at restaurants.
- Life events and holidays are marked with baked goods, often based in tradition.

Mathematics Connection

The term "proportions" is used throughout this chapter. Ensure that the students understand this concept.

Help the students to understand that proportions remain constant, regardless of how large or how small the recipe, sample, yield, and so on. A proportion is a portion of the whole. A whole is represented as 100 percent.

A visual of a pie graph might help here. The proportions in the example pie graph shown are 25 percent, 33 percent, 39 percent, 3 percent. No matter the size of the chart, the proportions remain the same:

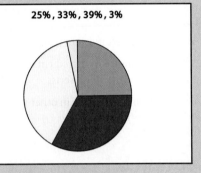

25%, 33%, 39%, 3%

It can be shown in various sizes to illustrate this point. Or a concentric circle could be applied within the pie chart and the proportions would still be constant.

No matter how large or how small the chart is, the proportions of 25 percent, 33 percent, 39 percent, 3 percent remain constant.

Ask the students to provide real-life examples from their experience that might help illustrate this point.

One example might be frozen juice concentrate. No matter how much juice you want, you use the proportional recipe of 3 parts water to 1 part juice concentrate.

Study Questions

After studying Section 8.1, you should be able to answer the following questions:

- What are the main ingredients used in baking?
- What are the primary percentages needed for proper baking?
- What are the basic types of dough used in baking?

Baker's Ingredients

Nearly all bakery products are prepared using a common list of ingredients that fall into eight categories:

- **Strengtheners**, such as flour and eggs
- **Fats/shortenings**, such as butter and oils
- **Sweeteners**, such as sugars and syrups
- **Flavorings**, such as vanilla and nuts
- **Chemical, organic, and physical leaveners**, such as baking powder, baking soda, yeast, and steam
- **Thickeners**, such as cornstarch, flour, and eggs
- **Liquids**, such as water, milk, cream, eggs, honey, molasses, and butter
- **Additives**, such as food coloring

In baking, **strengtheners** provide stability and ensure that the baked item doesn't collapse once it is removed from the oven. Flour is a main ingredient used in baking. There are six popular types of wheat flour, as described in Table 8.1 on the following page.

Shortenings/fats make baked goods moist, add flavor, and keep baked items fresh longer. Any fat, such as oil or butter, acts as a shortening in baking. The more thoroughly mixed the fat, the more it will affect the item's overall texture. Fats that are rubbed or rolled into doughs tend to separate the dough into large layers, creating a flaky texture. When the fat is thoroughly creamed together with the other ingredients, the resulting texture of the baked item will be smooth, soft, and more cake-like.

504

Vocabulary Terms

- **Strengtheners:** Agents that provide long molecules to give structure to baked goods.
- **Fats/shortenings:** Lipid agents that make baked goods tender by "shortening" long structure molecules.
- **Sweeteners:** Sugar or sugar substitutes added for sweet flavors. Sugars also lend color.
- **Flavorings:** Extracts, alcohols, oils, or other additives for taste and aroma.
- **Chemical, organic, and physical leaveners:** Agents that add air bubbles to lighten the structure.
- **Thickeners:** Agents that can add long molecules to increase the structure to add body to liquids.
- **Liquids:** Water and other water-soluble liquids to dissolve, moisten, and mix.
- **Additives:** Colorings, conditioners, stabilizers, and preservatives.

Table 8.1: Types of Wheat Flour

	Type of Flour	Description
	All-purpose flour	This flour falls between pastry and bread flour. It is good to use in cookies, biscuits, and general production work.
	Bread flour	As its name suggests, this a strong flour that is used for making breads, hard rolls, and any product that needs high gluten for a strong texture. **Gluten** (gloo-ten) is a protein found in flour. The more bakers mix, work, and knead yeast doughs, the more the gluten becomes elastic and stretchy. When baked, it helps provide the firm structure and light, even texture needed in bread production.
	Cake flour	This flour has a low-gluten content, a very soft, smooth texture, and a pure white color. Use cake flour for cakes and other delicate baked goods.
	Durum flour	This is a hard, wheat flour used to make breads; its gluten content is a little higher than that of typical bread flour.
	Pastry flour	This flour is not as strong as bread flour and not as delicate as cake flour. Use pastry flour for baking cookies, pie pastry, and some sweet yeast doughs, biscuits, and muffins. It feels like cake flour, but has the creamy color of bread flour.
	Semolina flour	This is a type of durum flour, but it is more coarsely ground than the flour used to make most breads. It has a fine texture with a high gluten content and is primarily used to make pastas and certain Italian pastries.

Sweeteners include refined sugars, sugar syrups, molasses, brown sugar, corn syrup, honey, and malt syrup (usually used in yeast breads). Sweeteners add flavor and color to baked goods. They also help the shortening blend with other ingredients and make the product soft and tender. When a product containing refined sugars is baked, the heat causes the sugar to turn a light brown color. This process is called **caramelization** and occurs whenever sugar is used as an ingredient in baked items.

505

Table 8.1: Types of Wheat Flour

- This table elaborates on the types of wheat and the qualities of their flours. It might be helpful to review information on grains from Level 1.

- Part of experiencing bread differences can be gently tearing the bread from the crust.
- The bread must be very fresh for the differences to show.

Discuss

- Discuss the explanation of gluten that is found in Table 8.1.
- Help students understand that flour has gluten already in it.
- Kneading bread helps the gluten form into a structure.
- Kneading does not add or create more gluten.

Vocabulary Terms

- **Sweeteners:** Sugars and artificial sweeteners that add flavor and color and help with blending and structure.
- **Carmelization:** The browning that results from heating sugar.

Teaching Tips

- Table 8.1 presents several types of flours.
- If possible, have a sample of each type of flour in the classroom.
- The students can see and feel the characteristics of the flour.
- Again, if possible, have a taste test available, including a food product for tasting made from each type of flour.
- Especially interesting is the different texture of white bread made from bread, all-purpose, and durum flours.
- Part of the tasting experience should include noting the textures of the crusts made from the various flours.

Table 8.2: Types of Leaveners

- A brief review of chemistry principles will help students conceptually understand leavening agents and their actions.

Homework Activity: Leaveners Venn Diagram Graphic Organizer

Mathematics Connection, Literacy Connection, 21st-Century Skills—Use Systems Thinking

Using the information in Table 8.2, have the students create a Venn diagram graphic organizer about leavening agents.

There should be four overlapping circles.

The common traits will be in the overlapping areas and the differences will be in the unique areas.

Here is an example of such a diagram. The students might find even more information to include:

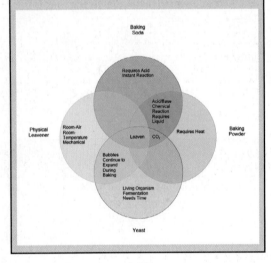

Leaveners are necessary in baking because they allow the dough or batter to rise. It is important to measure all leavening agents very carefully. Even small changes can produce major defects in baked products. Leaveners fall into three categories: chemical, organic, and physical. Table 8.2 describes each leavener.

Table 8.2: Types of Leaveners		
	Leavener	**Description**
	Baking powder	This is a very versatile leavener. It is a mixture of baking soda and an acid with an inactive material, like starch. Because there is acid in the baking powder, the pastry chef does not need to add any acid to the batter for leavening to take place. Leavening occurs when liquid and heat are added.
	Baking soda	Both baking soda and baking powder are chemical leaveners. Baking soda (sodium bicarbonate) releases carbon dioxide gas when mixed with a liquid and an acid. For example, baking soda will leaven a batter when mixed with an acid such as lemon juice, yogurt, or buttermilk. Other less reliable reactants are honey, molasses, cocoa, and chocolate. Because heat is not necessary for the leavening process to occur, bake the item right away to prevent the gases from escaping and leavening the item too soon.
	Physical leaveners	Introducing air into the batter is another way to leaven a baked item. The air expands during baking and leavens the product. Pastry chefs use two methods to introduce air into batter: creaming and foaming. In the **creaming method**, beat the fat and sugar together. Use the creaming method most often in cake and cookie making. In the **foaming method**, beat eggs, with or without sugar. Use whole egg foams in sponge cakes, and egg white foams in angel food cakes, meringues, and soufflés.
	Yeast	An organic leavener, yeast is a microscopic fungus used often in baking. When yeast is mixed with carbohydrates (such as sugar and flour) it **ferments**, or produces carbon dioxide gas and alcohol. Yeast works in much the same way that the chemical leaveners do, by releasing carbon dioxide gas, causing the bread dough to rise.

Thickeners include gelatin, flour, arrowroot (a powdered starch made from a tropical root), cornstarch, and eggs. Thickeners, combined with the stirring process, determine the consistency of the finished product. For example, custard cooked over direct heat and stirred constantly will result in a sauce; the same custard recipe cooked (without stirring) in a bain-marie, which is a water bath used to cook foods gently by surrounding the pan with simmering water. Then, it will set into a firm custard that can be sliced.

Vocabulary Terms

- **Leaveners:** Biological or chemical agents that create bubbles of carbon dioxide gas. When resisted by a dough or batter structure, these bubbles cause the dough or batter to rise.

- **Thickeners:** Chemical agents that form long chains or a matrix to give structure and thickness to a food product.

Flavorings, such as cocoa, spices, salt, and extracts, affect a baked item's taste and color. Cocoa is the basis of all chocolate desserts, and therefore absolutely vital to any dessert menu. Spices used most often in baking are cinnamon, nutmeg, mace, cloves, ginger, caraway, cardamom, allspice, anise, and poppy seed. Salt plays an important role in baking. It improves the texture of breads and controls how yeast ferments in bread doughs. **Extracts** are flavorful oils taken from such foods as vanilla, lemon, and almond. A few drops of extract will greatly enhance the flavor of baked goods. Flavorings need to be measured accurately so that the flavor of the spice or extract will not overwhelm the flavor of the finished baked product.

Liquids are one of the most important elements used in baking. The liquid used in baking can be water, milk, cream, molasses, honey, or butter. Liquid is used in baking to provide moisture to the product and to allow the gluten to properly develop. Water is the most basic and common form of liquid used in baking. Often, milk products such as whole milk, buttermilk, cream, or dried milk are used. Milk provides the baked product with flavor, nutritional value, and texture. Honey, molasses, eggs, and butter also act as liquids in baking by contributing moisture to the baked item, as well as a unique taste and texture.

[fast fact]

Did You Know . . . ?
Yeast has been used in baking for a long time. The ancient Egyptians used it to bake bread 4,000 years ago. As a matter of fact, some people think that humans probably used yeast before the development of a written language.

[nutrition]

Gluten Sensitivity
Gluten is a protein found in wheat and other grains. When kneaded or worked, gluten protein develops into long strands that stretch and hold a structure. This is why kneaded bread can rise without the bubbles of carbon dioxide bursting through the dough. If yeast dough is not kneaded, the carbon dioxide production from yeast is a bit too vigorous for the dough to resist it. It will be flat. Gluten is responsible for the pleasantly chewy elastic quality of yeast breads.

Some individuals have an intestinal sensitivity to gluten. A disorder called "Gluten-sensitive enteropathy" (GSE), also called "Celiac Disease" or "Celiac Sprue," is caused by gluten, which approximately 1 to 2 percent of the population suffers from. The interior lining of the small intestine becomes inflamed in the presence of gluten. Pain and diarrhea result. These individuals can avoid gluten in the diet and improve their symptoms.

In normal individuals, there is no health benefit to avoiding gluten in the diet. Gluten sensitivity is not the same as a wheat allergy. Although there is some discussion and controversy on the subject, research still supports that gluten is perfectly safe for unaffected individuals.

507

Discuss

- Students might have experience with vanilla extract.
- They might realize that vanilla is added to foods that are not only "vanilla" flavored.
- Can students think of examples of foods that have vanilla extract?
- Vanilla and other extracts are often carried in an alcohol medium. Why?
- Alcohol helps extract the essential aromatic compounds from vanilla beans. The flavor is alcohol-soluble.
- The FDA requires a specific alcohol content for vanilla extract.

Teaching Tips

- Be careful telling high school students about the alcohol content of large quantities of vanilla extract that might be stored in the school pantry.
- Any alcohol-containing products in intoxicating quantities should be in locked storage.

Fast Fact:
Did You Know . . . ?

Perhaps the class would enjoy discussing all the various techniques, processes, discoveries, and experiments that had to occur to create a modern loaf of yeast bread.

Nutrition:
Gluten Sensitivity

Protein structures are an interesting area of food chemistry. Science-oriented or advanced students might like to research this aspect of food science a bit further.

Vocabulary Terms

- **Flavorings:** Give taste and sometimes color to baked goods and other foods.
- **Extracts:** Oils with essential flavorings of a food item, such as almond or lemon.
- **Liquids:** Moisture added to mix batters and doughs.

Table 8.3: Formula for Soft Rolls Using Baker's Percentages

- If possible, find a recipe for rolls and put the percentages to work!

Discussion

- "If I have a pound of flour, that would be my 100 percent proportion for a baking formula." Show students a pound of flour. Assess for understanding.

- "If my formula now calls for 50 percent sugar, how much sugar would this be if 1 pound is 100 percent?" The answer is ½ pound. Assess for understanding:

  - Example: 0.5 lb sugar ÷ (1 lb flour × 100 percent) = 50 percent sugar

    This can be turned around to calculate the weight of sugar:

  - Example: 50 percent sugar × (1 lb flour × 100 percent) = 0.5 lb sugar

    0.5 can be expressed as ½ lb.

  - Remind the students that "percent" means "per 100," or "divided by 100." Every percentage is actually another way of expressing the decimal "100ths," or two places to the right of the decimal point.

  - Example: 50 percent ÷ 0.50 = $^{50}/_{100}$.

Teaching Tips

- Use classroom discussion to ascertain the math numeracy and literacy of the students.

- Work with the class according to their math readiness.

- Some students might not understand percentages. The pizza analogy in the text is good for helping them to understand percentages. For formulas, help the students to see that this requires using another pizza in reference (or comparison) to the first.

- Some students might not be able to discuss proportions with clear understanding.

- The concept of relative percentages might need practice.

- If individual students require more assistance, enlist the help of a math teacher.

- Conversions between fractions, decimal expressions, and percentages might also need clarification for students.

- Use as many real-life visuals and manipulatives as possible. Talk might be confusing to some students.

Baker's Measurements

Standardized recipes for bakery products are called **formulas**, and they are set up a bit differently than those for other food items. Proportions for each ingredient are given in the form of percentages. A percentage indicates a part of a whole. For example, a pizza with four pieces is divided into quarters. Each slice is 25 percent of the pizza. Two slices, half the pizza, is 50 percent, and three slices is 75 percent. The whole pizza is 100 percent.

In baking, flour always has a proportion of 100 percent, and the percentages of all other ingredients are calculated in relation to the flour. These are known as **baker's percentages**. In this way, pastry chefs can convert recipes to give larger or smaller yields by changing ingredient amounts while keeping proportions and percentages the same. The formula for baker's percentages is expressed like this:

Weight of ingredient ÷ (Weight of flour × 100 Percent) = Percent of ingredient

Table 8.3 shows a formula for soft rolls using baker's percentages. Although the example in Table 8.3 doesn't include directions, usually the formula also shows the various directions given in a bakeshop recipe, such as mixing, yeast fermenting time, scaling, and baking temperature.

Table 8.3: Formula for Soft Rolls Using Baker's Percentages

Soft Yeast Dinner Rolls	Baker's Percentages
Active dry yeast, 2 ounces	4.5%
Water (temperature controlled), 1 pound 8 ounces	54.5%
Bread flour, 2 pounds 12 ounces	100%
Salt, 1 ounces	2.3%
Granulated sugar, 4 ounces	9%
Nonfat dry milk powder, 2 ounces	4.5%
Shortening, 2 ounces	4.5%
Unsalted butter, softened, 2 ounces	4.5%
Eggs, 3.2 ounces (2 eggs)	7.3%
Egg wash, as needed	
Total dough weight: 5 pounds 4 ounces	

Vocabulary Terms

- **Formulas:** Recipes with percentages of ingredients.

- **Baker's percentages:** Baking recipes that can easily have the yield scaled up or down.

- **Yield:** The quantity, or number of servings, a recipe makes.

- **Sifting:** Passing dry powders through a sieve to loosen clumps and add air.

Understanding baker's percentages makes it easy to calculate the weight of any ingredient or to convert a formula to a new **yield**. A yield is how much of something is produced.

To calculate the weight of a particular ingredient, change the ingredient percentage to decimal form by moving the decimal point two places to the left. Then, multiply the weight of the flour by this decimal to get the weight of the ingredient. For example, if a formula calls for 20 percent sugar and the pastry chef is using 10 pounds of flour, how much sugar does the chef need by weight?

Example: 20 percent = 0.20

10 pounds flour × 0.20 = 2 pounds sugar

To convert a formula to a new yield, change the total percentage to decimal form by moving the decimal point two places to the left. Then, divide the desired yield by this decimal figure to get the weight of the flour. If necessary, round off this number to the next highest figure. Use the weight of flour and remaining ingredient percentages to calculate the weights of the other ingredients. Check recipes carefully to see whether ingredients are to be scaled before or after sifting. **Sifting** is very important in baking. Dry ingredients must be sifted before they are mixed into the dough or batter. Sifting adds air to flour, cocoa, and confectioner's sugar; removes lumps; and filters out any impurities.

Safe Baking
The principles of food safety and sanitation apply to the making of baked goods, too. Dough must be handled frequently, whether the pastry chef uses machinery or kneads the dough by hand. The various stages of baking require different tools and stations of the kitchen; therefore, cross-contamination should be a concern. Always follow safe foodhandling procedures:

- Keep hands away from the face, hair, and body.
- Wash hands whenever changing from one task to another—especially from raw foods to ready-to-eat foods.
- Keep work areas clean.
- Handle and clean all foods properly. Keep waste away from edibles.
- Keep pest control a high priority; rodents and insects can thrive on a diet of grains and flour, which are essential baking ingredients.

In-Class Activity: Working with Baker's Percentage Formulas

Mathematics Connection

Using the sample recipe in Table 8.3, scale the recipe several ways for different yields. Use the math examples to perform the required math.

Example: To double the yield, you would multiply each ingredient amount by 2. This is not so difficult. The 2 ounces of dry yeast would become 4 ounces, and so on. Multiply everything by the factor of increased yield.

However, if the desire is to make the dough using 10 pounds of flour, then the conversions need to use the percentages. For dry yeast:

4.5 percent = 0.045

0.045 dry yeast × 10 lb = .45 lb dry yeast

The conversion of pounds to ounces is 16 ounces = 1 pound.

To convert this to ounces, multiply 16 oz × .45 = 7.2 oz dry yeast

The recipe can also be decreased.

For example, if the baker would like to use 1 pound of flour:

0.045 dry yeast × 1 = 0.045 lb dry yeast

16 oz × 0.045 lb dry yeast = .72 oz dry yeast

ServSafe Connection: Safe Baking

Some bakers like to use gloves for the process.

CUSTOMIZED INSTRUCTION

Mathematics Connection

More Advanced Students

Accomplished math or chemistry students might be interested in applying the principles of dimensional analysis to these baker's percentage equations. Dimensional analysis is a process of unit conversions used in chemistry that places all the operations into one equation. This method is sometimes also known as "reducing" or "factor label" or "unit factor label" or "unit conversions."

The setup looks like this, with the units of measure labeled:

$$10 \text{ lb.} \left(\frac{4.5\%}{100\%} \right) \left(\frac{16 \text{ ounces}}{1 \text{ lb}} \right) = 7.2 \text{ ounces}$$

Keep in mind that the 10 lb is a whole number and not a portion, so it acts as a numerator.

Note that the units lb and % each appear in both numerator and denominator, so they cancel.

Please recall that the vertical line means "divided by."

The operations can now be performed with or without a calculator in the correct order as follows: $10 \times 4.5 \div 100 \times 16 \div 1 = 7.2$

The only units that remain after canceling are ounces, so 7.2 indicates the number of ounces: 7.2 ounces.

Although perhaps difficult to grasp at first, dimensional analysis simplifies the operations, eliminates repetitive equations, and keeps the units in order. Practicing this is worth a try.

Sifting breaks up clumps, and baking soda and baking powder tend to clump. They taste very soapy in a clump.

Discussion

- Sifting used to be required to remove debris from flour and other dry ingredients. Why is it still done? Flour today is clean. What are the advantages of sifting flour?

- What are the advantages of sifting dry ingredients together?

- What if there are still clumps of baking soda or other dry ingredients remaining in the bottom of the sifter? What should be done with those ingredients?

Teaching Tips

- Clumps should never be dumped into the dry ingredients.

- If they can be forced through the sifter and broken up, they can join the rest of the dry ingredients.

- If there is a large amount of any ingredient remaining in the sifter that might alter the recipe, break it up and sift it through.

- If there is a negligible amount of any ingredient remaining in the sifter, discard it.

Essential Skills
Sifting: Why it Matters

If you have ever tasted soap in your mouth, you can appreciate the need to sift dry ingredients.

It used to be necessary to sift flour to remove little twigs or stones or other items that might have infiltrated it, but most flour is free of debris today. Also, most commercial recipes call for weights of flour rather than dry measures (cups) of flour, so sifting is irrelevant in measuring—a given weight of dry flour will weigh the same whether it is sifted or not. If it is sifted, it will have more volume, but not more weight. See Figure 8.1.

Why does sifting matter, and what does this have to do with soap? Soap is alkaline, giving it a nasty, bitter taste. Baking soda is also alkaline, and tastes like soap. Baking soda tends to form small clumps, especially in humid conditions. Sifting the dry ingredients together forces the clumps of soda to break apart as they pass through the sieve. This prevents little clumps from remaining whole in the final product. One little clump of soda in a muffin will taste like a mouthful of soap—probably not the flavor you want.

In addition, sifting adds air to the flour, making it lighter and fluffier. This is important for many recipes, especially cakes and light baked goods.

Figure 8.1: Sifting flour.

Figure Focus

Figure 8.1: Flour and dry ingredients should be sifted carefully to prevent flying flour landing on surfaces.

Summary

In this section, you learned the following:

- There are eight main categories of ingredients used in baking:

  - Strengtheners provide stability and ensure that the baked item doesn't collapse once it is removed from the oven. Flour is a main ingredient used in baking.

  - Shortening makes baked goods moist, adds flavor, and keeps the baked item fresh longer. Any fat, such as oil or butter, acts as a shortening in baking.

  - Sweeteners include refined sugars, sugar syrups, molasses, brown sugar, corn syrup, honey, and malt syrup (usually used in yeast breads). Sweeteners add flavor and color to baked goods. They also help the shortening blend with other ingredients, and make the product soft and tender.

  - Leaveners are necessary in baking because they allow the dough or batter to rise. Leaveners fall into three categories: chemical, organic, and physical. Baking soda and baking powder are the main chemical leaveners; yeasts comprise the organic leaveners; the basic physical leaveners are air and steam.

  - Thickeners include gelatin, flour, arrowroot (a powdered starch made from a tropical root), cornstarch, and eggs. Thickeners, combined with the stirring process, determine the consistency of the finished product.

  - Flavorings, such as spices, salt, and extracts, affect a baked item's taste and color.

  - Liquids are one of the most important elements used in baking. The liquid used in baking can be water, milk, cream, molasses, honey, or butter. Liquid is used in baking to provide moisture to the product and to allow the gluten to properly develop.

  - Additives include substances such as food coloring, which may add to the appearance of baked goods.

- Standardized recipes, or formulas, for bakery products are set up a bit differently than those for other food items. Proportions for each ingredient are given in the form of percentages. In baking, flour always has a proportion of 100 percent, and the percentages of all other ingredients are given in relation to the flour. These are known as baker's percentages. Understanding baker's percentages makes it easy to calculate the weight of any ingredient or to convert a formula to a new yield, which is how much a recipe produces.

511

Summary

- Remind students to review the following:
  1. Baker's ingredients
  2. Baker's measurements

Section 8.1
Review Questions

1. Leaveners help baked goods to rise.

2. Flour is the most basic strengthener.

3. Thickeners include gelatin, cornstarch, arrowroot, eggs, and flour.

4. The baker's percentage is based on the weight of flour used, which represents 100 percent.

5. Each student will have a unique opinion about this.

6. Students can list any ten of the ingredients from seven main categories of ingredients, and the list should include at least one from each category:

- Flour

- Shortening
- Butter
- Oil
- Lard

- Sugar
- Sugar syrup
- Molasses
- Brown sugar
- Corn syrup
- Honey
- Malt syrup
- Artificial sweeteners

- Baking soda
- Baking powder
- Dry yeast

- Gelatin
- Arrowroot
- Corn starch
- Eggs

- Milk
- Cream

- Salt
- Spices
- Vanilla extract
- Other flavoring extracts

Section 8.1 Review Questions

1. What category of ingredients helps baked goods to rise?
2. What is the most basic strengthener?
3. List three examples of thickeners.
4. What is a baker's percentage based on?
5. Gale Gand says that she "absolutely loves the ingredients, how reliable they are, how predictable pastry is." What does this mean to you? What is she saying?
6. Kabob's neglect of dessert service is due in part to a lack of dessert preparation. Miguel and Chef Kate simply never gave it a lot of thought. As a first step in the right direction, they want to make sure their pantry is well stocked for dessert preparation. What ingredients would you suggest they purchase? List 10 items you feel they absolutely must have on hand.
7. What is durum flour? Research this. When is it used? Why? What are its other names?
8. Why do you think baker's percentages are all based around flour?

512

7. Durum flour is made from durum wheat, which is a hard wheat that is high in gluten. It is used for chewy breads, pasta, and other baked goods that benefit from its elasticity, sheen, and fine finish. It is also called semolina flour.

8. Flour is the most abundant ingredient in most baked goods.

Section 8.1 Activities

1. Study Skills/Group Activity: Weighing Flour

Divide into groups depending upon the number of scales available in your classroom. Using a scientific gram scale, tare the weight of an empty measuring cup. Fill the same cup with packed flour and level the top. Weigh the cup and flour. Note the weight. Sift the flour into a bowl. Loosely fill the one cup measure with the sifted flour and level the top. Weigh the cup and the flour. Is there a difference in the weight? Is there flour remaining in the bowl? What are your conclusions?

2. Activity: Artificial Sweeteners

Investigate online the baking qualities of artificial sweeteners. Does artificial sweetener perform the same in baking as sugar or honey? Write a paragraph about your findings.

3. Critical Thinking: Parker House Rolls

Describe the *mise en place* for making Parker House rolls. Create a flow chart of the recipe method.

513

CUSTOMIZED INSTRUCTION

Science Connection

More Advanced Students

Determine the percentage difference in weight between the sifted and the unsifted flour.

---

2. Each student will have a unique answer depending on the sweetener he or she chooses. Have students provide their sources and references that support their work. Check their sources for accurate information.

3. The *mise en place* would be the same as for other white rolls. The Parker House technique is an off-center fold of the roll before baking. The recipe at the end of the chapter for soft yeast dinner rolls can be used as a guide.

Section 8.1 Activities

1. The activity is more specifically described here:

CUSTOMIZED INSTRUCTION

Science Connection

Less Advanced Students, Special Needs Students, ESOL Students

Needed:

1 lb flour

3 bowls

Scales (sensitive, or gram scales from the science department)

1 cup dry measuring cups

Paper towel

Blade spatula for leveling flour

Sifter

Group the students in pairs, partnering a less advanced student with either an ESOL student (of any ability level) or a special needs student (regardless of accommodation required; hearing impaired will require an interpreter).

The less advanced student acts as "lead" and verbally explains the process as they perform the following experiment. The ESOL and special needs students can participate in the hands-on functions.

Place the empty 1 cup dry measure on the scales and zero, or "tare", the scales.

Divide the 1 pound of flour equally between two bowls, each bowl containing ½ pound of flour.

Sift one of the ½ pound bowls of flour into the empty bowl.

Carefully fill the measuring cup with unsifted flour.

Weigh the flour to the furthest decimal available on the scales (some measure hundredths of grams).

Record exact weight to the furthest decimal.

Return the flour to the unsifted bowl and completely knock out the remaining flour.

Gently remove remaining flour with a dry paper towel.

Carefully fill the measuring cup with sifted flour.

Weigh the flour to the furthest decimal available on the scales.

Record exact weight to the furthest decimal.

Compare the two weights.

Is there a weight difference between the unsifted and the sifted flour?

Each student should express a conclusion about sifting flour.

Section 8.2
Yeast Breads

Introduce the Section

a. There are several types of yeast-bread dough that will be introduced in this section.

b. Yeast bread preparation follows time-honored techniques.

c. Yeast bread techniques are ancient, and yet continue to be innovative.

d. Small variations in technique can change a bread.

Vocabulary Review

a. Direct students to the key terms.

b. Pronounce each word, and have the students repeat the pronunciation out loud.

c. Discuss the definition of each word.

Teach

Discuss

- Ask students how many of them have eaten yeast bread in the last 24 hours.

- Yeast breads are one of the most common, and most cross-cultural, foods on the planet.

In-Class Activity:
Cross-Cultural Varieties of Lean and Rich Breads

Literacy Connection, 21st-Century Skills—Global Awareness

Divide the students into groups.

Have each group find five types of yeast breads from any nation or culture.

Have the students identify:

- The name of the bread (for example, challah).

- The nation or culture.

- The use of the bread (daily fare, special celebration, etc.).

- Whether or not the bread is a lean dough or a rich dough.

Present findings to the class.

Vocabulary Terms

- **Lean dough:** A dough with little or no fat or sugar.

- **Rich dough:** A dough with shortening or other fat, plus other rich ingredients like eggs or milk.

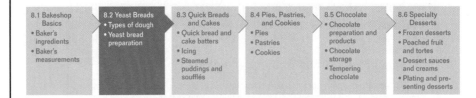

8.1 Bakeshop Basics	8.2 Yeast Breads	8.3 Quick Breads and Cakes	8.4 Pies, Pastries, and Cookies	8.5 Chocolate	8.6 Specialty Desserts
• Baker's ingredients • Baker's measurements	• Types of dough • Yeast bread preparation	• Quick bread and cake batters • Icing • Steamed puddings and soufflés	• Pies • Pastries • Cookies	• Chocolate preparation and products • Chocolate storage • Tempering chocolate	• Frozen desserts • Poached fruit and tortes • Dessert sauces and creams • Plating and presenting desserts

SECTION 8.2 YEAST BREADS

Yeast breads consist of some very familiar breads. Hard rolls for sandwiches, loaves of French and Italian bread for dinner, or soft dinner rolls that might be served at a restaurant all fall under the category of yeast bread. This section discusses the different types of dough that make up these breads as well as the basic steps in yeast bread preparation.

Study Questions

After studying Section 8.2, you should be able to answer the following questions:

- What are the two basic types of yeast bread dough?

- What are the two basic methods used to make yeast breads?

- What are the 10 basic steps to making yeast bread?

Types of Dough

Yeast is a living organism that acts as a leavener—that is, it makes baked goods rise. Breads that use yeast are called yeast breads. Yeast breads are divided into two categories: lean doughs and rich doughs. Doughs are simply a mixture of flour, liquid, and a leavener. Yeast bread dough obviously always includes a leavener. Other ingredients can be used as well when creating a dough. The texture of dough is stiff but still pliable.

Lean doughs are made with flour, yeast, water, and salt. They have very little or no sugar or fat. Breads made from lean dough tend to have a chewy texture and a crisp crust. French bread and hard rolls are examples of lean doughs.

Rich doughs are made with the addition of shortening or tenderizing ingredients such as sugars, syrups, butter, eggs, milk, and cream. Introducing these ingredients changes the bread's overall texture, as well as the way the dough is handled. Rich doughs should have a cake-like texture after baking. Parker House rolls, cloverleaf rolls, soft rolls, and Danish are examples of rich doughs.

514

Bakers most often use two primary methods to make yeast breads: straight-dough method or sponge method. The **straight-dough method** (also called the straight-mix method) can be used for all types of doughs—lean, rich, and sponge. When using the straight-dough method to mix dough, the baker can combine all ingredients at the same time, or he or she might mix the yeast with warm water first, at a temperature of 138°F. (Some yeasts require a different temperature.) After mixing the dough, the baker kneads until it is elastic and smooth. Different doughs will require different kneading times. **Kneading** (NEED-ing) dough is important because it develops the gluten in the dough and gives the dough the stretch and give it needs to develop the proper texture. See the Essential Skills below for a step-by-step guide to the straight-dough method.

Essential Skills
The Straight-Dough Method

❶ Combine all ingredients in a bowl.

❷ Mix the dough until it starts to catch (when the ingredients cling together).

❸ Knead the dough until it is smooth and springy. See Figure 8.2a.

❹ Remove the dough to an oiled bowl.

❺ Let it rise. See Figure 8.2b.

❻ Punch it down.

❼ Scale, or size, it to the appropriate size.

❽ Remove it to a floured workbench and rest covered.

❾ Shape and place the dough in pans. See Figure 8.2c.

❿ Proof it (let it rise a second time).

⓫ Bake.

Figure 8.2a: Step 3— Knead the dough.

Figure 8.2b: Step 5—Let the dough rise.

Figure 8.2c: Step 9— Place dough in pans.

Teaching Tips

- The various methods of dough mixing should be demonstrated in the classroom to the students.

- If there is a mirror, perhaps the students can see from where they sit.

- If the school is equipped, an overhead document camera and screen could also make the process visible to the students.

- If there is no mirror or camera, gather the students around so they can see and experience the various methods as much as possible.

Essential Skills: The Straight-Dough Method

The size of the "bowl" depends on the size of the operation or bakery. The dough can be made in a bowl for a few servings, up to a large drum for a major bread producer. Regardless of the size of the batch of dough, the straight-dough mixing method remains the same.

Vocabulary Terms

- **Straight-dough method:** A bread mixing method that mixes all the ingredients at once.

- **Kneading:** Working bread dough to develop a gluten protein molecular web-like structure.

Figure Focus

Figure 8.2a: Kneading dough by hand. This can also be done with a dough hook in a large mixer.

Figure 8.2b: A measured and floured portion of kneaded dough resting, awaiting the next step.

Figure 8.2c: Dough rising in a pan.

Reinforce and Review

- The temperature referred to here is the room temperature, or the temperature in the proofing box.

- There is some heat generated by the yeast growth, but dough needs to be a in warm place to rise.

- Large-scale bakeries will have large proofing boxes.

Homework Activity:
Homework Activity: Sourdough In Song and Story
Literacy Connection
Sourdough has played a role in American history.
Because a crock of sourdough can travel well, Western pioneers often carried sourdough starters.
San Francisco has a lush Gold Rush and sourdough history that is influenced by the Bay Area climate.
The Alaskan Gold Rush also has a rich sourdough tradition.
The Amish of Pennsylvania and Indiana use a sourdough starter as a gift of friendship.
Sourdough shows up elsewhere, too.
Research and explore an aspect of sourdough in the United States. Write a poem, song, skit, or story about some aspect of sourdough in the United States. Present your creation to the class, either individually or in groups.

Vocabulary Terms

- **Sponge method:** A two-stage method for mixing bread dough, beginning with yeast and a portion of ingredients. This mixture grows and creates a sponge-like curd.

- **Sponge:** The yeast, flour, and liquid curd that is actively growing, ready for the addition of more ingredients.

- **Sourdough:** A sour-tasting dough or batter made with a special fermented yeast culture called a starter.

- **Starter:** The fermented yeast mixture that is portioned out for sourdough baked goods. A portion always remains as starter and is "fed" for future use.

- **Proof:** The second raising of dough, usually done in the baking pan or on the baking stone.

Bakers also use the **sponge method** to mix yeast doughs. The first stage of this method involves mixing the yeast, half of the liquid, and half of the flour to make a thick batter called a **sponge**. After the sponge rises and doubles its size, add the remaining fat, liquid, salt, sugar, and flour. Knead the dough and leave it to rise. Breads made with the sponge method have a lighter texture and more unique flavor than breads made using the straight dough method.

Sourdough is another type of bread made with yeast batter. However, sourdough breads are leavened with something called a **starter**, a mixture of water, yeast, and all-purpose flour that has been fermented (usually overnight) until it has a sour smell.

Once yeast dough has been mixed and left to rise, the baker will need to punch it down, or fold it over, by pushing the dough down in a few places. This will expel some of the carbon dioxide and redistribute the yeast evenly. Figure 8.3 shows dough rising in a baking pan.

Once the dough is in the pan, the baker leaves it to **proof**, or rise a second time. Proofing, the final rise of the yeast product before baking, should be between 95°F and 115°F. The product should continue proofing until it is about twice its original size and bounces back when lightly touched.

Some products are proofed in a specific piece of equipment called a proofer or a proofing cabinet or box. This allows for specific control of temperature and moisture for optimal rise of the product.

Figure 8.3: Dough rising in a baking pan.

Figure Focus
Figure 8.3: The pan on the left has dough that has been kneaded and portioned, and allowed to rest before being put in the pan. The pan on the right is the same dough after the proofing, or second rising, ready to bake.

[fast fact]

Did You Know . . . ?
Sourdough was likely the first form of leavening dough used for baking. It was eventually replaced during the Middle Ages by barm leaven, which is created in the beer-making process. Both were eventually replaced as the baker's most popular choice by cultured yeast in the late nineteenth century after Louis Pasteur's discovery of the fermentation process.

[nutrition]

Bran, Phytic Acid, and Yeast
Phytic acid is a compound found in the bran portion of grains. Bran is not digestible by humans. The phytic acid it contains binds to such healthful mineral nutrients as iron, magnesium, and zinc. So when the body excretes the bran, it excretes these essential nutrients as well. Phytic acid is sometimes called an "anti-nutrient" because it can prevent the absorption of mineral nutrients from food.

The good news: Adding yeast to products that contain bran prevents the excretion of these nutrients. Yeast helps break down phytic acid. As the phytic acid breaks down, so does its capacity to bind to essential nutrients that the body needs. That's why yeast-leavened whole grain breads are a good source of minerals such as iron, magnesium, zinc, and others.

[ServSafe Connection]

Making Bread in the Danger Zone
Yeast is a fungus. It is a pathogen that grows under favorable conditions of warmth, air, and moisture. It reproduces itself by budding new yeast cells off of old ones. As it grows, it gives off carbon dioxide gas. It is the formation of this gas that makes yeast a useful leavener. Baker's yeast is also a friendly microbe, not a pathogen, and serves a positive purpose in food science.

However, take note of the conditions that are good for yeast growth: warmth, air, and moisture. As you'll recall, athogens also grow under these same circumstances. In fact, yeast dough must be kept in the danger zone to proof! It's the same zone. You want to create great baked goods—but that's it. Understanding this temperature range will help you keep your food better and safer.

Yeast Bread Preparation

There are 10 basic steps in making yeast breads. The Essentials Skills box on the following page shows the steps and provides a brief description and illustration of each.

517

**Fast Fact:
Did You Know . . . ?**

Sourdough starter, a wet curd, was anciently stored in earthen pots. It still is.

**Nutrition:
Bran, Phytic Acid, and Yeast**

It is clear to see that nutrition is not a simple, nor always intuitive, science. Nutrition advice and guidance can be provided to a restaurant or foodservice operation by a registered dietitian.

**ServSafe Connection:
Making Bread in the Danger Zone**

Keeping all surfaces, bowls, pans, and bread-making equipment clean and sanitized is essential. Everything grows, both good microbes and bad, in the temperature zone needed for bread yeast growth.

Teaching Tips

- If at all possible, take the students on a field trip to a bakery.
- If not, perhaps the students could arrange to visit a bakery operation on their own.
- At the bakery, the students should observe how and where the yeast dough is proofed.

Essential Skills: Making Yeast Breads

Encourage students to discuss the following:

- The ancient science of bread-making has required and time-tested steps.

- Attempting to shortcut the process in the interests of time usually does not work.

- Bread recipes are very specific and sensitive to small changes.

- Additionally, very small differences in ingredients, proportions, and methods produce vast changes in the finished products.

- Bread recipes must be carefully developed and recorded, then faithfully followed.

- Even weather conditions can affect the end result.

Discuss

- Ask students how many shapes of yeast breads there are.

- Discuss and, if possible, show pictures of various shapes.

- There are rounds, baguettes, loaves, braids, twists, rings, rolls, rolls made in muffin tins, and so on.

- Perhaps students can think of other shapes that have not been mentioned.

Essential Skills
Making Yeast Breads

❶ **Scaling ingredients:** Measure all ingredients accurately.

❷ **Mixing and kneading ingredients:** Mixing combines the ingredients, distributes the yeast, and develops the gluten. To further develop the gluten, knead the dough until it is smooth and elastic. See Figure 8.4a.

Figure 8.4a: Step 2—Knead the dough.

Figure 8.4b: Step 3—Fermentation.

❸ **Fermentation:** During fermentation, the yeast acts on sugars and starches in the dough to produce carbon dioxide and alcohol. Carbon dioxide gas gets trapped in the gluten. This is also known as **pushing up.** See Figure 8.4b.

Figure 8.4c: Step 4—Punching down the dough.

Figure 8.4d: Step 5—Divide the dough.

❹ **Punching down:** Gently fold down the dough to expel and redistribute gas pockets in the dough. Punching also relaxes the gluten and evens the temperature. See Figure 8.4c.

❺ **Portioning:** Divide the dough into pieces of uniform weight, according to the product. Weigh portions on a portion scale to ensure uniform size and weight. See Figure 8.4d.

Figure 8.4e: Step 6—Shape the dough into round balls.

Figure 8.4f: Step 8—Proofing the dough.

❻ **Rounding:** After portioning, shape the dough into smooth, round balls. The outside layer of gluten becomes smooth. This holds in the gases and makes it easier to shape the dough. See Figure 8.4e.

❼ **Shaping:** Now it is possible to shape the dough into a variety of forms, depending on the desired type of bread.

❽ **Proofing:** Proofing is the final rise of the shaped yeast dough just before baking. Keep the dough in a warm, draft-free area or in a proofing box, and allow it to double in size. See Figure 8.4f.

518

Figure Focus

Figures 8.4a–8.4h: Review with the students the steps to making yeast bread. If possible, have students make bread in class, or at home.

❾ **Baking:** Load the ovens carefully because proofed doughs are fragile until they become set by baking. The dough can sink or dent if care isn't taken at this stage. Common baking temperatures are between 400°F and 425°F. A golden brown crust color normally indicates the loaves are done. See Figure 8.4g.

Figure 8.4g: Step 9—Bake the bread.

Figure 8.4h: Step 10—Cool the bread.

❿ **Cooling and storing:** Remove loaves from their pans and place them on racks to allow air circulation. Cool yeast products at room temperature. For storage, wrap cooled breads in moisture-proof bags to slow down staling. Breads must be thoroughly cool before wrapping or moisture will collect inside the bags. See Figure 8.4h.

When using fresh yeast, keep it refrigerated until it is time to use it. It should look creamy and white and have a fresh, yeasty smell. If the yeast has a sour odor, or is brown and has a slimy film, discard it immediately. Using only the freshest yeast will help ensure a quality baked product.

Some yeast breads are glazed or washed before baking. The glazes or washes are used to change the color or texture of the bread. Rye bread is often washed with egg. Washes can also help to attach toppings to the top of the dough. Examples of toppings include oats and seeds.

[on the job]

The Baker's Corner

While baking is very much like a science, it's not an exact one. Every great baker has gone through trial and error in perfecting the finished product. Below are a few helpful troubleshooting hints straight from the bakeshop:

- If the baked item tastes strongly of yeast, one of the following things happened to the dough:
  - It was not allowed sufficient time to proof before baking.
  - It was made with too much yeast.
- Doughs without sufficient salt will have a bland flavor.
- On the other hand, too much salt can kill yeast, which will make the product heavy and dense.
- If the dough is pale after baking, one of the following things happened:
  - It was not completely baked.
  - It was baked at too low a temperature.

519

Reinforce and Review

- Rye bread is made from rye, which is a grain that is darker than wheat and has less gluten.

- Rye bread is made from a mixture of rye flour and wheat flour.

- Rye also has a full-bodied, slightly grassy flavor.

- Caraway seeds are often mixed into rye bread dough.

- The caraway seeds are not the rye. Rye bread does not always have caraway seeds, either.

On the Job: The Baker's Corner

Becoming acquainted with the science and art of bread-making requires practice, attention, and mentoring. There are food science principles that can be learned as students gain practical experience.

Essential Skills: Making Lighter Stone-Ground Whole Wheat Bread

If dough is put into an oven that is still too cool, the short gluten structure will allow the yeast gases to expel before they do the work of raising the structure.

Too hot an oven will burn the crust while the inside will be too dense to cook entirely.

It's a delicate balance with a whole-grain dough.

Trial and error with the exact conditions of a kitchen's own ovens and the region's climate will determine how to ensure success.

Reinforce and Review

- Slice warm whole wheat bread carefully with a sharp bread knife to prevent smashing the warm loaf.

- Turn the loaf onto its side and start the sawing motion in the air before making contact with the bread.

- Let the knife blade gently "bite" into the crust and do the work without pressure.

Essential Skills
Making Lighter Stone-Ground Whole Wheat Bread

Whole wheat flour has the bran and germ still in the mix, ground with the rest of the wheat kernel. It will develop a gluten structure as it is kneaded, just like white flour. However, the bran cuts the gluten somewhat, reducing the long strands to shorter gluten lengths. This gives whole wheat bread a heavier, denser crumb than white bread.

To lighten a whole wheat loaf, follow these steps:

❶ Use as little flour as possible to start the mixing process.

❷ Add flour slowly, just enough to keep the dough workable. On a humid day, the dough will take more flour, and the bread will be heavier. See Figure 8.5a.

❸ Let it rise once, punch it down, and shape it into loaves. See Figure 8.5b.

❹ Let it rise again in a greased loaf pan until it is almost double in size. To a gentle touch, the dough should feel light and not as elastic anymore.

❺ Make sure the oven temperature is accurate, and always put the dough into a preheated oven. In the initial phase of baking, the carbon dioxide from the yeast will expand and bring the dough to its greatest volume. Then, the heat will kill the yeast and denature (cook) the gluten in its structure. No more rising will occur. If the oven temperature is correct, it will bake through the center without burning the crust.

❻ Remove the loaf from the pan to cool to protect the crust from becoming soggy.

❼ Serve while still warm for best taste. See Figure 8.5c.

Figure 8.5a: Step 2— Add the flour slowly.

Figure 8.5b: Step 3— Let the dough rise once.

Figure 8.5c: Step 7—Serve warm.

520

Figure Focus

Figure 8.5a: Proper kneading is especially important for whole wheat dough so that it won't be too heavy.

Figure 8.5b: Proofing can make the loaf lighter.

Figure 8.5c: An inviting slice of whole wheat bread.

Summary

In this section, you learned the following:

- Yeast is a living organism that acts as a leavener; that is, it makes baked goods rise. Breads that use yeast are called yeast breads. Yeast breads are divided into two categories—lean doughs and rich doughs:

  - Lean doughs are made with flour, yeast, and water. They have very little or no sugar or fat. Breads made from lean dough tend to have a chewy texture and a crisp crust. French bread and hard rolls are examples of lean doughs.

  - Rich doughs are made with the addition of shortening or tenderizing ingredients such as sugars, syrups, butter, eggs, milk, and cream. Introducing these ingredients changes the bread's overall texture, as well as the way the dough is handled. Rich doughs should have a cake-like texture after baking. Parker House rolls, cloverleaf rolls, soft rolls, and Danish are examples of rich doughs.

- Yeast breads are most often made using two primary methods—the straight-dough method or the sponge method:

  - Bakers use the straight-dough method for all types of doughs: lean, rich, and sponge. When using the straight-dough method to mix dough, a baker can combine all ingredients at the same time, or he or she may mix the yeast with warm water first, at a temperature of 138°F. (Some yeasts require a different temperature.) After the dough is mixed, it must be kneaded until it is elastic and smooth.

  - Bakers use the sponge method to mix yeast batters. In the first stage of this method, mix the yeast, liquid, and half of the flour to make a thick batter called a sponge. After the sponge rises and doubles its size, add the remaining fat, salt, sugar, and flour. Knead the dough and leave it to rise. Breads made with the sponge method have a lighter texture and more unique flavor than breads made using the straight dough method.

- There are 10 basic steps in making yeast breads:

  1. Scaling ingredients
  2. Mixing and kneading ingredients
  3. Fermentation
  4. Punching down
  5. Portioning
  6. Rounding
  7. Shaping
  8. Proofing
  9. Baking
  10. Cooling and storing

521

Summary

- Remind students to review the following:
  1. Types of dough
  2. Yeast bread preparation

Section 8.2
Review Questions

1. Two basic kinds of bread dough are lean and rich.

2. Lean dough does not have oil, butter, or other fat in it.

3. Straight dough is mixed all at once. The sponge method creates a yeast and flour sponge with a portion of the ingredients. The rest are added in the next phase of mixing.

4. These are the ten steps of making yeast breads:
   1. Scaling ingredients
   2. Mixing and kneading ingredients
   3. Fermentation
   4. Punching down
   5. Portioning
   6. Rounding
   7. Shaping
   8. Proofing
   9. Baking
   10. Cooling and storing

5. Each student's answer will be unique.

6. This answer will require information from Chapter 5.

7. This answer will be based on the opinion of each individual student.

8. Students should mention that bread would be flat, tough, and heavy.

Section 8.2 Review Questions

1. What are the two basic kinds of yeast bread dough?

2. Discuss one way in which the two kinds of yeast bread dough are different.

3. Describe the two basic methods used to make yeast breads.

4. List the 10 basic steps to making yeast bread.

5. Gale Gand notes that she likes the fact that her pastry kitchen makes the first impression of the meal. Select two specific types of bread that would be served at dinner. Why do you think these breads would make a good first impression?

6. Using a make-or-buy analysis, do you think it would be beneficial for Kabob to make their own bread or to buy it from a trusted vendor? Support your rationale.

7. Compare and contrast the sponge method and the straight-dough method of yeast making. What are the pros and cons of both? Which do you think produces a higher quality product? Why?

8. Why is proofing so important? What would happen if this step were skipped? Write a paragraph explaining your findings.

522

Section 8.2 Activities

1. Study Skills/Group Activity: Yeast Colony

Work in teams of two or more. Grow a yeast colony in warm water and observe its changes over a 30-minute period. Note the temperature of the water used. Measure the size of the colony every five minutes. Record observations, including smell.

2. Independent Activity: History of Yeast Bread

What is the history of yeast bread making? How was the process invented? Create a time line based upon your findings.

3. Critical Thinking: Moldy Bread

Breads can become unsafe when moldy. Investigate mold formation in yeast breads and how to prevent it. Write two paragraphs about your findings.

523

Section 8.2 Activities

1. Level 1, Chapter 2 in the teacher's edition has a formalized yeast colony experiment ("The Growth of Microbes" on p. 82) that can be accessed for this activity, if desired, for more support.

2. Each answer will be a bit different. Note that the students take the process back to historically ancient times. Also check that the timeline is mathematically and visually correct, rather than haphazard or messy. The connection to math is subtle but important as the students calibrate their timeline in a meaningful way.

3. The students might recommend or warn against adding preservatives to bread, depending on their personal leanings and their research. Encourage students to provide their sources of information. Recommend that they check out the Food and Drug Administration list of additives that are generally recommended as safe.

Section 8.3
Quick Breads and Cakes

Introduce the Section

a. Quick breads are batter breads that are not kneaded.

b. Cakes are tender, baked batter desserts.

c. There are mixing methods that produce the best results.

Vocabulary Review

a. Direct students to the key terms.

b. Pronounce each word, and have the students repeat the pronunciation out loud.

c. Discuss the definition of each word.

Teach

Discuss

- Cakes and quick breads are baked chemistry projects.

- Their success depends on properly mixing the correct ingredients.

- There is minimal mixing and no kneading. Even though they are made with flour, gluten is not developed.

Vocabulary Terms

- **Quick breads:** Chemically leavened breads that are not kneaded.

8.1 Bakeshop Basics	8.2 Yeast Breads	8.3 Quick Breads and Cakes	8.4 Pies, Pastries, and Cookies	8.5 Chocolate	8.6 Specialty Desserts
• Baker's ingredients • Baker's measurements	• Types of dough • Yeast bread preparation	• Quick bread and cake batters • Icing • Steamed puddings and soufflés	• Pies • Pastries • Cookies	• Chocolate preparation and products • Chocolate storage • Tempering chocolate	• Frozen desserts • Poached fruit and tortes • Dessert sauces and creams • Plating and presenting desserts

SECTION 8.3 QUICK BREADS AND CAKES

Quick breads and cakes are staples in the American diet. There's a quick bread or cake appropriate for just about any time of day. Your local coffeehouse, for example, will normally serve a wide variety of both. In the morning, you're likely to see a bigger selection of quick breads in the form of scones and muffins. Later in the day and into the evening, you're likely to see a wider variety of cakes instead. In this section, you'll learn about the various forms of quick breads and cake batters, as well as how they're prepared and served.

Study Questions

After studying Section 8.3, you should be able to answer the following questions:

- What are quick breads and cake batters, and how are they prepared?

- What are the three basic purposes for icing, and what are various types of icing?

- What are steamed puddings and soufflés?

Quick Breads and Cake Batters

Quick breads and cakes are popular snack and dessert items and are usually easy and quick to make. Quick breads and cakes use the same mixing methods.

Quick breads, such as biscuits, scones, and muffins, differ from yeast breads. As their name suggests, quick breads can be prepared faster. Quick breads use chemical leaveners rather than organic ones, and therefore don't require a rising period.

A batter is a semi-liquid mixture containing flour, liquid, and other ingredients. Unlike a dough, which is stiff but pliable, a batter is usually thin enough to be poured. A batter typically has more fat and sugar than a dough. Table 8.4 on the following page shows the four basic methods of preparing quick bread and cake batters.

524

Table 8.4: The Four Methods for Preparing Quick Bread and Cake Batters

	In the **creaming method**, cream the fat and sugar together to produce a very fine crumb and a dense, rich texture. A yellow butter cake is an example of a cake made with the creaming method.
	In the **foaming method**, a foam of whole eggs, yolks, or whites provides the structure for cakes with a light texture, such as angel food and chiffon cakes.
	In the **straight-dough method**, as discussed in the previous section, the baker combines all ingredients and blends them into a batter at once. Cornbread and blueberry muffins are examples of quick breads made with the straight-dough method.
	Bakers use the **two-stage method** to prepare **high-ratio** cakes. High-ratio cakes are called that because they contain more sugar than flour in the recipe. In other words, there is a higher ratio of sugar to flour than in other doughs and batters. (As discussed in Section 8.1, baker's measurements assign all ingredients a percentage in proportion to the amount of flour used.) In the two-stage method, combine a softened or melted shortening with the dry ingredients. Then, add and blend in one-half of the liquid being used in the recipe. Gradually add the remaining liquid to the mixture. High-ratio cakes made using the two-stage method have a very fine crumb, and are quite moist. Devil's food cake is one popular item prepared with the two-stage method.

The mixing technique for biscuits and scones, called the biscuit method, differs from the four mixing methods described above. Instead of combining all the ingredients at once, rub or cut in the fat into the flour until the mixture is mealy or bumpy in appearance. This produces a stiff batter with a slightly chewier texture than that of more cake-like items. Sometimes this batter is kneaded, but only very briefly because the dough will be tough if overworked.

[fast fact]

Did You Know . . . ?
Scones originated in Scotland. The first historical mention of the word was by a Scottish poet in the 1500s. Originally, scones were round and flat and made of unleavened oats. They didn't transform into the quick breads we eat today until baking powder became widely available.

525

Table 8.4:
The Four Methods for Preparing Quick Bread and Cake Batters

- In all methods, the mixing should be the optimal time according to the recipe. Overmixing can make quick breads and cakes tough.

Reinforce and Review

- The "biscuit method" mentioned, which is used for biscuits and scones, bears more similarity to pie crust and pastry mixing than to batter breads.

- The students will have a greater understanding of mixing fat into flour after the section on pie crusts.

- However, biscuits and scones are often chemically leavened like quick breads, which pie crusts are not.

- They also serve a place in cuisine similar to muffins or rolls, rather than desserts.

Vocabulary Terms

- **Creaming method:** The method that creams fat and sugar first, before liquid and dry ingredients are added.

- **Foaming method:** A cake made with an egg foam structure.

- **Straight-dough method:** The method involving mixing all batter ingredients at once.

- **Two-stage method:** Mixing fat with dry ingredients and a portion of the liquid, then adding the remaining liquid. Makes a fine crumb and is good for high-sugar cakes.

- **High-ratio cakes:** Cakes with a higher ratio of sugar to flour.

Fast Fact:
Did You Know . . . ?

The name "scone" does not always apply to a sweet biscuit-type quick bread. In the mountain states of the United States, a scone is made of squares of deep-fried yeast dough. These types of scones are served with whipped honey butter, or with powdered sugar and jam.

Nutrition:
The Muffin Exposé

Commercially prepackaged muffins should have a Nutrition Facts panel disclosure. Those made in a bakery might not. Recipe analysis software can calculate the nutrition data, which can make the disclosure available to any guest who might request the information.

Trends:
Flourless Chocolate Cake: A Decadent Dessert Statement

This dessert is usually baked in a cake-shaped pan in a bain-marie to add moisture to the baking process.

Discuss

- The generic term "topping" is sometimes substituted for icing, frosting, glaze, sauce, condiments, garnishes, and even meat and cheese options on a pizza.

- Do you think all these things should be lumped into one term?

- Is it more efficient or less so?

- Does it describe these things accurately or not?

- Is efficient communication that which uses the fewest words, or that which is the most accurate?

- Encourage the students to be specific and accurate when they refer to icings, coatings, and other enhancements.

Vocabulary Terms

- **Icings:** Frostings, coatings, or glazes for cakes and pastries.

[nutrition]

The Muffin Exposé

A muffin is not often thought of as a dessert, but as a bread; perhaps a light breakfast bread for a buffet or quick snack. It is certainly not often thought of as an entire meal. However, many commercial muffins contain as much or more fat and sugar than the same quantity of cake and as many calories as an entire meal!

It is not unusual for a commercially prepared, single-serving, 6-ounce blueberry muffin to contain more than 600 calories.

So while muffins are definitely tasty and satisfying, like all foods, they should be consumed in moderation.

[trends]

Flourless Chocolate Cake: A Decadent Dessert Statement

Although the percentage of the population that cannot tolerate gluten is small, gluten-free cooking for them is necessary. This concern has given rise to a dessert phenomenon: the Flourless Chocolate Cake. Quickly becoming a favorite around the United States, it has taken on an identity of its own beyond its humble dietetic beginnings.

Hardly a cake at all, this dish is rooted in eggs, sugar, and butter. The egg mixture is loaded with semi-sweet chocolate. The mixture is baked, which brings structure and firmness to the eggs. It resembles a cake because it is baked in a cake pan and inverted to remove and cool. It retains its shape for slicing, and it stores well, covered, for up to a week in the refrigerator without decreasing in quality.

A flourless chocolate cake may be topped with a berry ganache, a scoop of fruit sorbet, or a simple dusting of cocoa powder and powdered sugar. It is rich, smooth, chocolaty, and very bold.

Icing

Icings, or frostings, are sweet coatings for cakes and other baked goods. Icings have three main functions:

1. They improve the keeping qualities of the cake by forming a protective coating around it.

2. They contribute flavor and richness.

3. They improve appearance.

It is important to always use top-quality flavorings and ingredients for icings so that they will enhance the cake rather than detract from it. Icing should be light and delicate; it should not overwhelm the flavor of the cake. In general, use heavy frostings on heavy cakes, and use light frostings on light cakes. For example, frosting an angel food cake with a heavy fudge icing would cause the cake to collapse. Table 8.5 on the following page shows a number of different types of icings.

526

Table 8.5: Types of Icings

	Buttercream: A very popular icing made of sugar and fat (usually butter or shortening, although shortening often has an unpleasant mouthfeel). Most often used on cakes, in different colors and flavors. Should be used at room temperature.
	Foam: Also called boiled icing, foam icings are made with hot sugar syrup. Bakers often use it on cakes, such as lemon or chocolate. Use it the day it is made and apply it in thick layers.
	Fondant: Smooth and creamy. Cook fondant by combining sugar, water, and a glucose or a corn syrup. Bakers often use it on éclairs, petits fours, cakes, and napoleons. It becomes a shiny, nonsticky coating when dried.
	Fudge: Use cocoa/chocolate, sugar, butter, and a liquid (water or milk) to make fudge icings. Use it on cupcakes, layer, and sheet cakes. Apply it while still warm. Fudge holds well in storage.
	Ganache: This is a French term referring to a smooth mixture of chocolate and cream. Used to cover cakes or tortes. Also used to make truffles.
	Glaze: This icing can be a simple corn syrup glaze, or it can include a fruit or chocolate. Glazes add moisture, shine, and sometimes flavor to bakery products. They are usually drizzled rather than spread.
	Royal icing: Also called decorator's icing, royal icing is almost always used only for decorations. It dries brittle and is an uncooked icing. Make it from confectioners' sugar and egg whites, and color it with food coloring if desired.

527

Table 8.5: Types of Icings

- Icings come in several varieties. Decisions about which icing to use are often visually artistic choices rather than purely flavor or texture choices.

Vocabulary Terms

- **Buttercream:** Fat (butter is best) and confectioner's sugar icing that can be colored, flavored, or both. It is spread with a thin-blade spatula or piped from a bag.

- **Foam:** Boiled sugar syrup icing.

- **Fondant:** A corn-syrup based, candy-type sheeting that is cooked, spread, and cooled and can be applied over a cake for a smooth finish that encases that cake.

- **Fudge:** A cooked chocolate confection that can be spread while warm. A brown-sugar variant without chocolate is called penuche.

- **Ganache:** A rich mixture of chocolate and cream.

- **Glaze:** An icing that is drizzled rather than spread or piped. It might harden a bit on the surface, but stays moist underneath.

- **Royal icing:** A mixture of confectioner's sugar and egg white that can be colored. It dries hard and smooth.

The chimney is actually a vertical extension of the sides of the soufflé dish for support.

Teaching Tips

- Talking about soufflés is not as effective as making them with the students.

- There might be enough time in a class period to try one.

- This chapter does not have a specific recipe for a soufflé, so find one that works well in your local climate and at your altitude.

- Be sure and have a camera ready to photograph each soufflé as it comes out of the oven.

- Take photos a few moments later, if possible, to show the students the life span of a puffy creation like this.

Vocabulary Terms

- **Steamed puddings:** A steamed, cake-like batter dessert often served with a sauce or glaze.

- **Soufflés:** A baked egg structure.

Steamed Puddings and Soufflés

Steamed puddings and dessert soufflés are made of batters that require special handling. **Steamed puddings** are more stable than soufflés because of the greater percentage of eggs and sugar in the batter. Baked custard and chocolate sponge pudding are examples of steamed puddings.

Soufflés (soo-FLAYZ) rely on egg whites and are not as stable as puddings. Soufflés are lightened with beaten egg whites and then baked. Baking causes the soufflé to rise like a cake. As the soufflé rises, the moisture evaporates and the light batter sets temporarily. Chocolate soufflé and almond soufflé are examples of dessert soufflés.

Essential Skills
How to Make a Dessert Soufflé

❶ Prepare a base according to the recipe and have it at room temperature. See Figure 8.6a.

❷ Coat the molds with butter and sugar. Make a chimney and adhere it to the mold, then coat it with butter and sugar to ensure even rising. See Figure 8.6b.

❸ Add any desired flavoring to the base.

❹ Whip the egg whites to a medium peak and fold them into the base. See Figure 8.6c.

❺ Fill the molds and level the tops. See Figure 8.6d.

❻ Bake the soufflé on a sheet pan in a hot oven.

❼ Serve it immediately with whipped cream or the appropriate sweet sauce. See Figure 8.6e.

Figure 8.6a:
Step 1—
Prepare the base.

Figure 8.6b:
Step 2—
Attach the chimney to the mold.

Figure 8.6c:
Step 4—
Whip the egg whites.

Figure 8.6d:
Step 5—
Fill the molds.

Figure 8.6e:
Step 7—
Serve immediately.

528

Figure Focus

Figure 8.6a: The soufflé base is prepared.

Figure 8.6b: The pan has a chimney added to extend the sides upward.

Figure 8.6c: Egg whites are whipped until peaks form.

Figure 8.6d: Fold egg whites into the base.

Figure 8.6e: A soufflé ready for a guest.

[ServSafe Connection]

Handling Custard-Based Pies

Pastry cream is a spoonable custard made with egg yolks. It can be the foundation for cream pie fillings, like banana cream pie. It is rich, smooth, and sweet. It pairs beautifully with delicate, mild banana or coconut. It is topped with a lightly sweetened whipped cream in a single-crust, flaky, non-sweet pie shell.

Custards must be handled carefully because they contain cream and egg yolks. Hold them at 41°F or below, refrigerated in a covered container. As custard pies sit in the cooler, the moisture of the filling makes even the best pie crust a bit soggy. It is best to store the custard separately and fill the baked shell just before serving the pie, if possible. Ideally, there will be no leftovers.

[on the job]

Keeping a Soufflé Light and Fluffy: The Life of a Pastry Chef

A soufflé is a very light, puffy, warm dish. It is made by folding a thick, flavored white sauce base into stiffly beaten egg whites. It is baked at a moderate temperature (usually 350°F) in a buttered, straight-sided round ceramic baking dish set in a water bath.

Baking the soufflé causes it to expand and rise. As the heat bakes the egg in place, the fluffiness is set. It comes out light and airy. Or at least it should! A pastry chef, who is in charge of desserts in the commercial kitchen, needs to take great care in preparing soufflés, as they can fall, or collapse, for a variety of reasons:

- The sauce base may be too thick or the egg whites may be overbeaten and too stiff. Both of these will require too much handling to fold the two together, which causes air to be lost from the mixture.
- If it is baked too hot, the outside will rise and harden before the inside cooks. It will be mushy inside, and the structure will fall over.
- Opening the oven and altering the baking temperature can cause heat to escape the structure too early, making it fall.

All soufflés will fall a little bit as they cool. Serve a soufflé very soon after baking, while it is in its glory and the guests can be impressed. Part of the joy of this dish is the presentation of the beautifully light, puffy wonder. The fastest way to upset a pastry chef is let a soufflé sit too long before service. The grand soufflé will soon be a shrunken shadow of itself!

ServSafe Connection: Handling Custard-Based Pies

If it appears that leftovers might be a problem, consider making individual tarts. Then the shells can be filled individually as the guests are ready to eat them.

On the Job: Keeping a Soufflé Light and Fluffy: The Life of a Pastry Chef

Try baking a soufflé and see how easy or difficult it is.

Use a recipe that is adapted to your locale.

Discuss

- If you were able to make soufflés with the class, did the students enjoy the experience?
- Have them do a "postmortem" discussion about the experience.
- Debrief them, compare notes, and let their thoughts settle.
- You might find their excitement level high when the beautiful creation comes out of the oven.
- Did they enjoy eating it? That is the ultimate test: Is it good food?
- During the debriefing, students might have "down to earth" opinions and ideas for next time.
- Their attitudes are just like the soufflé itself: Exciting and high, then more stable and settled.

Summary

- Remind students to review the following:
1. Quick breads and cake batters
2. Icing
3. Steamed puddings and soufflés

Summary

In this section, you learned the following:

- Quick breads and cakes are popular snack and dessert items and are usually easy and quick to make. Quick breads and cakes use the same mixing methods. Quick breads can be prepared faster than yeast breads. Quick breads use chemical leaveners rather than organic ones, and therefore don't require a rising period. There are four basic methods for preparing quick bread and cake batters:

  - Straight-dough method

  - Creaming method

  - Two-stage method

  - Foaming method

- The mixing technique for biscuits and scones, known as the biscuit method, differs from the four mixing methods mentioned above. Instead of combining all the ingredients at once, rub or cut a fat into the flour until the mixture is mealy or bumpy in appearance.

- Icings are sweet coatings for cakes and other baked goods. The types of icings are buttercream, fondant, foam, fudge, royal icing, and glaze. Icings have three main functions:

  - They improve the keeping qualities of the cake by forming a protective coating around it.

  - They contribute flavor and richness.

  - They improve appearance.

- Steamed puddings and dessert soufflés are made of batters that require special handling. Steamed puddings are more stable because of the greater percentage of eggs and sugar in the batter. Soufflés rely on egg whites and are not as stable as puddings. Lighten soufflés with beaten egg whites and then bake. Baking causes the soufflé to rise like a cake. As the soufflé rises, the moisture evaporates and the light batter sets temporarily.

Section 8.3 Review Questions

1. Explain one difference between a quick bread and a yeast bread.

2. Describe two preparation methods for quick breads and cakes.

3. List the three main functions of icing.

4. Why are steamed puddings more stable than soufflés?

5. Gale Gand talks about "piping buttercream." On what kinds of pastries would you pipe buttercream frosting?

6. One customer reviewer suggested putting a soufflé on the menu. Gauging Kabob's customers' discontent with the dessert creativity and selection against Chef Kate's and Miguel's time and skill levels, would you agree with this suggestion or not? Explain your answer.

7. What role does buttermilk play in leavening quick breads? Do all quick bread recipes have buttermilk? What other ingredients could serve this same purpose?

8. If you were making a dessert menu and had to choose between putting a steamed pudding on the menu or a soufflé, which would you choose and why?

Section 8.3 Review Questions

1. There are several differences: Chemical leavening vs. yeast leavening; Very light mixing vs. kneading; Immediate baking vs. rising time; Tender crumb vs, elastic texture. Students might have additional ideas.

2. See Table 8.4 for specifics.

3. The primary functions of icing are protection, flavor, and appearance. Students might express these ideas in slightly different language.

4. Steamed puddings have more whole eggs and sugar in the batter. Also, they are not dependent on the delicate mechanical leavening of beaten egg whites.

5. Students might have some creative ideas about this. Most typical would be decorated cakes and cupcakes.

6. Each student will have a unique answer. With the delicate, labor-intensive preparation and need for timely serving, this might not be the best dessert choice for Kabob. However, there might be students who make a strong case in favor of offering soufflé.

7. Buttermilk provides acid to react with baking soda to produce carbon dioxide, which will leaven the bread batter. Milk with a little vinegar or lemon juice will do the same thing. Also, fruit juices or even certain types of puréed fruits might provide enough acid for this reaction to occur. Even cream of tartar could be used. Not all recipes have buttermilk, or even acid. If the recipe uses only baking powder, there doesn't need to be additional acid. Baking powder has the acid in it, and the reaction is activated by heat and moisture.

8. The students will have various opinions about this. The steamed pudding is more stable, but the soufflé is more spectacular.

Section 8.3
Activities

1. Tunnels are holes or channels made by escaping gas bubbles. When the gluten is overly developed, the batter structure does not allow the gas bubbles to evenly float to the top. They have to "dig their way out."

2. This is a good, simple activity. It teaches the importance of time planning and remaining on task while baking. It doesn't work to activate the chemical leavening, and then leave the batter sitting to do something else. This is one reason why the baking pans should be prepared and the oven preheated before the batter is mixed.

3. The scone is a small British quick bread (or cake if recipe includes sugar) of Scottish origin. Scones are especially popular in the United Kingdom, Canada, Australia, New Zealand, Ireland, and the United States, but are eaten in many other countries. British scones are often lightly sweetened, but may also be savory—for instance, cheese scones. In the United States, scones are drier, larger, and typically sweet, sometimes including pieces of fruit or chocolate.

Section 8.3 Activities

1. Study Skills/Group Activity: Good Batter, Bad Batter

Overmixing quick bread batter causes tunnels to form in the product. Divide into groups. One group should make a "bad example" muffin with overmixed batter. Slice it open and observe the tunnels. Another group should make a "good example" of a properly mixed muffin. Slice it open to observe the crumb. Compare the two products. Sample them and compare the tenderness.

2. Independent Activity: Leavening Experiment

Baking soda and acid leavening begin to react immediately upon mixing. Mix 1 tablespoon of buttermilk with 1 teaspoon of baking soda. Time the duration of the reaction. How long did it take until the bubble stopped forming? How far in advance of baking can leavenings be activated?

3. Critical Thinking: Scones of the World

Scones are different foods in different regions. Find at least two different types of bread products called scones. Describe the products and the regions they are from.

532

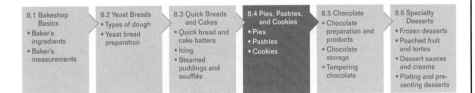

SECTION 8.4 PIES, PASTRIES, AND COOKIES

"As American as apple pie," the saying goes. And it's true to a large extent. Pie is an integral part in just about any festivity in this country, from graduation parties to Thanksgiving. Americans take pie seriously, and so any smart restaurant or foodservice operation should do the same. And for those who may not be the biggest pie fans, there's usually a tempting array of pastries and cookies just an arm's length away. This section will address pies, pastries, and cookies.

Study Questions

After studying Section 8.4, you should be able to answer the following questions:

- What kind of dough is used in pie crusts and how is pie crust made?
- What kind of doughs are used for pastries?
- What kind of dough is used for cookies and what are the seven makeup methods of cookie preparation?

Pies

Pies, croissants, and Danish pastries are all popular baked goods. Pastry chefs make pies using a basic pie dough called **3-2-1 dough**. It's called this because it is made of three parts flour, two parts fat, and one part water (by weight). When it is properly made, the crust is flaky and crisp and often referred to as *pâte brisée* (paht breeze AY). It is important to use pastry flour and work the dough as little as possible. Both the fat and liquid should be cold when mixed into the dough. Pastry chefs use shortening, butter, or lard for the fat, and for the liquid, usually water or milk. When using milk, decrease the amount of fat in the overall formula in proportion to the amount of fat in the dairy.

533

Section 8.4
Pies, Pastries, and Cookies

Introduce the Section

a. Pies are made with a classic pie crust pastry.

b. Pastries have specific types of dough for the type of pastry.

c. Cookies are a very popular and simple dessert option, especially for a quick lunch. Many of the students will have experience with making cookies.

Vocabulary Review

a. Direct students to the key terms.

b. Pronounce each word, and have the students repeat the pronunciation out loud.

c. Discuss the definition of each word.

Teach

Discuss

- "As American as apple pie." Have students heard this statement before reading it in the textbook?

- Have they eaten apple pie? Do they like apple pie?

- Say to the class, "Isn't wheat flour a magical thing?" See how the students respond.

- It can develop gluten and be elastic for bread. It can form a cohesive batter and bake into a fine crumb for cakes and quick breads. It can also form a rollable crust that is tender with golden flakes. It all depends on what it's mixed with and how it's mixed.

Reinforce and Review

- Pie crusts are a special variety of pastry: tender, not kneaded, and flaky.

- Pie crusts themselves are usually not sweet. They help temper the sweetness of the fillings.

- A good pie crust is flavorful yet mild, flaky and light, and golden brown.

Vocabulary Terms

- **3-2-1 dough:** Pie crust with the ratio of 3 parts flour, 2 parts fat, 1 part water.

The essence of pie crust is light handling and rolling to maintain the flakes, caused by fat preventing the gluten from forming long strands. The fat keeps it "short," which is why it's called "shortening." Overmixing will defeat the purpose and develop the gluten, causing it to be tough.

Reinforce and Review

- The cutting process of mixing solid fat into flour is the same process used when making biscuits and scones, as mentioned earlier.

- The cutting keeps the fat in small pieces.

- During baking the pieces melt, forming tiny divisions or layers, which are perceived as "flakes."

- Biscuits, scones, and pie crusts should be tender and flaky, not tough or heavy.

- Biscuits and scones are leavened.

- Pie crusts are not leavened, so they remain flat.

- If a pie crust bubbles up during baking, it is because air was trapped underneath it or within it. Good rolling, then weighing down the crust with filling, helps prevent this.

- A few tiny air holes pierced in the crust helps when baking an unfilled pie shell. So do weights (and see the next page for "baking blind" and "docking").

Essential Skills
Making Pie Dough

1. Dissolve the salt in water.
2. Cut the fat into the flour. See Figure 8.7a.
3. Add the cold water and mix together.
4. Chill the dough.
5. Turn the dough out onto a floured work surface. See Figure 8.7b.
6. Roll out the dough. See Figure 8.7c.
7. Cut the dough and fill the pie pan. See Figure 8.7d.
8. Bake or fill, add a top crust, and bake. See Figure 8.7e.

Figure 8.7a: Step 2—Cut the fat into the flour.

Figure 8.7b: Step 5—Place the dough on a floured surface.

Figure 8.7c: Step 6—Roll out the dough.

Figure 8.7d: Step 7—Fill the pie pan.

Figure 8.7e: Step 8—Add the top crust.

The making of pie crust is an art. When a pastry chef makes the crust properly, it is flaky, tender, and flavorful, the perfect compliment to the filling. A poorly made pie crust is heavy and tough. The magic of the crust is in the "shortening" of the gluten fibers of the wheat flour. Make pie crust by cutting a solid fat into the flour. Properly done, this creates very small pieces of the fat covered in the flour. When rolling a pie crust, handle the dough quickly. During the baking process, the fat particles melt and form flaky, tender layers. Over handling creates tough crusts. Remember, kneading and working dough makes the gluten fibers longer and chewier. That's not what anyone wants in a pie crust.

Some pies rely on a crumb crust for both flavor and texture to compliment the filling. Crumb crusts are a bit simpler to make, and contribute a nutty, buttery flavor that highlights cheesecake or frozen fillings. Make the crumb from crumbled graham crackers, nuts, or cookies. Mix it with butter, sugar, and cinnamon, if desired, and press it into the pie pan; then bake the crust alone or with the filling.

In general, bake pies just until they begin to take on a golden color. If they begin to brown too much before they are done baking, top the pie loosely with aluminum foil near the end of the baking process.

Many pies use fruit fillings. Prepare these fillings using sliced and peeled fresh fruit that is either poached with a liquid or allowed to cook as the entire pas-

Figure Focus

Figure 8.7a: Cutting the fat into the flour.

Figure 8.7b: Gently and barely mixing the dough without kneading.

Figure 8.7c: Quickly rolling out the dough without overworking.

Figure 8.7d: Placing the crust into the pie pan.

Figure 8.7e: Completing the top of the pie before baking.

try bakes. Cornstarch, tapioca, or arrowroot may be added to thicken the fruit filling. Cooks sometimes use lower-grade fruits in baked pies and puddings.

Baking blind is the procedure for preparing a prebaked pie shell. Prepare the dough, roll it out, fit it into the pan, and then **dock** (or pierce) it in several places with a fork. Then cover the pastry with parchment paper and bake it with an empty pie pan, baking weights, or even dry rice or beans on top of it to keep the crust nice and flat as it bakes. Once the pie shell is baked, fill it with custard, pudding, or fresh fruit filling. These are fillings that will not be cooked in the shell; they are precooked as necessary. Refrigerate the pie to set and then serve it cold, often with whipped cream or meringue on top. Examples include chocolate cream pie, banana cream pie, and lemon meringue.

Cheesecake is similar to pie, but unique in many respects. Pastry chefs usually bake it from a cream cheese or **quark** (a cheese that is a lot like sour cream) and egg batter on a crumb crust, using a springform pan. This pan has straight sides rather than the angled sides of a pie pan. But unlike a cake pan, the sides open and can be removed when the cheesecake is done. See Figure 8.8. Slice cheesecake and serve it like a pie. Add fruit, chocolate, or sauces for variety.

Figure 8.8: A springform pan is ideal both for delicate confections and for flourless chocolate cakes and creamy cheesecakes.

In the United States, an unbaked cheesecake is also popular. Make it by coagulating sweetened condensed milk with an acid such as lemon juice. Cream cheese and/or sour cream are often part of this recipe as well. This version is not as delicate or fine as the traditional baked cheesecake.

535

Vocabulary Terms

- **Baking blind:** Baking a pie shell for filling later. It is covered and can't be observed during baking.
- **Dock:** Piercing the pie shell before baking.
- **Quark:** A mild, fresh cheese dairy product.

Figure Focus

Figure 8.8: This type of pan comes apart, so that it comes "off" the cheesecake. This way the cheesecake isn't disturbed.

[fast fact] **Did You Know...?**
A 1-ounce chocolate chip cookie has approximately twice as many calories and grams of fat as a one-ounce slice of blueberry or apple pie. The chocolate chip cookie has approximately 140 calories and 8 grams of fat, compared to roughly 70 calories and 3½ grams of fat for the slice of blueberry or apple pie.

[on the job] **Making Great Pies**
Making a great pie takes some patience, time, and testing in the kitchen. Every great baker has gone through trial and error in perfecting the finished product. Below are a few helpful troubleshooting hints straight from the baker's corner:

- If the dough has been rolled out unevenly, the thicker portions may appear moist, indicating that the dough is not fully baked. To help prevent uneven rolling, use dowel rods on the sides of the dough. This helps ensure uniform consistency and more even cooking.
- The dough should be flaky. If the dough has been underbaked, the texture may be gummy or rubbery. If it has been overbaked, the crust may be tough.

Lard gives a very flaky crust, while shortening gives a more mealy crust. Most mass-produced, commercially made pie crusts use shortening, which is cheaper but yields a product that is inferior to pie crusts made using lard.

Reinforce and Review

- Students will note that many of the same ingredients are used in pie crust and pastry dough.
- The differences between the different foods are not in the ingredients.
- Mixing order and method make a difference, as do handling techniques.
- Even temperature, humidity, and equipment make a difference.
- Observe an expert pastry chef make it look easy, and then try it yourself.

Vocabulary Terms

- **Roll-in dough:** A dough that is rolled and folded into layers.

Pastries

While chefs use 3-2-1 dough for making pie crusts, they use the **roll-in dough** method (also called laminated dough) to make Danish, croissant, and puff pastry. Proper mixing methods, rolling techniques, and temperature control are necessary to produce a flaky, quality product. Roll the dough out into a large rectangle. Then fold it over in thirds, spread it with butter, chill, and roll it out again. Fold it the appropriate number of times to create the right shape for the item. There are a few guidelines to follow in working with this dough:

- Keep the dough chilled.
- Use a sharp knife when shaping and cutting edges.
- Mark the dough with a small indentation to help avoid overrolling.
- Do not run the roller over the dough's edge.
- Chill puff pastry items before baking them.
- Save puff pastry scraps for use in other smaller items.

Puff pastry is an elegant product also called *pâte feuilletée* (paht PHOO e tay) (feuilletée means squares), and it can be used in both sweet and savory applications.

Pastry chefs also commonly use other doughs, such as phyllo and *pâte à choux*, for pastries. Use **phyllo** (FEE-low) dough to prepare baklava, a dessert made of thin pastry, nuts, and honey. Make *pâte à choux* (paht ah SHOE) by combining water (or another liquid), butter, flour, and eggs into a smooth batter. Some familiar desserts that use *pâte à choux* include éclairs, cream puffs, and **profiteroles** (pro-FIT-uh-rolls), which are small round pastries made from *pâte à choux* filled with ice cream. Figure 8.9 shows a variety of pastries made with puff pastry, phyllo, and *pâte à choux*.

Figure 8.9: Pastries made with puff pastry, phyllo, and *pâte à choux*.

Essential Skills
Making Roll-In Dough

❶ Combine ingredients, usually shortening, flour, and water.

❷ Loosely blend the dough. See Figure 8.10a.

❸ Shape into a ball.

❹ Roll into a rectangle. See Figure 8.10b.

❺ Fold into thirds and roll again. See Figure 8.10c.

❻ Cut the dough into shapes called for in the recipe. See Figure 8.10d.

Figure 8.10a: Step 2—Blend the dough.

Figure 8.10b: Step 4—Roll the dough.

Figure 8.10c: Step 5—Fold the dough into thirds.

Figure 8.10d: Step 6—Cut the dough into shapes.

Discuss

- Can the students think of any examples of puff pastry used for a savory dish?
- Perhaps they have tasted sweets made with puff pastry or phyllo dough.

Essential Skills: Making Roll-In Dough

In Austria and southern Germany, this type of dough is used for traditional *Apfelstrüdel*.

Rather than rolling it, it is worked over the fists. It becomes so thin you can read a newspaper through it.

It is rolled over itself to form the layers of crust for the dessert.

Vocabulary Terms

- **Puff pastry:** A delicate layered pastry crust that can be used for sweet or savory dishes.
- *Pâte feuilletée:* Another name for puff pastry.
- **Phyllo:** A type of crispy layered pastry.
- *Pâte à choux:* An egg batter-type pastry.
- **Profiteroles:** Ice cream pastry.

Figure Focus

Figure 8.9: These pastries are each delicate and tender, yet flavorful and rich.

Figure 8.10a: Blend the dough until it is smooth.

Figure 8.10b: Roll out the dough evenly.

Figure 8.10c: Fold the dough.

Figure 8.10d: After it's folded, cutting the dough makes layered pieces.

ServSafe Connection:
How to Care for Cheese Danish

Second-day Danish that has been refrigerated can be gently warmed through, but not warm enough to melt or cook the cheese filling.

Nutrition:
Budgeting for Desserts

Beautiful desserts are not generally "snack foods," nor should they be. They are a complete course of a fine meal. They are a special indulgence for guests to enjoy in a relaxed, unhurried, and congenial way.

Discuss

- Students might realize that cookies are efficient desserts to make.

- See if they understand why they are efficient. (You can make so many of them at a time.)

- Perhaps students will consider that this is cost-effective in many cases.

- Help students realize that there is great skill involved in making fine cookies, even if they seem simple and commonplace to bake.

- However, students probably have enough experience with cookies to be able to describe a truly bad cookie.

- What are the traits of a truly bad cookie? Students might mention these things, among others:

  - Burnt
  - Underdone
  - Tough
  - Boring
  - Too sweet
  - Icing too thick
  - Too crispy and fragile
  - Lump of baking soda
  - Stale
  - Greasy

- As a class, see if students can brainstorm ways to remedy these various problems.

- Assure them that if they don't understand the remedies yet, they will after studying the textbook.

- Encourage them to bake cookies at home after studying their text.

[ServSafe Connection]

How to Care for Cheese Danish

Danish pastry is a yeast dough shortened with butter. Pastry chefs use this dough to make individual rolls filled with fruit, nuts, chocolate, or mild cheese (like cream cheese or quark). It is tender and flaky, but chewy and elastic. It has the best qualities of both bread and pastry.

Danish pastry is best eaten fresh, but may be stored for a day. It is subject to mold. Storing cheese Danish causes a problem. Due to the protein and fat content of the mild cheese, it should be refrigerated. However, refrigeration dries and toughens the pastry.

You must refrigerate Danish according to typical storage guidelines for TCS food, but the best approach is to try to carefully match your needs to a daily delivery of freshly made Danish. In a perfect world, there won't be any left over to store.

Cookies

Pastry chefs make most cookies from rich dough. Typically, rich dough uses the same creaming method as quick breads and cake batters, but with the liquid and the flour added at the same time. The creaming of the dough determines the texture of the cookie and how much it will spread in the pan during baking.

Cookies should be decorative and appetizing. Due to their high sugar content, cookies are best when they are baked in convection ovens. In a convection oven, the air is pulled in by the fan, then gently pushed out through the holes, so it creates a gentler environment for baked goods that tend to burn quickly because of their high sugar content. Table 8.6 on the following page describes the seven makeup methods for cookies.

[nutrition]

Budgeting for Desserts

Fat and/or sugar are high in many desserts, which can cause a problem if people eat them too often. However, everyone needs calories, fat, and some simple carbohydrates. So, it's okay to allocate some of a daily allowance of calories, fat, and sugar to delicious, beautiful, and well-made desserts—especially on a special occasion!

Table 8.6: Types of Cookies

	Bagged: Make bagged cookies by forcing soft dough through a pastry bag. Varieties include ladyfingers, macaroons, and tea cookies.
	Bar: Make bar cookies by baking three or four bars of dough the length of the baking pan, and then slicing them into small bars. One variety is biscotti.
	Dropped: Make dropped cookies, such as chocolate chip and oatmeal, from a soft dough and drop them from a spoon or scoop onto the cookie sheet.
	Icebox: Make icebox cookies by rolling dough into a log, chilling it, and then slicing it just before baking. Butterscotch icebox cookies and chocolate icebox cookies are examples.
	Molded: Mold stiff dough by hand into any shape to make molded cookies. Peanut butter cookies are an example.
	Rolled: Rolled cookies are made more often at home than in commercial kitchens because they take a lot of work. Cut these cookies from a stiff dough that has been rolled out on a baking board. Varieties include decorated sugar cookies and shortbread.
	Sheet: Pour the batter into the entire baking pan and then slice it into individual squares or rectangles after baking. Brownies are usually made this way. Other types of sheet cookies include butterscotch brownies or blondies.

539

Table 8.6: Types of Cookies

Encourage students to discuss the following:

- Which cookies are they most familiar with?
- Which are the easiest to make?

Teaching Tips

- Teaching teenagers about cookies doesn't need much textbook support. Have fun.

Vocabulary Terms

- **Bagged:** Cookies made from piped dough.
- **Bar:** Cookies made from a long piece of dough, sliced after baking.
- **Dropped:** Cookies made by spoonfuls of dough.
- **Icebox:** Cookies made from chilled dough.
- **Molded:** Cookies shaped by hand or in a mold.
- **Rolled:** Cookies made from rolled and cut dough.
- **Sheet:** Cookies made from spreading dough, baking it, and slicing it into servings.

Summary

- Remind students to review the following:
  1. Pies
  2. Pastries
  3. Cookies

Summary

In this section, you learned the following:

- Make pie crusts using a basic pie dough called 3-2-1 dough. It's called this because it is made of three parts flour, two parts fat, and one part water (by weight). Made properly, the crust is flaky and crisp. It is important to use pastry flour and work the dough as little as possible. Make sure both the fat and liquid are cold when mixed into the dough. The fats used are shortening, butter, or lard, and the liquid is usually water, milk, or cream. Many pies use fruit fillings. Prepare these fillings using sliced and peeled fresh fruit that is either poached with a liquid or allowed to cook as the entire pastry bakes.

- Use the roll-in dough method for Danish, croissant, and puff pastry. Proper mixing methods, rolling techniques, and temperature control are necessary to produce a flaky, quality product. Roll the dough out into a large rectangle. Then, fold the dough over in thirds, roll it out again, and then fold it the appropriate number of times to create the shape the recipe calls for. Pastry chefs also commonly use other doughs, such as phyllo and *pâte à choux,* for pastries. Use phyllo dough to prepare baklava, a dessert made of thin pastry, nuts, and honey. Make *pâte à choux* by combining water (or another liquid), butter, flour, and eggs into a smooth batter.

- Pastry chefs make most cookies from rich dough. Typically, rich dough uses the same creaming method as quick breads and cake batters, but with the liquid and the flour added at the same time. The creaming of the dough determines the texture of the cookie and how much it will spread in the pan during baking. Cookies should be colorful and appetizing. Due to their high sugar content, cookies are best when they are baked in convection ovens. There are seven makeup methods for cookies: dropped, bagged, rolled, molded, icebox, bar, and sheet.

Section 8.4 Review Questions

1. What kind of dough is pie usually made of?

2. What are the ingredients and proportions in 3-2-1 dough?

3. What is roll-in dough used to make?

4. List three makeup methods for cookies and describe each of them.

5. Gale Gand talks about baking pumpkin pies for Thanksgiving. Find recipes for two other traditional holiday pies served around Thanksgiving. Find at least two different recipes for each pie and compare them. How are they alike? How are they different?

6. One thing Chef Kate and Miguel are certain of is that they want to have one house-made pie on the new menu. Which pie would you select for them and why? Remember to take into account cost, appeal, and labor.

7. Why is the roll-in dough method useful in making lighter pastries?

8. Why is lard better to use in pie-crust making than shortening?

541

Section 8.4 Review Questions

1. Pie crusts are usually made from 3-2-1 dough.

2. By weight, 3-2-1 dough is 3 parts flour, 2 parts fat, and 1 part water.

3. Roll-in dough makes Danish, croissants, and puff pastry.

4. Each method is described in Table 8.6.

5. Each student's findings will be different.

6. Each student's answer and opinion will be different.

7. More air is incorporated between the layers.

8. Students might need to research this for more information than is found in the text. The lard fat is saturated and hard at room temperature, but does not have the milk solids of butter (which can burn). Tiny particles of lard melt as the dough is baking in a way perfect for making flaky layers of crust. Shortening is a hydrogenated vegetable fat, so it is saturated but has a lower melting point. It can turn a crust slightly soggy in comparison. However, a shortening crust can still be very good.

Section 8.4
Activities

1. Students might need to do some additional research to learn about emulsified shortening. It is also known as cake, icing, or high-ratio shortening. Emulsifying means that it can mix with water, whereas other fats separate from water. It can mix better with sugar and liquid than regular shortening. It gives a fine and smooth texture to cakes. It can keep cakes and icings moist and stable, resistant to separation. However, it should be used in icings and high-ratio cakes where the recipe contains a large percentage of sugar.

2. Here is some information about *Linzer Augen*, pronounced LINT-zer OW-gan. *Linzer* means from the city of Linz ("lintz"). *Augen* means "eyes." These cookies look sort of like eyes, as they are a flat butter cookie topped with raspberry or apricot jam, then topped with a ring of cookie dough and baked. They are then dusted with confectioner's sugar.

   There are cookies from all over the world that the students might research.

3. Use the information in Table 8.6 as a starting point for this research.

Section 8.4 Activities

1. Study Skills/Group Activity: Comparing Shortenings

In kitchen stations, compare the characteristics of regular and emulsified shortening. Compare the plasticity (spreadability), melting point, weight by volume, feel, and any other traits that might be considered. Why would emulsified shortening be best for light, high-ratio cakes?

2. Independent Activity: Cookies of the World

Research a traditional cookie from a foreign country. For example, you might select a cookie from Austria called the *Linzer Augen*. Describe the cookie, where it is from, and how it is made.

3. Critical Thinking: Cookie Makeup Methods

Research two cookie makeup methods. How does each work? Why is each used? What kinds of cookies are produced though each method? Then, compare and contrast the two in one-page report.

542

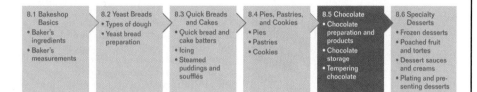

SECTION 8.5 CHOCOLATE

Chocolate has a long and colorful history. The Mayans believed it was a divine food from the gods. The French once thought it to be a dangerous drug. And many people and cultures throughout the ages have associated chocolate with love and romance, which seems especially appropriate given how many people simply love eating it. In fact, chocolate is more popular than ever. There are more varieties and types of chocolate available than ever before. Restaurant and foodservice operations can capitalize on this trend, but chefs need to know the basics of chocolate first. This section covers how chocolate is made, stored, and tempered.

Study Questions

After studying Section 8.5, you should be able to answer the following questions:

- How is chocolate made?
- How is chocolate stored?
- How is chocolate tempered?

Chocolate Preparation and Products

Chocolate is produced from cocoa beans picked from cacao trees. Americans usually think of chocolate as a sweet, used in cookies, candies, cakes, and other desserts. However, chocolate is very versatile and can be used in many main dishes.

To make chocolate, processors roast the cocoa beans, as shown in Figure 8.11 on the following page. Machinery loosens the outer shells and cracks the beans

543

Section 8.5
Chocolate

Introduce the Section

a. Chocolate is a food that evokes romance, mystery, and even love.

b. Chocolate is usually included on any dessert menu.

c. Knowing how to handle, store, and cook with chocolate is a foundation of dessert craft.

Vocabulary Review

a. Direct students to the key terms.

b. Pronounce each word, and have the students repeat the pronunciation out loud.

c. Discuss the definition of each word.

Teach

Discuss

- Chocolate is actually a South American bean product that has flavorful solids and rich fat.

- Chocolate also has very mild drug properties, due to theobromine and traces of caffeine.

- The "theo" part of theobromine means "gods," and chocolate is nicknamed the food of the gods.

Table 8.7:
Chocolate and Related Products

- Each aspect of Table 8.7 involves industrial food science know-how.

Reinforce and Review

- Chocolatiering is a science, skill, craft, art, and entire industry.

- A chef can build an entire career on chocolate.

Teaching Tips

- If there is any access, a tour of a chocolate factory or processing plant would be valuable.

- Perhaps a local chocolatier would be willing to guest lecture the class.

- A video presentation about chocolate making would also be effective.

- There are also Web sites by chocolatiers that show the process of making chocolate from harvesting and processing of cacao beans and working with chocolate, all the way to manufacture of the finished product. At the time of publication, two such sites of interest are www.demel.at (translate page to English, or choose the English option or the New York location) and www.amanochocolate.com.

- Cocoa powder is shelf-stable, whereas cocoa butter itself is vulnerable to deterioration.

Vocabulary Terms

- **Nibs:** Pieces of cocoa beans.

- **Chocolate liquor:** Cocoa bean paste.

- **Cocoa butter:** The fat, or lipid, portion of cocoa beans.

- **Cocoa powder:** Ground chocolate solids.

Figure 8.11: Roasted cocoa beans.

into small pieces, called nibs. Nibs are the basis of all cocoa products. The cocoa beans are then crushed into a paste that is completely unsweetened, called chocolate liquor. Chocolate liquor may be ground (possibly with other ingredients, such as sweeteners or flavorings) to give it an even smoother texture, or it may be pressed to separate the liquid from the solid materials. The liquid is cocoa butter, which can be combined with chocolate liquor to make eating chocolate, or flavored and sweetened to make white chocolate. The solids are further ground to form cocoa powder. For a full list of chocolate products, see Table 8.7.

Table 8.7: Chocolate and Related Products

Type	Description	Purchase Form
Chocolate, bittersweet	Solid chocolate made with 35–50% chocolate liquor, 15% cocoa butter, and 35–50% sugar; interchangeable with semi-sweet chocolate; may have added ingredients, such as nuts, fillings, stabilizers, emulsifiers, and/or preservatives	Solid, in blocks, bars, chunks, and chips
Chocolate liquor	Chocolate-flavored portion of the chocolate; obtained by grinding and liquefying chocolate nibs	(See Chocolate, unsweetened)
Chocolate, semi-sweet	Solid chocolate made with about 45% chocolate liquor, 15% cocoa butter, and 40% sugar; interchangeable with bittersweet chocolate; may have added ingredients	Solid, in blocks, bars, chunks, and chips
Chocolate, unsweetened (bitter or baking)	Solid chocolate made with about 95% chocolate liquor, 5% cocoa butter, and 5% sugar and other flavorings	Solid, in blocks or bars
Cocoa	Chocolate from which all but 10–25% of the cocoa butter has been removed	Powder, in bulk and cans
Cocoa, breakfast	Cocoa with at least 22% cocoa butter	Powder, in bulk and cans
Cocoa butter	Vegetable fat portion of chocolate; removed for cocoa; added for chocolate	Wrapped in plastic at room temperature
Cocoa, Dutch process	Cocoa from which all but 22–24% of the cocoa butter has been removed; treated with alkali to reduce its acidity	Powder, in bulk and cans
Cocoa, instant	Cocoa that has been precooked, sweetened (usually about 80% sugar), and emulsified to make it dissolve more easily in liquid; may have powdered milk added	Powder, in bulk and cans
Cocoa, low-fat	Cocoa with less than 10% cocoa butter	Powder, in bulk and cans

544

Figure Focus

Figure 8.11: From harvesting cacao beans to finishing fine chocolate, the process is highly specialized.

Essential Skills
Tasting Chocolate

Because chocolate is such a key ingredient in so many dishes, it is important to get a sense of what the various types of chocolate taste like so you know how each type of chocolate will affect the overall flavor profile of a dish. Tasting is much different from eating. There's more to it than simply popping a piece of chocolate into your mouth and chewing it until it's gone. In fact, the less chewing you do during a tasting the better. Below are simple guidelines to follow when taste-testing chocolate:

❶ Get situated in a quiet, distraction-free environment, so you can concentrate fully on the taste, texture, and smell of each piece of chocolate. See Figure 8.12a.

❷ Have a notepad on hand to write down your immediate impressions.

Figure 8.12a: Step 1—Get ready to taste the chocolate.

❸ Make sure your palate is clean for each taste. Have a glass of water on hand to cleanse your palate of any residual food or taste. A piece of bread or unsalted crackers also help to wipe out lingering tastes. See Figure 8.12b.

❹ Never taste cold chocolate, as the chill masks the true flavors of the chocolate.

❺ Allow the chocolate to dissolve slowly in your mouth. Do not bite into it right away. Ideally, you won't bite or chew it all. Instead just let it melt in your mouth.

❻ Note how the flavor evolves over time. How does it taste when it first touches your tongue? How does the taste change as it begins to melt? How does it finish after it's fully dissolved?

Figure 8.12b: Step 3—Make sure your palate is clean.

❼ Keep a record of all of this, making sure to note the type of chocolate, how it looked, smelled, and tasted at the beginning and end. Keeping such a record will help you refine your use of chocolate in your dishes, which will help you refine your menu overall.

545

Figure Focus

Figure 8.12a: Chocolate for tasting is in small pieces, but enough for a good evaluation.

Figure 8.12b: Water is a good way to cleanse the flavor of a sample before trying another sample.

In-Class Activity: A Chocolate Cutting (Tasting)

Science Connection

The students can taste samples of various types and brands of chocolate.

Will the chocolate be evaluated for color, flavor, mouthfeel, aroma, finish, depth, sweetness, and other features? Determine evaluation criteria in advance and make a standard form.

Identify the pieces by number only.

Have water available for the students to drink between samples.

Have a really good time!

ServSafe Connection: Can Chocolate Go Bad?

Cocoa powder does not have the fat or sugar content of chocolate, so it can be stored on a shelf for a long time. The flavor remains stable for at least a year.

Vocabulary Terms

- **Bloom:** A harmless yet unsightly white coating appearing on chocolate under adverse conditions.

Chocolate Storage

To store chocolate, wrap it carefully, and keep it in a cool, dry, well-ventilated area. Do not refrigerate chocolate. Refrigeration causes moisture to condense on the surface of the chocolate. In hot, humid weather, however, refrigeration or freezing may be necessary to prevent flavor loss.

Sometimes a white coating, called **bloom**, appears on the surface of the chocolate, shown on Figure 8.13. The bloom indicates that some of the cocoa butter has melted and then recrystallized on the surface. This has no effect on the quality, but it does detract from the chocolate's visual appeal. Properly stored, chocolate will last for several months. Cocoa powder stored in tightly sealed containers in a dry place will keep almost indefinitely, although most operations use a one-year rule for keeping this product.

Figure 8.13: Chocolate with bloom.

[ServSafe Connection]

Can Chocolate Go Bad?

Chocolate is not prone to growing microbes, so it does not have to be stored in the refrigerator. It can be stored on the shelf at room temperature for a year. After that, the fats can lose their smoothness and become a bit grainy or mealy.

If the storage is too hot, however, the fat in chocolate can oxidize and become rancid. Rancid chocolate might give you a stomachache if swallowed, but you probably wouldn't get that far, as it would taste and smell off. Follow these guidelines for storing chocolate:

- Carefully wrap chocolate to prevent unwanted pests from eating it.
- If it has melted and rehardened, check for rancidity.
- If the chocolate contains nuts, it shortens the shelflife to that of the particular nut. Six months is the maximum for a chocolate bar with fresh roasted nuts at room temperature.
- Storing chocolate in the refrigerator or freezer can alter the smoothness of it, but it is still safe to eat, even if it has a whitish bloom on it. However, it might not melt as evenly, or have the same mouthfeel.
- Cocoa powder is very stable. Once a container is opened, it can usually be stored until it's used up, but a year is a good guideline. Keep the container closed and/or covered. Unopened airtight containers of cocoa can be stored indefinitely.

546

Figure Focus

Figure 8.13: Bloom on chocolate does not look good, but it is not harmful. It can be caused by humid weather, or by freezing and thawing chocolate.

Tempering Chocolate

Handle chocolate very carefully when using it in cooking. Chocolate contains two distinct types of fat that melt at different temperatures. Cooks melt chocolate in a process called **tempering**, melting the chocolate by heating it gently and gradually. This ensures that both fats melt smoothly, harden evenly, and have a good shine. To temper chocolate, chop the chocolate into coarse pieces and place it in a **double boiler**, a stainless steel bowl over water simmering on very low heat. Figure 8.14 shows a commercial double boiler. It is important not to get water into the chocolate, or it will become grainy.

Figure 8.14: A double boiler for melting chocolate.

Reinforce and Review

- A double boiler works to protect the chocolate from overheating.

- Double boilers heat with steam that transfers heat from the stovetop pan to the upper pan or bowl.

- The upper pan or bowl does not come in direct contact with the boiling water or the stovetop.

- The steam rises when the water reaches 212°F (at sea level), gently warming the upper pan to this degree and not beyond.

- The trick to using a double boiler is making sure the lower pan does not boil dry. If this happens, the entire system can overheat.

- In addition to chocolate, double boilers are useful for reheating hollandaise sauce or other things that need gentle warming.

Vocabulary Terms

- **Tempering:** Carefully and slowly melting chocolate over a double boiler.

- **Double boiler:** A bowl or pan that fits over a stovetop pan for simmering water. The steam heat from the water gently transfers heat to the bowl or pan on top without overheating it.

Figure Focus
Figure 8.14: A picture of a double boiler with a large bowl-type top portion.

Reinforce and Review

- It is important to carefully and closely monitor temperature and warming of chocolate.

- Tempering chocolate is a delicate process that will be worth the effort.

Nutrition:
Is Dark Chocolate Really Nutritious?

Antioxidants are more abundant in fresh fruits and vegetables than in dark chocolate. Milk chocolate does not have the same antioxidants as dark chocolate. Enjoy it for what it is!

Once the temperature of the chocolate reaches 105°F, remove it from the heat. Add more chocolate pieces and stir until the temperature drops to 87°F. Then place the pot back on the heat to raise the temperature to 92°F. Make sure that the tempered chocolate does not become grainy or scorched. If it does, discard it. Tempered chocolate will coat items with an even layer and then harden into a shiny shell.

To coat a food item, dip it directly into the tempered chocolate, or place it on a rack over a clean tray and pour the chocolate over it. Tempered chocolate can be drizzled or piped out into designs with a piping bag for decoration, or can be used as a glaze.

[nutrition]

Is Dark Chocolate Really Nutritious?
Dark chocolate's health benefits are often trumpeted, so let's separate fact from fiction.

It's definitely not a smart, healthful strategy to eat lots of chocolate, which is high in fat and sugar. But it is true that dark chocolate contains some antioxidants. Antioxidant chemicals help fight the damaging effects of aging. They also fight cancer and other illnesses. So while there are certainly better food sources for antioxidants than chocolate, it's nice to know that a piece of dark chocolate now and then is helping you towards that end.

Chocolate also has an insignificant amount of caffeine. It has more of a compound called theobromine, caffeine's weaker chemical cousin. Theobromine can cause a slight sense of energetic euphoria and may be slightly addictive—perhaps that's why some chocolate lovers actually describe themselves as "addicts."

So is chocolate good for you? A little bit, maybe, but don't go overboard. As always, use moderation and good sense in maintaining a healthy diet.

Summary

In this section, you learned the following:

- Chocolate is produced from cocoa beans picked from cacao trees. Chocolate is very versatile and can be used in many main dishes, such as Chicken Mole or chicken with chocolate sauce. To make chocolate, processors roast the cocoa beans. Machinery loosens the outer shells and cracks the beans into small pieces, called nibs. Nibs are the basis of all cocoa products. The cocoa beans are then crushed into a paste that is completely unsweetened, called chocolate liquor. Chocolate liquor may be ground (possibly with other ingredients, such as sweeteners or flavorings) to give it an even smoother texture, or it may be pressed to separate the liquid from the solid materials. The liquid is cocoa butter, which can be combined with chocolate liquor to make eating chocolate, or flavored and sweetened to make white chocolate. The solids are further ground to form cocoa powder.

- To store chocolate, wrap it carefully, and keep it in a cool, dry, well-ventilated area. Do not refrigerate chocolate. Refrigeration causes moisture to condense on the surface of the chocolate. In hot, humid weather, however, refrigeration or freezing may be necessary to prevent flavor loss. Properly stored, chocolate will last for several months. Cocoa powder stored in tightly sealed containers in a dry place will keep almost indefinitely, although most operations use a one-year rule for keeping this product.

- Chocolate contains two distinct types of fat that melt at different temperatures. Cooks melt chocolate in a process called tempering, melting the chocolate by heating it gently and gradually. This ensures that both fats melt smoothly, harden evenly, and have a good shine. To temper chocolate, chop the chocolate into coarse pieces and place it in a double boiler, a stainless steel bowl over water simmering on very low heat. It is important not to get water into the chocolate. Once the temperature of the chocolate reaches 105°F, remove it from the heat. Add more chocolate pieces and stir until the temperature drops to 87°F. Then place the pot back on the heat to raise the temperature to 92°F. Make sure that the tempered chocolate does not become grainy or scorched. If it does, discard it. Tempered chocolate will coat items with an even layer and then harden into a shiny shell.

549

Summary

- Remind students to review the following:
  1. Chocolate preparation and products
  2. Chocolate storage
  3. Tempering chocolate

Section 8.5
Review Questions

1. Cocoa butter is made by extracting the fat from cocoa beans.

2. Nibs are tiny pieces of cocoa beans.

3. Refrigerating chocolate can cause the fat portion to crystallize, which can cause bloom.

4. There are two types of fat in chocolate.

5. The students will each have a different answer for this.

6. Each student will have an opinion on this.

7. The chocolate can become grainy, which ruins the mouthfeel. It can also become scorched, which ruins the flavor.

8. The students can research this information in greater detail than what is offered in the text. The process is very old and began in South America. Europeans did not know about chocolate until after Christopher Columbus and the other early explorers came to the Americas.

Section 8.5 Review Questions

1. How is cocoa butter made?

2. What are nibs?

3. Why should you avoid refrigerating chocolate if possible?

4. How many types of fat are in chocolate?

5. Gale Gand specifically mentions dipping truffles in melted chocolate and placing each in cocoa powder. Research a dessert recipe for something else that can be dipped in melted chocolate.

6. Miguel and Chef Kate are thinking about putting a chocolate dessert on the menu. What kind of dessert would you choose for them and why?

7. The process for tempering chocolate is very intricate. What do you think would happen if you heated it all at once without following the process described in the text? Do you think the texture would change? If so, how? Do you think the taste would change? Explain your rationale.

8. What is the history behind chocolate making? Who first discovered the process for making modern chocolate? How many steps are involved?

550

Section 8.5 Activities

1. Study Skills/Group Activity: Blooming Stations

Set up stations for causing "bloom" to happen to chocolate: A steam station, an ice station, a cold-air (refrigerator) station, and a warm-air station. (Be sure to be careful with the heat source!) Expose one freshly made chocolate drop to each condition. Note your findings and compare with the rest of the class.

2. Independent Activity: Perfect Chocolate-Dipped Strawberry

In class, have a contest to produce The Perfect Chocolate-Dipped Strawberry. Rate the product from 1 to 5 on the following criteria: quality of the berry, ease of eating, smoothness of the chocolate, appearance, and shine of the cooled chocolate.

3. Critical Thinking: White Chocolate

Research white chocolate. What is it? How is it made? Write a one-page report about white chocolate and its common uses in cuisine.

551

Section 8.5 Activities

1. Set up this activity to be done in groups. Have students keep careful records. Have students evaluate the various station results for bloom. Are some bloom station conditions worse for the chocolate than others? Remind students that bloom is not harmful to eat.

2. This activity is best done in the late spring when strawberries are in season. It is possible to purchase strawberries at other times of year, however.

3. Each student's answers will be different. They should include the basic fact that white chocolate is not really chocolate. Sometimes it is made from cocoa butter; however, most commercially available white chocolate is made of a hardened oil and flavorings.

Section 8.6
Specialty Desserts

Introduce the Section
a. Frozen desserts come in several varieties.
b. Desserts include specialty sauces and creams that are part of dessert creations.
c. There is a growing demand for low-sugar and sugarless desserts for guests with diabetes.

Vocabulary Review
a. Direct students to the key terms.
b. Pronounce each word, and have the students repeat the pronunciation out loud.
c. Discuss the definition of each word.

Teach

Discuss
- Guests enjoy frozen desserts in the summertime.
- Do they only sell in the summertime?
- Do you only eat frozen desserts when the weather is hot?

Reinforce and Review
- There are several types of frozen desserts from various cuisines.
- Some frozen desserts are low in fat, but others are quite high in fat.

Vocabulary Terms
- **Ice cream:** Frozen and aerated cream custard and flavorings.

SECTION 8.6 SPECIALTY DESSERTS

The dessert specialties described in this section are as ageless as they are timeless. Ice cream and frozen treats are staple American desserts, enjoyed by kids and adults alike. Poached fruit and tortes have been favorites for centuries, and the wide variety of dessert creams and sauces enhance the taste of most any dish. In this section, each of these items are discussed, as are the best ways to plate and present desserts, a skill no successful foodservice operation can or should overlook.

Study Questions

After studying Section 8.6, you should be able to answer the following questions:

- What are the different types of frozen desserts?
- What are poached fruit and tortes?
- What are dessert sauces and creams?
- How should desserts be plated and presented?

Frozen Desserts

Ice cream has a long history as a dessert favorite. To be accurately labeled "ice cream," ice cream must contain a certain amount of milkfat. Vanilla ice cream must contain no less than 10 percent milkfat; other flavors must contain at least 8 percent milkfat. Quality ice cream has a custard base (cream and/or milk and eggs), melts readily in the mouth, and does not weep, or separate, when it softens at room temperature. Ice cream can be served as part of a larger dish, on its own, or in one of its many forms (ice cream bar, ice cream float, ice cream sundae, etc.).

552

CUSTOMIZED INSTRUCTION

Literacy Connection, 21st Century Skills—Think Creatively

Less Advanced Students

Have students name and describe five flavors of ice cream, sherbet, frozen yogurt, sorbet, or gelato.

All words should be correctly spelled.

They can use flavors that are already on the market, or make some up.

ESOL Students

Have students name and correctly spell five flavors of ice cream.

Have them cut out or draw very simple color pictures of what the ice cream would look like.

Have them write a simple description (color, flavor, etc.).

All words should be correctly used and spelled.

Special Needs Students

Have students identify possible flavors for five photos or drawings of ice cream.

For example, a dish of pink ice cream could be strawberry, bubble gum, or another pink flavor.

If appropriate, have students write the name of the ice cream flavor, correctly spelled.

More Advanced Students

Have students create five new flavors of ice cream, sherbet, frozen yogurt, sorbet, or gelato.

Have them name the new flavors.

Have them describe the special ingredients in the frozen dessert.

All words should be correctly spelled.

Gelato is an Italian version of ice cream that is gaining in popularity. It's made with most of the same ingredients as ice cream, but does not contain eggs. Gelato is often made with whole milk, but rarely with cream.

Sherbets and sorbets are frozen mixtures of fruit juice or fruit purée. **Sherbet** contains milk and/or egg for creaminess; **sorbet** contains no dairy, just fruit juice or purée with sweeteners and other flavors or additives. Serve sorbet as a first course, as a palate cleanser between courses, or as a dessert. Serve sherbets as a dessert item, as a rule.

Frozen yogurt contains yogurt in addition to the normal ice cream ingredients, such as sugar or other sweeteners, gelatin, coloring, and flavors. Make frozen yogurt with non-fat or low-fat yogurt. Frozen yogurt both freezes and melts more slowly than ice cream. Figure 8.15 shows various frozen desserts.

[fast fact]

Did You Know . . . ?
Americans consume approximately 23 quarts of frozen desserts each year. That's more than a pint a week for every man, woman, and child in the United States.

Figure 8.15: Frozen desserts: ice cream, gelato, sorbet, sherbet, and frozen yogurt.

553

Discuss

- Ask students to discuss and describe their favorite types of frozen desserts.
- Can they verbally describe their own experiences with ice cream, sherbet, and other frozen desserts?
- Do they have the descriptors to meaningfully express the characteristics of the desserts?

Reinforce and Review

- Gelato is sold in stores, little shops, carts, and stands in Italy.
- There are usually several flavors laid out in slabs in a temperature-controlled display case.
- Gelato is served with a scoop or a blade-style spoon into cones or cups.
- Gelato is more elastic than ice cream, due to stabilizers.
- The most popular flavors of gelato include chocolate, lemon, pistachio, cherry, and spumoni.

Fast Fact:
Did You Know . . . ?

The Pacific Northwest beats the rest of the nation in per capita ice cream consumption, so they aren't just drinking coffee in Portland or Seattle.

Vocabulary Terms

- **Sherbet:** A frozen fruit and milk dessert.
- **Sorbet:** A dairy-free frozen fruit ice.
- **Frozen yogurt:** A yogurt-based ice cream-type dessert that substitutes yogurt and perhaps thickeners for cream.

Figure Focus

Figure 8.15: Even lower-calorie frozen desserts can be delicious. Ask students what some of their favorites are.

Nutrition: Sugar-Free Ice Cream

Legal artificial sweeteners are not considered harmful by the Food and Drug Administration. For a diabetic guest, they are certainly less harmful than regular sugar.

Reinforce and Review

- Foods with artificial sweeteners, soy, and other substitutions used to be considered useful for sick people, not for "regular" people.

- Our culture is shifting as people recognize the benefits of new formulations.

- Sometimes they genuinely are improvements for flavor, health, nutrition, price, storage, convenience, religious dietary laws, and even disease accommodation.

- Poached fruit need not be poached only in water.

- Fruit juices, light wines, and liqueurs can be used to simmer fruit.

What's New: Cream-Free Ice Cream?

Kosher dietary guidelines preclude combining meat and milk or their derivatives in the same dish or even meal.

Vocabulary Terms

- **Poached fruit:** Fruit that is gently heated or simmered in liquid until tender.

[nutrition]

Sugar-Free Ice Cream

Diabetes is on the increase in the United States. A treatable, yet life-altering and life-threatening disease, diabetes requires diligent attention to a low-sugar diet. Persons with diabetes cannot properly digest dietary sugar because their bodies don't produce insulin, a hormone that controls sugar glucose in the blood. They must carefully select their food accordingly. Does this rule out desserts completely? In most cases, yes, unless the desserts are adapted to the needs of the diabetic customer.

Artificial sweeteners have opened new horizons of cuisine to diabetics. Aspartame, saccharine, sucralose, acesulfame K, and neotame are all available to consumers now. Desserts made with these ingredients can be sweet and delicious.

Each sugar substitute performs differently in baking, boiling, holding, refrigeration, freezing, etc. Some stay deliciously sweet under a particular set of circumstances, while others might go bitter. Research the best alternative sweetener for a given recipe. Seek out ways to include some sugar-free high-quality desserts for your diabetic customers. The word will spread!

[what's new]

Cream-Free Ice Cream?

Soy beans can be finely ground and made into a smooth emulsion with oil and water. This is called soy milk. This milk can be coagulated and pressed into a semi-solid form. In Asian cuisine, this form is called **tofu**. Tofu can be used as a substitute for cheese, cream, or milk in recipes if handled correctly. Tofu contains no dairy, no meat, and no eggs.

David Mintz, a Manhattan restaurateur, served only kosher menu items at his deli. But he wanted to expand his menu to include mixed dishes (like lasagna) that combine milk products and meat, which is not kosher. He experimented with tofu and learned to seamlessly substitute it for the dairy foods. The customers could not tell the difference, to the point that some kosher guests were offended. He assured them that what they were eating was, indeed, kosher.

He saw the potential for a frozen ice cream-like dessert made from tofu. After much experimentation, trial, and error, he developed delicious Tofutti®. That was 30 years ago. Since then, the value of soy-based desserts has been realized on a large scale, and there are now soy-based frozen desserts accessible at most any supermarket. Soy-based desserts are more than just kosher. They are cholesterol-free, dairy-free, lactose-free, egg-free, and vegan. What a great invention!

Poached Fruit and Tortes

To **poach fruit**, combine fruit with a liquid, usually a mixture of sugar, spices, and wine. Heat the fruit and liquid together until the fruit is tender. Test for doneness with a fork; the fruit is fully poached when it is easy to pierce. The greater the amount of sugar in the poaching liquid, the more firm fruit will be when it is done. Handle poached items with care for easier plating. Poached fruits include favorites such as peach Melba and pears belle Hélène. Use fruits that are firm enough to hold their shape during cooking. Good fruits to use for poaching are apples and pears. Figure 8.16 shows a pear poaching in spiced red wine.

A **torte** is an elegant, rich, many-layered cake often filled with buttercream or jam. Normally, pastry chefs use génoise (zhen-WAAHZ), French sponge cake, in preparing a torte. Split it into layers, and then top each layer with the buttercream or jam filling. Place the layers back together, coat the entire cake with simple syrup, then frost it. Figure 8.17 shows a torte being prepared.

Figure 8.16: Pear poaching in spiced red wine.

Figure 8.17: Preparation of a torte.

Dessert Sauces and Creams

Chefs use sauces to add flavor, moisture, and eye appeal to desserts. Vanilla sauce, also known as **crème Anglaise** (krem an-GLAYZ), shown in Figure 8.18 on the following page, is a classic accompaniment to soufflés and steamed puddings. It is a light, vanilla-flavored custard sauce made from milk, egg yolks, and sugar. Handle it carefully; it is quite delicate. It is especially important to assemble all the necessary equipment before preparing the sauce. If the sauce begins to overheat it can **curdle**, or develop lumps. It may be possible to save it by straining it immediately into a container set in an ice-water bath, as shown in Figure 8.19 on the following page. Other popular sauces include caramel, butterscotch, chocolate, and fruit sauces.

Fruit sauces can be raw or cooked, depending upon the desired flavor. A **coulis** is a fruit sauce made from fresh berries or other fruits. If cooked at all, it is cooked just lightly to activate a thickener. Strain out seeds and skins with a chinois, and thicken the remaining pulp with cornstarch, arrowroot, or even a light pectin. Keep cooking to an absolute minimum to maintain the fresh flavor of the sauce. Use coulis to top ice cream, cheesecake, or other dessert items. A coulis can be spooned on or piped through a tip. If piped, it should be thick enough to form a bead. A **fruit syrup**, by contrast, is a cooked sugar-based juice. The sugar itself provides the thickening as the liquid boils and is reduced. Use fruit syrups to garnish desserts and ice cream or to complement breakfast items.

555

Vocabulary Terms

- **Torte:** A light sponge cake layered with fruit, jam, buttercream, or a combination of these.

- **Crème Anglaise:** Vanilla sauce.

- **Curdle:** Broken or lumpy texture.

- **Fruit sauces:** Raw or cooked sauce made of fresh fruit.

- **Coulis:** A fresh berry or fruit sauce, raw or barely cooked.

- **Fruit syrup:** A cooked, sugar-based fruit juice.

Figure Focus

Figure 8.16: Fruit does not need to be poached in water.

Figure 8.17: A torte is different than a layer cake, and usually has fruit.

Teaching Tips

- Remind students that they learned about sauce principles in Chapter 6.

- Help students realize that sauces are not always savory or specific to main dish menu items or vegetables.

Reinforce and Review

- Some sauces and creams make ordinary dessert foods divinely extraordinary.

- Many dessert sauces can be purchased ready-made.

- They can be extra special if they are made fresh in house.

- Sabayon sauce is made just before serving.

Vocabulary Terms

- **Caramel sauce:** Caramelized sugar and butter, sometimes with cream.

- **Butterscotch-flavored sauce:** Caramel sauce with vanilla and brown sugar added.

- **Chocolate sauce:** Several different sauces that all are based on chocolate.

- **Sabayon (zabaglione):** A fragile wine dessert sauce.

- **Pastry creams:** A thicker version of custard for filling éclairs and other pastries.

Figure 8.18: Crème Anglaise is a flavorful sauce.

Figure 8.19: Curdled crème Anglaise can be saved by straining it immediately into a container set in an ice-water bath.

When pastry chefs cook sugar and caramelize it with butter, the result is **caramel sauce.** Sometimes they add cream, but the basic principles are the same. The greater the heat, the darker the caramel. The ideal color is an amber golden brown. Also, the longer the cooking time, the more the sugar crystal will develop, so the harder the caramel will be. Be careful not to overcook a caramel sauce, or it will become too thick. Add vanilla and brown sugar to the caramel recipe to create **butterscotch-flavored sauce.** This is a bit more full flavored than the milder caramel.

Chocolate sauce is a family of sauces and syrups with cocoa or melted chocolate as the base. There is usually some butter and corn syrup in the recipe to maintain the flowing liquid quality of the sauce. Some chocolate sauces will harden again when cooled, such as a chocolate fondue. Those that are truly a syrup will remain liquid when cold; these are the types that work best as an ice cream topping. For a hardened chocolate shell over ice cream, use a special formulation of chocolate with a saturated oil. A drizzle of chocolate sauce is a welcome addition to just about any dessert.

Any of these sauces can be prepared in advance; however, **sabayon** (sa-by-ON), or **zabaglione** (zah-bahl-YOH-nay), is one sauce that is too delicate to be made ahead of time and held. Sabayon is a fragile foam of egg yolks, sugar, and Marsala wine. Whip it constantly as it cooks over simmering water until it becomes thick and light.

Pastry creams, also called *crème pâtissière*, have greater density than custards and are frequently used as the filling for pastries such as éclairs. Use these creams as a soufflé base as well. Cook eggs, sugar, flour or cornstarch, milk, and/or cream together into a very thick, smooth mixture. Pastry cream, as a basic preparation, is part of the *mise en place* for many kitchen desserts. Figure 8.20 shows a variety of pastries with cream.

556

Figure Focus

Figure 8.18: Crème Anglaise is very smooth and can be poured.

Figure 8.19: Straining and cooling a curdled sauce to remove lumps and save the sauce.

Figure 8.20: Three fruit creme puffs with raspberries, blueberries, and kiwi (left). Mango mille-feuille dessert garnished with fresh kiwi and mint (right).

Make delicate **Bavarian creams** by combining three basic ingredients: vanilla sauce, gelatin, and whipped cream. Combine the vanilla sauce with the dissolved gelatin. Then, cool this mixture over an ice-water bath until it mounds slightly when dropped from a spoon. Fold whipped cream into the mixture and pour it into molds. Use Bavarian creams as single items, or as fillings for a variety of pastries.

Essential Skills
Making Crème Anglaise (Vanilla Sauce)

❶ Carefully scale or measure all ingredients. See Figure 8.21a.

❷ Heat the milk or milk/cream combination with some of the sugar to just below a boil. See Figure 8.21b.

❸ Combine the eggs with the remainder of the sugar.

❹ Temper (gently heat) the eggs with the hot milk and return the mixture to the pan. See Figure 8.21c.

❺ Stirring constantly, cook the sauce over low heat, or pour the tempered egg mixture into custard cups and bake in a bain-marie until the custards are set. See Figure 8.21d.

Figure 8.21a: Step 1—Measure all of the ingredients.

Figure 8.21b: Step 2—Heat the milk to below boil.

Figure 8.21c: Step 4—Return the mixture to the pan.

Figure 8.21d: Step 5—Stir constantly.

557

This sauce has several techniques, including stovetop techniques and even baking with a bain-marie.

Discuss

- Fresh fruit can be a delicious dessert alone or as part of an item.

- In the Professional Profile, Chef Gand suggested using ripe, flavorful fruit.

- Ask students if they use and enjoy fresh, ripe, flavorful fruit in season.

- Discuss fruits, what is grown locally, where it is harvested and purchased, and so on.

Vocabulary Terms

- **Bavarian cream:** A vanilla sauce that is lightened by whipped cream and stabilized with a little gelatin.

Figure Focus

Figure 8.20: Various types of desserts made with creams, pastry, and fruit. They all look appealing.

Figure 8.21a: The premeasured ingredients.

Figure 8.21b: Gently heating the milk or cream and sugar.

Figure 8.21c: Mixing the eggs into the sauce according to the procedure (off heat), then returning to heat.

Figure 8.21d: Tending and carefully stirring the sauce.

Separation does not always mean spoilage with egg custards.

Reinforce and Review

- When fluid is bound in a protein structure, as in egg custard, it eventually leaks out.

- Improper or impatient baking can increase this process.

- Syneresis is not dangerous, and the liquid that exudes from custard is clear and sweet. However, it is not ideal.

Discuss

- Why should everything on a plate be edible?

- Can the same food be more appetizing or less so by the appearance?

- Do students have examples of things that make a food look less appealing?

- What ideas do students have for improving their plating skills?

Vocabulary Terms

- **Syneresis:** Water loss as it exudes from a baked egg custard or other protein custard.

[on the job]

Syneresis vs. Curdling: How to Evaluate the Safety of Egg-Based Desserts

Cooked eggs or egg yolks in a sauce or custard can coagulate, or cook unevenly. This is called curdling, but it's not the same curdling that milk does when it turns sour. Eggs curdling in cooking can affect the quality of the product, but do not make it unsafe to consume. Overheating stirred cooked custard can cause curdling problems.

When a chef cooks stirred egg custard with a starch, such as cornstarch, the egg portion does not curdle as readily. The starch provides a chemical protection. The result is a smoother product that can actually be gently boiled in preparation.

When a custard is baked, the protein of the eggs forms a structure. Baked custard almost looks like golden-opaque gelatin. This structure is soft and holds water chemically within. As the custard is cut and served, or as it sits and ages, some of the watery liquid leaks from the gel structure. This is called **syneresis**. It is safe to eat.

Baking a custard too hot and too fast affects the amount of water held in the structure, and increases the syneresis. It can also make the protein structure tough. The key to a smooth custard that doesn't weep watery liquid is lower heat and patience. Serve it after it gently cools or store it in the refrigerator.

Plating and Presenting Desserts

Food presentation is an art, and good plate presentation results from careful attention to colors, shapes, textures, and arrangement of food on the plate. Plate presentation involves the ability to visually please the guest while ensuring that the visual enhancements also complement the taste of the dish. Guests eat first with their eyes (appearance), then their noses (smell), and finally their mouths (taste). All foods must work together to form a pleasing work of art on the plate.

There are two areas of presentation technique: first, the food itself, and second, the plate, platter, or dish as a whole. Figure 8.22 on the following page shows a range of dessert platings, from the uninspired to the elegant. When plating desserts, keep the presentation simple. Everything on the plate should be edible. Fruit sauces shouldn't envelope the whole dessert. Instead, use sauces in moderation to add a note of visual appeal while enhancing the flavor of the main dessert, not overwhelming it. Sometimes, a dessert calls for a shallow pool of sauce at the center of the dish; sometimes just a swirl of sauce on the plate or the dessert item itself is enough.

558

Figure 8.22: A range of dessert platings: chocolate cake (good), chocolate cake with cherry and chocolate sauce (better), chocolate cake with chocolate shavings and sauce (best).

Chocolate piping is a popular dessert garnish. Like dessert sauces, it's used for visual appeal and taste enhancement as shown in Figure 8.23.

It is also important to think about how to arrange the food on the plate. For example, should the dessert be in the center of the plate or slightly to the side? If the dessert is round or square, it might be better in the center, whereas a slice of cake or torte might present better slightly to the side. Finally, it's best to place dessert decoration in threes, because that tends to be appealing to the eye.

Figure 8.23: Chocolate being piped onto a tuiles.

Summary

In this section, you learned the following:

- Ice cream must contain a certain amount of milkfat. Vanilla ice cream must contain no less than 10 percent milkfat; other flavors must contain at least 8 percent milkfat. Quality ice cream has a custard base (cream and/or milk and eggs), melts readily in the mouth, and does not weep, or separate, when it softens at room temperature.

- Sherbets and sorbets are frozen mixtures of fruit juice or fruit purée. Sherbet contains milk and/or egg for creaminess; sorbet contains no dairy products. Serve sorbet as a first course or as a palate cleanser between courses. Serve sherbets as a dessert item, as a rule.

- Frozen yogurt contains yogurt in addition to the normal ice cream ingredients, such as sugar or other sweeteners, gelatin, coloring, and flavors. Make

559

Reinforce and Review

- Garnishes are used to make desserts look as pretty as they taste. A beautifully decorated cake is a gift to all who see it and eat it. It adds to any celebration.

- Remind students, however, that dessert garnish can be overdone, and this will distract from the finished product.

Figure Focus

Figure 8.22: All of these photos show the same dessert. The plating lends a different flare and feeling to each.

Figure 8.23: Piped chocolate is nearly always a welcome addition to a dessert.

Summary

- Remind students to review the following:
  1. Frozen desserts
  2. Poached fruit and tortes
  3. Dessert sauces and creams
  4. Plating and presenting desserts

yogurt with either non-fat or low-fat yogurt. Frozen yogurt both freezes and melts slower than ice cream.

- To poach fruit, combine fruit with a liquid, usually a mixture of sugar, spices, and wine. Then, heat the fruit and liquid together until the fruit is tender. The greater the amount of sugar in the poaching liquid, the more firm the fruit will be when it's done. Poach fruits that are firm enough to hold their shape during cooking. Good fruits to use for poaching are apples and pears.

- A torte is an elegant, rich, many-layered cake often filled with buttercream or jam. Chefs normally use génoise, French sponge cake, in preparing a torte. Split it into layers, and top each layer with the buttercream or jam filling. Then, place the layers back together, coat the entire cake with simple syrup, and frost it.

- Use sauces to add flavor, moisture, and eye appeal to desserts. Vanilla sauce, also known as crème Anglaise, is a classic accompaniment to soufflés and steamed puddings. It is a light, vanilla-flavored custard sauce made from milk, egg yolks, and sugar. Other popular sauces include caramel, butterscotch, chocolate, and fruit sauces. Any of these sauces can be prepared in advance; however, sabayon, also called zabaglione, is one sauce that is too delicate to be made ahead and held. Sabayon is a fragile foam of egg yolks, sugar, and Marsala wine. Whip it constantly as it cooks over simmering water, until it becomes thick and light.

- Pastry creams have greater density than custards and are frequently used as the filling for pastries such as éclairs. These creams may also be used as a soufflé base. Cook eggs, sugar, flour or cornstarch, milk, and/or cream together into a very thick, smooth mixture. Pastry cream, as a basic preparation, is part of the *mise en place* for many kitchen desserts. Make delicate Bavarian creams by combining three basic ingredients: vanilla sauce, gelatin, and whipped cream. Combine the vanilla sauce with the dissolved gelatin. Then cool this mixture over an ice-water bath until it mounds slightly when dropped from a spoon. Fold whipped cream into the mixture and pour it into molds. Use Bavarian creams as single items or as fillings for a variety of pastries.

- Food presentation is an art, and good plate presentation results from careful attention to colors, shapes, textures, and arrangement of food on the plate. Plate presentation involves the ability to visually please the guest while ensuring that the visual enhancements also complement the taste of the dish. There are two areas for presentation techniques: first, the food itself, and second, the plate, platter, or dish as a whole. When plating desserts, keep the presentation simple. Everything on the plate should be edible. Fruit sauces shouldn't envelope the whole dessert. Instead, use sauces in moderation to add a note of visual appeal while enhancing the flavor of the main dessert, not overwhelming it. Chocolate piping is a popular dessert garnish. It is also important to think about how to arrange the food on the plate. Finally, it's best to place dessert decoration in threes, because that tends to be appealing to the eye.

560

Section 8.6 Review Questions

1. List four types of frozen desserts.

2. Name two fruits that are good for poaching.

3. What are the three main ingredients in vanilla sauce?

4. What are the two main criteria for dessert plate presentation?

5. Gale Gand mentions the need for improvisation, a new take on a traditional idea. How might you change the presentation of a traditional frozen dessert such as ice cream, sorbet, or frozen yogurt?

6. Part of the problem with Kabob's dessert menu is not just the quality of the food, it is also the quality of the presentation. What are three tips you could give Miguel and Chef Kate in plating and presenting their desserts?

7. Why does quality vanilla ice cream require a minimum of 10 percent milkfat, while all other ice creams require a minimum of 8 percent?

8. Write up a garnishing specification sheet for each of the three dessert items below. Make sure to include the type of plate or bowl that should be used, how the food should be arranged on the plate, and any garnish that you would use and where.

- Chocolate torte
- Vanilla ice cream
- Strawberry shortcake

561

Section 8.6 Review Questions

1. The students should choose four from among ice cream, sherbet, gelato, sorbet, frozen yogurt, frozen custard, and soy-based frozen desserts.

2. Peaches and pears were mentioned in this chapter. Cherries, berries, and other fruits can be poached as well.

3. Vanilla sauce includes milk, egg yolks, sugar, and vanilla.

4. Everything on the plate should be edible, and it should look appealing and visually please the guest.

5. Each student will have ideas about this.

6. Each student will have an opinion about this.

7. The answer to this is not clearly given in the text. However, vanilla ice cream does not have other flavors to "hide behind," so the creamy mouthfeel and subtle aroma of milkfat contributes to the flavor experience. There might be other reasons the students come up with. They might want to research this further.

8. Each student will have creative ideas, and some might be quite innovative.

Section 8.6
Activities

1. Crème brûlée is "broiled crème," and is a mild and smooth custard that is caramelized on the top to form a crunchy shell. A small culinary blow torch accomplishes the task.

2. Petit fours are small pieces of cake and perhaps a filling covered with smooth fondant and decorated. They are usually bite-sized and pretty, often pastel colored.

3. The students should include "overrun," which is the introduction of air to the mix during freezing. It is usually expressed as a percentage, based on the increased volume the aerated ice cream has as compared to the original mix. If ice cream is not stored at optimal temperatures it can partially thaw and lose some of the air. If it refreezes, it will crystallize and lose its smoothness and creamy mouthfeel. Students can find more information on this topic.

Section 8.6 Activities

1. Study Skills/Group Activity: Making Crème Brûlée

As a class, observe a demonstration of creating a crème brûlée, prepared with a culinary blow-torch to caramelize the top. Then break up into groups of three or four and try to replicate the process.

2. Independent Activity: Petits Fours

What are petits fours? Cookies? Cakes? Pastries? Candy? When are they served? How are they made? Write a paragraph about petits fours. Include a color drawing of one of your own design. Label the parts, including flavors.

3. Critical Thinking: Keeping Ice Cream Cold

Research online the best temperatures for freezing ice cream. How does air in the product affect taste and texture? What happens when ice cream is not stored at optimal temperatures? Why is this so? Write a one-page report of your findings.

Case Study Follow-Up *Dessert Dilemma*

Miguel and Chef Kate have received poor customer feedback on their dessert options. They are trying to resolve this dilemma.

1. After having read this chapter, do you think dessert is just as vital an aspect of menu planning as other courses? Why or why not?

2. If you had to suggest a five-item dessert menu especially tailored to Kabob's needs and means, what would you suggest? Why?

3. Take the five items you just suggested and create a presentation spec for each one. Make sure to include all sauces, garnish, and plateware that should be used.

563

Case Study Follow-Up

1. Students will have their own ideas. Hopefully, they will have decided that desserts are a vital aspect of menu planning for a successful operation.

2. Students will come up with a unique mix. There should probably be a chocolate offering, and perhaps something frozen.

3. Students' creativity will be displayed with this assignment.

Apply Your Learning

Converting Measurements

A 6 pound yield, using 3 pounds flour, will yield approximately 10 shells.

Figure this recipe for 5 shells instead of 10. Students should be able to divide the formula by half. They can multiply it by .5, 50 percent, or divide by 2.

Advanced students might want to set up a dimensional analysis equation.

Bread and Culture

Each student's answer will be unique.

Selling Double-Acting Baking Powder

Double-acting baking powder has an acid-base reaction between baking soda (sodium bicarbonate) and monocalcium phosphate monohydrate (an acid powder) immediately upon contact with liquid. Another powder in the baking powder is called SAS, or sodium aluminum sulfate. When SAS is heated with water, it forms sulfuric acid, which reacts with the remaining sodium bicarbonate, another acid-base reaction. Each acid-base reaction gives off carbon dioxide gas bubbles to leaven the product. Therefore bubbles form when the batter is mixed, and then more bubbles form during baking.

Now, students can come up with a way to explain this information in a creative, informative, and fun way.

Apply Your Learning

Converting Measurements

Sometimes, it is easy to forget that what you learn in math class is the same math you will need in chemistry classes, food classes, and daily life. Math is important in the commercial kitchen in order to accurately read, use, and convert recipes.

Convert the following recipe for pie crust to yield 10 shells:

Yields: 6 pounds
Pastry flour, 3 pounds
Salt, 1 ounce
Granulated sugar, 3 ounces
All-purpose shortening, 1 pound 14 ounces
Water (cold), 14 fluid ounces

1. Sift the flour, salt, and sugar together in a bowl.
2. Cut the shortening into the flour mixture until the desired consistency (flaky or mealy) is reached.
3. Gradually add the cold water, mixing gently until the dough holds together. Do not over mix or add too much water.
4. Cover the dough with plastic wrap and chill thoroughly before using.

Since this is a real situation you will be faced with in the restaurant and foodservice industry, do not rely on your instructor to walk you through this problem. Show your work, and write out the verbal explanation for each step.

Bread and Culture

Bread is involved in many traditional and cultural events and ceremonies. Research one. Share with the class the type of bread you chose, how it is made, the culture it comes from, the significance it has in that culture, and the kind of ceremony in which it is used.

Selling Double-Acting Baking Powder

Research and learn how double-acting baking powder works. Why does it act as a leavening agent? What makes it different from baking soda and vinegar? Does it make baking easier and/or more successful? How?

564

Create a brief brochure or sales document as if you were selling double-acting baking powder to people who had never used it. Include artwork, recipes, chemical equations, or whatever else you want. Make sure the brochure answers all the questions asked in the first paragraph.

Critical Thinking **The Upper Crust**

People can be very particular about their pie crusts, and it is wise in the restaurant and foodservice industry to have a sense of what your particular likes and dislikes are as well. Make a homemade pie and sample a few different slices of store-bought pie, paying close attention to the crusts. Note textures: Is it crumbly or flaky? Note tastes: Is it sweet? Sour? Salty? Savory? After you've done your taste-testing research, write a one-page summary of what you've found, and, most important, what your favorite type of crust is.

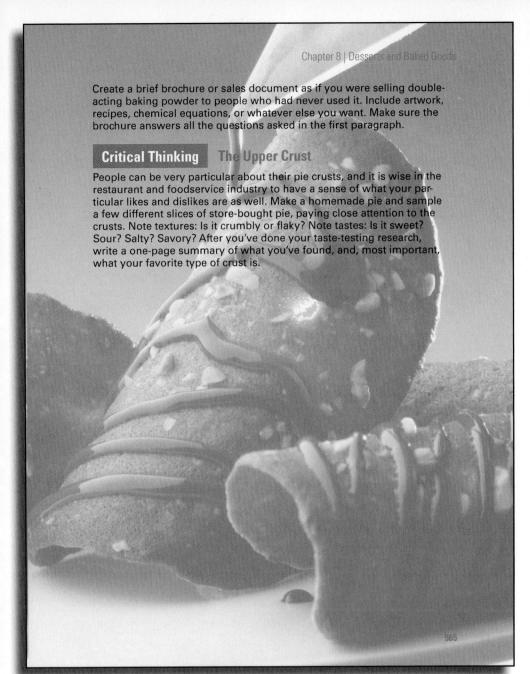

565

Critical Thinking **The Upper Crust**

Each student should try this either in class or at home. Most commercial crusts are mixed with shortening in a machine, which can make the crust have a crumb texture instead of a flake texture.

Exam Prep Answers

1. A
2. C
3. A
4. A
5. D
6. A
7. A
8. A
9. A
10. C

Exam Prep Questions

1 What allows the dough or batter to rise?

   A. Leaveners

   B. Sweeteners

   C. Shortenings

   D. Strengtheners

2 In baking, ingredients are given percentages in relation to

   A. eggs.

   B. milk.

   C. flour.

   D. sugar.

3 What are the two types of dough used for yeast breads?

   A. Rich dough and lean dough

   B. Flaky dough and flat dough

   C. Sweet dough and salty dough

   D. Milk-based dough and water-based dough

4 What is the first step in yeast bread preparation?

   A. Scaling

   B. Proofing

   C. Rounding

   D. Fermentation

5 A scone is an example of a

   A. cake.

   B. soufflé.

   C. yeast bread.

   D. quick bread.

6 Steamed puddings are more stable than soufflés because they have a

   A. greater percentage of eggs and sugar in the batter.

   B. smaller percentage of eggs and sugar in the batter.

   C. greater percentage of milk and flour in the batter.

   D. smaller percentage of milk and flour in the batter.

7 What are the ingredients and proportions in 3-2-1 dough?

   A. Three parts flour, two parts fat, one part water

   B. Three parts fat, two parts water, one part flour

   C. Three parts water, two parts flour, one part fat

   D. Three parts flour, two parts water, one part fat

8 What is the basis of all cocoa products?

   A. Cocoa nibs

   B. Cocoa butter

   C. Cocoa liquor

   D. Cocoa powder

9 When tempering chocolate, the chocolate is heated

   A. gently the entire time.

   B. rapidly the entire time.

   C. rapidly at first and then gently.

   D. gently at first and then rapidly.

566

⑩ For a product to be accurately labeled vanilla ice cream, it must contain at least what percentage of milkfat?

- A. 1
- B. **5**
- C. 10
- D. 15

Soft Yeast Dinner Rolls

Yield: 64 Rolls, approximately 1.25 ounces each
Method: Straight dough
Fermentation: 1 hour
Proofing: 30 to 45 minutes
Cooking time: 15 minutes

Ingredients

2 oz	Active dry yeast	2 oz	Shortening
1 lb 8 oz	Water (temperature controlled)	2 oz	Unsalted butter, softened
2 lb 12 oz	Bread flour	3.2 oz (2)	Eggs
1 oz	Salt	As needed	Egg wash
4 oz	Granulated sugar		Total Dough Weight: 5 pounds, 4 ounces
2 oz	Non-fat dry milk powder		

Directions

1. Preheat oven to 400°F.
2. Dissolve the yeast in the water in a bowl. Combine the flour, salt, sugar, milk powder, shortening, butter, and eggs in the bowl of a mixer fitted with a dough hook.
3. Add the water and yeast mixture to the mixer bowl; stir to combine.
4. Knead on medium speed 10 minutes or until the dough reaches 77°F.
5. Transfer the dough to a lightly greased bowl, cover, and place in a warm spot. Allow to rise until doubled, approximately 1 hour.
6. Punch down the dough. Let it rest a few minutes to allow the gluten to relax.
7. Divide the dough into 1¼ ounce portions and round. Shape as desired and arrange on paper-lined sheet pans. Proof until doubled in size.
8. Carefully brush the proofed rolls with egg wash. Bake at 400°F until medium brown, approximately 12 to 15 minutes.

Recipe Nutritional Content

Calories	100	Cholesterol	10 mg	Protein	3 g
Calories from fat	20	Sodium	180 mg	Vitamin A	2%
Total fat	2 g	Carbohydrates	17 g	Vitamin C	0%
Saturated fat	1 g	Dietary fiber	< 1 g	Calcium	2%
Trans fat	0 g	Sugars	2 g	Iron	6%

Nutritional analysis provided by FoodCalc®, www.foodcalc.com

567

Recipe

Soft Yeast Dinner Rolls

- These rolls can be shaped into Parker House or other shapes.

Recipe

Flourless Chocolate Cake

- Perhaps the students realize that this isn't actually a cake at all. It is more like firm custard loaded with dark chocolate.

Flourless Chocolate Cake
Yield: 21 servings
Method: Egg foam

Ingredients

1 lb	Unsalted butter	As needed	Powdered sugar
27 oz	Dark chocolate	As needed	Vanilla and chocolate custard sauce
2 lb	Eggs, separated	Total batter weight: 5 pounds 2 ounces	
7 oz	Granulated sugar		

Directions

1. Preheat oven to 400°F.
2. Melt the butter and chocolate over a bain marie.
3. Whisk the egg yolks in the melted chocolate.
4. Whip the egg whites until shiny. Add the granulated sugar and whip until very stiff. Fold into the chocolate. Pour the batter unto a full-size hotel pan that is lined with butter parchment.
5. Bake at 400°F for 10 minutes. Lower the oven temperature to 350°F and continue baking until done, approximately 40 minutes.
   Note: A cake tester will not come out clean, even though the cake is done.
6. Invert the cake onto the back of a sheet pan and remove the hotel pan. Cool completely, and then dust with powdered sugar. Serve garnished with vanilla or chocolate custard sauce.

Recipe Nutritional Content

Calories	460	Cholesterol	240 mg	Protein	8 g
Calories from fat	300	Sodium	70 mg	Vitamin A	20%
Total fat	34 g	Carbohydrates	33 g	Vitamin C	0%
Saturated fat	13 g	Dietary fiber	2 g	Calcium	4%
Trans fat	0 g	Sugars	29 g	Iron	8%

Nutritional analysis provided by FoodCalc®, www.foodcalc.com

568

Linzer Tart

Yield: 8-10 Servings

Ingredients

8 oz	Unsalted butter (softened)	.14 oz (1 tsp)	Baking powder
8 oz	Granulated sugar	.14 oz (2 tsp)	Cinnamon, ground
1.3 oz (2)	Egg yolks	.04 oz (½ tsp)	Cloves, ground
4 oz	Orange zest (fine grate)	.05 oz (¼ tsp)	Salt
.2 oz	Lemon zest (fine grate)	14 oz	Raspberry preserves
11 oz	All-purpose flour	Total dough weight: 2 pounds 3 ounces	
6 oz	Hazelnuts (ground fine)		

Directions

1. To make dough, cream together the butter and sugar until light and fluffy. Add the egg yolks and the orange and lemon zest. Beat until well combined.
2. In another bowl, mix together the flour, hazelnuts, baking powder, cinnamon, cloves, and salt. Add the dry mixture all at once to the creamed mixture and mix briefly, until just combined. (This dough looks more like cookie dough than pastry.) Wrap in plastic and chill until firm, at least 4 hours or overnight.
3. Divide the dough in half. On a generously floured board, briefly knead one piece of dough and flatten it with the palm of your hand. Gently roll the dough and flatten out to ¼ inch thick. Use it to line a 9- or 10-inch tart pan with a removable bottom. This rich dough patches easily. Chill approximately 10 minutes.
4. Roll out the second piece of dough to form a 12-inch × 4-inch rectangle. Using a sharp knife or pastry wheel, cut lengthwise strips in parallel lines, ½ inch wide.
5. Remove the lined tart shell from the refrigerator and spread the raspberry preserves evenly over it. To create the lattice pattern with the pastry strips, first lay some strips in parallel lines, ½ inch apart. Then lay a second row of strips at a 45 degree angle to the first. Press the strips to the edge of the crust to seal.
6. Bake at 350°F until the crust is golden brown and the filling is bubbly in the center, approximately 45 minutes. Set aside to cool.

Recipe Nutritional Content

Calories	280	Cholesterol	45 mg	Protein	3 g
Calories from fat	20	Sodium	60 mg	Vitamin A	6%
Total fat	14 g	Carbohydrates	37 g	Vitamin C	6%
Saturated fat	6 g	Dietary fiber	2 g	Calcium	4%
Trans fat	0 g	Sugars	20 g	Iron	8%

Nutritional analysis provided by FoodCalc®, www.foodcalc.com

569

Recipe

Linzer Tart

- This is pronounced LINT-zer tart.

Chapter 9 Overview

Chapter 9 introduces students to sustainable practices in the restaurant and foodservice industry, as well as the challenges and opportunities involved in introducing and following them.

Section 1: The first section describes sustainability and frames a discussion about the importance of water conservation.

Section 2: This section builds on the previous section, introducing energy conservation and efficiency.

Section 3: Section 3 discusses alternate forms of waste management in the restaurant and foodservice industry.

Section 4: This section describes a variety of sustainable food practices and addresses growing consumer demand for sustainably produced menu items.

Advance Preparation	
Review	Sections 9.1–9.4
	Chapter 6
	Book 1, Chapters 3, 7, and 8
Contact	A guest speaker from a local utility company
	A guest speaker from a local "green" building
	A guest speaker from a local building authority
	A guest speaker who is a LEED expert
	A guest speaker from a food rescue program or from a restaurant or foodservice organization that participates in that program
	A guest speaker who is a local food producer, such as a farmer or cheese maker
Prepare	Obtain an incandescent lightbulb, an LED lightbulb, and a CFL lightbulb, as well as a lamp with which they can be used
	Obtain images of "green" buildings
	Obtain photographs of open- and closed-system fish farms

ServSafe Connection
Page 607

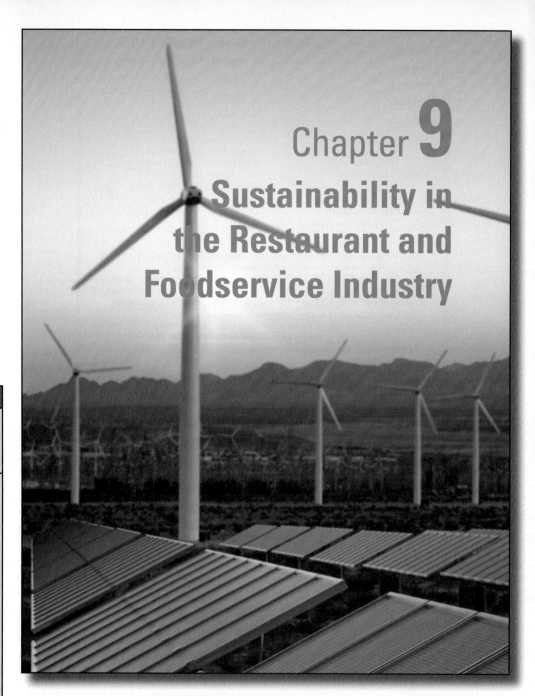

Chapter **9**
Sustainability in the Restaurant and Foodservice Industry

CUSTOMIZED INSTRUCTION OPTIONS			
Less Advanced Students	**More Advanced Students**	**ESOL Students**	**Special Needs Students**
Pages 577, 615	Pages 580, 609	Pages 593, 606	Pages 582, 606

CHAPTER TOOLS			
21st-Century Skills	**Mathematics**	**Science**	**Literacy**
Pages 576, 577, 579, 580, 581, 582, 587, 588, 589, 590, 591, 592, 593, 595, 601, 602, 603, 606, 609, 611, 614, 615, 617, 619, 623, 624, 626	Pages 573, 581, 582, 588, 589, 601, 615, 617	Pages 576, 579, 587, 590, 591, 592, 603, 609, 611	Pages 573, 576, 577, 579, 580, 581, 582, 587, 588, 589, 590, 591, 592, 593, 595, 601, 602, 603, 606, 609, 611, 614, 615, 617, 619, 623, 624, 626

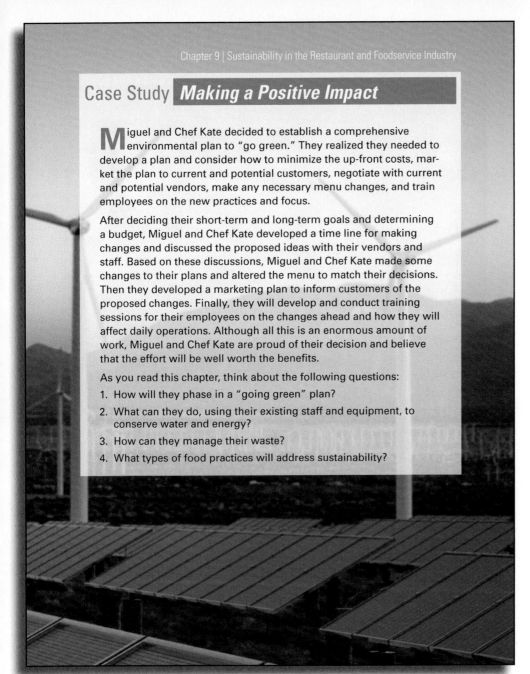

Case Study *Making a Positive Impact*

Miguel and Chef Kate decided to establish a comprehensive environmental plan to "go green." They realized they needed to develop a plan and consider how to minimize the up-front costs, market the plan to current and potential customers, negotiate with current and potential vendors, make any necessary menu changes, and train employees on the new practices and focus.

After deciding their short-term and long-term goals and determining a budget, Miguel and Chef Kate developed a time line for making changes and discussed the proposed ideas with their vendors and staff. Based on these discussions, Miguel and Chef Kate made some changes to their plans and altered the menu to match their decisions. Then they developed a marketing plan to inform customers of the proposed changes. Finally, they will develop and conduct training sessions for their employees on the changes ahead and how they will affect daily operations. Although all this is an enormous amount of work, Miguel and Chef Kate are proud of their decision and believe that the effort will be well worth the benefits.

As you read this chapter, think about the following questions:

1. How will they phase in a "going green" plan?
2. What can they do, using their existing staff and equipment, to conserve water and energy?
3. How can they manage their waste?
4. What types of food practices will address sustainability?

Case Study
Making a Positive Impact

- Encourage students to discuss ways in which the employees might react to the new environmental plan. How will their duties be affected? What about their morale? How can Miguel and Chef Kate achieve employee "buy-in"? Relate this to Chapters 7 and 8 in Level 1.

- What effects might the new plan have on regular and potential guests? How might customers respond, either positively or negatively?

- Does the environmental plan that Miguel and Chef Kate have developed make sense? How do students think it could be improved?

- Encourage students to describe the restaurant's vision statement, mission statement, and code of ethics under this new way of doing business.

- Note that there are follow-up questions about the case study at the end of the chapter.

- This activity could be done in groups, as a class, or as a homework assignment.

Discuss	Why do students think that George W. McKerrow, Jr., has posted a plaque reading "Would you eat this?" over the expediting window at his operation? What effect might this have on quality?
	What characteristics do students identify in McKerrow that might have contributed to his success in the restaurant and foodservice industry?
	When is it time for a poorly performing business to change its operation style or even close for good?
	Encourage students to discuss the importance of attitude in the restaurant and foodservice industry and elsewhere. How does it relate to professionalism?
Reinforce and Review	Passion for the work is a fundamental component of success in the restaurant and foodservice industry. Although passion alone does not guarantee success, its absence almost always leads to failure.
	Concentrating on the basics and maintaining a positive attitude can help weather the inevitable storms.
Teaching Tips	After retiring from one restaurant group, McKerrow cofounded a second. Encourage students to discuss why he might have made this choice.

[professional profile]

George W. McKerrow Jr.

President and CEO, Ted's Montana Grill and We're Cookin' Inc. (which owns Canoe and Aria in Atlanta)

❝ *We all look good together and we all look bad together! I also have a plaque at the Expo window that reads, 'Would you eat this?'* ❞

I fell in love with the restaurant industry at 16 when I got my first job at Uncle John's Pancake House. I was a buser, dishwasher, and cook. I liked the excitement and the opportunity. It just felt right.

After graduating from Ohio State University with a B.S. in political science, I bought the Log Cabin Supper Club in West Virginia. In 1974, I joined the Victoria's Station restaurant chain, moving up to southeast regional manager. I opened the first LongHorn Steakhouse as a neighborhood restaurant in 1981, a time when Atlanta had few choices in casual dining.

You know, when I started LongHorn Steakhouse, I was full of pride and drive. But we practically failed before we ever opened our doors. Still, I believed in what I was doing and figured out a way to continue my dream. When we did our preopening, 400 of my closest friends came for free food and drink; however, on opening day, only 14 people came for lunch and 21 for dinner. We had a very slow first six months.

I did everything I could in the restaurant to make it successful, and I never gave up. I said hello and goodbye to every guest. I concentrated on the basics and kept a positive attitude. Soon sales began to grow, and we became the place to go for great food, great service, and a great attitude. We got positive write-ups in the local paper. Our big break came when Atlanta got shut down by a snowstorm, and we were one of few businesses that stayed open for our guests. Folks knew we were committed, and that's what really put us on the map. The rest is history!

That single location evolved into RARE Hospitality International, which owns LongHorn Steakhouse and The Capital Grille and was sold to Darden Restaurants in October, 2007. Before that time, I had retired from RARE Hospitality and in 1996 I co-founded We're Cookin' Inc. This restaurant group now has two award-winning, fine-dining restaurants in Atlanta: Aria and Canoe.

In addition to serving on the board of directors for the National Restaurant Association (1997–2003) and the Culinary Institute of America (1996–2002), George McKerrow received the first Lifetime Achievement Award from the Georgia Restaurant Association in 2007 for his years of service to Georgia's restaurant industry. In October 2008, he was inducted into The Atlanta

Hospitality Hall of Fame by the Atlanta Convention & Visitors Bureau. Nation's Restaurant News has called him a "dinner-house legend" and credits him with giving "birth to an entire casual-dining segment" more than 20 years ago when he founded LongHorn Steakhouse Inc.

In the restaurant business, I believe simple is always best. It's always about the food, the service, and the attitude. We don't need to overcomplicate or over analyze this. People bring their hard-earned money to a restaurant to have fun, relax, and enjoy a quality meal. We're all here to serve those basic needs.

My advice to you: Learn the basics. Try to stay loyal to one company as long as you can. And remember, the harder you work, the luckier you get!

About Sustainability

Our industry uses about five times more energy than most other businesses because we're open long hours. We require more energy to produce our products (good food), and we create significantly more waste than most businesses. However, we can and do find ways to conserve, and thereby become more sustainable. The good news is that we've been responsive, and we're always finding ways to reinvent ourselves in this area. It's just the right thing to do.

Once we open our minds to simple ideas like conserving energy and water, using better and more sustainable building products and practices, recycling, composting, using less plastic, and simply using more sustainable products in all areas of restaurant operations, it all works to our and the planet's benefit.

At Ted's Montana Grill, we try to focus our energy on not only being a great restaurant company, but also embracing being a good "world citizen." In fact, our mantra is to, "Eat great. Do good." The positive motivation we get from being more environmentally sensitive and influencing other businesses to change their practices is what gives us pride. If we can change the way one person feels one day at a time, we will over time make an impact. Millions of small efforts can create great success for all of us in coexisting on our planet, in our businesses, and in our personal lives.

9.1 Introduction and Water Conservation	9.2 Energy Conservation	9.3 Waste Management	9.4 Sustainable Food Practices
• History of sustainability • The need for water conservation • What this industry can do	• The importance of energy efficiency • What this industry can do • Building for efficiency	• Reusing • Reducing • Recycling • Getting started	• Local sourcing • Sustainable seafood • Coffee • Animal products • Organic food • The emerging landscape

573

Professional Profile (cont.)

Discuss	Why are sustainable practices so important in the restaurant and foodservice industry? How can small changes, if practiced industry-wide, generate huge results? What does it mean to be a "world citizen"? How might it affect how a company does business? McKerrow and his colleagues receive positive motivation from their ecological sensitivity and the influence they exert on other businesses. To what extent is this pride related to professionalism? To take it a step further, is following sustainable practices an inherent part of professionalism? McKerrow notes, "The harder you work, the luckier you get!" Encourage students to discuss this concept. Can people really create their own luck, or is what is commonly called "luck" really just being professional and motivated?
Reinforce and Review	Learn the basics: Simple is always best. The restaurant and foodservice industry uses about five times more energy than most other industries because of the long hours worked and the resources consumed. Small efforts, when practiced over time and in sufficient number, can have a significant impact.
Teaching Tips	Engage students in a discussion of simplicity: What does it really entail, and how is it consistent with providing excellent guest services?

Homework Activity: Small Actions, Big Effects

Mathematics Connection, Literacy Connection

George McKerrow notes that making small changes can produce significant results. Each student should identify one small lifestyle change he or she can make that would be considered a sustainable practice: recycling cans and bottles instead of placing them in the garbage, consuming fewer food items that have nonrecyclable packaging, taking shorter showers at slightly cooler temperatures, and so on. Students should then make the change for one week.

Students should record the effects of this change on their daily lives. Is the selected change simple to make, or does it require more effort? How does the student feel about making the change? In what ways is making this change a step toward sustainability? Each student should write a brief essay addressing these issues.

Focus and Engage

Discuss

- How can students work independently to promote sustainable habits in the restaurant and foodservice industry? In what ways do individual efforts differ from group efforts?

- Discuss whether it is important for restaurant and foodservice operations to observe sustainable practices. What are the advantages and disadvantages, both in the short term and in the long term?

- What is the relationship between sustainability and finances, both for small restaurants and for the American economy?

Reinforce and Review

- Environmental responsibility for the restaurant and foodservice industry is an ongoing and challenging process.

- Sustainable practices in the restaurant and foodservice industry include using resources more efficiently, reducing waste, and increasing the use of renewable resources.

- Many environmentally sound behaviors can have the added benefits of saving money and attracting customers.

Teaching Tips

- Should the restaurant and foodservice industry—the largest private-sector industry in the United State—lead the way in the conservation and sustainable use of natural resources? Why or why not? Divide the class into two groups, assigning each one side of this argument. The two teams could debate the issue, research and report on specific issue areas, or create multimedia presentations defending their assigned position.

Section 9.1 Introduction and Water Conservation

Introduce the Section

a. Discuss the role that the restaurant and foodservice industry, as a major employer and consumer of resources, can play in conserving natural resources, paying special attention to the importance of water use.

b. Describe the history of the conservation and sustainability movements in the United States and their relevance to contemporary efforts.

SECTION 9.1 INTRODUCTION AND WATER CONSERVATION

What does environmental responsibility mean for the restaurant and foodservice industry? How can a restaurant or foodservice establishment provide top-quality service to customers and use resources efficiently? As you grow in your career, what choices can you make to ensure that your operation is taking care of its customers, its profits, and the planet?

With approximately 945,000 operations in the United States, the restaurant and foodservice industry has the opportunity to lead the way in the conservation and sustainable use of resources. Environmental responsibility for this industry is an ongoing process that continually challenges businesses to use resources more efficiently, reduce waste, and increase the use of renewable resources as new technologies and practices become available. Many of the practices you'll learn about in this chapter also have two other important potential benefits: They may save money and attract customers. In many cases, these practices increase profits for the business and reduce costs to the environment, so everybody wins.

Study Questions

After studying Section 9.1, you should be able to answer the following questions:

- What are the definitions of sustainability and conservation?
- Why is water conservation important?
- What can a foodservice operation do to use water efficiently?

History of Sustainability

In the last few years, more and more people have been discussing "going green." The concept of protecting and preserving the environment has actually been around in the United States for longer than one might think. As early as 1864, the U.S. Congress began creating national parks. The founding of private organizations such as the Audubon Society and the Sierra Club also date back to the late nineteenth century. Throughout the twentieth century, lawmakers and environmentalists worked to control pollution from burgeoning mining and oil sites, and to protect endangered species and woodlands.

574

c. Discuss the objectives for the section.

Vocabulary Review

a. Direct students to the key terms.
b. Pronounce each word, and have the students repeat the pronunciation out loud.
c. Discuss the definition of each word.

Teach

Discuss

- What does "going green" mean? How can different people interpret it in different ways, and why?

- Are students surprised to learn of the long history of the American conservation movement? Why or why not? How do students think this movement might have evolved over the decades, and why?

The U.S. government founded the **Environmental Protection Agency** (EPA) in 1970. The EPA is a federal agency whose mission is to protect human health and the environment. Much of the EPA's focus in recent years has been on finding ways to preserve natural resources such as water and energy. It researches new technologies, makes recommendations about business practices, and promotes practices that use energy and other resources as efficiently as possible.

The EPA defines **sustainability** as practices that meet current resource needs without compromising the ability to meet future needs. In other words, people should use a resource in ways today that don't hurt the future ability to use that same type of resource. Similarly, **conservation** is the practice of limiting the use of a resource.

Restaurant and foodservice operations rely on many natural resources throughout the course of their daily business. Depending on the establishment and the area, these may include water, natural gas, wind power, nuclear energy, hydroelectric power, and/or solar power just to keep the lights on and the water running. Other natural resources, such as paper and steel, are essential to basic hospitality operations.

The Need for Water Conservation

Water resources in the United States are found in two forms: surface water and groundwater. Surface water includes all of the water that is on top of the earth's surface, from lakes and oceans to the snow on mountain caps. Groundwater is what you find beneath the earth's surface, the water that the earth has absorbed. Almost 75 percent of the earth's surface is covered with water, but only 1 percent of that can be used by humans, either as groundwater or as freshwater. Although the earth is mostly water, oceans contain 97 percent of it, and polar ice contains 90 percent of the rest. Much more water is beneath the earth's surface than on it, although it is always very close to the top.

Many people rely on groundwater through the use of public and private wells. These wells pump the water from aquifers (underground reservoirs) to the surface. About 40 percent of the United States relies on groundwater for its public supply to households and businesses. Some areas receive almost all of their supply from groundwater. For example, San Antonio, Texas, relies solely on groundwater for all of its water needs. See Figure 9.1 on the following page.

When rainfall is less than usual or a well is pumped at a faster rate than before, the level of the groundwater can go down. Then the wells may "go dry," which means they are pumping air instead of water.

575

Teaching Tips

- Do students know their community's water sources? Does the area rely primarily on groundwater or surface water? Encourage students to discuss why this might matter.

Vocabulary Terms

- **Environmental Protection Agency (EPA):** A federal agency, founded in 1970, with the mission of protecting human health and the environment.

- **Sustainability:** Practices that meet current resource needs without compromising the ability to meet future needs.

- **Conservation:** The practice of limiting the use of a resource.

Reinforce and Review

- The U.S. Congress began creating national parks in 1864, an early example of the importance of conservation.

- Both the Sierra Club and the Audubon Society were founded in the late nineteenth century.

- Throughout the twentieth century, lawmakers and environmentalists have worked to control pollution and protect endangered species and locales.

Teaching Tips

- Encourage students to select an environmental issue from the nineteenth, twentieth, or twenty-first century and research its history and importance. Make sure students identify how concern about these issues reflected popular social needs of the time.

- Ask students what they perceive to be "natural resources." Why might responses vary?

Discuss

- The EPA is a federal agency, part of the executive (presidential) branch of government. Can its mission and agenda be affected by whichever political party holds the presidency, or is it immune to political pressure due to the nature of its work? How might its research and recommendations be changed, if they are based on scientific fact?

Reinforce and Review

- The U.S. government founded the EPA in 1970; today, much of its focus has been on finding ways to preserve natural resources, such as water and energy.

- According to principles of sustainability, people should use resources in ways that don't compromise future abilities to use those same resources.

- Restaurant and foodservice operations rely on a wide variety of natural resources to meet daily operational needs.

- Water resources in the United States are found in surface water (all the water atop the earth's surface, including snow) and groundwater (all the water that has been absorbed into the earth).

- Only 1 percent of all water can be used by humans; 97 percent of water is stored in the oceans, and much of the rest is stored in polar ice.

- During periods of low rainfall or excessive use, wells and aquifers can "go dry" due to the lack of available water.

Discuss

- Explain how short-term and long-term water shortages can affect schools and communities. What effects might these shortages have on the restaurant and foodservice industry?

Reinforce and Review

- The effects of a disappearing water supply can be devastating: decreased food supply with increased prices; fewer businesses and more unemployment; environmental conditions can change, affecting human and community health; and severe population imbalances can arise, due to environmental immigration.

- By 2013, it is expected that 36 states will experience some form of water shortage, and preventative restrictions are already in place in a number of areas.

- Countries around the world are imposing restrictions on water use to encourage businesses and residents to use water more carefully and thoughtfully.

Teaching Tips

- Relate environmental refugees to economic refugees. Explain that just as economic conditions can force people to move to new areas looking for work, environmental conditions can force people to move as well. Often, economic and environmental issues combine forces, as in the U.S. Great Depression.

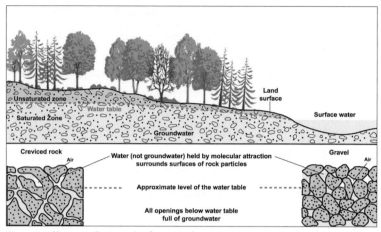

Figure 9.1: How groundwater and surface water function.

The effects of a disappearing water supply can be devastating:

- Crops and animals no longer have the water they need, which limits the food supply and raises prices.
- With the loss of supply and profits, businesses and farms close.
- Unemployment rises in affected industries.
- Brushfires and dust storms may increase.
- In severe cases, residents may leave, causing some towns to die and others to become overpopulated.

It might be difficult to picture these results happening in the United States. But by 2013, water managers in 36 states expect a local, regional, or statewide water shortage to affect their residents. Many areas already have water restrictions in place. One example is California, where drought has been a major factor in the last few years. Many farms have been forced to reduce their size and number of workers because their water supply has been limited.

Currently, many of the consumer restrictions in the United States limit the amount of lawn watering and car washing that residents may do. But the restrictions could get much tighter as water shortages continue. Many European countries are currently trying to ban all "unnecessary" consumer water usage.

576

Figure Focus

Figure 9.1: When rain falls on land, it might sink into the surface and seep below the water table, becoming groundwater. Alternately, it can flow downhill and into surface water.

**Homework Activity:
Environmental Refugees**

Science Connection, Literacy Connection, 21st-Century Skills—Reason Effectively, Information Literacy, Communicate Clearly, Initiative and Self-Direction

Throughout the centuries, climate and other environmental changes have forced people to leave their homes and travel to new lands in search of food, shelter, and employment. As water shortages become more pervasive, it is expected that the number of environmental refugees will continue to increase.

Research the issue of environmental refugees. Globally, what regions have been most affected, and in what ways? Select a particular state or geographic area that has experienced environmental changes that have resulted in environmental migration and describe the challenges it has faced.

Write a one-page report discussing your findings.

**Homework Activity:
Economy, Environment**

Literacy Connection, 21st-Century Skills—Make Judgments and Decisions, Information Literacy, Communicate Clearly, Work Independently

It often happens that environmental conditions are entwined with economic conditions. Sometimes, one improves as the other declines, and sometimes both rise and fall together.

Research the U.S. Great Depression and the Dust Bowl. How were the two events related? Looking back now, what impact did each experience have on American society? Some examples include changes in agricultural practices and large-scale migration to the West Coast.

Write a one-page report discussing your findings.

In Australia, some businesses aren't allowed access to the public water supply unless they can prove that they are reducing their usage. In places of long-lasting droughts, such as East Africa, famine and disease affect vast parts of the population. By 2025, four billion people—about half the world's population—could live in "severe water stress" conditions.

The United States uses more than 345,000 million gallons of freshwater every day. On average, Americans and Canadians use more than 100 gallons of water a day per person just for personal use. Compare that to residents of the United Kingdom, who use about a third of that. Residents of African countries use even less—sometimes as little as three gallons. See Figure 9.2.

Average Daily Domestic Water Use (Per Capita)

Gallons of water per person per day

North America — 92
Europe — 53
Sub-Saharan Africa — 3-4

Figure 9.2: United States residents use more freshwater per day than residents of other countries.

Most people realize that hot water uses energy, but supplying and treating cold water requires a significant amount of energy, too. American public water supply and treatment facilities consume about 56 billion kilowatt-hours per year, enough electricity to power more than 5 million homes for an entire year.

Water conservation is a critical principle of sustainability. Restaurant and foodservice operations have a responsibility to use as little water as needed to keep their patrons safe and happy. Many steps are actually easy to do and ultimately help to lower utility costs and benefit the community.

[fast fact]

Did You Know...?
If all of the earth's water fit into a gallon bottle, the fresh water available for human use would equal just over one tablespoon.

577

Figure Focus

Figure 9.2: Why do students think that North Americans use so much more water than residents of other continents?

Discuss

• How is it possible that Americans use more than 100 gallons of fresh water apiece each day? What might account for all this use?

Reinforce and Review

• The United States uses more than 345,000 million gallons of fresh water every day; on average, Americans and Canadians use over 100 gallons of water per day per person for personal use.

• American public-water supply and treatment facilities use enough electricity each year to power more than 5 million homes for a year.

• Water conservation is a critical principle of sustainability; because restaurant and foodservice operations typically use a great deal of water, it is important for them to identify ways in which they can conserve this resource.

Teaching Tips

• Encourage students to monitor their water use in the classroom: Set up tracking sheets by each sink so students can record how much water they use for each activity.

Fast Fact: Did You Know . . . ?

Encourage students to discuss the following:

• What are some practical ways to increase the percentage of water available for human use?

• How can fresh water be reused? For instance, what other uses can students think of for soapy dishwater?

• What are some ways students can reduce their use of fresh water without changing their habits too much? For instance, taking a slightly shorter shower or turning off the faucet while brushing teeth or shaving can significantly reduce fresh water consumption over time.

CUSTOMIZED INSTRUCTION

Literacy Connection, 21st-Century Skills—Critical Thinking and Problem Solving, Think Creatively, Work Independently, Flexibility and Adaptability

Less Advanced Students

Imagine using only 3 gallons of fresh water each day for all your needs. How might this change your behaviors?

Encourage students to discuss the following:

- How might these water conservation techniques affect guests? Do students think that the majority of guests will even notice these efforts?

- Why do students think that the other steps Snappy Salads has taken to conserve resources, such as milk paint and biodegradable containers, might or might not attract guests? What type of guests do you think might be the operation's target market and why?

- Would the same conservation techniques be successful in more traditional operations, where more cooking is done? Why or why not?

Discuss

- What food safety principles could be involved in water conservation? What pathogens can thrive in water?

- How can the restaurant and foodservice industry capitalize on its conservation of resources in its marketing campaigns?

Reinforce and Review

- Although there are many steps an operation can take to conserve water, these should never be taken at the expense of guests or of basic food safety principles. Appropriate conservation techniques can save water, protect food, and satisfy customers.

- To conserve water, food should be thawed under refrigeration, not under running water; this requires planning for future services.

- Scrape or soak dirty equipment before washing it to prevent multiple trips through the dishwashing machine.

Teaching Tips

- Encourage students to implement the suggestions on this page and the next page in the classroom kitchen where appropriate.

[sustainability in action]

Snappy Salads

With two locations in Dallas, Texas, Snappy Salads works hard to reduce its water usage. Each unit uses about half the amount of water used in an operation of similar size that doesn't practice conservation.

The company's water-saving program includes using low-flow toilets and infrared faucets in restrooms, as well as a large triple-basin sink for dishwashing. As a restaurant that offers mostly salads, little cooking equipment is needed, so the decision to hand-wash dishes actually saves both water and energy costs.

Over time, Snappy Salads has built conservation into other aspects of its operations. The dining rooms use tables made from reclaimed wood, have walls painted with milk paint, and feature low-wattage lighting. Menus are printed on recycled paper, containers are made from biodegradable corn, and utensils are made from potato starch. Employees wear shirts made from organic cotton, hemp, or corn.

What This Industry Can Do

Water is an important resource for the restaurant and foodservice industry. Chefs need it to make the food, servers need it for customers, and employees need it to keep everything clean. Industry professionals can never compromise the safety and well-being of their guests when trying to find ways to save water. Remember, the water a restaurant or foodservice operation needs must be potable—safe to drink. Still, restaurant and foodservice operations can make some simple choices that can save water, protect food, and satisfy customers:

- Thaw food in the cooler. Plan ahead of time to put frozen food in the cooler for thawing instead of placing it under running water in the sink.

- Soak and scrape first. Dirty cookware and dishes should be pre-cleaned by scraping or soaking off as much food as possible in standing water rather than a running flow. See Figure 9.3. Then foodhandlers won't have to run the items through the dishwasher a second or third time.

Figure 9.3: To conserve water, preclean cookware and dishes.

Figure Focus

Figure 9.3: Presoaking utensils not only decreases energy and water use, but increases the dishwasher's efficiency, as soaked utensils typically only need to run through the dishwashing machine once instead of two or three times.

- Keep water temperature at the right level. Use a thermometer to make sure water is not hotter than needed. Water in a dishwasher should be at a temperature determined by the manufacturer. Water for hand washing should be at 110°F.

- Load dishwashers correctly. Make sure racks are full but not stuffed before sending them through. Figure 9.4 shows properly and improperly loaded dishwasher racks.

Figure 9.4: Dishwashers should be properly loaded and full but not stuffed, as in the second picture.

- Repair leaks quickly. A faucet leaking just a tenth of a gallon of water a minute can waste 50,000 gallons or more of water a year. Make sure that everyone in the operation reports leaks. Then, make sure any leaks are repaired as soon as possible. See Figure 9.5.

- Don't automatically serve water. Customers who would like to have water will request it. This policy helps avoid customers receiving water they don't plan to drink.

- Sweep the outside areas. Don't use water hoses to clean sidewalks and parking lots. Instead, blow or sweep the areas. Also, use timers on any outside sprinklers.

- Train employees to conserve. Managers must do more than set policies about water conservation. They must show their employees why it is important and how each person can make a difference. Then they need to follow up, to make sure everyone is conserving.

Figure 9.5: A leaky faucet wastes water.

579

Discuss

- Which of the tactics described on this page and the previous page do students think will be most effective in conserving water in a restaurant or foodservice operation? Why?

- How can these techniques be adapted for home use?

Reinforce and Review

- Water should be hot, but not hotter than necessary: Handwashing water should be at 110°F, and dishwashing water should be at manufacturer-recommended temperatures.

- Dishwashers should be loaded correctly to ensure that every item is cleaned thoroughly.

- Water should be served to guests upon request.

- Restrict the amount of water used to clean and maintain the exterior of the property.

- Leaks should be promptly reported and repaired; leaked water should be retained for other purposes where appropriate.

- As always, proper training and follow-up are paramount.

Teaching Tips

- Encourage students to look around the campus for examples of water waste. How can these issues be resolved?

Homework Activity: Banning the Bottle

Science Connection, Literacy Connection, 21st-Century Skills—Critical Thinking and Problem Solving, Information Literacy, Communicate Clearly, Initiative and Self-Direction

Some communities around the world have banned bottled water, arguing that bottling water increases both water waste and overall pollution, as the bottles must be made, filled, and shipped. Research these bans and their effects. Do you support or oppose these bans? Why?

Write a one-page report describing the bans and their effects, as well as why you support or oppose these bans.

Figure Focus

Figure 9.4: Can students readily identify the bottom picture as showing an overstuffed dishwashing rack? Why might overloading be an inefficient use of resources?

Figure 9.5: Most foodservice staff members eventually learn how to make small repairs in different parts of the facility. Why might learning to fix leaks and perform other minor repairs be a step toward conservation?

Discuss

- What other technologies or tactics can students envision that might also conserve water, besides the ones discussed in the text?

Reinforce and Review

- Some water-saving technologies that restaurant and foodservice operations can use include low-flow spray valves, low-flow toilets, waterless urinals, sink aerators, energy-efficient dishwashers, on-demand water heaters, and connectionless steamers.

- Although many of these items can be expensive to install and maintain, they can be considered an investment in the facility; often, the cost can be repaid in full or in part through lower utility bills, tax incentives, rebates, and business credits.

- On-demand water heaters and connectionless steamers are particularly effective ways of conserving water and energy, as they only require energy when needed.

Teaching Tips

- Encourage students to discuss what types of operations might choose to install such equipment and why.

CUSTOMIZED INSTRUCTION
Literacy Connection, 21st-Century Skills— Creativity and Innovation, Critical Thinking and Problem Solving, Initiative and Self-Direction, Social and Cross-Cultural Skills, Leadership and Responsibility
More Advanced Students
You are the general manager of a local restaurant and have decided your facility needs to conserve more water. Design a training program for your employees addressing some aspect of water conservation, such as water service or loading the dishwasher. Develop a 5-minute training session on the chosen subject and present it to the class.

Restaurant and foodservice operations owners also have opportunities to buy equipment and design their facilities to better conserve water. Here are a few examples of water-saving technology that can be used in restaurant and foodservice operations:

- **Low-flow spray valves:** These valves reduce the amount of water coming out of sink sprayers. Some states actually require them for all purchases of new spray valves.

- **Low-flow toilets and waterless urinals:** Conventional toilets use 3.5 to 5 gallons per flush. Low-flow toilets use as little as 1.3 gallons per flush.

- **Sink aerators:** An aerator adds air to a water flow. They can save as much as a gallon per minute in kitchen and restroom sinks. See Figure 9.6.

Figure 9.6: A sink aerator reduces water consumption.

- **Energy-efficient dishwashers:** Some of the newest dishwashers use less than a gallon of water per dish rack. Using a chemical rinse instead of a water rinse is also an option.

- **On-demand water heaters:** The average water heater heats up to 70 gallons of water and holds it in a tank. When the user turns the faucet on, the hot water flows through the pipes, and the tank refills with cold water to be heated. But when nobody is using hot water, the heater is still working to keep the water hot. Tankless water heaters heat water only when needed. Place them close to the sink and run water through a heating unit to produce the needed hot water. Figure 9.7 is a tankless water heater.

Figure 9.7: A tankless water heater reduces energy consumption and costs.

- **Connectionless steamers:** These cookers use almost 90 percent less water than conventional steamers. They don't connect to a continuous water line. Instead, they use a manually filled reservoir to recirculate steam rather than vent it. This closed system saves both water and the energy needed to cool the venting steam.

580

Figure Focus

Figure 9.6: How does adding air to water help conserve water?

Figure 9.7: Tankless water heaters take up less space than conventional water heaters, an important point in a crowded facility.

Many of the items in the preceding list require an investment that usually pays back over time through lower utility costs. Also, tax incentives, rebates, and business credits based on the purchase of these items are often available from local, state, and federal agencies.

[fast fact]

Did You Know...?
Did you know that Americans use 18.5 gallons of water, per person, per day, just flushing the toilet?

[on the job]

Employment Sustainability
As restaurant and foodservice businesses have begun thinking about what "sustainability" really means to their organizations, many have realized that a responsibility to the community includes making a commitment to the satisfaction and development of their employees. It just makes sense: The companies are strengthening their staff's skills and encouraging education and dialogue. This, in turn, leads to happier, better-served customers, more profits, and a stronger community as a whole.

For example, McDonald's Corporation focuses on creating "a diverse and inclusive" culture. It has multiple employee networks, including the Women's Leadership Network and McDonald's African American Council. All employees are offered seminars, workshops, and presentations that promote and explore diversity.

Another example is the multi-unit chain Burgerville, which offers coaching and mentoring programs to its staff with a focus on leadership and community. Employees can also take advantage of tuition reimbursement for completing coursework.

Essentials Skills
Water Conservation

Around the country, restaurant and foodservice owners and operators have found ways to conserve water and lower operating costs with a few simple strategies. From educating employees to updating appliances, they have a number of ways to make their kitchen and business a model of water conservation.

Step 1: Know Water Usage

Tracking water usage from month to month is as easy as reading a water bill or checking the meter. Not only will this make operators more aware of how much water gets used, but they'll see the savings add up as their bill decreases. Figure 9.8a on the following page is an example of a water meter.

581

Encourage students to discuss the following:

- How can low-flow toilets reduce water use? Can they be as efficient as conventional toilets?

- Many toilets in commercial facilities now have a two-part flushing system: The lever is pulled up to eliminate liquid waste and pushed down to eliminate solid waste, with different amounts of water used for each flush. How might these be more or less efficient than conventional toilets?

- Other commercial facilities have installed toilets that use infrared sensors to determine when to flush. How might these be more or less efficient than conventional toilets?

**On the Job:
Employment Sustainability**

Encourage students to discuss the following:

- How is "employment sustainability" related to the concepts of onboarding, training, and professional development, as discussed in Level 1, Chapter 8 and elsewhere?

- Link "employment sustainability" to diversity, as discussed in Level 1, Chapter 8.

- Why is it important for employers to provide coaching, mentoring, and other educational opportunities for their staff? Why might some employers choose not to provide some or all of these options?

**Essential Skills:
Water Conservation**

How can simply knowing a business's water usage provide incentives to use less water?

**Homework Activity:
Water, Water**

Mathematics Connection, Literacy Connection, 21st-Century Skills—Reason Effectively, Information Literacy, Initiative and Self-Direction

If possible, look at your home water bill. Call the water company to find out the average usage for similar households. Is your household use above or below the average? How do you explain the difference?

Write a one-paragraph report on your findings.

Essential Skills:
Water Conservation (cont.)

Encourage students to discuss the following:

- Describe some elements that would be used to train employees on proper water conservation.

- If half of all water use in a restaurant occurs in the kitchen, much of the other half occurs in the dining room. How can the dining room use less water while still providing excellent customer service?

- In what ways can students conserve more water in the classroom kitchen?

CUSTOMIZED INSTRUCTION

Mathematics Connection, Literacy Connection, 21st-Century Skills—Critical Thinking and Problem Solving, Communicate Clearly, Adapt to Change

Special Needs Students

How many ways do you use water each day? Which uses would you consider essential and which would you consider inessential? Why?

Figure 9.8a: Step 1—Know water usage.

Step 2: Educate Employees

Reducing water use is a team effort, so enlist the aid of employees:

- Inform personnel of policy changes.

- Invite them to make suggestions for water-saving measures.

- Post signs reminding employees to practice smart water use. See Figure 9.8b.

- Train employees to watch for leaky pipes, clogged nozzles, or similar inefficiencies.

CONSERVE WATER

Turn off all taps after use
Report any leaks immediately

Protect the environment by saving water

Figure 9.8b: Step 2—Educate employees.

Step 3: Conserving in the Kitchen

Half of all water use in a restaurant occurs in the kitchen. Here are a few tips to save water and cut costs:

- Switch to low-flow faucets. A low-flow faucet can cut water use by a third without significantly losing performance.

- Only run the dishwasher when completely full.

- Ask customers whether they would like water before serving it to them. A single glass of water actually uses closer to three glasses of water altogether: one when it is filled and two more when it is washed. Since many patrons order a beverage other than water, this single change can make a noticeable difference in water usage.

582

Figure Focus

Figure 9.8a: This meter indicates that 2,422 gallons of water have been used at this facility. In your community, how much money might this cost?

Figure 9.8b: Labels and signs like this are often posted in facilities that use significant amounts of water to remind employees that they should conserve resources.

Summary

In this section, you learned the following:

- Sustainability refers to all the practices that meet current resource needs without compromising the ability to meet future needs. For example, use a resource in ways today that don't hurt the future ability to use that same type of resource. Conservation is the practice of limiting the use of a resource.

- Water conservation is important because droughts reduce water levels and many parts of the world are already experiencing water shortages. Without water, crops and animals will die, which limits the food supply and raises prices; businesses and farms may close; brushfires and dust storms increase; and residents may move out of areas, thus overpopulating other areas.

- To use water efficiently, restaurant and foodservice operations should do the following:

  - Thaw food in coolers instead of running it under hot water.

  - Soak and scrape dirty cookware and plates in standing water instead of running water.

  - Keep water temperature at correct level for both the dishwasher and water for handwashing.

  - Load dishwashers correctly.

  - Repair leaks quickly.

  - Don't automatically serve water to guests. Ask them first whether they would like water.

  - Sweep outside areas instead of rinsing with a hose.

  - Train employees to conserve water.

  - Use low-flow spray valves, low-flow toilets, sink aerators, energy-efficient dishwashers, on-demand water heaters, and connectionless steamers.

583

Summary

- Remind students to review the following:
  1. The history of sustainability
  2. The need for water conservation
  3. What the restaurant and foodservice industry can do

Section 9.1
Review Questions

1. Conservation is the practice of limiting the use of a resource; sustainability is the group of practices that meet current resource needs without compromising the ability to meet future needs. Conservation is therefore a component of sustainability.

2. Water drought can have several devastating effects on a community, including a limited food supply, increased food prices, business closures, rising unemployment, increased possibility of brushfires and dust storms, and population migration away from the affected area.

3. Back-of-the-house staff can thaw food in the cooler, soak and scrape equipment before washing it, maintain appropriate water temperatures, load dishwashers correctly, sweep outside areas, and train one another to conserve.

4. Students may answer in a variety of ways so long as they appropriately defend their responses.

5. Students may answer in a variety of ways so long as they appropriately defend their responses.

6. Miguel and Chef Kate might consider low-flow spray valves, low-flow toilets and waterless urinals, sink aerators, energy-efficient dishwashers, on-demand water heaters, and connectionless steamers.

7. Students may answer in a variety of ways so long as they appropriately defend their responses.

8. Students may answer in a variety of ways so long as they appropriately defend their responses.

Section 9.1 Review Questions

1. Explain the difference between conservation and sustainability.

2. List the effects that a water drought could have on a community.

3. Give three examples of actions that back-of-the-house staff could take to reduce water usage.

4. Explain a situation in which you shouldn't try to reduce the amount of water you would normally use for a task.

5. George McKerrow states that, "Our industry uses about five times more energy than most other businesses, as we're open long hours. We require more energy to produce our products (good food), and we create significantly more waste than most businesses. We can and do find ways to conserve, and thereby become more sustainable. The good news is that we've been responsive, and we're always finding ways to reinvent ourselves in this area." What types of water conservation efforts would you expect to see at Ted's Montana Grill?

6. Restaurant owners have opportunities to buy equipment and design their facilities to better conserve water. What water-saving technology should Chef Kate and Miguel consider?

7. What do you think is the most compelling reason for a restaurant to use sustainable practices and why?

8. Why do you think Americans use more water per day than any other nation? Name three ways you could reduce the amount of water you use each day.

584

Section 9.1 Activities

1. Study Skills/Group Activity: Stress on the System

Work with two or three other students to research the current water restrictions or guidelines in three states from different regions. Be sure to include at least one of these states: California, Florida, Texas, or Colorado. Then, create a report showing how the restrictions vary by region of the country. Account for any major differences you see.

2. Activity: Down the Drain

Research the cost to purchase a conventional toilet and a low-flow toilet. Note how much water each uses to flush once. Then find out the cost of water per 1,000 gallons in your area. Comparing the total amount of water needed to flush each toilet 25,000 times, calculate how much water and money you would spend for each toilet. Which toilet would you choose for your operation and why? Write a paragraph of your conclusions.

3. Critical Thinking: Conserve Water

To conserve energy and cut costs, your restaurant plans to reduce water use by one-third during the coming year. What are some ways you can achieve this goal?

585

Section 9.1 Activities

1. Students should explain what the water restrictions or guidelines are and why they have been enacted. They should also explain why different regions have developed different plans for dealing with water scarcity.

2. Student should research these costs and determine the best choice for their foodservice operations, describing and defending their selections.

3. Students should develop a plan for reducing water consumption at their restaurants. Answers may vary but should include training as a component of the program.

Section 9.2
Energy Conservation

Introduce the Section

a. Explain why energy efficiency is such a critical issue for the United States in general and for the restaurant and foodservice industry in particular.

b. Identify some steps that the restaurant and foodservice industry can take to reduce its energy consumption, both in existing and new facilities.

c. Discuss the objectives for the section.

Vocabulary Review

a. Direct students to the key terms.

b. Pronounce each word, and have the students repeat the pronunciation out loud.

c. Discuss the definition of each word.

Teach

Discuss

- What are some historical and cultural reasons that the United States uses the most energy of any country in the world?

- What examples of renewable energy resources are used in your community? Why are they important?

Reinforce and Review

- Much of the energy used in the United States is nonrenewable, which means that it cannot be renewed and that it could be used up.

- Americans spend approximately $8 billion each year to cook, store, hold, and serve food. Increasing energy efficiency can reduce these costs.

- Many nonrenewable energy resources are fossil fuels, such as natural gas, coal, propane, and petroleum.

Vocabulary Terms

- **Fossil fuels:** Fuels that are formed from plant or animal remains buried deep in the earth.

9.1 Introduction and Water Conservation	9.2 Energy Conservation	9.3 Waste Management	9.4 Sustainable Food Practices
• History of sustainability	• The importance of energy efficiency	• Reusing	• Local sourcing
• The need for water conservation	• What this industry can do	• Reducing	• Sustainable seafood
• What this industry can do	• Building for efficiency	• Recycling	• Coffee
		• Getting started	• Animal products
			• Organic food
			• The emerging landscape

SECTION 9.2 ENERGY CONSERVATION

The United States uses the most energy of any country in the world. Restaurants and foodservice operations also use tremendous amounts of energy. To cook, store, hold, and serve food, Americans spend approximately $8 billion a year. Energy efficiency is the key to reducing use and cost.

Study Questions

After studying Section 9.2, you should be able to answer the following questions:

- What is the difference between renewable and nonrenewable sources of energy?

- Why is energy efficiency important?

- How can a restaurant or foodservice operation become energy efficient?

- What steps can an operation take to construct a more sustainable building?

The Importance of Energy Efficiency

Much of what people use to power cities, homes, and businesses comes from energy that isn't renewable, meaning we could run out of it eventually. Many nonrenewable energy sources are **fossil fuels,** fuels that are formed from plant or animal remains buried deep in the earth. Examples of fossil fuels include natural gas, coal, propane, and petroleum (also called crude oil). See Figure 9.9 on the following page for examples.

586

In addition to air pollution, one of the effects on the environment are greenhouse gas emissions, which are caused by the burning of fossil fuels. The burning of fossil-based energy sources to make electricity and manufacture fuel releases greenhouse gases. These gases, which include carbon dioxide and water vapor, trap the sun's heat in the earth's atmosphere. Some of this heat is necessary to keep us warm. But some scientists predict that over time, an increase in the volume of greenhouse gases could raise the earth's average surface temperature, affecting both the climate and the population. Although there are a range of opinions on climate science, many scientists believe that human activity affecting the atmosphere is "very likely" an important driving factor.

Renewable energy sources do not rely on a finite supply of a resource, directly emit greenhouse gases, or contribute to air pollution. They can be replenished quickly. See Figure 9.10. The most common examples of renewable energy include the following:

- **Water (hydropower):** Energy comes from directing, harnessing, or channeling moving water. The amount of available energy in moving water is determined by how quickly it moves. Fast-moving water produces a large amount of energy, such as that in Niagara Falls. This is the most common form of renewable energy in the United States.

- **Wind:** To produce energy, wind flows over the blades of wind machines causing lift, which then causes them to turn. The blades are connected to a drive shaft that turns a generator to produce electricity.

Figure 9.9: Fossil fuels include coal and propane.

Figure 9.10: Solar and wind power are examples of renewable energy sources.

587

Figure Focus

Figure 9.9: Why do many countries rely on fossil fuels to meet their energy needs? What are some advantages and disadvantages of this?

Figure 9.10: How can wind and solar energy reduce dependence on conventional fuels? What are their advantages and disadvantages?

Discuss

- Does an operation's use of renewable resources change the way in which it actually uses energy to meet its needs? Why or why not?

- What renewable energy resources do students see as the most practical and efficient? Why?

Reinforce and Review

- Burning fossil fuels to provide energy results in both air pollution and greenhouse gas emissions.

- Over time, an increase in the volume of greenhouse gases accumulated in the earth's atmosphere can increase the planet's average surface temperature, affecting climate and population.

- Renewable energy sources, such as water (hydropower) and wind, can be replenished quickly.

- The amount of available energy in moving water is determined by how quickly it moves.

- To produce energy, wind flows over the blades of wind machines, which forces them to turn, thereby generating electricity.

Teaching Tips

- Encourage students to debate whether renewable or nonrenewable resources are more efficient and desirable. Why might a restaurant choose to rely on one or the other, or a combination of the two?

Homework Activity: Human and Climate Science
Science Connection, Literacy Connection, 21st-Century Skills—Critical Thinking and Problem Solving, Communicate Clearly, Be Self-Directed Learners
Does human activity affect climate change? Despite much study, scientists, politicians, and the public cannot agree. What do you think? Discuss your beliefs on climate change in a one-page essay, defending your position.

Vocabulary Terms

- **Renewable energy sources:** Energy resources that do not rely on finite supplies of particular resources, directly emit greenhouse gases, or contribute to air pollution.

Discuss

- Does the use of renewable resources always mean saving money? In what ways can introducing renewable energy sources increase costs, at least in the short term?

- In what ways can students practice energy conservation at school? What about at home?

Reinforce and Review

- Solar energy can be converted to electricity either through the use of "solar cells" or by converting the energy to steam.

- Geothermal energy is the heat produced within the earth.

- Biomass contains stored energy from the sun through photosynthesis.

- Restaurant and foodservice operations can reduce their energy costs, which can reach five times as much per square foot as energy costs in other types of commercial enterprises, through either conservation or efficient use.

- Americans can reduce pollution and emissions and save money by using renewable energy resources and efficiently using nonrenewable resources.

Teaching Tips

- Encourage students to think of ways to reduce energy consumption in the classroom kitchen.

Fast Fact: Did You Know . . . ?

Encourage students to discuss the following:

- Why is the United States compared to Qatar, instead of to another country? (Note: Qatar leads the world in per-capita energy consumption.)

- Why is energy consumption here measured by barrels of oil?

- Qatar is in the Middle East. What effect might its geographical situation have on its oil consumption?

Homework Activity: Barrels of Money

Mathematics Connection, Literacy Connection, 21st-Century Skills—Use Systems Thinking, Information Literacy, Communicate Clearly

What is the current price of a barrel of oil? If the United States consumes 19.6 million barrels of oil per day, how much does it spend on oil consumption in a week? In a year?

- **Solar:** Solar energy can be converted to electricity in two ways: 1). Photovoltaic (PV devices) or "solar cells" change sunlight directly into electricity. 2). Solar power plants generate electricity when the heat from solar collectors is used to heat a fluid, which then produces steam that is used to power a generator.

- **Geothermal:** This energy is heat inside the earth. People can use the steam and hot water produced inside the earth to heat buildings or generate electricity. The water is replenished by rainfall, and the heat is continuously produced inside the earth.

- **Biomass:** Biomass contains stored energy from the sun through photosynthesis. Examples of biomass fuels are wood, crops, manure, and some types of garbage. When burned, the chemical energy in biomass is released as heat. For example, the wood burned in a fireplace is a biomass fuel.

Monetary costs are another important factor when talking about energy usage. Energy costs have been climbing throughout the last decade at an increase of 6 to 8 percent a year. Some restaurants use five times more energy per square foot than any other type of commercial building.

Owners and operators can reduce energy usage in a restaurant or foodservice operation in two ways:

1. Conservation

2. Efficient use

[fast fact]

Did You Know...?
Overall, North America is the biggest user of energy in the world. The United States, with a population of about 301,140,000 (in 2007), alone consumes 19.6 million barrels per day. In comparison, Qatar, with a population of a little over 907,000 (in 2007), uses 108,900 barrels per day!

Conserving energy means using less energy. An example is turning off a light when leaving a room. Using energy efficiently means using technology in ways that allow the same function to be performed while using less energy. An example is using a compact fluorescent lightbulb instead of an incandescent bulb. (More discussion about this topic will come later.)

Through a combination of renewable energy and the efficient use of nonrenewable sources, Americans can help to reduce the amount of pollution and emissions in the atmosphere and save money that can contribute to other parts of the economy. The restaurant and foodservice industry has a significant opportunity to lead the way in using energy efficiently and responsibly. Add the

588

---

fact that energy is among the top expenses in an operation's operating budget, and energy conservation and energy efficiency can have quite an impact on both the bottom line and the environment.

Did You Know...?
Utility costs consume approximately 2.5 to 3.4 percent of a restaurant's total sales each year. Any reduction in energy use can have a significant impact on the bottom line. For example, by leaving a broiler off for one extra hour a day, the average restaurant could save $450 a year.

What This Industry Can Do

To better understand the energy choices an operation can make to become more efficient, first try to understand how an operation typically uses its energy. See Figure 9.11.

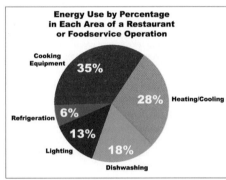

Energy Use by Percentage in Each Area of a Restaurant or Foodservice Operation

Cooking Equipment 35%
Heating/Cooling 28%
Dishwashing 18%
Lighting 13%
Refrigeration 6%

Figure 9.11: Energy use by percentage in each area of a restaurant or foodservice operation.
Source: National Restaurant Association

Every restaurant and foodservice operation should have an energy efficiency plan based on its usage needs. This enables management to see where it can make a difference. Many utility companies and energy-related organizations, such as ENERGY STAR (a program from the EPA and the U.S. Department of Energy), offer free online tracking programs that compare month-to-month energy usage. Many utility companies also offer energy-auditing services, sometimes at no cost.

589

Fast Fact:
Did You Know . . . ?

Encourage students to discuss the following:

- Is it realistic to think that foodservice staff members will pay the close attention to reducing energy consumption that their managers expect? Why or why not?

- In what ways can reducing utility consumption and costs benefit a restaurant or foodservice operation? What disadvantages can students identify?

- How can restaurant or foodservice operations that are open 24 hours a day conserve energy?

Discuss

- Are the percentages demonstrated in Figure 9.11 in line with student expectations? Why or why not? What categories would students have expected to be larger or smaller consumers of energy and why?

- How can tracking utility expenses enable an operation to change both its own bottom line and the environment?

Reinforce and Review

- Energy is among the top expenses in a restaurant's budget, so conservation and efficient use are critical.

- Every foodservice operation should develop an energy efficiency plan, based on its usage needs.

- ENERGY STAR, a program developed jointly by the EPA and the U.S. Department of Energy, offers free resources to help managers track their energy use.

Teaching Tips

- Encourage students to draw their own pie charts demonstrating what they perceive to be the consumption of energy in the classroom kitchen, using the five categories listed in Figure 9.11.

Homework Activity:
Black Gold

Mathematics Connection, Literacy Connection, 21st-Century Skills—Reason Effectively, Use Systems Thinking, Communicate Clearly, Information Literacy, Work Independently

Qatar consumes 108,900 barrels of oil each day. Select another country in the Middle East. How much oil does it consume daily?

Calculate the per-capita daily consumption of oil in each country. Which is greater? What factors might explain your findings?

Discuss

- Many of the suggestions offered here to reduce energy savings require no new technology, just some simple changes in habits. Why might a restaurant or foodservice operation not have taken these steps already?

Reinforce and Review

- Many utility companies can help a restaurant or foodservice operation understand its energy costs and usage by conducting an energy audit.

- Many steps that can increase an operation's efficiency and save money are commonsense measures, such as turning off unnecessary lights or equipment, cleaning and maintaining equipment regularly, and only operating machinery like dishwashers and ovens when they are fully loaded.

- Operations that can afford to invest in energy-saving equipment can conserve even more resources.

Teaching Tips

- Encourage students to apply these steps for energy conservation to the classroom kitchen.

- Consider inviting a representative from a local utility company to discuss energy conservation.

Homework Activity: Incentives to Change

Literacy Connection, 21st-Century Skills— Solve Problems, Communicate Clearly, Information Literacy, Work Independently

What incentives to install energy-conserving technology are available in your area, either for households or for businesses? Research local utility providers to learn what benefits they offer.

Describe your findings in a one-page report.

Homework Activity: Renewing the World

Science Connection, Literacy Connection, 21st-Century Skills—Use Systems Thinking, Communicate Clearly, Create Media Products, Work Independently

Which form of renewable energy do you find most interesting? Research this energy source to learn more about it.

Create a poster or slide-show presentation to share the information you have learned.

After they understand how much energy an operation is using, managers can begin to make efficiency improvements. Then they will see the impact on the operation's expenses. Planning ways to save energy does not have to be a complicated or overly expensive process. Some steps don't require any investment and are basically just good common sense:

- Turn off lights when not in use. Make sure that lights in closets, storerooms, restrooms, offices, and even dining areas are always turned off when not in use. Use timers if lights have them, especially for parking lots and other outdoor lighting that doesn't need to be on during daylight hours.

- Make sure loads are full. This applies to using any dishwasher, washing machine, or oven.

- Power down idle equipment. Powering down just one computer every night and on weekends can save up to $80 a year. This also holds true with nonessential kitchen appliances, copiers, front-of-the house computer systems, and other office equipment. Also, unplug electronic equipment, coffee machines, and small equipment when they're not in use. Many of these types of equipment are using electricity when turned off but still plugged in.

- Seal off unused areas. Reduce the energy used for heating and cooling by sealing off unused areas and keeping exterior doors closed. In cold weather, open up window treatments to take advantage of the natural energy of the sun. In warm weather, save energy and keep rooms cooler by leaving window treatments closed.

- Reduce idle times. Put in place a set start-up and shutdown schedule for the broiler, fryer, and range. This reduces both preheating and idle times.

- Clean and maintain equipment regularly. Clean and maintain heating and cooling equipment to ensure that they are running at their most efficient. This includes coolers, water heaters, plumbing, and all other major equipment. Something as simple as replacing a gasket or cleaning out some dust could make a big cost difference.

Operations that can invest in the latest energy-efficient technology have many opportunities for savings. Many utility companies across the United States offer mail-in rebates, loan programs, and tax incentives to businesses that invest in energy-efficient technology:

- Replace incandescent lighting. Compact fluorescent lightbulbs (also called CFLs) can be used in many parts of a restaurant or foodservice operation. Some examples are inside coolers and in kitchen ventilation hoods.

590

According to ENERGY STAR, if every restaurant in the United States replaced only one incandescent lightbulb with a CFL, the industry would avoid 570 million pounds of carbon dioxide emissions going into the atmosphere each year and would save almost $38 million a year. However, the style of light produced by CFLs is probably only good for back-of-the-house functions. Many restaurants choose not to use CFLs in dining or bar areas because the light they emit is often deemed too harsh for intimate settings, even when dimmed. These lights are very useful in professional kitchens, though.

Figure 9.12: Energy-efficient lightbulbs pay for themselves by reducing energy consumption. From top to bottom, we see a compact fluorescent lightbulb, an LED (a Light Emitting Diode) lightbulb, and an energy efficent incandescent lightbulb.

■ Consider using LED lightbulbs, which are also becoming more widely available as replacements for incandescent bulbs. Although the price is currently much higher for LED bulbs, their expected lifetimes are greater than 30,000 hours, close to four years. (In comparison, incandescent bulbs typically last between 1,000 to 2,000 hours, or two to three months.) The softness of the light is also closer to that of incandescent bulbs than the light produced by CFLs. They have the potential to work in all areas of the operation, not only the back of the house. Figure 9.12 shows a CFL, LED, and incandescent bulb.

■ Purchase energy-efficient equipment. Equipment labeled with the ENERGY STAR seal is energy efficient. See Figure 9.13. Most categories of restaurant and foodservice kitchen equipment have ENERGY STAR options, as do many computer systems for the front of the house and the office. Although these items can cost more to purchase, they typically save money over the long term. Energy-efficient fryers, for example, offer shorter cook times, meaning preparers can cook more food per hour while spending less on the energy used per hour.

Figure 9.13: Equipment labeled with the ENERGY STAR seal is energy efficient.

591

Discuss

- Installing CFL lightbulbs throughout the back of the house can be a wise investment for an operation. What arguments might convince a skeptical restaurateur to replace incandescent bulbs with CFLs?

- Similarly, using CFLs or LED lightbulbs might be a wise choice for households. Would the same arguments used to convince the restaurateur work to convince consumers? Why or why not?

Reinforce and Review

- LED and CFL lightbulbs, both of which conserve energy as well as money, are becoming increasingly available for use in restaurant and foodservice operations.

- CFL lightbulbs emit a very bright light that can be very effective in the back of the house, whereas LED lightbulbs produce a light more similar to incandescent light and are therefore suitable for all parts of a restaurant or foodservice operation.

- Energy-efficient equipment, used everywhere from the kitchen to the office, is typically labeled with the ENERGY STAR logo.

Teaching Tips

- Turn off the classroom lights and demonstrate the light produced by incandescent, CFL, and LED lightbulbs in turn so that students can recognize the different effects produced by each.

Homework Activity: Seeing Clearly
Science Connection, Literacy Connection, 21st-Century Skills—Critical Thinking and Problem Solving, Communicate Clearly, Information Literacy, Work Independently
How do CFL and LED lightbulbs work? Explain the science behind each of these forms of alternative technology. What makes these light sources different from standard incandescent lightbulbs?
Discuss your findings in a one-page report.

Figure Focus

Figure 9.12: Why might a restaurant or foodservice operation choose one type of lightbulb over another?

Figure 9.13: What other labels or seals are commonly found on restaurant equipment? (Note: NSF and UL are typical; see Level 1, Chapter 3.)

Discuss

- Following the energy-saving techniques outlined here can help an operation conserve valuable resources, as well as dollars. However, the techniques only work if they are performed correctly. Besides training staff members, what can management do to reinforce correct behaviors?

- Besides the steps listed here, what other suggestions do students have that can help restaurants—or households—save money and energy?

Reinforce and Review

- Restaurant and foodservice operations can save money on energy bills by using a timer on their water heaters and by only heating water to the minimum standards for safety required in their communities.

Sustainability in Action: Solar Power in Florida

Encourage students to discuss the following:

- Potential guests to a restaurant often base their impressions of the operation's menu and service style on their impressions of the restaurant's physical exterior. How might the presence of solar panels affect a guest's impressions of the restaurant?

- Estela's uses wastewater to cool its facility. What other uses can students identify for repurposed waste?

- Half of all electrical power in Florida is used to run air conditioning systems. In what other ways can residents of hot climates cool themselves and their homes?

Homework Activity: Light up Your Life

Science Connection, Literacy Connection, 21st-Century Skills—Reason Effectively, Communicate Clearly, Information Literacy, Work Independently

What is a photovoltaic module, or, as it is more commonly known, a solar panel? How does it work, and under what circumstances is it a valuable tool? In what ways does using solar panels help reduce consumption of nonrenewable energy sources?

Describe your findings in a one-page paper.

- Heat water in smarter ways. Restaurant and foodservice operations spend a lot of money to heat water. Take some easy actions to save money on this task. Two examples are using a timer on the water heater (shutting it down close to the end of the day) and making sure to heat the water to the minimum required temperature for the task. Many times, this means following the local laws about minimum temperatures for dishwashing and handwashing.

[sustainability in action]

Solar Power in Florida

One restaurant in Brandon, Florida, has found a way to beat the heat and harness the bright sun's rays. Estela's Mexican Restaurant was the first restaurant in the world to use solar energy and recycled kitchen water to power its cooling system.

In Florida, where the hot sun shines for many days during the year, half of all electrical power is used to run air conditioning units. The system used by Estela's draws most of its power from solar panels on the roof that turn sunlight into electricity. See Figure 9.14. The air conditioning unit uses recycled wastewater from the kitchen for the water required by the system to cool the building.

Not only has Estela's saved money on its power bill, it has also seen an increase in business. According to owner Scott Jorgensen, business increased by 10 percent once the new system was installed. "People are willing to support restaurants that are environmentally friendly," he says.

Figure 9.14: Solar panels turn sunlight into electricity.

Figure Focus

Figure 9.14: How might solar panels be more or less effective, depending on where in the United States they are located?

Essential Skills

Better Lighting

The average restaurant has its lights on for 16 to 20 hours a day, an expense that eats into profits. Help the environment and the bottom line by learning ways to make lighting better and cheaper.

Switch to Compact Fluorescent Lamps

Compared with regular incandescent bulbs, CFLs last 10 times as long, while using only one-third the energy. Replacing a single, regularly used incandescent bulb with a CFL will save an average of $6 per year in electricity and bulb replacement costs.

Update Older Fluorescent Fixtures

Many establishments, especially those older than 10 years, have outdated fluorescent light fixtures. The most common fluorescent fixture uses T12 lamps (tubes), a lamp style created in the 1940s. Though functional, T12 lamps have been surpassed in efficiency with newer technologies, such as T8 or T5 lamps. This switch may require converting the light fixtures, but utility companies and state organizations often offer rebates to help offset the cost.

Use a Shutdown Schedule

A simple strategy to cut down on power use is to use a shutdown schedule. As part of the closing routine, have a checklist that ensures every unneeded light gets turned off when the restaurant is closed.

Install Motion Sensors

In closets, coolers, and break rooms, it can be easy to forget to turn off a light. These little mistakes can become expensive additions to operating expenses. In areas that are often unoccupied, install a motion sensor that shuts off lights when a room is empty. These little devices will pay for themselves quickly, both in terms of energy and convenience.

Another investment that an operation can make in this area is to make sure the water heater and pipes coming from it are insulated. This helps to reduce heat loss when the water travels from the tank through the pipes and out the faucet. Another possibility is to locate the water heater as close to the usage point as possible. This reduces the distance the water has to travel to get to the faucet.

The final step in making sure a restaurant or foodservice operation is actually saving both energy and money is to track utility bills from month to month.

593

Essential Skills: Better Lighting

Encourage students to discuss the following:

- Why does the average restaurant or foodservice operation have its lights on during so much of the day? Are there ways in which fewer lights can be used for certain periods?

- Utility companies often offer rebate programs or other incentives to convince business owners to switch to technologies that conserve more energy. Why might these companies operate such programs, when doing so can cut into their own profits by reducing utility consumption?

- The use of motion detectors can conserve wasted energy. What other benefits can installing motion sensors have for a restaurant or foodservice establishment?

Homework Activity: Energy Efficiency

Literacy Connection, 21st-Century Skills—Reason Effectively, Communicate Clearly, Information Literacy, Work Independently

Research the ENERGY STAR program. What benefits does it offer? How can it help restaurant and foodservice operations save money and conserve resources?

Describe your findings in a one-page report.

CUSTOMIZED INSTRUCTION

Literacy Connection, 21st-Century Skills—Reason Effectively, Communicate Clearly, Information Literacy, Work Independently

ESOL Students

What types of renewable and nonrenewable energy resources are most commonly used by households in your community of origin? Are these the same resources that are most commonly used in your current community? To what do you attribute any similarities or differences?

Prepare a brief report describing your findings.

Discuss

- What difficulties might be involved with either designing a green building from scratch or remodeling an existing building to make it green?

- Why do commercial buildings consume so much energy, especially electricity? What are some ways in which even nongreen buildings can conserve resources?

Reinforce and Review

- Commercial buildings consume 36 percent of all energy and 64 percent of all electricity used in the United States.

- Businesses can dramatically increase net income by cutting energy consumption by 30 percent.

- The first step toward a green building, whether a brand new design or a retrofit, is adopting a green strategy that focuses on energy savings.

- Energy rebates, tax incentives, and other financial assistance is available for green building projects from national, state, and local authorities and utility companies.

Teaching Tips

- If there are any notable green buildings in your community, consider inviting a representative from the building's owners to speak to the class on how the project was developed.

- Consider inviting a speaker from a local building authority to discuss government incentives for green building.

[sustainability in action]

Culver's Restaurants

With 376 locations in 17 states, Culver's Restaurants knows that fuel is a major expense for the company and its franchisees. After seeing costs rise dramatically in recent years, the company decided to find ways to cut use and cost.

To cut electricity use, Culver's put timers on inside and outside lights, replaced neon signs with LED lights, and installed compact fluorescent bulbs. The chain also switched to low-energy LED exit signs, costing $1,000 less to run than typical exit signs. New cooking hood systems were installed, and Culver's management believes this has made a significant difference by keeping the kitchens cooler.

For water conservation, Culver's installed low-flow spray valves that cost $40 each. Culver's says the new valves pay for themselves in a year and save an estimated 123,000 gallons of water a year per store. Most recently, Culver's installed recycling centers at its family restaurants. The company is teaching guests to separate their recyclables.

One Culver's location took conservation a step further by becoming the first restaurant in the United States to heat water using leftover cooking oil. It was a challenge, company officials report. No other restaurant had attempted this before, and the restaurant had to work closely with fire marshals and health inspectors. But their work paid off. In the first month, the restaurant saved $270 on energy and fuel costs. A year and a half later, the system is still saving money.

Building for Efficiency

Buildings are among the top energy users in the United States. The EPA reports that commercial buildings consume 36 percent of all energy and 64 percent of all electricity used in the United States. Experts say that a business can increase its net operating income by 5 percent with just a 30 percent decrease in its building's energy consumption. An energy-efficient "green" building also adds value to the overall operation and investment.

A **"green" building** is one that has been designed, built, renovated, or reused so that the structure conserves energy, uses resources more efficiently, and reduces the overall impact on the environment. Figure 9.15

Figure 9.15: A "green" building is a sustainable building.

594

Vocabulary Terms

- **"Green" building:** A building that has been designed, built, renovated, or reused so that the structure conserves energy, uses resources more efficiently, and reduces the overall impact on the environment.

Figure Focus

Figure 9.15: What visual cues are there in this photograph that suggest that this is a green building? Why?

is an example of a "green" building. The first step toward becoming a green building is adopting a green strategy that focuses on energy savings. For some, that means building a green, energy-efficient certified restaurant from the ground up. For others, going green means retrofitting a current building to meet energy-efficiency standards.

Whether a green building starts from the ground up or is part of a remodel, owners often can find financing to fund or offset their efforts through energy rebates, tax incentives, and deductions available from national, state, and local agencies.

New Construction

Designing and constructing a new building from scratch affords the best opportunity for making an operation efficient and environmentally friendly. Some contractors and architects are LEED (Leadership in Energy and Environment Design) certified, meaning they have been trained in building facilities that comply with national standards for green construction, including sustainable site development, water savings, materials selection, and indoor environmental quality.

[trends]

Reflective Roofs

Buildings under construction and older establishments being refurbished can benefit from new energy-conserving roofing trends. Some restaurants have planted edible gardens atop their buildings, while others have replaced traditional shingles with metal. Both are types of "cool roofs" that are designed to reduce the amount of heat a building absorbs and thereby reduce energy costs. Other "cool roofs" are made by replacing or covering the existing roof with white or pale materials, including paint, polyurethane, and even clay tiles.

Cool roofs last longer than traditional roofing materials since they don't break down as quickly during hot weather. They can reduce surface temperatures by up to 80°F, so air-conditioning usage—typically a big drain on energy resources—can be drastically lower inside the building. Construction costs are also affected since less insulation may be needed in buildings with cool roofs. A final advantage is that cool roofs can help keep city temperatures lower by reducing the amount of trapped heat in the area. The more cool roofs in a community, the cooler the surrounding air will be. Because of these benefits, financial incentives are often available for those planning to convert from traditional to cool roofs.

Site selection is an important aspect of green building. A site with easy access to public transportation will help both customers and staff to save money and energy from driving. Placing buildings in spots that can optimize natural light and then designing to capitalize on the light will save costs. Brownfield sites may also be a good choice. A **brownfield site** is a previously abandoned

595

Vocabulary Terms

- **Brownfield site:** A previously abandoned industrial site that, once cleaned up, can be repurposed for commercial business use.

Discuss

- Why is materials selection an important part of designing a green building?

- "Location, location, location" is a popular saying in real estate. How is it relevant to constructing green buildings?

Reinforce and Review

- Designing and constructing a new building offers the best opportunity for making an operation efficient and environmentally friendly.

- LEED-certified architects and contractors have been trained to build facilities that comply with national standards for green construction.

- Site selection is important in green building: Locations near public transportation that are open to natural light are often good options, as might be brownfield sites.

Teaching Tips

- Show students some examples of buildings that were built "green," identifying sustainable or environmentally sound elements.

Trends: Reflective Roofs

Encourage students to discuss the following:

- Besides energy conservation, what other benefits might cool roofs have for a restaurant or foodservice establishment?

- Why is roofing a major focus of remodelers looking to incorporate green building principles?

- In designing a new facility or remodeling an existing building, how can restaurateurs incorporate green principles into their operations' walls? What effects can these efforts have on the business itself as well as on the neighborhood?

Homework Activity: Building Green

Literacy Connection, 21st-Century Skills— Critical Thinking and Problem Solving, Communicate Clearly, Information Literacy, Work Independently

What is the U.S. Green Building Council? What does it do, and what are its goals? Who are its members, and why?

Write a brief report on your findings.

Discuss

- What safety issues might be involved with cleaning up and building on brownfield sites? What factors might deter building?

- What challenges and opportunities might restaurant and foodservice operations face when renovating or remodeling their facilities?

Reinforce and Review

- Building on a brownfield site not only protects undeveloped land, but also might qualify an operation for tax incentives and other savings.

- Building renovations are opportunities to improve energy efficiency and reduce costs.

- Sustainable renovations typically involve researching energy savings, working with LEED experts, and budgeting for green improvements.

- Although green building practices might increase the cost of construction, over time much of these costs are recouped through lower operational costs.

Teaching Tips

- Consider inviting a LEED expert to speak to the class.

What's New: LEED Certification

Encourage students to discuss the following:

- What other questions, besides the ones included here, do students think should be asked about building sites and new construction to ensure sustainable building?

- Why might builders and architects choose to earn LEED certification for a building, instead of simply following sustainable construction practices?

- Why are buildings that exhibit innovative design or those that are regional priorities eligible to earn more points toward certification than other new buildings?

industrial site that, once cleaned up, can be repurposed for commercial business use. Developing on one of these sites not only saves undeveloped land but may also qualify an operation for tax incentives and property savings. Figure 9.16 is an example of a brownfield site.

Figure 9.16: Brownfield sites are land that was previously used for industrial or commercial purposes. The land may be contaminated with hazardous waste or pollution.

Renovations to Existing Buildings

For restaurant and foodservice operations in an existing building, renovations are an opportunity to improve energy efficiency and reduce costs. Renovating with sustainable practices in mind includes the following:

- Research energy savings. Look for incentives and tax breaks available for energy upgrades such as purchasing solar lights. Check with the utility company for free energy audits.

- Work with LEED experts. A LEED-certified architect or contractor will suggest improvements or perhaps even manage the renovation.

- Budget for green improvements. Building for energy efficiency can affect the upfront costs of construction. Owner/operators are more likely to save money in operating costs over the life of the building.

[what's new]

LEED Certification

LEED (Leadership in Energy and Environmental Design) certification is rapidly becoming popular in construction and renovation circles. This rating system, offered through the U.S. Green Building Council, gives third-party assurance that builders have adhered to specific construction standards. For example, is the site sustainable? Is alternative transportation readily available? Has light pollution been reduced? Has a brownfield site been used as a construction site? What about the environmental effects on workers inside the building? Or the amount and type of energy used, both to construct and to maintain the facility? Were local materials used in construction?

Buildings gain "points" toward certification levels, such as Certified, Silver, Gold, and the highest, Platinum, based on their performance according to these standards. Additional points may be awarded to projects demonstrating innovative design or that are regional priorities. The ultimate goal is to make the completed construction more profitable while simultaneously reducing its environmental impact. Although this program began in the United States, LEED projects may now be found in 30 nations.

596

Figure Focus

Figure 9.16: Can students identify any brownfield sites in the area? How might these be used commercially?

Table 9.1 lists many of the green materials and strategies that an operation can use to build or renovate green.

Table 9.1: Building Green

Green Materials	Strategies
Insulation	• Insulate exterior walls, floors, and ceilings to maximize heating and cooling. • Install windows that offer natural ventilation. Use double-paned windows to help with insulation.
Landscaping	• Add greenery to absorb heat and lower temperatures around the building. Plant native or adapted trees and plants and use recycled mulch to retain water around the plants. • Create a green roof of plants to insulate against cold and hot temperatures, absorb energy, and reduce water flow.
Lighting	• Install skylights and windows to save on lighting and heating costs. Use blinds to control the light. • Install timers, motion sensors, and dimmers to help control the amount of light used.
Nonwood and wood products	• Use wood composites made of agricultural waste and nonwood materials. • Use wood certified by the Forest Stewardship Council, which means it came from a sustainable, well-managed forest.
Recycled materials	• Use recycled flooring, bricks, stones, and paving materials for both exteriors and interiors. • Find ways to incorporate used structural steel, plumbing fixtures, and cabinets. • Recycle your used construction materials to keep it out of landfills.

[sustainability in action]

Spoons Coffee Café

A restaurant or foodservice operation's building doesn't have to be new to feature environmentally friendly construction elements. Spoons Coffee Café, a fast-casual restaurant and coffee roaster in Baltimore's historic Federal Hill, boasts plenty of energy-efficient features. Yet, the building is 120 years old.

Owners Deborah and Bernard Kayes decided in 2006 to adopt environmental practices. They wanted to stop depleting the earth's resources and saw they could save money by conserving water and energy and cutting down on waste. One of their first changes was to replace the building's black tar roof with aluminum-coated rubber. The "cool" roof reflects up to 80 percent of the sun's rays, lowering the inside temperature. As a result, the cooling system doesn't have to work as hard to cool the restaurant's interior in hot weather.

A year later, Spoons switched energy sources. Today, 100 percent of the restaurant's energy comes from wind power. Other green features include recycled furniture and equipment, as well as no-VOC (volatile organic chemicals) paint. New appliances and

Table 9.1: Building Green

- What would a restaurant or foodservice operation built according to these standards look like? What patrons would it be likely to attract? What type of food might it offer?

- How might using green building materials, including recycled and repurposed products, affect food safety issues? Is there a relationship between the two?

- How can appropriate landscaping help to lower an operation's energy costs? How might it affect the operation's other costs?

Sustainability in Action: Spoons Coffee Café

Encourage students to discuss the following:

- What special challenges might be involved in remodeling a century-old building in a historic location?

- Why might the owners have chosen to take incremental steps when adopting environmental business practices?

- Why might the Kayes have decided to use 100 percent wind power for their operation's energy needs? What other renewable energy sources might have been more or less appropriate?

Encourage students to discuss the following:

- Spoons has taken many steps toward becoming a "green" restaurant. What should be its next move?

- How can purchasing locally and organically grown ingredients be part of an overall green business plan?

- Spoons is not just a café, but a coffee roaster. Because Spoons is located in Maryland—not renowned for its coffee plantations—what are some inherent challenges to sustainability that Spoons must face?

Summary

- Remind students to review the following:
  1. The importance of energy efficiency
  2. What the restaurant and foodservice industry can do
  3. Building for efficiency

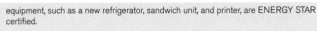
equipment, such as a new refrigerator, sandwich unit, and printer, are ENERGY STAR certified.

A member of the U.S. EPA Green Power Partnership, Spoons has a comprehensive recycling program for glass, cardboard, plastic, and metal. All food and biodegradable waste are composted. Spoons buys nontoxic cleaning products, recycles ink cartridges, and uses biodegradable paper products and take-out packaging, as well as eco-friendly menus. The neighborhood cafe replaced paper-towel dispensers with automatic hand dryers and its dishwashing station features a low-water, prerinse spray valve.

In addition to its conservation and waste-reduction efforts, Spoons buys local and organic ingredients when possible. The staff educates customers about the restaurant's conservation efforts and promotes Spoons' green initiatives on menus and in-store signs.

Summary

In this section, you learned the following:

- Renewable energy sources do not rely on a finite supply of a resource, directly emit greenhouse gases, or contribute to air pollution. They can be replenished quickly. Water, wind, solar, geothermal, and biomass are the most common examples. Many nonrenewable energy sources are fossil fuels. Fossil fuels are formed from plant or animal remains buried deep in the earth. Examples of fossil fuels include natural gas, coal, propane, and petroleum (also called crude oil).

- Restaurant and foodservice operations can become energy efficient by turning off lights when not in use; fully loading dishwashers, washing machines, and ovens; powering down idle equipment; sealing off unused areas; reducing idle time; cleaning and maintaining equipment regularly; replacing incandescent lighting; purchasing energy-efficient equipment; and heating water in smart ways.

- To construct a more sustainable building, operations should research energy savings, work with LEED experts, and budget for green improvements.

598

Section 9.2 Review Questions

1. Why is it important to reduce the use of fossil fuels?

2. List three renewable energy sources and describe how they work.

3. Give three examples of inexpensive actions you can take to reduce energy usage in a restaurant or foodservice operation.

4. What types of lightbulbs could be used in a restaurant or foodservice operation to reduce energy usage?

5. What is a brownfield site?

6. George McKerrow states, "At Ted's Montana Grill, we try to focus our energy on not only being a great restaurant company, but also embracing being a good 'world citizen.'" Research the types of actions taken at Ted's Montana Grill to reduce energy usage.

7. How can Miguel establish processes to ensure that Kabob is more energy efficient?

8. As the owner of a small café, you have decided that you can spend a few hundred dollars to improve the energy efficiency of your dining area. What would you choose to do and why?

9. You plan to build a 200-seat restaurant and have found an excellent site near the river and close to a popular tourist attraction. However, you learn that the property is a brownfield site. Knowing this, why might you choose to build or not to build on this particular site?

599

Section 9.2 Review Questions

1. It is important to reduce the use of fossil fuels to control air pollution and limit the emission of greenhouse gases.

2. Students can choose to describe three of the following energy sources: water, wind, solar, geothermal, or biomass.

3. Student responses may vary but should be clearly related to reductions in foodservice energy usage.

4. Using LED and CFL lightbulbs can help restaurant and foodservice operations cut energy costs.

5. A brownfield site is a previously abandoned industrial site that, once cleaned up, can be repurposed for commercial business use.

6. Students should research Ted's Montana Grill and report on the ways in which it controls energy use.

7. Students may respond in a variety of ways so long as their answers clearly describe ways in which Kabob can use energy more wisely.

8. Students may answer in a variety of ways so long as they appropriately defend their responses.

9. Students may answer in a variety of ways so long as they appropriately defend their responses.

Section 9.2 Activities

1. Students should clearly describe their lighting strategies for the various parts of the facility, identifying ways in which these strategies are energy efficient.

2. Students should present a cogent assessment of the locally available options for renewable energy. If few or no options are available in this area, students could instead be asked to assess the locally available conventional energy sources.

3. Students should research foodservice energy costs and strategies for reducing energy consumption. The presentation should be made to the entire class and should be both persuasive and informative.

Section 9.2 Activities

1. Study Skills/Group Activity: Lighting Plan

With two or three other students, design an energy-efficient lighting strategy for a restaurant. You should include plans for the kitchen, storage, office, parking, and dining areas.

2. Independent Activity: Renewable Energy Options

Write a one-page description of the renewable energy options available in your area. Possible sources of information include your city or county government, local utility providers, and nonprofit groups.

3. Critical Thinking: Menu that Reduces Energy Usage

Research different ways to reduce energy in a restaurant. Make a presentation to an imaginary restaurant owner trying to persuade him or her to "go green."

600

SECTION 9.3 WASTE MANAGEMENT

The statistics are staggering. The United States uses an average of 580 pounds of paper per person per year. Americans throw out enough aluminum in just three months to rebuild all commercial airplanes. As for food, approximately 100 billion pounds a year of uneaten, prepared food ends up in incinerators or landfills. This accounts for up to 20 percent of all commercially prepared food. These mountains of garbage and decomposing food not only take up space but produce volumes of methane that escapes into the atmosphere. Landfills make up 34 percent of all methane emissions. According to the EPA, processing wasted food costs the country $1 billion a year.

The restaurant and foodservice industry is in a unique position to reduce the amount of waste ending up in landfills. Efficient waste management also often leads to better operating efficiency and lower energy and water costs. A good plan focuses on three types of efforts:

- Reducing
- Reusing
- Recycling

Study Questions

After studying Section 9.3, you should be able to answer the following questions:

- What are some ways to reduce total waste in an operation?
- What items can a restaurant or foodservice operation reuse?
- What items can a restaurant or foodservice operation reduce?
- What items can a restaurant or foodservice operation recycle?

601

Homework Activity: Wasting Away

Mathematics Connection, Literacy Connection, 21st-Century Skills—Think Creatively, Critical Thinking and Problem Solving, Communicate Clearly, Information Literacy, Work Independently

For many people, it is easier to identify waste at home than it is in the workplace. After all, when food or other resources are wasted at home, the cost of the waste comes directly from the household budget. So, why do households waste food?

Research the percentage of food wasted each year by households. What are some reasons for this waste? How much does it cost? How can this waste be reduced?

Discuss your answers in a one-page essay.

Section 9.3
Waste Management

Introduce the Section

a. Describe the role played by the restaurant and foodservice industry in contributing to and helping manage waste-management issues.

b. Explain the separate yet related roles played by reusing, reducing, and recycling in the workplace.

c. Discuss the objectives for the section.

Vocabulary Review

a. Direct students to the key terms.

b. Pronounce each word, and have the students repeat the pronunciation out loud.

c. Discuss the definition of each word.

Teach

Discuss

- Why is so much commercially prepared food discarded?

- Why do Americans consume and discard so much paper and aluminum annually?

Reinforce and Review

- Up to 20 percent of all commercially prepared food—approximately 100 billion pounds—ends up in American landfills and incinerators each year.

- Processing wasted food costs the United States $1 billion each year.

- Efficient waste management can reduce waste, encourage better operating efficiency, and reduce energy and water costs.

- A good plan for efficient waste management focuses on reducing, reusing, and recycling.

Teaching Tips

- Encourage students to consider how waste management efforts in the classroom kitchen could be improved.

Discuss

- What other ideas do students have for reusing or repurposing food waste? For example, some coffee shops donate used coffee grounds to community gardens; restaurants might compost their food scraps and use the finished product to enrich their own herb and vegetable gardens; and so on.

Reinforce and Review

- One way to manage foodservice waste is to consider reusing or repurposing food that otherwise would be discarded, either for the establishment's own needs or for donation to another organization.

- If food has been safely held and has maintained its quality, it can be repurposed for another use.

- After food is on a customer's table, it cannot be reused; once it has left the kitchen, it has left the controlled environment.

- Appropriate methods for reusing food include serving the food in its original format, repurposing the food into another format, or donating the food to a local food rescue program.

- Food rescue programs are nonprofit organizations that receive mainly prepared and perishable food items as donations, and then distribute the food to local organizations, which then redistribute the food to families and individuals.

- Food banks are similar to food rescue programs, except they primarily collect and redistribute nonperishable foods.

Teaching Tips

- If there is a food rescue program in your area, consider inviting a guest speaker from the program or from a restaurant or foodservice operation that participates in the program.

Homework Activity:
Food for Thought

Literacy Connection, 21st-Century Skills—Communicate Clearly, Information Literacy, Initiative and Self-Direction

Are there food rescue programs or food banks in your area? How do they operate, and whom do they serve? Who donates food or other resources to these programs? What role do these organizations play in your community?

Write a one-page report discussing these operations and their work.

Reusing

One way to manage the amount of waste that an operation produces is to look at reusing or repurposing items that employees would otherwise throw away. Sometimes the operation itself is able to reuse the items. Other times, donations to other organizations help to reduce the amount of waste an operation is producing.

Repurposing Food

Repurposed food is food that customers did not eat, but that back-of-the-house staff prepared, cooked, cooled, and held safely. Most of the time, repurposed food was prepared in advance for customers but not sold. Safety and quality are obviously the key components to making sure this food can actually be repurposed.

Before considering any food for repurposing, ensure that the food was prepared and held in a controlled environment. A **controlled environment** is one in which food has been within the kitchen's control and has been kept safe from cross-contamination and time-temperature abuse. Food should be in a controlled environment from the time it is received until it reaches the customer. After food is on a customer's table, it cannot be reused.

Management can reuse food in three ways—two of them within the restaurant or foodservice operation:

1. Serve the food in its original format.

2. Repurpose the food into another format. For example, unused cooked chicken breasts can be used to make chicken salad.

3. Donate food to local food rescue programs, which are located in many communities. These food rescue programs are nonprofit organizations that receive mainly prepared and perishable food items from food establishments. Then they distribute the food to local food banks or soup kitchens, which in turn distribute the items to individuals and families. Food banks have a similar operation, but they collect and distribute primarily nonperishable food. Some shelters and soup kitchens may also accept food.

The restaurant and foodservice operation is responsible for safe handling the food before it is accepted by the rescue program. Work with the food rescue program to determine what food it will accept. As a general rule, food rescue programs accept only unserved food that can be safely transported and reused. They do not accept foods that spoil easily. Work with the food rescue program to determine who will transport the food. Most

602

Vocabulary Terms

- **Repurposed food:** Food that customers did not eat, but that back-of-the-house employees prepared, cooked, cooled, and held safely.

- **Controlled environment:** An environment in which food has been within the kitchen's control and has been kept safe from contamination.

programs offer free pickup and have employees and volunteers who have been trained in safe foodhandling procedures.

In some communities, you might be able to donate food scraps to local farms or zoos to produce animal feed. Typically, the scraps need to be refrigerated and covered until pickup.

Opportunities for Reuse in the Operation

Another way to reduce waste is to reuse. This can be as simple as printing on both sides of paper and reusing cardboard boxes, plastic containers, or glass bottles. Also reuse by purchasing goods manufactured from recycled materials.

Restaurant and foodservice operations have many opportunities to incorporate reused materials as part of their facility design and customer offerings. Possibilities include the following:

- Use recovered or reclaimed wood. Install flooring made from salvaged wood. Typical sources of this wood include old barns, large factories no longer in use, and even decks and wine barrels.

- Purchase used furniture and equipment.

- Buy new furniture made from recycled metal or other material.

- Install countertops containing recycled paper or plastic.

- Use recycled paper for menus, signs, and stationer.

- Use biodegradable dinnerware such as plates, cups, and utensils. Often, these items are made from sugarcane or cornstarch. See Figure 9.17.

Figure 9.17: An example of a biodegradable cup.

Donations

Worn but usable items are frequently accepted by many types of charity organizations and homeless centers. Uniforms, furniture, and appliances are popular and appreciated donations. Other opportunities for donations include the following:

- If you have unwanted, used computer monitors, hard drives, and systems, check with the equipment manufacturers. Most hardware companies have

603

Figure Focus
Figure 9.17: In what settings is biodegradable dinnerware appropriate?

Discuss

- In what ways can students reuse or repurpose items in the classroom kitchen to reduce waste?

- In what ways is waste expensive? Every time a still-useful item is discarded, money is discarded, too. Encourage students to discuss the relationship between waste and costs, both for restaurant and foodservice operations and for households.

Reinforce and Review

- Some communities allow restaurant and foodservice operations to donate food scraps to local farms or zoos.

- Opportunities for reuse can include purchasing goods made from recycled items, printing and copying documents using both sides of a sheet of paper, and using reclaimed building materials in new construction and renovations.

- Used but still usable items that might otherwise be discarded can often be donated to charitable organizations; similarly, purchasing used rather than new furniture and equipment for the operation itself can also save money as well as reduce waste.

Teaching Tips

- Encourage students to identify steps they can take at home, school, or work to reuse items and reduce waste.

- Consider holding a clothing drive, recycling drive, or other activity to encourage students to think more deeply about how useful items are often wasted.

Homework Activity: Biodegradable Dishes
Science Connection, Literacy Connection, 21st-Century Skills—Reason Effectively, Communicate Clearly, Information Literacy, Initiative and Self-Direction
Learn more about biodegradable dinnerware. What materials are commonly used to produce it? What types of operations are likely to offer it to their customers? How do the costs of manufacturing or purchasing these items differ from conventional disposable dinnerware? Write a one-page report answering these questions, adding any other relevant information.

Discuss

• What other steps related to "reducing" can restaurants make that can lower costs?

• How can smart planning be used in other ways throughout a foodservice environment?

Reinforce and Review

• Opportunities for recycling older electronics include rebates or discounts on new purchases or "e-cycling" programs.

• Reclaimed cell phone programs donate phones to a variety of needy populations.

• Used cooking oil can be used as biodiesel fuel to operate vehicles or, as in the case of Culver's, heat the water needed by the restaurant or foodservice operation.

• Restaurant and foodservice operations can limit the waste they produce by planning smartly.

• Smart planning involves accurate production forecasting and, where appropriate, bulk purchasing.

Teaching Tips

• Encourage students to identify ways in which they can reduce waste in the classroom kitchen.

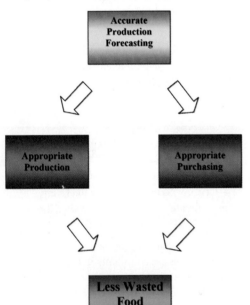

take-back programs in place, often offering cash rebates or discounts on new equipment. In some areas, "e-cycling" programs will pick up used electronics or offer a local drop-off center.

■ Old cell phones can go to reclaimed phone programs operated by homeless shelters, centers for battered women, and military-support groups.

■ Used cooking oil can be converted to biodiesel fuel for powering automobiles and farm machinery. In fact, a number of restaurants already use their own leftover oil and grease as fuel to run their delivery trucks or store vehicles.

[fast fact]

Did You Know...?
In 1996, the U.S. government enacted the Bill Emerson Good Samaritan Food Donation Act. This law protects companies and organizations that donate food to nonprofit organizations from criminal and civil liability. The goal of the law is to protect companies who donate food "in good faith," should that food eventually cause unintentional harm.

The National Restaurant Association is a partner with the Food Donation Connection, which helps to link restaurant and foodservice companies with nonprofit companies that can distribute food donations. Many states also provide tax incentives for companies who make food donations.

Reducing

Another component of a waste management system is waste reduction. Simply put, a restaurant or foodservice operation can take steps to limit the amount of garbage it makes. Reducing is both a benefit to the environment and to the bottom line: Less waste often means the operation is making better choices about food production and storage.

The key to reducing waste is smart planning. Accurate production forecasting can help to limit overproduction, which leads to less wasted food. It also helps buyers to purchase the right amount of food, leading to fewer products expiring in storage.

For those products with a longer shelf life, buyers can make bulk purchases as storage space allows, which helps to reduce the number of containers in use. Asking suppliers to consolidate their packing and shipping can also reduce excess packaging.

604

Fast Fact:
Did You Know . . . ?

Encourage students to discuss the following:

• Why do students think that the 1996 Food Donation Act is necessary? Why do donors need to be protected?

• How can "good faith" be established in a court of law?

• Why might states provide tax incentives for companies making food donations?

[sustainability in action]

The Rockfish

As part of the group of restaurants owned by Ocean Pro Industries, a company that also works in seafood distribution, The Rockfish of Annapolis, Maryland, continues to expand its sustainable practices every year, under the guidance of an environmental coordinator.

The company's recycling program began at a time when the county didn't offer recycling for businesses. The operation found a recycling facility that would take its recycled waste for $12,000 a year. Then to help smaller businesses in the community that couldn't afford an extra $1,000 a month to recycle, the operation set up big bins for cardboard, aluminum, plastic, glass, and newspaper and told fellow business owners that The Rockfish would buy them a beer when they dropped off their recycling. The operation then took the items to the recycling plant, which eventually began accepting the waste for free. Later, the company struck a deal with a farm 12 miles away to take almost all the restaurant's waste, except for nonbiodegradable plastic, glass, sanitary gloves, and straws.

The Rockfish added two rain barrels on the roof and nine in the parking lot to slow storm water runoff. The rain barrels provide water for rain gardens, which also slow runoff. The gardens of marsh grasses create little ecosystems in the parking lot and keep about 200 gallons of polluted water from every rainfall or snow from entering the bay.

Today, about 12 of The Rockfish's 15 seafood options are sustainable, and a quarter of its wines come from certified organic wineries that don't use pesticides. The Rockfish has also offered eco-themed events for the community to learn more about sustainable practices at home.

Recycling

Recycling transforms waste into valuable resources. Figure 9.18 is a recycle symbol. When recycling, sort and collect empty plastic bottles and containers, cardboard boxes, old newspapers, discarded cans, and other disposables for processing and converting into new, useable products. For example, old jeans can become wall and ceiling insulation, used office paper can transform into cups, and discarded beverage bottles can turn into glass tiles. Figure 9.19 shows some examples of easily recycled items.

Figure 9.18: The recycle symbol.

Figure 9.19: Materials that can easily be recycled.

Encourage students to discuss the following:

- Why might a restaurant or foodservice operation choose to employ an environmental coordinator? What responsibilities might this person hold?

- What do students think motivates The Rockfish to take such proactive steps toward protecting the environment?

- Several of The Rockfish's initiatives, such as protecting the local bay, are specific to its community. What elements of The Rockfish's environmental plan might be appropriate for operations in your community?

Discuss

- What items do students commonly put into garbage bins instead of recycling? What are some incentives that would increase recycling?

- What obstacles prevent restaurant and foodservice operations from recycling? What incentives could help them begin or expand recycling efforts?

Reinforce and Review

- Recycling transforms waste into valuable resources.

- A variety of used items, including glass bottles, cloth, and paper, can be recycled into useful products.

Teaching Tips

- If a recycling program exists on your campus, talk with its coordinator about its efficiency, and talk with students about ways to expand the program.

Figure Focus

Figure 9.18: Where is this logo commonly located? What role does it serve?

Figure 9.19: What other items commonly used in restaurant and foodservice operations can be easily recycled?

Discuss

- Which of the items on this list are commonly used in the restaurant and foodservice industry? In schools? In households?

- Why do some communities offer recycling for certain products, such as batteries or even paint, but others do not?

Reinforce and Review

- A wide variety of goods can be recycled, including metal, glass, plastic, and paper waste.

- Some items, such as batteries or cooking grease, can only be recycled in certain communities or by certain companies.

- Recycling prevents pollution, reduces greenhouse gases, and saves energy; it can also generate revenue for the business.

CUSTOMIZED INSTRUCTION

Literacy Connection, 21st-Century Skills—Solve Problems, Use Systems Thinking, Communicate Clearly

Special Needs Students

What items can households recycle in your area? Do you choose to recycle? Why or why not?

CUSTOMIZED INSTRUCTION

Literacy Connection, 21st-Century Skills—Critical Thinking and Problem Solving, Communicate Clearly, Information Literacy, Interact Effectively with Others

ESOL Students

What recycling opportunities are available in your community of origin? How are these similar to or different from those available in your current home? Why do you think this is the case?

Give a brief presentation to the class addressing this topic.

Homework Activity: Recycling Without Borders

Literacy Connection, 21st-Century Skills—Make Judgments and Decisions, Communicate Clearly, Information Literacy, Work Independently, Interact Effectively with Others

Every community has different opportunities for recycling, based on local demand. Select some other city or town in the United States and research the recycling options available there.

Prepare a brief oral report on your findings.

Typical materials that can be recycled include the following:

- Newspapers
- Paper bags and carry-out drink trays
- Office paper
- Corrugated cardboard
- Metal food containers
- Aluminum cans and foil wrap
- Milk cartons/jugs
- Juice cartons
- Glass bottles and jars
- Plastic bottles, cutlery, straws, and butter containers
- Film plastics, plastic wrap, plastic shopping bags
- All beverage containers
- Bottle caps

Some communities and companies also offer recycling for these items:

- Fluorescent lightbulbs
- Cooking oil, grease
- Cell phones
- Acid and NiCd (nickel-cadmium) batteries
- Uniforms
- Used furniture and appliances
- Computer equipment and ink cartridges

Recycling offers both environmental and operational benefits. It helps to prevent pollution, reduce greenhouse gases, and save energy. It can also generate additional revenue for the business.

606

[sustainability in action]

The Fresh Sourdough Express Bakery and Café

The owners of The Fresh Sourdough Express Bakery and Café, which is located in Homer, Alaska (approximately 220 miles from Anchorage), began their conservation efforts when the restaurant opened in the early 1980s, well before the sustainability movement was so widespread. Its guiding philosophy is to weigh the impact that every business practice has on the natural environment.

The operation practices the three Rs: recycle, reduce, and reuse. From the time the bakery and café opened, the operation has composted the restaurant's waste; recycled paper, aluminum, glass, and other items; powered down unused equipment and lights; and grown and purchased locally raised food. It also recently added low-flow spray nozzles and toilets; replaced old seals and gaskets; and switched to compact florescent lightbulbs, full spectrum lighting, and energy-efficient ballasts and hand dryers.

The Fresh Sourdough Express Bakery and Café buys local organic food to avoid shipping food to Alaska. The restaurant grinds its own organic grains and cooks its nutritionally dense food with organic, wild, and local ingredients. The staff wear organically grown cotton T-shirts.

[ServSafe Connection]

Handling Recyclables

Store recyclables in clean, pest-proof containers. See Figure 9.20. Keep them as far away from your building as local regulations allow. Bottles, cans, paper, and packaging give pests food and shelter.

Figure 9.20: An effective recycling container.

Getting Started

Much like water and energy conservation in an operation, a recycling program requires some planning. Before beginning to recycle, take the following steps:

1. Audit the trash. Make a list of the things the operation throws away every day. Identify what can and cannot be recycled.

2. Select a recycling manager. Choose an employee to oversee the program, track results, and report progress on a regular basis.

607

Figure Focus
Figure 9.20: What makes this recycling container effective?

Sustainability in Action:
The Fresh Sourdough Express Bakery and Café

Encourage students to discuss the following:

· What particular challenges might exist to recycling in Alaska? What opportunities might there also be?

· The restaurant purchases locally and organically grown foods. How might this affect its menu?

· This restaurant's guiding principle is "to weigh the impact that every business has on the natural environment." Is this philosophy a sensible one? How might restaurants in your community apply it?

ServSafe Connection:
Handling Recyclables

Encourage students to discuss the following:

· What makes a recyclables container "pest-proof"?

· What are some other ways in which pests can be denied access to an operation?

· Why is it essential to keep pests out of a restaurant?

Discuss

· How can a trash audit save a restaurant or foodservice operation money? How can it help conserve resources?

Reinforce and Review

· A good recycling program, like other business operations, requires a clear and thoughtful plan.

· A trash audit is used to identify materials that are discarded daily, both as waste and as recyclables.

· A recycling manager is responsible for overseeing training and implementation of the recycling program and for tracking and reporting its results.

Teaching Tips

· Consider assigning (or electing) a recycling manager for the classroom kitchen. Encourage students to describe this person's responsibilities.

Discuss

- Is it always appropriate to have recycling containers visible to guests in the dining room? Under what circumstances might that be a good or bad decision?

- What other components of a good foodservice recycling plan can students identify?

Reinforce and Review

- Always handle recyclables in ways that help to reduce pests and protect equipment and food from contamination.

- In some communities, recycling large amounts of certain commodities can earn money, so collaborating with neighboring businesses in a recycling program can generate income.

- Employee training is a significant component of a successful recycling plan.

- Many people, including young adults, select restaurants in part based on the operation's sustainability practices, so it is important for restaurants to publicize their efforts.

Teaching Tips

- What components of this recycling plan can be useful in the classroom kitchen?

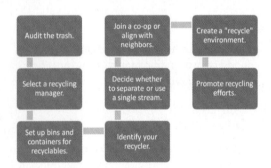

3. Set up bins and containers for recyclables and waste. Clearly identify and color-code containers for recyclables. Use blue or yellow for recyclables (like glass, metals, and plastics). Keep paper separate in a separate blue container. Use green for organics and black for garbage. See Figure 9.21. Cut holes in container lids and use clear, biodegradable plastic bags to see recyclables. Post signs on or above recycle bins with pictures and simple, concise instructions. Don't forget to include bins in the dining rooms of restaurants or foodservice operations where you clear your own plate. Let customers get in on the act.

Figure 9.21: Sort recyclables and waste in marked bins.

Remember to handle bags of recyclables in ways that help to reduce pests and protect equipment and food from contamination. When storing full bags for pickup, follow all of the procedures used for nonrecyclable garbage.

4. Identify your recycler. Check with your waste hauler/recycler to identify the types of recycling programs offered in your area. Although some communities have curbside recycling pickup, the type of materials picked up varies. Some items, such as cooking oil and batteries, cannot be processed curbside and require a different type of recycling process.

5. Decide whether to separate or use a single stream. Based on the curbside pickup program, the operation may be able to single-stream common recyclables. This means no sorting of recyclables. All designated recyclable materials go in one bin, and a recycling facility sorts them later.

6. Join a co-op or align with neighbors. Recycling large amounts of glass, paper, and aluminum cans generates substantial revenues from recyclers who pay for uncontaminated goods. To reap these financial benefits, form a co-op or recycling alliance with other restaurants or businesses in the area. Chain operators can get the same benefits by developing a central collection point for recyclables.

7. Create a recycle environment. Train employees on the importance of recycling. Show them what to recycle and what to discard. Involve customers if applicable.

8. Promote recycling efforts. Let customers and the community know how the restaurant or foodservice operation is recycling and helping the environment. In a 2008 National Restaurant Association survey, 44 percent of the participants said that they are likely to make a restaurant choice based on an operation's sustainability practices. The number is even higher for young adults.

608

Figure Focus

Figure 9.21: What colors are your local recycling bins? What items are put into each?

Composting

Do not dump or wash down inedible food scraps, such as plate scrapings and vegetable peels, into garbage disposals. Instead, compost them, turning food throwaways and biodegradable products into organically decomposed material used for growing plants and conditioning lawns and gardens. See Figure 9.22.

Figure 9.22: Food waste can be recycled as compost.

Composting, or biological decomposition, is a natural form of recycling that occurs when organic material decomposes (or composts) to form organic fertilizer. Compost is created by putting organic wastes—food leftovers, yard trimmings, and biodegradable products—in proper ratios and then into piles, rows, or vessels and adding bulking agents to accelerate the breakdown of organic materials.

Composting is also a process that can transform wasted food into an environmentally useful commodity. For example, in San Francisco, kitchen trimmings, plate scrapings, and compostable material from more than 2,000 restaurants are composted each day. Instead of 300 tons of restaurant food waste going into landfills, a composting operation turns the restaurant garbage into premium, high-priced compost sold to California vineyards.

Not all food waste can be composted because some of it can cause serious odors and/or attract pests. Make sure to separate items appropriately. Table 9.2 lists items that can and cannot be composted.

Table 9.2: Composting

DO Compost	DON'T Compost (generally)
• Cardboard rolls and clean paper	• Dairy products
• Coffee grounds and filters	• Fats, grease, or oils
• Food scraps	• Meat, fish bones, or related scraps
• Fruits and vegetables	• Papers with nonbiodegradable inks
• Kitchen trimmings	• Unwaxed cardboard
• Leftover bakery goods	
• Paper napkins or other paper products soiled with food	
• Salt, pepper, sugar, and straw paper wrappers	
• Soiled boxboard, paper bags, and paper tray liners	
• Tea bags, egg shells, and nut shells	
• Waxed paper, waxed cardboard	

609

CUSTOMIZED INSTRUCTION

Science Connection, Literacy Connection, 21st-Century Skills—Critical Thinking and Problem Solving, Communicate Clearly, Information Literacy, Work Independently

More Advanced Students

What is vermicompost? Explain the science of using worms to compost organic material. Under what conditions is this an appropriate way to compost?

Discuss this information in a one-page report.

Figure Focus

Figure 9.22: Under the right conditions, almost any type of organic material can be used to make compost.

Discuss

- Why might a restaurant or foodservice operation choose not to compost its food waste?

- Compost is often known as "black gold" in the gardening community. Why is this the case?

Reinforce and Review

- Food scraps and certain other kitchen waste can be turned into compost, used to provide nutrients and water to growing plants.

- Compost is created by putting organic wastes in proper ratios and then into piles, rows, or vessels and adding bulking agents to accelerate the breakdown of organic materials.

Teaching Tips

- Encourage students to discuss why composting might or might not be appropriate in the classroom kitchen.

Table 9.2: Composting

- Why do students think that animal products are in the "don't" list?

- How long do students think that certain items, like nut shells and waxed cardboard, might take to break down?

- What are some ways that a restaurant can save its food scraps for compost without creating food safety concerns?

Homework Activity: Break It Down

Science Connection, Literacy Connection, 21st-Century Skills—Critical Thinking and Problem Solving, Communicate Clearly, Information Literacy, Work Independently

How do organic materials—like wood, eggshells, or cotton—break down to become compost? Research and describe the processes involved in biological decomposition. For instance, how long does decomposition take? What conditions does it require? Why must some organic materials be composted in different ways or not at all?

Discuss your findings in a two-page report.

Vocabulary Terms

- **Composting:** A natural form of recycling that takes place when organic material decomposes to form an organic fertilizer; also, a process that can transform wasted food into an environmentally useful commodity.

Discuss

- Why might a company choose to compost rather than recycle certain items, like paper, and vice versa?

- What is the biggest problem with a composting program? What is its biggest benefit?

Reinforce and Review

- A successful composting operation requires time, money, space, and commitment.

- If properly administered, a composting program can help the environment by providing organic materials to farmers and reducing overall waste.

- Operating a composting plan might require certain permits from local authorities, including the health department.

Teaching Tips

- If the campus does not have a "kitchen garden," perhaps consider talking with campus and district administrators about whether such a program might be successful.

Making a Plan

Composting may not work in every operation. It can be expensive. Some of the most efficient composting systems require special equipment and resources, including water, labor, and electricity. Simpler systems still need equipment, containers, and signage. Waste companies and haulers also sometimes charge additional fees for transporting composting materials.

Time and commitment are also essential. Staff need training on how to compost, as well as extra time to separate food scraps and compost materials from other wastes, such as paper. If not handled properly, composted material can cause odors and attract pests. The system should be placed where odors will not bother customers, staff, or neighbors.

Those choosing to compost will help improve the environment by providing organic materials that enhance the soil, help reduce pollution caused by the incineration of waste, and improve water-holding capacity. See Figure 9.23. But most importantly, composting helps remove tons of waste from waste stream and water treatment plants and diverts reusable organic matter from landfills.

Setting up a composting plan is the smartest way to ensure that a restaurant or foodservice operation will handle this process effectively. Consider these guidelines when putting together a plan:

- Ensure adequate space for a composting system and bins.

- Find a hauler to transport composted material to a compost processor.

- Obtain the proper permits for composting in the local area and be sure to follow all requirements, policies, and standards. This will help to ensure composting in an environmentally safe way.

- Train employees on how to separate items for composting. Ask customers to help if the operation has a self-service aspect.

- Talk with like-minded neighbors. Collectively, the businesses might be able to save some money on transport and processing fees.

Figure 9.23: Compost is used to improve soil structure and provide nutrients.

Figure Focus

Figure 9.23: Ask students if any of them compost at home. If possible, set up a small compost system at the school.

[sustainability in action]

Composting with Kitchen Waste

The Rio Grande Mexican Restaurant made big changes to help the environment and improve the local communities in which it operates. To cut down on garbage and waste from its restaurants, the Colorado chain began composting much of its garbage.

Compost uses decomposed paper, food, and other organic matter to provide nutrients to gardening soil. The garbage is mixed with manure and special microbes that help to break down the garbage into nutrient-rich mulch. The result is a rich brown substance that looks like soil. When mixed into soil and used for gardening or farming, compost helps to give plants more nutrients, develop healthy root systems, and fight off disease.

The Rio makes compost with its own garbage. The restaurants collect all of their cardboard, napkins, order tickets, and other paper products. They also collect certain food scraps that the kitchens would normally throw away. They keep 700 pounds of garbage out of the landfill every single week. Instead, this garbage is turned into nutrient-rich compost that helps local farmers grow healthier crops.

Summary

In this section, you learned the following:

- Operations can reduce total waste by reducing, reusing, and recycling.

- Restaurant and foodservice operations can recycle empty plastic bottles and containers, cardboard boxes, old newspapers, paper bags, Styrofoam, paper bags, and plastic cutlery.

- Restaurant and foodservice operations can reuse repurposed food that was not eaten by customers but that was prepared, cooked, cooled, and held safely; use recovered or reclaimed wood; purchase used furniture and equipment; install countertops containing recycled paper or plastics; buy new furniture made from recycled metal or other materials; use recycled paper for menus, signs, and stationery; and use biodegradable dinnerware such as plates, cups, and utensils.

- Restaurant and foodservice operations can reduce by limiting the garbage they make. They can do this by accurate production forecasting, purchasing what they have storage room for, and asking suppliers to reduce their packaging and shipping.

611

Sustainability in Action: Composting with Kitchen Waste

Encourage students to discuss the following:

- Why do restaurants choose to compost, given some of the inconveniences associated with it?

- How is composting ultimately a form of providing excellent guest service? For example, farms receive nutrient-rich ingredients for compost, which is then used to grow stronger and more nutritious crops, which are then sold to restaurants and served to guests.

- How is compost different from soil? Why does it help plants thrive?

Summary

- Remind students to review the following:
  1. Reusing
  2. Reducing
  3. Recycling
  4. How to get started on recycling

Homework Activity: Compost Composition

Science Connection, Literacy Connection, 21st-Century Skills—Think Creatively, Reason Effectively, Information Literacy, Create Media Products, Work Independently

What does finished compost look like? Draw a diagram of the finished product, identifying important components like air pockets, bits of leaves or straw, and so on.

Homework Activity: Choices in Composting

Literacy Connection, 21st-Century Skills—Make Judgments and Decisions, Information Literacy, Communicate Clearly, Work Independently

There are many ways to compost organic material, ranging from high-tech commercial facilities to simple piles of leaves in a backyard. Identify and describe two distinct types of composting. What are their similarities and differences? Why might one method be chosen over another?

Discuss your conclusions in a one-page report.

Section 9.3 Review Questions

1. Student answers may vary; many possible items are found on p. 606.

2. Food can be repurposed by serving it in its original format, repurposing it into another format, or donating it to a local food rescue program.

3. Accurate production forecasting helps limit overproduction, which leads to less wasted food. It also helps buyers purchase the right amounts of food, leading to fewer products expiring in storage.

4. Benefits of composting include providing soil enhancements and reducing overall waste.

5. Students should research and report on Ted's Montana Grill and its recycling efforts.

6. Students may answer in a variety of ways.

7. Students may answer in a variety of ways so long as they defend their responses appropriately.

8. Accurate production forecasting helps a restaurant meet its environmental goals by reducing overproduction, overpurchasing, and overall waste.

Section 9.3 Review Questions

1. List ten items in a restaurant or foodservice operation that could be recycled.

2. Name three ways to repurpose food in a restaurant or foodservice operation.

3. Explain the importance of accurate production forecasting to sustainability.

4. What are the benefits of composting?

5. Research the types of recycling efforts currently in practice at Ted's Montana Grill.

6. Kabob currently recycles plastic containers, but it wants to increase its recycling efforts. What other materials should it consider recycling?

7. Why might or might not a restaurant choose to start a recycling program?

8. How does production forecasting relate to a restaurant's environmental goals?

100% Biodegrad

612

Section 9.3 Activities

1. Study Skills/Group Activity: Making a Plan

Working with two or three other students, talk to your school cafeteria about what it does in terms of reducing, reusing, or recycling. What can it do to improve?

2. Independent Activity: Promoting Your Efforts

Design a table tent for your dining room that highlights the steps your restaurant has taken to repurpose leftover food.

3. Critical Thinking: Compost

You would like to compost the waste from your 30-seat seafood restaurant, but you're not sure how to start. Make a list of all the items your restaurant currently throws away instead of composting. Research your local government rules governing composting in your area. Based on this information, plan a composting system and develop some ways to train your employees on the new system. Write a two-page essay covering this information.

613

Section 9.3 Activities

1. Students should talk with campus foodservice staff about their recycling, reducing, and reusing efforts and report their findings, as well as identify any possible improvements.

2. Students should develop a creative table tent that describes their operations' repurposing efforts.

3. Students should identify compostable materials that are otherwise wasted (the list does not need to be comprehensive) and research how these items could be appropriately composted in your community. They should develop a composting plan based on these regulations, and then describe some components of appropriate employee training on the new plan.

Section 9.4
Sustainable Food Practices

Introduce the Section

a. Explain the role of purchasing as a component of both sustainable practices and cost-conscious practices.

b. Describe the environmental implications of conventional and sustainable production methods for some common foods.

c. Discuss the objectives for the section.

Vocabulary Review

a. Direct students to the key terms.

b. Pronounce each word, and have the students repeat the pronunciation out loud.

c. Discuss the definition of each word.

Teach

Discuss

• Why might offering locally produced foods, such as vegetables or cheeses, help attract guests to a restaurant or foodservice operation?

• In what ways can offering these items benefit both the operation and the community?

Reinforce and Review

• Over the last 10 years, both chefs and consumers have become increasingly conscious of the issues involved in sustainable food production.

• In a recent National Restaurant Association survey, more than 1,600 chef members of the American Culinary Federation ranked local produce as the top food trend.

• Restaurant and foodservice operations can often attract customers by offering foods produced locally.

• There is no established rule about what makes an item or a source "local."

Teaching Tips

• Consider inviting a local food producer to speak to the class.

Vocabulary Terms

• **Local source:** A supplier offering food produced in the surrounding growing region.

9.1 Introduction and Water Conservation	9.2 Energy Conservation	9.3 Waste Management	9.4 Sustainable Food Practices
• History of sustainability	• The importance of energy efficiency	• Reusing	• Local sourcing
• The need for water conservation	• What this industry can do	• Reducing	• Sustainable seafood
• What this industry can do	• Building for efficiency	• Recycling	• Coffee
		• Getting started	• Animal products
			• Organic food
			• The emerging landscape

SECTION 9.4 SUSTAINABLE FOOD PRACTICES

Research studies throughout the past 10 years have shown that consumers are increasingly interested in where their food comes from and how it is produced. And chefs agree: More than 1,600 chefs ranked local produce as the top food trend in a 2009 survey by the National Restaurant Association. So how can the industry respond to this interest? Where will it make the most sense for an operation to focus on sustainable food? This section discusses some of the issues associated with sustainable food production and what options a restaurant or foodservice operation has for offering these types of products.

Study Questions

After studying Section 9.4, you should be able to answer the following questions:

■ What steps should you take if you decide to offer locally sourced food to your customers?

■ What must you consider if you decide to offer sustainably produced seafood on your menu?

■ What are the issues surrounding sustainably produced coffee, animal products, and organic food?

Local Sourcing

As sustainability continues to grow, featuring food produced by an operation's local region can be a powerful tool to attract customers. A **local source** offers food produced in the surrounding growing region. There is no hard and fast rule about what exact distance makes a source local. For example, one vendor

614

Homework Activity: Across the Miles

Literacy Connection, 21st-Century Skills—Critical Thinking and Problem Solving, Communicate Clearly, Information Literacy, Work Independently

What is the "100-mile diet"? Would it be easy or difficult for you to follow these prescriptions? Why or why not?

Share your thoughts in a one-page essay.

may sell produce from its farm in a neighboring town, while another may offer dairy products from a location in a neighboring state. Depending on the region and the considerations of the purchaser, both products might still be considered "local." The spirit of the concept is to purchase food that comes from a relatively close source and supports the surrounding economy and communities.

Many environmental advocates also point to local sourcing as a way to reduce the amount of travel that some food products must make. This travel is commonly called **food miles.** In the course of growing, processing, packaging, and sale, some foods might travel anywhere from one mile to thousands of miles.

Until recently, the focus of food miles has been on the environmental impact of the travel, specifically on how much fossil fuel is used in the shipment of the food from place to place. But the issue of food miles is a complex one. Some opportunities demonstrate obvious benefit to reducing travel impact; for example, in the summer, buying strawberries that were just picked from a local, sustainable farm rather than purchasing berries from a vendor that is shipping the produce from 2,000 miles away. But other purchases may not offer such clear benefit. Recently, some researchers have shown that food miles may not simply be about distance traveled. For example, a study by Lincoln University in New Zealand shows that producing lamb on the temperate and fertile lands of New Zealand and then sailing the product to the United Kingdom results in far less energy impact than raising the lambs in the United Kingdom, where feed must be used and energy needs during the animals' life spans are far different. The lamb from New Zealand will travel 11,000 food miles, but the use of fossil fuels and emission of greenhouse gases isn't nearly as great as the British lamb traveling fewer than even 100 miles.

A restaurant or foodservice operation that wants to buy food from local sources needs to be prepared and focused on specific goals:

1. Start small and look for logical opportunities. The first step in local sourcing is to decide what "local" means to the specific restaurant or foodservice operation and then look at the menu. From what regions is the operation willing to buy? Where on the menu does a local product make the most sense? Most operations cannot source all products locally, whether it is because of cost, location, or practicality. But most likely, it can find at least a few options through farmers' markets or by talking with a supplier about its interest in local products.

2. Research and network. The more time spent researching options and talking with other individuals interested in local sourcing, the more likely it is that a manger will find others working toward the same goals. Evaluate each option to better understand the true effect of each choice. Many cities already have collectives of restaurants that work together to find local

615

Discuss

- What does "local" mean? Does it matter where food is produced, as long as it tastes good?
- How can committing to purchasing only locally grown foods affect a restaurant or foodservice operation's menu?

Reinforce and Review

- The spirit of local sourcing is to purchase food that comes from a relatively close source and supports the surrounding economy and communities.
- Depending on the situation, local sourcing can also limit the number of food miles required to prepare and serve a meal, thereby reducing the amount of energy and the cost used to provide the food.
- Food miles are not the only standard by which to judge the sustainability of an item; the methods used to produce the item are also important.
- The first step in pursuing a local-sourcing plan is determining what "local" means in that specific instance.
- Purchasing from local suppliers typically involves research and networking to learn who offers what products in what amounts.

Teaching Tips

- Encourage students to discuss the relationship between locally sourced items and healthy eating. For instance, what foods would be excluded from a locally sourced diet in your area?

CUSTOMIZED INSTRUCTION
Mathematics Connection, Literacy Connection, 21st-Century Skills—Solve Problems, Information Literacy, Be Self-Directed Learners
Less Advanced Students
Select three of your favorite foods. Where is each produced? How far does it travel to reach you?

Vocabulary Terms

- **Food miles:** The amount of travel a specific food item must take from its production site to its consumption site.

Discuss

- Do any restaurant or foodservice operations in the area feature locally grown foods? What types of customers do they attract? What dishes are they known for preparing?

Reinforce and Review

- Nonprofit organizations can help connect restaurants and local purveyors; in communities with farmers' markets, conversations with the suppliers might be all that is necessary to find new sources.

- Many operations that rely on locally sourced foods change all or part of their menus more frequently than those that do not.

- Many guests and potential guests respond favorably to operations that offer locally sourced foods; using the sources' names on menus and in promotional materials can help raise the profile of both the operation and the supplier.

Teaching Tips

- If any nearby restaurants serve locally sourced foods, obtain menus and share them with the class as part of a discussion of what foods are produced nearby.

Trends:
Farm to Table

Encourage students to discuss the following:

- Is the growing popularity of the "farm-to-table" movement a trend, or is it here to stay? Why or why not?

- How can farmers' markets and community-supported agriculture programs link producers with consumers, at both the wholesale and the retail levels?

- Is eating locally produced food healthier than eating globally sourced foods? Is it always better for the environment?

suppliers. Some areas may have nonprofit organizations working to connect local farmers and buyers. Simply talking to the farmers at a market can also go a long way toward learning what is available, and then the farmers also better understand what your operation wants. Many operations work with farmers to increase the amount of a crop available. Some large companies, including Chipotle, even invest in the development of sustainable agriculture to better support their volume needs.

3. Stay flexible. Many operations that locally source products revise their menus on a regular basis to account for what is seasonally available. This doesn't mean that the entire menu must change (although some operations do this). A manageable starting point might be to focus on specials that correlate with what can be bought locally—for example, heirloom tomato salad in the summer or pumpkin soup in the autumn.

4. Promote local efforts. It pays to let customers know that the menu features locally produced ingredients. Mention the name of the farm on the menu and train servers to talk about the operation's efforts to support local companies as part of their menu presentation. More casual operations might use table tents, posters, or creative names for dishes to show their sourcing efforts.

[trends]

Farm to Table

An increasing trend in many parts of the country is for restaurants and other foodservice establishments to purchase local ingredients such as meat, vegetables, and even dry goods like flour. Some restaurants, like Meriwether's (Oregon) and Blue Hill at Stone Barns (New York), even maintain their own gardens or farms to ensure that their customers receive the freshest available foods, some of which may be unique to the area. Many restaurants hold "farm dinners," in which as many ingredients as possible come from a local farm partner. Overall, this "farm-to-table" movement, pioneered in this country by Alice Waters, has helped protect many smaller farms and has generated significant interest in traditional foodways.

This is tied into a local-foods movement that is becoming increasingly popular in the United States and Europe. Patronage of farmers' markets and community-supported agriculture (CSA) projects continues to rise as consumers are ever more curious about the origins of their food. Local growers and foragers use these outlets to provide produce, meat, dairy, and other ingredients to their customers.

A related trend is the "locavore" movement: people choose to eat only or primarily foods produced within a specific radius from their homes.

616

Sustainable Seafood

When last measured in 2007, global seafood production topped 140 billion tons. The Food and Agriculture Organization of the United Nations (FAO) estimates that by 2030, more than 40 million additional tons will be needed to meet global demand.

Americans spend more than 7 percent of their food dollars on seafood. This amounts to almost $70 billion a year. Restaurants account for two-thirds of all seafood revenue in the United States, while an additional 24 percent is made through retail outlets. Table 9.3 lists the most popular seafood in the United States and consumptions rates per person.

Table 9.3: Most Popular Seafood in the United States	
Seafood	**Consumption Rates per Person, 2008**
1. Shrimp	4.10 pounds
2. Canned tuna	2.80 pounds
3. Salmon	1.84 pounds
4. Alaska pollock	1.34 pounds
5. Tilapia	1.19 pounds

Source: National Fisheries Institute

The FAO also reports that 75 percent of the world's fish species have been fully fished, overfished, or depleted within the last 15 years. The reason for this is not entirely clear but is definitely complex. As the world's population has increased, so has the demand for food like seafood. Diets continue to change, with some populations more recently focusing on the nutritional value of seafood.

617

Discuss

- How can the menu choices a restaurant or group of restaurants makes affect fishing choices?

Reinforce and Review

- Some factors that contribute to the depletion of fish stocks include overfishing, bycatch, bottom trawling, habitat damage, and pollution.

- Some fishing equipment targets specific species and sizes, whereas other equipment catches everything in the target area.

- Fishermen work to reduce bycatch, which takes time and energy from catching the intended species and injures or kills other species; bycatch accounts for about 40 percent of the global marine catch.

- Farming and development can affect marine environments by polluting and damaging habitats.

- Efforts to divert water, such as by building dams, can also result in the destruction of marine habitats.

Vocabulary Terms

- **Overfishing:** Harvesting yields of fish that outpace the species' ability to replenish its population.

- **Bycatch:** Fish and seafood that are caught unintentionally.

- **Trawlers:** Fishing boats that pull large nets through the ocean, catching most of what is in their paths regardless of species or size.

- **Bottom trawling:** Scraping along the ocean floor with a net, disturbing or destroying marine life.

- **Habitat damage:** The damage done to specific marine environments, often through development or farming.

- **Dead zone:** An area of water in which the oxygen has been depleted, and the sea life destroyed, by the algae blooms that result from the runoff of nutrients and waste from farming.

In addition, some technological advances in fishing and environmental changes have produced new effects:

- **Overfishing:** Some species are being caught at a faster rate than they can reproduce. Recent advances in tracking equipment and fishing gear have allowed boats to catch larger yields of fish than in years past, outpacing the fish's ability to replenish its population.

- **Bycatch:** Some fishing gear will catch other species in addition to the species that is targeted in a given region. For example, **trawlers** are fishing boats that pull large nets through the water (called "trawls"), catching everything that is too big to escape through the mesh of the nets. See Figure 9.24. These fish are sometimes too small, too young, or undesirable for sale. Marine life such as seals,

Figure 9.24: A trawler is used for commercial fishing.

whales, dolphins, sea turtles, and seabirds can also be accidentally caught in the gear. Fishermen try to reduce bycatch because it takes time and energy away from catching the target species. Fishery managers work to develop more efficient gear and to close areas where the probability of bycatch is high. Still, a study group of the global conservation group WWF (World Wildlife Fund) estimates the amount of bycatch is at least 38 million tons each year, or about 40 percent of the global marine catch.

- **Bottom trawling:** This involves pulling trawls across the bottom of the sea floor, where the heavy equipment scrapes against it. This scraping can muddy the water with loose sediment, destroy coral and other sea life, and dislodge rocks or other chunks of the floor. The fishing method itself also affects the ability of marine life to survive.

- **Habitat damage:** Some scientists point to farming and development on land having an effect on coastal waters and aquatic ecosystems. For example, nutrients and waste from farming can reach bodies of water through runoff from the land. When these nutrients reach high enough levels, they can create very large algae blooms. These blooms deplete the oxygen in the water, which dooms the species in the area. Another term for the effect of these blooms is **dead zones**. Dead zones now exist throughout the world.

- **Carbon emissions, pollution, shoreline development, and dams and water diversions:** These can all have an impact on the natural patterns of marine life and coastal waters.

618

Figure Focus

Figure 9.24: Besides trawling, in what other ways can fish and seafood be harvested?

Available Options

Fisheries in the wild are still producing billions of tons of fish each year. But the sharp increase in demand for seafood over the last few decades has led to an equally strong increase in the production of farm-raised fish. **Aquaculture** is the production of seafood under controlled conditions. See Figure 9.25. According to researchers at the National Academy of Sciences, aquaculture now accounts for 50 percent of the fish consumed globally—an integral element for meeting global demand. A restaurant and foodservice operation seeking out vendors that provide environmentally sustainable seafood can enjoy both farm-raised and wild-caught options.

Figure 9.25: Aquaculture produces 50 percent of the fish consumed globally.

The key to choosing seafood from sustainable fisheries is research. To help restaurateurs and consumers determine which species of fish are in strong supply and caught or produced with sustainable practices in mind, some conservation groups offer guides for understanding which species and locations are viable for sustainable purchase. These groups typically combine government research, opinions from fishery and farm experts, and information from local scientists about current populations and sustainable practices. Typically, they offer recommendations for which species to purchase, which species are good substitutes for others, and which species to avoid. The guides are not definitive; one fishery may have a sustainable population of a "species to avoid" while another does not. Talking with a reputable supplier about its seafood sourcing policies and species diversity is still the best process for understanding sustainable seafood options available to a specific operation. Table 9.4 offers examples of guides and the organizations that create them.

Table 9.4: Organizations and Publications

Organization	Publication
Monterey Bay Aquarium	*Seafood Watch*
National Oceanic and Atmospheric Administration	*FishWatch*
New England Aquarium	*Celebrate Seafood*
Seafood Choices Alliance	*The Good Catch Manual*

619

Figure Focus

Figure 9.25: Is aquaculture appropriate for all types of seafood? Why or why not?

Discuss

- When designing a menu, which is a more important consideration: a species' sustainability or consumer demand for it? Why?

Reinforce and Review

- Wild fisheries produce billions of tons of fish per year, but aquaculture now accounts for 50 percent of global seafood consumption.

- The key to choosing seafood from sustainable fisheries is research.

- Some conservation groups report their findings to the public about which species and locations can be fished sustainably, which can help guide purchases.

- Talking with a reputable supplier about its seafood sourcing policies and species diversity is the best process for understanding the sustainable seafood options available to a particular restaurant or foodservice operation.

Table 9.4: Organizations and Publications

- Why are there so many organizations and publications dedicated to seafood sustainability?

- What makes the National Oceanic and Atmospheric Administration (NOAA) different from the other groups in this table? (Note: It is the only member of the list that is a federal agency.)

- How do aquaria play a role in sustaining seafood populations?

Homework Activity: Saving Seafood

Literacy Connection, 21st-Century Skills— Critical Thinking and Problem Solving, Communicate Clearly, Information Literacy, Work Independently

Research one of the seafood conservation groups mentioned in this chapter to learn more about its goals, policies, and assessment standards. Why is this organization's work important?

Describe what you have learned in a brief report.

Vocabulary Terms

- **Aquaculture:** The production of seafood under controlled conditions.

Discuss

- Why might a given fishery decide to adopt sustainable practices?

- How can a manager determine whether a fishery is in fact following sustainable practices?

Reinforce and Review

- After deciding which species they will purchase, restaurant and foodservice managers must investigate fisheries to ensure that sustainable practices are followed and that populations are appropriately managed.

- Critical information for managers to know about wild fisheries includes whether the fish population is strong and well managed, where the fish are caught, and how the fish are caught.

- Strong, well-managed fisheries following sustainable practices can usually provide enough seafood so that operations can purchase consistently.

- The Marine Stewardship Council researches fisheries to identify and certify those that are sustainable.

- The United States produces 800 million pounds of farmed seafood each year.

After deciding which varieties of seafood the restaurant or foodservice operation wants to purchase, managers can take the next step of reviewing the fisheries themselves to make sure that the companies involved are following sustainable practices and that the fish populations are well managed.

Fish in the Wild

For wild fisheries, the critical questions for purchasers regarding sustainable practices are as follows:

1. Does the fishery have a strong population that is well managed? A fishery with a healthy population will most likely be able to provide a consistent product. Consider that although some species may be in strong supply now, if the fish cannot reproduce at a fast-enough rate, the population may deplete very quickly. Restaurants looking for sustainable seafood may need to consider how much of a certain fish is available over a certain time frame to better forecast menu needs and changes.

2. Where was the fish caught? Some seafood species are in robust supply in one area but not in another. For example, cod has a strong supply in the Pacific Ocean, but not in the Atlantic.

3. How was the fish caught? Fisheries that use nonselective fishing methods may have a large percentage of bycatch or may potentially cause damage to the ocean floor.

Fisheries with well-managed, healthy populations are typically a good source of sustainable seafood for restaurants and foodservice operations because purchasers will be able to order the seafood consistently according to menu needs.

Farmed Fish

Aquaculture has grown from a small industry in 1970 to one that produces more than 45 million tons of seafood every year. The United States is responsible for the production of approximately 800 million pounds each year. Catfish, for example, is a popular farm-raised fish produced by many Gulf Coast states.

Regulations for fish farms vary across the world, and some farms follow more environmentally-minded practices than others. Some scientists believe that certain aquaculture practices can have a negative impact on the surrounding ecological system.

[trends]

The Sustainable Alaskan Pollock

Anyone who has eaten a fried-fish sandwich recently has probably eaten Alaskan pollock. This mild-flavored whitefish is popular throughout the world, with more than three billion pounds of it fished annually. See Figure 9.26. It is also frequently used by American quick-service restaurants that appreciate its abundance and relatively low price.

According to the National Marine Fisheries Service, the agency responsible for monitoring pollock populations, numbers of Alaskan pollock in the eastern Bering Sea are currently below target levels (2008). Harvest limits have been adjusted to correspond with the decrease in population levels. Alaskan pollock is caught by midwater trawls, which have minimal impact on the sea floor. Although bycatch in this fishery is estimated to be around 1 to 2 percent, all of the incidental catch is counted toward the catch limit. The practice of stripping pollock for roe and discarding the fish is prohibited in the Alaskan pollock fishery.

In February 2005, the Bering Sea Aleutian Islands pollock fishery was certified as sustainable by the Marine Stewardship Council (MSC). This fishery is responsible for 93 percent of the pollock caught in the United States. The smaller Gulf of Alaska fishery was also certified by MSC in April 2005. Although the primary fisheries are now certified as sustainable, several conservation organizations and scientists remain concerned that current fishing levels significantly reduce an important food source for the endangered Steller sea lion and the Northern fur seal. To reduce competition for resources, large near-shore areas around the sea lion rookeries of these areas are now off limits to trawling.

Sources: *Sourcing Seafood: A Professional's Guide to Procuring Ocean-Friendly Fish and Shellfish.* Seafood Choices Alliance and www.fishwatch.noaa.gov.

Figure 9.26: Alaskan pollock is popular throughout the world.

Open systems use a natural body of water to produce the fish. Farms can be located in many places, including oceans, lakes, bays, and rivers. Farmers produce the fish in sea cages or net pens, which allow water to flow through

621

Figure Focus
Figure 9.26: What can students determine about this fish from its photograph?

Discuss

- What images come to mind when students consider "farmed fish"?

- Should there be globally established rules for aquaculture practices? Why or why not?

Reinforce and Review

- Some scientists believe that certain aquaculture practices can be detrimental to surrounding marine habitats.

- Fish farms produce animals in sea cages or net pens within an open body of natural water, known as an open system.

- A potential downside to farming within an open system is that the animals' waste and leftover medications can pollute the surrounding ecosystem, which can potentially endanger marine life in the area.

Teaching Tips

- Obtain photographs of open and closed system aquaculture projects to help students understand the differences between the two.

Vocabulary Terms

- **Open systems:** Natural bodies of water used by a farm to produce fish.

Discuss

- What are some reasons why farmed fish are more desirable than wild-caught fish, and vice versa?

Reinforce and Review

- One benefit to open-system aquaculture is that popular shellfish filter their surrounding water, improving the quality of the marine environment.

- Closed systems recondition and reuse the water used to produce fish and therefore require more management and attention than open systems.

Essential Skills: Following Through on Sustainable Seafood

Encourage students to discuss the following:

- Switching to sustainably harvested seafood is both time-consuming and potentially expensive. Why do some restaurant and foodservice operations choose to make this change? What types of operations are more likely to purchase sustainable seafood?

- How might purchasing sustainable seafood contradict a local sourcing policy? How can the two coexist?

- Why is it important to train servers and other front-of-the-house staff to talk knowledgably about an operation's use of sustainable seafood?

Vocabulary Terms

- **Closed system:** A fish farm that is not in a natural body of water.

without losing any of the fish. A potential downside to an open system is that both the waste that the fish produce and any medicine needed to care for them flow into the body of water, which can pollute the water and alter or possibly harm the wild fish in the area.

On the other hand, some seafood produced in open systems actually filter the surrounding water. Oysters, clams, and mussels all eat the plankton in the water, thus improving the water quality. Farmers raise these species in bags or cages with minimal impact on the surrounding ecosystem.

Essential Skills
Following Through on Sustainable Seafood

After researching the types of sustainable seafood that the restaurant or foodservice operation would like to purchase, purchasers should follow through to make sure vendors can and do provide what is requested.

❶ Determine the best plan for the operation. Before choosing which species you want to feature on the menu, think about what will work best for the operation. Does the purchasing team have the capacity to do the research and follow-up? Will the staff have the skills to work with a variety of seafood? Will customers pay for the new menu item? Some of the team will need to spend more time on procurement and training, and some certified species are significantly more expensive than conventionally caught products.

❷ Tell the supplier about sustainability goals. The more suppliers understand about what an operation wants, the more likely is they'll be able to get it. Confirm the information found through research and ask suppliers questions about what kinds of sustainable seafood they can provide. They usually know what's available both locally and elsewhere.

❸ Keep track of where seafood comes from. By using a chart or some other form of monitoring, the staff will know what's on the menu and why. This is also helpful when handling customer questions about menu items.

❹ Promote sustainability efforts. Customers are increasingly attracted to operations that make sustainable efforts. If the restaurant or foodservice operation offers sustainable seafood, add a line to the menu about it. Identify seafood dishes by species and encourage and train servers to talk about these dishes. Make sure they know which species are similar in taste and texture so customers will understand what they're ordering.

Closed systems recondition and reuse the water in the farm, which doesn't need to be placed in or sometimes even near a natural body of water. Closed systems require much more management than open systems do, and they frequently require more energy usage as well. An additional consideration is that some farms require a large volume of wild-caught fish to feed the farmed ones. In some cases, an aquaculture operation might end up using more fish to make fishmeal than it actually produces. Other farming systems may rely on alternative feeding options that have little effect on the wild population.

Farm-raised fish can be a wholesome and attractive option for any restaurant or foodservice operation looking for sustainable seafood. Many seafood guides address concerns for both farmed and caught seafood. Some trade associations, such as the Global Aquaculture Alliance, have begun to issue eco-labels for certified sustainable farms.

Coffee

The National Coffee Association reported in 2009 that more than 54 percent of American adults drink coffee every day, averaging well over two cups per person. Americans buy and drink more coffee than any other country in the world. So it makes sense that the beverage is a true staple on menus of almost all American restaurant and foodservice operations.

Worldwide, coffee production now accounts for approximately 30 million acres of farmland spread over 60 countries. In the last decade, a sharp increase in global demand has rapidly changed the volume of coffee being produced. To meet this growing demand, some farms have shifted to agricultural methods that allow for more trees and more rapid production. Brazil, for example, nearly doubled its already considerable export in five years.

Conservationists and scientists have recently begun studying the environmental effects of modern coffee-production methods versus more traditional practices. On newer, monocultured farms, the larger forest is cleared or thinned to make room for more crops known as **sun coffee**. These farms require strict management and frequent intervention through fertilizers and pesticides to maintain healthy crops. In recent years, the abundant crop of sun coffee has helped to meet the global demand for affordable coffee and helped farmers to increase their profits.

On the other hand, some scientists who study the effects of coffee farms on biodiversity, such as those at the Sustainable Agriculture Network and the Smithsonian Migratory Bird Center, have connected sun coffee farms to the decline in rainforest habitats and the migratory bird population in Latin America. With fewer tall trees of the rainforest available, some birds may not be able to survive their migration period, lacking food and shelter. These same

623

**Homework Activity:
Coffee Countries**

Literacy Connection, 21st-Century Skills—Critical Thinking and Problem Solving, Communicate Clearly, Information Literacy, Work Independently

How many brands of coffee are available at your local supermarket? What countries produce these coffees? What information does that give you about the coffee trade?

Write a brief essay reporting your findings.

Discuss

- How much coffee do class members drink each day? Each week? Encourage students to relate their own habits to the increasing demand for coffee.
- Is there a "good" or "bad" method of coffee production? Why or why not?

Reinforce and Review

- Closed systems often require more energy to operate than open systems.
- Some closed farms use wild-caught fish to feed the growing farmed fish; in some cases, a farm might consume more total fish than it can produce.
- Trade associations, like the Global Aquaculture Alliance, now certify farms as sustainable.
- Americans buy and drink more coffee than any other country in the world.
- Coffee production accounts for 30 million acres of land in 60 countries; rapidly increasing global demand has resulted in new agricultural techniques that can produce more coffee more quickly and on less land.
- Sun coffee plantations require substantial management, including the use of pesticides and fertilizers, to produce abundant crops.
- Shade coffee farms not only provide coffee, but they provide habitat for migratory birds and other species.

Teaching Tips

- Encourage students to relate the demand for coffee to the price of coffee.

Vocabulary Terms

- **Sun coffee:** Coffee produced on newer, monocultured farms in areas where the forest has been cleared or thinned.
- **Shade-grown coffee:** Coffee produced on traditional farms within forested areas, so the coffee trees are shaded.

Discuss

- Why has there been such a significant increase in both global food demand and demand for animal foods?

- Why has the debate over industrialized animal farming practices become so prominent in recent years?

Reinforce and Review

- Shade-grown coffee farms usually receive little direct management, owing in large part to the biodiverse environments in which they appear.

- Shade-grown coffee can be an attractive way to preserve biodiversity in tropical rainforests as well as preserve and advance local economies.

- Offering shade-grown coffee is more expensive for a restaurant or foodservice operation than offering sun coffee, but it is an easy way for an operation to differentiate itself from the competition and to explore sustainability.

- As general food demand has increased worldwide, the demand for animal food products has increased as well.

- Industrialized animal farming practices can provide a high volume of meat for a low price, but they can also consume large amounts of energy and water while producing large amounts of waste and carbon dioxide; moreover, these practices are sometimes characterized as inhumane.

- Some restaurant and foodservice operations purchase animal foods that have been produced with more humane and sustainable techniques.

Teaching Tips

- Relate the material on animal products to the material in Chapter 6.

In-Class Activity: Coffee Options

Literacy Connection, 21st-Century Skills—Make Judgments and Decisions, Communicate Clearly, Interact Effectively with Others

If you were a restaurant or foodservice manager, would you serve shade-grown coffee or sun coffee in your establishment? What factors might affect your decision?

scientists favor the more traditional method of **shade-grown coffee** forests that offer numerous benefits to a local ecosystem. By this method, coffee trees grow under taller rainforest trees, whose larger leaves shade the crop. The forests are frequently home to many wildlife species, including amphibians and birds, and a large variety of trees. The habitat is essentially left to itself, and the coffee trees often grow without fertilizer or pesticides.

Although no definition exists for "sustainable" coffee, environmentalists have focused on shade-grown coffee as an attractive way to preserve biodiversity in tropical rainforests. Shade-grown coffee also helps local coffee-producing economies to remain stable, since the farmers can often also sell the other crops and products that can grow on the diversified farm.

As with most sustainable food products, restaurant and foodservice operations must consider the costs of the coffee that they plan to offer. Shade-grown coffee is typically more expensive than sun coffee. However, for those operations that plan to feature sustainable food products on their menus, coffee is a simple place to start. A number of popular coffee purveyors already offer sustainably produced brands to the restaurant and foodservice market. Some organizations, including the Smithsonian Migratory Bird Center and the Rainforest Alliance, offer certifications for sustainable coffee.

Animal Products

The demand for animal food products has sharply increased along with general global food demand over the last few decades. Farmers and ranchers needed to find more productive agricultural practices to meet that demand. Industrialized farming of beef, pork, and poultry transformed the volume of product available, the price of the meat, and its availability worldwide.

On the other side of the issue, critics have targeted industrialized farming for its possible effects on the environment. In the concentrated space of an industrial farm, which can be quite large geographically, farmers sometimes confine a large number of animals to very close quarters. The practice produces equally large volumes of waste and carbon dioxide and requires significant energy and water. These farms are also scrutinized by animal rights groups, who have considered some kill methods and living conditions on these farms inhumane.

These issues have become more prominent in the last decade. Some restaurant and foodservice operations, both large and small, look for ways to procure animal products that are produced with more environmentally friendly and humane practices. For example, both Burger King and McDonald's have worked with suppliers to change the slaughtering methods of poultry and the

624

acquisition of eggs, which has helped to change and improve conditions on a larger scale. Chefs such as Alice Waters, Dan Barber, and Rick Bayless also lead considerable efforts to increase the use and availability of sustainable animal products in their regions.

Much like the other products discussed in this section, restaurant and foodservice operations seeking out sustainably produced animal products must do some research and talk to their suppliers. The key to buying these products is asking the right questions: What conservation practices does the farm use? How is waste handled? In some cases, purchasers might even be able to visit a few suppliers' farms to see for themselves.

[sustainability in action]

Elevation Burger

Based in Falls Church, Virginia, this fast-casual operation is committed to the use of environmentally sustainable and nonhazardous operating practices. To meet that goal, Elevation Burger started in 2002 by increasing the percentage of products with a healthy profile and using many organic or naturally raised ingredients. Today, the company uses only grass-fed beef.

Elevation Burger donates its old fryer oil to individuals who turn it into diesel fuel, saving money on removing waste and helping to recycle it. The company also follows many U.S. Green Building Council standards, including electric appliances that expel less heat than their gas counterparts, which results in less energy use overall.

[trends]

Understanding the Lingo

When talking about sustainably-produced animal products, it helps to know what some recently coined terms generally mean. Sometimes one person's understanding of a term is not the same as another's:

- Free range: The USDA defines "free range" as allowing an animal access to an outdoor area. This may not mean that the chickens are allowed to roam across the pasture, as some marketing suggests. Free range can also refer to pigs and cattle.

- Cage free: This term is a voluntary one and has no regulated definition. It refers to the practice of growing chickens in open barns without wire cages.

- Grass fed: This term is also voluntary and usually refers to cattle but can also apply to pork and lamb. Typically, a grass-fed animal eats a variety of grasses and legumes. Many times, the term is used to identify animals that haven't been industrially farmed, where the typical diet includes grains, soy, and other supplements.

625

Discuss

- Can students identify these chefs? Why are they important? (Note: These individuals are all famous for their leadership and their commitments to sustainably produced foods: Alice Waters/Chez Panisse, Dan Barber/Blue Hill, Rick Bayless/Topolobampo.)

Reinforce and Review

- As when making other decisions about switching to sustainably-produced ingredients, managers must research their options and talk with suppliers when selecting animal foods.

- The key to buying sustainably produced animal foods is asking the right questions.

Teaching Tips

- Encourage students to relate the questions managers should ask when purchasing animal products to the questions managers should ask when purchasing other sustainably produced foods.

Sustainability in Action: Elevation Burger

Encourage students to discuss the following:

- What is grass-fed beef, and why does it matter? Does an animal's food source affect its level of sustainability? Does it affect its taste?

- What special challenges might a fast-casual operation face when engaging in sustainable practices?

- How can purchasing food from an operation that observes sustainable practices help individuals follow more sustainable practices in their own lives?

Trends: Understanding the Lingo

Encourage students to discuss the following:

- How are terms such as these used to market particular products? How might this mislead consumers?

- What other words or phrases are commonly used to sell foods, for instance, "natural" or "value"? How can terms like these relate to the image that a company wishes to project? How can they relate to the consumer's self-image?

- How can consumers know for certain what practices are used to produce their foods? Is it important to know this information?

Discuss

- How do consumers decide whether or not to spend more money to purchase organic goods?

- In some cases, restaurant and foodservice organizations must choose between buying locally produced items and organically produced items. Why might they choose one over the other?

Reinforce and Review

- Organic farmers typically conserve soil and water, do not use pesticides or synthetic fertilizers to grow crops, and do not use antibiotics or growth hormones to treat animals.

- The term "organic" is regulated by the USDA.

- In recent years, U.S. sales of organic products have experienced average growth of 15 to 20 percent annually. By 2008, sales approached $25 billion.

- Organic items are often more expensive than conventionally produced foods, although some consumers are willing to pay higher prices for what they consider to be better options.

Table 9.5: Organic and Conventional Farming Methods

- What benefits do organic farming methods have over conventional methods, and vice versa? How might the best aspects of each method be combined?

- How do an organic farm's costs differ from those on a conventional farm?

- Which method of farming is more efficient, in which ways?

Homework Activity: Greasy Goodness

Literacy Connection, 21st-Century Skills—Reason Effectively, Communicate Clearly, Information Literacy, Work Independently

What is biodiesel? How and by whom is it used? How is it made? In what ways does using biodiesel help to conserve nonrenewable resources?

Discuss this information in a brief report.

Vocabulary Terms

- **Organic:** Foods (or other products) that have been produced without pesticides or synthetic fertilizers.

Organic Food

Organic food is generally defined according to agricultural practices as products that have been produced without pesticides or synthetic fertilizers. Organic farmers usually conserve soil and water and don't treat animals with antibiotics or growth hormones. The designation of "organic" is regulated by the USDA through the National Organic Program. It can refer to almost any agricultural product, including fruits, vegetables, dairy products, meat, and grains.

Table 9.5 shows some typical differences between organic and conventional farming methods.

Table 9.5: Organic and Conventional Farming Methods		
Method	**Organic**	**Conventional**
Fertilizing crops	Natural materials, such as compost or manure, are used.	Chemical-based materials are used.
Managing weeds	Tilling, mulching, and hand weeding are common.	Chemical herbicides help to kill weeds.
Managing insects	Insects that can help keep the crops healthy are brought into the fields. Farms might also use traps or try to disrupt the mating patterns of native pests.	Insecticides are sprayed to kill pests and manage diseases.
Managing growth and diseases	Emphasis is on clean surroundings, grazing, and healthy diets to minimize disease and encourage growth.	Have clean surroundings and healthy diets, but both crops and animals can receive antibiotics, hormones, and preventive medications.

The market for organic food has exploded in the last two decades. U.S. sales of organic food and beverages were approximately $1 billion in 1990. By 2008, sales approached $25 billion. Growth of the organic market has averaged 15 to 20 percent a year. In contrast, the conventional food market has grown by 2 to 3 percent a year, although its total sales are still far larger.

Price is a concern when considering organic products. An organic item can cost anywhere from 10 to 40 percent higher than its conventional counterpart; some niche products go even higher. The market, however, is somewhat volatile. As the market continues to expand, more large-volume companies have entered the production sphere, lowering some of the pricing. Recent studies have shown that some customers are willing to pay the higher price, although generally the debate over whether to pay a "premium" for organic food and how it fits into a household budget continues.

626

Did You Know...?

Through a third-party accrediting organization, a restaurant or foodservice operation can apply for and receive an organic certification through the USDA's National Organic Program. The process to achieve the certification is complex. Operations must maintain highly detailed records that track their ingredients' progress through the supply chain. The food must also be handled following strict guidelines related to chemical exposure and processing. At least 95 percent of the food must also be certified organic in its own right.

As of early 2010, less than a dozen operations in the United States were certified organic. Still, those that have gone through the process cite high customer loyalty and strong business.

Sources: *Nation's Restaurant News*, www.usda.gov

The Emerging Landscape

The movement toward sustainable food practices and conservation as a whole continues to grow and change at a rapid pace. Each year, the number of independent certifications as well as government-created standards increases, serving to create better communication but also leading to confusion as to what each label and standard means. Studies and scientific findings are submitted almost every day. Our understanding of agriculture and the environment and our affect on each continues to evolve. Making the right decisions about sustainability for a business isn't always easy. Changes that can save money and resources in the long run can be very expensive in the short term. Managers and owners must analyze their choices carefully, keeping both the present and the future of their businesses in mind.

Both independent and chain operations have already begun to explore and sometimes even expand the reach of sustainable practices. Restaurant owners, farmers, processors, suppliers, and manufacturers are all working to develop smarter technology, more environmentally friendly practices, and sustainable, profitable operations. The key to understanding the issues and deciding what to do about them is staying involved. Research, talk to other people interested in sustainability, and get involved in shaping the future of restaurant and foodservice operations to come. Young members of this industry are in a perfect position to help lead the way. Keep learning throughout your career. Stay abreast of new developments—including financial incentives—that can help save money and conserve resources. And don't get discouraged; remember, every little bit helps.

627

**Fast Fact:
Did You Know . . . ?**

Encourage students to discuss the following:

- Why might a restaurant or foodservice establishment choose to become certified organic?

- Why does the USDA administer the National Organic Program, not the FDA?

- What marketing techniques might the certified operations use to promote their unusual status?

Discuss

- How can members of the restaurant and foodservice industry continue to learn about sustainability issues throughout their careers?

- When it comes to sustainability and conservation, is it better to make sweeping changes all at once or to make small, incremental changes over a period of years? What are the advantages and disadvantages of each approach?

Reinforce and Review

- Independent certifications and government standards can enhance communication, but also cause confusion.

- Making sustainability-related decisions can be difficult, especially as transitional and short-term expenses can be significant.

- The key to understanding sustainability-related decisions and making the right choices is staying involved.

Summary

- Remind students to review the following:
  1. Local sourcing
  2. Sustainable seafood
  3. Coffee
  4. Animal products
  5. Organic food
  6. The emerging landscape

Summary

In this section, you learned the following:

- A local source offers food produced by the surrounding growing region. The spirit of the concept is to purchase food that comes from a relatively close source and supports the surrounding economy and communities.

- The FAO reports that 75 percent of the world's fish species have been fully fished, overfished, or depleted within the last 15 years. Fisheries in the wild still produce billions of tons of fish each year. But the sharp increase in demand for seafood over the last few decades has led to an equally strong increase in the production of farm-raised fish. Aquaculture is the production of seafood under controlled conditions.

- For those operations that plan to feature sustainable food products on their menus, coffee is a simple place to start. Of course, they must consider the costs of the coffee that they plan to offer. Shade-grown coffee is typically more expensive than sun-grown coffee.

- As with other products, restaurant and foodservice operations seeking out sustainably produced animal products must do some research and talk to their suppliers. They should find out what conservation practices the farm uses and how waste is handled.

- Organic food is generally defined according to agricultural practices as products that have been produced without pesticides or synthetic fertilizers. Organic farmers also usually conserve soil and water and avoid treating animals with antibiotics or growth hormones. However, organic food does tend to be more expensive.

- Restaurant owners, farmers, processors, suppliers, and manufacturers are all working to develop smarter technology, more environmentally friendly practices, and sustainable, profitable operations.

Section 9.4 Review Questions

1. What is aquaculture? Why is it important to seafood demand?

2. What is organic food? Why do some companies prefer to use organic food?

3. Describe the pros and cons of local sourcing.

4. Why would an operation choose to purchase a conventionally produced product?

5. Research the menu at Ted's Montana Grill. Can you determine from where it purchases its food?

6. Chef Kate is interested in using local sources for produce. What are the pros and cons of making this decision?

7. How would you define a "local source" for an operation in your hometown? From what areas and/or regions would you purchase your products?

8. What items would you focus on if you decided to begin purchasing a few sustainable food products for a small diner?

629

Section 9.4 Review Questions

1. Aquaculture is the production of seafood under controlled conditions. It accounts for 50 percent of the fish consumed globally.

2. Organic food is produced without pesticides or synthetic fertilizers. Some companies prefer to use organic ingredients because of their positive effects on the environment.

3. Advantages of local sourcing include supporting the local economy and communities, limiting the food miles that some ingredients must travel, increasing opportunities for marketing and promotion, and reducing the amount of resources consumed. Disadvantages include limited ingredient options, the need for increased research and networking, and potentially higher ingredient costs.

4. Conventionally produced products might be less expensive, more consistent, and more readily available than organically produced foods.

5. Students should base their assessments on the menu items available at the time of research.

6. Advantages of local sourcing include supporting the local economy and communities, limiting the food miles that some ingredients must travel, increasing opportunities for marketing and promotion, and reducing the amount of resources consumed. Disadvantages include limited ingredient options, the need for increased research and networking, and potentially higher ingredient costs. Chef Kate must weigh both advantages and disadvantages to make the correct decision.

7. Student answers may vary.

8. Student answers may vary but should be logical and clear.

Section 9.4
Activities

1. Students will need to research prices for conventional and organic products to complete this project.

2. Students will need to research a fish or shellfish of their choice and provide the information that would be necessary to make a decision on the item's sustainability. Many fish and shellfish are found in multiple bodies of water, but students need only focus on a single site.

3. Students may not be able to interview farmers or other individuals, especially if the site they have selected is distant, in which case they should rely on any available resources for information.

Section 9.4 Activities

1. Study Skills/Group Activity: Food Cost

Create a breakfast menu for a café that has five entrées. Price out the ingredients if conventional products are purchased. Then price out the same ingredients purchasing organic items. Show the difference in prices as a percentage.

2. Independent Activity: Harvest

Select a fish or shellfish and research its location, annual harvest, harvest technique, annual sales, total population, and any other information related to determining whether this item is sustainably harvested. If wild, where is it found and when? If farmed, where is it grown? You are not being asked to determine whether the item is being sustainably harvested; you are simply reporting the information that a scientist would use to make that decision. Write a one-page essay on your findings.

3. Critical Thinking:

Research the effects of either an aquafarm operation or a large animal product farm on the surrounding environment. The sources to compare and contrast should include the farmers themselves, the local water company and environmentalists, U.S. government statistics of the area as a whole, and so on.

630

Case Study Follow-Up *Making a Positive Impact*

Miguel and Chef Kate developed a time line for making changes and discussed the proposed ideas with their vendors and staff. Based on these discussions, Miguel and Chef Kate made some changes to their plans and altered the menu to match their current "going green" focus. Now they are developing and conducting training sessions for their employees on the changes ahead and how they will affect daily operations.

Questions to consider:

1. How might they phase in a "going green" plan?

2. What can they do, using their existing staff and equipment, to conserve water and energy?

3. How can they manage their waste?

4. What types of food practices will address sustainability?

5. How might they announce the changes to their guests? Should they do any market research before they commit to a revised menu?

6. How can they monitor and help to adjust the behaviors of their staff in terms of recycling and conservation?

631

Case Study Follow-Up

1. Students should develop a plan to cover at least three elements of conservation or sustainability. They should include employee training in their plans.

2. Students should identify some simple ways to conserve energy and water; they can use methods discussed in the text.

3. Students should point out some waste management techniques that include at least two sustainability-related methods.

4. Student answers may vary but should be related to sustainability issues.

5. Student answers may vary but should include employee training.

6. Student answers may vary but should be clear and logical.

Apply Your Learning

Reducing Utility or Disposal Costs

Students might need to contact local utility companies to determine how much rates might fall, based on changes in behavior. In some instances, this information—either the amount of a typical utility bill or the amount utility rates would fall, depending on the behavioral change made—might not be readily available. In these cases, teachers should assign hypothetical utility costs or percentage savings to students.

For instance, Student A might be assigned an imaginary electricity bill of $250 for a school, whereas Student B might be assigned an imaginary garbage bill of $600 for a restaurant. Student A might choose installing CFL lightbulbs to reduce monthly costs, so the teacher might assign that student a 2 percent drop in electricity rates. Student B might choose composting to reduce monthly costs, so the teacher might assign that student a 5 percent drop in garbage rates.

Going Green

Students should research and report on a restaurant or foodservice company of their choice.

Marine Litter

Students should research and report on this topic.

Critical Thinking Sustainability Trade-offs

Student answers may vary so long as they defend their positions appropriately.

Chapter 9 | Foundations of Restaurant Management & Culinary Arts

Apply Your Learning

Reducing Utility or Disposal Costs

Research an average water, electricity, or garbage removal bill at your school or at a restaurant. Choose one way to reduce the cost of the monthly bill and show the decreases mathematically.

Going Green

Research a local, regional, or national restaurant or foodservice company that has a reputation for being "green." What sustainable practices does this company use, and how are these practices promoted? What effect does this activity have on current and potential consumers? Could the company take other steps to become more "green"? Discuss your findings in a two-page essay.

Marine Litter

What is a "plastic island" or "floating garbage patch"? Research this topic and discuss ways that the restaurant or foodservice industry can work toward preventing the spread of marine litter. Write a two-page report on your findings.

Critical Thinking Sustainability Trade-offs

Moving to more sustainable methodology can lead to cost savings in both the short term and the long run, but not always. And, installing sustainable technologies can be expensive. What is the trade-off between making a profit and practicing sustainability? Is there a trade-off at all? Must businesses always sacrifice one or the other? Explain your thoughts in a two-page essay.

632

Exam Prep Questions

❶ Limiting the use of a resource is called

A. globalization.

B. conservation.

C. sustainability.

D. responsibility.

❷ What percentage of the earth's surface water can be used by humans?

A. 1

B. 5

C. 10

D. 15

❸ How can dirty dishes be handled to preserve safety and conserve water?

A. Scrape food off quickly under a running flow.

B. Soak the dishes in standing water in the sink.

C. Run each rack of dishes through the dishwasher once.

D. Load each rack for the dishwasher beyond its capacity.

❹ Sink aerators help to conserve water by

A. recirculating steam.

B. adding air to a water flow.

C. restricting the time a tap can be on.

D. heating water only when it is needed.

❺ The electricity produced by using steam or hot water produced inside the earth is known as

A. hydropower.

B. solar collection.

C. photosynthesis.

D. geothermal energy.

❻ Which energy source is renewable?

A. Propane

B. Manure

C. Crude oil

D. Natural gas

❼ Where is the most energy used in a restaurant or foodservice operation?

A. Refrigeration

B. Dishwashing

C. Heating/cooling

D. Cooking equipment

❽ Of the areas of a restaurant or foodservice operation listed here, which would be the best place for using compact fluorescent lightbulbs?

A. Host stand

B. Restrooms

C. Prep areas

D. Dining room

❾ Which item should be included in an operation's composting program?

A. Fish bones

B. Fats and oils

C. Coffee grounds

D. Unwaxed cardboard

❿ In aquaculture, the water in an open system

A. flushes away bycatch.

B. recirculates after being reconditioned.

C. circulates from cage to cage through trawlers.

D. flows from a natural body of water through the farm.

633

Exam Prep Answers

1. B
2. A
3. B
4. B
5. D
6. B
7. D
8. C
9. C
10. D

Chapter 10 represents North and South America, which have almost every type of climate, providing vast varieties of foods.

Section 1: This section reviews the cultures and cuisines of North America, which includes the United States and Mexico.

Section 2: This section covers the cultures and cuisines of Central America and the Caribbean.

Section 3: This section reviews the cultures and cuisines of South America.

Advance Preparation	
Review	Sections 10.1–10.3
Contact	Computer lab
Prepare	Maps
	Globe of the world
	Paper
	Art supplies (pens, colored pencils, crayons, etc.)

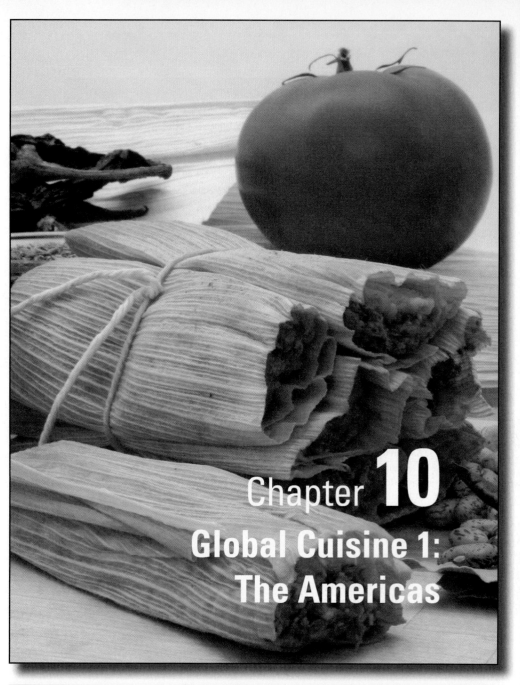

Chapter 10
Global Cuisine 1: The Americas

CUSTOMIZED INSTRUCTION OPTIONS

Less Advanced Students	More Advanced Students	ESOL Students	Special Needs Students
Pages 653, 680	Pages 653, 680	Pages 653, 680	Pages 653, 680

CHAPTER TOOLS

21st-Century Skills	Mathematics	Science	Literacy
Pages 639, 643, 644, 648, 653, 656, 668, 680	Page 668	Page 639	Pages 643, 648, 653, 680

ServSafe Connection

Page 641

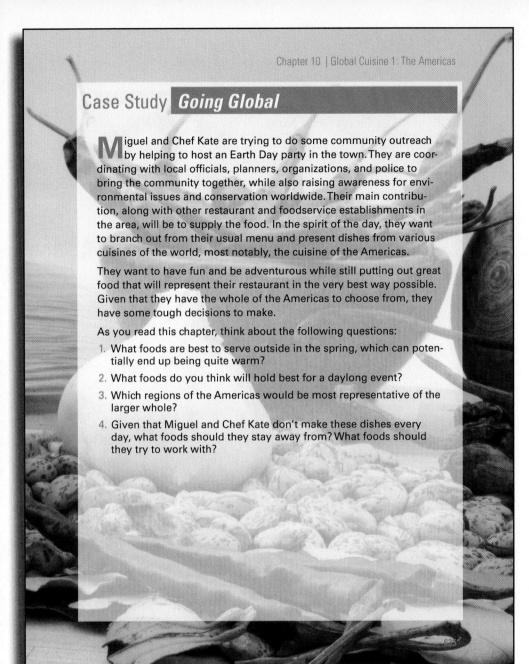

Case Study *Going Global*

Miguel and Chef Kate are trying to do some community outreach by helping to host an Earth Day party in the town. They are coordinating with local officials, planners, organizations, and police to bring the community together, while also raising awareness for environmental issues and conservation worldwide. Their main contribution, along with other restaurant and foodservice establishments in the area, will be to supply the food. In the spirit of the day, they want to branch out from their usual menu and present dishes from various cuisines of the world, most notably, the cuisine of the Americas.

They want to have fun and be adventurous while still putting out great food that will represent their restaurant in the very best way possible. Given that they have the whole of the Americas to choose from, they have some tough decisions to make.

As you read this chapter, think about the following questions:

1. What foods are best to serve outside in the spring, which can potentially end up being quite warm?

2. What foods do you think will hold best for a daylong event?

3. Which regions of the Americas would be most representative of the larger whole?

4. Given that Miguel and Chef Kate don't make these dishes every day, what foods should they stay away from? What foods should they try to work with?

Case Study
Going Global

- Help students see that "The Americas" includes many completely different areas.

- "America" applies to the entire two continents.

- Note that there are follow-up questions about the case study at the end of the chapter.

- This activity could be done in groups, as a class, or as a homework assignment.

Professional Profile

Discuss	Perhaps the students realize that Rick Bayless is not Mexican. Many chefs are not natives of the regions from which they draw their inspiration and menus.
Reinforce and Review	It is possible to specialize in a certain global cuisine by having a love for it and practicing it. Encourage students to think of other chefs who specialize in cuisines other than their native ones.
Teaching Tips	Rick Bayless quotes Julia Child. Do the students know who Julia Child is? Discuss her influence on French cuisine's popularity in the United States.

[professional profile]

Rick Bayless

Chef/Owner of Frontera Grill, Topolobampo, and XOCO

❝*I am the fourth generation of a restaurant family—it is in my blood! At age 14, I fell in love with Mexico and that has never changed. Having grown up in the industry, I am primarily self-taught, although travels in Mexico and learning about the food from Mexicans have fine-tuned my skills and preferences.*❞

In 1987, I founded the Frontera Grill and Topolobampo. Now, my line of salsas, grilling sauces, and organic chips can be found coast to coast. I try to share my love for Mexico through the Public Television series *Mexico—One Plate at a Time*, and through my six cookbooks.

Locally, with my staff, we started the Frontera Farmer Foundation in 2003 to attract support for small Midwestern farms. Each year, grants are given to our local farmers for capital improvements to their family farms. And recently, we took an additional step, launching the Frontera Scholarship—a full-tuition scholarship that will send a Mexican-American student to Kendall Culinary College to study the culinary arts.

For those of you interested in entering this field, remember to cook what you are passionate about and to make it your own. I learned from many Mexican grandmothers, but I took what they taught me and made the food that I loved and then made it my own.

International cuisine offers endless opportunities. Travel! See as much as you can. Then decide what you truly care about.

Remember:

❝Find something you're passionate about and keep tremendously interested in it.❞

— Julia Child

About Global Cuisine

When I first opened Frontera Grill 23 years ago, my goal was to share the love and passion that I had for Mexico with Chicago and beyond. I had always hoped that the United States would clamor for authentic Mexican food...not the stuff that we all thought it was—gooey cheese, runny beans, and combo platters. So to still have lines outside my restaurant today makes me feel honored.

Mexican food is healthy, flavorful, and is no longer considered low on the totem pole of cuisine. I would like to think that I had something to do with that.

636

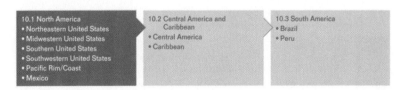

10.1 North America	10.2 Central America and Caribbean	10.3 South America
• Northeastern United States • Midwestern United States • Southern United States • Southwestern United States • Pacific Rim/Coast • Mexico	• Central America • Caribbean	• Brazil • Peru

SECTION 10.1 NORTH AMERICA

North American cuisine is a melting pot, based upon the diversity of the natural resources of the continent and the variety of the native and immigrant populations. There is no single "American" flavor in the region from Canada to Mexico, Pacific to Atlantic. However, each region has traditional dishes, flavors, ingredients, and cooking methods. Each is worthy of attention. There are coastal zones with abundant seafood; Asian pockets with fusion influences; the vast mountains, plateaus, and plains with beef, wheat, potatoes, and corn; Southern cuisine with African influences; and Mexican food with both native and Spanish flavors, to name just a few. North American cuisine began with the Native Americans and soon fused with the first European settlers at Plymouth, so the Northeastern United States is a good place to begin.

Study Questions

After studying Section 10.1, you should be able to answer the following questions:

- What are the cultural influences and flavor profiles of the Northeast?
- What are the cultural influences and flavor profiles of the Midwest?
- What are the cultural influences and flavor profiles of the South?
- What are the cultural influences and flavor profiles of the Southwest?
- What are the cultural influences and flavor profiles of the Pacific Coast/Rim?
- What are the cultural influences and flavor profiles of Mexico?

637

Teach

Discuss

- Ask students where their families come from, if they want to share.
- Ask them if they have favorite or traditional dishes from where their parents grew up.
- Even the seemingly "plain" American foods are part of a cuisine that is not familiar in some parts of the world.
- Macaroni and cheese would seem very unusual in India or China.
- North American cuisine is worthy of study as its own cuisine.

Focus and Engage

Discuss

- Have students ever had a taco? Then they have eaten Mexican food.
- What about corn on the cob? Then they have eaten Native American food.
- There are very few "pure" cuisines left in the world.
- There are still some on the American continents, but most of them have other influences.

Section 10.1 North America

Introduce the Section

a. There are several regions of North American cuisine:
  - The Northeast—New England and Eastern Canada
  - The Midwest—The Great Plains from Oklahoma north to central Canada
  - The South—From Virginia to the border of Texas
  - The Southwest—Texas, New Mexico, and Arizona
  - The Pacific Coast/Rim—California, Oregon, Washington, British Columbia, and north to Alaska
  - Mexico—The entire country with all its regions

b. Each region has its own cultural influences and flavor profiles.

c. Discuss the objectives for the section.

Vocabulary Review

a. Direct students to the key terms.
b. Pronounce each word, and have the students repeat the pronunciation out loud.
c. Discuss the definition of each word.

Although mild, the flavors are full. Think Yankee pot roast, which has a mild yet full spectrum.

Chapter 10 | Foundations of Restaurant Management & Culinary Arts

Northeastern United States

[flavor] Flavor Profile

Traditional New England recipes are not highly seasoned. The flavors are deep and rich, and tend to be more mild than spicy.

Cultural Influences

New England is in the northeast corner of the United States, situated along the Atlantic seaboard where it has access to a large supply of fresh seafood. Figure 10.1 provides a map of the region. Because this region was the location of some of the earliest settlements of the United States, Native Americans had an influence on New England cuisine. They introduced early European settlers to many foods, such as the region's wild game, corn, and vegetables.

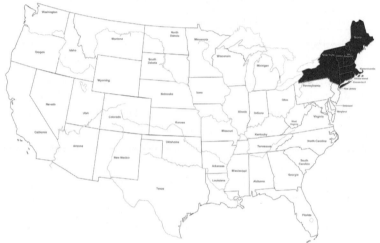

Figure 10.1: The Northeast region of the United States includes Maine, New Hampshire, Vermont, Massachusetts, Rhode Island, Connecticut, and New York.

638

Figure Focus

Figure 10.1: Understanding the geography of a region can help understand the agriculture and animal life and the resulting cuisine.

The Native Americans of upstate New York and other parts of the Northeast had a nutritious diet based upon sophisticated agricultural techniques. Using a system known as "Three Sisters," the Iroquois cultivated a diet of corn, beans, and squash. First, corn was planted in mounds and grew a few inches. Then pole beans and ground squashes were added around the corn. The beans climbed the cornstalks for support. The squashes covered the ground to control the weeds and hold moisture, while their fallen leaves made mulch. The corn and beans provided carbohydrate energy and combined to form a complete protein for the diet. The squash provided vitamins and minerals. All could be stored for two years and could be cooked in one pot. This one-pot method of cooking is still prevalent in the region today, which produces bean dishes, chowders, and stews.

When the Pilgrims settled in New England, they wrote about the "fruits of the sea," referring to the abundance of fish. Cape Cod was so named due to the abundance of cod in the area. The seafood in the territory became the main ingredient in most recipes. Lobster, for example, was actually so abundant that it was a food typically eaten by the lower classes. Over the course of its 500-year history, New England has also been influenced by the Puritans, Portuguese, Irish, and Italians who came over from Europe.

New England culinary influences can be seen throughout the United States, partly because many groups migrated from the Northeast, taking culinary traditions with them. In the nineteenth century, herbs and spices were a luxury for only the upper classes. That history is still at play today as even the flavors of this regional cuisine tend to be more basic, involving simple preparations and milder spices.

Regional Ingredients and Dishes

New England cooking is characterized by simple recipes and extensive use of seafood, starches, and dairy products, including cheese and cream. The **New England boiled dinner** is a very popular, classic menu item in this region and includes corned beef brisket (beef that is cured in a salt brine, often with spices), boiled potatoes, cabbage, and root vegetables like onions, carrots, or parsnips, as shown in Figure 10.2.

Seafood is abundant in the Northeast region, so many

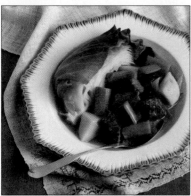

Figure 10.2: A New England boiled dinner is a popular, classic meal.

Discuss

- The ancient "Three Sisters" technique is important to learn.

- It will appear again in other regions, and binds the Americas together.

- The Three Sisters appears in the Northeast.

- It then appears again much further south where the Mayans and others were settled.

- Hold off discussion of that aspect until it appears again. For now, help the students gain a solid understanding of what it is.

- The students might be able to identify the protein sources in Three Sisters.

- The Three Sisters were cooked in one pot, like a stew.

- One-pot cooking is seen throughout New England cuisine.

In-Class Activity: The Three Sisters

Science Connection, 21st-Century Skills— Global Awareness

Science is often taught through artistic illustrations, to the point where science illustrating is a career unto itself.

Using artistic illustration, have the students draw a picture of the Three Sisters, the agricultural technique used by the Native Americans.

Vocabulary Terms

- **New England boiled dinner:** Corned beef and vegetables boiled together in a single pot.

Figure Focus

Figure 10.2: One-pot cooking is an ancient method.

Reinforce and Review

- Maple syrup has chemical characteristics that contribute to its desirability.

- Maple sugar naturally occurs in the sap of the sugar maple tree.

- This maple sugar sap contains sucrose, the disaccharide found in white table sugar.

- However, when the sap sugar is dissolved and heated with water, some of the sugar inverts.

- Invert sugar is hydrolyzed, which means it is broken apart by a chemical reaction with water, and it is cleaved from a disaccharide into the two monosaccharides.

- When sucrose inverts, it becomes free glucose and free fructose in the solution.

- In maple syrup, some of the sugar is inverted.

- The invert sugar in solution tastes sweeter than sucrose.

- Less maple syrup is needed than sucrose to achieve the same level of sweetness.

- In addition, maple syrup has a distinctively delicious flavor!

Techniques:
Northeastern United States Cooking Methods

Sand-pit cooking is also seen in the Polynesian islands.

Nutrition:
Red, White, and Clam Chowder

Similar names and clams are most of what the two chowders really have in common. They are otherwise very different foods.

Vocabulary Terms

- **New England clam chowder:** Cream soup with clams, potatoes, onions, and celery.

- **Bisque:** An opaque creamy soup made from crustacean shells.

dishes are centered around this ingredient. **New England clam chowder** is perhaps the most familiar version of a thick clam soup, creamy, white, and mild. Seafood bisque and lobster stew are also common dishes that are distinct from each other. While the stew is a thick soup with lobster meat, a **bisque** is made from the lobster shells, extracting all the color and flavor before straining the shells away. Other Northeast favorites include fresh Atlantic salmon, flounder, and boiled shellfish, such as crab legs or whole lobsters.

New England is also known for its maple syrup. Blueberries, cranberries, and Concord grapes are staple fruits in the area. Baked beans and apple cider can be enjoyed any time of year, and root vegetables such as squash and pumpkin are markers of the region.

[techniques]

Northeastern United States Cooking Methods

The clambake is a cooking method introduced by Native Americans, where fish, corn, and vegetables are cooked in a pit dug in wet sand. Today, the clambake has been modified to a one-pot method that can be used in any home or backyard. Boiling, baking, broiling, and frying are also frequent methods of cooking.

[nutrition]

Red, White, and Clam Chowder

Clam chowder is a thick, creamy soup made from milk, clams, onions, potatoes, and salt pork. It is a delicious meal in itself, originating in New England but now served nationwide. It is especially popular on both the Atlantic and Pacific coasts.

But not all clam chowder is white and creamy. The other main contender is Manhattan clam chowder, a Portuguese variant introduced in the fish markets of New York City. Manhattan clam chowder is tomato based and full of vegetables along with the clams.

Fisherman's Wharf in San Francisco on the Pacific Coast is home to many seafood restaurants. Both types of clam chowder feature prominently on the menus, with the Manhattan style being especially good with San Francisco sourdough bread.

While both taste delicious, their nutritional values do differ. Manhattan clam chowder is a fairly low-fat food, while New England clam chowder is higher in fat. Also, red chowder has phytochemicals (chemical compounds such as beta-carotene that occur naturally in plants), which are absent from the New England style. The two soups may be cousins, but only distant ones. Figure 10.3 on the following page shows the two types of chowder side by side. Table 10.1 compares some of the nutritional content of the two types of clam chowder.

640

Figure 10.3: Manhattan clam chowder (left) and New England clam chowder (right) are familiar New England dishes.

Table 10.1: Nutritional Content of Clam Chowder		
	Manhattan Clam Chowder	**New England Clam Chowder**
Serving size	8-ounce bowl	8-ounce bowl
Calories	134 calories	228 calories
Total fat	30 calories from fat	116 calories from fat
Calories from fat	3 grams total fat	13 grams total fat
Cholesterol	14 milligrams cholesterol	45 milligrams cholesterol

[ServSafe Connection]

The Safety of the Boiled Dinner

New England boiled dinner, Yankee pot roast, and other classics are one-pot meals with vegetable and meat simmered together for several hours in moist, low heat.

Covered steam kettles and slow cookers do a good job, but check the temperatures to make certain that the initial warming of the food is fast enough for safety. The food should reach a temperature above 140°F within 4 hours. Check it this way: Heat water in the cooker, lid on, for 4 hours. If the water reaches 185°F, it will heat food quickly enough.

When using the cooker, do not remove the lid unless absolutely necessary. Opening the cooker drops the temperature of the food by about 10 degrees. Do not put frozen foods into the cooker or the temperature might remain too low for too long. Start the foods on a high temperature setting for the first hour, and reduce it for the rest of the slow-cooking.

641

Figure Focus

Figure 10.3: Although both soups are made from clams, the two chowders are very different nutritionally.

Discuss

- Ask students why they think so many cultures converged on the Midwest.

- Of the countries listed, what would these settlers find in the Midwest that was familiar to them?

- What differences would they find?

- If students have studied U.S. history, perhaps they have opinions about the Louisiana Purchase and its influence on immigration in the eighteenth century.

- What influence did this immigration have on cuisine?

Midwestern United States

[flavor]
Flavor Profile
Midwestern cuisine is generally hearty, but light handed with seasonings, preferring sage, dill, caraway, mustard, and parsley to bold and spicy flavors.

Cultural Influences

The Midwest region of the United States consists of states in the center of the country. Figure 10.4 shows a map of this region. These states are known for their grassy plains, lakes and streams, and changes of season. The climate and conditions are good for raising cattle and growing grains and vegetables. Midwestern cuisine usually showcases simple and hearty dishes that make use of locally grown food.

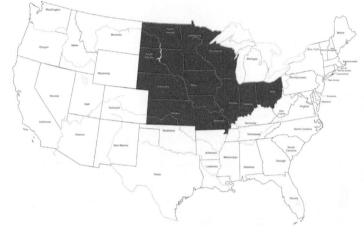

Figure 10.4: The Midwest region of the United States includes Ohio, Indiana, Illinois, Missouri, Kansas, Iowa, Wisconsin, Minnesota, Wisconsin, North Dakota, and South Dakota.

Midwestern cuisine has many cultural influences from people who immigrated from Germany, Britain, Italy, Hungary, and Scandinavia. In the early 1700s, Germans started to arrive, bringing sauerkraut and sausages. They also

642

Figure Focus

Figure 10.4: There are vast prairies in the Midwest, providing lots of farming and grazing land.

introduced the tradition of serving meals family style. The British began arriving in the late 1700s and brought *pasties* (PASS-tees), or meat pies, bread pudding, and roasts with potatoes. The Italians brought pastas and native cheeses, and the Hungarians brought goulash. The Scandinavians introduced **lefse** (potato bread) and meatballs. Together these various cultural influences bring a diverse range of tastes to the region.

Regional Ingredients and Dishes

Foods in the Midwest are simple and hearty. The vast farmland in the region provides an abundance of fresh produce. Excellent dairy foods are produced in the Midwest, including fine cheddar cheese varieties. Milk, sour cream, and ice cream are very popular in recipes and alone. Figure 10.5 shows a variety of Midwestern dairy products.

Food from the central part of the continent is sometimes called "meat-and-potatoes" or "comfort food." It is probably the food that most people associate with the United States. Beef or pork roasts, sausage, turkey, and ground meats are typical proteins. These meats are often prepared by simply roasting them with potatoes and vegetables. Ground beef is common for meatloaf and casseroles. Ground beef is also the basis for the hamburger, a German name for the very American sandwich. Macaroni and cheese, pork chops and gravy, mashed potatoes, chicken-fried steak, green bean casserole, chicken and dumplings, and bean soup are all popular dishes as well. Each of these dishes is based upon foods that are plentiful and easy to purchase in the Midwest. Some of these dishes are quite filling, a holdover from the dietary needs of folks who worked hard on their farms in the summers and withstood freezing weather in the winters.

Figure 10.5: Midwestern dairy products include milk, sour cream, and cheese.

Kansas City, Missouri, in particular is famous for its barbecue. Other regions of the country have delicious barbecue dishes as well, of course, but Kansas City couples terrific barbecue sauces and techniques with local corn-fed, high-quality beef and pork for a very special result. Pork and beef are cooked slowly over slow-burning wood fires. Kansas City barbecue features dry rubs for meat prior to cooking. The famous Kansas City barbecue sauces are applied at the table.

643

Vocabulary Terms

- *Pasties*: Traditional British foods including meat pies, bread puddings, and roasts with potatoes.
- **Lefse:** Potato bread.

Figure Focus
Figure 10.5: Dairy products are a major part of Midwestern cuisine.

Techniques:
Midwestern United States Cooking Methods

"Chicken fry" doesn't necessarily have anything to do with chicken.

Trends:
Entertainment Concept Dining

Each of these trends features a concept from the Americas.

Flavor Profile

The flavors of the southern regions of the United States become distinctive favorites for many diners.

In-Class Activity:
Entertainment Concept Dining Ideas

21st-Century Skills—Financial, Economic, Business, and Entrepreneurial Literacy

Divide the students into groups of four or five.

Together, have them design an entertainment concept dining restaurant experience.

They should have a theme, entertainment ideas, menu ideas, service ideas, costume ideas for the serving staff, and ideas for the restaurant's décor. They will also need one advertising idea.

Have them write the concepts as a business proposal.

Each group of students can present its proposal to the class.

Vocabulary Terms

· **Tidewater cuisine:** From Virginia and North Carolina's Tidewater region, cuisine influenced by the Native Americans who taught European settlers to plant corn and introduced them to native squashes, plums, berries, greens, game, and seafood, including fish and oysters.

[techniques]

Midwestern United States Cooking Methods
The cooking techniques used in the Midwestern United States include barbecue, chicken-fry, pickling, and canning.

[trends]

Entertainment Concept Dining
Building on global concepts, restaurants in the United States are starting to offer not only food, but a whole new world to take in. Entertainment dining is a growing trend in the restaurant industry.

In the United States, outlets like The Rainforest Cafè, The Mayan Restaurant, and Dave & Buster's offer a full experience for the entire family. The Rainforest Cafè takes a tropical theme one better by re-creating the rainforest in a family-friendly, fun environment. Whether it's indoor cliff diving at the Mayan or interactive online games from Dave & Buster's, there is something for everyone in concept dining. The family no longer just goes out to eat; they go on a global adventure.

Southern United States

[flavor]

Flavor Profile
The flavor profiles of the southern regions vary from the highly flavored and spicy Cajun dishes to the more mild but full-flavored cuisine of the Tidewater region. In all cases, they are fresh flavors that speak of the local ingredients.

Cultural Influences

The southern United States is often defined as Virginia, North Carolina, South Carolina, Georgia, Florida, Alabama, Mississippi, Louisiana, Arkansas, and Tennessee. This is a large and, in many places, fertile land that provides a wide variety of food. Due to the wide expanse of this region, it's easiest to discuss the cuisine in three parts: the Tidewater region of Virginia and North Carolina; the Low Country of South Carolina, Georgia, and northeastern Florida; and the Gulf Coast area of the Mississippi Delta and Louisiana. Figure 10.6 on the following page shows a map of this region.

Tidewater cuisine was influenced by the Native Americans who taught European settlers to plant corn and introduced them to native squashes, plums, berries, greens, game, and seafood, including fish and oysters. These native foods were then combined with the pigs, cattle, sheep, chickens, wheat, and cabbages that

644

the British settlers brought over from England. The English settlers also brought with them cooking methods from both the upper class and the tavern. The other major influence came from enslaved Africans who brought native African foods such as yams, black-eyed peas, and okra. They also contributed their cooking methods and familiarity with Native American foods, such as peanuts, tomatoes, and peppers, which were not widely used in Europe.

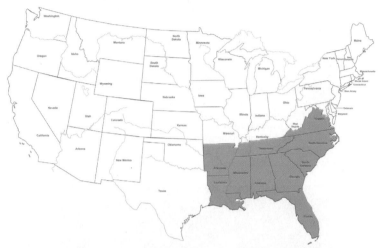

Figure 10.6: The Southern region of the United States includes the Tidewater, the Low Country, and the Delta.

Low Country cuisine had many of the same cultural influences as Tidewater, but the cuisine is also influenced by the warmer climate and rice plantations combined with the busy port of Charleston, where pickles and relishes of the warmer climates became standard fare.

Florida is a Low Country Southern state with some of its own unique cuisine. Cuban flavors inform southern Florida cooking with spices of garlic, oregano, bay leaves, and cumin. Beans, potatoes, and rice blend with seafood and peppery heat to form a unique palate that includes tropical fruits, seafood, and even alligator.

Two of the primary cuisines of the Gulf Coast region, Cajun and Creole, were the result of migration, the geography of the region, and the influence of conquerors. Louisiana has been influenced by its Native American heritage, the influx of Spanish, French, English, Italian, and German immigrants; and Africans, who have deeply affected the culture and cuisine of this region.

645

Discuss

- How many different cuisines can you identify in the South?
- How did each one come to be?
- What has influenced the cuisine of Florida?

Vocabulary Terms

- **Low Country cuisine:** South Carolina, Georgia, and northern Florida Atlantic seaboard cuisine.

Figure Focus

Figure 10.6: There are some close neighboring and overlapping areas of the cuisine areas of the South.

Discuss

- Perhaps students are aware of concepts from social studies and history classes.

- Religion has been a major factor in causing large groups of people to move to new places.

- How has this influenced the cuisine of the New Orleans, Louisiana area?

Vocabulary Terms

- **Creole:** A French-African mix of cuisines in the New Orleans area.

- **Cajun:** The cuisine of the French Canadian Acadians who settled in the Mississippi Delta area.

Creole (KREE-ole) developed in the city of New Orleans in the homes of the rich French and Spanish land owners. It is the blending of French grand cuisine principles with the cooking techniques of the enslaved Africans. The techniques are then applied to local and imported foods and seasoning. These recipes often still carry the French or African names that inspired them. Just as the word Creole was used to describe a person of mixed ethnicities—African and generally French—the cuisine is a mix of cultures and food. Creole cooking is found in the areas along the Gulf Coast and into Florida. It is rather spicy with some heat, and it includes Caribbean elements and spices.

Cajun is a style of cooking from the swamps and bayous of southwestern Louisiana, shown in Figure 10.7. The people who developed this cooking style were French Acadian Catholics who originally settled in Nova Scotia. They were forced to relocate after England gained control of Canada. They returned to France where they continued to be persecuted for their religious beliefs. When France took control of Louisiana they saw an opportunity and immigrated to New Orleans. From New Orleans they settled into the bayous west of the city. The name "Cajun" comes from a way of pronouncing "Acadian." They adapted their heritage of French cooking to the bounty of the swamp. They used the native laurel (bay), pepper grass (for a pepper flavor), thistle (instead of celery), and wild onion and garlic to prepare the seafood, freshwater fish, and game native to the region.

Figure 10.7: Cajun cooking comes from the bayous of southwestern Louisiana.

Regional Ingredients and Dishes

Tidewater dishes include fried chicken, crab cakes, and oyster on the half shell, as illustrated in Figure 10.8 on the following page.

646

Figure Focus

Figure 10.7: The food available in the swamp was used to substitute for foods that were already familiar to the Acadians.

Figure 10.8: Dishes from the Tidewater region include fried chicken, crab cakes, and oysters.

One popular Low Country dish is **low country boil**, which is a well-spiced, one-pot dish, generally consisting of shrimp, smoked sausage, red potato, and corn. Hoppin John, shrimp and grits, and she-crab soup are also popular.

Both Cajun and Creole cuisines frequently incorporate what's called the **trinity**, which means a unity of three. In this case, the trinity is a form of mirepoix that blends celery, onions, and green bell peppers instead of the carrots that are traditional in mirepoix. Trinity is considered foundational to Louisiana cooking.

Creole dishes include Creole **gumbo**, which is not roux based like Cajun gumbo and often contains tomato, shrimp remoulade, and seafood Creole.

Cajun dishes include **jambalaya**, which is a spicy rice dish with chicken, andouille sausage, shrimp, crayfish, trinity, other vegetables, herbs, broth, and seasonings. **Andouille** (an-DOO-ee) is pork sausage with a strong, smoky, garlicky taste. **Gumbo** is a hearty soup with trinity and shrimp, thickened with brown roux containing okra (a seed-pod vegetable that helps gel the gumbo), and *filè*, a thickener made from dried sassafras leaves. Figure 10.9 shows these unique dishes. True Cajun cuisine is more spicy than Creole, but not as overwhelmingly hot as is often expected by Louisiana visitors.

Figure 10.9: Cajun dishes include jambalaya, andouille, and gumbo.

Reinforce and Review

- Gumbo is often thickened with okra.

- It can also be thickened with filè powder.

- Some gumbos are thickened with roux.

Teaching Tips

- Crayfish, crawfish, and crawdads are all the same thing.

Vocabulary Terms

- **Low country boil:** Another example of a one-pot meal.

- **Trinity:** New Orleans type of mirepoix.

- **Gumbo:** A sauce-based one-pot meal that is usually served over rice.

- **Jambalaya:** Another one-pot meal, but with several different proteins, which usually includes crayfish and andouille.

- **Andouille:** Cajun sausage.

- *Filè:* A thickener made from dried sassafras leaves.

Figure Focus

Figure 10.8: Delicacies of the Eastern seaboard area.

Figure 10.9: Spicy dishes from the New Orleans area.

Techniques:
Southern United States Cooking Methods

Nearly all the cuisine cooking methods of the world are born of local necessity and innovation. Each region has its own climate and resources. Historically, this has dictated the crops and herds that could thrive in the region. Humans had to determine a way to meet their nutritional needs using what was available. All the populations that survived managed to do this. Humans also like to enjoy food, so spices and flavorings have evolved to meet this desire while meeting the need for life-sustaining nutrition.

What's New:
GMO Food

There are many facets to the conversation about GMO processes.

In-Class Activity:
The GMO Debate

Literacy Connection, 21st-Century Skills— Reason Effectively

Divide the class into two teams.

Label one team "Pro" (affirmative) and the other team "Con" (negative).

Have them research and debate this statement: "Resolved: All food crops should be Genetically Modified Organisms."

Students should research their arguments and present their cases as a persuasive speech with a time limit. Each side will get to cross-examine the other team, also against a time limit. Each side will also have a timed chance for rebuttal.

This might not fit the exact demands of a formal debate, but the students can benefit from teaching each other about the various views.

[techniques]

Southern United States Cooking Methods

The cooking techniques used in the southern United States cover the full range of techniques used in Western cookery. The one that is somewhat a hallmark of the region is one-pot cookery, in which a full meal is prepared in one pot. Everything is well spiced and carries an exquisitely blended flavor and aroma.

[what's new]

GMO Food

GMO means "genetically modified organism." When DNA was discovered in the 1950s, it became apparent that scientists could adjust the building blocks and recombine them to create different traits. This concept has grown into the genetic engineering industry. Humulin, a synthetic form of insulin, was developed through this process, called recombinant DNA, and has been a huge benefit to individuals with diabetes. More very promising therapies are in development for multiple sclerosis, cystic fibrosis, and others.

The same technology is used to create food crops that are more productive, more nutritious, and resistant to diseases and pests. Millions of acres worldwide, including land in developing nations, are now farmed using GMO seeds. Common GMO crops include corn, soybeans, and rice, as shown in Figure 10.10. Solutions to world hunger problems may include GMO crops.

However, there is controversy with GMO and food crops. The technology is expensive, and the new seed lines are patented. Some are genetically encoded to prevent the seeds from being fertile after the first planting. A farmer cannot develop seed stock, but must purchase new seeds every year. This is a multibillion-dollar global industry.

The profit potential leaves some folks in fear of GMO. Also, environmental groups are wary of the pollens and crossbreedings that occur in the plant world. What if there is something harmful in the new products? What if there are allergens or pollens not yet identified?

The United States is a leader in the use of GMO crops, but there are pockets in the United States where strong environmental concerns have outlawed them locally. African governments are encouraging their use, but there is still fear from the population. Canadian and Australian states are mixed on their acceptance. There is GMO use in Asia. The European Union is avoiding their use while taking a slow approach toward acceptance, and is studying the matter in various committees.

What is your opinion of GMO?

Figure 10.10: GMO food crops: Can you tell the difference?

648

Figure Focus
Figure 10.10: GMO food crops can be modified for any number of traits; some of these will be readily visible, whereas others will not.

Essential Skills
Making the Trinity

Trinity means a unity of three. Trinity is a form of mirepoix that is used in Cajun and Creole cuisines. Instead of carrots, celery, and onions, the carrots are replaced by green bell pepper. Gumbo and Jambalaya are two classic Creole dishes based on trinity. Trinity is considered foundational to Louisiana cooking. Here is the process for making trinity:

❶ Dice two parts celery. See Figure 10.11a.

❷ Dice two parts onion. See Figure 10.11b.

❸ Dice one part green bell pepper. See Figure 10.11c.

❹ Over medium-low heat, slowly sautè all three in a pan with olive oil.

❺ Stir occasionally and add a few tablespoons of water as ingredients reduce in size and blend together.

❻ When celery, onion, and green peppers all look similar to each other, the trinity is complete, usually about 30 minutes or so.

Figure 10.11a:
Step 1—Dice the celery.

Figure 10.11b:
Step 2—Dice the onion.

Figure 10.11c:
Step 3—Dice the green bell pepper.

Southwestern United States

[flavor]

Flavor Profile
Southwestern flavors are smoky and spicy.

Cultural Influences

The Southwest is composed of Texas, Arizona, and New Mexico. Figure 10.12 on the following page shows a map of this region. Much of the cuisine of the Southwest has been heavily influenced by Mexican culture, heritage, and cooking methods, all of which will be discussed in greater detail later in the chapter. The first contributors to the formation of Southwestern cuisine were the Native Americans, who had to adapt to the arid weather conditions and scarce vegetation in the desert and mountains. The use of edible plants such as pine nuts, beans, corn, and prickly pear (cactus) became the foundation of Southwestern cuisine. Aztec Indians and Spanish colonists introduced the use of different meats like rabbit,

649

Essential Skills:
Making the Trinity

Green pepper substitutes for carrots. The flavor is quite different.

Flavor Profile

Southwestern flavors are influenced by Mexico.

Discuss

- If you have ever eaten a taco, you have had a Southwestern-influenced menu item.

- The American-style, Mexican-influenced cuisine of the Southwest can be found all over North America now.

- Tortillas and spices are features of the cuisine.

Figure Focus

Figure 10.11a: Celery may be dirty at the root. Be sure to clean the celery before dicing it.

Figure 10.11b: The horizontal cuts do the dicing so the onion is not just sliced.

Figure 10.11c: Remove seeds and pith before chopping green pepper.

- Perhaps students are fans of salsa.

- Salsa has passed ketchup as the single most popular condiment in the United States.

- Salsas come in many varieties, not just those including tomatoes and peppers.

- Ask students if they eat salsa as part of their regular diet.

- Ask them how they use the salsa.

- Perhaps they would like to know that tomato salsa is nutritious, and is a source of beta carotene and lycopene.

> **Techniques:**
> **Southwestern United States Cooking Methods**
>
> Cooking with fire and smoke is popular in the Southwest.

Vocabulary Terms

- **Tex-Mex:** Southwestern cuisine featuring ground meats.

- **Cal-Mex:** Southwestern cuisine featuring shredded meats

- **Salsa:** A vegetable sauce, usually with tomatoes, peppers, and spices, usually served cold.

---

deer, and wild turkey to the Southwestern natives. Prominent Mexican influences include the use of a variety of chili peppers. Other cuisines have spun off of the Southwestern cuisines, such as **Tex-Mex** and **Cal-Mex**. In Cal-Mex, meats are shredded, while with Tex-Mex the meats are generally ground.

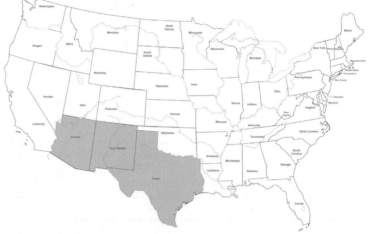

Figure 10.12: The Southwest region of the United States includes Texas, Arizona, and New Mexico.

Regional Ingredients and Dishes

Beef and pork are commonly used meats. Offal meat, such as heart, kidneys, liver, tripe, sweetbreads, and tongue, is also used in Southwestern cuisine. Corn, beans, cactus, nuts, cumin, avocados, rice, citrus, and chili, ancho, and chipotle peppers are common ingredients.

> **[techniques]**
>
> **Southwestern United States Cooking Methods**
> The cooking techniques used in the Southwestern United States include grilling, smoking, and barbecue.

Salsa is a signature dish of the Southwest. The word means sauce in Spanish. Although salsa can be smooth and thin in consistency, it is usually a chunky sauce that

Figure Focus
Figure 10.12: Parts of the United States border Mexico in the Southwest. Mexican flavors influence their cuisine.

may even resemble a relish. Salsa can be cooked or fresh, can be made with vegetables and/or fruits, and can be hot and spicy or mild. It has become an umbrella term with a broad application, but usually has a foundation of fresh chopped red or green tomatoes. Figure 10.13 illustrates the wide variety of salsas available.

Figure 10.13: Types of salsa include Salsetta Rossa Cruda (left) and Salsa Casera, chopped raw vegetables (right).

Barbecue is also common in the region. Whole **barbecued** chicken, pulled pork, and ribs—cooked with the heat of a fire, sometimes after a marinade, spice rub, or basting sauce has been applied—are popular dishes. Texas alone has several different varieties of barbecue methods and specialties. Throughout the Southwest, barbecued meat is a favorite. Chili, a thick blend of kidney, red, or pinto beans with meat and seasonings, will be on most any Southwestern menu.

[on the job]

Spanish in the Americas

Knowing how to speak Spanish in the Western Hemisphere is a good idea. Spanish is the official language of every nation of the Americas except Canada, The United States, Suriname, Guyana, some Caribbean islands, and Brazil. In fact, it is estimated that between 325 and 400 million people speak Spanish as their native language. That means that there are more native Spanish speakers in the world than any other language, with the exception of Mandarin Chinese.

The United States has no official language but is mostly an English-speaking country with a large Spanish-speaking portion of the population. Spanish is very common in California, the Southwest, Texas, and Florida, and is spreading rapidly throughout the Pacific Northwest, Intermountain West, and Midwestern states. It is estimated that 35 million U.S. residents speak Spanish, making it the second most common language in the United States This number is continuing to grow.

Both English and Spanish are commonly spoken in restaurant and foodservice kitchens across the country. Knowing both languages can be an invaluable tool on the job. Being able to communicate with most anyone in an establishment, or being able to serve as translator for customers or fellow employees will help anyone wanting to work in management, as a chef, or even as a server.

If you want to learn Spanish, start taking classes in school. Local community colleges and adult education programs also frequently provide Spanish classes. And if those options don't work, try a self-learning guide, online program, or recorded lessons.

651

Flavor Profile

There are many Asian influences in the Western United States.

Discuss

• "Fusion" does not necessarily mean Asian.

• Fusion cuisine means that two different types are brought together into a single menu or dish.

• Perhaps students can give some examples of fusion dishes or menus.

• Mexican pizza or Southwestern-style pizza might be something they have heard of.

Vocabulary Terms

• **Fusion cuisine:** A combination of two or more regional cuisines to form new dishes.

[fast fact]

Did You Know . . . ?

Barbecue is a noun, a verb, and an adjective. It describes several pieces of cooking equipment; an event; a place; several styles of various types of cooked meat; a method of cooking anything; an unlimited array of sauces, spices and marinades; and even a flavor of potato chips.

So just what exactly is barbecue? As you can see, it means a number of different things, but there is one element common to all barbecue: smoke.

To barbecue something is to cook it over wood fire or coals, using the smoke as part of the cooking process. Because of the smokiness of the process, it is done outdoors. The cooking may take a few minutes, or last up to 18 hours. It can also include cooking food on an outdoor gas grill with a closed lid to retain the smoke. Anything from a tiny Japanese hibachi to a huge fire pit dug into the ground can become a barbecue as long as very hot smoke meets meat.

Barbecue is also a flavor for sauces. Many Southwestern barbecue sauces are tomato and molasses based, but sauces with mayonnaise or vinegar are also found around the United States. The sauce can be a marinade, a last-minute glaze, or a table sauce. Do not baste with a tomato-based sauce throughout the cooking process, because it burns the sauce on the meat. Barbecue flavor for potato chips and other snacks means a sweet-sour-smoky-tomato taste.

Vegetables and fruits such as summer squash, bell peppers, pineapple, apples, and onions can also be grilled on a barbecue. This makes good use of the heat while imparting a rich, smoky flavor to the vegetables. Bread, corn, potatoes, and even apple pie can be cooked with the smoky heat of a barbecue and be all the better for it. Again, smoke is the common thread tying all of these variations together.

Pacific Rim/Coast

[flavor]

Flavor Profile

Asian fusion flavors range from sweet and sour to bland due to the influences of Thai and Chinese cuisines. The Thai and Chinese believe that food should be served in its natural state. Additional Pacific Coast flavors are based in seafood, sourdough bread, and local fruits and vegetables.

History and Cultural Influences

This is a vast region, including all of the Pacific Coast shoreline of the United States as well as the islands all along the coast in the Pacific Ocean. Figure 10.14 on the following page shows a map of the mainland American states included in the region. The food of this region is sometimes referred to as Asian fusion or Euro-Pacific. Awareness of this cuisine was created around the early 1970s when many eclectic styles of fusion cuisine became popular. Chef Wolfgang Puck helped popularize fusion cuisine. It is a style of cooking and presenting food that combines the ingredients and techniques of Asian and West Coast cuisines. In Hawaii, Chef Roy Yamaguchi was credited with creating and developing Pacific Rim cuisine in particular.

652

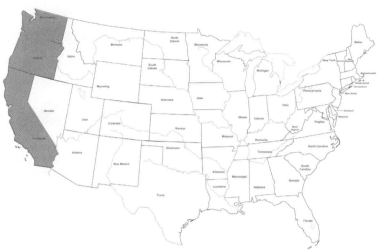

Figure 10.14: The Pacific Rim/Coast region includes California, Oregon, and Washington as well as Alaska and Hawaii.

Common Ingredients and Dishes

Seafood ingredients are used in abundance. Salmon, halibut, mussels, and oysters are all commonly used in dishes. Other staples include poultry, coconut, bananas, pineapple, tropical fruits, fruit salsas, avocadoes, red onions, tomatoes, cucumbers, sesame seeds, basil, cilantro, wasabi, citrus fruits, annatto seed oil, and cardamom. One hallmark example of Asian fusion is Chef Sammy Choy's wasabi cheesecake appetizer, a sweet/spicy creation with a macadamia-nut crust. This single dish exemplifies the fusion of a Euro-American concept by combining the Asian flavor of wasabi with a distinctly Hawaiian crust. These principles are carried out in many dishes along the Pacific Coast, including the easy-to-find Asian chicken salad.

Pacific cuisine is not limited to Asian influences. San Francisco, for example, has a singular cuisine style that revolves around seafood and sourdough bread. The cooler, more even-keeled climate of the Bay Area creates the environment for what some feel is the perfect sourdough starter. Both the seafood and the bread are heavily influenced by Italian cooking principles from the Italians who settled throughout the city and the Bay Area. Spanish and Portuguese cuisine made an impact as well, along with Asian and Native Californian inflections.

653

Figure Focus

Figure 10.14: The western United States has enjoyed Asian influences along the Pacific Coast.

Reinforce and Review

- Berries are full of flavor and very popular.

- Many berries are full of noticeable seeds.

- They are often more acceptable for certain menu items if they are seeded.

- A *chinois* can be used for this purpose.

- Whole, plump, ripe, sweet berries are beautiful garnishes.

Techniques:
Pacific Coast/Pacific Rim Cooking Methods

Light flavors of fresh fruit and vegetables infuse Pacific cuisine.

Nutrition:
Got SPAM?

Hawaii is a place full of culinary surprises. Ask students if they have ever tried SPAM.

Continuing north to Oregon and Washington, increased rainfall and fertile soil create an area where trees, flowers, and berries grow like weeds. Pacific Northwest salmon, halibut, and crawfish are popular local items. Marionberry cobbler is a restaurant favorite. Marionberries are a blackberry hybrid developed in Marion County, Oregon, as shown in Figure 10.15. Farther north in Seattle, the coffee culture is very strong. However, people also enjoy a steaming hot cup of clam juice on a chilly afternoon in the harbor. In Seattle, Western Canada, and on up to Alaska, some form of salmon is found on most local menus.

Figure 10.15: Marionberries developed in Marion Country, Oregon.

[techniques]

Pacific Coast/Pacific Rim Cooking Methods
Pacific Coast/Pacific Rim cooking methods include stir-frying, grilling, and baking.

[nutrition]

Got SPAM®?
When you think of SPAM, shown in Figure 10.16, you might think of canned meat, Monty Python, and unwanted email. But now add "tropical paradise" to the group. Hawaii is the top market for SPAM in the world. World War II altered many things in the Pacific Islands, cuisine being one of them. During the war, Hawaiians relied upon U.S. military barges of supplies for many commodities, including protein from SPAM canned meat from the Hormel Food Corp.

Figure 10.16: SPAM hits the shelves back in 1937 and has become an American institution.

SPAM appears on the local classic Hawaiian plate lunch: meat, two scoops of white rice, one scoop of macaroni salad. This meal is loaded with calories (more than 1,000), fat, and sodium—well over half the daily allowance of all three! Meanwhile, it contributes protein and carbohydrates, but very few other nutrients.

Plate lunch is so common that the phrase, "Have you eaten rice yet?" means, "Do you want to go to lunch?" The option for "Hapa-style" plate lunch increases the fiber and a few vitamins by mixing a scoop of brown rice and a scoop of white. SPAM is served at McDonald's and Burger King outlets in the Hawaiian Islands.

654

Figure Focus

Figure 10.15: Berries are a wonderful addition to a summer menu.

Figure 10.16: Hormel's classic canned meat product was especially useful during World War II.

Mexico

Flavor Profile
The flavors of Mexico are spicy hot and earthy. Most of the flavors originate from vegetarian sources, but meat, poultry, and seafood feature prominently in modern Mexican cuisine.

Cultural Influences

Mexico is a vast country with various climates and regions. Figure 10.17 shows a map of the region. Mexico has regions of mountains, plains, deserts, rainforests, and vast coastlines. It is fairly warm throughout, except for the highest elevations, so crops can grow in some regions of the country year-round.

Figure 10.17: Mexico is a vast region.

Mexico was colonized by Spain during a time when the area was dominated by two powerful native cultures: the Aztecs and the Mayas. The Spanish were not

655

Flavor Profile
Mexican flavors aren't exactly like the American concept of Mexican food.

Discuss

- Do students recall from social studies and history classes the main Native Americans of Mexico, Central American, and South America?

- The native nations discussed in this chapter include:
  - The Aztec civilization in Mexico
  - The Mayan civilization in Mexico and Central America
  - The Incan civilization in western South America

- These ancient civilizations developed foods that still influence the cuisines of the region, the continent, the hemisphere, and the world.

Figure Focus

Figure 10.17: Help students notice the variety of regions and terrains: coastal, mountains, plains, and tropics.

Discuss

- Talk with the students about peppers.

- Why do they think that peppers are such an integral part of Mexican cuisine?

- Are there other cuisines that they know of that feature peppers so prominently?

- They will learn of more in this chapter and the next one.

- Introduce the pronunciation for comale: "koh-MAHL" or "koh-MAH-lay."

In-Class Activity:
Tortilla Brainstorm

21st-Century Skills—Work Effectively in Diverse Teams

Divide the students into four teams.

Have each team think of a completely new way to serve a tortilla.

The students should specify whether or not they have chosen corn or flour tortillas.

Any meal of the day, any course of the meal is fair game.

For example, students might suggest a fried corn tortilla, salted, rolled, and cooled as an ice cream cone. Students will have their own ideas and creations.

Vocabulary Terms

- **Comale:** A cooking surface for tortillas.

- **Masa:** Corn meal created by chemically treating corn with alkali to remove the husks

---

always well received because they focused on conquering the local populations. The conflict between the Spanish colonizers and the Aztec and Mayan natives continued for many years. Modern-day Mexico is a Spanish-speaking nation of people who are a mix of Spanish, Aztec, and Mayan descent.

Today, Mexican cuisine derives from those ancient Aztec and Mayan cultures, which were very sophisticated in their food preparation. There are techniques and nutritional considerations that the Aztec and Mayan people integrated into their cooking methods and diets that scientists didn't fully understand until the twentieth century; and there's more discovery likely to come. In short, Mexican tacos and enchiladas are just the beginning of the bold and broad palate of our neighbors to the south.

Regional Ingredients and Dishes

Corn has been a staple food of Mexico for centuries. The technique of chemically treating corn with alkali to remove the husks and create a corn meal called *masa* was an ancient food science breakthrough. It increased the palatability, digestibility, and absorbability of this foundational food. The simple, daily handmade corn tortilla was a benchmark in food processing long before the arrival of the Europeans and their influences. It is similar in significance to the development of breads in other nations, all of which are marvels of biochemistry.

Figure 10.18: A modern comales.

Corn tortillas were originally cooked without fat on a **comale,** or a round, flat griddle made of stone or earthenware. Modern comales are cast iron or made of another metal, and are still commonly used in the Mexican kitchen. Figure 10.18 shows a modern comale. Tortillas today are fried with or without fat, but are still made from masa.

The ancient Mexican diet was usually vegetarian, perhaps supplemented with seafood in the coastal regions. Meat products were rare, and dairy products were introduced by the Europeans. Some meat and dairy are now incorporated into traditional dishes; shredded meat, melted cheese, or sour cream are all common now. But it is still difficult to think of Mexican food without tortillas, beans, some sort of pepper, and perhaps guacamole, all of which are original to the cuisine.

Peppers are a major flavoring agent of Mexican food in all regions. The varieties of peppers themselves vary from area to area, but they are commonly called

656

Figure Focus
Figure 10.18: Cooking a tortilla.

---

chiles, or chili peppers. These are more pungent and spicier with capsaicin than typical green bell peppers. A jalapeño pepper is the flagship, familiar throughout the world as a Mexican flavor. Other peppers include the relatively mild poblano (or ancho when it's dried), the spicy serrano, and the very hot habañero peppers, which some say are the hottest peppers of all. Hot, spicy peppers are perhaps the notable flavor of Mexico. But, there are subtleties far beyond the heat of peppers.

Seafood, beef, pork, and chicken are very typical in modern Mexican food. Also, a traveler might encounter goat, iguana, or grasshopper on the menu in certain locales. Offal meats, such as heart and kidney, are also used in Mexican dishes, a favorite being menudo, a tripe (stomach organ) soup that is very spicy and cooks slowly over several hours or even days. Meat pieces and seasonings are also made into Mexican *salchichas,* or sausages, including chorizo (pork) and *butifarra* (dried pork).

Mole means sauce or mixture and can sometimes be used as a suffix on words to describe the sauce. The most familiar example of this is guacamole or "avocado mixture." However, cooked mole is also a feature in Mexican cuisine. Mole is a slow-cooked sauce that is elegant in its complexity of flavors. It is rich and dark with a smoky or tobacco type of flavor. The most notable variety is Mole Poblano, which is made with dried fruits and ancho chilis. Sometimes chocolate is melted in, giving it a sweet yet smoky flavor and a rich brown color. *Mole Negro,* shown in Figure 10.19, from Oaxaca (Wah-HAH-Ka), has a smoky, earthy tobacco quality imparted by local *chihuacle negro* chilis. Other moles come in various colors: *Mole Verde* is a green sauce of toasted pumpkin seeds, tomatillos (a fruit related to the tomato family), and cilantro; and *Mole Amarillo* is a yellow variety of tomatillo sauce.

Figure 10.19: Mole Negro.

Mexican Cooking Methods
Mexican cooking methods include griddle frying with or without fat (comale), grinding, and fire roasting.

Reinforce and Review

- "Mole" can be used as a word, or as the ending of a word, as in "guacamole."

- Guacamole is popular outside of Mexico.

- In the United States, guacamole is often used as a dip or party food.

- In Mexican cuisine, guacamole is used as a condiment.

- Guacamole traditionally added important vitamins and fats to the diet.

- Guacamole is still a rather simple mashed avocado mixture.

- Introduce the pronunciation for mole: "MOH-lay."

Techniques: Mexican Cooking Methods

The various cooking methods are holdovers from primitive techniques.

Vocabulary Terms

- **Mole:** A Mexican sauce; there are several varieties.

Figure Focus
Figure 10.19: The rich, brown, smoky Mole Negro.

Summary

- Remind students to review the following:
  1. Northeastern United States—culture, ingredients, and dishes
  2. Midwestern United States—culture, ingredients, and dishes
  3. Southern United States—culture, ingredients, and dishes
  4. Southwestern United States—culture, ingredients, and dishes
  5. Pacific Rim/Coast—culture, ingredients, and dishes
  6. Mexico—culture, ingredients, and dishes

Summary

In this section, you learned the following:

- New England is in the northeast corner of the United States situated along the Atlantic Seaboard, so it has access to a large supply of fresh seafood. Because this region was the location of some of the earliest European settlements of the United States, Native Americans had an influence on New England cuisine. It has also been influenced by the Puritans and Portuguese, Irish, and Italian immigrants who came over from Europe. Traditional New England recipes are not highly seasoned. The flavors are deep and rich and tend to be more mild than spicy. One-pot cookery is common in the region.

- The Midwest region of the United States consists of states in the center of the country. These states are known for their grassy plains, lakes and streams, change of seasons, and a good climate and conditions for raising cattle and growing vegetables. Midwestern cuisine usually showcases simple, hearty dishes that make use of locally grown food. Midwestern cuisine has many cultural influences because people immigrated to this area from Germany, Britain, Italy, Hungary, and Scandinavia. The food is generally hearty, but can be prepared with a light hand with seasonings ranging from sage, dill, caraway, mustard, and parsley to bring out bold and spicy flavors. Barbecue, chicken-frying, pickling, and canning are popular cooking methods of the region.

- Due to the wide expanse of this region, it's easiest to discuss Southern cuisine in three parts: the Tidewater region of Virginia and North Carolina; the Low Country of South Carolina, Georgia, and northeastern Florida; and the Gulf Coast area of the Mississippi Delta and Louisiana. The flavor profiles of Southern regions vary from the highly flavored and spicy Cajun food to the more mild but full-flavored food of the Tidewater region. In all cases, the flavors are fresh and typical of local ingredients. The cooking techniques used in the southern United States cover the full range of techniques used in Western cookery. One that is somewhat of a hallmark of the region is one-pot cookery, in which a full meal is prepared in one pot. Everything is well spiced and carries an exquisitely blended flavor and aroma.

- The Southwest is composed of Texas, Arizona, and New Mexico. Much of the cuisine of the Southwest has been heavily influenced by Mexican culture, heritage, and cooking methods. The flavor profile of Southwestern cuisine is typically smoky and spicy, and the cooking methods consist of grilling, smoking, and barbecuing.

- Sometimes referred to as Asian fusion or Euro-Pacific, Pacific Rim cuisine was created around the early 1970s when many eclectic styles of fusion cuisine become popular. Pacific Rim cuisine is a combination of the cuisine of many different countries along the Pacific Coast. It is a style of cooking and presenting foods that combines the ingredients and techniques of Asian and West Coast cuisines. Additional Pacific Coast flavors are based in seafood, sourdough bread, and local fruits and vegetables.

- Mexican cuisine derives from ancient Aztec and Mayan cultures, which were very sophisticated in their food preparation. Mexican tacos and enchiladas are just the beginning of the bold and broad palate of our neighbors to the south. The flavor profile of Mexican cuisine is spicy hot and earthy. Most of the flavors originate from vegetarian sources, but meat, poultry, and seafood feature prominently in modern Mexican cuisine. Cooked mole is a feature in Mexican cuisine.

659

Section 10.1
Review Questions

1. One-pot cooking is a notable cooking method in the Northeast.

2. The Midwest flavors are much milder than those in Southwestern cuisine.

3. The South includes the Tidewater, Low Country, and Gulf Coast regions.

4. Stir-frying, grilling, and baking are often used in Pacific Rim/Coast cuisine.

5. Each student will have a unique answer that does not need to be limited to the cuisines covered thus far in the text.

6. Each student will have a unique answer, but possible answers include New England clam chowder or Manhattan clam chowder, New England boiled dinner, barbecued meat (dry-rub), meatloaf, and so on.

7. Each student will do research and present his or her own opinions and findings.

8. Students may have a variety of ideas. It's possible to combine all the southern spicy areas, all the northern meat areas, and the western fusion areas. They could also combine the fusion sections of Pacific Rim/Coast and Southwest, then all of the Eastern seaboard and Gulf Coast where seafoods are featured, then the Midwestern milder meat and dairy region.

Section 10.1 Review Questions

1. What is the most notable cooking method of the Northeast?

2. How does the flavor profile of the Midwest compare to the Southwest?

3. What are the three regions of the Southern United States?

4. List three cooking methods commonly used in Pacific Rim/Coast cuisine.

5. Rick Bayless notes that you should "cook what you are passionate about." He learned from "many Mexican grandmothers." In what kinds of food are you most interested? What have you been exposed to through your family and friends?

6. Miguel and Chef Kate have decided that in order to best represent the northern parts of North America, they need to pick at least one dish from the Northeast or Midwest. Which dish would you suggest they choose? Why?

7. Pick one region of North America and describe how the culture has influenced the cuisine. What influence do you feel has had the biggest impact on the cuisine of this region today? Report your findings and opinion in two paragraphs.

8. If you had to combine the six regions of North America discussed in this section into three regions, what regions would you combine and why? Explain your rationale based on geography, regional ingredients, or cultural influences.

660

Section 10.1 Activities

1. Study Skills/Group Activity: Clambake!

A clambake has become an American tradition involving a large social gathering and party atmosphere. What is the origin of the word? What region is it from? In a small group, explain the origin of the word, what region it originated in, and what a traditional clambake was like. Then, plan a clambake including the location, food, safety, menu, presentation, and cleanup.

2. Activity: Looking Deeper Into the South

Pick one subsection of the Southern United States—Low Country, Tidewater, or the Gulf Coast region—and research the cuisine. Be sure to include ethnic and racial influences, geographic influences, and ingredients native to the particular region you choose. Report your findings in a three-paragraph summary. Add two recipes from the region.

3. Critical Thinking: Taste of North America

Create a six-course meal using one dish from each of the six regions of North America discussed in this section. You will need to include the full recipe for each of the six dishes you incorporate. Be sure to consider how the dishes will work with each other in terms of taste, texture, and the sequence in which they are served. Each dish should reflect what you feel is the essence of each region's cuisine.

661

Section 10.1 Activities

1. Students should do some research into the cooking method, the traditional menu, and so on.

2. The subregions of the South are specifically influenced by their geography, native plants and wildlife, and ethnic origins of inhabitants.

3. This assignment will be time consuming. It will also help students synthesize all of the information they have read in this section.

Section 10.2
Central America and the Caribbean

Introduce the Section
a. There are cultural influences that infuse Caribbean cuisine with many different flavors and foundations.
b. Central American cuisine has grown out of both poverty and the availability of tropical fruits.
c. Discuss the objectives for the section.

Vocabulary Review
a. Direct students to the key terms.
b. Pronounce each word, and have the students repeat the pronunciation out loud.
c. Discuss the definition of each word.

Teach

Discuss
- Many students have never considered Central American cuisine as being different than Mexican.
- There are many tropical influences in Caribbean and Central American cuisines.
- Central America and the Caribbean have different cuisines.
- Perhaps the students have heard of jerk spice. If so, they have heard of Caribbean cuisine.
- If they have eaten a banana, they have probably eaten food from Central America.

Reinforce and Review
- The Caribbean was the first part of the Americas with permanent European settlers.
- Christopher Columbus arrived on the island of Hispaniola, now the location of Haiti and the Dominican Republic.
- Several European nations settled in the Caribbean.
- African slaves were also brought to the region.
- The Caribbean is currently a popular tourist and cruise ship destination, and is influenced by popular chefs.
- Central America has experienced less tourism and fewer European settlers.
- Central America has pockets of ancient and traditional cultures.

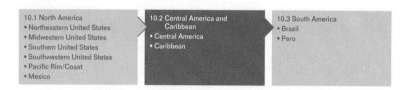

10.1 North America
- Northeastern United States
- Midwestern United States
- Southern United States
- Southwestern United States
- Pacific Rim/Coast
- Mexico

10.2 Central America and Caribbean
- Central America
- Caribbean

10.3 South America
- Brazil
- Peru

SECTION 10.2 CENTRAL AMERICA AND THE CARIBBEAN

The Caribbean has an overlapping collection of cuisine influences from past and present residents. There are native, Spanish, English, French, Dutch, and African foods and techniques fused with the local tropical and ocean foods. A varied array of foods and preparation methods is the result. Food may be different even on the same island. For example, on the island of Hispaniola, the Spanish settled the Dominican Republic on the eastern side, and the French settled Haiti on the west. Each side now has its own cuisine.

Often overlooked, but interesting in its own right, is the cuisine of Central America. While it has definitely been influenced by Mexico and the Caribbean, there are unique qualities to the corn, rice, and bean diet of this region. Sadly, many of them derive from poverty and the struggles and adaptations that it requires. Tourism and immigration have not been historically strong in this region, so outside influences are not as prevalent as they are in other places. This has kept the native diet fairly pure and unchanged in some villages for centuries.

Study Questions

After studying Section 10.2, you should be able to answer the following questions:

- What are the cultural influences and flavor profiles of Central America?
- What are the cultural influences and flavor profiles of the Caribbean?

Central America

[flavor]

Central American Cuisine Flavor Profile
Central American flavors are mild and earthy accompanied by the sweetness of tropical fruit.

662

Flavor Profile

Tropical fruit of Central America includes the bananas that are sold in the United States.

Cultural Influences

Central America includes Guatemala, El Salvador, Belize, Honduras, Nicaragua, Costa Rica, and Panama. Figure 10.20 shows a map of this region. It is located on the land between the southern border of Mexico and the northern border of Colombia, which is also the defining division of South America. Tropical weather, beaches, and volcanic mountain terrain are hallmarks of Central America. The culture differs from Mexico in important ways, including a larger remnant of the original native Mayan populations. These Mayan tribes are distinct from each other and have their own languages and religions to this day.

Figure 10.20: Central America includes Guatemala, El Salvador, Belize, Honduras, Nicaragua, Costa Rica, and Panama.

The influence of the Spanish conquerors of the sixteenth and seventeenth centuries was profound in these regions as well as Mexico and the Caribbean. Spanish is the official language of every Central American country except Belize, where English is spoken. Political and economic conflicts have long kept Central America off many vacationers' must-see lists, but now this is changing and the newly evolving cuisines of the region reflect that.

Since the main trade has historically been fruit (especially bananas), these countries are nicknamed "The Banana Republics." Bananas, pineapples, cacao

663

Figure Focus
Figure 10.20: The regions discussed here are tropical.

- Have students ever tasted typical Central American dishes such as *curtido*?

- There is some overlap with Mexican foods.

Vocabulary Terms

- *Cacao*: A tropical tree that grows seed pods that produce the beans that are ground to make cocoa powder (which is then made into chocolate).

- *Gallo pinto*: A Central American bean and rice dish.

- *Curtido*: A typical Central American relish made form cabbage, onions, and carrots in vinegar.

(chocolate), organic dyes, and coffee beans have been the main exports. **Cacao** is a tropical tree that grows the seed pods that produce the beans that are ground to make cocoa powder, which is made into chocolate.

Common Ingredients and Dishes

Central American cuisine is an interesting transition point between classic Mexican food and the more varied array of foods in South America. It is influenced by Spanish and Caribbean dishes without as much West African flavor. There are still original remnants of the Mayan diet. Tropical fruits, vegetables, and starches are simple to prepare and provide much of the daily fare. The most common features are rice, beans, coconuts, yuca, and some spices. Although chili peppers are found, they are not as prominent a cuisine element as they are in either Mexico or some South American countries.

Curtido is a typical Central American relish that is made from cabbage, onions, and carrots in vinegar. It originated in El Salvador and spread to its neighbors. It is served as a condiment on various dishes, including *pupusas*, a stuffed corn tortilla.

Gallo pinto, which literally means "painted chicken," has nothing to do with either paint or chickens. It is a mix of white rice and black beans, cooked separately and then fried together in coconut oil. The blend of colors makes it look similar to the markings on a local variety of hen. Gallo pinto is eaten nearly every day, often for breakfast, plus with later meals. It is affordable and offers a complete protein. The addition of coconut oil adds both saturated and mono-unsaturated fats to the diet, which can have both a positive and negative impact on heart health.

Figure 10.21: Tamales may be steamed in banana leaves.

Corn tortillas and masa harina are staples in Central America as they are in Mexico. Tamales of this region may be steamed in banana leaves instead of corn husks, as shown in Figure 10.21. Tamale fillings are made from various combinations of pork, chicken, raisins, carrots, peas, onions, corn kernels, rice, and tomatoes. The mixture is placed inside the corn meal dough, wrapped in leaves or husks, and steamed. Sometimes starchy plantain bananas are used for the dough rather than cornmeal. A corn-flour version, a bit more refined, is popular in Guatemala at Christmas.

Figure Focus

Figure 10.21: Corn husks are used for tamales in Mexico, and banana leaves are often used in Central America.

[techniques]

Central American Cooking Methods

Central American cooking methods include griddle-frying and steaming.

[nutrition]

Yuca

Yuca, yucca, cassava, manioc, and tapioca are all the same thing! They are names for the starchy root of the cassava plant, shown in Figure 10.22. A food staple in many tropical parts of the world, these roots are rich in carbohydrates (starch for energy), calcium, phosphorus, and vitamin C. Yuca provides for a balanced, adequate diet in many parts of Central America, South America, and the Caribbean.

Yuca is used boiled or fried, as Americans might use a potato. The flour is used for baking and as a thickener. Little pearls are used to thicken milk and sugar in tapioca pudding. It is an efficient crop, providing a lot of energy output for minimal energy input. Since it has no connection to wheat at all, it can be used by individuals with gluten-sensitive enteropathy (Celiac Disease) or wheat allergy.

Figure 10.22: The cassava plant is a staple crop in Africa, Asia, and South America.

665

Techniques:
Central American Cooking Methods

Central American cooking methods have been used since ancient time, like Mexican techniques.

Nutrition:
Yuca

Many different cultures across the world depend on yuca for calories and nutrients. Ask students if they've ever tasted yuca.

Figure Focus

Figure 10.22: Cassava roots are used for food.

In El Salvador and Guatemala, a *pupusa* might be perfect for a quick lunch on the go. Ask students if they've ever tasted a *pupusa*.

Teaching Tips

- *Pupusas* would be interesting for students to make in class.

- Students might also like to try making *curtido* a day or two in advance of the *pupusas*.

Essential Skills
Making Pupusas

Originally a Salvadoran food, the *pupusa* has migrated next door to Guatemala, other Central American countries, and farther north, all the way to Canada. A **pupusa** looks like a fat homemade tortilla. It is actually a stuffed, pan-fried corn biscuit filled with cheese, beans, pork, or chicken and perhaps even bacon. It's topped with *curtido* (a pickled cabbage relish) and a simple tomato salsa, and eaten handheld. Here is a recipe to make *pupusas*:

❶ Mix 2 parts masa harina with 1 part water in a mixing bowl. Knead well, adding more water a little at a time if needed to make moist but firm dough. See Figure 10.23a.

❷ Set aside for a few minutes to let it rest.

❸ Roll the dough into a log and cut into approximately 8 equal portions.

❹ Roll each portion into a ball and then press an indentation into each ball with your thumb.

❺ Fill the indentation with filling of choice, then completely enclose it with dough.

❻ Carefully press each filled dough ball until it is about 5 or 6 inches wide and ¼ inch thick.

❼ On an ungreased pan heated at medium-high heat, cook each *pupusa* about 2 minutes on each side, or until lightly browned. See Figure 10.23b.

Figure 10.23a: Step 1— Knead the dough.

Figure 10.23b: Step 7—Cook *pupusa* 2 minutes on each side.

666

Figure Focus

Figure 10.23a: Be sure not to add too much water to the dough.

Figure 10.23b: *Pupusas* are often sold by open air vendors.

Did You Know...?
Central America has a combined population of approximately 42 million people.

Caribbean

Flavor Profile
Caribbean flavors are sweet and tropical, while the meat is richly spiced and smoky.

Cultural Influences

Christopher Columbus himself could not have realized all the changes his arrival would have upon the American continent. It all began on the island of Hispaniola, where he first set foot on American soil in 1492. He thought he had landed in the East Indies, but he had actually arrived at an island in the Caribbean. It would be some time before he had any idea that there were two enormous land masses, the North and South American continents—in the nearby region. The island Columbus and his crew landed on is now the home of two nations: Haiti, settled by the French, and The Dominican Republic, settled by Spain.

The Caribbean natives knew their land and their food supply. They knew what to grow and how to use it. The newcomers had to learn to use the native foods. In addition, they brought their own foods and cooking skills. When African slaves arrived, they also brought their foods and skills to the new land. Together, these Carib-Euro-African influences created the varied and vast cuisine of the tiny island nations of the Caribbean. A map of the Caribbean is shown in Figure 10.24 on the following page. Perhaps nowhere else on earth are there blended more distant and far-flung influences than this region.

As small as the tiny island nations are, each cuisine carries the stamp of its original colonizer. The Dutch-settled islands have quite different flavors and foods than the Spanish-settled islands, for example. Each cuisine has a sensibility from the settlers' homeland that mixed with the African influences in a tropical oceanic setting.

667

Fast Fact: Did You Know...?
There are seven Central American nations.
Guatemala is the largest, and it is twice as large as the next largest country.

Flavor Profile
Tropical fruit greatly influences Caribbean cuisine.

Reinforce and Review

- After Columbus discovered a route to the Caribbean, European settlers arrived and established settlements.
- There were native people on the islands when Europeans arrived.
- Many of the natives died when they contracted new illnesses from Europeans.

In-Class Activity:
The Tropics—Earth Math

Mathematics Connection, 21st-Century Skills—Global Awareness

The Tropic of Cancer is a latitudinal line around the Northern Hemisphere. The Tropic of Capricorn is a similar line around the Southern Hemisphere. The Equator is halfway between the two Tropic lines.

The region between the two Tropic lines is called "tropical" or "the tropics." This includes the Equatorial region. Tropical fruit and other tropical foods grow here.

Some of the region just beyond those lines with similar climate is also thought of as "tropical" because palm trees grow, although technically these areas would be "subtropical" (Los Angeles or Florida, for example).

Have the students use a globe, a map, or online resources to discover the latitudes of the tropics. Have them verbalize the locations of the tropics in correct nomenclature, while pointing to the tropic lines on a map or globe.

The Tropics exist at 23°, 26' 22" N and S of the Equator. The students should be able to verbalize what those numbers mean.

These are the measurements of latitude, which are horizontal when considering the Earth with the poles top and bottom. The lines of latitude do not intersect, and run east–west around the girth, with the Equator as the central and 0° line.

Each line of latitude is approximately 60 nautical miles apart. It is referenced using a number and the term "degree" and a superscript symbol (°). The area between degrees is referenced in "minutes" with the symbol ' and "seconds" with the symbol ". There are 60 minutes between each degree and 60 seconds between each minute.

The lines of longitude run north–south and all intersect at the poles. They are at right angles, or 90° to the lines of latitude. They are also 60 nautical miles wide at the Equator, but narrow as they proceed toward the poles where they intersect.

Climate zone locations are determined by the degrees of latitude. Students probably already realize that the Equator is very hot, the poles are very cold, and the climate zones range between the two.

The student should be able to verbalize these concepts, which are the mathematical interpretation of planet Earth.

Figure 10.24: The Caribbean consists of many island nations.

Modern history has influenced cuisine even more. Many Caribbean islands have become resorts and tourist stops for cruise ships. This brings chefs and restaurants to further broaden the palate of the region. However, the largest island, Cuba, has been politically and socially isolated from the rest of the hemisphere for decades. Its cuisine has not had the recent influx of new flavors that the others have experienced. Politics and food go hand-in-hand, especially in the Americas.

Regional Ingredients and Dishes

Caribbean cooking has influenced the entire planet, because barbecue originated in this region. The technique of spicing meat and roasting it over a smoky wood fire may not have first happened here, but this is where it was first noticed and appreciated by the rest of the world. In Jamaica, meat is seasoned with a spicy dry rub called **jerk spice**, which helps preserve the meat, and allows it to marinate in the flavors. Traditional jerk spice was a local mixture of allspice, Scotch bonnet peppers (a very hot relative of the habañero chili), marjoram, cinnamon, and other local herbs (which varied depending upon the chef). Europeans added garlic and rum to the mix, and recently dry mustard and

668

Figure Focus

Figure 10.24: The Caribbean islands are home to a wide variety of cultures.

Vocabulary Terms

- **Jerk spice:** A Jamaican dry rub for barbecued meat.

other additions have added a deeper color. When it is roasted, the flavor of the chili and garlic and other spices permeates the entire cut of meat. Figure 10.25 shows a typical way to serve a jerk-spiced entrèe. Even the jerk spice blend is an example of a melting pot—the roasting method came from Africa, the spices grew in the Caribbean, and the garlic was a European contribution.

The Caribbean is a tropical zone. The beauty of tropical islands includes the abundance of fresh fruits and seafood. The fresh seafood of the region includes crustaceans, marlin, and other very meaty, flavorful fish. Coconuts and cashews are native plants, while peanuts were brought from Africa.

African cuisine included many mashed starchy staples. This has brought mashed yams and yuca (cassava) to Caribbean cuisine. Plantains are a type of starchy banana that is also mashed as a savory side dish both in the Caribbean and in tropical parts of the American continents.

Modern Caribbean people put their own stamp on even the most European foods. For example, a simple raw carrot is juiced and then mixed with cream and sugar for a delicious refreshing Jamaican beverage. It's just called carrot juice, and shown in Figure 10.26, but it's sometimes flavored with a little bit of vanilla for a sweet and creamy flavor.

A ham-and-cheese sandwich becomes a *Cubano* by adding roasted pork and pickles and then grilling it like a panini on *pan Cubano*, or Cuban

Figure 10.25: Grilled jerk spiced chicken is a typical Caribbean dish.

Figure 10.26: Caribbean carrot juice consists of raw carrot juice, cream, and sugar.

669

Reinforce and Review
- African cuisine heavily influences Caribbean and Creole cuisines, plus others elsewhere (soul food cuisine elements).
- Africans were brought to these regions for the slave trade after the Europeans arrived.
- They brought some of their familiar foods and cooking methods.
- These elements have fused and blended with the cuisines of the other cultures.
- These same cuisine elements are still found in Africa.

Vocabulary Terms
- *Cubano:* A ham, cheese, pork, and pickle grilled sandwich on Cuban bread.
- *Pan Cubano:* Sandwich roll from Cuba.

Figure Focus
Figure 10.25: Jerk spice is applied before roasting.

Figure 10.26: Caribbean carrot juice is a mixture of carrot juice, cream, and sugar.

Reinforce and Review

- *Sofrito* is used to flavor rice.

- Without the *sofrito*, rice is bland.

- *Sofrito* is found throughout Puerto Rico.

- Although *sofrito* has peppers in it, it is not especially hot.

Techniques:
Caribbean Cooking Methods

Barbecue grills are often homemade oil drums with a metal grate over the fire.

What's New:
What's Stevia?

Stevia is sold in the United States.

Vocabulary Terms

- **Sofrito:** A Puerto Rican foundational cooked sauce.

---

bread, which is a simple white yeast roll with a crease down the center. *Cubanos* are popular throughout Cuba and southern Florida as a quick lunch.

Even the concepts of mirepoix and trinity are seen in Puerto Rican *sofrito*, which is a mix of salt pork, ham, onions, garlic, green peppers, jalapeño, tomato, oregano, and cilantro. **Sofrito** is cooked slowly together and then used as a foundation in soups and stews. It is even used to flavor basic rice or beans.

[techniques]

Caribbean Cooking Methods

Caribbean cooking methods include barbecue, frying, and stewing.

[what's new]

What's Stevia?

Stevia is a food sweetener developed from a subtropical plant also called stevia, shown in Figure 10.27. The dried plant leaves produce a sweetener that is 300 times as sweet as sugar. Therefore, much less is required, so the caloric contribution is negligible. Individuals can use stevia to sweeten their foods without elevating their blood sugar or insulin requirements or consuming the calories of sugar.

Sweeteners are important for their performance in food, not just for their flavor. Stevia performs well, but while it is legal for sale in the United States as a "naturally sweet herb," it cannot be marketed as a sweetener because it does not have FDA approval. However, it is legal in foods in Japan and other parts of Asia, Australia, New Zealand, and South American countries. The FDA has not yet completed studies on the safe consumption of stevia as a widely used sweetener, but research and use in other countries has thus far shown positive results.

Figure 10.27: The stevia plant is used to produce one of the low calorie sweeteners.

Figure Focus

Figure 10.27: Stevia is regarded as a promising sweetener.

[fast fact]

Did You Know . . . ?

Steel drums that store 55 gallons of oil or water have been used for decades in the Caribbean. It is believed they are an abandoned remnant of World War II supplies. These drums are cut down and used for barbecue grills. A wood fire is built under a metal mesh laid across the top. The drums are used to roast jerk chicken and jerk pork for purchase along the roadside.

In addition, residents without running water take frequent trips to the local reservoir and fill the drums with fresh water for culinary, hygiene, and household use. The drums can also be used to create a home shower by mounting the drum up high, and installing a spigot and showerhead.

As more and more families install water cisterns and pumps into their residences, the steel drums become surplus. Probably originating on the island of Trinidad, but spreading to Jamaica, the drums are used as musical instruments. The bottom of the drum is cut out and tuned by hammering the shape to sound a certain note when struck with a bamboo stick or the hand. Several drums together can play tunes. Steel drum bands perform at carnivals and elsewhere around the islands.

Summary

In this section, you learned the following:

- Central American cuisine is an interesting transition point between classic Mexican food and the more varied array of foods in South America. It is influenced by Spanish and Caribbean dishes, without as much West African flavor. Tropical fruits, vegetables, and starches are simple to prepare and provide much of the daily fare. The most common features are rice, beans, coconuts, yuca, and some spices. Although chili peppers are used in Central America, they are not as prominent a cuisine element as they are in Mexico or some South American countries. The flavor profile tends to be more mild and earthy, and common cooking methods include griddle-frying and steaming.

- Caribbean cooking has influenced the entire planet, because barbecue originated in this region. The technique of spicing meat and roasting it over a smoky wood fire may not have first and only happened here, but this is where it was first noticed and appreciated by the rest of the world. The beauty of tropical islands includes the abundance of fresh fruits and seafood. The fresh seafood of the region includes crustaceans, marlin, and other very meaty flavorful fish. Caribbean flavors are sweet and tropical, while the meat is richly spiced and smoky. Barbequing, frying, and stewing are all common cooking methods in the Caribbean.

671

**Fast Fact:
Did You Know . . . ?**

Steel drums are now found throughout the Caribbean islands.

Summary

- Remind students to review the following:
    1. Central America—culture, ingredients, and dishes
    2. Caribbean—culture, ingredients, and dishes

Section 10.2
Review Questions

1. Central American cuisine is tropical and earthy.

2. Central American techniques include griddle-frying and steaming.

3. Caribbean food is smoky, spiced, and tropical.

4. Barbecue is originally from the Caribbean. The cuisine is also tropical.

5. Students might need to do some extra research, and can choose many different spices, including peppers, cocoa, vinegar, cinnamon, allspice, cilantro, cumin, and oregano.

6. This will require outside research by students. The first aspect is to make the *pan Cubano* roll. Then the pork must be roasted and ready at the correct time to make the sandwiches.

7. Each is made from ingredients that grow well in the local area. The combination gets spicier the further south you travel. Mirepoix is made in the north with the mild ingredients of carrots, celery, and onion. Trinity trades the sweet and earthy carrot for the bold flavor of green bell pepper. *Sofrito* is made with jalapeño peppers, which add heat, in addition to added meat and more herbs and spices.

8. Each student will respond with personal opinions and thoughts.

Section 10.2 Review Questions

1. What is the flavor profile of Central American cuisine?
2. What are common cooking methods of Central American cuisine?
3. What is the flavor profile of Caribbean cuisine?
4. What are common cooking methods used in Caribbean cuisine?
5. Are there herbs and spices that are commonly used in classic Mexican, Central American, and Caribbean cooking? What is the history behind two of these herbs or spices?
6. Chef Kate and Miguel have decided that a good dish for them to make would be the Cubano. It's a good representation of the region, and it doesn't require a lot of work to serve or to eat. The trouble is, they're unfamiliar with the process of exactly how to make it. Write out exactly what equipment and ingredients they will need, as well as the process for making this sandwich.
7. Compare mirepoix, trinity, and *sofrito*. How do the ingredients and flavor profiles of each reflect the cultures they derive from?
8. Which aspect of Caribbean cuisine best fits your thoughts about the region as a whole: the sweet tropical fruit profile or the more spicy, savory side? Explain why you made the choice that you did in a paragraph.

Section 10.2 Activities

1. Study Skills/Group Activity: Caribbean Time Line

Working in small groups, create a time line highlighting the prominence of the various ethnic and racial groups who have inhabited the Caribbean. Your group will need to start, of course, with the native peoples and then mark the arrival of the various explorers as well as African slaves. Detail what influences each group brought to what we now know as Caribbean cuisine. Compare and contrast your findings with the time lines created by other groups.

2. Independent Activity: Looking Deeper into Jerk

Often, the evolution of a region's cuisine reveals a lot about its history. Research jerk seasoning. Where does the name derive from? Why was the mixture originally created? How and why has it changed over the years? Report your finding in a one-page report.

3. Critical Thinking: Caribbean Meal

Create a three-course meal focusing on Caribbean cuisine. Include an appetizer, entrèe, and a dessert. Be sure to include the recipes for each course that you choose.

673

Section 10.2 Activities

1. There is some outside research required, and the students should divide the tasks for this assignment. They might want to consult a history or social studies text or resource.

2. Jerk spice is a signature dish of Jamaica. It brings a very powerful and full-spectrum flavor to barbecued meat.

3. This activity will require outside research. Each student's meal will be different.

Section 10.3
South America

Introduce the Section

a. There are many cultural and geographic areas of South America.

b. There will be a brief overview of the continent, and then focus on two countries.

c. Supplemental information could be added as desired.

d. Discuss the objectives for the section.

Vocabulary Review

a. Direct students to the key terms.

b. Pronounce each word, and have the students repeat the pronunciation out loud.

c. Discuss the definition of each word.

Teach

Discuss

- Contrary to what some might believe, there are very few tortillas in South American cuisine.

Vocabulary Terms

- **Quinoa:** Flour from the grain-like goosefoot plant.

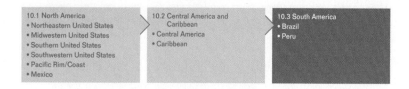

10.1 North America
- Northeastern United States
- Midwestern United States
- Southern United States
- Southwestern United States
- Pacific Rim/Coast
- Mexico

10.2 Central America and Caribbean
- Central America
- Caribbean

10.3 South America
- Brazil
- Peru

SECTION 10.3 SOUTH AMERICA

When you think of South American cuisine, you probably think more of tacos than of wienerschnitzel. However, the cuisine of South America is truly an international mix of concepts that began with native tribal foods to which the influences of Spain, Portugal, Italy, Germany, and Switzerland have been added. Currently, Asian cultures are being incorporated into South America, bringing their signature dishes with them as well.

The entire continent is varied and vast. It begins with tropical and equatorial regions in the north that are hot and humid. Venezuela, Colombia, Ecuador and Brazil are green and lush with jungles, rainforests, coastlines, and mountains. Figure 10.28 on the following page shows a map of the region. Some native cultures are still strong in villages of this region. The cuisine is heavily influenced by both the Spanish and the natives. Tropical fruits are plentiful. Corn, beans, and rice are typical.

The western side of South America is made of the countries of Peru, Chile, and Bolivia. The Andes Mountains define this region, both geographically and culturally. They run the length of the continent and are very high (the highest point is 22,000 feet) and very harsh. Chile is a long, narrow nation between the western Andes to the Pacific coast. Most of the population is near the seaports, with native, Spanish, and northern European settlers. There are even German-speaking sections of Chile and other South American countries from migrations late in the 1800s. Tropical fruit supplements a diet of seafood, rice, and beans that might also include llama meat and **quinoa** (the high-protein dried fruits and seeds of the goosefoot plant used as a food staple and ground into flour).

Bolivia neighbors the eastern border of part of Chile in the Andes. It is a very high-altitude country of the Altiplano, or High Plain, which is a high, dry plateau region. Potatoes, rice, beans, and yuca are the staples of Bolivia. Guinea pig meat is included in the diet as well.

Also neighboring the Andes on the eastern side is Argentina, named for its silver mines that attracted the Spanish conquistadors. Argentina extends to the Atlantic coast. The climate in this region is temperate with vast grasslands similar to the plains of the United States. Cattle ranches and wheat fields thrive here. Argentina is famous for its beef, and it is a major part of the diet.

674

Figure 10.28: The South American continent consists of the countries of Venezuela, Colombia, Ecuador, Brazil, Bolivia, Uruguay, Paraguay, Guyana, Suriname, Chile, Argentina, and Peru.

675

Reinforce and Review

- The terrain of South America still determines the diet to a great extent.

- There are some very untouched areas, especially in the Amazon rainforests and the high Andes Mountains.

- Tortillas are not as common in South America as they are in Central America and Mexico, but hot peppers are found throughout the continent.

- Much of South America was settled by the Spanish, but Portuguese, Dutch, and French people settled some of the regions.

- The English and Germans and other Europeans are also represented in South America.

Figure Focus
Figure 10.28: The South American continent is vast.

Discuss

- In what ways are the Portuguese influences in Brazil different than the Spanish influences in other parts of South America?

- In what ways are they the same?

- Students could read the text in the book together for some information, or they could read silently in advance of the discussion.

Flavor Profile

The cuisine of Portugal is still a major influence in Brazil.

Also in this region of the continent are Paraguay and Uruguay. Uruguay is perhaps the melting pot of South America, with populations of nearly every nationality and philosophy. Many northern and eastern European communities exist within Uruguay, and they have mixed with the native populations to produce a culture that differs from most South American countries. Both Uruguay and Paraguay have climates ranging from the temperate zones at their southern borders to the subtropical, which increases the variety of foods in the diet.

Hot peppers are used in South American cuisine, including many varieties that are not found elsewhere in the world. The northern regions along the Atlantic coast were settled by the Dutch, the French, and the English along with the Spanish, so there is a unique flavor in each of the small nations of Guyana (English), Suriname (Dutch), and French Guiana. West African slaves were also brought here to work sugar, coffee, and cacao plantations. Peanuts, collards, okra, and black-eyed peas are all African additions. There are many varieties of potatoes throughout South America in colors ranging from purple to red to white, with cooked textures varying from waxy to mealy to crispy. Domesticated animals, introduced by the Spanish, increased the protein options beyond the use of seafood, guinea pig, iguana, wild fowl, and game to include goats, pigs, and beef cattle. No matter how varied the cultures and the cuisines, the common features to all are beans and rice.

Study Questions

After studying Section 10.3, you should be able to answer the following questions:

- What are the cultural influences and flavor profiles of Brazil?
- What are the cultural influences and flavor profiles of Peru?

Brazil

[flavor]

Flavor Profile

Brazilian cuisine features savory and spicy roasted meats with tropical fruits and Portuguese influences.

Cultural Influences

Brazil is unique among all the nations of South America. As Figure 10.29 on the following page shows, it is the largest nation of the continent by far, fifth largest by area in the world. The northern portion is the Amazon River valley and

676

- Brazil is in the tropical zone, so there are tropical fruits that grow in Brazil.

- Citrus fruits also grow in Brazil.

- Their citrus fruits are shipped throughout the world.

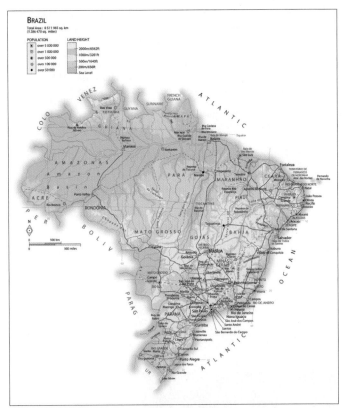

Figure 10.29: Brazil is the largest country in South America.

rainforest, still populated by native communities, some of which have never been contacted by outsiders. They live on local plants, insects, and wild game in their own societies with their own languages. The Amazon rainforest extends beyond the river and into the other nations in northeastern South America. The Amazon itself begins in the Peruvian Andes.

The most important aspect of this region is the vegetation itself. This rainforest has been called "the lungs of the planet" because of the enormous oxygen output of so much growth. Layer upon layer of plants and trees grow in this fertile zone.

677

Figure Focus
Figure 10.29: Brazil is larger than Australia and a little smaller than the continental United States.

Churrasco is a specialty of Brazilian cooking.

Reinforce and Review

- Yerba matè and guarana are quite strong with their caffeine-like qualities.

- They also have nutritional and health-promoting aspects.

- However, when made into soda pop, they have the same drawbacks as other sweetened sodas.

Brazil was settled by Portugal as a colony, so the language and customs are Portuguese. Even though Portugal is a neighbor of Spain, the two countries have different sensibilities. Portugal introduced the western world to citrus fruits, which were also brought to the New World and grow in Brazil. Portuguese cuisine includes tomato-based fish stews, which influenced the Brazilian *Moqueca de Peixe*, a version with coconut milk added. This same influence is found in Manhattan clam chowder in the United States (without the coconut milk, of course). West African slaves were brought to Brazil for agricultural work, and their influence is also felt throughout the settled areas as well, with the use of okra and other African foods.

Regional Ingredients and Dishes

Portuguese-bred Brazilian cuisine is not based upon corn and tortillas like many of its South American neighbors. Tropical fruits like bananas are a staple of the daily diet. Meat roasted on skewers over fire (churrasco), as shown in Figure 10.30, is a specialty. A bean stew called feijoada (FEY-oo-da) is a hallmark item in both Portugal and Brazil.

[techniques]

Brazilian Cooking Methods
Brazilian cooking methods include churrasco (roasting skewered meat over fire), stewing, and incorporating fresh tropical produce.

Figure 10.30: Churrasco is cooked over fire.

Beverages common to Brazil as well as Uruguay are yerba matè tea and guarana. Both are stimulants similar to and stronger than coffee. A typical breakfast in Sao Paolo, the largest city in Brazil, would simply be one of these beverages and a plain white roll. In parts of Brazil, pinto beans (brown beans) will be daily fare; in other areas it will be black beans. Rice and beans are common, and meat is served even in poverty-stricken areas.

678

Figure Focus

Figure 10.30: Entire restaurants are designed around churrasco skewered meats.

Did You Know . . .?

The World Health Organization, or WHO, is the public health arm of the United Nations. It was founded in 1948 and is headquartered in Geneva, Switzerland. It includes delegates from 193 member nations. The purpose of WHO is to improve the quality of life and longevity of all humans on earth.

Food distribution has become a global enterprise. Fresh and processed foods are flown to the far reaches of the globe within hours. Restaurants that feature a cuisine from a particular region can have authentic and native ingredients delivered daily.

This accessibility demands some global safety precautions. WHO's Department of Food Safety and Zoonoses (zōh-UH-nuh-seez)—diseases that can spread from animals to humans—is currently studying the world food markets to develop global food safety standards and quality controls. These controls can help safeguard the health of consumers of imported food. In addition, they help to improve the flavor, nutrition, and freshness of any food purchased from any country.

WHO produces publications periodically on its findings. As it determines the safety issues and solutions, it influences public policy within the participating nations. WHO publications and positions are available in the food safety section of its Web site at www.who.int.

[fast fact]

Essential Skills
Cracking Coconuts

Coconut and coconut milk are commonly used in Brazilian cuisine. But while a coconut is easy to find, it's not necessarily as easy to access. The shell of a coconut is very hard. However, knowing a few easy tips can make the process of opening a coconut faster, cleaner, and safer.

❶ Hold the coconut over a large bowl in one hand so that the middle (fattest part) rests in the middle of your palm.

❷ Whack the coconut with the back of a cleaver—that is, the blunt (nonsharp) side— a few times all around the center of the shell until it cracks open easily into two almost equally sized halves. See Figure 10.31.

❸ The juice from the coconut will fall into the bowl, and you're ready to go.

Figure 10.31: Step 2—Whack the coconut with the back of a cleaver.

Did You Know . . .?

South America is the world's fourth-largest continent (below Asia, Africa, and North America, and above Antarctica, Europe, and Australia). It is divided into twelve countries: Argentina, Bolivia, Brazil, Chile, Colombia, Ecuador, Guyana, Paraguay, Peru, Suriname, Uruguay, and Venezuela, plus the overseas administration of French Guiana.

[fast fact]

679

Fast Fact:
Did You Know . . . ?

The World Health Organization is concerned with both nutrition and food safety.

Essential Skills:
Cracking Coconuts

The liquid that pours out of a coconut is not coconut milk; it is coconut water.

Fast Fact:
Did You Know . . . ?

The South American continent is vast. It begins above the Equator and proceeds south toward the Antarctic Circle.

Figure Focus
Figure 10.31: Cleaving a coconut.

Potatoes are ancient cuisine elements of Peru and the high Andes.

CUSTOMIZED INSTRUCTION

Literacy Connection, 21st-Century Skills—Access and Evaluate Information, Global Awareness

Access the following article:

Bon Appétit magazine, January 2009, "Lima: The Next Great Food City," by Daniel Duane.

This article covers the various cuisines, fusions, and influences in Peru. It also discusses Peruvian influences on other cuisines of the world.

Have students read all or your selection of parts of it aloud in the classroom.

If students have language or reading challenges, select passages that are in keeping with their ability level.

After students have read the information, jigsaw the various aspects of this article. Have students present their findings to the class.

More Advanced Students

Track the various historical influences on the cuisine of Peru. What were the events that brought different cultures to Lima?

Less Advanced Students

What are the various influences that Peruvian cuisine has provided to the rest of the world?

Special Needs Students

Chef Acurio now has 20 restaurants in South America and has opened one in San Francisco. How many miles is San Francisco, California from Lima, Peru?

ESOL Students

Has the native culture of the ESOL student been part of the history of Peruvian cuisine? Has the cuisine of the native culture been influenced by Peru?

Have students share some information about their native culture with the class.

Peruvian Cuisine

[flavor]

Flavor Profile

Peruvian cuisine features mild staples of fish, potatoes, and other local foods with the addition of hot peppers.

Figure 10.32: Peru is in northwestern South America.

680

Figure Focus

Figure 10.32: Peru is on the Pacific Coast, high in the Andes Mountains and down to the shore.

Cultural Influences

Peru sits in northwestern South America on the Pacific coast and extends up into the rugged Andes mountains, as the map in Figure 10.32 on the previous page shows. Lima, the largest city, has a large and growing Asian population in addition to the Spanish and native mixed populations and communities from other parts of the world. The cuisine incorporates these Chinese and Japanese influences, in addition to the Euro-African-American flavors found throughout South America.

Historically, the native populations developed sophisticated methods for coping with their extreme environment that are a marvel even now. The western native tribes that descended from the Incas learned to tame and farm the Andean highlands. They terraced the steep hillsides to hold the rain and level the land for planting. Narrow stripes of terracing extended up the mountain farms, as shown in Figure 10.33. It was an ingenious coping mechanism developed by the highly advanced ancient Incan civilization. They raised corn, rice, beans, and potatoes, and still do.

Regional Ingredients and Dishes

Cuisine in Peru fuses many South American flavors with Chinese concepts and haute cuisine techniques. **Ceviche**, shown in Figure 10.34, is a citrus and fish mixture common to most of the Latin American coastal regions, but it's a signature dish in Peru. In the city of Lima it is called *chebiche*, and key lime juice, rather than heat cooking, is used to denature the protein. Chunks of meaty fish varieties are served with onions, salt, peppers, and potatoes.

Potatoes are many and varied in Peru. They come in more than 3,000 sizes, shapes, and colors! Peruvian purple

Figure 10.33: The terraced agricultural system of Peru began with the Incas.

Figure 10.34: Ceviche (*Chebiche*) is common to Peru.

681

Reinforce and Review

- The very high Andes Mountains extend down the western side of the South American continent, not far from the Pacific coast.

- The Incan people were adapted to living in the high Andes.

Vocabulary Terms

- **Ceviche:** A citrus and fish mixture common to most of the Latin American coastal regions.

Figure Focus

Figure 10.33: Terracing for agriculture was a needed adaptation on the mountainsides.

Figure 10.34: A fresh-tasting Peruvian specialty.

Reinforce and Review

- Machu Picchu is an ancient Incan terraced city perched very high in the areas of the Andes.

- It is located an elevation of 8,000 feet above sea level.

Techniques:
Peruvian Cooking Methods

Did students realize that mashed potatoes were actually a Peruvian contribution to their diet?

Nutrition:
Cherimoya

If at all possible, try and obtain a cherimoya for the students to taste, and have the students research cherimoyas.

Fast Fact:
Did You Know . . . ?

Peruvian cooking includes many ways of preparing many varieties of potatoes.

---

potatoes are making a showing in the United States recently. Potatoes are served in soups, salads, and meat dishes, and are prepared in any number of ways, including boiled, fried, baked, steamed, mashed, and stuffed. *Papa rellena* is a deep-fried mashed potato dumpling filled with ground beef, raisins, onions, and spicy hot aji peppers. Ancient Peruvian potatoes are the original progenitors of all the familiar varieties used today.

[techniques]

Peruvian Cooking Methods

Peruvian cooking methods include marinating, mashing boiled starches, frying, grilling, and braising.

[nutrition]

Cherimoya

The author Mark Twain made quite sarcastic comments about things he didn't particularly enjoy. And he was seldom lavish in praise for something good. However, Mr. Twain himself said that cherimoya was "the most delicious fruit known to men." High praise, indeed.

Cherimoya is grown around the world, but only in moderately high-altitude, tropical areas. The lower part of Bolivia is one such place, and cherimoya is a popular fruit there. It is a green bulbous fruit with a white flesh and dark seeds that grows on a shrub throughout South America, including the Andes Mountains foothills. Figure 10.35 shows the cherimoya fruit.

Cherimoya is a good source of vitamin C. At 20 mg/100 grams of fruit, it contains as much vitamin C as potatoes, melons, and berries. It tastes like a cross between a banana, a pineapple, an apple, a berry, and custard. So many great flavors rolled into one!

Figure 10.35: A cherimoya.

[fast fact]

Did You Know . . . ?

The potato, which can be found in just about any cuisine today, was first cultivated as long as 10,000 years ago in southern Peru. High in the Andes Mountains, tribes in ancient Peru found that the potato was a very nutritious food that could be easily domesticated and stored for long periods of time. These early crops are the ancestors to nearly 5,000 modern worldwide varieties of potato.

In 1537, Spanish conquistadors exploring Peru brought the potato to Europe. Even though potato plants are easily grown, the food was rejected by most Europeans. The potato is a member of the poisonous nightshade family, and parts of the plant, such as

---

Figure Focus

Figure 10.35: The cherimoya's rich and creamy pulp, with a hint of a sweet flavor, makes it an excellent dessert fruit.

the leaves, can cause illness or death when eaten. Not understanding that the potato itself could be safely eaten, people ignored the nutritious crops for several decades.

Eventually, the potato gained acceptance as a food for the poor. In France and Ireland, the potato became a staple food for the lower classes. In 1708, Scottish and Irish settlers brought the potato back to the Americas and introduced the crop to North America.

The acceptance of the potato in France led to many new preparations and uses for potatoes. French fries, though, weren't actually invented in France, but in Belgium. The fried strips of potato were so popular that during Thomas Jefferson's term as president, they were added to the White House menu.

In the United States, the most recognizable variety of potato is the Idaho potato. The most common variety of Idaho potato, which is grown in the Rocky Mountain valleys of that state, is the Russet Burbank, which is known for its long-bodied tuber and the white, starchy flesh inside. The soil and climate of Idaho combine with a long growing season to produce potatoes that are unique for their size and their flavor.

Summary

In this section, you learned the following:

- Brazil was settled by Portugal as a colony, so the language and customs are Portuguese. Portugal introduced the western world to citrus fruits, which were brought to the New World and grown in Brazil. Portuguese cuisine includes tomato-based fish stews, which influenced the Brazilian *Moqueca de Peixe,* a version with coconut milk added. This same influence is found in Manhattan clam chowder in the United States. West African slaves were brought to Brazil for agricultural work, and their influence is also felt throughout the settled areas with the use of okra and other African foods. A cooking method unique to the region is churrasco. Savory and spicy roasted meats are often featured in the cuisine, with tropical fruits and Portuguese influences.

- Peru sits in northwestern South America on the Pacific coast and extends up into the rugged Andes mountains. The cuisine incorporates Chinese and Japanese influences in addition to the Euro-African-American flavors found throughout South America. Historically, the native populations developed sophisticated methods for coping with their extreme environment that are a marvel even now. They terraced the steep hillsides to hold the rain and level the land for planting. Narrow stripes of terracing extended up the mountain farms. It was an ingenious coping mechanism developed by the highly advanced ancient Incan civilization. They raised corn, rice, beans, and potatoes, and still do. The dishes often rely on the mild staples of fish, potatoes, and other local foods with the addition of hot peppers for spice. Mashing boiled starches is common in Peru, as is marinating and frying.

683

Summary

- Remind students to review the following:
  1. South America—overall culture and ingredients
  2. Brazil—culture, ingredients, and dishes
  3. Peru—culture, ingredients, and dishes

Section 10.3 Review Questions

1. Portugal has had the strongest influence on Brazilian cuisine.

2. Roasting and stewing are common cooking methods in Brazil.

3. They are often mashed, but boiling or frying would also be correct answers.

4. Potatoes and beans are Peruvian staples. Students could also mention rice, corn, fish (coastal), and peppers.

5. Students should concentrate on a combination of rice and beans.

6. Each student will have an idea about this. They might need to do some outside research.

7. Either answer could be correct. The meat-based diet of Brazil's vast population and area is coupled with the meat diet of Argentina. Paraguay, Uruguay, and some of the other areas have meat-based diets as well. However, the potato—a gift from Peru—is so ubiquitous throughout North and South America that it might be chosen, too.

8. Each student will identify different things. Students might mention the complementary proteins that are found in Mexican food, and also seen in the beans and rice dishes of South America. Because Mexico is part of North America, this can connect the two continents. Seafood also connects the two continents, as there are vast coastlines along both sides with much access to fish and other seafood. The plains of both continents are ideal for grazing beef, so beef is common on both continents. Tropical fruit is found more in south than the north, as the north only has a small section of tropics north of the Equator (Tropic of Cancer) in Central America and the Caribbean. The south has some of that tropic as well, plus the Equatorial area and the tropic south of it as well (Tropic of Capricorn).

Section 10.3 Review Questions

1. What European country has had the strongest influence on the cuisine of Brazil?

2. What is a common cooking method of Brazil?

3. How are starches often prepared in Peruvian cuisine?

4. Name two staple ingredients in Peruvian cuisine.

5. We know that individual recipes are altered based on local produce or specific cooking methods. Identify two dishes that are served in some form in all three countries of Brazil, Peru, and Mexico. Explain how each country's version of these dishes is similar to the others, and how they differ.

6. Miguel and Chef Kate feel as if they have enough meat dishes on their menu, and so they want a vegetarian dish to represent Peru. Choose a dish that you feel would not only taste great but also represent the essence of the country well. It must also be fairly simple in preparation and hold well given the circumstances under which it is being served. Explain why you chose the dish that you did.

7. Which cuisine do you feel best captures the "essence" of South America: the meat-based cuisine of Brazil or the potato-based cuisine of Peru? Explain your rationale.

8. What similarities do you see between the cuisines of South America and North America? What are some differences? Explain your answer in two paragraphs.

684

Section 10.3 Activities

1. Study Skills/Group Activity: Mapping South America

In small groups, create a map of South America that is highlighted by the ingredients, signature dishes, and cooking methods of each region.

2. Independent Activity: Midwest-Brazil Connection

Compare and contrast the cuisine of the Midwestern United States with the cuisine of Brazil. What are the similarities? What are the differences? Why would there be similarities or differences? Write two paragraphs.

3. Critical Thinking: South American Seafood Dinner

Create a three-course seafood menu, using ingredients and cooking techniques from South America. Be sure to include the full recipe for each course you create.

685

Section 10.3 Activities

1. If this will take too long for the class period, jigsaw the assignment by assigning regions to each group. When they are done, assemble a large completed map for display in the classroom.

2. This will be interesting for the students. They should note the similarity in meat, often beef, as a main dish. A main difference should be tropical foods. Plus, Brazil has a coastline and seafood, unlike the Midwest. The Midwest does have the Great Lakes, which have great freshwater fish.

3. This will require some outside research.

Case Study Follow-Up

1. It would be appropriate for the students to choose cuisines of various regions to highlight global awareness. They might also include some dishes from native cultures. Finally, at least one menu option could be a complementary protein item, perhaps based on Three Sisters, tortillas, beans and rice, or another successful dietary strategy of Native Americans.

2. Practice would help. They will need to do a trial run or two before actually trying to serve a new dish at an Earth Day party.

3. Each student will have an opinion, and should be able to defend it. The most global possibilities are probably the Pacific Rim/Coast of North America, with American, Asian, and Mexican flavors, plus fresh vegetables and fruit, including citrus. Another would be Brazil, with African and Portuguese influences. The Caribbean might have more nationalities influencing a small area than any other portion of the Americas.

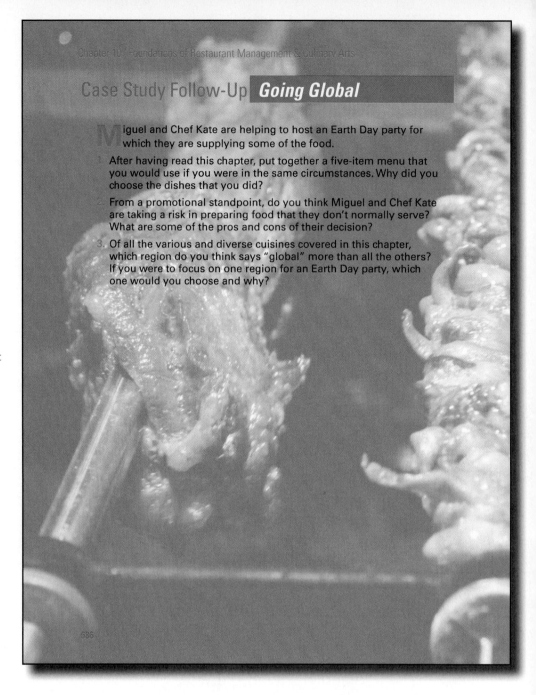

Case Study Follow-Up *Going Global*

Miguel and Chef Kate are helping to host an Earth Day party for which they are supplying some of the food.

1. After having read this chapter, put together a five-item menu that you would use if you were in the same circumstances. Why did you choose the dishes that you did?

2. From a promotional standpoint, do you think Miguel and Chef Kate are taking a risk in preparing food that they don't normally serve? What are some of the pros and cons of their decision?

3. Of all the various and diverse cuisines covered in this chapter, which region do you think says "global" more than all the others? If you were to focus on one region for an Earth Day party, which one would you choose and why?

Apply Your Learning

Compare and Contrast

Compare and contrast the cuisine of the Northeastern United States with the cuisine of Peru. Supplement the information in the text with additional research. Create a two-circle Venn diagram to display your result. Common characteristics will be in the overlap of the two circles.

Language and the Culinary Arts

Create a chart of the various nations and regions of the Western Hemisphere and their languages. What might this tell you about the European settlers of each nation or region? How does this information relate to the cuisine of each nation or region? Total the number of nations or regions that speak each of the following languages: English, Spanish, Portuguese, French, and Dutch.

Some Like It Hot

Hot peppers are used in the various cuisines of the Americas. What causes these foods to taste hot? What effect do they have on the body? Are they safe? Are there risks and/or benefits to eating hot foods? Research and create a chart answering these questions.

Critical Thinking   A Selling Script

Pick one region discussed in this chapter and design a one-page promotional brochure for it on the computer. Discuss the geography, the people, the cultural influences, and the cuisine. Remember, you're promoting this region, so you want to not only know the details of the region, but frame them in a way that will sound appealing to potential visitors.

687

Apply Your Learning

Compare and Contrast

Students should definitely have potatoes, and probably corn, in the Venn overlap. They will come up with other ideas as well.

Language and the Culinary Arts

Students might want to consult history resources for this assignment. When settlers arrive in a new place, they still talk and they still eat.

Some Like It Hot

Students will research capsaicin and other chemical compounds that lend heat to chili peppers. The greater the capsaicin content, the greater the heat. Another chemical they might research is peperine, the heat from black pepper. Students might learn that in addition to tasting "hot" and "burning," these substances actually cause some heart rate and blood pressure response (increase, usually), and can even trigger the release of endorphins. That helps explain their popularity!

Critical Thinking   A Selling Script

The students can be creative with this.

Exam Prep Answers

1. C
2. B
3. B
4. B
5. D
6. C
7. B
8. D
9. B
10. A

Exam Prep Questions

1 The flavor profile of the cuisine in the Northeastern United States can best be described in general as

A. sweet and sour.

B. salty and savory.

C. deep, rich, and mild.

D. sharp, pungent, and bitter.

2 The foods of the Midwestern United States can best be described as

A. sweet and sour.

B. simple and hearty.

C. light and nutritious.

D. delicate and complex.

3 What are the ingredients of the trinity?

A. Red peppers, onions, and carrots

B. Celery, onions, and green peppers

C. Scallions, garlic, and yellow peppers

D. Carrots, orange peppers, and scallions

4 What country has had a strong influence on Southwestern cuisine?

A. France

B. Mexico

C. Portugal

D. Puerto Rico

5 The flavors of Pacific Rim/Coast cuisine can best be described as

A. spicy.

B. hearty.

C. simple.

D. eclectic.

6 *Comales* used in Mexican cooking are

A. clay plates.

B. ceramic pots.

C. cast-iron pans.

D. pewter pitchers.

7 *Gallo pinto*, of Central American cuisine, is a staple dish that consists of

A. black beans and tomatoes.

B. white rice and black beans.

C. pulled chicken and brown rice.

D. white beans and pulled chicken.

8 A hallmark of Caribbean cooking is meat that is

A. served raw.

B. stewed and pulled.

C. stuffed with cheese.

D. richly spiced and smoky.

9 The cooking technique of churrasco in Brazil involves

A. steaming meats over a fire pit.

B. roasting skewered meat over fire.

C. marinating meat before griddle-frying.

D. stewing meat slowly for long periods of time.

10 What signature dish of Peru mixes key lime citrus juice with raw fish?

A. Ceviche

B. Sashimi

C. Feijoada

D. *Papa rellena*

New England–Style Clam Chowder

Yield: 3.5 quarts
Prep Time: 50 minutes

Ingredients

2 qt	Canned clams with juice	1 qt	Milk
1½ qt	Water or fish stock	8 fl oz	Heavy cream
1 lb 4 oz	Potatoes, small dice	To taste	Salt and pepper
8 oz	Salt pork, small dice	To taste	Tabasco sauce
2 oz	Whole butter	To taste	Worcestershire sauce
1 lb	Onions, small dice	To taste	Fresh thyme
8 oz	Celery, small dice	As needed	Fresh parsley for garnish
4 oz	Flour	As needed	Carrot, julienned, for garnish

Directions

1. Drain the clams, reserving both the clams and their liquid. Add enough water or stock so that the total liquid equals 2 quarts.
2. Simmer the potatoes in the clam liquid until nearly cooked through. Strain and reserve the potatoes and the liquid.
3. Render the salt pork with the butter. Add the onions and celery to the rendered fat and sweat until tender but not brown.
4. Add the flour and cook to make a blond roux.
5. Add the clam liquid to the roux, whisking away any lumps.
6. Simmer for 30 minutes, skimming as necessary.
7. Bring the milk and cream to a boil and add to the soup.
8. Add the clams and potatoes, and season to taste with salt, pepper, Tabasco sauce, Worcestershire sauce, and thyme.
9. Garnish each serving with fresh parsley and julienned carrot as desired.

Recipe Nutritional Content

Calories	430	Cholesterol	95 mg	Protein	24 g
Calories from fat	230	Sodium	740 mg	Vitamin A	30%
Total fat	26 g	Carbohydrates	24 g	Vitamin C	40%
Saturated fat	12 g	Dietary fiber	2 g	Calcium	20%
Trans fat	0 g	Sugars	6 g	Iron	105%

Nutritional analysis provided by FoodCalc®, www.foodcalc.com

689

Recipe

New England-Style Clam Chowder

- This recipe helps the students develop technique skills with roux.

Recipe

Jamaican Jerked Pork Chops

- Help students appreciate the interesting combination of spices. Cinnamon, allspice, and nutmeg are not just for sweets, but some students might be new to the concept.

Jamaican Jerked Pork Chops

Yield: 10 Servings
Prep Time: 10 minutes for marinade.
Marinate overnight.
20 minutes to cook.

Ingredients

2	Habañero chilis, stemmed, chopped	1½ tsp	Allspice, ground
8 oz	Scallions, chopped	1½ tsp	Nutmeg, ground
2 Tbs	Thyme, dried	1 Tbs	Cinnamon, ground
1 Tbs	Sugar	4 fl oz	Olive oil
2 tsp	Salt	1 fl oz	Cider vinegar
1 tsp	Ground black pepper	4 lbs	Pork Chops, boneless

Directions

1. In a food processor, combine all ingredients (except the pork) and purée.
2. Using gloves, rub the jerk sauce into the pork chops and marinate over night.
3. The next day, grill the jerked pork chops for 7 to 9 minutes per side. The meat should be tender and cooked through.

Recipe Nutritional Content

Calories	500	Cholesterol	165 mg	Protein	24 g
Calories from fat	240	Sodium	580 mg	Vitamin A	10%
Total fat	27 g	Carbohydrates	06 g	Vitamin C	15%
Saturated fat	7 g	Dietary fiber	2 g	Calcium	4%
Trans fat	0 g	Sugars	2 g	Iron	10%

Nutritional analysis provided by FoodCalc®, www.foodcalc.com

690

Ceviche of Scallops

Yield: 10 Servings
Prep Time: 15 minutes for marinade and prepping vegetables.
Marinate 4 to 12 hours. Serve chilled.

Ingredients

1 lb 4 oz	Sea scallops, muscle tab removed, thinly sliced*	½ oz	Jalapeño pepper, fine dice or julienne
10 oz	Tomato concasse	1 tsp	Garlic clove, mashed to paste
6 fl oz	Lemon or lime juice	1.2 oz	Cilantro, chopped
3 oz	Red onion rings, thinly sliced	10 fl oz	Guacamole
2 oz	Scallions, bias-cut		
2 fl oz	Olive oil		

*If necessary, substitute scallops with a less expensive fish.

Directions

1. Combine all the ingredients. Marinate the scallops for a minimum of 4 hours to a maximum of 12 hours before service.
2. Serve the ceviche cold, with guacamole, on chilled plates.

Recipe Nutritional Content

Calories	150	Cholesterol	20 mg	Protein	17 g
Calories from fat	90	Sodium	190 mg	Vitamin A	20%
Total fat	11 g	Carbohydrates	7 g	Vitamin C	20%
Saturated fat	1 g	Dietary fiber	1 g	Calcium	12%
Trans fat	0 g	Sugars	2 g	Iron	18%

Nutritional analysis provided by FoodCalc®, www.foodcalc.com

691

Recipe

Ceviche of Scallops

- The fish isn't "raw" even though it is uncooked. It is denatured with acid rather than heat.

Chapter 11 Overview

Chapter 11 follows from Chapter 10, introducing students to the cultures and cuisines of four major regions.

Section 1: The first section discusses European cultures and foodways, focusing on France, Spain, and Italy.

Section 2: This section describes Mediterranean food patterns, focusing on Morocco, Greece, and Tunisia.

Section 3: This section explores the cultures and cuisines of the Middle East, especially in Egypt, Iran, and Saudi Arabia.

Section 4: This section discusses Asian cultures and food patterns, focusing on China, Japan, and India.

Advance Preparation	
Review	Sections 11.1–11.4 Chapters 9, 10 Level 1, Chapter 1
Contact	Owners or chefs of restaurant and foodservice operations and stores specializing in the cuisines discussed in this chapter
Prepare	Maps and images of the countries and regions under discussion Images of a tandoori oven

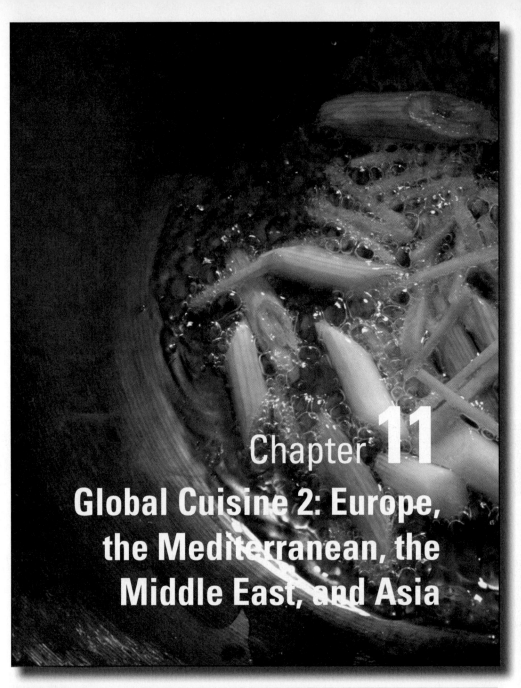

Chapter 11

Global Cuisine 2: Europe, the Mediterranean, the Middle East, and Asia

CUSTOMIZED INSTRUCTION OPTIONS			
Less Advanced Students	**More Advanced Students**	**ESOL Students**	**Special Needs Students**
Pages 700, 742	Pages 707, 746	Pages 721, 746	Pages 700, 703, 742

CHAPTER TOOLS			
21st-Century Skills	**Mathematics**	**Science**	**Literacy**
Pages 693, 696, 697, 699, 700, 702, 703, 704, 705, 706, 707, 711, 712, 713, 715, 716, 719, 720, 721, 725, 726, 728, 729, 730, 731, 734, 738, 739, 740, 741, 742, 743, 745, 746, 747, 748	Pages 699, 726	Pages 699, 713, 741, 742, 746, 748	Pages 693, 696, 697, 699, 700, 702, 703, 704, 705, 706, 707, 711, 712, 713, 715, 716, 719, 720, 721, 725, 726, 728, 729, 730, 731, 734, 738, 739, 740, 741, 742, 743, 745, 746, 747, 748

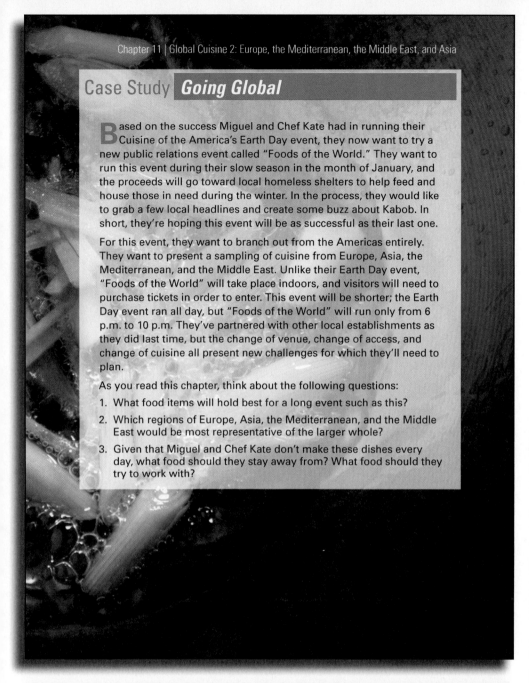

Case Study | *Going Global*

Based on the success Miguel and Chef Kate had in running their Cuisine of the America's Earth Day event, they now want to try a new public relations event called "Foods of the World." They want to run this event during their slow season in the month of January, and the proceeds will go toward local homeless shelters to help feed and house those in need during the winter. In the process, they would like to grab a few local headlines and create some buzz about Kabob. In short, they're hoping this event will be as successful as their last one.

For this event, they want to branch out from the Americas entirely. They want to present a sampling of cuisine from Europe, Asia, the Mediterranean, and the Middle East. Unlike their Earth Day event, "Foods of the World" will take place indoors, and visitors will need to purchase tickets in order to enter. This event will be shorter; the Earth Day event ran all day, but "Foods of the World" will run only from 6 p.m. to 10 p.m. They've partnered with other local establishments as they did last time, but the change of venue, change of access, and change of cuisine all present new challenges for which they'll need to plan.

As you read this chapter, think about the following questions:

1. What food items will hold best for a long event such as this?

2. Which regions of Europe, Asia, the Mediterranean, and the Middle East would be most representative of the larger whole?

3. Given that Miguel and Chef Kate don't make these dishes every day, what food should they stay away from? What food should they try to work with?

Case Study
Going Global

- Encourage students to explore relationships between the cuisines of the Americas and the cuisines of the other countries that will be represented at this event.

- Discuss what ingredients are commonly associated with these regions and why.

- Help students identify some ways to market this event. Who do Miguel and Chef Kate hope to attract to this fundraiser? How might those attending differ from the crowds participating in the previous Earth Day event?

- What other establishments and organizations might be interested in partnering with Kabob?

- What difficulties might Miguel and Chef Kate face in planning and executing this event?

- Note that there are follow-up questions about the case study at the end of the chapter.

- This activity could be done in groups, as a class, or as a homework assignment.

Homework Activity:
Festival Focus

Literacy Connection, 21st-Century Skills— Communicate Clearly, Information Literacy, Initiative and Self-Direction

Does your community celebrate any cultural festivals, such as the event planned at Kabob? Identify a local gathering and describe it: When it is held, what it celebrates, what cultural groups sponsor it, what activities typically occur, and other relevant information. In what ways does this event support the notion of "community"?

If your community does not hold any such festivals, research and report on a festival held elsewhere.

Write a one-page report describing the festival and its effects on the local community.

In-Class Activity:
Create a Celebration

Literacy Connection, 21st-Century Skills—Creativity and Innovation, Critical Thinking and Problem Solving, Initiative and Self-Direction, Communication and Collaboration, Social and Cross-Cultural Skills

Working in groups of two or three, identify some characteristics you all share—some aspects of your common culture. Devise a celebration of your group's culture. What will it emphasize and why? What foods will be served? What activities will occur? How many people are expected to attend?

Draw up an action plan for your cultural celebration. If possible, the class should conduct a "culture fair" so that class members can see one another's work.

Discuss	Lina Fat notes that restaurant and foodservice employees often say, "This isn't my real job." What does the term "real job" mean in this context? What does it mean in terms of professionalism?
	Fat was trained as a pharmacist but is now a restaurateur. What skills might she have learned in her previous field that have helped her succeed?
	Similarly, what skills can one learn in restaurant and foodservice professions that can be used to advance careers in other areas?
Reinforce and Review	Cooking is a combination of science and creativity.
	The skills learned in the restaurant and foodservice industry can be adapted to other professions and can help us learn to discipline ourselves as well.
	There is something to learn in every job that can help to prepare you for a future career.
Teaching Tips	This is the last chapter in the text. Encourage students to relate Lina Fat's vision of professionalism with those offered by other individuals profiled in this book and in Level 1.
	How have the various "Professional Profiles" in Levels 1 and 2 helped students expand their understandings of the restaurant and foodservice industry?
	In Level 1, Chapter 1, students were encouraged to think about their own skills, interests, and passions and how these could help identify career paths. In what ways have students' skills, interests, and passions changed since then? What events or experiences contributed to these changes?

[professional profile]

Lina Fat
Restaurateur, Fat City Inc.

❝ The curtain is up. Bring out your smile, and keep your troubles at home. It's showtime. ❞

I basically fell into this industry when my father-in-law decided to open another restaurant in Old Sacramento. He called it China Camp to commemorate the Chinese immigrants. I helped with that opening as the opening chef. After that, we opened Fat City and then expanded into San Diego. Our latest, Fat's Asia Bistro in Folsom, was opened in 2005. My current position is now vice president, Director of Food.

My educational background? Well, I have a doctor of pharmacy degree from the University of California, San Francisco Medical Center. Cooking, however, is a combination of science and creativity. After training and working in the science field, I was very happy to be able to explore my creative side.

You know, the skills learned in the restaurant business can be adapted to other professions and can help us to discipline ourselves as well. My oldest son told other guests a story at one of our dinner parties. He had been working part time in one of our restaurants since he was 17 as a dishwasher, a buser, and finally a server. He continued when he attended the University of California, Davis, before his dental training at the University of Pacific Dental School. Presently, he is an endodontist, and he recalled one Friday when he was working in his dental office. All the chairs were filled with patients and the waiting room was also filled with emergency patients. He had an important dinner function at 7:30 p.m. An elderly gentleman came in, insisting that he needed to have his emergency taken care of and that he would wait as long as needed. My son was trying to think about how he could accommodate all these patients at a reasonable time. He said he remembered his server training and organized his patients in the chairs, just like tables of customers in the restaurant. He noted the stages of dental care at each chair and organized his service systematically to accommodate every patient, including the elderly gentleman. He was able to accomplish that and still have plenty of time before his dinner engagement.

I am sure every restaurateur has heard from employees who say that "this is not my real job. I am attending such and such college." I would remind them that there is always something to learn from every job that will help to prepare them for their future careers. In the restaurant business, we learn about organization; public relations; and human relations with guests, other employees, and management as well as finance. If all students would think about each job position as a learning skill for their future, they would find more satisfaction in their studies or in their jobs.

694

Teaching Tips

- Use maps or other images when introducing each section to students to help them understand relevant geographies.

- Throughout this chapter, encourage students to relate information that they have learned in other courses, especially history, to the material in the textbook.

- Make sure students understand that this material is simply a broad overview and does not delve deeply into the cuisines or cultures of any one country.

Focus and Engage

Discuss

- Encourage students to discuss why the countries covered in this chapter are relevant to American cuisines.

- Why is it important to study a country's history and cultures along with its cuisines?

Foodservice operation is a part of the entertainment business. I get instant grati-fication when seeing and knowing my guests enjoyed a good day or evening with good food and service. To succeed in the hospitality business and to maintain longevity, one must really enjoy people. Numbers and the bottom line are very important, but genuine interest and caring about your guests' satisfaction is what will help to maintain your business for a long time.

About Global Cuisines

I enjoy every cuisine as long as it is prepared well in taste and texture. The United States is known as a melting pot of many people from different cultures. Since the beginning, our cuisine has been an adaptation of many cuisines from around the world from Britain to the American Indians; from Europe to Asia. Examples are the East Coast influence from Britain and Europe; Southern States from France, American Indians, and Africa; West Coast States from Spain, Mexico, and Asia. Global cuisine is not new; it is really our roots.

11.1 Europe	11.2 The Mediterranean	11.3 The Middle East	11.4 Asia
• France	• Morocco	• Egypt	• China
• Italy	• Greece	• Iran	• Japan
• Spain	• Tunisia	• Saudi Arabia	• India

SECTION 11.1 EUROPE

With 50 countries and more than 730 million residents, the continent of Europe spans an enormous range of cultures and cuisines. Abundant resources exist for those who want to learn more about these countries and their culinary tradi-tions. However, for reasons of space, only a few can be included here. France, Italy, and Spain have been selected to demonstrate how both physical geography and cultural influences can affect the development of a country's cuisines.

695

Professional Profile (cont.)

Discuss	In what ways is the restaurant and foodservice industry similar to the entertainment industry? In what ways is it different?
	Lina Fat demonstrates a clear passion for customer service. In what ways have students experienced such passion, either on the giving or the receiving side?
	Is the United States a melting pot or a salad bowl? Which metaphor better describes American culture and society? Which better describes American eating patterns?
Reinforce and Review	Foodservice is like entertainment: To succeed in this industry, one must really enjoy working with people.
	Global cuisine is not new. It is a reflection of American heritage.
Teaching Tips	Encourage students to discuss why different cultures have influenced the cuisines of different American regions, linking this discussion to the material covered in Chapter 10.

Section 11.1 Europe

Introduce the Section

a. Explain the importance of studying European culture and history in terms of understanding American society.
b. Explain why France, Spain, and Italy are ap-propriate selections to introduce the breadth of European cuisines.
c. Discuss the objectives for the section.

Vocabulary Review

a. Direct students to the key terms.
b. Pronounce each word, and have the students repeat the pronunciation out loud.
c. Discuss the definition of each word.

Teach

Discuss

- In what ways has European history affected American history?
- How can a society's geography affect its consumption patterns?
- How can a country's politics affect what its people eat?

Reinforce and Review

- Europe consists of 50 countries, and far more cuisines.

Teaching Tips

- Encourage students to explore cuisines not addressed in this chapter by researching print and online sources, dining at "ethnic" restaurants, and trying appropriate recipes.

- Consider asking owners or chefs from local restaurants or stores specializing in the cuisines discussed in this chapter to speak to the class.

Discuss

- Why did each new invader have a different cuisine? What can be deduced about a society based on knowledge of its people's eating habits?

- What can Figure 11.1 tell us about what foods might be popular in various parts of contemporary France?

- Why do many Americans associate French food with "fancy" food? Is this appropriate? Why or why not?

Reinforce and Review

- France's cultures and cuisines have been shaped by its numerous invaders and settlers over the centuries.

- Important contributors to French culture and cuisine include the Gauls, the Romans, and the Moors.

Teaching Tips

- Provide students with images, such as maps of what would later become France as it appeared under various rulers.

Flavor Profile

Encourage students to discuss the following:

- What does it mean to say that a cuisine reflects "fresh and refined" dishes? What examples can students identify, either in France or in the United States?

- In what ways does reduction typify French cuisines?

- Historically and culturally, why might traditional French cuisines not incorporate many strong spices?

Homework Activity: A Statement of Principles

Literacy Connection, 21st-Century Skills— Critical Thinking and Problem-Solving, Access and Evaluate Information, Initiative and Self-Direction

In what ways have the cooking principles emphasized in this course reflected French culinary traditions? Is this important? Why or why not?

Discuss your opinions in a two-paragraph essay.

Study Questions

After studying Section 11.1, you should be able to answer the following questions:

- What are the cultural influences and flavor profiles of France?
- What are the cultural influences and flavor profiles of Italy?
- What are the cultural influences and flavor profiles of Spain?

France

Cultural Influences

France's culture and cuisine have been shaped by the numerous invaders, peaceful and otherwise, who have passed through over the centuries. (See Figure 11.1.) The Gauls introduced farming around 1500 BCE and the Romans emphasized fishing and hunting upon their arrival nearly 1500 years later. The Moors invaded in 718 AD, bringing a number of new ingredients (galangal, caraway, and cinnamon, for instance) and techniques to the region.

Figure 11.1: The cuisine of France has been shaped by the many groups that have traveled through and settled in the country.

[flavor] Fresh and refined dishes are typical of French cuisine. Food items taste of themselves without overwhelming or complex spices. This preference is shown by the use of reduction, a process by which stocks and sauces are simmered or boiled to remove excess water and concentrate flavors.

696

Figure Focus

Figure 11.1: How do students think that France's proximity to so many other countries has affected its cultures and its cuisines?

But perhaps the event that most profoundly affected the development of French cuisine was the 1533 AD marriage of Henri II to the Italian Catherine de'Medici. As a member of Florence's powerful ruling family, Catherine was used to the finer things in life, which included cuisine. She was so disappointed in the simple, rustic food popular in France at that time that she brought in cooks from Italy. In fact, she and her employees are credited with introducing roux and forks to France, as well as refining sauces and increasing the use of vegetables.

The Industrial Revolution of the nineteenth century began to break down regional barriers throughout France as improvements in transportation allowed products to be shipped nationwide. These changes, along with advances in technology, gave chefs new opportunities for demonstrating their

Figure 11.2: A brigade is a group of workers assigned a specific set of tasks.

skills and creativity. The resulting development of **haute cuisine**, characterized by highly refined dishes and the creation of a strictly disciplined brigade system (a hierarchy of specialized roles in the kitchen), soon spread throughout the globe (see Figure 11.2). "French" soon became synonymous with both "fine dining" and "fancy." Most French people, however, maintained their traditional, regional eating habits.

Haute cuisine eventually became "**cuisine classique**" and later "**nouvelle cuisine**" (noo-vehl kwee-ZEEN), as chefs in the late twentieth century embraced lighter dishes and simpler flavors—in a sense, returning to their roots. Contemporary French cuisine blends new and old as well as regional and global, and France continues to be esteemed as a culinary capital.

Regional Ingredients and Dishes

Each of France's regions has a unique gastronomic identity, characterized largely by its geography. Brittany, in Northwest France, is renowned for its seafood (especially oysters) and its buckwheat crêpes (KREIPS). Nearby Normandy,

697

- How might the French Revolution of 1789 have affected French cultures and cuisines?

- How might the seemingly simple act of introducing a fork to France have required a profound transformation of upper class eating habits?

- How did the transportation advances of the Industrial Revolution help to codify and spread "French cuisine"?

- Why did most French people maintain traditional, regional eating patterns, despite changes in technology and transportation that offered new foods and new ways of eating them?

- Why might Brittany, in northwest France, be known for its seafood and for buckwheat?

Reinforce and Review

- The 1533 AD marriage of Henri II to the Italian Caterina de'Medici had a profound effect on the development of contemporary French cuisines; among other things, she and her court are credited with introducing roux, forks, and refined sauces.

- The Industrial Revolution broke down regional barriers across France, improving both transportation and technology.

- Over the course of a century, haute cuisine, cuisine classique, and nouvelle cuisine helped to define international impressions of French food.

Teaching Tips

- Relate this discussion to the material in Level 1, Chapter 1, about the history of the restaurant and foodservice industry.

Vocabulary Terms

- **Haute cuisine:** A style of eating characterized by elaborately conceived and presented dishes requiring a highly skilled kitchen and dining-room staff.

- **Cuisine classique:** A modification and simplification of haute cuisine, usually associated with Escoffier and characterized by multiple courses of rich foods.

- **Nouvelle cuisine:** A lighter, more delicate cuisine evolved from cuisine classique, commonly incorporating nontraditional flavors and techniques.

Figure Focus

Figure 11.2: Escoffier originally developed the brigade system, still used in kitchens worldwide.

Homework Activity:
French Foods

Literacy Connection, 21st-Century Skills—Reason Effectively, Communicate Clearly, Information Literacy, Work Independently
Students should each identify and research a dish that they believe to be characteristically French. They should explain its origins, ingredients, and cooking method.
Students should present an oral report describing the dish to the class.

Discuss

- Explain how U.S. culinary regions relate to French culinary regions. For instance, how is the American Northeast similar to the French northeast? What foods and cooking methods are popular in which regions?

- What is the U.S. culinary capital? Why?

Reinforce and Review

- Famous French regional dishes include choucroute, *boeuf bourguignonne*, ratatouille, bouillabaisse, and cassoulet.

- Important French ingredients include pork and pork fat, foie gras, *poulet de Bresse*, saffron, and Dijon mustard.

- Lyon is located in Burgundy, which is in southeast France; it is the country's culinary center.

Teaching Tips

- Encourage students to identify other ingredients and dishes that they consider to be typically "French." How is the "nationality" of a dish determined?

Techniques: French Cooking Methods

Encourage students to discuss the following:

- Which of these cooking methods are commonly used in American kitchens?

- How have French culinary traditions informed American traditions?

- What other methods of cooking are popular in France?

Vocabulary Terms

- **Foie gras:** The engorged liver of a specially fattened goose or duck, which is seared or poached.

- *Poulet de Bresse:* A famously flavorful blue-legged chicken native to Bresse, in Burgundy.

- **Cassoulet:** A hearty casserole of beans and meat, popular in southwest France.

- **Duck confit:** Salted pieces of duck, subsequently poached in duck fat.

- *Jambon de Bayonne:* A mild pork ham.

a dairy stronghold, is famous for its cheeses, particularly *Pont l'Évêque* and Camembert, and its apples. Northeast France, with its bitterly cold winters, specializes in hearty, cold-weather dishes, especially the famous choucroute (shoo-KROOT), which is sauerkraut served with a variety of meats, mostly pork. In fact, pork fat appears prominently in many regional dishes, and pork charcuterie (sausages, pâtés, and terrines) is extremely popular. An Alsatian specialty is **foie gras** (FWA gra), the engorged liver of a specially fattened goose or duck, which is seared or poached. See Figure 11.3.

Lyon, the country's culinary center, is in southeast France; famous restaurants like Fernand Point's La Pyramide and Paul Bocuse's Restaurant Paul Bocuse are located nearby. This region is Burgundy, home to Dijon mustard, *boeuf bour-guignonne* (BEUF boor-gee-NYON), and the famous ***poulet*** (poo-LAY) ***de Bresse***, a blue-legged chicken of renowned tenderness and flavor. Provence is a Mediterranean region, offering such food items as ratatouille, a summer vegetable dish, and bouillabaisse, a hearty fish soup made with saffron. Southwest France is renowned for **cassoulet** (ka-soo-LAY), a rich dish of beans and meat. Different towns have different versions, which include such ingredients as sausages and preserved goose. Foie gras is also found here, as are **duck confit** (kohn-FEE) (salted pieces of duck, poached in duck fat), black truffles (the edible body of a group of fungi), and ***jambon*** (zhan-BAWN) ***de Bayonne***, a mild local ham.

Figure 11.3: Foie gras is a popular French cuisine.

[techniques] French Cooking Methods

French cooking methods include braising, sautéing, *sous-viding*, deglazing, reducing, and confiting.

Figure Focus

Figure 11.3: Foie gras is used in a variety of ways in French cuisine; here, it is seared and served atop beef tenderloin, then garnished with a turned mushroom cap and sliced truffles in the famous dish *Tournedos Rossini*, named for the composer Gioacchino Rossini

Moreover, France is home to the mother sauces: *espagnole*, velouté, béchamel, hollandaise, and tomato. Other characteristically French foods include soufflés, which are light egg dishes puffed by hot air; frogs' legs; and beurre blanc, a light and fragile butter sauce. A classic preparation is pot au feu, a one-pot dish made of meat (usually beef), poultry (usually chicken), and vegetables cooked in a rich broth. The liquid is strained, made into a sparklingly clear consommé, and served as a first course, with the meat and vegetables presented as a second course.

[nutrition]

Confit

The technique of confiting has been used since ancient times to preserve meat, particularly poultry, in order to ensure food supplies for winter. Typically, the preparer cuts up the meat, salts it heavily, and poaches it, often in its own fat, until tender and fully cooked. The preparer preserves the meat in the cooking fat until it is eaten. The fat protects the meat from oxygen so that it does not spoil, but the preparer should store the item in a cool place, ideally under refrigeration. To serve, remove the meat from the fat and wipe it clean. Since the meat is fully cooked, diners can eat it cold; for instance, shredded atop a salad. Alternately, pan-sear or broil the meat, particularly to crisp the skin of confited poultry.

Although cooked and stored in fat, confited meats themselves tend to be quite lean. Even if fatty meat is confited, the fat melts away during the poaching process. Wipe away fat clinging to the surface before eating. Although it appears to be unhealthy, confited meat is actually quite nutritious and provides a vital source of protein during long, cold winters.

Contemporary chefs often confit nontraditional items, including vegetables and fruits. Olive oil is often used as the cooking and storing fat, and the items are not always salted. Unlike confited meat, confited produce tends to retain quite a bit of fat. Fruits and vegetables are very absorbent and soak up a great deal of fat. However, these items are generally eaten in very small amounts and therefore contribute a relatively small addition of fat to the total intake.

Italy

Cultural Influences

In 415 BCE, Greek invaders introduced olives, honey, and nuts to southern Italy (see Figure 11.4 on the following page) where they remain prominent ingredients today. In fact, olive oil is one of the two major cooking fats of Italy; the other is butter, more commonly found in northern Italy. Subsequently, Arab occupiers brought food like citrus, saffron, pasta, and couscous to Italy. Sicily, an island near the toe of the country's "boot," is especially known today for its use of these items, although each is used throughout Italy.

699

Discuss

- How is pot au feu similar to olla podrida? How are the two dishes different? What other one-pot dishes are popular in other cultures around the world?

- Why do students think that olive oil predominates in southern Italy, whereas butter is used in northern Italy?

Reinforce and Review

- France is home to the five mother sauces: *espagnole*, velouté, béchamel, hollandaise, and tomato.

- Pot au feu is a one-pot dish combining meat, poultry, and vegetables cooked in a rich broth, then strained and served in two separate courses.

- The two major cooking fats in Italy are butter, used in the north, and olive oil, used in the south.

- Greek invaders introduced olives, honey, and nuts to what is now southern Italy, and later Arab occupiers brought citrus, couscous, pasta, and saffron.

Teaching Tips

- Work with students as they practice the concept of confiting a variety of ingredients, such as meat, fruit, or vegetables.

- What ingredients do students consider traditionally "Italian"? Which of these ingredients actually originated in contemporary Italy?

Homework Activity: Famous Figures—France

Literacy Connection, 21st-Century Skills—Work Creatively with Others, Use Systems Thinking, Information Literacy, Communication and Collaboration, Social and Cross-Cultural Skills

Working in small groups, research a famous figure in French cuisine, not including Escoffier or Carême. Prepare and present a group report discussing this individual's life and contributions to cuisine.

Alternately, present a report describing an important development in French culture and how it affected the country's cuisines.

Homework Activity: Confit

Science Connection, Mathematics Connection, Literacy Connection, 21st-Century Skills—Critical Thinking and Problem Solving, Communicate Clearly, Information Literacy, Work Independently

Find a recipe for confited meat. What ingredients does it require? What type of fat does it use, and how might that affect the flavor of the finished product?

Explain the science involved in confiting. How do the salt and the fat work to preserve the item?

Convert the recipe you have selected to feed 4, 10, and 45 guests. Be sure your work is accurate.

Discuss

- In what ways are French and Italian historical experiences similar? How are they different?

- Think about your favorite "Italian" dishes. What ingredients first used in the Americas are required to make them? In what ways are these dishes still "Italian"?

Reinforce and Review

- The Roman Empire, which colonized much of the known world at the time, was responsible for introducing a wide range of ingredients and ideas to contemporary Italy.

- Other ingredients, like lemons, coffee, and rice, were first brought to the region by travelers and traders, not colonizers.

- For centuries, Venice was a major trading community, linking Europe with the Middle East and Asia.

- The new foods brought back from the Americas through the Columbian Exchange dramatically affected Italian dining patterns.

Teaching Tips

- Encourage students to imagine and describe a world in which the Columbian Exchange never took place.

CUSTOMIZED INSTRUCTION
Literacy Connection, 21st-Century Skills—Reason Effectively, Communicate Clearly, Information Literacy
Less Advanced Students
What ingredients entered the Old World as a result of the Columbian Exchange? What ingredients entered the New World? How were these cuisines affected?

CUSTOMIZED INSTRUCTION
Literacy Connection, 21st-Century Skills—Make Judgments and Decisions, Communicate Clearly
Special Needs Students
What are some of your favorite foods? Which ones were originally American, but came to Europe as part of the Columbian Exchange?

Vocabulary Terms

- **Columbian Exchange:** The exchange of ingredients, ideas, and other resources between the Old World and the New World.

Not all those who brought new ingredients to the region invaded it. In fact, soldiers of the Roman Empire brought many new food techniques and ideas back to Italy from other conquered regions. The European Crusaders crossed and recrossed the area, bringing buckwheat and lemons back from what is today the Middle East. The Spanish brought rice, which they had obtained from their own Arab colonizers. And Venice was a trading center for centuries; coffee, sugar, and many spices first entered Italy through Venetian ports. The "**Columbian Exchange**," named for explorer Christopher Columbus, brought many new foods to Europe, such as tomatoes, peppers, potatoes, corn, and beans, all of which rapidly found homes in Italian cuisine. See Figure 11.5. No other parts of Europe welcomed this exchange like Italy. Although for centuries most Europeans refused to eat tomatoes, fearing that they were poisonous, tomatoes were grown and eaten in Italy as early as 1544 AD.

Figure 11.4: Italy has been a prominent cultural force since the ninth century AD.

Figure 11.15: The "Columbian Exchange" brought economic opportunities and agricultural exchanges between Europe and the Americas.

700

Figure Focus

Figure 11.4: What characteristics of Italy's geographic position might have affected the development of its cuisines?

Figure 11.5: Which ingredient involved in the Columbian Exchange had the most profound effects on European culture and society? Why?

[flavor]

Traditionally, Italian food has been characterized as "*la cucina povera*" (the cuisine of poverty). Simple, filling, and delicious dishes are made by using all ingredients as carefully as possible. Olive oil, semolina, and the extravagant use of vegetables define this cuisine.

[fast fact]

Did You Know...?
Europeans erroneously thought that tomatoes were poisonous because the acid in the tomatoes reacted to the pewter used for service or tableware. The acid could cause the lead to leech out, resulting in lead poisoning.

Regional Ingredients and Dishes

Modern Italy did not become a unified country until 1861, so regional culinary traditions generally persist today. Northern Italy, close to Alpine Europe, is known for its abundant use of meat, especially beef, and dairy products such as milk, cheeses, and butter. Hearty starches, like polenta, potato gnocchi, and risotto are common, particularly during cold weather. *Risotto alla Milanese* is a northern rice dish made with saffron and often served with osso buco, a braised veal shank. Other northern dishes include minestrone alla Genovese, a thick vegetable soup finished with pesto, a hallmark of Genoa's cuisine; and ***bollito misto*** (boh-LEE-toh MEES-toh). It is a Piemontese stew including a variety of meat with vegetables subsequently cooked in the resulting broth (the words mean "mixed boil"). Another northern dish is ***bagna cauda*** (BAHN-yah KOW-dah), an olive oil-based dipping sauce flavored with anchovy and garlic and served warm with raw vegetables, especially cardoons, a member of the artichoke family.

The cuisine of central Italy is characterized by simple, fresh flavors with an emphasis on seasonality. Beef, goat, and lamb are often grilled, spit-roasted, or stewed. ***Bistecca alla Fiorentina***, an enormous grilled steak (similar to a T-bone), at least two inches thick, is a Tuscan specialty. ***Saltimbocca*** (sahl-tihm-BOH-kuh) ***alla Romana***, a popular Roman dish, is made of pounded scallops of veal sautéed with fresh sage and prosciutto. Fresh seafood is also important due to the vast coastlines. *Brodetto* may be the oldest Mediterranean fish soup, predating the French bouillabaisse (BOOL-yuh-BAYZ). The region is also known for its vegetables, fruits, and legumes, particularly white beans and tomatoes.

701

Teaching Tips

- Saltimbocca means "jump in the mouth"—it refers to the exciting combination of flavors that virtually leap in the diner's mouth.

Vocabulary Terms

- ***Bollito misto:*** A rich stew containing a mixture of meat and vegetables, cooked in a succulent broth.

- ***Bagna cauda:*** A dipping sauce made of olive oil, anchovy, and garlic, served with raw vegetables.

- ***Bistecca alla Fiorentina:*** A thick beefsteak that has been grilled.

- ***Saltimbocca alla Romana:*** Pounded and breaded veal, sautéed with sage and prosciutto.

Discuss

- In what ways has the Italian climate affected the country's culinary habits? Compare this to French cuisines.

- Why is dried pasta used almost exclusively in the south, whereas fresh pasta is used almost exclusively in the north?

- Broadly speaking, which Italian cuisines (north, central, or south) best characterizes what we think of as "Italian" food in the United States? Why might this be the case?

Reinforce and Review

- Southern Italy is known for its use of non-cow's-milk cheeses, fresh seafood and vegetables, and locally produced olives and olive oil.

- Popular southern Italian dishes include *vitello tonnato, spaghetti alla vongole,* macaroni with tomato sauce, pizza, and *pasta con le sarde.*

- Dried pasta, made with semolina flour and water, is common throughout the south; fresh pasta, which uses softer flour and eggs, is used in the north.

- Emilia-Romagna, in northern Italy, is famed for the high-quality ingredients it produces, including *prosciutto di Parma, aceto balsamico tradizionale,* and Parmigiano-Reggiano.

Homework Activity:
Emilia-Romagna

Literacy Connection, 21st-Century Skills—Reason Effectively, Communicate Clearly, Information Literacy, Initiative and Self-Direction

The region of Emilia-Romagna is known worldwide for its high-quality balsamic vinegars, cheeses, and cured meat. Select one of its famous products and research it, identifying its characteristics, manufacturing process, and culinary uses.

Discuss your findings in a one-page report.

Vocabulary Terms

- *Vitello tonnato:* A Neapolitan dish made with cold veal, served with a sauce made of tuna.

- *Pasta con le sarde:* A dish of dried pasta, combined with a sauce made of sardines, raisins, and fennel and topped with fresh sardines.

Southern Italy with its mountainous and arid climate is perfect for goats and sheep, used both to make cheeses and as foods in their own rights. The famous *mozzarella di bufala*, made of the milk of water buffaloes, comes from here (see Figure 11.6). Fresh vegetables and seafood are also important, as is the use of local olives and olive oil. A famous dish is **vitello tonnato** (vee-TEHL-loh tohn-NAH-toh), a Neapolitan dish of cold veal with tuna sauce. Another Naples dish is *spaghetti alla vongole*, or with clams. Macaroni in tomato sauce originated in nearby Campania. Naples was also the birthplace of pizza. The southern islands of Sicily and Sardinia have similar culinary traditions, although they incorporate more sweet flavors into their savory dishes. **Pasta con le sarde**, a dish of pasta in a sardine sauce with raisins and fennel and topped with fresh sardines, is a good example of this tradition of *agrodolce* (sour-sweet), a remnant of Arabian influence.

Although pasta is widely used throughout Italy, dried pasta is found in the south, made with semolina flour and water. Fresh pasta made with eggs and a softer wheat flour is common in the north. Emilia-Romagna, a northern province, is renowned for its famous exported foods like *prosciutto* (proh-SHOO-toh) *di Parma* (a type of cured ham), *aceto balsamico tradizionale* (artisanal balsamic vinegar), and Parmigiano-Reggiano (the famed "Parmesan cheese"). Truffles are also found in Italy, with white truffles in northern Piemonte and black truffles in southern Umbria.

Figure 11.6: *Mozzarella di Bufala* is handmade in southern Italy. From left to right: curdled and cut mozzarella, heating the curds, shaping the mozzarella, and finished mozzarella.

702

Figure Focus

Figure 11.6: At some restaurant and foodservice operations, mozzarella cheese is made by hand to order throughout service. What might this indicate about these operations?

Homework Activity:
TomAYto, TomAHto

Literacy Connection, 21st-Century Skills—Critical Thinking and Problem Solving, Communicate Clearly, Information Literacy, Initiative and Self-Direction

Tomatoes were considered to be poisonous in many European cultures, so it took centuries for them to become established as valuable ingredients in some areas.

Research the history of tomatoes in the United States. When and where were they first eaten? In what ways were they originally used? What is the annual tomato consumption in the United States today?

Report your findings in a brief essay.

[techniques]

Italian Cooking Methods

Italian cooking methods include braising, boiling, roasting (either on a spit or in a wood-burning oven), grilling, and deep-frying.

[on the job]

Food Policy Analysts

Food policy analysts (FPAs) typically work for research institutes; nonprofit organizations; or state, local, or even international governments. Food policy analysts are in many ways like other types of policy analysts. They review proposed policies or legislation and explain what would happen if the policies or legislation were enacted. They organize, review, research, and revise these rules, making sure that newly proposed ideas are legal and that the new ideas promote the organization's mission and goals. If the new proposals do not meet these criteria, policy analysts offer alternative proposals for consideration.

What's special about food policy analysts is that they focus on the importance of food to the world. They may study the effects of new import-export laws on agriculture, or they may study the effects of proposed anti-hunger plans in a particular region. Some FPAs focus on security issues, such as global food shortages and possible political instability. Generally speaking, FPAs must know any national and international laws and policies that can affect food.

Food policy analysts usually have bachelor's degrees, often in political science, public policy, or economics. Many have master's or doctoral degrees. Some experience in policy analysis, even schoolwork, is generally required. Career paths may include heading a major nonprofit organization or appointment to a political position. In fact, it has even been suggested that a "Secretary of Food" be added to the U.S. Cabinet, which advises the president on a variety of issues.

[fast fact]

Did You Know...?

Pizza, as we know it today, originated in Naples, Italy, sometime around the sixteenth century. It was considered street food for people of lesser means and was flavored with garlic, oil, anchovies, and mozzarella cheese.

703

Techniques: Italian Cooking Methods

Encourage students to discuss the following:

- Based on what you have learned about Italian cuisines, which of these cooking methods would most likely be used in which regions of Italy? Why?

- How are these cooking methods similar to those popularly used in France? How would you explain that?

- What special equipment and skills are needed to operate either a spit or a wood-burning oven? How might the flavors of foods roasted in these ways differ from the flavors of foods cooked in a conventional gas or electric oven?

On the Job: Food Policy Analyst

Encourage students to discuss the following:

- What makes the work of food policy analysts so important?

- In what ways do food policy analysts affect our daily eating patterns?

- How can access to food be considered a national security issue?

Fast Fact: Did You Know . . . ?

Encourage students to discuss the following:

- Why do students think that strong-tasting ingredients like garlic and anchovy were used to flavor these early pizzas?

- When it was originally developed, pizza was considered an inexpensive food for the poor. How does this fit into the earlier discussion of "*la cucina povera*"?

- How has pizza changed from its early beginnings? Is it still considered street food, or food for the less wealthy? What do we think of when we think of pizza?

Homework Activity: Famous Figures—Italy

Literacy Connection, 21st-Century Skills—Work Creatively with Others, Use Systems Thinking, Information Literacy, Communication and Collaboration, Social and Cross-Cultural Skills

Working in small groups, research a famous figure in Italian cuisine. Prepare and present a group report discussing this individual's life and contributions to cuisine.

Alternately, present a report describing an important development in Italian culture and how it affected the country's cuisines.

CUSTOMIZED INSTRUCTION

Literacy Connection, 21st-Century Skills—Reason Effectively, Communicate Clearly

Special Needs Students

What is your favorite type of pizza? Why? Do you know the origins of your favorite pizza toppings?

Homework Activity: Italian Foods

Literacy Connection, 21st-Century Skills—Reason Effectively, Communicate Clearly, Information Literacy, Work Independently

Students should each identify and research a dish that they believe to be characteristically Italian. They should explain its origins, ingredients, and cooking method.

Students should present an oral report describing the dish to the class.

Discuss

- Compare and contrast the lingering effects of the Arabian occupation on France and Spain. In what culture was it the most significant?

- What ingredients or dishes do students consider characteristically "Spanish"? Why?

- Why do students think that French and Italian cuisines have been more popularly accepted in the United States than Spanish cuisine?

Reinforce and Review

- Historically, Spain's peninsular location provided many opportunities for trade and conquest, but it also left the region vulnerable to conquest by others, such as the Romans, the Visigoths, and the Arabs, all of whom left their marks on Spanish cuisine.

- Arabs had a profound impact on Spanish cuisine, introducing an enormous range of foods like sugarcane, citrus and other fruit, and spices (notably saffron).

- The "medieval green revolution" was a drastic improvement in the efficiency of agricultural practices, due to the introduction of Arabian technology, which resulted in much higher levels of public nutrition.

- Both Sephardic Jews and Arabs coexisted in Spain; both cuisines shared a love for sweet-and-sour combinations.

Flavor Profile

Encourage students to discuss the following:

- What does it mean to say that a cuisine is "earthy and complex"?

- In what ways might Spain's history explain the flavors popular there today?

- How are the characteristic flavors of French, Italian, and Spanish cuisines similar? How do they differ?

Homework Activity: Spanish Foods

Literacy Connection, 21st-Century Skills— Reason Effectively, Communicate Clearly, Information Literacy, Work Independently

Students should each identify and research a dish that they believe to be characteristically Spanish. They should explain its origins, ingredients, and cooking method.

Students should present an oral report describing the dish to the class.

Spain

Cultural Influences

Spain is bordered on several sides by water, allowing easy trade with both nearby neighbors and distant lands (see Figure 11.7). Spain has historically been a strong naval power, and its government sponsored many expeditions in search of gold, spices, and new lands to conquer.

However, Spain's history is also one of occupation. Spain was at one time a Roman province; occupied

Figure 11.7: Spain, with its strong naval presence and government-sponsored expeditions, spread cultural and culinary knowledge to neighboring countries.

by Visigoths, a Germanic people; and controlled by Arabs. An Arabian influence on Spanish cuisines persists today. The Arabs introduced citrus fruits (including the famous Valencian oranges), almonds, sugarcane, rice, saffron, and a wide variety of vegetables and spices. More important, perhaps, was the "medieval green revolution" brought about by the introduction of irrigation methods. During the same period, Sephardic Jews were building a complex cuisine of their own in Spain, which bore certain similarities to the sweet-and-sour dishes introduced by the Arabs.

[flavor] Spanish favors are earthy and complex, with unusual flavor combinations and contributions from a number of cultures.

Figure Focus

Figure 11.7: What countries might have a strong influence on Spanish culture and cuisine? Why?

Regional Ingredients and Dishes

Spain's geography covers a wide variety of terrains, so naturally its regional cuisines vary considerably. One constant is the *cocido*, a boiled one-pot meal incorporating meat, legumes (usually beans), and green vegetables. Every region (and many a town) has its own version of this dish, which likely originated in Roman times.

The northern regions are notable for seafood cookery, often including cod or salt cod. Elvers, which are baby eels, are also popular. These and other seafood, including octopus and spider crabs, are often cooked in a bath of olive oil. Galicia, in the northwest, has a Celtic-influenced cuisine unknown in the rest of Spain, while Basque cuisine reflects its proximity to the Pyrenees Mountains and to France. A famous Austrian dish is *fabada*, a thick soup of fava beans, pig trotters, pork fat, and blood. Toward the east, Catalan cooking is an entire cuisine unto itself; many dishes are based on game or seafood. A popular sauce is *picada*, made with toasted and ground nuts, toasted bread, garlic, and fresh herbs.

The northern interior is famous for agriculture. *Pimientos del piquillo*, sweet red peppers, are grown here; they are fire-roasted and then peeled and jarred. Wheat and a wide variety of fruits and vegetables also thrive here, including the beans of Ávila. Aragon is noted for dishes cooked *al chilindrón*, or with a sauce of tomatoes, onion, and peppers. *Castilla-Leon* is known for hearty, plain food, like roast suckling pig, tortillas (thick egg dishes, similar to the Italian frittata), and blood sausages. Farther south, the central plains are sheep-producing lands known for *manchego* cheese. Saffron and garlic are also cultivated here. In the western part of this region, Extremadura is home to *jamón Ibérico*, a famous Spanish cured ham, and *pimentón de la Vera*; both products are legally protected from imitation. Figure 11.8 depicts a variety of important ingredients used in Spanish cuisine.

Figure 11.8: Important ingredients to Spanish cuisine include cheese, ham, olives, saffron, and garlic.

The southeast coast is famous for citrus, saffron, and rice production. **Paella** (pi-AY-yuh), which originated in Valencia but now has countless varieties, is based on rice, olive oil, and saffron cooked in one pot over an open flame. Other ingredients may include chicken, rabbit, snails, seafood, green beans, peas, or sausage among others. Southern Spain also produces cured hams, and, since it is coastal, it's known for seafood fried in olive oil. Gazpacho (gahz-PAH-choh)

705

Figure Focus

Figure 11.8: Why are cured pork products, like *jamón Ibérico* and *prosciutto di Parma*, popular in warmer regions?

Discuss

- How are French, Spanish, and Italian foods all related? How are they different?
- Do students think that France, Spain, and Italy are representative of European cuisines? Why or why not?

Reinforce and Review

- A *cocido* is a boiled, one-pot meal incorporating meat, vegetables, and legumes, found throughout Spain.
- The coast of northern Spain is famous for seafood, especially cod and elvers; across the north, Galician, Basque, and Catalan cuisines all differ significantly.
- Central Spain is known for agriculture. Wheat, sheep, and a wide variety of vegetables and fruit are produced and widely consumed here, often featured in hearty but simple dishes.
- Southeastern Spain is known for citrus, saffron, and rice; overall, southern Spain is famous for its seafood and cured hams.

Vocabulary Terms

- **Paella:** A dish with numerous variations, involving rice, olive oil, and saffron cooked in a wide, shallow pan over an open fire.

Discuss

- What characteristics of Spanish cuisine are most prominent? If you had to select one word to describe it, what would it be and why?

- Spanish chefs are at the forefront of a worldwide revolution in gastronomy, introducing radical new culinary techniques and flavors. How might this be related to Spain's rich history of exploration and trade?

Reinforce and Review

- "White" gazpacho, which preceded the Columbian Exchange, was made with garlic, almonds, and grapes.

- Tapas are small savory snacks, usually associated with bar food; originally, the term referred to a slice of bread laid over the top of one's wine glass to prevent insect contamination.

Fast Fact: Did You Know . . . ?

Encourage students to discuss the following:

- Is saffron so expensive because it is comparatively rare and difficult to produce, or because people like its taste so much?

- Saffron's high price has also led to adulteration and fraud. What other ingredients might be susceptible to similar concerns?

- What dishes are characterized by the use of saffron?

Techniques: Spanish Cooking Methods

Encourage students to discuss the following:

- How are Spanish cooking methods similar to French and Italian cooking methods?

- Olive oil is used liberally in Spanish cuisine. What cooking techniques are best suited to its use?

- Why is paella-making considered a separate technique?

---

originated here long before the Columbian Exchange brought tomatoes or peppers; early versions included garlic, almonds, and even white grapes. Tortillas are also popular here, as are tapas, which are small, usually savory snacks associated with bar food. In fact, the original "tapa" was a slice of bread laid over one's wine glass to prevent insects from entering it.

[fast fact]

Did You Know...?
Saffron is the world's most expensive spice (by weight). A pound of saffron requires 50,000 to 75,000 saffron crocus flowers. See Figure 11.9.

Figure 11.9: Saffron flowers.

[techniques]

Spanish Cooking Methods
Spanish cooking methods include braising, baking, boiling, and—of course—making paella.

706

Homework Activity: One-Pot Wonders

Literacy Connection, 21st-Century Skills—Critical Thinking and Problem Solving, Communicate Clearly, Information Literacy, Work Independently

Many of the cuisines discussed in this chapter are known for their one-pot dishes. Identify a famous one-pot dish and research it. What are its primary characteristics and ingredients? Where is it traditionally eaten and by whom? What other cultures might have influenced its development?

Discuss your findings in a one-page report.

Figure Focus

Figure 11.9: Only the slender pistils are used to produce saffron; they must be removed by hand.

Essential Skills
Escabeche

This is a classic preparation of fried fish that dates back to at least the fourteenth century. *Escabeche* (es-keh-BEHSH) has been found in many countries, including Spain, France, Algeria, and the Philippines. To prepare, cool and cover the fish with a vinegar-based marinade, which is often spicy.

1. Brine the chosen fish fillets in saltwater for 30 minutes.
2. Toast aromatics (garlic, bay leaf, and so forth) in hot olive oil. See Figure 11.10a.
3. Sear the brined fish on each side and then set aside to cool. See Figure 11.10b.
4. Sweat onions in the hot oil and then add vinegar, broth, and other seasonings.
5. Reduce the liquid and strain.
6. Pour the hot marinade over the fish, cool, and store in the refrigerator.
7. Marinate for 24 hours before eating. See Figure 11.10c.

Figure 11.10a: Step 2—Toast aromatics in hot olive oil.

Figure 11.10b: Step 3—Sear brined fish on each side.

Figure 11.10c: Step 7—Marinate before serving.

707

Essential Skills: Escabeche

Encourage students to discuss the following:

- How is *escabeche* similar to and different from ceviche?
- Why did the technique of escabeche develop? (Note: The acid and spices in the marinade helped to preserve the cooked fish.)
- What might seeing the term "*escabeche*" on a menu indicate about an operation?

Homework Activity: Portuguese Cuisines

Literacy Connection, 21st-Century Skills—Reason Effectively, Communicate Clearly, Information Literacy, Work Independently

What foods are popular in Spain's neighbor, Portugal? How are its cuisines similar to and different from Spain's? What might account for these similarities and differences?

Write a brief report describing your findings.

CUSTOMIZED INSTRUCTION

Literacy Connection, 21st-Century Skills—Critical Thinking and Problem Solving, Communicate Clearly, Information Literacy, Work Independently

More Advanced Students

Research the Basque region of Europe, investigating its history, language, and cuisine. What is its flavor profile? What ingredients, cooking techniques, and dishes are most popular?

Discuss your findings in a one-page report.

Figure Focus

Figure 11.10a: Why are the aromatics toasted?

Figure 11.10b: How does brining the fish affect its flavor and texture?

Figure 11.10c: Why is it important to heat the marinade before pouring it over the seared fish?

Summary

- Remind students to review the following:
  1. France—culture, ingredients, and dishes
  2. Italy—culture, ingredients, and dishes
  3. Spain—culture, ingredients, and dishes

Summary

In this section, you learned the following:

- France's culture and cuisine have been shaped by the numerous invaders, peaceful and otherwise, who have passed through over the centuries. Perhaps the event that most profoundly affected the development of French cuisine was the 1533 AD marriage of Henri II to the Italian Catherine de'Medici. She was so disappointed in the simple, rustic food popular in France at that time that she brought in cooks from Italy. The Industrial Revolution of the nineteenth century began to break down regional barriers throughout France as improvements in transportation allowed products to be shipped nationwide. These changes, along with advances in technology, gave chefs new opportunities for demonstrating their skills and creativity. The result was the development of haute cuisine, characterized by highly refined dishes. The flavor profile of French cuisine consists of fresh and refined food items that taste of themselves without overwhelming or complex spices. Reduction, deglazing, and confiting are signature French cooking methods.

- In 415 BCE, Greek invaders introduced olives, honey, and nuts to southern Italy, where they remain prominent ingredients today. In fact, olive oil is one of the two major cooking fats of Italy; the other is butter, more commonly found in northern Italy. Not all those who brought new ingredients to the region invaded it. In fact, the Roman Empire, which fanned out from contemporary Italy, introduced new foods, techniques, and ideas from the regions its soldiers had conquered. Traditionally, Italian food has been characterized as "*la cucina povera*" (the cuisine of poverty), which is simple, filling, and delicious dishes made by using all ingredients as carefully as possible. Olive oil, semolina, and the extravagant use of vegetables define this cuisine. Braising, roasting, and grilling are common cooking methods in Italy.

- Spain is bordered on several sides by water, allowing easy trade with both nearby neighbors and distant lands. The Columbian Exchange, named for explorer Christopher Columbus, brought many new food items to Spain, such as tomatoes, peppers, and beans. However, Spain's history is also one of occupation. Spain was at one time a Roman province occupied by a Germanic people, the Visigoths, and also controlled by Arabs. Arabian influence on Spanish cuisines persists today. The flavor profile is earthy and complex, with unusual flavor combinations. Braising, baking, and paella are common cooking methods in Spain.

Section 11.1 Review Questions

1. List three signature cooking methods in French cuisine.

2. Explain one way in which French and Italian cuisines differ.

3. What is the flavor profile of Spanish cuisine?

4. What is one cooking method that is particularly Spanish?

5. Lina Fat mentions that she likes any cuisine that is "well prepared in taste and texture." Think of one specific French, Italian, and Spanish dish that she might like. What is special about the texture or taste of each dish?

6. Miguel and Chef Kate have decided that in order to best represent Europe they need to make one dish each from France, Italy, and Spain. Which dishes would you suggest they choose? Why?

7. Do you think French cuisine's association with being highly refined is deserved? In what ways does it make sense? In what ways has it become a stereotype?

8. Explain the impact of the "Columbian Exchange" on European cuisine, most notably that of France, Spain, and Italy.

709

Section 11.1 Review Questions

1. Signature French cooking methods include braising, sautéing, *sous vide*, deglazing, reducing, and confiting.

2. Students may identify and explain a difference of their choosing, so long as it is accurate.

3. Spanish flavors are earthy and complex, with unusual flavor combinations and contributions from a number of cultures.

4. *Escabeche* is a particularly Spanish culinary technique.

5. Students may identify any of a variety of dishes so long as they can identify the specific characteristics of the dishes they choose.

6. Students may suggest any of a variety of dishes as long as they can support and defend their choices.

7. Students may answer in a variety of ways so long as they can logically defend their responses.

8. Students should focus on the culinary aspects of the Columbian Exchange, discussing these clearly and accurately.

Section 11.1 Activities

1. Students may choose any European country besides France, Italy, and Spain and should produce a group presentation describing its cuisine, including common ingredients, representative cooking methods, and any other information about the country's cuisine that the students consider important.

2. Students will need to research one of the four cooking methods suggested to learn about its history and significance.

3. Students should explain the science behind processing food without air, including any food safety issues.

Section 11.1 Activities

1. Study Skills/Group Activity: Unexplored Europe!

Working with two or three other students, select a European country that is not covered in this chapter. Prepare a group presentation, including a handout, on this country's cuisine.

2. Activity: Researching Methods

Select one of the following cooking methods: reduction, deglazing, paella, or confit. Then, research where the method originated, why it first was used, and how the process works today. Finally, explain a modern dish in which this cooking method is used. Your findings should be summarized in a one-page report.

3. Critical Thinking: The Ethics of *Sous-Viding*

Research the history of *sous-viding*. How did it come about? What are the pros and cons of cooking in this manner? Write a two-page report describing your research.

710

SECTION 11.2 THE MEDITERRANEAN

It can be difficult to determine which countries actually belong in this region. France, Italy, and Spain all border the Mediterranean Sea, and all have regions with "typical" Mediterranean foodways. Moreover, the Mediterranean Sea is long enough that countries from Morocco to Syria can be legitimately included in this category. However, this text focuses on three countries—Morocco, Greece, and Tunisia—that reflect traditional Mediterranean cuisines.

Study Questions

After studying Section 11.2, you should be able to answer the following questions:

- What are the cultural influences and flavor profiles of Morocco?
- What are the cultural influences and flavor profiles of Greece?
- What are the cultural influences and flavor profiles of Tunisia?

Morocco

Cultural Influences

The countries of North Africa, known collectively as the **Maghreb**, share a fairly similar set of cultural influences. Morocco, as shown in Figure 11.11, has been a center for trade since the twelfth century, when the Phoenicians established trading posts on the coast, through which sausage was introduced to the region. The Carthaginians followed suit a few centuries later, bringing with them wheat and semolina. The native Berbers developed couscous from semolina, creating what would become their staple starch. But the Arabs, who occupied Morocco during the seventh century, had perhaps the most pronounced and long-lasting

711

Homework Activity:
Moroccan Foods

Literacy Connection, 21st-Century Skills—Reason Effectively, Communicate Clearly, Information Literacy, Work Independently

Students should each identify and research a dish that they believe to be characteristically Moroccan. They should explain its origins, ingredients, and cooking method.

Students should present an oral report describing the dish to the class.

Section 11.2
The Mediterranean

Introduce the Section

a. Explain the importance of studying Mediterranean culture and history in terms of understanding American society.
b. Explain why Morocco, Greece, and Tunisia are appropriate selections to introduce the breadth of Mediterranean cuisines.
c. Discuss the objectives for the section.

Vocabulary Review

a. Direct students to the key terms.
b. Pronounce each word, and have the students repeat the pronunciation out loud.
c. Discuss the definition of each word.

Teach

Discuss

- Why are France, Spain, and Italy categorized here as "European," not "Mediterranean"? What are the pros and cons of this approach?

- Encourage students to explore why Morocco has historically been a logical choice for a trading center.

Reinforce and Review

- Morocco has been a trade center since the twelfth century BCE, so a variety of cultures have influenced its development and its cuisine.

- The Phoenicians, who established trading posts in present-day Morocco, also introduced sausage to the region.

- The Carthaginians subsequently brought wheat and semolina to the area. The native Berbers used semolina to develop couscous, which became a staple starch.

Teaching Tips

- Provide a map to enable students to understand where Morocco is situated with respect to Europe and the Middle East.

Vocabulary Terms

- **Maghreb:** The countries of North Africa that share a similar set of cultural influences.

Discuss

- Arab occupiers introduced the same ingredients and culinary concepts to multiple regions, including Morocco, Spain, and France. Why have the cuisines of these three countries developed so differently?

Reinforce and Review

- Arab occupiers had the most significant effects on Moroccan cuisine, introducing characteristic ingredients like saffron, ginger, cumin, and cinnamon, and initiating the practice of combining sweet and sour flavors.

- Under the Ottoman Empire, the use of sweets and pastries was revolutionized as sugar and honey came to prominence.

- Spanish influences arrived with the expulsion of the Moors in 1492. These new arrivals also introduced innovative agricultural techniques, such as irrigation, and were shortly followed by the results of the Columbian Exchange.

- Other European influences arrived later, as Morocco was occupied by the British, French, and Spanish.

Flavor Profile

Encourage students to discuss the following:

- In what ways does a country's cuisine reflect its culture?

- What flavors and ingredients do students perceive as particularly "Moroccan"?

- Morocco is located just a few miles from Spain. In what ways are the two countries' flavor profiles similar and different?

Homework Activity: Famous Figures—Morocco

Literacy Connection, 21st-Century Skills—Work Creatively with Others, Use Systems Thinking, Information Literacy, Communication and Collaboration, Social and Cross-Cultural Skills

Working in small groups, research a famous figure in Moroccan cuisine. Prepare and present a group report discussing this individual's life and contributions to the cuisine.

Alternately, present a report describing an important development in Moroccan culture and how it affected the country's cuisines.

Vocabulary Terms

- *Pastilla:* A delicacy made by layering sheets of delicate *warqa* with almonds and pastry cream.

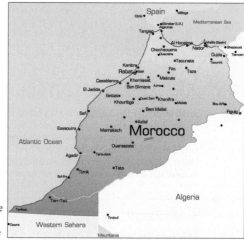

Figure 11.11: Morocco has been a center of trade since about 1500 BCE.

effect on Moroccan cuisine. They introduced saffron, ginger, cumin, and cinnamon, as well as the principle of combining sweet and sour tastes. All of this radically transformed the somewhat bland cuisine of the area and established a distinctive culinary tradition.

Other colonizers followed. Around the fourteenth century, the Ottoman Empire brought new developments in pastries and sweets, apparent today in the prominent use of sugar and honey in very sweet dessert items. *Pastilla* (pah-STEE-yuh) is a delicacy made by layering sheets of delicate pastry, known as *warqa*, with almonds and pastry cream. The Spanish expulsion of Moors and Jews in 1492 caused many to flee to nearby Morocco and Tunisia, where they and their foodways were welcomed. These newcomers brought with them agricultural techniques, such as irrigation, that were perfectly suited to the North African climate. Soon after, the Columbian Exchange introduced new products like tomatoes and peppers. Much later, Morocco was occupied by the British, French, and Spanish in turn. In 1912, it became a French protectorate, but became independent in 1956. These European influences brought new ingredients to Morocco, such as pasta and tea. When combined with mint, tea became an important part of the Moroccan culture.

[flavor] Sweet, sour, and spicy, the complex Moroccan cuisine has been influenced by a variety of occupiers and trading partners for thousands of years. Rich, full-flavored stews, steamed dishes, and roasts dominate the cuisine.

712

Figure Focus

Figure 11.11: Given Morocco's location, do students think its cuisine would be similar to that of other African countries? Why or why not?

Regional Ingredients and Dishes

Two spice mixtures are particularly representative of Moroccan cuisine: *la kama* and *ras-el-hanout*. **La kama** is a blend of black pepper, turmeric, ginger, cumin, and nutmeg used to season soups and stews. *Ras-el-hanout* is used throughout the Maghreb; the exact ingredients frequently vary, but some common additions include rose petals, black peppercorns, cardamom, clove, and fennel. Use this mixture to flavor rice, stews, and *tagines*.

Tagines are also commonly eaten in Morocco. They are meat stews cooked for a long time, usually based on lamb, fish, game, or chicken, and often served with preserved lemon, another popular flavor in Morocco. Chefs of this cuisine often combine sweet and savory ingredients in the same dish. The word "*tagine*" also refers to the earthenware or metal cooking vessel used to make these stews. It has two parts: a shallow basin and a tall, conical lid, which allows for the dish to self-baste as steam is trapped and then condenses to form water (see Figure 11.12). At major festivals, several *tagines* may be served, one after the other. Traditionally, the final *tagine* is made of lamb, honey, and onions.

Figure 11.12: Moroccan *tagine* with raisins, almonds, and honey.

Couscous (KOOS-koos) is the national dish of Morocco. Chefs steam the tiny grains in a **couscoussière**, a specialized earthenware or metal vessel (see Figure 11.13). They place raw couscous in a perforated pot, which they then place atop another pot containing simmering water, stock, or stew. Couscous is usually served with a spicy stew; diners form the grains into balls and eat them by hand. Chicken, raisins, and chickpeas are popular stew ingredients.

Figure 11.13: A *Couscoussière* is a double boiler used to make couscous and stews.

713

Figure Focus

Figure 11.12: Although traditionally made of heavy clay, contemporary *tagines* are often made of cast iron, which also allows slow, even cooking to take place.

Figure 11.13: *Couscoussières* and *tagines* are essential components for cooking authentic Moroccan cuisine.

Discuss

- Why do students think that lamb plays such a prominent role in Moroccan celebrations and everyday meals?

- Compared to the European countries discussed in this chapter, why did Moroccan cuisine undergo so few changes after the Columbian Exchange?

Reinforce and Review

- *B'stilla* can be understood as a savory version of *pastilla*: Although it contains sugar, *warqa*, and crushed almonds, its main ingredient is spicy stewed pigeon.

- *Choua*, *meshoui*, and *harira* are all lamb dishes, but the latter is an everyday stew, whereas the two former are festival fare.

Teaching Tips

- Monitor students as they make couscous.

Vocabulary Terms

- ***B'stilla***: Stewed and spiced pigeon, layered with *warqa*, sugar, and crushed almonds and formed into a pie.

- ***Choua***: Steamed forequarter lamb, flavored with cumin.

- ***Meshoui***: A whole roasted lamb.

- ***Harira***: A thick stew of chickpeas, rice, meat, and vegetables.

Essential Skills:
Couscous

Encourage students to discuss the following:

- Why is it important to soak couscous in cold water before steaming it? What effect might hot water have?

- What might contemporary Moroccan cuisine be like if semolina had never been brought to the region?

- Besides onions, what other aromatic ingredients and spices might be appropriate in couscous?

Several other dishes are also popular for festivals. **B'stilla** (similar to the *pastilla* mentioned previously) is a pie of minced stewed pigeon flavored with *ras-el-hanout* that is layered with *warqa*, a thin sheet of pastry resembling phyllo, as well as with sugar and crushed almonds. Some pies can have up to fifty layers. **Choua** and **meshoui** are also common. The first is a steamed forequarter of lamb, flavored with cumin, while the latter is a whole roasted lamb. **Harira**, on the other hand, is an everyday dish. It is a thick stew of chickpeas, rice, meat (usually lamb), and vegetables, eaten with salad or bread.

Essential Skills
Couscous

Morocco's national dish, couscous, is also found throughout the countries of Northern Africa. Instead of a *couscoussière*, put a small-holed metal colander (or a regular metal colander lined with cheesecloth) into a stockpot, using aluminum foil as a lid.

❶ Add couscous to cold water and let it swell for 10 minutes. See Figure 11.14a.

❷ Place the couscous in the colander over a stockpot half filled with water.

❸ Steam the couscous for 10 minutes, and then remove the colander and empty the water. See Figure 11.14b.

❹ Sauté onions and aromatics in the stockpot, and then add chunks of meat and a large amount of water. See Figure 11.14c on the following page.

❺ Return the couscous-filled colander to the top of the stockpot, cover it with foil, and simmer 30 minutes.

❻ Add a disjointed chicken to the stockpot and simmer another 30 minutes.

❼ Add vegetables to the stockpot and simmer until tender.

❽ Place the couscous in the center of a serving platter, and then push it outward, creating a cavity in the center.

❾ Place the meat and vegetables into the center of the platter and serve. See Figure 11.14d on the following page.

Figure 11.14a: Step 1—Add couscous to cold water.

Figure 11.14b: Step 3—Steam the couscous.

714

Figure Focus

Figure 11.14a: Soaking couscous in a glass vessel enables the cook to monitor the swelling of the individual grains.

Figure 11.14b: Steaming couscous, rather than boiling it, helps it develop a light and fluffy texture.

Figure 11.14c: Step 4 —Sauté onions and aromatics in the stockpot.

Figure 11.14d: Step 9—Place the meat and vegetables into the center of the platter and serve.

[techniques]

Moroccan Cooking Methods

Moroccan cooking methods focus on *tagine*, *couscoussière*, steaming, and spit-roasting.

Greece

Cultural Influences

In ancient times, the Greeks were extremely interested in cuisine. In fact, some scholars believe that **Archestratos**, writing in 330 BCE, produced one of the world's first cookbooks. Good chefs were prized, and scholarly treatises were written on the art and science of cookery. The ancient Greeks were also explorers. By 2000 BCE, they had established trade relationships with the Minoans in Crete and later rivaled the Phoenicians for dominance in the area. Subsequently,

[flavor]

The flavors of Greece are fresh, clean, and simple. Olive oil, lemon, and mountain herbs are characteristic flavoring agents.

715

Vocabulary Terms

- **Archestratos:** A Greek writer believed by some to have produced the world's first cookbook.

Figure Focus

Figure 11.14c: Sautéing aromatic ingredients helps bring out their flavors.

Figure 11.14d: Couscous is typically served on a platter or in a large bowl, to encourage communal dining.

Discuss

- What ingredients and foods do students consider to be typically "Greek"? Why?

- In ancient times, Greeks were profoundly interested in food and cuisine, prizing chefs and ingredients. How might this relate to contemporary American culture?

Reinforce and Review

- In ancient times, Greeks prized their chefs and wrote scholarly treatises on cuisine.

- By 2000 BCE, Greeks had begun to trade with the Minoans and subsequently rivaled the Phoenicians for control of the area.

Discuss

- Olives and olive oil are fundamental to Greece, both its cooking and its culture. Can students identify other ingredients that are so closely linked with a particular culture?

Reinforce and Review

- Greece's culinary reputation encouraged the occupying Romans to take Greek chefs and to facilitate the flow of culinary ideas and ingredients between the two regions.

- The Ottomans, whose empire later controlled Greek territory, were strongly influenced by Persian cuisine and introduced spicy, fruity elements to Greek cuisine.

- Greece's unusual physical geography limited contact by Europeans while facilitating trade with other regions.

- The Columbian Exchange introduced tomatoes and peppers, both of which became important ingredients.

- Olive trees have made a fundamental, basic, and lasting contribution to both Greek cuisine and Greek character; olive oil is the universal fat, and local olives are both consumed and exported.

Teaching Tips

- Use a map to identify particular aspects of Greece's physical geography that influence its cuisine, such as the mountains, islands, and coastlines.

Figure 11.15: In ancient times, Greece was the home of good chefs and scholarly works written on the science of cookery.

Roman occupiers (knowing a good thing when they saw it) employed Greek chefs in their homes in both occupied Greece and imperial Rome. During these periods of trading and occupation, culinary goods and ideas were exchanged between Greece and its neighbors/captors.

The Ottoman Empire took over the region in the fifteenth century. The Ottomans, who had been strongly influenced by Persian cooking techniques, brought spicy, fruity elements to the region. Their rule lasted nearly four centuries (independence came in 1829), long enough that even today Greek and Turkish cuisines, both the dishes and the names, are very similar. During this period, the Columbian Exchange brought what would become important products, like tomatoes and peppers, to Greece.

Greece, as shown in Figure 11.15, a mountainous country, is surrounded on most sides by the Mediterranean and Aegean Seas; these factors have strongly affected its culinary culture. On the one hand, the presence of the mountains prevented the filtration of European influences into the country. On the other hand, trading vessels crossing the Mediterranean could readily stop in Greek territory to exchange both ideas and ingredients.

Regional Ingredients and Dishes

Greece's abundant olive trees, which thrive in the dry, rocky terrain, have perhaps made the most basic contribution to its cuisine and to its culture. Olives have been cultivated in Greece for thousands of years and are considered essential to the country's well-being. Olive oil is the universal fat, and cured olives, especially kalamata and *Naphlion* olives, are both widely eaten and exported. Figure 11.16 on the following page shows a variety of Mediterranean olives.

716

Figure Focus

Figure 11.15: How might Greece's geography contribute toward the development of many regional cuisines rather than a single dominant cuisine?

In this region, food preparers commonly use herbs since so many flourish in the Mediterranean climate. Oregano, dill, and thyme are especially popular. Garlic is also prevalent, and food preparers use milder spices, like cinnamon and cloves, in meat dishes in northern Greece. People in this region, commonly gather *horta*, or wild greens, and eat them raw or lightly steamed.

Figure 11.16: Types of olives, shown clockwise from left, include kalamata, niçoise, Moroccan oil-cured, manzanilla, and picholine.

One dish that has become synonymous with Greece is **moussaka** (MOO-sah-kah), a casserole of lamb and eggplant that is often covered with a layer of béchamel sauce or beaten egg before baking. Lamb and eggplant are both common ingredients in Greece. The mountainous regions are excellent for goat and sheep cultivation, and eggplant and other vegetables thrive in the Mediterranean heat. Food preparers often stuff vegetables with other vegetables or lamb. Seafood is also very important due to the vast coastline; octopus, squid, and a variety of finfish are popular with diners. Products like feta, yogurt, and other popular protein sources are derived from goats' milk and sheep's milk.

Olive oil and lemon juice are the two most important flavoring agents used in Greek cuisine. Chefs almost always flavor dips and sauces with one or both, and olive oil and lemon juice are crucial elements in livening up what could otherwise be a bland cuisine. Popular dips include hummus and *taramasalata*. **Hummus** consists of puréed chickpeas seasoned with lemon juice, olive oil, and sesame-seed paste. *Taramasalata's* main ingredient is smoked cod roe, which is also puréed and combined with lemon juice, bread, and olive oil. These dips are often part of *mezze* (meh-ZAY), Greece's version of hors d'oeuvres or antipasto. The two primary sauces are *skorthalia* and *avgolemono* (ahv-goh-LEH-moh-noh). The first is a combination of olive oil, garlic, and bread that accompanies fried fish or cooked vegetables; The latter is a lemony egg sauce that is often used to finish seafood soups and stews.

To make **baklava** (BAHK-lah-vah), a highly honey-sweetened pastry, layer thin sheets of phyllo dough with chopped nuts, bake in large sheets, and cut into

717

- How do dishes like moussaka, a definitive Greek dish, reflect foreign influence on Greek cuisine?

- Many of the countries discussed so far have had a tradition of small dishes, such as *mezze* or tapas. What other characteristics do these countries share?

- How does baklava resemble typical Moroccan desserts? What explains the similarity?

Reinforce and Review

- Herbs are widely used in Greek cuisine because so many, such as oregano, thyme, and dill, grow so well in the climate.

- Wild greens, collectively called *horta*, are commonly gathered and eaten; eggplant is also a popular vegetable.

- Olive oil and lemon juice are the two most important flavoring ingredients in Greek cuisine.

- Common proteins include goat, lamb, seafood, and dairy products. Vegetables are extremely popular and grow profusely.

Teaching Tips

- Bring a variety of olives (or olive oils) to class so that students can observe and taste them.

Vocabulary Terms

- **Moussaka:** A casserole of lamb and eggplant that is often covered with a layer of béchamel sauce or beaten egg before baking.

- **Hummus:** A dip of puréed chickpeas seasoned with lemon juice, olive oil, and sesame-seed paste.

- *Mezze:* Greece's version of hors d'oeuvres or antipasto.

- *Skorthalia:* One of two major Greek sauces, a combination of olive oil, garlic, and bread that accompanies fried fish or cooked vegetables.

- *Avgolemono:* One of two major Greek sauces, a lemony egg sauce often used to finish seafood soups and stews.

- **Baklava:** A highly sweetened pastry layering phyllo dough with chopped nuts.

Figure Focus

Figure 11.16: Of the five olives pictured here, only Kalamata olives are Greek: Niçoise and Picholine olives are French, Manzanilla olives are Spanish, and Moroccan oil-cured olives are produced in Morocco.

Discuss

- Greece is part of the European continent, but many of its food traditions originated in the Middle East or North Africa. What might this indicate about the Mediterranean?

- The "Mediterranean diet" is a set of healthy eating practices based on regional cuisines. In what ways is the traditional Greek diet nutritious? Would you choose to follow it? Why or why not?

Reinforce and Review

- Phyllo, *warqa*, and *malsoufa* are all regional names for paper-thin sheets of dough, used in both sweet and savory preparations.

- Wheat has been cultivated for thousands of years in the Mediterranean, so flatbreads are common throughout the Mediterranean and Middle East; in Greece, the pita, with its easily stuffed pocket, is most popular.

Teaching Tips

- Assist students in making baklava, using either homemade or purchased phyllo.

Techniques:
Greek Cooking Methods

Encourage students to discuss the following:

- Many European and Mediterranean cuisines share similar cooking methods. What might explain that?

- What are some reasons that baking is so popular in Greece?

- How does Greece's physical geography promote the prevalent cooking methods?

Trends:
Gastro-Tourism

Encourage students to discuss the following:

- How would you market your community to gastro-tourists?

- Have you ever traveled somewhere just to eat? Why might such journeys be so important to some people?

- If you were to become a "gastronaut," where would you go, and why? Would you travel with an established agency or explore on your own? What are the pros and cons of each approach?

---

diamonds. This phyllo dough, which is used in savory preparations as well, is identical to Morocco's *warqa* and Tunisia's *malsoufa* (see Figure 11.17). This is not the only bread-like product, though. Owing to centuries of wheat cultivation, an enormous variety of flatbreads is present not only in Greece, but throughout the

Figure 11.17: *Warqa*, phyllo, and *malsoufa* are different names for same thing.

Mediterranean and Middle East. Pita is the most popular in Greece. Open the circular bread to form a pocket for stuffing or leave it intact to dip into other food items, especially while enjoying *mezze*.

[techniques]

Greek Cooking Methods

Greek cooking methods include boiling, simmering, spit-roasting, and baking.

[trends]

Gastro-Tourism

Gastro-tourists, or "gastronauts," travel for the sole purpose of experiencing the food and drink of a particular area. People have traveled to taste different food items for centuries, but it is becoming increasingly popular today, thanks in part to television channels like the Food Network and the Travel Channel, which highlight gastro-tourism.

The National Restaurant Association and the Travel Industry Association of America recently did a joint survey that found that 25 percent of leisure travelers base their travel plans on food. Some travel agencies also specialize in gastro-tourism, and a number of countries are now establishing official programs to promote regional specialties and unusual ingredients.

Cooking schools are also getting in on the act. Tourists can now attend culinary programs in a wide variety of countries that work with the International Culinary Tourism Association. Alternatively, travelers can simply pick a country and cuisine that appeals to them and then experience it by exploring the markets, shops, and restaurants there. The options are limitless.

718

Figure Focus

Figure 11.17: Baklava is a highly sweetened pastry made with nuts; the phyllo (filo) sheets used to prepare it are known in other parts of the Mediterranean as *warqa* and *malsoufa*.

[fast fact]

Did You Know...?
Olive oil has uses that go way beyond the culinary. Olive oil is also used in cosmetics, pharmaceuticals, and soaps. It was even used as a fuel in traditional oil lamps.

Tunisia

Cultural Influences

The Tunisian experience of occupation and colonization is very similar to the Moroccan experience up until modern times (see Figure 11.18). The two share a common colonial heritage with the rest of the Maghreb; a series of traders, refugees, and occupiers arrived on their shores, bringing with them their own food, techniques, and recipes. Even the two countries' final colonial experience was similar: Tunisia was placed under French government in 1881, some 30 years before Morocco, but both gained independence in 1956.

Figure 11.18: Tunisia has a culture and cuisine very similar to that of Morocco.

Regional Ingredients and Dishes

Clear connections can be made between French and Tunisian food. A popular salad, made of roasted peppers and tomatoes and garnished with tuna and hard-boiled egg, is known as **salade composé** (suh-LAHD com-poh-ZAY), a French name. Another common dish is **chakchouka** (SHAK-shoo-ka), a ratatouille (a vegetable dish of southern France) made with brown sugar and

[flavor]
Tunisia cuisine features spicy and pungent flavors like chili and ginger. Vegetables and seafood are important elements of this cuisine.

719

Figure Focus
Figure 11.18: Tunisia is in the center of the north African coastline, in the heart of the Mediterranean Sea.

Discuss

- What effect did the Columbian Exchange have on Tunisian cuisine?

- How do the spicy condiments used in Tunisian cuisine relate to the complex moles used in Mexican cuisine?

Reinforce and Review

- Many Tunisian dishes have French names or histories, such as *brik à l'oeuf*.

- Spicy flavors predominate in Tunisian cuisine: Although *harissa* is the most popular condiment, *tabil*, *chermoula*, and *ras-el-hanout* are also widely used.

- Other popular ingredients in Tunisian cuisine include ginger, pickled lemon, spicy *merguez* sausage, lamb, couscous, flatbreads, and a wide array of vegetables.

- As in Morocco, highly sweetened desserts are popular, with honey, dates, and other fruits in demand.

- Tunisian cuisine differs from other Mediterranean and Maghreb states in both its ingredients and its cooking methods: Wild boar, edible fungi, and spiny lobsters are all popular foods, and although *tagines* and couscous are commonly made, their cooking methods differ from those used in Morocco.

- In particular, Tunisian *tagines* stand out from their counterparts in other countries: These dishes are thick stews combined with beaten egg, baked until set, and cut into large squares.

Teaching Tips

- Divide students into groups to make *harissa*, *tabil*, or *chermoula*. Hold a taste test to see which condiment students prefer and why.

Vocabulary Terms

- **Harissa**: A highly spiced condiment made of chilis, coriander, garlic, and olive oil, used throughout Tunisian cuisine.

- **Tabil**: A spicy condiment made of chilis, coriander, caraway, and garlic, used to flavor beef or veal.

- **Chermoula**: A mixture of puréed onion and garlic mixed with pungent spices, like chili and saffron.

topped with beaten egg. Finally, *brik à l'oeuf*, tuna and hard-boiled egg wrapped in *malsouga* and baked or fried, is another French name for a popular appetizer.

Spicy condiments are a major component of Tunisian cuisine. Food preparers often serve grilled steaks with a spicy condiment. Tunisians enjoy *ras-el-hanout* here as in the rest of the Maghreb, but more important is **harissa** (hah-REE-suh), a highly spiced paste of chilis, coriander, garlic, and olive oil guaranteed to enliven any meal. A similar preparation is **tabil** (TAY-bul), which combines chilis, coriander, caraway, and garlic and is often used to flavor beef or veal. **Chermoula** is a mixture of puréed onion and garlic mixed with pungent spices like chili and saffron. Ginger and pickled lemon are also tremendously popular flavors here.

Many ingredients in the Tunisian pantry are similar to those elsewhere in the Maghreb: lamb, spicy *merguez* sausage, flatbreads, a wide variety of vegetables, and especially couscous. The strong regional preference for sweet foods is found here as well, expressed as a passion for honey and fruits, especially dates. But Tunisia parts ways with its companions in other aspects.

Northwest Tunisia is known for its wild boar and edible fungi, both of which are popular ingredients. Fishermen catch spiny lobsters off the island of Galita. Cooking methods differ, too. Tunisian cooks prepare couscous by steaming it in a covered pot until it becomes tender and moist, while Moroccans use a *couscoussière* to ensure that the couscous will be fluffy and light. To make what is called a *tagine* in Tunisia, first make a stew (usually of veal or lamb, plus onion and sweet spices), then thicken it with a starchy food like chickpeas or potatoes, add vegetables and herbs for still more flavor, and finally add egg and cheese to the mix. Bake the dish until it is set, and then turn it onto a platter to be cut into squares. *Tagine* is a common dish in both Tunisia and Morocco, as seen in Figure 11.19.

Figure 11.19: Here we see both Moroccan and Tunisian *tagines*.

Figure Focus

Figure 11.19: How do either Moroccan or Tunisian *tagines* resemble dishes popular in other cuisines?

Homework Activity:
Famous Figures—Tunisia

Literacy Connection, 21st-Century Skills—Work Creatively with Others, Use Systems Thinking, Information Literacy, Communication and Collaboration, Social and Cross-Cultural Skills

Working in small groups, research a famous figure in Tunisian cuisine. Prepare and present a group report discussing this individual's life and contributions to cuisine.

Alternately, present a report describing an important development in Tunisian culture and how it affected the country's cuisines.

Tomatoes are particularly prominent in the Tunisian diet, as are eggs, olives, and pastas. Seafood (not just tuna and spiny lobster) is abundant. Grilling with lemon juice or deep-frying are popular cooking techniques. *Poisson* (pwah-SOHN) *complet* is a specialty: grill, sauté, or deep-fry the desired fish and then serve with potato chips and a mixture called *tastira*. This is made of grilled peppers, onion, garlic, and tomato, all chopped finely and topped with a poached egg.

[techniques]

Tunisian Cooking Methods

Tunisian cooking methods include steaming, simmering, grilling, roasting, and—of course—using a *tagine*.

[nutrition]

Mediterranean Diet

During the 1990s, Dr. Walter Willett of Harvard University presented research results indicating that people living in the Mediterranean area, although consuming relatively high amounts of certain fats, actually had much less cardiovascular disease than people consuming the typical American diet with roughly the same amounts of different fats. The Mediterranean diet, as it came to be known, emphasizes the abundant consumption of fruits, vegetables, and grains, along with olive oil. "Mediterranean dieters" consume animal proteins, especially red meat, in small quantities, and enjoy dairy products and wine in moderation. Of course, this is not the diet consumed by all Mediterranean people, but the label has stuck nonetheless.

Olive oil, the major fat consumed, is thought to be an important factor in the low rates of cardiovascular illness, as are the high quantity of plant fiber, low amount of saturated fat, and low intake of processed food. Olive oil contains monounsaturated fatty acids, which makes it a heart-healthy fat. Genetics and lifestyle may also play a role. Other research has found that risks for developing cancer, diabetes, Parkinson's disease, and Alzheimer's disease are lower for those following this diet. One study, the Lyon Diet Health Study, found that the Mediterranean diet was associated with a 70 percent decrease in mortality from all causes. For these reasons, as well as the weight loss typically associated with it, the Mediterranean diet became wildly popular outside its homeland and continues to be important today.

721

CUSTOMIZED INSTRUCTION

Literacy Connection, 21st-Century Skills—Critical Thinking and Problem Solving, Communicate Clearly, Information Literacy, Work Independently

ESOL Students

Which of the cooking methods discussed in this section are also used in your cuisine of origin? Are similar ingredients and cooking vessels used? How are the Mediterranean flavor profiles discussed in this section similar to or different from the flavor profile of your cuisine of origin?

Write a brief essay discussing your thoughts.

Discuss

- What are the possible origins of *poisson complet*? Why do you think these ingredients and flavors are arranged in such a way? Does the dish sound appealing? Why or why not?

- How do the cuisines of Tunisia, Greece, and Morocco compare to those of France, Spain, and Italy? Consider both ingredients and cooking methods. Should these latter three countries be considered part of the Mediterranean, based on what you have learned? Why or why not?

Reinforce and Review

- Tomatoes, olives, eggs, pastas, and seafood are all popular Tunisian ingredients.

- Grilling and deep-frying are popular cooking techniques.

Teaching Tips

- Relate the use of tomatoes, olives, and pasta to Italian cuisine to demonstrate the breadth of the Mediterranean.

Techniques: Tunisian Cooking Methods

Encourage students to discuss the following:

- How are Tunisian cooking methods similar to and different from those used in Morocco and Greece?

- What can Tunisian cooking methods indicate about the country's geography and natural resources?

- Why do students think that the Tunisian and Moroccan *tagines* have evolved so differently?

Nutrition: Mediterranean Diet

Encourage students to discuss the following:

- Why is olive oil considered to be a "healthy" fat?

- One study found that the Mediterranean diet is associated with a 70 percent decrease in mortality from all causes. What might explain these results?

- If the Mediterranean diet is associated with so many health benefits, why do the majority of people worldwide choose not to follow it?

Summary

- Remind students to review the following:
  1. Morocco—culture, ingredients, and dishes
  2. Greece—culture, ingredients, and dishes
  3. Tunisia—culture, ingredients, and dishes

Summary

In this section, you learned the following:

- Morocco has been a center for trade since the twelfth century when the Phoenicians established trading posts on the coast and introduced sausage to the region. The Arabs, who occupied Morocco during the seventh century, had perhaps the most pronounced and long-lasting effect on Moroccan cuisine. They introduced saffron, ginger, cumin, and cinnamon, as well as the principle of combining sweet and sour tastes. All of this radically transformed the somewhat bland cuisine of the area and established a distinctive culinary tradition. Other colonizers followed. Around the fourteenth century, the Ottoman Empire brought new developments in pastries and sweets. The Columbian Exchange introduced new products like tomatoes and peppers. European influences brought new ingredients to Morocco, such as pasta and tea. Moroccan cuisine is sweet, sour, spicy, and complex. Signature cooking methods are *tagines* and *couscoussières*.

- In ancient times, the Greeks were extremely interested in cuisine. Good chefs were prized, and scholarly treatises were written on the art and science of cookery. The Ottoman Empire took over the region in the fifteenth century. The Ottomans, who had been strongly influenced by Persian cooking techniques, brought spicy, fruity elements to the region. During this period, the Columbian Exchange brought what would become important products, like tomatoes and peppers, to Greece. The flavor profile is fresh, clean, and simple. Olive oil, lemon, and mountain herbs are characteristic flavoring agents. Boiling, simmering, and spit-roasting are all common cooking methods.

- The Tunisian experience of occupation and colonization is very similar to the Moroccan experience up until modern times. The two share a common colonial heritage with the rest of North Africa; a series of traders, refugees, and occupiers arrived on their shores bringing with them their own foods, techniques, and recipes. Tunisia was placed under French government control in 1881 AD, some 30 years before Morocco, but both gained independence in 1956. Clear connections can be made between French and Tunisian food. The Tunisian flavor profile is spicier and more pungent. Chili and ginger are commonly used, and vegetables and seafood are important elements of this cuisine. Grilling, simmering, and *tagine* are common cooking methods.

722

Section 11.2 Review Questions

❶ What is the flavor profile of Moroccan cuisine?

❷ What are two common cooking methods of Moroccan cuisine?

❸ What are two staple ingredients in Greek cuisine?

❹ What are two ingredients commonly used in Tunisian cuisine?

❺ The Arabs had perhaps the most pronounced and long-lasting effect on Moroccan cuisine. They introduced saffron, ginger, cumin, and cinnamon, as well as the principle of combining sweet and sour tastes. Identify two Moroccan dishes that combine sweet and sour tastes. What spice or ingredient causes the sweet taste in each? What causes the sour taste?

❻ Chef Kate and Miguel have decided to create a *tagine* dish from the Mediterranean. They are trying to decide between the Moroccan version and the Tunisian version. Explain to them the difference between the two so they can make a more informed decision.

❼ How does Tunisian cuisine compare to Moroccan cuisine?

❽ Why do you think the flavor profile of Greek cuisine is characterized as "fresh, clean, and simple"? Explain the common ingredients and preparations in Greek cuisine that would allow for such a description.

723

Section 11.2 Review Questions

1. The Moroccan cuisine is sweet, sour, and spicy.

2. Common Moroccan cooking techniques include *tagine*, making couscous, steaming, and spit-roasting.

3. The two staple ingredients in Greek cuisine are olive oil and lemon juice.

4. Ingredients commonly used in Tunisian cuisine include tomatoes, eggs, olives, pasta, seafood, lamb, *merguez* sausage, flatbreads, couscous, honey, dates, and chilis.

5. *B'stilla*: Sweetness from sugar, sourness from *ras-el-hanout*; Festival *tagine*: Sweetness from honey, sourness from onion and *ras-el-hanout*.

6. Moroccan *tagines* are prepared in a vessel called a *tagine*: It has a conical top and a shallow basin and is used to make rich meat stews, often seasoned with *ras-el-hanout* or preserved lemon. Tunisian *tagines* are lightly sweetened meat and vegetable stews, thickened with chickpeas or potatoes, and combined with egg and cheese before baking until set; these *tagines* are served cut into dense squares.

7. Students should explain the similarities and differences between the two cuisines.

8. Students should discuss common ingredients, dishes, and cooking methods in defense of the Greek flavor profile.

Section 11.2 Activities

1. Students should describe the most important aspects of their chosen country's cuisine when creating their media products.

2. Students should research couscous and how it has spread and evolved. They should write a cogent paper describing their findings, making sure to answer the questions asked in the activity.

3. Students should research olive oil and its effects on Mediterranean history and cultures. Those choosing to present their findings as a chart should be sure to provide as much information as those writing the two-page paper would have to include.

Section 11.2 Activities

1. Study Skills/Group Activity: Exploring the Mediterranean

Working with two or three other students, select a Mediterranean country that is not covered in this chapter. Create a poster or Web page about the country's cuisine, important ingredients, and typical dishes.

2. Independent Activity: Looking Deeper into Couscous

Often, the evolution of a region's cuisine can tell a lot about its history. Research couscous. Where does the name derive from? Why was it originally created? How and why has it changed over the years? How does it differ in different countries? There are different colors of couscous. Do they taste different? Report your findings in a one-page report.

3. Critical Thinking: The History of Olive Oil

Research the role olive oil has played in Mediterranean history. How has it shaped the region in both economic and cultural ways? Describe your findings in a two-page paper or in a chart.

724

SECTION 11.3 THE MIDDLE EAST

Some Middle Eastern countries border the Mediterranean and several share similar culinary characteristics with Mediterranean nations. This can cause some confusion over boundary lines. A commonly drawn distinction is that Mediterranean cuisines are often sea-based, and Middle Eastern cuisines are often land-based. This section follows that pattern.

Study Questions

After studying Section 11.3, you should be able to answer the following questions:

- What are the cultural influences and flavor profiles of Egypt?
- What are the cultural influences and flavor profiles of Iran?
- What are the cultural influences and flavor profiles of Saudi Arabia?

Egypt

Cultural Influences

Egypt, as shown in Figure 11.20, is part of the "Fertile Crescent." The rich Nile Valley and its delta are prime agricultural land, and the river floods annually to ensure a consistent harvest. However, most of the country is desert, and Egypt today imports more than 60 percent of its food. Most people still adhere to traditional diets, although they are influenced to some extent by the variety of cultures that have controlled or been controlled by Egypt throughout the centuries.

725

Homework Activity:
Egyptian Foods

Literacy Connection, 21st-Century Skills—Reason Effectively, Communicate Clearly, Information Literacy, Work Independently

Students should each identify and research a dish that they believe to be characteristically Egyptian. They should explain its origins, ingredients, and cooking method.

Students should present an oral report describing the dish to the class.

Homework Activity:
Famous Figures—Egypt

Literacy Connection, 21st-Century Skills—Work Creatively with Others, Use Systems Thinking, Information Literacy, Communication and Collaboration, Social and Cross-Cultural Skills

Working in small groups, research a famous figure in Egyptian cuisine. Prepare and present a group report discussing this individual's life and contributions to cuisine.

Alternately, present a report describing an important development in Egyptian culture and how it affected the country's cuisines.

Section 11.3
The Middle East

Introduce the Section

a. Explain the importance of studying Middle Eastern culture and history in terms of understanding American society.

b. Explain why Egypt, Iran, and Saudi Arabia are appropriate selections to introduce the breadth of Middle Eastern cuisines.

c. Discuss the objectives for the section.

Vocabulary Review

a. Direct students to the key terms.

b. Pronounce each word, and have the students repeat the pronunciation out loud.

c. Discuss the definition of each word.

Teach

Discuss

- Just as it can be difficult to determine whether a country belongs to Europe or to the Mediterranean, it can be difficult to determine whether a country belongs to the Mediterranean or to the Middle East. What factors do we use in making these decisions?

- What dishes, ingredients, and cooking methods do students identify with the Middle East? Why?

- In what ways might Mediterranean cuisines resemble Middle Eastern cuisines?

- Egypt imports over 60 percent of its food from other countries. How might this affect its cuisine?

Reinforce and Review

- Although Egypt is part of the Fertile Crescent and contains some rich agricultural soil, the country is predominantly desert and must import the majority of its food.

- Most Egyptians adhere to traditional diets, influenced to a varying extent by the cultures that have controlled or been controlled by Egypt over the centuries.

Teaching Tips

- Use a map to help students understand how Egypt has been affected by such a variety of other cultures and why it imports much of its food.

- Which cuisine that has been discussed so far in this chapter most closely resembles that of Egypt? Why?

- Egypt has a long coastline. Why does it have an agriculture-based cuisine?

- Why are Egyptian flavors so simple, unlike the more complex flavors of the neighboring Maghreb?

Discuss

- Why have European cuisines and ingredients had such a small effect on Egyptian diets?

Reinforce and Review

- Although Egypt was once a colonial power in its own right, it was subsequently invaded and governed by various cultures until it became independent from Great Britain in 1956.

- Peoples who occupied or governed Egyptian territory included the Libyans, Nubians, Assyrians, Greco-Macedonians, Romans, Arabs, Turks, and British.

- Like some of the other cultures discussed in this chapter, both the Islamic Empire and the Ottoman Empire occupied Egypt at different times.

- Traders and colonizers introduced foods like rice, fruit, garlic, tahini, and chickpeas.

- The three staple ingredients in Egyptian cuisine are onions, wheat, and olives.

Homework Activity: Time on Their Side

Mathematics Connection, Literacy Connection, 21st-Century Skills—Critical Thinking and Problem Solving, Communicate Clearly, Information Literacy, Create Media Products, Work Independently

Create a timeline showing key points in Egyptian history, such as its occupation of or by other peoples and the construction of the pyramids. The timeline should include at least ten key points.

Chapter 11 | Foundations of Restaurant Management & Culinary Arts

[flavor] Egypt's agriculture-based cuisine follows traditional foodways, especially in its heavy use of olive oil and wheat. Bread, vegetables, and legumes are central to the typical Egyptian diet, and most flavorings are simple and straightforward: lemon juice, parsley, and sesame.

Egypt became an international power about 3,500 years ago, overpowering neighboring regions and some Mediterranean areas. However, Egypt was also in turn invaded by Libyans, Nubians, and Assyrians, all of whom were later expelled. Egypt was governed by various invaders for more than 2,000 years; Greco-Macedonians, Romans, Arabs, and ultimately Turks all played a role. Egypt was absorbed by the Islamic Empire in 639 AD and by the Ottoman Empire in 1517 AD. Traders and colonizers introduced new foods, such as rice and a variety of fruits from India, China, and Persia. Garlic, tahini, and chickpeas all remain staple parts of the Egyptian cuisine today.

Figure 11.20: Egypt has an agriculture-based cuisine, emphasizing the use of olive oil and wheat.

In 1914, Egypt briefly became a British protectorate before declaring independence in 1922. A 1952 revolution against the Kingdom of Egypt, which had resulted from its remaining ties to Britain, established full independence in 1956. European culinary habits appear to have had only a limited effect on Egypt's cuisine with the major exception of macaroni with béchamel sauce, a popular dish with penne pasta and a layer of spiced meat and onions.

All in all, Egyptian cuisine resembles that of other parts of the Middle East and the Mediterranean, but it maintains its own identity. Onions, which have been an essential ingredient since the pyramids were constructed, remain fundamental to contemporary diets, as do wheat and olives.

726

Figure Focus

Figure 11.20: Egypt is bordered by two seas. How might this have affected its trading patterns and ultimately its cuisine?

Homework Activity: Trading Up

Literacy Connection, 21st-Century Skills—Reason Effectively, Communicate Clearly, Information Literacy, Work Independently

Egypt imports over 60 percent of its food each year. Where does it get this food? Who are its primary trading partners? What foods does it import?

Report your findings in a single paragraph.

Regional Ingredients and Dishes

Despite changing economic and demographic patterns, Egyptians still eat much as they always have, enjoying fish and seafood along the coast and in Alexandria, but savoring a soil-based cuisine everywhere else. Vegetables, legumes, and wheat are heavily used. Unique among Middle Eastern countries, Egyptian cuisine is predominantly vegetarian and even vegan. The national dish is *ful medames*. To make *ful medames*, soak, boil, and simmer fava beans eight to ten hours and then mix with oil or clarified butter, onions, and spices such as coriander, cumin, and caraway. Alternatively, add garlic and tahini. Egyptians usually eat *ful medames* as a breakfast dish; it has enough calories to fuel a long day of labor. Make Egyptian falafel with fava beans by crushing them and forming a patty before deep-frying. Falafel is made with chickpeas in most other countries.

As in other countries, flatbreads are popular. A common variety in Egypt is *eish baladi*, which is sprinkled with **duqqa** (DOO-ka), a spice mixture that often includes sesame, dried mint, coriander, and cumin, among others. *Eish baladi* and other flatbreads may be dipped into **baba ghanoush** (bah-bah gah-NOOSH), a combination of eggplant, chickpeas, lemon juice, parsley, cumin, and olive oil that has relatives throughout the Middle East. Either of these may be considered street food. **Shawarma**, shredded meat served in a pita with tahini and analogous to the Greek gyros, may also be a street food (see Figure 11.21).

Melohkia refers both to a muci-laginous green vegetable and a soup flavored with this vegetable. This is a working-class dish that can be made more elaborate with garlic, coriander, and even rabbit. *Kushari* is also a common dish made with rice, lentils, and macaroni. At the other end of the scale, *hamam mahshi* consists of pigeon stuffed with rice or wheat and

Figure 11.21: Egyptian shawarma is analogous to the Greek gyros.

herbs and then roasted or grilled. Although Egyptians who live inland don't eat much animal protein, favorites include pigeon, eggs, and even camel, which is tenderized with crushed onion and cumin before cooking.

727

Discuss

- Egypt is unique among Middle Eastern countries in enjoying a cuisine that is mostly vegetarian. What factors might account for this difference?

- What does it mean to describe a dish as "working-class"?

- Does *ful medames* sound like a typical American breakfast dish? What dishes does it resemble?

Reinforce and Review

- Contemporary Egyptians enjoy a traditional diet. Although seafood is consumed along the coast, the rest of the country follows a predominantly vegetarian—even vegan—diet, relying on vegetables, legumes, and wheat.

- The national dish is *ful medames*, made with fava beans, onions, and spices and consumed as a breakfast dish.

- Although most other cultures make falafel with chickpeas, Egyptians use fava beans in this dish.

- Flatbreads, often sprinkled with spice mixtures and dipped into vegetable purées, are popular throughout Egypt.

- Inland Egyptians consume little animal protein, although eggs, pigeon, and camel are favorites.

Teaching Tips

- Assist students making baba ghanoush in the classroom kitchen.

Vocabulary Terms

- *Duqqa:* A spice mixture that typically includes sesame, dried mint, coriander, and cumin.

- *Baba ghanoush:* A purée of eggplant, chickpeas, lemon juice, parsley, cumin, and olive oil.

- **Shawarma:** Shredded meat served in a pita with tahini.

Figure Focus

Figure 11.21: What meats do students think might be commonly used to make shawarmas?

Essential Skills: Flatbreads

Encourage students to discuss the following:

- Why are flatbreads so popular throughout so much of the world? What cuisines are not associated with flatbreads? What might account for this?

- What might happen if the water used to make the dough is too warm?

- How do flatbreads made of wheat differ from flatbreads made of corn?

Homework Activity: Flatbreads

Literacy Connection, 21st-Century Skills—Critical Thinking and Problem Solving, Communicate Clearly, Information Literacy, Be Self-Directed Learners

Many cuisines worldwide have a tradition of flatbread consumption. Identify a flatbread from a cuisine not discussed in this textbook and describe its ingredients, where it is commonly eaten, its method of manufacture, and other relevant information. Include and discuss at least two recipes for making the flatbread. How do they differ?

Discuss your findings in a one-page report, appending the recipes.

Essential Skills
Flatbreads

Leavened flatbreads made of wheat are common to many culinary traditions throughout the Mediterranean, the Middle East, and Asia.

1. Combine sugar and yeast with warm water and stir until dissolved; cover and allow to froth.
2. Combine flour and salt, and then add yeast mixture and any dairy or flavoring ingredients desired. See Figure 11.22a.
3. Knead the dough until a smooth ball forms. See Figure 11.22b.
4. Thinly coat the dough with oil and cover it with a towel to double in size.
5. Divide the dough into portion-sized balls. See Figure 11.22c.
6. Roll the dough into circles and brush it with melted butter or oil. See Figure 11.22d.
7. Bake or pan-fry until it is puffed and lightly browned. See Figure 11.22e.

Figure 11.22a: Step 2—Add the water and yeast mixture.

Figure 11.22b: Step 3—Knead the dough.

Figure 11.22c: Step 5—Divide the dough in half with a knife.

Figure 11.22d: Step 6—Brush the dough with melted butter or oil.

Figure 11.22e: Step 7—Bake or pan-fry it until puffed and lightly browned.

728

Figure Focus

Figure 11.22a: What effect might adding dairy products have on the finished flatbread?

Figure 11.22b: When kneading the dough, be sure that all ingredients are fully incorporated and smooth.

Figure 11.22c: If desired, the portions can be weighed to ensure uniformity.

Figure 11.22d: What effect might brushing fat onto the prepared dough have on the finished flatbread?

Figure 11.22e: How might the finished flatbread appear and taste differently, depending on whether it was baked or pan-fried?

[techniques]

Egyptian Cooking Methods
Egyptian cooking methods include baking (clay ovens), braising, and roasting.

Iran

Cultural Influences

Iran, or Persia, is one of the world's oldest continuous civilizations, having been established around 7000 BCE (see Figure 11.23). Although around 500 BCE it was a territorial power controlling land from Russia to Egypt and from Greece to India. Iran was later occupied itself, falling to the Islamic Empire around 652 BCE. However, Iranians adopted Islam without adopting Arabian practices, maintaining a distinct Persian identity.

A bigger influence on Iranian culture and cuisine came from its presence on the ancient Silk Road between China and modern Italy. This Silk Road was a conduit for both ideas and ingredients such as long-grain rice, citrus fruits, and eggplant, all of which remain essential in the Iranian diet today. Persia reciprocated by sharing its own ingredients, like rosewater, pomegranates, and spinach, with other cultures.

Figure 11.23: Iran is one of the world's oldest continuous civilizations.

[flavor]

The key word for Iranian cuisine is "balanced." A good mixture of vegetables, dairy products, meat, herbs, and vegetables is presented at every meal. Pungent ingredients and sweet-and-sour combinations are popular in this very complex and aromatic cuisine.

729

Figure Focus

Figure 11.23: Like Egypt, Iran is bounded by two separate bodies of water. How might this have affected the development of its cuisine?

Homework Activity:
Iranian Foods

Literacy Connection, 21st-Century Skills—Reason Effectively, Communicate Clearly, Information Literacy, Work Independently

Students should each identify and research a dish that they believe to be characteristically Iranian. They should explain its origins, ingredients, and cooking method.

Students should present an oral report describing the dish to the class.

Techniques: Egyptian Cooking Methods

Encourage students to discuss the following:

- How might baking in a clay oven produce a different dish than baking in a conventional oven?

- How does Egypt's unique cuisine affect its cooking methods?

- In what ways are Egyptian cooking methods similar to those used in the Mediterranean? What accounts for those similarities?

Discuss

- How might Iranian cuisine have developed differently if the Silk Road had taken a different path?

- How might both Egypt and Iran be said to be culturally distinct from other Middle Eastern nations? Given these differences, what makes them appropriate representatives of the Middle East?

Reinforce and Review

- Iran, or Persia, is one of the world's oldest continuous civilizations; although once a colonial power, it was subsequently occupied by the Islamic Empire.

- Iranians adopted Islam without adopting other Arabian practices and behaviors, maintaining a distinctly Persian society and identity.

- A major influence on the development of Iranian cuisine was its presence on the Silk Road between China and modern-day Italy; this brought such contemporary staples as eggplant, long-grain rice, and citrus fruit while spreading the use of rosewater, spinach, and pomegranates.

Teaching Tips

- Review a map of the region with students to help them understand the significance of the Silk Road in spreading cultural influences.

Flavor Profile

Encourage students to discuss the following:

- Why is "balance" an important part of Iranian cuisine? How does it reflect the broader Iranian culture?

- Of the cultures and cuisines studied thus far, here and in Chapter 10, which does Iran most resemble?

- Why might Iranian cuisine be expected to incorporate sweet-and-sour elements?

Discuss

- As in Greece, Iranian cuisine relies heavily on lemon, stuffed vegetables, lamb, wheat, and sweet desserts. What other similarities between the two cuisines and cultures can you identify, and how can you explain them? What are some notable differences?

- Three major methods of rice cookery have developed in Iran. What does that signify about the culture and about the cuisine?

- How is the Iranian preference for balanced flavors reflected in its traditional meal patterns?

Reinforce and Review

- Iranian food relies on a combination of traditional ingredients, like wheat and lamb, and recent imports, like rice and lemon.

- A traditional Iranian meal includes rice, meat, and a mixture of onion, vegetables, herbs, and nuts; these dishes are served with an array of fresh vegetables, dairy products, and bread.

- The three major types of rice cookery practiced in Iran are *polo, katteh,* and *damy.*

- *Polo* is made using the soak-boil-steam technique, also known as the "three-step method."

- Stuffed meat and vegetables, known as *dolmehs,* are popular, as are kebabs and other lamb dishes.

- Desserts are very sweet, often inspired by French traditions, although others adhere to more traditional patterns.

Teaching Tips

- Divide the students into groups and assign each group one version of Iranian rice cookery. Afterward, encourage students to taste the finished products, identifying which they prefer and why.

Vocabulary Terms

- *Katteh:* One of three major methods of rice cookery in Iran, this method uses raw rice to create a moist, clumpy product, traditionally a breakfast dish in the north.

Regional Ingredients and Dishes

Iranian food relies on traditional ingredients, such as wheat and lamb, into which more recent imports, such as rice and lemon, have been incorporated. The basic meal pattern is to have rice, a meat, and some combination of onion, vegetables, herbs, and nuts. Cooks often combine the meat and onion mixture as a stew and ladle it over the rice. Serve this dish with a platter of fresh herbs (which may include tarragon, costmary, dill, and mint), *panir* (a feta-like cheese), bread, cucumber, tomato, onion, yogurt, and lemon juice to achieve the balance of flavors so important in Persian cuisine (see Figure 11.24).

Figure 11.24: The traditional condiments for an Iranian meal.

Three major types of rice cookery are practiced in Iran. *Chelow,* or parboiled white rice, is gently steamed with other ingredients, like vegetables or dried fruit, to produce *polo.* If *polo* is prepared properly, a desirable golden crust known as *tah-dig* forms on the bottom of the pan. *Polo* is made by the characteristic soak-boil-steam technique, producing a light, fluffy rice. **Katteh** is made with raw rice, which absorbs all the liquid in the pot and is, therefore, moist and clumpy. *Katteh* is a traditional breakfast dish in the Gilan Province in the north. Finally, *damy* is made like *katteh,* except that other ingredients like legumes or grains are added with the raw rice.

Stuffed meat and vegetables, known as *dolmehs,* are popular, as are kebabs, ground meat molded around a stick and grilled. Kebabs are often served with leavened wheat flatbreads such as *taftun* or *sangak.* A similar dish common in central Iran is *biryani* in which ground lamb is cooked in a pan over an open fire before it is served with *taftun. Fesenjan,* a casserole of lamb cooked with walnut sauce and flavored with pomegranate, is also common in that area.

Desserts tend to be extremely sweet, and many are inspired by French pastries, such as the Napoleon, similar to the mille-feuille (meel-FWEE) and flavored

730

Figure Focus

Figure 11.24: Iranian meals typically incorporate a number of side dishes and garnishes.

Homework Activity:
Famous Figures—Iran

Literacy Connection, 21st-Century Skills—Work Creatively with Others, Use Systems Thinking, Information Literacy, Communication and Collaboration, Social and Cross-Cultural Skills

Working in small groups, research a famous figure in Iranian cuisine. Prepare and present a group report discussing this individual's life and contributions to cuisine.

Alternately, present a report describing an important development in Iranian culture and how it affected the country's cuisines.

---

with rosewater. Others may even include meat, as in *koresht-e-mast*, a yogurt stew incorporating sugar, minced lamb or chicken, saffron, and orange peels, served at weddings and celebrations in central Iran. Baklava is also popular in Iran.

Important flavoring elements include nuts, especially walnuts, pistachios, and almonds; fruits, such as pomegranates, dates, mulberries, and citrus fruits; rosewater; saffron; and sumac, an acidic "berry" used in dried or powdered form throughout the region (see Figure 11.25). Traditionally, the fat of fat-tailed sheep or clarified butter were the most commonly used fats in Iran, but today vegetable oils are more often used. Vegetables and seafood play a prominent role in Iranian cuisine. Northern Iran is known for producing caviar, made of salted fish roe.

Figure 11.25: Iranian cuisine uses many flavors, such as cinnamon, cardamon, and coriander.

[techniques]

Iranian Cooking Methods
Iranian cooking methods include the three-step rice method (soak-boil-steam), braising, grilling, and baking.

[fast fact]

Did You Know...?
Tahini originated in ancient Persia, which is now known as Iran. The first mention of it is found in an Arabic cookbook circa the thirteenth century.

731

- What other cuisines share the Iranian tendency to combine savory and sweet ingredients in dessert dishes?

- Explain why many Iranian desserts exhibit French influence.

Reinforce and Review

- Some Iranian desserts, like *koresht-e-mast*, include meat as well as other savory ingredients.

- Important flavoring elements in Iranian cuisine include nuts, fruits, rosewater, saffron, and sumac.

- Vegetable oils have largely replaced animal fats in Iranian cooking.

- Vegetables are important in Iranian cuisine, as is seafood.

Teaching Tips

- Bring a sample of tahini to class for students to taste.

Techniques:
Iranian Cooking Methods

Encourage students to discuss the following:

- Why is the three-step method of rice cooking so important in Iranian cuisine?

- How are common Iranian cooking methods similar to and different from common Egyptian methods? How do each country's cooking methods reflect its culture?

Fast Fact:
Did You Know . . . ?

Encourage students to discuss the following:

- What is tahini? How is it used?

- What other cuisines also use tahini?

Figure Focus

Figure 11.25: Iranian flavors tend to be complex and rich, with no single flavor dominating the whole. What other cuisines share this tendency?

Homework Activity:
Iranian Ingredients

Literacy Connection, 21st-Century Skills—Critical Thinking and Problem Solving, Communicate Clearly, Information Literacy, Initiative and Self-Direction

Research an ingredient that is popular in Iran but is used less often in the United States, such as sumac, tahini, or rosewater. Describe it, including its flavor, how it is manufactured, the dishes in which it is used, and other characteristics you think relevant. If possible, taste or cook with the selected ingredient.

Discuss your findings in a one-page report.

Discuss

- The Egyptian national dish, *ful medames*, is a simple vegetarian or vegan dish eaten for breakfast, whereas the Saudi Arabian national dish, *khouzi*, is an elaborate and extravagant meat-based dish served at large gatherings and festivals. How do these two dishes demonstrate each country's culinary culture? What do they indicate about the breadth of Middle Eastern cuisine?

Reinforce and Review

- Like most other cuisines (and cultures), Saudi Arabian foodways have been influenced by trade as well as by occupation.

- The Persian Empire introduced rosewater and saffron; the Greco-Macedonian Alexander the Great later conquered the region, and both Indian and Greek foods were introduced.

- Like Iran, contemporary Saudi Arabia was conquered by the Islamic Empire; unlike Iran, the region became more or less assimilated into Arabian traditions.

- Typical Saudi Arabian meals include communal platters heaped with rice and garnished with meat and vegetable dishes, flatbreads, and freshly made pickles.

- *Khouzi* is considered by some to be the Saudi Arabian national dish: A whole lamb is stuffed and cooked, then served with rice that has been combined with clarified butter and almonds.

- Common flavorings include *baharat*, made with black pepper, cardamom, coriander, cassia, clove, nutmeg, and paprika; *loomi*, or dried *Omani* lime; and cinnamon.

Teaching Tips

- Use a map to help students understand Saudi Arabia's location in the Middle East.

Flavor Profile

Encourage students to discuss the following:

- How does "vegetal" differ from "vegetable"?

- How is the Saudi Arabian flavor profile similar to the Iranian flavor profile? What might explain that?

- In what ways is Saudi Arabian cuisine similar to Maghreb cuisine?

Saudi Arabia

Cultural Influences

The food of this region has been influenced by a variety of sources, including trade with the Horn of Africa, India, Iraq, and the Mediterranean (see Figure 11.26). The Persian Empire, which occupied the area around 550 BCE, introduced ingredients like saffron and rosewater, while Alexander the Great's regime brought Greek and Indian food to the region. The Islamic Empire later incorporated contemporary Saudi Arabia into both its territory and culinary traditions.

Figure 11.26: Saudi Arabian food has been influenced by trade with Africa, India, Iraq, and the Mediterranean.

Regional Ingredients and Dishes

The typical Saudi Arabian meal involves a large communal platter heaped with rice and garnished with meat and vegetable dishes, flatbreads, and fresh pickles. *Khouzi*, which may be the country's national dish, typifies this ideal. To make *khouzi*, bake or spit-roast a whole lamb stuffed with chicken, egg, rice, saffron, and onions, and serve it on a bed of rice flavored with almonds and clarified butter. Flavor the stuffing with *baharat*, a common spice mixture made with black pepper, cardamom, coriander, cassia, clove, nutmeg, and paprika; it is floral and aromatic, without any "hot" flavors.

Baharat is one of two extremely popular seasonings in Saudi Arabia; the other is *loomi*, or dried *Omani* lime, which lends an acidic flavor to meat dishes. Another important flavor is cinnamon, which is used in meat dishes. Other

[flavor] Saudi Arabia has a complex, herby, and vegetable/plant-based cuisine. Fruity and mildly acidic flavors are popular, as are mixtures of sweet and savory spices.

Figure Focus

Figure 11.26: Like Egypt and Iran, Saudi Arabia is bounded by water on two sides. How might this have affected its cultural and culinary development?

characteristic ingredients include saffron, tamarind, tomato (used for a tangy, fruity acidity), and tahini. As in nearby countries, lemon juice and olive oil are widely used.

Vegetables are prominent and include eggplant, cucumbers, zucchini, and okra (see Figure 11.27). Rice is the most popular grain, but wheat, including bulgur and couscous, are also common. Dates are extremely important and have been cultivated in Saudi Arabia for more than 4,000 years. Use them in both sweet and savory items, although date molasses is primarily used in desserts. Figs, melons, and pomegranates are also common fruits. Fresh herbs are used abundantly in Saudi Arabian cuisine, including parsley, mint, and cilantro. Dairy products, usually made from sheep's milk, include *laban* (yogurt) and *labneh* (strained yogurt). They are usually put into dishes or served as accompaniments, not consumed on their own. Seafood, especially prawns, is widely consumed in coastal areas, but not elsewhere.

Figure 11.27: Vegetables of the Saudi diet.

A common lamb dish, one that falls under the category of "street food," is *kebab meshwi*, or ground lamb molded around a stick and grilled. Bread commonly accompanies kebabs and shawarma (similar to the Egyptian shawarma and Greek gyro). *Mafrooda*, a leavened wheat flatbread, is a popular choice, but hollowed-out rolls are also used. Roasted chicken dishes are also popular street food.

[techniques]

Saudi Arabian Cooking Methods
Saudi Arabian cooking methods include baking, spit-roasting, grilling, and pickling.

733

- How did the Columbian Exchange affect Saudi Arabian cuisine? Was this significant?

- Compare the Saudi Arabian spice mixture *baharat* to spice mixtures commonly used in other countries.

- In what ways is Saudi Arabian cuisine more typically Middle Eastern than that of Egypt or Iran?

Reinforce and Review

- Other common flavoring ingredients include saffron, tamarind, tomato, tahini, lemon juice, and olive oil.

- Common vegetables include eggplant, cucumbers, zucchini, and okra; dates, which have been cultivated in the region for thousands of years, are extremely popular, as are figs, melons, and pomegranates.

- Rice is the most popular grain, although wheat is common.

- Fresh herbs are used abundantly, especially parsley, mint, and cilantro.

- Sheep's-milk products are popular ingredients and garnishes, not served alone; other animal proteins include lamb, chicken, egg, and—in coastal areas—seafood.

Teaching Tips

- Work with students to make fresh vegetable pickles, using some combination of vegetables and flavorings common in Saudi Arabia.

**Techniques:
Saudi Arabian Cooking Methods**

Encourage students to discuss the following:

- Why might pickling be an important cooking method in Saudi Arabia?

- Explain why grilling and spit-roasting are popular throughout much of the Middle East and Mediterranean.

Figure Focus

Figure 11.27: Which of these vegetables entered Saudi Arabia through the Columbian Exchange?

Nutrition:
Fat-Tailed Sheep

Encourage students to discuss the following:

- How has the use of fat from fat-tailed sheep made the traditional nomad diet more nutritious?

- What other benefits can fat-tailed sheep provide?

- Why is global demand for lean meat increasing?

Homework Activity:
Saudi Arabian Foods

Literacy Connection, 21st-Century Skills—Reason Effectively, Communicate Clearly, Information Literacy, Work Independently

Students should each identify and research a dish that they believe to be characteristically Saudi Arabian. They should explain its origins, ingredients, and cooking method.

Students should present an oral report describing the dish to the class.

Homework Activity:
Famous Figures—Saudi Arabia

Literacy Connection, 21st-Century Skills—Work Creatively with Others, Use Systems Thinking, Information Literacy, Communication and Collaboration, Social and Cross-Cultural Skills

Working in small groups, research a famous figure in Saudi Arabian cuisine. Prepare and present a group report discussing this individual's life and contributions to cuisine.

Alternately, present a report describing an important development in Saudi Arabian culture and how it affected the country's cuisines.

[nutrition]

Fat-Tailed Sheep

Fat-tailed sheep account for a quarter of the world's sheep. They are found throughout most of Africa, the Middle East, and parts of Asia (see Figure 11.28). These animals store fat in their tails. This tail fat is desirable for cooking. It is soft because it is kept away from the body's heat and surrounded by cooler air. Therefore, it melts more quickly than harder fats. Harder fats are also slightly less enjoyable when eaten. Hard fat has a higher melting point than soft fat, meaning that it hardens more quickly than soft fat. So as food cools, the hard fat they are cooked in begins to congeal, making them disagreeable to eat. Soft fat is much less likely to cause this result.

Historically, these large pieces of mutton-flavored fat were essential to nomad nutrition since fat was otherwise not a major component of the traditional diet. Although the use of tail fat has declined in recent years, these sheep are still common today. Their meat is lean (since most of the fat accumulates in the tail), and global demand for leaner meat continues to increase. The fat-tailed sheep is, therefore, quite versatile. It has provided fat when that was nutritionally desirable, and now it provides lean protein when that is nutritionally desirable. No wonder fat-tailed sheep account for so much of the world's sheep population!

Figure 11.28: Fat-tailed sheep account for a quarter of the world's sheep.

Summary

In this section, you learned the following:

- Egypt is part of the "Fertile Crescent." The rich Nile Valley and its delta are prime agricultural land, and the river floods annually to ensure a consistent harvest. However, most of the country is desert, and Egypt today imports more than 60 percent of its food.

734

Figure Focus

Figure 11.28: Fat-tailed sheep are characteristically leaner-bodied than other sheep, as demonstrated in this photograph.

- Most people still adhere to traditional diets, although influenced to some extent by the variety of cultures that have controlled or been controlled by Egypt throughout the centuries. Egypt was absorbed by the Islamic Empire in 639 and by the Ottoman Empire in 1517. Traders and colonizers introduced new food items such as rice and a variety of fruits from India, China, and Persia. Garlic, tahini, and chickpeas remain staple parts of the Egyptian cuisine today. Onions, which have been an essential ingredient since the pyramids were constructed, remain fundamental to contemporary diets, as do wheat and olives. Egypt's agriculture-based cuisine follows traditional foodways, especially in its heavy use of olive oil and wheat. Bread, vegetables, and legumes are also central to the typical Egyptian diet, and most flavorings are simple and straightforward: lemon juice, parsley, and sesame. Baking in clay ovens, braising, and roasting are common cooking methods.

- Iran, or Persia, is one of the world's oldest continuous civilizations, having been established around 7000 BCE. Iranians adopted Islam without adopting Arabian practices, maintaining a distinct Persian identity. A major influence on Iranian culture and cuisine came from its presence on the ancient Silk Road between China and modern Italy, a conduit for both ideas and ingredients such as long-grain rice, citrus fruits, and eggplant, all of which remain essential in the Iranian diet today. Persia reciprocated by sharing its own ingredients—like rosewater, pomegranates, and spinach—with other cultures.

- The key word in Iranian cuisine is "balanced." A good mixture of vegetables, dairy products, meat, herbs, and vegetables is presented at every meal. Pungent ingredients and sweet-and-sour combinations are popular in this very complex and aromatic cuisine. Popular cooking methods are the three-step rice method of soak-boil-steam; braising; and grilling.

- The food of Saudi Arabia has been influenced by a variety of sources, including trade with the Horn of Africa, India, Iraq, and the Mediterranean. The Persian Empire, which occupied the area around 550 BCE, introduced ingredients like saffron and rosewater, while Alexander the Great's regime brought Greek and Indian food to the region. The Islamic Empire later incorporated contemporary Saudi Arabia into both its territory and culinary traditions. The flavor profile is complex, herby, and vegetal. Fruity and mildly acidic flavors are popular, as are mixtures of sweet and savory spices. Common cooking methods are grilling, spit-roasting, and pickling.

735

Summary

- Remind students to review the following:
  1. Egypt—culture, ingredients, and dishes
  2. Iran—culture, ingredients, and dishes
  3. Saudi Arabia—culture, ingredients, and dishes

Section 11.3
Review Questions

1. Egyptian cuisine is predominantly vegetarian or vegan.

2. Iranian cuisine is balanced, using pungent ingredients and sweet-and-sour combinations; the cuisine is very complex and aromatic.

3. The three-step rice cooking method is soak-boil-steam.

4. Saudi Arabian cuisine is complex, herby, and vegetal, with fruity and mildly acidic flavors and mixtures of sweet and savory spices.

5. Students should research Saudi Arabian cuisine to identify pickled dishes.

6. Students may suggest a variety of dishes so long as they properly support their selections.

7. Students may choose any of the three cuisines discussed, although it will be more difficult to defend Iranian and Egyptian cuisines.

8. Students have been encouraged to discuss this issue throughout the text; their responses should sum up any classroom discussions as well as their own judgment after reading the text.

Section 11.3 Review Questions

1. How is the cuisine of Egypt unique among most of the other Middle Eastern countries?

2. What is the flavor profile of Iranian cuisine?

3. What is the three-step method for cooking rice in Iranian cuisine?

4. What is the flavor profile of Saudi Arabian cuisine?

5. Pickling is one of the common cooking methods in Saudi Arabia. Identify two dishes that are prepared by pickling and provide the recipes.

6. Miguel and Chef Kate feel as if they have enough meat dishes on their menu, so they want a vegetarian dish to represent Egypt. Choose a dish that you feel would not only taste great and represent the essence of the country well, but is also simple in preparation and will hold well given the circumstances under which it's being served. Explain why you chose the dish that you did.

7. Which cuisine do you feel best captures the "essence" of the Middle East? Explain your rationale.

8. What similarities do you see between the cuisine of the Middle East and that of the Mediterranean? What are some differences? Explain your answer in two paragraphs.

736

Section 11.3 Activities

1. Study Skills/Group Activity: Exploring the Middle East

Working with two or three other students, select a Middle Eastern country that is not covered in this chapter. Pick a typical recipe and then research its origins. Prepare the dish for your classmates, along with a brief presentation of your findings.

2. Independent Activity: Comparing Cuisines

Compare and contrast the cuisine of Greece with the cuisine of Saudi Arabia. What are the similarities? What are the differences? Why would there be similarities or differences? Write two paragraphs.

3. Critical Thinking: Middle Eastern Dinner

Create a three-course menu using ingredients and cooking techniques of the Middle East. Be sure to include the full recipe for each course you create and a full explanation of the cooking method you chose.

737

Section 11.3 Activities

1. Students should prepare the selected dish for their classmates, explaining its history and why it is typical of its country's cuisine.

2. Student answers will vary, but they should be logical and properly supported.

3. Student answers will vary. Students should submit copies of the recipes they choose and explain why the cooking methods used are appropriate.

Section 11.4
Asia

Introduce the Section

a. Explain the importance of studying Asian culture and history in terms of understanding American society.

b. Explain why China, Japan, and India are appropriate selections to introduce the breadth of Asian cuisines.

c. Discuss the objectives for the section.

Vocabulary Review

a. Direct students to the key terms.

b. Pronounce each word, and have the students repeat the pronunciation out loud.

c. Discuss the definition of each word.

Teach

Discuss

- It is as difficult to determine the precise boundaries of Asia as it is to determine the boundaries of the Mediterranean or the Middle East. Why does this present such a challenge? Does a country fit into one category or another based on its citizens' opinions and identities, so that if the people think they're Mediterranean, then they are Mediterranean? Why or why not?

- What comes to mind when students think of "Chinese food"? Why?

Reinforce and Review

- The Chinese were the first to control fire and use it to cook food.

- Traditionally, foods in China carry meaning or symbolism that goes beyond simple nourishment.

- Chinese cuisine is based on the philosophy of yin and yang, which is part of the Tao.

- Foods should not be forced to become what they are not: They should be kept in their most natural and pure states.

Teaching Tips

- Encourage students to discuss Asian cuisines that they have experienced, either at home or in restaurants. What have some characteristics of these meals been?

- Remind students that this is simply an introduction to Asian cuisines and should not be taken as all-encompassing.

11.1 Europe	11.2 The Mediterranean	11.3 The Middle East	11.4 Asia
• France	• Morocco	• Egypt	• China
• Italy	• Greece	• Iran	• Japan
• Spain	• Tunisia	• Saudi Arabia	• India

SECTION 11.4 ASIA

As with the Mediterranean and the Middle East, it can be difficult to determine the actual borders of Asia. Some feel that Asia includes not only the entire Middle East, but a significant part of the Mediterranean as well, extending as far west as Cyprus. Other definitions may include or exclude Australasia, Oceania, the Middle East, and the Mediterranean. Even using the most restrictive parameters, though, Asia contains a huge amount of the world's population and hundreds of its languages, so it's no surprise that so many of the continent's cuisines are world renowned. This section focuses on three of the best known in the United States: Chinese, Japanese, and Indian.

Study Questions

After studying Section 11.4, you should be able to answer the following questions:

- What are the cultural influences and flavor profiles of China?

- What are the cultural influences and flavor profiles of Japan?

- What are the cultural influences and flavor profiles of India?

China

Cultural Influences

China has a long, extensive history with food (see Figure 11.29 on the following page). The Chinese were the first to control fire and apply it to the cooking of food. Traditionally, foods in China have meaning beyond the nourishment they provide. Chinese cuisine is based on the yin and yang philosophy of the **Tao** (DOW), the belief that a single guiding principle orders the universe. Foods should not be forced to become something they are not and should be kept in

738

Homework Activity: Chinese Foods

Literacy Connection, 21st-Century Skills—Reason Effectively, Communicate Clearly, Information Literacy, Work Independently

Students should each identify and research a dish that they believe to be characteristically Chinese. They should explain its origins, ingredients, and cooking method.

Students should present an oral report describing the dish to the class.

Vocabulary Terms

- **Tao:** The belief that a single guiding principle orders the universe.

[flavor] Ginger, green onion, soy, and garlic are key flavors in Chinese cuisine. Two coexisting principles, "eat to live" and "eat for pleasure," describe grains as a source of nourishment, and vegetables and meat as sources of enjoyment.

their most natural and pure states. The Chinese believe that every food has an inherent character ranging from hot to cold. For example, cooked soybeans are hot, vinegar is mild, and spinach is cold. The Chinese often say that they eat the symbol, not the nourishment.

Chinese religious belief divides the world into five parts: earth, wood, fire, metal, and water. These correspond to the five flavors: sweet, sour, bitter, pungent, and salty. Each of these affect different parts of the body: stomach, liver, heart, lungs, and kidneys. Such relations among the natural elements of nature, food, and the human body lead to the Chinese principle of balance. Unlike a western meal with its division of meat, starch, and green vegetables, a Chinese recipe carefully combines *tan* (grains and rice) with *ts'ai* (vegetables and meat). Think for a moment of broccoli beef or sweet-and-sour pork; these classic dishes are good examples of combining *tan* and *ts'ai*.

Figure 11.29: In China, cuisine is based on the yin and yang philosophy.

Buddhism, in particular, has been a fundamental influence on Chinese lifestyles and cuisine. This religion emphasizes balance, serenity, and peace, which has led to the rise of vegetarianism and the simultaneous development of a number of innovative meat substitutes, especially those based on bean curd, in order to respect the lives of animals, which would otherwise be eaten. However, vegetarianism has not prevailed in all parts of China. In the north, for instance, Mongolian invasions have left a notable taste for lamb and mutton, and fresh seafood is essential in the coastal south and southeast.

739

Figure Focus
Figure 11.29: China's extreme size has enabled a number of regional cuisines to develop.

Homework Activity: Famous Figures—China

Literacy Connection, 21st-Century Skills—Work Creatively with Others, Use Systems Thinking, Information Literacy, Communication and Collaboration, Social and Cross-Cultural Skills

Working in small groups, research a famous figure in Chinese cuisine. Prepare and present a group report discussing this individual's life and contributions to cuisine.

Alternately, present a report describing an important development in Chinese culture and how it affected the country's cuisines.

Flavor Profile

Encourage students to discuss the following:

- What is the difference between eating to live and eating for pleasure? How are the two principles related?

- Is it possible to receive all the nourishment a healthy body requires from grains? Why or why not?

- Which is usually the most enjoyable and satisfying component of a meal: the grain, the vegetable, or the meat? Why?

Discuss

- What does it mean to "eat the symbol, not the nourishment"?

- Why is it important to have some understanding of Chinese religious beliefs when discussing Chinese culinary traditions?

Reinforce and Review

- The Chinese believe that every food has an inherent character, ranging from hot to cold.

- Chinese religious belief divides the world into five parts, each of which has a corresponding flavor and affects a corresponding body part: earth/sweet/stomach, wood/sour/liver, fire/bitter/heart, metal/pungent/lungs, and water/salty/kidneys.

- These relations among the elements of nature, food, and the human body lead to the Chinese principle of balance.

- Chinese meals and recipes combine *tan* and *ts'ai* to provide balance.

- Buddhism, which emphasizes balance, serenity, and peace, has had a profound impact on Chinese cuisines, including the rise of vegetarianism and the development of meat substitutes.

Teaching Tips

- Make sure students understand how vast China's landmass is to give them a sense of the importance of regional cuisines.

Vocabulary Terms

- *Tan:* Grains and rice.
- *Ts'ai:* Vegetables and meat.

Discuss

- Why have certain Chinese cuisines become more popular than others in the United States?

Reinforce and Review

- Trade has been a major influence on Chinese cuisines. The presence of the Silk Road allowed interaction as far west as Italy and as far south as India, introducing ginger, eggplant, and peppers.

- After 1911, when China opened its border to Western influences, trade across the Pacific Ocean brought European-style desserts and cooking equipment to China.

- China has the largest population in the world, with one of the largest landmasses. Three regional cuisines that have been influential in the United States include Mandarin, Szechwan-Hunan, and Canton.

- Chopsticks are the primary eating utensils in China, so stir-frying—in which foods are cut into small pieces before cooking—is very popular.

- Some common Chinese cooking techniques that are less known in the United States include velveting, lacquering, and red-cooking.

Vocabulary Terms

- **Velveting:** Pieces of meat are coated with cornstarch and egg whites before stir-frying, to retain moisture and improve sauce adherence.

- **Lacquered meats:** Larger items of meat are coated with multiple layers of a flavorful, sweet marinade before being roasted.

- **Red-cooking:** Meat or fish is stewed in a broth of soy sauce and water to develop a rich color and succulent taste.

Homework Activity: Duck, Duck, Goose

Literacy Connection, 21st-Century Skills—Critical Thinking and Problem Solving, Communicate Clearly, Information Literacy, Work Independently

What is Peking duck? How is it produced? What special equipment is needed to prepare it? How and with what is it eaten? Why is it important in Chinese cuisine and culture?

Discuss your findings, including any other material you consider relevant, in a one-page paper.

Trade has been another major factor in Chinese cuisines. Like so many other countries in this chapter, China was on the Silk Road, with well-established trade routes west to Rome and south to India. Ginger, eggplant, and peppers were introduced through this network (see Figure 11.30). After China opened its borders to western influences in 1911, trade across the Pacific Ocean swelled as the Chinese discovered European-style desserts and cooking equipment.

Figure 11.30: The Silk Road is a well-known trading route of ancient Chinese civilization.

China has the largest population in the world. The country is vast with many different climates: the cold mountains in the north, the coastal regions in the southeast, and the desert steppe in the west. A number of different languages and dialects as well as native cooking styles have developed over the centuries. Three of these cuisines are especially important to us since they are the most well known in the United States: **Mandarin**, **Szechwan-Hunan**, and **Canton**. It's best to discuss Chinese cuisine in the context of these three regions.

Regional Ingredients and Dishes

Before discussing specific regions, some general notes should be mentioned about Chinese cuisine as a whole. First, chopsticks, and to a lesser extent spoons, are the primary eating utensils of China. Therefore, carefully present dishes with no large pieces that could prove inconvenient to eat. Even foods cooked whole, like steamed fish, are sliced in the kitchen before presentation. The use of chopsticks fits well with the common technique of stir-frying; ingredients that are cut into small pieces for quick cooking are easily picked up with chopsticks.

Some unusual cooking methods should be noted here as well. For **velveting,** coat prepared meats with cornstarch and egg whites before stir-frying to retain moisture and improve sauce adherence. Prepare **lacquered meats** by brushing multiple layers of a flavorful, sweet marinade onto a cut of meat before roasting it. Finally, for **red-cooking,** stew meat or fish in a broth of soy sauce and water to develop a rich color and succulent taste.

740

Figure Focus

Figure 11.30: How has the Silk Road influenced culinary traditions in other cultures?

Mandarin

Mandarin is the cuisine of the northern region of China. Mandarin cuisine refers to the elaborate and delicate specialties prepared for the elite members of the imperial court in Peking. Typical ingredients include soy bean paste, dark soy sauce, rice wine, and onions, including garlic, leeks, scallions, and chives. Unlike other parts of China, northern China favors wheat, not rice, as the standard starch. Foods such as dumplings, noodles, and steamed buns filled with pork or minced garlic and scallions are frequently found on the menu. This region is famous for bird's nest soup, Peking duck, and *moo shu* pork (see Figure 11.31).

Figure 11.31: Bird's nest soup, Peking duck, and *moo shu* pork are traditional Mandarin dishes.

Szechwan-Hunan

The cuisine from the neighboring provinces of Szechwan and Hunan is best known for its hot, spicy food. The introduction of hot chili peppers 150 years ago from South America greatly changed the cooking style of this region. Once again, balance is an important factor in the cuisine. A well-trained chef uses the hot spices to enhance the flavor of food. As the heat fades away, the underlying five flavors described by the Tao should come forward.

Aside from chilis, cooks also use Szechwan pepper, garlic, scallions, five-spice powder (a blend of anise seed, Szechwan pepper, fennel seed, cloves, and cinnamon), mushrooms, ginger, and fennel. The primary meat items used are chicken and pork. Due to its distance from the sea, fish plays a very small part in Szechwan-Hunan cuisine. Examples of this cuisine with which most are familiar are *kung pao* chicken (Hunan) and hot and sour soup (Szechwan).

Canton

The city of Canton is situated on the Pearl River, 90 miles inland from the South China Sea. Because of this important location, it became an international trading center. This cuisine was the first to be introduced to the United States. The

741

Discuss

- Why is wheat preferred in northern China, when rice is preferred elsewhere?
- Relate Chinese and Iranian conceptions of balance. How are they similar?

Reinforce and Review

- Mandarin is the cuisine of imperial northern China, so its roots are elaborate and delicate. Common ingredients include soybean paste, dark soy sauce, rice wine, onions, pork, and duck.
- Wheat is the preferred starch of Mandarin cuisine; it appears as noodles, dumplings, and steamed buns.
- Famous Mandarin dishes include bird's-nest soup, Peking duck, and *moo shu* pork.
- Szechwan-Hunan cuisine is known for hot, spicy flavors, although the concept of balance remains important; other popular ingredients include Szechwan pepper, garlic, scallions, five-spice powder, mushrooms, ginger, fennel, chicken, and pork.
- Five-spice powder is a blend of anise seed, Szechwan pepper, fennel seed, cloves, and cinnamon.
- Famous Szechwan-Hunan dishes include *kung pao* chicken and hot and sour soup.
- Canton is located on the Pearl River, an important center for international trade; unsurprisingly, its cuisine was the first to be introduced to the United States.

Homework Activity: A-Choo!

Literacy Connection, 21st-Century Skills—Reason Effectively, Communicate Clearly, Information Literacy, Work Independently

Research Szechwan, or Sichuan, pepper. Investigate its culinary uses, its flavor, its production, other common names, and other information that you consider relevant.

Discuss your findings in a one-page paper.

Homework Activity: It's Soy Good

Science Connection, Literacy Connection, 21st-Century Skills—Critical Thinking and Problem Solving, Communicate Clearly, Information Literacy, Work Independently

Research the role of soy sauce in Chinese cuisine. What types of soy sauce are commonly available? What are their characteristics, and how are they used? What impact does the use of soy sauce have on the Chinese diet, from a flavor standpoint? What about from a nutritional perspective?

Discuss this information in a one-page report.

Figure Focus

Figure 11.31: What characteristics of each dish can students identify that mark the items as Mandarin?

Reinforce and Review

- Cantonese immigrants brought their culinary traditions to the United States during the nineteenth century.

- Cantonese cuisine strives for color harmony as well as a balance of yin and yang.

- Famous Cantonese dishes include sweet-and-sour pork, egg foo yung, and lemon chicken.

Teaching Tips

- Divide students into groups to practice the technique of red-cooking.

Essential Skills: Red-Cooking

Encourage students to discuss the following:

- Why is red-cooking popular throughout China, not just in a particular region?

- What ingredients might be particularly well-suited to this cooking technique? Which might not work so well?

- Why is sugar added to the cooking meat and vegetables? Compare this to some other cuisines discussed in this chapter.

Homework Activity: Rice

Science Connection, Literacy Connection, 21st-Century Skills—Critical Thinking and Problem Solving, Communicate Clearly, Information Literacy, Work Independently

Discuss the importance of rice in Asian cuisines, from both a nutritional and a cultural perspective. Why is it so prevalent, and why is it so respected? How much rice is consumed annually in Asia, and which types are most popular? What role does rice play in nutrition? How is rice typically prepared?

Discuss these and any other aspects of rice you consider important in a one-page paper.

CUSTOMIZED INSTRUCTION

Literacy Connection, 21st-Century Skills— Solve Problems, Communicate Clearly, Information Literacy, Work Independently

Less Advanced Students

Besides rice, what other starches are consumed in Asia? Where do these predominate?

Chinese men who immigrated to California during the gold rush and later to work on the building of the transcontinental railroad brought with them their cooking techniques. Many of their native dishes remained the same. The cuisine of this region strives for color harmony as well as a yin and yang balance. The most notable dishes are sweet-and-sour pork, egg foo yung, and lemon chicken.

Essential Skills
Red-Cooking

Red-Cooking, a long, slow braising in a mixture of soy sauce and water, is a common technique throughout much of China for the flavorful, moist stew it produces.

❶ Sweat ginger and other aromatics in hot oil. See Figure 11.32a.

❷ Add chunks of meat and sear. See Figure 11.32b.

❸ Add water, dark soy sauce, and broth and bring to a boil.

❹ Cover and simmer one hour or longer.

❺ Add vegetables, light soy sauce, more dark soy sauce, and brown sugar.

❻ Simmer uncovered 30 minutes or until the vegetables are tender and meat pieces are extremely tender but still intact.

❼ If desired, remove the meat and vegetables, strain out aromatics, and reduce the sauce.

❽ Serve hot with rice or noodles. See Figure 11.32c.

Figure 11.32a: Step 1—Sweat ginger and aromatics in hot oil.

Figure 11.32b: Step 2—Add meat and sear.

Figure 11.32c: Step 8—Serve hot with rice or noodles.

Figure Focus

Figure 11.32a: Ginger, garlic, and scallions are popular aromatics in much of China.

Figure 11.32b: Properly searing the meat will help develop the appropriate color and flavor in the finished dish.

Figure 11.32c: The finished product takes on a rich reddish color with a pronounced sheen.

CUSTOMIZED INSTRUCTION

Literacy Connection, 21st-Century Skills—Make Judgments and Decisions, Communicate Clearly

Special Needs Students

Have you ever eaten Chinese foods? Which ones? Which flavors were especially prominent?

[techniques]

Chinese Cooking Methods
Chinese cooking methods include stir-frying, steaming, red-cooking, lacquering, and velveting.

[fast fact]

Did You Know...?
Soy sauce, which originated in China, is a liquid made by fermenting soybeans and roasted wheat or barley in brine. Its use as a condiment traces back at least 2,500 years.

Japan

Cultural Influences

Japan's close neighbors, China and Korea, have traditionally played major roles in its culture through both trade and religion (see Figure 11.33). Buddhism entered from China in the sixth century, and meat eating and animal slaughter were soon (although ineffectually) banned. In the twelfth century, Zen Buddhism, tea, and frying also arrived, radically changing Japanese culture. An entire set of ceremonies, as well as an entire cuisine (*cha kaiseki*), soon arose around tea drinking, and a vegetarian cuisine in keeping with Zen Buddhism (*shojin ryori*) quickly developed.

Figure 11.33: Japan's cuisine and culture has been influenced by trade with China and Korea.

743

Figure Focus
Figure 11.33: How does Japan's geographic position affect its cuisines?

**Homework Activity:
Japanese Foods**

Literacy Connection, 21st-Century Skills—Reason Effectively, Communicate Clearly, Information Literacy, Work Independently

Students should each identify and research a dish that they believe to be characteristically Japanese. They should explain its origins, ingredients, and cooking method.

Students should present an oral report describing the dish to the class.

**Techniques:
Chinese Cooking Methods**

Encourage students to discuss the following:

- Most of the other cuisines discussed in this chapter have used cooking methods that are common in the United States. Why are some common Chinese cooking techniques relatively unknown here?

- How does steaming help to reinforce the principle that foods should be kept in their most natural and pure states?

- How does lacquering resemble barbecuing? Compare the two cooking techniques.

**Fast Fact:
Did You Know . . . ?**

Encourage students to discuss the following:

- What other culinary uses do soybeans have?

- Why are soybeans so commonly used throughout Chinese cuisine?

- In what other cuisines are soy products widely used?

Discuss

- Russia is geographically near to Japan. Why have its cuisine and culture had so little effect on Japan?

Reinforce and Review

- China and Korea have significantly influenced Japanese culture through both trade and religion.

- The introduction of Buddhism resulted in the banning of meat eating and animal slaughter in Japan.

- In the twelfth century, the arrival of Zen Buddhism, tea, and frying radically changed Japanese culture, resulting in the development of two new cuisines.

- *Cha kaiseki* is the cuisine of tea drinking, and *shojin ryori* is the vegetarian cuisine following the tenets of Zen Buddhism.

Teaching Tips

- Use a map to demonstrate Japan's physical proximity to Korea, China, and Russia.

Vocabulary Terms

- *Cha kaiseki*: A ritualized cuisine in which meals are served in the context of a formal tea ceremony.

Flavor Profile

Encourage students to discuss the following:

- How is the Japanese flavor profile similar to and different from the Chinese flavor profile?

- Why is soy such an important ingredient in Japanese cuisine?

- Explain why strong flavors, like ginger and wasabi, might be necessary to Japanese cuisine.

[flavor] Characteristic flavors of Japanese food include ginger, miso (a fermented soybean paste), shoyu (soy sauce), wasabi (a hot herb similar to horseradish), and most important, dashi. Dashi is a flavorful broth made of dried, smoked, and cured bonito (a type of tuna), and dried *konbu* (a type of seaweed). Soy, tea, and rice are all essential ingredients.

Trade with Westerners has also affected Japanese culture. During the sixteenth and early seventeenth centuries AD, explorers and traders, especially Portuguese, introduced ingredients like tomatoes, sweet potatoes, and peppers. They also introduced cooking techniques like baking and deep-frying, which was quickly adopted as tempura (tehm-POOR-uh). However, the country was closed to Westerners in the early seventeenth century as a result of interference in political affairs. Japan was almost entirely isolated until it reopened to trade in 1853 AD. Today, Japanese cuisine is strongly influenced by Western cultures and cuisines.

Regional Ingredients and Dishes

Although Japan is an island nation, the cuisine is largely based on agriculture. Rice cultivation is fundamental to the society itself. The word for cooked rice, **gohan** (goh-HAHN), also means meal, demonstrating its essential nature to the cuisine. The other major agricultural product is soybeans. They are used in a variety of culinary forms, with tofu (TOH-foo), shoyu (SHOH-yoo), and miso (MEE-soh) being perhaps the most prominent. With rice providing the carbohydrates and soy providing the protein and fat, the Japanese could enjoy a virtually complete protein and adequate calorie diet with just these two ingredients. However, plenty of other foods are available to the Japanese despite the country's space limitations. A broad range of seafood, including sea vegetables, is part of the diet. Other important flavors include wasabi, sesame, vinegar, daikon radish, and shiitake mushrooms (see Figure 11.34 on the following page).

The Japanese prioritize quality over quantity in their food, prizing each ingredient individually. Visual appeal is as important as the food itself, so preparation and presentation are meticulous. This stems from the Zen Buddhist principle of **wabi sabi**, which means quiet simplicity merged with quiet elegance. Accordingly, seasonality, even microseasonality, is an important principle in Japanese cuisine. Ingredients are used only at their peak, both to extract maximum enjoyment for the diner and to show respect for the item's life cycle.

744

Discuss

- Like Japan, Egypt is considered to have an agriculture-based cuisine despite its long coastline. How are the two cuisines and cultures similar and different?

- How does the use of a single word for both "cooked rice" and "meal" signal the importance of rice in Japanese society?

- How is the principle of *wabi sabi* related to the Chinese conception of balance?

Reinforce and Review

- Trade with Westerners, especially the Portuguese, introduced ingredients like tomatoes, sweet potatoes, and peppers, and brought cooking techniques like baking and deep-frying.

- Despite Japan's 200-year closure to Westerners, today it is strongly influenced by Western culture and cuisines.

- Japanese cuisine is fundamentally based on agriculture. Rice cultivation is essential to Japanese culture, and soybean cultivation is also very important.

- Soybeans are used to make tofu, shoyu (soy sauce), and miso.

- Together, rice and soy could provide a virtually complete protein and adequate calorie diet with no other foods necessary.

- Other important ingredients include seafood and sea vegetables, wasabi, sesame, vinegar, daikon radish, and shiitake mushrooms.

- The Japanese prioritize quality of food over quantity, prizing visual appeal, seasonality, and respect for ingredients.

Vocabulary Terms

- *Gohan:* The Japanese word for both "cooked rice" and for "meal."

- *Wabi sabi:* A Zen Buddhist principle of quiet simplicity merged with quiet elegance.

Sea vegatables   Wasabi   Sesame

Vinegar (rice)   Daikon   Shiitake

Figure 11.34: Common Japanese flavors.

[techniques]

Japanese Cooking Methods
Japanese cooking methods focus on tempura, sushi, sashimi, bento, steaming, *nabemono* (one-pot dishes), teriyaki, *tsukemono* (salt-pickling), and *yakimono* (grilling and pan-frying).

Northern Japan, Hokkaido, produces not only most of the seafood consumed domestically, but also cultivates sheep and a wide variety of vegetables. Wheaten ramen noodles were developed here. Farther south lies the rice belt, where various mountain vegetables as well as *maitake* mushrooms are also found. Buckwheat soba noodles are popular here, as are hot-pot dishes using local seafood. Tokyo and its surrounding area are famous for *nigiri-sushi* (seasoned rice topped with raw fish), seafood, and soybean products (see Figure 11.35 on the following page). Kansai, in the west, produces a wide variety of food: vegetables, rice, fruit, and the famous Kobe beef. *Sukiyaki*, a dish of beef and vegetables cooked in shoyu, originated here, and udon noodles are a specialty. In the south, Kyushu grows a number of different vegetable and fruit crops, including onions and strawberries, and is a major producer of shiitake mushrooms.

745

Discuss
- What geographic characteristics influence Japanese cuisines?

Reinforce and Review
- Hokkaido, northern Japan, produces most of the seafood consumed in Japan, as well as a wide variety of vegetables; wheaten ramen noodles were developed there.
- In the rice belt, mountain vegetables and *maitake* mushrooms are also produced; buckwheat soba noodles and hot-pots using local seafood are popular.
- Tokyo and its environs are famous for *nigiri-sushi*, seafood, and soybean products.
- Kansai, in the west, produces vegetables, fruit, rice, and Kobe beef; *sukiyaki* and udon noodles are specialties.
- Southern Kyushu grows a wide variety of vegetables and fruit, including onions, strawberries, and shiitake mushrooms.

Teaching Tips
- Bring a variety of soy-based ingredients to class so students can taste them.
- Make instant dashi and encourage students to taste it.

Techniques:
Japanese Cooking Methods

Encourage students to discuss the following:

- Which of these techniques are commonly used in the United States?
- How might *nabemono* resemble one-pot dishes from other cuisines?
- How can respect for ingredients be demonstrated through one's cooking methods?

Figure Focus
Figure 11.34: What do these ingredients have in common?

Homework Activity:
Kobe Beef

Literacy Connection, 21st-Century Skills—Critical Thinking and Problem Solving, Communicate Clearly, Information Literacy, Work Independently

What is Kobe beef? Explain how the cattle are raised and how their meat differs from conventionally produced beef in flavor, appearance, and texture. Describe suitable cooking methods, and investigate the growing popularity of Kobe beef in the United States.

Produce a one-page report on your findings.

Homework Activity:
Famous Figures—Japanese

Literacy Connection, 21st-Century Skills—Work Creatively with Others, Use Systems Thinking, Information Literacy, Communication and Collaboration, Social and Cross-Cultural Skills

Working in small groups, research a famous figure in Japanese cuisine. Prepare and present a group report discussing this individual's life and contributions to cuisine.

Alternately, present a report describing an important development in Japanese culture and how it affected the country's cuisines.

Nutrition: Tofu

Encourage students to discuss the following:

- Why are soybeans and soy products consumed in so many parts of Asia?

- What nutrients do soy foods provide?

- What are some cooking methods that are appropriate for tofu?

CUSTOMIZED INSTRUCTION

Science Connection, Literacy Connection, 21st-Century Skills—Critical Thinking and Problem Solving, Communicate Clearly, Information Literacy, Work Independently

More Advanced Students

Traditionally, the tongue was believed to identify four basic tastes: salty, sweet, sour, and bitter. However, scientific advances have shown that the tongue can recognize other tastes as well, such as spicy or floral.

An important development in the study of taste was the discovery of umami, a meaty or savory sensation. This concept is important in contemporary Japan and is becoming more popular worldwide.

Research umami, including foods in which it is found, its uses, and other information you consider relevant. Write a two-page report describing umami's scientific and culinary importance.

CUSTOMIZED INSTRUCTION

Literacy Connection, 21st-Century Skills—Reason Effectively, Communicate Clearly, Work Independently

ESOL Students

Some of the cuisines discussed in this chapter have been based on underlying religious or philosophical guidelines. Is your cuisine of origin based on principles like these? If so, describe them in a brief essay.

Futomaki   Hosomaki   Uramaki

Nigiri-sushi   Inari   Temaki

Figure 11.35: Types of sushi, including nigiri-sushi.

[nutrition]

Tofu

Soybeans and rice are the two staple agricultural products of many Asian diets. Soybeans provide protein and fat. Rice provides needed carbohydrates. Soybean protein absorption is improved by making the fermented soybean curd, tofu (see Figure 11.36).

Tofu, or bean curd, is a soft or firm cheese-like product, high in available protein and versatile enough to handle nearly any cooking method. To make tofu, soak soybeans in water and then grind and boil them. After a careful straining, combine the resulting warm liquid with either calcium sulfate or lye, which causes the proteins to solidify. Then pour or ladle this soft substance into molds and press it to develop the desired amount of firmness. The tofu is now ready to sell, cook, or even eat as is. When combined with rice, it can make a nearly perfect meal from a nutritional standpoint.

Figure 11.36: Tofu.

Figure Focus

Figure 11.35: Is sushi always made of raw fish? What are some other common ingredients?

Figure 11.36: Fresh tofu is available in firm, silken, or dried form, and is made from soy milk.

India

Cultural Influences

Since the fourth century, Hinduism has evolved as the dominant faith in India (see Figure 11.37). Hinduism promotes vegetarianism and discourages meat consumption. Today, 80 percent of Indians belong to the Hindu faith. But India has had many cultural influences.

In the eighth century, the Islamic Empire spread into northern India, where several separate kingdoms were eventually established. In 1562 AD, these were unified as the Moghul Empire. This culture was strongly influenced by Persia, and rulers emulated the Persian cuisine with the Indian

Figure 11.37: Indian culture and cuisine were strongly influenced by Persia.

ingredients at hand. Lamb and even kebabs (kuh-BOB) were popularized, as were polos and biryanis. Meat dishes cooked with cream, nuts, and dried fruits also became prominent. All these remain part of contemporary Indian cuisine.

Trade affected the development of Indian cuisine as well. The Arabs were able to control the lucrative spice trade from the seventh century onward, as they were the only traders with a clear-cut path to India. They brought food items from along the Spice Road in exchange. In 1498 AD, however, Vasco da Gama discovered a sea route to India, breaking the Arab stranglehold. The Portuguese

[flavor] Complex, aromatic, and subtle spice mixtures characterize Indian cuisine. Grains, legumes, and vegetables are combined in both spare and luxurious ways, using a wide variety of cooking techniques.

747

Figure Focus

Figure 11.37: Like China, India has an extremely large landmass and therefore a number of regional cuisines.

Teaching Tips

- Use a map to help students understand the various cultures and climates that compose India.

Homework Activity: Famous Figures—India

Literacy Connection, 21st-Century Skills—Work Creatively with Others, Use Systems Thinking, Information Literacy, Communication and Collaboration, Social and Cross-Cultural Skills

Working in small groups, research a famous figure in Indian cuisine. Prepare and present a group report discussing this individual's life and contributions to cuisine.

Alternately, present a report describing an important development in Indian culture and how it affected the country's cuisines.

Discuss

- Religious beliefs have profoundly affected many Asian cuisines. What culinary traditions in other regions of the world have been influenced by religions?

- How can trade monopolies affect a region's economics and culture?

Reinforce and Review

- Hinduism is the dominant faith in India, accounting for 80 percent of the population; it promotes vegetarianism and discourages meat consumption.

- The Islamic Empire occupied much of what is now northern India; this region later became the Moghul Empire.

- The Moghul Empire was strongly influenced by Persian culture, and Persian cuisine was mimicked with Indian ingredients; lamb, kebabs, elaborate rice dishes, and meat dishes cooked with cream, nuts, and dried fruit became and remain popular.

- For centuries, Arab traders monopolized the Indian spice trade, bringing with them the ingredients and techniques they encountered along the route.

- In 1498, Vasco da Gama discovered a sea route to India, opening the region to multiple trading partners.

Homework Activity: Indian Foods

Literacy Connection, 21st-Century Skills— Reason Effectively, Communicate Clearly, Information Literacy, Work Independently

Students should each identify and research a dish that they believe to be characteristically Indian. They should explain its origins, ingredients, and cooking method.

Students should present an oral report describing the dish to the class.

Flavor Profile

Encourage students to discuss the following:

- Based on the flavor profiles discussed in this chapter and Chapter 10, what other cuisines does India's resemble? Why?

- Why is there relatively little meat consumption in India? How might this affect its flavor profile?

- What do students think of when they think about "Indian food"? What ingredients do they expect to encounter?

Reinforce and Review

- Once the sea route to India had been found, subsequent explorers brought ingredients like peppers, potatoes, and cashews, all of which became important in Indian cuisine.

- The British left the most profound impact on Indian cuisine. The British East India Company traded spices, so its employees were extremely interested in food, and under the British Raj a new Anglo-Indian cuisine developed.

- India is the second-most populous country in the world, and therefore offers a wide variety of ingredients, flavors, and cooking techniques.

- Turmeric, cumin, coriander, and red pepper are commonly used in curry dishes.

- Kashmir retains many Moghul culinary traditions; hearty, dry meat dishes, such as *rogan josh*, are popular.

- Common Kashmiri ingredients include masalas, lamb, sheep, goat, saffron, ghee, and dried fruit.

Teaching Tips

- Students should understand that "curry" is a generic term, with no fixed meaning.

Homework Activity:
Hello, Dal-ly!

Science Connection, Literacy Connection, 21st-Century Skills—Critical Thinking and Problem Solving, Communicate Clearly, Information Literacy, Work Independently

Research the importance of dal in India, both from a nutritional and a cultural perspective. What varieties of dal are commonly consumed in India, and in what ways? How does dal contribute both flavor and nutrition to the Indian diet?

Describe your research in a one-page paper.

Vocabulary Terms

- **Masala:** A mixture made by grinding and frying a combination of spices at the time of use; these mixtures are common in Kashmiri cuisine.

- **Garam masala:** A popular masala made with strong-tasting spices, like black cardamom, black pepper, and clove.

---

were followed by other explorers (from Britain, France, Holland, Denmark, and Spain), bringing new ingredients like peppers, potatoes, and cashews.

The British left the most profound impact of all on Indian cuisine. In the early eighteenth century, the British East India Company was formed to compete in the spice trade. It rapidly became very successful, causing its senior employees to become decadent and food obsessed. Having defeated their rivals by the middle of the next century, the British established a new empire, the British Raj. They introduced cutlery, dining tables, and French cooking techniques to India, blending the latter with Indian methods to develop a distinctly Anglo-Indian cuisine. Today, a strong relationship persists between the two countries, although India gained independence some 60 years ago.

Regional Ingredients and Dishes

As the second-most populous country in the world, India has an enormous diversity of ingredients, flavors, and cooking techniques, so only a very few can be addressed here. Of course, most of us think of curry when we think of traditional Indian cooking. Curry is not really a spice; it is a dish. Some specific spices used in curry dishes include turmeric, cumin, coriander, and red pepper.

Kashmir, in Northern India, retains many of the foodways left behind by the Moghuls. Hearty, dry dishes are popular, often based on goat, lamb, or sheep. *Rogan josh* is a popular dish, a rich combination of steamed lamb in a spicy yogurt sauce, enriched with ground almonds. **Masalas** (mah-SAH-lahs), spice mixtures that preparers grind and fry before they add them to dishes, are important in Kashmiri cuisine (see Figure 11.38). **Garam masala** (gah-RAHM mah-SAH-lah) is particularly enjoyed; it includes a variety of strong-tasting spices such as black cardamom, black pepper, and clove, so it is generally considered too overpowering to use in fish or vegetable dishes. Saffron, ghee (a clarified semi-fluid butter), and dried fruits are also common.

Figure 11.38: The various spices that comprise Masala spice mixture.

748

Figure Focus

Figure 11.38: What spices can students identify?

Homework Activity:
Regional Cuisines

Literacy Connection, 21st-Century Skills—Critical Thinking and Problem Solving, Communicate Clearly, Information Literacy, Work Independently

Each student should select (or be assigned) a different region of India and research its cuisine, including principal ingredients, flavor profiles, cultural influences on cuisine, and important dishes.

Write a one-page report describing the region's cuisine.

The nearby Punjab enjoys a cuisine based on wheat, vegetables, and dairy. Many Punjabis belong to the vegetarian Sikh religion, though other residents consume meat. Tandoori cookery is important here, as in Kashmir. One famous dish is *raan mussalam*, or leg of lamb roasted in a tandoori (tahn-DOOR-ee) with a marinade of papaya and yogurt. Delhi, on the other hand, mixes Moghul and Punjabi cuisine, so a characteristic dish is a spicy korma, which is seafood or meat cooked with a spicy, yogurt-based sauce, usually reserved as a celebratory food.

In the region of Rajasthani, cuisine emphasizes the use of dals, or pulses, although it is not an especially vegetarian state. Cooks of this region often marinate skewered meat in yogurt and spices before grilling, as in the Middle East, and elaborate chicken and meat dishes with rice are popular for festivals. In Gujarat, however, the presence of Jainism, an ancient religion, ensures a healthy vegetarian cuisine. Stir-fried vegetables with mustard and chili or saucy curries served with chutney are typical. Finally, West Bengal is noted for its use of *panchphoron*, or "five-spice." It is a pungent combination of cumin, fennel, fenugreek, mustard, and onion seed. *Mangsho jhol*, a lamb curry, is popular here, as are cheese patties cooked in syrup (see Figure 11.39).

An important cooking method in northern India is **dum**, a type of steaming in which preparers cover the cooking pot and seal it with strips of dough. They place the pot directly over heat with hot coals atop it. This concept is also found in European peasant cuisines.

Figure 11.39: Tasty *chum-chums* are cheese patties cooked in syrup.

Tropical southern cooking tends to be lighter and hotter than its northern counterpart. Goa, an island overtaken by the Portuguese in the early days of colonialism, retains several characteristics of Portuguese cuisine today, such as the use of pork, vinegar, and cashews. Fish curry is prominent, as is vindaloo (VIHN-dah-loo), a spicy meat stew with hot peppers and vinegar. Kerala, the only state in India where it is legal to sell beef, uses a wide variety of spices and tropical flavors—coconut, ginger, cardamom—in its cuisine. Seafood and stews are popular.

Some other important culinary elements include flatbreads and crackers, like chapati (chah-PAH-tee), naan (NAHN), paratha (pah-RAH-tah), and *poppadum* (PAH-pah-duhm). These may be made of lentils, chickpeas, or wheat. Dal,

749

Figure Focus
Figure 11.39: *Chum-chums* are traditional sweets from Bengal, in western India.

- What similarities and differences can you identify in Chinese and Indian cuisines?
- How are Indian flatbreads similar to and different from the flatbreads used in other cuisines we have discussed?

Reinforce and Review
- The Punjab cuisine is based on wheat, vegetables, and dairy; tandoori cookery is popular, as in *raan mussalam*, although many Punjabi belong to the vegetarian Sikh religion.
- Kormas, meat or seafood cooked with a spicy yogurt sauce, are popular celebratory items in Delhi, which combines Moghul and Punjabi cuisines.
- Rajasthani cuisine emphasizes the use of dals; popular foods include skewered, marinated, and grilled meat and elaborate chicken and meat dishes.
- The Jain population in Gujarat enjoys a vegetarian cuisine; popular items include stir-fried vegetables with mustard and chili.
- West Bengal is known for *panchphoron*, a spice mixture including cumin, fennel, fenugreek, mustard, and onion seed, and for its *mangsho jhol*, a lamb curry.
- Southern cooking tends to be lighter and hotter than northern cooking.
- Goa retains the culinary traditions of its Portuguese occupiers, such as the use of pork, vinegar, and cashews; fish curries and spicy meat vindaloos are popular.
- Kerala, the only state in India where the sale of beef is legal, incorporates many spices and tropical flavors, such as coconut, cardamom, and ginger, into its cuisine, and seafood and stews are popular.
- Throughout India, flatbreads and crackers are popular. These may be made of lentils, chickpeas, or wheat.

Teaching Tips
- Provide images of a tandoori oven and explain to students how these are operated.

Vocabulary Terms
- **Dum:** A type of steaming in which preparers cover the cooking pot and seal it with strips of dough; popular in northern India and also used in some European peasant traditions.

Discuss

- Why have dal become so prominently used throughout India? Compare the Indian use of dal to the Egyptian use of fava beans.

Reinforce and Review

- Dal are the dried legumes and pulses popular throughout India and much of the Middle East.

- *Pulao* is a one-pot dish of vegetables, fruit, nuts, spices, meat or fish, and sometimes yogurt, reserved for special occasions and originating in Persian times.

- Another Persian dish, today used for celebrations, is biryani. This one-pot meal uses basmati rice, meat, vegetables, and spices.

- *Tarka* is the technique of scattering whole or ground spices into hot fat until they pop, flavoring the oil.

- *Bhuna* is similar to stir-frying, but with a small amount of water added

- Korma is a yogurt-based braise incorporating spices and nuts.

- *Talana* involves deep-frying items that have been dunked into a legume-based batter.

Teaching Tips

- Students have now reached the end of the second year of the program. Encourage them to discuss what they have learned over the last two years. What information was particularly helpful? What do they think was overlooked or omitted? Do they believe that this program is a good introduction to the restaurant and foodservice industry?

Techniques: Indian Cooking Methods

Encourage students to discuss the following:

- Why does *talana* use a legume-based batter instead of a flour-based batter?

- When meat is braised using the korma method, what role does the yogurt play?

- What other cuisines have cooking methods similar to these?

---

or dried legumes and pulses, are virtually ubiquitous throughout India, as they are in many parts of the Middle East. *Pulao* and biryani reflect their Persian ancestry. *Pulao* is a one-pot dish of vegetables, fruit, nuts, spice, and meat, fish, and/or yogurt. Biryani, also a one-pot meal, involves basmati rice, meat, vegetables, and spices. Both are elaborate dishes, reserved for special occasions.

Finally, some cooking techniques uncommon outside India should be noted. *Tarka* is the technique of scattering dry whole or ground spices into hot oil or ghee until they pop, flavoring the oil. *Bhuna* is similar to stir-frying, but with a small amount of water added. Korma is a yogurt-based braise including spices and nuts, using meat or seafood (for celebrations). *Talana* involves deep-frying items after dunking them in a legume-based batter.

[techniques]
Indian Cooking Methods

Indian cooking methods include steaming, *dum*, tandoor, *tarka*, *bhuna*, korma, and *talana*.

[what's new?]
Technology and Rice Cultivation

Rice is a staple food throughout much of the world. It is grown in more than 100 countries in a wide range of environments. Perhaps 100,000 varieties exist, although "only" 8,000 have been used for food in contemporary times.

Traditionally, the best varieties provided small but regular yields if managed properly. Because of its importance, research in rice breeding and cultivating is ongoing in an effort to find varieties that can combine high yields and nutritional value with growing conditions and requirements suited to particular areas. The "Green Revolution" of the 1960s and 1970s was a part of this work, resulting in the much-planted IR36 variety.

But growing rice remains a blend of ancient and modern technologies. In much of southern and eastern Asia, rice is grown the traditional way. Tiny, terraced fields are usually flooded with water from either rainfall or irrigation. The fields are then planted with rice seedlings and are cultivated and harvested by hand. This method helps preserve traditional local habitats.

In other places with larger fields and more money available, germinated rice seeds are tossed over a prepared field from an airplane, and computers and heavy equipment are used to manage and harvest the crop. New technologies and new rice varieties are on the horizon as researchers and farmers seek to provide more food for a rapidly growing global population.

750

What's New: Technology and Rice Cultivation

Encourage students to discuss the following:

- Why is it important to combine traditional and contemporary methods of rice growing?

- How many kinds of rice can students identify?

- How many rice-growing countries can students identify?

Summary

In this section, you learned the following:

- Chinese cuisine is based on the yin and yang philosophy of the Tao, which is the belief that a single guiding principle orders the universe. Foods should not be forced to become something they are not and should be kept in their most natural and pure states. The Chinese believe that every food has an inherent character ranging from hot to cold. Chinese religious belief divides the world into five parts: earth, wood, fire, metal, and water. These correspond to the five flavors: sweet, sour, bitter, pungent, and salty. Each of these affect different parts of the body: stomach, liver, heart, lungs, and kidneys. Such relations among the natural elements of nature, food, and the human body lead to the Chinese principle of balance. Ginger, green onion, soy, and garlic are key flavors in Chinese cuisine. Two coexisting principles, "eat to live" and "eat for pleasure," describe grains as a source of nourishment and vegetables and meat as sources of enjoyment. Chinese cooking methods are varied, including velveting, lacquering, and stir-frying.

- Japan's close neighbors, China and Korea, have traditionally played major roles in its culture through trade and religion. Buddhism entered from China in the sixth century, and meat eating and animal slaughter were soon (although ineffectually) banned. In the twelfth century, Zen Buddhism, tea, and frying also arrived, radically changing Japanese culture. Trade with Westerners has also affected Japanese culture. Today, Japanese cuisine is strongly influenced by Western cultures and cuisines. Characteristic flavors of Japanese food include ginger, miso, shoyu, wasabi, and most important, dashi. Soy, tea, and rice are all essential ingredients. Popular Japanese cooking methods include tempura, sushi, and teriyaki.

- Since the fourth century, Hinduism has evolved as the dominant faith in India. Hinduism promotes vegetarianism and discourages meat consumption. Today, 80 percent of Indians belong to the Hindu faith. But India has had many other cultural influences. The British left the most profound impact of all on Indian cuisine. They introduced cutlery, dining tables, and French-cooking techniques to India, blending the latter with Indian methods to develop a distinctly Anglo-Indian cuisine. Complex, aromatic, and subtle spice mixtures characterize Indian cuisine. Grains, legumes, and vegetables are combined in both spare and luxurious ways, using a wide variety of cooking techniques. Tandoor, *khuma*, and korma are among many varied cooking methods in India.

751

Summary

- Remind students to review the following:
  1. China—culture, ingredients, and dishes
  2. Japan—culture, ingredients, and dishes
  3. India—culture, ingredients, and dishes

Section 11.4
Review Questions

1. Chinese cooking methods include stir-frying, steaming, red-cooking, lacquering, and velveting.

2. Characteristic Japanese flavors include ginger, miso, shoyu, wasabi, and dashi.

3. Indian cooking methods include steaming, *dum*, tandoor, *tarka*, *bhuna*, korma, and *talana*.

4. The flavor profile of Indian cuisine is complex, aromatic, and subtle.

5. Students may answer in various ways, as long as they clearly and logically defend their positions.

6. Students may suggest a variety of dishes, but their selections should be suitable for the pro-posed festival: easy to serve, easy to maintain quality and safety over time, and so on.

7. Student responses may vary as long as they clearly and logically defend their answers.

8. Student responses may vary as long as they prop-erly support their arguments.

Section 11.4 Review Questions

1. What are three signature Chinese cooking methods?

2. Name three flavors characteristic of Japanese cuisine.

3. What are three signature Indian cooking methods?

4. How would you explain the flavor profile of Indian cuisine?

5. Chinese cuisine is based on the yin and yang philosophy of the Tao, the belief that a single guiding principle orders the universe. Foods should not be forced to become something they are not and should be kept in their most natural and pure states. How do you think Lina Fat would view this philosophy? Why?

6. Miguel and Chef Kate want to include a dish for their event that is distinctly Japanese. What dish would you suggest for them? Explain your rationale.

7. In what way do you feel Japanese cuisine has been most influenced by China?

8. Of the three cuisines covered in this section, which two do you feel are most similar to each other? Why? Explain your choice in two paragraphs.

Section 11.4 Activities

1. Study Skills/Group Activity: Exploring Asia

Working with two or three other students, select an Asian country that is not covered in this chapter. Compare its cuisine to the cuisine of a country discussed in this section (China, Japan, or India). Write a two- or three-paragraph report on your findings.

2. Independent Activity: Researching Korma

Often the evolution of a region's cuisine can tell a lot about its history. Research the Indian cooking method korma. From where does the name derive? Why was it originally created? How and why has it changed over the years? Report your findings in a one-page report.

3. Critical Thinking: Asian Dinner

Create a three-course menu using ingredients and cooking techniques of Asia. Be sure to include the full recipe for each course you create.

Section 11.4 Activities

1. Student answers may vary but should clearly compare the selected cuisine to a cuisine discussed in this section.

2. Students should research korma and discuss its history and evolution.

3. Student answers will vary. Students should submit copies of the recipes they choose and explain why the cooking methods used are appropriate.

Case Study Follow-Up

1. Students should be able to justify their selections.

2. Student responses will vary, as long as they can logically and clearly defend their positions.

3. Student answers will vary, but their choices should be adequately supported.

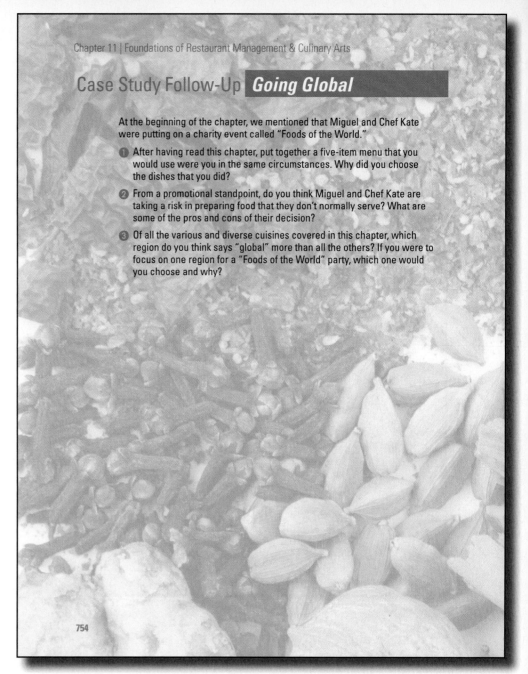

Case Study Follow-Up   *Going Global*

At the beginning of the chapter, we mentioned that Miguel and Chef Kate were putting on a charity event called "Foods of the World."

1. After having read this chapter, put together a five-item menu that you would use were you in the same circumstances. Why did you choose the dishes that you did?

2. From a promotional standpoint, do you think Miguel and Chef Kate are taking a risk in preparing food that they don't normally serve? What are some of the pros and cons of their decision?

3. Of all the various and diverse cuisines covered in this chapter, which region do you think says "global" more than all the others? If you were to focus on one region for a "Foods of the World" party, which one would you choose and why?

754

Apply Your Learning

Portioning

Select a recipe that is typical of one of the countries discussed in this chapter. For instance, you could choose a risotto recipe since risotto is characteristically served in Italy. Provide the quantities of each ingredient used and the number of portions served. Now calculate the correct quantities of each ingredient needed to produce (a) 3 portions, (b) 12 portions, and (c) 25 portions. Please show your work, including the original recipe.

Revisiting Trade Routes

Two historic trade events mentioned frequently in this chapter are the Columbian Exchange and the Silk Road. Research how they started, how they evolved over time, and how they affected the cuisines of those countries that were involved. Write a two-page report summarizing your findings.

Cured Meat

Many cuisines discussed in this chapter involve cured meat, or meat that is often not cooked before eating. Why would this be safe? Why would these techniques be used instead of cooking? Select a cured meat that is used in one of these cultures and describe in two paragraphs the process for manufacturing it.

Now obtain a piece of cured meat from a local grocery or delicatessen. What are its characteristics? How do its appearance, texture, and aroma differ from an equivalent piece of raw meat? How do its appearance, texture, aroma, and flavor differ from an equivalent piece of cooked meat? Describe your findings in three paragraphs.

Critical Thinking | Globalized Cuisine

How has globalization changed international eating patterns? How has agricultural production changed? What sustainability issues have emerged from these changes? How have health concerns shifted? Consider and research these issues and any others that you deem relevant and write a two-page paper on your findings.

Apply Your Learning

Portioning

Students should demonstrate proficiency in recipe conversion.

Revisiting Trade Routes

Students should discuss both the Columbian Exchange and the Silk Road, focusing primarily on how these affected regional cuisines.

Cured Meats

Student should discuss both the processes involved in the proper manufacture of cured meats and the historical and cultural reasons for curing meats. They should also be able to observe and identify a number of differences among cured, raw, and cooked meat.

Critical Thinking | Globalized Cuisine

Students should incorporate the material from Chapter 9 in their responses where appropriate. Their reports should clearly identify and discuss the effects of globalization on regional eating patterns.

Exam Prep Answers

1. B
2. B
3. D
4. D
5. C
6. B
7. D
8. B
9. C
10. D

Exam Prep Questions

❶ What is haute cuisine?
   A. Mild and bland food
   B. Highly refined dishes
   C. Hot and peppery food
   D. Simple, rustic cooking

❷ What kind of flour is most frequently used in Italian cuisine?
   A. Durham
   B. Semolina
   C. Bleached
   D. All-purpose

❸ What two words best characterize the flavor profile of Spanish cuisine?
   A. Rich and mild
   B. Simple and light
   C. Hot and peppery
   D. Earthy and complex

❹ What starch is most commonly used in Moroccan cuisine?
   A. Rice
   B. Lentils
   C. Potatoes
   D. Couscous

❺ What two ingredients are the two most important flavoring agents in Greek cuisine?
   A. Garlic and butter
   B. Lemon and butter
   C. Olive oil and lemon
   D. Peppers and olive oil

❻ *Ful medames* is the national dish of
   A. China.
   B. Egypt.
   C. Tunisia.
   D. Saudi Arabia.

❼ What one word best describes Iranian cuisine?
   A. Mild
   B. Spicy
   C. Complex
   D. Balanced

❽ What are the three steps involved in the three-step rice cooking method of Iran?
   A. Boil, bake, rinse
   B. Soak, boil, steam
   C. Steam, bake, chill
   D. Soak, sauté, bake

❾ The Chinese cooking method of velveting involves doing what to meat?
   A. Marinating it in soy sauce and ginger overnight
   B. Chopping it up and frying it quickly on high heat
   C. Coating it in cornstarch and egg white before frying
   D. Marinating it in crushed garlic for one hour before roasting

❿ What two words best describe the flavor profile of Indian cuisine?
   A. Light and spicy
   B. Mild and earthy
   C. Simple and piquant
   D. Complex and aromatic

756

Paella Valencia (Europe)

Yield: 10 servings
Prep Time: 50 minutes

Ingredients

80 fl oz	Chicken stock	4 oz	Carrots, diced
4 fl oz	Tomato sauce	1½ oz	Garlic, minced
2 tsp	Saffron	8 oz	Peas
1 tsp	Salt	2 lb 8 oz	Rice, short grain
2 fl oz	Olive oil (extra virgin)	20 each	Mussels
2 lb	Chicken meat (boneless and diced)	20 each	Clams
1 lb	Chorizo, diced	20 each	Shrimp
8 oz	Onions, diced	4 each	Lemons, halved
8 oz	Green peppers, diced	5 oz	Roasted red pepper, julienne

Directions

1. Heat the stock, tomato sauce, saffron, and salt in a large saucepan over medium heat.
2. In a paella pan over medium heat, heat the oil and sauté the chicken and chorizo until browned, about 7 to 8 minutes.
3. Add the vegetables and sauté for another 2 minutes.
4. Add the rice and stir to coat. Add the stock mixture, adjust seasoning, bring to a simmer, and cook for 8 minutes over medium-low heat.
5. Arrange the shellfish and the peas on the rice and continue cooking for another 5 minutes.
6. Remove from heat, squeeze the lemons over the top, cover, and let sit for 5 minutes.
7. Garnish with the julienne red pepper and serve.

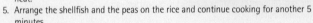

Recipe Nutritional Content

Calories	760	Cholesterol	160 mg	Protein	28 g
Calories from fat	300	Sodium	1400 mg	Vitamin A	40%
Total fat	33 g	Carbohydrates	56 g	Vitamin C	45%
Saturated fat	10 g	Dietary fiber	3 g	Calcium	8%
Trans fat	0 g	Sugars	9 g	Iron	25%

Nutritional analysis provided by FoodCalc®, www.foodcalc.com

757

Recipe

Paella Valencia

- Many non-Spaniards view paella as Spain's national dish, but most Spaniards consider it to be a regional Valencian dish. Valencians, in turn, regard paella as one of their symbols.

Recipe

Chicken *Tagine*

- *Tagine* refers both to the cooking pot as well as a stew cooked in it. This is a classic dish prepared in Northern Africa, especially Morocco. The *tagine* itself consists of two parts: a round pot (traditionally clay), and a conical cover with a small hole that allows some steam to escape.

Chicken *Tagine* (Mediterranean)

Yield: 10 servings
Prep Time: 50 minutes

Ingredients

3 (about 3 lb each)	Chicken	1 tsp	Cumin seed, toasted and ground
1 Tbs	Salt	¼ tsp	Saffron
1½ tsp	Ground black pepper	8 fl oz	Chicken stock
3 fl oz	Olive oil, extra virgin	4 Tbs	Parsley, chopped
30 each	Cipollini onions, blanched and peeled	50 each	Green olives
½ oz	Garlic cloves, thinly sliced	2 each	Preserved lemons
½ oz	Ginger, peeled and thinly sliced		

Directions

1. Cut the chicken into 6 pieces. Season the chicken parts with salt and pepper. Heat the oil over medium-high heat in a large rondeau and sauté the chicken until a light golden color. Work in batches if necessary. Remove the chicken from the pan and reserve.
2. Add the onions to the pan and sauté until they take on a light brown color, about 8 minutes.
3. Add the garlic and ginger and sauté until aromatic. Stir in the saffron and cumin.
4. Add a small amount of liquid and begin the braising process. Adjust the seasoning with salt and pepper, if necessary. Cover the pan and braise over low heat until the chicken is cooked through.
5. In the last 15 minutes, add the parsley, olives, and lemons.
6. Serve immediately.

Recipe Nutritional Content

Calories	550	Cholesterol	160 mg	Protein	37 g
Calories from fat	310	Sodium	1100 mg	Vitamin A	10%
Total fat	34 g	Carbohydrates	8 g	Vitamin C	10%
Saturated fat	8 g	Dietary fiber	2 g	Calcium	6%
Trans fat	0 g	Sugars	3 g	Iron	15%

Nutritional analysis provided by FoodCalc®, www.foodcalc.com

758

Hummus bi Tahini (Middle East)

Yield: 32 fluid ounces
Prep Time: Overnight soaking. 2 hours next day.

Ingredients

12 oz	Chickpeas, soaked overnight	4½ oz	Tahini
5 fl oz	Lemon juice	As needed	Salt
3 each	Garlic cloves, crushed in salt	As needed	Paprika
3 fl oz	Olive oil, extra virgin	1 oz	Parsley, chopped

Directions

1. After soaking the chickpeas overnight, boil them in water until tender, about 1 to 2 hours. Drain the chickpeas, reserving the cooking liquid. In a food processor, blend the chickpeas with about 4 fluid ounces of cooking liquid until they become a smooth paste.
2. Add the lemon juice, garlic, olive oil, tahini, and salt. Process until well incorporated.
3. Adjust seasoning and texture with water, if necessary. Garnish with paprika and parsley and serve.

Recipe Nutritional Content

Calories	2100	Cholesterol	0 mg	Protein	4 g
Calories from fat	1370	Sodium	780 mg	Vitamin A	0%
Total fat	159 g	Carbohydrates	139 g	Vitamin C	2%
Saturated fat	22 g	Dietary fiber	40 g	Calcium	2%
Trans fat	0 g	Sugars	21 g	Iron	6%

Nutritional analysis provided by FoodCalc®, www.foodcalc.com

Recipe

Hummus bi Tahini

- Many cuisine-related sources describe hummus as one of the oldest known prepared foods, with a long history in the Middle East stretching back to antiquity. In reality, this is folklore; its historical origins are unknown.

Recipe

Tandoori-style Chicken

- Tandoori refers to the super-hot clay oven used to cook a lot of Indian bread and meat. You probably do not have a tandoori oven at home, but you can replicate the effect by cooking the chicken directly under a very hot broiler.

Tandoori-style Chicken (Asia)

Yield: 10 servings
Prep Time: 12 hour marinate. 20 minutes next day

Ingredients

8 oz	Nonfat yogurt	1 Tbs	Coriander, ground
1 fl oz	Water	½ tsp	Saffron
2 oz	Ginger, minced	½ tsp	Cayenne, ground
1 Tbs	Cumin, ground	4 each	Garlic cloves, minced
1 Tbs	Cardamom, ground	10 each (about 3 lb 12 oz)	Chicken breasts

Directions

1. Mix the yogurt, water, and seasonings together.
2. Place the chicken breasts in the yogurt mixture and marinate under refrigeration for 12 hours.
3. Remove the chicken from the marinade and allow any excess to drain away. Place the chicken presentation-side down on the grill.
4. Grill over medium-high heat for 3 minutes undisturbed. Turn the chicken over and complete cooking until done, about 3 or 4 minutes more, or until it reaches an internal temperature of 170°F.

Recipe Nutritional Content

Calories	300	Cholesterol	145 mg	Protein	28 g
Calories from fat	60	Sodium	135 mg	Vitamin A	6%
Total fat	6 g	Carbohydrates	2 g	Vitamin C	2%
Saturated fat	2 g	Dietary fiber	0 g	Calcium	6%
Trans fat	0 g	Sugars	2 g	Iron	6%

Nutritional analysis provided by FoodCalc®, www.foodcalc.com

760

Appendix A
Staying Connected with the National Restaurant Association throughout Your Career

The National Restaurant Association has the resources and tools to support you throughout your education and career in the restaurant and foodservice industry. Through scholarships, educational programs, industry certifications, and member benefits, the Association is your partner now and into the future:

- **Scholarships:** The Association's philanthropic foundation, the National Restaurant Association Educational Foundation (NRAEF), offers scholarships to college students through its **NRAEF Scholarship Program**. These scholarships can help pave your way to an affordable higher education and may be applied to a culinary, restaurant management, or foodservice-related program at an accredited college or university. We encourage you to investigate the opportunities, which include access to special program scholarships for ProStart students who earn the National Certificate of Achievement, as well as ManageFirst Program® students. You may be awarded one NRAEF scholarship per calendar year—make sure you keep applying every year! The NRAEF partners with state restaurant associations to offer student scholarships. Check with your state to see if they offer additional scholarship opportunities. The NRAEF also offers professional development scholarships for educators. Visit www.nraef.org/scholarships for information.

761

- **College education**: As you research and apply to colleges and universities to continue your industry education, look for schools offering the National Restaurant Association's **ManageFirst Program**. Just like *Foundations of Restaurant Management & Culinary Arts*, the ManageFirst Program and curriculum materials were developed with input from the restaurant and foodservice industry and academic partners. This management program teaches you practical skills needed to face real-world challenges in the industry, including interpersonal communication, ethics, accounting skills, and more. The program includes the ten topics listed below, plus ServSafe® Food Safety and ServSafe Alcohol®:

  - Controlling Foodservice Costs

  - Customer Service

  - Food Production

  - Hospitality and Restaurant Management

  - Human Resources Management and Supervision

  - Inventory and Purchasing

  - Managerial Accounting

  - Menu Marketing and Management

  - Nutrition

  - Restaurant Marketing

  You can also earn the ManageFirst Professional® (MFP™) credential by passing five required ManageFirst exams and completing 800 work hours in the industry. Having the MFP on your resume tells employers that you have the management skills needed to succeed in the industry. To learn more about ManageFirst or to locate ManageFirst schools, visit www.managefirst. restaurant.org.

- **Certification**: In the competitive restaurant field, industry certifications can help you stand out among a crowd of applicants.

  The National Restaurant Association's **ServSafe** Food Protection Manager Certification is nationally recognized. Earning your certification tells the industry that you know food safety and the critical importance of its role— and enables you to share food safety knowledge with every other employee.

Through ServSafe Food Safety, you'll master sanitation, the flow of food through an operation, sanitary facilities, and pest management. ServSafe is the training that is learned, remembered, shared, and used. And that makes it the strongest food safety training choice for you. For more information on ServSafe, visit www.ServSafe.com.

The challenges surrounding alcohol service in restaurants have increased dramatically. To prepare you to address these challenges, the National Restaurant Association offers **ServSafe Alcohol**. As you continue to work in the industry, responsible alcohol service is an issue that will touch your business, your customers, and your community. Armed with your ServSafe Alcohol Certificate, you can make an immediate impact on an establishment. Through the program, you'll learn essential responsible alcohol service information, including alcohol laws and responsibilities, evaluating intoxication levels, dealing with difficult situations, and checking identification. Please visit www.ServSafe.com/alcohol to learn more about ServSafe Alcohol.

- **National Restaurant Association membership**: As you move into the industry, seek out careers in restaurants that are **members of the National Restaurant Association and your state restaurant association.** Encourage any operation you are part of to join the national and state organizations. During your student years, the National Restaurant Association also offers student memberships that give you access to industry research and information that can be an invaluable resource. Students in the ProStart program receive a complimentary student membership; ask your educator for details. For more information, or to join as a student member, visit www.restaurant.org.

- **Management credentials**: After you've established yourself in the industry, strive for the industry's highest management certification—the National Restaurant Association's **Foodservice Management Professional**® (FMP®). The FMP certification recognizes exceptional managers and supervisors who have achieved the highest level of knowledge, experience, and professionalism that is most valued by our industry. You become eligible to apply and sit for the FMP Exam after you've worked as a supervisor in the industry for three years. Passing the FMP Exam places you in select company; you will have joined the ranks of leading industry professionals. The FMP certification is also an impressive credential to add to your title and resume. For more information on the Foodservice Management Professional certification, visit www.managefirst.restaurant.org.

Make the National Restaurant Association your partner throughout your education and career. Take advantage of the Association's scholarship, training, certification, and membership benefits that will launch you into your career of choice. Together we will lead this industry into an even brighter future.

763

Appendix B

Handling a Foodborne-Illness Outbreak

Foodborne-illness is the greatest threat to a foodservice operation's customers. As a manager, you'll need to know what to do if some of your customers get sick. Handling a foodborne-illness outbreak involves the following three steps:

1. Preparing
2. Responding
3. Recovering

Preparing for a Foodborne-Illness Outbreak

As you know by now, the first step to preventing outbreaks is to put a food safety program in place. That program must train all staff on the policies and procedures that will keep food safe in your operation, such as personal hygiene and good cleaning and sanitizing.

But even with your best efforts, an outbreak might happen. How you respond to it can make the difference between your operation surviving or closing. Successful managers create tools that will be helpful in the event of an outbreak and that increase the chance of overcoming it.

One such tool is a foodborne-illness incident report form. This form will help you document the following critical pieces of information:

- When and what the customer ate at the operation

- When the customer first became ill

- Medical attention received by the customer

- Other food eaten by the customer

Get legal help when developing your form and make sure you teach staff how to fill it out the right way. Whenever a customer reports getting sick from food eaten at your operation, fill out the form. Don't wait for more than one customer to report something.

Another tool you'll need is an emergency contact list. This list should contain contact information for the local regulatory authority, testing labs, and the operation's management team.

Finally, your operation should determine who will be in charge if a foodborne-illness outbreak happens. You should also identify who will speak to the media—there should be one person to handle all of the contact with journalists.

Responding to a Foodborne-Illness Outbreak

In a foodborne-illness outbreak, you may be able to avoid a crisis by quickly responding to customer complaints. Here are some things you should consider when responding to an outbreak.

IF	Then
A customer calls to report a foodborne-illness.	• Take the complaint seriously and express concern. Do not admit or deny responsibility. • Complete the foodborne-illness incident report form. • Evaluate the complaint to determine if there are similar complaints.
There are similar customer complaints of foodborne-illness.	• Contact the operation's management team. • Identify common food items to determine the potential source of the complaint. • Contact the local regulatory authority to help with the investigation.
The suspected food is still in the operation.	• Put the suspected food somewhere away from other food. Put a label on it to prevent selling it. • If possible, get samples of the suspected food from the customer.
The suspected outbreak is caused by an ill staff member.	• Do not allow the staff member to continue to be in the operation until he or she has recovered.
The regulatory authority confirms that your operation is the source of the outbreak.	• Cooperate with the regulatory authority to resolve the crisis.
The media contacts your operation.	• Follow your communication plan. Let your spokesperson handle all communication.

Recovering from a Foodborne-Illness Outbreak

The final step in preparing for a foodborne-illness outbreak is developing procedures to recover from one. Think about what you need to do to make sure that the operation and the food are safe. This is critical for getting your operation running again. Consider the following in your recovery plan:

- Work with the regulatory authority to resolve issues.

- Clean and sanitize all areas of the operation so the incident does not happen again.

- Throw out all suspected food.

- Investigate to find the cause of the outbreak.

- Establish new procedures or revise existing ones based on the investigation results. This can help to prevent the incident from happening again.

- Develop a plan to reassure customers that the food served in your operation is safe.

Appendix C
Identifying Pests

Despite a foodservice manager's best efforts to prevent infestations, pests may still get into an operation. Remember, the best way to deal with pests is to work with a pest control operator (PCO). To work with a PCO effectively, you must be able to determine the type of pests you are dealing with. Record the time, date, and location of any signs of pests and report them to your PCO. Early detection means early treatment.

Cockroaches

Roaches often carry pathogens. Most live and breed in dark, warm, moist, and hard-to-clean places. You can often find them in sink and floor drains, in spaces around hot water pipes, and near motors and electrical devices in equipment. If you see a cockroach in daylight, you may have a major infestation. Generally, only the weakest roaches come out during the day. There are several types of roaches that can infest your operation. See the illustrations below.

American

German

Brown-banded

Oriental

769

If you think you have a roach problem, check for the following signs:

- **Odor.** Usually there will be a strong, oily odor.

- **Droppings.** Roach feces look like grains of black pepper.

- **Egg cases.** These are capsule-shaped. They may be brown, dark red, or black, and may appear leathery, smooth, or shiny.

Rodents

Rodents are a serious health hazard. They eat and ruin food, damage property, and spread disease. A building can be infested with both rats and mice at the same time. Rodents hide during the day and search for food at night. Like other pests, they reproduce often. Typically, they do not travel far from their nests. Mice can squeeze through a hole the size of a nickel to enter a facility, while rats can fit through half dollar-sized holes. Rats can jump 3 feet (1 meter) in the air and can even climb straight up brick walls. There are several types of rodents that can infest your operation. See the illustrations below.

Roof rat

Common house mouse

Norway rat

Here are some signs that there are rodents in the operation:

- **Gnaw marks:** Rats and mice gnaw to get at food and to wear down their teeth, which grow continuously.

■ **Tracks:** Rodents tend to use the same pathways through your operation. If rodents are a problem, you may see dirt tracks along light-colored walls.

■ **Droppings and urine stains:** Fresh droppings are shiny and black. See figure at right. Older droppings are gray. Rodent urine will "glow" when exposed to a black (ultraviolet) light.

■ **Nests:** Rats and mice use soft materials, such as scraps of paper, cloth, hair, feathers, and grass to build their nests. The photo at right shows an example of a mouse's nest.

■ **Holes:** Rats usually nest in holes located in quiet places. Nests are often found near food and water and may be found next to buildings.

Illustrations courtesy of Orkin, Inc.

Appendix **D**
Building a Career

This appendix reviews some of the career information provided in Year 1, *Chapter 12: Building a Successful Career in the Industry* including information about the job search, sample résumés and cover letters, portfolios, school applications and scholarships, and the interview process.

The Job Search

Job hunting can be both exciting and stressful. The job market is the ideal place to tell others about your abilities, talents, and dreams. Search job ads in online job search engines and job banks by keyword, discipline, and location. These sites are usually more current than traditional classified ads, since posts are frequently updated. Most online job sites allow job seekers to post their résumés online for free. Some sites require job seekers to complete an online résumé or questionnaire as well.

The steps for searching for a job include the following:

1. Decide what characteristics your desired job should have, including the hours and days desired, as well as job responsibilities. Although finding a job that matches your list exactly is unlikely, generally knowing the desired job characteristics will help.

2. Determine which areas may be open to compromise. Willing to work part of the weekend? How late is too late to catch a ride? Think about what trade-offs can be made to accept a job.

3. Gather and organize the information needed for applying. Compile a work history (if possible), including complete contact information for each of your previous employers. Make sure all personal contact information is at hand. Talk with people about being references and review all past training and skills.

4. Create the documents needed for applying—a résumé, reference list, customizable cover letter, and portfolio.

5. Identify the search methods. Examples include the Internet, newspapers, and friends.

6. Choose the businesses to contact. Create a list of their addresses and contact information.

7. Research each business chosen. Knowing as much as possible about the business makes for a better prepared interview and shows an eagerness to work for the business.

8. Contact the businesses chosen in whatever method they've indicated. If applying in person, be sure to dress professionally and be prepared with all application documents.

9. When a potential employer makes contact, decide on an interview time. Don't be late! Ask questions during the interview to make sure that the job meets all your needs.

10. After sending a résumé or applying, call the business once a week to ask about open positions and check the status of an application (if the business hasn't initiated a follow-up contact). Keep searching.

Sample Résumés and Cover Letters

A résumé is a written summary of experience, skills, and achievements that relate to the job being sought. A résumé is not a life story. It is like a sales brochure that tells an employer why the applicant is the best person to hire for the job. Use these basic tips to create a successful résumé:

- Include all important information such as name, address, telephone number, and email address in case the résumé gets separated from the cover letter.

- Use active language.

- Avoid using buzzwords or jargon.

- Show off accomplishments. Employers want to know what the applicant has accomplished, not what his or her responsibilities or duties were. If possible, quantify achievements with percents or dollars.

- Put work experience first unless just entering the job market; then showcase education first. List degrees, GPA, honors, scholarships, and accomplishments.

- Include professional references that can speak about your accomplishments. Grab the potential employer's attention!

- Leave white space and use headings and section breaks. See Figure D.1. Visual layout is important. If it looks unprofessional or cluttered, a résumé will not impress the employer.

Faith Fitzpatrick
110 West 84th Street
Funtown, USA 50094
Phone: 123-456-7890
E-mail: ffitz@notmail.net

Objective

 To work as a part-time server at Uptown Grille

Work Experience:

2009-present, Busperson, Blue Bird Café, Funtown, USA

- Clear tables quickly and set correctly
- Refill water and other beverages during dinner service
- Assist servers in serving food, as needed

Related Experience:

- Help serve food at high school café (sponsored by Foodservice Class)
- Organized junior class bake sale
- Developed new recipe for low-fat chocolate chip cookies sold at annual bake sale
- Used computer program to type recipes for class cookbook
- Volunteer kitchen worker at community Thanksgiving dinner

Related Skills and Abilities

- Strong customer service, teamwork, and interpersonal skills
- Ability to use word-processing and spreadsheet programs
- Dedicated to maintaining a clean dining area and adhering to all safety and health guidelines
- Work well with others

Education

- Senior at Funtown High School
- Currently taking food, management, and health and safety procedures classes in Foodservice school-to-career program.

References Available on Request

Figure D.1: A sample résumé.

- Keep the length of a résumé to one to two pages. The employer needs just enough information about accomplishments to make a decision about an interview.

- Edit and proofread any résumé or cover letter before sending it out.

When sending a résumé to a potential employer, send a cover letter along with it. A cover letter is a brief letter in which applicants introduce themselves to an employer. The following are tips for writing a cover letter:

- **Attention:** Grab a reader's attention in the first paragraph to make sure the person keeps on reading. State the reason for writing the letter.

- **Interest:** Hold the reader's interest by mentioning the source of his or her name as a contact or how the job opening or company became of interest.

- **Desire:** Tell the reader what you want to do for his or her company. List qualifications and the reasons for the application. See Figure D.2.

- **Action:** End the letter by mentioning meeting in an interview.

Ms. Linda Brown
Manager
Uptown Grille
75 East Pleasant Street
Funtown, USA 50094

January 5, 2011

Dear Ms. Brown:

I am applying for the position of part-time server with the Uptown Grille that I read about in Sunday's *Anytown Daily*. This position offers a great opportunity for me to continue my career in foodservice. I am a senior at Anytown High School, where I'm enrolled in a new program that combines food preparation classes with health and safety procedures as well as business management courses. Currently, I work as a busperson at the Blue Bird Café, so I have learned some of the basics of customer service and have received food safety training.

For your review, I am enclosing a copy of my résumé that shows my qualifications. I am hard-working, dependable, and honest, with a pleasant disposition and outgoing personality. My references can testify to these characteristics.

I am sure that once you have had a chance to review my résumé and meet with me, you will agree that my enthusiasm and willingness to learn will help me become an ideal server at Uptown Grille. You can reach me Monday through Friday after 3:30 p.m. or at any time on Saturday and Sunday at 123-456-7890.

I look forward to hearing from you at your earliest convenience. Thank you for your consideration.

Sincerely,

Faith Fitzpatrick
110 West 84th Street
Funtown, USA 50094
Phone: 123-456-7890
Email: ffitz@notmail.net

Figure D.2: A sample cover letter.

Portfolios

A portfolio is a collection of samples that showcase interests, talents, contributions, and studies. A portfolio displays an applicant's finest efforts and is a good self-marketing tool to show potential employers. The following is a list of items a portfolio may include:

- Lists or samples of skills and abilities (such as the list of competencies learned at worksites)

- Samples of work

- Examples of problems solved (at school, in the community, with friends)

- Examples demonstrating teamwork

- Examples showing leadership and responsibility

- Important experiences and what was learned from them

- Certificates of recognition and reward (the certificate received upon successful completion of this program and a high school diploma are two examples)

- Newsletters or announcements (with name or group highlighted)

- Essays, reports, and papers (those with high grades or positive teacher remarks)

- Letters of thanks you've received; particularly ones that highlight your motivation and work ethic

- Résumé

- Audio or videotapes that display abilities

- Test scores

- Original recipes

- Letters of recommendation from past employers or groups

Make sure that portfolios are complete, neat, and well-organized. Include a cover page that gives the following:

- Full name, address, and phone number

- Career objectives

- A brief description of the contents

Select samples that highlight the applicant's best talents. Each sample should be accompanied by a brief explanation of why it is important. Type information whenever possible. Include clean photocopies of letters and other important documents or certificates.

A portfolio is best displayed in a three-ring binder or folder. It's a good idea to use three-ring clear plastic sleeves to hold samples. A portfolio should be about 10 pages in length and easy to carry to interviews. A portfolio that is sloppy, too long, or too big does not make a good impression.

School Applications and Scholarships

In addition to asking for your name and address, college or trade school applications require education information. The application may also require that applicants state the program or course of study they are applying for and ask them to complete a short essay. When writing the essay, remember that the person reviewing the application is looking for signs that the applicant will be successful. If the essay is open-ended, write about successes and future goals. Ask parents or a teacher to review your essay drafts. It is always a good idea to have an essay proofread by someone who is particularly strong in grammar and composition.

It's important to remember that the process of completing college applications has stages with strict deadlines. Applications and essays must be delivered to schools within a specified time frame. Essays take time to write. Also be aware of the time it will take for a school district to provide grades to application schools.

A scholarship is a grant or financial aid award to a student for the purpose of attending college. A large number of available scholarships aren't awarded each year just because no one applies, so the first step in being awarded a scholarship is simply to apply. Applicants who meet the base criteria for the scholarship should apply and let the awarding organization make the decision. They should not assume that they will not get a scholarship. Only by not applying do students guarantee that they won't get any scholarships.

To find scholarships:

- Contact the financial aid office of the school to find out what types of scholarships the school offers and how to apply for them.

- Search the Internet. Some Web sites collect and organize scholarship information. Narrow the search based on potential majors, but don't overlook scholarships that might be available to all students. Also consider searching for scholarships based on ethnicity or disability.

- Talk with a guidance counselor. Share findings and ask about any local scholarships that might be available.

Scholarship applications are similar to college applications in that they always have deadlines. Some also require applicants to answer questions or submit an essay. Add these due dates to the continuing list of application deadlines.

Some states and schools also have financial aid to offer students. This includes grants, educational loans, and work study (working as a student for the school). To qualify for financial aid at any school that receives federal funds (almost all of them), the student and the student's parents will need to complete the Free Application for Federal Student Aid (FAFSA). Get information about the FAFSA and the submission deadlines at www.fafsa.ed.gov. This application is used by the federal government to determine the total amount of financial aid for which an applicant qualifies. In most cases, students should automatically apply for financial aid and let the school determine whether they qualify. Remember that educational loans do have to be repaid, so students should minimize borrowing if possible.

The Interview

Most job interviews last about an hour, depending on the job level. Most interviewers try to help applicants relax and feel comfortable. The potential employer will ask questions to get to know the applicant better and to see whether the applicant's talents would be a suitable match for the job available. The potential employer has a job position to fill and wants to hire someone capable of doing the job or learning it quickly. The interviewer also wants to know whether the applicant will fit in with the restaurant or foodservice team and the organization as a whole.

Think of the interview as a chance to visit a workplace, to learn more about an interesting job, and an opportunity to meet new people. It's important to make a good impression, but it's also important to be true to yourself.

Bring the following to the interview:

- Portfolio, including résumé

- Names, addresses, and phone numbers of three people as references, personal and professional

- Birth certificate or valid passport; Social Security card; driver's license or state-issued ID; green card or proof of ability to work in the United States

The steps to be taken before an interview, during the interview, and after the interview are shown in Table D.1.

Table D.1: Interview Steps	
Before the interview	• Know the route to the job. Take a preview trip to the interview site. Consider traffic. • If you're taking public transportation, bring enough money and allow time for delays. • Know what materials to take. • Review important interview questions and responses. • Practice aloud. • Bring a pen that writes clearly and a clean notebook. • Write down the name, address, and telephone number of the interviewer. • Give yourself enough time to get ready. • Get a good night's sleep. • Arrive at the interview 15 minutes before the appointment. • If you are going to be late, call the interviewer. • Good luck and relax!
During the interview	• Smile, look interested, and pay attention. • Sit with back straight; lean back in the chair. • Practice good listening skills. • Never say unkind or negative things about previous bosses or coworkers. • Be an interactive participant. Avoid answering questions too quickly, which makes the answers appear to be not thought out. • Ask questions. • Look confident (and feel confident). • Sell yourself! Explain how your skills and abilities make you the ideal person for the job.
After the interview	• Write a brief thank-you note to the interviewer as soon as possible. • Follow up with a phone call to the interviewer. • Congratulate yourself on doing your best!

Glossary

Chapter 1

albumen: White part of an egg, which consists of protein and water.

basted egg: Egg that has been fried and then steamed in a covered pan.

black tea: Tea in which the leaves have been fermented.

bread: Basic component of the sandwich, bread serves as an edible container for the food inside and also provides bulk and nutrients.

butter substitute: Any alternative used to replace butter in a recipe. Examples include margarine, olive oils, and soy-based oils.

caffeine: Stimulant that occurs naturally in coffee and tea.

canapé (CAN-uh-pay): Small, open-faced cold sandwich that is a type of hors d'oeuvre. They usually are made from bread or toast cutouts, English muffins, crackers, melba toasts, and tiny unsweetened pastry shells.

chalazae (kuh-LEY-zuh): Membranes that hold an egg yolk in place.

clarified butter: Butter that is created when the chef or manufacturer heats butter and then removes milk solids and water.

club sandwich: Three slices of toasted bread spread with mayonnaise and filled with an assortment of sliced chicken and/or turkey, ham, bacon, cheese, lettuce, and tomato.

cold sandwich: Sandwich consisting of two slices of bread or two halves of a roll, a spread, and a filling.

crêpe (CRAPE or CREPP): Very thin pancake-type item with a high egg content. The result is a delicate, unleavened griddlecake.

curdling: Process in which dairies make cheese by separating a milk's solids from its liquid.

deep-fried sandwich: Sandwich made by dipping it in beaten egg (sometimes with bread crumbs) and then deep-frying. Cook the sandwich on the griddle or in the oven to reduce fat and make it less greasy.

filling: Basic component of the sandwich, the filling provides the primary flavor and generally is protein-based, but it doesn't have to be.

French toast: Sliced bread (preferably day old) dipped in an egg-and-milk mixture and cooked on a lightly oiled griddle or flat pan.

fried egg: Egg that has been fried in cooking fat at 145°F for at least 15 seconds. If it is going to be held for a few minutes, it should be cooked at 155°F. The yolk should be cooked to whatever doneness the customer requests.

frittatas: Flat omelet that may be made in individual portions or in larger quantities.

green tea: Tea in which the leaves are not fermented.

grilled (or **toasted**) **sandwich:** Another type of hot sandwich in which the outside of the bread is buttered and browned on the griddle or in a hot oven.

hard-cooked egg: Product made by simmering, and then **shocking,** eggs.

hashed brown potatoes, or **hash browns**: Potatoes prepared by steaming or simmering them in lightly salted water and then peeling, chilling, and shredding. Shredded potatoes are cooked on a lightly oiled griddle on medium heat to a light golden brown on both sides.

home fries: Raw potatoes that have been peeled and then sliced, diced, or shredded and then cooked on a well-oiled griddle or pan-fried until golden brown and cooked though.

homogenization (huh-MAH-juh-ni-ZAY-shun): Process in which milk is strained through very fine holes to break down fat and then blended into one fluid.

hors d'oeuvre (or DERV): Hot or cold bite-sized finger food that is served before a meal.

hot cocoa: Popular breakfast drink made from cocoa powder or shaved chocolate and sugar stirred into heated milk or water.

hydrogenate: To combine with, treat with, or expose to the action of hydrogen.

margarine: One of the most common butter substitutes, this manufactured food product often contains no milk products. Margarine is made of vegetable oils and animal fats with added flavoring, emulsifiers, colors, preservatives, and vitamins.

mise en place: Condition in which everything needed to prepare a particular item or use for a particular service period is ready and at hand.

multi-decker sandwich: Sandwich with more than two slices of bread (or rolls) with several ingredients in the filling.

omelet: Dish made by slightly beating eggs and then cooking them in a skillet with a filling, such as cheese, mushrooms, onions, or ham.

open-faced hot sandwich: Sandwich made by placing one slice of buttered or unbuttered bread or roll on a serving plate with hot meat or other filling and covering it with a hot topping, such as sauce or cheese. Some are broiled quickly if the cheese needs melting or the topping should be crisped.

over easy egg: Egg that has been fried on the bottom, turned over, and then fried very lightly on its top side.

pancake: Griddlecake made from a medium-weight pour batter.

panini (PAH-nee-nee): Sandwich made by grilling on a panini press, which compresses the sandwich and warms the ingredients without adding additional fat to the outside of the sandwich.

pasteurization (pass-cher-i-ZAY-shun): Process in which milk is heated to kill microorganisms that cause spoilage and disease without affecting its nutritional value.

pizza: Hot, open-faced Italian pie with a crisp yeast-dough bottom.

Plugrá: European-style butter that is low in moisture and high in butterfat. Regular butter is 80 percent butterfat and 20 percent water and milk solids; Plugrá is 82 percent butterfat. It is slow-churned, which helps to create a creamy texture.

poached egg: Egg that has been shelled (removed from the shell) and simmered in water. A properly poached egg should be tender and well shaped, meaning the yolk is centered and the white is not rough or ragged.

pooled eggs: Eggs that are cracked open and combined in a container. Cook them immediately after mixing, or store them at 41°F or lower.

processed cheese: Cheese product that manufacturers make by grinding, blending, and forming one or more natural cheeses. Emulsifiers help to make the product uniform. It's also pasteurized to prevent it from aging.

Pullman loaf: Sandwich loaf of sliced white bread that is the most frequently used sandwich bread.

quiche (KEESH): Savory egg custard baked in a crust.

ramekins (RAM-uh-kins): Small, ceramic, oven-proof dishes.

ripened cheese: Some cheeses are ripened by external bacteria put into curds (Brie, bleu, Roquefort, Camembert). Others are ripened by bacteria naturally in the curds (Swiss, Havarti).

scrambled eggs: Eggs that have been blended until the yolks and whites are combined and then cooked over gentle heat while constantly stirring and scraping from the bottom and sides of the pan to keep them creamy and to prevent burning.

shirred egg: Variety of a baked egg.

shocking: Process of putting something in cold water immediately after cooking it to stop the cooking.

smoke point: Point at which an oil or fat begins to burn.

soufflé (soo-FLAY): Baked dish made with eggs that can be savory or sweet.

spread: Basic component of the sandwich that serves three main purposes: to prevent the bread from soaking up the filling, to add flavor, and to add moisture.

submarine sandwich: Usually a cold sandwich served on a long, sliced roll with several types of cheese, meat, lettuce, tomato, onion, and various other toppings. These sandwiches may also be referred to as a sub, grinder, hero, or hoagie.

Swedish pancake: Pancake made with a slightly sweetened batter that is a bit heavier than a crêpe batter. Cook these pancakes on a flat griddle or in a special fluted pan.

tea sandwich: Small, cold sandwich usually served on bread or toast, trimmed of crusts, and cut into shapes.

tea: Breakfast beverage that is generally less expensive than coffee, although some rare teas can be quite expensive. One cup of tea has about half the caffeine contained in a cup of coffee. Tea is served either very hot or iced.

trans fat: Short for transformed fat, this fat Is artificially created when manufacturers hydrogenate liquid oils to make the oils solid, so they have longer shelf lives.

unripened cheese: Fresh cheeses, including cream cheese and cottage cheese, that have not been ripened with either naturally occurring bacteria or added external bacteria.

up (sunny-side up): Egg that is fried only on the bottom.

waffle: Cake-like breakfast dish made from a medium-weight pour batter similar to pancake batter, but with more egg and oil. Cook waffles in a specially designed waffle maker, or iron, that creates grid-like holes or specialty designs.

wrap sandwich: Sandwich made on any type of flat bread—for example, tortillas, cracker bread, or rice paper wrappers—and spread with a hot or cold sandwich filling and then rolled up.

yolk: Yellow part of an egg, which contains protein, fat, and lecithin, a natural emulsifier (thickener).

Chapter 2

additive: Chemical that might occur naturally or be synthetic, but is chemically identical to natural substances. Additives are added to food as a result of processing, production, or packaging.

adequate intakes (AIs): Similar to RDAs, AIs also identify daily intake levels for healthy people. AIs are typically assigned when scientists don't have enough information to set an RDA.

amino acids: Chemical compounds that have special functions in the body, including supplying nitrogen for growth and maintenance.

antibiotic: Medicines that prevent bacterial infections.

calorie: *See* **kilocalorie**.

carbohydrate: Body's main energy source; this type of nutrient provides the body with four kilocalories of energy per gram of food eaten and helps the body use protein and fat efficiently.

cardiovascular diseases: Diseases that affect the heart and blood vessels and include hypertension, strokes, and heart attacks. Collectively, they are the number one cause of death in the United States.

certified organic: Products that meet the requirements of their certifying organization. The "certified organic" name applies to farming and processing techniques that are simple, nontoxic, and sustainable. If a label is USDA "certified organic," it will apply to these standards.

cholesterol: White, waxy substance produced in the liver that helps the body carry out its many processes.

coagulate: This is when a substance thickens and congeals.

785

complementary proteins: Two or more incomplete protein sources that together provide adequate amounts of all the essential amino acids.

complete proteins: Proteins that contain all the essential amino acids in the right amount. Good sources of complete proteins are meat, poultry, fish, eggs, and dairy products.

complex carbohydrate: This energy source contains long chains that include many glucose molecules. They are found in plant-based foods such as grains, legumes, and vegetables. They provide a long-lasting source of energy.

conventional product: Product grown using approved USDA and FDA agricultural methods. The methods allow the use of certain fertilizers, pesticides, hormones, and drugs that are recognized as safe. Most of the food in the supermarket and from restaurant and foodservice suppliers comes from conventional producers.

diabetes mellitus: Condition in which the body cannot regulate blood sugar properly.

***Dietary Guidelines for Americans 2005*:** Document published jointly by the Department of Health and Human Services and the USDA that offers science-based advice for healthy people over the age of two about food choices to promote health and reduce risk for major chronic diseases. Like the recommended dietary allowances, these dietary guidelines apply to diets eaten over several days, not to single food items or meals.

Dietary Reference Intakes (DRIs): Recommended daily nutrient and energy intake amounts (that is, what a person needs to consume) for healthy people of a particular age range and gender. They are the guides for nutrition and food selection.

essential amino acids: Nine amino acids that have to be obtained from food each day.

essential fatty acid: Required for good nutrition, these nutrients are used to make substances that regulate vital body functions. They are also needed for normal growth, healthy skin, and healthy cells.

fat: Usually refers to both fats and oils, although basic differences exist between the two. Fats are solid at room temperature and often come from animals.

fat-soluble vitamin: Vitamins A, D, E, and K, which are found in food containing fat. They're stored in the liver and body fat. The body draws on these stored vitamins when needed.

fiber: Substance found in plant food, such as whole grains, fruit, vegetables, nuts, and legumes, that promotes digestive health and regularity.

foam: Sauce that has been aerated and then spooned onto the dish.

food additive: Substance or combination of substances present in food as a result of processing, production, or packaging.

genetically modified organism (GMO): Plant or animal whose genetic makeup has been altered.

glucose: Very important simple sugar; glucose is the primary source of energy and the only source of energy for the brain and nervous system. Good sources of glucose are fruit, vegetables, and honey.

786

GMO (genetically modified organism): Plant or animal whose genetic makeup has been changed.

herbicide: Weed killer.

hormones: Special chemical messengers made by bodies that regulate different body functions. This term might also refer to substances injected into animals to make them grow.

hydrogenation: Process in which fats are combined with, treated with, or exposed to hydrogen to alter their physical properties and make them stay fresh longer.

incomplete protein: Food that lacks one or more of the essential amino acids. Food from plant sources are incomplete proteins.

insoluble fiber: Fiber that does not dissolve in water. It was once referred to as roughage ("ruff-ij") because it is rough. It acts like a stiff broom to clean and scrub the digestive tract so we can eliminate wastes from our systems more easily.

insulin: Hormone produced in the pancreas that allows glucose, or blood sugar, to travel throughout the body for energy use.

iodized salt: Table salt that has been enriched with iodine as a nutritional supplement.

iron-deficiency anemia: Condition caused by lack of iron in a person's blood.

kilocalorie: Energy needed to heat 1 kilogram (about 2.2 pounds) of water by approximately 1°C. In nutrition, the unit of measurement for energy is the kilocalorie, but it is more commonly called a **calorie.**

Kosher salt: Has no additives, so it has a purer flavor than table salt. It is usually coarser than table salt, which means it has larger crystals.

lacto-ovo-vegetarian: Person who consumes vegetarian items plus dairy products and eggs.

lacto-vegetarian: Person who consumes vegetarian items plus dairy products.

lipids: Another word for fat, lipids are a group of molecules that include fats, oils, waxes, steroids, and other compounds.

malnutrition: Condition that occurs when a body does not get enough nutrients.

malnutrition: Physical condition caused by a lack of nutrients or an imbalance of nutrients.

mineral: Inorganic element essential to nutrition that is classified as major or trace, according to how much is needed in the diet. Even though some minerals are needed in very tiny amounts, getting the right amount is important to good health. Minerals are part of body structures and are also needed for body functions.

natural: Legally meaningless as a term. Food products labeled as "natural" may or may not have any organic ingredients or processing.

nutrients: Components of food that are needed for the body to function.

nutrition: Study of the nutrients in food and how they nourish the body.

obese: Describes a person who has excessive body fat; a person has traditionally been considered to be obese if they are more than 20 percent over their ideal weight.

organic: Generally, the term refers to products that have been produced without pesticides or synthetic fertilizers. Soil and water are also usually conserved. Animals don't receive antibiotics or growth hormones.

osteoporosis: Condition in which the bones gradually lose their minerals, becoming weak and fragile.

overweight: Describes a person who has a weight greater than what is generally considered healthy; identifies a range of weight that has been shown to increase the likelihood of certain diseases and other health problems.

oxidation: Chemical process that causes unsaturated fats to spoil. Heat, light, salt, and moisture help speed up oxidation.

pesticide: Chemical that kills insects and other plant pests.

phyllo dough: Thin layers of pastry dough used in various Greek and Near Eastern sweet and savory preparations.

phytochemical: Also known as a phytonutrient, this type of chemical aids the body in fighting or preventing diseases.

portion control: Controlling the quantity of particular foods by using appropriately sized servings.

protein: Composed of large complex molecules that contain long chains of amino acids, protein is a class of nutrients that can supply energy to the body. Proteins are needed to build new cells and repair injured ones. If used for energy, proteins can provide four calories of energy per gram to the body.

Recommended Dietary Allowances (RDAs): Daily nutrient standards established by the U.S. government; the average daily intakes that meet the nutrient requirement of nearly all healthy individuals of a particular age and gender group. The nutrients recommended are protein, eleven vitamins, and seven minerals.

reduction: Simmering a stock made from vegetables, meat, poultry, or fish until it is about one-third of the original volume. In the process of reduction, the stock develops body, and its flavors intensify.

rock salt: Less refined than table salt and not meant to be eaten. It is used in ice cream makers and as a bed for certain items, such as oysters or clams on their shells.

sea salt: Extracted from the ocean using evaporation techniques. It is usually not refined, so it contains additional minerals and other elements found in sea water, which affect the flavor.

simple carbohydrate: Contains one or two sugars. Sugars are called simple carbohydrates because their chemical structure is relatively simple compared to starch and fiber, which are complex carbohydrates.

soluble fiber: Fiber that dissolves in water, slows down the release of sugar into the blood, and helps lower cholesterol levels in the blood.

table salt: The most common salt found on every table. It is refined to remove other minerals and impurities. It is processed to give it a fine, even grain, and a small amount of starch to keep it from forming clumps.

trans fatty acid: Result of taking a liquid fat and making it solid. This is achieved through a process called hydrogenation.

vegan: Person who follow the strictest diet of all and will consume no dairy, eggs, meat, poultry, fish, or anything containing an animal product or byproduct. They consume only grains, legumes, vegetables, fruit, nuts, and seeds.

vegetarian: Person who consumes no meat, fish, or poultry products. *See also* **lacto-vegetarian**, **lacto-ovo-vegetarian**, and **vegan**.

vitamins: Chemical compounds found in food that are needed for regulating metabolic processes, such as digestion and the absorption of nutrients.

water-soluble vitamins: Vitamins C and B, which are found in food such as oranges and grapefruit. These vitamins are vulnerable to cooking and may be destroyed by heat or washed away by steam or water.

Chapter 3

as-purchased (AP) method: Used to cost an ingredient at the purchase price *before* any trim or waste is taken into account.

average check method: Way to price a menu in which the total revenue is divided by the number of seats, average seat turnover, and days open in one year.

average sales per customer: Calculated by the total dollar sales divided by the total number of customers.

beverage costs: One of four main cost categories that a restaurant or foodservice operation needs to effectively manage.

business volume: Amount of sales an operation is doing for a given time period.

closing inventory: Inventory at the end of a given period.

contribution margin method: Way to price a menu in which an operation must know the portion costs for each item sold. An operation can determine the average contribution margin needed to cover

overhead and yield a desired profit at an expected level of sales volume.

contribution margin: Portion of dollars that a particular menu item contributes to overall profits.

controllable costs: Costs subject to change based on how the operation is doing; the operation has a certain amount of control in how it spends on these aspects of the operation.

conversion factor: Number to multiply ingredients by in order to convert a recipe to serve a different number of people. For example, if your chili recipe serves eighty and you need to serve forty: $40 \div 80 = 0.5$. The conversion factor is 0.5.

cost control: A business's efforts to manage how much it spends.

cost: Price an operation pays out in the purchasing and preparation of its products or the providing of its service.

crew schedule: Chart that shows employees' names and the days and times they are supposed to work.

edible-portion (EP) method: Used to cost an ingredient *after* trimming and removing waste so that only the usable portion of the item is reflected.

employee turnover: Number of employees hired to fill one position in a year's time.

fixed costs: Costs that need to be paid regardless of whether the operation is making or losing money. Fixed costs, in contrast to variable costs, do not change based on the operation's sales.

food cost: Actual dollar value of the food used by an operation during a certain period.

food costs: One of four main cost categories that a restaurant or foodservice operation needs to effectively manage.

food production chart: Form that shows how much product should be produced by the kitchen during a given meal period.

forecast: Prediction of sales levels or costs that will occur during a specific time period.

full-line supplier: Company that provides equipment, food, and supplies and usually has programs available to their customers that help with controlling costs.

historical data: Information about past performance that a manager uses to forecast foodservice sales and costs.

inventory: Dollar value of a food product in storage; can be expressed in terms of units, values, or both.

invoice: Document from a vendor that lists such details as items purchased, date of order, purchaser, and sales price; also called a bill.

labor costs: One of four main cost categories that a restaurant or foodservice operation needs to effectively manage.

master schedule: Template, usually a spreadsheet, showing the number of people needed in each position to run the restaurant or foodservice operation for a given time period.

moving average technique: Also called the smoothing technique, this involves averaging together sales information for two or three recent and similar periods. The average can produce a forecast that is more likely to be accurate, since it is not based solely on one period that might have had unique circumstances.

noncontrollable costs: *See* **fixed costs.**

opening inventory: Physical inventory at the beginning of a given period (such as the month of April).

operating budget: Financial plan for a specific period of time that lists the anticipated sales revenue and projected costs and gives an estimate of the profit or loss expected for the period.

operational standards: Specifications of an operation with regard to products. If an item must be redone to meet standards, this costs money, not only in terms of wasted product that increases food cost, but also in terms of productivity that increases labor cost.

overhead costs: One of four main cost categories that a restaurant or foodservice operation needs to effectively manage.

These costs can include insurance, utilities, or an operation's lease or mortgage on the building.

physical inventory: Process of counting and recording the number of each item in the storeroom.

pilfering: Stealing that occurs when employees illegally take inventory items for their personal use.

point-of-sale (POS) systems: Computerized cash register system.

price point: Price that appears on a menu and that takes into consideration the cost of purchasing and preparing a menu item.

production sheet: Sheet that lists all menu items that are going to be prepared for a given date.

profit-and-loss report: Compilation of sales and cost information for a specific period of time. This report shows whether an operation has made or lost money during the time period covered by the report.

quality standards: Specifications of an operation with regard to products and service.

recipe cost card: Tool used to calculate the standard portion cost for a menu item.

recipe yield: Process of determining the number of portions that a recipe produces.

revenue: Income from sales before expenses, or costs, are subtracted.

sales history: Record of the number of portions of every item sold on a menu.

semivariable costs: Costs that can change based on sales.

standard portion cost: Exact amount that one serving, or portion, of a food item should cost when prepared according to the item's standardized recipe.

standardized recipes: Guidelines and instructions that are followed every time a menu item is prepared.

straight markup pricing method: Way to price a menu in which an operation multiplies raw food costs by a predetermined fraction.

total food cost percentage: Relationship between sales and the cost of food to achieve those sales.

variable costs: Costs that can change based on sales.

variances: Changes that have occurred over time. Observing variances is a good way to analyze what happened and to develop a plan of how to correct the problem.

Chapter 4

accompaniment salad: Also known as a side salad, this salad is served with the main course of the meal.

base: Usually a layer of salad greens that line the plate or bowl in which a salad will be served.

body: Main ingredients of a salad.

bound salad: A salad type in which salad ingredients such as meat, poultry, fish, egg, or starch such as potato, pasta, or rice are cooked and then "bound" with some type of heavy dressing such as mayonnaise.

brunoise (BROON-wah): Cuts of uncooked, unseasoned red pepper that add color, but do nothing to enhance flavor.

combination salad: Incorporates a combination of any of the four salad types: green, bound, vegetable, or fruit.

composed: Type of green salad in which the ingredients are not mixed together prior to plating.

consommés (CON-suh-mays): Rich, clarified stocks or broths.

dauphinoise potatoes: Croquettes of potatoes mixed with pastry or bread crumbs and formed into shapes.

dessert salads: Salads that are usually sweet and that often contain fruits, sweetened gelatin, nuts, cream, and whipped cream.

dollop (DOLL-up): Small glob of a soft food item, such as sour cream.

duchesse potatoes: Puréed cooked potatoes with egg yolks and butter, which are formed into small shapes or used as a garnish and baked until golden brown.

emulsified (uh-MUL-si-fide) vinaigrettes: Dressings that have gone through the emulsion process to keep them from separating.

emulsifier: Ingredient that can permanently bind unlike ingredients, such as oil and vinegar, together on a molecular level.

emulsion: Mixture of ingredients that permanently stays together.

fruit salad: Mixed fruit with a slightly sweet or sweet/sour dressing to enhance the flavor.

garnish: Object that enhances the appearance of a salad while also complementing the overall taste. A garnish should be something that will be eaten with the body, functioning as a flavor component.

gougères (GOO-jere): Small, finger-sized pastries filled with ingredients such as mushrooms, beef, or ham.

guacamole (gwah-kuh-MOE-lee): Avocado dip of Aztec origin.

hummus: Chick pea with garlic and tahini (from the Middle East).

intermezzo salad: Intended to be a palate cleanser after a rich dinner and before dessert.

main course salads: Large enough to serve as a full meal, these salads also contain protein ingredients, such as meat, poultry, seafood, egg salad, beans, or cheese.

mayonnaise: The most stable and thickest emulsified dressing; contains a higher ratio of oil to vinegar and a greater quantity of egg yolks than is required for an emulsified vinaigrette.

mayonnaise-based: Type of dressing that is typically creamy.

napping: Coating or drizzling lightly with sauce.

salad dressings: Liquids or semi-liquids used to flavor salads. They act as a sauce that holds the salad together.

salsa: Peppers, such as jalapeño or serrano, onions, and tomatoes (from Mexico).

starter salad: Served as an appetizer to the main meal, this salad is smaller in portion and consists of light, fresh, crisp ingredients to stimulate the appetite.

string work: Garnish consisting of thin strings used decoratively.

suspension: Temporary mixture of ingredients that eventually separates back into its unique parts.

tossed: Type of green salad in which the ingredients are mixed together prior to plating.

tourner: Method of cutting food, usually vegetables, that results in a small shape with a pleasant appearance for the food being served.

vegetable salad: Salad in which cooked and/or raw vegetables are combined with either a heavy dressing to bind it or are tossed with a lighter dressing.

vinaigrette (vin-uh-GRETT) dressing: In its simplest form, this type of dressing is made of oil and vinegar. Vinaigrettes are lighter, thinner dressings often used on more delicate ingredients, such as greens and vegetables.

Chapter 5

bids: Specialized, written price lists created for the restaurant by a supplier.

buyer: Person responsible for purchasing food items, beverages, and/or equipment and supplies. An operation might have more than one buyer.

capital: Assets that an operation has at its disposal.

cash position: Amount of funds available to an operation at any given time.

channel of distribution: Particular businesses that buy and sell a product as it makes its way from its original source to a retailer.

competitive position: Ability to attract customers and make a profit among other operations offering similar products.

credit memo: Written record that ensures the vendor will credit the operation for a rejected item.

daily food cost sheets: Ongoing records of daily and monthly food costs for an operation.

form value: Price savings created when a buyer purchases bulk quantities of food instead of individually portioned servings.

formal purchasing method: Purchasing method in which buyers prepare purchase specifications for the items they want. These specifications are then sent to several suppliers for bids.

franchise: People who are granted a license to market a company's goods or services in a certain area.

gross profit: Profit before all other costs are deducted.

humidity: Amount of water moisture in the air or in a contained space such as a refrigerator.

impinger oven: Conveyer-belt-style oven used to toast bread products.

informal purchasing method: Purchasing method in which buyers ask for verbal price quotes from a variety of suppliers before making a decision.

intermediary sources: Wholesalers, distributors, and suppliers.

inventory shrinkage: Difference between the total cost of food and the cost of goods issued during the period.

inventory: Record of all products an operation has in storage and in the kitchen.

investment: Use of money for future profit.

invoice: Supplier's bill listing the actual goods delivered by the supplier.

issuing: Official procedures employees use when taking an item out of the storeroom and putting it into production.

JIT ("just in time") format: When buyers determine the amount of an item needed prior to the next delivery, with the goal that the chefs will have used up the majority of the previous order by the time the new delivery arrives.

kickbacks: Money or other goods received by a person in exchange for purchasing from a specific vendor.

leaders: Items that sell well.

losers: Items that don't sell well.

make-or-buy analysis: This analysis helps to balance how much food a kitchen produces with the quality standards of the operation and enables the operation to decide whether it should make an item from scratch or buy a ready-made version.

nonperishable products: Items that generally, due to packaging or processing, do not readily support the growth of bacteria.

overproduction: Making too much food.

par stock: The ideal amounts of inventory items that an operation should have at all times.

perishable products: Food products sold or distributed in a form that will spoil or decay within a limited period of time.

perpetual inventory method: Method in which employees record items when they are received and then when they are used up.

physical inventory method: Employees review the entire stock physically on a regular basis.

pilfering: Stealing that occurs when employees illegally take inventory items for their personal use.

place value: Differences in price of a product depending on where it needs to be shipped.

primary sources: Farmers and ranchers who raise produce and livestock; also manufacturers, and distillers.

product specifications: *See* **specifications**.

production records: Records that help to forecast buying needs and include production sheets, daily food cost sheets, and sales mix records.

production sheet: Form that lists all menu items that the chefs will prepare on a given day.

purchase order: Legally binding written document that details exactly what the buyer is ordering from the vendor.

quality standards: Specifications of an operation with regard to products and service.

quote: Notice of a price that a supplier gives to a buyer during the purchasing process.

receiving: Inspecting, accepting, and, in some cases, rejecting deliveries of goods and services.

reorder point, or ROP: When an inventory item reaches this point, the buyer knows to reorder that item to keep it in stock. The reorder point can be used with the par stock figure to help maintain proper inventory when suppliers do not deliver regularly.

requisition (WREK-kwi-ZI-shun) form: Formal request for an item or service needed that is sent to company headquarters. Once headquarters approves the purchase and notifies the buyer, then the buyer can place the order.

retailers: Operations that sell their products directly to the public.

sales mix records: Way of tracking each item sold from the menu.

service value: Additional convenience services that a vendor provides to its customers.

specifications: Set by the chef, manager, and/or owner, **specs** are a way of communicating quality standards to potential vendors; they are easy to follow when purchasing brand-name items such as alcohol or condiments.

staples: Items for which the demand is constant.

stockouts: Running out of a menu item.

supply and demand: As the demand for an item goes up, supply goes down; this can impact the cost of an item.

time value: Price retailers pay for the convenience of selecting the time of delivery from suppliers.

transportation value: Cost of choosing a quick but expensive form of transport to get goods delivered.

vermin: Small disease-carrying animals, such as lice, fleas, or mice that are difficult to control.

Chapter 6

à point (ah PWAH): Point in cooking at which pressing the meat with the back of a form yields a slight amount of "give;" any juices are colorless.

aging: Between 48 and 72 hours that butchers hang meat to allow the muscles to relax, which helps lengthen the muscle fibers and increases the tenderness of the meat.

bard: Technique in which the chef ties a layer of fat (bacon or pork fatback) around a roast; used for meats that have little or

no natural fat cover in order to protect and moisten them during cooking.

boning: Separating meat from bones.

bouillabaisse (BOO-ya-base): French seafood stew made with assorted fish and shellfish, onions, tomatoes, white wine, olive oil, garlic, saffron, and herbs.

butterflying: Butchering technique in which a piece of meat is cut lengthwise nearly in half so that it opens out and lies flat.

795

carryover cooking: Term for what occurs when heat absorbed during the cooking process continues to cook food even after it's removed from the oven or stovetop.

cephalopods: Shellfish with a single internal shell and tentacles.

charcuterie: In French, "cooked flesh;" refers to specially prepared pork products, including sausage, smoked ham, bacon, pâté, and terrine.

contribution margin: The marginal profit per unit sale.

crustaceans: Shellfish with an outer skeleton and jointed appendages.

deveining: Process of removing a shrimp's digestive tract.

fabrication: Process of butchering primal cuts into usable portions, such as roasts or steaks.

fin fish: Fish with a backbone that can live in freshwater or in the ocean.

flatfish: Fin fish that are oval and flat in shape and have two eyes on the front part of the head.

forcemeat: Mixture of lean ground meat and fat that is emulsified, or forced together, in a food grinder and then pushed through a sieve to create a very smooth paste.

game meat: Meat from animals that are not raised domestically.

garde manger (gard mawn-ZHAY): Department typically found in a classical brigade system kitchen and/or the chef who is responsible for the preparation of cold foods.

graded: Levels assigned to meat's quality, which is based primarily on its overall flavor characteristics and tenderness.

IQF: The abbreviation for the term "individually quick frozen."

Kosher meat: Meat specially slaughtered to comply with Jewish dietary laws.

marbling: Lines of fat within the lean flesh portion of the meat.

meat: Beef, veal, lamb, mutton, or pork.

mirepoix (meer-PWAH): Combination of chopped aromatic vegetables.

mollusks: Shellfish with one or two hard shells.

mousseline (moose-uh-LEEN): Forcemeat that is delicately flavored and lightened with cream and egg whites.

offal (OH-fel) meat: Organ meat from hogs, cattle, or sheep.

paupiettes (po-pee-EHT): Thin, rolled fillets filled with stuffing.

poultry: Chicken, turkey, duck, geese, guinea, and pigeon protein sources.

primal cuts: Primary divisions of meat produced by the initial butchering of animal carcasses.

quality grade: Measures the flavor characteristics of meat products. The USDA evaluates meat for traits that indicate its tenderness, juiciness, and flavor.

retail cuts: Cuts of meat that are ready for sale.

round fish: Fin fish with a round body shape and one eye on each side of the head; they swim upright in salt water or freshwater.

sausages: Originally referred to ground pork that the preparer forced into a casing made from the lining of animal intestines. Today, many other ingredients are used to make sausage including game, beef, veal, poultry, fish, shellfish, and even vegetables.

shellfish: Fish with an outer shell but no backbone that live primarily in salt water.

shucking: Opening or removing of a mollusk's shell.

truss: Tying the legs and wings to a bird's body.

yield grade: Measures the proportion of edible or usable meat after being trimmed of bones or fat.

Chapter 7

a la carte menu: Menu that prices each item separately.

advertising: Paying to present or promote an operation's products, services, or identity. Advertising can be conducted through multiple mediums.

aesthetic: The way an operation looks and feels to the customers.

apparel and branded merchandise: An operation's name and/or logo on T-shirts or other garments, mugs, pencils, stuffed animals, etc.

average check method: Menu pricing method in which managers divide the total revenue by the number of seats, average seat turnover, and days open in one year.

average contribution margin: *Total contribution margin of all menu items ÷ Total number sold = Average contribution margin.*

California menu: Lists all meals available at any time of day.

carryout and door hanger menus: Paper menus for customers to use outside of the restaurant; door hanger menus for hanging on doorknobs or handles.

communication mix: All the ways an operation actively tries to reach, or communicate, with its desired customers.

community relations: Interacting with people in the local area to create awareness of and trust for an operation.

contemporary marketing mix: Consists of the product-service mix, presentation mix, and communication mix.

contribution margin method: Menu pricing method that uses operation-wide data to determine a dollar amount that must be added to each major menu item's food cost. There are two steps to the formula:

(Total nonfood cost + Target profit) ÷ Number of customers = Contribution margin

Contribution margin + Food cost = Menu price

cooperative sales promotions: When two or more sponsors develop complementary promotions or offer complementary promotion materials.

customer driven: Marketing strategy that is driven by satisfying the wants and needs of the customer.

cyclical menu: A menu in which chefs or managers change menu items after a certain period of time.

demographic segmentation: Marketing that looks at the personal makeup of individuals in a given location.

demographics: Ways in which researchers categorize or group people; for example, by age, income levels, geographic location, and so on.

direct mail: Mass mailing of coupons, menus, advertising about a promotion, etc., to customers in a particular area.

direct marketing: Making a concerted effort to connect directly with a certain segment of the market.

dogs: Menu items that are unpopular and unprofitable.

du jour menu: Lists the menu items that are available on a particular day.

email: Electronic mail targeted to a particular market.

experimental method: Marketing strategy in which an operation might try out a product for a limited time or with a limited group of people in order to judge the response.

fixed menus: Menu that offers the same items every day.

flyers: Paper notices that are distributed in a specific location or to a targeted group to create awareness of a certain promotion or menu item.

focus group: Specific, small group of people used to determine how well a product or service might do on a larger scale.

food percentage method: Menu pricing method in which an operation sets the percentage of menu price that the food cost must be and then calculates the price that will provide this percentage using the following formula:

Item food cost ÷ Food cost percentage = Menu price

frequent shopper program: Provides a benefit in exchange for continuing patronage; often free food items or substantial discounts.

geographic segmentation: Marketing that includes such factors as where consumers live, where they work, and what kind of transportation they use.

lifestyle segmentation: Marketing strategy that looks at the activities, hobbies, interests, and opinions of a given location.

limited menu: Menu that offers only a few items.

margin: Difference between the amount of money left over from the sale of food or beverages (after preparation costs) and the amount needed to pay for other overhead, like rent and heat.

market segmentation: When marketers break down a large market into smaller groups of similar individuals that make up that market.

market trends: Responses to consumers' changing attitudes about food, service, or aesthetics. They can also be responses to broader trends, such as political issues to do with energy conservation and recycling, or economic upswings or downturns that can greatly affect the behavior of a given market.

market: Group of people who desire that product or service.

marketing mix: Combination of all the factors that go into creating, developing, and selling a product.

marketing plan: List of steps an operation must take to sell a product or service to a specific market.

marketing: The process of communicating a business's message to its market.

mass marketing: Treating everyone in the market as having the same needs and wants.

media relations: Relationships that marketers maintain with media outlets.

media vehicles: Particular publications or radio stations.

menu boards: Menus written with chalk on a blackboard, or even on a wall in the dining room, that is visible to all the patrons.

menu engineering: Breaks down a menu's components to analyze which items are making money and which items are selling; helps management make decisions about which menu items to leave alone, which to increase or decrease in selling price, which to promote, and which to eliminate.

menu mix percentage: *Item number sold ÷ Total number of purchases = Menu mix percentage.*

merchandising materials: Table tents and other display items in the restaurant.

observational method: Marketing strategy in which an operation observes how customers react in a natural setting toward a product.

personal selling: Face-to-face interactions between service staff and guests; well-trained service staff can also go a long way in communicating an operation's message.

plow horses: Menu items that are popular but less profitable.

point-of-purchase (POP) materials: Menu boards, video, print pieces, and other display items near the point of purchase, where customers make their decisions about what to buy; can be at the counter or at the table.

positioning: Creating within the marketplace a clear, specific identity for both a product and the operation that offers that product.

premiums: Free or reduced-price merchandise, such as a pen or cup that shows the name and location of the restaurant, usually given away or sold for a reduced price with the purchase of a food item.

premiums: Token gifts or giveaway items, such as pens, stationary, children's toys, mugs, T-shirts, or magnets that display the restaurant name and location or phone number.

presentation mix: All the elements that make the operation look unique.

press kit: Also called a media kit; a packet of information given to media representatives to answer questions they might have about a business or organization.

press release: Also called a news release; a brief presentation of promotional information written to sound like a news article.

prix fixe menus: Offers multiple menu items at one price. Often, customers are offered multiple courses for a single set price.

product usage: Marketing strategy that segments the market according to what products or services are popular in a given geographic area.

product-service mix: All of the food and services offered to customers.

profitability: Defined as the amount of money remaining for an operation after expenses, or costs, are paid.

promotional mix: Ways in which marketing communicates with an operation's market.

public relations (PR): Process by which an operation interacts with the community at large.

publicity: Attention an operation receives.

puzzles: Menu items that are unpopular but very profitable.

sales mix analysis: An analysis of the popularity and profitability of a group of menu items.

sales promotions: Limited, or short-term, incentives to entice customers to patronize an operation.

sales volume: Number of times the item is sold in a time period.

sales volume percentage: Managers use sales volume information to compare the number of each menu item sold to the total number of items sold on the entire menu in the same time period, which means each menu item's sales can be expressed as a percentage of total sales.

samples: Free, small tastes of food items, providing customers a risk-free opportunity to try a new item.

sampling: Marketing strategy in which an operation tests a product with a specific, small group of people, sometimes called a **focus group**.

set dollar amount markup: Menu pricing method in which a fixed dollar amount is added to the food cost of an item. Managers must know the food cost and the dollar amount of the markup:

Food cost + Markup = Menu price

The markup is calculated based on the following:

Profit per menu item + Labor cost per menu item + Operating cost per menu item = Markup

set percentage increase method: Menu pricing method that builds on the set dollar amount markup method and takes it a step further. Managers calculate the markup and then determine what the percentage markup is in comparison to the items' food costs.

Food cost × Percentage = Markup

Markup ÷ Food cost = Percentage

signage: Menu boards, directional signs, and other signs that indicate where the operation is located and/or the items it serves.

special pricing: Limited-time reduced prices offered through specials, deals, coupons, or other programs; saves customers money and creates a low-risk opportunity to try a new item.

spoken menu: This is when servers memorize the menu and relay it verbally to the customers.

stars: Menu items that are both popular and profitable.

straight markup pricing: Menu pricing method in which managers mark up the costs according to a formula to obtain the selling price.

survey method: Marketing strategy in which a marketer gathers information using questionnaires.

SWOT analysis: Also called a situation assessment; identifies a restaurant or foodservice operation's **S**trengths, **W**eaknesses, **O**pportunities, and **T**hreats.

table d'hote menu: Similar to a prix fixe menu, it bundles various elements of the menu into one package.

target market: People an operation intends to pursue as customers.

target marketing: Treating people as different from each other and trying to make a focused appeal to a distinct group of customers.

value proposition: Statement of the value an operation's target customers will experience when they purchase its products and services.

Chapter 8

3-2-1 dough: Used for pies, this dough is made of three parts flour, two parts fat, and one part water.

all-purpose flour: Flour that falls between pastry and bread flour in regard to texture.

baker's percentages: Flour always has a proportion of 100 percent, and the percentages of all other ingredients are calculated in relation to the flour.

baking blind: Procedure for preparing a prebaked pie shell.

baking powder: Versatile leavener that is a mixture of baking soda and an acid with an inactive material, like starch.

baking soda: Sodium bicarbonate; a chemical leavener that releases carbon dioxide gas when mixed with a liquid and an acid.

Bavarian creams: Delicate creams made by combining three basic ingredients: vanilla sauce, gelatin, and whipped cream.

biscuit method: Instead of combining all the ingredients at once, rub or cut in the fat into the flour until the mixture is mealy or bumpy in appearance. This produces a stiff batter with a slightly chewier texture than that of more cake-like items.

bloom: White coating that sometimes appears on the surface of the chocolate and indicates that some of the cocoa butter has melted and then recrystallized on the surface.

bread flour: Strong flour that is used for making breads, hard rolls, and any product that needs high gluten for a strong texture.

butterscotch-flavored sauce: Vanilla and brown sugar added to caramel.

cake flour: Flour with a low gluten content; a very soft, smooth texture; and a pure white color.

caramel sauce: Cooked sugar caramelized with butter.

caramelization: Occurs whenever sugar is used as an ingredient in baked items; the heat causes the sugar to turn a light brown (caramel) color.

chocolate liquor: Cocoa beans crushed into a paste that is completely unsweetened.

chocolate sauce: Family of sauces and syrups with cocoa or melted chocolate as the base.

cocoa butter: Liquid from pressed cocoa liquor.

cocoa powder: Solid from pressed cocoa liquor that is ground down.

coulis: Fruit sauce made from fresh berries or other fruits.

creaming method: Beating fat and sugar together in order to introduce air into a batter as a leavener.

creaming method: Process of mixing the fat and sugar together to produce a very fine crumb and a dense, rich texture.

crème anglaise (krem an-GLAYZ): Vanilla sauce for desserts.

curdle: Lumps that develop when exposed to too much heat.

dock (or pierce): To pierce a pie crust in several places with a fork.

double boiler: Stainless-steel bowl over water simmering on very low heat.

durum flour: Hard wheat flour used to make breads; its gluten content is a little higher than that of typical bread flour.

extracts: Flavorful oils taken from such foods as vanilla, lemon, and almond.

ferments: Producing carbon dioxide gas and alcohol.

flavorings: Cocoa, spices, salt, extracts, and so on that affect a baked item's taste and color.

foaming method: Beating eggs, with or without sugar, in order to introduce air into a batter as a leavener.

foaming method: Creating a foam of whole eggs, yolks, or whites provides the structure for the cake. This is used to make cakes with the lightest texture, such as angel food and chiffon cakes.

formulas: Standardized recipes for bakery products.

frozen yogurt: Frozen dessert that contains yogurt in addition to normal ice cream ingredients, such as sugar or other sweeteners, gelatin, coloring, and flavors.

fruit sauces: Dessert sauce made from raw or cooked fruit.

fruit syrup: Cooked sugar-based juice.

gluten (GLOO-ten): Protein found in flour.

high-ratio cake: Cake that contains more sugar than flour in the recipe.

ice cream: Frozen dessert with a custard base that must contain no less than 10 percent milk fat (vanilla) or 8 percent milk fat (all other flavors), melts readily in the mouth, and does not weep, or separate, when it softens at room temperature.

802

icings: Also called frostings, icings are sweet coatings for cakes and other baked goods.

kneading (NEED-ing): Manipulating dough to develop the gluten and give the dough the stretch and give it needs to develop the proper texture.

lean doughs: Made with flour, yeast, water, and salt; they have very little or no sugar or fat.

leaveners: Necessary in baking; they allow the dough or batter to rise.

liquids: One of the most important elements used in baking; the liquid used in baking can be water, milk, cream, molasses, honey, or butter.

nibs: Small pieces of cocoa beans that are the basis of all cocoa products.

pastry creams: Also called crème pâtissière, these creams have greater density than custards and are frequently used as the filling for pastries such as éclairs.

pastry flour: Flour that is not as strong as bread flour and not as delicate as cake flour.

pâte à choux (paht ah SHOE): Made by combining water (or another liquid), butter, flour, and eggs into a smooth batter.

pâte feuilleteée (paht PHOO e tay): Feuilletée means squares. This is another name for puff pastry.

phyllo (FEE-low): Dough used to prepare baklava.

physical leaveners: Introducing air into a batter to leaven a baked item.

poached fruit: Combination of fruit with a liquid, usually a mixture of sugar, spices, and wine.

profiteroles (pro-FIT-uh-rolls): Small, round pastries made from pâte à choux filled with ice cream.

proof: To allow dough to rise a second time.

puff pastry: Elegant product also called pâte feuilletée; (feuilletée means squares) that can be used in both sweet and savory applications.

pushing up: When carbon dioxide gas gets trapped in the gluten during fermentation.

quark: Cheese that is a lot like sour cream.

quick breads: Popular snack and dessert item that is usually easy and quick to make. Quick breads use chemical leaveners rather than organic ones and, therefore, don't require a rising period.

rich doughs: Made with the addition of shortening or tenderizing ingredients such as sugars, syrups, butter, eggs, milk, and cream.

roll-in dough: This method (also called laminated dough) is used to make Danish, croissant, and puff pastry.

semolina flour: Type of durum flour, but it is more coarsely ground than the flour used to make most breads. It has a fine texture with a high gluten content and is primarily used to make pastas and certain Italian pastries.

sherbets: Frozen mixtures of fruit juice or fruit purée that contain milk and/or egg for creaminess.

shortenings: Any fat, such as oil or butter, that acts as a shortening in baking.

sifting: Adds air to flour, cocoa, and confectioner's sugar;, removes lumps, and filters out any impurities.

sorbet: Frozen mixtures of fruit juice or fruit purée that contain no dairy and contain sweeteners and other flavors or additives.

soufflés (soo-FLAYZ): Soufflés are lightened with beaten egg whites and then baked. Baking causes the soufflé to rise like a cake. They rely on egg whites and are not as stable as puddings.

sourdough: Type of bread made with yeast batter and leavened with a **starter.**

sponge method: Used to mix yeast doughs. The first stage of this method involves mixing the yeast, half of the liquid, and half of the flour to make a thick batter called a sponge. After the sponge rises and doubles its size, the remaining fat, liquid, salt, sugar, and flour are added.

starter: Mixture of water, yeast, and all-purpose flour that has been fermented until it has a sour smell (usually overnight).

steamed puddings: More stable than soufflés because of the greater percentage of eggs and sugar in the batter. Baked custard and chocolate sponge pudding are examples of steamed puddings.

straight-dough method: Also called the straight-mix method; this method can be used for all types of doughs—lean, rich, and sponge. The baker can combine all ingredients at the same time, or he or she might mix the yeast with warm water first.

strengtheners: Provide stability and ensure that a baked item doesn't collapse when it is removed from the oven.

sweeteners: Refined sugars, sugar syrups, molasses, brown sugar, corn syrup, honey, and malt syrup.

syneresis: Watery liquid that leaks from a custard as it is cut and served or as it sits and ages. It is safe to eat.

tempering: Melting by heating it gently and gradually.

thickeners: Gelatin, flour, arrowroot (a powdered starch made from a tropical root), cornstarch, and eggs. Thickeners, combined with the stirring process, determine the consistency of the finished product.

tofu: Soy milk that has been coagulated and pressed into a semisolid form.

torte: Elegant, rich, many-layered cake often filled with buttercream or jam.

two-stage method: Used to make high-ratio cakes. The first stage is to combine a softened or melted shortening with the dry ingredients. The second stage is to add and blend in one-half of the liquid being used in the recipe and then gradually add the remaining liquid to the mixture.

yeast: An organic leavener, yeast is a microscopic fungus used often in baking. When yeast is mixed with carbohydrates (such as sugar and flour), it ferments.

yield: How much of something is produced.

zabaglione (zah-bahl-YOH-nay): Also called **sabayon** (sa-by-ON); a sauce that is too delicate to be made ahead of time and held. It is a fragile foam of egg yolks, sugar, and Marsala wine.

Chapter 9

aquaculture: Production of seafood under controlled conditions.

bottom trawling: Pulling trawls across the bottom of the sea floor, where the heavy equipment scrapes against it.

brownfield site: Previously abandoned industrial site that, once cleaned up, can be repurposed for commercial businesses.

bycatch: Other species caught in some fishing gear in addition to the species that is targeted in a given region.

closed systems: Fish farms that recondition and reuse the water in the farm, which doesn't need to be placed in or sometimes even near a natural body of water.

composting: Biological decomposition; a natural form of recycling that occurs when organic material decomposes (or composts) to form organic fertilizer.

conservation: The practice of limiting the use of a resource.

controlled environment: Environment in which food has been within the kitchen's control and has been kept safe from cross-contamination and time-temperature abuse.

dead zones: Very large algae blooms that deplete the oxygen in the water, which dooms the species in the area.

Environmental Protection Agency (EPA): Founded in 1970; a federal agency whose mission is to protect human health and the environment.

food miles: Amount of travel that some food products must make.

fossil fuels: Fuels that are formed from plant or animal remains and buried deep in the Earth.

green building: Building that has been designed, built, renovated, or reused so that the structure conserves energy, uses resources more efficiently, and reduces the overall impact on the environment.

local source: Offers food produced by the surrounding growing region.

open systems: Fish farms that use a natural body of water to produce the fish.

organic: Food that is generally defined according to agricultural practices as products that have been produced without pesticides or synthetic fertilizers.

overfishing: Catching a species at a faster rate than it can reproduce.

renewable energy sources: Energy sources that do not rely on a finite supply of a resource, directly emit greenhouse gases, or contribute to air pollution.

repurposed food: Food that customers did not eat, but that back-of-house staff prepared, cooked, cooled, and held safely.

shade-grown: Coffee forests that offer numerous benefits to a local ecosystem. By this traditional method, coffee trees grow under taller rainforest trees, whose larger leaves shade the crop.

sun coffee: Crop produced on newer, monocultured farms, in which the larger forest is cleared or thinned to make room for more crops.

sustainability: Practices that meet current resource needs without compromising the ability to meet future needs.

trawlers: Fishing boats that pull large nets through the water (called "trawls"), catching everything that is too big to escape through the mesh of the nets.

Chapter 10

andouille (an-DOO-ee): Pork sausage with a strong, smoky, garlicky taste.

barbecued: Meat cooked with the heat of a fire, sometimes after a marinade, spice rub, or basting sauce has been applied.

bisque: Soup made from lobster shells, extracting all the color and flavor before straining them away.

Cajun: Style of cooking from the swamps and bayous of southwestern Louisiana.

comale: Round, flat griddle made of stone or earthenware.

Creole (KREE-ole): Developed in the city of New Orleans in the homes of the rich French and Spanish land owners. It is the blending of French grand cuisine principles with the cooking techniques of the enslaved Africans and then applied to local and imported foodstuffs and seasoning.

curtido: Typical Central American relish that is made from cabbage, onions, and carrots in vinegar.

fusion cuisine: Style of cooking and presenting food that combines the ingredients and techniques of Asian and West Coast cuisines.

gallo pinto: Literally means "painted chicken," but has nothing to do with either paint or chickens. It is a mix of white rice and black beans, cooked separately and then fried together in coconut oil.

gumbo: Hearty soup with trinity and shrimp, thickened with brown roux containing okra (a seed-pod vegetable that helps gel the gumbo), and filé, a thickener made from dried sassafras leaves.

jambalaya: Spicy Creole rice dish with chicken, andouille sausage, shrimp, crayfish, trinity, other vegetables, herbs, broth, and seasonings.

jerk spice: Used to be a local mixture of allspice, Scotch bonnet peppers (a very hot relative of the habañero chili), marjoram, cinnamon, and other local herbs. Europeans added garlic and rum to the mix, and recently dry mustard and other additions have added a deeper color.

Low Country boil: Well-spiced, one-pot dish, generally consisting of shrimp, smoked sausage, red potato, and corn.

Low Country cuisine: From the Low Country of South Carolina, Georgia, and northeastern Florida, cuisine influenced by the warmer climate and rice plantations combined with the busy port of Charleston, where pickles and relishes of the warmer climates became standard fare.

mole: Sauce or mixture and can sometimes be used as a suffix on words to describe the sauce.

New England boiled dinner: Very popular, classic menu item in New England that includes corned beef brisket (beef that is cured in a salt brine, often with spices), boiled potatoes, cabbage, and root vegetables like onions, carrots, or parsnips.

New England clam chowder: The most familiar version of a thick clam soup, creamy, white, and mild.

pupusa: A stuffed corn tortilla.

quinoa: The high-protein dried fruits and seeds of the goosefoot plant used as a food staple and ground into flour.

salsa: Signature dish of the Southwest. The word means sauce in Spanish. Although salsa can be smooth and thin in consistency, it is usually a chunky sauce that may even resemble a relish.

sofrito: Mix of salt pork, ham, onions, garlic, green peppers, jalapeño, tomato, oregano, and cilantro that is cooked slowly together and then used as a foundation in soups and stews.

Tidewater cuisine: From Virginia's and North Carolina's Tidewater region, cuisine influenced by the Native Americans who taught European settlers to plant corn and introduced them to native squashes, plums, berries, greens, game, and seafood, including fish and oysters.

trinity: Form of mirepoix that blends celery, onions, and green bell peppers instead of the carrots that are traditional in mirepoix. Trinity is considered foundational to Louisiana cooking.

Chapter 11

Archestratos: Wrote around 330 BCE and produced one of the world's first cookbooks.

cha kaiseki: Japanese cuisine centered around tea drinking.

cassoulet: Rich dish of beans and meat.

Columbian Exchange: Named for explorer Christopher Columbus, the trading that took place between the Roman Empire and Europe that brought many new foods to Europe, such as tomatoes, peppers, and beans.

couscoussiere: Specialized earthenware or glass cooking vessel used in Moroccan cuisine.

cuisine classique: Later called "nouvelle cuisine (noo-vehl kwee-ZEEN)," this cuisine developed as chefs in the late twentieth century embraced lighter dishes

and simpler flavors—in a sense, returning to their roots. Based on the works of Auguste Escoffier.

duck confit: Salted pieces of duck, poached In duck fat.

gohan: Japanese word for cooked rice.

haute cuisine: Type of cuisine characterized by highly refined dishes and the creation of a strictly disciplined brigade system (a hierarchy of specialized roles in the kitchen).

jambon de Bayonne: Mild local ham of Southwest France.

lacquered meats: Brushing multiple layers of a flavorful, sweet marinade onto a cut of meat before roasting it.

Maghreb: Countries of North Africa.

nouvelle cuisine: Type of cuisine developed as chefs in the late twentieth century embraced lighter dishes and simpler flavors. Differs from cuisine classique in that the dishes are even lighter and more delicate, and there is an increased emphasis on presentation.

poulet de Bresse: Blue-legged chicken of renowned tenderness and flavor.

red-cooking: Stewing meat or fish in a broth of soy sauce and water to develop a rich color and succulent taste.

reduction: Process of thickening or intensifying the flavor of a liquid mixture such as a soup, sauce, wine, or juice by evaporation.

Saltimbocca alla Romano: Popular Roman dish, made of pounded scallops of veal sautéed with fresh sage and prosciutto.

Szechwan-Hunan: Chinese cuisine from the neighboring provinces of Szechwan and Hunan best known for their hot, spicy foods.

tagines: Commonly eaten in Morocco, these meat stews are cooked for a long time and are usually based on lamb, fish, game, or chicken, and often served with preserved lemon.

tan: Grains and rice in Chinese cuisine.

Tao: Belief that a single guiding principle orders the universe.

ts'ai: Vegetables and meat in Chinese cuisine.

velveting: Coating prepared meats with cornstarch and egg whites before stir-frying to retain moisture and improve sauce adherence.

wabi sabi: Buddhist principle that means quiet simplicity merged with quiet elegance.

Index

Raspberry Sauce, 281
receiving, 326–329
    cheese, 15
    dairy, 200
    dried goods, 200
    eggs, 22
    fish, 200
    food costs, 165
    meat, 200
    milk, 10
    nutritious practices, 109–110
    poultry, 385
    produce, 200
    specialty produce, 200
recipe cost card, 168–169
recipe substitutions, 125
recipe testers, 174
recipe yields, 171–174
Recommended Dietary Allowances, 100
recycling, 605–607
red cabbage, 221
red-cooking, 740, 742
reducing, 604–605
reflective roofs, 595
refrigerated storage, 111
rendering fat, 374
renewable energy sources, 587
reorder point, 316
repurposing food, 602–603
requisition forms, 318
research methods, 447–450
restaurant PR specialists, 458
retail cuts, 357
retailers, 291
reusing, 602–604
revenue, 147
rice, 85, 88, 750
rice milk, 7, 9
rich doughs, 514
rinds, cheese, 16
ripened cheese, 15–16
rock salt, 123
roll-in dough, 536–537
rolled cookies, 539
rolled omelet, *see* omelets
rolls, soft, 508, 567
Romaine lettuce, 221
Roquefort, 15
round fish, 397, 405–406
roux, 118
royal icing, 527
rubs, meats, 371

S

sabayon, 556
safety
    eggs, 34
    meat, poultry, and seafood, 418
    sandwiches, 56, 59
    tea, 47
safflower oil, 245
saffron, 706
salads, 219–242
    accompaniment, 234–235
    base, 221
    body, 221–222
    bound, 224–225, 230–231

salads, *cont.*
    cleaning, 236–239
    combination, 224–226
    composed, 225, 228–229
    designing, 226
    dessert, 234–235
    dressings, 221–222, 243–250
        colloids, 251
        emulsified vinaigrette, 244–245, 247, 249
        emulsifiers, 246
        emulsions, 245–246, 251
        matching, 249
        mayonnaise, 244, 248–250
        mayonnaise-based, 244, 247, 249
        oils, 245
        ordering on side, 249
        solutions, 251
        suspensions, 244, 251
        vinaigrettes, 244, 246, 249, 280
    fruit, 224–225, 233
    garnishes, 221–222, 257–272
        bottles, 272
        brunoise, 257
        color, 267
        cucumber fans, 267
        cucumbers, 262–263
        desserts, 269–270
        dollops, 271
        flowers, 272
        French, 268–269
        fried leeks, 262
        fried parsley, 261–262
        frosted grapes, 264–265
        gougères, 271
        lemons, 265
        mushroom caps, 263
        napping, 269–270
        pickles, 264
        plate presentation, 259–260
        platters, 266
        preparation, 261–265
        radishes, 263
        scallion brushes, 264
        scoops, 272
        soups, 271–272
        string work, 269
    gelatin, 231–232
    green, 224–225
    greens, 220–221, 224, 237
    ingredients, 220–224
    intermezzo, 234–235
    main course, 234–235
    mayonnaise-based, 58
    plating, 236
    prepackaged, 237–238
    preparation, 227–232
    presentation, 226
    service, 233–236
    starter, 234
    storing, 236–239
    tossed, 225, 228
    types of, 224–226
    vegetable, 224–225, 229–230
    vegetables, 223
salad dressings, 119
salad spinner, 238
sales, 485–491

Photo Credits

All photographs and images in this product are presented for educational purposes only and should not be considered actual materials or settings.

Vincent Cannon/**Abshier House**
17-19, 23, 83, 87-88, 91, 95, 147-150, 152-153, 157, 165, 169, 172, 176, 186-188, 190-191, 193, 201, 235, 244, 255, 287, 297, 304, 315, 319, 356, 361, 404, 417, 435, 438-439, 442, 449, 472, 474, 479-480, 482, 495, 576-577, 589,

Alisa Alering and David A.J. Ripley
48, 75, 317, 546, 582

Lew Robertson/**AP Wide World Photos**
457, 496

Paul Sakuma/**AP Wide World Photos**
654

Sherrie Blondin
xiv-1

Rob Brinson
572

Maren Caruso
636

Centers for Disease Control and Prevention
101

Comstock Images
185

Corbis RF
544

D.K. Bonatti, Christopher Columbus reaching New World. © Historical Picture Archive/**Corbis**
700

© **Culinary Institute of America**
358, 405, 556

© **Dorling Kindersley**
26-28, 30, 32, 35, 86, 90, 113, 124, 226, 230, 233, 259, 263-265, 274, 370, 381, 405, 515, 522, 638, 642, 645, 650, 653, 655, 666, 672, 677, 680, 690, 714-715, 740

Peter Anderson © **Dorling Kindersley**
31-32, 518, 520

Martin Brigdale © **Dorling Kindersley**
374

Martin Cameron © **Dorling Kindersley**
535

Demetrio Carrasco © **Dorling Kindersley**
678, 686-687

Andy Crawford © **Dorling Kindersley**
175

Philip Dowell © **Dorling Kindersley**
506

Neil Fletcher and Matthew Ward © **Dorling Kindersley**
706

Steve Gorton © **Dorling Kindersley**
237

Stephen Hayward © **Dorling Kindersley**
228

Will Heap © **Dorling Kindersley**
31, 175

Sian Irvine © **Dorling Kindersley**
363

Hugh Johnson © **Dorling Kindersley**
679, 684

Dave King © **Dorling Kindersley**
74, 121, 222, 229, 265, 277, 388, 393, 406, 505, 557, 692-693, 715, 724, 731, 742

Lisa Linder © **Dorling Kindersley**
234

Andrew McKinney © **Dorling Kindersley**
429

David Munns © **Dorling Kindersley**
25, 27, 30, 33, 391

David Murray © **Dorling Kindersley**
233, 417, 506, 528

David Murray and Jules Selmes © **Dorling Kindersley**
33, 35, 116, 120, 226, 230-231, 236-237, 239, 263, 266, 272, 279, 355, 370, 405, 528, 647, 649

Ian O'Leary © **Dorling Kindersley**
42, 272, 370, 405-406, 417, 421, 505, 515-516, 528, 555, 557, 559, 564-565, 669, 673, 691, 728, 737, 741, 752

Roger Phillips © **Dorling Kindersley**
505, 717

Russell Sadur © **Dorling Kindersley**
17

Howard Shooter © **Dorling Kindersley**
40, 520, 714, 728

Simon Smith © **Dorling Kindersley**
520, 523

Clive Streeter © **Dorling Kindersley**
73, 297, 385, 537, 651

David Thelwell © **Dorling Kindersley**
226

Andrew Whittuck © **Dorling Kindersley**
93

Philip Wilkins © **Dorling Kindersley**
553

Jerry Young © **Dorling Kindersley**
40, 116, 263, 267, 270, 275, 362, 374, 528

Bill Freeman
284

Robert Fried/Robertfriedphotography.com
657

Getty Images, Inc. – Stockbyte/Royalty Free
436, 445

Ron Chapple/**Getty Images, Inc. – Taxi**
648

John Feingersh/**Getty Images, Inc. – Blend Images**
iii

Mitch Hrdlicka/**Getty Images, Inc. – Photodisc/Royalty Free**
234

Ryan McVay/**Getty Images, Inc.**
iv, 697

828

Doug Menuez/**Getty Images, Inc. – Photodisc/Royalty Free**
469, 494

Josh Mitchell/**Getty Images, Inc. – Stone Allstock**
362

Skip Nall/**Getty Images, Inc. – Photodisc/Royalty Free**
455, 497

John A. Rizzo/**Getty Images, Inc. – Photodisc/Royalty Free**
234

Bob Thomas/Stone/**Getty Images, Inc.**
204, 210

Courtesy of the **Golden Corral Corporation**
461

Anita Govic
78

Robert Harbison
v

Bob Daemmrich/**The Image Works**
450

Courtesy of **Intuit**
159

© **istockphoto.com/gregdh**
297, 304

Martin Jacobs/FoodPix/**Jupiter Images – PictureArts Corporation**
639

Bob Knight Photography
4

Victor S. Krebneski
502

Used with the permission of **The Manitowoc Company, Inc.**
311

Courtesy **McDonald's Corporation**
(Photographer: Bill Parrish)
432

Steve Adams/Creative Eye/**MIRA.com**
388, 394, 422

Owned or licensed by the **National Restaurant Association**
Cover, i, 4, 20, 41, 78, 116, 144, 154, 171, 192, 199, 205, 209, 218, 238, 284, 301-302, 326, 328, 333, 341, 350, 357, 399, 432, 436, 448, 457, 461, 473, 487, 502, 572, 579, 636, 694

Ken Hively/**Newscom**
666

John Obal
350

Ann Hagen Griffiths/**Omni-Photo Communications, Inc.**
457

Ronnie Padgett
218

Pearson Education/PH College
352, 380, 396

Richard Embery/**Pearson Education/PH College**
14, 34-35, 55, 63, 65, 116, 120-121, 123, 222, 225, 227, 229, 231, 234, 238, 246-247, 250, 262, 264, 270, 272, 276, 280-281, 354, 358-359, 362, 364, 366, 368-369, 371-372, 381, 383-386, 389, 391, 427-428, 506, 510, 512, 515, 518, 527-528, 534, 537, 547, 551, 553, 555, 557, 568, 621, 649, 707, 728

Vincent P. Walter **Pearson Education/PH College**
65, 216-217, 228, 386, 405, 519, 578

Peter Bowater/**Photo Researchers, Inc.**
49

Kent Foster/**Photo Researchers, Inc.**
648

Prof. P. Motta, Department of Anatomy, University "La Sapienza," Rome/Science Photo Library/**Photo Researchers, Inc.**
102

Joseph Nettis/ **Photo Researchers, Inc.**
310

Rosenfeld Images Ltd./**Photo Researchers, Inc.**
7

Mary Kate Denny/**PhotoEdit, Inc.**
459

Jeff Greenberg/**PhotoEdit, Inc.**
436, 446

David Young-Wolff/**PhotoEdit, Inc.**
20

Stewart Cohen/**Photolibrary.com**
59

Eurelios/**Phototake NYC**
357

Eric Rector
734

The Ritz-Carlton Hotel Company, L.L.C.
295

Gavin Hellier/**Robert Harding World Imagery**
681

James McConnachie © **Rough Guides**
367

Greg Roden © **Rough Guides**
681, 685

Shutterstock.com
ix, 2-3, 14, 19-21, 24, 28-29, 34-35, 37-38, 40-41, 43-45, 49, 51-54, 61-70, 76-77, 82-86, 88, 90-91, 95-98, 107-110, 114-115, 117-118, 121-123, 126, 131-136, 142-143, 147-148, 162-163, 175, 182-183, 196-197, 211-213, 221, 223, 225, 232, 234-235, 241-244, 251-258, 261, 282-283, 287, 291, 299, 301, 305, 308, 310, 323-324, 328, 335, 342-345, 348-349, 359-360, 363, 365-367, 377-378, 385-386, 400-402, 408, 413-415, 420, 423-424, 430-431, 438, 441, 451, 455, 461, 466-467, 478-479, 482, 495, 500-501, 518-519, 525-527, 531-532, 539-542, 545, 550, 553, 556, 559, 561-563, 567, 570-571, 579-587, 591-596, 599-600, 603-613, 618-619, 629-632, 634-635, 641, 643, 646-647, 654, 656, 660-665, 668-670, 675, 682, 689, 696, 698-705, 709-713, 716, 718-720, 723, 726-727, 729-730, 732-733, 736, 739, 741-749, 753-760

Stephen Ivy/**Sodexo**
144

Dallas and John Heaton/**The Stock Connection**
46

U.S. Department of Agriculture
128

U.S. Environmental Protection Agency ENERGY STAR Hotline
591

U.S. Food and Drug Administration
403

U.S. Geological Survey
576

Jeff Zaruba/**Zaruba Photography**
vi

829